The **Rough Gu**

D0497377

Portugal

written and researched by

Jules Brown, Mark Ellingham, John Fisher, Matthew Hancock and Graham Kenyon

with additional updating by
Jens Finke, Brendon Griffin, Sally Schafer and James Stewart

ROUGH
GUIDES

NEW YORK • LONDON • DELHI

www.roughguides.com

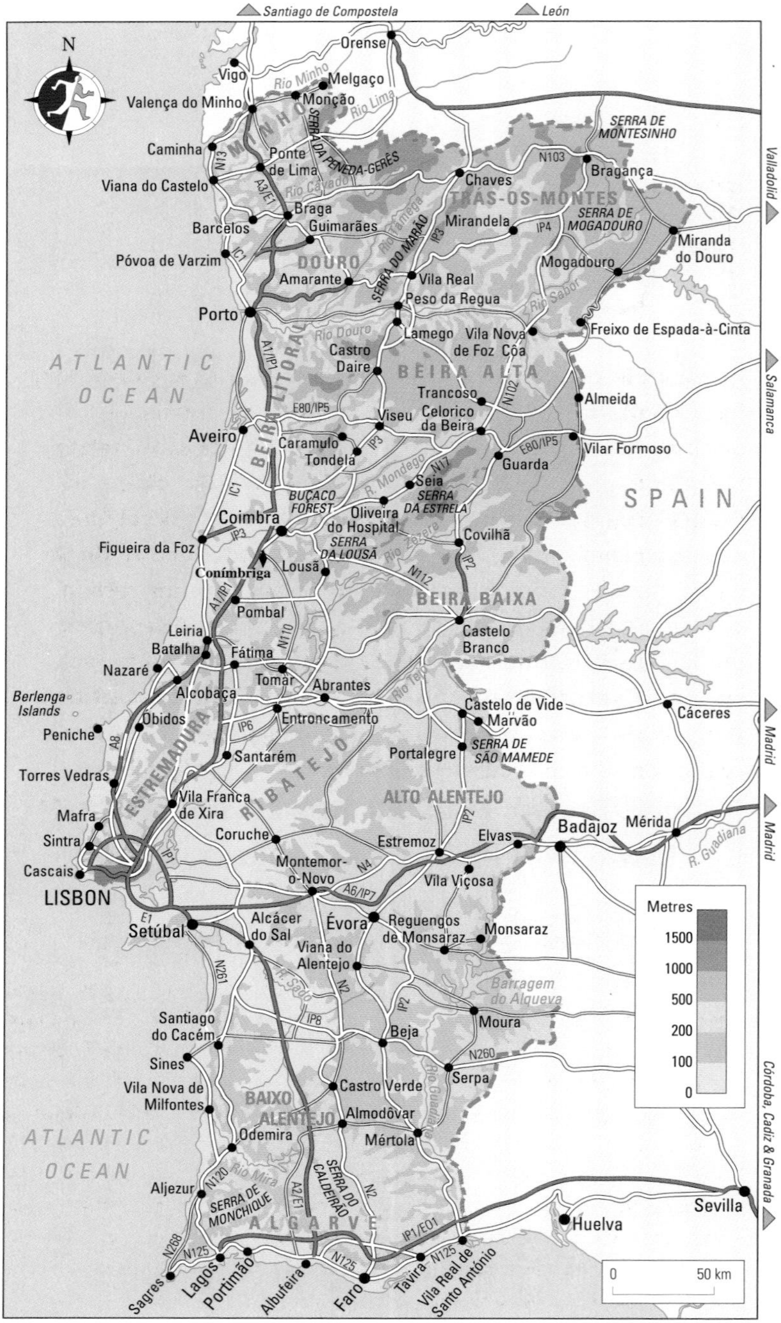
Santiago de Compostela
León
Valladolid
Salamanca
Madrid
Madrid
Córdoba, Cadiz & Granada
N
ATLANTIC OCEAN
ATLANTIC OCEAN
SPAIN
Orense
Vigo
Melgaço
Rio Minho
Monção
Valença do Minho
Rio Lima
MINHO
SERRA DA PENEDA-GERÊS
SERRA DE MONTESINHO
Caminha
N13
Ponte de Lima
Viana do Castelo
A3/E1
Rio Cávado
N103
Bragança
Chaves
TRÁS-OS-MONTES
SERRA DE MOGADOURO
Braga
Barcelos
Guimarães
Rio Tâmega
IP3
Mirandela
IP4
Miranda do Douro
Póvoa de Varzim
IC1
DOURO
SERRA DO MARÃO
Mogadouro
Amarante
Vila Real
Peso da Regua
Rio Sabor
Porto
Rio Douro
Lamego
Vila Nova de Foz Côa
Freixo de Espada-à-Cinta
A1/IP1
BEIRA LITORAL
Castro Daire
BEIRA ALTA
N102
Trancoso
Almeida
E80/IP5
Viseu
Celorico da Beira
Aveiro
Caramulo
Tondela
IP3
E80/IP5
Vilar Formoso
Guarda
R. Mondego
N17
Seia
IC1
BUÇACO FOREST
SERRA DA ESTRELA
Coimbra
Oliveira do Hospital
IP3
Covilhã
Figueira da Foz
SERRA DA LOUSÃ
Rio Zêzere
Conímbriga
Lousã
IP2
N112
A1/IP1
BEIRA BAIXA
Pombal
N110
Castelo Branco
Leiria
Batalha
Fátima
Nazaré
Tomar
Rio Tejo
Alcobaça
Abrantes
Berlenga Islands
Castelo de Vide
Cáceres
Óbidos
Entroncamento
Marvão
IP6
Peniche
A8
ESTREMADURA
SERRA DE SÃO MAMEDE
Santarém
Portalegre
Torres Vedras
RIBATEJO
ALTO ALENTEJO
Vila Franca de Xira
IP2
Mafra
Badajoz
Mérida
Coruche
Sintra
Elvas
Estremoz
R. Guadiana
IP1
Cascais
Montemor-o-Novo
N4
Vila Viçosa
LISBON
A6/IP7
E1
Alcácer do Sal
Évora
Reguengos de Monsaraz
Monsaraz
Setúbal
Metres
1500
1000
500
200
100
0
Viana do Alentejo
N261
R. Sado
N2
Barragem do Alqueva
IP2
Santiago do Cacém
IP8
Moura
Beja
N260
Sines
Serpa
Rio Guadiana
Vila Nova de Milfontes
Castro Verde
BAIXO ALENTEJO
Almodôvar
Odemira
Mértola
Rio Mira
N120
SERRA DO CALDEIRÃO
A2/E1
N2
Aljezur
SERRA DE MONCHIQUE
Sevilla
ALGARVE
Huelva
IP1/E01
N268
N125
N125
N125
Sagres
Lagos
Portimão
Albufeira
Faro
Tavira
Vila Real de Santo António
0
50 km

Introduction to

Portugal

Portugal is an astonishingly beautiful country; the rivers, forests and lush valleys of the north are a splendid contrast to its contorted southern coastline of beaches, cliffs and coves. If you've come from the arid plains of central Spain, Portugal's dry southern Alentejo region doesn't promise any immediate relief, but – unlike Spain – you don't have to travel very far to witness so total a contrast that it's hard, at first, to take in. Suddenly the landscape is infinitely softer and greener, with flowers and trees everywhere. Life also seems easier-paced and the people more courteous; the Portuguese talk of their nation as a land of *brandos costumes* – gentle ways.

For so small a country, Portugal sports a tremendous cultural diversity. There are highly sophisticated resorts along the coast around Lisbon and on the well-developed Algarve in the south, upon which European tourists have been descending for almost fifty years. Lisbon itself, in its idiosyncratic way, has enough diversions to please city devotees – firmly locked it into modern Europe without quite jettisoning its most endearing, rather old-fashioned, qualities. But in the rural areas – the Alentejo, the mountainous Beiras, or northern Trás-os-Montes – this is often still a conspicuously underdeveloped country. Tourism and European Union membership have changed many regions – most notably in the north, where new road-building scythes through the countryside – but for anyone wanting to get off the beaten track, there are limitless opportunities to experience smaller towns and rural areas that still seem rooted in the last century.

▲ Monument of the Discoveries, Lisbon

In terms of population and customs, differences between the **north and south** are particularly striking. Above a roughly sketched line, more or less corresponding with the course of the Rio Tejo (River Tagus), the people are of predominantly Celtic and Germanic stock. It was here, in the north at Guimarães, that the Lusitanian nation was born, in the wake of the Christian reconquest from the North African Moors. South of the Tagus, where the Roman, and then the Moorish, civilizations were most established, people tend to be darker-skinned (*moreno*) and maintain more of a Mediterranean lifestyle (though the Portuguese coastline is, in fact, entirely Atlantic). **Agriculture** reflects this divide as well, with oranges, figs and cork in the south, and more elemental corn and potatoes in the north. Indeed, in places in the north the methods of farming date back to pre-Christian days, based on a mass of tiny plots divided and subdivided over the generations.

More recent events are also woven into the pattern. The 1974 Revolution, which brought to an end 48 years of dictatorship, came from the south, an area of vast estates, rich landowners and a dependent workforce; while the later conservative backlash came from the north, with its powerful religious authorities and individual smallholders wary of change. But more profoundly even than the Revolution, it is **emigration** that has altered people's attitudes and the appearance of the countryside. After Lisbon, the largest Portuguese community is in Paris, and there are migrant workers spread throughout France, Germany and North America. Returning, these emigrants have brought in modern ideas and challenged many traditional rural values. New ideas and cultural influences have arrived, too, through Portugal's own immigrants from the old African colonies of Cape Verde,

▼ Cork trees

Fact file

• Portugal is the most south-westerly country in mainland Europe; its only **neighbour** is Spain with which it shares one of the longest and most established borders in Europe.

• The country occupies an **area** of approximately 92,000 square kilometres with a surprisingly diverse **landscape** – from the steep mountains of the north to the arid plains of the Alentejo and the wetlands of the south-east coast. The entire **coastline** of 1,793km gives on to the Atlantic Ocean.

• **Tourism** is the country's largest industry, though the greatest proportion of the population works in **agriculture**. Twenty-six percent of land remains arable, with a further thirty-six percent made up of forests and woodland. Portugal's most important **exports** are textiles, wine, especially port from the north of the country, and cork – over fifty percent of the world's wine corks come from Portugal.

• Apart from brief periods of Spanish occupancy, Portugal has been an independent country since 1140. It became a **republic** in 1910 and is now a **parliamentary democracy** divided into eighteen regions, together with two autonomous regions (the islands of Madeira and the Azores). It joined the **EU** in 1986 and, despite rapid economic growth, remains one of the EU's poorest countries, with a **GDP** of around sixty-six percent that of the four leading European economies. Lisbon is officially the European capital with the lowest **cost of living.**

Mozambique and Angola, while the country's close ties with Brazil are also conspicuously obvious.

The greatest of all Portuguese influences, however, is **the sea**. The Atlantic dominates the land not only physically, producing the consistently temperate climate, but mentally and historically, too. The Portuguese are very conscious of themselves as a seafaring race; mariners like Vasco da Gama led the way in the discovery of Africa and the New World, and until comparatively recently Portugal remained a colonial power, albeit one in deep crisis. Such links long ago brought African and South American strands into the country's culture: in the distinctive music of fado, blues-like songs heard in Lisbon and Coimbra, for example, or the Moorish-influenced Manueline architecture that provides the country's most distinctive monuments.

▼ Coffee and pastéis de nata

This "glorious" history has also led to the peculiar national characteristic of *saudade*: a slightly resigned, nostalgic air, and a feeling that the past will always overshadow the possibilities of the future. The years of isolation under the dictator Salazar, which yielded to democracy after the 1974 Revolution, reinforced such emotions, as the ruling elite spurned influences from the rest of Europe. Only in the last three decades, with Portugal's entry into the European Union, have things really begun to change and the Portuguese are becoming increasingly geared toward Lisbon

▲ Café, Lisbon

and the cities. For those who have stayed in the countryside, however, life remains traditional – disarmingly so to outsiders – and social mores seem fixed in the past. Women still wear black if their husbands are absent, as many are, working in France, or Germany, or at sea.

The Golden Age

For over a hundred years, in the period spanning the fifteenth to sixteenth centuries, Portugal was one of the richest countries in the world, an economic powerhouse that controlled a trading empire spreading from Brazil in the west to Macau in the east. It was Vasco da Gama's discovery of a sea route to India in 1498 that kick-started the **spice trade**, shooting Portugal – already doing well from **African gold** and **slavery** – into the top league of wealthy nations. Its maritime empire reached a peak during the reign of Manuel I "The Fortunate" (1495–1521), the so-called Golden Age that also produced Luís de Camões and Gil Vicente, two of Portugal's

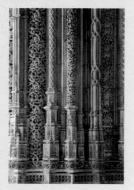

greatest writers, along with the new, exuberant Manueline architectural style. Portugal was to hit the jackpot again in the seventeenth century, when enormous gold reserves were discovered in Brazil, but changing markets and over-indulgence soon reduced its financial clout, and after the **Great Earthquake** of 1755 the country sank into economic obscurity. Nevertheless, the physical legacy of Portugal's empire remains in the surviving buildings and monuments of the Golden Age, such as Lisbon's **Torre de Belém** and **Mosteiro dos Jerónimos**, while **Portuguese** itself is the world's fifth most-spoken language.

Where to go

▼ Praia de Faro

The obvious place to start a visit to Portugal is the capital, **Lisbon**, which contains a selection of just about everything the country has to offer within its vicinity: historical monuments from the Golden Age, superb beaches nearby and a cool hilltop retreat just to the north in **Sintra**, along with neighbourhood grill houses, hip nightclubs and traditional city quarters. Further north on the Rio Douro (River Douro), **Porto** is the country's second city and the economic heart of the nation, though perhaps best known for its port wine lodges. It certainly beats to a faster work rhythm than the rest of the country but the city nevertheless retains an earthy, typically Portuguese welcome for outsiders.

These are the only cities of any size in Portugal, but the country's cultural and historical past is also reflected in smaller towns, especially the university towns of **Coimbra** and **Évora**, in the country's first capital

The missing lynx

Portugal's traditional farming techniques, combined with a lack of major industrialization, have historically helped protect the kind of wildlife that has become endangered elsewhere on the continent. A handful of the world's two hundred remaining **Iberian lynx**, for example – a relative of the tiger and Europe's only native big cat – survive in the Serra da Malcata park which straddles the Spanish border, while another rare species, the Iberian wolf, lives in the mountainous interior and the north of Portugal. However, as a predatory animal that still arouses fear and suspicion, the latter creature is often shot on sight. Furthermore, as Portuguese agriculture has been modernized in recent years, so the habitats of both these species have become increasingly threatened. Conservation attempts are offering hope, however, ironically, in the tourist areas of the Algarve and Lisbon: a new **lynx reserve** is planned in the hills of the Algarve to boost numbers of this handsome, spotted cat, while the Centro de Recuperação de Lobo Ibérico north of Mafra, just outside Lisbon, is doing sterling work in conserving the much-feared wolf.

of Guimarães, and at **Braga**, the religious centre. But, with its miles of Atlantic coastline, Portugal is most famous for its beaches. The safest and most alluring of these are in the **Algarve**, and though this has led to large-scale development, you can still escape the crowds in the east of the region on the offshore islands around **Tavira** and along the west coast north of **Sagres**. Other less-developed but more exposed beaches can be found up the entire west coast of Portugal, with small-scale, thoroughly Portuguese resorts such as **Vila Nova de Milfontes** on the Alentejo coast, **Nazaré** and the **Pinhal de Leiria** resorts in Estremadura, and the **Costa da Prata** resorts in the Beira Literal. Crowds are even thinner along the Costa Verde around **Viana do Castelo**, but by the time you are this far north the sea is decidedly chilly for much of the year.

Most of Portugal's population lives on the coastline and to see a more rural, traditional side of Portugal involves heading inland. The most dramatic and verdant scenery lies in the north around the sensational gorge and valley of the **Rio Douro** and in the wild mountainous national parks of the Serra da Estrela, Peneda-Gerês and Montesinho. Some of the rural villages in **Trás-os-Montes** or the **mountain Beiras** region still live a startlingly traditional existence firmly rooted in subsistence farming. By contrast,

Food from afar

Portugal's former status as an important trading nation has had a far greater influence on world cuisine than is often realized. Along with **port**, the Portuguese are credited with introducing several dishes that today are quintessentially Eastern. The Japanese **tempura** method of deep-frying food was introduced to the Japanese by sixteenth-century Portuguese traders and missionaries, while the fiery curry-house mainstay **vindaloo** derives from a *vinho* (wine) and *alho* (garlic) sauce popular with the Christian community in Portuguese Goa. Indeed, the use of **chillis** in the East only began when the Portuguese started to import them from Mexico. Another, less exotic, Portuguese export is **marmalade** (although Portuguese *marmelada* is actually made from quince).

Despite this global culinary influence, however, it is only recently that the Portuguese themselves have embraced food with anything other than solid Portuguese ingredients. Nowadays, along with the ubiquitous grilled **chicken** and **sardines**, you'll find restaurants serving dishes deriving from Portugal's former colonies, such as Angolan *mufete* (beans with palm oil and fish), chicken *piri piri* (chicken in chilli sauce), which originated in **Angola** and **Mozambique**, Asian *caril de camarão* (shrimp curry) and **Brazilian** dishes such as *feijoada* (bean stew).

the wide-open plains of the flat southern **Alentejo** are an agricultural area of endless olive and cork groves scattered with some of Portugal's prettiest whitewashed villages. Here the fierce sun and parched landscape pro-

▼ Tavira

motes a far more laid-back lifestyle than in the greener hills of the north and centre. All along the border with Spain you'll find fantastic fortified border settlements, from **Valença do Minho** in the north to **Mértola** in the south, most of them barely touched by tourism.

When to go

A weather map of endless suns sums up the situation across the whole of Portugal in summer, certainly between June and September, when the only daytime variation across the country is a degree or two further up the scale from 30°C. At this time, and especially in July and August, Portugal's coastal resorts are at their busiest and prices correspondingly reach their peak.

But, with such a verdant landscape, it should be no real surprise that Portugal also has a fairly high level of rainfall, most of it from November to March. The **north** of Portugal is particularly wet, and in the higher areas showers

▲ Grilled sardines

are possible more or less throughout the year. In **central and southern Portugal**, especially on the coast, it is mild all year round and, although it can be cloudy in winter, when the sun does break through it is delightfully warm.

Perhaps the best times of year to visit are in late **spring** – for the dazzling flowers – and early **autumn**, when the weather is warm but not too hot and the summer crowds have thinned out. Swimmers, however, should note that the official swimming season in Portugal lasts from around June to mid-September; outside these months, outdoor pools close and few beaches are manned with lifeguards. Some hotels, restaurants, campsites and water parks also only open from around Easter to September.

In **winter**, in the north things can get pretty chilly, especially inland where snow is common along the mountainous border areas in January and February. But, if you don't mind the odd tourist facility being closed, crisp, sharp sunshine makes winter a highly appealing time to visit the middle and south of the country. In Lisbon, the Alentejo and Algarve there are dramatic reductions in hotel prices and, in February, the almond blossom lights up the countryside. This is the time when you'll see the country at its most Portuguese, with virtually no tourists around.

Average temperatures and rainfall

Daytime temperatures (°C) and average monthly rainfall (mm)

	Jan	Mar	May	Jul	Sep	Nov
Lisbon						
Max °C	14	18	22	27	25	17
Min °C	8	10	13	17	16	12
Rainfall	111	109	44	3	33	93
Porto (Costa Verde)						
Max °C	13	15	19	25	24	17
Min °C	5	7	10	15	14	8
Rainfall	159	147	87	20	51	148
Faro (Algarve)						
Max °C	15	18	22	28	26	19
Min °C	9	11	14	20	19	13
Rainfall	70	72	21	1	17	65

40

things not to miss

It's not possible to see everything that Portugal has to offer in one trip – and we don't suggest you try. What follows is a selective taste of the country's highlights: outstanding buildings and historic sights, natural wonders and vibrant events. They're arranged in five colour-coded categories, which you can browse through to find the very best things to see and experience. All highlights have a page reference to take you straight into the guide, where you can find out more.

01 Velha Universidade, Coimbra Page **215** • The country's oldest and most prestigious university adds a certain cachet to the city of Coimbra.

02 Pilgrimage to Fátima

Page **184** • Every May and October, thousands of devout Catholics descend to a giant square by the basilica to commemorate the Apparitions of the Virgin Mary.

04 Wines of the Ribatejo

Page **201** • Once you develop a taste for the fruity Portuguese varieties, you may find you want nothing else.

03 Coastline, Lagos

Page **593** • Explore the extraordinary shaped rocks and grottoes by boat from the historic Algarve port of Lagos.

05 Parque Natural de Montesinho

Page **476** • Bucolic unspoilt countryside dotted with traditional villages.

06 **Corgo train line** Page **452** • One of Portugal's great rides, the Corgo train line winds through spectacular gorges from Peso da Régua to Vila Real.

xiv

07 **Pinhal de Leiria** Page **178** • Little-visited, pine-fringed coastline with superb wave-battered beaches.

08 Convento de Cristo, Tomar Page **190** • Extraordinary former headquarters for the Knights Templars.

10 Parque Nacional da Peneda-Gerês Page **430** • Wild mountain terrain for walks and cycling.

ACTIVITIES | CONSUME | EVENTS | NATURE | SIGHTS |

11 Pastéis de Belém Page 99 •

These delicious flaky custard tartlets have been made and served for over a century at the *Antiga Confeitaria de Belém*.

12 Tram #28, Lisbon Page 69 •

The capital's best tram route, winding through all the historic districts.

13 Citânia de Briteiros Page 397 •

Step back to pre-Roman times at the magnificent Celtic hill fort.

14 Festa de São João

Page 299 • Expect to be pounded with plastic hammers at one of the country's most important saint's days, especially in Porto.

15 Mosteiro Palácio Nacional de Mafra Page
139 • With 5200 doors and 2500 windows, this lavish palace-convent nearly bankrupted the country when it was built in the eighteenth century.

17 Rio Douro valley Page
364 • Take a boat trip from Porto up one of the loveliest river valleys in the country.

18 Bom Jesus do Monte
Page **395** • Portugal's most photographed church, reached up a series of winding steps.

16 Ponte de Lima Page 424 • The
beautiful riverside town of Ponte de Lima is well-known for its quality rural accommodation.

19 **Museu de Arte Contemporânea de Serralves, Porto** Page
318 • Contemporary art from Warhol, Pollock and company in a wonderful building
remodelled by Portugal's leading architect, Álvaro Siza Vieira.

20 **Alfama, Lisbon** Page **91** • A village in the heart of the capital, with streets so
narrow and precipitous that few cars can enter.

21 Ericeira Page **156** • Hang out at this world-championship surfing beach.

22 Bacalhau Page **41** • Dried cod is the country's national dish, and with over 365 ways of cooking it, one of them is sure to be to your taste.

23 Azulejos Page **94** • Beautiful glazed tiles grace buildings and monuments throughout the country – the national collection in Lisbon has some fine examples.

24 **Bairro Alto, Lisbon** Page **80** • The capital's big night out – touring the bars, clubs and restaurants of the funky Bairro Alto neighbourhood.

25 **Óbidos** Page **164** • Picture-book walled town that was once the traditional bridal gift of Portuguese kings.

26 **Fado** Page **633** • Mariza, pictured, is one of the most critically acclaimed performers of Portugal's most famous musical genre.

27 **Museu Gulbenkian, Lisbon** Page **96** • One of Europe's greatest treasure chests of arts from ancient times to the twentieth century.

28 Alcobaça Page **172** • An impressive twelfth-century Cistercian monastery.

30 Ilha de Tavira Page **565** • Escape the Algarve crowds on the extensive sandspit beach on Tavira island.

29 Monsanto Page **290** • One of the country's most ancient hilltop settlements seems to grow out of the very rocks it's built upon.

31 Feira de Barcelos Page **400** • The country's liveliest and most colourful market shows that rural traditions are alive and well.

32 Serra da Estrela Page **270** • The highest mountains in Portugal conceal remotevillages and challenging hiking trails.

33 Porto's riverfront Page **298** • The historic riverside bairro of Ribeira is now a UNESCO World Heritage Site.

34 Guimarães
Page **381** •
The first capital of Portugal is a beguiling place of cobbled streets and historic buildings.

35 Conímbriga Page **220** •
The most important Roman site in Portugal.

36 Sintra Page **129** • The hilltop retreat near Lisbon is one of the most scenic in the country, surrounded by opulent palaces and country estates.

37 Pousadas
Page **145** • The country's pousadas (government-run hotels) make superb use of historic buildings, like the dramatic conversion of the Castelo de Palmela.

38 **Estádio da Luz, Lisbon** Page **120** • Portugal's most stunning sports stadium hosts top-class football matches throughout the season.

39 **Monsaraz** Page **510** • Many of the ancient houses in the fortified hilltop village of Monsaraz have been converted into atmospheric guest houses.

40 **Évora** Page **495** • UNESCO-protected university town complete with Roman temple, Moorish alleys and medieval walls.

Contents

Using this Rough Guide

We've tried to make this Rough Guide a good read and easy to use. The book is divided into six main sections, and you should be able to find whatever you want in one of them.

Colour section

The front colour section offers a quick survey of Portugal. The **introduction** aims to give you a feel for the country, with suggestions on where to go. We also tell you what the weather is like and include a basic country fact file. Next, our authors round up their favourite aspects of Portugal in the **things not to miss** section – whether it's the outdoors, amazing sights or a special hotel. Right after this comes a full **contents** list.

Basics

The **basics** section covers all the **pre-departure** nitty-gritty to help you plan your trip. This is where to find out which airlines fly to your destination, what paperwork you'll need, what to do about money and insurance, Internet access, food, public transport, car rental – in fact just about every piece of **general practical information** you might need.

Guide

This is the heart of the Rough Guide, divided into user-friendly chapters, each of which covers a specific region. Every chapter starts with a list of **highlights** and an **introduction** that helps you to decide where to go. Likewise, introductions to the various towns and smaller regions within each chapter should help you plan your itinerary. We start most town

accounts with information on arrival and accommodation, followed by a tour of the sights, and finally reviews of places to eat and drink, and details of nightlife. Longer accounts also have a directory of practical listings. Each chapter concludes with **public transport** details for that region.

Contexts

Read **contexts** to get a deeper understanding of what makes Costa Rica tick. We include a brief **history** of the country, an overview of its **environment** and **wildlife**, and a detailed further reading section that reviews dozens of **books** relating to Portugal.

Language

The **language** section gives useful guidance for speaking Spanish, Tico-style, and vocabulary you might need on your trip, including a comprehensive menu reader. Here you'll also find a glossary of words and terms particular to Costa Rica.

small print + Index

Apart from a **full index**, which includes maps as well as places, this section covers publishing information, credits and acknowledgements, and also has our contact details in case you want to send in updates and corrections to the book – or suggestions as to how we might improve it.

Map and chapter list

Contents

Contexts

609–647

Language

648–658

small print and Index

673–688

Basics

Basics

Getting there

The most convenient way of reaching Portugal, tucked away in the southwest corner of Europe, is to fly. There are regular international services to Lisbon, Faro and Porto, though travellers from outside Europe may find it cheaper to fly via London and arrange onward travel from there – in particular, there are no direct flights to Portugal from Australia or New Zealand. If you want to see some of France or Spain en route, or are taking a vehicle, there are various overland combinations of ferry, rail and road to consider, though bear in mind that these will nearly always work out pricier than flying, and that car rental in Portugal is relatively inexpensive. European rail passes might save you some money, but most of the major ones need to be purchased before you leave (see p.30 for more). If you're looking for more than just a flight, package holidays and tours can be good value, whether it's an Algarve beach holiday or escorted walking tour – and travel agents and specialist tour operators can also provide car rental, hotel bookings and other useful services.

Air fares are seasonal, with the highest – for flights from Europe or North America – in July and August, and at Christmas and New Year. Fares drop during the "shoulder" seasons – September and October, mid-March to June, and the ten days or so before Christmas. The rest of the year is low season. Coming from Australia and New Zealand, low season runs from February to mid-June and from September to mid-November; shoulder season is January and from mid-June to end-August; high season is mid-November to end-December. Note that advertised fares rarely include **airport taxes**, which can add £25–60 (€35–90/ US$45–105) to a return fare.

The cheapest flights from the UK and Ireland are usually with no-frills **budget** and **charter airlines**, especially if you're prepared to book several weeks (or months) in advance, or chance a last-minute deal. Budget airline tickets tend to be sold direct (by phone or internet) on a one-way basis, and you may find the outward or return leg of your journey significantly more expensive depending on demand. The flights also all have fixed dates, while return tickets with charter airlines may limit your stay to one month. The major **scheduled airlines** are usually (though not always) more expensive, but tickets remain valid for at least three months (often a year), and have a degree of

flexibility should you need to change dates after booking. You can cut costs by going through a **specialist flight** or **discount agent**, who may also offer charter flights, and special student and youth fares, plus a range of other travel-related services. An increasingly popular option is to **buy tickets online**: most airlines and discounters offer this service (indeed, many are internet-only) and, even if you prefer dealing with your local travel agent, the internet is invaluable for tracking down special offers and last-minute deals.

Booking flights online

Many airlines and discount travel websites offer you the opportunity to book your tickets online, cutting out the costs of agents and middlemen. The websites listed below all offer good deals and useful price comparisons.

Ⓦ **www.airline-network.co.uk** Discounter for UK scheduled flights, including TAP, BA and Monarch.

Ⓦ **www.cheapflights.co.uk,** Ⓦ **www .cheapflights.com,** Ⓦ **www.cheapflights.ca,** Ⓦ **www.cheapflights.com.au** Access to third-party search and booking engines, useful for tracking down specific flights and routes.

Ⓦ **www.farebase.net** Particularly useful for UK charter deals and holiday packages, with a great search engine.

Ⓦ **www.hotwire.com** US site with last-minute deals for over-18s; no refunds or changes.

Ⓦ **www.kelkoo.co.uk** Fast searches and bookings on a range of UK scheduled and charter flights, particularly competitive for BA, TAP and charter carrier Excel.

Ⓦ **www.lowestfare.com** Easy-to-use site for cheap flights from the US.

Ⓦ **www.opodo.co.uk** Owned by nine major European airlines; a reliable source of low fares on scheduled flights.

Ⓦ **www.portugal.com** Online US agency offering riding, walking and biking holidays, thematic tours, golfing, accommodation, car rental and flights.

Ⓦ **www.searstravel.ca** Good prices on scheduled flights from Canada through New York, and direct from New York.

Ⓦ **www.travel.com.au**, Ⓦ **www.travel. co.nz** Comprehensive online travel company with discounted fares from Australia/New Zealand.

Ⓦ **www.travelocity.com** US site with discount fares plus car rental and accommodation.

Ⓦ **www.zuji.com.au** Hot fares on major airlines from Oz, and handy fare comparisons.

From Britain

Flying to Faro, Lisbon or Porto takes two to three hours from airports around the UK. Given the plethora of budget and charter airlines serving the Algarve, Faro is generally the cheapest destination and, even in high season, return fares under £100 are common. Booking as early as possible – months in advance – is the key to a good price. But even if you miss the best deals, you're unlikely to part with more than £150–200 for a return flight to Portugal. Of course, if you leave it too late, or want a fully flexible ticket, you could spend as much as £400.

Flights

Budget airline easyJet has a daily year-round services to **Faro** from various airports (routes listed below), with prices directly related to seat availability, so as planes fill up the very low advertised fares (from under £40 return, plus taxes) gradually increase. Bmibaby has a similar setup, but only flies once a week in summer from Nottingham East Midlands, while Monarch's "scheduled" arm of its service has a daily flight from Gatwick. Seats on all three can be booked three to four months ahead. British Airways also has daily scheduled flights from Gatwick, starting at similarly low prices, and with the advantage

of being bookable up to a year in advance. Other scheduled airlines flying direct from the UK to Faro include Portuguese national airline TAP and Portugália.

The logic gets fuzzier with "flight-only" **charters**; Excel Airways and First Choice have good-value tickets whenever you book (from £100–120 return), but for Thomson Flights (Britannia), Monarch and Airtours, booking late is the trick. Their last-minute deals, departing from virtually every regional airport in the country, can cost as little as £75 return from London (£20–40 more from regional airports), though more realistically you'll pay £150–250 for a standard return bought in advance. Charters usually only operate in summer, the exceptions being First Choice's flights, and ones from Gatwick and Manchester.

There are fewer charters and low-cost outfits flying to **Lisbon and Porto**, but British Airways flights can be as cheap as those to Faro if you buy your ticket early. Flying BA from Heathrow to Lisbon starts at £92 return in high season, or £36 return from Gatwick to Porto. Even within a few weeks of departure, you should be able to find a high-season seat for around £150. Other airlines flying into Lisbon include Portugália (from Manchester) and TAP (from Heathrow), while direct flights to Porto are also operated by Iberia (from Gatwick), TAP (Heathrow), and Portugália (Manchester). If direct flights are full, most European airlines offer indirect flights from London or Manchester via their hubs, averaging a journey time of 5–6 hours: Lufthansa, via Frankfurt, is often good value.

Airlines

Airtours ☎0870/238 7788, Ⓦwww.airtours .co.uk. Charters to Faro: high season, 2–3 weekly from Gatwick, Manchester and Stansted, and fortnightly from Birmingham, Bristol, Cardiff, Edinburgh, Glasgow, Leeds, Liverpool, Newcastle, Norwich and Nottingham East Midlands, in low season every fortnight from Gatwick and Manchester.

Bmibaby ☎0870 264 2229, Ⓦ www.bmibaby. com. Weekly to Faro from Nottingham East Midlands, summer only, with handy connections from Dublin.

British Airways ☎0870/850 9850, Ⓦwww .britishairways.com. Daily to Faro and Porto from

Gatwick (except Sat in winter for Porto), and daily to Lisbon from Heathrow.

easyJet ☎0871/750 0100, ⓦwww.easyjet .com. Daily to Faro from Bristol, Nottingham East Midlands, Gatwick, Luton and Stansted.

Excel Airways ☎0870/998 9898, ⓦwww .excelairways.com. Twice-weekly summer charters to Faro from Gatwick, Birmingham, Manchester and Nottingham East Midlands.

First Choice ☎0870/850 3999, ⓦwww .firstchoice.co.uk. Year-round charters to Faro: weekly from Glasgow and Luton, twice-weekly from Birmingham and Nottingham East Midlands, three times a week from Bristol, Gatwick, Manchester and Stansted.

Lufthansa ☎0845/773 7747, ⓦwww.lufthansa .com. Daily from Heathrow to Lisbon or Faro via Frankfurt.

Monarch ☎0870/040 5040, ⓦwww.flymonarch .com. Daily scheduled flights from Gatwick to Faro, and once or twice weekly summer charters from Birmingham, Cardiff, Edinburgh, Glasgow, Leeds, Newcastle, Nottingham East Midlands and Stansted.

PGA Portugália ☎0870/755 0025, ⓦwww .flypga.com. Weekdays from Manchester to Faro, Lisbon and Porto, also weekends to Faro and Lisbon.

TAP ☎0845/601 0932, ⓦwww.tap-airportugal .pt. Daily from Heathrow to Faro, Lisbon and Porto. Online auction Thurs 9am-midnight GMT.

Thomson Flights ☎0800/000747, ⓦwww .thomsonflights.com. Summer charters to Faro: twice weekly from Cardiff, Gatwick, Liverpool, Luton and Manchester; once a week from Birmingham, Bristol, Edinburgh, Glasgow, Humberside, Newcastle, Norwich, Nottingham East Midlands and Teesside.

Discount flight and travel agents

Dial-A-Flight ☎0870/333 4488, ⓦwww .dialaflight.com. Efficient online search accessing rock-bottom fares to Lisbon and Porto as well as Faro.

eBookers ☎0870/814 0000, ⓦwww.ebookers .com. Low fares on scheduled flights, plus a range of other travel services.

Flightcentre ☎0870/499 0040, ⓦwww .flightcentre.co.uk. Guaranteed rock-bottom fares worldwide; perfect if you're flexible about dates and connections.

North South Travel ☎01245/608291, ⓦwww .northsouthtravel.co.uk. Friendly, competitive travel agency discounting fares to all destinations; profits support projects in the developing world.

STA Travel ☎0870/160 6070, ⓦwww.statravel .co.uk. Low-cost under-26 specialists; older customers welcome.

Travel Bag ☎0870/890 1456, ⓦwww.travelbag .co.uk. Great prices on most scheduled flights, often cheaper than charters or budget airlines; also handles car rental and insurance.

Travelcare ☎0870/112 0085, ⓦwww.travelcare .co.uk. Part of the Co-op group; extremely cheap packages, charters, scheduled flights and hotels, and last-minute deals.

Package holidays and tours

Standard **package holidays** (available from any high-street travel agent) concentrate on the Algarve's beaches, with accommodation usually in large resort hotels or villas; note that some companies only take two-week bookings in high season. Summer prices start at around £350 per person (including flights) for a week's bed and breakfast at a modest hotel or villa near the beach, though you'll have to search hard; more usual for week-long holidays is £400–700, including flights, with prices based on two people travelling together. In low season, last-minute deals can bring the cost of a week's or ten days' accommodation and flights into the £100–200 range.

Several companies also offer **fly-drive holidays** based around accommodation in historic manor houses and *pousadas* (upwards of £500 per person for a week, including flights and car), whilst others offer sporting holidays (mainly tennis and golf) and more specialized tours such as bird-watching, horse-riding, hiking, biking and wine tours. Summer **golfing packages** based in a three- or four-star hotel start at £500 a week, whilst other **specialized holidays** average £100–200 a day, depending on the style of accommodation. Most specialist tour operators should be able to arrange flights, insurance and car rental, and are flexible about extending flights, allowing you to indulge in some independent travel as well. The list of specialist operators below is of mainly smaller companies, directed towards arranging holidays for individuals.

Holiday and specialist tour operators

Abreu Tours ☎020/7313 2617, ⓦwww .abreu-tours.com. *Pousada* bookings, tailor-made holidays and fly-drive packages.

Arblaster & Clarke ☎01730/893344, ⓦwww
.winetours.co.uk. Sophisticated wine tour specialists
offering: four nights in Lisbon and Alentejo in
February; a romantic eight-day port wine cruise on a
sailing ship from Bilbao; or a seven-day Douro Walk
(and train ride), staying at port wine *quintas*. Land
accommodation in four-star hotels with meals at fine
restaurants.

ATG Oxford ☎01865/315678, ⓦwww.atg-oxford
.co.uk. Stylish five- and eight-day walking trips
through Alentejo, Minho and Lisbon region, staying
at intimate four- and five-star hotels, manor houses
and *pousadas*. There's an emphasis on fine food and
prices are reasonable for the quality.

Caravela ☎0870 443 8181, ⓦwww.caravela
.co.uk. TAP airline's touring arm covers most options,
from luxury golfing packages (from £750 a week at
a five-star hotel, including flights and car rental) and
Douro river cruises to fly-drive *pousada* holidays and
city breaks.

Destination Portugal ☎01993/773269 ⓦwww
.destination-portugal.co.uk. Long-established,
value-for-money agency offering flights and car
rental, golfing breaks, personalized thematic tours
(culture, history, wine) and accommodation bookings
at four-star hotels, *pousadas* and manor houses.

Equitour ☎01608/819182, ⓦwww.equitour
.co.uk. Classic horse-riding breaks throughout the
year in Alentejo and around Lisbon, with optional trail
riding. Accommodation is by the stables.

First Choice ☎0870/850 3999, ⓦwww
.firstchoice.co.uk. Major charter holiday operator for
the Algarve, mainly self-catering in villa complexes.
Very good last-minute deals, especially in winter.

GreyPower Travels ☎00-351/229 448 839,
ⓦwww.greypowertravels.com. Family-run tour
operator based in Porto, specializing in group tours
for over-55s, with one-week programmes in northern
Portugal and Galicia, the accent on history and culture.

Jonathan Markson Tennis ☎020/7603 2422,
ⓦwww.marksontennis.com. Three-star apartment
accommodation and intensive tuition at the Praia
da Luz Ocean Club near Lagos for wannabee tennis
stars – the week-long courses include 15 hours of
coaching.

Light Blue Travel ☎01223 568904, ⓦwww
.lightbluetravel.co.uk. Upmarket Algarve operator
combining a huge selection of villas and hotels
for tennis packages based at Vale do Lobo Tennis
Academy, with more mainstream villa and beach
resort holidays.

Limosa Holidays ☎01263/578143, ⓦwww.
limosaholidays.co.uk. Bird-watching in Alentejo,
Algarve and Madeira, including a ten-day
"Undiscovered Portugal" trip in May. There's some
walking involved. Price includes flights, minibus

transport and full board at modest local hotels and
restaurants.

Longshot Golf ☎0870/609 0995, ⓦwww
.longshotgolf.co.uk. One of the best golfing
specialists, with the emphasis on three- and seven-
day packages at resorts in the Algarve and around
Lisbon.

Magic of Portugal ☎0800/980 3378, ⓦwww
.magictravelgroup.co.uk. A build-your-own-holiday
setup, with a good selection of moderately priced
villas with pools, plus year-round golfing packages
and self-drive tours.

Portuguese Affair ☎020/7385 4775, ⓦwww
.portugueseaffair.com. High-quality but value-for-
money villa holidays in the Algarve, Alentejo, Minho
and Sintra. Also handles flights and car rental.

Pure Vacations ⓦwww.purevacations.com/surf.
Affordable week-long surfing holidays, with basic villa
accommodation. Prices are with breakfast or half-
board and include local transport and optional tuition,
but not flights. Summer only to Peniche and Lagos, all
year to Sagres.

Ramblers Holidays ☎01707/331133, ⓦwww
.ramblersholidays.co.uk. Good-value one- and
two-week walking trips in the eastern Algarve
(based at Tavira), Alentejo, Lisbon, the Douro valley
and northern parks. The emphasis is on nature,
and accommodation is in simple hotels. Several
departures weekly throughout the year.

Rough Tracks ☎070/0056 0749, ⓦwww
.roughtracks.com. Relaxed point-to-point cycling
jaunts (5–6hr a day) in and around Gerês, and from
Lisbon to Faro, with accommodation in local pensions
and hotels. Prices are based on half-board and
exclude flights. Monthly departures between April and
July and from Sept to Nov.

Something Special ☎0870/165 2603, ⓦwww
.somethingspecial.co.uk. Huge selection of Algarve
villas, most with pools.

Thomson Villas with Pools ☎0870/166
0367, ⓦwww.thomsonvillas.co.uk. Vast selection
of Algarve villas (at Vilamoura, Albufeira, Silves
and Carvoeiro) to suit most budgets, and can be
packaged online with reasonably priced flights.

Travel Club of Upminster ☎01708/225 000,
ⓦwww.travelclub.org.uk. Long-established
family-run travel agency offering accommodation in
four- and five-star beach resorts as well as villas.

Travellers Way ☎01527 559000, ⓦwww
.travellersway.co.uk. One-stop agency for quality
villa vacations, golf and riding holidays.

By train

London to Lisbon by train takes at least 24
hours via the Channel Tunnel, and closer

to 40 hours if you use the cross-Channel ferry. It's usually more expensive than flying, even if you qualify for under-26 or over-60 discounts, or buy a railpass (see "Getting around", p.29), and as such is generally a last resort unless you're planning to stop off in France or Spain.

The cheapest standard **return fare** for the London–Lisbon routing from London Charing Cross, over the Channel by ferry and with no couchette reservation in Spain, is at least £200, and involves transferring stations in Paris (from Nord to Austerlitz). Tickets are valid for two months and allow stops anywhere along the pre-specified route; dates can be freely changed after booking. The quicker route from London Waterloo, using the Channel Tunnel's Eurostar train service, starts at £250 return, including obligatory seat reservations on the *TGV Atlantique* (from Paris Montparnasse to the Spanish border at Hendaye/Irún) and couchette (optional) on the overnight *Sud-Expresso* (from the border to Lisbon). Through tickets on either route can be bought from your nearest UK mainline station, or from one of the agents listed on p.31.

By bus

Eurolines (☎0870/514 3219, ⊛www.eurolines.co.uk) operates various services to Portugal, but it's a long journey (35–38hr depending on your destination) from the UK. There are at least two bus changes involved: one at Lille in France, the other at Serrano in Spain. Buses leave daily from London Victoria: Lisbon costs £148 return, Faro £168, and reductions are available for under-26s and over-60s – tickets can be bought online or from any National Express agent. Alternatively, if you make your own way to Paris, to the Porte de Charenton terminus, there are daily buses to Lisbon and Porto and fairly regular services to most other towns in Portugal. Coming back, you can join these buses at any stage, provided you've made an advance reservation. Tiring though these journeys are, they're comfortable enough, and broken by frequent rest and meal stops. As long as you take plenty to eat, drink and read (and some euros to use along the way), you should emerge relatively unscathed.

By car, ferry and Eurotunnel

Drivers have over a dozen **ferry routes** from the UK to choose from, mainly to France but also to northern Spain (see list below). The 60–90 minute Dover to Calais hop is the cheapest crossing, the 18–35hr sailings to Spain the most expensive, though the latter will shave at least a day from the total driving time, as it's just a day's drive from Spain to Portugal. Using the Channel crossings and taking the quickest route (by motorway through Bordeaux, and again by motorway across Spain), the drive will take two days, though you'll arrive pretty exhausted. Count on at least three days, ideally four or five, to get off the motorways and really enjoy the journey.

Fares are at a premium Thursday to Sunday between mid-July and the end of August, whilst the cheapest tickets are for night sailings. In general, you can expect to pay £250–275 in high season for a two-week return from Dover or Newhaven for a car with two adults and two children, or £300–350 on Hoverspeed's catamaran service. Sailing from other English ports, expect to pay £200–450 return depending on the season, whilst motorcyclists will cough up £100–180 return.

A quicker alternative to the ferries for drivers is the **Eurotunnel** shuttle train via the Channel Tunnel (☎0800/096 9992, ⊛www.eurotunnel.com). The service runs continuously between Folkestone and Coquelles, near Calais (up to four departures an hour, every 2hr at night; journey time 35–45min). It's possible to turn up and buy your ticket at the toll booths, though at peak periods booking is advisable. As with the ferries, it's cheaper to travel midweek and at night (10pm–6am), while July and August attract premiums. A standard one-way ticket for a car in June, including passengers, is £165; the same for July and August weekends is £180 for a fixed-date fare booked months in advance, or £275 for more flexibility.

The best way of cutting down the driving time to Portugal is to catch a ferry to either Santander or Bilbao in northern Spain. Brittany Ferries sails from **Plymouth to Santander** (March–Nov 1–2 weekly; 18–24hr), and P&O Ferries from **Portsmouth to Bilbao** (2

Overland from Spain

Combining a trip to Portugal with Spain is simple, especially if you leave from Madrid, Bilbao, Málaga or Santiago de Compostela: tickets on easyJet from the UK to any of these can cost as little as £24 return if bought months in advance, though £120–200 is more likely. There are also cheap flights on Aer Lingus from Ireland to Alicante, Madrid and Valencia. Bus and train connections from Madrid, Málaga, Santiago de Compostela and Seville to Portugal are easy, with rewarding stops en route. Rail passes (see p.30) are valid on all the routes below, but you'll be liable for supplements on many trains. There are of course numerous other border road crossings, but if you're in a rental car remember to check whether you're covered to take the vehicle between countries.

From Madrid (Chamartin station), the overnight *Lusitânia Comboio Hotel* takes 10hr 30min to Lisbon, arriving in time for breakfast. The train has seats and couchettes, plus one- and two-bed cabins complete with showers. Prices start at €53 one-way, €85 return (or €74/€119 with a bed); change at Entroncamento in Portugal for Coimbra and Porto. Tickets can be bought at Chamartin, or through the Spanish railway company's website (ⓦ www.renfe.es; it's under "Trenhotel Lusitânia"). If you want to see the glorious countryside on this line in daylight your best bet is to start at the Spanish city of **Badajoz**, on the train line from Madrid. This lies 5hr 30min from Lisbon and is a close neighbour of Elvas, the first stop the train makes in Portugal, while other stops are at Portalegre and Abrantes.

Another scenic route – the one taken by the *Sud-Expresso* from the French border at Hendaye/Irún – passes through **Salamanca**, entering Portugal at Vilar Formoso in Beira Alta, and calling at Portugal's highest town, Guarda. The sun should have risen well before reaching Portugal, leaving you with a lovely ride past Guarda and the stark, boulder-strewn landscape beyond; change at Coimbra for Porto. Tickets for the entire Hendaye–Lisbon journey cost €62 one-way, €99 return, and again can be bought through the RENFE website (look for "Surex"); the cost from Salamanca is €45 one-way, €73 return.

From **northern Spain**, two trains a day connect Vigo in Galicia to Porto (around 3hr 30min), passing the border at Tuy/Valença on the River Minho, then following the river and coast down via Vila Praia de Âncora, Viana do Castelo and Barcelos.

From Málaga you are well placed to head for the Algarve and, if you have the time, you could take in a loop through the great Andalusian cities of Granada, Córdoba and Seville (though note that the Málaga–Granada and Granada–Córdoba journeys are quicker by bus). At Córdoba, you're back on the main train line to Seville from where daily **buses** run to the Portuguese border at Ayamonte/Vila Real de Santo António, for onward transport by bus or train along the Algarve coast.

From North America

The only direct non-stop services between North America and Portugal are from New York (JFK or Newark) to Lisbon, or Toronto to Lisbon or Porto, a flight time of seven hours; from all other cities you'll need to get a connecting flight via New York or a European airport. If you want to fly to Porto or Faro, TAP can organize onward flights from Lisbon, while some of the European airlines, such as BA, Lufthansa and Air France, fly direct to Porto and/or Faro from their home hubs. Another option is to take advantage of cut-price tickets between the US and London (from $600–700 return east coast, $1000 west coast), with airlines like Virgin, American Airlines, British Airways and United, and then make your way from there, as the onward flight from London to Portugal can cost as little as US$150 return (see "From Britain: Flights" for all the details). This is also an option from Canada (Toronto and Montreal to London from CDN$1000–1100, Vancouver from CDN$1400), especially from Vancouver, whose indirect Lisbon services are fairly pricey. Weekly direct flights from Toronto to Lisbon and Porto are operated by Azorean operator SATA, connecting with flights on Continental, and in Portugal with Portugália and TAP.

Flights

Direct flights **from New York** to Lisbon are operated by American Airlines (in conjunction with TAP) and Continental; return flights on either can be picked up for under $1000 in high season. Indirect flights via a European hub can be $100 cheaper, and journey times are 11 to 13 hours. Currently good value are British Airways and Delta, with American Airlines/TAP and Continental not far behind. Low season fares can be 30 to 50 percent cheaper, so long as you're not pernickety about connection times.

All flights to Portugal from **central USA** and the **west coast** involve changing planes, either in New York or in Europe. From the Pacific Coast, expect to pay around about $300 on top of the New York fare; from Chicago, the extra cost is around $250. The actual fare depends in large part on connection times: you pay more for shorter waits (ideal flight time from LA being 15–16hr), and less for longer routings, sometimes with two stops (which can push journey times to 17–22hr). Cheapest airlines are usually BA, American Airlines/TAP and Continental.

There are no direct flights **from Canada** to Portugal; most airlines route through New York or Europe. Flight times from Montreal and Toronto to Lisbon are around 10–12 hours; 14–15 hours is the best you can hope for from Vancouver. From Toronto, Continental via New York has high season returns starting at CDN$1560, while British Airways and partners (Air Canada and bmi) have fares under CDN$1900. From Montreal, TAP (in conjunction with United and Air Canada) is the best bet, with high-season fares via London starting under CDN$1400. From Vancouver, Lisbon in one-hop is served by KLM, BA (with bmi or Air Canada) and others, but fares start at CDN$2200 and frequently top CDN$3000.

Airlines

American Airlines ☎1-800/433-7300, ⓦwww .aa.com. Daily service direct from New York to Lisbon and London.
British Airways ☎1-800/AIRWAYS, ⓦwww .britishairways.com. Daily direct from New York to London, with connections from all over Canada and the US. Also New York, other US cities and Vancouver via London to Lisbon, Porto and Faro. Code shares with Air Canada and bmi.
Continental Airlines ☎1-800/231-0856, ⓦwww.continental.com. Newark to Lisbon via

London (code sharing with TAP), connections from Toronto and elsewhere.
Delta ☎1-800/241-4141, ⓦwww.delta.com. Indirect from New York to Lisbon.
Northwest/KLM International ☎1-800/447-4747, ⓦwww.nwa.com, ⓦwww.klm.com. Vancouver to Lisbon with one stop.
SATA Canada ☎416/515-7188, ⓦwww.sata.pt. Weekly from Toronto to Lisbon and Porto.
TAP (Air Portugal) ☎1-800/221-7370, ⓦwww .tap-airportugal.pt. Code shares with Continental for New York to Lisbon; Montreal to Lisbon via London (in conjunction with United and Air Canada).
United Airlines ☎1-800/538-2929, ⓦwww .united.com. Daily direct from New York to London.
Virgin Atlantic ☎1-800/862-8621, ⓦwww.virgin -atlantic.com. Daily direct from New York to London.

Discount flight and travel agents

Educational Travel Center ☎1-800/747-5551 or 608/256-5551, ⓦwww.edtrav.com. Low-cost fares worldwide, student/youth discount offers, car rental, accommodation, tours and rail passes.
Flightcentre US ☎1-866/WORLD-51, ⓦwww .flightcentre.us, Canada ☎1-888/WORLD-55, ⓦwww.flightcentre.ca. Guaranteed rock-bottom fares worldwide, and last-minute deals.
New Frontiers/Nouvelles Frontières ☎1-800/677-0720, ⓦwww.newfrontiers.com. Discount packages and flights.
Now Voyager ☎212/459-1616, ⓦwww .nowvoyagertravel.com. Quirky courier flight broker.
Orbitz ☎1-888/656-4546, ⓦwww.orbitz.com. At-a-glance fare comparisons and bookings on all major airlines from the States to London or Lisbon, with great follow-up customer service. US only.
STA Travel US ☎1-800/329-9537, Canada ☎1-888/427-5639, ⓦwww.statravel.com. Independent travel specialists; also student IDs, travel insurance, car rental and rail passes.
Student Flights ☎1-800/255-8000 (US) or 480/951-1177, ⓦwww.isecard.com/studentflights. Student/youth fares, plus student IDs and rail and bus passes.
Travel Avenue ☎1-800/333-3335, ⓦwww .travelavenue.com. Full-service travel agent; discounts given as rebates.
Travel Cuts US ☎1-800/592-CUTS, Canada ☎1-888/246-9762, ⓦwww.travelcuts.com. Long-established student-travel organization.

Package holidays and tours

Standard **package holidays and tours** from North America tend to concentrate on the cultural side of things, including port wine cruises along the Douro River, and historically themed tours with overnight accommodation in upmarket *pousadas* and manor houses. These holidays can also be done as fly-drive packages. Given the volatility of flight prices, costs are usually quoted excluding flights, though all operators can book flights for you.

High-season "no-flight" prices start at around US$450 for a seven-night self-drive holiday, with overnights in good four-star hotels or manor houses, and $500–600 for specialist wine-, cultural- or historically-themed tours, either self-drive or by minibus. More **exclusive tours**, ranging from ten nights to over two weeks, staying in top-notch *pousadas* and manor houses, start at $1000 for all meals included; the same with flights included would be at least $1500. All-inclusive **golfing and tennis packages** start at around $800 a week without flights. The list of specialist operators below is of mainly smaller companies, directed towards arranging holidays for individuals. For more Portuguese specialists, see ⓦ www.atop .org. Some UK-based operators will also take "no-flight" bookings from North America; see p.13.

Specialist tour operators

Abreu Tours Ⓣ 1-800/223-1580 or 212/760-3301, ⓦ www.abreu-tours.com. Portuguese travel agency handling everything from *pousada* bookings and tailor-made holidays to land/air packages.

Cross-Culture Ⓣ 1-800/491-1148 or 413/256-6303, ⓦ www.crosscultureinc.com. Small-group cultural tours all over Portugal.

Easy Rider Tours Ⓣ 800/488-8332, ⓦ www .easyridertours.com. Off-the-beaten-path bike tours throughout spring and autumn, either in eastern Alentejo, along the coast between Lisbon and the Algarve, or in the Minho's vinho verde region. Accommodation is in modest hotels.

EC Tours Ⓣ 1-800/388-0877, ⓦ www.ectours .com. Luxury yet affordable year-round tours, including fly-drive and *pousada* accommodation.

Europe Through the Back Door Ⓣ 425/771-8303, ⓦ www.ricksteves.com. Excellent travel club running good-value "free-spirited tours" by bus to Spain and Portugal.

GreyPower Travels Ⓣ 001-351/229 448 839, ⓦ www.greypowertravels.com. Family-run tour operator based in Porto, specializing in group tours for over-55s, with one-week programmes in northern Portugal and Galicia, the accent on history and culture.

Magellan Tours Ⓣ 1-856/786-6969, ⓦ www .magellantours.com. Upmarket Portugal specialists arranging golfing trips, cruises, wine tours, *pousada* and manor house accommodation, fly-drive holidays, and Lisbon city breaks.

Maupintour Ⓣ 1-800/255-4266, ⓦ www .maupintour.com. Various luxury tours of Portugal and Spain featuring luxurious accommodation in *pousadas* and five-star hotels.

Pinto Basto Tours Ⓣ 1-800/526-8539, ⓦ www .pousada.com. Fly-drive holidays and customized special interest trips, including hiking, watersports and Douro river cruises, all featuring *pousadas* and small, characterful hotels.

Untours (Idyll) Ⓣ 1-888/868-6871, ⓦ www .untours.com. All-in-one agent offering a blend of independent travel and guided tour over 2 or 4 weeks, based in apartments in Sintra. Profits fund community projects.

From Australia and New Zealand

Although there are no direct flights from Australia or New Zealand to Portugal, airlines offer through tickets with their partners via European or Asian hubs. Whichever you choose, keep an eye on connection times; some, like the British Airways/Qantas combo, are slick and take under 26 hours, but others – usually cheaper – may see you twiddling your thumbs in a departure lounge for up to a day. If you're planning several stopovers en route, consider a **Round-the-World** (RTW) ticket, which is valid for a year. The BA/Qantas "European Explorer" ticket (A$2400–3200) gives you three stopovers in Asia and Europe, including Portugal, while other more flexible RTW tickets cost A$3270–4680 depending on the start date.

High-season returns **from Australia** to Lisbon average A$2100–3000, though rock-bottom deals – often with obscure East Asian airlines such as Air China, China Airlines, China Eastern Airlines and Vietnam Airlines – can be found for A$1450–1750. Of the major carriers, consistently cheapest are Air France, KLM and their partners, while Singapore and Cathay Pacific are also good value. Flying into London instead is usually cheaper than flying to Lisbon, but not so much as to guarantee saving money overall. The lowest London fares start at about A$1500 return, though with a major airline it's more likely to be in the A$1750–2300 range, depending on your departure city. See p.12 for details of flights from the UK to Portugal.

High-season economy return fares **from New Zealand** to Lisbon are pretty stable, starting at NZ$2450 (Cathay Pacific Airways/Crossair), levelling out at NZ$2600–3000. From Christchurch or Wellington you'll pay around NZ$200 more; cheapest is usually Air New Zealand/Lufthansa. In contrast, fares to London are volatile, varying significantly between airlines, though averaging NZ$2400–3000 from Auckland and NZ$2600–2900 from Christchurch. Shopping around might get this down to around NZ$1800, and overall the cheapest airlines are Emirates, Air New Zealand (code-sharing with Lufthansa), JAL, Singapore, Cathay (code-sharing with Crossair), and KLM, while other airlines worth keeping tabs on include Korean Air and SriLankan. Fares on Qantas/BA invariably weigh in at the upper end of the scale.

Only a couple of Antipodean **tour operators** specialize in Portugal, though both are flexible enough to cover most possibilities and budgets. Prices vary enormously given the volatility of airfares. For "no-flight" packages, expect to pay upwards of A$900 or NZ$1000 for an eight-day cultural holiday with transport by minibus or rental car, staying full board at *pousadas* and manor houses. For more choice, some UK-based operators will also take "no-flight" bookings; see pp.13–14.

Airlines

Air China Australia ☏02/9232 7277, ⓦwww.airchina.com.cn.
Air France Australia ☏1300/361400, New Zealand ☏09/308 3352, ⓦwww.airfrance.com.
Air New Zealand Australia ☏132476, ⓦwww.airnz.com.au, New Zealand ☏0800/737 000, ⓦwww.airnz.co.nz.
British Airways Australia ☏1300/767177, New Zealand ☏0800/274847 or 09/356 8690, ⓦwww.britishairways.com.

Cathay Pacific Australia ☏131747, New Zealand ☏0508/800 454 or 09/379 0861, ⓦwww.cathaypacific.com.
China Airlines Australia ☏02/9244 2121, New Zealand ☏09/308 3371, ⓦwww.china-airlines.com.
China Eastern Airlines Australia ☏02/9290 1148, ⓦwww.ce-air.com.
Emirates Australia ☏1300/303 777 or 02/9290 9700, New Zealand ☏09/377 6004, ⓦwww.emirates.com.
KLM Australia ☏1300/303747, New Zealand ☏09/309 1782, ⓦwww.klm.com.
Qantas Australia ☏131313, New Zealand ☏0800/808767 or 09/357 8900, ⓦwww.qantas.com.
Singapore Airlines Australia ☏131011, New Zealand ☏0800/808 909, ⓦwww.singaporeair.com.
Vietnam Airlines Australia ☏02/9283 1355, ⓦwww.vietnamairlines.com.

Travel agents and tour operators

Flightcentre Australia ☏133133, ⓦwww.flightcentre.com.au, New Zealand ☏0800/243544, ⓦwww.flightcentre.co.nz. Guaranteed rock-bottom fares worldwide; perfect if you're flexible about dates and connections.
Holiday Shoppe New Zealand ☏0800/808480, ⓦwww.holidayshoppe.co.nz. Great deals on flights and holidays; the online selection is limited though.
Ibertours Australia ☏1800/500016, New Zealand ☏0800/444843, ⓦwww.ibertours.com.au. Classy escorted and solo tours, including on foot, through Spain, Portugal and Morocco. Emphasis on history, culture and gastronomy, with nights in *pousadas* and manor houses, though they're happy arranging overnights at cheaper places. One or trips weekly throughout the year.
Silke's Travel Australia ☏1800 807 860 or 02/8347 2000, ⓦwww.silkes.com.au. Specialist agency for gay and lesbian travellers.
STA Travel Australia ☏1300/733035, ⓦwww.statravel.com.au; New Zealand ☏0508/782872, ⓦwww.statravel.co.nz. Low-cost under-26 specialists; older customers welcome; good online search engine.
Trailfinders Australia ☏02/9247 7666, ⓦwww.trailfinders.com.au. Well-informed and efficient agents for independent travellers.

Red tape and visas

EU citizens need only a valid passport or identity card to enter Portugal, and can stay indefinitely. Citizens of Canada, the US, Australia and New Zealand do not need a visa for stays of up to 90 days. Most other nationals will have to apply for a visa from a Portuguese embassy or consulate – there's a full list at ⊛www .min-nestrangeiros.pt/mne/estrangeiro. Entry conditions can change, however, so check the situation before leaving home on ⊛www.eurovisa.info.

If necessary, an **extension to your stay** can be arranged once you're in the country. Extensions are issued by the nearest District Police headquarters or the Foreigner's Registration Service – **Serviço de Estrangeiros e Fronteiras** (⊛www.sef.pt) – which has branch offices in most major tourist centres. You should apply at least a week before your time runs out and be prepared to prove that you can support yourself without working (for example by keeping your bank exchange forms every time you change money). Extended stay visas are also available through Portuguese consulates.

Portuguese embassies and consulates abroad

Australia 23 Culgoa Circuit, O'Malley ACT 2606 ☎02/6290 1733, ℮embportcamb@internode

.on.net. Plus consulates in Sydney, Melbourne, Brisbane, Adelaide, Darwin and Fremantle.
Canada 645 Island Park Drive, Ottawa K1Y 0B8 ☎613/729-0883, ℮embportugal@embportugal -ottawa.org. Plus consulates in Vancouver, Montreal and Toronto.
Ireland Knocksinna House, Knocksinna, Foxrock, Dublin 18 ☎01/289 4416, ℮ptembasseydublin@tinet.ie.
New Zealand Nearest embassy is in Canberra, Australia. Consulates: PO Box 305, 33 Garfield St, Parnell, Auckland ☎09/309 1454; and PO Box 1024, Suite 1, 1st floor, 21 Marion St, Wellington ☎04/382 7655.
UK 11 Belgrave Sq, London SW1X 8PP ☎020/7235 5331, ℮london@portembassy .co.uk.
USA 2125 Kalorama Rd NW, Washington DC 20008 ☎202/328-8610, ℮embportwash@attglobal. net. Plus consulates in New York, Boston and San Francisco.

Health

Portugal poses few health problems for the visitor, and the worst that's likely to happen to you is that you might fall victim to an upset stomach. As an EU country, Portugal has free reciprocal health agreements with other member states. EU citizens don't need an E111 form (available from main post offices) on a temporary visit – simply show your passport at a health centre or hospital.

No **inoculations** are required, though you'll want to make sure you're up to date with your tetanus jab. **Tapwater** is generally safe to drink, although most visitors and indeed

Portuguese prefer bottled water, especially in summer, and this is recommended if you have a sensitive stomach. Under no circumstances should you drink warm, cloudy or discoloured tapwater, and avoid ice in less salubrious-looking bars and cafés. Otherwise, just use common sense: wash and peel fruit and vegetables, and avoid eating snacks that appear to have been sitting in display cabinets for too long. **Mosquitoes** can be a menace in the summer, especially in the Algarve, but – except for very rare and isolated cases – malaria is absent. Mosquito-to-repellent lotion and coils are widely sold in supermarkets and pharmacies. Take care to use a high-factor **sun cream** as the sun is extremely powerful.

For minor complaints go to a **farmácia** (pharmacy); most have a green neon cross outside. There's one in virtually every village and English is often spoken. Pharmacists are highly trained and can dispense drugs that would be prescription-only in Britain or North America. Generic drugs are widely available. Opening hours are usually Monday to Friday 9am to 1pm and 3 to 7pm, Saturday 9am to 1pm. Local papers carry information about 24-hour or nighttime pharmacies (*farmácias de serviço*) and the

details are also posted on every pharmacy door. Condoms – *preservativos* – are widely available from street vending machines, and in pharmacies and supermarkets. In more rural places you may have to ask and the pharmacist will set out an array on the counter, in the best formal Portuguese manner.

In an **emergency**, dial ☎112 (free); the ambulance service (*ambulância*) is run by volunteers and is also free. A **hospital** is the first port of call; details are given in the "Listings" sections at the end of each major town or city account. Standards of care are perfectly adequate once you get past the waiting room, and cases are dealt with according to urgency. Basic hospital treatment is free for EU citizens, though you'll have to pay for X-rays, lab tests and the like. Contact details of **English-speaking doctors** can be obtained from British or American consular offices or, with luck, from the local tourist office or a major hotel; consultation fees average €20–30. There's also a British Hospital in Lisbon (see "Listings", p.123).

Insurance

Although EU health care privileges apply in Portugal, it's essential to take out a travel insurance policy before travelling to cover against loss, theft and illness or injury. Before paying for a new policy it's worth checking whether you're already covered: some all-risks home insurance policies may cover your possessions when overseas, and many private medical schemes include cover when abroad.

Even so, you still might want to contact a specialist travel insurance company, or consider the travel insurance deal we offer (see below). A typical travel insurance policy usually provides cover for the loss of baggage, tickets and – up to a certain limit – cash or cheques, as well as cancellation or curtailment of your journey. Most of them exclude so-called dangerous sports unless an extra premium is paid: in Portugal this can mean scuba diving, windsurfing, trekking and kayaking. Many policies can be chopped and

changed to exclude coverage you don't need - for example, sickness and accident benefits can often be excluded or included at will. If you do take medical coverage, ascertain whether benefits will be paid as treatment proceeds or only after you return home, and if there is a 24-hour medical emergency number. When securing baggage cover, make sure that the per-article limit – typically under £500/$750 and sometimes as little as £250/$400 – will cover your most valuable possession.

Rough Guides travel insurance

Rough Guides Ltd offers a low-cost travel insurance policy, especially custom-ized for our statistically low-risk readers by a leading British broker, provided by the American International Group (AIG) and registered with the British regulatory body, GISC (the General Insurance Standards Council). There are five main Rough Guides insurance plans: No Frills for the bare minimum for secure travel; Essential, which provides decent all-round cover; Premier for comprehensive cover with a wide range of benefits; Extended Stay for cover lasting four months to a year; and Annual Multi-Trip, a cost-effective way of getting Premier cover if you travel more than once a year. Premier, Annual Multi-Trip and Extended Stay policies can be supplemented by a "Hazardous Pursuits Extension" if you plan to indulge in sports considered dangerous, such as scuba diving or trekking. For a policy quote, call the Rough Guide Insurance Line: toll-free in the UK ☏0800/0150906 or +44 1392 314 665 from elsewhere. Alternatively, get an online quote at ⓦwww.roughguides .com/insurance.

If you need to make a claim, you should keep receipts for medicines and medi-cal treatment, and in the event you have anything stolen, you must obtain an **official statement** from the police (a *formulário de participação de roubo*); police stations are included in "Listings" throughout the guide.

Information, maps and websites

You can request a wide range of free brochures and maps from ICEP Portugal (the Portuguese trade and tourism agency) in your home country, or consult their website ⓦwww.portugal.org. Portugal's official tourism website ⓦwww.portuga-linsite.com is another good place to start for basic country information.

Information offices

In Portugal itself you'll find a tourist office, or **turismo**, in almost every town. Most are listed in the guide (with full opening hours and con-tact details) and are usually helpful and frien-dly; at least one member of staff in each office will usually speak English, and often other languages, too. Note that the official opening times given in the guide do not always apply, particularly in more rural places where offices are short-staffed. Aside from the help they can give in finding a room (some will make bookings, others simply supply lists), they often have useful local maps to supplement the ones in this book and leaflets that you won't find in the national offices.

In addition, there's a national **telepho-ne enquiries service** (Contact Center ☏808/781 212, Mon–Fri 8am–7pm), whose English-speaking operators give information about museums and their opening times, transport practicalities and timetables, hotels and restaurants (no prices given or bookings made), and hospitals and police stations, among other information. Calls are charged at local rates.

ICEP Portugal offices abroad

Canada 60 Bloor St West, Suite 1005, Toronto, Ontario N3W 3B8 ☏416/921-7376, ⓔicep .toronto@icep.pt.

Ireland 54 Dawson St, Dublin 2 ℡01/670 9133, brochure line ℡1800/943131, ℮info@icep.ie. **UK** Portuguese Embassy, 11 Belgrave Sq, London SW1X 8PP ℡020/7201 6666, brochure line ℡0845/355 1212, ℮tourism@portugaloffice.co.uk. **USA** 590 Fifth Avenue, 4th Floor, New York, NY 10036-4702 ℡212/719-3985, ℮tourism@portugal.org.

Portugal on the internet

There's a lot of information about Portugal in English available on the internet, and the websites listed below are a useful starting point, whether you want to find out local festival dates or the best wine vintages. The country's newspapers all have their own websites too (see p.47), which, while in Portuguese, can be useful sources of information.

General sites

ⓦ **www.algarvenet.com** A detailed site dedicated to the Algarve, covering everything from tourist sites to weather and shopping.
ⓦ **www.maisturismo.pt** Search engine for hotels of all categories throughout Portugal, plus manor houses and other rural tourism choices.
ⓦ **www.paginasamarelas.pt** The Portuguese Yellow Pages. Telephone numbers can also be found through ⓦ www.118.pt.
ⓦ **www.portugalvirtual.pt** Comprehensive directory of everything from hotels to shops, tourist sites and businesses.

Food and wine

ⓦ **www.gastronomias.com** An encyclopedia of Portuguese gastronomy, with thousands of recipes organized by region, plus restaurant reviews, and features on cheese and wine. Only some pages have English translations.
ⓦ **www.infoportwine.com** An independent port wine site, with up-to-date practical advice and reviews for travelling along the Douro.
ⓦ **www.ivp.pt** Everything you every wanted to known about port wine, from the official Instituto dos Vinhos do Douro e do Porto.
ⓦ **www.vinhoverde.pt** The official site for vinho verde, with information about producers, labels, regional history and attractions.

Sport and leisure

ⓦ **www.algarvegolf.net** Provides a full rundown of all the Algarve's golf courses.

ⓦ **www.portuguesesoccer.com** Independent soccer magazine in English, with reports on games, fixtures and links to official club websites.
ⓦ **www.sailing.org/sailingclubs/por.asp** The International Sailing Federation site has links to all Portugal's major sailing clubs.
ⓦ **www.surfingportugal.com** All the news and information (in Portuguese) you need for surfing in Portugal.

Culture

ⓦ **www.blitz.pt** Online Portuguese magazine on contemporary underground sounds, including interviews, concert reviews and music clips.
ⓦ **www.ipmuseus.pt** The Portuguese Museums Institute: info on over 100 museums, special events, and links to their websites.
ⓦ **www.ippar.pt** Instituto Português do Patromónio Arquitectónico website (Portuguese only) has lots on Portugal's historical buildings, including a calendar of events held in them.
ⓦ **www.juliopereira.pt** An attractive introduction to traditional Portuguese music, with some text in English.
ⓦ **http://paginas.fe.up.pt/~fado** Comprehensive site dedicated to Portugal's most famous musical genre, with details on everything from singers to how to tune a fado guitar.
ⓦ **www.portugal.org/tourism/calendar.shtml** Comprehensive, annually updated festival and events calendar.
ⓦ **www.uc.pt/artes/6spp** Six centuries of Portuguese painting (in Portuguese only), with reproductions from most major artists' works.

Maps

The best country map is the waterproof and untearable **Rough Guide Map: Portugal** (1:350,000), while also good is Michelin's Portugal (1:400,000, #440), and Geo Centre's Euro Map Portugal and Galicia (1:300,000). The Portuguese National Tourist Office and the turismos in larger towns can also provide you with a reasonable map of the country (1:600,000), which is fine for everything except mountain roads. Similar maps and more detailed regional plans can be bought at most service stations in cities, larger towns and along major highways. Rough Guides also produces a map of **Lisbon** (marked with shops, bars, hotels and restaurants, local transport routes and the surrounding area), and Michelin's Lisboa Planta Roteiro is pretty good too. For the

Algarve, get a copy of the Rough Guide Map: The Algarve (1:100,000). For **northern Portugal**, the best is Turinta's North of Portugal map (1:250,000).

The Geocid **website** at ⊛http://geocid-snig .igeo.pt offers high-resolution satellite and aerial topographic images, and innumerable maps of almost all of Portugal. For **walking and hiking**, the best maps are the 1:25,000 topographic plans belonging to the so-called "Série M888", produced by the Instituto Geográfico do Exército (⊛www.igeoe. pt). You can order them online from the Institute, or from shops in Portugal; see below. Just as useful are the institute's 1:50,000 "Série M782" plans. Sheets from either series cost €6. Many local tourist offices produce **walking leaflets and books**, while also worth looking out for is the annual *Passo-a-passo* guidebook (€5) published by the Federação Portuguesa de Campismo, Av. Coronel Eduardo Galhardo 24D, 1199-007 Lisboa (⊕218 126 890, ⊛www .fcmportugal.com), which details both short and long itineraries across the country, many of them waymarked.

Map outlets

Portugal

Econauta Rua João Freitas Branco 24-3º, 1500-359 Lisbon ⊕217 220 210, ⊛www.econauta.com.
Instituto Geográfico do Exército Av. Dr. Alfredo Bensaúde, 1849-014 Lisbon ⊕ 218 505 300, ⊛www.igeoe.pt.
Livraria Simões Rua do Alportel 86-A, 8000-293 Faro ⊕ 289 826 618, ⊕ 289 829 204.
Porto Editora Praça Dona Filipa de Lencastre 42, 4050-259 Porto ⊕ 222 007 681, ⊛www .portoeditora.pt.

UK and Ireland

Blackwell's Map Centre 50 Broad St, Oxford OX1 3BQ ⊕ 01865/793 550, plus branches in Bristol, Cambridge, Cardiff, Leeds, Liverpool, Newcastle, Reading and Sheffield ⊛ http://maps. blackwell.co.uk.
The Map Shop 30a Belvoir St, Leicester LE1 6QH ⊕0116/247 1400, ⊛www.mapshopleicester.co.uk.
National Map Centre 22–24 Caxton St, London SW1H 0QU ⊕ 020/7222 2466, ⊛ www.mapsnmc .co.uk.
National Map Centre Ireland 34 Aungier St, Dublin ⊕ 01/476 0471, ⊛ www.mapcentre.ie.

Stanfords 12–14 Long Acre, London WC2E 9LP ⊕020/7836 1321, ⊛www.stanfords.co.uk. Also at 39 Spring Gardens, Manchester ⊕0161/831 0250, and 29 Corn St, Bristol ⊕0117/929 9966.
Travel Bookshop 13–15 Blenheim Crescent, London W11 2EE ⊕ 020/7229 5260, ⊛www .thetravelbookshop.co.uk.
Traveller 55 Grey St, Newcastle-upon-Tyne NE1 6EF ⊕0191/261 5622, ⊛www.newtraveller.com.

USA

110 North Latitude Online store, US ⊕ 336/369-4171, ⊛www.110nlatitude.com.
Book Passage 51 Tamal Vista Blvd, Corte Madera, CA 94925, and in the San Francisco Ferry Building ⊕1-800/999-7909 or 415/927-0960, ⊛www .bookpassage.com.
Distant Lands 56 S Raymond Ave, Pasadena, CA 91105 ⊕1-800/310-3220, ⊛www.distantlands .com.
Globe Corner Bookstore 28 Church St, Cambridge, MA 02138 ⊕1-800/358-6013, ⊛www.globecorner.com.
Longitude Books 115 W 30th St #1206, New York, NY 10001 ⊕1-800/342-2164, ⊛www .longitudebooks.com.

Canada

Map Town 400 5 Ave SW #100, Calgary, AB, ⊕2P 0L6 ⊕1-877/921-6277 or 403/266-2241, ⊛www.maptown.com.
Travel Bug Bookstore 3065 W Broadway, Vancouver, BC, V6K 2G9 ⊕604/737-1122, ⊛www.travelbugbooks.ca.
World of Maps 1235 Wellington St, Ottawa, ON, K1Y 3A3 ⊕1-800/214-8524 or 613/724-6776, ⊛www.worldofmaps.com.

Australia

Mapland 372 Little Bourke St, Melbourne ⊕03/9670 4383, ⊛www.mapland.com.au.
Map Shop 6–10 Peel St, Adelaide ⊕08/8231 2033, ⊛www.mapshop.net.au.
Map World 371 Pitt St, Sydney ⊕02/9261 3601; 900 Hay St, Perth ⊕08/9322 5733; Jolimont Centre, Canberra ⊕02/6230 4097; and 1981 Logan Road, Brisbane ⊕07/3349 6633, ⊛www .mapworld.net.au.

New Zealand

Auckland Map Centre National Bank Centre, 209 Queen St, Auckland ⊕09/309 7725, ⊛www.mapcentre.co.nz.
Mapworld NZ 173 Gloucester St, Christchurch ⊕0800/627967, ⊛www.mapworld.co.nz.

Costs, money and banks

The cost of living in Portugal has been edging up ever since its entry into the European Union in 1986 but, for tourists, it remains one of the cheapest places to travel in Europe. Accommodation, transport, food and drink are cheaper than in northern Europe or North America – and, on the whole, better value than in Spain. The only things that are markedly more expensive are telephone calls.

Currency

Portugal is one of the twelve European Union countries to use the **euro** (€). Euro notes are issued in **denominations** of 5, 10, 20, 50, 100, 200 and 500 euro, and coins in denominations of 1, 2, 5, 10, 20 and 50 cents and 1 and 2 euro. The coins feature a common EU design on one face but different country-specific designs on the other. No matter the design, all coins and notes can be used in the member states.

At the time of writing, the **exchange rate** was around €1.45 to £1 (€1=£0.69), or €0.78 to $1 (€1=$1.27). Up-to-the-minute rates are displayed at ⓦ www.xe.com.

Average costs

On average, if you're prepared to camp and picnic (or always choose the very cheapest hotels and cafés) you could reasonably expect to survive on a **daily budget** of €25, though you won't have much change for actually doing anything. On €50 per person per day, you can afford a basic room for the night, two meals in modest restaurants, drinks in the evening, entry to a museum or two, and a bus or train ride – if you're just visiting Lisbon and the Algarve you can add

twenty percent to these figures. The biggest single cost is usually accommodation – travelling out of season (when many hotels drop their prices) and with a companion (to share rooms) will always save you money. Conversely, if you are going to stay exclusively in resort hotels, *pousadas* or manor houses, and eat in fancier restaurants, you're looking at a daily budget of more like €120.

Eating out can be very cheap, and sometimes costs even less than putting together a picnic. You can always get a substantial basic meal for around €8, or €5–6 if you choose the day's set menu at the cheapest *tascas* and *adegas*. Even dinner in the smartest of restaurants is unlikely to cost more than €30 a head. A bottle of house wine rarely comes to more than €5, and the same bottle in supermarkets might be three times cheaper, whilst a bottle or glass of beer in a bar is less than €1. Even **transport** is not going to break the bank, especially since most distances are fairly short. A second-class train journey from Porto to Lisbon, or Lisbon to the Algarve, for example, starts at €16, whilst the same journey by bus costs €18–23. **Valued added tax** (known as IVA), set at 19 percent for most tourist-related services, is usually included in advertised prices, though some car rental outfits especially like to keep it separate to appear cheaper than they really are.

Banks and exchange

You'll find a **bank** (*banco*) or savings bank/building society (*caixa*) in all but the smallest towns. The major banks are Atlântico, Banco Espírito Santo, BPI, and Millennium (BCP); the main *caixa* is Caixa Geral de Depósitos. Standard **opening hours** are

Tipping

Simple cafés, restaurants and bars don't charge for service; leaving small change is fine. In more upmarket restaurants you'll either be charged, or should leave, around ten percent of the bill. Hotels include a service charge but porters and maids will expect something; taxi drivers won't.

27

Monday to Friday 8.30am to 3pm, remaining open at lunchtimes when everything else is closed. In Lisbon and larger Algarve resorts, some banks may also open in the evening to change money, while others have installed automatic exchange machines for various currencies. **Exchange bureaux** (*câmbios*), which you'll find in Lisbon, Porto and the Algarve, tend to have longer working hours, closing on weekdays at around 6pm, and also open on Saturdays. Changing cash in banks is quick and easy, and shouldn't attract more than a €3 commission. However, it's unwise to carry all your money as cash, so consider the alternatives.

By far the easiest way to get money in Portugal is to use your bank debit card or credit card and a personal identification number (PIN) to withdraw cash from an **ATM** (known as a *Multibanco*). You'll find them in even the smallest towns, and also at petrol stations along major routes. Instructions are available in English, and the daily withdrawal limit depends on your bank or credit card company, usually €200 a day. The amounts withdrawn on debit cards are not liable to interest payments, and the flat transaction fee is usually quite small – your bank can advise on this. You'll also need to check with your domestic bank whether you can use your debit card directly in shops, etc, as not all systems are available in Portugal.

Credit cards can also be used over the counter, with MasterCard and Visa accepted just about everywhere, though as ever American Express is more restricted – we've noted hotels in the guide that don't accept plastic. Remember that all cash advances on credit cards are treated as loans, with interest accruing daily from the date of withdrawal; there may also be a transaction fee on top of this.

Travellers' cheques are not widely accepted, and can attract outrageous commission in banks (upwards of €13 per transaction). It might be worth considering them as a back-up if your plastic is lost, stolen or swallowed by an ATM, in which case be sure to keep the purchase agreement and a record of cheque serial numbers safe and separate from the cheques themselves. In the event that cheques are lost or stolen, most companies claim to replace them within 24 hours. The issuing company will expect you to report the loss immediately to the police, and to them.

Discounts and discount cards

A **Euro<26 card** (Ⓦwww.euro26.de) is worth having for European residents under 26 – it'll get you free or reduced admission to many museums and sights, discounts on bus and train tickets (on distances over 90km), and reductions in numerous shops and restaurants, campsites and youth hostels, cinema tickets and some car rental. The card is available from USIT in Ireland (p.17), and in the UK from STA (p.13). The card is also sold in Portugal (€8, valid for a year) at post offices, youth hostels, and at branches of the Caixa Geral de Depósitos bank. Ask for a *Cartão Jovem*; you'll need a photo and your passport. Of much less use is an **ISIC** card (International Student Identity Card, Ⓦwww.isiccard.com), which is rarely accepted, even if you attempt an explanation in Portuguese.

Senior travellers in Portugal are also entitled to a range of benefits. Many sites and museums give generous discounts to over-65s and it is always worth showing your senior citizen's card or another form of ID when asking for tickets. On trains seniors get thirty-percent discounts if they ask for a *bilhete terceira idade*, and there's fifty-percent off a *Bilhete Turístico* rail pass (see p.30). Look out, too, for seasonal promotions for over-65s at the country's *pousadas* (see pp.35–36).

Getting around

Portugal is not a large country and you can get almost everywhere easily and efficiently by train or bus. Trains are often cheaper, and some lines very scenic, but it's almost always quicker to go by bus – especially on shorter or less obvious routes. Approximate times and frequencies of most journeys are given in the "Travel details" section at the end of each chapter; local connections and peculiarities are pointed out in the text. With car rental rates among the lowest in Europe, driving around Portugal is an option worth thinking about, though you may find you need nerves of steel to drive on some Portuguese roads. There are also internal flights from Lisbon to most regional capitals (including Porto, Bragança, Faro and Viseu), and fares are reasonable, though most tourists don't choose to fly around the country.

Trains

Comboios de Portugal (CP) operates all trains. Services are generally efficient, but be aware that rural train stations can sometimes be miles from the town or village they serve – Portalegre station and town are 12km distant, for example. Most lines have now been modernized, which means faster journey times, but although several of the old **narrow-gauge mountain railways** of the north have been phased out, the highly picturesque Tâmega, Corgo, Tua Valley and Douro lines are still terrific routes. **Timetables** (*horários*) for individual lines are available from stations, and on the CP website, ⓦwww.cp.pt. Complete timetables are sold at stations for €5.

Most **trains** are designated *Regionais* (R) or *Suburbanos*, and stop at most stations en route. The faster *Interregionais* (IR) stop only at major stations, and have first- and second-class cars (with compartments for six or eight passengers respectively as well as normal seating). Similar is the weekly overnight *Comboio Azul* ("Blue Train"), connecting Porto with Faro. The next category up, *Intercidades* (IC), are faster and more expensive, whilst even faster, more luxurious and pricey are the *Alfa Pendulares* (AP), which speed along three routes: Lisbon to Braga via Santarém, Coimbra, Aveiro and Porto; Lisbon to Guarda via Castelo Branco and Covilhã; and Lisbon to Faro. **Seat**

reservations are obligatory on IC and AP trains (up to 30 days in advance), while rail pass holders will pay supplements to use these faster trains.

Tickets

Train travel is inexpensive and most visitors simply buy a **ticket** every time they make a journey; always turn up at the station with time to spare since long queues often form at the ticket desk. Major stations now also have ticket machines, which take credit cards. If you end up on the train without a ticket you could be liable for an on-the-spot fine. However, smaller regional stations are sometimes unstaffed, in which case just hop on and pay the ticket inspector on board. First-class is called *primeira classe* or *conforto*; second-class is *segunda classe* or *turística*.

Return **fares** on journeys over 91km are twenty percent cheaper than two singles, and it's cheapest to travel on "Blue Days" – ie, avoiding Friday afternoons, Sunday afternoons, Monday mornings, national holidays and the day preceding a national holiday. Children under four travel free, while under-12s pay half (ask for a *bilhete meio*). There are thirty-percent **discounts** for senior citizens (over-65, ID required; ask for a *bilhete terceira idade*) and to Euro<26 card-holders, valid on all on journeys over 91km (though not on AP trains, nor on some weekend IC trains).

PORTUGAL: TRAINS

N

ATLANTIC
OCEAN

SPAIN

▲ La Coruña
Vigo
Tuy
Valença
Caminha
Viana do Castelo
Braga
Barcelos
Guimarães
Mirandela
Lousado
Amarante Vila Real
Porto
Régua Tua Pocinho
Espinho
Sernada
Vilar
Formoso
Aveiro
Nelas
Salamanca,
Madrid & Paris
Pampilhosa
Guarda
Cantanhede
Sta. Comba Dão
Figueira da Foz
Coimbra
Covilhã
Lousã
Fundão
Pombal
Serpins
Leiria
Castelo Branco
Tomar
Abrantes
Caldas
da Rainha
Marvão-
Beira
Torres
Vedras
Entroncamento
Santarém
Portalegre
Setil
Sintra
Cacém
LISBON
Vendas
Novas
Elvas
Madrid
Cascais
Barreiro
Badajoz
Mérida & Madrid
Setúbal
Casa
Branca
Évora
Alcácer
do Sal
Ermidas-
Sado
Beja
Funcheira
Vila Real de
Sto. António
Silves
Lagos
Tunes
Sevilla
Portimão
Faro
Tavira
Olhão

0   50 km

Rail passes

A rail pass may save you money, though you'll still pay supplements and reservation fees. Realistically, though, they are only worth considering if you plan to travel very extensively by train in Portugal, or are visiting the country as part of a wider tour of Europe. Note that some have to be bought before leaving home, while others can only be bought in the country itself. The agencies listed below can provide up-to-date information, prices and bookings, as can many of the travel agencies (like STA Travel, Trailfinders or USIT) and specialist tour operators covered in "Getting there".

CP sells its own pass, the **Bilhete Turísti-co**, valid for first-class travel on all trains for 7 days (€110), 14 days (€187) or 21 days (€275); under-12s and over-65s pay half; it's available to anyone at major Portuguese train stations. EU residents can also buy a

Eurodomino pass for Portugal, allowing 3–8 days unlimited rail travel in one calendar month, which gives more flexibility than CP's *Bilhete Turístico* at comparable prices. Prices for under-26s (2nd class) start at £36/€48 for 3 days, up to £77/€103 for 8 days. Over-26s pay 15 to 20 percent more, or 50 percent more for the first-class version. Passes must be bought prior to your departure.

The **Inter-Rail Pass** is also only available to EU residents, comes in over-26, cheaper under-26, and half-price child versions, and covers 29 European countries (including Turkey and Morocco) grouped together in eight zones. Passes are available for one zone for 16 days (under-26s £159/€210, over-26s £223/€299), two zones in 22 days (£215/€289, £303/€409), and all zones in one month (£295/€399, £415/€559). Portugal is zoned with Spain and Morocco. Inter-Rail passes do not include travel between Britain and the continent, although Inter-Rail Pass holders get discounts on cross-Channel ferries and the London-Paris Eurostar service.

For non-EU residents, the only choice is a **Eurail pass**, which must be purchased before arrival in Europe, and allows unlimited first-class train travel in 17 countries for a set period of between 15 days and 3 months. Under-26s will save around thirty percent with a **Eurailpass Youth**, valid for second-class travel. A scaled-down version, the **Eurail Selectpass**, allows travel in up to 5 adjoining countries for 5–15 days within a two-month period, while cheaper still, if you're travelling with up to five companions, is a joint **Eurailpass Saver**.

Rail contacts

Europrail International US & Canada ☏1-888/667-9734, ⓦwww.europrail.net.
International Rail UK ☏0870/751 5000, ⓦwww.international-rail.com.
Rail Europe UK ☏0870/584 8848, ⓦwww.raileurope.co.uk; US ☏1-877/257-2887, Canada ☏1-800/361-RAIL, ⓦwww.raileurope.com.
Rail Plus Australia ☏1300/555 003 or 03/9642 8644, ⓦwww.railplus.com.au.

Buses

Buses shadow many of the main train routes as well as linking most of the country's smaller towns and villages. It's almost always quicker to go by bus if you can, though you'll pay slightly more than for the equivalent train ride. Comfortable express buses operate on longer routes, for which it's wise to reserve tickets in advance.

All bus services are run by private companies, though a national network of **express coaches** (Rede Expressos) combines services from a number of different companies (there's a route map at ⓦwww.rede-expressos.pt). The variety of companies can be a cause of confusion, as two buses going to the same destination may leave from different terminals and companies may be unwilling to volunteer information about their rivals.

Local **bus stations** are the place to pick up timetables and reserve seats on long-distance journeys but, as companies, addresses and routes change every year, it's advisable to check first with the local turismo. Be aware that bus services are considerably less frequent – occasionally non-existent – at weekends, and that rural services may be timed to fit with school schedules, meaning early morning departures, sometimes only during term times.

Driving

You'll obviously have a great deal more freedom if you take or rent a car to drive around Portugal, though it's worth bearing in mind that Portugal has one of the highest accident rates in Europe. Road surfaces are improving, but even **major roads** (prefixed EN – *Estrada Nacional* – or just N) are often narrow and full of dangerous bends. But it's not so much the quality of roads but the driving that is lethal, reckless overtaking being the main problem. You'll need to check your mirror every few seconds to make sure someone isn't right up your exhaust pipe.

A massive EU-funded road construction programme has made previously remote areas of the country such as Trás-os-Montes and Beira Alta far more accessible, via a network of main **highways** (numbers prefixed "IP"), similar in speed to motorways; there are plans to convert some into toll roads. The **motorway** (*auto-estrada*) network itself (numbers prefixed with "A") is privately owned by BRISA and comprises a network of **toll roads** expanding outwards from a central spine that links the Algarve with Lisbon and Porto. The advantages are far less traffic and faster journeys, though you pay for the privilege – using the stretch from Lisbon to Porto, for example, costs around €15. Traffic on smaller roads will be much heavier and slow journeys stuck behind trucks are common.

As car ownership has increased massively over recent years, towns and beach resorts can no longer cope with the traffic, so in summer you'll have endless problems finding **parking** space. Mid-range and budget hotels tend not to have car parks, in which case you can expect to spend ages looking for a space, often ending up on the outskirts of town. Coimbra is notoriously bad, and has pioneered a park-and-ride scheme in response; Porto is heading the same way, having constructed huge car parks at metro stations on the city's outskirts. When parking in cities, do as the locals do and use the empty spaces pointed out to you. A tip of €0.50 to the man doing the pointing will pay them for "looking after" your car. Parking on any town's main streets between 8am and 8pm weekdays needs paying for; keep small coins handy for the ticket machines nearby. The price varies, but averages €0.40 an hour.

Traffic drives on the right: **speed limits** are 50kph in towns and villages, 90kph on normal roads, and 120kph on motorways and inter-regional highways, not that you'd ever guess from the antics of fellow motorists. Oncoming cars flashing their headlights at you usually means traffic police or radar trap ahead. At road junctions, unless there's a sign to the contrary ("*Não tem prioridade*"), vehicles coming from the right have right of way – a senseless rule that allows anyone to cut in. Thankfully, most drivers use common sense to interpret this rule. **Petrol** (*gasolina*) costs around €1.20 a litre for unleaded (*sem chumbo*) 98-octane, a little less for diesel (*gasóleo*).

Driving licences from most countries are accepted, so there's no need to get an international one before you leave. Many **car insurance** policies cover taking your car to Portugal; check with your insurer when planning your trip. However, you're advised to take out extra cover for motoring assistance in case your car breaks down, and **motoring organizations** like the RAC (UK ☎0800/550055, ⓦwww.rac.co.uk) or the AA (UK ☎0870/600 0371, ⓦwww.theaa .co.uk) can help. Alternatively, you can get 24-hour assistance from the **Automóvel Clube de Portugal** (☎707 509 510, ⓦwww.acp.pt), which has reciprocal arrangements with foreign automobile clubs. If you're stopped by the **police** in Portugal, they'll want to see your documents: personal ID or passport, driving licence, and papers for the car. It pays to be patient and courteous.

Car rental

Car rental agencies can be found in all the major towns and at the airports in Lisbon, Porto and Faro; details are given in the guide. **Rates** start at €30–50 a day with unlimited mileage, theft, collision damage and super collision damage waivers (see below). You may find it cheaper and easier to arrange car rental in conjunction with your flights; Avis, for instance, have cheap deals for TAP passengers. Minimum age for rental is 21, though up to and including the age of 24 you'll have to pay a supplement – no more than €7.50 per day.

When picking up your car, check the brakes and tyre tread and, if you're renting locally, insurance coverage. As you might have gathered, **collision insurance** is a good idea. Without it, you'll be liable for up to several thousand euros of costs should the vehicle be damaged, and this includes even minor scratches (ensure that all visible damage on a car you're picking up is duly marked on the rental sheet, usually in the form of a diagram). The standard supplement is CDW (Collision Damage Waiver; €7–20 per day depending on the style of car), and reduces your liability to a few hundred euros. For an additional daily fee (Super CDW), you're completely covered, save for a small (usually €50) excess charge. Keep the receipts of any repairs you make along the way – you may be able to get some money back from the company.

Finally, it can't be stressed enough that foreign and rental cars are common targets of **theft**. Don't leave anything visible in an unattended car.

Car rental agencies

Alamo US ☎ 1-800/462-5266, ⓦ www.alamo .com.

Auto Europe US and Canada ☎ 1-888/223-5555, ⓦ www.autoeurope.com.

Avis UK ☎ 0870/606 0100, ⓦ www.avis.co.uk; Republic of Ireland ☎ 021/428 1111, ⓦ www.avis .ie; US ☎ 1-800/230-4898, Canada ☎ 1-800/272-5871, ⓦ www.avis.com; Australia ☎ 1300/137498 or 02/9353 9000, ⓦ www.avis.com.au; New Zealand ☎ 09/526 2847 or 0800/655111, ⓦ www .avis.co.nz; Portugal ☎ 800 201 002, ⓦ www.avis .com.pt.

Budget UK ☎ 0870/153 9170 or 0870/156 5656, ⓦ www.budget.co.uk; Republic of Ireland ☎ 09/0662 7711, ⓦ www.budget.ie; US ☎ 1-800/472-3325, Canada ☎ 1-800/268-8900, ⓦ www.budget.com; Australia ☎ 1300/794344, ⓦ www.budget.com.au; New Zealand ☎ 09/976 2222 or 0800/652227, ⓦ www.budget.co.nz.

easyCar ☎ 0906/333 3333, ⓦ www.easycar .co.uk.

Europcar UK ☎ 0870/607 5000, ⓦ www.europcar .co.uk; Republic of Ireland ☎ 01/614 2888, ⓦ www.europcar.ie; Australia ☎ 1300/131390, ⓦ www.deltaeuropcar.com.au.

Hertz UK ☎ 0870/844 8844, ⓦ www.hertz.co.uk; Republic of Ireland ☎ 01/676 7476, ⓦ www.hertz .ie; US ☎ 1-800/654-3131, Canada ☎ 1-800/263-0600, ⓦ www.hertz.com; Australia ☎ 133039 or 03/9698 2555, ⓦ www.hertz.com.au; New Zealand ☎ 0800/654321, ⓦ www.hertz.co.nz.

Holiday Autos UK ☎ 0870/400 0099, ⓦ www .holidayautos.co.uk; Republic of Ireland ☎ 01/872 9366, ⓦ www.holidayautos.ie; Australia ☎ 1300/554432, ⓦ www.holidayautos.com.au; New Zealand ☎ 0800/144040, ⓦ www .holidayautos.co.nz.

Thrifty ☎ 01494/751 600, ⓦ www.thrifty.co.uk; Republic of Ireland ☎ 1800/515 800, ⓦ www .thrifty.ie; US and Canada ☎ 1-800/847-4389, ⓦ www.thrifty.com; Australia ☎ 1300/367227, ⓦ www.thrifty.com.au; New Zealand ☎ 0800/737070, ⓦ www.thrifty.co.nz.

Taxis

Travelling by taxi in Portugal is relatively cheap by European standards, and worth considering for trips across major towns and for shorter journeys in rural areas where other means of transport are limited.

Generally, taxis are metered, so an average journey across Lisbon or Porto shouldn't cost more than €6. Minimum fare is around €2, and additional charges are made for carrying baggage (€1.50 per item), travelling at weekends or between 9pm and 6am (20 percent extra), and for calling a cab by phone (€0.75). You can also negotiate an hourly fare, though there are minimum rates: just under €10 in Porto, for instance.

Bikes, mopeds and motorbikes

Bicycles are a great way of seeing the country, though anywhere away from the coast – especially north of Lisbon and inland from the Algarve's beaches – is hilly, and you'll also find pedalling hard work across the burned plains of southern Alentejo. Several special shops, plus hotels, campsites and youth hostels, **rent bikes** for around €10 a day; the major ones are listed in the text.

Portugal's woeful road accident statistics mean that **defensive riding** is essential. Fitting a rear-view mirror to the handlebars is a definite advantage, as is reflective and fluorescent clothing (or sashes) at night. In general, it's best to assume that drivers will not obey road signs or regulations – just be prepared. Obviously, minor country roads have far less traffic to contend with, but locals know them backwards and so speeding – even around blind corners – is the norm. For more information on cycling abroad, contact the UK's national cycling organization, the CTC (☎ 0870/873 0061, ⓦ www.ctc.org.uk).

Collapsible bikes can be taken for free on regional and interregional **trains** (ie, the slow ones), so long as they're dismantled and stowed in a bag or other cover. Normal bikes can only be carried on one of two daily regional trains (€2 fee) along the following lines: Porto–Valença, Porto–Régua, Porto–Coimbra, Coimbra–Entroncamento, Lisbon–Tomar and Vila Real de Santo António–Faro. More details are available at ⓦ www.cp.pt/servicos/cir/p_comboio -bicicleta.html.

You can also rent **mopeds**, **scooters** and low-powered (80cc) **motorbikes** in many resorts, with costs starting at around

€25 a day. You need to be at least 18 (and over 23 for bikes over 125cc), and to have held a full licence for at least a year. Rental should include helmet and locks along with third-party insurance. A helmet and valid licence are, of course, obligatory. Check all cables and brakes before setting off, and go easy.

Accommodation

In almost any Portuguese town you can find a basic pension (*pensão*) offering a double room for around €20–30. The only accommodation that you're likely to find cheaper than this is a simple room in a private home, while you can expect to pay more for accommodation in Algarve resorts in high season, or in Lisbon, where an average room is likely to cost €30–40. Moving upmarket, you're often spoilt for choice, with some wonderful manor houses and a network of comfortable state-run hotels, or *pousadas*, scattered about the country, all at prices that beat the rest of Europe hands down. Even in high season you shouldn't have much of a problem finding a bed in most Portuguese regions. However, Lisbon and the Algarve are often a very different matter, with all rooms booked up for days ahead. Advance reservations here are advised, especially if you're arriving late.

When asking for a room, a *quarto duplo* has two **single beds**, and a *quarto casal* has a large **double bed** for a couple. A **single room** – *quarto solteiro* or *individual* – is a little cheaper, but almost always proportionately more expensive per person than if you were to share. Ask to see the room before you take it, even in upmarket places, and don't be afraid to ask if there's a cheaper one (rooms without private showers or bathrooms are often considerably less). *Tem um quarto mais barato?* ("Do you have a cheaper room?") is the relevant phrase. Be prepared to pay more for a room with a view when next to a river or the sea (though not always that much more).

Lastly, a word of warning: between November and April, give or take a month, nighttime temperatures throughout Alentejo and Trás-os-Montes can plummet to

Accommodation price codes

All establishments listed in this book have been categorized according to the price codes outlined below. They represent the price for the **cheapest available double/twin room in high season**. Effectively this means that most places with a **1** or **2** category will be without private bath or shower, though there's usually a washbasin in the room. In places with a **3** category and above, you'll probably be getting private facilities and often a TV, while many of the cheaper places may also have more expensive rooms with bath/shower if you ask. Price codes are not used for youth hostels (see p.37), where we give the euro rate for a dorm bed instead.

1	under €25	**4**	€56–75	**7**	€126–150
2	€26–35	**5**	€76–100	**8**	€151–200
3	€36–55	**6**	€101–125	**9**	over €201

below freezing, and even along the coast temperatures of under 5°C are common. However, few pensions have any form of **heating** other than the odd plug-in radiator, so check out the facilities before taking a room, or you'll find yourself wearing the entire contents of your luggage for the night. Similarly, in the height of summer check for some kind of **cooling**, be it a fan or air conditioning, as nights can remain very warm.

Private rooms

Rooms let out in **private houses** – *dormidas* – are most commonly available in seaside resorts. They are sometimes advertised, or more often hawked at bus and train stations, while the local turismo may also have a list of available rooms. Rates average €15–20 for a double/twin, though on the Algarve in high season expect to pay up to twice as much. It's always worth haggling over prices, especially if you're prepared to commit yourself to a longish stay, but don't expect too much success in summer. Given the absence of any formalized system, room quality and facilities vary greatly; some are no more than a bed in a converted attic, others come with modern bathrooms, TVs and air conditioning. Always ask where the room is before you agree to take it – you could end up miles from the town centre or beach. Get the owner to write down the agreed price too, if possible, to avoid the possibility of overcharging. Breakfast is not usually included.

Pensions

The main budget travel standby is a room in a **pensão** (plural *pensões*), which tend to occupy old – and often pleasingly characterful – buildings, sometimes with owners to match. Rooms rarely come with bathrooms or indeed much else other than the bed(s), an electric heater, a heavy and almost never used wardrobe, and perhaps a chair or table. Breakfast is not normally available. Rates average €15–25 for a double/twin. Similar to a *pensão*, and generally at the cheaper end of the scale, is a **hospedaria** or **casa de hóspedes** – boarding house – which tends to fall into one of two categories: solemnly religious places catering primarily for pilgrims en route to Fátima or

Santiago de Compostela, or dictinctly dodgy dosshouses in red-light districts. Neither provide much more than beds and heaters in spartan rooms.

Slightly more upmarket than a *pensão* is a **residencial** (*residenciais* or *residências*), whose more modern rooms tend to have en-suite bathrooms equipped with showers, some with bathtubs, plus TVs, heaters and sometimes phones and air conditioning. They're officially graded in three categories and rates range from €20–50 double, depending on season, location and facilities. Breakfast is often included, but don't expect much more than a few white buns or slices of bread with butter and jam, and coffee.

Hotels, inns and pousadas

A one-star **hotel** usually costs about the same as a higher-grade *residencial*, and often doesn't show any notable difference in standards. Prices for two- and three-star hotels, though, see a notable shift upwards, with en-suite doubles running from €40–70, though older establishments may have one or two cheaper rooms without en-suite bathrooms. One- and two-star hotels tend to serve continental-style breakfasts; more substantial breakfasts, sometimes taking the form of regal buffets, are provided at three-star places and up.

There's a dramatic shift in rates as you move into the four- and five-star hotel league, where you'll pay anything from €100 to €300, and the very fanciest places, on the Algarve and in Lisbon, can pretty much charge what they like. For this, you get a double room kitted out with all mod cons (cable or satellite TV, direct dial phones, modem sockets, air conditioning and hairdriers), plus the run of the establishment's facilities, usually including a swimming pool, restaurant, bar, room service and private parking.

For more charm, *estalagems* and *albergarias* – **inns** – offer similar standards of comfort in more attractive and intimate surroundings, often in converted town manor houses. There's also a chain of over forty **pousadas**, government-run hotels that have often been converted from old monasteries or castles, or located in dramatic countryside settings. Most are traditionally, though elegantly, furnished and make full use of the cloisters, ramparts, chapels and other features of the original buildings. Many also have swimming pools, lovely gardens and excellent restaurants. Prices vary considerably depending on the season, day (more expensive Fri and Sat nights), location, size and position of the room, but expect to pay €130–200 in summer, or €90–150 in low season. Look out for seasonal promotions, too, especially for over-65s, who receive discounts of around 35 percent. We've detailed most of the *pousadas* in the guide but for a full list contact any major tourist office or consult the *pousadas* organisation, **Pousadas de Portugal**, Av. Santa Joana Princesa 10, 1749-090 Lisbon ☏218 442 001, ⓦwww .pousadas.pt; accepts online bookings.

Country and manor houses

An increasingly popular alternative in the three- to four-star hotel price range is to stay in one of the many country and manor houses throughout Portugal promoted by the tourist board as **Turismo no Espaço Rural** (TER). You may also encounter the following terms: "TR" or Turismo Rural (country houses); "CC" or Casas no Campo (simpler country houses); "AT" or Agro-Turismo (farmhouses, often in working farms); and "TH" or Turismo de Habitação or Turihab (old manor houses and palaces).

There are now hundreds of properties available, all of which have had their facilities and accommodation inspected and approved by the government tourist office. In terms of atmosphere and luxury, they are often unbeatable and their equivalent in other European countries would command in excess of double the price; rates currently range from €60–100 for a double/twin room. Many will provide typical dinners made from local ingredients, sometimes accompanied by wine and other produce made on the estate, and almost all are founts of advice and information about local matters. Even if dinner is not available – or you prefer not to eat with the family – large breakfasts are invariably included. Many also offer suitably rural activities like fishing, rambling, horse riding and wine-tasting.

Properties vary from simple **farmhouses** (*casas rústicas*), offering just two or three rooms on a bed-and-breakfast basis, to **country manors** (*casas antigas*), often dating from the sixteenth to eighteenth centuries and complete with period furnishings. **Quintas** or **herdades** are farm estate houses, and you can even stay in **palaces** (*palácios*), owned by Portuguese aristocrats who have allowed their ancient seats to become part of the scheme.

Once a property has passed government inspection, its owners can choose to join one of several marketing organizations (see list below). You can of course book directly with the houses themselves (details in the guide), or via specialist holiday operators in your own country (see "Getting there" for details).

Country and manor house contacts

ANTER (Associação Nacional de Turismo no Espaço Rural), Rua 24 de Julho 1, 7000 Évora ☏ & ⓕ 266 744 555. A wide choice of places, mainly from Lisbon southwards.
CENTER (Central Nacional de Turismo no Espaço Rural), Pr. da República, 4990-062 Ponte de Lima ☏ 258 931 750, ⓦ www.center.pt. Umbrella organization handling reservations for several schemes, including the village tourism project at Soajo in Peneda-Gerês, plus Casas no Campo, Aldeias de Portugal and Solares de Portugal. Mainly in Minho but also in and around the Douro Valley and Beiras, Trás-os-Montes, around Lisbon and Azores. Three-night minimum, book at least 3 days in advance. Credit cards accepted.
PRIVETUR ⓦ www.manorhouses.com. Over 100 properties countrywide, including manor houses, estalagems, cottages and *pousadas*. The website provides full descriptions and booking information for each.

Villas

Virtually every area of the country – certainly near the coast – has some sort of **villa** or **apartment** available for rent, from simple one-room studios to luxurious five- or six-bed houses complete with garden and swimming pool. Holiday and specialist tour operators in your own country (see "Getting there") can provide full details of properties across Portugal, though note that in summer the best places are booked up months in advance. You can expect to pay at least €60 a night in high season for a two-person apartment, or up to €200 a night for a top villa – and the minimum rental period in summer is usually a week. Outside peak period you should be able to turn up and bag somewhere for the night for between 25 and 50 percent less – the local turismo will probably be able to help.

Youth hostels

There are over 40 **youth hostels** (*pousadas de juventude*) in Portugal, most open all year round. Prices, which almost always include breakfast whether you take it or not, depend on the location and season: the price for a dormitory bed runs from €7.50–12.50 a night in low season (Jan to mid-June and mid-Sept to Dec), and from €9–15 in high season (mid-June to mid-Sept); double/twin rooms, where available, go for €20–45, according to location, season and whether there's a bathroom. Add on a little extra if you need to hire sheets and blankets. The most expensive hostels are in Lisbon, Porto and on the Algarve.

Check-in time is officially 6pm, though some may be willing to admit you earlier. Check-out time is noon. The rural ones have a **curfew** (11pm or midnight); ones in Lisbon, Porto and the Algarve are open all hours. All require a valid Hostelling International (HI) card, available from your home-based youth hostel association (see below), or from the individual hostel on your first night. Among the **best hostels** in Portugal are those at Vilarinho das Furnas (in Peneda-Gerês National Park), Penhas de Saúde (in the Serra de Estrela), Areia Branca (on the beach, close to Peniche), Oeiras (on the seafront near Lisbon), Viana do Castelo (in an old sailing ship), Alcoutim (northeastern Algarve), Lagos and Leiria (the latter perhaps the best of the lot).

Youth hostel associations

Australia Australia Youth Hostels Association
☏ 02/9261 1111, ⓦ www.yha.com.au.
Canada Hostelling International Canada
☏ 1-800/663-5777 or 613/237-7884, ⓦ www.hihostels.ca.
England and Wales Youth Hostel Association
☏ 0870/870 8868, ⓦ www.yha.org.uk.
New Zealand Youth Hostelling Association
☏ 0800/278 299 or 03/379 9970, ⓦ www.yha.co.nz.
Northern Ireland Hostelling International Northern Ireland ☏ 028/9032 4733, ⓦ www.hini.org.uk.
Portugal *Movijovem*, Lisbon ☏ 217 232 100,
ⓦ www.pousadasjuventude.pt.
Republic of Ireland Irish Youth Hostel Association
☏ 01/830 4555, ⓦ www.irelandyha.org.
Scotland Scottish Youth Hostel Association
☏ 0870/155 3255, ⓦ www.syha.org.uk.
USA Hostelling International-American Youth Hostels ☏ 301/495-1240, ⓦ www.hiayh.org.

Camping

Portugal has around two hundred authorized campsites, many in very attractive locations and, despite their often large size (over 500 spaces is not uncommon), they can get extremely crowded in summer. The most useful campsites are noted in the text, and unless otherwise stated are open all year. The **Roteiro Campista** (ⓦ www.roteiro-campista.pt) booklet detailing the country's campsites is available from most Portuguese tourist offices and from bookshops and newsstands, while the website has an online list of campsites.

Most of the larger campsites have spaces for campervans/RVs and caravans, and will also have permanent caravans and bungalows for rent. Charges are per person and per caravan or tent, with showers and parking extra; even so, it's rare that you'll end up paying more than €6 a person, although those operated by the **Orbitur** chain (ⓦ www.orbitur.pt) – usually with bungalows on site as well – are more expensive.

A few sites require an **international camping carnet** and, if you're planning to do a lot of camping, it's a good investment. The carnet gives discounts at member sites and serves as useful identification: many campsites will take it instead of your passport, and it covers you for third-party insurance when camping. The carnet is available in the UK and Ireland (£4.50/€10) to members of the AA, the RAC, the CTC (cycling organisation), or the Camping and Caravanning Club (☏ 024/7669 4995, ⓦ www.campingandcaravanningclub.co.uk). In the US and Canada, the carnet (US$10) is available from home motoring organizations, or from Family Campers and RVers (FCRV; ☎1-800/245-9755 or 716/668-6242, ⓦwww.fcrv.org).

Camping outside official grounds is legal except in the Algarve, and with certain restrictions. You're not allowed to camp: "in urban zones, in zones of protection for water sources, or less than 1km from camping parks, beaches, or other places frequented by the public". What this means in practice is that you can't camp on tourist beaches, but with a little sensitivity you can pitch a tent for a short period almost anywhere in the countryside. That said, fly camping is prohibited in all Portugal's natural parks, in an attempt to reduce littering and – crucially – fire damage. If you're caught, don't expect too many favours; it'll be a long time before rangers forget the catastrophic forest fires of 2003 and 2004.

Eating and drinking

Portuguese food is excellent and inexpensive. Virtually all cafés and simple restaurants will serve you a basic meal for around €5–6, while for €15–25 you have the run of most of the country's establishments. Servings tend to be huge. Indeed, you can usually have a substantial meal by ordering a *meia dose* (half portion), or *uma dose* (a portion) between two. Meals are often listed like this on the menu and it's normal practice; you don't need to be a child. Beware, however, of eating anything you haven't explicitly asked for (bread, olives, etc) and expecting it to be free: it won't be. Lunch is usually served from noon–3pm, dinner from 7.30pm onwards; don't count on being able to eat much after 10pm outside cities and tourist resorts. Snacks and small meals can be found throughout the day in bars, cafés and pastry shops. Useful words and terms are covered below, but for a full eating and drinking glossary see p.652.

Foreign restaurants have yet to make much of an impression in Portugal, though you'll find pizzerias and Chinese establishments in the oddest of places. **Fast food**, whilst popular with Portuguese youth and families, is – in town centres at least – conspicuous by its absence. Whilst McDonalds and company do now cover most of the country, they're mainly found on the outskirts of towns or in shopping centres.

Portuguese table **wines** are dramatically inexpensive and of a good overall quality. Even the standard *vinho da casa* that you get in the humblest of cafés is generally a very pleasant drink, and ascending the scale you'll be surprised at the quality of wines on offer at very moderate prices. But it's fortified port, of course, and Madeira that are Portugal's best-known wine exports.

Breakfast, snacks and sandwiches

For **breakfast** it's best to head to a café, a *pastelaria* (pastry shop) or a *confeitaria* (confectioners), where you'll be able to order a croissant, some toast (*uma torrada*; a doorstep with butter) or some sort of cake or pastry (see p.42) washed down with coffee. If there's food displayed on a counter and you see anything that looks appealing, ask for *uma coisa destas* ("one of those").

Classic Portuguese **snacks**, available throughout the day, include *croquetes* (deep-fried meat patties), *pastéis* or *bolinhos de bacalhau* (cod fishcakes), *iscas de bacalhau* (battered cod fishcakes with egg), *chamuças* (samosas), *bifanas* (a thin slice of grilled or fried pork on bread), and *prego no pão* (steak sandwich), which when served on a plate with a fried egg on top is a *prego no prato*. In the north you'll also find *lanches* (pieces of sweetish bread stuffed with ham) and *pastéis de carne* or *pastéis de Chaves* (puff pastries stuffed with sausage meat).

Among **sandwiches** (*sandes* or *sanduíches*), common fillings include cheese, ham, *presunto* (smoked ham) and *chouriço* (smoked sausage). *Sandes mistas* are a combination of ham and cheese; grilled, they're called *tostas*. Better places offer the same on wholewheat or rye; ask for a *tosta mista com pão caseiro* or *com pão integral*. You may also see blackboard lists of dishes, or a sign reading **petiscos** or **comidas**, which are Portugal's answer to Spain's tapas. Usually served cold, these are little dishes that range from the simple and sublime to the truly unspeakable: not only prawns, sardines, snails, grilled octopus, marinaded chicken livers, *tremoços* (pickled lupin seeds) and *pimentos* (marinaded fried sweet peppers), but also *orelhas de porco* (crunchy pig's ears – nice if you like cartilage), and *túberos* (marinated boiled pig's testicles).

Restaurants and meals

Apart from straightforward **restaurants** (*restaurantes*), you could end up eating a meal in one of several other venues. A *tasca* is a small neighbourhood tavern, while a *casa de pasto* is a cheap, local dining room usually with a set three-course menu, mostly served at lunch only. A *cervejaria* is literally a "beer house", more informal than a restaurant, with people dropping in at all hours for a beer and a snack. In Lisbon they're often

wonderful tiled caverns specializing in seafood. Also specializing in seafood is a *marisqueira*, while a *churrasqueira* specializes in char-grilled meat, especially chicken, pork chops and sausages.

Wherever you eat, it's always worth taking stock of the **prato do dia** (dish of the day) if you're interested in sampling local specialities. The **ementa turística** is worth checking out, too – not a "tourist menu", but the set meal of the day, sometimes with a choice of two starters and two main courses, plus a glass of beer or a small carafe of wine. It can be very good value, though smarter restaurants sometimes resent the law that compels them to offer the *ementa turística*, responding with stingy portions and excessive prices.

The one thing to watch for when eating out in Portugal is the plate of **appetizers** placed before you when you take a table and before you order. These can be quite elaborate little dishes of olives, cheese, sardine spread and *chouriço*, or can consist of little more than rolls and butter, but what you eat is counted and you will be charged for every bite. *Não quero isto* ("I don't want this") should get the waiter to take it away. When you want **the bill**, ask for *a conta*.

Restaurants listed in this guide have each been given a price category: inexpensive (less than €10), moderate (€10–18), expensive (€18–30), or very expensive (over €30). This is the price per person you can expect to pay for a three-course meal, or equivalent, including drinks. Obviously, in many restaurants, the listing is only a guide to average costs, since you will almost

Vegetarian Portugal

Traditional Portuguese cuisine is tough on strict **vegetarians**, and egg dishes, salads and soups will be the main choices available on most menus. Virtually every meal ordered in a restaurant also comes with rice and salad. It's always worth asking whether a restaurant has a good cheese board (*tábua de queijos*): while some cheeses contain animal rennet (*coalho animal*), labels listing *cardo* (thistle flower rennet) among the ingredients are safe. In Lisbon, Porto and some parts of the Algarve, there are **vegetarian restaurants**, even macrobiotic ones, together with Chinese, Italian and Indian establishments where you should be able to put together a non-meat meal. Also, most towns have **health food shops** where you can find cereal bars, gluten-free biscuits, organic dried fruit and the like, whilst for picnics you're spoiled for choice, with a wealth of fruit, bread, cakes and pastries widely available.

always be able to eat more cheaply (choosing the *prato do dia*, skipping dessert) or more expensively (eating seafood, quaffing vintage port).

Dishes and specialities

Many meals start with one of Portugal's extraordinarily inexpensive **soups**. The thick vegetable *caldo verde* – a cabbage-and-potato broth, sometimes with ham – is as filling as dishes come, and at its best in the north. In the south the traditional mainstay is *sopa à alentejana*, a garlic and bread soup with a poached egg in it.

On the coast, **seafood** is pre-eminent: crabs, prawns, crayfish, cuttlefish, squid, clams and huge barnacles are all fabulous, while **fish** on offer always includes mullet,

---

Smoked meats and sausages

Traditionally, pork took pride of place in Portuguese cooking, attested to by prehistoric stone *porcas* – carvings of sows or boars – found in the north of the country. To last out the year, much of the slaughtered animal was preserved as smoked legs of ham and spiced sausages – *enchidos* ("stuffed things") or *fumeiros* ("smoked things"). Some *enchidos* have to be cooked, but many can be eaten raw and are great for picnics.

Alheiras, azedos and farinheiras These have their roots in the Inquisition, when Jews felt obliged to mimic the Catholic passion for sausages while avoiding pork, although nowadays most of them are far from kosher. *Alheiras* are based on bread and chicken, the best from Mirandela in Trás-os-Montes, and are served grilled or steamed. The superior *alheiras de caça* contain game fowl such as partridge. *Azedos* are a more meaty variant and a little sour, whilst *farinheiras* from Beira Baixa and Alentejo are more floury, and seasoned with paprika, wine or oranges. All need cooking.

Buchos and maranhos *Bucho* ("stomach"), from Trás-os-Montes, is Portugal's haggis, usually stuffed with pork, rice and bits of cartilage, and seasoned with wine and garlic. *Maranhos*, from Beira Baixa, are similar but contain goat's meat or mutton, tempered with garlic, wine, onion, parsley and mint.

Chouriço or linguiça The most common of the *enchidos*, eaten raw or grilled over flaming alcohol (*chouriço assado*). The best are from Alentejo, Guarda, Lamego, Montemor-o-Novo and Trás-os-Montes. The stuffing varies from coarsely chopped pieces of the less digestible parts of pigs to finer blends flavoured with herbs and wine (*chouriço de vinho*). *Chouriço doce*, served as a boiled starter, is a variant from Trás-os-Montes containing almonds, cinnamon and syrup.

Moiras A cross between *morcelas* and *chouriço*, famously from Lamego, made with wine and onion, and having a strong, bitter taste. Can be eaten raw but best cooked.

Morcelas or sangueiras Similar to black pudding, these are filled with blood and fat, and an intense aroma of cumin and cloves. Traditionally eaten with cornflour polenta (*farinha de milho*), the best and least fatty are from Guarda.

Paio (or palaios, paínhos or paiolas) The largest pieces of meat go into these – *paio*, especially from Beira Baixa, contains a more or less solid chunk of prime smoked and seasoned ham, delicious on bread.

Presunto King of the *fumeiros* and Portugal's challenge to Parma ham: smoked leg of pork preserved in sea salt and cured for months or years, often found hanging in local *tascas* and *adegas*. Eaten as an appetizer in very thin slices, or as a stuffing for trout (*truta recheada com presunto*).

Salpicão Similar in quality to *paio* in that it contains prime meat rather than noses and trotters, virtually fat-free, and can be sliced like cured bacon. There are many varieties, variously seasoned with wine, salt, paprika, bay leaves, garlic or even orange peel. Eaten sliced with bread, or in stews and *feijoada*. Mainly from Beiras, Alentejo and Rio Douro.

tuna and scabbard fish. The most typical Portuguese fish dish is that created from **bacalhau** (dried, salted cod), which is much better than it sounds. It's virtually the national dish with reputedly 365 different ways of preparing it – roasted with onions and potatoes, served with boiled egg and black olives, baked in cream, made into a pie, char-grilled or cooked in a traditional copper *cataplana*, the list is endless. Almost every restaurant in the country boasts a *bacalhau* dish, and some cook little else.

Grilled or barbecued **sardines**, provide one of the country's most familiar and appetizing smells, and in the Algarve and elsewhere you should definitely try a **cataplana**, named after the wok-like lidded copper vessel in which it's cooked. The

Portuguese cheese

There's a huge range of regional Portuguese cheese, a sizeable quantity of which is still handmade (the label D.O.P. guarantees that it was made in its traditional area). A *queijo de cabra* or *cabreiro* is goats' cheese, sheep is *ovelha*, cow is *vaca*, while a mixture of these is *queijo de mixtura*. Hard cheese is *queijo de pasta dura*, soft is *de pasta mole*, cured is *curado* (not necessarily to maturity), and buttery is *amanteigado*.

Queijo Alentejano Small hard rounds of matured cheese (typically Alentejan) made from goat or sheep's milk, often referred to as *Queijo Seco* (dry cheese). They're curdled with thistle flowers (*cardo* or *coalha-leite*) instead of rennet, and pressed and turned daily for several months. Look for *Queijo de Nisa* from northern Alentejo (similar to Parmesan) and *Queijo de Serpa* from the south – strong, tart and available young (soft) or mature (hard).

Queijo da Serra (or Queijo Serrano) Unctuous, aromatic cotton-girdled beauty from the Serra da Estrela. It's not matured for long, and consequently has an almost liquid texture. The cloth simply keeps the cheese in one place, so don't try to slice it (at least in public): the traditional method is to cut out a hole on top and scoop up the contents by spoon.

Azeitão A gorgeous sheep's milk cheese from Estremadura, which crumbles slightly when you cut it and has a pleasantly astringent taste.

Queijo de Ovelha Churra A hard cheese made with milk from the rugged sheep of southern Trás-os-Montes, especially around Vila Flôr. The soft, delicate flavour comes from the rennet used for coagulation. Stronger variants are sold in Alto Douro and Trás-os-Montes, cured with salt, olive oil and paprika.

Queijo Queimoso (or Picante) Rich and piquant (*queimoso* means "burning") mix of goat/sheep's milk, similar to Roquefort. The best is from the Serra da Gardunha in Beira Baixa. Less pungent is the paprika-covered *pimentão*, made from cows' milk.

Rabaçal Slightly slightly tart cheese, a splendidly refined blend of sheep's milk and cows' milk, at its best from Ansião in the Serras de Penela, near Coimbra.

Queijo de Tomar Tiny semi-hard matured cheese from Ribatejo.

Queijo da Ilha de São Jorge The best of the Azores' acclaimed cows' milk cheeses, with a Swiss look and flavour. It's also the heaviest, weighing in at over 7kg; it's sold in wedges. *Queijo da Ilha Branca* is similar. There are other good cows' milk cheeses from the Minho.

Queijo fresco (or requeijão) *Queijo fresco* is strained, lightly pressed curds of cows' milk one or two days old, whilst *requeijão* is unpressed curds of sheep's milk, vaguely similar to cottage cheese. Both are neutral in taste.

Chèvre A recent introduction styled on the soft French cylindrical goats' cheeses, primarily from Ribatejo and Minho.

Flamengo *Flamengo* ("Flemish") is a direct copy of Dutch Edam, complete with the red wax. The best is *Limiano*, from Ponte de Lima in Minho. *Flamengo* is also industrially produced in rectangular blocks and sold sliced as *queijo em barra* or *queijo em fatias*.

best *cataplanas* are made with seafood, as is **arroz de marisco**, a bumper serving of mixed seafood in a gloopy rice – *cataplanas* and *arroz* dishes are usually served for a minimum of two people. Other seafood specialities include a **caldeirada de peixe**, basically a fish stew, and the bread-based stew called an **açorda**, at its best served with shellfish.

On the whole, **meat dishes** are less special, though they're often enlivened by the addition of *piri-piri* (chilli) sauce, either in the cooking or provided on the table. Simple grilled or fried steaks of beef and pork are common, while chicken is on virtually every menu – at its best when barbecued (*no churrasco*). Also ubiquitous is *porco à alentejana* (pork cooked with clams), which originated, as its name suggests, in Alentejo. *Leitão* – spit-roast suckling pig – is distinctly Portuguese, too, at the centre of many a communal feast, particularly in Beiras. It's either served sliced and cold, or – better – just off the coals.

However, steel yourself for a couple of special dishes that local people might entice you into trying. Porto's *tripas* (tripe) dishes incorporate beans and spices but the heart of the dish is still recognizably chopped stomach-lining; while *cozido à portuguesa*, widely served in restaurants on a Sunday, is a stomach-challenging boiled "meat" stew in which you shouldn't be surprised to turn up lumps of fat, cartilage or even a pig's ear. Other traditional dishes use pig's blood as a base – the word to look for is *sarrabulho* – though the addition of cumin, paprika and other spices can turn these into something quite delicious.

Accompanying nearly every dish will be **potatoes**, either fried in the case of most meat dishes or boiled if you've ordered fish. The distinction is less marked in tourist resorts on the Algarve and elsewhere, but trying to get chips to come with your grilled trout or salmon in a rural town simply invites incomprehension – fish comes with boiled potatoes and that's that. Most dishes are also served with a helping of rice and salad. Other **vegetables** rarely make an appearance, though you might find sliced tomato served with your fish, and heavily boiled carrots, broccoli or cabbage and the like accom-

panying meat stews. Any restaurant can also provide a **mixed salad** (*salada mista*) of lettuce, tomatoes, onions and olives, but as these tend to be enormous (and you'll probably get some salad anyway), think twice about ordering one as an appetizer.

For **dessert**, you'll almost always be offered either fresh fruit, the ubiquitous Olá, Miko or Gelvi ice cream lists, *pudim flan* (crème caramel), *arroz doce* (rice pudding) or *torta da noz* (almond tart). The presence of home-made desserts on a restaurant's menu is a good indicator of how seriously they take their food, but no restaurant will have the range of cakes and pastries you'll find in a pastry shop (see below). **Cheese** is widely available, but you won't have much to choose from unless you're eating upmarket or travelling off the beaten track, especially in Alentejo, Beiras and southern Trás-os-Montes.

Pastries, cakes and sweets

Pastries (*pastéis*), buns (*bolinhos*), rolls (*tortas*), tarts (*tartes*) and cakes (*bolos*) are serious business in Portugal, at their best in *confeitarias* and *casas de chá* (tearooms), though you'll also find them in cafés and *pastelarias*. There are hundreds of local specialities, in many places known as *doces conventuais* ("convent desserts"), thanks to the gastronomic inspiration of nuns past.

Some particularly delightful confections include *pastéis de nata* (custard tarts), *queijadas de Sintra* (Sintra "cheesecakes", not that they contain any cheese), *palha de ovos* (egg pastries) from Abrantes, *bolo de anjo* ("angel cake", with a super-sweet fluffy topping), *mil-folhas* (big light millefeuille pastries nicknamed "Salazar" on account of the late dictator's puffed up self-importance), *bolinhos* made with beans (*feijão*), carrot (*cenoura*) or pumpkin (*chila*), *bolos de arroz* (rice-flour muffins), *suspiros* ("sighs" – meringues), and a range of almond biscuits and marzipan (*bolinhos de maçapão*) from the Algarve. The incredibly sweet egg-based *ovos moles* wrapped in wafers – most famously from Aveiro – are completely over-the-top, as are *pastéis de Tentúgal* (millefeuille rolls containing more *ovos moles*). Equally filling is *broa de mel* – a heavy but soft bread made from cornflour and honey, found mainly in the north. *Broa doce* is similar but contains dried fruit.

Markets and fruit

A **market** (*mercado*) is the best place to put together a picnic: fruit, dried fruit and vegetables, nuts, bread, smoked meat and cheese, olives, biscuits and cakes. Every town has its own market, usually open Monday to Saturday mornings, sometimes also in the afternoons. The choice is usually widest on Saturdays, while on Mondays fish can be difficult to find. Portuguese **fruit** is a particular joy, especially in the Algarve and the region around Alcobaça, though any market should turn up some excellent local produce (ask for *frutas da região*), usually given away by their smaller size and more battered appearance. You may even find officially certified *biológico* – organic – produce, though it has yet to make much of an impact on mainstream food-buying habits.

In **spring** cherries are a delight, when you can also sample *anonas* from Madeira (sugar apples or sweetsops; there's a second harvest in Oct/Nov), plus strawberries and early apples and pears from Alcobaça. Particularly good **summer** fruits are melons, peaches and apricots, and exotics from the Algarve including Barbary figs, guavas and mangoes, plus *nêsperas* or *magnórios* (loquats or medlars, especially in June). The grapes arrive in late summer and **autumn**, especially black Moscatel and a welter of local white varieties. Pears, apples, plums and figs are also good at this time, including the long black figs called *bêberas* (don't eat the sap in the stem, which will blister your lips).

Winter is the time for citrus fruits, pomegranates, and immensely sweet *dióspiros* (persimmon or date-plums; tomato-like spheres with pulp like liquidized jam, eaten with a spoon). Winter and early spring is also the time for chestnuts (*castanhas*), which you can buy roasted from street vendors around the country. Available year-round are delicious finger-sized bananas from Madeira, and sweet and aromatic pineapples from the Azores.

Wines

Portugal is now an internationally recognized centre of vinicultural excellence, and the output from some of its regions – notably Alentejo, Bairrada, Dão, Estremadura, Ribatejo and the Douro – has garnered a strong following. Portuguese wine lists (ask for the *lista de vinhos*) don't just distinguish between *tinto* (red), *branco* (white) and *rosé*, but between *verde* ("green", meaning young, acidic and slightly sparkling) and *maduro* ("mature", meaning the wines you're probably accustomed to). You'll find a decent selection from around the country in even the most basic of restaurants, and often in half-bottles, too. In humbler places, the house wine is served in jugs – and can be surprisingly easy to knock back.

Some of the best-known **maduros** are reds from the Douro, Palmela, and the Dão region, a roughly triangular area between Coimbra, Viseu and Guarda, around the River Dão. Tasting a little like burgundy, and produced mainly by local co-operatives, they're available throughout the country. Among other smaller regions offering interesting wines are Colares (near Sintra), Bucelas in the Estremadura (crisp, dry whites), Valpaços from Trás-os-Montes, and Reguengos from Alentejo (with the strength and full-body typical of that region).

The light, slightly sparkling **vinhos verdes** – "green wines", in age not colour – are produced in quantity in the Minho. They're drunk early as most don't mature or improve with age, but are great with meals, especially shellfish. There are red and rosé *vinhos verdes*, though the whites are the most successful. Particularly good are those made from the Alvarinho grape variety in Monção and Melgaço, along the River Minho. Also worth seeking out are *vinhos verdes de quinta*, which are produced solely with grapes from one property (*quinta*), along the lines of the French chateaux wines: look for labels saying "Engarrafado pelo Viticultor (or Produtor)" and "Engarrafado na Propriedade (or Quinta)".

Otherwise, Portuguese **rosé wines** are known abroad mainly through the spectacularly successful export of Mateus Rosé, Saddam Hussein's favourite tipple before he was toppled. This is too sweet and aerated for most tastes, but other rosés – the best is Tavel – are definitely worth sampling.

Portugal also produces an interesting range of sparkling, **champagne-method wines**, known as *espumantes naturais*. They are designated *bruto* (extra dry), *seco* (fairly dry), *meio seco* (quite sweet) or *doce* (very sweet). The best of these come from the Bairrada region, north of Coimbra, though Raposeira wines – a little further north from near Lamego – are more commonly available.

Fortified wines

Port (*vinho do Porto*), the famous fortified wine or *vinho generoso* ("generous wine"), is produced from grapes grown in the vineyards of the Douro valley and mostly stored in huge wine lodges at Vila Nova de Gaia, facing Porto across the River Douro. You can visit these for tours and free tastings; see p.321 for all the details. Even if your quest for port isn't serious enough to do this, be sure to try the dry white aperitif ports, still little known outside the country.

Madeira (*vinho da Madeira*), from Portugal's semi-autonomous Atlantic island province, has been exported to Britain since Shakespeare's time – it was Falstaff's favourite drink, known then as sack. Widely available, it comes in four main varieties: Sercial (a light dry aperitif), Malvasia (very sweet, heavy dessert wine), Vermelho (a sweeter version of Sercial) and Boal or Malmsey (drier versions of Malvasia). Each improves with age and special vintages are greatly prized and priced. Also worth trying are the sweet white wines from **Setúbal**, which – like port and Madeira – also come as yearly vintages.

Spirits (licor)

The national **brandy** is arguably outflanked by its Spanish rivals – which are sold almost everywhere – but the native spirit is available in two major labels (Macieira and Constantino), each with loyal followings. It's frighteningly cheap. Portuguese **gin** is weaker than international brands but again ridiculously inexpensive. Be warned that the typical Portuguese measure of spirits is equivalent to at least two shots in Britain or North America.

Local firewaters – generically known as **aguardente** – include *bagaço* (the fieriest, made from grapes), *aguardente de figo*

(made from figs, with which it shares similar qualities when drunk to excess), *ginginha* (made from cherries), and the very wonderful *Licor Beirão* (a kind of cognac with herbs). In the Algarve, the best-known firewaters are *medronho*, made from the strawberry tree and which tastes a bit like schnapps, and *amarginha*, made from almonds. Other local spirits include *brandymel*, a honey brandy, *licor de bolota* (made from acorns) and *licor de ameixa* (a plum brandy).

Beer

Portugal's main **beer** (*cerveja*) brands, found nationwide, are Sagres and Super Bock. The other two brands are Cristal and Cintra, not that there's much to distinguish any of them. The standard offerings are pretty decent European-style lagers. Sagres and Super Bock also come in non-alcoholic versions, and both also have *preta* (black) variants, being quite palatable dark beers half way between Irish stout and British brown ale. Pils and Pilsner Ice are occasionally available in smarter bars, and Sagres Green is a shandy.

When drinking **draught beer**, order *um imperial* (or *um fino* in the north) if you want a regular glass, and *uma caneca* for half a litre. If you prefer bottled beer, ask for *uma garrafa*.

Coffee, tea and soft drinks

Coffee (*café*) comes either black, small and espresso-strong (*uma bica* in the south, or simply *um café*); black, small but weaker (*um carioca*); small and with milk (*um garoto* in Lisbon and the south, *um pingo* in the north); or large and with milk but weak (*um galão* or *um meia de leite*, mixing it about half-half in a glass). For white coffee that tastes of coffee and not diluted warm milk, ask for *um café duplo com um pingo de leite*.

Tea (*chá*) is a big drink in Portugal (which originally exported tea-drinking to England) and you'll find wonderfully elegant tea houses (*casas de chá*) dotted around the country. It's usually served plain; *com leite* is with milk, *com limão* with lemon, but *um chá de limão* is hot water with lemon rind. **Herbal teas** are known as *infusões*; most places have at least some bags. The most common are *cidreira* (lemon-balm), *tília* (linden) and *lúcia-lima* (lemon verbena).

All the standard **soft drinks** are available. Local varieties include the Tri Naranjus range of still fruit drinks and fizzy Sumol; both are loaded with chemicals. Healthier is fresh orange juice (*sumo de laranja*), which – rather surprisingly for an orange-producing country – can be awkward to find; adding the word *natural* should get you the real thing. *Sumo de limão* is lemonade. Lastly, **mineral water** (*água mineral*) is everywhere, either still (*sem gás*) or carbonated (*com gás*). Asking for *água da torneira* gets you tapwater, usually perfectly drinkable if heavily chlorinated.

Post, phones and the internet

The Portuguese telephone network is expensive by European standards, though using prepaid telephone cards from independent operators helps reduce the cost. The mobile phone network spans most of the country, internet access is widespread, and the postal service is usually efficient.

Postal services

Post offices (*correios*) are normally open Monday to Friday 8.30am to 6pm, the smaller ones closing for lunch. Larger branches sometimes open on Saturday mornings, while the main Lisbon and Porto offices have longer hours. Offices are invariably understaffed, so you'll find it's quicker to buy stamps from coin-operated vending machines inside the offices, or from newsagents. Letters or cards should take three or four days to arrive at destinations in Europe, and seven to ten days elsewhere. *Correio azul* is the equivalent of airmail or first-class, and theoretically (but not always in practice) takes two or three days to Europe, five elsewhere.

You can have **poste restante** (general delivery) mail sent to you at any post office in the country. Letters should be marked "Poste Restante", and your name, ideally, should be written with your surname first, in capitals and underlined. To collect, you need to take along your passport – look for the counter marked *encomendas*. If you're expecting mail, ask the clerk to check for letters under your first name as well as surname.

Telephones

All calls are most easily made using **public telephones**, which you'll find in all but the most remote villages. Most are card-operated, though a small number also work with coins. **Cards** (*cartões telefónicos*) are available from post offices, newsagents, tobacconists and kiosks. Those from Portugal Telecom (Telecom Card PT) cost €3, €6 or €9 and go in the slot; much cheaper are *cartões virtuais* ("virtual cards"), which use PIN numbers and can be used from any fixed line phone. There are several competitors, and currently cheapest for long-distance and international calls is Onicard, available in denominations of €5, €10 and €20. Most overseas phone companies also provide telephone charge cards, allowing you to call from Portugal using a PIN number and have the bill charged to your home account. While this might be convenient, charges tend to be higher than simply using a Portuguese phone card. Phoning from hotels invariably attracts even more inflated prices – check the rates before you pick up the handset.

You'll also find pay phones in bars and cafés, and in some turismo offices and newsagents. Rates are higher than in public

Useful telephone numbers

All Portuguese phone numbers have nine digits. Ones beginning with a 2 are normal land lines, charged according to distance: local, regional, and national. Numbers starting with 800 are free; 808 are local rate calls. Mobile numbers (starting with 9) are expensive to call.

Directory enquiries (national) ☏118
Directory enquiries (international) ☏177
Emergency services (free) ☏112

Operator (national) ☏12118
Operator (international; free) ☏171
Telegrams (international) ☏1582
Tourist enquiries (local rate) ☏808 781 212

phones and you can't use cards. If you need quieter surroundings you're better off in one of the **phone cabins** found in post offices and in offices of Portugal Telecom, usually next door – tell the clerk where you want to call and pay afterwards. Except in Lisbon, Porto and some places in the Algarve, telephone offices are closed in the evening.

The **cheap rate** for international and national calls operates Monday to Friday 9pm to 9am, and all day weekends and holidays. International **reverse charge** (collect) calls (*chamada à cobrar no destinatário*) can be made from any phone by dialling a special number for each country; details from the international operator on ☏171. For reverse charge calls within Portugal, ring ☏120.

Calling home from Portugal

To the UK: dial ☏00 + 44 + city/area code minus initial zero + number.
To Ireland: dial ☏00 + 353 + city/area code minus initial zero + number.
To North America: dial ☏00 + 1 + city/area code minus initial zero + number.
To Australia: dial ☏00 + 61 + city/area code minus initial zero + number.
To New Zealand: dial ☏00 + 64 + city/area code minus initial zero + number.

Calling Portugal from abroad

From the UK: dial ☏00 + 351 + number (nine digits).
From Ireland: dial ☏00 + 351 + number (nine digits).
From North America: dial ☏001 + 351 + number (nine digits).
From Australia: dial ☏0011 + 351 + number (nine digits).
From New Zealand: dial ☏00 + 351 + number (nine digits).

Mobile phones

If you want to use your mobile phone abroad, you'll need to check with your provider whether it's feasible, and what the charges are. Most mobiles in the UK and Ireland, Australia and New Zealand use GSM, which works in Portugal, though it's unlikely that a mobile bought for use in the US will work outside the States. If you are taking your own phone, you'll have to inform your phone provider before going abroad to get international access switched on (there may be a charge for this). You will also be charged extra for incoming calls when abroad, as the people calling you will be paying the usual (domestic) rate. If you want to retrieve messages while you're away, you may also have to ask your provider for a new access code. Overall, it's much easier – and possibly also cheaper, over a week or two – simply to **buy a phone** (*um telemóvel*) in Portugal. Basic models cost around €80, including a €20–30 credit. You might also be able simply to buy a replacement SIM card for your own phone, though this depends on the model and service provider – Vodafone has shops all over Portugal, for example, including at Lisbon airport.

Internet access

Internet cafés can be found in the larger towns and resorts, most charging around €1.50–2.50 per hour. Larger post offices have internet posts which you can access by credit card (around €3 per hr) or by buying a prepaid net card. Some turismos, municipal libraries (often in the town hall) and youth centres (*institutos da juventude*) offer half an hour's free access, while others make a charge. See the guide for specific details of where to go to get online.

The media

Foreign language newspapers (including the *International Herald Tribune*, British tabloids and the daily and weekly European editions of British broadsheets) can be bought in the major cities and resorts, usually a day late. One or two domestic English-language magazines and newspapers pop up from time to time on the Algarve, none of them especially informative but occasionally useful for finding work.

The Portuguese press

The most established Portuguese daily **newspapers** are the Lisbon-based *Diário de Notícias* (ⓦwww.dn.pt) and Porto's *Jornal de Notícias* (ⓦwww.jnoticias.pt). They have their uses for listings information, even if you have only a very sketchy knowledge of the language. The stylish *Público* (ⓦwww.publico.pt) has good foreign news and regional inserts and fairly easy-to-read listings. For an interesting view of the country's culture, try the weekly *JL* (*Jornal de Letras*). For fans of Portuguese sport (basically football), *A Bola*, *O Jogo* and *O Recorde* record the daily ins and outs of teams and players.

TV and radio

Portuguese **television** has four domestic stations – RTP1, 2:, SIC and TVI. The best is 2:, which has excellent films from all over the world, documentaries, daily coverage of the arts, and in-depth news. The other three channels are far more downmarket, heavy on adverts, gameshows, reality TV, and imported American and British series and films (nearly always subtitled rather than dubbed). You also get a full diet of *telenovelas* (soaps), based on the Brazilian model but now mostly home grown, which make for compelling if trashy viewing, even if you don't understand a word. Most bars and many hotels also have cable and satellite TV. Sports channels are popular in bars, mainly for football.

Portugal has a plethora of national and local **radio** stations, many of which play all the latest international hits as well as distinctive local sounds. RDP's Antenna 2 is the most serious of the lot. The BBC World Service, with hourly news, is at 6195, 12095 or 15485 KHz bands (frequencies vary throughout the day). Voice of America is sporadically audible on 96.9 and 100.5 FM, and at 972, 1296 or 9770 KHz.

Opening hours and public holidays

Most stores and businesses, plus smaller museums and rural post offices, close for a good lunchtime break – from around 12.30pm to 2.30 or 3pm. Banks are the exception, staying open during the week over lunchtime. Restaurants tend to close one day a week, usually Sunday or Monday; details are given throughout the book.

Shops generally open at 9/9.30am, and upon re-opening after lunch keep going until 6/7pm. Most will also open on Saturday mornings, especially in towns and cities. Larger **shopping centres and malls** stay open seven days a

Public holidays

January 1	New Year's Day (*Dia Um de Janeiro*)
Shrove Tuesday	February/March Carnival (*Carvaval*)
Good Friday	March/April (*Sexta Feira Santa*)
April 25	Liberty Day, commemorating the 1974 Revolution (*Vinte Cinco de Abril*)
May 1	Labour Day (*Dia do Trabalhador*)
Corpus Christi	End-May/early-June (*Corpo de Deus*)
June 10	Portugal Day (*Dia de Portugal*)
August 15	Feast of the Assumption (*Festa da Assunção*)
October 5	Republic Day (*Dia da Instauração da República*)
November 1	All Saints' Day (*Dia de Todos os Santos*)
December 1	Celebrating independence from Spain in 1640 (*Dia da Restauração*)
December 8	Immaculate Conception (*Imaculada Conceiçaõ*)
December 25	Christmas Day (*Natal*)

week, often until midnight. **Museums, churches** and **monuments** generally open from around 10am to 12.30pm and 2 to 6pm, though the larger ones stay open through lunchtime. Almost all museums and monuments, however, are closed on Mondays (or Wednesdays for palaces).

The other things to watch out for are **national public holidays** (see list above) when almost everything is closed and transport services are much reduced. There are also local festivals and holidays (see next section), when entire towns, cities and regions grind to a halt: for example June 13 in Lisbon and June 24 in Porto.

Festivals

Portugal maintains a remarkable number of folk customs, which find their expression in local carnivals (*festas*) and traditional pilgrimages (*romarias*). Some of these have developed into wild celebrations lasting days or even weeks and have become tourist events in themselves; others have barely strayed from their roots.

Every region is different, but in the north especially there are dozens of village **festivals**, everyone taking the day off to celebrate the local saint's day or the harvest, and performing ancient songs and dances in traditional dress for no one's benefit but their own. Look out, too, for the great **feiras**, especially at Barcelos in the Minho. Originally they were simply markets, but as often as not nowadays you'll find a combination of

agricultural show, folk festival, amusement park and, admittedly, tourist bazaar.

The festival list is potentially endless and only the major highlights are picked out in the **festival calendar** below. For more details on what's going on around you, check with the local turismo or buy either of the annual *Borda d'Água* or *Seringador* booklets (available from stationers or tobacconists), which are old-style almanacs detailing saints' days, star signs, eclipse predictions, gardening tips and, most importantly, all the country's annual fairs. Alternatively, consult ⓦ www.portugal.org/tourism/calendar.shtml. Local town hall websites often carry details of local festivities: the addresses are usually in the following format, ⓦ www.cm-nameoftown.pt.

Among major **national events**, Easter week, and the Santos Populares festivities associated with St Anthony (June 12/13), St John (23/24 June) and St Peter (June 28/29) stand out. All are celebrated throughout the country with religious processions. Easter is most magnificent in Braga, where it is full of ceremonial pomp, while the saints' festivals tend to be more joyous affairs. In Lisbon, during St Anthony, the Alfama becomes one giant street party. In Porto, where St John's Eve is the highlight of a week of celebration, everyone dances through the streets all night, hitting each other over the head with leeks or plastic hammers.

Events calendar

January
6: Epiphany (*Dia de Reis*) The traditional crown-shaped cake *bolo rei* (king's cake) with a lucky charm and a bean inside is eaten; if you get the bean in your slice you have to buy the cake next year.

February
Carnaval Many areas now have Rio-like parades, and Lisbon and towns in the Algarve are good destinations. But Carnaval has much older traditions steeped in spring-time fertility rites, and for a glimpse of what it was like before thongs and spangles, the masked merry-making at the *Entrudo dos Comprades* (p.362), near Lamego, is superb.

March/April
Easter (*Páscoa*) Religious processions in most places, most majestically in Braga, and at São Brás de Alportel in the Algarve (the *Festa das Tochas*). The *Festa da Mãe Soberana* in Loulé, also in the Algarve, is one of the country's largest Easter festivals. Another good location is Tomar, where the floral crosses of the procession are ceremoniously destroyed afterwards.

May
Early May: Queima das Fitas The "burning of the ribbons", celebrating the end of the academic year, reaches its drunken apogee in Coimbra.

13: Fátima (*Peregrinação de Fátima*) Portugal's most famous pilgrimage commemorates the Apparitions of the Virgin Mary (see p.185); also in October.

End of May (or early June), Corpus Christi *Vaca das Cordas* is a "running of the bull" ceremony in Ponte de Lima with roots in classical mythology (see p.425).

June
First 2 weeks: Feira Nacional da Agricultura Held at Santarém, for 10 days from the first Friday, with dancing, bullfighting and an agricultural fair.
First weekend: Festa de São Gonçalo Prominent saint's day celebrations in Amarante (see p.349).
Santos Populares (Popular Saints) Celebrations in honour of Santo António (St Anthony, June 12–13), São João (St John, 23–24) and Pedro (St Peter, 28–29) throughout the country.

July
First 2 weeks: Festa do Colete Encarnado Held in Vila Franca de Xira, with Pamplona-style running of bulls through the streets.

August
Third weekend: Romaria da Nossa Senhora da Agonía Viana do Castelo's major annual religious celebration, plus carnival and fair (see p.410).

September
First week: Romaria de Nossa Senhora dos Remédios The annual pilgrimage in Lamego comes to a head at the end of the first week, though events start in the last week of August (see p.356–357).
Second & third weekends: Feiras Novas The "New Fairs" – a traditional festival and market – held in Ponte de Lima.

October
First 2 weeks: Feira de Outubro More bull-running and fighting in Vila Franca de Xira.
13: Fátima The second great pilgrimage of the year at Fátima.

November
First 2 weeks: Feira Nacional do Cavalo The National Horse Fair, held in Golegã (see p.197).
11: São Martinho Celebrations in honour of St Martin, with roots in pre-Christian harvest festivals: coincides with the first tastings (*magustos*) of the year's wine, roast chestnuts and *Água Pé* – a weak wine made from watered-down dregs. At its

most traditional in northern Trás-os-Montes, Beira Baixa (particularly Alcains), Golegã (see above), and Penafiel east of Porto.

December
24: Christmas (*Natal*) The main Christmas celebration is midnight Mass on December 24,

followed by a traditional meal of *bacalhau*, turkey or – bizarrely in Trás-os-Montes – octopus.
31: New Year's Eve (*Noite de Ano Novo*) Individual towns organize their own events, usually with fireworks at midnight, and the New Year is welcomed by the banging of old pots and pans.

Sports and bullfighting

Portugal is famous as the home of some of Europe's top golf courses and tennis centres. Watersports are also popular, in particular surfing and windsurfing, while away from the coast the countryside provides ample opportunity for horse-riding, hiking and fishing. The country's national sport, however, is football and at times during the season (September to May) more than half the nation will be tuned to the radio or watching that week's big match at a stadium or on TV. Bullfighting, too, has a loyal following, and the spectacle has a very distinct identity from its Spanish cousin. For further information – and addresses of operators promoting sporting holidays – contact ICEP Portugal (see pp.24–25) for a copy of their *Sportugal* brochure.

Participatory sports

Although Portugal boasts some top-class **golf courses**, exclusivity is often the key word. The best way to guarantee a round is to go on a special golf-holiday package or stay at one of the hotels or villas attached to golf clubs. Green fees are usually around €60–90 per round. For more information on the country's courses, see the excellent ⓦ www.portugalgolf.pt and ⓦ www.algarvegolf.net.

Tennis courts are a common feature of most of the larger Algarve hotels, their attraction being that you can play year-round. If you want to improve your game, the best intensive coaching is at the Vale do Lobo Tennis Academy (packages organized by Light Blue Travel ⓦ www.lightbluetravel .co.uk) or the Praia da Luz Ocean Club near Lagos (Jonathan Markson Tennis ⓦ www .marksontennis.com).

Horse-riding stables dotted around throughout the country offer one-hour or full-day rides into the surrounding countryside,

as well as dressage – best experienced on Lusitano horses. Prices start from around €20 for an hour's trek, rising to around €80–100 for a full day, which usually includes a picnic lunch. For details of Centros Hípicos (riding schools) in a particular area, contact the local tourist office; traditionally at the heart of Portugal's equestrian traditions is Ribatejo province and its capital, Santarém.

Adventure and "extreme" sports are increasingly popular, with activities ranging from paragliding, rappel and abseiling to canoeing, rafting and caving. Main areas of interest are the Serra da Estrela, and the mountains of the north, for which Porto acts as a major base: the big operators there are Arrepio, Rua Prof. Antão Almeida Garrett 229, Porto (ⓣ & ⓕ 228 303 940), and Trilhos, Rua de Belém 94, Porto (ⓣ 225 504 604, ⓦ www.trilhos.pt).

Skiing is usually possible from November to February, sometimes March, in the Serra da Estrela. The slopes, with five ski lifts, lie just below the Serra's highest point, Torre. Access is easiest from Covilhã town. The lifts, ski school, and ski and snowboard rental are operated by Turistrela (☎707 275 707, ⓦwww.turistrela.pt). Use of the lifts is €12.50 weekdays, €20 weekends; Turistrela also offers half-board ski packages, starting at around €110 for two nights and three days.

Watersports

The biggest **windsurfing** and **surfing** destinations are Guincho and Praia Grande, north of Lisbon, though the winds and currents here require a high level of expertise. Ericeira on the Estramadura coast is another popular centre and frequently hosts pro competitions, as does Peniche in Estremadura, Espinho south of Porto (popular with bodyboarders), and Figueira da Foz near Coimbra. The west coast of the Algarve, round Arrifana, is excellent for beginners. Windsurf boards are available for rent on most of the Algarve beaches for around €10 a half-day, and at the more popular northern and Lisbon coast resorts. A couple of good websites (in Portuguese) are: ⓦwww.beachcam.pt for surf-savvy weather and wave height forecasts and events, and ⓦwww.surfingportugal.com, home to the Federação Portuguesa de Surf, which organizes competitions.

Laser-class **sailing** boats are usually available for rent at marinas, with lessons arranged by municipal organizations; asking for the local *clube naval* should get you in the right direction.

Scuba diving for beginners is best off Praia do Carvoeiro near Lagoa in the Algarve, where Tivoli Diving (☎282 351 194, ⓦwww.tivoli-diving.com) and Divers Cove (☎282 356 594, ⓦwww.diverscove.de) offer PADI-accredited tuition in English; a five-dive Open Water course costs around €300. For experienced divers, both also offers night and wreck dives; standard dives with equipment rental are around €35. On the west coast, conditions can be more trying, with a strong undertow, though the more sheltered waters between Lisbon and Cascais are the haunt of Aquadive, based at Paço d'Arcos (☎214 413 562, ⓦwww.aquadive.pt), which offers PADI tuition and night dives. Experienced divers should appreciate the wrecked German U-1277 submarine off Matosinhos: contact Mergulhomania (☎934 837 434, ⓦwww.mergulhomania.com). For a good

selection of links to dive shops and clubs, see ⓦwww.scubaspots.com.

Football

Portuguese **football** has a long and often glorious tradition of international and club teams. The much-vaunted *Geração de ouro* ("Golden generation"), with Figo as the star player, never quite fulfilled its early promise, though came close to glory in the 2004 European Championships, held in Portugal. They were beaten in the final by surprise winners Greece. The build-up to the championships saw the construction of several new stadiums, including the Estádio do Dragão in Porto, and Benfica's Estádio da Luz.

The leading clubs, inevitably, hail from the country's big cities, Porto and Lisbon. Over the last decade, **FC Porto** has swept up just about every title available, including the national Superliga title (seven in nine years, at the time of writing), the European UEFA Cup in 2003, and – its crowning glory – Europe's Champions League title in 2004. By contrast, Lisbon-based **Benfica**, who experienced a similar golden age in the 1960s when Mozambique-born striker Eusébio was at his masterful height, has been depressingly quiet of late, its vast legion of fans still yearning for a return to the golden days. The other big team is **Sporting**, also from Lisbon.

Just about every Portuguese supports one of these three teams, paying scant attention to the lesser, local outfits. Of these, Boavista (Porto's second team), Sporting Braga and Guimarães are the most successful. Ticket prices for league matches depend on who's playing: a clash between two big names averages €15–40 depending on the seat location, whilst a game between a big name and a lesser-known team is about half that. Matches are given due prominence in the local press. Indeed, national papers *A Bola*, *O Jogo* and *O Recorde* deal with little else. The Superliga season runs from the end of August to mid-May, most matches being held on Saturdays.

Bullfights

The Portuguese **bullfight** (*tourada*) is neither as commonplace nor as famous as its Spanish counterpart. In Portugal the bull isn't

B

killed, but instead wrestled to the ground in a colourful and skilled display. After the fight, however, the bull is usually injured and it is always slaughtered later in any case. If you choose to go – and we would urge visitors not to support the events put on simply for tourists on the Algarve – these are the basics.

A **tourada** opens with the bull, its horns padded or sheared flat, facing a mounted *toureiro* in elaborate eighteenth-century costume. His job is to provoke and exhaust the bull and to plant the dart-like *farpas* (or *bandarilhas*) in its back while avoiding the charge – a demonstration of incredible riding prowess and elegance. Once the beast is tired the *moços-de-forcado*, or simply *forcados*, move in, an eight-man team dressed in "seven dwarfs" hats. Their task is to immobilize the bull. It appears a totally suicidal mission – they line up behind each other across the ring from the bull, while the front man shouts and gesticulates to persuade the bull to charge them. In theory, the front man leaps between the charging bull's horns while the rest grab hold and try to subdue it, but in practice it often takes two or three attempts, the first tries often resulting with one or more of the *forcados* being tossed spectacularly into the air.

The great Portuguese bullfight centre is **Ribatejo**, where the animals are bred. If you want to see a fight, it's best to witness it here, amid the local aficionados, or as part of the festivals in Vila Franca de Xira and Santarém. The season lasts from around April to October. Local towns and villages in the Ribatejo also feature bull-running, through the streets, at various of their festivals.

There is a small band of Portuguese bullfighters and fans, mostly in the town of **Barrancos** in southern Alentejo, who claim the Spanish model as their own, and spent the 1990s defying the forces of law and order by publicly killing bulls in the ring. Their defiance has finally met with legal approval, allowing the practice in areas where this was traditional.

Crime and personal safety

By European standards, Portugal is a remarkably crime-free country, though there's the usual petty theft in the cities and larger tourist resorts, particularly in the form of pickpockets on public transport and in main transport terminals, something for which Lisbon has a reputation. Rental cars are also prey to thieves: remove any rental company stickers and, wherever you park, don't leave anything visible in the car (preferably, don't leave anything in the car at all). In an emergency, dial ☎112.

There are two main police forces: the metropolitan **Polícia de Segurança Pública** (PSP) and the more rural **Guarda Nacional Repúblicana** (GNR). Either handle incidents involving tourists; their contacts are given in "Listings" throughout the guide. You can't count on English being spoken and since tourists can usually muster only a few basic words of Portuguese, confusion can easily arise. To this end, showing deference is wise: the Portuguese still hold respect dear, and the more respect you show a figure in authority, the quicker you'll be on your way.

If you are unlucky enough to be robbed, don't resist. Hand over your valuables and run. If you do have anything stolen, you'll need to go to the police – primarily to file a **report** (*formulário de participação de roubo*), which your insurance company will require before they'll pay out for any claims.

Portugal is rarely a dangerous place for **women travellers** and you only need to be particularly wary in parts of Lisbon at night (around Cais do Sodré, at the top end of Avenida da Liberdade, on the metro and on the Cais do Sodré–Cascais train line), in the darker alleys near the river in Porto, and in streets immediately around train stations in the larger towns (traditionally red-light districts). In some Algarve resorts, like seaside resorts the world over, men congregate on the pick-up. If you are on your own or feel uncomfortable anywhere, you should be able to get around at night by taxi. On the whole, though, the country is formal to the point of prudishness. People may initially wonder why you're travelling on your own – especially inland and in the mountains, where Portuguese women rarely travel unaccompanied – but once they have accepted that you are a crazy foreigner you're likely to be welcomed and adopted.

Travellers with disabilities

Portugal is slowly coming to terms with the needs of travellers with disabilities, but you should not expect much in the way of special facilities. There is now ramped access to the more expensive hotels and to some museums and public buildings, while adapted WCs can be found at train stations, airports and major shopping centres. Beyond that, people are generally always ready to help and will go out of their way to make your visit as straightforward as possible.

Your first port of call in any town should be the local turismo, which will invariably find you suitable **accommodation** and, in smaller towns, may be able to organize your needs. It's worth bearing in mind that many *pensões* and *residenciais* are located on the first floor and up, and don't have lifts. However, most four- and five-star hotels have lifts, wheelchair ramps and specially adapted bedrooms and bathrooms, while many manor houses and farmhouses have guest rooms on the ground floor, while more recent conversions have tended to install lifts. *Pousadas* (pp.35–36) do not generally have any special facilities, though staff are used to requests of all kinds and will do their best to help.

Transport is the other potential problem. Whilst wheelchair access is usually possible as far as the platform (even if you have to wait for someone to come with a key to start the lift, not always in working order), getting from the platform on to the train is difficult. Arriving early is the best tactic, to give you enough time to get on without rushing. Lisbon's **metro** is not recommended, either in terms of access or for the crowds that throng it at rush hour. Porto's metro is more accessible, though outside the centrally located underground stations, where platforms are at the same level as the train doors, getting on and off will require assistance. **Self-drive vehicles** with automatic gear-shifts are available from the larger car rental companies, and there are reserved disabled parking spaces in main cities, where the Orange Badge is recognized.

Portugal's **medieval town centres** – specifically their steps and cobblestone alleys – pose their own problems. The good news is that a number of attractive medieval towns and villages have been rehabilitated as part of central Portugal's *Aldeias Históricas* scheme, which for some has also meant the construction of smooth wheelchair-accessible pathways alongside the cobbles, as is the case at Castelo Rodrigo, for instance.

Useful contacts

Portugal

ARAC Rua Dr. António Cândido 8, 1097 Lisbon ☎213 563 836, ℻213 563 737. Provides information on rental companies that have cars with adapted controls.

Secretariado Nacional Para a Reabilitação e Integração das Pessoas com Deficiência Av. Conde de Valbom 63, Lisbon ☎217 929 500, ⊚www.snripd.mts.gov.pt. Government organization producing comprehensive regional accessible tourism guides (in Portuguese only: *Guia de Turismo Acessível*), featuring disabled-friendly travel agents, restaurants, transport facilities, clubs etc.

Wheeling Around the Algarve Rua Casa do Povo 1, Apartado 3421, 8135-905 Almancil ☎289 393 636, ⊚www.disabledholidaydirectory.co.uk. Private company organizing accessible holiday accommodation, transport (including adapted cars and vans), and sporting/leisure activities in the Algarve. All facilities are personally inspected before recommendation.

UK and Ireland

Access Travel 6 The Hillock, Astley, Lancashire M29 7GW ☎01942/888 844, ⊚www .access-travel.co.uk. Small tour operator handling flights, transfer and accommodation suitable for the disabled – Algarve holidays only.

Holiday Care 2nd floor, Imperial Building, Victoria Rd, Horley, Surrey RH6 7PZ ☎0845/124 9971 or 020/8760 0072, ⊚www.holidaycare.org.uk. Provides free lists of accessible accommodation abroad.

Irish Wheelchair Association Blackheath Drive, Clontarf, Dublin 3 ☎01/818 6400, ⊚www.iwa.ie.

Useful information provided about travelling abroad with a wheelchair.

Tripscope Alexandra House, Albany Rd, Brentford, Middlesex TW8 0NE ☎08457/585 641, ⊚www .tripscope.org.uk. Registered charity providing a telephone information service with free advice on international transport for those with a mobility problem.

North America

Access-Able ⊚www.access-able.com. Online resource for travellers with disabilities.

Directions Unlimited 123 Green Lane, Bedford Hills, NY 10507 ☎1-800/533-5343 or 914/241-1700. Travel agency specializing in bookings for people with disabilities.

Mobility International USA 451 Broadway, Eugene, OR 97401 ☎541/343-1284, ⊚www .miusa.org. Information and referral services, access guides, tours and exchange programmes.

Wheels Up! ☎1-888/389-4335, ⊚www .wheelsup.com. Provides discounted airfare, tour and cruise prices for disabled travellers, also publishes a free monthly newsletter and has a comprehensive website.

Australia and New Zealand

ACROD (Australian Council for Rehabilitation of the Disabled) PO Box 60, Curtin ACT 2605; ☎02/6282 4333, ⊚www.acrod.org.au. Provides lists of travel agencies and tour operators for people with disabilities.

Disabled Persons Assembly 4/173-175 Victoria St, Wellington, New Zealand ☎04/801 9100, ⊚www.dpa.org.nz. Resource centre with lists of travel agencies and tour operators for people with disabilities.

Travelling with children

As Portuguese society largely revolves round family life, the country is very child-friendly and families will find it one of the easiest places for a holiday. The two main worries for parents in Portugal are cars – which as a rule don't observe pedestrian crossings, certainly not outside the Algarve – and the strong sun. Keep young children covered up between 11am and 3pm, make them wear a hat, and always apply a high-factor sun screen.

Most **hotels and pensions** can provide an extra bed or a cot (*um berço*) if notified in advance. There is usually no charge for children under six who share their parents' room (or under-3s in some of the stingier four- and five-star places), while discounts of up to fifty percent on accommodation for six- to eight-year-olds are not uncommon. Baby-sitting and child supervision is available at most four- and five-star places, though you'll have to pay.

Children are welcome in all **cafés and restaurants** at any time of the day, irrespective of whether or not they sell alcohol. Indeed, waiters often go out of their way to spend a few minutes entertaining restless children; tots may even find themselves being carried off for a quick tour of the kitchens while parents finish their meals in peace. Highchairs and child menus are scarce – though restaurants happily do half portions, which are still probably too much for most children to finish. In addition, restaurants rarely open much before 7.30pm,

so kids will need to adjust to Portuguese hours; local children are still up at midnight. Specific **changing facilities** in restaurants, cafés and public toilets are largely non-existent, and when you do find them – such as in larger shopping centres – they are usually part of women's toilets only.

For those with **babies**, fresh milk (*leite do dia*) is sold in larger shops and supermarkets; mornings are best as it tends to sell out by mid-afternoon. Smaller shops and cafés stock UHT. Nappies/diapers (*fraldas*) are widely available in supermarkets and pharmacies, as are formula milk, babies' bottles and jars of baby food – though don't expect the full range of (or indeed any) organic choices you might be used to at home.

Most **museums, sights and attractions** don't usually charge for small children, while under 12s get in for half price. On **public transport**, under-5s go free while 5–11 year-olds travel half price on trains but pay full fare on metros and buses.

Directory

Addresses Most addresses in Portugal consist of a street name and number followed by a storey, eg. Avenida da República 34-3° (US, fourth floor). An "esq" or "E" (for *esquerda*) after a floor number means you should go to the left; "dir" or "D" (for *direita*) indicates to the right; *esquina* means

corner or junction; R/C stands for *rés-do-chão* (ground floor). In rural areas, the address may simply consist of a house or building name followed by the area. *Apartado* followed by a number is a PO Box, not a physical address. In this guide, we've also used the followng abbreviations:

Av. (for Avenida, avenue), Pr. (Praça, square); Trav. (Travessa, alley).

Beaches Beware of the heavy undertow on many of Portugal's western Atlantic beaches (southward in summer, northward in winter) and don't swim if you see a red or yellow flag. The EU blue flag indicates that the water is clean enough to swim in – sadly, not always the case – and that the beach has lifeguards. The sea is warmest on the eastern Algarve, but remains chilly outside summer.

Cinemas Films are almost always shown with the original (usually English) soundtrack with Portuguese subtitles. Listings are in local newspapers or on boards placed somewhere in the central square of every small town; don't expect film names to be literal translations of the original – whoever's in that line of work seems to prefer titles based on Roget's entries for "fatal" and "dangerous". Screenings are cheap, with reduced prices at matinées and on Mondays. The website @ www.7arte.net reviews and lists the latest releases.

Complaints If you feel strongly enough to want to make a formal complaint about a restaurant, café, hotel or tour operator, ask for the *livro de reclamações* (complaints book) – every establishment, however humble, is obliged to keep one. If you really get nowhere, the local turismo is as good a place as any to vent your frustration.

Dress Churches require "modest dress", which just means you shouldn't wear shorts or flimsy tops.

Electricity Mains voltage is 220V, which works fine with equipment intended for 240V. Plugs are the European two round pin variety; adaptors are sold at airports and at *drogarias* – hardware stores.

Emergencies Call ☏112 for the emergency services. If you're involved in a road accident, use the nearest roadside orange-coloured SOS telephone – press the button and wait for an answer.

Gay and lesbian Though traditionally a conservative society, Portugal has become increasingly tolerant of homosexuality, at least in the cities and in the Algarve. In more rural areas, however, old prejudices are engrained and coming out is still a problem for many. As there is no mention of homosexuality in law, gays have the same rights as heterosexuals by default and the legal age of consent is 16. The best contact is the Lisbon-based Centro Comunitário Gay e Lésbico de Lisboa, Rua de São Lázaro 88, 1150-333 Lisbon (Mon–Sat 4–8pm; ☏ 218 873 918, @ www.ilga-portugal.oninet.pt), which organizes

gay events, mainly in the capital, but can also help with information and contacts. Another good website is @ www.portugalgay.pt. Both sites have English versions. The biggest scene is in Lisbon, which has a number of gay bars and clubs, plus the gay-friendly *Anjo Azul* hotel (see p.73).

Laundry There are very few self-service launderettes, but loads of *lavandarias*, where you can get your clothes washed, mended, and ironed (overnight) at fairly low cost, paid by item or by kilo. Some only do dry-cleaning (*limpeza a seco*).

Left luggage You can often leave bags at a train or bus station for a small sum while you look for rooms. On the whole the Portuguese are highly trustworthy, and even shopkeepers and café owners will keep an eye on your belongings. Or try the local turismo, which may agree to look after your bags for a while.

Swimming pools Each sizeable town has a swimming pool (*piscina*), usually outdoors, but you'll find that they are often closed from September to May.

Time Portugal is in the same time zone as the UK, following GMT in winter. Clocks go forward an hour at the end of March and back an hour at the end of October. If you're coming from France or Spain, turn your watch back one hour.

Toilets Public toilets are neither numerous nor obvious, though a number of cities including Porto and Lisbon have installed French-style coin-operated automated toilets, usually in main squares. Cafés and pastry shops are handy in an emergency, though you'll have to order something first, and sometimes ask for the key (*por favor, a chave do banheiro*). The "facilities" at cheaper cafés and bars may leave you somewhat dazed. A sign reading *Sanita, Retretes, Banheiro, Lavábos* or *WC* will head you in the right direction, then it's *homens* or *cavalheiros* for men and *senhoras* or *mulheres* for women.

Working in Portugal Portugal has employment problems of its own, and without a special skill you're unlikely to have much luck finding any kind of long-term work, especially without having mastered the language. All workers should register with the Serviço de Estrangeiros e Fronteiras (ask at the nearest police station), and non-EU passport holders must apply for a work permit before they enter Portugal. For more information, see Jonathan Packer's *Live and Work in Spain and Portugal*, or Sue Tyson-Ward's *How to Live and Work in Portugal*, both slanted towards ex-pats but packed with practical advice.

Guide

Guide

Lisbon and around

CHAPTER 1 # Highlights

✳ **Bairro Alto** Don't miss a night out in Lisbon's "upper town", packed with vibrant bars, clubs and restaurants. See p.80

✳ **Alfama** Explore the city's oldest quarter, though be warned – getting lost here is half the fun. See p.90

✳ **Museu Nacional do Azulejo** The splendid *azulejo* (tile) museum traces the history of this most Portuguese of art forms. See p.93

✳ **Museu Gulbenkian** An awe-inspiring collection of priceless art and antiquities. See p.96

✳ **Mosteiro dos Jerónimos** The magnificent Manueline monastery houses the tomb of Vasco da Gama. See p.99

✳ **Antiga Confeitaria de Belém** Enjoy a tasty custard tart in Belém's most traditional pastry shop-café. See pp.106–107

✳ **Lux** Dance till dawn at one of Europe's coolest clubs. See p.115

✳ **Estádio da Luz** The country's finest sports arena is the home of its most famous football club, Benfica. See p.120

✳ **Palácio National, Sintra** A splendid royal retreat in the summer residence of kings. See p.130

✳ **Castelo de Palmela** Stay the night in the converted castle at Palmela, now a luxurious *pousada*. See p.145

△ Torre de Belém

Lisbon and around

There are few cityscapes as startling and eccentric as that of **Lisbon** (Lisboa). Built on a switchback of hills above the broad Tejo estuary, its quarters are linked by an amazing network of cobbled streets with outrageous gradients, up which crank trams and funiculars. Down by the river, the outstretched arms of a vast, Rio-like statue of Christ embrace one of the grandest of all suspension bridges and a fleet of cross-river ferries. For visitors, it's hard not to see the city as an urban funfair, a sense heightened by the brooding castle poised above the Alfama district's medieval, whitewashed streets, the fantasy Manueline architecture of Belém, the vibrant mosaics of the central Rossio square, and the adventurous contemporary architecture in the Parque das Nações. Gentler than any port or capital should expect to be, and defiantly human in pace and scale, Lisbon is immediately likeable.

For much of the last century, the city stood apart from the European mainstream, an isolation that ended abruptly with the 1974 Revolution, and the subsequent integration into the European Community (now the European Union) just over a decade later. Over the past hundred years, central Lisbon's population has more than doubled to over a million, one tenth of all Portuguese, with numbers boosted considerably after the Revolution by the vast influx of **refugees** – *retornados* – from Portugal's former African colonies of Angola, Cabo Verde, São Tomé e Principe, Guinea-Bissau and Mozambique. The *retornados* imposed a heavy burden on an already strained economy, especially on housing, but their overall integration is one of the modern country's chief triumphs. Portuguese Brazilians and Africans have had a significant effect on the capital in particular, and alongside the traditional fado clubs of its Bairro Alto and Alfama quarters, Lisbon now has superb Latin and African bands, and a panoply of international restaurants and bars.

The 1755 Great Earthquake destroyed many of Lisbon's most historic buildings. The Romanesque **Sé** (cathedral) and the Moorish walls of the **Castelo de São Jorge** are fine early survivors, however, and there is one building from Portugal's sixteenth-century Golden Age – the extraordinary **Mosteiro dos Jerónimos** at Belém – that is the equal of any in the country. Two major museums demand attention, too: the **Fundação Calouste Gulbenkian**, a combined museum and cultural complex with superb collections of ancient and modern art, and the **Museu Nacional de Arte Antiga**, which is effectively Portugal's national art gallery. The main contemporary highlight is the **Oceanário** (Europe's second-largest ocean-arium) out at the **Parque das Nações** Expo site, and there are numerous

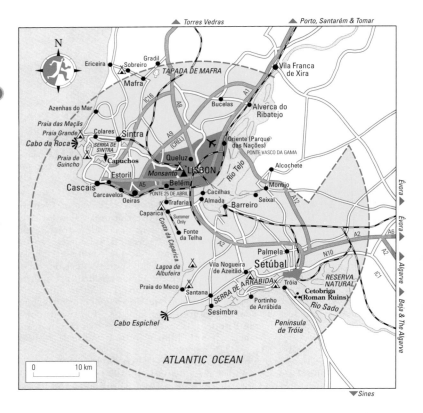

smaller museums throughout the city too, but more than anything perhaps, it's the day-to-day life on display in the streets, avenues and squares that makes the city so enjoyable – from the shoe shiners of the Rossio to the multitude of Art Nouveau shops and cafés.

It would take a few days to do Lisbon justice, though it's better still to make the capital a base for a week or two's holiday, taking day trips and excursions out into the surrounding area. There's no need to rent a car; you can see almost everything by public transport. The beach suburbs of **Estoril** and **Cascais** are just half an hour's journey away to the west, while to the south, across the Tejo, are the miles of dunes along the **Costa da Caparica**. Slightly further south lies the port of **Setúbal**, featuring one of the earliest Manueline churches, and nearby is the resort of **Sesimbra** – a popular day trip for Lisboans. To the north is the Rococo **Palácio de Queluz** and its gardens, which you can see en route to **Sintra**, to the northwest, whose lush wooded heights and royal palaces make up Byron's "glorious Eden". Finally, further north, the extraordinary palace-monastery at **Mafra** marks a first step into the province of Estremadura.

Lisbon

Physically, central **LISBON** is an eighteenth-century city: elegant, open to the sea and carefully planned. The description does not extend to its modern expanse, of course – there are suburbs here as poor and inadequate as any in Europe – but remains accurate within the old central boundary of a triangle of hills. This "lower town", the **Baixa**, was the product of a single phase of building, carried out in less than a decade by the dictatorial minister, the Marquês de Pombal, in the wake of the earthquake that destroyed much of central Lisbon in 1755.

The **Great Earthquake**, which was felt as far away as Jamaica, struck Lisbon at 9.30am on November 1 (All Saints' Day) 1755, when most of the city's population was at Mass. Within the space of ten minutes there had been three major tremors and the candles of a hundred church altars had started fires that raged throughout the capital. A vast tidal wave swept the seafront, where refugees were seeking shelter and, in all, 40,000 of the 270,000 population died. The destruction of the city shocked the continent, prompting Voltaire, who wrote an account of it in his novel *Candide*, into an intense debate with Rousseau on the operation of providence. For Portugal, and for the capital, it was a disaster that in retrospect seemed to seal an age.

Before the earthquake, eighteenth-century Lisbon had been arguably the most active port in Europe. The city had been prosperous since Roman, perhaps even Phoenician, times. In the Middle Ages, as **Moorish** Lishbuna, it thrived on its wide links with the Arab world, while exploiting the rich territories of the Alentejo and Algarve to the south. The country's reconquest by the Christians in 1147 was an early and dubious triumph of the Crusades, its one positive aspect being the appearance of the first true Portuguese monarch **Afonso Henriques**. It was not until 1255, however, that Lisbon took over from Coimbra as the capital.

Over the following centuries Lisbon was twice at the forefront of European development and trade, on a scale that is hard to envisage today. The first phase came with the great **Portuguese discoveries** of the late fifteenth and sixteenth centuries, such as Vasco da Gama's opening of the sea route to India. The second was in the opening decades of the **eighteenth century**, when the colonized Brazil yielded both gold and diamonds. These phases were the great ages of Portuguese patronage. The sixteenth century was dominated by Dom Manuel I, under who the flamboyant national architectural style known as **Manueline** (see box on p.191) developed. Lisbon takes its principal monuments – the tower and monastery at Belém – from this era. The eighteenth century, more extravagant but with less brilliant effect, gave centre stage to **Dom João V**, best known as the obsessive builder of Mafra, which he created in response to Philip II's El Escorial in Spain.

In the nineteenth and early twentieth centuries the city was more notable for its political upheavals – from the assassination of Carlos I in 1908 to the Revolution in 1974 – than for any architectural legacy, though the Art Nouveau movement made its mark on the capital. In the last two decades, however, Lisbon has once more echoed to the sounds of reconstruction on a scale not seen for two hundred years. The influx of EU cash for economic

64

LISBON

Airport ◄ | ◄ Roma Metro | ◄ Campo Grande & Museu da Cidade | ◄ Avenida da República

AREEIRO

CAMPO PEQUENO

AV. JOÃO XXI

PR. DR FRANCISCO DE SÁ CARNEIRO

AREEIRO Ⓜ

PR. DE LONDRES

AV. ALMIRANTE REIS

ALAMEDA Ⓜ

AV. DA IGREJA

ARROIOS Ⓜ

AV. ALMIRANTE REIS

PENHA DE FRANÇA

RUA MORAIS SOARES

ACCOMMODATION

13Yda Sorte	L
Alegria	N
Avenida Alameda	F
Barco do Tejo	U
Britania	I
Canadá	A
Dom Carlos	H
Dom Sancho I	K
Florescente	P
As Janelas Verdes	V
Lapa Palace	S
Lisboa Plaza	M
Miraparque	E
Pascoal de Melo	D
Portuense	O
Pousada de Juventude	B
Ritz Four Seasons	G
Sana Classic Rex	C
Suíço Atlântico	J
Veneza	Q
VIP Orion Eden	R
York House	T

Entrecampos Station

Praça de Touros

Culturgest

R. DO ARCO DO CEGO

Bus Station

SALDANHA Ⓜ

AV. DUQUE D'ÁVILA

AV. DEFENSORES DE CHAVES

AV. B. DU BOCAGE

Feira Popular

CAMPO PEQUENO

AVENIDA CINCO DE OUTUBRO

AVENIDA DA REPÚBLICA

PR. DUQUE SALDANHA

Museu Dr A. Gonçalves

PICOAS Ⓜ

R. DONA ESTEFÂNIA

ESTEFÂNIA

RUA GOMES FREIRE

AV. ELIAS GARCIA

AV. VIS. DE VALMOR

AV. DUQUE D'ÁVILA

AV. MIGUEL BOMBARDA

AV. JOÃO CRISÓSTOMO

R. M. DE SÁ DA BANDEIRA

PARQUE Ⓜ

AV. FONTES PEREIRA DE MELO

AV. DE BERNA

Museu Gulbenkian

Centro de Arte Moderna

S. SEBASTIÃO Ⓜ

RUA R. ORTIGÃO

PR. DE ESPANHA

PRAÇA DE ESPANHA Ⓜ

AV. DOS COMBATENTES

AV. COLUMBANO BORDALO

SETE RIOS Ⓜ

AV. ANTÓNIO AUGUSTO DE AGUIAR

AVENIDA SIDÓNIO PAIS

Pavilhão dos Desportos

Parque Eduardo VII

Estufas

RUA MARQUES DE FRONTEIRA

RUA CASTILHO

RODRIGO DA FONSECA

AV. J. A. DE AGUIAR

PR. DO MARQUÊS DE POMBAL (ROTUNDA)

Fundação Arpad-Sziznes

CAMPOLIDE

AV. E. D. PACHECO

AVENIDA CALOUSTE GULBENKIAN

RUA DAS

Amoreiras

RUA DAS

◄ Zoo | Aqueduto das Águas Livres ▼

CAFÉS & RESTAURANTS

A Linha d'Água	3
Bica do Sapato	10
Botequim do Rei	4
Casa da Comida	6
Casanova	11
Jardim do Marisco	12
Os Tibetanos	8
Picanha	9
Portugáila	5
Ribadouro	7
Rodizio Grill	1
Versailles	2

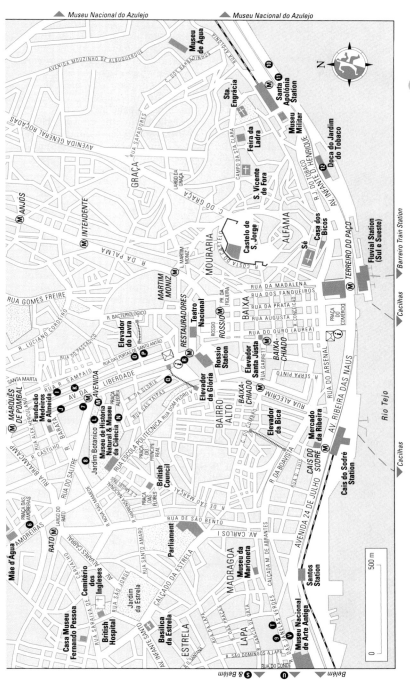

Museu Nacional do Azulejo

Museu Nacional do Azulejo

N

AVENIDA MOUZINHO DE ALBUQUERQUE

Museu de Água

FUNICULAR DOS BARBADINHOS

RUA DOS BARBADINHOS

Sta. Engrácia

M Santa Apolónia Station

AVENIDA GENERAL ROÇADAS

RUA DOS SAPADORES

Barreiro Train Station

Museu Militar

ANJOS M

RUA SAPADORES

GRAÇA

R. J. DO TOBACO P. J. DE HENRIQUE

Doca do Jardim do Tobaco

Cacilhas

LARGO DA GRAÇA

C. DO GRAÇA

Feira da Ladra

CAMPO DE STA. CLARA

S. Vicente de Fora

AV. INFANTE D. HENRIQUE

INTENDENTE M

R. DA PALMA

C. DO CASTELO

MOURARIA

Castelo de S. Jorge

ALFAMA

Casa dos Bicos

TERREIRO DO PAÇO

Fluvial Station (Sul e Sueste)

RUA GOMES FREIRE

L. MARTIM MONIZ

Sé

Cacilhas

MARTIM MONIZ

COSTA DO CASTELO

RUA DA MADALENA

RUA DOS FANQUEIROS

M

R. BACTERIOLOGICO

Teatro Nacional

RUA DA PRATA

BAIXA

RUA DA CONCEIÇÃO

RUA LUCIANO CORDEIRO

RUA DO PASSADIÇO

RESTAURADORES

RUA AUGUSTA

Elevador do Lavra

M

Rossio Station

RUA DO OURO (AUREA)

PRAÇA DO COMÉRCIO

RUA DAS PORTAS DE SANTO ANTÃO

RUA B SAMPAIO

i

M

ROSSIO

M

RP DA FIGUEIRA

i

SANTA MARTA

LIBERDADE

Elevador da Glória

Rossio

Elevador Santa Justa

BAIXA-CHIADO

AV. DA

Fundação Medeiros e Almeida

7

M

AVENIDA

PRAÇA DA ALEGRIA

R. DA GLÓRIA

RUA GARRETT

BAIXA-CHIADO

MARQUÊS DE POMBAL M

RUA ALEX HERCULANO

R. BARATA

R. DAS TAIPAS

M

R. SERPA PINTO

RUA DA ARSENAL

Rio Tejo

Jardim Botânico

8

Museu de História Natural & Museu da Ciência

BAIRRO ALTO

RUA DOM PEDRO V

Elevador da Bica

Mercado da Ribeira

R. DO SALITRE

RUA ESCOLA POLITÉCNICA

PRAÇA DO PRÍNCIPE REAL

M

AV. RIBEIRA DAS NAUS

British Council

PRAÇA DAS FLORES

R. DO ALECRIM

CAIS DO SODRÉ

Cacilhas

RATO M

LARGO DO RATO

R. SÃO MARÇAL

Cais do Sodré Station

AMOREIRAS

PRAÇA DAS AMOREIRAS

6

RUA DE SÃO BENTO

R. DE SÃO PAULO

Mãe d'Água

RUA BRAAMCAMP

RUA DO SALITRE

R. DE SÃO BENTO

Parliament

AV CARLOS I

AVENIDA 24 DE JULHO

Santos Station

Cemitério dos Ingleses

MADRAGOA

Museu da Marioneta

Casa Museu Fernando Pessoa

British Hospital

CALÇADA DA ESTRELA

RUA SANTO AMARO

Jardim da Estrela

LAPA

Museu Nacional de Arte Antiga

Basílica da Estrela

ESTRELA

9

Belém

Belém & Belém

500 m

0

65

regeneration in the 1980s was followed by works associated with Lisbon's status as **European City of Culture** in 1994 and its hosting of the **Expo** in 1998. The city now has a major new transport infrastructure, including Europe's longest bridge, and new rail and metro lines, while the **European Championships** of 2004 – with Lisbon in the spotlight again – bequeathed the city two newly constructed football stadia. The streets of the Chiado, burned out in a devastating fire in 1988, have been beautifully restored to their original design, while the old riverfront has also been given a new lease of life, with once-derelict warehouses converted into thriving cafés and clubs. If this non-stop rebuilding and renovation has somewhat diminished the erstwhile lost-in-time feel of the city, it has also injected a wave of optimism that has made Lisbon one of Europe's most exciting capitals.

Arrival and information

On arrival, the first place to head for is Rossio, the main square of the lower town, easily reached by public transport and with much of the city's accommodation within walking distance. On the western side of the adjoining Praça dos Restauradores is the main Portuguese tourist board in the **Palácio da Foz** (daily 9am–8pm; ☎213 463 314, ⊛www.portugalinsite.pt) – useful for information on destinations outside Lisbon – though the main Lisbon tourist office, the **Lisbon Welcome Centre** is down by the riverfront in Praça do Comércio (daily 9am–8pm; ☎210 312 810/5, ⊛www.atl-turismolisboa.pt), and can supply accommodation lists, bus timetables and maps. In summer, smaller "Ask Me" kiosks are dotted round town near the main tourist sights, such as in Largo Martim Moniz, on Rua Augusta and within the Castelo de São Jorge.

By air

The **airport** (☎218 413 700, ⊛www.ana-aeroportos.pt) is twenty minutes north of the city centre and has a tourist office (daily 8am–midnight; ☎218 450 660), ATMs, 24-hour exchange bureau and car rental agencies.

The easiest way into the centre is by **taxi** and, depending on traffic conditions, a journey to Rossio should cost €7–10. Note that you'll be charged €1.60 extra for baggage, and that fares are slightly higher between 10pm and 6am, at weekends and on public holidays. The tourist office at the airport also sells **taxi vouchers**, priced according to the zone or destination you are travelling to (€11/13.20 for the central zone (day/night), €14/16.80 for zone 2, to Belém for example, and €35/42 to Estoril and Cascais). The vouchers allow you to jump the queue for airport taxis and establish the cost beforehand, but otherwise they work out more expensive than normal rides.

Alternatively, catch the #91 **Aerobus** (every 20min, 7am–9pm; €2.50, free from the Welcome Desk for TAP passengers; ☎966 298 558), which departs from outside the terminal and runs to Praça do Marquês de Pombal, Praça dos Restauradores, Rossio, Praça do Comércio and Cais do Sodré train station. The ticket, which you buy from the driver, gives you one day's travel on the city's buses and trams. Cheaper **local buses** (#44 or #45, every 10–15min, 6am–midnight; €1) leave from outside the terminal – a little beyond the Aerobus stop – to Praça dos Restauradores and Cais do Sodré station, though these are less convenient if you have a lot of luggage.

By train

Long-distance trains from Coimbra, Porto, northern Portugal, Madrid and Paris arrive at **Estação Santa Apolónia** (☎218 884 142), which is a fifteen-minute walk east of Praça do Comércio (and on the Gaivota metro line from late 2005). Buses #9, #39, #46 or #90 run to Praça dos Restauradores or Rossio. At the station there's a helpful information office (daily 8am–4pm; ☎218 821 604) and an exchange bureau. An increasing number of trains call at **Estação do Oriente** (☎800 201 820), 5km east of the centre at Parque das Nações, on the Oriente metro line, convenient for the airport and for the north or east of Lisbon. There are connecting trains to Santa Apolónia from here, as well as bus links to towns north and south of the Tejo.

There are plans to open a new rail bridge over the Rio Tejo and to extend the commuter rail route under the Ponte 25 de Abril so it links up with the Algarve line, but for the time being trains from the Algarve and the south of Portugal still terminate opposite Lisbon at **Barreiro** (☎212 073 028), on the far bank of the river. From the station here you catch a ferry (included in the price of the train ticket) to **Estação Fluvial** (also known as Sul e Sueste), next to Praça do Comércio (on the Gaivota metro line from late 2005). Buses #9, #39, #80 and #90 run up from Fluvial to Rossio, through the Baixa.

Local trains – from Sintra or Queluz – emerge right in the heart of the city at **Estação do Rossio** (☎213 433 747), a mock-Manueline complex with the train platforms an escalator-ride above street-level entrances. The station is complete with shops, ATMs, and left-luggage lockers. Services from Cascais and Estoril arrive at the other local station, **Cais do Sodré** (☎213 424 780), on the Caravela metro line – you can either walk the 500m east along the waterfront to Praça do Comércio or take any of the buses heading in that direction.

By bus

Various bus companies have terminals scattered about the city, but the main terminal is at **Avenida João Crisóstomo** (metro Saldanha), 2.5km north of Rossio, which has an information office (6am–10pm) that can help with all bus arrival and departure details. This terminal is also where most **international bus services** arrive. You can usually buy tickets if you turn up half an hour or so in advance, though for the summer express services to the Algarve and Alentejo coast it's best to book a seat (through any travel agent) a day in advance. An increasing number of bus services also use the **Oriente** transport interchange at Parque das Nações on the Oriente metro line. See "Listings" for contact details for all city bus terminals.

By car

Driving into Lisbon can take years off your life, and if it's the beginning or end of a public holiday weekend should be avoided at all costs. Heading to or from the south on these occasions, it can take over an hour just to cross the Ponte 25 de Abril, a notorious traffic bottleneck. **Parking** is also very difficult in the centre. Pay-and-display bays get snapped up quickly, and many unemployed people earn tips for guiding cars into available spaces (give a small tip – a euro should do it – to avoid finding any unpleasant scratches on your car when you return).

You'd be wise to head straight for an official **car park**: central locations include the underground ones at Restauradores; Parque Eduardo VII; Parking Berna on Rua Marquês de Sá da Bandeira near the Gulbenkian; and the Amoreiras complex on Avenida Engenheiro Duarte Pacheco. Expect to pay around €8–10 per day. Wherever you park, do not leave valuables inside: the break-in rate is extremely high.

If you are **renting a car** on arrival, for touring outside Lisbon, the best advice is to wait until the day you leave the city to pick it up; you really don't need your own transport to get around Lisbon. See "Listings" on p.123 for car rental companies and remember to leave plenty of time if returning your car to the airport: paperwork is time-consuming.

City transport and tours

Most places of interest are within easy walking distance of each other, but you'll probably need to use Lisbon's **public transport system** at some stage. As well as the tram, bus, *elevador* (funicular), ferry or metro, taxis are widely used and are among the cheapest in Europe. Although Lisbon ranks as one of the safer European cities it does have its share of pickpockets, so take special care of your belongings when using the metro and buses. If you want to see the city quickly, or just get a different view, consider taking a **tour** – we pick out the highlights below.

Public transport in the city is operated by **Carris** (☏213 613 078, ⓦwww .carris.pt). You can just buy a single **ticket** (*bilhete simples*) each time you ride, but it's much better value to buy one of the available **travel passes**. You will first need a *Sete Colinas Card* (Seven Hills Card; €0.50), which allows access to the electronic barriers on the metro. You can then load the card with a **day pass** (*bilhete um dia*; €2.85), which allows unlimited travel on buses, trams, *elevadores* and the metro until midnight of that day; there's also a **five-day pass** (*bilhete cinco dias*; €11.85). For longer stays, you will need a *Lisboa Viva Card* (€5), on which you can load a 30-day pass (€22.85). Cards and passes are available at main metro stations, at kiosks next to the Elevador Santa Justa, and in Praça da Figueira, among other places.

If you're planning some intensive sightseeing, consider a **Cartão Lisboa** (Lisbon Card; €13.25 for one day, €22.50 for two, or €27.50 for three), which entitles you to unlimited rides on buses, trams, metro and *elevadores* and entry to around 25 museums, including the Gulbenkian and Museu de Arte Antigua, plus discounts of around 25 to 50 percent at other sights and attractions. It's available from all the main tourist offices, including the one in the airport.

The metro and local trains

Lisbon's **metro** – the Metropolitano – is the quickest way to reach outlying sights, including the Gulbenkian museum, the zoo and the Oceanarium. Three new stations on the Gaivota line are still not operational, but should be by the end of 2005. The most central metro stations are those at Restauradores, Rossio and Baixa-Chiado, all in Zone 1, and it is unlikely that you'll need to stray from the central zone. The **hours of operation** are daily from 6.30am to 1am and tickets cost €0.65/€1 per journey (Zone 1/2), or €6/9 for a ten-ticket *caderneta* – sold at all stations. If you think you're going to use the metro a lot, buy a one-day pass as detailed above.

The local train line from **Cais do Sodré** station runs west along the coast to Belém (€0.95), or to Estoril and Cascais (€1.30 to either). You can also buy a five-day pass on the Cascais train line (€10.40), which is worth considering if

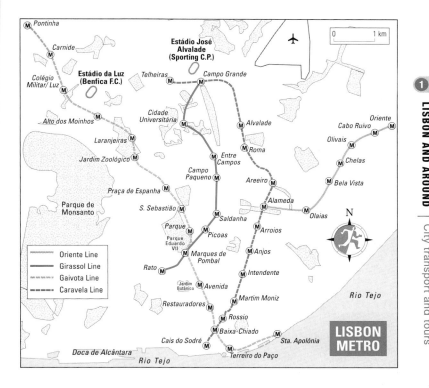

you are staying in Carcavelos, Estoril or Cascais. Other local trains depart from the central **Rossio** station to Queluz (€0.90) and Sintra (€1.40 one way, or a five-day pass €11.20).

Trams, elevadores and buses

At the slightest excuse you should ride one of Lisbon's **trams** (*eléctricos*). Ascending some of the steepest gradients of any city in the world, the five tram routes are worth taking for the sheer pleasure of the ride alone. The best route is #28, which runs from Graça to Prazeres, though the most interesting stretch is from São Vicente to the Estrela gardens, passing through Rua da Conceição in the Baixa.

The three funicular railways and one street lift – each known as an **elevador** – offer quick access up to Lisbon's highest hills and the Bairro Alto (see box below for their routes). Otherwise, **buses** (*autocarros*) run just about everywhere in the Lisbon area, filling in the gaps to reach the more outlying attractions. Most trams, buses and *elevadores* run every ten to fifteen minutes throughout the day, from around 6.30am to midnight: stops are indicated by a sign marked *paragem*, which carries route details. Clubbers can take advantage of the *Madrugada* ("Dawn Service") **night buses**, which operate from 12.30–5am. Most services run to and from Cais do Sodré station, and useful routes include the #201 (Belém via the docas) and the #208 (Parque das Nações).

Tram and elevador routes

Trams

#12 circles the Castelo de São Jorge via the Alfama, Pr. da Figueira and Largo Martim Moniz.

#15 A modern "supertram" from Pr. da Figueira to Algés via Belém; buy tickets in advance or take exact change for automatic ticket machines.

#18 from Rua da Alfândega via Pr. do Comércio and Cais do Sodré to the Palácio da Ajuda.

#25 from Rua da Alfândega to Campo Ourique via Pr. do Comércio, Cais do Sodré, Lapa and Estrela.

#28 from Graça to Prazeres, via the Alfama, Baixa, Chiado, São Bento and Estrela.

Elevadores

Elevador da Bica: links Calçada do Coimbro in Barrio Alto to Rua da Boavista near Cais do Sodré station.

Elevador da Glória: links the Bairro Alto with the west side of Pr. dos Restaura-dores.

Elevador de Santa Justa: a lift, rather than a funicular, taking you from Rua do Ouro, on the west side of the Baixa, up to a walkway by the ruined Carmo church; due to reopen shortly.

Elevador do Lavra: links Rua São José, just off Av. da Liberdade, to the back of the Hospital de São José.

Individual **tickets** (*bilhetes*, also known as BUCs, pronounced *books*) for buses, trams and *elevadores* can be bought on board (tram #15 has an automatic ticket machine and does not issue change) and cost €1.10/€2.20 for zone 1/2. It's much cheaper to buy tickets in advance (either individually or in blocks of ten) from kiosks around the main bus terminals, such as in Praça do Comércio and Praça da Figueira. These cost €0.65 each, and are valid for one journey within a single travel zone (so a journey across two travel zones – say, from the city centre to Belém – requires two tickets, costing €1.30). Punch the ticket in the machine next to the driver when you board. Travel passes (see p.68) are also valid on all buses, trams and *elevadores*.

Taxis

Lisbon's cream or (older) black-and-green **taxis** are inexpensive, as long as your destination is within the city limits; there's a minimum charge of €1.90 and an average ride across town will cost around €6. Fares are higher from 10pm to 6am, at weekends and on public holidays. All taxis have meters, which should be switched on, and tips are not expected. A green light means the cab is occupied. Outside the rush hour taxis can be hailed quite easily in the street, or alternatively head for a **taxi rank**, found outside the stations, at Rossio, at the southern end of Avenida da Liberdade, and at Estação Fluvial – you can expect to queue during morning and evening rush hours. At night, your best bet is to ask a restaurant or bar to call a cab for you, or phone yourself (which entails an €0.80 extra charge): try Rádio Taxis ☎218 119 000, Autocoope ☎217 932 756 or Teletáxi ☎218 111 100.

Ferries

Ferries cross the Rio Tejo at various points, offering terrific views of Lisbon. From **Praça do Comércio** (Estação Fluvial), there are crossings to Cacilhas (every 15min, Mon–Fri 6.10am–9.45pm, Sat & Sun 6.15am–9.50pm; €0.65 one-way), Barreiro for train connections to Algarve and the south (every 20–30min, same hours; €1.50) and Montijo (every 30min, Mon–Fri 6.30am–11.30pm, Sat 7am–10pm, Sun 9.45am–10pm; €1.65). From **Cais do Sodré**, car ferries also cross to Cacilhas (every 5–10min, daily 5.30am–2.30am; €0.65), while ferries run **from Cacilhas** to Parque das Nações (Mon–Fri 6 daily, Sat & Sun 8 daily; €1.50). From **Belém** there are services to Trafaria (every 30–60min, Mon–Sat 6.30am–11.30pm, Sun 7.30am–11.30pm; €60), from where you can catch buses to Caparica.

Tours

Public transport is good fun but can be crowded, so if you want more space or are pushed for time, it is worth considering one of the various organized tours of the city. The turismos have more information about any of the tours covered below.

Bus tours Carris (☎966 298 558) operates two open-top bus tours: the one-hour Circuito Tejo (hourly 11am–4pm; board-at-will day-ticket €13) takes passengers around Lisbon's principal sites, with clearly marked stops across the city; while the Oriente Express tour (3 departures daily; €13) departs from Pr. do Comércio to Parque das Nações. A four-hour Sintra tour (€40, ☎213 582 334) departs daily at 2pm from Pr.do Comércio, travelling via Cascais, Guincho and Cabo da Roca. Art Shuttle (☎213 959 818) has a hop-on hop-off minibus service that visits Lisbon's main sites every 15 minutes or so (May–Sept; €6 for 12hr, €12 for 24hr).

River cruises Cruises up the Rio Tejo depart from Estação Fluvial (daily 11am & 3pm; 2hr 30min; €15; ☎218 820 348). The price includes a drink and a bilingual commentary and, at weekends, the boat stops at Parque das Nações and Belém.

Taxi tours Taxis can be booked for three-hour tours of the city (€60), or for half-day (€77/127) or full-day (€80/130) excursions to Sintra and Cascais. Call ☎218 450 660.

Tram tours Circuito Colinas (Hills Tour; March–Oct hourly 9am–6pm; Nov–Feb departures at 11am, 1.30pm & 3.30pm; €16; ☎966 298 558) takes passengers on a ninety-minute ride in an antique tram from Pr.do Comércio, around Alfama, Chiado and São Bento.

Accommodation

Lisbon has scores of small, inexpensive **pensões** (pensions), often located in tall tenement buildings in the city centre. There are dozens of possibilities alone around Rossio, Praça dos Restauradores and Praça da Figueira, with the cheaper places found on streets parallel to Avenida da Liberdade, such as Rua das Portas de Santo Antão and Rua da Glória. The Baixa grid, including the more upmarket area of the Chaido, has a fair selection of places, too, though rooms in the Bairro Alto – handy for the nightlife – can be both hard to come by and noisy. The most atmospheric part of town, around the Alfama and the castle, has some very attractive choices, though *pensão* prices here are higher. **Hotels** tend to be located outside the historic centre, particularly along Avenida da Liberdade, around Parque Eduardo VII and Saldanha, and in the prosperous suburb of Lapa. Lisbon also has several **youth hostels**, including one right in the city centre and another out at the Parque das Nações, while the closest **campsite** is 6km west of the centre, with others sited close to regional beaches.

The airport information desk, or either of the tourist offices in town, will establish whether or not there's space at a city *pensão* or hotel. They won't reserve the room for you but will supply telephone numbers if you want to call yourself. Don't be unduly put off by some fairly insalubrious staircases, but do be aware that rooms facing onto the street can be unbearably noisy. Although air conditioning is standard in the better establishments, you'll have to rely on opening windows in cheaper places, which adds to the noise level. The humbler guest houses also often lack central heating, which can make them pretty chilly during the cool winter nights.

At Easter, and between June and September, rooms can be hard to find without an **advance reservation** and prices are at their highest – though August can be less expensive as many people head for the beach. At peak times, be prepared to take anything vacant and look around the next day for somewhere better or cheaper. During the rest of the year you should have little difficulty finding a room, and can even try knocking the price down, especially if you're able to summon up a few good-natured phrases in Portuguese.

Rossio and Praça da Figueira

The following are marked on the Baixa map on p.78.

Hotel Avenida Palace Rua 1 de Dezembro ☏213 460 151, ⓦ www.hotel-avenida-palace.pt. Lisbon's grandest downtown hotel has an elegant nineteenth-century style with modern touches, and very comfortable rooms sporting high ceilings, traditional furnishings and marble bathrooms. Artists Gilbert and George often stay here. Breakfast included. ❾

Pensão Coimbra e Madrid Pr. da Figueira 3-3° ☏213 424 808, ⓕ213 423 264. Large, decently run (if faintly shabby) *pensão*, above the *Pastelaria Suíça*. Superb views of Rossio, Pr. da Figueira and the castle from the street-honkingly noisy front-facing rooms. Others vary in attraction, so you might need to ask to see one or two before you make your choice. No credit cards. ❷, en-suite ❸

Residencial Gerês Calç. da Garcia 6 ☏218 810 497, ⓕ218 882 006. The beautifully tiled entrance hall sets the tone in one of the city's more characterful central guest houses, located on a steep side street just off the Rossio. The varying-sized rooms are simply furnished but clean, and all have TVs. ❸, en-suite ❹

Hotel International Rua da Betesga 3 ☏213 240 990, ⓕ213 290 999. You know this is a smart central hotel as soon as you see the red-carpeted lift, and if you get one of the (albeit small) rooms with a balcony overlooking the town, you won't be disappointed. Rooms have air conditioning, TV and a safe. Breakfast included. ❹

Hotel Metrópole Rossio 30 ☏213 469 164, ⓦ www.almeidahotels.com. Very centrally located period hotel, with most of the comfortable rooms (as well as the airy lounge bar) offering superb views over Rossio and the castle. However, you pay for the location, and the square can be pretty noisy at night. Buffet breakfast included. ❼

Hotel Mundial Rua Dom Duarte 4 ☏218 842 000, ⓦ www.hotel-mundial.pt. Central four-star hotel with nearly 300 air-conditioned rooms, all decorated in contemporary colours. There's a rooftop restaurant and terrace with amazing views too. Disabled access. Parking. Buffet breakfast included. ❾

Hotel Portugal Rua João das Regras 4 ☏218 877 581, ⓕ218 867 343. An amazing old hotel that has suffered from an appalling conversion; the high decorative ceilings upstairs have been chopped up under wall partitions. For all that, there are comfortable rooms, an ornate TV room and a fine *azulejo*-lined staircase. Breakfast included. ❹

Baixa and Chiado

The following are marked on the Baixa map on p.78.

Hotel Borges Rua Garrett 108 ☏213 461 951, ⓕ213 426 617. A traditional hotel in a handy position for Chiado's shops and cafés, though the rooms are very ordinary and the hotel often fills with tour groups. ❹

Hotel Duas Nações Rua da Vitória 41 ☏213 460 710, ⓕ213 470 206. Classy, pleasantly faded, nineteenth-century hotel in the Baixa grid with a secure entrance and friendly reception. Rooms are simply furnished but comfortable and clean. ❹

Residencial Insulana Rua da Assunção 52 ☏213 427 625, ⓕ213 428 924. On the top floor of an old Baixa building, above a series of under-wear shops, this decent *residencial* has smart en-suite rooms and English-speaking staff. The bar overlooks a quiet pedestrianized street. ❹

Hotel Lisboa Regency Chiado Rua Nova do
Almada 114 ☎ 213 256 100, ⓦ www
.regency-hotels-resorts.com. Stylish hotel designed
by Álvaro Siza Viera – the architect responsible for
the Chiado redevelopment – with Eastern-inspired
interior decor. The cheapest rooms lack much of a
view, but the best ones have terraces with stunning castle vistas, a view you get from the bar terrace too. Rooms are not huge but are plush and
contemporary. Breakfast included. ❽
Pensão Prata Rua da Prata 71-3° ☎ 213 468
908. You need mountaineering experience to
climb the stairs to this *pensão*, which offers small,
basic rooms in a family-run apartment. Toilets are
shared, but some rooms have showers, the others share a clean bathroom. No credit cards. ❷,
en-suite ❸

Bairro Alto and Príncipe Real

*The following are marked on the Bairro Alto map
on pp.82–83.*
Hotel Anjo Azul Rua Luz Soriano 75 ☎ 213 478
069, ⓔ anjoazul@mail.telepac.pt. This is the city's
first exclusively gay hotel, in a tastefully refurbished, blue-tiled town house right in the heart
of the nightlife. There are just twelve simple but
attractive rooms, so it is best to book ahead. ❷,
en-suite ❸
Residencial Camões Trav. do Poço da Cidade 38-1°
☎ 213 467 510, ⓕ 213 464 048. Small *residencial*
with a mixed bag of rooms – some have a balcony,
and the more expensive ones have a private bathroom. Breakfast provided April–Oct only. ❸
Casa de São Mamede Rua da Escola Politécnica
159 ☎ 213 963 166, ⓕ 213 951 896. Superb seventeenth-century town house with period fittings,
a bright breakfast room and even a grand stained-
glass window. Rooms are rather ordinary but come
with private bathroom and TV. ❺
Pensão Duque Calç. do Duque 53 ☎ 213 463
444, ⓕ 213 256 827. Near São Roque church,
down the steps off Largo T. Coelho heading down
to Rossio, so clear of the nightlife noise. It has
basic but spotless rooms, with shared bathrooms.
No credit cards. ❷
Pensão Globo Rua do Teixeira 37 ☎ 213 462
279. Located in an attractive house, the rooms
are simple but clean and reasonably large (though
those at the top are a little cramped). It's in a
good location, near the clubs but in a quiet street.
Cheaper rooms come without showers (or even
windows), the more expensive ones have showers
and views. ❷
Pensão Londres Rua Dom Pedro V 53 ☎ 213 462
203, ⓕ 213 465 682. Great old building with high

ceilings and pleasant enough rooms spread across
several floors; some of the larger ones fall into
the next price category. A few rooms come with
cubby-hole bathrooms. Gay friendly, though not
exclusively so. ❸
Pensão Luar Rua das Gavéas 101-1° ☎ 213 460
949. Calm, polished interior and decently furnished
rooms (with and without shower), which are
somewhat noisy. Some are also much larger than
others, so ask to see. ❸

Lapa

*To reach these hotels (marked on the general map
of Lisbon on pp.64–65), take bus #40 or #60 or
tram #25 from Pr. do Comércio.*
Barco do Tejo Trav. do Cruz da Rocha 3 ☎ 213
977 055, ⓕ 213 956 946. Run by a characterful
bevy of English-speaking staff and set in a quiet
side street, this simple *pensão* is within walking
distance of the docks and the Museu Nacional de
Arte Antiga. Spotless rooms, each with their own
shower. ❸
As Janelas Verdes Rua das Janelas Verdes 47
☎ 213 218 200 ⓦ www.heritage.pt. This discreet
eighteenth-century town house is just metres from
the Museu Nacional de Arte Antiga. There are well-
proportioned rooms with marble-clad bathrooms,
period furnishings, and a delightful walled garden
with a small fountain where breakfast is served in
summer. The top-floor rooms have stunning river
views. ❾
Lapa Palace Hotel Rua do Pau de Bandeira 4
☎ 213 949 494, ⓦ www.orient-express.com. A
stunning nineteenth-century mansion in the heart
of the Diplomatic Quarter, with lush gardens,
health club and five-star facilities. Rooms – which
cost around €375 a night – are luxurious, particularly within the Palace Wing, where the decor
is themed from Classical to Art Deco. In summer,
grills are served in the gardens by the pool. Disabled access. Buffet breakfast included. ❾
Residencial York House Rua das Janelas Verdes
32 ☎ 213 962 435, ⓦ www.yorkhouselisboa.
com. Installed in a seventeenth-century convent,
rooms come with rugs, tiles and four-poster beds.
The best are grouped around a beautiful interior
courtyard, where drinks and meals are served in
summer. The highly rated restaurant is also open
to non-residents. Buffet breakfast included. ❾

Alcântara

Pestana Palace Rua Jau 54 ☎ 213 615 600,
ⓦ www.pestana.com. See map on p.100. Set in
an early twentieth-century palace full of priceless
works of art, most of the spacious and contemporarily furnished rooms at this superb five-star hotel

are in tasteful modern wings that stretch either side of luxuriant gardens. Prices start at about €300 a night. There are indoor and outdoor pools, a sushi bar, health club and restaurant. A superb buffet breakfast is served in the ballroom. ❾

Alfama and Castelo

The following are marked on the Alfama and Castelo map on p.89.

Pensão Ninho das Águias Costa do Castelo 74 ☎218 854 070. Beautifully sited *pensão* in its own view-laden terrace garden on the street looping around the castle – this is one of the most popular budget options in Lisbon, so book well in advance. Climb up the staircase and past the bird cages. Rooms are bright but spartan, and those with private bath cost €5 more. ❸

Pensão São João de Praça Rua de São João de Praça 97-2° ☎218 862 591, ⓕ218 881 378. Located immediately below the cathedral in a beautiful town house with street-facing balconies, this has bags of character even if it is slightly shabby. ❸, en-suite ❹

Sé Guest House Rua São João de Praça 97-1° ☎218 864 400, ⓕ263 271 612. In the same building as the São João de Praça but a bit more upmarket. Wooden floors throughout, bright, airy rooms with communal bathrooms, and friendly, English-speaking owners. ❹

Albergaria Senhora do Monte Calç. do Monte 39 ☎218 866 002, ⓔsenhoradomonte@hotmail. com. Comfortable, modern hotel in a beautiful location, close to Largo da Graça, with views of the castle and Graça convent from its south-facing rooms – the more expensive rooms have terraces. Parking available or tram #28 passes close by. Breakfast served on a fine terrace. ❼

Solar do Castelo Rua das Cozinhas 2 ☎218 870 909, ⓦwww.heritage.pt. Lisbon's latest boutique hotel is a beautiful eighteenth-century mansion abutting the castle walls on the site of the former palace kitchens, parts of which remain. Just fourteen bright, modern rooms cluster round a tranquil Moorish courtyard, where breakfast is served in summer. ❾

Avenida da Liberdade, Restauradores and around

The following are marked on the map of Lisbon on pp.64–65.

Residencial 13 da Sorte Rua do Salitre 13 ☎213 531 851, ⓕ213 956 946; metro Avenida. Translates as "Lucky 13", and it's certainly an attractive option in a good location. The en-suite rooms are well decorated, and have TVs and minibars. ❸

Residencial Alegria Pr. Alegria 12 ☎213 220 670, ⓔmail@alegrianet.com; metro Avenida. Great position, facing the leafy square, with spacious, spotless rooms with TVs. ❸

Hotel Britania Rua Rodrigues Sampaio 17 ☎213 155 016, ⓦwww.heritage.pt; metro Avenida. A smart four-star hotel with good-sized rooms and a classic 1940s Deco interior designed by Cassiano Branco. A fine buffet breakfast is included. ❽

Hotel Dom Carlos Av. Duque de Loulé 121 ☎213 512 590, ⓦwww.domcarloshoteis.com; metro Marquês de Pombal. Decent three-star hotel, with fair-sized rooms, all with bath, TV and minibar. There's also a downstairs bar where breakfast is served. ❻

Residencial Dom Sancho I Av. da Liberdade 202 ☎213 548 648, ⓔdsancho@iol.pt; metro Avenida. One of the few inexpensive options right on the Avenida, set in a grand old mansion with high ceilings and decorative cornices – though the front rooms are noisy. The large en-suite rooms come with TVs and air conditioning, and price includes breakfast. ❹

Residencial Florescente Rua das Portas de Santo Antão 99 ☎213 426 609, ⓕ213 427 733; metro Restauradores. One of this pedestrianized street's best-value options, where many of the rooms are spick-and-span and come with TV and small bathroom. However, others are windowless and less appealing. ❹

Hotel Lisboa Plaza Trav. Salitre 7 ☎213 218 200, ⓦwww.heritage.pt; metro Avenida. Just off the Avenida, and in front of a theatre park, this bright, polished, four-star hotel has marble bathrooms, bar, restaurant and botanical garden views from rear rooms. A substantial buffet breakfast is included. Disabled access. ❽

Pensão Portuense Rua das Portas de Santo Antão 151–153 ☎213 464 197, ⓔrportuense@net. sapo.pt; metro Restauradores. Welcoming and good-value guest house just off the pedestrianized stretch. The rooms are all en suite. ❸

Hotel Suíço Atlântico Rua da Glória 3–19 ☎213 461 713, ⓔh.suisso.atlantico@grupofbarata.com; metro Restauradores. Tucked around the corner from the elevator, just off the Avenida, this provides standard mid-range accommodation. Rooms have showers, and some have a balcony overlooking the seedy Rua da Glória. The intriguing mock-baronial bar is the best bit. Breakfast included. ❹

Hotel Veneza Av. da Liberdade 189 ☎213 522 618, ⓦwww.3Khoteis.com; metro Avenida. Built in 1886, the distinguishing feature of this former town house is an ornate staircase, now flanked by modern murals of Lisbon. The rest of the hotel is more ordinary, with standard en-suite rooms containing minibars and TVs. Breakfast included. Parking.

VIP Orion Eden Pr. dos Restauradores 18–24 ℡ 213 216 600, Ⓦ www.viphotels.com; metro Restauradores. Compact studios and apartments sleeping up to four people, in the impressively converted Eden Theatre. Get a ninth-floor apartment with a balcony and you'll have the best views and be just below the rooftop pool and breakfast bar. All studios come with dishwashers, microwaves and satellite TV. Disabled access. ❻, larger apartments ❽

Praça Marquês de Pombal and Saldanha

The following are marked on the map of Lisbon on pp.64–65.

Residencial Avenida Alameda Av. Sidónio Pais 4 ℡ 213 532 186, Ⓕ 13 526 703; metro Parque or Marquês de Pombal. Very pleasant three-star *pensão* with air-con rooms, all with bath and park views. Breakfast included. ❹

Residencial Canadá Av. Defensores de Chaves 35-1-4° ℡ 213 513 480, Ⓕ 13 542 922; metro Saldanha. Excellent value for money: largish, airy rooms with private bathrooms (and satellite TV) plus a sunny breakfast room and lounge area. It's very handy for the bus station. ❹

Miraparque Av. Sidónio Pais 12 ℡ 213 524 286, Ⓔ miraparque@esoterica.pt; metro Marquês de Pombal or Parque. An attractive building with a traditional feel overlooking Parque Eduardo VII. The reception can be a bit brusque, but there's a decent bar and restaurant, and all the spacious, if slightly old-fashioned, rooms come with TV. Breakfast included. ❺

Residencial Pascoal de Melo Rua Pascoal de Melo 127–131 ℡ 213 577 639, Ⓕ 13 144 555; metro Arroios or Saldanha. This airy three-star *residencial* has a bright *azulejo*-lined entry hall. Small but well-decorated rooms have bathrooms, TVs and balconies that face the street. ❸

Ritz Four Seasons Rua Rodrigo da Fonseca 88 ℡ 213 811 400, Ⓦ www.fourseasons.com; metro Marquês de Pombal. This vast modern building is one of the grandest and – at €450 a double – one of the most expensive hotels in Lisbon. Rooms are huge, with classy marble bathrooms, great beds and terraces overlooking the park, while public areas are replete with marble, antiques, old masters and overly attentive staff. There's also a fitness centre, spa, highly rated restaurant and internet facilities. Disabled access. Excellent buffet breakfast. ❾

Sana Classic Rex Rua Castilho 169 ℡ 213 882 161, Ⓦ www.sanahotels.com; metro Marquês de Pombal. Smart hotel with in-house restaurant and small but well-equipped rooms, complete with TV, minibar and baths. The front rooms have large balconies overlooking Parque Eduardo VII. Breakfast included. ❽

Youth hostels

Pousada de Juventude da Almada Quinta do Bucelinho, Pragal, Almada ℡ 212 943 491, Ⓦ www.pousadasjuventude.pt. On the south side of the Tejo – with terrific views back over Lisbon – this is not particularly convenient for sightseeing in the city (take a train from Entrecampos or Sete Rios to Pregal, the first stop after Ponte 25 de Abril), but is within striking distance of the Caparica beaches. There are over twenty four-bedded dorms and thirteen twin rooms with their own loos, plus a games room, disabled access and internet facilities. Dorms from €12.50, rooms ❸, apartments ❹

Pousada de Juventude de Catalazete Estrada Marginal, Oeiras ℡ 214 430 638, Ⓦ www .pousadasjuventude.pt. A small, attractive hostel, overlooking the beach at Oeiras, between Belém and Cascais, with accommodation in four- or six-bedded dorms or simple twin rooms. Either take bus #44 direct from the airport, or the train from Cais do Sodré to Oeiras station, then a taxi for the last 2km. Reception is open 6am–11pm and there's a midnight curfew, although you can get a pass to stay out later. Dorm rooms from €11, rooms ❷

Pousada de Juventude de Lisboa Rua Andrade Corvo 46 ℡ 213 532 696, Ⓦ www .pousadasjuventude.pt; metro Picoas. See map on pp.64–65. This is the main city hostel, set in a rambling old building, with a small bar (6pm–midnight) and canteen. Thirty rooms sleeping 4 or 6 (with shared bathrooms), or doubles with private shower rooms. There's also a TV room on the top floor, and breakfast is included in the price. Disabled access. Dorms €15, rooms ❸

Lisboa Parque das Nações Rua de Moscavide 47–101, Parque das Nações ℡ 218 920 890, Ⓦ www.pousadasjuventude.pt; metro Oriente. See map on p.104. Five minutes walk northeast of Parque das Nações, towards the new bridge, this well-equipped modern youth hostel has 18 four-bedded dorms and ten double rooms. There's also a pool table and disabled access. Dorms from €12.50. rooms ❸

Campsites

Parque Municipal de Campismo Estrada da Circunvalação, Parque Florestal de Monsanto ℡ 217 623 100, Ⓕ 217 623 106. The main city campsite – with disabled facilities, a swimming pool and shops – is 6km west of the city centre, in the expansive hilltop Parque de Monsanto. The entrance is on the park's west side. Bus #43 runs here from Pr. da Figueira via Belém. Though the campsite is secure, take care in the park after dark.

Orbitur Costa de Caparica Av. Afonso de Albuquerque, Quinta de Santo António, Monte de Caparica ☎ 212 901 366, ⓦ www.orbitur.pt. In a good position a short, tree-shaded walk from the beach, this is one of the few campsites in Caparica open to non-members, but tents, caravans and bungalows are crammed in cheek by jowl.

Facilities are good, but it's not for those looking for solitude.

Orbitur Guincho N247, Lugar da Areia, Guincho ☎ 214 870 450, ⓦ www.orbitur.pt. Attractive campsite set among pine trees close to Guincho beach, which is served by bus from Cascais. The site, with its own tennis courts, minimarket and café, also has bungalows and caravans for rent. Orbitur members get a ten-percent discount.

Camping Praia Grande Praia Grande ☎ 219 290 581, ⓔ wondertur@ip.pt. Well-equipped campsite less than 1km from the beach at Praia Grande, west of Sintra. Bus #441 runs from Sintra train station.

The City

Eighteenth-century prints show a pre-quake Lisbon of tremendous opulence, its skyline characterized by towers, palaces and convents. There are glimpses of this still – the old Moorish hillside of Alfama survived the destruction, as did Belém – but these are isolated neighbourhoods and monuments. It is instead the Marquês de Pombal's perfect Neoclassical grid that covers the centre, Europe's first great example of visionary urban planning. Giving orders, following the earthquake, to "Bury the dead, feed the living and close the ports", the king's minister followed his success in restoring order to the city with a complete rebuilding. The lower town, the **Baixa** – still the heart of the modern city – was rebuilt according to Pombal's strict ideals of simplicity and economy. In an imposing quarter of ramrod-straight thoroughfares, individual streets were assigned to each craft and trade, with the whole enterprise shaped by grand public buildings and spacious squares.

At the Baixa's southern end, opening onto the Rio Tejo, is the broad, arcaded **Praça do Comércio**, with its grand triumphal arch as well as ferry stations for crossing the river and tram terminus for Belém. At the Baixa's northern end – linked to the Praça do Comércio by almost any street you care to take – stands Praça Dom Pedro IV, popularly known as **Rossio**, the main square since medieval times and the only part of the rebuilt city to remain in its original place, slightly off-centre in the symmetrical design. Rossio merges with Praça da Figueira and Praça dos Restauradores and it is these squares, filled with cafés and lively with buskers, business people, and streetwise hawkers and dealers, which form the hub of Lisbon's daily activity. At night the focus shifts to the **Bairro Alto**, or upper town, high above and to the west of the Baixa, and best reached by funicular (the Elevador da Glória) or – when it reopens – by the great street elevator, the Elevador de Santa Justa. Between the two districts, halfway up the hill, **Chiado** is Lisbon's most elegant shopping area. East of the Baixa, the landmark **Castelo de São Jorge** surmounts an even higher hill, with the **Alfama** district – the oldest, most fascinating part of the city with its winding lanes and anarchic stairways – sprawled below.

From Rossio, the main, tree-lined **Avenida da Liberdade** runs north to the city's central park, **Parque Eduardo VII**, beyond which spreads the rest of the modern city: the **Museu Gulbenkian** is to the north; the Amoreiras shopping complex to the west; and mundane shopping streets to the east. No stay in Lisbon should neglect the futuristic oceanarium in the **Parque das Nações**,

5km to the east, or the waterfront suburb of **Belém**, 6km to the west, which is dominated by one of the country's grandest monuments, the Mosteiro dos Jerónimos. En route to Belém lies Lisbon's other main museum, the **Museu de Arte Antiga**, close to the rejuvenated docks at **Alcântara.**

The Baixa

At the southern, waterfront end of the **Baixa** (pronounced *Bye-sha*), the **Praça do Comércio** was the climax to Pombal's design, surrounded by classical buildings and centred on an exuberant bronze of Dom José – the reigning monarch during the earthquake and the capital's rebuilding. The metro station is named **Terreiro do Paço**, after the royal palace (*paço*) that once stood on this spot – the original steps still lead up from the river. Ironically, Portugal's royals came to a sticky end in the square; in 1908, alongside what was then the Central Post Office, King Carlos I and his eldest son were shot and killed, clearing the way for the declaration of the Republic two years later. Nowadays the square is one of the city's main venues for New Year's Eve festivities.

At the western side of the square lies the **Lisbon Welcome Centre** (daily 9am–8pm), which acts as the tourist office as well as housing a café, internet centre, shops, restaurant and exhibition hall, all buried in a series of rooms between the square and neighbouring Rua do Arsenal, where there is another entrance. North of Praça do Comércio, the largely pedestrianized Rua Augusta is marked by a huge arch, **Arco da Rua Augusta**, depicting statues of historical figures, including Pombal and Vasco da Gama. Beyond here you'll encounter buskers and street artists, banks and business offices, though this area was also the site of Lisbon's earliest settlement. Building work on the Banco Comercial Português at Rua dos Correeiros 9 revealed Roman walls and a mosaic floor, which can be viewed from the tiny **Núcleo Arqueológico** (book in advance for visits, Thurs 3–5pm, Sat 10am–noon & 3–5pm; free; ☎213 211 700).

Many of the streets in the Baixa grid take their names from traditional crafts and businesses once carried out here, such as Rua da Prata (Silversmiths' Street), Rua dos Sapateiros (Cobblers' Street), Rua do Ouro (Goldsmiths' Street, now better known as Rua Aurea) and Rua do Comércio (Commercial Street). Although the trades have largely disappeared, tiled Art Deco shopfronts and elaborately decorated *pastelarias* still survive here and there, while Rua da Conceição retains its shops selling beads and sequins.

At the western end of Rua de Santa Justa in the upper reaches of the Baixa, it's hard to avoid Raul Mésnier's **Elevador de Santa Justa** (May–Sept Mon–Fri 8.30am–10.30pm, Sat & Sun 9am–10.30pm; Oct–April daily 9am–7pm; ticket office above the entrance, €1), one of the city's most eccentric structures. Built in 1902 by a disciple of Eiffel, a giant lift whisks you 32m up the innards of a latticework metal tower before depositing you on a platform high above the Baixa. The exit at the top of the *elevador* – which leads out beside the Bairro Alto's Convento do Carmo – has been closed for some time now for structural work, but this should not deter you from taking the trip up to the rooftop café, which has great views over the city.

Rossio and Praça da Figueira

Rossio (officially Praça Dom Pedro IV) – at the northern end of the Baixa grid – is Lisbon's oldest square and, though shot through with traffic, remains the liveliest. The square itself is modest in appearance, but very much a focus for the city, sporting several popular cafés, most of which have outdoor seating.

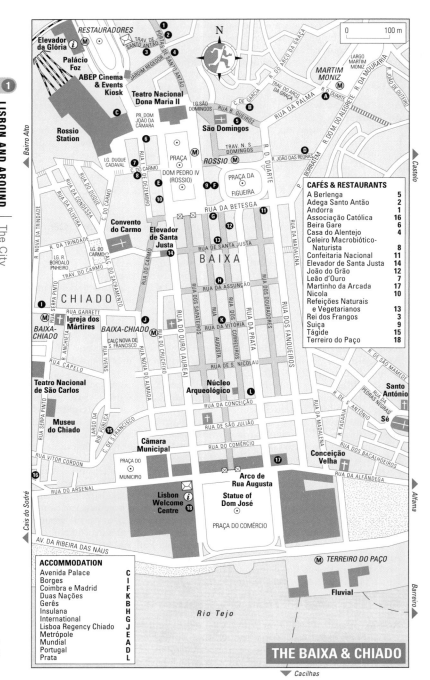

CAFÉS & RESTAURANTS

A Berlenga	5
Adega Santo Antão	2
Andorra	1
Associação Católica	16
Beira Gare	6
Casa do Alentejo	4
Celeiro Macrobiótico-Naturista	8
Confeitaria Nacional	11
Elevador de Santa Justa	14
João do Grão	12
Leão d'Ouro	7
Martinho da Arcada	17
Nicola	10
Refeições Naturais e Vegetarianos	13
Rei dos Frangos	3
Suiça	9
Tágide	15
Terreiro do Paço	18

ACCOMMODATION

Avenida Palace	C
Borges	I
Coimbra e Madrid	F
Duas Nações	K
Gerês	B
Insulana	H
International	G
Lisboa Regency Chiado	J
Metrópole	E
Mundial	A
Portugal	D
Prata	L

THE BAIXA & CHIADO

The square's single concession to grandeur is the **Teatro Nacional de Dona Maria II**, built along the north side in the 1840s. Here, prior to the earthquake, stood the Inquisitional Palace, in front of which public hangings, *autos-da-fé* (ritual burnings of heretics) and even bullfights used to take place. The nineteenth-century statue atop the central column is of Dom Pedro IV (after whom the square is officially named), though curiously it's a bargain adaptation: cast originally as Maximilian of Mexico, it just happened to be in Lisbon en route from France when news came through of Maximilian's assassination.

The **Igreja de São Domingos**, immediately to the east in Largo São Domingos, was where the Inquisition read out its sentences. It was gutted by a fire in the 1950s, but has now been fully restored. The road and square outside the church, at the bottom of Rua das Portas de Santo Antão, is a popular meeting place. The local African population hangs out on the street corner, while Lisbon's lowlife frequent the various **ginginha bars**, which specialize in lethal measures of cherry brandy. Resist the urge to eat the proffered cherry itself – they've been soaked in alcohol for years and provide a kick usually only available from expensive drugs. South, past the church, the street runs into **Praça da Figueira**, the square adjacent to Rossio. It contains some of the main city bus and tram stops and, like Rossio, is centred on a fountain and lined with shops.

Chiado

On the west side of the Baixa, stretching up the hillside towards the Bairro Alto, the area known as **Chiado** – the *nom de plume* of the poet António Ribeiro – suffered great damage from a fire that swept across the Baixa in August 1988. Many old shops in Rua do Crucifixo were destroyed, but following restoration their soaring new marble facades consciously mimic the originals.

Chiado remains one of the city's most affluent quarters, focused on the fashionable shops and old café-tearooms of the Rua Garrett. Of these, **A Brasileira**, Rua Garrett 120, is the most famous, having been frequented by generations of Lisbon's literary and intellectual leaders. The street's **Igreja dos Mártires** (Church of the Martyrs) occupies the site of the Crusader camp during the Siege of Lisbon. The church was later built on the site of a burial ground created for the English contingent of the besieging army. Music recitals are often held in the church; check the local press for details.

Just beyond, Rua Serpa Pinto veers steeply downhill to the **Museu do Chiado** (Tues 2–6pm, Wed–Sun 10am–6pm; €3, free on Sun until 2pm). Opened in 1994, this stylish building, with a pleasant courtyard café and rooftop terrace, incorporates the former Museum of Contemporary Art, whose original home was damaged in the Chiado fire. The new museum was constructed around a nineteenth-century biscuit factory, which explains the presence of the old ovens. The three floors display the work of some of Portugal's most influential artists since the nineteenth century. Highlights include the beautiful sculpture *A Viúva* (The Widow) by António Teixeira Lopes and some evocative scenes of the Lisbon area by Carlos Botelho and José Malhoa. Look out also for the wonderful decorative panels by José de Almada Negreiros, recovered from the San Carlos cinema.

Around Cais do Sodré

A ten-minute walk west of the Baixa grid, along the riverfront or the parallel **Rua do Arsenal** (a road packed with shops selling dried cod, cheap wine, port and brandy) is **Cais do Sodré** station and metro, from where trains run out to Estoril and Cascais, and ferries cross to Cacilhas. It's not the most elegant of areas, but it's certainly full of character. *Varinas* – fishwives from Alfama – and groups of *retornados* from Cabo Verde and other former colonies bargain for wares and cart off great basketfuls of fish on their heads.

The **Mercado da Ribeira** (market Mon–Sat 6am–2pm; flower market Mon–Sat 3–7pm) is located in the domed building on Avenida 24 de Julho, just beyond Cais do Sodré. This is Lisbon's main market, featuring an array of local characters selling fish and meat of all shapes and sizes, alongside tables full of fruit and vegetables. The upper level serves as a centre for regional arts and gastronomy and, though squarely aimed at tourists, the **Loja de Artesenato** (daily 10am–10pm) specializes in art and crafts from Lisbon and the Tejo valley, and doubles as an exhibition space and shop. The upper level also has various food stalls (daily 10am–11pm) selling superb fresh bread, cheese, wines and *petiscos* (snacks), as well as a restaurant specializing in regional food. A central stage hosts live music at weekends (Fri & Sat 10pm–1am), from jazz to folk.

A short walk behind the market is the precipitous **Elevador da Bica** (entrance on Rua de São Paulo; Mon–Sat 7am–10.45pm, Sun 9am–10.45pm; €1), a funicular railway leading up to the foot of the Bairro Alto. Take a left at the top and then the second left down Rua M. Saldanha and you'll reach the **Miradouro de Santa Catarina**, with spectacular views over the city next to a handy drinks kiosk with outdoor tables.

Bairro Alto

By day, the narrow seventeenth-century streets of the upper town, or **Bairro Alto** – high above the central city, to the west of the Baixa – have a quiet, residential feel, with children playing and the elderly sitting in doorways. Two of the city's most interesting churches – the Convento do Carmo and Igreja de São Roque – are located on the fringes, making the quarter well worth a morning or afternoon's exploration. At night, its character changes entirely, as it's here that you'll find many of the city's best bars, restaurants and fado clubs. Many of the Bairro Alto's most interesting thoroughfares lie west of Rua da Misericórdia, a confusing network of cobbled streets, whose buildings are often liberally defaced with grafitti. But renovation and gentrification along streets like Rua do Norte, Rua Diário de Notícias, Rua da Atalaia and Rua da Rosa have wrought major changes in the last few years.

You can approach the Bairro Alto on two amazing feats of engineering in the form of its funicular-like trams, originally powered by water displacement, and then by steam, until electricity was introduced. Most conveniently, the **Elevador da Glória** (daily 7am–1am; €1), built in 1885, links the quarter directly with Praça dos Restauradores, departing from just behind the Palácio da Foz tourist office. The **Elevador da Bica** (see "Around Cais do Sodré" above) climbs up to Rua Loreto at the foot of the Bairro Alto. A third approach, by the Elevador de Santa Justa (see p.77), has its exit at the side of the Convento do Carmo – but this has been closed for structural works for some time.

From the Elevador da Glória to São Roque

The Elevador da Glória drops you at the top of the hill on Rua de São Pedro de Alcântara, from whose adjacent gardens there's a superb view across the city to the castle. Immediately across the road is the **Solar do Vinho do Porto** (Port Wine Institute), a good place to stop and taste Portugal's finest tipple

Eça de Queirós

Halfway down the Rua do Alecrim, in the Bairro Alto, stands a bizarre statue of a frock-coated, moustachioed man who looks down with a rather bemused expression at the half-naked woman sprawled in his arms. The man is **Eça de Queirós** (1845–1900), who in a series of outstanding novels turned his unflinching gaze on the shortcomings of his native land; the woman is presumably Truth – the quality for which his work was most often praised during his lifetime.

While Eça's earliest novels, like *The Sin of Father Amaro* (1875 – recently modernized and made into an acclaimed Mexican film) and *Cousin Bazilio* (1878), reveal a clear debt to French naturalism in their satirical intent, his mature writings offer a more measured critique of contemporary Portuguese society. Novels like *The Maias* (1888) and *The Illustrious House of Ramires* (1900) work by gradually building up a picture of decadence and inertia, through an assemblage of acutely observed vignettes tinged with a sardonic but always affectionate humour.

Eça's cosmopolitan outlook was both a result of his background and of the fact that he was extremely well travelled. Born out of wedlock, he was brought up by his paternal grandparents in the north of Portugal in an atmosphere of Liberal political ideas. At Coimbra University, where he studied law, he was part of a group of young intellectuals (known as the "Generation of 1870") dedicated to the idea of reforming and modernizing the country. His adult years were spent as a career diplomat and for much of the 1870s and 1880s he was in England, first as consul in Newcastle upon Tyne and then in Bristol.

Oddly enough, it was at Newcastle that Eça wrote much of his masterpiece, *The Maias*, a complex portrayal of an aristocratic, land-owning family unable, or unwilling, to adapt to changing times. Focusing on three generations of male family members, Eça brilliantly conveys what he sees as a peculiarly Portuguese indolence and hedonism that inevitably acts as curb to good intentions – a condition that becomes a metaphor for the country's inwardness and lack of ambition.

The Maias is the Lisbon novel *par excellence*, conjuring up an extraordinarily powerful sense of place. Whether it's the leafy quiet of the Janelas Verdes district where Ramalhete, the Maia family home, is situated, the bustle of the Chiado, or the faded grandeur of the São Carlos Opera House (all places that have changed little over the last 100 years), the essential charm of the city is beautifully conveyed. Best of all is a description of a seemingly carefree, day trip to Sintra, in which a mundane errand and a romantic assignation are poignantly interwoven in a way that reveals Eça at his subtle best.

(see p.115), while a turn to the left from the *elevador* takes you downhill and round the corner to the **Igreja de São Roque** (daily 8.30am–5pm; free), in Largo Trindade Coelho. From the outside, this looks like the plainest church in the city, its bleak Renaissance facade (by Filipo Terzi, architect of São Vicente) having been further simplified by the earthquake. Nor does it seem impressive when you walk inside until you look at the succession of side chapels, each lavishly crafted with *azulejos* (some emulating reliefs), multicoloured marble, or Baroque painted ceilings.

However, the highlight of a visit is the **Capela de São João Baptista**. It was one of the most bizarre commissions of its age and, for its size, is estimated to be the most expensive chapel ever constructed. It was ordered from Rome in 1742 by Dom João V to honour his patron saint and, more dubiously, to requite the pope, whom he had persuaded to confer a patriarchate upon Lisbon. Designed by the papal architect, Vanvitelli, and using the most costly materials available, including ivory, agate, porphyry and lapis lazuli, it was actually

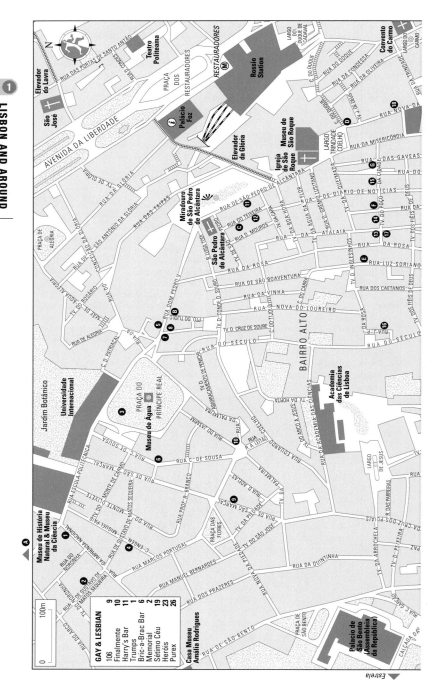

0		100m

GAY & LESBIAN

106	9
Finalmente	10
Harry's Bar	11
Trumps	1
Bric-a-Brac Bar	6
Memorial	2
Sétimo Céu	19
Heróis	23
Purex	26

Casa Museu
Amália Rodrigues

Museu de História
Natural & Museu
da Ciência

Jardim Botânico

Universidade
Internacional

PRAÇA DO
PRÍNCIPE REAL

Museu de Água

BAIRRO ALTO

Academia
das Ciências
de Lisboa

Miradouro
de São Pedro
de Alcântara

São Pedro
de Alcântara

Museu de
São Roque

Igreja
de São
Roque

LARGO
TRINDADE
COELHO

Elevador
da Glória

Palácio
Foz

PRAÇA DOS
RESTAURADORES

RESTAURADORES

Rossio
Station

Teatro
Politeama

Elevador
do Lavra

São
José

AVENIDA DA LIBERDADE

Convento
do Carmo

Palácio de
São Bento
(Assembleia
da República)

N

Estrela

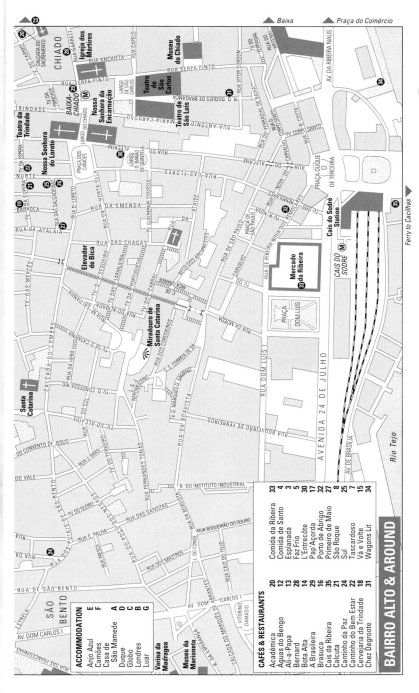

▲ Baixa   ▲ Praça do Comércio

Ferry to Cacilhas

BAIRRO ALTO & AROUND

ACCOMMODATION

Anjo Azul	E
Camões	F
Casa de São Mamede	A
Duque	D
Globo	C
Londres	B
Luar	G

CAFÉS & RESTAURANTS

Académica	20	Comida da Ribeira	33
Águas do Bengo	12	Comida de Santo	4
Ali-a-Papa	13	Esplanada	3
Bernard	28	Faz Frio	5
Bota Alta	14	L'Entrecôte	30
A Brasileira	29	Pap'Açorda	17
Brasuca	16	Porto de Abrigo	32
Cais da Ribeira	35	Primeiro de Maio	27
Calcuta	21	São Roque	8
Cantinho da Paz	24	Sul	25
Cantinho do Bem Estar	22	Tascardoso	7
Cervejaria da Trindade	18	Vá à Volte	15
Chez Degroote	31	Wagons Lit	34

erected at the Vatican for the pope to celebrate Mass before being dismantled and shipped to Lisbon. Take a close look at the four "oil paintings" of John the Baptist's life and you'll discover that they are in fact mosaics, intricately worked over what must have been years rather than months.

Next to the church, the associated **Museu de São Roque** (May–Oct Tues–Sun 10am–5pm; Nov–April daily 10am–noon & 1–5pm; €2.50, free Sun) displays sixteenth- to eighteenth-century paintings and the usual motley collection of vestments, chalices and bibles bequeathed to the church over the centuries, including treasure from the Capela de São João Baptista.

Convento do Carmo

Further south, it's a couple of minutes' walk down to the pretty **Largo do Carmo**, with its outdoor café facing the ruined Gothic arches of the **Convento do Carmo**. Once the largest church in the city, this was half-destroyed by the earthquake but is perhaps even more beautiful as a result. In the nineteenth century its shell was adapted as a chemical factory but these days it houses the splendid **Museu Arqueológico do Carmo** (Tues–Sun: April–Sept 10am–6pm; Oct–March 10am–5pm; €2.50, free on Sun), whose miscellaneous collection is one of the joys of the city, housing many of the treasures from monasteries that were dissolved after the 1834 Liberal revolution. The entire nave is open to the elements, with columns, tombs and statuary scattered in all corners. Inside, on either side of what was the main altar, are the main exhibits, centring on a series of tombs of great significance. Largest is the beautifully carved, two-metre-high stone tomb of **Ferdinand I** while nearby, the tomb of **Gonçalo de Sousa**, chancellor to Henry the Navigator, is topped by a statue of Gonçalo himself, his clasped arms holding a book to signify his learning. Other noteworthy pieces include a fifteenth-century alabaster relief, made in Nottingham, and sixteenth-century Hispano-Arabic *azulejos*. There's also a model of the convent before it was ruined, an Egyptian sarcophagus (793–619 BC), whose inhabitant's feet are just visible underneath the lid, and, more alarmingly, two pre-Columbian mummies which lie curled up in glass cases, alongside the preserved heads of a couple of Peruvian Indians.

Praça do Príncipe Real and around

At the north end of Rua do Século, or a pleasant ten-minute walk uphill from the top of Elevador da Glória along Rua Dom Pedro V, lies the attractive **Praça do Príncipe Real**, one of the city's loveliest squares, laid out in 1860 and surrounded by the ornate homes of former aristocrats – now largely offices. The central pond and fountain is built over a covered reservoir that forms the **Museu da Água Príncipe Real** (Mon–Sat 10am–6pm; €1.25). Steps lead down inside the nineteenth-century reservoir where you can admire the water and view the temporary exhibits from a series of walkways winding among the columns, usually accompanied by ambient music.

From here it is a short walk along Rua Escola Politécnica to the classical building housing the city's natural science museums; alternatively take bus #15 or #58 from Cais do Sodré station. The **Museu de História Natural** (Mon–Fri 10am–noon & 1–5pm, closed Aug; free) exhibits a rather sad collection of stuffed animals tracing the evolution of Iberian animal life, while the adjoining **Museu da Ciência** (Mon–Fri 10am–1pm & 2–5pm, Sat 3–6pm; closed Aug; €2) includes an imaginative interactive section amongst its otherwise pedestrian geological displays.

Beyond the museums lies the entrance to the enchanting **Jardim Botânico** (May–Oct Mon–Fri 9.30am–7pm, Sat & Sun 10am–8pm; Nov–April same hours until 6pm; €1.50). Laid out in 1873, the gardens are almost completely invisible from the surrounding streets, and form an oasis of twenty thousand exotic plants from around the world – each one neatly labelled.

São Bento

São Bento, downhill and east from the Bairro Alto, was home to Lisbon's first black community – originally slaves from Portugal's early maritime explorations. However, the area today is best known for the Neoclassical parliament building, the **Palácio de São Bento** (or Palácio da Assembléia), originally a Benedictine monastery before the abolition of religious orders in 1834. It can only be visited by prior arrangement (☎213 919 000), though you get a good view of its steep white steps from tram #28, which rattles right by.

A little way uphill from here, Rua de São Bento 193 is the house where Portugal's most famous fado singer lived from the 1950s until her death in 1999. The house has been preserved as the **Casa Museu Amália Rodrigues** (Tues–Sun 10am–1pm & 2–6pm; €2), tracing the life and times of the daugher of an Alfama orange seller who became an internationally famous singer. Revered in her lifetime, her death resulted in three days of national mourning, and her record covers, film posters and everyday belongings are lovingly displayed here.

Estrela

Situated on another of Lisbon's hills, the district of **Estrela** lies 2km west of Bairro Alto – a thirty-minute walk or a short ride on tram #28 from Praça Luís de Camões in Chiado, or bus #13 from Praça do Comércio. Its main point of interest for the visitor is the **Basílica da Estrela** (daily 8am–1pm & 3–8pm; free), a vast domed church and *de facto* monument to late-eighteenth-century Neoclassicism. Below the church is the **Jardim da Estrela**: Lisbon takes its gardens seriously, even the small patches amid squares and avenues, and these are among the most enjoyable in the city, a quiet refuge occasionally graced with an afternoon band. There's a pool of giant carp, too, and a café with outside tables.

Through the park and on Rua de São Jorge is the gate to the post-Crusader **Cemitério dos Ingleses** (English cemetery; ring loudly for entry) where, among the cypresses, lies Henry Fielding, author of *Tom Jones*, whose imminent demise may have influenced his verdict on Lisbon as "the nastiest city in the world".

A little uphill from here, the **Casa Museu Fernando Pessoa,** Rua Coelho da Rocha 16 (Mon–Wed 10am–6pm, Thurs 1–8pm, Fri 10am–6pm; free), was home to Portugal's best-known poet for the last fifteen years of his life (see box below). The building is now a cultural centre containing a few of Pessoa's personal belongings, such as his glasses and diaries, and exhibits of artists who have been influenced by Pessoa. There's also Almada Negreiros' famous painting of the writer on display, depicting him in his distinctive spectacles and black hat.

From the stop in front of the Basílica da Estrela you can catch the #25 tram down the steep Rua de São Domingos à Lapa, getting off where the tram veers left into Rua Garcia de Orta. Here, you're only a five-minute walk from the Museu Nacional de Arte Antiga (see p.86); staying with the tram takes you to Praça do Comércio and back into the Baixa.

Fernando Pessoa

"Whether we write or speak or do but look
We are ever unapparent. What we are
Cannot be transfused into word or book."

Fernando Pessoa (1888–1935) is now widely recognized not just as Portugal's greatest poet of the twentieth century but as one of the major – and strangest – figures of European Modernism. Born in Lisbon, Pessoa spent most of his childhood in Durban, South Africa, where he received an English education and wrote his earliest poems – in English. He returned to Portugal in 1905 and spent most of his adult life working as a translator for various commercial firms. The rest of his time was devoted to literature. He founded a short lived artistic magazine *Orpheu* in 1915 with fellow poet Mario de Sá-Carneiro, contributed to several other magazines, and rapidly became a conspicuous figure in the Baixa cafés where he wrote.

Much of Pessoa's work is concerned with the evasive nature of the self and, perhaps in recognition that personality can never be fixed, his work was created under a number of different identities, or "heteronyms". Each of his poetic alter egos had a fully worked out history, vision and style of their own – he even went so far as to have calling cards printed for his English heteronym, Alexander Search. By a marvellous piece of poetic serendipity, *pessoa* actually means "person" in Portuguese, a word that in turn derives from *persona* – the mask worn by Roman actors. Of the many heteronyms that Pessoa adopted, three were responsible for his finest poems. They are the nature poet, Alberto Caeiro; the classicist, Ricardo Reis; and the ebullient modernist, Álvaro de Campos. All three made their first appearance in 1914, and to some extent their histories intertwine with each other but with Caeiro regarded as the master by the other two. They share an obsessive introspection and a morbid fascination with interior and exterior reality that makes Pessoa one of the most telling of existential artists.

Pessoa died a year after the publication of *Mensagem* (Message), a series of patriotic and mystical poems dealing with Portuguese history. Written for a national competition (which he didn't win), this was the only volume of his Portuguese verse to appear during his lifetime. What he left was a large trunkload of manuscripts and typescripts, often in quite fragmentary form. These include the unclassifiable *Livro do Desassossego* (Book of Disquiet) written under the heteronym Bernardo Soares, a quasi-autobiography, consisting of aphorisms, anecdotes, and philosophical rumination, that has a directness and self-centredness that is both exhilarating and irritating by turns. It is in the piecing together and editing of these scraps of writing that the posthumous reputation of the enigmatic Pessoa has been built.

Museu Nacional de Arte Antiga

The **Museu Nacional de Arte Antiga**, Rua das Janelas Verdes 95 (Tues 2–6pm, Wed–Sun 10am–6pm; €3; ⓦ www.mnarteantiga-ipmuseus.pt), Portugal's national gallery, is situated in the wealthy suburb of Lapa, a kilometre south of Estrela. To get here directly, take bus #40 or #60 from Praça do Comércio, or bus #27 or #49 on the way to or from Belém. The core of the museum – comprising renowned fifteenth- and sixteenth-century Portuguese works – is beautifully displayed in a converted seventeenth-century palace; the garden and café (hours as for museum) are worth a visit in their own right. The palace was built over the remains of the Saint Albert monastery, most of which was razed in the 1755 earthquake, although its beautiful chapel can still be seen today.

The Portuguese School

Nuno Gonçalves and his fellow painters of the Portuguese school span that indeterminate and exciting period of the late-fifteenth century when Gothic art was giving way to the Renaissance. Their works, notably Gregório Lopes' *O Martírio de São Sebastião* (Martydom of St Sebastian), and those by Frei Carlos, are exclusively religious in concept, and particularly interesting in their emphasis on portraiture – transforming any theme, even a martyrdom, into a vivid observation of local contemporary life. Stylistically, the most significant influences upon them were those of the Flemish, Northern Renaissance painters: Jan van Eyck, who came to Portugal in 1428, Memling and Mabuse (both well represented here) and Rogier van der Weyden.

The acknowledged masterpiece, however, is Gonçalves' **Panéis de São Vicente** (St Vincent Altarpiece; 1467–70), a brilliantly marshalled canvas depicting the saint – Lisbon's patron – receiving homage from all ranks of its citizens. On the two left-hand panels are Cistercian monks, fishermen and sailors; on the opposite side the Duke of Bragança and his family, a helmeted Moorish knight, a Jew (with book), a beggar, and a priest holding St Vincent's own relics (a piece of his skull, which is still displayed in the Sé). In the epic central panels the moustachioed Henry the Navigator, his nephew Afonso V (in green), and the youthful (future) Dom João II, pay tribute to the saint. Among the frieze of portraits behind them, that on the far left is reputed to be Gonçalves himself; the other central panel shows the Archbishop of Lisbon.

Later Portuguese painters – from the sixteenth to the eighteenth century – are displayed too, most notably works by António de Sequeira and Josefa de Óbidos (see p.165).

The rest of the collection

After Gonçalves and his contemporaries the most interesting works are by **Flemish and German** painters – Cranach, Bosch (represented by a fabulous *Temptation of St Anthony*) and Dürer – and miscellaneous gems by Raphael, Zurbarán and Rodin. But exhibits more likely to delay you are those in the extensive **applied art** sections. Here, on Level 1, you'll find Portuguese furniture and textiles to rival the European selection in the Gulbenkian and, on Level 2, an excellent collection of **silverware** and **ceramics**. Also on Level 2, the **Oriental Art** collection shows the influence of Indian, African and Oriental designs. Other colonially influenced exhibits include inlaid furniture from Goa and a superb series of late sixteenth-century **Japanese screens**, showing the Portuguese landing at Nagasaki, complete with Pinnochio-like noses.

The Sé and around

Lisbon's cathedral – the **Sé** (May–Sept Tues–Sat 10am–7pm, Sun 2–7pm; Oct–April until 6pm; free) – stands stolidly above the Baixa grid. Founded in 1150 to commemorate the city's reconquest from the Moors, it has a suitably fortress-like appearance, similar to that of Coimbra, and in fact occupies the site of the principal mosque of Moorish Lishbuna. Like so many of the country's cathedrals, it is Romanesque – and extraordinarily restrained in both size and decoration. The great rose window and twin towers form a simple and effective facade, but inside there's nothing very exciting: the building was once splendidly embellished on the orders of Dom João V, but his Rococo whims were swept away by the earthquake and subsequent restorers.

You need to buy tickets for admission to the Baroque **Sacristia** (same hours as cathedral; €5) with its small museum of treasures, including the relics of St

Vincent, brought to Lisbon in 1173 by Afonso Henriques, having arrived in Portugal from Spain in a boat piloted by ravens. For centuries the descendants of these birds were shown to visitors but the last one died in 1978, despite receiving great care from the sacristan. Nevertheless, ravens are still one of the city's symbols. The ticket price also allows access to the decaying thirteenth-century **cloister** (closed Sun), or you can visit the cloisters alone for €2.50.

Opposite the Sé is the church of **Santo António** (daily 9am–7.30pm; free), said to have been built on the spot where the city's adopted patron saint was born. His life is chronicled in the neighbouring museum (Tues–Sat 10am–1pm & 2–6pm, Sun 10am–1pm; €1, free on Sun).

South to the river

Winding down south from the cathedral, towards the river, you'll find the church of **Conceição Velha** on Rua da Alfândega, severely damaged by the earthquake but still in possession of its flamboyant Manueline doorway. It's an early example of the style, hinting at the brilliance that later emerged at Belém. Five minutes walk further east, on Rua dos Bacalhoeiros, stands the curious **Casa dos Bicos** (Mon–Fri 9.30am–5.30pm; free), set with diamond-shaped stones. The building was built in 1523 for the son of the Viceroy of India, though only the facade of the original building survived the earthquake. It sees fairly regular use for cultural exhibitions; at other times, you can look round the remains of Roman fish preserving tanks and parts of Lisbon's old Moorish walls (demolished in the fifteenth century), which were excavated during renovation work in the 1980s.

On the riverfront just east of here, across the busy Avenida Infante Dom Henrique, lies the **Jardim do Tobaco** dockland development. Facing one of the broadest sections of the Tejo, there are fine views from the outdoor tables of its upmarket restaurants.

Up to the Castelo

From the Sé, Rua Augusto Rosa winds upward towards the castle, past sparse ruins of the **Teatro Romano** (57 AD), set behind a grille just off to the left at the junction of ruas de São Mamede and Saudade. The finds excavated from the site can be visited at the small adjacent **Museu do Teatro Romano** (entrance on Patio de Aljube; Tues–Sun 10am–1pm & 2–6pm; free), which has multimedia explanations about the theatre's history. Further up the hill you reach the **Igreja da Santa Luzia** and the adjacent **Miradouro da Santa Luzia**, from where there are fine views down to the river.

Just beyond, at Largo das Portas do Sol 2, is the Fundação Espírito Santo Silva, home of the **Museu de Artes Decorativas** (Tues–Sun 10am–5pm; €5) a seventeenth-century mansion stuffed with what was once the private collection of banker Ricardo do Espírito Santo Silva, who offered it to the nation in 1953. On display are unique pieces of furniture, major collections of silver and porcelain, paintings, textiles and *azulejo* panels – in short, some of the best examples of seventeenth- and eighteenth-century applied art in the country. The museum also has a courtyard café.

Over the road from the **terrace-café** in Largo das Portas do Sol, the views are tremendous – a solitary palm rising from the stepped streets below, the twin-towered facade of Graça convent, the dome of Santa Engrácia, and the Tejo beyond. Catch your breath here for the final push up to the castle, higher up the hill to the northeast. Signposts keep you on the right track as the roads wind confusingly ever higher.

Tram #28 runs from Rua da Conceição in the Baixa, past the Sé and Santa Luzia, to Largo das Portas do Sol. Coming from Rossio, **bus** #37 from Praça do Comércio follows a similar route, cutting off at Santa Luzia and climbing to one of the castle entrances.

Castelo de São Jorge

A small statue of Afonso Henriques, triumphant after the siege of Lisbon, stands at the main entrance to the **Castelo de São Jorge**. An important victory, leading to the Muslim surrender at Sintra, this was not, however, the most Christian

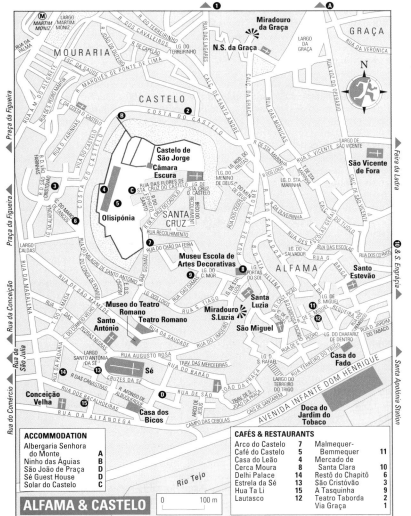

ACCOMMODATION
Albergaria Senhora do Monte	A
Ninho das Águias	B
São João de Praça	D
Sé Guest House	D
Solar do Castelo	C

CAFÉS & RESTAURANTS
Arco do Castelo	7	Malmequer-Bemmequer	11
Café do Castelo	5	Mercado de Santa Clara	10
Casa do Leão	4		
Cerca Moura	8	Restô do Chapitô	6
Delhi Palace	14	São Cristóvão	3
Estrela da Sé	13	A Tasquinha	9
Hua Ta Li	15	Teatro Taborda	2
Lautasco	12	Via Graça	1

ALFAMA & CASTELO

0   100 m

or glorious of Portuguese exploits. A full account of the siege survives, written by one Osbern of Bawdsley, an English priest and Crusader, and its details, despite the author's judgemental tone, direct one's sympathies to the enemy.

The attack, in the summer of 1147, came through the opportunism and skilful management of Afonso Henriques, already established as "King" at Porto, who persuaded a large force of French and British Crusaders to delay their progress to Jerusalem for more immediate and lucrative rewards. The Crusaders – scarcely more than pirates – came to terms and in June the siege began. Osbern records the Archbishop of Braga's demand for the Moors to return to "the land whence you came" and, more revealingly, the weary and contemptuous response of the Muslim spokesman: "How many times have you come hither with pilgrims and barbarians to drive us hence? It is not want of possessions but only ambition of the mind that drives you on." For seventeen weeks the castle and inner city stood firm but in October its walls were breached and the citizens – including a Christian community coexisting with the Muslims – were forced to surrender.

The pilgrims and barbarians, flaunting the diplomacy and guarantees of Afonso Henriques, stormed into the city, cut the throat of the local bishop and sacked, pillaged and murdered Christian and Muslim alike. In 1190 a later band of English Crusaders stopped at Lisbon and, no doubt confused by the continuing presence of Moors who had stayed on as New Christians, sacked the city a second time.

The Castelo

The impressively sited **Castelo** (daily: March–Oct 9am–9pm; Nov–Feb 9am–6pm; free) is perhaps Lisbon's most splendid monument, an enjoyable place to spend a couple of hours, wandering amid the ramparts looking down upon the city. Beyond the main gates stretch gardens and terraces, walkways, fountains and peacocks, all lying within old Moorish walls that have been zealously over-cleaned. At first the Portuguese kings took up residence within the castle – in the *Alcáçova*, the Muslim palace – but by the time of Manuel I this had been superseded by the new royal palace on Terreiro do Paço. Of the *Alcáçova* only a much-restored shell remains. This now houses **Olisipónia** (daily 10am–1pm & 2–5.30pm; €1.50), a multimedia exhibition detailing the history of the city. Portable headsets deliver a 35-minute commentary presenting aspects of Lisbon's development through film, sound and image, and while it glosses over some of the less savoury chapters of the past – such as slavery and the Inquisition – it's a useful introduction to the city. Built into the ramparts, the Tower of Ulysses contains a **Câmara Escura** (daily 10am–1.30pm & 2.30–5pm, every 30min, weather permitting; €2), a periscope focusing on sights round the city with English commentary – though the views are almost as good from the neighbouring towers.

Crammed within the castle's outer walls is the tiny medieval quarter of **Santa Cruz**, still very much a village in itself, though currently undergoing substantial redevelopment. Just below the castle's eastern entrance sprawls the old **Mouraria** quarter, to which the Moors were relegated on their loss of the town. North of the castle, meanwhile, Calçada da Graça leads up to the Graça district and the **Miradouro da Graça** from where the views across the city are stunning.

Alfama

The oldest part of Lisbon, stumbling from the walls of the castle down to the Rio Tejo, **Alfama** was buttressed against significant damage in the 1755 earthquake by the steep, rocky mass on which it is built. Although none of its

△ Alfama town house

houses dates from before the Christian conquest, many are of Moorish design and the kasbah-like layout is still much as Osbern the Crusader described it, with "steep defiles instead of ordinary streets … and buildings so closely packed together that, except in the merchants' quarter, hardly a street could be found more than eight foot wide". In Arab-occupied times Alfama was the grandest part of the city, and continued to be so after the Christian reconquest, but following subsequent earthquakes the new Christian nobility moved out, leaving it to the local fishing community. Today, although an increasing number of tourist-orientated fado restaurants is in evidence, the quarter retains a largely traditional life of its own: you can eat at local prices in the cafés, the flea market (see below) engulfs the periphery of the area twice a week, and this is very much the place to be during the June "Popular Saints" festivals (above all on June 12), when makeshift cafés and stalls appear on every corner.

Ruas de São Miguel and São Pedro

The alleys and passageways are known as **becos** and **travessas** rather than **ruas**, and it would be impossible (as well as futile) to try and follow any set route. Life continues here much as it has done for years: kids playing ball in tiny squares and chasing each other up and down precipitous staircases; people buying groceries and fish from hole-in-the-wall stores; householders stringing washing across narrow defiles and stoking small outdoor charcoal grills. At some point in your wanderings around the quarter, though, head for the **Rua de São Miguel** – off which are some of the most interesting **becos** – and for the (lower) parallel **Rua de São Pedro**, the main market street leading to the lively Largo do Chafariz de Dentro, right at the bottom of the hill. Here you'll find the **Casa do Fado e da Guitarra Portuguesa** (daily 10am–1pm & 2–6pm; €2.50), an engaging museum outlining the history of fado and Portuguese guitar by way of wax models, pictures, sounds and descriptions of the leading characters and styles of this very Portuguese music. It's an excellent introduction to fado and worth seeing before you visit a fado house. There's also a good shop for fado CDs and a small café.

São Vicente de Fora

East of the castle, the name of the church of **São Vicente de Fora** (Tues–Fri 9am–6pm, Sat 9–7pm, Sun 9am–12.30pm & 3–5pm; free) – "of the outside" – is a reminder of the extent of the sixteenth-century city walls. Located where Afonso Henriques pitched camp during his siege and conquest of Lisbon, the church was built during the years of Spanish rule by Philip II's Italian architect, Felipe Terzi, its severe geometric facade an important Renaissance innovation. Through the cloisters, decorated with **azulejos**, you can visit the old monastic refectory, which since 1855 has formed the **pantheon of the Bragança dynasty** (Tues–Sun 10am–5.30pm; €4). Here, in more or less complete sequence, are the bodies of all Portuguese kings from João IV, who restored the monarchy, to Manuel II, who lost it and died in exile in England in 1932. Among them is Catherine of Bragança, the widow of Charles II and (as the local guide points out) "the one who took the habit of the fifth o'clock tea to that country". You can enjoy tea and other beverages at the monastery café, which has a roof terrace commanding superb views over the Alfama and the Tagus.

Feira da Ladra and Santa Engrácia

The **Feira da Ladra**, Lisbon's rambling and ragged flea market, fills the Campo de Santa Clara, at the eastern edge of Alfama on Tuesdays and Saturdays

(6am–3pm). Though it's certainly not the world's greatest market, it does turn up some interesting things: oddities from the former African colonies, old prints of the country, and inexpensive clothes and CDs. Out-and-out junk – broken alarm clocks and old postcards – is spread on the ground above the church of Santa Engrácia, and half-genuine antiques at the top end of the *feira*. To get here, tram #28 runs from Rua da Conceição in the Baixa to São Vicente (see above), and bus #12 runs between Santa Apolónia station and Praça Marquês de Pombal.

While at the flea market, take a look inside **Santa Engrácia** (Tues–Sun: May–Oct 10am–6pm; Nov–April 10am–5pm; €2, free Sun 10am–2pm), the loftiest and most tortuously built church in the city. Begun in 1682 and once a synonym for unfinished work, its vast dome was finally completed in 1966. Since 1916, the church has been the **Panteão Nacional** housing the tombs of eminent Portuguese figures, including former presidents, the writer Almeida Garrett and Amália Rodrigues, Portugal's most famous fado singer. You can go up to the dome, and look down on the empty church and out over the flea market, port and city.

Museu Nacional do Azulejo

About 1.5km east of Santa Apolónia station is the **Museu Nacional do Azulejo** (Tues 2–6pm, Wed–Sun 10am–6pm; €3, free on Sun) at Rua Madre de Deus 4, one of most appealing of Lisbon's small museums. Installed in the church and cloisters of Madre de Deus, a former convent dating from 1509, the museum traces the development of tile-making from Moorish days to the present. This is a fascinating story (see feature on p.94) and the museum contains a hugely impressive collection of **azulejos** covering the main styles of tile from the fifteenth century to the present day. The church itself has a Baroque interior, installed after the earthquake of 1755, and it still retains striking eighteenth-century tiled scenes of the life of St Anthony. But most of the museum is set in the church cloisters, which house many more delights, including Portugal's longest *azulejo* – a wonderfully detailed 36-metre panorama of Lisbon, completed in around 1738 – and fascinating examples of the large *azulejo* panels known as **tapetes** (carpets).

Don't miss out on the opportunity of a drink in the lovely garden **café** at the museum. You can come here directly by bus: #104 from Praça do Comércio or #105 from Praça da Figueira.

Avenida da Liberdade, Parque Eduardo VII and Amoreiras

To the north of the Baixa is the city's principal park – the **Parque Eduardo VII**. The easiest approach is by metro (to Marquês de Pombal or Parque) or bus (to Marquês de Pombal), though you could also walk up the main **Avenida da Liberdade** in about twenty minutes, which would give you the chance to make a couple of stops along the way. The bottom end of Avenida da Liberdade, just above metro Restauradores, has some of the city's nicest outdoor cafés, with esplanade tables in the green swathes that split the avenue. Running parallel, to the east, the pedestrianized Rua das Portas de Santo Antão is well known for the seafood restaurants that line it, waiters hovering by every doorway attempting to entice you in. Avenida da Liberdade ends in a swirl of traffic at the landmark roundabout of **Praça do Marquês de Pombal** (otherwise known as Rotunda).

Portuguese azulejos

Lisbon has some fine example of **azulejos** – brightly coloured, decorative ceramic tiles – and you can see a variety of styles spanning five hundred years decorating houses, shops, monuments and even metro stations. The craft was brought over by the Moors in the eighth century – the word "azulejo" derives from the Arabic *al-zulecha* meaning "small stone". The Koran prevents the portrayal of living forms – hence the typically geometric Moorish designs – and the craft developed using thin ridges of clay to prevent the lead-based colours from running into each other. Early Portuguese tiles were produced using the same techniques – see the early sixteenth-century geometric tiles in the Palácio Nacional in Sintra – and because of these ridges the Catholic Portuguese were able to design figurative images. Portuguese *azulejos* developed their own style around the mid-sixteenth century when a new Italian method – introduced to Iberia by Francisco Niculoso – enabled images to be painted directly onto the clay thanks to a tin oxide coating which prevented running.

At first, religious imagery was the favoured form – such as those in the Bairro Alto's Igreja de São Roque – but during the seventeenth century decadent and colourful images were all the rage. Wealthy Portuguese began to commission large *azulejos* panels displaying battles, hunting scenes and fantastic images influenced by Vasco da Gama's voyages to the east. Later, Dutch Delftware techniques made it possible to add much more detail to each tile. Large *azulejos* panels were also commissioned for churches – these often covered an entire wall and became known as *tapetes* (carpets) because of their resemblance to large rugs.

By the late seventeenth century, blue and white tiles influenced by Dutch tile-makers, were popular with Portugal's aristocracy, and their favoured images were flowers and fruit – there are examples in Lisbon's Palácio dos Marquêses de Fronteira. The early eighteenth century saw artist masters being highly trained to compete with international rivals, producing elaborately decorated multicoloured ceramic mosaics, culminating in Rococo themes.

After the Great Earthquake, more prosaic tiled facades, often with Neoclassical designs, were considered good insulation devices, as well as protecting buildings from rain and fire. By the mid-nineteenth century, *azulejos* were being mass-produced to decorate shops and factories, while the end of the century saw the reappearance of figurative designs, typified by the work in the *Cervejaria da Trindade*, a vaulted beer-hall in the Bairro Alto. Art Deco took hold in the 1920s, while more modern works can be admired in Lisbon's underground stations – Campo Pequeno, Colégio Militar and Cidade Universitária, among others. But though there remain individual artists maintaining the hand-painted tradition, the majority of today's tiles continue to be less impressive mass-produced items, pale imitations of the old figurative or geometric designs.

Fundação Medeiros e Almeida

Once the Avenida da Liberdade was the exclusive address for some of Lisbon's most respected figures, and you can experience a taste of this opulence at the **Fundação Medeiros e Almeida**, Rua Rosa Araújo 41 (Mon–Sat 1–5.30pm; €5), set in the former home of art collector António Medeiros (1895–1986). Parts of the house have been kept as they were when he lived there, while other rooms display his priceless collection of works, including 2000-year old Chinese porcelain, an important collection of sixteenth- to nineteenth-century watches, and dazzling English and Portuguese silverware. There are sumptuous eighteenth-century **azulejos** in the Sala de Lago, a room also filled with bubbling decorative fountains.

Parque Eduardo VII

At the top of the avenue lies the formal **Parque Eduardo VII**. On the west side, at the northern end, are the **Estufas** (daily: April–Sept 9am–5.30pm, Oct–March 9am–4.30pm; €1.50), huge planthouses filled with tropical plants, pools and endless varieties of palms and cacti. Rock and classical concerts and exhibitions are occasionally held in the **Estufa Fria** ("cool house"); others are held at the tile-fronted **Pavilhão dos Desportos** at the opposite side of the park. You can walk uphill to a viewpoint, which affords fine views over the city, and over the grassy hillock beyond (with its olive trees, lake and café) to the Gulbenkian museum (see below), or alternatively take bus #51, which runs from Belém to the museum via the top of the park.

Casa-Museu Dr. Anastácio Gonçalves

Five minutes east of the park, near metro Saldanha, is the **Casa-Museu Dr. Anastácio Gonçalves** (Wed–Sun 10am–6pm, Tues 2–6pm; €2), on Rua Pinheiro Chagas. Set in the Casa Malhoa, a Neo-Romantic building with Art Nouveau touches – such as its beautiful stained-glass window – the house was constructed for the painter José Malhoa in 1904 and retains many of its original fittings. It now holds the private art collection of ophthalmologist, Dr. Antastácio Gonçalves, Calouste Gulbenkian's doctor. When he died in 1964, Gonçalves left a collection not quite as sumptuous as the Armenian, but amongst his 2000 works of art are paintings by Malhoa himself, Chinese porcelain from the sixteenth-century Ming dynasty, and furniture from England, France, Holland and Spain dating from the seventeenth century.

Amoreiras and around

West of the park, up Avenida Engenheiro Duarte Pacheco, is Lisbon's post-modernist shopping centre, **Amoreiras** (daily 10am–midnight), a wild fantasy of pink and blue designed by Tomás Taveira in the 1980s, and sheltering ten cinema screens, sixty cafés and restaurants, 250 shops and a hotel. Most of the shops here stay open until midnight (11pm on Sun); the heaviest human traffic is on Sunday, when entire families descend on the complex for an afternoon out. To get here directly by bus, take the #11 from Rossio/Restauradores.

Rua das Amoreiras runs down to the delightful **Praça das Amoreiras**, dominated on its west side by the soaring wall of the **Aqueduto das Águas Livres**. Opened in 1748, the aqueduct stood firm during the 1755 earthquake, bringing a reliable supply of drinking water to the city for the first time. On the south side of the square the **Mãe d'Água** water cistern (Mon–Sat 10am–6pm; €2) marks the end of the line for the aqueduct, with the reservoir contained within a cathedral-like stone building with gothic lion heads. It now hosts occasional exhibitions. The entrance to the acqueduct itself is around a kilometre north of Praça das Amoreiras, at Calçada da Quintiha 6 in Campolide (bus #58 from Rossio; March–Nov daily 10am–6pm; €2.50), where you can walk right over the 60-metre-high central section, which takes about 15 or 20 minutes.

On the east side of Praça das Amoreiras, set in a former eighteenth-century silk factory, the **Fundação Arpad Siznes-Viera da Silva** (Mon & Wed–Sat noon–8pm, Sun 10am–6pm; €2.50) is a gallery dedicated to the works of two painters and the artists who have been influenced by them: the Hungarian-born Arpad Siznes (1897–1985) and his Portuguese-born wife Maria Helena Viera da Silva (1908–92). The foundation shows the development of both the artists' works, with Viera da Silva's more abstract, subdued paintings contrasting with the colourful, more flamboyant Siznes, whose *Enfant au cerf-volant* shows the clear influences of Miró, who was a friend of his wife.

Fundação Calouste Gulbenkian

The **Fundação Calouste Gulbenkian** is the great cultural centre of Portugal – and it is a wonder that it's not better known internationally. Located a few minutes' walk north of Parque Eduardo VII, the foundation is set in its own grounds, and features a museum whose collections take in virtually every great phase of Eastern and Western art – from Ancient Egyptian scarabs to Art Nouveau jewellery, Islamic textiles to French Impressionist paintings. In a separate building, across the park, the Centro de Arte Moderna concentrates largely on Portuguese works, touching on most styles of twentieth-century art.

Astonishingly, all the main museum exhibits were acquired by just one man, the Armenian oil magnate **Calouste Gulbenkian** (1869–1955), whose legendary art-market coups included buying works from the Leningrad Hermitage after the Russian Revolution. In a scarcely less astute deal made during World War II, Gulbenkian literally auctioned himself and his collections to the European nations: Portugal bid security, an aristocratic palace home (a marquês was asked to move out) and tax exemption, to acquire one of the most important cultural patrons of the century.

Today, in the capital alone, the Gulbenkian Foundation runs an orchestra, three concert halls and two galleries. It also finances work in all spheres of Portuguese cultural life – there are Gulbenkian museums and libraries in the smallest towns – and makes charitable grants to a vast range of projects. To reach the main entrance of the complex, on Avenida de Berna, take bus #31 or #46 from Restauradores, #51 from Belém (not weekends), or the metro to Praça de Espanha or São Sebastião. The admissions desk of the museum has a schedule of current activities.

Museu Gulbenkian

The objects in the **Museu Gulbenkian** (Av. de Berna; Tues 2–6pm, Wed–Sun 10am–6pm; €3, combined ticket with Museu de Arte Moderna €5, free on Sun, Ⓦwww.gulbenkian.pt) aren't immense in number but each themed collection contains pieces of such individual interest and beauty that you need frequent unwinding sessions – well provided for by the basement **café-bar** and tranquil gardens.

It seems churlish to hint at highlights, but they must include the entire contents of the small **Egyptian room**, which covers almost every period of importance from the Old Kingdom (2700 BC) to the Roman period. Particularly striking are the bronze cats from 664–525 BC and the Head of Sestrostris III from the XIIth dynasty (2026–1785 BC). Fine **Roman** statues, silver, glass and intricate gold jewellery, along with coins from ancient **Greece** come soon after. **Mesopotamia** produced the earliest forms of writing, and two cylinder seals – one dating from before 2500 BC – are on display, along with architectural sculpture from the Assyrian civilization. **Islamic arts** are magnificently represented by ornamented texts, opulently woven carpets, glassware (such as the fourteenth-century mosque lamps from Syria) and Turkish *azulejos*. There is some stunning fourteenth-century Syrian painted glass and some superbly intricate eighteenth-century silk coats from **Persia**. These are followed by remarkable illuminated manuscripts and ceramics from **Armenia**, porcelain from **China**, and beautiful **Japanese** prints and lacquer-work.

European art includes work from all the major schools, beginning with a group of French medieval ivory diptychs (in particular the six scenes depicting the life of the Virgin) and a thirteenth-century version of St John's prophetic *Apocalypse*, produced in Kent and touched up in Italy under Pope Clement IX.

From fifteenth-century Flanders, there's a pair of panels by van der Weyden, and from the same period in Italy comes Ghirlandaio's *Portrait of a Young Woman*. The seventeenth-century collection yields two exceptional portraits – one by Rubens of his second wife, *Helena Fourment*, and Rembrandt's *Figure of an Old Man* – plus works by van Dyck and Ruisdael. Eighteenth-century works featured include a good Fragonard, and a roll-call incorporating Gainsborough, Sir Thomas Lawrence and Francesco Guardi. Finally Corot, Manet, Monet, Degas and Renoir supply a good showing from nineteenth- to twentieth-century France.

Sculpture is poorly represented on the whole, though a fifteenth-century medallion of *Faith* by Luca della Robbia, a 1780 marble *Diana* by Jean-Antoine Houdon, and a couple of Rodins all stand out. Elsewhere, you'll find **ceramics** from Spain and Italy; **furniture** from Louis XV to Louis XVI; eighteenth-century works from **French goldsmiths**; fifteenth-century Italian bronze **medals** (especially by Pisanello); and assorted Italian tapestries and textiles, including a superb fifteenth-century red velvet parasol from Venice. The last room consists of an Art Nouveau collection, with 169 pieces of fantasy jewellery by **René Lalique**; look for the amazing bronze and ivory Medusa paperweight (1902) and the fantastical *Peitoral-libélula* brooch, half woman, half dragonfly, decorated with enamel work, gold, diamonds and moonstones.

Centro de Arte Moderna

To reach the **Centro de Arte Moderna** (main entrance on Rua Dr. Nicolau de Bettencourt; hours as main museum; €3, combined ticket with Museu Gulbenkian €5, free on Sun) walk through the gardens, which are enlivened by some specially commissioned sculptures. The centre features some big names on the twentieth-century Portuguese scene, including **Almada Negreiros** (1873–1970), the founder of *modernismo* (look out for his self-portrait, set in the café *A Brasileira*), Amadeu de Sousa Cardoso and Guilherme Santa-Rita (both of Futurist inclinations), and **Paula Rego** (one of Portugal's leading contemporary artists; see feature below). There are also works by American abstract-expressionist Arshile Gorky and by various British artists, including Anthony Gormley – notably his prostrate sculpture of a man. Next to the museum, don't miss the perennially popular self-service **restaurant** (see p.112).

Paula Rego

Paula Rego (born 1935) shot to international prominence in 1990 when she was appointed as the National Gallery Artist in Residence in London, and she is now considered one of the world's leading figurative painters. Although she has spent most of her life in England – she married English artist Vic Willing – her formative years were spent in Salazar's Lisbon, where she was born. Her sheltered childhood was passed in the confines of a wealthy family home and she still feels bitter about the way her mother became a "casualty" of a society which encouraged wealthy women to be idle, leaving work to their servants. Her women are portrayed as typical of the servants of her childhood: stocky and solid. Other adults are usually viewed with the unsentimental eye of a child, and she avoids graceful forms, preferring hairy, bony yet powerful female figures. Power and dominance are major themes of her work; she revives the military outfits of post-war Portugal for her men and dresses many of her women like dolls in national costume. Several of her pictures convey sexual opposition, the result perhaps of a background dominated by the regimes of the Roman Catholic church and a military dictatorship. Her images are rarely beautiful, but are undoubtedly amusing, disturbing and powerful. Her work is often displayed at galleries and temporary exhibitions around Lisbon.

Outer Lisbon

Few visitors explore anything of Lisbon beyond the Gulbenkian, unless for a trip to the Sporting or Benfica football stadiums. However, there are a couple of diverting attractions out beyond the landmark Praça de Touros (bullring) at Campo Pequeno, including the **Museu da Cidade** – devoted to the city's history – and the **Museu Rafael Bordalo Pinheiro**, housing an ornate series of ceramics by the famous nineteenth-century artist. These are both on the route of the #1 bus, which runs from Cais do Sodré via Rossio. Over to the northwest, further peripheral attractions are provided by the **Jardim Zoológico** (the city's zoo, around 2km north west of the Gulbenkian), and by the nearby **Palácio dos Marquêses da Fronteira** (a further 1km northwest of the zoo).

Museu da Cidade and Museu Rafael Bordalo Pinheiro

Just south of metro Campo Grande, the **Museu da Cidade** (Tues–Sun 10am–1pm & 2–6pm; €2, free on Sun) is installed in the eighteenth-century Palácio Pimenta, in the northwestern corner of Campo Grande. Its principal interest lies in an imaginative collection of prints, paintings and models of pre-1755 Lisbon. A death-defying crossing of the road leads you to another lovely mansion housing the **Museu Rafael Bordalo Pinheiro** (Tues–Sun 10am–1pm & 2–6pm; €1.50), dedicated to the nineteenth-century caricaturist and ceramicist. Upstairs exhibits include his amazing collection of ornate dishes crawling with crabs and lobsters, frogs and snakes. The paintings, cartoons and sketches downstairs are of less interest.

Jardim Zoológico

The **Jardim Zoológico**, at Estrada de Benfica 158–160 (daily: April–Sept 10am–8pm, Oct–March 10am–6pm; €11.50; ⓦ www.zoolisboa.pt) has been greatly improved over recent years and makes for an enjoyable day out, especially if you have children. There's a small *teleferico* or cable car (daily from 11am until 30min before closing time), which offers a fine aerial view of many of the enclosures, a reptile house (11am–30min before closing time), a boating lake and various animal "shows" – sealions, macaws and the like – as further diversions. Just by the entrance, the **Animax** amusement park has further rides to shed parents of a few euros. Bus #31 links Restauradores with the Jardim Zoológico via Praça Marquês de Pombal, or simply take the metro to Jardim Zoológico.

Palácio dos Marquêses da Fronteira

Palace enthusiasts should make every effort to visit the seventeenth-century **Palácio dos Marquêses da Fronteira**, Largo de São Domingos de Benfica 1 (tours daily Mon–Sat: June–Sept at 10.30am, 11am, 11.30am & noon; Oct–May at 11am & noon; €7.50, gardens only €3; reservations advised ☎217 782 023), which is around twenty minutes' walk west from the zoo; bus #46 from Restauradores (via the zoo) also passes nearby. After the view of the bland housing development on neighbouring Rua de São Domingos de Benfica, the fantastic gardens of this small, pink country house, complete with topiary, statues and fountains, represent something of an oasis. Inside, there is period furniture along with more stunning *azulejos* dating back to the seventeenth century, with some particularly vivid ones showing the battles during the Restoration Wars with Spain.

Belém and around

It was from **Belém** (pronounced **Ber-layng**) in 1497 that Vasco da Gama set sail for India, and here too that he was welcomed home by Dom Manuel, "The Fortunate" (**O Venturoso**). Da Gama brought back with him a small cargo of pepper, but it was enough to pay for his voyage several times over. The monastery subsequently built here – the Mosteiro dos Jerónimos – stands as a testament to his triumphant discovery of a sea route to the Orient, which amounted to the declaration of a "Golden Age". Built to honour the vow Dom Manuel made to the Virgin in return for a successful voyage, it stands on the site of the hermitage founded by Henry the Navigator, where Vasco da Gama and his companions had spent their last night ashore in prayer. The monastery was partly funded by a levy on the fruits of da Gama's discovery – a five-percent tax on all spices other than pepper, cinnamon and cloves, whose import had become the sole preserve of the Crown. The Rio Tejo at Belém has receded with the centuries, for when the monastery was built it stood almost on the beach, within the sight of moored caravels and of the Torre de Belém, guarding the entrance to the port. This, too, survived the earthquake and is the other showpiece Manueline building in Lisbon.

Both monastery and tower lie in what is now a pleasant waterfront suburb, 6km west of the city centre. It is also home to a small group of museums, and some fine cafés and restaurants, notably the historic *Antiga Confeitaria de Belém* (see pp.106–107). You can get here by **tram** (signed Algés) – the fast supertram #15 runs from Praça da Figueira via Praça do Comércio (20min) – or by the Oeiras train from Cais do Sodré to Belém station. At Belém, a road train, the **comboio turístico** (10am–noon & 2–5pm; €3), departs roughly hourly from in front of the Mosteiro dos Jerónimos, running up to the Torre de Belém and back. When planning your trip keep in mind that quite a few of the sights at Belém are **closed on Mondays**.

Mosteiro dos Jerónimos

Even before the Great Earthquake of 1755 the **Mosteiro dos Jerónimos** (daily: June–Sept 10am–6.30pm, Oct–May 10am–5pm, restricted access Sat mornings and during Mass; free) was Lisbon's finest monument. Begun in 1502, and more or less completed when its funding was withdrawn by João III in 1551, the monastery is the most ambitious and successful achievement of Manueline architecture (see box on p.191). It is less flamboyantly exotic than either Tomar or Batalha – the great culminations of the style in Estremadura – but, despite a succession of master-builders, it has more daring and confidence in its overall design. This is largely the achievement of two outstanding figures: **Diogo de Boitaca**, perhaps the originator of the Manueline style with his Igreja de Jesus at Setúbal, and **João de Castilho**, a Spaniard who took over the construction from around 1517.

It was Castilho who designed the **main entrance** to the church, a complex, shrine-like hierarchy of figures centred around Henry the Navigator (on a pedestal above the arch). In its intricate and almost flat ornamentation, it shows the influence of the contemporary Spanish style, Plateresque (literally, the art of the silversmith). Yet it also has distinctive Manueline features – the use of rounded forms, the naturalistic motifs in the bands around the windows – and these seem to create both its harmony and individuality. Just inside the entrance lie the stone **tombs** of Vasco da Gama (1468–1523) and the great poet and recorder of the discoveries, Luís de Camões (1527–70).

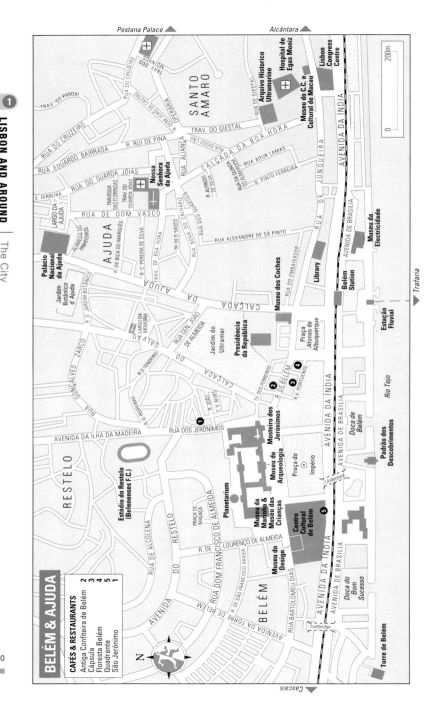

BELÉM & AJUDA

CAFÉS & RESTAURANTS

Antiga Confiteira de Belém	2
Cápsula	3
Floresta Belém	4
Quadrante	5
São Jerónimo	1

Pestana Palace ▲

Alcântara ▲

200m

0

Hospital de
Egas Moniz

Lisbon
Congress
Centre

Arquivo Histórico
Ultramarino

Museu do C.C. e
Cultural de Macau

SANTO
AMARO

TRAV. DOS
MOINHOS

RUA DO CRUZEIRO

RUA D. JOÃO DE CASTRO

R. GUERRA

TRAV. DO PARDAL

TRAV. DO GIESTAL

CALÇADA DA BOA HORA

RUA DIOGO CÃO

AVENIDA DA ÍNDIA

RUA DE GIESTAL

RUA DO CRUZEIRO

RUA EDUARDO BAIRRADA

R. RUI DE PINA

RUA ALIANÇA

RUA ADUR LAMAS

RUA DA QUINTA
DO ALMIRANTE

R. ALFREDO
DE SILVA

R. PINTO FERREIRA

AVENIDA DE BRASÍLIA

RUA DO GUARDA JÓIAS

TRAVESSA
DAS FLORINDAS

TRAV. DO
GUARDA JÓIAS

Nossa
Senhora
da Ajuda

RUA NOVA DO CALHARIZ

RUA DE JUNQUEIRA

G. FERREIRA

LARGO DA
AJUDA

RUA DE DOM VASCO

RUA DOS QUARTÉIS

Museu da
Electricidade

ALMEIDA DO PINHEIROS

R. DE BICA DO MARQUES

R. PEREIRA DE SILVA

TR. DE D. VASCO

RUA ALEXANDRE DE SÁ PINTO

Palácio
Nacional
da Ajuda

AJUDA

R. D. JARDIM BOTÂNICO

R. PEREIRA DE SILVA

TRAV. DE BOA HORA

Museu dos Coches

RUA DO EMBAIXADOR

Library

Belém
Station

Jardim
Botânico
d'Ajuda

CALÇADA DA AJUDA

LARGO DA
MEMÓRIA

RUA GEN. JOÃO DE ALMEIDA

Jardim do
Ultramar

Presidência
da República

Praça
Afonso de
Albuquerque

Estação
Fluvial

Rio Tejo

Trafaria ▼

GALVÃO

R. D. TENDEIRINO

R. J. PRIMPRAS

TV. DOS FERREIROS

R. D. BELÉM

R. V. PORTUENSE

CALÇADA

DO

GALVÃO

R. JOÃO
C. S. ALVES

RESTELO

GONÇALVES ZARCO

RUA

R. D. PRIMPRAS

RUA DOS JERÓNIMOS

Mosteiro dos
Jerónimos

AVENIDA DE BRASÍLIA

Padrão dos
Descobrimentos

AVENIDA DA ILHA DA MADEIRA

Estádio do Restelo
(Belenenses F.C.)

Museu de
Arqueologia

Praça do
Império

Doca de
Belém

Planetarium

PRAÇA DE
MALACA

AVENIDA DE BRASÍLIA

R. DE ALCOLENA

RUA DE FRANCISCO DE ALMEIDA

R. DE
LOURENÇO DE ALMEIDA

Museu da
Marinha &
Museu das
Crianças

Centro
Cultural
de Belém

AVENIDA DA ÍNDIA

Undersea

Footbridge

RESTELO

DO

AVENIDA

R. DE SÃO FRANCISCO XAVIER

Museu do
Design

Torre de Belém

RUA DOM FRANCISCO DE BELÉM

RUA BARTOLOMEU DIAS

BELÉM

AVENIDA DA TORRE DE BELÉM

AVENIDA DA ÍNDIA

Footbridge

AVENIDA DE BRASÍLIA

Doca do
Bom
Sucesso

Cascais ▼

N

The breathtaking sense of space inside the church places it among the great triumphs of European Gothic. Here, though, Manueline developments add two fresh dimensions. There are carefully restrained tensions between the grand spatial design and the areas of intensely detailed ornamentation. And, still more striking, there is a naturalism in the forms of this ornamentation that seems to extend into the actual structure of the church. Once you've made the analogy, it's difficult to see the six central columns as anything other than palm trunks, growing both into and from the branches of the delicate rib-vaulting.

Another peculiarity of Manueline buildings is the way in which they can adapt, enliven, or encompass any number of different styles. Here, the basic structure is thoroughly Gothic, though Castilho's ornamentation on the columns is much more Renaissance in spirit. So too is the semicircular apse, added in 1572, beyond which is the entrance to the remarkable double **cloister** (same hours as church; €4.50, free Sun 10am–2pm). Vaulted throughout and fantastically embellished, this is one of the most original and beautiful pieces of architecture in the country. Again, it holds in balance Gothic forms and Renaissance ornamentation and is exuberant in its innovations, such as the rounded corner canopies and delicate twisting divisions within each of the arches. These lend a wave-like, rhythmic motion to the whole structure, a conceit extended by the typically Manueline motifs drawn from ropes, anchors and the sea. In this – as in all aspects – it would be hard to imagine an artistic style more directly reflecting the achievements and preoccupations of an age.

In the wings of the monastery are two museums. The **Museu de Arqueologia** (Tues 2–6pm, Wed–Sun 10am–6pm; €3, free Sun morning), to the west of the main entrance, has a few fine Roman mosaics unearthed in the Algarve and occasional interesting exhibits, but is largely unexceptional. In contrast, the enormous **Museu da Marinha** (Tues–Sun: April–Sept 10am–6pm, Oct–March 10am–5pm; €3), with its entrance opposite the Centro Cultural de Belém, is more interesting, packed not only with models of ships, naval uniforms and a surprising display of artefacts from Portugal's oriental trade and colonies, but also with real vessels – among them fishing boats and sumptuous state barges – a couple of seaplanes and even some fire engines. It also incorporates the **Museu das Crianças** (same hours as Museu da Marinha, but from 11am; €1.50 extra), a children's museum, with imaginative interactive displays designed to raise children's awareness of fear and the unknown.

Torre de Belém

Still washed on three sides by the sea, the **Torre de Belém** (Tues–Sun: June–Sept 10am–6.30pm, Oct–May 10am–5pm; €3) stands 500m west of the monastery, fronted by a little park with a café. Whimsical, multi-turreted and with a real hat-in-the-air exuberance, it was built over the last five years of Dom Manuel's reign (1515–20) as a fortress to safeguard the approach to Lisbon's harbour. Before the Great Earthquake shifted the course of the water, it stood virtually in the centre of the river. As such, it is the one completely Manueline building in Portugal, the rest having been adaptations of earlier structures or completed in later years.

Its architect, **Francisco de Arruda**, had previously worked on Portuguese fortifications in Morocco and the Moorish influence is very strong in the delicately arched windows and balconies. Prominent also in the decoration are two great symbols of the age: Manuel's personal badge of an armillary sphere (representing the globe) and the cross of the military Order of Christ, once the Templars, who took a major role in all Portuguese conquests. Though worth entering for the views from the roof, the tower's interior is unremarkable except for a "whispering gallery". It was used into the nineteenth century as a prison, notoriously by Dom Miguel (1828–34), who kept political enemies in the waterlogged dungeons.

Padrão dos Descobrimentos

Walking back along the waterfront, towards the monastery, you can't miss the **Padrão dos Descobrimentos** (Monument to the Discoveries; June–Sept Tues–Sun 9am–6.30pm, Nov–May Tues–Sun 9am–5pm; €2), an angular slab of concrete in the shape of a caravel which was erected in 1960 to commemorate the 500th anniversary of the death of Henry the Navigator. Henry appears on the prow with Camões and other Portuguese heroes. Within the monument is a temporary exhibition space, with interesting changing exhibits on the city's history. The entrance fee also lets you climb right up to the top for some fine views of the Rio Tejo and Torre de Belém.

Centro Cultural de Belém, Museu do Design and Museu dos Coches

Across from the monument, on the western side of Praça do Imperio, an underpass leads to the **Centro Cultural de Belém** (Ⓦwww.ccb.pt), which puts on regular cultural exhibitions and concerts as well as hosting live entertainment over the weekend – jugglers, mime artists and the like. For the best views of the surroundings, drop into the café, whose garden esplanade overlooks the river and the Monument to the Discoveries.

The centre also houses the **Museu do Design** (daily 11am–8pm, last entry 7.15pm; €3.50), whose collection is displayed chronologically in three sections entitled "Luxo" (Luxury), "Pop" and "Cool". It comprises design classics – furniture to jewellery – spanning the period from 1937 to today, which were amassed by former stockbroker and media mogul Francisco Capelo. Exhibitions are occasionally rotated, but there are usually chairs by Charles and Ray Eames and Phillipe Starck on display, plus 1970s bean bags, an amazing Joe Colombo Mini Kitchen, works by the Memphis Group and contemporary designs by Tomas Tavira and Álvaro Siza.

At the corner of Belém's other main square – Praça Afonso de Albuquerque, a few minutes' walk east from the monastery along Rua de Belém – you'll find the far more traditional **Museu dos Coches** (Tues–Sun 10am–5.30pm; €3). Housed in the attractive former riding school of the president's palace, the Presidência da República, it contains one of the largest collections of saddlery and coaches in the world – heavily gilded and sometimes quite beautifully painted.

North of here lies the leafy **Jardim do Ultramar** (daily 10am–5pm; free), a green oasis with hothouses, ponds and towering palms – the entrance is on Calçada do Galvão. In the southeastern corner of the gardens lies the Portuguese President's official residence, the pink **Presidência da República** (closed to the public).

East to Ponte 25 de Abril

Heading back over the railway footbridge to the riverside from Praça Afonso de Albuquerque, past the ferry station, it is possible to walk the 2km along the relatively traffic-free gardens all the way from Belém to the towering Ponte 25 de Abril. En route is the extraordinary redbrick **Museu da Electricidade** (Tues–Fri & Sun 10am–12.30pm & 2–5.30pm, Sat 10am–12.30pm & 2–8pm; €3), an early twentieth-century electricity generating station with cathedral-like windows. The electricity museum's highlights include its original enormous generators, steam turbines and winches – all looking like something out of the science-fiction film *Brazil*. There are also temporary exhibitions.

North of the railway line, just beyond the high-tech **Lisbon Congress Centre** on the main Rua da Junqueira 30, it is another ten minutes' walk to the **Museu do Centro Científico e Cultural de Macau** (Tues–Sun 10am–5pm, Sun noon–6pm; €3). This museum is dedicated to Portugal's trading links with the Orient and its former colony of Macau, which was handed back to Chinese rule in 1999. There are model boats and audio displays detailing early journeys, and exhibits of Chinese art from the sixteenth to the nineteenth centuries, including an impressive array of opium pipes and ivory boxes.

Palácio da Ajuda

Jump on bus #14, from central Belém or Calçada da Ajuda behind the Museu dos Coches, for the short ride uphill to the **Palácio da Ajuda** (Mon, Tues & Thurs–Sun 10am–5pm; €4, free Sun morning 10am–2pm). The palace was built by those crashingly tasteless nineteenth-century royals, Dona Maria II and Dom Ferdinand, and like their Pena Palace folly at Sintra, it's all over-the-top aristocratic clutter. The banqueting hall, however, is quite a sight; likewise the lift, decked out with mahogany and mirrors. Next to the palace is the attractive **Jardim Botânico d'Ajuda** (Mon, Tues & Thurs–Sun 9am–dusk; €1.50), one of the city's oldest botanical gardens – a fine example of formal Portuguese gardening boasting some great views over Belém. Tram #18 will get you back from the palace to Praça do Comércio, or take bus #60 to Praça da Figueira.

Parque das Nações

Parque das Nações – the Park of Nations – the former Expo 98 site, 5km to the east of the city, remains a huge attraction for Lisboans who come here en masse at weekends. The main highlight is the oceanarium, though there are plenty of other attractions, from water gardens to cable car, as well as a diverse array of bars, shops and restaurants, many overlooking Olivais docks and the astonishing 17km-long Vasco da Gama bridge. This part of Lisbon's riverfront is slowly being transformed into a large-scale business and residential zone, with the aim of redirecting the city's sprawling suburbs in a more planned fashion to the east.

Oriente metro deposits you in the bowels of the **Estação do Oriente**, a stunning glass-and-concrete bus and train interchange designed by Spanish architect Santiago Calatrava. As you exit the station, head through the Vasco da Gama shopping centre to the main **Posto de Informação** (daily 9.30am–8pm; ☎218 919 333, ⓦwww.parquedasnacoes.pt), which has details of current events. If you want to visit more than a couple of things, it may be worth buying a *Cartão do Parque* (€15.50, valid one month), which allows unlimited access to the main sights (including the oceanarium) and discounts at other attractions.

A **road train** trundles anticlockwise round the whole park (daily 10.30am–7pm, every 20min; €2.50), starting and finishing in front of the Pavilhão Atlântico. From here, you can also **rent bikes** (from around €5/hr), a good way to get round the flat, traffic-free lanes. It is not too taxing, however, to walk to the principal attractions, especially if you take advantage of the cable car (see below).

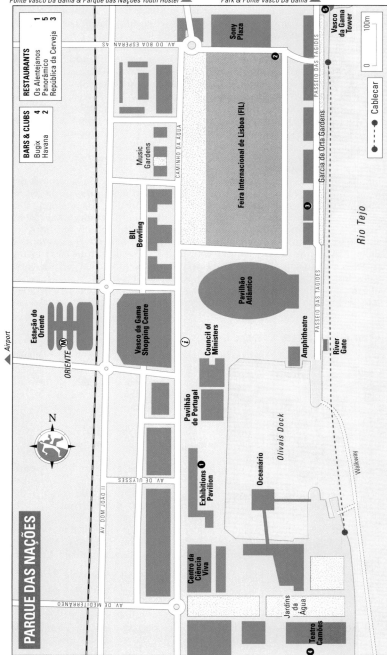

PARQUE DAS NAÇÕES

N

Ponte Vasco Da Gama & Parque das Nações Youth Hostel

Park & Ponte Vasco Da Gama

Airport

Lisbon

RESTAURANTS
Os Alentejanos 1
Panorâmico 5
República da Cerveja 3

BARS & CLUBS
Bugix 4
Havana 2

AV DO BOA ESPERAN AS

Sony Plaza

PASSEIO DAS TAGIDES

Vasco da Gama Tower

CAMINHO DA ÁGUA

Music Gardens

Feira Internacional de Lisboa (FIL)

Garcia de Orta Gardens

Rio Tejo

- - - ● Cablecar

0   100m

BIL Bowling

Estação do Oriente
Ⓜ
ORIENTE

Vasco da Gama Shopping Centre

Pavilhão Atlântico

PASSEIO DAS TAGIDES

ⓘ

Council of Ministers

Amphitheatre

River Gate

AV DE ULYSSES

AV DOM JOÃO II

Pavilhão de Portugal

Olivais Dock

Walkway

Exhibitions Pavilion ❶

Oceanário

AV DE MEDITERRÂNEO

Centro da Ciência Viva

Jardins da Água

Teatro Camões ❹

Oceanário de Lisboa

At weekends in particular, hour-long queues to get in the futuristic **Oceanário de Lisboa** (daily 10am–7pm; €10; Ⓦ www.oceanario.pt) are not uncommon, so it is worth getting here early. Designed by Peter Chermayeff, and resembling a set from a James Bond film, Europe's second-largest oceanarium contains around 25,000 fish and marine animals. Its main feature is the enormous central tank, the size of four Olympic-sized swimming pools, which you can look into from different levels to get close-up views of the sharks and rays. Perhaps even more impressive are the re-creations of various ocean ecosystems, such as the Antarctic tank containing frolicking penguins, and the Pacific tank, where otters bob about and play in the rock pools. These areas are separated from the main tank by invisible acrylic sheets, which give the impression that all the marine creatures are swimming together in the same space. On the darkened lower level, smaller tanks contain shoals of brightly coloured tropical fish and other warm water creatures. Find a window free of the school parties and the whole experience becomes the closest you'll get to deep-sea diving without getting wet.

The rest of the park

Children like the **Centro da Ciência Viva** (Centre for Live Science; Tues–Fri 10am–6pm, Sat & Sun 11am–7pm, last entry 1hr before closing; €5), which is run by Portugal's Ministry of Science and Technology (which shares the premises). There are permanent interactive exhibits here, including holograms, plus a cybercafé with thirty terminals offering free internet access. Behind the centre lies the **Jardim da Água** (Water Garden), crisscrossed by ponds linked by stepping stones, with enough fountains, water gadgets and pumps to keep kids occupied for hours.

On the riverfront, the **Teatro Camões** is the park's main venue for theatre, classical music and opera. Beyond here, a narrow walkway leads across Olivais docks below the **cable car** (June–Sept Mon–Fri 10am–9pm, Sat & Sun 11am–8pm; Oct–May Mon–Fri 10am–8pm, Sat & Sun 11am–7pm; €3.50 one way, €5.50 return) which shuttles you to the northern side of the park, with commanding views on the way.

The cable car drops you just beyond the **Jardim Garcia de Orta**, a leafy waterside garden displaying plant species from Portugal's former colonies. But the main draw on this side of the park is the elevator ride to the top of the **Torre Vasco da Gama** (daily: June–Sept 10am–9pm, Oct–May 10am–6pm; €2.50). The tower was once part of an oil refinery, and the viewing platform at the top gives a 360° panorama over Lisbon, the Tejo and into the Alentejo to the south. There's also a pricey restaurant at the top. Opposite the tower is the **Sony Plaza**, Lisbon's largest purpose-built outdoor arena, which hosts concerts and sports events. When there are no events scheduled it hosts **Adrenalina**, a small adventure park zone (charges for individual attractions) featuring skateboard ramps, climbing walls, trampolines and a Skycoaster, a kind of bungee-swing suspended 35m up; there are also bouncy castles and inflatables for younger children.

Heading back towards Olivais docks you'll pass the **Pavilhão Atlântico** (Atlantic Pavilion), Portugal's largest indoor arena and another venue for touring bands and sporting events. Opposite stands the elegant **Pavilhão de Portugal** (Portugal Pavilion), designed by Álvaro Siza Vieira, Portugal's best-known architect, and featuring a distinctive sagging concrete roof. It now houses the Council of Ministers (a forum for Portugal's MPs).

Eating

Lisbon has some of the best-value cafés and restaurants of any European city, serving large portions of good Portuguese food at sensible prices. A **set menu** (**ementa turística**) at lunch or dinner will get you a three-course meal for €10–13, though you can eat for considerably less than this by sticking to the ample main dishes and choosing the daily specials. **Seafood** is widely available – there's an entire central street, Rua das Portas de Santo Antão, as well as a whole enclave of restaurants across the Rio Tejo at Cacilhas that specialize in it. This is the only time you'll need to be careful what you eat if you're on a tight budget as seafood is always pricier than other menu items.

Lisbon's **cafés** are its pride and joy, ranging from atmospheric turn-of-the-century artists' haunts to Art Deco wonders. The capital, naturally, also features some of the country's best and most expensive **restaurants**, specializing for the most part in a hybrid French-Portuguese cuisine, as well as some beautifully tiled **cervejarias** (beer halls). If you tire of the local food, Lisbon has a rich vein of inexpensive foreign restaurants, in particular those featuring food from the former colonies: Brazil, Mozambique, Angola, Cape Verde, Macão and Goa.

Cafés

The cafés listed below are good for breakfast, coffee and cakes or just a beer during the afternoon. Most stay open into the evening, too, with a few – like **A Brasileira** and **Cerca Moura** – also on the late-night bar-crawl circuit. All are open daily unless stated otherwise.

Baixa and Chiado

The following are marked on the Baixa and Chiado map on p.78.

Bernard Rua Garrett 104 ☎211 373 133. Old-style café with an ornate interior offering superb cakes, ice cream and coffees, and an outdoor terrace on Chiado's most fashionable street. Closed Sun.

A Brasileira Rua Garrett 120 ☎213 469 547. Opened in 1905 and marked by a bronze of Fernando Pessoa outside, this is the most famous of Rua Garrett's old-style coffee houses. Livens up at night with a more youthful clientele swigging beer outside until 2am, though the interior is its real appeal.

Confeitaria Nacional Pr. da Figueira 18 ☎213 424 470. Opened in 1829 and little changed since, with a stand-up counter selling pastries and sweets below a mirrored ceiling. There's a little side room for sit-down coffees and snacks and a few outdoor tables.

Elevador de Santa Justa Café Rua de Santa Justa. The drinks and snacks are inevitably over-priced, but a visit is worthwhile for the stunning views of the Baixa from the rooftop platform of this iron latticework lift, built in 1902.

Nicola Rossio 24 ☎213 460 579. This grand old place is not quite what it was following restoration, but is still a good stop for breakfast. Outdoor seats

are always at a premium. Closed Sat afternoon, and all day Sun.

Suíça Rossio 96 ☎213 214 090. Famous for its cakes and pastries; you'll have a hard job getting an outdoor table here, though there's plenty of room inside – the café stretches across to Pr. da Figueira where the best tables are.

Bairro Alto and Cais do Sodré

The following are marked on the Bairro Alto map on pp.82–83.

Académica Largo do Carmo 1–3, Bairro Alto ☎213 469 092. Tables in one of the city's nicest, quietest squares, outside the ruined Carmo church. Also does light lunches – the grilled sardines are hard to beat.

São Roque Rua Dom Pedro V 57C, Bairro Alto ☎213 224 358. Relaxed, ornate corner *pastelaria* where you can enjoy coffee and croissants.

Wagons-Lit Estação Fluvial, Cais do Sodré. Simple café with lovely outdoor tables facing the river, a great place for a drink and popular with ferry commuters from the terminal next door.

Belém

Antiga Confeitaria de Belém Rua de Belém 90

☎ 213 637 423. See map on p.100. Excellent tiled pastry shop and café, which has been serving superb *pasteis de Belém* (flaky tartlets filled with custard-like cream) since 1837; an unmissable place during a visit to Belém.

Alfama

Cerca Moura Largo das Portas do Sol 4 ☎ 218 874 859. See map on p.89. Stunning views of the Alfama from its esplanade; a good resting place as you climb up and down the hilly streets. Open till 2am, 8pm on Sun.

Parque Eduardo VII and Saldanha

The following are marked on the Lisbon map on pp.64–65.
Botequim do Rei Parque Eduardo VII. Tranquil park café by a little lake, with outdoor seats surrounded by geraniums. Closed Mon.
Versailles Av. da República 15A, Saldanha ☎ 13 546 340; metro Saldanha. A fine traditional café where a fleet of waiters circle the starched tablecloths beneath chandeliers.

Restaurants

There are hundreds of restaurants throughout the city, with concentrations in all the areas in which you're likely to be sightseeing. Restaurants in the **Baixa**, in particular, are good for lunch as most have inexpensive set menus catering for office employees. In **Belém**, Rua Vieira Portuense, near the monastery, has a terrace of *tascas* and restaurants with outdoor seats that are always busy at lunchtime (those further from the monastery tend to be the best value). Out at the **Parque das Nações**, the riverfront Passeio das Tágides is one long line of moderately priced bars and restaurants specializing in international cuisine, from Israeli to Cuban. The *docas* at **Alcântara** also have a range of international restaurants, while the waterside places at **Doca do Jardim do Tobaco** and by **Santa Apolónia** station tend to specialize in upmarket Portuguese and fusion cuisine. By night the obvious place to be is the **Bairro Alto**, which houses several of the city's most fashionable restaurants, as well as plenty of other more basic value-for-money venues.

Options for **vegetarians** are somewhat limited in Lisbon, though *Celeiro Macrobiótico-Naturista* (p.109), *Refeições Naturais e Vegetarianos* (p.109) and *Os Tibetanos* (p.112) are worth seeking out. Indian restaurants also offer good vegetarian options, as do some of the museum cafés, notably at the Centro de Arte Moderna at the Gulbenkian (p.112).

Restaurants listed are open daily for lunch and dinner, unless otherwise stated. Note that many are **closed** on Sunday evenings or Mondays, while on Saturday nights you should reserve a table for the more popular places. The listings below have been coded into four **price categories**: inexpensive (less than €10), moderate (€10–18), expensive (€18–30), and very expensive (over €30) – the average price per person you can expect to pay for a meal, including drinks.

Baixa

The following are marked on the Baixa map on p.78.
Andorra Rua das Portas de Santo Antão 82 ☎ 213 426 047. Occupying a raised bit of the street, the *Andorra* specializes in *açorda* and *arroz de marisco*, plus fresh fish and steaks, served at its well-positioned outdoor tables. It's not particularly cheap, but it is good for people watching. Moderate.
Associação Católica Trav. Ferragial 1. Go through the unmarked door and head to the top floor for this self-service canteen offering different dishes each day. The chief attractions are the low prices and the fine rooftop terrace with views over the Tejo. Open Mon–Fri noon–3pm. No credit cards. Inexpensive.
Beira Gare Rua 1° de Dezembro 5. Long-standing snack-bar restaurant opposite Rossio station serving stand-up Portuguese snacks or cheap meals night and day in the back diner. No credit cards. Inexpensive.
A Berlenga Rua Barros Queiróz 29. A *cervejaria* with a window stuffed full of crabs and seafood.

△ Igreja da Jesus, Setúbal

Early-evening snackers at the bar munching prawns give way to local diners eating meals chosen from the window displays. Expensive.

Casa do Alentejo Rua das Portas de Santo Antão 58 ☎ 213 469 231. Extravagantly decorated building which is as much a private club dedicated to Alentejan culture as mere restaurant. The courtyard is stunning, as is the period furniture, a perfect backdrop for sound Alentejan dishes such as *carne de porco à alentejana* (grilled pork and clams). Moderate.

Celeiro Macrobiótico-Naturista Rua 1° de Dezembro 65 ☎ 213 422 463. This health-food supermarket with basement self-service restaurant offers tasty vegetarian spring rolls, quiches and the like. Closes 6pm, and at weekends. Inexpensive.

João do Grão Rua dos Correeiros 220–228, ☎ 213 424 757. Established Baixa restaurant with an *azulejo*-covered interior, outdoor seats on a pedestrianized stretch and reliable Portuguese food, including some interesting salads. Moderate.

Leão d'Ouro Rua 1° de Dezembro 105 ☎ 213 469 195. Very attractive *azulejo*-lined restaurant specializing in seafood (which can push the price up) and grilled meats. Get there early or reserve a table. Moderate.

Martinho da Arcada Pr. do Comércio 3 ☎ 218 879 259. Beautiful restaurant in the arcade, little changed from the beginning of the twentieth century when it was frequented by writer Fernando Pessoa. The food is well-presented traditional Portuguese, but you can always just call in for a coffee and *pastel de nata* in the attached stand-up café, which has outdoor tables under the arches. Closed Sun. Expensive.

Refeições Naturais e Vegetarianos Rua dos Correeiros 205, 2°. Atmospheric self-service canteen with a daily changing menu of vegetarian hot and cold meals – usually crepes, rissoles and rice dishes – on the second floor of a Baixa town house. Closes 7pm and weekends. Inexpensive.

Rei dos Frangos/Bom Jardim Trav. de Santo Antão 11–18 ☎ 213 424 389. The "king of chickens" has branches on two sides of an alleyway connecting Restauradores with Rua das Portas de Santo Antão. It is the place for spit-roast chicken – whole ones with fries cost about €8. Inexpensive.

Adega Santo Antão Rua das Portas de Santo Antão 42. Very good value *adega* with a bit of local character: a bustling bar area and tables inside and out offering great grilled meat and fish. Closed Mon. Inexpensive.

Tágide Largo Academia das Belas Artes 18–20 ☎ 213 420 720. One of Lisbon's most renowned traditional restaurants, serving superb regional dishes in a dining room with sweeping city views. Book ahead, especially for a window seat. Closed Sat & Sun. Expensive.

Terreiro do Paço Pr. do Comércio ☎ 210 312 850. Stylish restaurant right on the square, serving high-quality meat and fish dishes accompanied by wine in glasses the size of pumpkins. Intimate downstairs tables are separated by wooden screens, though upstairs is nicer, under a brick-vaulted ceiling. Saturday lunch specials feature *cozido* (boiled meat stews), while Sunday brunch concentrates on Portuguese specialities like *bacalhau* or *coelho* (rabbit). Closed Sun evening. Expensive.

Chiado, Cais do Sodré and around

The following are marked on the Bairro Alto map on pp.82–83.

Cais da Ribeira Armazem A, Porta 2 ☎ 213 463 611. Attractive converted warehouse with river views around the back of Cais do Sodré serving superior fish, meat and seafood dinners, straight from the market. Dinner only except Sun; closed Mon. Expensive.

Chez Degroote Rua dos Duque de Bragança 4 ☎ 213 472 839. Romantic spot in a tastefully restored town house, with soaring ceilings and shuttered windows. Specialities include various beef dishes and some great starters. It's popular with a gay clientele but not exclusively so. Closed Sat lunch and all day Sun. Moderate.

A Comida da Ribeira Mercado da Ribeira. Upstairs in the market building, this is a very popular Sunday lunch spot, and a great place at any time for well-priced regional dishes. Inexpensive.

L'Entrecôte Rua do Alecrim 121 ☎ 213 428 343. The place to eat steaks washed down with fine wines. There's a relaxed, informal atmosphere in the spacious, wood-panelled interior. Set menus are around €15, though it's easy to spend more if you wade through the a la carte menu. Expensive.

Porto de Abrigo Rua dos Remolares 16–18 ☎ 213 460 873. Old-style tavern-restaurant serving market-fresh fish at reasonable prices; the *arroz de polvo* (octopus rice) is good. Closed Mon. Moderate.

Bairro Alto

The following are marked on the Bairro Alto map on pp.82–83.

1° de Maio Rua da Atalaia 8 ☎ 213 426 840. Buzzing *adega* with good-value dishes of the day and sizzling meat and fish specials. Closed Sat dinner & all Sun. Inexpensive.

Águas do Bengo Rua do Teixeira 1 95 ☎ 213

477 516. African music restaurant owned by Angolan musician Waldemar Bastos. The menu features unusual-for-Lisbon tropical dishes – like chicken cooked in palm oil – and there's seafood too, though, this can push your dinner into the expensive category. If you're lucky and he's about, Waldemar will play a tune or two. Dinner only, closed Mon. Moderate.

Ali-a-Papa Rua da Atalaia 95 ☏ 213 472 116. Moroccan restaurant with an attractive interior. The couscous and tajine dishes are good value. Closed Tues. Moderate.

Bota Alta Trav. da Queimada 37 ☏ 213 427 959. This attractive old tavern with quirky, boot-themed decor (its name means "high boot") attracts queues for its large portions of traditional Portuguese food. It's always packed and the tables are crammed in cheek by jowl; try to get there before 8pm. Closed Sat lunch and all day Sun. Moderate.

Brasuca Rua João Pereira da Rosa 7 ☏ 213 220 740. Well-established Brazilian restaurant in a great old building down hill from the Bairro Alto. Dishes include a good *feijoada moqueca* (chicken and bean stew) and *picanha* (slices of garlicky beef). Closed Mon from Nov–April. Moderate.

Calcuta Rua do Norte 17 ☏ 213 428 295. Very popular Indian restaurant at the foot of the Bairro Alto, with modern decor and a largely young clientele. Lots of chicken, seafood and lamb curries, tandooris, good vegetarian options and a reasonable set menu. Closed Sun. Moderate.

O Cantinho do Bem Estar Rua do Norte 46. The decor borders on the kitsch, with fake chickens and a tiled roof over the kitchen, but the "canteen of well-being" lives up to its name with friendly service. Rice dishes and generous salads are the best bet; the passable house wine comes in ceramic jugs. Moderate.

Comida de Santo Calç. Engenheiro Miguel Pais 39 ☏ 213 963 339. Rowdy, late-opening Brazilian restaurant serving cocktails and classic dishes. Expensive.

Esplanada Pr. do Príncipe Real ☏ 962 311 669. Glass pavilion in the square with outdoor seats under the shady trees. Great for lunch, as it does a good range of tortillas, quiches and vast wholemeal sandwiches. Inexpensive.

Faz Frio Rua Dom Pedro V 96 ☏ 213 461 860. A traditional restaurant, replete with tiles and private cubicles, serving huge portions of *bacalhau*, seafood paella and other daily specials. Moderate.

Pap'Açorda Rua da Atalaia 57–59 ☏ 213 464 811. Famous restaurant attracting arty celebrities who enjoy the agreeable surroundings of a dining room converted from an old bakery, now hung with chandeliers. *Açorda* – the house speciality

– is a sort of bread and shellfish stew, seasoned with fresh coriander and a raw egg. Reservations recommended. Closed Mon. Expensive.

Sul Rua do Norte 13 ☏ 213 462 449. Idiosyncratic restaurant and tapas bar that – as its name suggest – serves all types of food from the south, ie southern Portugal/Spain/Italy, southern Africa and South America. The lower level houses a neat bar with classy wines and bar snacks. Closed Mon. Moderate.

Tascardoso Rua Dom Pedro V 137 ☏ 213 427 578. Go through the stand-up bar and down the stairs for the tiny eating area, where excellent tapas-style meats and cheeses plus good-value hot dishes are available. Inexpensive.

Cervejaria da Trindade Rua Nova da Trindade 20 ☏ 213 423 506. Huge vaulted beer hall-restaurant – the city's oldest, dating from 1836 – with some of Lisbon's loveliest *azulejos* on the walls. It specializes in shellfish, though other dishes are also good, as is the beer. There's a patio garden. Moderate.

Vá e Volte Rua do Diário de Notícias 100 ☏ 213 4 27 888. Friendly family diner serving large plates of fried/grilled fish or meat. The food is not spectacular but prices are good and there are outside seats in summer. Closed Mon. Moderate.

São Bento, Lapa and around

Unless otherwise stated, the following are marked on the Bairro Alto map on pp.82–83.

Cantinho da Paz Rua da Paz 4, São Bento ☏ 213 969 698. Near the parliament building, this offers excellent Goan dishes such as shark soup, prawn curry and some vegetarian options. It's on a side street just off tram route #28. Moderate.

Picanha Rua das Janelas Verdes 47, Lapa ☏ 213 975 401. See Lisbon map, pp.64–65. Just up from the Museu de Arte Antiga, with an intimate, ornately tiled interior, Picanha has multilingual service and specializes in *picanha* (thin slices of beef) accompanied by black-eyed beans, salad and potatoes. Great if this appeals to you (as that's all they do) and for a fixed-price of around €14 you can eat as much of the stuff as you want. Closed Sat & Sun lunch. Moderate.

Varina da Madragoa Rua das Madres 34, ☏ 213 965 533. A very traditional place with lots of *azulejos* and great Portuguese food; *bacalhau* is the speciality. Closed Sat lunch and all day Sun & Mon. Moderate.

Alcântara and the docas

Alcântara Café Rua Maria Luísa Holstein 15, Alcântara ☏ 213 637 176. Expensive designer bar-restaurant blending industrial and modern architecture. One of the city's trendiest in decor and clientele. Dinner and drinks only, until 3am. Expensive.

Espalha Brasas Armazém 12, Doca de Santo Amaro ☏213 962 059. Tapas and superb grilled meats can be enjoyed at outdoor riverside tables, or head for the bright upstairs room, which offers great views over the river. Expensive.

The Sé, Alfama and Castelo

The following are marked on the Alfama and Castelo map on p.89.

Arco do Castelo Rua do Chão da Feira 25 ☏218 876 598. Cheerful place specializing in Goan dishes, like a tempting shrimp curry, Indian sausage and spicy seafood. Closed Sun. Moderate.

Café do Castelo Castelo de São Jorge. Set inside the castle walls, this offers good-value buffet lunches – all you can eat for around €7 – as well as drinks. Its outdoor tables are beautifully positioned under shady trees with peacocks for company. Inexpensive.

Casa do Leão Castelo de São Jorge ☏218 875 962. Couldn't be better sited, within the castle walls and with an outdoor summer terrace, offering a superb city view. Service is slick – this is rated one of the city's best restaurants – and the menu highlights classic Portuguese dishes such as *caldeirão de cabrito* (goat stew); tourist menu around €28. Very expensive.

Delhi Palace Rua da Padaria 18–20 ☏218 884 203. Unusual Indian-run restaurant offering curries, pizza and pasta in an *azulejo*-covered interior. Full marks for innovation at least, though the prawn curry is really good. Closed Mon. Moderate.

Estrela da Sé Largo S. António da Sé 4 ☏218 870 455. Beautiful restaurant with wooden booths built in the nineteenth century for discreet trysts. It serves tasty dishes like *alheira* (sausage) and salmon. Closed weekends. Moderate.

Hua Ta Li Rua dos Bacalhoeiros 115 ☏218 879 170. Highly rated Chinese restaurant, particularly popular at Sun lunch when reservations are advised. There's good-value seafood (which pushes prices up to moderate) alongside all the usual Chinese dishes. Inexpensive.

Lautasco Beco do Azinhal 7 ☏218 860 173. There are tables in a pretty courtyard with fairy lights, making this a particularly romantic spot for a night out. The *cataplana* is recommended. Reservations advised. Closed Sun & Dec. Expensive.

Malmequer-Bemmequer Rua de São Miguel 23–25, at Largo de São Miguel ☏218 876 535. Charcoal-grilled meat and fish (try the sole) served

up amidst cheery, flowery decor. The set menu costs around €13. Closed Tues lunch & all day Sun. Moderate.

Mercado de Santa Clara Campo de Santa Clara, east of São Vicente de Fora ☏218 873 986. Above the old market building and by Feira da Ladra, this characterful restaurant offers award-winning cuisine and river views. It specializes in beef and meat dishes, though there's a small fish selection which can push it into the expensive range. Closed all day Mon and Sun evening. Moderate.

São Cristóvão Rua de São Cristóvão 28–30 ☏218 885 578. Small, earthy Cape Verdean restaurant which somehow squeezes in a band for live African music on weekends, while serving dishes such as *galinha caboverdiana* (chicken with coconut milk). Inexpensive.

A Tasquinha Largo do Contador Mor 5–7. Considering its position, on the main route up to the castle, this lovely *tasca* has remained remarkably unaffected by tourism, with a few tables in its traditional interior and a fine outdoor terrace. Closed Sun. Moderate.

Teatro Taborda Costa do Castelo 75 ☏218 860 104. Fashionable theatre cafe-restaurant with fine views from the terrace. The menu makes a change, offering fresh vegetarian dishes and Greek salads. Open from 2pm, closed Mon. Moderate.

Via Graça Rua Damasceno Monteiro 9B ☏218 870 830. Unattractive new building but an interior offering stunning panoramas of Lisbon. Superbly cooked specialities include spider crab, clam *cataplana* and lobster. Closed all day Sun, and Sat lunch. Expensive.

Santa Apolónia and Doca Jardim do Tobaco

The following are marked on the Lisbon map on pp.64–65.

Bica do Sapato Armazém B, Cais da Pedra à Bica do Sapatas ☏218 810 320. Part-owned by actor John Malkovich and attracting Lisbon's glitterati, this is a very swish warehouse conversion with an outside terrace facing the river opposite Santa Apolónia. The menu features a long list of international dishes – lunchtime ciabatta sandwiches to crab ravioli and sushi. Closed Mon lunch & all day Sun. Expensive.

Casanova Loja 7 Armazém B, Cais da Pedra à Bica do Sapato ☏218 877 532. The modest *Casanova* offers pizza, pasta and crostini accompanied by fine views from its outside terrace. It's phenomenally popular and you can't book, so turn up early. Closed all day Mon & Tues lunch. Moderate.

Jardim do Marisco Av. Infante Dom Henrique, Doca Jardim do Tobaco Pavilhão AB ☎ 218 824 240. Best positioned of the row of warehouse-restaurants in the Doca Jardim do Tobaco development. No prizes for guessing the speciality: the counter groans under the weight of crabs, giant prawns and shellfish. There's an upstairs terrace with great river views. Expensive.

Avenida da Liberdade and outer Lisbon

The following are marked on the Lisbon map on pp.64–65.

Casa da Comida Trav. das Amoreiras 1 ☎ 213 885 376; metro Marquês de Pombal. Just below one of Lisbon's loveliest square sits one of the city's top restaurants, with a long list of salads, pastas and superb fish – feast on *tamboril com molho de limão e alho frances* (monkfish with leeks and lemon sauce) or *crepes de camarão* (shrimp crepes). Closed Sat & Mon lunch, & all day Sun. Very expensive.

Centro de Arte Moderna Fundação Calouste Gulbenkian, entrance by Rua Dr. N. de Bettencourt; metro São Sebastião. Join the lunchtime queues at the museum restaurant for good-value hot or cold dishes. There are excellent salads for vegetarians; you get a choice of four or six varieties. Closes 5.30pm & Mon. Inexpensive.

Cervejaria Portugália Av. Almirante Reis 117 ☎ 218 851 024; metro Arroios. The original beer-hall-restaurant where you can either snack and drink at the bar, or eat fine *mariscos* or steak in the dining room. It's a popular family outing and always busy. Moderate.

A Linha d'Água Parque Eduardo VII; metro São Sebastião. Right at the top of the park, this sleek glass-fronted café faces a small lake, a lovely spot for a drink or good-value buffet lunch. Closes at 6pm. No credit cards. Inexpensive.

Ribadouro Av. da Liberdade 155 ☎ 213 549 411; metro Avenida. The Avenida's best *cevejaria*, serving a decent range of grilled meat and fresh shellfish (but no fish). If you don't fancy a full meal, order a beer with a plate of prawns at the bar. Moderate.

Rodizio Grill Campo Pequeno 79 ☎ 217 939 760; metro Campo Pequeno. A *rodizio* is a Brazilian buffet, and if you're looking for quantity, €20 spent here gets you unlimited stabs at twelve types of barbecued meat and various salads. Expensive.

Os Tibetanos Rua do Salitre 117 ☎ 213 142 038; metro Avenida. Located in the Buddhist Centre, this stripped-pine restaurant has superb, unusual veggie food, like a tasty vegetarian paella. Closed Sat and Sun. Inexpensive.

Belém

The following are marked on the Belém map on p.100.

Càpsula Rua Vieira Portuense 74 ☎ 213 648 768. Tiled interior with upstairs seating and outside tables catering to tourists tucking into tuna steaks, trout and the like. Closed Mon evening & all day Tues. Moderate.

Floresta Belém Pr. Afonso de Albuquerque 1. One of the best-value places on this stretch, attracting a largely Portuguese clientele, especially for weekend lunches. Great salads, grills and fresh fish inside or on a sunny outdoor terrace. Closed Sat. Moderate.

Quadrante Centro Cultural de Belém ☎ 213 612 400. Good-value self-service food (salads, sandwiches and rice dishes), which you can enjoy on the roof-garden terrace providing exhilarating views over Belém and the river. Inexpensive.

São Jerónimo Rua dos Jerónimos 12 ☎ 213 648 797. Rustic-style dining by the side of the monastery, with excellent fish dishes. Its speciality is *migas*, a garlicky bread stew from the Alentejo region. Closed Sat. Moderate.

Parque das Nações

The following are marked on the Parque das Nações map on p.104.

Os Alentejanos Cais dos Argonautas ☎ 218 956 116; metro Oriente. Great wooden barrels and hams dangling from the ceiling and waiters in broad-rimmed hats give a jolly feel to a restaurant specializing in regional food from the Alentejo district – *petiscos* (olives, cheeses, *presunto* ham), *açorda* with seafood, and the thick red wines are the best bets. Moderate.

Restaurante Panorâmico Torre Vasco da Gama ☎ 218 939 550; metro Oriente. An exclusive tower-top restaurant with fantastic views, and decent Portuguese and international food – though you're paying for the setting. Closed Mon, & Sun evening. Very expensive.

República da Cerveja Passeio das Tágides 2–26 ☎ 218 922 590; metro Oriente. One of the best positioned of the riverside restaurants. Steaks and German cuisine can be washed down with some fine international beers, though the local Super Bock saves a few euros. There's live music Thursday to Saturday night. Expensive.

Drinking and nightlife

The traditional centre of Lisbon's nightlife is the **Bairro Alto**, with its cramped streets, ageing taverns, designer bars, fado houses and restaurants. The quarter hosts one of Europe's biggest weekly parties, with up to 50,000 people descending on the maze of streets over the weekend, drifting from bar to club before heading out to those around the docks for the small hours. Several Bairro Alto clubs are extremely low key, revealing their presence simply by a streetlight and a slot in the door for the attendant to inspect customers. Don't be intimidated by this: just knock and walk in – and straight out, if you don't like the look of the place. Other downtown areas are not really on the bar and club circuit – you'll be hard pushed to find a bar open late at night in the **Baixa**, though the **Alfama** and **Graça** have a few places catering for the crowds leaving the excellent local restaurants.

Instead, as the night progresses, Lisboetas seek out the classy venues along **Avenida 24 de Julho**, around Santos station, or a little further west at **Alcântara** docks, near Ponte 25 de Abril. To the east, the world-famous club *Lux* typifies the city's most up-and-coming area along the riverfront by **Santa Apolónia** station. The **Parque das Nações** (metro Oriente) also has a lively bar and club scene. For all these outlying areas, you'll need a taxi or nightbus to get you back to town again. **Gay and lesbian nightlife** focuses on the Bairro Alto and Praça do Príncipe Real, where a generally laidback group of clubs and bars attracts people of all ages. For more information on the gay and lesbian scene in Lisbon, see "Listings", p.123.

Drinks are uniformly expensive in all fashionable bars and clubs – from €4 for a beer – but the plus-side is that very few charge admission. Instead many places have a "minimum consumption" policy, designed to stop people dancing all night without buying a drink, which many Portuguese would happily do. Mostly, these fees are at the whim of the doorman, who will relax it if it's a quiet night, or whack it up if it's busy or if he doesn't like the look of you. Generally, you can expect to pay anything from €10 to €50; keep hold of your ticket as drinks will be stamped on it to ensure you consume enough (otherwise you pay on exit).

Friday and Saturday nights tend to be overcrowded and expensive everywhere, while on Sunday, especially in the Bairro Alto, places often close to sleep off the weekend excesses. None of the places listed below open much before 10pm unless otherwise stated; all are open until at least 2am, with most doing business much later than that; 3–4am is normal, 7am not unheard of. Unless stated otherwise, the following are open daily.

Baixa and Chiado

The following are marked on the Bairro Alto bars and clubs map on p.114.

Bicaense Rua da Bica Duarte Belo 38–42. Small, fashionable bar on the steep street used by the Elevador da Bica, with jazzy and Latin sounds and a moderately priced list of bar food. Closed Sun.

Español Calç. Nova de São Francisco 2. A little slice of fashionable Spain, with high bar stools, spinning ceiling fans and outdoor tables on a steep stepped street. Great tapas served with your drinks.

Caffè Rosso Galerias Garrett, Rua Ivens 53–61, entrance on Rua Garrett ☎213 471 524. Court-yard café and bar in the renovated shop galleries off Rua Garrett. It's a relaxed spot with seats under huge square canopies, while downstairs there's a huge room with modernist seats and lighting.

Cais do Sodré

Irish Pub O'Gilins Rua de Remolares 8–10 ☎213 421 899. The oldest and best of Lisbon's Irish bars, with a pleasant, light burnished wood interior and live music from Thurs to Sat. Pub quizzes on Sun too.

Jamaica Rua Nova do Carvalho 8 ☎213 421 859. Set on a seedy road this characterful club attracts

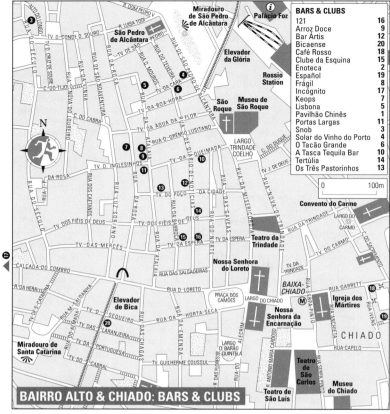

▲ **①**, **②** & *Praça do Príncipe Real*

BARS & CLUBS

121	16
Arroz Doce	9
Bar Ártis	12
Bicaense	20
Café Rosso	18
Clube da Esquina	15
Enoteca	2
Español	19
Frágil	8
Incógnito	17
Keops	7
Lisbona	5
Pavilhão Chinês	1
Portas Largas	11
Snob	3
Solar do Vinho do Porto	4
O Tacão Grande	6
A Tasca Tequila Bar	10
Tertúlia	14
Os Três Pastorinhos	13

BAIRRO ALTO & CHIADO: BARS & CLUBS

a very mixed clientele, from sailors to students; music is predominantly retro, with reggae on Tues. Closed Sun.

Bairro Alto

The following are marked on the Bairro Alto bars and clubs map above.

121 Rua do Norte 117–119. Laidback lounge bar with low, comfy seats, aboriginal art and ambient sounds. Closed Sun & Mon.

Arroz Doce Rua da Atalaia 117–119 ☎213 462 601. A nice, normal bar in the middle of the otherwise frenetic nightlife. The owners are friendly and it's a good spot for an early or late beer, or try "Auntie's" sangria. Closed Sun.

Bar Ártis Rua do Diário de Notícias 95 ☎213 424 795. Jazz bar with arty posters on the wall and marble table tops. The snacks here

are good too (try the chicken toasties). Closed Mon.

Clube da Esquina Rua da Barroca 30 ☎213 427 149. Lively corner bar with ancient radios on the wall and DJs spinning discs on a good, old-fashioned turntable. Great for people watching.

Enoteca Rua da Mãe de Água ☎213 422 079. Downhill from Praça do Prícipe Real, this extraordinary wine bar is set in the bowels of a nineteenth-century bathhouse. Serves upmarket wines and other drinks, along with *petiscos* (snacks). Closed Mon.

Frágil Rua da Atalaia 126 ☎213 469 578. An icon of cool for years before the owner opened *Lux* (see p.115). Partly gay, definitely pretentious, this continues to be a fashionable destination – it's best after 1am. Ring the bell to get in.

Incógnito Rua dos Poiais de São Bento 37

☎213 908 755. Appropriately named, as the only indication that there's anything inside is a pair of large metallic doors. Once within, you'll find the low-lit dance floor downstairs booming with retro sounds, though Wed is more cutting edge. Opens 11pm, closed Mon, Tues & Sun.

Keops Rua da Rosa 157–159 ☎213 428 773. Friendly music bar with doors open onto the streets, and a candlelit interior, playing the latest sounds most nights. Closed Sun.

Lisbona Rua da Atalaia 196 ☎213 471 412. Earthy, local bar with its share of quirky regulars, but its chequerboard tiles covered in soccer memorabilia, old film posters and graffiti also lure in the Bairro Alto fashionistas. Inexpensive beer, too. Closed Sun.

Pavilhão Chinês Rua Dom Pedro V 89 ☎213 424 729. A wonderfully decorated bar, lined with mirrored cabinets full of ludicrous and bizarre artefacts from around the world, including a room full of old war helmets. Drinks include a long list of speciality cocktails.

Portas Largas Rua da Atalaia 105 ☎218 466 379. Atmospheric, black-and-white tiled *adega* with cheapish drinks, music from fado to pop, and a varied, partly gay crowd, which spills out onto the street on warm evenings. Often a starting point for clubbers moving on to *Frágil* opposite.

Snob Rua do Século 178 ☎213 463 723. Appropriately named upmarket bar-restaurant towards Principe Real, full of media people. It's a good spot for cocktails or a late-night light meal (the steaks are recommended).

Solar do Vinho do Porto Rua de São Pedro de Alcântara 45 ☎213 475 707. Opened in 1944, the Port Wine Institute's Lisbon base lures in visitors with over 300 types of port, starting at around €1 a glass and rising to €25 for a glass of forty-year-old JW Burmester. Drinks are served at low tables in a comfortable eighteenth-century mansion, and though the waiters are notoriously snooty and the cheaper ports never seem to be in stock, it's still a good place to kick off an evening. Closed Sun.

O Tacão Grande Trav. da Cara 3. Barn-like bar that pulls in a young crowd into thumping rock, beer and free peanuts.

A Tasca Tequila Bar Trav. da Queimada 13–15. Colourful Mexican bar which caters to a good-time crew downing tequilas, margaritas and wicked Brazilian caiphirinhsa.

Tertúlia Rua do Diário de Notícias 60 ☎213 462 704. Relaxed café-bar with inexpensive drinks, papers to read, background jazz and varied art exhibitions that change fortnightly. If you fancy the urge to play, there's a piano for customers too. Closed Sun.

Os Três Pastorinhos Rua da Barroca 111 ☎213 464 301. Welcoming music bar with great dance sounds and an off-kilter feel; gets very busy at weekends. Closed Sun.

Alfama and Graça

Costa do Castelo Calç. do Marquês de Tancos 1B ☎218 884 636. Beautifully positioned sunny terrace-café with Baixa views, a long list of cocktails and a restaurant serving mid-price Mozambiquan dishes. There's live (usually Brazilian or jazz) music on Thurs and Fri nights, and poetry readings on others. Closed Mon & Tues.

Esplanada da Graça Largo da Graça ☎217 427 508. Kiosk-bar underneath the Miradouro da Graça, with great views and, as it gets later, pumping music. A good place for a drink at sunset.

Rêsto do Chapitô Costa do Castelo 7 ☎218 867 334. Multi-purpose venue incorporating a theatre and circus school, moderately priced restaurant (evenings only) and a tapas bar attracting Lisbon's bohemian set. The outdoor esplanade commands terrific views over the Alfama. Opens 7.30pm weekdays, weekends at noon; closed Mon.

Santa Apolónia

Lux Armazéns A, Cais da Pedra a Santa Apolónia ☎218 820 890, ⓦ www.luxfragil.com. This three-storey converted meat warehouse has become one of Europe's most fashionable places to be seen, attracting the likes of Prince and Cameron Diaz. Part-owned by actor John Malkovich, it was the first place to venture into the docks opposite Santa Apolónia station. There's a rooftop terrace with amazing views, a middle floor with various bars, comfy chairs and sofas, amazing projection screens, and music from pop to jazz and dance; while the downstairs dance floor descends into frenzy at times. The club is also increasingly on the circuit for visiting bands. Closed Mon.

Avenida 24 de Julho

Kapital Av. 24 de Julho 68 ☎213 955 963. Well-established hotspot, with three sleekly designed floors full of *queques* (yuppies) paying high prices for drinks and listening to the latest dance sounds. There's a great rooftop terrace. Open till 6am, until 4am on Sun and Mon.

Kremlin Escadinhas da Praia 5 ☎216 087 768. Packed with flash, young, raving Lisboans. Tough door rules, and don't bother showing up before 2am. Open till 7am, and till 9am on Fri and Sat; closed Sun & Mon.

Alcântara and the docas

Blues Café Rua Cintura do Porto de Lisboa,

Doca de Alcântara ⊕ 213 957 085. Converted dockside warehouse serving Cajun food in the restaurant (until 12.30am) in Lisbon's only blues club. Live music on Mon and Thurs, club nights on Fri and Sat from 2.30am. The advertised minimum consumption of €150 is designed to put off the hoi polloi; take it with a pinch of salt. Closed Sun.

Doca de Santo Doca de Santo Amaro ⊕ 213 963 535, Large, palm-fringed club, bar and restaurant with a great cocktail bar on the esplanade.

Docks Club Doca de Alcântara ⊕ 213 950 856. Another thriving warehouse conversion funded by nightclub mogul Pedro Luz; now a dance temple for Lisbon's moneyed set. Tues night is "ladies night" with free drinks for women; Thurs night features Latin music. Closed Sun.

Havana Armazéns 5, Doca de Santo Amaro ⊕ 213 979 893. Cuban-themed bar-restaurant with wicker chairs, Latin sounds and salsa lessons on request, usually undertaken in the bar area.

Paradise Garage Rua João de Oliveira Miguens 48 ⊕ 213 544 452. Large, ultra-trendy club on a tiny side road opposite Alcântara Terra station, spinning various sounds from disco to garage. It is also becoming a major venue for visiting bands. Opens 11.30pm; closed Mon–Wed & Sun.

Queens Rua Cintura do Porto de Lisboa, Armázem H Naves A–B ⊕ 213 955 870. Pedro Luz launched this club as a "high-tech gay disco", but it has always successfully attracted a large following of beautiful people of all sexual persuasions. It's a huge, pulsating place – there's an excellent sound system – which can hold 2500 people. Closed Sun & Mon.

Salsa Latina Gare Marítima de Alcântara ⊕ 213 950 555. A bar-restaurant and club just outside the docks in a fantastic 1940s maritime station, offering salsa Tues to Sat (lessons on Tues and Thurs) and live music at weekends. Alternatively, just come and admire the terrace views. Closed Sun.

Parque das Nações

Bugix Rua D. Fuas Roupinho ⊕ 218 951 181. The in-spot in the Parque at present, with live music at midnight and pulsating dance sounds from 2–5am Thurs–Sat. The rest of the week it is a relatively quiet restaurant serving moderately priced Portuguese food. Diners pay half the €10 entry fee. Closed Mon.

Havana Rua da Pimenta. Lively Cuban bar with an airy interior and outdoor seating. After 11pm it turns into more of a club.

Gay and lesbian bars and clubs

The following are marked on the Bairro Alto map on p.114.

106 Rua São Marçal 106, Príncipe Real ⊕ 213 427 373. Ring on the bell for admission to this friendly gay bar. Fridays often feature leather nights.

Bric-a-Brac Bar Rua Cecílio de Sousa 82–84, Príncipe Real ⊕ 213 428 971. On a steep road beyond Praça do Prinçipe Real, this cruisy gay club has a large dance floor, "dark room" and various bars. Free entry and occasional drag shows.

Finalmente Rua da Palmeira 38, Príncipe Real. A well-known place with a first-class disco and lashings of kitsch. Weekend drag shows (at 2am) feature skimpily dressed young senhoritas camping it up to high-tech sounds.

Harry's Bar Rua de São Pedro de Alcântara 57–61, Bairro Alto ⊕ 213 460 760. A tiny front-room bar, with waiter service, bar snacks and an eclectic clientele – often including a late-night contingent from the nearby gay clubs. Ring the bell for admission.

Heróis Calç. do Sacramento 14, Chiado. Popular gay bar with modern decor, that also serves decent light meals. Open from 10pm, from 5pm on Sun.

Memorial Rua Gustavo Matos Sequeira 42, Príncipe Real ⊕ 213 968 891. Lesbian and bi club, with floor shows some nights; otherwise a low-key place, with disco and "romantic" sounds. Closes Sun at 8pm, & closed Mon.

Purex Rua das Salgadeiras 28, Bairro Alto. Small and friendly dance bar, popular with lesbians, with upbeat sounds Thurs–Sun nights. Closed Mon.

Sétimo Céu Trav. de Espera 54, Bairro Alto ⊕ 213 466 471. Popular with gays and lesbians, this is an obligatory stop for beers and caipirinhas served by the Brazilian owner. The great atmosphere spills out onto the street. Closed Sun.

Trumps Rua da Imprensa Nacional 104B ⊕ 213 971 059. Popular gay club with a reasonably relaxed door policy. Packed from Thurs to Sat, which sees a good lesbian turnout, a bit cruisy midweek. Drag shows on Sun and Wed.

Live music

Although tourist brochures tend to suggest that live music in Lisbon begins and ends with **fado** – the city's most traditional music – there's no reason to miss out on other forms. Portuguese **jazz** can be good (there's a big annual International Jazz Festival at the Gulbenkian in the summer), and **rock** offers an occasional surprise (look out for emerging bands at the March Super Bock Rock festival). For Lisboans, **African music** from the former colonies of Cabo Verde, Guinea Bissau, Angola and Mozambique is always popular, as is **Brazilian and Latin** music, with major artists touring frequently.

There's often a crossover between musical styles at many of the places listed below; it's always worth checking the listings magazines (see "Arts and culture" below) and posters around the city to see what's on. Note, too, that many of the bars listed in the previous section put on live bands on certain nights of the week. There's a charge to get into most music clubs, which usually covers your first drink, and most of them stay open until around 4am, often later. Touring bands and artists also play at a variety of larger venues (listed below). You can usually get advance **tickets** from the APEB kiosk (daily 9am–9.30pm) at the corner of Praça dos Restauradores (near the post office), which also has ticket and programme details for all the city's cinemas and theatres. Tickets can also be purchased from the book-and-music store FNAC (Rua do Cruicifixo 103, Chiado) as well as from the venues themselves.

Fado

Fado is often described as a kind of working-class blues, although musically it would perhaps be more accurate to class it as a kind of light operetta, sung to a viola accompaniment (for more on its roots see p.633). Alongside Coimbra (which has its own distinct tradition), Lisbon is still the best place to hear it, in the fado clubs in the Bairro Alto, Alfama and elsewhere – either at a *casa de fado* or in an *adega típica*. There's no real distinction between these places: all are small, all serve food (though you don't always have to eat), and all open around 8pm, get going toward midnight, and stay open until 3 or 4am. Their drawbacks are inflated minimum charges – rarely below €15 – and, in the more touristy places, extreme tackiness. Uniformed bouncers are fast becoming the norm, as are warm-up singers crooning Beatles' songs, and photographers snapping your table. We've highlighted some of the more authentic experiences.

Adega Machado Rua do Norte 91, Bairro Alto ℗ 213 224 640. One of the longest-established Bairro Alto joints, as the photo portraits on the wall testify (heads of state included). The minimum consumption of €16 builds to around €25 a head if you sample the fine Portuguese cooking. Closed Mon.

Adega Mesquita Rua do Diário de Notícias 107, Bairro Alto ℗ 213 219 280. Another of the big Bairro Alto names, with better-than-average music and traditional dancing as well as singing. The food is poor though. Minimum consumption €16.

Adega do Ribatejo Rua do Diário de Notícias 23, Bairro Alto ℗ 213 468 343. Great little *adega*, with one of the lowest minimum charges, enjoyable food and fado that locals describe as "pure

emotion". The singers include a couple of professionals, the manager and – best of all – the cooks. Minimum charge €10. Closed Sun.

Clube do Fado Rua de São João da Praça 92–94, Alfama ℗ 218 852 704. Intimate place with stone pillars, an old well and a mainly local clientele. Attracts small-time performers, up-and-coming talent and the occasional big names. Minimum charge around €12.

Mercado da Ribeira Av. 24 de Julho. The revamped Cais do Sodré market forms the backdrop to Fri and Sat night music sessions (from 10pm), which vary from fado to jazz and folk. Acoustics aren't great and don't expect top performers, but it's an atmospheric place.

Parreirinha d'Alfama Beco do Espírito Santo

1, Alfama ☎ 218 868 209. One of the best fado venues, just off Largo do Chafariz de Dentro, often attracting leading stars and a local clientele. Reservations are advised when the big names appear. Minimum charge is around €15, up to around €30 with food.

O Senhor Vinho Rua do Meio à Lapa 18, Lapa ☎ 213 972 681. Famous club sporting some of the best singers in Portugal, which makes the €20 minimum charge (rising to around €40 with a meal) pretty reasonable. Reservations are advised. Closed Sun.

A Severa Rua das Gáveas 55, Bairro Alto ☎ 213 468 314. A city institution, named after a nineteenth-century gypsy singer. Big big fado names and big prices. Minimum consumption around €18. Closed Thurs.

Taverna do Embuçado Beco dos Cortumes 10, Alfama ☎ 218 865 088. First opened in 1966, this well-established *adega* has a cosy feel. Attracts some big-name visitors, and the food is good. Minimum charge around €18, Closed Sun.

A Taverna do Julião Largo do Peneireiro 5, Alfama ☎ 218 872 271. Authentic fado house in the heart of the Alfama with a great house singer. Around €12 minimum charge.

Timpanas Rua Gilberto Rola 24, Alcântara ☎ 213 972 431. This is one of Lisbon's most authentic options, well away from the tourist scene. Closed Wed.

African and Brazilian

B.leza Largo Conde-Barão 50, Santos ☎ 213 963 735. Live African music on most nights in this wonderful sixteenth-century building, with a dance floor, Cape Verdean food and table service. Closed Sun.

Chafarica Calç. de São Vicente 81, Alfama ☎ 218 867 449. Tiny, pricey Brazilian bar with live music from 11pm. Closed Sun.

Luanda Trav. Teixeira Júnior 6, Alcântâra ☎ 213 633 959. With a smart chrome-and-wood interior, this is one of the biggest and most popular of African clubs. Big with the Bairro Alto crowd, who like ending a night here. Closed Tues, and Mon–Wed from Oct–April.

Pê Sujo Largo de São Martinho 6–7, Alfama ☎ 218 866 144. The "dirty foot" is just up from the Sé. There's an outdoor wooden terrace and live bands most nights which result in massive table-banging sessions if the audience approves. Closed Mon.

Jazz

Hot Clube de Portugal Pr. de Alegria 39, off Av. da Liberdade ☎ 213 621 740; metro Avenida. The city's best jazz venue – a tiny basement club that hosts local and visiting artists. Closed Sun & Mon.

Speakeasy Armazém 115, Cais das Oficinas, Doca de Alcântara ☎ 213 957 308. Docklands jazz bar and restaurant hosting some big and up-and-coming names, usually on Tues–Thurs after 11pm. Closed Sun.

Large venues

Aula Magna Reitoria da Universidade de Lisboa, Alamada da Universidade ☎ 217 967 624; metro Cidade Universitaria. The student union venue, which feels like a lecture hall; seating only.

Coliseu dos Recreios Rua das Portas de Santo Antão, Baixa ☎ 213 240 580, 🌐 www.coliseulisboa.com; metro Restauradores. Main indoor city-centre rock, pop and classical venue set in a lovely domed building, originally opened in 1890 as a circus.

Pavilhão Atlântico Parque das Nações ☎ 218 918 440, 🌐 www.pavilhaoatlantico.pt; metro Oriente. Big name stars play at Portugal's largest indoor venue, which holds up to 17,000 spectators.

Sony Plaza Parque das Nações ☎ 218 918 440, 🌐 www.pavilhaoatlantico.pt; metro Oriente. The Parque's main outdoor venue holds up to 10,000 people for summer concerts and New Year's Eve extravaganzas.

Arts and culture

Most major cultural events in the city – including just about every **classical music** concert – are sponsored either by the Fundação Calouste Gulbenkian, Culturgest or the Centro Cultural de Belém, all of which have a full annual programme. Tickets range from €5 to €30, though there are also frequent free concerts and recitals at the São Roque church in Bairro Alto, the Sé, the Basílica da Estrela, São Vicente de Fora and the Igreja dos Mártires. For details of **ballet** performances, consult the website of the renowned Lisbon-based Companhia Nacional de Bailado (ⓦ www.cnb.pt).

Classical music aside, there's a fair amount of other entertainment in Lisbon, including several **theatres**, though productions are almost exclusively in Portuguese. **Cinema** is a better bet for most tourists, as virtually all cinemas show original-language films with Portuguese subtitles, and ticket prices are low (around €5–8; cheaper on Mon). We've picked out a couple of interesting art-house venues below, though for mainstream Hollywood movies you only need to head for any major shopping centre: there are multi-screen complexes at Amoreiras, Edifício Monumental (metro Saldanha), El Corte Inglês (metro São Sebastião), Vasco da Gama in Parque das Nações (metro Oriente) and Colombo Shopping Centre (metro Colégio Militar-Luz).

To find out **what's on**, pick up a schedule of exhibitions, concerts and events from the reception desks at the Gulbenkian and the Belém Cultural Centre. The best **listings** are in *Agenda Cultural*, a free monthly magazine produced by the town hall, which details current exhibitions and shows (in Portuguese). *Follow Me Lisboa* is a watered-down English-language version produced by the local tourist authorities – both are available from the tourist offices. For other listings and previews of forthcoming events, get hold of *Público*, the *Diário de Notícias* or *O Independente* **newspapers**, or consult the ABEP kiosk at the corner of Restauradores (daily 9am–9.30pm), though remember that the Portuguese titles for films are not always direct translations.

Cinema

Instituto da Cinemateca Portuguesa Rua Barata Salgueiro 39 ☎ 213 596 266; metro Avenida. The national film theatre, with twice-daily shows, ranging from contemporary Portuguese films to anything from Truffaut to Valentino. It also has its own small cinema museum.

Quarteto Rua das Flores Lima 1, off Av. Estados Unidos ☎ 217 971 244; metro Entre Campos. Art-house cinema with four screens.

São Jorge Av. da Liberdade 175 ☎ 213 103 400; metro Avenida. Most central cinema for mainstream movies, though sometimes closed for temporary exhibitions and fairs.

Classical music and opera

Centro Cultural de Belém Pr.do Império, Belém ☎ 213 612 400, ⓦ www.ccb.pt. Has both a large and small auditorium for a range of music, from jazz to classical.

Culturgest Av. João XXI 63, Campo Pequeno ☎ 217 905 155, ⓦ www.cgd.pt. Large modern arts complex with two auditoriums.

Fundação Calouste Gulbenkian Av. de Berna ☎ 217 823 000, ⓦ www.gulbenkian.pt. There are three concert halls (including an outdoor amphitheatre) at the Gulbenkian, with performances ranging from jazz to chamber to classical.

Teatro Nacional de São Carlos Rua Serpa Pinto 9, Chiado ☎ 213 468 408, ⓦ www.saocarlos.pt. The opera season runs from September to June and, in addition, there's a regular classical music programme.

Theatre

Lisbon Players Rua da Estrela 10, Lapa ☎ 213 961 946. Check out performances by this amateur but highly rated English-speaking theatrical group consisting largely of expat actors.

Teatro Nacional de Dona Maria Rossio, Baixa ☎ 213 472 246, ⓦ www.teatro-dmaria.pt. Regular performances of Portuguese and foreign plays.

Sports

Football is the biggest game in Lisbon, and it's easy to get match tickets (see below), while summer season **bullfights** are the other main spectacle. Otherwise, you're going to need to travel out of the capital for sports, either for **golf**, on the upmarket courses around Estoril (consult Ⓦwww.portugalgolf.pt), or **watersports**, namely surfing at Caparica (see pp.141–142) and windsurfing at Guincho (p.129) and Ericeira (p.156).

Football

Benfica – Lisbon's most famous football team – have a glorious past (the great Eusébio played for the team in the 1960s), though they have been struggling of late to keep up with city rivals Sporting. The awesome **Estádio da Luz**, Avenida Gen. Norton Matos (Ⓣ217 210 522 or 214 153 815, Ⓦwww.slbenfica.pt; metro Colégio Militar-Luz), was completely rebuilt in preparation for the 2004 European Championships; it was here that Portugal lost in the final to Greece in front of 65,000 disbelieving spectators.

   Sporting Lisbon (officially called Sporting Club de Portugal), Benfica's traditional city rivals, play at the nearby **Estádio José Alvalade** (Ⓣ217 516 010 or 217 516 000, Ⓦwww.sporting.pt; metro Campo Grande), also purpose built for Euro 2004 and featuring state-of-the-art stadium-design, with a capacity of 54,000. Top-division action can also be caught at the Estádio do Restelo, Avenida do Restelo, Belém (Ⓣ213 010 461, Ⓦwww.cfbelenenses.pt), home of **Belenenses**, though they last won the title back in 1946.

   The **Portuguese Cup Final** is held every May at the Estádio Nacional (National Stadium; Ⓣ214 197 212), Praça da Maratona, Cruz Quebrada (bus #6 from Algés or train to Cruz Quebrada from Cais do Sodré). The stadium holds up to 55,000 but is pretty run-down and soulless – it was not among the eight stadiums selected as venues for the 2004 European Championships.

   Daily soccer tabloid *Bola,* available from any newsagent or newspaper kiosk, has fixtures, match reports and news, as does the website Ⓦwww .portuguesesoccer.com. To buy advance **tickets** for big games – which cost between €20 and €40 – go to the kiosks (not the turnstiles) at the grounds.

Bullfights

Bullfights take place most Thursdays (April–Sept) at the principal **Praça de Touros do Campo Pequeno**, just off Avenida da República (Ⓣ217 932 093; metro Campo Pequeno). Built in 1892, the beautiful building has a capacity of 9000, making it one of the largest bullrings in the world. Tickets cost €15–60, depending on where you sit, and the spectacle takes place in the evening. There are less frequent fights at Cascais in summer, or you can travel out of Lisbon to Vila Franca de Xira (see p.202) and surrounding towns and villages for more traditional events.

Festivals and events

Lisbon's main festivals are in June, with fireworks and street-partying to celebrate the **Santos Populares** – ie saints António (Anthony; June 13), João (John; June 24) and Pedro (Peter; June 29). Celebrations of each begin on the previous evening; Santo Antonio is the largest, taking over just about every square in Alfama and with a parade down Avenida da Liberdade. Also in June, the **Festas da Lisboa** presents a series of city-sponsored events, including free concerts, exhibitions and culinary contests.

On the cultural front, there's the annual **Sintra Music Festival** (July and August; Ⓦ www.cm-sintra.pt) – which embraces the **Noites de Bailado** ballet festival at the Palácio de Seteais – offering top performances by internationally known orchestras, musicians and dance groups. Events are held in various venues in Sintra, as well as at Queluz, Cascais and Estoril. Lisbon's Instituto da Cinemateca Portuguesa and Quarteto cinemas are the venues for the **Troia International Film Festival** (June; Ⓦ www.festroia.pt), which showcases movies from countries which produce fewer than 21 films per year, subtitled in Portuguese. Another annual event is the **Gay Film Festival**, held at various cinemas in September (Ⓦ www.lisbonfilmfest.org).

February sees the **Fado/Harbour Festival**, which combines fado with music from other port cities from around the world. Other events include a **carnival** celebration (February/March), usually at Parque das Nações; free street entertainment in the Baixa as part of the **Baixanima** festival (July–Sept); the **Festival dos Oceanos** (Oceans Festival, August), celebrating the city's links with the ocean through special events, regattas and parades; the **Festival do Vinho** (November), with events and tastings to celebrate the wine harvest; and more vibrant celebrations on **New Year's Eve**, with fireworks and all-night partying in Praça do Comércio and at the Parque das Nações.

At Estoril, and a lot better than it sounds, is the state-run **Feira Internacional Artesanato** (Handicrafts Fair), when crafts of all kinds, from every region of the country, are on display – if you buy anything, bargain at length. The fair runs through July and August, from around 5pm until midnight, with foodstalls included in the attractions. A similar international handicrafts fair takes place in July at the **Feira Internacional de Lisboa** (Ⓦ www.fil.pt), Lisbon's main exhibitions hall in the Parque das Nações.

Shops and markets

The Bairro Alto and Chiado are the main centres for alternative designer clothes and crafts, while international designer names are fast appearing along Avenida da Liberdade. Antique shops are concentrated along Rua do Alecrim in Chiado, Rua Dom Pedro V in the Bairro Alto, and along Rua de São Bento, between Rato and São Bento. As well as all these areas, don't miss the city's **markets** and major **shopping centres** (listed below) or the Feira da Ladra **flea market** in the Alfama (see pp.92–93). Traditional **shopping hours** are Monday to Friday 9am to 7pm (some shops close for an hour at lunch), Saturday 9am to 1am. However, many of the Bairro Alto shops are open afternoons and evenings only, usually 2 to 9pm or so. Many larger shops, especially in shopping centres, open all day until 11pm or midnight, some even on Sundays. Unless otherwise stated, the shops listed below are closed Saturday afternoon and all day Sunday, though the shopping centres are all open daily.

Other than traditional **ceramics and carpets**, perhaps the most Portuguese of items to take home is a **bottle of port**: check out the vintages at the *Solar do Vinho do Porto* (see p.115), where you can also sample the stuff. Alternatively, buy port or the increasingly respected **Portuguese wines** from one of the specialist shops listed below, or from any delicatessen or supermarket.

Antiques, arts and crafts

Casa do Turista Av. da Liberdade 159; metro Avenida. Crammed with regional arts, crafts, ceramics, T-shirts and some rather fine toy trams.

Fábrica Sant'ana Rua do Alecrim 95, Chiado. If you're interested in Portuguese tiles – *azulejos* – check out this factory shop, founded in 1741, which sells copies of traditional designs and a great range of pots and ceramics.

Fábrica Viúva Lamego Largo do Intendente 25; metro Intendente. Highly rated *azulejo* factory-shop producing made-to-order designs or reproduction antiques. Closed Sat in July & Aug.

Loja de Artesenato Mercado da Ribeira, Av. 24 de Julho; metro Cais do Sodré. Specializing in art and crafts from Lisbon and the Tejo valley, it doubles as an exhibition space. Closed Sun.

Santos Ofícios Rua da Madalena 87, near the Sé. Small shop stuffed with a somewhat touristy collection of regional crafts including some attractive ceramics, rugs, embroidery, baskets and toys. Closed Sun. There's another branch at the Lisbon Welcome Centre (entrance on Rua do Arsenal; daily 10am–8pm).

Books and music

Casa do Fado e da Guitarra Portuguesa Largo do Chafariz de Dentro 1. Alfama. The museum contains an excellent selection of fado CDs and cassettes, and staff give expert advice.

FNAC Rua do Crucifixo 103, Chiado. A good range of English-language books, along with an extensive music department and computer equipment. Also has a desk selling tickets to major events. There's another branch at Loja 103A, Colombo Shopping Centre (see below).

Livraria Bertrand Rua Garrett 73, Chiado. Portugal's oldest general bookshop, opened in 1773, once the meeting place of the literary set. Today it has a good range of novels in English, plus a range of foreign magazines. Closed Sun morning.

Livraria Britânica Rua de São Marçal 83, Bairro Alto. Well-stocked English-language bookshop, which caters mainly to the British Council nearby.

Livraria Portugal Rua do Carmo 70–74, Baixa. Excellent Portuguese bookshop that features many of the books reviewed on pp.640–645.

Clothes and accessories

Aba Salazar Rua do Carmo 87, Chiado. One of the country's best-known designer's main Lisbon outlet, with adventurous styles mostly for women.

Espaço Fátima Lopes Rua da Atalaia 36, Bairro Alto. Flagship store for Lisbon's biggest names in fashion; bold, colourful and confident clothes to reflect the mood of Portugal's wannabees.

José Dias Sobral Rua de São Paulo 218, Cais do Sodré. Founded in 1880 and barely changed since, this traditional workshop at the foot of the Elevador da Bica sells quality leather belts, briefcases and shoe-laces.

Luvaria Ulisses Rua do Carmo 87a, Chiado. Quality gloves from this superb, ornate shoebox of a shop, with gloves neatly tucked into rows of boxes.

Markets

Mercado 31 de Janeiro Rua Eng. Viera da Silva; metro Picoas or Saldanha. Features everything from fresh fish and flowers to arts and crafts. Mon–Sat 7am–2pm.

Mercado da Ribeira Av. 24 de Julho, Cais do Sodré. One of Lisbon's most atmospheric covered markets, with a great fish hall. Mon–Sat: food 6am–2pm; flower market 3–7pm.

Numismatists' market Pr. do Comércio, Baixa. Old coins and notes from Portugal and its former colonies. Sun morning.

Parque das Nações Estação do Oriente, Level 2. Changing markets take place weekly above the metro station. The first Sun of the month sees a stamps, coins and collectibles fair; the second Sun has handicrafts; the third antiques; and the fourth decorative arts. Sun 10am–7pm.

Praça de Espanha Characterful, downmarket affair near the Gulbenkian, with stalls selling African music CDs, cheap clothes and general tat. Mon–Sat 9am–6pm.

Shopping centres

Armazéns do Chiado Rua do Carmo 2, Chiado ⓦ www.armazensdochiado.com. This well-designed shopping centre sits on six floors above metro Baixa-Chiado. The top floor has a series of cafés and restaurants, most offering great views over town.

Centro Colombo Av. Colégio Militar-Luz ⓦ www .colombo.pt; metro Colégio Militar-Luz. Iberia's largest shopping complex boasts 400 international and national stores, restaurants, cinemas and play areas.

Centro Comércial Mouraria Largo Martim Moniz, Mouraria. The city's most atmospheric shopping centre, with six levels (three underground) featuring a motely collection of Indian fabrics, Oriental and African foods, and ethnic cafés.

Centro Vasco da Gama Av. Dom João II, Parque das Nações ⓦ www.centrovascodagama.pt; metro Oriente. Three floors of national and international stores under a glass roof permanently washed by running water. Also restaurants, children's areas and disabled access.

El Corte Inglês Av. António Augusto de Aguiar ⓦ www.elcorteingles.pt; metro São Sebastião. Giant Spanish department store spread over nine floors, selling everything from gourmet foods, clothes and sports goods to CDs, books and toys.

Tivoli Forum Av. da Liberdade; metro Avenida. Flash marble-fronted shopping emporium sheltering the likes of DKNY, French Connection & Adolfo Dominguez. Also has a Pingo Doce supermarket (daily 8.30am–9pm), cafés and a juice bar.

Wine and food

Casa Pereira da Conceição Rua Augusta 102–104, Baixa. Art Deco 1930s shop selling aromatic coffee beans and teas.

Manuel Tavares Rua da Betesga 1A, Baixa. On the edge of Rossio, this small, century-old shop has a great selection of chocolate and national cheeses, plus a basement stuffed with vintage wines and ports. Closed Sun and (from Oct–June) Sat afternoon.

Napoleão Rua dos Fanqueiros 70, Baixa, junction with Rua da Conceição. Great range of port and wine, with knowledgeable, English-speaking staff. Closed Sun.

Listings

Airlines Air France, Av. 5 de Outubro 206 ☏ 217 900 202; Alitalia, Pr. Marquês de Pombal 1–5° ☏ 213 536 141; British Airways, airport ☏ 808 200 125; Iberia, Rua Rosa Araújo 2 ☏ 213 558 119; KLM, Campo Grande 220B ☏ 217 955 010; Lufthansa, airport ☏ 214 245 155; TAP, Estação do Oriente, metro Oriente ☏ 218 958 310; Varig, Pr. Marquês de Pombal 1 ☏ 213 136 830.

Banks Most main branches are in the Baixa and surrounding streets. Standard banking hours are Mon–Fri 8.30am–3pm. ATMs can be found throughout Lisbon, including at the airport, the main stations and in all the main squares.

Buses The main terminal is at Av. João Crisóstomo ☏ 707 223 344 (metro Saldanha) for international and most domestic departures, including express services to the Algarve and Alentejo. Other bus terminals include: Praça de Espanha (metro Praça de Espanha) for Transportes Sul do Tejo (☏ 217 262 740) services to Caparica, Sesimbra and places south of the Tejo, and Setu-balase (☏ 265 525 051) to Setúbal; Parque das Nações (metro Oriente) for AVIC services (☏ 218 940 238) to the northwest coast, and Renex services (☏ 218 956 836) to the Minho and Algarve; and Campo Grande 5 (metro Campo Grande) for Mafrense Empresa Barraqueiro (☏ 217 582 212) services to Mafra and Ericeira. You can buy advance bus tickets from most travel agents.

Car rental Alamo/Nacional, Av. Alvares Cabral 45B ☏ 213 703 400, Rato; Auto Jardim, Rua Luciano Cordeiro 6, east of Av. da Liberdade ☏ 213 549 182 and airport ☏ 218 463 187; Avis, Campo Grande 390 ☏ 217 547 800; Budget, Rua Cas-tilho, west of Av. da Liberdade 167B ☏ 213 860 516 and airport ☏ 218 478 803; Europcar, Santa Apolónia station ☏ 218 861 573 and airport ☏ 218

401 176; Hertz, Rua Castilho 72, west of Av. da Liberdade ☏ 213 812 430 and airport ☏ 218 463 154; Nova Rent, Largo Monterroio Mascarenhas 9, Amoreiras ☏ 213 845 270.

Embassies and consulates Australia, Av. da Liberdade 198–2° ☏ 213 101 500 (metro Avenida); Canada, Av. da Liberdade 196–200 ☏ 213 164 600; Ireland, Rua da Imprensa à Estrela 1–4° ☏ 213 929 440; UK, Rua de São Bernardo 33 ☏ 213 124 000, ⓦ www.uk-embassy.pt (metro Rato); USA, Av. das Forças Armadas ☏ 217 273 300 (metro Jardim Zoológico).

Gay and lesbian Centro Comunitário Gay e Lèsbi-ca de Lisboa (Lisbon Gay and Lesbian Community Centre; Rua de São Lazaro 88, Largo Martim Moniz ☏ 213 873 918, ⓦ www.ilga-portugal .oninet.pt; Mon–Sat 4–8pm) organizes events and can help with information – their excellent website is in English and Portuguese.

Hospital British Hospital, Rua Saraiva de Carvalho 49 ☏ 213 955 067 has English-speaking staff and doctors on call from 8.30am to 9pm. In an emergency, call ☏ 112.

Internet Central options include Ponto Net, above the Lisbon Welcome Centre, Pr. do Comércio, Baixa ☏ 210 312 815 (daily 9am–8pm); Web Café, Rua do Diário de Notícias 16, Bairro Alto ☏ 213 421 181 (daily 4pm–2am); and Cyberica, Rua Duques de Bragança 7 Chiado ☏ 213 421 707 (daily 11am–midnight).

Language courses Portuguese language courses are run by the Cambridge School, Av. da Liberdade 173 ☏ 213 124 600, ⓦ www.cambridge.pt; and International House, Rua do Marquês Sa da Bandeira 16, metro São Sebastião ☏ 213 151 496.

Laundry The self-service Lava Neve, Rua da Alegria 37, Bairro Alto ☏ 213 466 195 (Mon

9am–1pm & 3–7pm, Tues–Fri 10am–1pm & 3–7pm, Sat 9am–1pm) is good value at €5 for 5kg of laundry.

Left luggage There are 24hr lockers at the airport (in level 1 of car park 1), and at Rossio, Cais do Sodré and Santa Apolónia stations (around €2–5 a day), and a left-luggage office at the bus terminal on Av. João Crisóstomo (Mon–Fri 6.30am–8pm, Sat & Sun 9am–1pm & 2–6pm).

Lost property For anything lost on public transport, call ☎213 558 457 (metro), ☎213 224 000 (ferries) or ☎213 463 181 (trains).

Newspapers There are several newsstands around Rossio and Restauradores – such as the one attached to the ABEP ticket kiosk – which sell foreign-language papers, as do the lobbies of many of the larger hotels.

Pharmacies City pharmacies are open Mon–Fri 9am–1pm & 3–7pm, Sat 9am–1pm. Local papers carry information about 24-hour pharmacies and the details are posted on every pharmacy door.

Police The tourist police station is the Foz Cultura building in Palácio Foz, Restauradores ☎213 421 634 (daily 24 hours). You need a report from here in order to make a claim on your travel insurance.

Post office The main post office is at Pr. dos Restauradores 58 ☎213 238 700 (Mon–Fri 8am –10pm, Sat & Sun 9am–6pm), from where you can send airmail and *correio azul* (express mail – the fastest service). There's a 24-hour post office at the airport. Stamps can also be purchased from some – but not all – newsagents.

Swimming pools The most central option is the pool in the Atheneum club at Rua das Portas de Santo Antão 110, next to the Coliseu (☎213 421 365; Mon–Fri 3.30–4.30pm & 9–10pm, Sat 3.30–7pm; €3.50).

Telephones There's a telephone office next to the post office in Pr. dos Restauradores (see above). There's a second office on the corner of Rossio (no. 65; 8am–11pm). You can also make international calls from any phone booth.

Trains See p.67 for details of Lisbon's various stations. Timetables and train information are available from individual stations and on ⓦ www .cp.pt. Always check departure times and stations in advance: many intercity services require a seat reservation (particularly to Coimbra/Porto), which you can do prior to departure, though allow yourself plenty of time.

Travel agencies Marcus & Harting, Rossio 45–50 ☎213 224 550, is a good, central option for bus tickets and general travel information. USIT Tagus, Rua Camilo Castelo Branco 20 ☎213 525 986, specializes in discounted student tickets and sells ISIC cards.

Around Lisbon

The most straightforward way to escape the city is to head for the string of beach resorts west along the coast from Belém, which can be reached by train from Cais do Sodré. At places like **Oeiras** and **Carcavelos**, and above all at **Estoril** and **Cascais**, the beaches are good even if the water quality isn't. For better sands and a cleaner ocean you'll have to head north to **Guincho**, or cross the Tejo by ferry to reach the **Costa da Caparica**, a 30km stretch of dunes to the south of the capital. Further south still, there are good, clean beaches at **Sesimbra** and in the Parque Natural da Arrábida, a superb unspoilt craggy reserve, while the large town of **Setúbal** is noted for its Igreja de Jesus, the earliest of all Manueline buildings. There's reasonably priced accommodation at all these places, as well as a youth hostel at Oeiras and campsites at Guincho, Costa da Caparica and Arrábida. But, as you might imagine, all the beach resorts in the Lisbon area get very crowded at weekends and throughout August.

Basing yourself in Lisbon, you also could take in a fair part of the provinces of Estremadura (Chapter 2) and Alentejo (Chapter 8) on day-trips. Indeed, some of those regions' greatest attractions lie within a 50km or so radius of the capital – such as the palaces of **Queluz** or **Mafra** – and are best seen on a day-trip. However, the beautiful town of **Sintra**, the most popular excursion from Lisbon, demands a longer look, and reveals a different side if you stay overnight. Bear in mind that most of the Sintra palaces are closed on Mondays, and those at Queluz and Mafra on Tuesdays.

West to Estoril and Cascais

Stretching for over 30km west of Lisbon, the Estoril coast makes for an enjoyable day out, drifting from beach to bar and strolling along the lively seafront promenades. Sadly, the water itself has suffered badly from pollution and, though steps are being taken to clean it up, most beaches fail to get a blue flag. Nonetheless, the coast retains its attractions, particularly at the main resorts of **Estoril** and **Cascais** – the latter, in particular, makes a pleasant alternative to staying in Lisbon, and is well placed for trips to Sintra or to the wild Guincho beach.

The **Linha de Cascais train** leaves every twenty minutes from Cais do Sodré station (Mon–Thurs & Sun 5.30am–1.30am, Fri & Sat 5.30am–2.30am; €1.30), stopping at the beaches of Oeiras, Carcavelos and stations beyond. If you are staying in Cascais or Estoril, note that there are hourly buses to both resorts to and from Lisbon airport. By road, the **N6** coastal highway passes through most of the centres along the seafront, often as the Avenida Marginal; the faster **A5 motorway** (Auto-Estrada da Oeste) is an inexpensive toll road running from Lisbon to Estoril – drive west past Amoreiras and follow the signs.

Oeiras to São João

The first suburb of any size after Belém is **OEIRAS**, where the Rio Tejo officially turns into the sea. The riverside walkways are being improved and the beach here has recently been cleaned up, though most people still swim in the ocean pool alongside the sands. Unless you're staying at the youth hostel (see p.75), however, the only reason for a stop here would be to see the **Palácio do Marquês de Pombal**, erstwhile home of the rebuilder of Lisbon. The house is now an adult education centre and the park is not technically open to visitors. However, if there's nothing special going on, the guard should be able to show you the attractive formal gardens, or you can peer over the walls at its massive grotto.

The next stop, **CARCAVELOS**, has the most extensive sandy beach on this part of the coast. Swimmers chance the waters in high summer, and at other times it's a lively spot for beach soccer, surfing and blowy winter walks. To reach the beach, it's a ten-minute walk from the station along the broad Avenida Jorge V. There are plenty of beachside cafés and bars; *Perola*, on the promenade at the west end of the beach, offers inexpensive food and great sea views. Try to visit Carcavelos on Thursday morning, when the town hosts a huge **market**; turn right out of the station and follow the signs. Street upon street is taken over by stalls selling cheap goods, clothes (many with brand-name labels) and ceramics.

Along the last stretch of the Linha de Cascais, the beaches improve rapidly and you reach the beginning of an esplanade that stretches virtually uninterrupted to Cascais. **SÃO PEDRO** has a superb beach, just down from the station, and **SÃO JOÃO** is flanked by two lovely stretches of sand. The whole seafront here is pretty animated in the summer months, swarming with young surfers and Portuguese holidaymakers frequenting the numerous cafés and restaurants.

Estoril

ESTORIL gained a postwar reputation as a haunt of exiled royalty and the idle rich, and it continues to maintain its pretensions towards being a "Portuguese Riviera", with grandiose villas and luxury hotels. It is little surprise then that the town's touristic life revolves around its golf courses and **Casino** (daily 3pm–3am; free; ⓦ www.casino-estoril.pt). The latter requires some semblance of formal attire, but once inside you'll find roulette, card games, slot machines, restaurants, shops, nightly shows at 11pm and even an art gallery.

The casino sits at the far end the **Parque do Estoril**, a lovely stretch of fountains and exotic trees, surrounded by Estoril's nicest bars and restaurants. The resort's fine sandy beach, **Praia de Tamariz**, is backed by a seafront promenade that stretches all the way to Cascais, a twenty-minute stroll. From July to mid-September, a free fireworks display takes place above Estoril's beach every Saturday night at midnight.

Practicalities

The **train station** is on Estoril's through-road, with the beach accessible by underpass. Across the main road from the station, at the bottom of the park, you'll find the very helpful **turismo** (Mon–Sat 9am–8pm, Sun 10am–6pm; ⓣ 214 663 813, ⓦ www.estorilcoast-tourism.com), which can provide advice on private rooms and details of the area's various golf clubs.

There's a fair amount of local **accommodation**, with the best budget choice the pleasant rooms at the *Pensão-Residencial Smart*, Rua José Viana 3 (ⓣ 214 682 164, ⓔ residencial.smart@netcabo.pt; breakfast included; ❹). It's east of the park – turn right out of the station, turning left when you reach Avenida Bombeiros Voluntarios, which runs up behind the *Hotel Paris*.

Deck Bar, Arcadas do Parque 21 (ⓣ 214 680 366; open till 2am; closed Mon) is a nice outdoor **restaurant** and café just behind the tourist office, overlooking the western side of the park. *Jonas Bar*, on the seafront between Cascais and Estoril, is a fun spot day or night, selling cocktails, juices and snacks. However, the best place to eat is the expensive *Cimas* (also known as the *English Bar*) at Avenida Sabóia 9 (ⓣ 214 680 413; closed Sun), just west of the square in Monte Estoril, between Cascais and Estoril. Originally named after the Englishman who built the mansion in the 1940s, it has a fine wood-panelled interior, sea views and top-quality fish, meat and game.

Cascais

At the end of the train line, **CASCAIS** is a major resort, with three fairly good beaches along its esplanade, a flash marina and a fort (closed to the public) that guards the harbour. It is positively bursting at the seams in summer, especially at weekends, but despite the commercialism it's not too large or difficult to get around, and has a much younger, less exclusive, feel than Estoril. It even retains some vestiges of its previous existence as a fishing village.

You'll find the main concentration of bars and nightlife – and consequently most of what makes Cascais tick as a town – on Rua Frederico Arouca, the main pedestrian thoroughfare. The local **fish market** near here is worth a look (Mon–Sat from around 8am), while for a wander away from the crowds, cross over the main Avenida and stroll up beyond Largo 5° de Outubro into the old, and surprisingly pretty, west side of town, at its most delightful in the streets around the graceful **Igreja da Assunção**.

Cascais' other attractions are all to the west of the centre. Beyond the church lies the pleasant **Parque Municipal da Gandarinha**, in whose southern

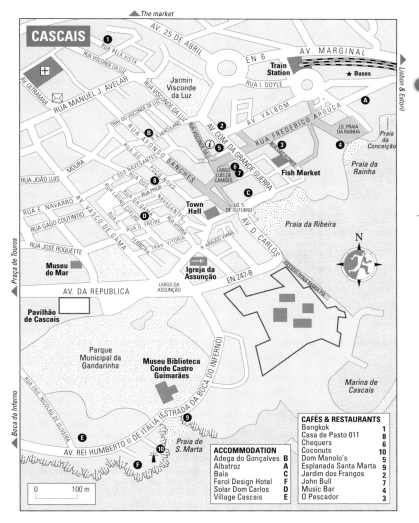

CASCAIS

The market

AV. 25 DE ABRIL

EN 6 · AV. MARGINAL

Train Station

★ Buses

RUA I. DOYLE

Lisbon & Estoril

RUA BELA VISTA

RUA VISCONDE DA LUZ

AV. ULTRAMAR

RUA MANUEL J. AVELAR

Jarmin Visconde da Luz

RUA VISCONDE DE LUZ

TRAV. DO VISCONDE DE LUZ

RUA AFONSO SANCHES

A.HERCULANO

RUA DO VISCONDE DA LUZ

AV. COM. DA GRANDE-GUERRA

AV. VALBOM

RUA FREDERICO AROUCA

RUA VISCONDE DA LUZ

RUA FRESTELOS

LG. PRAIA DA RAINHA

Praia da Conceição

Praia da Rainha

RUA JOÃO LUIS

MOURA

RUA DO

T. DOS NAVEGANTES

RUA DOS

POÇO NOVO

RUA PRIOR

RUA PRIOR

LARGO LUIS DE CAMÕES

Fish Market

RUA LATINO COELHO

RUA DA GAMA

RUA DOS NAVEGANTES

RUA VITORIA

RUA G. FREIRE

Town Hall

LG 5 DE OUTUBRO

Praia da Ribeira

RUA E. NAVARRO

RUA GAGO COUTINTIO

AV. VASCO DE GAMA

RUA JOSÉ ROQUETTE

FERREIRA

TRAV. VITORIA

R. ARAUJO VIANA

AV. D. CARLOS

PASSEIO DONA MARIA PIA

N

Praça de Touros

Museu do Mar

LARGO DA ASSUNÇÃO

Igreja da Assunção

EN 247-8

AV. DA REPUBLICA

Pavilhão de Cascais

Parque Municipal da Gandarinha

Museu Biblioteca Conde Castro Guimarães

Marina de Cascais

Boca da Inferno

RUA FRE. NICOLAU DE OLIVEIRA

ESTRADA DA BOCA DO INFERNO

EN DE ITÁLIA (ESTRADA DA BOCA DO INFERNO)

Praia de S. Marta

AV. REI HUMBERTO II DE ITÁLIA

0 ——— 100 m

ACCOMMODATION

Adega do Gonçalves	B
Albatroz	A
Baía	C
Farol Design Hotel	F
Solar Dom Carlos	D
Village Cascais	E

CAFÉS & RESTAURANTS

Bangkok	1
Casa de Pasto 011	8
Chequers	6
Coconuts	10
Dom Manolo's	5
Esplanada Santa Marta	9
Jardim dos Frangos	2
John Bull	7
Music Bar	4
O Pescador	3

reaches stands the mansion of the counts of Guimarães, preserved complete with its nineteenth-century fittings as the **Museu Biblioteca Conde Castro Guimarães** (Tues–Sun 10am–5pm; €1.60); most days, there's someone around to give you a guided tour of the furniture, paintings and antiques that the count bequeathed to the nation. On the north side of the park, opposite the Pavilhão de Cascais, signs point you to the modern **Museu do Mar** (Tues–Sun 10am–5pm; €1.30), an engaging little collection of model boats, sea-related artefacts, old costumes and pictures.

Taking the coastal road, it's about twenty minutes' walk west to the **Boca do Inferno** – the "Mouth of Hell" – where waves crash against caves in the cliff face. The viewpoints above are always packed with tourists (as is the very tacky market on the roadside) but, frankly, the whole affair is rather unimpressive except in stormy weather. It's a pretty walk, however, past the little beach at **Praia de Santa Marta,** which has a nice café (see below) on the terrace above.

Practicalities

From the **train station** it's just a short walk into town; **buses** to Guincho, Cabo da Roca and Sintra leave from the stands outside the station (there are local bus timetables posted in the turismo, too). Walk down Rua Frederico Arouca and cross the main avenue for the **turismo** (Mon–Sat 9am–7pm, Sun 10am–6pm; ☎214 868 204), set in an old mansion on Rua Visconde da Luz, where the staff will usually phone around on your behalf for private rooms (❸). **Accommodation** prices in July and August are very high but most of the places listed below will drop room rates by up to forty percent out of season.

At night, Cascais shows itself off in the smart **pubs, bars and cafés** around Largo Luís de Camões, down the steps on the west side of the main avenue. They nearly all serve food (none of it particularly memorable), but the suntrap square is a pleasant (if expensive) place to sit and drink. On summer nights the bars throw open their doors, turn up the music and, come closing time at 2am, the square is full of bleary-eyed drinkers dancing and shouting the words to tunes they never realized they knew.

There's a lively **market** every Wednesday on Rua do Mercado, off Avenida 25 de Abril, and there are Sunday evening **bullfights** during summer in the Praça de Touros, Avenida Pedro Alvares Cabral, in the west of town some 2km from the centre.

Hotels and pensions

Adega do Gonçalves Rua Afonso Sanches 54 ☎214 831 519. Basic rooms and shared facilities above the restaurant. It's in a handy location but is guaranteed to be noisy. Downstairs, the *adega* is not yet overwhelmed by tourists, serving huge portions of good food at moderate prices; the grilled fish is recommended. ❷

Hotel Albatroz Rua Frederica Arouca 100 ☎214 847 380, ⓦwww.albatrozhotels.com. Built in the nineteenth century as a royal retreat, €300 or so will get you a room in one of Portugal's finest seaside hotels, with glorious views from some rooms (which you pay extra for). There's also a lovely swimming pool on the ocean terrace, and more views from the restaurant. Big winter reductions. Breakfast included. Parking. ❾

Hotel Baía Av. Com. da Grande Guerra ☎214 831 095, ⓦwww.hotelbaia.com. Modern seafront hotel overlooking the beach and harbour. There are over 100 rooms, many with a sea view (book ahead in summer for these), and a great rooftop covered pool and bar. Breakfast included. ❻

Farol Design Hotel Av. Rei Humberto II de Italia ☎214 823 490, ⓦwww.cascais.org. Right on the seafront, this designer hotel has a modern wing moulded onto a sixteenth-century villa, and the decor mixes traditional wood and marble with modern steel and glass. Rooms aren't huge but most have sea views and terraces; there's also a fashionable bar, restaurant (serving nouveau Portuguese cuisine) and outdoor pool facing the rocks. Breakfast included. Parking. ❾

Solar Dom Carlos Rua Latina Coelho 8 ☎214 828 115, ⓦwww.solardomcarlos.com. This very attractive sixteenth-century mansion is the best mid-range option in town, so book ahead. It's on a quiet backstreet with cool tiling throughout and a welcoming air. Bright, pretty rooms, garden and even an old royal chapel. Breakfast included. ❹

Village Cascais Rua Frie Nicolau de Oliveira ☎214 826 000, ⓦwww.vilagale.pt. Superbly positioned next to Parque da Gandarinha, near an unspoilt part of coast, this large modern complex is set in palm-studded grounds. Good for families, the spacious rooms have satellite TV and minibar, and there's also a downstairs bar and restaurant. Breakfast included. Parking. ❽

Restaurants

Bangkok Rua da Bela Vista 6 ☎214 847 600. Sublime Thai cooking in a traditional town house, beautifully decorated with inlaid wood and oriental furnishings. Specials include lobster in curry paste and assorted Thai appetizers; expect to pay upwards of €30. Very expensive.

Casa de Pasto 011 Trav. dos Navegantes 11. With just half a dozen tables, this local grill-house attracts crowds thanks to its bargain-priced, and very tasty, fish and meat dishes and house wine. The service is slow, so sit back and enjoy. Closed Sun. No credit cards. Inexpensive.

Dom Manolo's Av. Com. da Grande Guerra11 ☎214 831 126. Busy grill-house serving superb chicken and chips; add a salad, local wine and home-made dessert and you'll still pay only around €10. Inexpensive.

Esplanada Santa Marta Praia de Santa Marta. Charcoal-grilled fish served on a tiny terrace overlooking the sea and beach. Closed Sun & Mon. Moderate.

Jardim dos Frangos Av. Com. da Grande Guerra 66. Permanently buzzing with people and sizzling with the speciality grilled chicken, which is devoured by the plateload at indoor and outdoor tables. Inexpensive.

O Pescador Rua das Flores 10 ☎214 832 054. One of several places close to the fish market, this offers superior fish meals and good service. Closed Sun. Expensive.

Bars and clubs

Chequers Largo Luís de Camões 7 ☎214 830 926. Lively English-style pub, especially once the pumping rock music strengthens its grip.

Coconuts Av. Rei Humberto II de Itália 7 ☎214 844 109. Club on the road to Boca do Inferno with a great little seaside terrace, attracting a mix of fashionable locals and clubbing tourists. Guest DJs on Thursdays. Opens 11pm, closed Mon, Tues & Sun.

John Bull Pr. Costa Pinto 31 ☎214 833 319. Backing onto the Largo Luís de Camões, this English-style pub fills up early with a good-time crowd.

Music Bar Largo da Praia da Rainha 121 ☎214 820 848. One of the few bars in town with decent sea views, which you can take in sitting at tables on the patio above the beach. Also serves decent meals. Closed Mon Oct–April.

Praia do Guincho

Buses from outside Cascais train station (daily 7.15am–7.15pm, every 1–2hr; €2) run the 6km west to **PRAIA DO GUINCHO**, a great sweeping field of beach with body-crashing Atlantic rollers. It's a superb place for surfing and windsurfing – legs of the World Windsurfing Championships are often held here in August – but also a dangerous one. The undertow is notoriously strong and people are drowned almost every year. To add to that, there's absolutely no shade and on breezy days the wind cuts across the sands. Even if you can't feel the sun, you need to be very careful.

The beach is flanked by half a dozen large, moderately priced **terrace-restaurants**, all with standard fish-dominated menus and varying views of the breaking rollers. There's no budget **accommodation** – in fact, quite the opposite. At the deluxe-class *Fortaleza do Guincho* (☎214 870 491, Ⓦwww .guinchotel.pt; ❾) you can stay in a converted fort with a Michelin-starred restaurant. There are 27 tastefully decorated rooms with sea views and others gathered round the internal courtyard; a limousine service takes guests to and from the airport on request. More affordable is *Estalagem O Muchaxo* (☎214 870 221, Ⓦwww.muchaxo.com; ❺), a highly attractive place, with a seawater pool, stone-flagged bar and picture windows looking out across the beach from the highly rated restaurant; sea-view rooms here are priced a category higher. The well-equipped Orbitur **campsite** (see p.76) is about 1km back from the main part of the beach; follow the signs from the coast road.

Sintra and around

As the summer residence of the kings of Portugal, and the Moorish lords of Lisbon before them, Sintra's verdant charms have long been celebrated. British travellers of the eighteenth and nineteenth centuries found a new Arcadia in its cool, wooded heights, recording with satisfaction the old Spanish saying: "To see the world and leave out Sintra is to go blind about." Byron stayed here in 1809 and began *Childe Harold*, his great mock-epic travel poem, in which the "horrid crags" of "Cintra's glorious Eden" form a first location. Writing home, in a letter to his mother, he proclaimed the village:

... perhaps in every aspect the most delightful in Europe; it contains beauties of every description natural and artificial. Palaces and gardens rising in the midst of rocks, cataracts and precipices, convents on stupendous heights, a distant view of the sea and the Tagus ... it unites in itself all the wildness of the Western Highlands with the verdure of the South of France.

That the young Byron had seen neither of these is irrelevant: his description of Sintra's romantic appeal is exact – and still telling two centuries later. Sintra is home to two of Portugal's most extraordinary palaces, some lavish private estates and a Moorish castle with breathtaking views over Lisbon. Within reach, too, are semi-tropical gardens and small-scale resorts on a craggy coastline boasting Europe's most westerly point. Move mountains and give yourself the best part of two full days here.

The Town

SINTRA loops around a series of green and wooded ravines making it a confusing place in which to get your bearings. Basically, though, it consists of three distinct and separate settlements: **Estefânia,** around the train station; the attractive main town of **Sintra–Vila;** and, 2km to the east, the separate village of **São Pedro de Sintra**. It's Sintra-Vila and its environs that have most of the hotels and restaurants, and the main sights, including the extraordinary landmark of the Palácio Nacional. Distinguished by its vast pair of conical chimneys, this dominates the central square around which the old town is gathered.

Palácio Nacional
The **Palácio Nacional** – or Paço Real (Mon, Tues & Thurs–Sun 10am–5.30pm; €3, free Sun morning) – was probably already in existence under the Moors. It takes its present form, however, from the rebuilding and enlargements of Dom João I (1385–1433) and his fortunate successor, Dom Manuel, heir to the wealth engendered by Vasco da Gama's inspired explorations. The palace's style, as you might expect, is an amalgam of Gothic – with impressive roofline battlements – and the latter king's Manueline additions, with their characteristically extravagant twisted and animate forms. Inside, the Gothic–Manueline modes are tempered by a good deal of Moorish influence, adapted over the centuries by a succession of occupants. The last royal to live here, in the 1880s, was Maria Pia, grandmother of the country's final reigning monarch – Manuel II, "The Unfortunate".

Today the palace is a museum (it's best to go early or late in the day to avoid the crowds). Highlights on the lower floor include the Manueline **Sala dos Cisnes**, named for the swans painted on its ceiling, and the **Sala das Pegas**, which takes its name from the flock of magpies (*pegas*) painted on the frieze and ceiling. They are holding in their beaks the legend *por bem* (in honour) – reputedly the response of João I, caught by his queen, Philippa (of Lancaster), in the act of kissing a lady-in-waiting. He had the room decorated with as many magpies as there were women at court in order to satirize and put a stop to their gossiping. A succession of state rooms climaxes in the **Sala das Brasões**, its domed and coffered ceiling emblazoned with the coats of arms

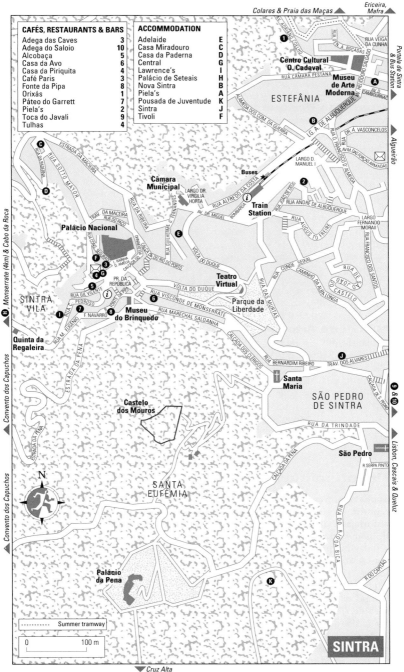

Colares & Praia das Maças ▲

Ericeira,
Mafra ▲

CAFÉS, RESTAURANTS & BARS

Adega das Caves	3
Adega do Saloio	10
Alcobaça	5
Casa da Avo	6
Casa da Piriquita	4
Café Paris	3
Fonte da Pipa	8
Orixás	1
Páteo do Garrett	7
Piela's	2
Toca do Javali	9
Tulhas	4

ACCOMMODATION

Adelaide	E
Casa Miradouro	C
Casa da Paderna	D
Central	G
Lawrence's	I
Palácio de Seteais	H
Nova Sintra	B
Piela's	A
Pousada de Juventude	K
Sintra	J
Tivoli	F

Portela de Sintra & Bus Station ▶

▶ Algueirão

Centro Cultural
O. Cadaval

Museu
de Arte
Moderna

ESTEFÂNIA

Câmara
Municipal

Buses

LARGO D.
MANUEL I

Train
Station

Palácio Nacional

Teatro
Virtual

Parque da
Liberdade

◀ Monserrate (4km) & Cabo da Roca

SINTRA
VILA

Museu
do Brinquedo

Quinta da
Regaleira

SÃO PEDRO
DE SINTRA

Santa
Maria

◀ Convento dos Capuchos

Castelo
dos Mouros

São Pedro

N

SANTA
EUFÉMIA

◀ Convento dos Capuchos

◀ Lisbon, Cascais & Queluz

Palácio
da Pena

---------- Summer tramway

0   100 m

SINTRA

▼ Cruz Alta

of 72 noble families. Look out for the gallery above the palace chapel, built perhaps on the old mosque. In a room alongside, the deranged Afonso VI was confined for six years by his brother Pedro II; he eventually died here in 1683, listening to Mass through a grid, Pedro having seized "his throne, his liberty and his queen". Finally, you pass through the **kitchens**, their roofs tapering into the giant chimneys.

Museu do Brinquedo and Teatro Virtual

Just round the corner from the Palácio Nacional is a fascinating private toy collection housed in a former fire station on Rua Visconde de Monserrate, now the impressive **Museu do Brinquedo** (Tues–Sun 10am–6pm; €3; @ www. museu-do-brinquedo.pt). The huge array of toys over three floors is somewhat confusingly labelled, but look out for the 3000-year-old stone Egyptian toys, as well as the Hornby trains from the 1930s, and some of the first ever toy cars, produced in Germany in the early 1900s. Perhaps the most interesting section is that on early Portuguese toys, containing papier-mâché cars, tin-plate animals, wooden trams and trains, as well as a selection of 1930s beach toys, including beautifully painted buckets and the metal fish that appears on the museum brochure.

A hundred metres or so southeast of the toy museum, off Volta do Duque on the leafy slopes of the Parque da Liberdade, the **Teatro Virtual** (June–Sept Tues–Fri 10am–12.30pm & 2–6pm, Sat & Sun 2–6pm; Oct–May same hours until 5.30pm; €1.50) is a tiny cinema projecting a virtual re-creation of the Portuguese discoverers and their early voyages to Japan.

Museu de Arte Moderna

Northeast of the train station, in Estefânia, it's worth making the detour to visit the superb **Museu de Arte Moderna** on Avenida Heliodoro Salgado (Tues –Sun 10am–6pm; €3, free on Thurs; @ www.berardomodern.com). Occupying Sintra's former casino, the 1920s building spreads over three floors and houses parts of the collection of tobacco magnate Joe Berardo. Only twenty of the works are shown at any one time; the rest of the space is used for temporary exhibits, which change every two or three months. Depending on when you visit, you can see pieces by Jackson Pollock, David Hockney, Roy Lichtenstein and Andy Warhol, while the top-floor restaurant offers great views over the Pena palace.

Practicalities

Trains depart every fifteen minutes from Lisbon's Rossio station (45min journey; €1.40 one-way, or a five-day pass €11.20). There's a small turismo desk at **Sintra station** (daily 9am–7pm), while local **buses** depart across the street from the train station, with services to and from Cascais, Colares, Cabo da Roca, the Sintra beaches, Estoril and Mafra. However, Sintra's main **bus station** is at Portela, opposite the train station of the same name, the stop before Sintra.

It's a ten- to fifteen-minute walk from Sintra station to Sintra-Vila and around twenty minutes from Sintra-Vila to São Pedro. The useful #434 **bus service** (daily departures every 40min; €3.50) runs on a circular route from Sintra station to Sintra-Vila, the Castelo dos Mouros, Palácio da Pena and back. A **day rover ticket** (€7) is valid on any Scotturb bus, including the #403, which goes from Sintra to Cascais via Cabo da Roca. There are **taxis** outside the train station and in Praça da República, near the Palácio Nacional; check the price first for every journey since the meters aren't always used. It costs roughly €15 return to Pena or Monserrate with an hour's stopover, or around €35 return to the Convento dos Capuchos.

The efficient and helpful **turismo** (daily: June–Sept 9am–8pm; Oct–May 9am–7pm; ☏219 231 157, ⓦwww.cm-sintra.pt) lies just off the central Praça da República. You'll also find a **post office** and **bank** on the square.

There's a country **market** – with antiques and crafts, as well as food – in São Pedro's main square on the second and last Sunday of every month. Sintra's annual **festa** in honour of St Peter is held on June 28 and 29, while in July and August the **Sintra Music Festival** puts on classical performances in a number of the town's buildings, as well as the lovely gardens of the *Palácio de Seteais* hotel. The end of July also sees the **Feira Grande** in São Pedro, with crafts, antiques and cheeses on sale.

Accommodation

There's a fair range of **accommodation** available including a network of private rooms (best booked through the turismo; ❷), half a dozen *pensões* and hotels, and upmarket bed and breakfast in several local *quintas*, or manor houses. The local youth hostel is located in the hills above São Pedro de Sintra, while the nearest campsite is at Praia Grande (see p.76). Sintra is a popular resort and you should book ahead or turn up early in the day if you intend to stay, especially if you're here during one of the town's festivals when accommodation will be scarce.

Pensions, quintas and hotels

Residencial Adelaide Rua Guilherme Gomes Fernandes 11 ☏219 230 873. Very clean if spartan en-suite rooms; the quieter rooms face a patio at the rear. ❷

Casa Miradouro, Rua Sotto Mayor 55 ☏219 235 900, ⓦwww.casa-miradouro.com. Renovated mansion in terraced gardens, 500m beyond the Palácio Nacional, with terrific views of coast and castle. Five stylishly furnished rooms with bath. Breakfast included. Parking. ❼

Casa da Paderna Rua da Paderna 4 ☏219 235 053. Highly attractive accommodation in a small old house reached down a steep cobbled track, just north of Sintra-Vila. Great views up to Quinta da Regaleira. Rooms with bath cost €15 more. Breakfast included. ❺

Hotel Central Pr. da República 35 ☏219 230 964, ⓔhotelcentral@netcabo.pt. Comfortable nineteenth-century hotel, opposite the Palácio Nacional, with polished wood and tiles throughout. Triple rooms available, too, and good off-season discounts. Breakfast included. ❺

Lawrence's Hotel Rua Consigliéri Pedroso 38–40 ☏219 105 500, ⓔlawrences@mail.telepac. pt. Lays claim to being the oldest hotel in Iberia, first opened in 1764 and restyled as a five-star establishment by Dutch owners in 1999. There are only eleven spacious rooms and five suites, all relatively simply furnished in traditional style, and

a highly rated restaurant serving traditional Portuguese cuisine (open to non-residents; expensive; reservations advised). Breakfast included. ❾

Palácio de Seteais 1km west of town ☏219 233 200, ⓦwww.tivolihotels.com. The "Seven Sighs Palace", completed in the last years of the eighteenth century and entered through a majestic Neoclassical arch, is now an immensely luxurious hotel – a night here will set you back around €280. The giant rooms have period furniture and comfy beds – it's popular with honeymooners – while the landscaped gardens have their own pool. Breakfast included. Parking. ❾

Pensão Nova Sintra Largo Afonso d'Albuquerque 25, Estefânia ☏219 230 220, ⓕ219 107 033. Very smart *pensão* in a big mansion, which also has a raised café-terrace overlooking the busy street. Modern rooms, all with TV, bath and shiny marble floors. Breakfast included. ❹

Piela's Av. Desiderio Cambournac 1–3, Estefânia ☏219 241 691. On a main road close to the market, this renovated town house has good rooms with bath, TV and air conditioning. Some smaller rooms are priced a category lower. ❹

Residencial Sintra Trav. dos Alvares, São Pedro ☏219 230 738, ⓔpensao.residenciasl. sintra@clix.pt. Fantastic place with a rambling garden, swimming pool and huge rooms which can easily accommodate extra beds – so it's ideal for families or groups. ❺

Hotel Tivoli Pr. da República ☏219 237 200,

ⓦwww.tivolihotels.com. A modern building right in the middle of the historic centre, with fine views from the balconies of the comfortable en-suite rooms. There's also an in-house restaurant. Rates drop in winter. Parking. Breakfast included. ❾

Youth hostel
Pousada de Juventude de Sintra Santa

Eufémia, São Pedro de Sintra ☎19 241 210, ⓦwww.pousadasjuventude.pt. The comfortable hostel is 6km by road from the train station; it's best if you catch bus #435 to São Pedro, from where it's just a 2km walk. Meals are served if you can't face the hike down into town and back. Dorm rooms from €10.50, rooms ❷

Eating and drinking

There are some fine **cafés** and **restaurants** scattered about the various quarters of Sintra. With a couple of honourable exceptions the most mundane are in the centre, near the palace or around the train station; the best concentration is at São Pedro, a twenty-minute walk from town. Local specialities include *queijadas da Sintra* – sweet cheese pastry-cakes. If you're out for the day, take a **picnic**: refreshments out of town are exorbitantly priced. You can stock up on supplies at the morning fruit and vegetable **market**, a short walk from the station opposite the Museu de Arte Moderna. For a drink, *Fonte da Pipa,* Rua Fonte da Pipa 11–13, is a laidback **bar** (open from 9pm) next to the lovely fountain (*fonte*) that the street is named after.

Sintra-Vila

Adega das Caves Rua de Pendora 2 (café) & 8 (restaurant). Bustling café-bar beneath *Café Paris*, attracting a predominantly youthful local clientele; the neighbouring restaurant (closed Mon) has good value Portuguese grills. Moderate.

Alcobaça Rua das Padarias 7–11 ☎219 231 651. The best central choice for a decent, straightforward Portuguese meal. Plain, tiled dining room with friendly service and large servings of grilled chicken, *arroz de marisco*, clams and steak for around €15 a head.

Casa da Avo Rua Visconde de Monserrate 46 ☎219 231 280. Basic eating-house with few pretensions but the house wine is cheap enough and it's hard to fault dishes like *caldeirada* (fish stew). There's a decent bar attached, too. Closed Thurs. Inexpensive.

Casa da Piriquita Rua das Padarias 1 ☎219 230 626. On the uphill alley across from the *Café Paris*, this smoky tearoom and bakery is always busy with locals queueing to buy *queijadas da Sintra* and the similarly sticky *travesseiros*. Closed Wed. Its more modern sister branch, up the hill at no. 18 (closed Tues) has a big outdoor terrace. Inexpensive.

Café Paris Largo Rainha D. Amélia ☎219 232 375. The highest-profile café in town, opposite the Palácio Nacional, which means steep prices for underwhelming food. However, it's a great place to sit and nurse a drink in the sun. Expensive.

Páteo do Garrett Rua Maria Eugénia Reis F. Navarro 7. Bar-restaurant with a darkened interior, though the lovely, sunny patio has great views over the village. It serves standard Portuguese

meals, or just pop in for a drink. Closed Wed, & Jan–April. Moderate.

Tulhas Rua Gil Vicente 4 ☎219 232 378. Imaginative cooking in a fine building, converted from old grain silos. The speciality is veal with Madeira. Closed Wed. Expensive.

Estefânia

Orixás Av. Adriano Coelho 7 ☎219 241 672. Brazilian bar, restaurant, music venue and art gallery in a lovely building complete with waterfalls and outdoor terrace. The buffet costs around €30, but you'll be here all night and with live Brazilian music thrown in, it's not bad value. Open for lunch and dinner at weekends, dinner only Tues–Fri, closed Mon. Expensive.

Piela's Rua João de Deus 70–72 ☎219 241 691. Budget meals and late-night drinks in a friendly café-restaurant, over the tracks from the station. Inexpensive.

São Pedro de Sintra

Adega do Saloio Trav. Chão de Meninos ☎219 231 422. Around five minutes from São Pedro's main square, close to Rotunda do Ramalha, this fine grill-restaurant has hospitable owners. Also does a good *arroz de marisco*. Closed Tues from Sept–April. Moderate.

Toca do Javali Rua 1º Dezembro 18 ☎219 233 503. Tables set up outside in summer amidst a lovely terraced garden, around 100m from São Pedro's main square. The cooking is superb at any time of year, with wild boar (*javali*) the house speciality. Closed Wed. Expensive.

Around Sintra

The **Castelo dos Mouros** and extraordinary **Palácio da Pena**, on the heights above the town, are the most obvious targets for visitors – the circular #434 bus from Sintra station or Sintra-Vila run throughout the day to both places. The nearby estate of **Quinta da Regaleira** is a popular attraction, too, and is a short walk from the town, though other local sights – including the gardens of **Monserrate** and the **Convento dos Capuchos** – will probably require a taxi ride (see "Practicalities", above). West of Sintra, the wine-growing centre of **Colares**, the beach at **Praia Grande** or the westernmost point in Europe, **Cabo da Roca**, can all be seen by public transport.

Castelo dos Mouros

From near the church of Santa Maria in Sintra, on the way to São Pedro, a stone pathway leads up to the ruined ramparts of the **Castelo dos Mouros** (daily: June–Sept 10am–7pm; Oct–May 10am–5pm; €3.50), around a thirty-minute

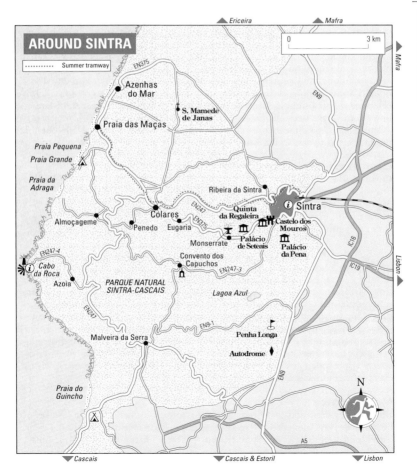

walk. Captured by Afonso Henriques with the aid of Scandinavian Crusaders, the Moorish castle spans two rocky pinnacles, with the remains of a mosque spread midway between the fortifications. You can still walk round the ruined ramparts and the views from here are extraordinary: south beyond Lisbon's Ponte 25 de Abril to the Serra de Arrábida, west to Cascais and Cabo da Roca, and north to Peniche and the Berlenga Islands.

Palácio da Pena

The upper gate of the castle gives onto the road up to Pena, opposite the lower entrance to the **Palácio da Pena** (Tues–Sun: mid-June to mid-Sept 10am–7pm, mid Sept–mid June 10am–5.30pm; €6, gardens only €3.30). You walk up through the gardens – a stretch of rambling woodland, with a scattering of lakes and follies – and at the top of the park, about twenty minutes' walk, the fabulous palace appears as a wild fantasy of domes, towers, ramparts and walkways, approached through mock-Manueline gateways and a drawbridge that doesn't draw. A compelling riot of kitsch, it was built in the 1840s to the specifications of Ferdinand of Saxe-Coburg-Gotha, husband of Queen Maria II, and it bears comparison with the mock-medieval castles of Ludwig of Bavaria. The architect, the German Baron Eschwege, immortalized himself in the guise of a warrior-knight on a huge statue that guards the palace from a neighbouring crag. Inside, Pena is no less bizarre, preserved exactly as it was left by the royal family on its flight from Portugal in 1910. The result is fascinating: rooms of concrete decorated to look like wood, statues of turbanned Moors nonchalantly holding electric chandeliers. Of an original convent, founded to celebrate the first sight of Vasco da Gama's returning fleet, a chapel and Manueline cloister have been retained.

Above Pena, past the statue of Eschwege, a marked footpath climbs for ten minutes or so to the **Cruz Alta**, highest point of the Serra de Sintra.

Quinta da Regaleira

Quinta da Regaleira (daily: June–Sept 10am–8pm; Oct & Feb–May 10am–6.30pm; Nov 10am–6pm; Dec & Jan 10am–5.30pm; 90min tours every 30min–1hr; reservations essential ☎219 106 650; €10, unguided visits €5) is just a five-minute walk out of town on the Seteais–Monserrate road. It's one of Sintra's most elaborate private estates, laid out at the turn of the twentieth century, and was declared a UNESCO World Heritage site in 1995. The estate was designed by Italian architect and theatrical set designer Luigi Manini for wealthy landowner António Augusto Carvalho Monteiro. The Italian's sense of the dramatic is obvious: the principal building, the mock-Manueline **Palaçio dos Milhões**, sprouts turrets and towers, though the interior is sparse apart from some elaborate Rococo wooden ceilings and impressive Art Nouveau tiles. The surrounding **gardens** are more impressive and shelter fountains, terraces, lakes and grottoes. The highlight is the Initiation Well, inspired by the initiation practices of the Knight Templars and Freemasons. Entering via a Harry Potter-style revolving stone door, you can walk down a moss-covered spiral stairway to the foot of the well and through a tunnel, which eventually resurfaces at the edge of a lake.

Monserrate

Beyond Regaleira and the *Palácio de Seteais* hotel, the road leads past a series of beautiful private *quintas* until you come upon **Monserrate** (daily: June–Sept 9am–7pm; Oct–May 9am–5pm; €3.50) – about an hour's walk from Sintra all told. With its Victorian folly-like mansion, and vast botanical park of exotic trees and subtropical shrubs and plants, Monserrate is one of the most romantic sights in Portugal. It would be easy to spend the whole day wandering around the paths laid out through the woods. The name most associated with Monserrate is that of **William Beckford**, author of the Gothic novel *Vathek* and the wealthiest untitled Englishman of his period. He hired the *quinta* here from 1793 to 1799, having been forced to flee Britain because of homosexual scandal – buggery then being a hanging offence. Setting about improving this "beautiful Claude-like place", he landscaped a waterfall and even imported a flock of sheep from his estate at Fonthill. In this Xanadu-like dreamland, he whiled away his days in summer pavilions, entertaining with "bevys of delicate warblers and musicians" posted around the grounds.

Half a century later, a second immensely rich Englishman, **Sir Francis Cook**, bought the estate. His fantasies were scarcely less ambitious, involving the construction of a great Victorian house inspired by Brighton Pavilion. Cook also spared no expense in developing the grounds and imported the head gardener from Kew, who laid out succulents and water plants, tropical ferns and palms, and just about every conifer known. Fernando II, who was building the Pena Palace at the time, was suitably impressed, conferring a viscountcy on Cook for his efforts. Cook's house is closed but you can still admire the exterior, with its mix of Moorish and Italian decoration (the dome is modelled on Brunelleschi's Duomo in Florence), and peer into a splendid series of empty salons.

Convento dos Capuchos

The **Convento dos Capuchos** (tours every 15–30min: May–Sept 9.30am–7pm Oct–April 9.30am–5pm; reservations essential on ☎219 237 300; €3.50) is a simply extraordinary hermitage with tiny, dwarf-like cells cut from the rock and lined in cork – hence its popular name of the "Cork Convent". Philip II, King of Spain and Portugal, pronounced it the poorest convent of his kingdom, and Byron, visiting a cave where one monk had spent 36 years in seclusion, mocked in *Childe Harold:*

Deep in yon cave Honorius long did dwell,
In hope to merit Heaven by making earth a Hell.

It's hard not to be moved by the simplicity of the place. It was occupied for three hundred years and finally abandoned in 1834 by its seven remaining monks. Some of the **penitents' cells** can only be entered by crawling through 70cm-high doors; here, and on every other ceiling, doorframe and lintel, are attached panels of cork, taken from the surrounding woods. Elsewhere, you'll come across a washroom, kitchen, refectory, tiny chapels, even a bread oven set apart from the main complex.

To get there, the most straightforward approach is by the ridge road from Pena – a distance of 9km. The minor road between Sintra, the convent and Cabo da Roca sports some of the country's most alarming natural rock formations, with boulders as big as houses looming out of the trees.

Colares

About 6km further west of Monserrate is **COLARES**, a hill village famed for its rich red wine made from grapes grown in the local sandy soil. The local producer, Adega Regional de Colares (☎219 288 082), hosts occasional concerts, tastings and exhibitions. In the village, head uphill (signed Penedo) for superb views back towards Sintra. Colares is easily reached on the Sintra–Cascais bus route (#403), while in summer, you can also take the **tram** (June–Sept; €1 return) from outside the Museu de Arte Moderna in Sintra, which runs to the coast at Praia das Maçãs via Colares, a fun way to get to the beach. Trams leave Friday to Sunday at 9.30am, 11.25am, 2.25pm, 4.25pm and 6.25pm, returning to Sintra at 10.20am, 1.20pm, 3.20pm and 5.20pm. In Colares there's a smart **restaurant** and teashop, *Colares Velho*, Largo Dr. Carlos Franca 1–4 (T 219 292 406; closed Mon).

Praia Grande and the coast

West of Colares, the road winds around through the hills to **PRAIA GRANDE**, the best beach on this section of coast, certainly for surfers, and with a row of handy cafés and restaurants spreading up towards the cliffs. There's a large, well-equipped **campsite**, *Camping Praia Grande* (T 219 290 581, E wondertur@ip.pt), less than 1km from the beach – bus #441 runs from Sintra train station runs here – as well as *Hotel Arribas* (T 219 289 050, W www-whotelarribas.com; breakfast included; ❻), a modern three-star plonked ungraciously at the north end of the sands. Rooms are enormous while the hotel boasts sea pools, a restaurant and café-terrace with great sea views.

Just north of Praia Grande is the larger resort of **PRAIA DAS MAÇÃS**, with a broad expanse of sand. Again, you can get here on bus #441 from Sintra train station or, in summer, the tram (see "Colares" above). The modern *Oceano*, on the main Avenida Eugénio Levy (T 219 289 490, E pensaooceano@iol.pt; breakfast included; ❹), is much the best place to stay. Of several **bars and restaurants**, *O Loureiro*, Esplanada Vasco da Gama (closed Thurs), has great-value seafood and overlooks the beach, or try the cheap and cheerful *Esplanada do Casino* opposite, with a seaside terrace. The bus continues another 2km to the north to **AZENHAS DO MAR**, a picture-book cliff-top town with a small beach and sea pool.

Cabo da Roca

CABO DA ROCA, 14km southwest of Colares, is officially the most westerly point in Europe; regular buses (#403) from either Sintra or Cascais train stations make the run throughout the year. It's an enjoyable trip, though the cape itself comprises little more than a lighthouse – below which foamy breakers slam the cliffs – a couple of stalls selling shells, a café and a **tourist office** (daily: 10am–6pm; Oct–May until 5pm; T 219 280 892). A cross at the cape carries an inscription by Luís de Camões ("Here …where the land ends, and the sea begins"), whose muse, for once it seems, deserted him.

Palácio de Queluz

The **Palácio de Queluz** (Mon & Wed–Sun 10am–5pm; €3) is one of Portugal's most sumptuous palaces, an elegant, restrained structure regarded as the country's finest example of Rococo architecture. Its low, pink-washed wings enclose a series of public and private rooms and suites, as well as rambling eighteenth-century formal gardens. Although preserved as a museum, it doesn't quite feel like one – retaining instead a strong sense of its past royal owners. It also hosts classical concerts in the summer months.

The palace lies on the Sintra train line, making it easy to see either on the way out (it's just twenty minutes from Lisbon's Rossio station; €0.90 one-way) or on the way back from Sintra. The station is called Queluz-Belas: turn left out of the station and walk down the main road for fifteen minutes, following the signs through the unremarkable town until you reach a vast cobbled square, Largo do Palácio, with the palace walls reaching out around one side. The square is also home to a local **turismo** (daily except Thurs 10am–12.30pm & 2–7pm; ☎214 350 039).

The Palace

The palace was built by Dom Pedro III, husband and regent to his niece, **Queen Maria I**, who lived here throughout her 39-year reign (1777–1816), quite mad for the last 27, following the death of her eldest son, José. William Beckford visited when the Queen's wits were dwindling, and ran races in the gardens with the Princess of Brazil's ladies-in-waiting. At other times fireworks displays lit up the ornamental canal and bullfights were held in the courtyards.

Visitors first enter the **Throne Room**, lined with mirrors surmounted by paintings and golden flourishes. Beyond is the more restrained **Music Chamber** with its portrait of Queen Maria above the French grand piano. Smaller quarters include bed and sitting rooms, a tiny oratory swathed with red velvet, and a **Sculpture Room**, whose only exhibit is an earthenware bust of Maria. Another wing comprises an elegant suite of public rooms – smoking, coffee and dining rooms – all intimate in scale and surprisingly tastefully decorated. The **Ambassador's Chamber**, where diplomats and foreign ministers were received during the nineteenth century, echoes the Throne Room in style, with one side lined with porcelain chinoiserie. In the end, though, perhaps the most pleasing room is the simple **Dressing Room** with its geometric inlaid wooden floor and spider's web ceiling of radial gilt bands.

The formal **gardens** are included in the ticket price. Low box hedges and elaborate (if weatherworn) statues spread out from the protection of the palace wings, while small pools and fountains, steps and terracing form a harmonious background to the building. From May to October, there is a display of horsemanship here every Wednesday at 11am.

You can still enjoy a meal in the palace's original kitchen, the **Cozinha Velha** (daily 12.30–3pm & 7.30–10pm; ☎214 350 232), which retains its stone chimney, arches and wooden vaulted ceiling, and sports copper pots, pans and utensils in every niche and alcove. The food – classic French-Portuguese – is not always as impressive as the locale, and you're looking at around €25 a head for a full meal (though there is a cheaper café in the main body of the palace). The kitchens are now part of the *Pousada Dona Maria I* (☎214 356 158, Ⓦ www.pousadas.pt; breakfast included; ❽), which gives you the chance to stay in one of 26 plush rooms in an annexe of the palace.

Mafra and around

Moving on from Lisbon or Sintra, **Mafra** makes an interesting approach to Estremadura. It is distinguished – and utterly dominated – by just one building: the vast monastery-palace which João V – the wealthiest and most extravagant of all Portuguese monarchs – built in emulation of El Escorial in Madrid. Around 5km beyond Mafra, **Sobreiro** is famed for its delightful craft village, a big draw for children.

Mosteiro Palácio Nacional de Mafra

Begun in 1717 to honour a vow made on the birth of a royal heir, the **Mosteiro Palácio Nacional de Mafra** (Mon & Wed–Sun 10am–5pm, last entry 4.30pm; €3) was initially intended for just thirteen Franciscan friars.

But as wealth poured in from the gold and diamonds of Brazil, João V and his German court architect, Frederico Ludovice, amplified their plans to include a massive basilica, two royal wings and monastic quarters for 300 monks and 150 novices. The result, completed in thirteen years, is quite extraordinary and, on its own bizarre terms, extremely impressive.

In style the building is a fusion of Baroque and Italianate Neoclassicism, but it is the sheer magnitude and logistics that stand out. In the last stages of construction more than 45,000 labourers were employed, while throughout the years of building there was a daily average of nearly 15,000. There are 5200 doorways, 2500 windows and two immense bell towers each containing over 50 bells. An apocryphal story records the astonishment of the Flemish bellmakers at the size of the order: on their querying it, and asking for payment in advance, Dom João retorted by doubling their price and his original requirement.

Parts of the monastery are used by the military but an ingenious cadre of guides marches you around a sizeable enough portion. The royal apartments are a mix of the tedious and the shocking: the latter most obviously in the **Sala dos Troféus**, with its furniture (even chandeliers) constructed of antlers and upholstered in deerskin. Beyond are the **monastic quarters**, including cells, a pharmacy and an infirmary with beds positioned so the ailing monks could see Mass performed. The highlight, however, is the magnificent Rococo **library** – brilliantly lit and rivalling Coimbra's in grandeur. Byron, shown the 35,000 volumes by one of the monks, was asked if "the English had any books in their country?" The **basilica** itself, which can be seen outside the tour, is no less imposing, with the multicoloured marble designs of its floor mirrored in the ceiling decoration.

Six kilometres north of Mafra on the Gradil road is the **Tapada de Mafra** (daily 9.30am–noon & 2–3.30pm; €4.50; ⓦ www.tapadademafra.pt), once the palace's extensive hunting grounds, now with walking trails for the public. At weekends, you can tour the park on a road train (Sat, Sun & public hols at 10.45am & 3pm; €9; reservations advised, ⓣ 261 817 050).

Practicalities

Mafrense **buses** run hourly from metro Campo Grande in Lisbon (1hr 30min) or from Sintra station (30min), stopping near the convent. The town of Mafra itself is dull, and with frequent buses heading on to the lively resort of Ericeira, 12km away, there seems no point in lingering. The **turismo** on Avenida 25 de Abril (daily: July–Sept 9.30am–7.30pm; Oct–June 9.30am–6pm, Sat & Sun all year closed 1–2.30pm; ⓣ 261 812 023) might be able to persuade you otherwise. For an inexpensive **restaurant** with good food try the *Solar d'El Rei,* Rua Detras dos Quintas, five minutes' walk from the palace.

Sobreiro

The small village of **SOBREIRO**, 5km northwest of Mafra on the road to Ericeira, is home to the **Aldeia Típica** (daily 10am–6pm), a craft village established by artist José Franco in 1945. As well as Franco's own work, the showroom sells other reasonably priced ceramics from all over the country, while children will enjoy looking round the traditional bakery, smithy, clockmaker, cobbler, schoolroom, distillery, wind- and water-mills and several other small museum-shops, all displaying various tools, furniture and artefacts collected over many years. The *adega* makes a splendid stop for lunch, serving local wine, bread and moderately priced meals.

The Lisbon–Mafra–Ericeira **bus** passes by every hour or so, while it's definitely worth a stop if you're driving on to Ericeira from Mafra.

South of the Rio Tejo

As late as the nineteenth century, the southern bank of the Tejo estuary was an underpopulated area used as a quarantine station for foreign visitors; the village of Trafaria was so lawless that the police visited it only when accompanied by members of the army. The huge **Ponte 25 de Abril**, a suspension bridge inaugurated as the "Salazar Bridge" in 1966 and renamed after the 1974 Revolution, finally ended what remained of this separation between "town and country". Since then, Lisbon has spilled over the river in a string of tatty industrial suburbs, the closest being **Cacilhas**, where locals come to eat seafood in a string of good restaurants. To the west, **Caparica** is the main resort on the Costa da Caparica, which stretches for some 20km to the south. On the other side of the peninsula, 50km south of the capital, the industrial city of **Setúbal** sustains one remarkable church and is a pleasant provincial base from which to explore the small town of **Palmela** and its medieval castle, or the River Sado and the **Parque Natural da Arrábida**. The coastal surroundings are particularly attractive, with several beaches within the *parque* and over the Sado estuary at **Tróia**, and one full-blown resort at **Sesimbra**.

Across the river: Cacilhas and the Cristo Rei

The most enjoyable approach to the Setúbal peninsula is to take the ferry from Lisbon's Estação Fluvial, by Praça do Comércio (see p.71 for schedules), to **CACILHAS**; there are also crossings from Cais do Sodré. The blustery ride grants wonderful views of the city, as well as of the Ponte 25 de Abril, though it's the **seafood restaurants** in the port that are as good a reason as any to make the crossing. Particularly good value is the *Escondidinho de Cacilhas* (closed Thurs), immediately on the right as you leave the ferry. Busier, and with better views, is the moderately priced riverside *Cervejaria Farol* (☎212 765 248; closed Wed), while if you head towards the bridge along the Cais do Ginjal you'll find two other atmospheric riverside restaurants: the pricey Brazilian *Atira-te ao Rio* (☎212 751 380; closed Mon), or the marginally cheaper *Ponto Final* (☎212 760 743; closed Tues), offering Portuguese staples and great views back to Lisbon.

Just past here is the foot of the **Elevador Panorâmico da Boca do Vento** (daily 8am–11.45pm; €1 return), a sleek modern elevator which whisks you up the cliff face to the old part of **Almada**; if the lift is in the wrong place, the guard will blow his whistle to alert the operator at the other end. From the top there are fantastic views over the river and city, while the surrounding streets are highly atmospheric.

Beyond Almada – best reached by bus #101 from Cacilhas – stands the **Cristo Rei** (daily: June–Sept 9am–7.30pm; Oct–May 9am–6pm; €2). Built in 1959, this relatively modest version of Rio's Christ-statue landmark has a lift that shuttles you up to a dramatic viewing platform, 80m above the ground. On a good day, Lisbon stretches out like a map below you, with the glistening roof of the Pena palace at Sintra in the distance.

From Cacilhas **bus station**, outside the ferry terminal, there are regular services to Costa da Caparica, Setúbal, Sesimbra and Vila Nogueira de Azeitão.

Caparica

Buses from Cacilhas (every 15–30min, daily 7am–9pm; 30min journey), or from Lisbon's Praça de Espanha (every 30min, daily 7am–12.45am;

40min–1hr), run to the beach resort of **CAPARICA**, at the northern end of the Costa da Caparica. It's hardly pretty, but it is a thoroughly lively Portuguese resort, crammed with restaurants, summer bars and discos, and it's here that most locals come if they want to laze around on the sand: foreign tourists are in a minority. In town, Rua dos Pescadores leads up from the central Praça da Liberdade (where you'll find the market, supermarkets and banks) to the beach, and is lined on both sides by café-restaurants with outdoor seating.

The **beach** itself stretches north towards Lisbon and south away into the distance, its initial stretch backed by apartments and cafés. The water is of good quality, though beware the dangerous undertow. A **mini-railway** (June–Sept daily every 20min; €3.50 return) runs along the 8km or so of dunes to Fonte da Telha – if you're after solitude you need only take it this far and walk. However, each of the twenty mini-train stops, based around one or two beach-cafés, has a very particular feel. Earlier stops tend to be family-oriented, later ones are on the whole younger and more fashionable, with nudity (though officially illegal) more or less obligatory, especially around stop 18–19, which is also something of a gay area.

Practicalities

In summer, **buses** stop at the bus park in town near the beginning of the sands. In winter, they use the station in Praça Padre Manuel Bernades, in which case it is best to get off at the first stop in Caparica, on the edge of the leafy Praça da Liberdade, five minutes back from the beach. From here, walk diagonally across the square, turn right and at Avenida da Liberdade 18 you'll find the **turismo** (Mon–Fri 9am–1pm & 2–5.30pm, Sat 9am–1pm; ☎212 900 071).

There are a growing number of **hotels and pensions** in Caparica, though they are relatively pricey and often full in summer. *Pensão Real*, Rua Mestre Manuel 18 (☎212 918 870, ℱ12 918 879; breakfast included; ➎) is one of the more reasonable central options, with some of the en-suite rooms featuring sea-facing balconies; or try *Residencial Capa-Rica,* Rua dos Pescadores 9 (☎212 900 242, ℯbenvindo.tours@mail.telepac.pt; breakfast included; ➒), some of whose bright en-suite rooms face the beach. There is also a string of **campsites**, packed out in summer. Your best bet is also the nearest, the well-equipped *Orbitur* (☎212 901 366, ⓦwww.orbitur.pt), complete with café and tennis courts – it's one of the few where camping club membership is not required.

Among the dozens of fish and seafood **restaurants**, a couple of recommended, moderately priced, choices include *O Borbas*, Praia da Costa (☎212 900 163; closed Tues evening & all day Wed), at the northern end of the beach, with beachside window seats, and *Primoroso* (closed Thurs), further along the seafront towards Lisbon, which serves an excellent *cataplana* at outdoor tables.

Setúbal

Some 50km south from Lisbon, **SETÚBAL** is Portugal's third port and a major industrial centre. It was once described by Hans Christian Andersen as a "terrestrial paradise" and, although those days are long gone, its pedestrianized centre and port are enjoyable enough for a short visit. If you're heading south, it's worth stopping at least for a look at the remarkable Igreja de Jesus and to enjoy the views from the Castelo São Filipe.

The Town

Setúbal's greatest monument is the **Igreja de Jesus** (Tues–Sun 9am–noon & 2–5pm, closed public hols; free) designed by Diogo de Boitaca and possibly the first of all Manueline buildings (see box on p.191). Essentially a late-Gothic structure, with a huge, flamboyant doorway, its interior design was transformed by Boitaca, who introduced fantastically twisted pillars to support the vault. The rough granite surfaces of the pillars contrast with the delicacy of the blue and white *azulejos* around the high altar, which were added in the seventeenth century. The adjacent Convento de Jesus now forms the **Museu de Setúbal** (Tues–Sat 9am–noon & 1.30–5.30pm; free) containing treasures from the church and town, though most of these seem to be permanently in storage.

The **Castelo São Felipe**, signposted off the western end of Avenida Luisa Todi, is half an hour's walk from town. Built on the orders of Spanish king Felipe II in 1590, it's a grand structure, harbouring an *azulejo*-lined chapel and protected by sheer walls of overpowering height. Legend has it that a series of secret tunnels connect the castle with the coast, but any proof was lost in the Great Earthquake of 1755. Part of the castle is now a *pousada* but the ramparts and bar are open to non-guests and there are superb views over the mouth of the Sado estuary and the Tróia peninsula.

The rest of town has little to detain you, though the pedestrianized shopping streets in the **old town** around Rua A. Castelões are handsome enough. On Largo Corpo Santo, take a peek inside the **Casa do Corpo Santo** (Tues–Fri 9.30am–5pm, Sat 9.30am–6pm; free), built in 1714 as part of the Cabedo family's palace and later used as a fisherman's fraternity. The upper floor has a painted ceiling, Baroque chapel and walls decked in superb *azulejos* showing

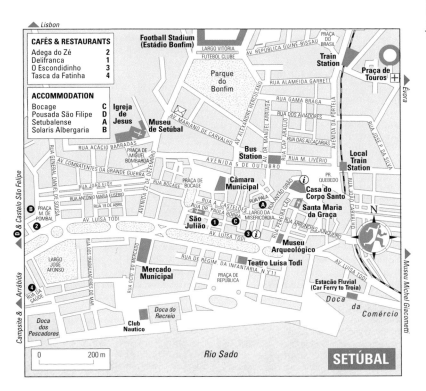

scenes of São Pedro, patron saint of fishermen. In the **Museu Arqueológico**, Avenida Luísa Todi 162 (Tues–Sat 9am–12.30pm & 2–5.30pm; closed Sat in Aug; €1.80) sparse finds from the city's Roman age are displayed along with a few dusty fishing boats and local handicrafts. The regional turismo (see below) nearby maintains the foundations of a Roman fish-preserving factory underneath its glass floor. Finally, a ten- to fifteen-minute walk east along Rua Arronches Junqueiro brings you to the **Museu Michel Giacometti** at Largo Defensores da República (Tues–Fri & Sun 9am–noon & 2–6pm; free), a museum of agricultural and trade implements collected by a Corsican ethnologist who was particularly interested in Portuguese culture.

Practicalities

The easiest way to Setúbal is to take the half-hourly Setubalase **bus** from Lisbon's Praça de Espanha, which takes around an hour; routes go via Ponte 25 de Abril or Ponte Vasco da Gama. There are also buses from Cacilhas (hourly; 50min–1hr). By car, the fast A2 from Ponte 25 de Abril whisks you to Setúbal in around forty minutes; it's about the same from Lisbon airport via Ponte Vasco da Gama. **Trains** from Lisbon (ferry to Barreiro, change for Palmela) drop you at Praça do Brasil, north of the town centre; local trains use the more central station at the eastern end of Avenida 5 de Outubro.

There are two **turismos** in Setúbal: the city one across from the local train station in the Casa do Corpo Santo, on Praça do Quebedo (daily 9am–7pm; ☎265 534 402), and the regional one, just off Avenida Luísa Todi at Travessa Frei Gaspar 10 (June–Sept Mon–Sat 9am–12.30pm & 2–7pm, Sun 9am–12.30pm; Oct–May Mon & Sat 9.30am–12.30pm & 2–6pm, Tues–Fri 9.30am–6pm; ☎265 539 120, ⓦwww.costa-azul.pt). Both hand out maps and can help with finding rooms. **Accommodation** is rarely a problem as there are plenty of hotels geared to business travellers. Good-value fish and seafood **restaurants** abound at the waterside around the Doca dos Pescadores. There are also plenty of places around the atmospheric **Mercado Municipal**; in midsummer, the market area is considerably expanded with clothes and touristy bric-a-brac. Nightlife in Setúbal revolves around the outdoor café-bars along Avenida Luísa Todi, which bustle with activity all evening. Alternatively, the **Teatro Luísa Todi** stages shows at weekends and often features art-house movies during the week.

The turismos can supply details of a range of privately organized **tours and activity sports** in the area including walking trips, jeep excursions, hot-air balloon flights and off-road driving. The highlight is the year-round **dolphin-watching** tour, organized by Vertigem Azul (daily 9.30am & 3pm, dependent on weather; €28 per person; ☎265 238 000, Ⓔvertigemazul@mail.telepac.pt), with trips to watch a resident colony of bottle-nosed dolphins, either in the Sado estuary or along the coast. For information on walking tours round Arrábida (see p.146), contact the **Parque Natural da Arrábida** office on Praça da República (Mon–Fri 9am–12.30pm & 2–5pm; ☎265 524 032).

Hotels and pensions

Residencial Bocage Rua de São Cristovão 14 ☎265 543 080, Ⓔresidencial.bocage@iol.pt. Attractive and well-maintained rooms with private bathrooms and TVs. Breakfast included. ❸

Pousada São Filipe Castelo São Filipe ☎265 523 844 or 218 442 001, ⓦwww.pousadas.pt. Built within the castle, the front rooms command superb views over the estuary, as does the surprisingly good-value restaurant. This is open to non-guests and serves good, if pricey, Portuguese and international cuisine. Parking. Breakfast included. ❽

Residencial Setubalense Rua Major Afonso Pala 17 ☎265 525 790, Ⓔres.setubalense @net-cabo.pt. Welcoming central residencial, with clean, simply furnished rooms, plus a bar for guests. Breakfast included. ❸

Solaris Albergaria Pr. Marquês de Pombal 12 ☎265 541 770, ✉albergaria.solaris@netc.pt. Set in an attractive tiled building; spruce rooms come with bath, cable TV and minibar. Breakfast included. ❹

Cafés and restaurants

Adega do Zé Av. Luísa Todi 588 ☎265 238 970. Unexotic-looking place but very popular thanks to excellent home cooking, including superb calamari and arroz dishes. Closed Mon. Inexpensive.

Delifranca Largo Dr. Francisco Soveral 20–22. Good for baguettes with interesting fillings – also has outdoor seats on the square. Inexpensive.

O Escondidinho Rua José António Januário da Silva 6. A tucked away local diner (its name means "the little hidden one") with outdoor tables. Serves good-value Portuguese grills and fish. Closed Sun. Inexpensive.

Tasca da Fatinha Rua da Saúde 58 ☎265 232 800. Good waterside restaurant, with piles of fresh fish delivered to your table straight from the grill. Closed Mon. Moderate.

Tróia

Setúbal's local beaches, reached by frequent ferries from the town, are on the **Península de Tróia**, a large sand spit that hems in the Sado estuary. The peninsula was settled by the Phoenicians and subsequently by the Romans, whose town of Cetobriga appears to have been overwhelmed by a tidal wave in the fifth century. There are some desultory remains, including tanks for salting fish, on the landward shore. Originally a wilderness of sand and wild flowers, Tróia must once have been magnificent, but it's now a heavily developed resort with its own golf course. Be prepared to walk for twenty minutes or so south along the beach to escape the worse of the development. The **car-ferries** depart daily from Setúbal (every 15min, 6am–11pm, hourly overnight; €1 per person, cars from €4.50); expect long queues for cars in summer. The crossing also provides a useful route into the Alentejo for anyone heading south.

Palmela

The small town of **PALMELA**, 10km north of Setúbal, is worth a quick visit for the views from its medieval **castle**, which on a clear day encompass Lisbon, Setúbal, the Sado estuary and Tróia. This is the centre of a wine-producing area, hence the town's major annual event: the Festa das Vindimas in September, celebrating the first of the year's wine harvest, with processions, fireworks, grape-treading and running of the bulls.

The former church in the castle has been restored and extended into a **pousada**, the *Castelo de Palmela* (☎212 351 226/218 442 001, ⓦwww .pousadas.pt; breakfast included; ❽). It's a fabulous place to stay, incorporating the original cloisters within the design, and boasting panoramic views from all points. The castle also incorporates a row of handicraft shops selling *azulejos*, cheese and the highly rated local wines, plus a café and a **museum** (Tues–Fri 10am–12.30pm & 2–5.30pm, Sat & Sun 10am–1pm & 3–5.30pm; free), which houses a small collection of archeological remains dating back to Moorish times. Opposite the museum is Palmela's **turismo** (Mon–Fri 10am–12.30pm & 2–5.30pm, Sat & Sun 10am–1pm & 3–5.30pm; until 8pm June–Sept; ☎212 332 122), which can provide you with details of other accommodation options in the area.

During the week there are ten **buses** a day to Palmela, four at weekends, from Lisbon's Praça de Espanha; the ride takes forty minutes. There are also buses every twenty minutes on the ten- to fifteen-minute run from Setúbal.

Parque Natural da Arrábida

Between Setúbal and Sesimbra lies the **Parque Natural da Arrábida**, whose main feature is the 500-metre granite ridge known as the Serra da Arrábida, visible for miles around and home to wildcats, badgers, polecats, buzzards and Bonelli eagles. The twisted pillars of Setúbal's Igreja de Jesus were hewn from here. If you want to explore the area on foot, **walking guides** are available from the park's main office in Setúbal (see p.144). Note, too, that from July to August, a one-way system operates on the narrow coastal road, which operates westwards only from 8am–7pm (though the inland N10 and N379-1 roads operate both ways).

In summer the coast road is served by three daily **buses** from Setúbal; year-round public transport is limited to those buses from Setúbal to Sesimbra that take the main road, well back from the coast. The bus passes through the town of **VILA NOGUEIRA DE AZEITÃO** where the main highlight is the **José Maria da Fonseca wine vaults and museum** on the main Rua José Augusto Coelho (Mon–Thurs 9.30am–noon & 2.15–4.15pm, Fri–Sat 10am–12.15pm & 2.15–4pm; free). A tour of the vaults, which lasts 45 minutes, includes a free tasting, and provides an interesting introduction to the local Setúbal Moscatel. Vila Nogueira de Azeitão can also be reached by **bus** from Lisbon's Praça de Espanha (hourly; 45min). There is a well-equipped **campsite**, *Picheleiros* (T 212 181 322), just outside town, complete with minimarket, café and children's playground.

Drivers should take the N379-1 from Azeitão to the **Convento da Arrábida** (Wed–Sun 3–4pm; at others times by appointment only; €3; T 212 180 520). Owned by the Fundação Orient, the convent was built by Franciscan monks in the sixteenth century. The convent's white buildings tumble down a steep hillside, offering stunning ocean views.

Around four kilometres south of the convent, the N10 winds down to the coast, reaching the tiny harbour village of **PORTINHO DA ARRÁBIDA**, which has one of the coast's best beaches. The harbour is guarded by a tiny seventeenth-century fort, now housing the **Museu Oceanográfico** (Tues–Fri 10am–4pm, Sat & Sun 3–6pm; €2), displaying marine animals from the region either live – in a small aquarium – or stuffed. At weekends, day-trippers head for the *Restaurant Beira Mar* (T 212 180 544; closed Wed & Sept–March) on the seafront, serving a good range of moderately priced fish and seafood. Certified divers can rent equipment from the *Centro de Mergulho* (T 212 183 197) diving school; the waters here are some of the clearest on the entire Portuguese coast.

Some 2km along the coast towards Setúbal you come to **Galapos**, a beautiful stretch of sand with beach cafés. Closer to Setúbal – and correspondingly more crowded – is the wide beach of **Figueirinha**, with the big sea-facing *Restaurante Bar Mar* – and the smaller **Praia de Albarquel**, with its beachside café and disco. Just beyond the beach by the main road, *Outão* (T 265 238 318, F 265 228 098) is a busy **campsite** set amongst trees.

Sesimbra

If you get up early enough in **SESIMBRA**, you'll still see fishermen mending their nets on the town's beach, but that's about as far as tradition stretches in this old fishing town. It's now a full-blown resort, with apartment buildings and hotels mushrooming in the low, bare hills beyond the narrow streets of the old centre. Sesimbra was an important port during the time of the Portuguese discoveries. Dom Manuel lived here for a while, and the town's fort, **Fortaleza** de **Santiago**, was built in the seventeenth century as an important part of Portugal's coastal defence. In the eighteenth century, Portuguese monarchs used the fort as a seaside retreat, though today it serves as a police station and prison.

The town is largely a day-trip and second-home destination for Lisbon residents and, although extremely busy in summer, it's still an admirable spot, with excellent swimming from the long beach and an endless row of café-restaurants along the beach road, each with an outdoor charcoal-grill. At high tide the beach splits into two, with a strand either side of the waterfront fort; offshore, jet skis and little ketches zip up and down under a clear blue sky.

A Moorish **Castelo** (Mon–Thurs & Sun 7am–7pm, Fri & Sat 7am–8pm; free) sits above Sesimbra, a short drive or a stiff half-hour climb from the centre. Within the walls are a pretty eighteenth-century church, and café and cemetery, while the battlements give amazing panoramas over the surrounding countryside and coastline. Back in the town, the only other sight lies just off Avenida da Liberdade (take the steps by *Restaurante Xurrex*), where the **Museu Municipal** (Mon–Fri 10am–12.30pm & 2–5.30pm; free) features scant archeological and historical finds from the area.

It's also a pleasant walk from the centre along the seafront Avenida dos Náufragos to the original fishing port, **Porto de Abrigo**, with its brightly painted boats, daily fish auctions, and stalls selling a superb variety of shellfish. Various **boat trips** operate out of the port. From June to September, usually daily, the Clube Naval (☎212 233 451, ⓦwww.naval-sesimbra.pt; €40) offers cruises on a traditional sailing boat, the *Santiago*. Between May and September, *Aquarama* (☎965 263 157; €15) runs daily "floating submarine" trips in a boat with a glass bottom, either up to Cabo Espichel or on night trips.

Practicalities

There are frequent **buses** to and from Lisbon's Praça de Espanha and Setúbal, and half-hourly services from Cacilhas. Coming from Lisbon in summer, it's usually much quicker to take the ferry across to Cacilhas and pick up a bus there, as the main bridge road is often jammed solid with traffic. In Sesimbra, you're dropped at the **bus station**, halfway up Avenida da Liberdade, a five-minute walk from the seafront. Walk down to the water, turn right past the fort, and the **turismo** (daily: June–Sept 9am–8pm; Oct–May 9am–12.30pm & 2–5.30pm; ☎212 288 540) is underneath the terrace, a step back from the seafront Avenida dos Náufragos. **Accommodation** can be hard to come by in high season. If you haven't booked in advance, your best bet is to try for private rooms through the turismo (❸).

At night, families crowd the line of **restaurants** east of the fort, along Avenida 25 de Abril, and round the little Largo dos Bombaldes. Cheaper places (meals under €15) abound in the back streets on either side of the central spine, Avenida da Nova Fortaleza. West of the fort along the avenue is also where most of the music **bars and cafés** are found, with the laidback *Bote Douro* at no.10 (closed Tues) and the sleek *Mareante* at no. 13 both popular hangouts. *A Galé*, Rua Capitão Leitão 5, on a raised terrace overlooking the sea, is a popular student haunt, while two **clubs** on Rua Prof. Fernandes Marques, just off the western seafront – the *Bolina* at no. 3 and *Central* at no. 11 – both get going at midnight (closed Mon; weekends only from Oct–May).

Hotels and pensions

Residencial Chic Trav. Xavier da Silva 2–6 ☎212 233 110. Very central choice, just back from the sea on a corner with Rua Candido dos Reis. It has bright rooms, some with restricted sea views. ❸

Residencial Náutico Bairro Infante D. Henrique 3 ☎212 233 233. Steeply uphill, this comfortable place is a little more secluded than most. Breakfast included. ❹

Sana Park Avenida 25 de Abril ☎212 289 000, ⓦwww.sanahotels.com. The best upmarket choice, a modern hotel with glass lifts, sauna and pool (open to non-guests), restaurant and groovy rooftop bar. The plush rooms are all en suite, though you'll pay a fair bit more for a sea view. Breakfast included. ❻, sea-view rooms ❽

Campsite

Forte do Cavalo ☎212 233 905. A well-located site just past the fishing port; closed Nov–April.

Restaurants

Marisqueira Filipe Av. 25 de Abril ☎212 231 653. Extremely popular seafood restaurant, and one of the more expensive places in town – €25

and upwards – but it serves great grilled fish, a bumper *arroz de marisco* plus some decent wines. Closed Wed. Expensive.

Nova Fortaleza Largo dos Bombaldes. On the edge of the square facing the beach with a great terrace. The prices are good for fish and the salads are nice. Closed Tues. Moderate.

A Sesimbrense Rua Jorge Nunes 17–19 ☎212 230 148. Bustling local just back from Largo dos Bombaldes (keep going past *Toni Bar*), serving no-nonsense soups, fish and grills with a TV for company. Closed Tues. Inexpensive.

A Tasca de Ratinho Rua Plinio Mesquita 17. Tucked up a side street behind Largo dos Bombaldes, this cosy place specializes in swordfish cooked in cream and port. There's a terrace overlooking the sea. Closed Thurs. Moderate.

Toni Bar Largo dos Bombaldes ☎212 233 199. For a quality fish or shellfish meal, the *Toni Bar* at the back of the square is hard to beat. Expensive.

Cabo Espichel and nearby beaches

Twice a day (both in the afternoon, making a brief day-trip feasible), buses make the 11km journey west from Sesimbra to **Cabo Espichel**, an end-of-the-world plateau lined on two sides by ramshackle arcaded eighteenth-century pilgrimage lodgings, with a crumbling chapel perched above the rocks at one end. The whole place has a rather desolate air that has made it a popular location for film directors, including Wim Wenders in *A Lisbon Story*. Beyond, wild and windswept cliffs drop almost vertically several hundred feet into the Atlantic; dinosaur footprints have been found on the nearby Praia dos Lagosteiros.

Four buses a day travel from Sesimbra beyond Cabo Espichel to the southern beaches of the surprisingly verdant and undeveloped Costa da Caparica (see p.62 for the northern section). A few kilometres to the north of Cabo Espichel is the village of **ALDEIA DO MECO**, from where a path cuts down to the superb beach of **Praia do Meco**. A large campsite, *Campimeco* (☎219 747 669, ☎219 748 728), complete with tennis courts, restaurant, pool and minimarket, lies northwest of here, just off **Praia das Bicas**. Like the other beaches on this coast, these are both prone to overcrowding in July and August, but can be almost deserted out of season, when the main drawback is the strong surf.

The calmest strip of beach is by the **Lagoa de Albufeira**, a little further south; the lagoon is extremely clean and excellent for windsurfing. There's another somewhat basic campsite, *Parque O Repouso*, 1km back from the lagoon (☎212 684 300; closed Oct–April), while just back from the beach overlooking the lagoon, *O Lagoeiro* (closed Mon) is the best place for grills, drinks or snacks.

Travel details

Trains

Cais do Sodré to: Belém (every 10min; 7min); Cascais (every 20min; 30min); Estoril (every 20min; 25min).

Fluvial, via Barreiro, to: Faro (4 daily; 5hr 30min–6hr; change for stations to Vila Real); Lagos (change at Tunes; 4–5 daily; 5–5hr 45min); Palmela (every 30min; 40min); Setúbal (every 30min; 55min); Tunes (for connections to western Algarve line; 4 daily; 4hr 15min).

Rossio to: Queluz (every 15min; 20min); Sintra (every 15min; 45min).

Santa Apolónia (note some services connect with Oriente trains) to: Abrantes (4 daily; 1hr 50min–2hr 15min); Coimbra (hourly; 2–3hr); Évora (2 daily; 3hr); Porto (hourly; 3hr 30min –4hr); Santarém (hourly; 50min–1hr 5min); Tomar (7 daily; 2hr).

International trains

Santa Apolónia/Oriente to: Badajoz (2 daily; 4hr 30min–5hr 30min); Biarritz (1 daily; 16hr); Bordeaux (1 daily; 18hr); Caceres (1 night train; 6hr); Madrid (1 night train; 10hr 40min); Paris (1 daily; 21hr); Salamanca (1 daily; 8hr); San Sebastián (1 daily; 14hr 15min).

Buses

The main local services are listed below, but express buses run daily to all main towns throughout the country. Mosty departures are from Lisbon's main bus terminal, though some services depart from a variety of other termini – see p.123 for more information.

Lisbon to: Costa da Caparica (every 30min; 40min–1hr); Ericeira (10 daily; 1hr 50min); Évora (hourly; 2hr–2hr 30min); Fátima (7 daily; 1hr 45min); Mafra (hourly; 1hr 30min); Nazaré (hourly; 1hr 50min); Palmela (Mon–Fri 10 daily, Sat & Sun 4; 40min–1hr); Peniche (9 daily; 1hr 45min); Porto (hourly; 3hr); Sesimbra (hourly; 1hr 30min–2hr); Setúbal (every 30min; 1hr); Tomar (2–4 daily; 1hr 45min); Torres Vedras (12 daily; 2hr); Vila Nogueira de Azeitão (hourly; 45min).

Estremadura and Ribatejo

ATLANTIC
OCEAN

N

SPAIN

△ Nazaré

2

Estremadura and Ribatejo

T he provinces of **Estremadura** and **Ribatejo** have played a crucial
role in each phase of the nation's history and have the monuments to
prove it. They are also now comparatively wealthy regions, both having
received substantial EU grants to help restructure agriculture. Although
they encompass a comparatively small area, the provinces boast an extraordinary concentration of vivid architecture: the monastery at **Alcobaça**, the
extraordinary abbey at **Batalha** and the headquarters of the Knights Templar
in **Tomar** – some of the most exciting buildings in Portugal – all lie within
a shallow triangle, easily accessible by bus or car. Other attractions are equally
compelling, from the completely walled medieval town of **Óbidos** to the
tremendous castle at elegant **Leiria**, while there's a different kind of fascination in visiting the shrine at **Fátima**, the country's (and, indeed, one of the
world's) most important pilgrimage sites.

The Estremaduran coast provides an excellent complement to all this,
and if you're simply seeking sun and sand it's not a bad alternative to the
Algarve. **Nazaré** and **Ericeira** are justifiably the most popular resorts, but
there are scores of less developed beaches, while ferries sail from **Peniche**
to the remote offshore bird sanctuary of the **Ilha Berlenga**. For isolated
beaches, you can also try the area around São Martinho do Porto or the
coastline west of Leiria, backed most of the way by the **Pinhal de Leiria**
pine forest. Inland, getting off the beaten track means going underground,
delving into the spectacular underground caverns that can be visited around
Mira de Aire.

Virtually all of these highlights fall within the boundaries of Estremadura, an area of fertile rolling hills that is perhaps second in beauty only to
the Minho. Although the flat, bull-breeding lands of Ribatejo (literally
"banks-of-the-Tejo") fade into the dull expanses of northwestern Alentejo, the valley of the **Rio Tejo** itself boasts some of Portugal's richest
vineyards, while many of its small towns host lively traditional festivals.
The wildest and most famous of these is the Festa do Colete Encarnado of
Vila Franca de Xira, with Pamplona-style bull-running through the
streets, though it's **Santarém**, the Ribatejo capital, that has the province's
longest history.

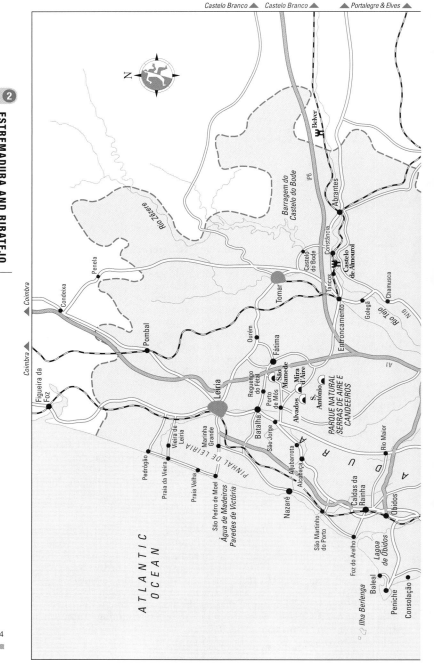

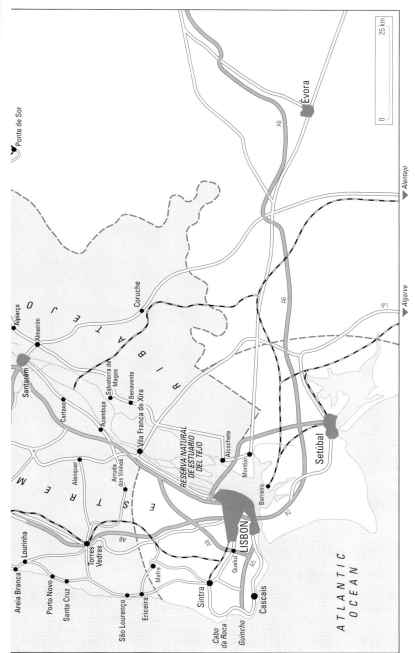

Ponte de Sor

Évora

A6

▼ Alentejo

▼ Algarve

IP1

Alpiarça

Almeirim

Coruche

Santarém

Cartaxo

Salvaterra de
Magos

Benavente

Azambuja

Vila Franca de Xira

R I B A T E J O

RESERVA NATURAL
DE ESTUARIO
DEL TEJO

Alcochete

Setúbal

Alenquer

Arruda
dos Vinhos

Montijo

Barreiro

A2

Areia Branca

Lourinha

Porto Novo

Santa Cruz

Torres
Vedras

A8

Mafra

LISBON

A9

Queluz

A5

Sintra

São Lourenço

Ericeira

Cabo
da Roca

Guincho

Cascais

E S T R E M A D U R A

A T L A N T I C
O C E A N

0   25 km

Ericeira

Perched on a rocky ledge thirty metres above a series of fine sandy beaches, **ERICEIRA** offers one of the few natural harbours between Cascais and Peniche. As a result, during the last century, the town became a major port, from where boats left to trade with countries as far away as Scotland and Brazil. The town's main claim to fame, though, is as the final refuge of Portugal's last monarch, Dom Manuel II – "The Unfortunate" – who, on October 5, 1910, was woken in his palace at nearby Mafra to be told that an angry Republican mob was advancing from Lisbon. Aware of the fate of his father and elder brother, he fled to the small harbour at Ericeira and sailed into the welcoming arms of the British at Gibraltar to live out the rest of his days in a villa at Twickenham. Baedeker's guidebook, published the same year, described Ericeira as "a fishing village with excellent sea bathing" and development has done little to change the town's original character. Although undeniably a busy resort in peak season, it remains a laid-back place of narrow lanes and whitewashed houses picked out in cobalt blue – it never feels completely besieged by tourists. It is especially lively on summer weekends, when people flock from Lisbon to enjoy the surprisingly buoyant nightlife, and is renowned by the Portuguese for excellent seafood – its very name is said to derive from the words *ouriços do mar* (sea urchin). You can see the tanks in which the shellfish are reared at the foot of the cliffs.

Praça da República, the small main square, is busy with sidewalk cafés and *pastelarias*, while bars and restaurants line Rua Dr. Eduardo Burnay, which leads from the square towards the town's main beach, **Praia do Sul**. The most central beach is that adjacent to fishermen's port, Porto de Pesca; it's often crowded and the water quality isn't as good as that of nearby beaches, but it offers safe bathing behind the port breakwater. To the north of town you'll find the **Praia do Norte** and the prettier, less crowded **Praia do São Sebastião**, the latter a fifteen-minute walk past the next headland and popular with surfers. Another option is to take a bus from Praça dos Navegantes to reach the series of untouched local beaches either further north or south: the World Surfing Championships have been held at **Praia da Ribeira d'Ilhas** (3km north), while at **Foz de Lizandro** (2km south) the river guarantees safe bathing whatever the sea state. However, the best local beach is perhaps the one at **São Lourenço**, a peaceful hamlet 5km north of Ericeira.

The surrounding coast is famous as the heartland of Portugese **surfing** – you can rent a wetsuit and board from Ultimar, Rua 5 de Outubro 25 (☎261 862 371; closed Sun afternoon) for €25 for 24 hours. Lessons (€25 per hour including equipment) are available from the surf schools Ribeira d'Ilhas Surfcamp (☎219 610 653, ⊛www.infortoldos.pt), at Praia da Ribeira d'Ilhas, and Na:onda (☎965 216 400, ✉naonda@sapo.pt) at Foz do Lizandro. Otherwise, if the sea is too rough, you might want to buy a day-pass for the **swimming pools** at the *Hotel Vila Galé* (daily 9.30am–7pm; €12 weekdays, €15 weekend), just beyond the pretty Parque Santa Marta.

Practicalities

Buses run virtually every hour to and from Mafra, 12km away, and there are also services to and from Lisbon and Sintra. You will be dropped in town at the top of Rua Prudêncio Franco da Trindade, which leads down to the main square. The **turismo**, at Rua Dr. Eduardo Burnay 46 (daily: July–mid-Sept 9.30am–midnight; mid-Sept–June 9am–7pm; ☎261 863 122,

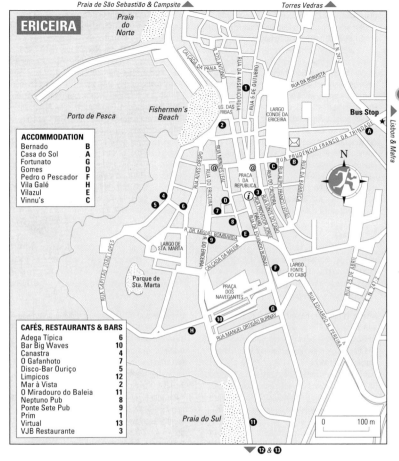

ERICEIRA

Praia de São Sebastião & Campsite ▲   Torres Vedras ▲

Praia do Norte

Porto de Pesca

Fishermen's Beach

Praia do Sul

ACCOMMODATION

Bernado	B
Casa do Sol	A
Fortunato	G
Gomes	D
Pedro o Pescador	F
Vila Galé	H
Vilazul	E
Vinnu's	C

CAFÉS, RESTAURANTS & BARS

Adega Típica	6
Bar Big Waves	10
Canastra	4
O Gafanhoto	7
Disco-Bar Ouriço	5
Limpicos	12
Mar à Vista	2
O Miradouro do Baleia	11
Neptuno Pub	8
Ponte Sete Pub	9
Prim	1
Virtual	13
VJB Restaurante	3

Bus Stop

0   100 m

Ⓦwww.ericeira.net), can help you to source **private rooms**, which are also advertised throughout town above bars and restaurants. **Internet** access is available free at the library on Rua Mendes Leal (Wed–Sat 10am–1pm & 2–7pm) and at Cyber Clube Eirceira, Praça da República (daily 11am –11pm).

Accommodation

Pensões and hotels are generally good value. The ones listed below are open all year round (not all are), while many should prove a good deal cheaper in winter. There's an excellent, well-equipped **campsite** at Parque Mil Regos, just beyond Praia do São Sebastião (Ⓣ261 862 706).

Hospedaria Bernado Rua Prudêncio Franco da Trindade 17 Ⓣ261 862 378, Ⓔhospedariabernado@iol.pt. Spotless small *pensão*, fairly close to the main square. ❸

Casa do Sol Rua Prudêncio Franco da Trindade 1 Ⓣ261 864 400, Ⓕ261 864 402. Homely, spacious, en-suite rooms in a grand house with shady gardens, but slightly blighted by its proximity to the main road. Breakfast included. No credit cards. ❹

Residencial Fortunato Rua Dr. Eduardo Burnay 7 ☎ 261 862 829, ✉ pensao.fortunato@iol.pt. Good views of Praia do Sul from west-facing rooms, but a little noisy in peak season. There's a range of modern accommodation (some rooms in the next price category up) – an annexe copes with the overflow – and a small wasteland car park opposite. Breakfast included. ❸

Residencial Gomes Rua Mendes Leal 11 ☎ & ℱ 261 863 619. A charming, good-value *residencial* in a rambling building, with faded decor and a whiff of eccentricity, but clean and friendly. All rooms share facilities. Breakfast included. American Express only. ❸

Hotel Pedro o Pescador Rua Dr. Eduardo Burnay 22 ☎ 261 864 302, ✉ hotel.pedro@mail.telepac. pt. Elegant small hotel gathered around a courtyard with a great bar. There's colourful tile work throughout, plenty of plants and a private patio. Breakfast included. ❹

Hotel Vila Galé Pr. dos Navegantes ☎ 261 869 900, ⊛ www.vilagale.pt. Ericeira's ritziest hotel is a slick, modern four-star affair on the seafront – sea views cost an extra €30. Spacious rooms are quietly elegant, with dark woods and tasteful fabrics. Breakfast included. Parking available. ❽

Hotel Vilazul Calç. da Baleia 10 ☎ 261 860 000, ⊛ www.hotelvilazul.net. All rooms have private bathrooms, air conditioning and televisions – it's worth paying €5 extra for a balcony and superb views to the sea. Serves great breakfasts (included). ❺

Residencial Vinnu's Rua Prudêncio Franco da Trindade 25 ☎ & ℱ 261 863 830. Clean, modern and airy – some of the rooms have small balconies. No credit cards. ❸

Eating

The lively *pastelarias* around Praça da República are recommended for lunch or tea-time indulgences. Despite its small size, Ericeira has a glut of good **restaurants**; the old-town alleys west of the square are a good hunting ground for more characterful eateries. Obviously, seafood is the best choice; the local speciality is *açorda de mariscos*, a sort of bread-based shellfish stew.

Adega Típica Rua Alves Crespo 3 ☎ 261 862 149. A cosy traditional restaurant – there's fado on Tuesday nights – serving good-value grilled meats and fish, plus an excellent range of local wines. Closed Thurs. Moderate.

Canastra Rua Capitão João Lopes 8A ☎ 261 865 367. A little pricey, but a highly recommended seafood restaurant in a harbourfront fisherman's house – reserve a table or be prepared to wait. Closed Wed. Expensive.

O Gafanhoto Rua da Conceição ☎ 261 861 514. A backstreet joint with no-frills decor and a small choice of meat and fish at budget prices. Closed Tuesday. Inexpensive.

Mar à Vista Largo das Ribas ☎ 261 862 928. A superb locals' place, with three basic nooks to dine in and the freshest seafood on the menu – the shellfish is highly rated. Arrive early or expect to wait. Closed Wed. Moderate.

O Miradouro do Baleia Praia do Sul ☎ 261 863 981. The best seafront dining in Ericeira, right before the breakers and with a large menu that includes *açorda de mariscos*. Moderate.

Prim Rua 5° de Outubro 12 ☎ 261 865 230. Small and friendly restaurant serving delicious grilled meat plus a few native dishes of the Brazilian owner, all at around €10 a dish and in belly-busting portions. Moderate.

VJB Restaurante Trav. do Jogos do Bola 3 ☎ 261 864 646. Relaxed bar-cum-restaurant just off Pr. da Républica, with a wide-ranging menu and mains at around €7. Moderate.

Nightlife

Ericeira after dark is surprisingly animated – its bars, clubs and proximity to the beaches attract an influx of young weekending Lisboans. In Ericeira itself, the bars around Praça dos Navegantes attract a young crowd, especially at weekends, but most of the "in" places are out of town.

Bar Big Waves Pr. dos Navegantes 22. One of the happening bars on the square near Praia do Sul. The place where locals start off the evening.

Limpicos Foz do Lizandro. This is one of the best of a group of trendy bars in this small beach resort 2km south of Ericeira – part of the night-time circuit for those with their own transport.

Neptuno Pub Rua Mendes Leal 12. A Portugese-style pub, with cocktails to complement the Sagres beer, and fados once a week. Closed Wed in winter.

Disco-Bar Ouriço Rua Capitao João Lopes 10. A conveniently located seafront disco, Portugal's second oldest (and whose music choice can be as dated).

Ponte Sete Pub Rua Dr. Miguel Bombarda. A hole-in-the-wall bar decorated with old rock memorabilia, with jazz and blues jam sessions at weekends.

Virtual Praia do Sul. Summer-only club popular with the surf crowd.

Torres Vedras

TORRES VEDRAS, 27km to the north and inland from Ericeira, took its name from the Duke of Wellington's famous defence lines (Linhas de Torres) in the **Peninsular War** against Napoleonic France. The "Lines" consisted of a chain of 150 hilltop fortresses, stretching some 40km from the mouth of the Rio Sizandro, directly west of Torres Vedras, to Alhandra, southeast of Torres Vedras, where the Tejo widens out into a huge lake. Astonishingly, they were built in a matter of months and without any apparent reaction from the French. Here, in 1810, Wellington and his forces retired, comfortably supplied by sea and completely unassailable. The French, frustrated by impossibly long lines of communication and by British scorching of the land north of the Lines, eventually retreated back to Spain in despair. Thus from a last line of defence, Wellington completely reversed the progress of the campaign – storming after the disconsolate enemy to effect a series of swift and devastating victories.

In view of this historical glory, modern Torres Vedras is disappointing. There are a few ruins of the old fortresses and a couple of imposing sixteenth-century churches but, bar a pleasant pedestrianized kernel of cobbled lanes, the town is swamped by a dull sprawl of recent buildings. Yet from the thirteenth to the sixteenth century, the **castle** (daily 10am–7pm; free) at Torres Vedras was a popular royal residence. It was here, in 1414, that Dom João I confirmed the decision to take Ceuta – the first overseas venture leading towards the future Portuguese maritime empire. The castle was eventually abandoned and then reduced to rubble by the earthquake of 1755. On the central Praça 25 de Abril, in the old Convento da Graça, is the **Museu Municipal** (Tues–Sun 10am–1pm & 2–6pm; €0.75), with a room devoted to the Peninsular War.

However, unless you get hooked on the local wine there's not much else to keep you in town, and you're probably better off taking one of the many buses out to the local beaches (see below) or on to Peniche or Óbidos. The **bus station** is just uphill from the **train station**, which is located at the end of the central Avenida 5 Outubro; at its end is Praça 25 de Abril, on the shoulder of which, at Rua 9 de Abril, is the **turismo** (Mon–Sat 10am–1pm & 2–6pm; ☎261 314 094, ⓦwww.cm-tvedras.pt). Both *O Gordo*, Rua Almirante Gado Coutinho 15 (☎261 323 079; moderate; closed Tues), and *Típico Adega do Miguel*, Avenida Dr. Raul Sarreira 35 (☎261 331 455; moderate; closed Sun), are good options for a **meal** if you're passing through. *Cafe Havaneza* serves coffee, cakes and snacks overlooking the main church on Plaça República.

North to Peniche

Thirteen kilometres east of Torres Vedras is the popular local resort of Praia de Santa Cruz, while smaller, quieter resorts lie along the coast to the north, many of them uncrowded outside public holidays or summer weekends. They are all easily reached on buses heading to Lourinhã or Peniche.

Praia de Santa Cruz

PRAIA DE SANTA CRUZ has a friendly, easy-going feel and two good beaches: **Praia Guincho** below the town; and the more secluded **Praia Formosa**, beneath cliffs to the south. In between is a "screaming rock" – partly covered by the tide – where air and water is forced through a hole in the rock at certain times to produce the distinctive sound. **Rooms** are available at the *Pensão-Restaurante Mar Lindo*, Trav. Jorge Cardoso (☎261 937 297; includes breakfast; ❹), some with sea views, and at the *Hotel de Santa Cruz*, Rua José Pedro Lopes (☎261 937 148; includes breakfast; ❹). There's a shady municipal **campsite** (☎261 930 150) on the main road north of the town, five minutes' walk from the sea, which, though large, fills up quickly in high summer.

Praia de Porto Novo

Five kilometres north of Santa Cruz, is the small bay of **PRAIA DE PORTO NOVO** whose beach has inevitably been developed but remains relatively unspoilt and low-key compared to neighbouring resorts. There are also a number of walking paths, which snake through the hills inland and offer a good day's hiking. In August 1808, British reinforcements were landed here, at the mouth of the River Maceira. They enabled Wellington, in his first serious encounter with the French, to defeat General Junot at the battle of Vimeiro, following which the French sued for peace. The fanciest **hotel** is the *Hotel Golf Mar* (☎261 980 800, ❼www.eav.pt; includes breakfast; ❼), which perches above the north of the bay – this is the place to organize local activities, from golf to windsurfing, and it has a pool. Alternatively, there are some reasonable **pensions** before the beach; *Residencial Promar* (☎261 984 220, ❺261 984727; includes breakfast; ❹) is a cut above its competitors.

Areia Branca and Consolação

Further north on the Peniche road, 21km from Torres Vedras, lies **AREIA BRANCA** ("White Sand"), a congenial small resort with a decent beach. The **youth hostel** here has a superb location overlooking the sands (☎261 422 127, ❼www.pousadasjuventude.pt; dorms €12.50), and there's also a pleasant **campsite** (☎261 412 199), or you can ask at the seafront **turismo** (Mon–Sat 10am–1pm & 2–6pm; ☎261 422 167) for a list of private rooms. Other accommodation choices include *Estalagem Areia Branca* (☎261 412 491; includes breakfast; ❺), near the beach, and *Residencial Restaurante Dom Lourenço*, on the way out of town to the north (☎261 422 809; includes breakfast; ❹), whose restaurant is an ever-reliable place to eat.

Despite the attractive sands, the sea at Areia Branca is not the cleanest and it's better to head 4km north to **CONSOLAÇÃO**, just south of Peniche, if you want to swim. The great swathe of beach here is popular with surfers, although the resort is far from pretty thanks to some gaudy development. However, there are only a few places to stay the night – you're better off heading for Peniche for accommodation.

Peniche

PENICHE, impressively enclosed by ramparts, is one of Portugal's most active fishing ports. As late as the fifteenth century the town was an island but the area has silted up and is now joined to the mainland by a narrow isthmus, with gently sloping beaches on either side. Unsightly development now stretches along the coast, but inside the walled town there is still much to appreciate, including the fortress, which dominates the south side of town. Peniche is also the embarkation point for the Ilha Berlenga (see p.163), while there's an enjoyable market on the *campo*, held on the last Thursday of the month. Tourism has undoubtedly introduced a tougher edge to the town – determined touts hawk rooms and a glut of seafood restaurants vie for the tourist euro – but, although the balance is changing, Peniche has yet to be seduced entirely from its fishing roots, and gangs of fishermen still repair nets at the harbourside. If you are in Peniche over the first weekend in August, you'll coincide with the festival of **Nossa Senhora da Boa Viagem** (Our Lady of Good Journeys), during which the statue of the Virgin is brought to the harbour by boat to be greeted by candle-bearing locals. After the village priest has blessed the fleet, there are fireworks, bands and dancing in the street.

The sixteenth-century **Fortaleza** (Tues–Sun 10.30am–12.30pm & 2–6pm; closes at 5pm in winter; €1.30) was one of the dictator Salazar's most notorious jails. Greatly expanded in the 1950s and 1960s to accommodate the growing crowds of political prisoners, it later served as a temporary refugee camp for *retornados* from the colonies. Today it houses a museum, with the familiar mix of local archeology, natural history and craft displays, among which you can still see the old cells (on the top floor), the solitary confinement pens (*segredos*) and the visitors' grille (*parlatório*).

Just outside the city walls, off the fine **north beach** of the peninsula, is a traditional boat yard. It's fascinating to watch shipwrights here manoeuvring huge timbers into position to form the skeletal framework of a new fishing vessel. Beyond the fortress, through the suburbs, it's a 45-minute walk to the tip of **Cabo Carvoeiro**, a rugged, rock-pillared peninsula topped by a lighthouse, where the *Nau dos Corvos* restaurant (no phone; moderate) has superb views and a good-value set menu. An alternative jaunt is to **Baleal**, an islet-village 5km to the north of Peniche, joined to the mainland by a narrow strip of fine sand. Frequent buses make the trip from town and it makes a good base in its own right, with a fine beach, laid-back atmosphere and relatively little development.

Practicalities

Buses pull in at the station on the isthmus just outside the town walls. It's a ten-minute walk into the centre across the Ponte Velha, which takes you to Rua Alexandre Herculano, where you turn left for the helpful **turismo** (daily: July & August 9am–8pm; Sept–June 10am–1pm & 2–5pm; ℡262 789 571, Ⓦwww.cm-peniche.pt). Nearly all of Peniche's hotels, bars and restaurants are on or just back from Rua Alexandre Herculano and Avenida do Mar, which lead down to the harbour by Largo da Ribeira. **Internet** access is at espaçaoInternet (Mon–Sat 10am–10pm, Sun 10am–7pm), before the second roundabout on Rua Dr. Joa de Matos Bilhau.

Accommodation

In summer (particularly in August) accommodation can be hard to find, without an advance reservation. You will be approached by people offering private rooms, but if you want more time to consider your options, and avoid the hard sell, head for the turismo who can help source accommodation. A limited number of options in Baleal offer a mellow alternative to Peniche, with the advantage of there being a beach on the doorstep.

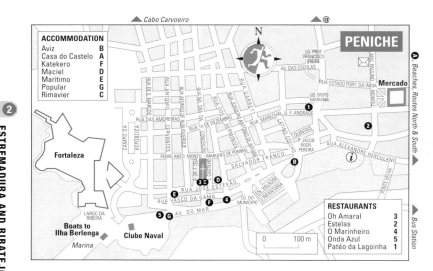

ACCOMMODATION

Aviz	B
Casa do Castelo	A
Katekero	F
Maciel	D
Marítimo	E
Popular	G
Rimavier	C

RESTAURANTS

Oh Amaral	3
Estelas	2
O Marinheiro	4
Onda Azul	5
Patéo da Lagoinha	1

Hotels and pensions

Residencial Aviz Pr. Jacob R. Pereira 7 ☎ 262 782 153. Good-value, if old-fashioned, *residencial* with clean, comfortable rooms, some with en-suite bathroom. ❸

Casa do Castelo Atouguia da Baleia, 5km east on N114 ☎ 262 750 647, ⊛ www.casa-do-castelo .com. An elegant seventeenth-century family home that tastefully blends modern style with antiques. It's set in lovely gardens with a swimming pool, and breakast is included. No credit cards. ❺

Katekero Av. do Mar 76 ☎ 262 787 107. One of the cheapest options in town. Rooms are spartan and basic, though all are spotless and some offer port views. No credit cards. ❷

Residencial Maciel Rua José Estêvão 38 ☎ 262 784 685, ⊛ www.residencial-maciel.com. The best budget option in town is a little classier than its neighbours, with spacious, characterful en-suite rooms. Breakfast included. ❸

Residencial Marítimo Rua José Estêvão ☎ 262 782 850. Set just back from the harbour, this *residencial* has simple rooms with private bathrooms. ❷

Residencial Popular Largo da Ribeira 40 ☎ 262 790 290, ⊛ www.apopular.com. Cosy, bright, modern rooms in a friendly place near the port – ask for a harbourside room for views (and to avoid the traffic noise). Breakfast included. ❸

Residencial Rimavier Rua Castilho 6–8 ☎ 262 789 459 Modern, clean en-suite rooms above a souvenir shop. Breakfast included. ❸

Campsites

Parque Municipal de Campismo Av. Monsenhor Bastos ☎ 262 789 529. East of Peniche centre, on the way into town after you've crossed the Rio Lagôa, and well placed for the bus station.

Camping Peniche Praia Estrada Marginal Norte ☎ 262 783 460, ⓕ 262 789 447. A fine private campsite, complete with pool, restaurant and internet access. It's on the north shore of the peninsula, 2km from the centre and near the sands of Praia Norte.

Eating and drinking

There is a fine array of **restaurants** along Avenida do Mar, most of them good value and serving huge portions. The snack bar in the Mercado (off Rua Arq. Paulino Montez) is just the ticket for breakfast or picnic provisions; visit in the morning and it's often full of fishwives swinging plastic bags of fish and sipping a *bica* as they exchange news. Your best bet for a lively drink and a view of the world going by is one of the harbourside bars.

Oh Amaral Rua Dr. Francisco Seia 7 ☎ 262 782 095. A little pricey, but this highly rated seafood place is worth it, especially if you feel like splash-

ing out on the house-special *frigideira* or *arroz de tamboril*. Moderate.

Estelas Rua Arq. Paulino Montez ☎ 262 782 435.

Surfing, diving and fishing

For **surfing**, there's equipment rental (around €15 per day) from Rip Curl, Rua Alexandre Herculano (☎262 787 206), and Supertubo-Art de Desporto (☎262 781 720), Rua Ernesto Moreira, east of the centre, while Baleal Surfcamp, Rua Amigos do Baleal 2, Baleal (☎261 769 277, ⓦwww.balealsurfcamp.com), also offers lessons. **Diving trips** are operated by Haliotis (☎262 781 160, ⓦwww.haliotis.pt), based in the *Hotel Praia Norte*, 1km north of Peniche centre; Mergulhão (☎262 789 045), on Rua António Cervantes; and Berlenga Sub, Largo da Ribeira 24 (☎262 189 619, ⓦhttp://clientes.netvisao.pt/mergus) – the best dives, in the gin-clear waters off Ilha Berlenga, cost around €50, although cheaper coastal dives are also available. For **sea fishing**, contact Nautipesca (☎917 588 358) or Julius (☎262 782 698 or 918 618 311, ⓦwww.julius-berlenga.com), both of which have booths at the harbour and charge around €35 per person per day (minimum ten people); prices will be higher for smaller groups. Julius also offers boat trips around the local coastline for €15 per person.

Acclaimed as the best restaurant in town by many, serving super-fresh seafood in a breezy modern dining room. Expensive.
O Marinheiro Av. do Mar ☎262 783 835.One of the finest of a line of restaurants – choose your fish from the day's catch displayed on ice and it's grilled over charcoal. Moderate.
Onda Azul Largo da Ribeira 38 ☎262 787 224.

Decent prices for seafood – sea bass for €8 or squid for €6.50 – in a spacious restaurant beside the port. Moderate.
Patéo da Lagoinha Largo Bispo de Mariana ☎939 096 171. Cheerful late-night bar-cum-restaurant with a courtyard garden, serving cheap dishes such as squid curry and good old spaghetti bolognaise. Inexpensive.

Ilha Berlenga

The **Ilha Berlenga**, 10km offshore and just visible from Cabo Carvoeiro, is a dreamlike place, rather like a Scottish isle transported to warmer climes. Just two-and-a-half square kilometres in extent, it is the largest island of a tiny archipelago, with a jagged coastline of grottoes, miniature fjords and extraordinary rock formations. In summer the sea is calm, crystal clear and perfect for snorkelling and diving – rare in the Atlantic.

The only people permitted to live here are a couple of dozen fishermen because the island has been declared a **natural reserve**, home to thousands upon thousands of sea birds, including gulls, puffins and cormorants, which perch in every conceivable cranny and seem intent on leaving their mark on every possible victim. Makeshift paths on the island are marked out with stones and guardians watch out for visitors straying into the prohibited areas and disturbing the birds.

The island

Human life revolves around the main landing dock, with its small fleet of fishing boats. The sandy beach looks (and is) idyllic – a golden notch in the cliffs – but quickly becomes crowded and noisy in peak season, even though the only buildings are a cluster of huts, a couple of basic shops, a minimarket and a lighthouse. Fortunately, the island is a delight to stroll and offers escape from the hubbub. Rowing boats can be hired at the jetty to explore the intricacies of the coastline, although you may prefer to go in something with a motor if there's any motion on the sea – you can get a guided **boat tour** for a few euros. Don't miss the Furado Grande, a fantastic tunnel 75m long, which culminates in the aptly named Cova do Sonho (Dream Cove) with its precipitous cliffs.

Accommodation is extremely limited, a choice between the pricey rooms at the bar-restaurant *Pavilhão Mar e Sol* (☎262 750 331; ❺) or dorm beds at the rudimentary **hostel** (☎262 785 263; €9) in the seventeenth-century Forte de São João Baptista, a short walk beyond the lighthouse, on an islet joined by the narrowest of causeways. It's essential to reserve in advance for either, and for the hostel you'll need to bring your own food (there is a kitchen) and sleeping stuff. There's also a **campsite** (☎262 789 571), which clings to the rocky slopes above the harbour – telephone in advance or book at the turismo in Peniche.

Getting there

The **ferry from Peniche** is operated by Viamar (☎262 785 646) and takes one hour – longer if the sea is rough. The service departs from the harbour below the fort, and operates from mid-May to mid-September, with two ferries a day in July and August (9am, 11.30am; return at 4.30pm and 6.30pm), and one a day at other times (10am; return at 4.30pm). A **return ticket** costs €17 and there's a limit of 300 tickets sold each day; one person can buy up to five at a time. In July and August the ticket office opens at 8pm to take bookings for the next day's ferry; if you want to be sure of a place, get there in good time. Outside these months, it's not usually a problem getting a ticket on the day of travel.

Other companies on the harbour front, such as Turpesca (☎262 789 960) and Julius (☎262 782 698 or 918 618 311, ⓦwww.julius-berlenga.com), operate **boat trips** (minimum four people; up to four departures a morning in peak season) all year round except in December. Tickets cost €15 for day-long excursions, including a pause at the island and a visit to the caves along the coastline. Note that you can use Turpesca for overnight stays on the island between June and September; the rest of the year it will only take day-trippers. If the weather is difficult, times will change and boats may be cancelled. In any case, those with weak stomachs should give breakfast a miss – as indicated by rows of buckets under the seats, it's a bouncy ride.

Óbidos

ÓBIDOS, 23km east of Peniche, is known as the "The Wedding City" and was the traditional bridal gift of the kings of Portugal to their queens. The custom was started in 1282 by Dom Dinis and Dona Isabel and the town seems hardly to have changed much in appearance since then. It is very small and completely enclosed by lofty medieval walls: streets are cobbled, whitewashed houses are framed with bright blue and yellow borders, and at all points steep staircases wind up to the ramparts, where you can gaze across a lovely rural landscape.

It wasn't always like this. Five hundred years ago, when Peniche was an island, the sea also reached the foot of the ridge on which Óbidos stands and boats were moored below its walls. However, by the fifteenth century the sea had retreated, leaving a fertile green plain and the distant Lagoa de Óbidos with its narrow, shallow entrance to the sea.

The town is touristy, of course, attracting visitors by the coach-load, while the surrounding area has sprouted a small flurry of modern development. However, you can escape the worst of the crowds on the perimeter walls which girdle the town – a narrow and at times hair-raising walkway with no handrails – and from this vantage point Óbidos seems to retain secrets of its own. The feeling is reinforced if you stay the night, when the town slowly empties of day-trippers and regains its impossibly picturesque charm.

The Town

The most striking building in town is Dom Dinis's massively towered **Castelo**, which has been converted into a splendid *pousada*. Below the castle, the principal focus is the parish church, the **Igreja de Santa Maria**, in the central Largo de São Pedro, venue of the wedding of the ten-year-old child king Afonso V and his eight-year-old cousin, Isabel, in 1444. It dates mainly from the Renaissance period, although the interior is lined with blue seventeenth-century *azulejos* in a homely manner typical of Portuguese churches. The *retábulo* to the right of the main altar was painted by **Josefa de Óbidos**, one of the finest of all Portuguese painters, and one of the few women artists afforded any reputation by art historians. Born in Seville in 1634, Josefa spent most of her life in a convent at Óbidos. She began her career as an etcher and miniaturist, and a remarkable handling of detail is a feature of her later full-scale religious works. Another of her paintings, a portrait of powerful priest Faustino des Neves, can be seen in the adjacent **museum** of archeology, furniture and devotional art in the old town hall (daily 10am–12.30pm & 2–6pm; €1.50).

There's an annual festival of ancient music from mid-September to mid-October, held in various venues around the town, including at the purpose-built **Casa da Música**, just inside Porta da Vila, the principal town gate at the far end of the main Rua Direita. The town is also busy on Tourist Day (one of the last two Sundays in August), when free wine is on offer. If you're on the hunt for souvenirs, rummage through the **craft shops** on Rua Direita, which include *Casa Mourisco* (ceramics, paintings and carvings) and the old people's handicrafts centre, which has a good variety of nicely made items.

Practicalities

Buses from Caldas da Rainha (6km to the north) and Peniche (24km west) stop outside the Porta da Vila, before which is the **turismo** (daily 9.30am–7.30pm; ☎262 959 231, ⓦwww.cm-obidos.pt). This hands out town plans that mark the restaurants and hotels, and also stocks information on nature walks in the locale, as does a **regional tourism office** at Rua Direita 84 (Mon–Fri 10am–noon & 2–6pm; ☎262 955 900). The **train station** is at the foot of the ridge; there is no ticket office here, so pay once you are on the train. If you are not too heavily laden, you can cross the tracks and climb the steps, which will bring you to the gate by the Castelo – at the opposite end of Rua Direita to Porta da Vila. Otherwise, follow the road and the easier gradients to reach the Porta da Vila. **Internet** access is available free of charge at espaçaoInternet (daily 10am–10pm), in the library on Rua Direita by the central square.

Óbidos's appeal to the heart also extends to its **accommodation**, which generally scores high on charm and comfort, especially in the historic town houses or classy country manors listed below. Most is priced at mid-range – budget travellers are advised to hunt out one of the handful of **private rooms** (usually ❸), advertised in the windows of a few houses and sometimes touted at the bus station. Alternatively, ask for advice at the turismo. **Restaurants** are mainly geared towards the day-trippers, so prices tend to be slightly higher than elsewhere and menus range from the predictable to the traditional.

Hotels and pensions

Casa d'Óbidos Quinta de Sâo José, 2km south of town ☎262 950 924, ⓕ262 959 970. Classy manor house in lovely gardens with a swimming pool. The price includes an excellent breakfast. ❺

Casa do Poço Trav. da Mouraria ☎262 959 358, ⓕ262 959 282. Downhill from the castle, a rambling, renovated house with only four snug double rooms, all en suite, gathered around a courtyard. Breakfast included. No credit cards. ❹

Hospedaria Casa da Raposeira Rua 1, Porta 11, Bairro da Raposeira, 500m west of turismo ☎262 959 662. Nothing special, but the clean and simple rooms here are the only option for those on a tight budget. No credit cards. ❷

Casa da Relógio Rua da Graça ☎262 959 282, ⓔcasa.relogio@clix.pt. Outside the walls, a former eighteenth-century mansion whose "clock" (*relógio*) is in fact a stone sundial on the facade. Six charmingly decorated en-suite double rooms offer good value for money. Breakfast included. ❹

Casa São Tiago do Castelo Largo de São Tiago ☎ & ⓕ262 959 587. A beautiful family house, furnished with antiques and exuding warmth, charm and homely comfort. Highly recommended for a romantic splurge. Breakfast included. ❺

Pousada do Castelo In the Castelo ☎262 955 080, ⓦwww.pousadas.pt. It's only small but this is one of the country's finest and priciest *pousadas*, with cosy rooms featuring four-poster beds and exposed stone walls. The restaurant is just as exclusive, serving high-class fare such as scallops with apple and watercress. Advance reservations advised for rooms and restaurant. Breakfast included. ❾

Estalagem do Convento Rua Dr. João de Ornelas ☎262 959 214, ⓦwww.estalagemdoconvento. com. A minor convent just outside the walls has been converted into a traditionally furnished hotel, while a small rear garden offers views over the surrounding countryside. There's also excellent patio dining in the restaurant (expensive; closed Sun dinner), which features a good-value *ementa turística* (€19). Breakfast included. ❺

Albergaria Josefa d'Óbidos Rua Dr. João de Ornelas ☎262 959 228, ⓦwww.josefadobidos .com. A large hotel in the shadow of the walls, decorated in traditional style but with modern comforts – rooms all have TVs and are air-conditioned. Breakfast included. ❹

Albergaria Rainha Santa Isabel Rua Direita ☎262 959 323, ⓔariso@oeste.online.pt. The carefully preserved facade hides an up-to-date hotel with lounge and bar. The rooms retain period features and some have balconies onto the main street. Hearty breakfasts included. ❺

Cafés and restaurants

Restaurante Alcaide Rua Direita, opposite Albergaria Rainha Santa Isabel ☎262 959 220. Attractive place serving excellent dishes, including sea bass or pork fillet with herbs. Arrive early – or book – if you want to eat on the balcony. Closed Wed. Expensive.

Casa de Ramiro Rua Porta do Vale ☎262 959 194. Just outside the walls, in an old house redesigned in Arabic style, serving aromatic grills. Closed Thurs & Jan–Feb. Moderate.

Restaurante O Conquistador Rua Josefa de Óbidos, off Rua Direita, near Porta da Vila ☎262 959 528. Try the roast *cabrito* or the stewed partridge, two of the pricier choices on a large menu. Closed Tues. Moderate.

Dom Jôao V Largo do Santuário do Senhor da Pedra, 2km south on the Caldas da Rainha road ☎262 959 134. Old-fashioned elegance and excellent traditional local cuisine. Closed Sat. Expensive.

Bar Lagar da Mouraria Rua da Mouraria ☎919 937 601. A nostalgic café for tea, coffee and pastries, fashioned with impeccable taste from an old house. Inexpensive.

Café-Restaurante 1 de Dezembro Largo Sao Pedro, next to the church ☎262 959 298. A good bet for a cheap(ish) meal of hearty pork and bean stew, plus all the usual omelettes and salads. Closed Sun. Moderate.

Caldas da Rainha

Six kilometres north of Óbidos, **CALDAS DA RAINHA** ("Queen's Spa") was put on the map by Dona Leonor. Passing in her carriage, she was so impressed by the strong sulphuric waters that she founded a hospital here, initiating four centuries of noble and royal patronage. That was in 1484, but the town was to reach the peak of its popularity in the nineteenth century when, throughout Europe, spas became as much social as medical institutions. English Gothic novelist William Beckford (recorded in his *Travels in Spain and Portugal*) found it a lively if depressing place – "every tenth or twelfth person a rheumatic or palsied invalid, with his limbs all atwist, and his mouth all awry, being conveyed to the baths in a chair".

Disappointingly little remains of the royal wealth poured into the spa, although once through the drab modern outskirts Caldas has a pleasant enough centre and offers a good break in the journey to Nazaré or Alcobaça. From the central **Praça da República**, which hosts a fruit market every morning, the royal spa hospital is a short walk downhill. There is a **museum** here (Tues–Sun 10am–12.30pm & 2–5pm; €2), but you can only bathe in the warm, sulphurous swimming pools under doctor's orders. Protruding from the back of the spa is the striking Manueline belfry of **Nossa Senhora do Pópulo**, the hospital church. There's a *Virgin and Child* by Josefa de Óbidos in the sacristy.

In the leafy Parque Dom Carlos I, the **Museu de José Malhoa** (Tues–Sun 10am–12.30pm & 2–5pm; €2) displays Malhoa's work and that of other late-nineteenth-century Portuguese painters. There are two other museums at the far edge of the park: the **Atelier Museu António Duarte** (Mon–Fri 9am–1pm & 2–6pm, Sat & Sun 10am–1pm & 2–6pm; €2, free Sun morning), devoted to the eminent sculptor; and, alongside, the much better **Museu da Cerâmica** (Tues–Sun 10am–12.30pm & 2–5pm; €2, free Sun morning), which contains some of the original work of local potter and caricaturist Rafael Bordalo Pinheiro – look for his series of life-sized ceramic figures representing the Passion. Indeed, Caldas remains famed for its traditional ceramics (including peculiar phallus-shaped objects) and the **Feira Nacional da Cerâmica** is held here during July or October in the Expooeste, an industrial part of town, northwest of the railway tracks.

Practicalities

It's a short walk from either the bus or train station to the main **turismo** (Mon–Fri 9am–7pm, Sat 10am–1pm & 3–7pm; ☎262 839 700, ⊛www.cm-caldas-rainha.pt), situated next to the town hall in Praça 25 de Abril. From here, Praça da República is a ten-minute walk away: take Rua Engheneiro Duarte Pacheo off the square, turn right on Rua Heróis da Grande Guerre, then left on pedestrianized Rua Almirante Cândido dos Reis. Due to the presence of the spa, there's a fair amount of **accommodation** around town, most of it reasonably priced, although nothing too exciting. The **cafés** around Largo Rainha Dona Leonor (a block south of Praça da República, reached via Rua da Liberdade) are a good bet for an evening drink and also for sampling the local sweet pastries, such as *trouxas de ovos*.

Hotels and pensions

Caldas Internacional Hotel Rua Dr. Figueirôa Rêgo 45 ☎262 832 307, ⊛www.hobai.pa-net.pt. The smartest (although rather characterless) hotel in town, with modern air-conditioned rooms, a swimming pool and its own parking. Breakfast included. ❺

Pensão Residencial Central Largo Dr. José Barbosa 22 ☎262 831 914. A trifle tatty, but there's a whiff of faded grandeur about this pleasant old *pensão*, the birthplace of painter José Malhoa. It's well located in a quiet square between Pr. da República and Largo da Rainha Dona Leonor. Breakfast included. ❸

Residencial Dom Carlos Rua de Camões 39A ☎262 832 551, @dcarlos.ali@netc.pt. Traditional old hotel, near the royal spa hospital and opposite the park. All rooms are en suite and have TVs, though front rooms can be noisy. Breakfast included. No credit cards. ❸

Residencial Europeia Rua Almirante Cândido dos Reis 64 ☎262 831 508, ℮residencialeuropeia @hotmail.com. Central and smart, though the heavy wooden furniture makes the rooms seem a bit dated. The entrance is in a shopping mall. There's a bar, and the price includes breakfast. American Express only. ❹

Residencial Rainha Dona Leonor Hermicício João Paulo II 9 ☎262 842 171, ⓦwww .donaleonor.com. A large, rather soulless hotel, but the rooms have satellite TV and are all en suite. Private parking. Breakfast included. ❹

Cafés and restaurants

Pasteleria Baia Rua da Liberdade 33 ☎262 832 349. Sit at the terrace on a small square to sample *trouxas de ovos* in one of Caldas' best cafés. Inexpensive.

Populus Parque Dom Carlos I, at Rua de Camões ☎262 845 840. An airy café favoured by students that's by far the most enticing spot for an al fresco lunch – good beef dishes cost around €8. Moderate.

Supatra Rua General Amílcar Mota, 1km out of centre, south on Óbidos road ☎262 842 920. A renowned Thai restaurant. Closed Mon. Expensive.

Zé do Barrete Trav. da Cova da Onça 16–18 t262 832 787. One of a number of good restaurants on a side street, midway down Rua Almirante Cândido dos Reis. Tempting spit-roasts and grills are the things to go for. Closed Sun. Moderate.

North to Nazaré

Heading north from Caldas da Rainha, buses and trains stay inland, touching the coast only at **São Martinho do Porto**, 13km south of Nazaré. However, if you have your own transport, you can bear northwest from Caldas along the N360, which takes you past the tranquil Lagoa de Óbidos, and then out along the coast via **Foz do Arelho** on a beautiful clifftop route – a much better option than taking the busy N8.

Foz do Arelho

At **FOZ DO ARELHO**, 9km west of Caldas, there's a fine lagoon beach, while the river threads down to another good beach at the ocean. Seafood restaurants line the sands, while Largo do Arraial, an attractive pedestrian square behind the lagoon, has a clutch of more elegant bars. There is a **campsite** (☎262 979 197) near the lagoon, plus some decent local **accommodation**: the modern and friendly *Penedo Furado*, on a side street 200m west of Largo do Arraial (☎262 979 610, ℮penedo_furado@clix.pt; includes breakfast; ❹); the stylish *O Facho* (☎262 979 110; includes breakfast; no credit cards; ❺), overlooking the Atlantic breakers at the road's end; and *Quinta da Foz* (☎262 979 369; includes breakfast; no credit cards; ❻), 1km before the village and only 500m from the lagoon, a lovely sixteenth-century country-house hotel with just five rooms.

São Martinho do Porto

SÃO MARTINHO DO PORTO is the main resort between Peniche and Nazaré, and one of the more developed spots along this stretch of Estremaduran coast. However, it's both low-key and largely low-rise and, compared with Peniche and Nazaré, an easy-going place favoured by families. Even so, in high season you will struggle to find a room – or even a place in the campsite.

The reason for São Martinho's success is its beach, a vast sweep of sand that curls around an almost landlocked bay to form a natural swimming pool, where sardine boats bob before the quay. This shelter makes it one of the warmest places to swim on the west coast, with the sands sloping down into calm, shallow water.

For something more bracing – or less crowded – there's a good northern beach on the open Atlantic coastline beyond the bay. (Beware of the Atlantic beaches beyond the bay; they can be dangerous.)

You can check with the **turismo** at the far end of seafront main drag, Avenida Marginal (May–Sept Mon–Fri 10am–1pm & 3–7pm, Sat & Sun 9am–1pm & 3–6pm; Oct–April Mon–Fri 10am–1pm & 2–6pm; ☎262 989 110) about the possibility of **accommodation** in private rooms. Alternatively, try *Residencial Atlântica*, Rua Miguel Bombarda 6 (☎262 989 151, ℉262 980 163; includes breakfast; no credit cards; ❺), an attractive place two blocks from the seafront; or nearby *Residencial Concha*, on Largo Vitorino Froís (☎262 985 010, ℉262 985 011; includes breakfast; ❺), which is a comfortable hotel with satellite TV and room balconies. There's also a **campsite**, *Colina do Sol* (☎262 989 764), 2km to the north, off the Nazaré road (N242), and more central but less attractive pitches in the *Baía Azul* caravan park (☎262 989 188) on Avenida Marginal.

The **restaurants** all serve solid home-cooked fare; one of the better options is the *Carvalho*, attached to the *Residencial Atlântica*. The seafood's good at *O Farol* (☎262 989 399), overlooking the beach on Avenida Marginal. *O Largo* at Largo Vitorino Froís 21 (no phone) is the place for moderately priced grilled meats and fresh fish; while *Café Baia* on Rua Vasco da Gama (☎262 989 129), behind the turismo, has a menu of cheap chicken and pork dishes.

Nazaré

After years of advertising itself as the most picturesque seaside village in Portugal, **NAZARÉ** has more or less destroyed itself. In summer, the crowds are far too heavy for the place to cope with and the enduring characteristics are not so much "gentle traditions" as trinket stalls and high prices with a touch of hard-edged hustle. While elderly local women still don traditional headscarves and embroidered aprons, their immense trays of fish have been replaced by signs touting rooms; the only nets mended on the beach are miniature souvenirs for tourists; and the sardine boats long ago dropped anchor in a new harbour, fifteen minutes' walk from the town. As long as you don't expect yesteryear nostalgia or a cosy village, and are steeled for peak-season crowds, Nazaré is enjoyable enough, with all the restaurants, facilities and knockabout cheer of a busy beach resort.

The village and beaches

The original settlement was not at Nazaré but at Sítio, 110m up the rock face above the present sprawl of holiday apartment buildings. It's a location that was the legacy of pirate raids, which continued well into the nineteenth century. However, legend has a different explanation, telling of a twelfth-century knight, Dom Fuas Roupinho, who, while out hunting, was led up the cliff by a deer. The deer dived into the void and Dom Fuas was saved from following by the timely vision of **Nossa Senhora da Nazaré**, in whose name a church was subsequently built.

You can reach the church and the surrounding Sítio district by taking the **funicular** (daily 7.15am–2am; €0.70 one-way), which rumbles up to a *miradouro* at the top. The shrine itself is unimpressive, despite an icon carved by St Joseph and painted by St Luke (a handy partnership active throughout Europe). However, the church hosts a well-attended *romaria* (Sept 8–10) with

Aleluia Av. da República 38 ☏ 262 561 967. A basic place but always busy with locals eating from a menu strong on fish or simply sipping a *bica*. Moderate.

Aquário Largo das Caldeiras 13 ☏ 262 561 070. One of a cluster of establishments in a pretty square, this bar-cum-restaurant has indoor pool tables and outdoor dining. Inexpensive.

Bartidor Rua das Abegoarias 9 ☏ 262 188 406. Excellent side-street seafood joint – try the delicious *arroz de lulas con camarão*, a rich rice-based stew of squid and shrimps. Moderate.

Casa Lazaro Rua Adrião Batalha 3 ☏ 262 551 293. Simple, tiled place by the seafront with shellfish specials – lobster, shrimp and spider crab – plus an excellent house wine. Moderate.

O Casalinho Pr. Sousa Oliveira 7 ☏ 262 551 328. Al fresco dining in the square, or in the bright dining room. Service is with a smile. Moderate.

A Celeste Av. da República 54 ☏ 262 551 695. Well-priced fish and steaks served overlooking the beach, plus egg-and-chip breakfasts. Moderate.

A Sardinha Largo de Nossa Senhora de Nazaré 45, Sítio ☏ 262 553 391. Unpretentious seafood restaurant near the church. Wait for a table to sample what some swear are the finest grilled sardines in the region. Moderate.

Listings

Ambulance Call ☏ 262 561 300.

Hospital The town hospital is up at Sítio on Rua do Alão ☏ 262 550 100.

Internet Access at espaçoInternet in the Centro Cultural, Av. Manuel Remigio (Mon–Fri 9.30am–1pm, 3–7pm & 9pm–midnight). More central terminals are at Online, Centro Commerical, Pr. Sousa Oliveira (Mon–Sat 10am–midnight, Sun 2pm–midnight). There is also a terminal in the post office (see below).

Pharmacy Farmácia Silvério and Farmácia dos Pescadores are both at the bottom of Rua Adrião Batalha, just up from the turismo.

Police Headquarters is on Av. Vieria Guimarães ☏ 262 551 268.

Post office Rua da Independência 2. Mon–Fri 9am–12.30pm & 2.30–6pm, Sat 9am–noon.

Surfing Clube Desportos Alternativos da Nazaré ☏ 964 304 736, ✉ cdan@mail.pt, offers surfing and bodyboarding lessons – a one-hour lesson costs €20 for one person or €12 per person for two.

Taxis You'll find them along Av. da República, or call ☏ 262 551 363.

Alcobaça

The Cistercian monastery at **ALCOBAÇA** was founded in 1153 by Dom Henrique to celebrate his victory over the Moors at Santarém six years earlier. Building started soon after and by the end of the thirteenth century it was the most powerful monastery in the country. Owning vast tracts of farmland, orchards and vineyards, it was immensely rich and held jurisdiction over a dozen towns and three seaports. Its church and cloister are the purest and the most inspired creation of all Portuguese Gothic architecture and, alongside Belém and Batalha, are the most impressive monuments in the country. The church is also the burial place of those romantic figures of Portuguese history, Dom Pedro and Dona Inês de Castro.

Not all of the monastery by any means is open to the public – and parts of it are currently occupied by an old people's home – but what there is to see could comfortably occupy a half-day's visit. Alcobaça itself is a small and fairly unmemorable town, but though it's no longer a hive of activity, it's not a bad place to stay the night. The ruined hilltop **castle** provides the best overall view of the monastery, otherwise the only other point of interest is the **Museu do Vinho** (Tues–Sun 9am–noon & 2–5.30pm; in winter Mon–Fri only; free), ten minutes' walk from the bus station on the Leiria road, which gives a fascinating glimpse into the area's wine-making and agricultural past. Guided tours last about an hour and provide opportunities to purchase local tipples.

Mosteiro de Alcobaça

The **Mosteiro de Alcobaça** (daily: April–Sept 9am–7pm; Oct–March 9am–5pm; last entry 30min before closing; €4.50, free Sun before 2pm, entry to church free), although empty since its dissolution in 1834 and marooned behind traffic on the town's main thoroughfare, still seems to assert power, magnificence and opulence. And it takes little imagination to people it again with monks, said once to have numbered 999. It was their legendary extravagant and aristocratic lifestyle that formed the common ingredients of the awed anecdotes of eighteenth-century travellers. Even English writer William Beckford, no stranger to high living, found their decadence unsettling, growing weary of "perpetual gormandizing . . . the fumes of banquets and incense . . . the fat waddling monks and sleek friars with wanton eyes". Another contemporary observer, Richard Twiss, for his part found "the bottle went as briskly about as ever I saw it do in Scotland" – a tribute indeed. For all the "high romps" and luxuriance, though, it has to be added that the monks enjoyed a reputation for hospitality, generosity and charity, while the surrounding countryside is to this day one of the most productive areas in Portugal, thanks to their agricultural expertise.

The abbey church

The main **abbey church**, modelled on the original Cistercian abbey at Citeaux in France, is the largest in Portugal. External impressions are disappointing, as the Gothic facade has been superseded by unexceptional Baroque additions of the seventeenth and eighteenth centuries. Inside, however, all later adornments have been swept away, restoring the narrow soaring aisles to their original simplicity. The only exception to this Gothic purity is the frothy Manueline doorway to the sacristy, hidden directly behind the high altar and encrusted with intricate, swirling motifs of coral and seaweed.

The church's most precious treasures are the fourteenth-century **tombs of Dom Pedro and Dona Inês de Castro**, each occupying one of the transepts and sculpted with a phenomenal wealth of detail. Animals, heraldic emblems, musicians and biblical scenes are all portrayed in an architectural setting of miniature windows, canopies, domes and towers; most graphic of all is a dragon-shaped Hell's mouth at Inês' feet, consuming the damned. The tombs are inscribed with the motto "Até ao Fim do Mundo" (Until the End of the World) and, in accordance with Dom Pedro's orders, have been placed foot to foot so that on the Day of Judgement the pair may rise and immediately feast their eyes on one another.

Pedro's earthly love for Inês de Castro, the great theme of epic Portuguese poetry, was cruelly stifled by high politics. Inês, as the daughter of a Galician nobleman, was a potential source of Spanish influence over the Portuguese throne and Pedro's father, Afonso IV, forbade their marriage. The ceremony took place nevertheless – secretly at Bragança in remote Trás-os-Montes – and eventually Afonso was persuaded to sanction his daughter-in-law's murder. When Pedro succeeded to the throne in 1357 he brought the murderers to justice, personally ripping out their hearts and gorging his love-crazed appetite for blood upon them. More poignantly, he also exhumed and crowned the corpse of his lover, forcing the entire royal circle to acknowledge her as queen by kissing her decomposing hand.

The kitchen

Alcobaça's feasting has already been mentioned but the **kitchen** – with its cellars and gargantuan conical chimney, supported by eight trunk-like iron columns – sets it in perspective. A stream tapped from the River Alcôa still runs straight through the room: it was used not only for cooking and washing but also to provide a constant supply of fresh fish, which plopped out into a stone basin. At the centre of the room, on the vast wooden tables, Beckford marvelled at:

... pastry in vast abundance which a numerous tribe of lay brothers and their attendants were rolling out and puffing up into a hundred different shapes, singing all the while as blithely as larks in a cornfield. "There," said the Lord Abbot, "we shall not starve. God's bounties are great, it is fit we should enjoy them."

And enjoy them they did, with a majestic feast of "rarities and delicacies, potted lampreys, strange Brazilian messes, edible birds' nests and sharks' fins dressed after the mode of Macau by a Chinese lay brother". As a practical test for obesity the monks had to file through a narrow door on their way to the refectory; those who failed were forced to fast until they could squeeze through.

The cloisters and Sala dos Reis

The **Claustro do Silencio** (Cloisters of Silence), notable for their traceried stone windows, were built in the reign of Dom Dinis, the "poet-king" who established an enduring literary and artistic tradition at the abbey. An upper storey of twisted columns and Manueline arches was added in the sixteenth century, along with – in its standard position opposite the refectory – a beautiful hexagonal lavatory.

The **Sala dos Reis** (Kings' Room), off the cloister, displays statues of virtually every king of Portugal up until Dom José, who died in 1777. Blue eighteenth-century *azulejos* depict the siege of Santarém, Dom Afonso's vow, and the founding of the monastery. Also on show here is a piece of war booty which must have warmed the souls of the brothers – the huge metal cauldron in which soup was heated up for the Spanish army before the battle of Aljubarrota in 1385 (for more of which, see "Batalha" on p.179).

Practicalities

The **bus station** is five minutes' walk from the centre of town, across the bridge; coming into town, bear right and head towards the abbey towers. There are reasonably frequent connections to Nazaré, Batalha and Leiria. A useful first stop is the **turismo** (daily: May–Sept 10am–1pm & 3–7pm; Oct–April 10am–1pm & 2–6pm; T 262 582 377) opposite the monastery on the central Praça 25 de Abril. It can supply maps of the town, advise on accommodation and onward transport, and provides **internet access** (free for first 15min).

Alcobaça has a limited but relatively inexpensive choice of **accommodation** around Praça 25 de Abril. **Restaurants** and **cafés** line the road that wraps around the monastery – the most pleasant spot for an al fresco lunch (if you can blank out the traffic) is the leafy Praça Dom Afonso Henriques.

Hotels and pensions

Challet Fonte Nova Palacete Rua da Fonte Nova T 262 598 300, W www.challetfontenova.pt. A superb boutique hotel with luxurious rooms – those on the first floor are classiest, those in an annexe have larger bathrooms – in an aristocratic nineteenth-century villa furnished with antiques. The house is secreted on a back street, and reached via Rua Eng. Duarte Pacheco beside the turismo. Breakfast and free bar included. **6**

Pensão Corações Unides Rua Frei António Brandão 39 T & F 262 582 142. Large rooms in a dated but friendly hotel just off Pr. 25 de Abril – those at the front can be noisy. The restaurant below is well thought of. Breakfast included. **3**

Hotel Santa Maria Rua Dr. Francisco Zagalo 20 T 262 590 160, F 262 590 161. A modern hotel whose front rooms have grandstand views of the monastery. Parking available, breakfast included. **4**

Cafés and restaurants

Celeiro dos Frades Rua Arcos Cister 2–6, under the arches alongside the abbey ☎ 262 582 281. Atmospheric dining beneath the arches of the "monks' barn", worth a visit just for a coffee or to try the house speciality *frango*. Closed Thurs. Moderate.

Frei Bernardo Rua Dom Pedro V 17–19 ☎ 262 582 227. A little touristy – there's folk dancing on some evenings – but tasty dishes nonetheless, served in portion sizes the decadent monks would have approved of. Try the lamb stew laced with red wine. Moderate.

O Telheiro Rua da Levadinha ☎ 262 596 029. A top-notch restaurant beyond the *Hotel Santa Maria*, decorated with *azulejos* and with a palm-fringed terrace. Choose from daily meat specials and the regional wine list. Closed Sat. Expensive.

Leiria

Thirty-five kilometres north of Alcobaça, a royal castle hangs almost vertically above the large town of **LEIRIA**, whose graceful old town is a place of cobbled streets, attractive gardens and fine old squares – cocooned within admittedly dull modern outskirts. If you are travelling around on public transport, you will probably want to make it your base for a couple of nights because the three big sites of northern Estremadura – Alcobaça, Batalha and Fátima – are easy day-trips by bus. As a student town Leiria also has enough good restaurants and bars to make the evenings go with a swing, while it's also handily poised for the fine beaches of the Pinhal de Leiria to the west.

Leiria was the main residence of Dom Dinis, who gave the town as a wedding gift to his beloved Queen Isabel, along with Óbidos, Abrantes, Porto de Mós and Trancoso. At the heart of the old town is **Praça Rodrigues Lobo**, surrounded by beautiful arcaded buildings and dominated by a splendidly pompous statue of the eponymous seventeenth-century local poet. In fact, Leiria's literary connections go back much further than this – in 1480, the town had one of Portugal's first printing presses, which was run by Jews who printed in Hebrew.

Leiria's **Castelo** (April–Sept Tues–Sun 10am–6.30pm; Oct–March Tues–Sun 9am–5.30pm; €2) was once one of the most important strongholds in Moorish Portugal, reconquered by Afonso Henriques as he fought his way south in 1135. The actual building you see today dates mostly from the fourteenth and eighteenth centuries. Within its walls stands a royal palace, with a magnificent balcony high above the Rio Lis, and a small museum (closed noon–1pm) containing the usual displays of armour and archeological finds. The walls also contain the church of **Nossa Senhora da Penha**, erected by João I in about 1400 and now reduced to an eerie, roofless shell. Nearby, on Largo de Sé, is the town's sixteenth-century **Sé**, which was built under the reign of Dom João III and has three naves. It was designed by Afonso Alvares, who worked on the São Roque in Lisbon.

Practicalities

The **train station** (services from Figueira da Foz and Lisbon) is 4km north of town, a cheap taxi ride away. Arriving by **bus**, you'll be dropped in the centre at a modern terminal on Avenida Heróis de Angola, but with another entrance on Praça Paulo VI. Across the Jardim Luís de Camões, on Praça Goa Damão e Diu, is the helpful **turismo** (daily: May–Sept 10am–1pm & 3–7pm; Oct–Apr 2–6pm; ☎ 244 814 770, ⓦ www.rt-leiriafatima.pt), which dispenses maps. Pricey metered **parking** is available on Largo de 5 Outubro and at the west end of Jardim Luís de Camões. Less central but cheaper is the large car park to

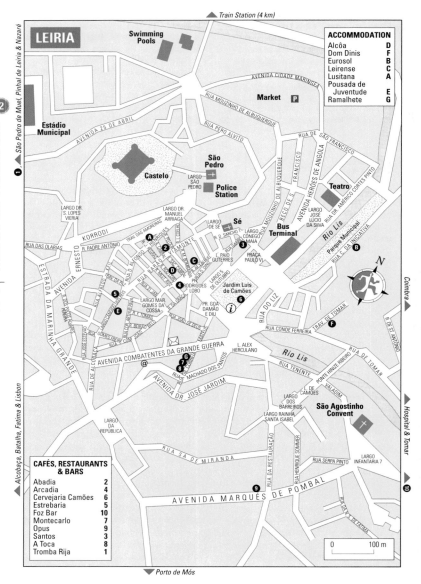

the north, beside the market, or you may strike lucky and find a free space in Largo Dr. Serafim Lopes Vieria, directly west of the castle.

Accommodation

For budget accommodation, make your way to Praça Rodrigues Lobo and look around here and on the narrow side streets, like Rua Mestre de Aviz and

Rua Miguel Bombarda. More cheap rooms are to be found in Largo Paio Guterres and Largo Cónego Maia, both near the cathedral. There's also a well-appointed **youth hostel** in town.

Hotels and pensions

Pensão Alcôa Rua Rodrigues Cordeiro 24–26 ☏244 832 690. Just off the main square with smallish, clean rooms with TVs. There's a good restaurant, too, and the price includes breakfast. No credit cards. ❸

Residencial Dom Dinis Trav. de Tomar 2 ☏244 815 342, ℻244 823 552. Across the bridge from the turismo, and with a drab exterior but more character inside. Rooms are double-glazed and have heating, there's a pleasant roof terrace and parking. Breakfast included. ❸

Eurosol Residence Rua Comissão da Iniciativa 13 ☏244 860 460, ⓦ www.eurosolresidence.com. Leiria's first four-star provides stylish, modern apartments (studios, one- and two-bedroom) that make an excellent base for forays to the region's attractions. It also offers a gym, swimming pool and parking. ❺

Pensão Residencial Leirense Rua Afonso de Albuquerque 6 ☏244 823 054, ℻244 823 073.

A firm favourite for some years, though service can be a little off at times. Excellent location, though, and good value for money. Breakfast included. ❸

Hospedaria Lusitana Rua D. Afonso Henriques 24 ☏244 815 698, ℻244 767 640. Homely en-suite rooms, spotless and with traditional dark wood furniture, in a friendly place near Largo Cândido dos Reis. No credit cards. ❷

Residencial Ramalhete Rua Dr. Correia Mateus 30 ☏244 812 802, ℻244 815 099. A large, bright *residencial* whose rooms are far more comfortable than the jaded exterior suggests; those at the rear are quieter. ❸

Youth hostel

Pousada de Juventude Largo Cândido dos Reis 9 ☏244 831 868, ⓦ www.pousadasjuventude.pt. One of the nicest in the country, fashioned from a grand old house retaining its period features. Dorm beds €11.

Eating, drinking and nightlife

Surprisingly, for such an otherwise agreeable town, Leiria's historic centre lacks good **restaurants**; a cluster of options on Rua Correia Mateus makes the best grazing ground. September is the ideal time to sample the region's cuisine, when the **Festival de Gastronomia** fills up the restored Mercado Sant'Ana on Rua Correia Mateus with row upon row of food stalls. The best place for a drink and a snack is at one of the **cafés** and **bars** around Largo Cândido dos Reis, which also give you the chance to take in Leiria's lively streetlife.

Cafés and restaurants

Pastelaria Arcadia Pr. Rodrigues Lobo no phone. Under the arches in the main square, making it a good place to people-watch at outdoor tables over breakfast or coffee. Inexpensive.

Cervejaria Camões Jardim Luís de Camões ☏244 838 628. Floor-to-ceiling windows provide pleasant views over the park to accompany snacks, drinks and tasty steaks, the latter pepped up with *queijo da serra* or garlic and ginger. Moderate.

Restaurante Montecarlo Rua Dr. Correia Mateus 32–34 ☏244 825 406. An unpretentious café-restaurant with a €9 *ementa turística*. Closed Sun. Inexpensive.

Pastelaria Santos Largo Paio Guterres ☏244 832 467. Small dishes of *bacalhau* and *porco* at low prices, plus the usual pastries and coffee. Inexpensive.

A Toca Rua Dr. Correia Mateus ☏244 832 221. Large portions of traditional well-cooked fare – the *bife a vaca* arrives sizzling in an earthenware dish and the *lulas grelhado* is excellent. It's the best restaurant on the street. Closed Sat. Moderate.

Tromba Rija Rua Professores Portela 22, Marrazes 22 ☏244 855 072. One of Portugal's most famous restaurants, a rustic charmer with *bacalhau* and roast *cabrito* that are worth every euro. It's located out of town on the Marrazes road; go west under the N1 and turn left after the Casa da Palmeira. Closed Sun & Mon. Expensive.

Bars

Abadia Rua Barão Viamonte 43. For the fashion-conscious, a slick late-night restaurant-bar with DJs.

Bar Estrebaria Largo Cândido dos Reis 23. Small but buzzy locals' bar on Leiria's favourite square.

Foz Bar Margem Esquerda do Rio Liz. Southeast of town, by the river. Dance music until 4am and occasional live bands.

Opus Av. Marqués de Pombal 23. A local institution which distributes its own magazine and booms to house and techno till 2am.

Listings

Ambulance Bombeiros Voluntários ☎ 244 832 122 or ☎ 244 881 120.

Banks and exchange Millennium has a branch on Pr. Rodrigues Lobo, others congregate on Pr. Goa Damão e Diu, facing the turismo. Cotacâbios at Rua Machalo Santos 31 has a currency exchange.

Car rental Avis, Av. D. José C. Silva (in Eurosol Residence) ☎ 244 827 131; Hertz, Av. Marquês de Pombal, Lote 2 ☎ 244 826 781; Raide, Av. Cidade Maringea, Arcadas D. João III ☎ 244 813 692.

Hospital Hospital Distrital de Sto André, Rua das Olhalvas ☎ 244 817 000.

Internet Arquivo bookshop, Av. Combatentes da Grande Guerra (Mon–Sat 9.30am–10.30pm, Sun 2.30–7.30pm).

Pharmacy Farmácia Baptista, Largo 5 de Outubro 33–34 ☎ 244 832 320.

Police Police headquarters is before the castle on Largo São Pedro ☎ 244 820 010.

Pinhal de Leiria and its beaches

Some of the most idyllic spots on the stretch of coast west of Leiria are in the **Pinhal de Leiria** (or Pinhal do Rei), a vast 700-year-old pine forest stretching from São Pedro de Moel to Pedrógão. Although there were always trees here, the "Royal Pine Forest" was planned by Dom Dinis, a king renowned for his agrarian reforms, to protect fertile arable land from the menacing inward march of sand dunes. It has since grown into an area of great natural beauty, with sunlight filtering through endless miles of trees and the air perfumed with the scent of resin. The **turismo** (Mon–Sat 10am–1pm & 3–7pm; ☎ 244 566 644) in the glass museum at Marinha Grande, 12km west of Leiria and halfway to the coast, can supply maps of the forest if you want to make your way through its grid-like tracks on foot. It's another 10km from Marinha Grande to the coast, where the **beaches** are, for the most part, superb – largely spared development and with pollution-free sea.

São Pedro de Moel and around

The nearest beach to Leiria is at **SÃO PEDRO DE MOEL**, 22km to the west, a laid-back resort where old buildings have been renovated and new ones erected with an eye for tradition. It's a pleasant place to stay, although the small town struggles with crowds in peak season. If the Atlantic breakers are too fierce to swim, you can try one of the swimming pools situated above the beach.

Buses from Leiria involve a change at Marinha Grande. There are regular buses in summer, but the service is less frequent outside the holiday season. **Accommodation** should be no problem, even in high season, since there are more than a dozen *pensões* and hotels. The seasonal **turismo** (May–Sept daily 10am–1pm & 3–7pm; ☎ 244 599 633) at the top of the village by the roundabout lists all options. Otherwise, try the seafront *Mar e Sol* (☎ 244 590 000, ⓦ www.hotelmaresol.com; includes breakfast; ❸), though it's a bit dated, or the friendly *Residencial D. Fernando I*, Rua D. Fernando I 19 (☎ 244 599 314; includes breakfast; no credit cards; ❹), a small place five minutes' walk north of the turismo. There are two **campsites**: the nearest is the *Orbitur* site (☎ 244 599 168, ⓦ www.orbitur.pt), just above the turismo, packed in season; while

1km to the north and less expensive is an *Inatel* site (☎244 599 289, ℻244 599 550; closed mid-Dec to mid-Jan).

Excellent **restaurants** abound, among them the superb *Brisamar*, Rua Dr. Nicolau Bettencourt 23 (☎244 599 520), and cheaper *A Fonte*, on Praçeta Afonso Lopes Vieira (☎244 599 479), both of which specialize in seafood, as does the more upmarket *A Concha*, Rua Duquesa de Caminha 16 (☎244 599 150; closed Thurs). However, for sunsets and sea views, *Estrela do Mar* (☎244 599 245; closed Thurs in winter) is hard to beat, situated right above the breakers on the main beach. For breakfast, try *Café Central* (no phone) on Rua Dr. Alfonso Leitão, where you can relax outside on wicker chairs.

South of São Pedro are other sheltered stretches of beach, like at **ÁGUA DE MADEIROS**, 3km away, where the friendly *Residencial Água de Madeiros* (☎244 599 324, ✉agua.madeiros@mail.telepac.pt; includes breakfast; ❺) sits above often deserted sands; there are just twelve rooms so advance booking is recommended. A further 3km south, wild campers congregate around **PAREDES DA VITÓRIA**, another quiet spot, though here you're no longer in the forest.

A couple of kilometres north of the lighthouse at São Pedro, **PRAIA VELHA** is a popular local beach – mainly because of the chance to swim in the small lake behind the beach. It's also worth a visit for its **restaurant**, *O Pai dos Frangos* (☎244 599 158), which prepares sensational mixed kebabs.

Praia da Vieira and Pedrógoã

Ten kilometres to the north of Praia Velha, **PRAIA DA VIEIRA** and the main town of **VIEIRA DE LEIRIA** (the latter 3km inland) are on the estuary of the Rio Liz and are notable for their fish restaurants. Praia da Vieira is served by a patchy bus service from Marinha Grande and has sprawled into a rather brash resort, saved by a superb beach. For accommodation, try first at the seafront *Estrela do Mar* (☎ & ℻244 695 404; breakfast included; ❸) or its sister hotel *Ouro Verde* (☎244 695 931; breakfast included; ❸) on the main road. Smarter rooms are available in *Hotel Cristal Veira Praia* (☎244 699 060, ✉cristalvieria@hoteiscristal.pt; breakfast included; ❺) on the seafront, and this also has a swimming pool and parking for guests. Alternatively, the seasonal **turismo** (Tues–Sun 10am–1pm & 3–7pm; ☎244 695 230) can recommend places to stay. Of the resort's several **restaurants**, one of the finest is *Solemar* beneath the *Estrela do Mar,* highly rated by locals.

PEDRÓGOÃ, 6km further to the north, also has a rash of modern development spread around another fantastic expanse of beach still used by fishermen to launch boats. There's a great **campsite** (☎244 695 403; closed mid-Dec to Jan) in the woods, while in town there are several restaurants and a seasonal **turismo** (July & Aug Tues–Sun 10am–1pm & 3–7pm; ☎244 695 411), which holds information about private rooms.

Batalha and around

Eleven kilometres south of Leiria, the Mosteiro de Santa Maria da Vitória, better known as **Batalha** (Battle Abbey), is the supreme achievement of Portuguese architecture – the dazzling richness and originality of its Manueline decoration rivalled only by the Mosteiro dos Jerónimos at Belém, with which it shares UNESCO world monument status. An exuberant symbol of national pride, it was built to commemorate the battle that sealed Portugal's independence after decades of Spanish intrigue.

With the death of Dom Fernando in 1383, the royal house of Burgundy died out, and there followed a period of feverish factional plotting over the Portuguese throne. Fernando's widow, Leonor Teles, had a Spanish lover even during her husband's lifetime and, when Fernando died, she betrothed her daughter, Beatriz, to Juan I of Castile, encouraging his claim to the Portuguese throne. João, Mestre de Aviz, Fernando's illegitimate stepbrother, also claimed the throne. He assassinated Leonor's lover and braced himself for the inevitable invasion from Spain. The two armies clashed on August 14, 1385, at the **Battle of Aljubarrota**, which despite its name was actually fought at São Jorge (see p.182), 10km northeast of Aljubarrota and just 4km south of present-day Batalha. Faced with seemingly impossible odds, João struck a deal with the Virgin Mary, promising to build a magnificent abbey in return for her military assistance. It worked: Nuno Álvares Pereira led the Portuguese forces to a memorable victory and the new king duly summoned the finest architects of the day.

The abbey has spawned a modern village and is rattled by the N1 highway from Lisbon to Coimbra, which runs across an embankment perilously close to the building. Despite years of campaigning, no plans to shift the road have been forthcoming, and the vibrations and fumes are gradually taking their toll. Furthermore, the abbey is showing its age; built largely of limestone, it's increasingly affected by acid rain.

The Abbey

The honey-coloured **Abbey** (daily: April–Sept 9am–6.30pm; Oct–March 9am–5.30pm; last entry 30min before closing; main church free, cloisters €4.50, free Sun before 2pm) was transformed by the uniquely Portuguese Manueline additions of the late fifteenth and early sixteenth centuries, but the bulk of the building was actually completed between 1388 and 1434 in a profusely ornate version of French Gothic. Pinnacles, parapets, windows and flying buttresses are all lavishly and intricately sculpted. Within this flamboyant framework there are also strong elements of the English Perpendicular style. Huge pilasters and prominent vertical decorations divide the main facade; the nave, with its narrow soaring dimensions, and the chapterhouse are reminiscent of church architecture in the English cathedral cities of Winchester and York.

Capela do Fundador

Medieval architects were frequently attracted by lucrative foreign commissions, but there is a special explanation for the English influence at Batalha. This is revealed in the **Capela do Fundador** (Founder's Chapel), directly to the right upon entering the church. Beneath the octagonal lantern rests the joint tomb of Dom João I and Philippa of Lancaster, their hands clasped in the ultimate expression of harmonious relations between Portugal and England.

In 1373, Dom Fernando had entered into an alliance with John of Gaunt, Duke of Lancaster, who claimed the Spanish throne by virtue of his marriage to a daughter of Pedro the Cruel, king of Castile. A crack contingent of English longbowmen had played a significant role in the victory at Aljubarrota and in 1386 both countries willingly signed the **Treaty of Windsor**, "an inviolable, eternal, solid, perpetual and true league of friendship". As part of the same political package Dom João married Philippa, John of Gaunt's daughter, and with her came English architects to assist at Batalha. The alliance between the two countries, reconfirmed by the marriage of Charles II to Catherine of Bragança in 1661 and the Methuen Commercial Treaty of 1703, has become the longest-standing international friendship of modern times – it was invoked by the Allies in World War II to establish bases on the Azores and the facilities of those islands were offered to the British Navy during the 1982 Falklands war.

The four younger sons of João and Philippa are buried along the south wall of the Capela do Fundador in a row of recessed arches. Second from the right is the **tomb of Prince Henry the Navigator**, who guided the discovery of Madeira, the Azores and the African coast as far as Sierra Leone. Henry himself never ventured further than Tangiers but it was a measure of his personal importance, drive and expertise that the growth of the empire was temporarily shelved after his death in 1460.

Concerted maritime exploration resumed under João II (1481–95) and accelerated with the accession of Manuel I (1495–1521). Vasco da Gama opened up the trade route to India in 1498, Cabral reached Brazil two years later and Newfoundland was discovered in 1501. The momentous era of burgeoning self-confidence, wealth and widening horizons is reflected in the peculiarly Portuguese style of architecture known (after the king) as Manueline (see box on p.191). As befitted the great national shrine, Batalha was adapted to incorporate two masterpieces of the new order: the Royal Cloister and the so-called Unfinished Chapels.

Claustro Real and Sala do Capítulo

In the **Claustro Real** (Royal Cloister), stone grilles of ineffable beauty and intricacy were added to the original Gothic windows by Diogo de Boitaca, architect of the cloister at Belém and the prime genius of Manueline art. Crosses of the Order of Christ and armillary spheres – symbols of overseas exploration – are entwined in a network of lotus blossom, briar branches and exotic vegetation.

Off the east side opens the early fifteenth-century **Sala do Capítulo** (chapterhouse), remarkable for the audacious unsupported span of its ceiling – so daring, in fact, that the Church authorities were convinced the whole chamber would come crashing down and employed condemned criminals to build it. The architect, Afonso Domingues, only finally silenced his critics by sleeping in the chamber night after night. Soldiers now stand guard here over Portugal's **Tomb of the Unknown Warriors**, one killed in France during World War I, the other in the country's colonial wars in Africa. The **refectory**, on the opposite side of the cloister, houses a military museum in their honour. From here, a short passage leads into the **Claustro de Dom Afonso V**, built in a conventional Gothic style, which provides a yardstick against which to measure the Manueline flamboyance of the Royal Cloister.

Capelas Imperfeitas

The **Capelas Imperfeitas** (Unfinished Chapels) form a separate structure tacked on to the east end of the church and accessible only from outside the main complex. Dom Duarte, eldest son of João and Philippa, commissioned them in 1437 as a royal mausoleum but, as with the cloister, the original design was transformed beyond all recognition by Dom Manuel's architects. The portal rises to a towering fifteen metres and every centimetre is carved with a honeycomb of mouldings: florid projections, clover-shaped arches, strange vegetables; there are even stone snails. The place is unique among Christian architecture and evocative of the great shrines of Islam and Hinduism: perhaps it was inspired by the tales of Indian monuments that filtered back along the eastern trade routes. It is a perfect illustration of the variety and uninhibited excitement of Portuguese art during the Age of Discovery.

The architect of this masterpiece was Mateus Fernandes, whose tomb lies directly outside the entrance to the Capela do Fundador. Within the portal, a large octagonal space is surrounded by seven hexagonal chapels, two of which contain the sepulchres of Dom Duarte and his queen, Leonor of Aragon. An ambitious upper storey – equal in magnificence to the portal – was designed by Diogo de Boitaca, but the huge buttresses were abandoned a few years later in 1533.

Practicalities

Buses (from Leiria, Fatima and Lisbon) stop on the central Largo 14 de Agosto de 1385, at the end of which the Batalha is visible, standing alone surrounded by a bare concrete expanse. There's a friendly **turismo** located directly opposite the abbey's entrance (May–Sept daily 9am–1pm & 3–7pm; Oct–April daily 9am–1pm & 2–6pm; ☎244 765 180), but not much else here except a sprinkling of tourist shops, bars and restaurants, which enjoy brisk business during the Fátima weekend in early October, when the place is packed.

The cheaper **accommodation** is snapped up quickly in high season. Either book ahead or look for private rooms above restaurants and bars. The best places for a snack or lunch are in the **cafés** that flank the concrete expanse on the southern side of the abbey.

Hotels and pensions

Residencial Batalha Largo da Igreja ☎244 767 500, ⓦwww.hotel-batalha.com. Comfortable, if a little dated – the rooms have air conditioning, minibar and satellite TV. Breakfast included. ❸
Casa do Outeiro Largo Carvalho 4 ☎244 765 806, ⓦwww.casadoouteiro.com. A small and stylish boutique hotel with a swimming pool. All 15 rooms are bright and modern and have a terrace. Breakfast included. ❹
Residencial Gladius Pr. Mousinho de Albuquerque 7 ☎244 765 760, ⓕ244 767 259. Charming en-suite rooms, with wicker furniture and tasteful modern fabrics – excellent value for money. No credit cards. ❸
Pousada do Mestre Afonso Domingues Largo Mestre Afonso Domingues ☎244 765 260, ⓦwww.pousadas.pt. Leisured luxury in the village's premiere address, where the elegant rooms are furnished with antiques. The restaurant (expensive, though €25 set-menu available) is

excellent, serving gourmet dishes like sea bass seasoned with coriander and olive oil. Breakfast included. ❼
Pensão Vitória Largo da Misericórdia ☎244 765 678. Small, basic rooms above a restaurant beside the bus station. ❶

Cafés and restaurants

Os Carlos Largo Goa, Damão e Diu 2 ☎244 768 207. Set back from the cafés before the abbey, this has good-value Portuguese food, though you'll push the boat out if you opt for the *lombinhona pedra guarnecido*, fillet steak grilled on stone (€15). Closed Tues. Moderate.
Mestre Afonso Largo Mestre Afonso Domingues 4 ☎244 765 601. A spacious bar-restaurant serving good grilled meats and snacks. Moderate.
Pastelaria Oliveira Pr. Dom João I no phone. A quieter spot from which to marvel at the abbey's splendour over decadent cakes and pastries. Inexpensive.

São Jorge: the battle site

The Battle of Aljubarrota was fought on a plain 10km northeast of Aljubarrota itself, at the small hamlet of **SÃO JORGE**, 4km south of Batalha. When the fighting was over a small chapel was built and remains at the entrance to the village today. The battle lasted only one hour, but it was a hot day and the commander of the victorious Portuguese forces, Nuno Álvares Pereira, complained loudly of thirst; a jug of fresh water is still placed daily in the porch of the chapel in his memory. Legend has it that Aljubarrota itself was defended by its baker, Brites de Almeida, who fended off the Castilian army with her baking spoon. This fearsome weapon dispensed with seven soldiers, whom Brites promptly baked in her oven.

The **Museu Militar** (Tues–Fri 2–5pm, Sat & Sun 10am–noon & 2–5pm; free) in São Jorge tackles the battle itself and the contemporary political intrigue, while nearby there's a frieze commemorating the battle with carved blocks of stone representing, it is said, the archers and foot soldiers.

None of this is really a good enough reason for a visit, although you can break your journey here on the way to or from Porto de Mós (see below), another 5km to the southeast.

Porto de Mós and around

Eight kilometres south of Batalha lies the small town of **Porto de Mós**, with its distinctive castle – it's also the nearest base from which to visit the fabulous underground caves at **Mira de Aire**. These lie within the **Parque Natural das Serras de Aire e Candeeiros**, a small but scenic national park to the south of Porto de Mós, which contains a mix of rugged limestone hills, crags and upland farmland divided by ancient stone walls. The N362 provides an alternative route through the park, running from Porto de Mós in the north all the way to Santarém, although the caves themselves are located in the more wooded eastern half of the park.

Porto de Mós

High above **PORTO DE MÓS**, nestled in the folds of the hills, a grandiose thirteenth-century castle stands guard. It was given to Nuno Álvares Pereira in 1385 by the grateful Dom João I, in recognition of his victory at Aljubarrota – significantly, the Portuguese army had rested here on the eve of the battle – and was later turned into a fortified palace reminiscent in scale of that at Leiria. Severely damaged in the earthquake of 1755, the **castle** (Tues–Sun 10am–12.30pm & 2–6pm; free) has been renovated piecemeal since, and now boasts rather too pristine electric-green tiled towers. The castle apart, the town itself is none too inspiring but it is the starting-point for a trip to the caves of Mira de Aire, 13km to the southeast.

The **bus terminal** is on the southern edge of town at Avenida Dr. Francisco Sá Carneiro. There are three buses to Porto de Mós from Leiria, via Batalha, and others from Alcobaça, Santarém and Nazaré (summer only), or from Batalha itself. Or you can catch any bus from Leiria or Batalha to Alcobaça/Caldas da Rainha and ask to be set down at São Jorge, just off the main N1, and take a local bus from there to Porto de Mós.

The **turismo** (May–Sept daily 10am–1pm & 3–7pm; Oct–Apr Mon–Sat 10am–1pm & 3–6pm; ☎244 491 323) is on Alameda Dom Afonso Henriques, in the local public gardens. **Cafés and restaurants** are gathered around the bus terminal, and while there's no real reason to stay you might be tempted by the serene *Quinta do Rio Alcaide* (☎244 402 124, @rioalcaide@mail.telepac.pt; ❹), a converted mill with self-catering apartments and a swimming pool, 1km out of town on the road to the caves (the N243).

Grutas de Mira de Aire

The largest, most spectacular and most accessible caves in Portugal are the **Grutas de Mira de Aire** (daily: April & May 9.30am–6pm; June & Sept

9.30am–7pm; July & Aug 9.30am–8pm; Oct–March 9.30am–5.30pm; €4.50; Ⓦ www.virtual-net.pt/grutasmiradeaire), ten minutes' walk from the bus stop in the drab textile town from which they take their name. Known locally for decades, but only open to the public since 1974, the caves comprise a fantasy land of spaghetti-like stalactites and stalagmites and bizarre rock formations with names like "Hell's Door", "Jelly Fish" and "Church Organ". Rough steps take you down and the excellent 45-minute guided tour (in Portuguese or French, even English on occasion) culminates in an extravagant fountain display in a natural lake 110m underground. You might have to wait some time for a group of acceptable size to gather. At the end of the tour, you emerge beside an aquatic park (summer only; use of its pools and slides is included in the entry fee for the caves), a great place to cool off and admire the views.

There are three daily **buses from Porto de Mós** to Mira de Aire, at 12.05pm, 2.30pm and 5.20pm. A return bus leaves Mira de Aire at 1.50pm, while the long-distance Nazaré–Torres Novas bus leaves Mira de Aire at 4.15pm and 5.15pm and stops in Porto de Mós. At weekends, there are buses from Porto de Mós at 12.05pm and 5.20pm, but no return service. A return trip by **taxi** from Porto de Mós will cost around €16, including a two-hour wait while you visit the caves.

Grutas da Moeda

East of Porto do Mós – though more easily reached from the Batalha–Fátima road (N356) – the labyrinthine **Grutas da Moeda** (daily: April–Sept 9am–6pm; Oct–March 9am–5pm; €4; Ⓦ www.grutasmoeda.com) at São Mamede are also well worth seeing, not least because one of the chambers has been converted into a bar with rock music, subtle lighting and stalactites nose-diving into your glass of beer. Buses between Batalha and Fátima can drop you off at the road junction, six kilometres west of Fátima, though without your own car it's best to arrange a taxi for the trip – again, you may have to wait for a group to form before you can enter the caves.

Fátima and around

FÁTIMA is the fountainhead of religious devotion in Portugal and one of the most important centres of pilgrimage in the Roman Catholic world. Its cult is founded on a series of six **apparitions of the Virgin Mary**, the first of which, on May 13, 1917, was to three peasant children from the village – while tending their parents' flock, they were confronted with a flash of lightning and "a lady brighter than the sun" sitting in the branches of a tree. According to the memoirs of Lúcia, the only child able to hear the Virgin's words and the only one to survive into her teens, the Lady announced: "I am from Heaven. I have come to ask you to return here six times, at this same hour, on the thirteenth of every month. Then, in October, I will tell you who I am and what I want."

News of the miracle was greeted with scepticism and only a few casual onlookers attended the second appearance, but for the third, July 13, apparition, the crowd had swollen to a few thousand. Although only the three children could see the heavenly visitor, Fátima became a *cause célèbre*, with the anticlerical government accusing the Church of fabricating a miracle to revive its flagging influence and Church authorities afraid to acknowledge what they feared was a hoax. The children were arrested and interrogated but refused to change their story.

By the date of the final appearance, October 13, as many as 70,000 people had converged on Fátima where they witnessed the so-called **Miracle of the Sun**. Eyewitnesses described the skies clearing and the sun, intensified to a blinding, swirling ball of fire, shooting beams of multicoloured light to earth. Apparently, lifelong illnesses were cured, the blind could see again and the dumb were able to speak. It was enough to convince most of the terrified witnesses. Nevertheless, the three children remained the only ones to see the Virgin and only Lúcia could communicate with her.

To her were revealed the three **Secrets of Fátima**. The first was a message of peace (this was during World War I) and a vision of Hell, with anguished, charred souls plunged into an ocean of fire. The second was more prophetic and controversial: "If you pay heed to my request," the vision declared, "Russia will be converted and there will be peace. If not, Russia will spread her errors through the world, causing wars and persecution against the Church" – all this just a few weeks before the Bolshevik takeover in St Petersburg, though not, perhaps, before it could have been predicted. After decades of speculation, the third secret was revealed in May 2000 by the Vatican. An angel "with a flaming sword in his left hand … [which] gave out flames as though they would set the world on fire" predicted the attempt on Pope John Paul II's life in 1981, fortelling of a "bishop clothed in white" who "falls to the ground, apparently dead, under a burst of gunfire". The announcement was made in Fátima during an emotional ceremony in front of more than 60,000 people. The complete text was released after "appropriate" preparation by the Vatican, whereupon conspiracy theorists pointed out inconsistencies in the commentary and Lúcia's handwriting, and muttered darkly about a forgery.

The Basilica and the Town

To commemorate the extraordinary events and to accommodate the hordes of pilgrims who flock here, a shrine was built, which has little to recommend it but size. The vast white **Basilica**, completed in 1953, and its gigantic esplanade are capable of holding more than a million devotees. Long Neoclassical colonnades flank the basilica and enclose part of the sloping esplanade in front. This huge area, reminiscent of an airport runway over which Gregorian chant wafts from flanking speakers, is twice the size of the piazza of St Peter's in Rome. On its left-hand side the original oak tree in which the Virgin appeared was long ago consumed by souvenir-hunting pilgrims; the small **Chapel of the Apparitions** now stands in its place with a new tree a few yards away. In the basilica the **tombs of Jacinta and Francisco** – Lúcia's fellow witnesses, both of whom died in the European flu epidemic of 1919–20 – are the subject of constant attention. Fátima is currently busying itself with another epic church behind the esplanade, the circular Igreja de Santissima Trindade, which, upon completion in 2007, will seat 9000 faithful pilgrims or, claim tourism authorities, have standing room for 300,000.

Whatever your feelings about the place, there is an undeniable atmosphere of mystery around it, perhaps created by nothing more than the obvious faith of the vast majority of its visitors. It's all at its most intense during the great **annual pilgrimages** on May 12–13 and October 12–13. Crowds of up to 100,000 congregate, most arriving on foot, some even walking on their knees in penance. Open-air Mass is celebrated at 5pm and an image of the Virgin is paraded by candlelight as priests move among the pilgrims hearing confessions. The fiftieth anniversary of the apparitions attracted one-and-a-half million worshippers, including Pope Paul VI and Lúcia, the latter again part of the vast crowds that greeted John Paul II here in 1982 and 1991. At the time of writing, Lúcia was still alive, crafting rosaries as a Carmelite nun, coccooned from the outside world in the Convent of Santa Teresa near Coimbra.

A multitude of hotels, car parks, hospices and convents have sprung up in the shadow of the basilica and, inevitably, the fame of Fátima has led to its commercialization. Seemingly with each year, the kitsch souvenir shops explore new territories of tackiness – look out for Fátima ballpoint pens, which tilt to reveal the Virgin in Glory. Business is particularly brisk on Sunday, when thousands of local families converge by bus, car, lorry and cart, often just for a family picnic. However, the shrine itself is not yet swamped. Make sure you catch the daily **torchlit procession** at dusk, which can be uplifting whatever your religious feelings; the procession is largest on the twelfth day of each month. There's another local pilgrimage site Reguengo do Fétal, 13km northwest, that's also host to a torchlit procession (lit by burning oil carried in shells) up to a hilltop sanctuary around October 3 each year.

The town's other attractions include the **Museu Arte Sacra e Etnologia** (Tues–Sun summer 10am–7pm, winter 10am–5pm; free) on Rua Francisco Marto, whose displays of devotional art and sculpture are organized by Christian narrative and ethnological region, and the **Museu de Cera** (daily: April–Oct 9.30am–6.30pm; Nov–March 10am–5pm; €4.50) on Rua Jacinta Marto, which relates the story of the miracle in 28 scenes of enjoyably grotesque wax figures. There is also a pleasant walk from the Rotunda de Santa Teresa de Ourém, on the outskirts of town, up to the place of the "**Apparitions of the Angel**", along which pilgrims follow the Stations of the Cross.

Practicalities

There are regular bus services to Fátima from Batalha (18km northwest), Leiria (25km northwest) and Tomar (35km east) making it an easy day-trip. The **bus** station is on Avenida Dom José Alves Correia da Silva, southwest of the basilica's esplanade. If you arrive by **train**, you'll need to get a local bus (there's not always an immediate connection) from Estação de Fátima, a hefty 25km east of town; the station is on the main Lisbon–Porto line. The **turismo** (daily: May–Oct 10am–1pm & 3–7pm; Nov–April 10am–1pm & 3–6pm; ☎249 531 139, ⓦ www.rt-leiriafatima.pt) is just off the main esplanade and through-road, Avenida Dom José Alves Correia da Silva, although it is expected to shift to an as yet undecided site in 2007. The esplanade slices the town in half; on its west side is the main pedestrian street, Rua Jacinta Marto, which becomes Rua Francisco Marto when it reappears on the eastern side.

Pensões abound in Fátima, but during the pilgrimages (when most accommodation is booked up months in advance and prices double) people camp around the back and sides of the basilica. However, outside the major pilgrimages and weekends there's enough **accommodation** to go round, because many of the older boarding houses are built on monastic lines, with over 100 rooms and private chapels. The huge modern hotels can also be bargains in low season. A glut of **restaurants** line Rua Francisco Marto and Rua de São José, all geared towards tourists and none particularly inspiring. Unpretentious budget options can be found on the unnamed road that loops behind the park off Rua Jacinta Marto.

Hotels and pensions

Casa das Irmãs Dominicanos Rua Francisco Marto 50 ☎249 533 317, ℮ casa-ir-dominicanas@clix.pt. Run by Dominican nuns, and the most atmospheric address in Fátima – there are crucifixes over the headboards in the spacious en-suite rooms. No credit cards. ❸

Residencial Santo Amaro Rua Francisco Marto 59 ☎249 530 170, ℮ hotelsantoamaro@clix.pt. Bright, modern rooms in a comfortable hotel away from the excesses of the main drag. Includes breakfast. ❹

Residencial São Paulo Rua de São Paulo 10 ☎ 249 531 572, ℻ 249 533 257. A modern giant on a quiet side street, away from the restaurants. Includes breakfast. No credit cards. ❷

Restaurants

Santa Cruz Rua Jacinta Marto 2 ☎ 249 533 858. On the corner with Rua de São José, with a pleasant outlook and reasonably priced mains costing around €7. Moderate.

Restaurante O Truão Rua da Capela, Boleiros ☎ 249 521 542. Follow signs to Minde to reach this rambling rustic-styled restaurant 4km from Fátima. The roast *cabrito* alone makes the trip worthwhile. Closed Mon. Expensive.

O Zé Grande Rua Jacinta Marto 32 ☎ 249 531 367. One of the less touristy options, serving traditional food with mountains of chips. Moderate.

Ourém

For a quieter overnight stop altogether than Fátima, you may prefer **OURÉM**, 12km to the east. Although the new town, Vila Nova de Ourém, is not worth the effort, Ourém **castle** (no set hours; free) is just 2km above it, crowning a hill above a cosy nest of lanes that form a medieval walled village. The town's heyday was in the fifteenth century, when the fourth count of Ourém, Don Afonso, built several grand monuments and converted the castle into a palace. The castle was virtually destroyed by Napoleon's forces, but is now largely restored; walk around its parapet, and you receive a marvellous, sweeping panorama, with the basilica of Fátima away to the west. The well-signed history trail round the old town will lead you to the cisterns, which, according to local legend, have never run dry. Look out also for the fifteenth-century fountain by the town gates.

The **turismo** (May–Sept Tues–Sun 10am–1pm & 3–7pm; Oct–April Tues–Sun 2–6pm; ☎ 249 544 654), to your right as you enter the old town, can provide maps and also arrange guides for visits to the small archeological museum. You can ask here about **private rooms**, or consider those at *Pensão Ouriense*, Avenida Dom Nuno Álvares Pereira (☎ 249 542 202; no credit cards; ❷). But really, it's the *Pousada Conde de Ourém* (☎ 249 540 920, ⓦ www.pousadas.pt; includes breakfast; ❼) that makes a stay here, fashioned from fifteenth-century buildings to create a stylish hotel with a pool.

Tomar

The Convento de Cristo at **TOMAR**, 34km east of Fátima, is an artistic *tour de force* which entwines the most outstanding military, religious and imperial strands in the history of Portugal. The Order of the Knights Templar and their successors, the Order of Christ, established their headquarters here and successive Grand Masters employed experts in Romanesque, Manueline and Renaissance architecture to embellish and expand the convent in a manner worthy of their power, prestige and wealth.

In addition, Tomar is a handsome small town in its own right, well worth a couple of days of slow exploration. Built on a simple grid plan, it is split in two by the Rio Nabão, with almost everything of interest on the west bank. Here, Tomar's old quarters preserve much of their traditional charm, with whitewashed, terraced cottages lining narrow cobbled streets that frame the convent above. This pleasing backdrop is seen to best effect during Tomar's famous **Festa dos Tabuleiros**, held only every four years (see box on p.189), when the entire town takes to the streets.

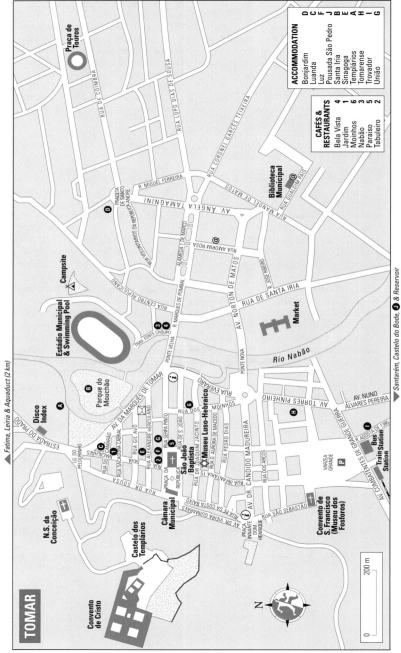

TOMAR

Coimbra, Pelinos & Hospital

Poço Redondo

Praça de Touros

RUA DE COIMBRA

RUA LOPO DIAS DE SOUSA

RUA CORONEL GARCES TEIXEIRA

R. MIGUEL FERREIRA

PRACETA DE SANTO ANDRÉ

RUA VOLUNTARIOS DA REPUBLICA

AV. ANGELA TAMAGNINI

RUA GUADOM PAIS

Biblioteca Municipal

RUA RANGEL DE MATOS

ALAMEDA 1 DE MARCO

RUA AMORIM ROSA

Campsite

RUA CENTRO REPUBLICANO

RUA MARQUES DE POMBAL

RUA DE SANTA IRIA

AV. NORTON DE MATOS

RUA DE JOSE RIBEIRO

Estádio Municipal & Swimming Pool

TRAV. FONTE CHOUPO

PONTE VELHA

PONTE NOVA

Market

Rio Nabão

Parque do Mouchão

AV. DA MARQUES DE TOMAR

RUA EVERARDO

RUA DE SANTA IRIA

Disco Index

ESTRADA DO PRADO

RUA DOS MOINHOS

AV. TORRES PINHEIRO

AV. NUNO ALVARES PEREIRA

Fatima, Leiria & Aquaduct (2 km)

N.S. da Conceição

LG. DO PELOURINHO

RUA DR SOUSA

RUA DO CAMARÃO

RUA SACADURA CABRAL

RUA GIL AVÔ

RUA ALEXANDRE HERCULANO

SILVA

RUA SERPA PINTO

RUA DR JOAQUIM JACINTO

Museu Luso-Hebraico

RUA DE S. JOÃO

São João Baptista

Câmara Municipal

PRAÇA DA REPUBLICA

RUA D. AURORA DE MACEDO

RUA INFANTARIA 15

RUA PEDRO DIAS

RUA DOS ARCOS

RUA D. COSTA BAIXO

AV. DR VIEIRA GUIMARÃES

PRAÇA INNANTE DOM HENRIQUE

RUA SÃO SEBASTIÃO

RUA D. CANDIDO MADUREIRA

VARZEA GRANDE

AV. COMBATENTES DE GRANDE GUERRA

RUA D. ACOSTA DE 1385

AV. COMBATENTES DE GRANDE GUERRA

Bus Station

Train Station

Convento de S. Francisco (Museu dos Fosforos)

Castelo dos Templários

Convento de Cristo

Santarém, Castelo do Bode, & Reservoir

N

0   200 m

The Festa dos Tabuleiros

Tomar is renowned throughout the country for its **Festa dos Tabuleiros** (literally, the Festival of the Trays). Its origins can be traced back to the saintly Queen Isabel who founded the Brotherhood of the Holy Spirit in the fourteenth century, though some believe it to derive from an ancient fertility rite dedicated to Ceres. Whatever its origins, it's now a largely secular event, held at four-yearly intervals. It's a five-day affair at the beginning of July, with the highlight – the parade of "trays" – on the final Sunday; the next event is in 2007.

The procession (Procissão dos Tabuleiros) consists of four hundred or so young women wearing white, each escorted by a young man in a white shirt, red tie and black trousers. Each woman carries on her head a tray with thirty loaves threaded on vertical canes, intertwined with leaves and colourful paper flowers, and crowned with a white dove – the symbol of the Holy Spirit. The resulting headdress weighs 15kg, and is roughly person-height – hence the need for an escort to lift and help balance it. As with other festivals, there's music and dancing in the streets, fireworks at dawn and dusk, and a bullfight the night before the procession. The day after the procession, bread, wine and beef are distributed to the local needy, following Isabel's injunction to "give bread to the poor" – needless to say, the bulls providing the beef have their own procession, three days before that of the *tabuleiros*.

The Town

On the central Praça da República stands an elegant seventeenth-century town hall, a ring of houses of the same period and the Manueline church of **São João Baptista**, remarkable for its octagonal belfry, elaborate doorway and six panels attributed to Gregório Lopes (1490–1550), one of Portugal's finest artists. Nearby, at Rua Joaquim Jacinto 73, is an excellently preserved fifteenth-century synagogue, now the **Museu Luso-Hebraico Abraham Zacuto** (daily 10am–1pm & 2–6pm; free), named after the Spanish astronomer, Abraham Zacuto, who prepared navigational aids for Vasco da Gama. The museum is particularly interesting in a town dominated for so long by crusading Defenders of the Faith and its stark interior, with plain vaults supported by four slender columns, houses a collection of thirteenth- to fourteenth-century Hebraic inscriptions. In 1496 Dom Manuel followed the example of the Reis Católicos (Catholic Kings) of Spain and ordered the conversion or expulsion of all Portuguese Jews. The synagogue at Tomar was one of the very few to survive so far south. Many Jews fled northwards, especially to Trás-os-Montes where Inquisitional supervision was less hawk-eyed.

Up on the hill to the north of the Convento de Cristo it's worth taking the time for a look around the unassuming but beautiful Renaissance church of **Nossa Senhora da Conceição** (daily 11am–6.45pm). It is attributed to Diogo de Torralva, architect of the Convento's Great Cloisters. Also of interest is the town **market**, held on Fridays, just off Rua de Santa Iria, while a touch of eccentricity is provided by the **Museu dos Fosforos** (Mon–Fri 10am–6pm, Sat–Sun 10am–1pm; free), inside the Convento de São Francisco, which claims its 40,000 collection of matchboxes is Europe's largest – although its boast of it being "a singular description of universal history and culture" is pushing it a bit. Out of town, the highlight is the impressive seventeenth-century **Pegões aqueduct**, built to supply the convent with water. The best place to see it – or walk along it – is 2km from town along the Leiria road.

Convento de Cristo

The **Convento de Cristo** (daily: June–Sept 9am–6.30pm; Oct–May 9am–5.30pm; last entrance 30min before closing; €4.50) is set among pleasant gardens (free) with splendid views, about a quarter of an hour's walk uphill from the centre of town. Founded in 1162 by Gualdim Pais, first and grandest Master of the Knights Templar, it was the headquarters of the Order and, as such, both a religious and a military centre.

One of the main objectives of the **Knights Templars** was to expel the Moors from Spain and Portugal, a reconquest seen always as a crusade – the defence of Christianity against the infidel. Spiritual strength was an integral part of the military effort and, despite magnificent additions, the sacred heart of the whole complex remains the **Charola** (also known as the Rotunda or Templars' Apse), the twelfth-century temple from which the knights drew their moral conviction. It is a strange place, more suggestive of the occult than of Christianity. At the centre of the sixteen-sided, almost circular, chapel stands the high altar, surrounded by a two-storeyed octagon. Deep alcoves decorated with sixteenth-century paintings are cut into the outside walls. The Templars are said to have attended Mass on horseback. Like almost every circular church, it is ultimately based on the Church of the Holy Sepulchre in Jerusalem, for whose protection the Order of the Knights Templar was originally founded.

Prince Henry and Dom Manuel's additions

By 1249 the reconquest in Portugal was completed and the Templars reaped enormous rewards for their service. Tracts of land were turned over to them and they controlled a network of castles throughout the Iberian peninsula. But as the Moorish threat receded, the knights became a powerful political challenge to the stability and authority of European monarchs.

Philippe-le-Bel, King of France, took the lead by confiscating all Templar property in his country and there followed a formal papal suppression of the order in 1314. In Spain this prompted a vicious witch-hunt and many of the knights sought refuge in Portugal, where Dom Dinis coolly reconstituted them in 1320 under a different title: the **Order of Christ**. They inherited all the Portuguese property of the Templars, including the headquarters at Tomar, but their power was now subject to that of the throne.

In the fifteenth and sixteenth centuries, the Order of Christ played a leading role in extending Portugal's overseas empire and was granted spiritual jurisdiction over all conquests. **Prince Henry the Navigator** was Grand Master from 1417 to 1460 and the remains of his palace in the Convento de Cristo can be seen immediately to the right upon entering the castle walls. Henry ordered two new *azulejo*-lined cloisters, the **Claustro do Cemitério** and the **Claustro da Lavagem**, both reached via a short corridor from the Charola.

Dom Manuel succeeded to the Grand Mastership in 1492, three years before he became king (1495–1521). Flush with imperial wealth, he decided to expand the convent by adding a rectangular **nave** to the west side of the Charola. This new structure was divided into two storeys: the lower serving as a chapterhouse, the upper as a choir. The **main doorway**, which leads directly into the nave, was built by João de Castilho in 1515, two years before Dom Manuel appointed him Master of Works at Belém. Characteristically unconcerned with structural matters, the architect adorned the doorway with profuse appliqué decoration. There are strong similarities in this respect with contemporary Isabelline and Plateresque architecture in Spain.

The crowning highlight of Tomar, though, is the sculptural ornamentation of the windows on the main facade of the **chapterhouse**. The richness and self-confidence of Manueline art always suggests the Age of Discovery, but here the connection is crystal clear. A wide range of maritime motifs is jumbled up in two tumultuous window frames, as eternal memorials to the sailors who established the Portuguese Empire. Everything is here: anchors, buoys, sails, coral, seaweed and especially ropes, knotted over and over again into an escapologist's nightmare.

Manueline architecture

With the new-found wealth and confidence engendered by the "Discoveries", came a distinctly Portuguese version of late Gothic architecture. Named after King Manuel I (1495–1521), the **Manueline style** is characterized by a rich and, often, fantastical use of ornamentation. Doors, windows and arcades are encrusted by elaborately carved stonework, in which the imagery of the sea is freely combined with both symbols of Christianity and of the newly discovered lands.

The style first appeared at the Igreja de Jesus (1494–98), in **Setúbal**, where each of the columns of the nave are made up of three strands of stone seemingly wrapped around each other like rope. This relatively restrained building is the work of Diogo Boitac, who later supervised the initial construction of the great Jéronimos monastery at **Bélem**, a few miles downstream from Lisbon. Commissioned by the king, this is a far more exuberant structure with an elaborately carved south portal opening onto a nave where the vaulting ribs seem to sprout out of the thin, trunk-like columns like leaves from a palm tree. Bélem was the point from which many of the Portuguese navigators set forth, and the new building was largely subsidized by the new, lucrative spice trade.

The Jéronimos monastery is the most unified expression of the new style, but Manuel I also commissioned lavish extensions to existing buildings, like the Convento do Cristo at **Tomar**. This is arguably the most brilliant and original expression of Manueline decoration. In particular, the famous chapterhouse window is a riot of virtuosic stone carving, in which twisted strands of coral, opulent flower heads and intricately knotted ropes are crowned by the royal coat of arms, the cross of the Order of Christ and two armillary spheres.

The armillary sphere – a navigational instrument – became the personal emblem of King Manuel, and frequently appears in Manueline decoration. It can be seen at the great abbey at **Batalha** in the screens set within the top half of the arches of the Claustro Real (Royal Cloister). The intricate tracery of these screens suggest Islamic filigree work and may well have been directly influenced by buildings in India. Beyond the church is a royal mausoleum begun by King Duarte and continued by King Manuel I but never completed. This octagonal building with seven radiating chapels is entered through a vast trefoil-arched portal that is smothered in a profusion of ornament (including snails and artichokes) that seems to defy the material from which it's carved.

Not all Manueline architecture was ecclesiastical: there were also palaces, like that of the Dukes of Bragança at **Vila Viçosa**, and castles, like the one at **Évora Monte** where the whole of the exterior is bound by a single stone rope. Most famous of all secular constructions is Lisbon's **Torre de Bélem**, a fortress built on an island in the Tejo which incorporates Moorish-style balconies, domed look-out posts, battlements in the form of shields, and even a carving of a rhinoceros.

Manueline architecture did not continue much beyond the fourth decade of the sixteenth century. In the reign of Manuel's successor, King João III, a more austere religious atmosphere prevailed in which the decorative excesses of the Manueline style were replaced by the ordered sobriety of Italian classicism.

△ Convento de Cristo, Tomar

The windows can only be fully appreciated from the roof of the **Claustro de Santa Bárbara**, adjacent to the Great Cloisters, which unfortunately almost completely obscure a similar window on the south wall of the chapterhouse.

A new style: João III

João III (1521–57) transformed the convent from the general political headquarters of the Order into a monastic community and he endowed it with the necessary conventual buildings: dormitories, kitchens and no fewer than four new cloisters (making a grand total of seven). Yet another, much more classical, style was introduced into the architectural melange of Tomar. So meteoric was the rise and fall of Manueline art within the reign of Dom Manuel that, to some extent, it must have reflected his personal tastes. João III on the other hand had an entirely different view of art. He is known to have sent schools of architects and sculptors to study in Italy and his reign finally marked the much-delayed advent of the Renaissance in Portugal.

The two-tiered **Great Cloisters**, abutting the chapterhouse, are one of the purest examples of this new style. Begun in 1557, they present a textbook illustration of the principals of Renaissance Neoclassicism. Greek columns, gentle arches and simple rectangular bays produce a wonderfully restrained rhythm. At the southwest corner a balcony looks out on to the skeletal remains of a second chapterhouse, begun by João III but never completed.

Practicalities

The **train** and **bus stations**, on Avenida Combatentes da Grande Guerra, are within easy walking distance of the centre. Head directly north and you'll soon hit Avenida Dr. Cândido Madureira, at the eastern end of which there's the **turismo** (daily: April–Sept Mon–Fri 10am–7pm, Sat & Sun 10am–1pm & 2–6pm; Oct–March daily 10am–1pm & 2–6pm; ☎249 322 427). It faces a fierce statue of Infante Dom Henrique and the gates of a park, which once formed the gardens of the Convento de Cristo. There's also a **regional turismo** at the bottom of Rua Serpa Pinto (Mon–Fri 9.30am–12.30pm & 2–6pm; ☎249 329 000), although the town office is more helpful. Tomar is pretty strict with its **parking** restrictions, though free parking is available on Varzea Grande beside the bus station.

Accommodation

Tomar has a good range of **accommodation** and finding a room should be pretty straightforward. There's a list of recommended places below, or you can ask at the tourist office about private rooms.

Hotels and pensions

Pensão Bonjardim Pr.de Santo André ☎249 313 195, ℻249 313 196. Some of the cheapest rooms in town, which are basic but adequate. Located a 15min walk from the centre in the new town. No credit cards. ❷

Residencial Luanda Av. Marquês de Tomar 15 ☎249 315 153, ℻249 322 145. Faces the river, so front rooms can be noisy but are brighter. All have air-con, TV and own bathroom. Includes breakfast. ❹

Residencial Luz Rua Serpa Pinto 144 ☎249 312 317, ⓦwww.residencialluz.com. Simple, old-fashioned rooms but good value and an excellent central location. Breakfast included. No credit cards. ❸

Pousada São Pedro Castelo do Bode, 13km southeast of town ☎249 381 159, ⓦwww.pousadas.pt. Overlooking the reservoir, this a great place to unwind, with quietly elegant rooms decorated with traditional furnishings and tasteful fabrics. Includes an excellent breakfast. ❻

Estalagem de Santa Iria Parque do Mouchão ☎249 313 326, ⓦwww.estalagemiria.com. At this classy island retreat by the river, the rooms have balconies onto the park, whose mature trees screen off the traffic. Its excellent restaurant is

Abrantes

ABRANTES is perched strategically above the Rio Tejo, 12km upstream of Constância. Hidden at the centre of a dreary modern town is a historic kernel of pretty narrow alleys and squares lined with crumbling houses. It looks its best in spring and summer when flowers on Rua da Barca and in the Jardim da República are in bloom; the views are also impressive.

The high point – in all respects – is the town's much-restored **Castelo** (Tues–Sun 10am–6pm; free), constructed in the early fourteenth century. As at Santarém, Romans and Moors established strongholds here and the citadel was again sharply contested during the Peninsular War. The chapel of **Santa Maria do Castelo** within the fort houses a motley archeological museum, its prize exhibits being three tombs of the Almeidas, Counts of Abrantes. From the battlements there are terrific views of the countryside and rooftops of Abrantes, and the gardens around its old town walls. The two large, whitewashed churches visible from here were both rebuilt in the sixteenth century.

Practicalities

There are two local **train stations**, both out of town, with useful services to towns in the lower Beiras and the Alto Alentejo. The main station is 2km south, across the Tejo, and all trains stop here – a taxi up the hill to the centre costs around €4. **Buses** stop a kilometre or so from the town centre in a depot on the way to the IP6 highway. The **turismo** (Mon–Fri 9am–6pm, Sat 10.30am–5.30pm; ☏ 241 362 555, Ⓦ www.cm-abrantes.pt) is in a booth before the town hall on Esplanade 1 de Maio.

Cheapest choice for **accommodation** in the centre is the rather tatty but pleasantly eccentric *Pensão Central*, Praça Raimundo Soares 15 (☏ 241 362 422; no credit cards; ❶). *Pensão Aliança*, Largo do Chafariz 50 (☏ 241 362 348; no credit cards; ❸), owned by the same proprietor, is slightly less characterful but has better facilities, with showers in some rooms; while *Pensão Lírios*, Praça Barao da Batalha 31 (☏ 241 362 142; includes breakfast; no credit cards; ❸), is another good choice carved out of a grand house. A kilometre out of town, just off the road to the IP6 highway, is the modern *Hotel de Turismo* (☏ 241 361 261, Ⓔ hotelabrantes@eol.pt; ❺), with its own tennis courts and pool.

There are a number of reasonable **restaurants** in Abrantes. *O Fumeiro* at Rua do Pisco 9 (☏ 241 363 983; closed Sun) serves good Portuguese staples, while *Grelha Nova*, Rua Montéiro de Lima 41 (☏ 241 365 539; closed Sat), is the place for good-quality grills. The locals' favourite is *A Cascata* (☏ 241 361 011; closed Mon), 3km out of town, at Alferrarede, near the second train station.

Castelo de Belver

The **Castelo de Belver** is one of the most famous in the country, its fanciful position, name and tiny size having ensured it a place in dozens of Portuguese legends. The name comes from *belo ver* (beautiful to see), the supposed exclamation of a medieval princess, waking up to look out from its keep at the river valley below. It dates from the twelfth century, when the Portuguese frontier stood at the Tejo, the Moors having reclaimed most of the territories to the south. Its founder was Dom Sancho I, who entrusted its construction and care to the knight-monks of the Order of St John.

The walls form an irregular pentagon, tracing the crown of the hill, with a narrow access path to force attackers into single file. Inside the castle chapel is a formidable fifteenth-century reliquary. All the pieces of bone were stolen during the French invasions in the nineteenth century, but fortunately for the villagers there was a casket of "spares" hidden away by the priest, and these substitutes are today paraded at the **Festa de Santa Reliquária**, held around August 18.

Although technically in the Alentejo, Belver is best approached from Abrantes, by public transport at least. Buses stop in the village square, while the train station is directly below the village beside the river. If you take the train north along the valley towards Castelo Branco, look out for the striking rock faces before Vila Velha de Ródão, known as the **Portas do Ródão** (Gates of Ródão).

Golegã and around

GOLEGÃ, on the west bank of the Tejo, midway between Tomar and Santarém, is a pleasant town, best known for its **Feira Nacional do Cavalo** (National Horse Fair), held during the first two weeks in November. The fair incorporates celebrations for St Martin's Day on November 11, when there's a running of the bulls and a grand parade in which red-waistcoated grooms mingle with gypsies. Culinary diversions include roasted chestnuts and barbecued chickens washed down with liberal quantites of *água-pé* (literally "foot water"), a light wine made by adding water to the crushed grape husks left after initial wine production. During the evening, people crowd into *Restaurante Central* on Largo da Imaculada Conceição, both to eat and to mingle with the haughty *cavaleiros* who have survived the bullfighting.

Golegã also boasts a couple of museums, most notably the **Casa-Museu de Fotografia Carlos Relvas**, opposite the Câmara Municipal at the top of Rua José F. Relvas (May–Sept daily 11am–12.30pm & 3–7pm; Oct–Mar Tues–Sat 10am–12.30pm & 3–6pm, Sun 3–7pm; free). Carlos Relvas was father of the Republican José Relvas (see "Alpiarça", below) and, ironically, godfather to King Carlos, who was assassinated by Republicans in 1908. The museum is an archive of Relvas' interest in the newly discovered art of photography and contains some 13,000 glass negatives. The house itself is worthy of being a museum piece, a fairy-tale building designed by Henrique Carlos Afonso and set in landscaped gardens. The town's other highlight is the sixteenth-century **Igreja Matriz**, with its Manueline door.

Your best bet for **accommodation** in Golegã is a room at the *Restaurante Central* (☎249 976 345), although they'll almost certainly be occupied during the fair. There's also a lovely **campsite** (☎249 976 222) close to the Igreja Matriz. Otherwise, you could drive the 12km southwest to the attractive west-bank riverside village of **Azinhaga** and stay at *Casa de Santo António da Azinhaga*, Rua Nova de Santo António (☎249 957 162, ⓕ249 957 122; includes breakfast; ❻). Here, you'll also find *Patio do Burgo* (☎249 957 216; closed Aug), a popular local restaurant serving traditional food.

South along the Tejo: the east bank

Golegã is one of the main crossing points to the **east bank** of the Rio Tejo – a bull-breeding territory of rich plains and riverside marshes. The N118 marks the most attractive route along the river, taking in several small historic towns, villages and *quintas* en route to Santarém, Vila Franca de Xira and Lisbon, although it's one to drive to rather then rely on local buses. Accommodation isn't plentiful, but you're unlikely to want to stop anywhere for any great length of time, except during the energetic annual festivals – when all available rooms will be booked up well in advance in any case.

CHAMUSCA, 9km from Golegã, is the most northerly of the east bank's bullfighting towns. Its Festa da Ascensão – six days of bull-running and bull-fighting – is held during the week incorporating Ascension Day (ie forty days after Easter). **ALPIARÇA**, 18km south of Chamusca, warrants a stop for **Casa Museu dos Patudos** (Mon–Fri 10am–5.30pm, Sat & Sun 10am–1pm & 2–5.30pm; €2.50), on Rua José Relvas south of town, which was originally the home of José Relvas (1858–1929). Musician, art collector, landowner, bullfighter, diplomat and politician, José is best known as the man who proclaimed the Portuguese Republic in Lisbon in 1910. The exterior of the house is striking, with a colonnade and outdoor staircases to the first floor. Inside, you'll find priceless collections of Portuguese paintings, porcelain, furniture, tapestries and over forty carpets from Arraiolos, including one embroidered in silk and dating from 1701.

Seven kilometres south of Alpiarça is **ALMEIRIM**, whose golden days were during the reign of the House of Avis (1383–1580), when the royal family – ensconced at Santarém, just 7km to the northwest – hunted from a summer palace on this stretch of riverside. Sadly, nothing remains of the palace today. *Restaurante Tonçinho,* Rua de Timor 2 (☎243 592 237; closed Thurs), one block behind the garage on the Coruche road (N114), is a good place for lunch, and you'll be able to sample local wines considered to be some of the region's finest. To visit the vineyards, the eighteenth-century *Quinta da Alorna* (☎243 570 700; €5 per person), 1km from Almeirim on the Lisbon road (N118), offers daily tours and tastings, though reservations must be made in advance.

Santarém

SANTARÉM, capital of the Ribatejo, rears high above the Rio Tejo, commanding a tremendous view over the rich pasturelands to the south and east. It ranks among the most historic cities in Portugal: under Julius Caesar it became an important administrative centre for the Roman province of Lusitania; Moorish Santarém was regarded as impregnable (until Afonso Henriques captured it by enlisting the aid of foreign Crusaders in 1147); and it was here that the royal *Cortes* (parliament) was convened throughout the fourteenth and fifteenth centuries. All evidence of Roman and Moorish occupation has vanished but, with its two exquisite churches, modern Santarém remains a pleasant enough place to visit – not least for the famous view from the *miradouro* known as the Portas do Sol.

The thinly populated agricultural plain above which Santarém stands is the home of Portuguese **bullfighting**: here, the very best horses and bulls graze in lush fields under the watchful eyes of *campinos*, mounted guardians. Agricultural traditions, folk dancing (especially the fandango) and bullfighting come together in the great annual **Feira Nacional da Agricultura**, held at Santarém for two weeks starting on the first Friday in June, while dishes from every region in Portugal are sampled at the **Festival de Gastronomia** (10–12 days, ending early Nov). In addition, a large **market** sprawls around the bullring on the second and fourth Sunday of every month.

The Town

At the heart of the old town is Praça Sá da Bandeira, overlooked by the many-windowed Baroque facade of the Jesuit **Igreja do Seminário** (1676), which serves as the town's cathedral. Rua Serpa Pinto or Rua Capelo e Ivens lead from here towards the signposted Portas do Sol, about fifteen minutes' walk, with the best of the churches conveniently en route.

First of these is the Manueline **Igreja de Marvila** (Tues–Sun 9am–12.30pm & 2–5.30pm, Sat & Sun open till 6.30pm) at the end of Rua Serpa Pinto, with brilliant seventeenth-century *azulejos* and a lovely stone pulpit comprising eleven

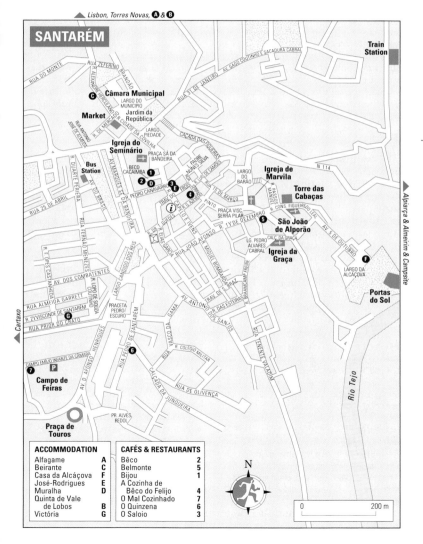

miniature Corinthian columns. From here, it's a short walk at right angles to the side of the church to the architectural highlight of Santarém, the early fifteenth-century **Igreja da Graça** (Tues–Sun 9.30am–12.30pm & 2.30–5.30pm). A spectacular rose window dominates the church and overlapping blind arcades above the portal are heavily influenced by the vertical decorations on the main facade at Batalha. Pedro Álvares Cabral, discoverer of Brazil in 1500, is buried within, but his rather austere tomb-slab is overshadowed by the elaborate sarcophagus of Pedro de Menezes, the first Governor of Ceuta, who died in 1437.

Continuing toward the *miradouro*, a third sidetrack is to the twelfth-century church of **São João de Alporão**, now an archeological museum (Tues–Sun 9.30am–12.30pm & 2–5.30pm; €2). Take a look at the flamboyant Gothic tomb of Duarte de Menezes who met his gruesome fate in 1464 – so comprehensively was he butchered by the Moors in North Africa that only a single tooth was recovered for burial.

Avenida 5 de Outubro eventually finishes at the **Portas do Sol** (Gates of the Sun; summer 9am–10pm, winter 9am–6pm) a large garden occupying the site of the Moorish citadel. Modern battlements look down on a long stretch of the Tejo with its fertile sandbanks and, beyond, a vast swathe of the Ribatejo disappears green and flat into the distance. A café here makes this a lovely spot for a mid-afternoon beer.

Practicalities

The **train station** lies a couple of hundred metres below the town. There are half-hourly buses into the centre, or you can walk in around twenty minutes. The **bus station** is more central, on Avenida do Brasil, and Rua Pedro Canavarro, across the gardens opposite, leads into Rua Capelo e Ivens, the main pedestrian street of the old town. Excellent free maps are available from the **turismo** at Rua Capelo e Ivens 63 (Mon 9am–12.30pm & 2–5.30pm; Tues–Fri 9am–7pm; Sat & Sun 10am–12.30pm & 2.30–5.30pm; ☎243 304 437, Ⓦ www.cm-santarem.pt).

Finding **accommodation** can be tough during festivals, when your best bet is to turn up early and source a private room through the turismo. Otherwise there should be little problem. Santarém is not blessed with an over-abundance of **restaurants**, though good central grazing areas are Rua Capelo e Ivens and Rua Dr. Jaime Figueiredo behind the market. Among local specialities look out for *fataça na telha*, mullet cooked on a hot tile.

⚓Hotels and pensions

Casa da Alcáçova Largo da Alcáçova ☎243 304 030, Ⓦ www.alcacova.com. An aristocratic mansion at the shoulder of the Portas do Sol, with equally jaw-dropping views. Elegant antiques and magnificent beds, including some four-posters, furnish the rooms. Parking available. Breakfast included. ❼

Hotel Alfageme Av. Bernardo Santareno 38 ☎243 370 870, Ⓦ www.hotelalfageme.com. Smart modern hotel just off the road towards Torres Novas, 500m northwest of the market. The rooms are all en suite, air-conditioned and double-glazed. Breakfast included. ❹

Residencial Beirante Rua Alexandre Herculano 3–5 ☎243 322 547, ℱ243 333 845. Somewhat spartan rooms, though all are en suite. Breakfast included. No credit cards. ❸

Pensão José Rodrigues Trav. do Frois 14 ☎243 323 088. With old furniture, and washstands and water-pitchers in rooms, this simple *pensão* is full of character or appallingly basic depending on your need for mod cons. No credit cards. ❷

Residencial Muralha Rua Pedro Canavarro 12 ☎243 322 399, ℱ243 329 477. Good-value, cheerful rooms near a surviving chunk of the city walls – hence the name. No credit cards. ❸

Quinta de Vale de Lobos Azóia de Baixo, 6km north on N3 ☎243 429 264, Ⓦ www.valedelobos.com. Four double/twin rooms and guest lounge in a nineteenth-century former farmhouse where the historian Alexandre

Herculano spent his final years. Surrounded by cedar and oak woods, it's set in lovely gardens with a swimming pool. Also has two cottages available, suitable for families. Breakfast included. ⑥

Residencial Victória Rua 2° Visconde de Santarém 21 ☎243 309 130, ⑤243 328 202. In a peaceful residential street, a 15min walk from the centre, with spacious, homely rooms, all with bath and TV. Breakfast included. No credit cards. ③

Restaurants

Bar do Bêco Bêco da Cacaimba 9–10 ☎243 322 937. Tucked down a cul-de-sac, this cosy bar-restaurant offers a soup and dish of the day, plus toasted sandwiches and snacks. Inexpensive.

Restaurante Belmonte Rua 1 Dezembro 3 no phone. Good steaks, plus occasional surprises such as paella in a friendly, family-run place. Moderate.

Pastelaria Bijou Pr. Sa da Bandeira ☎243 323 149. Perfect croissant-and-coffee spot opposite

the Seminário, the meeting point for young and old. Inexpensive.

A Cozinha do Bêco do Feleijo Bêco do Feleipo, off Rua Serpo Pinto ☎916 510 667. A tiny restaurant in a hidden square, with a small menu of bargain-priced dishes as well as a €4.50 dish of the day. Inexpensive.

O Mal Cozinhado Campo de Feiras ☎243 323 584. Small place where you may need to reserve a table, particularly on Friday, which is fado night. Some of the meat comes from bulls recently on duty in the nearby bullring, and, despite the name ("badly cooked"), meals are delicious. Closed Sun. Moderate.

O Quinzena Rua Pedro de Santarém ☎243 322 804. Simple dishes in a no-nonense *tasca* with a bullfighting obsession. Inexpensive.

O Saloio Trav. do Montalvo 11, off Rua Capelo e Ivens ☎243 327 656. Popular with local families, this cheap *tasca* is good value for money. Closed Sun. Inexpensive.

South along the Tejo: the west bank

The **west bank** of the Rio Tejo is highly developed south of Santarém, although away from the river it doesn't take long to get into the rolling hills. It's around an hour's journey on the motorway from Santarém to Lisbon but if you're in no hurry, you might want to detour to some of the Ribatejo's finest **vineyards** in towns like Cartaxo, Azambuja, Alenquer and Arruda dos Vinhos. In addition, the west bank city of **Vila Franca de Xira**, 45km downriver from Santarém, makes a rival (but unsubstantiated) claim to be the capital of the Ribatejo. It does, however, sit at the northern edge of the important wetlands of the **Reserva Natural do Estuario do Tejo**.

The wine towns

A good place to start exploring the Ribatejo wine trade is **CARTAXO**, 14km south of Santarém. Despite its enticing self-declaration as the "capital do vinho" the modern town is a dull and uninspiring affair, worth a visit

---

Ribatejo wines

Wine has been produced on the banks of the Tejo for around 2000 years, but it is only recently that modern wine-making techniques have ensured that the result is appreciated not only in local *tascas* but throughout Europe. The highly respected wines from the five denominations in the Ribatejo region – Almeirim, Cartaxo, Chamusca, Coruche and Santarém – can now be found in supermarkets outside Portugal, marketed under labels such as Ribatejo, Arruda and Liziria. Ribatejan **whites** are typically from the Fernão Pires or Trincadeira-das-Pratas grapes, which give rise to a dry, lemon-coloured and fruity wine. **Reds** tend to be from the Periquita, Tincadeira Preta and Castelão Nacional grapes, though Cabernet Sauvignon produces some of the best-tasting wines.

only for the fine **Museu Rural e do Vinho** (Mon–Fri 10.30am–12.30pm & 3–5.30pm, Sat & Sun 9.30am–12.30pm & 3–5.30pm; €0.75), housed in a *quinta* on the ringroad of Rua José Ribeiro da Costa (follow signs to "Adega Cooperativa Cartaxo"). There are exhibits about farming and wine-making, and you can taste and buy the local, full-bodied, fruity wine.

AZAMBUJA, 13km to the southwest, is known for its great reds made from the Periquita grape, but the town itself only really comes alive with the bull-running during its Feira do Maio, held during the last weekend in May. The Marquês de Pombal built a 26-kilometre long canal – the Vala de Azambuja – parallel to the river here, to drain the land when the Tejo was in flood. At its mouth are the ruins of the **Palácio das Obras Novas**, used as a staging post for the steamers plying from Lisbon north to Constância in the nineteenth century.

Perched on a hillside 17km to the west, **ALENQUER** sits in a major wine area; its refreshing, lemony-flavoured whites are definitely worth tasting. There is little else to delay you apart from the attractive upper town spreading up a steep hillside and boasting a **Franciscan convent** (open only on the first Sun of the month before morning and evening Mass) as its most prominent building. Founded in 1222 by Dona Sancha, daughter of Dom Sancho I, the convent is the oldest Franciscan house in Portugal and was built during the lifetime of St Francis of Assisi. It features a fine thirteenth-century doorway and Manueline cloisters, the latter added in 1557.

However, it is in the valleys around **ARRUDA DOS VINHOS**, 16km south of Alenquer, that the region's vineyards are at their most attractive. The fresh, beaujolais-style Arruda (also known as Arruta) red wines produced here are one of the reasons why Lisboans come to the village in their droves on Sundays. Many have lunch at the marvellous *O Fuso* (☎263 975 121), an *adega-restaurante* where vast slabs of meat and *bacalhau* are grilled over open fires.

Vila Franca de Xira

English Crusaders favoured the riverside location of **VILA FRANCA DE XIRA**, naming it Cornogoa after Cornwall, but today it's a largely drab indus-trial city; a poor second to Santarém in cultural attractions and only worth the effort of a visit for aficionados of the Portuguese bullfight. The rearing of bulls and horses dominates the local economy and the town celebrates its obsession in café names and statues, while posters everywhere announce forthcoming fights. The two great annual events are the **Festa do Colete Encarnado** ("Red Waistcoat Festival", a reference to the costume of the *campinos*) held over several days in the first two weeks of July; and the **Feira de Outubro** (October Fair), in the first two weeks of the month. On both occasions there are bullfights and a Pamplona-style running of the bulls through the streets – leading to the usual casualties among the bold (and drunk).

The **train station** and adjacent **bus station** are centrally located at one end of Avenida 25 de Abril, which runs north to the town's main thoroughfare, Rua Alves Redol. Accommodation is difficult to find during festivals – it's advisable to book well in advance or visit on a day-trip from Santarém or Lisbon. The **turismo**, at Rua Almirante Candido dos Reis 147 (Mon–Fri 10am–1pm 2–6pm, Sat 10am–1pm; ☎263 285 605), may be able to help; turn left from the station on Rua Serpa Pinto to locate it. Regular **accommoda-tion** includes the basic *Residencial Ribatejana*, Rua da Praia 2 (☎263 272 991; no credit cards; ②), next to the train station, and the smarter *Residencial Flora*, Rua Noel Perdigão 12 (☎263 271 272, ℻263 276 538; includes breakfast; ③), one block north from the train station and with a good restaurant. *O Copote* (no phone) in the station square, on the first floor above a bar, is an inexpensive **restaurant**. Better is *O Redondel* (⊕263 272 973; closed Mon), a classy place built into the Praça de Touros (bullring), although the full works here can easily add up to €20 per person.

Reserva Natural de Estuario del Tejo

To the south and southeast of Vila Franca de Xira, the banks of the Rio Tejo are classified as the **Reserva Natural de Estuário del Tejo**, providing protection for the thousands of wild birds that gather in the estuary. It is Portugal's most important wetland, but was somewhat disrupted by the construction of the enormous Vasco da Gama bridge. The reserve's headquarters are 35km south of Vila Franca in **ALCOCHETE**, right on the waterfront on the south side of the bridge at Avenida Combatentes 1 (Mon–Fri 9.30am–12.30pm & 2–5.30pm; ⊕212 341 742), from where information and advice are dispensed. Between October and April, you can also book tours of the wetlands from the headquarters. This is the best time to see the migrating bird species such as flamingoes, teal and avocet. During the summer, you'll spot nesting species such as black-winged stilt, purple heron and marsh harriers.

Travel details

Trains

Abrantes to: Castelo Branco (6 daily; 1hr 30min–2hr); Covilhã (5 daily; 2hr 30min–3hr 30min); Elvas (3 daily; 2hr 30min); Lisbon (8 daily; 1hr 35min–2hr 30min); Portalegre (4 daily; 1hr 35min).
Caldas da Rainha to: Figueira da Foz (7 daily; 1hr 30min–2hr 20min); Leiria (5 daily; 45min–1hr 10m); Lisbon (9 daily; 1hr 15min–2hr); São Martinho do Porto (5 daily; 9–20min); Torres Vedras (9 daily; 30–50min).
Leiria to: Caldas da Rainha (5 daily; 45min–1hr 10min); Figueira da Foz (6 daily; 45min–1hr 20min); Lisbon (4 daily; 2–3hr 20min); São Martinho do Porto (5 daily; 40–55min); Torres Vedras (4 daily; 1hr 14min–2hr 14min).
Lisbon to: Caldas da Rainha (9 daily; 1hr 15min–2hr); Leiria (5 daily; 2hr–3hr); Torres Vedras (9 daily; 45min–1hr 15min).
Santarém to: Castelo Branco (5 daily; 2hr 25min–3hr 10min); Covilhã (5 daily; 3hr 30min–4hr 20min); Lisbon (hourly; 1hr); Tomar (8 daily; 1hr).
Tomar to: Lisbon (7 daily; 2hr); Santarém (7 daily; 1hr).
Torres Vedras to: Caldas da Rainha (9 daily; 30–50min); Figueira da Foz (4 daily; 2hr 15min); Leiria (5 daily; 1hr 20min–2hr); Lisbon (8 daily; 40min–1hr 10min).
Vila Franca de Xira to: Lisbon (hourly; 30min); Santarém (hourly; 40min); Tomar (hourly; 1hr 30min).

Buses

Abrantes to: Coimbra (1 daily; 2hr 45min); Fátima (3 daily; 1hr 30min); Leiria (1 daily; 2hr); Lisbon (8 daily, 2hr 30min); Santarém (4 daily; 1hr 25min); Tomar (2–4 daily; 1hr 10min).
Alcobaça to: Batalha (5 daily; 30min); Leiria (4 daily; 45min); Lisbon (3 daily; 2hr); Nazaré (8 daily; 35min).
Batalha to: Fátima (4 daily; 25min); Leiria (5 daily; 15min); Lisbon (5 daily; 2hr).
Caldas da Rainha to: Foz do Arelho (9–10 daily; 20min); Leiria (4 daily; 1hr 55min); Lisbon (6 daily; 1hr 45 min); Nazaré (7 daily; 40min); Óbidos (6 daily; 20min).
Ericeira to: Lisbon (7 daily; 1hr 25min); Mafra (hourly, 20min); Sintra (12 daily; 45min).
Fátima to: Coimbra (5 daily; 1hr–1hr 30min); Leiria (9 daily; 25min); Lisbon (6 daily; 1hr 45min–2hr 15min); Porto (4 daily; 2hr 30min–3hr 30min).
Leiria to: Abrantes (1 daily; 1hr 50min); Alcobaça (4 daily; 50min); Batalha (5 daily; 15min); Coimbra (10 daily; 50min); Fátima (9 daily; 25min); Lisbon (9 daily; 1hr–2hr 10min); Porto de Mós (3 daily; 35min); Tomar (3 daily; 1hr 30min).
Nazaré to: Alcobaça (6 daily; 20min); Caldas da Rainha (7 daily; 40min); Leiria (10 daily; 1hr 10min); Lisbon (6 daily; 2hr); Óbidos (3 daily; 1hr); São Martinho do Porto (3 daily; 20min).
Óbidos to: Caldas da Rainha (6 daily; 20min);

Nazaré (7 daily; 1hr); Peniche (7–8 daily; 25–40min).

Peniche to: Areia Branca (6 daily; 30min); Caldas da Rainha (7 daily; 45min); Consolação (12 daily; 15min); Lisbon (9 daily; 1hr 45min); Óbidos (7–8 daily; 25–40min); São Martinho do Porto (3 daily; 1hr); Torre Vedras (8 daily; 50min).

Santarém to: Abrantes (6 daily; 1hr 25min); Fátima (9 daily, 1hr); Lisbon (12 daily; 1hr 15min); Ourem (1 daily; 1hr 10min); Tomar (2–6 daily;

1hr); Vila Franca de Xira (2–5 daily; 1hr 35min–2hr 20min).

Tomar to: Abrantes (2–4 daily; 1hr 10min); Coimbra (2 daily; 2hr); Fátima (2–4 daily; 45min); Leiria (3 daily; 1hr 10min–2hr); Lisbon (2–4 daily; 1hr 15min–2hr); Santarém (2–4 daily; 1hr 5min).

Vila Franca de Xira to: Évora (1 daily; 2hr); Lisbon (hourly; 50min); Santarém (2–5 daily; 1hr 35min–2hr 20min).

Coimbra and the Beira Litoral

COIMBRA AND THE BEIRA LITORAL

CHAPTER 3

Highlights

✳ **Velha Universidade, Coimbra** Wind your way up to the splendidly sited university, with its striking Baroque library. See p.215

✳ **Coimbra fado** Best listened to in a smoky bar, drink in hand, or with the atmospheric backdrop of an old-town alleyway. See p.218

✳ **Roman ruins at Conímbriga** Rove amongst Portugal's finest Roman remains. See p.220

✳ **Kayaking down the Mondego** Paddle between Penacova and Coimbra on the meandering Rio Mondego. See p.223

✳ **Mata Nacional do Buçaco** Explore the revered forest and stop for a meal in the luxurious *Palácio do Buçaco*. See p.223

✳ **Serra da Lousã** Hike through tiny villages in this little-visited mountain range. See p.226

✳ **Serra do Caramulo** Drive through the stunning mountain range, stopping off in Caramulo to visit the incongruous Museu do Automóvel. See p.230

✳ **Figueira da Foz** Be a proper tourist and bronze your limbs on this great swathe of beach. See p.233

✳ **Seafood in Aveiro** A host of fantastic restaurants in which to savour the region's delicious seafood. See p.238

△ Coimbra

3

Coimbra and the Beira Litoral

The province of Beira Litoral is dominated by the city of **Coimbra**, which, with Guimarães, Lisbon and Porto, forms the quartet of Portugal's historic capitals. Situated on a hill above the Rio Mondego, it's a wonderfully moody place, full of ancient alleys and lanes, spreading around the country's oldest university. As a base for exploring the region, the city can't be beaten, with Portugal's most extensive Roman site, **Conímbriga**, 16km to the southwest, and the castle at **Montemor-o-Velho**, 32km west, and the delightful spa town of **Luso** and ancient forest of **Buçaco** under an hour's journey to the north.

Beira's endlessly sandy coastline, from Figueira da Foz north as far as Porto, has been dubbed the **Costa de Prata** ("Silver Coast"). Although slowly succumbing to development, most noticeably around **Praia de Mira**, it remains one of the least spoiled coasts in Portugal, backed by rolling dunes and pine forests. The only resort of any real size is **Figueira da Foz** and even this remains thoroughly local in character. Inland, the villages and towns of the fertile plain have long been conditioned by the twin threats of floodwaters from Portugal's highest mountains, and silting caused by the restless Atlantic. Drainage channels were cut to make cultivation possible and houses everywhere are built on high ground. At **Aveiro**, positioned on a complex estuary site, a whole network of canals was developed to cope with the currents, and to facilitate salt production and the harvesting of seaweed.

The Beira region also hints at the river valley splendour to come, in the Douro and Minho, further north. Following the delightful **Rio Mondego** upstream from Coimbra, you'll come to see why it has been celebrated so often in Portuguese poetry as the "Rio das Musas" – River of the Muses. An equally beautiful road journey trails the **Rio Vouga**, from Aveiro, up to the pretty little town of **Vouzela**. To the north is the impressive convent at **Arouca**, and the *serras* of **Freita** and **Arada**, both peppered with remote hamlets and offering beautiful scenic routes for drivers. To the south lies the more accessible **Serra do Caramulo**, where the village of **Caramulo** makes a good base for mountain pursuits and boasts a pair of fascinating museums. Further south still brings you to the **Serra da Lousã** and the **Serra do Açor**, untamed mountain regions hosting a range of pretty settlements, inlcuding **Píodão**, an incredibly sited schist village.

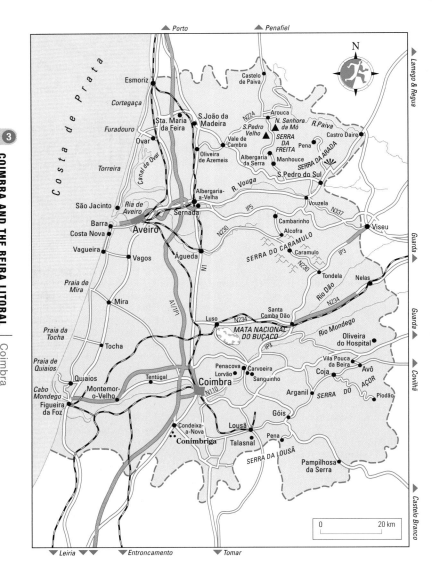

Coimbra

COIMBRA (pronounced *queem-bra*) was Portugal's capital for over a century (1143–1255) and its famous university – founded in 1290 and permanently established here in 1537 after a series of moves back and forth to Lisbon – was the only one in Portugal until the beginning of the last century. It remains highly prestigious and provides the greatest of Coimbra's monuments and buildings, most notably the renowned Baroque library. In addition, there are a remarkable number of other riches: two cathedrals, dozens of lesser churches, and scores of ancient mansions.

This roll-call of splendours is promoted zealously by the inhabitants of what – when all is said and done – is little more than a large, provincial town. There's an air of self-importance that whistles through both city and citizens, bolstered by Coimbra's long academic tradition and fed by shops, galleries and cafés that would sit easily in Lisbon. For visitors, this means that Coimbra can be a lot of fun: it's a very manageable size, with a population of around a hundred and fifty thousand, and its streets are packed with bars and taverns, at their busiest when the students are in town. The liveliest time to be here is in May, when the end of the academic year is celebrated in the **Queima das Fitas**, with late-night concerts, parades and graduates ceremoniously tearing or burning their gowns and faculty ribbons. Although the student's alcohol-fuelled antics can get rather excessive, this is when you're most likely to hear the genuine **Coimbra fado**, distinguished from the Lisbon version by its mournful pace and romantic or intellectual lyrics.

Arrival, information and city transport

There are three **train stations** – Coimbra A, Coimbra B and Coimbra Parque. Riverside **Coimbra A** (often just "Coimbra" on timetables, and known as Estação Nova) is right at the heart of things; express trains call only at **Coimbra B** (Estação Velha), 3km to the north, from where you pick up a local train into Coimbra A – just follow everyone else across the platform (you don't need another ticket). **Coimbra Parque**, southeast of the centre, is for services to and from Lousã, to the south.

The main **bus station** is on Avenida Fernão de Magalhães, about fifteen minutes' walk northwest of the centre. Almost all long-distance buses operate from here, as do international services to Spain, France and Germany. AVIC buses, operating along the Costa de Prata to and from Praia da Mira, stop at the station at Rua João de Ruão 18 on the way in from the main bus station. AVIC also runs buses to and from Condeixa-a-Nova and Conímbriga, which also make a stop at the top of Avenida Emídio Navarro, just before Coimbra A station. There are a couple of other bus companies, too, running local and national services – for all departure details, see "Listings", p.219.

Driving into Coimbra can be a nightmare, since most of the central streets are closed to cars. It's best to use one of the signposted **car parks** or stay at a hotel with car parking and then walk into town. If you do drive in, don't be confused by signs directing you to the Universidade Polo II (which is on the outskirts of town) – instead, follow signs to the city centre, before taking those to the main university.

Information and transport

For a free map, call at the **turismo** on the triangular Largo da Portagem, facing the Ponte Santa Clara (Easter–Sept Mon–Fri 9am–7pm, Sat & Sun 10am–1pm & 2.30–5.30pm; Oct–Easter Mon–Fri 9.30am–12.30pm & 2–5.30pm, Sat & Sun 10am–1pm; ☎239 488 120, ⓦwww.turismo-centro. pt). There are also tourist offices on Largo Dom Dinis (Mon–Fri 9am–6pm, Sat & Sun 9am–12.30pm & 2–5.30pm; ☎239 832 591), on Praça da República (Mon–Fri 10am–6.30pm; ☎239 833 202) and next to the main market (Mon–Fri 9am–6pm; ☎239 834 038).

You'll get most out of **walking** around the old quarter of Coimbra; indeed, you'll have no choice given the inaccessibility of most of the hillside alleys and

B & 4

CAFÉS & RESTAURANTS

Funchal	7
Galeria Santa Clara	16
Paço do Conde	6
O Pátio	1
Viela	12
Zé Carioca	3
Zé Manel	14
Zé Neto	7

BARS & CLUBS

Académico	9
Alcantara Mar	11
Cartola Esplanada Bar	5
Diligência	2
Quebra Costas	15
RMX	13
Scotch	17
Tropical	8
Via Latina	10
Vinyl	4

ACCOMMODATION

Antunes	L
Astória	K
Botânico	M
Bragança	E
Coimbra	H
Dómus	D
Flôr de Coimbra	G
Internacional	I
Kanimambo	A
Moderna	F
Oslo	C
Paris	J
Pousada de Juventude	B
Quinta das Lágrimas	N

Bus Station

Aveiro

AVENIDA FERNÃO DE MAGALHÃES

RUA DA FIGUEIRA DA FOZ

RUA DE AVEIRO

RUA PADRE ESTÊVÃO CABRAL

RUA PADRE ESTÊVÃO CABRAL

Local Buses

RUA DO ARNADO JOÃO MACHADO

LARGO DO ARNADO

Pingo Doce (Supermarket)

Igreja da Graça

RUA DA SOFIA

BAIXA

AVIC Buses

R. MARIO PAIS

DR. MANUEL RODRIGUES

Local Buses

Coimbra 'A'

AV FERNÃO DE MAGALHÃES

RUA DIREITA

RUA DOS OLEIROS

LARGO DAS OLARIAS

Igreja S. Tiago

Igreja de Santa Cruz

Police

R. OLÍMPIO NICOLAU RUI FERNANDES

RUA DE MONTARROIO

Mercado

RUA DA PONTE NOVA

Elevador

Sé Nova

RUA DOS ESTUDOS

Museu Machado de Castro

Sé Velha

Arco de Almedina

Palácio de Sub Ripas

VISCONDE DA LUZ

RUA FERREIRA BORGES

RUA FERNANDES TOMÁS

RUA DA LOUSA

RUA DA BAIXA

P

Avenida @ Cinema

AVENIDA SÁ DA BANDEIRA

RUA ANTERO DE QUENTAL

RUE NICOLAU CHANTERENNE

RUA ANTÓNIO JOSÉ DE ALMEIDA

RUA GUERRA JUNQUEIRO

RUA PADRE ANTÓNIO VIEIRA

RUA LOURENÇO A. AZEVEDO

Parque de Santa Cruz

PRAÇA DA REPÚBLICA

R. ALEXANDRE HERCULANO

R. GARRETT

RUA VENÂNCIO RODRIGUES

RUA OLIVEIRA MATOS

RUA DE TOMAR

Teatro Académico Gil Vicente

LARGO D. DINIS

RUA CASTRO MATOSO

LARGO DA PORTAGEM

Rio Mondego

AVENIDA DE CONIMBRIGA

Coimbra 'B' & Hotels Bus Station

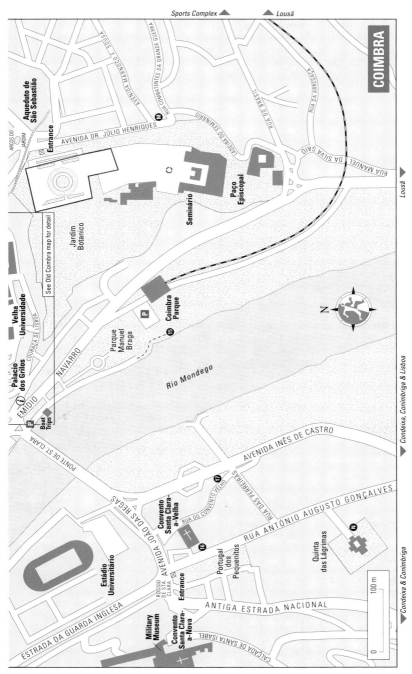

Sports Complex ▲   ▲ Lousã

COIMBRA

▶ Lousã

▶ Condeixa, Conimbriga & Lisboa

▶ Condeixa & Conimbriga

Aqueduto de São Sebastião

Entrance

AVENIDA DR. JÚLIO HENRIQUES

AVENIDA MARNÓCO E SOUSA

RUA COMBATENTES DA GRANDE GUERRA

LADEIRA DO SEMINÁRIO

RUA DA ARREGAÇA

RUA DR. BRASIL

RUA DA SILVA GAIO

RUA MANUEL DA SILVA GAIO

Jardim Botânico

Seminário

Paço Episcopal

See Old Coimbra map for detail

Velha Universidade

Palacio dos Grilos

COURAÇA DE LISBOA

NAVARRO

EMÍDIO

Boat Trips

PONTE DE ST CLARA

Parque Manuel Braga

Coimbra Parque

Rio Mondego

N

AVENIDA INÊS DE CASTRO

AVENIDA JOÃO DAS REGAS

Convento Santa Clara-a-Velha

RUA DO CONVENTO VELHO

RUA DAS FERREIRAS

RUA ANTÓNIO AUGUSTO GONÇALVES

Estádio Universitário

ESTRADA DA GUARDA INGLESA

ROSSIO DE STA CLARA

AVENIDA SANTA CLARA

Entrance

Portugal dos Pequenitos

Quinta das Lágrimas

Military Museum

Convento Santa Clara-a-Nova

ANTIGA ESTRADA NACIONAL

CALÇADA DE SANTA ISABEL

0   100 m

ARCOS DO JARDIM

211

streets. Tickets for **town buses** are sold on board (€1.30) but much better value are the three- or eleven-journey cards (called *senhas*; €1.50/5) which you buy from automatic machines dotted around town or from kiosks in Largo da Portagem, Praça 8 de Maio and Praça da República. Click your ticket in the machine by the driver as you board. Information on bus routes and timetables is available from the riverside café in front of the *Hotel Astória*, or the kiosk a little further up. There's also a **transport shop** near the market on Avenida Sá da Bandeira (Mon–Fri 7.30am–7.30pm, Sat 8am–1pm).

For a cheap **bus tour** of the city, #1 and #3 take in most of the sights. Alternatively, hop-on-hop-off, one-hour **open-top bus** tours visiting all the major sights are run by fun(tastic) Coimbra and leave from Largo da Portagem (Tues–Sun 10am–noon & 3–6pm on the hour; €6; ☏800 203 280).

Accommodation

Much of the city's accommodation is within a short walk of Coimbra A station. The cheaper *pensões* are concentrated in the rather sleazy Rua da Sota and the little streets between here and the central Praça do Comércio. More expensive places line Avenida Fernão de Magalhães and the riverside Avenida Emídio Navarro. There are also a couple of good options near Praça da República, including the **youth hostel**. What you won't find is much choice in the hilly streets of the old town. The nearest **campsite** is in Penacova, 22km northeast of town (see p.223), while the nearest **pousada** is 16km to the southwest at Condeixa-a-Nova (p.221).

Hotels and pensions

Pensão Residencial Antunes Rua Castro Matoso 8 ☏239 854 720, ⊛www.residencialantunes .pt.vu. A short walk from the bars and clubs around Pr. da República, this place is quiet, polished and good value; the high-ceilinged rooms are decently sized with bathrooms and TV. Breakfast included. Parking. ❸

Hotel Astória Av. Emídio Navarro 21 ☏239 853 020, ⊛www.almeidahotels.com. Perfectly placed (look for the landmark dome), classically upmarket and wonderfully old fashioned, with an Art Deco interior. The best rooms overlook the river. Breakfast included. ❺

Residencial Avenida Av. Emídio Navarro 37 ☏239 822 156, ℻239 822 155. A musty turn-of-the-twentieth-century pile on the riverside, with characterful rooms complete with broken chandeliers, sturdy old furniture and small, clean bathrooms. Bar, restaurant and TV lounge, too. Parking. ❸

Residencial Botânico Bairro de S. José 15 ☏239 714 824, ℻239 722 010. Quite far from the centre, but up near the botanical gardens, the en-suite rooms here are large and comfortable and the service is friendly. Family rooms available and there's also a bar. Breakfast included. ❹

Hotel Bragança Largo das Ameias 10 ☏239 822 171, ✉email.hbraganza@mail.telepac.pt. Bang opposite the train station, the pseudo-Stalinist

exterior of the *Bragança* is slightly alarming, but things pick up inside, where rooms are spacious, with parquet floors and tiled bathrooms, and service is polite. Breakfast included. Parking. ❹

Casa Pombal Rua dos Flores 18 ☏239 835 175, ℻239 821 548. Higgledy-piggledy Dutch-run town house near the university with lashings of atmosphere, a tiled dining room and small patio-garden. The plentiful breakfast is splendid and included in the rate. Thoroughly recommended. ❸

Residencial Coimbra Rua das Azeiteiras 55 ☏ & ℻239 837 996. Pleasant choice on a busy pedestrianized street in the heart of the city. Smart, en-suite rooms, friendly service and good breakfasts (included). ❸

Residencial Dómus Rua Adelino Veiga 62 ☏239 828 584, ℻239 838 818. On the nicest of the narrow streets across from the train station, this homely but slightly dated place (entrance hidden next to a rug store) has a wide variety of rooms, the best of which have shower, TV and air con. Breakfast included. ❷

Pensão Flôr de Coimbra Rua do Poço 5 ☏239 823 856, ℻239 821 545. Well-cared-for *pensão* with a good selection of rooms; the en-suite ones on the first floor are the better choice, those above are simple but economical. A tasty buffet breakfast is included, and there's also a restaurant (moderate; closed Sun) that serves up some great meat-free versions of Portuguese favourites (at least one vegetarian special daily), as well as a good selection of dishes for carnivores. ❷, en-suite ❸

Residencial Internacional Av. Emídio Navarro 4 ☎239 825 503, ℱ239 838 446. Facing the river, this once-grand, good-value hotel has small but comfortable rooms with high ceilings and smart bathrooms. Rooms at the front can be rather noisy. No credit cards. ❷

Residencial Kanimambo Av. Fernão de Magalhães 484 ☎239 827 151. Upstairs, in a slightly run-down apartment block, this is a good budget option near the bus station. Plain but adequate rooms (with and without shower) spread across two dark floors and accessed by lift. Breakfast included. ❶

Pensão Moderna Rua Adelino Veiga 49 ☎239 825 413, ℱ239 829 508. Set in an unlikely block of shops, the reception and corridors here are utilitarian, but the rooms are well furnished and comfortable, with bath and TV. Some have balconies overlooking the busy pedestrian street below. No credit cards. ❷

Hotel Oslo Av. Fernão de Magalhães 25 ☎239 829 071, ℮hoteloslo@sapo.pt. Pleasant, modern hotel with a restaurant and bar on the top floor. Clean and neat rooms, including some triples, and family rooms that sleep four. Breakfast included. Parking. ❹

Residencial Paris Rua da Sota 41 ☎239 822 732, ℱ239 820 569. Slightly shabby but cheap guest house a block back from the river; the friendly owner is happy to haggle over prices. Many of the decent-sized rooms have bathrooms, and the place is resplendent with plastic flowers and doilies. Breakfast included. No credit cards. ❶

Quinta das Lágrimas Off Rua António Augusto Gonçalves ☎239 802 380, ⓦwww .quintadaslagrimas.com. Situated across the river, this is Coimbra's grandest and most atmospheric choice. A plush stately house set in beautiful gardens and offering large, regally decorated rooms with all mod cons. Also has a swimming pool and a fine restaurant serving traditional Portuguese dishes accompanied by wines from the extensive cellar. Breakfast included. Parking. ❼

Youth hostel

Pousada de Juventude Rua Henrique Seco 14 ☎239 822 955, ⓦwww.pousadasjuventude.pt. Above Parque Santa Cruz, and close to the many pubs and clubs around Pr. da República, this is a decent modern hostel with nice 4–8-bedded dorms and private en-suite twin rooms, plus patio, kitchen and TV room. There's 24hr reception, but check in is only from 6pm–midnight. Buses #7 and #29 from Coimbra A run to the hostel. Dorm beds €11, rooms ❷

The City

Coimbra straddles a hilly site on the north bank of the Rio Mondego, with the **Velha Universidade** (Old University) crowning its summit. The slopes below are a convoluted mass of ancient alleys, centred on the medieval cathedral, the **Sé Velha**, and most things of interest are concentrated nearby on the hill itself or in the largely pedestrianized **Baixa**, or lower town, at its foot. This is the principal shopping area with numerous clothes shops and cafés. The western side of the old town is bounded by the main Rua Ferreira Borges and its continuation, Rua Visconde da Luz, which runs north from the café-filled Largo da Portagem to the **Igreja de Santa Cruz**. Off to the west, the narrow rat-runs and alleys that cut down to the train station contain budget restaurants, canteens, grocery stores, workshops, butchers and bakers.

On foot, the nicest approach to the old town proper is halfway along the main street, through the **Arco de Almedina**, an arch cut through the old city wall. Stepped streets climb beyond into the heart of old Coimbra, with attractive alleys off to either side revealing hidden courtyards, flower-decked balconies, cobbled dead-ends and glimpses of sky. Chances are you'll get lost as soon as you start to climb, but that's half the fun. If you don't feel up to it, take bus #1 to the Velha Universidade; from its balcony the city is laid out below you like a map. You could also cut the walking time by taking the **elevador** from the market on Avenida Sá da Bandeira (Mon–Sat 7.30am–11.30pm, Sat & Sun 9am–11.30pm) to Rua Padre António Vieira, a short walk from the Sé Nova; it costs the same as one bus journey and tickets can be bought at the transport shop next door (see "Information and transport", above).

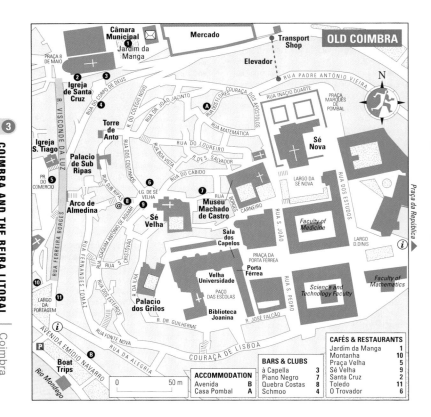

CAFÉS & RESTAURANTS

Jardim da Manga	1
Montanha	10
Praça Velha	5
Sé Velha	9
Santa Cruz	2
Toledo	11
O Trovador	6

BARS & CLUBS

à Capella	3
Piano Negro	7
Quebra Costas	8
Schmoo	4

ACCOMMODATION

Avenida	B
Casa Pombal	A

Igreja de Santa Cruz

Restraint and simplicity are simply not the words that spring to mind when considering the **Igreja de Santa Cruz** (Mon–Sat 9am–noon & 2–5.45pm, Sun 4–6pm; free), at the northern end of Rua Visconde da Luz. The church of the monastery that was founded on the site by São Teotónio, it predates even the Sé Velha, and it was here that the romantic history of Dom Pedro and Inês de Castro came to its ghoulish climax (see "Alcobaça", p.172). Nothing remains of the original design that has not been substantially remodelled, including the exuberant facade and interior eighteenth-century *azulejos*.

In the early sixteenth century, Coimbra was the base of a major sculptural school that included the French artists Nicolas Chanterene and Jean de Rouen (João de Ruão), as well as the two Manueline masters João de Castilho and Diogo de Boitaca, all of whom had a hand in rebuilding Santa Cruz. These artists designed a variety of projects, viewed via the sacristy (€2.50): **tombs** to house Portugal's first kings, Afonso Henriques and Sancho I; the elaborate **Sala do Capitulo**; and, most famously, the **Cloister of Silence**. It is here that the Manueline theme is at its clearest, with a series of airy arches decorated with bas-relief scenes from the life of Christ. You can ask to be shown the raised *coro*, accessed via a staircase from the cloister; above its wooden benches is a frieze celebrating the nation's flourishing empire.

Around the back of the church, the small **Jardim da Manga** is all that remains of the Manga fountain, once attached to the Santa Cruz monastery. At the rear is a good self-service restaurant (see p.217).

Sé Velha

The **Sé Velha** (Mon–Thurs & Sat 10am–6pm, Fri 10am–2pm, closed Sun; free), an unmistakable fortress-like bulk, squats about halfway up the hill in its own steeply shelving square. Begun in 1162, it's one of the most important Romanesque buildings in Portugal, little altered and seemingly unbowed by the weight of the years. The one significant later addition – the Renaissance Porta Especiosa in the north wall – has, in contrast to the main structure, almost entirely crumbled away. Solid and square on the outside, the cathedral is also stolid and simple within, the decoration confined to a few giant conch shells holding holy water and some unobtrusive *azulejos* from Seville around the walls. The Gothic tombs of early bishops and the low-arched cloister (€1; closed 1–2pm) are equally restrained.

Museu Machado de Castro and Sé Nova

Continuing up the northern side of the Sé Velha, along Rua Borges Carneiro, brings you to the **Museu Machado de Castro** (closed until 2007). The museum, named after an eighteenth-century sculptor, is housed in the former archbishop's palace and is positively stuffed with treasures: sculpture, paintings, furniture, and ceramics. Underneath lies the Roman **Cryptoportico** (no public access), a series of subterranean galleries probably used by the Romans as a granary and subsequently pressed into service for the foundations of the palace.

Across the way stands the unprepossessing **Sé Nova**, or New Cathedral (Tues–Fri 9am–noon & 2–5.30pm; free), a seventeenth-century Jesuit foundation which replaced the Sé Velha as cathedral in 1772.

Velha Universidade

From the Sé Nova, head up Rua de São João and turn right through the seventeenth-century **Porta Férrea**, the entrance to the main part the **Velha Universidade** (daily: April–Oct 9am–7.20pm; Nov–March 9.30am–5.30pm; €4 for university, library and Sala dos Capelos, €2.50 library only). Dating from the sixteenth century, when João III declared its establishment at Coimbra permanent, the buildings are set around a courtyard dominated by the Baroque clock tower nicknamed *A Cabra* – "the goat" – and a statue of the portly João III.

The elaborate stairway to the right of the main court leads into the administrative quarters and the **Sala dos Capelos**; tickets are sold here for visits to each of the main sections of the university. The hall itself – hung with portraits of Portugal's kings – is used for conferring degrees and has a fine wood-panelled ceiling with gilded decoration in the Manueline style. The highlight of this part of the building, though, is the narrow catwalk around the outside walls. The central door off the courtyard leads past the **Capela**, not the finest of Coimbra's religious foundations but one of the most elaborate – covered with *azulejos* and intricate decoration including twisted, rope-like pillars, a frescoed ceiling, and a gaudy Baroque organ.

To the left is the famous library, the **Biblioteca Joanina**, a Baroque fantasy presented to the faculty by João V in the early eighteenth century. Its rooms telescope into each other, focusing on the founder's portrait in a disconcertingly effective use of trompe l'oeil. The richness of it all is impressive, such as the expanse of cleverly marbled wood, gold leaf, tables inlaid with ebony, rosewood and jacaranda, Chinese-style lacquer work and carefully calculated frescoed ceilings. The most prized valuables, the rare and ancient books, are locked away out of sight and, despite their impressive multilingual titles, the volumes on the shelves seem largely chosen for their aesthetic value; no one seems likely to disturb the careful arrangement by actually reading anything.

Sadly, the other faculty buildings of the university are almost completely devoid of interest. Their lofty position atop the narrow, cobbled streets notwithstanding, too many are mere concrete excrescences dating from a modernization programme under Dr. Salazar. The wide spaces in between are tempered by modern sculpture of dubious quality, and only the lure of the student-frequented pavement bars on **Praça da República** – down the steep steps from Largo Dom Dinis – merit the diversion.

Jardim Botânico

Just down the hill from Largo Dom Dinis, ten minutes or so to the south, the **Jardim Botânico** (daily: April–Sept 9am–8pm; Oct–May 9am–5.30pm; €1.50, free weekdays) is worth a brief visit. Founded in the eighteenth century, these botanical displays once enjoyed a worldwide reputation and, even if they've seen better days, it's still very pleasant to stroll among the formally laid out beds of plants from around the world, but note that you're not allowed to picnic here. Nearby are the impressive remains of the sixteenth-century **Aqueduto de São Sebastião**.

The Santa Clara convents

Once home to the tomb of Coimbra's patron, saint-queen Isabel, the **Convento de Santa Clara-a-Velha**, a twenty-minute walk from the main town across the Ponte de Santa Clara, has suffered continually from its riverside position. From the first floods in the fourteenth century, various attempts were made to adapt to the unwanted water (such as adding successively higher floors), but by 1677 the nuns conceded defeat and moved up the hill to the Convento de Santa Clara-a-Nova, taking Isabel with them. Remarkably, the convent remained immersed in water and silt for more than three hundred years, with only the highest part visible. Between 1995 and 1999 the site was drained and the well-preserved convent is now accessible for **guided tours** (hourly Tues–Fri 4–8pm, Sat & Sun 2–7pm; in Portuguese, call ahead to arrange one in English ☏239 801 160; €3). A museum containing the many artefacts found during the restoration is planned at the site for 2006.

The **Convento de Santa Clara-a-Nova** (Tues–Sun 9am–noon & 2–5pm; cloister €1), higher up the hill and safe from the shifting river, was built in 1650; it doesn't have much of the charm of the old and the fact that the nuns' quarters now house a Portuguese army barracks doesn't help. Its two saving graces, which make the climb worthwhile, are **Isabel's tomb** – made of solid silver collected by the citizens of Coimbra – and the vast **cloister**, heady with honeysuckle, which was financed by João V, a king whose devotion to nuns went beyond the normal bounds of spiritual comfort. The army's presence exerts itself in a small, uninteresting **military museum** (daily 10am–noon & 2–5pm; €1.50), displaying bits and bombs retrieved from World War II.

Portugal dos Pequenitos and Quinta das Lágrimas

Between the two convents extends the parkland site of **Portugal dos Pequenitos** (daily: March–May 10am–7pm; June to mid-Sept 9am–8pm; mid-Sept to Feb 10am–5pm; €5), a theme park built in the 1950s where scale models of many of the country's great buildings are interspersed with "typical" farmhouses and sections on the overseas territories, heavy with the White Man's Burden. Historically and architecturally accurate it's not, but the place is great fun for children who can clamber in and out of the miniature houses.

A short distance beyond is a somewhat more sombre little park, the **Quinta das Lágrimas** (Garden of Tears; daily 9am–5pm; €0.75), in which, so legend has it, Inês de Castro was finally tracked down and murdered. The mansion here is now a luxury hotel (see p.213).

Eating

Down near the old town, the **cheapest meals** are to be found in the dives along Rua Direita in the Baixa, where if you're not too bothered about your surroundings – basement saloons and rough tables – you can eat for under €5. For a tad more sophistication, search out the atmospheric little **restaurants** tucked into the tiny alleys between Largo da Portagem, Rua da Sota and Praça do Comércio – Rua das Azeiteiras, in particular, has several good possibilities. Local specialities to try out are *chanfana* – kid goat slow-roasted in wine – and *pasteis de Santa Clara* (cream-filled pastries traditionally made at the Santa Clara convent). Vegetarians should examine the menu at the *Pensão Flór de Coimbra*.

Adega Funchal Rua das Azeiteiras 18–20 ☎239 824 137. This small restaurant serves generous helpings of chicken or mutton stew and the like in agreeable rustic surroundings. Closed Sat. Moderate.

Jardim da Manga Rua Olímpio Nicolau Rui Fernandes ☎239 829 156. Good, solid Portuguese standards on offer at a self-service restaurant where you can eat inside or more pleasantly on the small terrace, complete with fountain. Closed Sat. Inexpensive.

Adega Paço do Conde Rua Paço do Conde 1 ☎239 825 605. Great, locally renowned *churrasqueira* of cavernous proportions, with a dining room either side of a covered terrace. Around €9 for grilled meat or fish, salad, wine and coffee. Closed Sun. Inexpensive.

O Pátio Pátio da Inquisição ☎239 828 596. Good for lunch, this small restaurant on a tastefully renovated square has shaded outdoor dining on a little terrace, as well as seats inside. Good-value *pratos da dia* and slightly pricier seafood dishes. Moderate.

O Trovador Largo da Sé Velha 17 ☎239 825 475. Next to the old cathedral, this lovely wood-panelled and ceramic-tiled restaurant is reasonably priced, if rather limited in choice. It's a bit touristy, but that does mean you get regular fado sessions. Closed Mon. Moderate.

Viela Rua das Azeiteiras 33 ☎239 832 625. Simple tiled dining room with good food, overseen by a friendly proprietor. Tables also spill out around the back into the quiet Largo do Romal. The pork and chicken are both good. Inexpensive.

Zé Carioca Av. Sá da Bandeira 89 ☎239 835 450. Brazilian restaurant set in a series of small contemporarily styled dining rooms. The speciality is *rodízio de carnes nobres* (€16) a succession of delicious meats served up on sword-like skewers with an array of accompaniments. Also available are *bacalhau* with a Brazilian twist and a tasty *feijoada*. Live Brazilian music nightly. Lunch buffet €6.50. Closed Sun. Expensive.

Zé Manel Beco do Forno 12 ☎239 823 790. Tiny, atmospheric place, tucked away in a quiet street behind *Hotel Astória*. The walls are adorned with cartoons and poems, the service is brisk and friendly, and the simple food excellent. If you don't want to queue, turn up by 7pm. Closed Sat eve & Sun. Moderate.

Zé Neto Rua das Azeiteiras 8–10 ☎239 826 786. Portuguese grills and fries at budget prices, washed down with some of the least expensive house wine in town. Closed Sun. Moderate.

Drinking and nightlife

At some stage of the day, you should visit one of the traditional **cafés** and **coffee houses** along Rua Ferreira Borges and Rua Visconde da Luz, filled with package-laden shoppers. Praça da República, across town by the Parque de Santa Cruz, is also surrounded by café-bars, this time popular with students and staying open until 2am. Other fashionable **bars** are scattered across old and new parts of town, and the best are reviewed below; all stay open until 2am unless otherwise stated. Coimbra's **clubs** remain open much later; in some, you can expect the music to keep going until 7am. As a rule, you'll pay a minimum entrance fee of €2.50–5 in the clubs, as well as in bars where there's a DJ or live music.

You're most likely to catch **fado** during the student celebrations in May, though there are year-round performances in bars such as *Diligência* and *à Capella*, and even in some restaurants; those around the Sé Velha are good bets. From July to September there are also outdoor fado performances in the old town, which are advertised locally or you can find out more from the tourist office. For other **concerts** and events, watch for fly posters stuck up all over university buildings.

Cafés

Café Montanha Largo da Portagem. Best-sited of the square's cafés with a good view of the passing parade and bridge traffic. There's live music or poetry some evenings.

Café Santa Cruz Pr. 8 de Maio. Coimbra's most atmospheric and appealing café, set in part of the monastery buildings. It's hard to say which spot is more attractive – the vaulted stone interior or the outside tables. Also good for an evening drink.

Café Sé Velha Rua Joaquim António d'Aguiar 130–136. At the top of a particularly exhausting flight of steps a stone's throw from the cathedral, with outdoor terrace seating. Closed Sun.

Galeria Santa Clara Rua António Augusto Gonçalves 67. Excellent café-bar with attached gallery (daily 2–8pm), cool indoor seating and a large terrace overlooking Santa-Clara-a-Velha. Serves good cocktails, as well as herbal teas and snacks – they clock up your drinks on a card and you pay on the way out. Open until 3am Fri & Sat.

Pasteleria Toledo Largo da Portagem. Busy little café serving sandwiches, filling soups and divine *pasteis de Santa Clara*. Also has tables in the square outside.

Praça Velha Pr. do Comércio. Tables outside in a veritable suntrap of a square, just down the steps from the main street.

Bars

à Capella Rua do Corpo de Deus, Largo da Victória. In a former chapel, this stylish venue hosts excellent fado performances, accompanied by a grand piano.

Académico Pr. da República. This fashionable spot gets busy with a young studenty crowd.

Alcantara Mar Rua Alexandre Herculano. Compact, but extremely cool DJ bar attracting an older clientele who come for a civilized drink in the opulently decorated lounge area or to nod their heads knowingly at the bar to the quality house music. Dress up a little.

Cartola Esplanada Bar Pr. da República. Pretty plain but undeniably popular student favourite, next to the turismo, with esplanade seats and interior chrome fittings.

Diligência Bar Rua Nova 30. There's food, drink and fado every night in this atmospheric joint with cobblestone walls and candles, though the feelings of *saudade* (loss and longing), from which the music draws its spirit, will also be felt in your wallet.

Piano Negro Rua Borges Carneiro 19. Small and smoky, this unpretentious bar attracts a good-humoured international student crowd, listening to great jazz and chilled-out tunes.

Bar Quebra Costas Rua Quebra Costas 47. Small, stylishly laid-back bar tucked away on the steps leading down from the Sé Velha. A second branch, close to Coimbra Parque on the banks of the Mondego, is a great place for a riverside beer.

Schmoo Rua do Corpo de Deus 68. Tiny, funky bar tucked away up an old back street, with bright, simple decor and good DJs.

Tropical Pr. da República, corner of Rua Alexandre Herculano. Split-level bar packed with students at the weekends. The pavement tables soon get swamped, while the barman roves around with trays of ice-cold Super Bocks.

Clubs

RMX Rua Venâncio Rodrigues 11 & 19. A younger crowd hangs out at this popular, down-to-earth club where everyone is up for a good time. Music varies but tends towards chart hits and commercial dance.

Scotch Quinta da Ínsua. Young and lively club pumping out all sorts of dance music (depending on the night) to a cheerful, studenty crowd.

Via Latina Rua Almeida Garrett 1. Relaxed and trendy space near Pr. da República, covering two floors. Music changes nightly but includes house, hip-hop, drum 'n' bass and R&B. Open till 6.30–7am; closed Sun.

Vinyl Av. Afonso Henriques. Fashionable club favoured by the well-heeled glamour crowd. Usually showcases home-grown DJs as well as international names, such as Fatboy Slim.

Listings

Banks and exchange Banks and ATMs are grouped along the avenidas west and east of Coimbra A station, Av. Emídio Navarro and Av. Fernão de Magalhães. The *Hotel Astória*, Av. Emídio Navarro 21 (close to Largo da Portagem), will change currency outside bank hours, as will *Hotel Tivoli*, Rua João Machado.

Boat trips Basófias runs 75min trips up the Rio Mondego (departing from beside Parque Dr. Manuel Braga; ☎969 830 664, ⓦwww.basofias.com; €8), giving you a duck's-eye view of the old city. Trips depart Tues–Sun at 11am, 3pm, 4pm, 5pm & 6pm. O Pioneiro do Mondego arranges downriver kayak trips from the nearby town of Penacova to Coimbra (see p.223).

Buses Local buses are run by SMTUC ☎239 801 100. Most out-of-town services use the main bus station at the top end of Av. Fernão de Magalhães (information ☎239 855 270). AVIC, Rua João de Ruão 18 ☎239 823 769, ⓦwww.avic.pt), runs to the Costa de Prata resorts, Figueira da Foz, Aveiro, Condeixa-a-Nova and Conímbriga; Moisés Correia de Oliveira, Rua Rosa Falcão 10 (☎239 828 268), runs to Montemor-o-Velho and Figueira da Foz. RBL (☎239 855 270, ⓦwww.rblsa.com) run buses to Figueira da Foz, Leiria, Lousã, Luso, Penacova, Porto, Tondela and Viseu. For services to the mountain Beiras and the north, contact Rodo Norte, Bufete Teresinha, Av. Emídio Navarro ☎239 825 190, ⓦwww.rodonorte.pt.

Car rental Avis, Coimbra A station ☎239 834 786, ⓦwww.avis.com; Hertz, Rua Padre Estêvão Cabral ☎239 834 750, ⓦwww.hertz.com; Salitur, Rua Padre Estêvão Cabral ☎239 820 594.

Cinema Cinemas Millennium Avenida, Av. Sá da Bandeira 25 ☎239 826 342; also has a rooftop bar and great city views. Teatro Academico Gil Vicente, Pr. da República ☎239 855 630,

ⓦwww.uc.pt/tagv, has an arts cinema as well as a gallery, café and occasional classical and jazz concerts.

Hospital Centro Hospitalar de Coimbra, Quinta dos Vales – S. Martinho do Bispo ☎239 800 100.

Internet Central Modem, Escadas do Quebra Costas (daily 9am–4pm; ⓦwww.centralmodem.com); CiberEspaço, Galerias Avenida, Av. Sá da Bandeira (Mon–Sat 10am–midnight, Sun 1pm–midnight); Spacenet, Av. Sá da Bandeira 67 (Mon–Sat 10am–midnight, Sun 2pm–midnight).

Left luggage *Café Pasterlaria Cristal* (daily 6am–9.30pm), directly opposite the train station, will look after bags for €2 for 4 hours.

Market The main food market (Mon–Sat) is on Rua Olímpio Nicolau Rui Fernandes, close to the post office.

Police Main HQ at Rua Olímpio Nicolau Rui Fernandes ☎239 851 300, across from the post office.

Post office The main post office is at Av. Fernão de Magalhães 223, near Largo do Arnado (Mon–Fri 8.30am–6.30pm, Sat 9am–12.30pm); other central offices are on Rua Olímpio Nicolau Rui Fernandes, just below the market, and on Pr. da República (both same hours as main post office).

Taxis There are taxi ranks outside Coimbra A and B train stations, by the police headquarters near Pr. 8 de Maio, and in Pr. da República. To call a cab, ring Politaxis ☎239 499 090.

Train information ☎239 852 583, ⓦwww.cp.pt.

Travel agencies Inter Visa, Av. Fernão de Magalhães 11 ☎239 828 904, ⓔintervisacoimbra@mail.telepac.pt, sells international bus and flight tickets. Also try Viagens Mondego, Rua João de Ruão 16 ☎239 855 555, ⓦwww.viagensmondego.com, or Halcon Viages, Rua Visconde da Luz 75 ☎239 855 820.

Around Coimbra

There are several sights within easy reach of Coimbra that are worth a day-trip. Close by is the Roman city of **Conímbriga** and its fine mosaics, while west towards the coast stand the impressive ruins of the castle at **Montemor–o–Velho**.

To the northeast of the city the kayaking possibilities on the **Rio Mondego** and the attractive scenery around the hilltop town of **Penacova** are similarly enticing and, if you were looking for an overnight stop in the Coimbra countryside, this would be the best choice. All the destinations can be reached easily by public transport.

Conímbriga

The ancient city of **Conímbriga** (daily: March–Sept 9am–8pm; Oct–March 9am–6pm; €3, free Sun), 16km southwest of Coimbra, is by far the most important Roman site in Portugal. It was almost certainly preceded by a substantial Celto-Iberian settlement, dating back to the Iron Age, but the excavated buildings nearly all belong to the latter days of the Roman Empire, from the second to the fourth century AD. Throughout this period Conímbriga was a major stopping point on the road from Olisipo (Lisbon) to Bracara Augusta (Braga). Although by no means the largest town in Roman Portugal, it has survived better than any other – principally because when attacked its inhabitants abandoned Conímbriga, apparently for the comparative safety of Coimbra, and never resettled it. That the city came to a violent end is clear from the powerful wall thrown up right through its heart, a wall erected so hurriedly and determinedly that it even cut houses in two.

The site

It is the **wall**, with the Roman road leading up to and through it, that first strikes you. Little else, indeed, remains above ground level. In the urgency of its construction anything that came to hand was used and a close inspection reveals pillars, inscribed plaques and bricks thrown in among the rough stonework. Most of what has been excavated is in the immediate environs of the wall; the bulk of the city, still only partly excavated, lies beyond it.

What you can see is impressive enough though: houses with exceptional **mosaic floors**, some now unattractively covered to protect them from the elements; **pools** whose original fountains and water-ducts have been restored to working order (drop €0.50 into the machine in front of the fountains to watch them play); and a complex series of **baths** with their elaborate underfloor heating systems revealed. Beyond the wall, less work has been undertaken, but here, too, are evocative remains, particularly of the **aqueduct**, which fed the city with water, and the **forum**, with its shop entrances, and nearby **temple**. At the edge of the site, on a bluff above the steep valley – for many years Conímbriga's main defence – a series of **public baths** enjoy a stupendous view.

There are some explanatory notes in English posted across the site, but to make sense of it all, it's worth investing in the official **guidebook** sold at the entrance. In the summer you may find students on site to explain the finer points.

It's also worth stopping off in the excellent and inexpensive self-service **restaurant** (℡239 944 217) on site, which serves Roman and medieval recipes such as quail with grapes, as well as large salads.

The museum

The Conímbriga entrance fee (hang onto your ticket) includes entry to the excellent **Museu Monográfico de Conímbriga** (Tues–Sun: mid-March to Sept 9am–8pm; Oct to mid-March 9am–6pm), opposite the site entrance. On display are fascinating finds from the dig, presented thematically in cabinets detailing various trades (glass-making, ironmongery, weaving, even house-building) and aspects of daily life; the section on health and hygiene contains crude scalpels and needles, while nearby is a lovely collection of carved jade rings. On the other side of the museum, diagrams show how the finds relate to the site itself. Here, too, are displayed the larger spoils – statues of torsos, carved lintels, gargoyles from temples, monochromatic mosaics, remarkably bright mural fragments, and slabs, pillars and tombstones from the necropolis.

Practicalities

Only one or two **buses** run directly from Coimbra to Conímbriga and back each day, but there are more regular buses (roughly every 30min) to **CON-DEIXA-A-NOVA**, a nearby market town; both services run from the AVIC bus station in Coimbra or the stop near Coimbra A (see p.209). From the church at the edge of the main square it's a 2km walk to the site – follow the signposts. The last bus back leaves at 8.05pm. The town is a pleasant little place, with several cafés and bars around the square – *O Regional* does decent **meals** at reasonable prices; the speciality, roast kid, costs €9. For something more upmarket there's the restaurant in the elegant *Pousada de Santa Cristina* (℡239 944 025, ⓦ www.pousadas.pt; breakfast included; ❼), north of the main square, an elegant place set in peaceful grounds with a swimming pool. Condeixa is also the centre of the Beira's **hand-painted ceramics** industry and numerous local factories are open for visits – you'll pass a couple on the walk out along the main road to the site.

Montemor-o-Velho

Thirty-two kilometres west of Coimbra, the castle at **MONTEMOR-O-VELHO** broods over the flood plain of the Mondego. From the train, or driving along the N111, its keep and crenellated silhouette rival that of Óbidos, as does its early history. First the Romans, then the Moors, fortified this conspicuous rocky bluff; finally taken from the Moors at the end of the eleventh century, it became a favoured royal residence. It was here in 1355 that Dom Afonso IV met with his council to decide on the fate of Inês de Castro, and here, thirty years later, that João of Avis received the homage of the townspeople on his way to Coimbra to be acclaimed Dom João I.

Despite this royal attention, the town itself never prospered, and today there's little enough to see inside the **castle** (daily 9am–9pm; free) either, though the views from the walkways are stunning. The main attraction within the walls is the Manueline **Igreja de Santa Maria de Alcáçova**, said to have been designed by Diogo de Boitaca of Belém fame; it has a beautiful wooden ceiling, fine twisted columns and Moorish-style *azulejo* decoration.

If you can, aim to visit on the second or fourth Wednesday of the month, when Montemor's vast morning **market** spills across the plain in the lee of the castle. Families swarm in from the surrounding countryside, soon clogging up the congested central streets.

Practicalities

The **train station** is a 1km walk from town and castle; **buses** from Coimbra drop you much more centrally. There's no particular reason to require **accommodation**, given the proximity of Coimbra or indeed Figueira da Foz, just 13km further west. That said, the *Residencial Abade João*, Rua Combatentes da Grande Guerra 15 (℡239 689 458; breakfast not included but available; ❷), a beautiful, converted period town house, may persuade you to stop; it's just up the street to the left as you face the white town hall in the central Praça da República. The **turismo**, within the walls of the castle (daily: June–Sept 9am–9pm; Oct–May 10am–5pm; ℡239 680 380), could doubtless drum up more reasons to hang around, though there's no better excuse than a **meal** at the expensive *Restaurante Ramalhão* (℡239 689 435; closed Sun evening & Mon), Rua Tenente Valadim 24, where all the dishes – eel stew, chicken with rice, duck or rabbit – use ingredients grown, reared or caught around the town.

Penacova and the Rio Mondego

Northeast of Coimbra, the hilly, wooded valley of the **Rio Mondego** is a delight. The river is trailed by the minor N110 road, affording the occasional sweeping view of glistening water and improbably perched hamlets. Regular buses make the trip from Coimbra, while during the summer it's possible to rent a kayak to travel downriver from Penacova back to Coimbra (see below).

PENACOVA itself, 22km northeast of Coimbra, is a small town of some antiquity set high above the river, with stunning views of the valley. There is little enough to the place itself – a pint-sized square, a couple of cafés and restaurants, and the surrounding river and woods – though an oddity is the highly elaborate **toothpicks** (*palitos*) on sale. These are hand-carved from willow by local women and are beautiful artefacts; the more delicate ones are like feathered darts.

At Penacova, the road forks and drivers can make the most of the scenic surroundings by heading up the equally attractive N235 to Luso (see p.225). The IP3, meanwhile, sticks initially with the Mondego and forges on for Viseu, via Tondela (p.230), a roller-coaster of a main road with some very fast sections and more fine views.

Practicalities

The **bus** from Coimbra drops you in the main square, where you'll find the helpful **turismo** (Mon–Fri 9am–5pm, Sat & Sun 10am–1pm & 2–5pm; ℡239 470 300, ⓦwww.cm-penacova.pt), located in the town hall. This has a display of the locally made toothpicks, some of which are for sale.

Accommodation is usually easy enough to come by, with the plushest choice the four-star *Palacete do Mondego* (℡239 470 700, ⓦwww .palacete-penacova.net; breakfast included; ❺), Avenida Dr. Bissaya Barreto 3 (follow signs), set on a bluff high above the river. This former fort and chapel has 38 tastefully decorated rooms and fantastic views from its terrace, pool and stylish bar and restaurant. Equally agreeable is the lovely old *Casa do Repouso* (℡239 476 569, ℻239 476 568; breakfast included; no credit cards; ❸), Rua Cova do Barro 2, 100m up the hill from the turismo, with charming rooms and a beautiful garden. Otherwise, try the friendly, traditional *Pensão Avenida*, Avenida Abel Rodrigues da Costa (℡ & ℻239 477 142; no credit cards; ❷), down the hill from the main square, with a polished wood interior, sun-terrace and budget restaurant – the large, slightly musty rooms all come with shower.

For meals, the well-respected, if expensive, *O Panorâmico* (℡239 477 333) **restaurant** – next to the town hall and turismo – serves excellent *chanfana* as well as a selection of fish and game dishes. It has a glorious view down the valley and a very good wine selection. They also have a café (drinks and snacks, no meals) on the other side of the town hall, whose terrace revels in the same views.

There's a **campsite** (☎239 477 664; closed mid-Dec to mid-Jan), set on the opposite bank of the Mondego, a right turn after the bridge below town. There's another 3km northeast at Vila Nova (☎239 477 946), a left turn after the bridge, where you can fish in the river.

On the river

O Pioneiro do Mondego arranges downriver **kayak trips** to Coimbra (June–Sept daily; €18 per person; book in advance ☎239 478 385, ⓦwww .opioneirodomondego.com), leaving Penacova at 11am. It's a 25km (3–4hr) trip back to Coimbra and there's a free minibus from Coimbra at 10am to get you to Penacova in time for departure. Otherwise, Sportmargens in Penacova, Avenida 5° de Outubro 1 (☎239 477 143, ⓦwww.sportmargens.com), also organizes canoe trips (€15 per person) and rents out bicycles for the day (€10 per day).

The Mata Nacional do Buçaco and Luso

The Buçaco Forest – properly the **Mata Nacional do Buçaco** – is something of a Portuguese icon. The country's most famous and most revered woods were a monastic domain throughout the Middle Ages, and the site in the Peninsular War of a battle that saw Napoleon's first significant defeat. Today, they are a little overvisited, but remain an enjoyable spot for rambling. It's easy enough to visit the forest from Coimbra for an afternoon, or stop en route to Viseu, though there's also plentiful overnight accommodation at the enjoyable old spa town of **Luso**, just 3km from the forest.

The Forest

Benedictine monks established a hermitage in the midst of Buçaco forest as early as the sixth century, and the area remained in religious hands right up to the dissolution of the monasteries in 1834. The forest's great fame and beauty, though, came with the **Carmelite monks** who settled here in the seventeenth century, building the walls that still mark its boundary.

In 1643 Pope Urban VIII issued a papal bull threatening anyone who damaged the trees with excommunication; an earlier decree had already protected the monks' virtue by banning women from entering. The monks, meanwhile, were propagating the forest, introducing varieties new to Portugal from all over the world. Nowadays there are estimated to be more than seven hundred different types of tree, but the most impressive remain some of the earliest – particularly the mighty Mexican cedars.

Walls enclose the entire forest and **access** is via a number of gates (cars €2.50 May–Oct, free Nov–April). All non-express **buses** from Coimbra to Viseu take a short detour through the forest from Luso, stopping at the old royal forest lodge, now the swanky *Palácio do Buçaco*, and again by the Portas da Rainha (for the military museum).

The Palácio do Buçaco and the Convento dos Carmelitas

Built on the site of the old Carmelite monastery as a summer retreat for the Portuguese monarchy, the *Palácio do Buçaco* (☎231 937 970, ⓦwww.almeidahotels .com; breakfast included; ❾) was only completed in 1907, three years before the declaration of the Republic, so saw little royal use. It's an enormous imitation

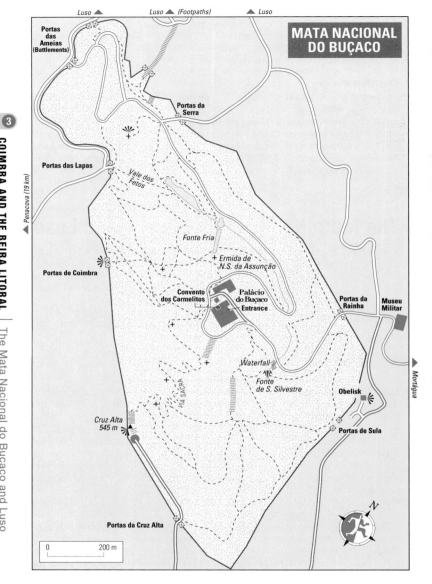

Luso ▲   Luso ▲ (Footpaths)   ▲ Luso

MATA NACIONAL DO BUÇACO

Portas das Ameias (Battlements)

Portas da Serra

Portas das Lapas

▲ Penacova (19 km)

Vale dos Fetos

Fonte Fria

✝ Ermida de N.S. da Assunção

Portas de Coimbra

Convento dos Carmelitos

Palácio do Buçaco
Entrance

Portas da Rainha

Museu Militar

Waterfall

Fonte de S. Silvestre

▲ Mortágua

Obelisk

VIA SACRA

Cruz Alta 545 m

Portas de Sula

Portas da Cruz Alta

N

0   200 m

Manueline construction, and rooms here are pricey, but anyone can stroll in and have a drink (their wine cellar is superb) or a meal (1–3pm & 8–10pm; set price excluding drinks €32.50–40).

You can also view what remains of the **Convento dos Carmelítas** (Mon –Sat 10am–12.30pm & 2–5.30pm; €0.50), and admire the sequence of *azulejos* depicting the Portuguese conquest of Ceuta and the Battle of Buçaco.

The Battle of Buçaco and the Museu Militar

The **Battle of Buçaco** (1810) was fought largely on the ridge just above the forest, and it marked the first serious reverse suffered by Napoleon in his campaigns on the Peninsula. The French under Massena launched a frontal assault up the hill on virtually impregnable Anglo-Portuguese positions, sustaining massive losses in what for the Duke of Wellington amounted to little more than a delaying tactic, which he exploited in order to give himself time to retreat to his lines at Torres Vedras. A small **Museu Militar** (Tues–Sun 10am–12.30pm & 2–5.30pm; €1), outside the forest near the Portas da Rainha, contains maps, uniforms and weapons from the campaign. Just above it, a narrow road climbs to the **obelisk** raised as a memorial to the battle, with vistas inland right across to the distant Serra da Estrela, from where the **Portas de Sula** leads back into the forest.

Walks around the forest

Buçaco is a lovely place to wander around, if not always the haven of peace the monks strove to create – at weekends and holidays the woods are packed with picnicking Portuguese. Walks (most of 1–2hr) are laid out everywhere: along the delightful **Vale dos Fetos** (Valley of Ferns) to the lake and cascading **Fonte Fria**, for example, or up Avenida dos Cedros to the **Portas de Coimbra**. But you can wander freely anywhere in the forest, and in many ways it's at its most attractive where it's wildest, away from the formal pathways and tour groups.

The **Via Sacra**, lined with seventeenth-century chapels in which terracotta figures depict the stages of Christ's journey carrying the cross to Calvary, leads from the *Palácio do Buçaco* to the **Cruz Alta**, a giant cross at the summit of the hill. From here, as from the Portas de Coimbra, there are magnificent panoramas of the surrounding country.

Luso

LUSO lies just 3km downhill from the forest, a pleasant hour's walk on shady paths. A spa town for the past hundred years or so, it still draws crowds of Portuguese, taking the waters as a cure for rheumatism and other complaints. As such places go, its series of elegant spa buildings and dated charm make it worth a brief stop.

Taking the waters at the **spa** (May–Sept; ☏231 937 910, ⦿www .termasdoluso.com), on the town's main thoroughfare Rua Emídio Navarro, can be fun; massage and hydrotherapy cost from €6.90–14.40 a go – the only serious expenditure is incurred if you see one of the spa's consultants. There's also a fine, Olympic-sized **swimming pool**, attached to the central *Grande Hotel de Luso* (see below), whose somewhat stiff admission fee (€10; mid-July to mid-Sept) is more than recompensed by a few hours' basking. Most locals, though, are here to picnic in the surroundings, taking the opportunity to fill bottles and plastic containers for free with spa water from the outdoor **Fonte de São João** (which also has its own *casa do chá*).

Practicalities

There are several **trains** a day from Coimbra to Luso; it's a fifteen-minute walk to town from the station – take the road on the left. More convenient are the **buses**, running Monday to Saturday from Coimbra bus station, that stop first at Luso (near the spa) and then at Buçaco.

The **turismo** (June–Aug Mon–Fri 9am–7pm, Sat & Sun 10am–1pm & 3–5pm; Sept–May Mon–Fri 9.30am–12.30pm & 2–6pm, Sat & Sun 10am –1pm & 3–5pm; ℡231 939 133, @jtluso-bussaco@mail.telepac.pt) is near the post office on the main street, Rua Emídio Navarro, and can help you find a private room (❶) or provide a list of local **accommodation**. Most of the town's *pensões* and hotels have **restaurants** attached, serving pasta as well as the usual fish and meat dishes, one of the best being that at the *Pensão Alegre*.

Hotels and pensions

Pensão Alegre Rua Emídio Navarro 2 ℡231 930 256, ⓦwww.alegrehotels.com. On the road up into the forest, this impressive building, once home to a count, is full of nineteenth-century style. Some of the characterful rooms have balconies and great views, and there's also a swimming pool in the pretty garden. Breakfast included. Parking. ❸

Pensão Astória Rua Emídio Navarro 144 ℡231 939 182. A stone's throw from the turismo, the *Astória* has a certain faded charm and a cute coffee shop and bar. Breakfast included. Parking. ❷

Casa de Hospedes Familiar Rua Ernesto Navarro 34 ℡231 939 612, ⒻF231 939 268. Closest choice to the forest, this charming old house offers a variety of rooms, a few with small balconies and some sleeping up to four people. Enthusiastically run by a friendly, English-speaking owner. Breakfast included. No credit cards. Parking. ❷

Grande Hotel de Luso Rua Dr. Cid de Oliveira 86 ℡231 937 937, ⒻF231 937 930. You can't fail to miss the yellow exterior of the *Grande Hotel* and inside it's also splendidly furnished. Most of the simple, tastefully designed rooms have balconies, and there's a heated indoor pool. Breakfast included. Parking. ❻

Residencial Imperial Rua Emídio Navarro 25 ℡231 937 570, ⒻF231 937 579. Just above the spa, this modern building provides very comfortable rooms furnished with sturdy new furniture – all have bathrooms and TV, while some rooms sleep four. There's a functional-looking restaurant below. Breakfast included. ❸

Campsite

Parque de Campismo ℡231 930 916, ⒻF231 930 917. Luso's campsite also has bungalows sleeping four (❸) and a swimming pool. It's about 2km out of town on the way to the football ground.

Restaurants

Lourenços Av. Emídio Navarro ℡231 939 747. Right in the middle of town, *Lourenços* has a snack-bar terrace and a smarter adjacent restaurant, the latter serving standard Portuguese fare as well as things like chicken in red wine or lasagne. Moderate.

Varanda do Lago Parque do Lago ℡231 930 888. Round past the *Grande Hotel* and down into the park, you can eat substantial meals in the glass-walled dining room here, or on the terrace overlooking the picturesque lake. Closed Mon. Moderate.

Serra da Lousã and Serra do Açor

Lying to the southeast of Coimbra and bordering the Serra da Estrela at its southwestern edge, the **Serra da Lousã** and the **Serra do Açor** form a rugged region abundant in wildlife and with some beautiful unexplored corners. Although only 25km from Coimbra, the handsome town of **Lousã** offers easy hikes into the mountains, while an hour's bus journey northeast brings you to **Góis**, a pretty village set in a river valley, and another gateway into the mountains. With your own transport, however, you can make real inroads into the area, specifically to the marvellous schist village of **Piódão**, high in the peaks.

Lousã

Easily accessible by train from Coimbra, **LOUSÃ** is a popular day-trip from the city, as well as a great starting point for excursions into the Serra da Lousã. Although not the diminutive village it once was, the attractive old centre remains fairly unchanged, with the modern town sprawling beyond. Wandering around the older streets, you pass a succession of intricately decorated **chapels** and **casas brasonadas** (heraldic mansions), while in the grand town hall on on the main square, a little local **museum** (free) doubles as the turismo (see below).

Lousã's real attraction, its miniature **castle**, lies a forty-minute walk or short drive southeast (uphill) of town. Take Rua de Sacadura Cabral out of the main square and then follow the sign for "CP Prado". At a small white building in the centre of the road, branch off to the right up Rua F. Lopes Fernandes. When you hit the main road turn right and continue for roughly 1.5km. Here, a tributary of the Mondego curls around a narrow gorge between two splendid wooded hills and on one sits the castle, whose stone keep provides views across the valley; on the other is a small hermitage dedicated to **Nossa Senhora da Piedade**. In summer, bathers brave the chilly river pool between the two, above which sits the *Burgo* restaurant (see below). On the opposite bank is a small drinks bar.

Practicalities

Trains run from Coimbra Parque station. There are two train stations at Lousã: get off at the first, **Lousã A**. From here, take the road at right angles to the rail

A hike to the mountain villages around Lousã

This three-hour, six-kilometre circular hike in the **Serra da Lousã** provides marvellous views and a fascinating glimpse of mountain village life. Although deserted in the 1950s as a result of rural emigration, and abandoned for the next forty years, the houses of the tiny villages are being renovated and repopulated, mainly to provide tourist accommodation – check with the turismo in Lousã for details of staying here.

From the *Burgo* restaurant near the pools below Lousã's castle, walk up the stone steps to the end of the picnic area, and follow the sign to Casal Novo and Talasnal. The steep rocky path climbs for 1km until it reaches a junction; follow the right-hand fork and after 700m or so you will emerge onto a wider track, which you should follow uphill until it joins a second similar track – turn left and continue the ascent. As the path comes clear of the trees your toil is rewarded by stunning views of the valley below. At the top of this path turn left and continue upwards where you'll meet an unsurfaced road; Talasnal is visible to your left – head right to sleepy **Casal Novo**, which spills down the hillside, and at the time of writing was inhabited by just one family.

Retrace your steps, ignoring the track you came up and continue in the direction of **Talasnal**, probably the most beautiful of the range's villages with a harmonious mix of ruined and restored cottages amidst stunning mountain views. Once you've wound round the side of the mountain you can descend to the entrance of the village. The narrow, higgledy-piggledy passageways are worth a wander and you may also be able to stop to eat in the sporadically open, but beautifully sited **restaurant** *Ti'Lena* (☏ 933 832 624; book ahead), serving local mountain cuisine in a restored schist house.

To exit the village, follow the stream downhill, passing numerous small dwellings in various states of repair to your left and right. Continue downwards on a path mostly marked by dry stone walls on both sides. When the trail meets a T-junction turn left downhill and cross the river via an old stone bridge. Follow the good, easily navigable path all the way back to the river pools, keeping an eye out for occasional fallen logs blocking the path and the dizzy drop to your right. A well-earned dip in the pools below the castle makes a refreshing end to the walk.

line and walk uphill to the centre. **Buses** stop in the main square, though to catch a bus on to Góis wait at the closest bench to the *Café Avenida* on Avenida do Brasil. You can ask in the café about bus information. The **turismo** (Mon–Fri 9am–12.30pm & 2–5.30pm, Sat 10am–12.30pm & 2.30–4pm, Sun 10.30am–1pm & 2.30–4pm; ☎239 990 376, ⓦwww.cm-lousa.pt) in the town hall is customarily helpful, and staff can supply you with a map of town and a rather out-of-date sketch map of the Serra da Lousã. There's free **internet access** (30min; Mon–Fri 9am–12.30pm & 2–5.30pm) in the municipal library on Avenida Coelho da Gama.

There's not much **accommodation**, but what there is is pretty good, and the town makes a peaceful overnight stop. The nearest **campsite** (☎239 971 141) to town is 8km away in Serpins, one stop further on the train line from Lousã. **Restaurants** are plentiful, while **cafés** put out tables around the modern Praça Sá Carneiro in front of the market. Incidentally, it was a pharmacist from Lousã who originally came up with the secret recipe for **Licor Beirão**, a herb-flavoured, sickly sweet sort of cognac, drunk all over Portugal.

Hotels and pensions

Pensão Bem Estar Av. Coelho da Gama 11 ☎239 991 445, ⓕ239 993 915. Round the corner from the main square this is a warren of bright rooms that come with TV, and washbasins if they aren't en suite. ❷

Residencial Martinho Rua Forças Armadas ☎239 991 397, ⓕ239 994 335. Simple, sunny en-suite rooms in an extension to the family house, with distant hill views and a log fire downstairs in winter. It's up the road from the square, past the *Bem Estar* and turn left. Breakfast included (though not up to much). Parking. ❸

Palácio da Lousã Contact Meliá hotels on ☎239 480 800, ⓦwww.solmelia.com. Just off the main square on the way to the castle, this impressive eighteenth-century building is currently being transformed into a boutique hotel.

Quintal de Além do Ribeiro Ceira dos Vales 4km northeast of Lousã ☎239 996 480, ⓦwww .wonderfulland.com/quintal. A well-run, homely collection of rustic rooms, some with kitchenettes and all with antique radios, peacefully set around a thoughtfully restored farmhouse, complete with simple bar, pretty garden and pool. Plentiful and delicious buffet breakfast. No credit cards. ❹

Cafés and restaurants

Borges Rua Dr. João Santos 2 ☎239 993 489. Basic but good grill-restaurant with a country feel, serving up veal chops, chicken and steaks (though some fish too), with quaffable local wine by the jug and home-made desserts. Closed Mon. Moderate.

Burgo Ermida da Senhora da Piedade ☎239 991 162. Up by the castle, *Burgo* enjoys a lovely setting and specializes in excellent local cuisine and wine, served in a dining room overlooking the river. Closed Mon. Expensive.

Casa Velha Pr. Sá Carneiro 14 ☎239 991 555. Set in the modern plaza in front of the market, *Casa Velha* offers good mountain cuisine and Portuguese standards, including a terrific *porco à alentejana*, though service can be rather indifferent and the wide-screen TV a distraction. Closed Tues eve, all Wed & last two weeks of July. Moderate.

Gato Rua Dr. João Santos 6 ☎239 994 640. Popular local dining room at the rear of a rustic bar, serving up great grills and fries as well as inexpensive daily specials. Closed Tues. Moderate.

O Sonho Largo A. Herculano no phone. Near the train station this dirt-cheap workers' bar with tables in a tiled back room serves a filling *prato do dia*, wine and coffee for under €5. Closed Sun. Inexpensive.

Vale da Perdiz Videira, Foz de Arouce, 6km northeast of town ☎239 995 595. Located in what looks like a residential house, but tastefully decorated inside in a traditional style. There is no menu – the English-speaking chef tells you what he's cooking that day and invariably you'll get a delicious three-course meal of local specialities, including wine, for €15. The *requeijão* cheese with pumpkin jam for dessert is exquisite, and service is impeccable. Book ahead. Closed Mon & Jan. Moderate.

Bars

94 Café Bar Av. São Silvestre 94. Small, convivial bar down some steps on the corner of the modern plaza, attracting a young crowd. Serves a tasty local port.

Cine Café Av. Dr. José Cardoso. Relaxed, friendly bar attached to the cinema with a large screen, often showing sports. Tables spill out onto the forecourt.

Góis and around

Sixteen kilometres northeast of Lousã the charming village of **GÓIS** is beautifully set on the Rio Ceira, accessed by an arched sixteenth-century bridge, which leads up to the central Praça da República. There's not a lot to occupy you here, beyond wandering the quaint old streets, perhaps seeking out the **Fonte de Pombal**, one square up from República and clad in Moorish tiles from Spain, and the nearby **Igreja Matriz**, which commands great views of the surrounding countryside and contains a very ornate Renaissance tomb. In summer, bathers congregate on the small sand **beach** in the river and you can rent a **canoe** to paddle downstream from here; contact Transerrano (☎235 778 938, ⊛www.transserrano.com) to arrange this. For more views of the village and nearby hills, climb up to the tiny **chapel** by the campsite, on the opposite bank of the river.

Practicalities

Buses arrive at the top of town in front of the fire station. Head down the cobbled road to the left to the central square, on which you'll find the very helpful **turismo** (June–Sept daily 9am–7pm; Oct–May Mon–Fri 9am–12.30pm & 2–5.30pm; ☎235 772 090, ⊛www.cm-gois.pt) where you can pick up a map of the village. There's only one **hotel**, the unsigned *Casa Santo António*, Rua de S. Antonio 18, just off the main square (☎235 770 120, ℮casa.antonio@netc.pt; ❸), which is well run and has modern en-suite rooms; you'll need to book ahead in summer. The town **campsite** (☎235 778 585, ℉235 770 129) enjoys a lovely position up the hill from the west bank of the river, and has barbecues and great views. There are **cafés** dotted round town including a riverside spot that serves snacks, but for a more substantial **meal** try tiny *Casa Ti Maria* (☎962 794 358), which serves inexpensive grills and is clean and friendly. There's a **supermarket** behind the fire station if you want to picnic on the tables by the river.

Around Góis

The mountains around Góis offer plenty of opportunity for **hiking** and other more adventurous pursuits; Transerrano (see above) arranges guided walks (€7.50–10) and guided climbing, kayaking and mountain-biking trips (€17.50–20). If you want to stay in some isolation you can rent the cosy *Casa da Cerejinha* (☎239 704 089, ⊛www.cerejinha.com; minimum 2-night stay in Aug; ❺) situated in the tiny village of **PENA**, 10km south of Góis. The beautifully renovated, but rather small, schist-built cottage has cooking facilities and sleeps four. The village is set on a pretty brook in a rocky valley rich with wildlife; it has no amenities but makes a fantastic base for hiking.

Piódão

From Góis, it's a beautiful ninety-minute drive via Arganil and Coja to **PIÓDÃO**, a fascinating traditional schist village, set on a steeply terraced mountainside in the **Serra do Açor**. It's 25km from Coja, yet was unconnected by road or to an electricity supply until the 1970s, so Piódão has changed somewhat over the intervening years with the advent of tourism. If you can get over the slight theme-park atmosphere, however, its narrow streets are great to explore, and the whole village affords superb valley views. The **turismo**, based in the small **museum** (daily 9–11am & 2–5pm; €1) on the main square at the bottom of the village, hands out an excellent "urban circuit" in English, to help you locate the main points of interest and navigate the confusing layout. The museum itself provides an insight into traditional village life with displays that cover emigration and economy, as well as daily toil. It's also possible to follow a couple of short **walks** from Piódão into the countryside – these are well signposted from the village.

Practicalities

For **accommodation**, try the imposing *Inatel Estalagem*, on the road into the village (☎235 730 100, ⓦwww.inatel.pt; ❹); it looks rather like a prison but the interior is comfortable enough, and there are good views from the restaurant. You can also rent a **room** overlooking the valley from the *Solar dos Pacheos* café on the main square (☎235 731 424, book one week in advance; no credit cards; ❷); they have more expensive rooms with kitchens (❸) or you can rent a whole cottage with two rooms (❹). The village's only **restaurant** *O Fontinha* (☎235 731 151), is basic and inexpensive, one road up from the main square, where there are also a couple of **cafés**.

The Dão valley and the Serra do Caramulo

The route northeast from Coimbra to Caramulo leads through the **valley of the Rio Dão**, heart of the region where Dão wines – some of the country's finest and richest reds – are produced. Where they're not covered with vineyards, the slopes are thickly wooded with pine and eucalyptus trees. It's a fine ride and though there's no overwhelming point of interest en route, you might stop for coffee at least in the small market town of Santa Comba Dão, a little over 50km from Coimbra.

Beyond here, the views from the main IP3 are of the spectacular **Serra do Caramulo**, breaking to the northwest. **Tondela** marks the eastern turn-off point for the mountains, accessed along the minor N230 which winds tortuously through a succession of tiny villages at the heart of the mountain range, before descending to Águeda, from where the fast main road runs due south to Coimbra. With your own transport, you could describe the circle from Coimbra, seeing Luso and Buçaco forest on the way. By bus, the same circuit is possible, though you'll need to change buses in Tondela and spend a night in the mountains at the pretty village of **Caramulo**, a twisting 19km from Tondela. Most of the other *serra* villages are little more than hamlets, surrounded by rhododendrons, brightly coloured azaleas and thick green shrubs growing wild on the hillside.

Tondela

Coming from Coimbra or Luso by public transport you need first to take the Viseu bus as far as the small, unassuming town of **TONDELA**, from where there are two daily buses (not weekends) on to Caramulo (and ultimately Águeda), a majestic if rather bumpy hour's drive straight across the centre of the Serra do Caramulo. The bus stops on the main square where you'll find the **turismo** (Mon–Fri 9am–12.30pm & 2–5.30pm; ☎232 811 121) and *Residencial Tondela*, Rua Dr. Simoes Carvalho (☎232 822 411, ⓕ232 813 443; no credit cards; ❷), which has adequate en-suite rooms. You shouldn't need to stay the night, but you might have time for lunch – there's a moderately priced **restaurant**, *O Solar* (☎232 813 897), across the square.

Caramulo

Tucked beneath the peaks of the high Beiras *serra*, **CARAMULO** makes a great walking base – the summit of the loftiest Serra de Caramulo peak, **Caramulinho** (1075m), is less than an hour's hike away. It's a small, somnolent place with some reasonable accommodation available - unfortunately the staggering views down into the valley are mostly blocked by development at the village's edge.

Aside from the great outdoors, it's the local museum, the **Museu do Caramulo** (daily 10am–1pm & 2–6pm; closes at 5pm in winter; €6; @www.museu-caramulo.net), on Avenida Abel de Lacerda, that's the main highlight. The principal display is the **Museu de Arte**, a wonderfully jumbled art collection, with everything from primitive religious sculpture to sketches by the greatest modern masters – minor works by Picasso and Dalí among them. There's an exquisite series of sixteenth-century Tournai tapestries depicting the earliest Portuguese explorers in India, full of weird animals and natives based on obviously very garbled reports. There's also a large *John the Baptist*, painted by sixteenth-century Viseu artist Grão Vasco, and quantities of furniture and china. Downstairs, and continuing next door, is the even more incongruous **Museu do Automóvel**, a superb collection of vintage cars and motorcycles, including some of the earliest Benz, Buggatti and Fiat models, an elegant series of Rolls-Royces and a pack of 1950s Harley Davidsons.

Practicalities

Buses drop you at the station at the top of the village, from where you can head downhill and left to the centre. The **turismo**, Avenida Dr. Abel de Lacerda (Mon–Sat 10am–12.30pm & 2–5pm; ☎232 861 437), is at the bottom of the village – take a left towards Tondela and it's on the left; staff can provide advice on walks in the area. **Accommodation** options are limited here, but there are some good-value **private rooms** (❶) next to the *Mercado Serrano* – walk up the main road past *Restaurante Marte* and take the left fork opposite the petrol station; enquire at the *mercado* which is past the chemist on the left. Otherwise, first choice is the excellent *Hotel do Caramulo*, Avenida Dr. Abel Lacerda (☎232 860 100, @www.hotel-caramulo.com; breakfast included; ❻), with superb amenities, including jacuzzi and hydrotherapy facilities, and unbeatable views towards the Serra da Estrela. The less inspiring *Estalagem do Caramulo* (☎232 861 291, ✉estalagemcaramulo@correio.agdo.pt; breakfast included; ❻), a kilometre along the Tondela road has a swimming pool and great views.

The best **restaurant** is the moderately priced *Casa do Monte* (☎232 861 558; closed Tues), Rua do Clube, signposted at the top of the village. It has views over the surrounding mountains, as well as a pretty garden bar, and serves delicious trout. The *Café-Restaurante Marte* on the main road (☎232 861 253) is a popular and less expensive option.

To book **mountain activities** such as canyoning (€50–75 per person) and canoeing (€55) or to rent a mountain bike (€20 per day) contact Desafios Caramulo (☎232 868 017, @www.desafios-caramulo.pt), based at the *Hotel do Caramulo*.

Along the Rio Vouga

The **Rio Vouga** is one of the most beautiful, somnolent rivers in the country and a fine route to follow if you feel like taking in a little of backwater Portugal. Bus services run from Coimbra or Aveiro and, on reaching the Vouga, follow the old train line along the river; you probably won't want to get off until **Vouzela**, though drivers will feel compelled to pause now and again to take in the views. Alternatively, you can approach from the south, from Caramulo, or from Viseu to the east, from where the minor N337 makes a particularly memorable approach.

Vouzela

VOUZELA is one of the most immediately attractive of Beira towns, a small place with an almost palpable sense of civic pride. The locals boast of the peculiar sweet cakes, or *pasteis de Vouzela* (only for the most sweet-toothed), richly flavoured traditional dishes such as *vitela de Lafões*, and the heady local *vinho Lafões* (similar to *vinho verde*). There's a *feira* on May 14 when flowers are strewn in the streets in honour of **São Frei Gil**, and everyone drives up into the hills to witness the blossoming of the rare *loendros*, a type of rhododendron peculiar to this area and which is now protected by law. Otherwise, note that there's a morning **street market** on the first Wednesday of the month, a good time to be in town.

The central **Praça da República** sports the striking *azelujo*-clad thirteenth-century parish church, downhill from which is the **Museu Municipal** on Praça Morais de Carvalho (Tues–Sun 10am–12.30pm & 2–5pm; free), housed in a former prison and containing a varied collection of religious artefacts, Romanesque stone fragments and local weaving and craftwork. Continuing down Rua São Frei Gil brings you to the low **Romanesque bridge** crossing a pretty stream, overhung by willow and bordered by small-town manor houses. Topping this scene is the **viaduct**, looping its way across the rooftops; for views over the village and to the surrounding Arada and Caramulo mountains, you can cross the viaduct from just beyond the bus station.

Practicalities

Buses drop you at the station just up from the centre – head downhill and turn right down Avenida João de Melo where you'll find the **turismo** at no. 23 (Mon–Fri 10am–7pm, Sat & Sun 10am–1pm & 2–5pm; reduced hours in winter; ☎232 771 515). Continuing down this street brings you to Praça da República, and the *Café Central*, a good place to sample *pasteis de Vouzela*.

There's **accommodation** at the *Casa das Ameias*, Rua São Frei Gil 43 (☎232 771 217, ⓦwww.ameias-viaromana.com; book ahead; breakfast included; ❺), which is elegantly decorated and has a small, pretty terrace at the rear, or the *Residencial Ferreira*, Rua Barão da Costeiro 3 (☎ & ⓕ232 771 650, ⓔlidiofer@net .sapo.pt; no credit cards; ❷), just down the hill from Praça da República, which has adequate en-suite rooms. Best of all, however, is *Casa de Fataunços* (☎ & ⓕ232 772 697, ⓔcasa.fatauncos@oninet.pt; breakfast included; ❺), 3km northeast of Vouzela in the village of the same name. It's a beautifully restored manor house with lovely rooms, gardens, a pool, tennis court and a small art gallery. There is also a municipal **campsite** with fine views (☎232 740 020, ⓕ232 740 027), 4km up the road towards Mortágua and **Senhora do Castelo**, a low hill that is the location for much merrymaking and picnicking on the first Sunday after August 5. There's a signpost pointing the way from Praça da República.

The town has a handful of decent **restaurants**, including *O Meu Menino*, Avenida Sidónio Pais 6 (☎232 771 335), a very large place, just down from the bus station and a good option for lunch. Or there's the simple, rustic and very friendly *Forno do Rei* at Rua Escolar 19 (☎232 772 722), around the corner from *Residencial Ferreira*, providing inexpensive local dishes.

Around Vouzela

With your own transport you can strike out from Vouzela up into the beautiful **Serra da Arada**. Head northeast for São Pedro do Sul and having passed through it and crossed a narrow bridge, take a left towards Castro Daire. On reaching the small village of São Felix follow signs to Sul and then Pena. From here the road begins to rise into the mountains and emerges on the heather-spotted mountain top with staggering views to the valley below. At the next junction take a left, then right, for **PENA**, 20km all told from Vouzela. The road winds precariously downhill, hugging the mountainside before reaching the tiny schist village (population, eight), where you can snack at the *Adega Tipica Pena* (no phone) and buy local honey and *aguadente*. After backtracking to the junction you can continue another 1km to the tiny mountain-top **São Macario** chapel, from where views unfold down the valley.

Another spectacular mountain route from Vouzela takes you over the **Serra da Freita** to Arouca, a 43-kilometre drive (see p.248 for route in reverse).

Figueira da Foz

FIGUEIRA DA FOZ is one of the liveliest towns on the west coast, a major resort and deep-sea fishing port sited at the mouth of the Rio Mondego. Roughly equidistant from Lisbon and Porto, and just over an hour by train from Coimbra, it attracts people from all over the country to its superb beaches and surf. That said, it's not the most initially alluring of beach resorts: there's a somewhat industrial approach from the south, and the town itself is resolutely modern, its long promenade backed by a line of anonymous apartment buildings. But most of the action, in fact, takes place away from the sands in the atmospheric backstreets, where a bubbling good humour prevails, even when the town is packed to the gills.

Arrival and information

The **train station** is a long 20- to 25-minute walk from the centre and beach. Keep walking along the river until you see the ocean and then cut into the town – a useful beachfront landmark is the concrete clock tower. The **bus station** is slightly closer to town, though it's still a fair walk downhill to São Julião church and the Jardim Municipal, from where the streets run straight to the beach. AVIC **buses to Buarcos** – the fishing village at the northern end of the bay, 2km from town – leave from directly outside the train station (Mon–Fri every 30min until 11pm, or 8.10pm Oct–May; hourly on Sat; 6 daily Sun), also making a stop on Rua da Liberdade in town. Buses stopping close to **Praia do Cabadelo** and the campsites – destination "Cova Gala" – leave from outside the Mercado Municipal (Mon–Fri every 30min till 8.10pm, Sat hourly till 6.10pm, Sun every 2hr till 6.10pm), as well as stopping across the road from the train station.

The large, bright **turismo** (daily: July & Aug 9am–midnight; Sept–June 9am–12.30pm & 2–5.30pm; ☏233 422 610, ⓦwww.figueiraturismo.com), Avenida 25 de Abril, is more helpful than most; there's another in Buarcos at Largo de Buarcos (July & Aug daily 9am–8pm; Sept–June Mon–Fri 9am–5.30pm; ☏233 433 019).

Orbitur & Foz do Mondego campsites (via bridge), Coimbra, Aveiro & Leira ▲ ▲ Train Station

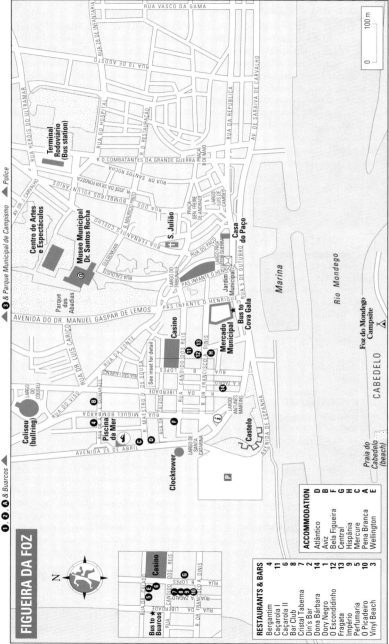

FIGUEIRA DA FOZ

N

RESTAURANTS & BARS

Bergantim	4
Caçarola I	11
Caçarola II	6
Bar Club	8
Cristal Taberna	7
Din's Bar	2
Dona Bárbara	14
Dory Negro	1
O Escondidinho	12
Fragata	13
Império	9
Hispânia	9
Perfumaria	5
O Picadeiro	10
Vinyl Beach	3

ACCOMMODATION

Atlântico	D
Aviz	B
Bela Figueira	F
Central	G
Hispânia	H
Mercure	C
Pena Branca	A
Wellington	E

Bus to ★ Buarcos

Casino

Accommodation

It can take time to find a room in Figueira in high season. You might well be met at the train station by people offering **private rooms** (➋), which – provided they're reasonably central – will be the best bargains in town. Otherwise, there are a couple of cheap *pensões* just in front of the train station on Rua Fernandes Tomás and Rua da República, but these are a long way from the beach. It's much better to head for the centre, where both **Rua Bernardo Lopes** and **Rua da Liberdade** are lined with possibilities, though many are booked well in advance. You'll also find that prices – already comparatively high in Figueira – tend to shoot through the roof in July and August.

Hotels and pensions

Hotel Apartmento Atlântico Av. 25 de Abril 20 ☎233 408 900, ✆233 408 901. Upmarket option in a modern, but slightly shabby, high-rise building with its own pool. Plainly decorated, en-suite apartments with kitchenette, many with sea views. Some sleep four (€120). Breakfast included. ➎

Residencial Aviz Rua Dr. Lopes Guimarães 16 ☎233 422 635, ✆233 420 909. The cheapest option in town, this chintzy but well-cared-for *pensão* with German-speaking owners offers small en-suite rooms with TV. Breakfast included. ➌

Pensão Bela Figueira Rua Miguel Bombarda 13 ☎233 422 728, ✆233 429 960. Near the main beach and town centre this cheap and cheerful place has small, unremarkable rooms with shower and TV. Noise can be a problem. The attached restaurant (dinner only; moderate) serves Indian and Portuguese food (try the shrimp curry), with meals also served on the terrace. Breakfast included. ➌

Pensão Central Rua Bernardo Lopes 36 ☎233 422 308, ⓦwww.pensaocentral.nafigueira.com. Airy, welcoming *pensão* approached up a flight of side-steps. Rooms are spacious with high ceilings and nice old furniture, and a couple share a grand street-facing balcony, though these are noisy. Breakfast included. No credit cards. ➌

Hotel Hispânia Rua Dr. Francisco António Dinis 61 ☎233 422 164, ✆233 429 664. A rambling old hotel with lots of natural light. Rooms are clean and come with showers. It's one of the few places in the centre with private parking. Breakfast included. ➍

Hotel Mercure Av. 25 de Abril 22 ☎233 403 900, ⓦwww.mercure.com. Next to the *Atlântico* on the seafront, this four-star chain hotel offers comfortable rooms, some with balcony, that are not bad value. ➎

Residencial Pena Branca Rua 5 de Outubro 42, Buarcos, 2km north of town ☎233 432 665, ✆233 421 892. In Buarcos, near the turismo, this is a splendid, high-quality setup whose en-suite rooms come equipped with phone, TV, fridge and balcony. There's a good regional restaurant below (☎233 401 570; moderate) with windows overlooking the beach – a great place for an *arroz de sardinha* or *caldeirada*. ➍

Hotel Wellington Rua Dr. Calado 23–27 ☎233 426 767, ✉hotelwellington@sabirhoteis.pt. Three blocks from the beach, the *Wellington* offers plush rooms with modern wooden furniture, bathrooms and cable TV. ➎

Campsites

Parque Municipal de Campismo 2km northeast of town ☎233 402 810, ✆233 402 818. Large and well equipped, with a swimming pool (July & Aug only; €3.50) and tennis courts. Follow the signs from town and beach, or take a taxi from the station.

Foz do Mondego Cabadelo ☎233 402 740, ⓦwww.fpcampismo.pt. Across the river mouth, and close to Cabadelo beach, this is by far the cheapest in the area. Closed mid-Nov to mid-Jan.

Orbitur Mata de Lavos, Gala, 4km to the south, across the estuary ☎233 431 492, ⓦwww.orbitur.pt. The most expensive site – though the ocean is much cleaner for swimming here. *Carrocel* (☎233 431 457; closed Mon), at Largo da Beira-Mar near the campsite, serves good, moderately priced food. Bus to Cova Gala.

The Town

Figueira's central streets form a tight little grid set back from the eastern end of the beach. Many are brimming with pavement cafés and strolling holidaymakers, while back along the river, on Passeio Infante D. Henrique is the **Mercado Municipal** (Mon–Sat 6am–3pm), good for fresh produce and just about anything else you might need. Otherwise, the town doesn't offer much in the way of sightseeing – the most impressive sights are the beaches – but there are a couple of places to scout around once you tire of the sands. On the edge of the town park, Parque das Abadias, the **Museu Municipal Dr. Santos Rocha** (June to mid-Sept Tues–Sun 9.30am–5.15pm; mid-Sept to May Tues–Fri 9.30am–5.15pm, Sat & Sun 2.15pm–5.15pm; €1.25), Rua Calouste Gulbenkian, has an impressive archeological section, as well as a large number of photographs of nineteenth-century bathing belles. Meanwhile, the inside walls of the **Casa do Paço** at Largo Prof. Vítor Guerra 4 (Mon–Fri 9.30am–12.30pm & 2–5.30pm; free), are covered with thousands of Delft tiles, part of a ship's cargo which somehow got stranded in Figueira.

The beaches

Figueira's **town beach** is enormous, not so much in length as in width: it's a good five-minute walk across the sand to the sea and unless you wear shoes or stay on the wooden walkways provided, the soles of your feet will have been burned long before you get there. There are cafés along the whole length of the beach, but since the busy main road and promenade are set well back from the water, there's no great sense of place. The best spot is at the **Buarcos** end of the beach, 2km away, where a huddle of pastel-coloured fishermen's houses sit amidst a rash of new concrete high-rises behind what remains of the old defensive wall.

If it's surfing you're after, head to **Praia do Cabadelo**, behind the mole on the south bank of the Mondego's river mouth (the bus drops you at the hospital 10min walk away). Escola de Surf da Figueira (☎966 470 489, ⓦwww .surfigueira.com), in a small hut behind the beach and opposite the campsite, offers a one-hour try-out lesson for €25, and they also rent surfing equipment and offer longer periods of tuition.

Eating, drinking, nightlife and entertainment

The centre of town is packed with snack bars, **cafés** and seafood **restaurants** offering *ementas turísticas* at reasonable prices. Several of the *pensões* also have good restaurants, notably the *Pena Branca* in Buarcos and the *Bela Figueira* in town (see "Accommodation" above).

Apart from the town's numerous **bars and clubs** (open from around 11pm until 4am or later in summer), nightlife centres on the **Casino** at Rua Bernardo Lopes 1 (daily 3pm–4am; ⓦwww.casinofigueira.com), for which semi-formal dress and an initial outlay on chips are compulsory. The slightly incongruous glass-bedecked building hosts a variety of **shows** – from rock bands to ballet – throughout the summer. Other musical events are staged at the **Centro de Artes e Espectáculos** (☎233 407 200, ⓦwww.figueiradigital.com/cae), up near the Museu Municipal Dr. Santos Rocha, in which you'll also find the cinema.

One of the best of the year's parties is **St John's Eve** (June 23 and 24) with bonfires on the beach and a "Holy Bathe" in the sea at dawn; while **bullfights** are often held during the summer season in the bullring on Largo do Coliseu (information from the turismo).

Restaurants

Caçarola I Rua Cândido dos Reis 65 ☎233 424 861. Basement shellfish restaurant with daily specials. To keep costs down, you could just sit at the bar and have a plate of prawns and a beer. Expensive.

Caçarola II Rua Bernardo Lopes 85–87 ☎233 426 930. Sister restaurant to *Caçarola I* and with its impressive array of seafood it's just as good, if not better. Open till 4am. Expensive.

Cristal Taberna Rua Académico Zagalo 28 ☎233

422 439. Great little restaurant specializing in *cataplanas*. Friendly service. Expensive.

Dory Negro Largo Caras Direitas 16, Buarcos ☎233 421 333. On the edge of Buarcos, this is a good place to come for fish, with dishes around the €8 mark. It's hidden out of sight from the sea, but has a little covered patio. Closed Tues in winter. Moderate.

O Escondidinho Rua Dr. Francisco António Dinis 62 ☎233 422 494. Hidden away (as the name suggests), this is worth seeking out for superb Goan food. The entrance is through a doorway opposite *Hotel Hispânia*, leading to a courtyard. Closed Mon & Tues. Moderate.

Fragata Rua Dr. Francisco A. Dinis 38 ☎233 429 882. Popular, small and simple restaurant-snack bar with fish and meat dishes. Inexpensive.

O Picadeiro Rua Dr. Francisco A. Dinis 80 ☎233 422 245. With tables on buzzy Rua Académico Zagalo, *O Picadeiro* is friendly and well run, serving excellent fish and meat dishes, and offering a comprehensive list of daily specials. Moderate.

Bars and clubs

Bar Club Rua Académico Zagalo. Unsigned but recognizable by its striped interior wall, this funky little bar has tables out on the street and a chilled atmosphere.

Din's Bar Areal de Buarcos. Right on the beach in Buarcos, *Din's* location is great for an ice-cold beer on the terrace whilst contemplating the waves.

Disco Bergantim Rua Dr. Lopes Guimarães 28. A long-standing favourite, right in the centre of town.

Dona Bárbara Rua Académico Zagalo 7. Established bar that's a little musty and cavern-like, playing classic rock and pop.

Império Rua Académico Zagalo. Bang next door to *Bar Club*, this place is slightly larger sporting Pop Art on the walls – there's a DJ most nights.

Perfumaria Rua Dr. Calado 37. Small, atmospheric and friendly bar on two levels, with a pool table and a good cocktail list.

Vinyl Beach Av. Dr. Mário Soares. Up next to the supermarket at the north end of Figueira, and close to the municipal campsite, this is a brand new sister club to *Vinyl* in Coimbra (see p.219).

Listings

Bike rental From Rotasmundo, Rua Miguel Bombarda 25 ☎233 411 635 (daily 9.30am–1pm & 2.30–6.30pm).

Car rental A. A. Castanheira, Rua Maestro David Sousa 103 ☎233 425 113; Salitur, Av. 25 de Abril 27 ☎233 425 395.

Hospital Hospital Distrital da Figueira da Foz, São Pedro ☎233 402 097.

Internet At Museu Municipal Dr. Santos Rocha (Tues–Fri 9.30am–5.15pm, Sat & Sun 2.15pm –5.15pm; free for 30min).

Police Av. Dr. Joaquim de Carvalho ☎233 407 560.

Post office Passeio Infante D. Henrique (Mon–Fri 9am–1pm & 2–6.30pm; ☎233 402 600).

Swimming pool Piscina da Mer (June–Sept 9am–6pm; €6.50) is an outdoor saltwater swimming pool on Av. 25 de Abril.

Taxis Available outside the train station ☎233 423 218; Pr. 8 de Maio ☎233 423 500; in Cabadelo or Gala call ☎233 431 431.

North of Figueira: to Praia de Mira

The coastline immediately **north of Figueira** is remarkable only for its air of total desertion. Beyond Buarcos, there's very little, and for long stretches hardly even a road. Off the main north–south road (IC1/N109) you can get to the coast at just three points before Aveiro: at **Quiaios**, **Tocha** and **Mira**, each with their respective beaches. If you're driving on to Aveiro stick with the minor coastal route beyond Praia de Mira, which is a pleasant run through farmland with dunes to one side and river to the other; this way, you'll pass through probably the nicest of this coast's small resorts, Costa Nova (see p.244).

Praia de Quiaios and Praia da Tocha

With a car you can find virtually empty beaches around either **QUIAIOS** or **TOCHA**, though the low-lying coastal plain offers no protection against the

Atlantic winds. For more sheltered leisure pursuits, aim for the inland lakes between the two beaches, particularly the large, pine-fringed **Lagoa da Vela**, where there are scores of picnic areas, and windsurfing and sailing schools.

Buses run irregularly from Figueira bus station up the N109, stopping at both Praia de Quiaios (25min) and Praia da Tocha (40min). There isn't any accommodation once you get to either beach other than the excellent **campsites**, *Orbitur Praia de Quiaios* (℡233 910 499) and *Praia da Tocha* (℡231 441 143).

Praia de Mira

Set on a small lagoon – the southernmost point of a system of waterways and canals centered on Aveiro – **PRAIA DE MIRA** is relatively well developed. There are infrequent direct buses from Aveiro and Coimbra but you'll usually have to change in Mira, the inland town 7km to the west. You couldn't exactly describe Praia de Mira as a beautiful place – its one extremely long main street, Avenida Cidade de Coimbra, spears towards the sea, lined by modern apartment buildings. But the beach that stretches to either side is seemingly endless and backed by dunes: ideal if your aims extend no further than beach-lounging and lazy walks.

Many places offer cheap, basic *dormidas* along the main street – look out for the signs, or ask in any bar. The **turismo**, in the boathouse-like building beside the lagoon (daily 9am–12.30pm & 2–6pm; ℡231 472 566) may be able to help with rooms, but is often closed out of season. Of the **pensões**, modern *Arco Íris* on Avenida do Mar (℡231 471 202; breakfast included; ❸), immediately on the left at the end of the main street, is a passable spot with a restaurant. Far preferable is the *Miratlântico* (℡231 471 262; breakfast included; ❷), 300m further along the seafront. It has pleasant, airy rooms with TV and bath – the front rooms are the best, with private balconies overlooking the beach.

There are two official **campsites** a short way from the village – the municipal *Parque de Campismo* (℡231 472 173; May–Sept) is closer and considerably cheaper, though less well equipped, than the *Orbitur* site (℡231 471 234; closed Dec & Jan), for which you go up the main street, turn left at the seafront and continue for a kilometre. Most appealing **restaurant** is the *Caçanito* (℡231 472 678; closed Mon), Avenida do Mar, which has a glass-fronted dining room that looks out over the ocean and dishes up relatively expensive seafood.

Aveiro and around

Although not visually striking, and without any major attractions, the small town of **AVEIRO** makes an excellent base for exploring the series of impressive beaches to its north and south. The centre is compact, with plenty of accommodation, and boasts a great range of excellent seafood restaurants as well as some lively bars. It was a thriving port throughout the Middle Ages, up until the 1570s, when the mouth of the Vouga silted up, closing its harbour and creating vast, fever-ridden marshes. Recovery began only in 1808 when a canal was cut through to the sea, reopening the port and draining much of the water; only the shallow lagoons you see today were left. These once formed the backbone of an industry based on vast **saltpans**, and although salt is still produced in this way, it is no longer the mainstay of the economy it once was.

The town's big annual event is the **Festa da Ria** (last two weeks of August), celebrated with boat races, folk dances, and competitions for the best decorated

△ Backstreets, Pena

barcos moliceiro, the flat-bottomed lagoon boats used to collect seaweed. The other major celebration is the **Festa de São Gonçalinho** (second week of January), held in honour of the patron saint of fishermen and single women. Those who have made vows during the year, either for the safe return of a fisherman or for the finding of a husband, climb to the top of a chapel and throw down loaves of bread to the crowd below; the aim is to catch as much as possible.

Arrival, information and accommodation

Aveiro is easily accessible by train from Porto or Coimbra, with the **train station** at the northeastern end of town, a fifteen-minute walk from the centre. Most **buses** use the train station forecourt and adjacent streets as their terminus; for information and tickets for long-distance services head to the nearby terminal on Rua Almirante Cândido dos Reis. Parking on the street in Aveiro costs roughly €0.30 per hour, or there are a few covered **car parks**, with the one under Praça Marquês de Pombal the most central.

The **turismo** is just up from the bridge in the town centre, in a beautiful Art Nouveau building at Rua João Mendonça 8 (June–Sept daily 9am–8pm; Oct–May Mon–Sat 9am–7pm; ☎234 420 760, ⓦwww.rotadaluz.pt). It supplies free maps and local bus timetables and can help with finding accommodation. **Bicycles** are a good way to explore the town and are available free from the *BUGA* kiosk just off Praça Humberto Delgado. You need to show your passport to get a bike, but are then free to use it around the town for a whole day. Otherwise, one-hour **boat trips** (hourly 10am–7pm June–Sept, book in advance Oct–May on ☎967 088 183; €7) by traditional boat around the lagoon leave from Rua Joâo Mendonça in front of the turismo.

Accommodation

You shouldn't have much trouble finding a **room** in Aveiro, except perhaps during the Festa da Ria in August, when you'd be wise to book ahead. There are several places immediately down from the train station, but they're a little far from things; in the centre, try the backstreets around the fish market for inexpensive *dormidas*. Those with transport have the option of staying **out of town** at one of the lagoon- or beach-resorts, although the beaches are easily accessible by public transport. The local **campsites** are also way out of town, at São Jacinto to the north, or to the south at Praia da Barra and Costa Nova (see "The lagoon and beaches", below).

Hotels and pensions

Residencial do Alboi Rua da Arrochela 6 ☎234 380 390, ⓦwww.residencial-alboi.com. This characterful converted house offers small doubles and triples with shower, overlooking a quiet street or a pretty patio at the back. Courteous staff. Best choice in its price range. Breakfast included. ❸

Hotel Arcada Rua de Viana do Castelo 4 ☎234 423 001, ⓕ234 421 886. Plain but comfortable rooms, pleasant staff and a central location in a grand building by the bridge with views over the canal. All rooms with either shower or bath and TV. Breakfast included. ❸

Pensão Avenida Av. Dr. Lourenço Peixinho 259 ☎234 423 366. Clean, well kept and good value for money, but it's a long walk from the centre. Rooms come with TV and shared bathrooms. No credit cards. Breakfast included. ❷

Residencial Beira Rua José Estêvão 18 ☎234 424 297. A welcoming *residencial* whose rooms are bright and homely, furnished with sturdy wooden furniture; some have bathrooms and all have cable TV. It's often full, so call ahead. Breakfast included. No credit cards. ❸

A Brasileira Rua Tenente Resende 47 ☎234 428 634. One of a handful of *dormidas* near the fish market, and rather tatty, although the small rooms themselves are clean and fine for a night. Breakfast included. No credit cards. ❶

Pensão Residencial Estrela Rua José Estêvão 4
℡234 423 818. An old, converted house whose
plant-filled staircase and polished wooden corridor
are rather grander than the smallish, but cool and
comfortable rooms, some of which are en suite.
Friendly owners, and big discounts out of season. No
credit cards. Breakfast not included but available. ❷
Hotel Imperial Rua Dr. Nascimento Leitão ℡234
380 150, ⓦwww.hotelimperial.pt. Unattractive
modern building with dowdy decor, but with fine
views of the lagoon from the top-floor terrace.
Breakfast included. Parking. ❹
Hotel Mercure Aveiro Rua Luís Gomes de Carvalho 23 ℡234 404 400, ⓦwww.mercure.com.
Very comfortable rooms (with bath and TV) in a
gracious, quiet town house. Near the station and
with its own parking. Breakfast not included but
available. ❹
Hotel Moliceiro Rua Barbosa de Magalhães
15–17, Largo do Rossio ℡234 377 400,

ⓦwww.hotelmoliceiro.com. The most expensive
choice in town, with very comfortable and excellently equipped rooms in a centrally located
building overlooking the canal. Limited parking.
Breakfast included. ❺
Palmeira Rua da Palmeira 7–11 ℡234 422 521,
ⓔr.palmeira@netcabo.pt. Pretty, modern, tiled
town house with attached dining room, in the old
quarter between the fish market and the Canal de
São Roque. Bright rooms, some with shower or
bath, and most with TV. Breakfast included. ❷

Youth hostel

Pousada de Juventude Rua das Pombas ℡234
420 536, ⓦwww.pousadasjuventude.pt. Aveiro's
hostel is situated inside a youth centre and is
small, far from the action and has no self-
catering facilities. Four double rooms available.
Bus #5 or #7 from the train station. Dorm beds
€10, rooms ❷

The Town

Aveiro casts off its rather workaday first appearances as soon as you reach the
bridge over the main canal. Handsome, pastel-coloured houses line Rua João
Mendonça on the north side, with a modern shopping area to the southeast.
More attractive is the old town around the **fish market**, behind which tiled
houses face each other across arms of the canal. Lagoon boats with raised prows
lie tied up along the quaysides.

There's only one sight of real note, the fifteenth-century **Convento de
Jesus**, on Avenida Santa Joana, which now houses the town museum (Tues
–Sun 10am–5.30pm; €2), whose finest exhibits all relate to Santa Joana, a
daughter of Afonso V who lived in the convent from 1475 until her death in
1489. Barred from becoming a nun because of her royal station and her father's
opposition, she was later beatified for her determination to escape from the
material world (or perhaps simply from an unwelcome arranged marriage).
Her tomb and chapel are strikingly beautiful, as is the convent itself, and there's
a fine collection of art and sculpture – notably a series of naive seventeenth-
century paintings depicting the saint's life.

Once you've seen this you may as well cross the road to the **Catedral**, whose
exterior concrete loggia and interior breeze-block walls make it resemble a
municipal swimming pool. Infinitely more pleasing is the **Igreja da Misericórdia**, back down towards the canal on Rua Coimbra, whose seventeenth
-century facade features blue snowflake-design tiles. The **Câmara Municipal**,
a century older, stands opposite, both buildings facing a declamatory statue of
Aveiro's famous son, the nineteenth-century politician José Estêvão Coelho
de Magalhães.

Eating, drinking and nightlife

There are some excellent restaurants in Aveiro, with **local specialities** including eels and shellfish from the lagoons and powerful Bairrada wine. The cheapest
eats are in the little *casas de pasto* in the old town streets around the fish market,
though there are also several regular restaurants in this area, too. While you're in

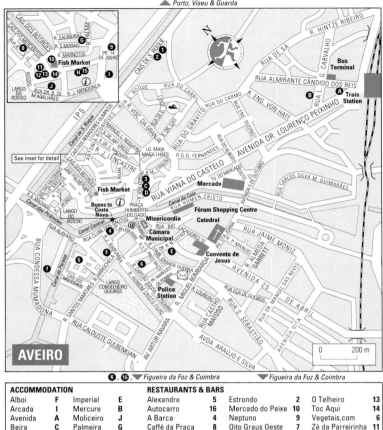

▲ Porto, Viseu & Guarda

AVEIRO

0   200 m

K, **16**, ▼ Figueira da Foz & Coimbra   ▼ Figueira da Foz & Coimbra

ACCOMMODATION				RESTAURANTS & BARS					
Alboi	F	Imperial	E	Alexandre	5	Estrondo	2	O Telheiro	13
Arcada	I	Mercure	B	Autocarro	16	Mercado do Peixe	10	Toc Aqui	14
Avenida	A	Moliceiro	J	A Barca	4	Neptuno	9	Vegetais.com	6
Beira	C	Palmeira	G	Caffé da Praça	8	Oito Graus Oeste	7	Zé da Parreirinha	11
A Brasileira	H	Pousada de		Cervejaria Rossio	12	Salpoente	1	Zico	3
Estrela	D	Juventude	K	Clandestino	15				

town, try some of the celebrated local **sweets**, especially *ovos moles*, candied egg yolks. At night, the liveliest place in town is the area immediately around the fish market, where young people crowd into the **bars** and spill out onto the tables scattered across the cobbles.

Cafés and restaurants

Alexandre Cais do Alboi 14 ☎ 234 420 494. A short walk along the canal, this is a well-regarded snack bar and adjacent restaurant with a local clientele, serving good Portuguese fish and meat dishes. Closed Thurs & mid-July to mid-Aug. Moderate.

A Barca Rua José Rabumba 5 ☎ 234 426 024. Intimate, long-running restaurant where diners can see the top-quality fresh fish and seafood

being prepared in the kitchen at the back. Dishes are simple and delicious and service is good. Go for the sea bass or sole. Closed Sat eve and Sun. Moderate.

Mercado do Peixe Largo da Praça do Peixe ☎ 234 383 511. In the rafters of the fish market, this trendy restaurant has crisp decor, attentive service and exceedingly fresh fish and seafood. The menu offers traditional local treats such as *caldeirada de enguias* (eel stew; €25 between 2) as well as more contemporary dishes, and there's a lunchtime buffet (Tues–Fri, €5.50). Great views out to the Ria or to the square below from the tiny terrace. Closed Sun eve and Mon. Expensive.

Neptuno Rua Mendes Leite 1 ☏ 234 424 566. Functional but decent little grill house serving large portions of chicken, home-made sausage, chops or fish. Around €10 for a *dose*. Closed Sun. Moderate.

Salpoente Cais de São Roque 83 ☏ 234 382 674. Ten minutes' walk north along the canal, this superior fish restaurant is set inside a renovated salt barn. There are crabs, fish and eels on the menu, as well as plenty of meat, while the restaurant has an enjoyable bar which opens at 11.30pm and has live music on Fri and Sat until 2.30am. Closed Sun. Expensive.

O Telheiro Largo da Praça do Peixe 20–21 ☏ 234 429 473. Excellent *adega* with wooden benches and tiled tables, and food cooked any way you like as long as it's chargrilled. *Lulas grelhados* (grilled squid) is superb. Closed Sat. Moderate.

Vegetais.com Rua Capitão Sousa Pizarro 23 ☏ 234 383 555. Small, modern, self-service vegetarian restaurant serving tasty dishes, mostly using meat substitutes, as well as home-made desserts. No alcohol, but there are great freshly squeezed juices. Also open for breakfast. Closed Sat. Inexpensive.

Zé da Parreirinha Trav. do Lavadouro 10 ☏ 234 426 137. Rough-and-ready *casa de pasto* with full meals for under €5. Just off Praça da Peixe. Closed Wed. Inexpensive.

Zico Rua José Estêvão 52 ☏ 234 429 649. Very popular local spot, with most dishes around €8. The menu changes daily, but there are always grills, local fish and good wine. Closed Sun. Moderate.

Bars and clubs

Autocarro Largo da Universidade. Funky bar, up by the university and youth hostel. It's partly set in an old red bus, with tables on a terrace outside.

Caffé da Praça Rua Antonio Santos Lé 18. Round the corner from the action on Praça do Peixe and up a set of stairs, this fashionable bar has very friendly staff and table service. Large windows overlook the canal.

Clandestino Rua do Tenente Resende 35. There's no sign but it's recognizable by its red interior and low-lighting. Friendly and warm atmosphere, with more tables upstairs and a DJ playing jazzy, mellow tunes.

Estrondo Cais de São Roque 73. Polynesian-style bar on the canal, open till 2–3am for cocktails and other drinks. Closed Mon.

Oito Graus Oeste Cais do Paraíso. Club with its own bar and terrace overlooking the Ria. Wed and weekends only.

Cervejaria Rossio Largo da Rossio 8A. Central *cervejaria* serving beer and good steak sandwiches until 2am. Closed Mon.

Toc Aqui Pr. do Peixe. One of a number of bars around the fish market, whose name (which isn't signed – it's the one with the blue facade) means "play here", and on more raucous nights, that's exactly what you can do with the instruments hung on the back wall.

Listings

Car rental Avis, Av. Dr. Lourenço Peixinho 350 ☏ 234 426 554; Salitur, Rua Almirante Cândido dos Reis 23B, Ap 3001 ☏ 234 371 897, ⓦ www.salitur.pt.

Hospital Hospital Infante Dom Pedro Aveiro, Av. Dr. Artur Ravara ☏ 234 378 300.

Internet Montra Digital de Aveiro, Pr. da República (9am–8pm) offers free access for 30min.

Police Pr. Marquês de Pombal ☏ 234 302 510.

Post office Pr. Marquês de Pombal ☏ 234 380 840 (Mon–Fri 8.30am–6.30pm).

Swimming pool Piscinas Sporting Clube de Aveiro, Rua de D. José I ☏ 234 480 191 (Mon–Sat 2–6pm; €5).

Travel agency Halcon Viages, Fórum Aveiro, 131B Batalhão Caçadores ☏ 234 404 170 (daily 10am–10pm).

The lagoon and beaches

There's no beach in Aveiro itself but the coast north and south is a more or less continuous line of sand, cut off from the mainland for much of the way by the meandering **lagoon**. Although developers have long caught on, and summer weekends can be crowded, the whole sand bar is still relatively little spoilt, and offers ample opportunity for beach lounging as well as fascinating walks along the lagoon's swampy edge, which boasts abundant birdlife. Note that the pine forests shelter several military bases, so stick to the roads and don't camp outside official sites. The easiest places to reach by **bus** are Praia da Barra, Costa Nova and São Jacinto – heading further north or south, you really need your own transport.

Praia da Barra and Costa Nova

Local **buses** from Aveiro (roughly hourly 7.05am–12.40am) depart from outside the train station, also stopping on Rua Clube dos Galitos, across the bridge from the turismo and about 150m down the canal on the right. They call at Barra first, then Costa Nova.

PRAIA DA BARRA is 9km west of Aveiro. Although less charming than Costa Nova, it has a greater choice of accommodation, as well as more restaurants and nightclubs, but prices can be steep. The best advice is to look out for signs for *quartos* once you arrive. The pick of the **accommodation** options is *Residencial Farol* on Largo do Farol (☎234 390 600, ✉ofarol@ciberguia.pt; breakfast included; ❹), with comfortable, brightly coloured rooms, situated above a pleasant café and billiards room – it's at the end of the main road and overlooked by the Iberian Peninsula's tallest lighthouse. Less polished *Residencial Marisqueira*, Avenida João Corte Real (☎234 369 262; breakfast included; ❹), and the slightly musty *Hotel Barra*, Avenida Fernandes Lavrador 18 (☎234 369 156, ✉hotel-barra@clix.pt; breakfast included; ❺), which has a pool and parking, are the back-up choices There's also a municipal **campsite** (☎234 369 425; closed Dec).

COSTA NOVA, 3km south of Barra, is an attractive ensemble of candy-stripe wooden buildings (plus the ubiquitous spread of newer concrete constructions), stuffed into the strip between beach and lagoon. The bus stops next to the wave-shaped **turismo** (July to mid-Sept Mon, Tues, Thurs & Fri 10am–1pm & 2–6pm, Wed, Sat & Sun 10am–8pm; ☎234 369 560), on Avenida José Estêvão Gafanha da Encarnação. You might strike lucky with private **rooms**, but otherwise there are two official places to stay: the excellent *Residencial Azevedo*, Rua Arrais Ança 16 (☎234 390 170, ✉234 390 171; breakfast included; ❹), where all rooms have terraces and you can rent a bike; and the huge **campsite** 1km to the south (☎234 393 220, ⓦwww.campingcostanova. com), complete with supermarket and disco and also offering rooms (❸) and bungalows (❺). **Restaurants** are dotted along the road facing the lagoon. *Dom Fernando* (☎234 369 525) is a good, reasonably priced *marisqueria*.

São Jacinto

If you want more than just a beach, then you need to head the 12km west to **SÃO JACINTO**. From Aveiro catch a bus bound for Forte da Barra (some signed Costa Nova will stop here too – ask the driver). Once at the port, São Jacinto is just a five-minute boat ride across the water (pay for the full journey on the bus). Unlike its neighbours along the coast, it's not really a resort at all, but rather a thriving little port with a handful of dockside café-restaurants. With a military base at one end and a forest of cranes cluttering the skyline, it's not beautiful, but there is an enormous – and undeveloped – dune-fringed **beach** twenty minutes' walk away: off the boat, walk to the right past the post office and turn left at *Restaurant Ferraz*. The beach is straight up the long road ahead, where you'll also find the *Restaurante Marluci* (☎234 331 217), which has a few **rooms** (❸), some with kitchens. There's a substantial Orbitur **campsite** (☎234 331 220, ⓦwww.orbitur.pt; closed Dec & Jan) with good facilities 5km out of São Jacinto on the road to Torreira. The best **restaurant** in

São Jacinto is *Restaurante A Peixara* (☎234 331 165; closed Mon) which serves simple fresh fish at reasonable prices; to find it take a left down Rua de Nossa Senhora das Areias from the main street.

Torreira

With your own transport you can continue the 13km north from São Jacinto to the lively little resort of **TORREIRA**, whose long sands face the tumbling Atlantic surf. The **turismo** is centrally located at Avenida Hintza Rirbaro 30 (Mon–Fri 9.30am–12.30pm & 2.30–5.30pm, Sat 2.30–5.30pm; ☎234 838 250). The best **accommodation** is undoubtedly the *Pousada da Ria*, Bico do Muranzel, on the road to Torreira from São Jacinto (☎234 860 180, ⓦwww .pousadas.pt; breakfast included; ❼), with swimming pool, tennis courts and rooms with lagoon-view balconies. But also good is the four-star *Estalagem Riabela*, at the north end of town (☎234 838 137, ⓦwww.riabela.com; breakfast included; ❹), which has similar amenities. The cheaper *Residencial Albertina*, Travessa Arrais Faustino (☎234 838 306, ⓕ234 838 206; ❷), is a popular, modern hotel by the beach with air-conditioned rooms and a bar. The municipal **campsite** (☎234 838 397) is 500m from the sea, and rents out bikes.

For **eating**, the moderately priced *Casa Passoiera* (☎234 838 632), on the main road, is highly recommended, serving good meat and fish. The *Estalagem Riabela* also has a decent grill-restaurant and live music.

Ovar, Furadouro and Santa Maria da Feira

The distinctive Ria countryside comes to an end around **Ovar**, 25km to the north of Aveiro, and there's no great reason to delay the drive or train ride straight to Porto. But Ovar itself is worth at least a coffee break, while the beach to the west at **Furadouro** is as good as anything that's gone before. Further inland, **Santa Maria da Feira** boasts a splendid castle and a good interactive science park.

Ovar

OVAR is an attractive market town on the main train line to Porto and 5km away from a fine beach at Furadouro (see below). It's known locally for its *pão-de-ló* sponge cake – every bit as good as it looks, and available at *pastelerias* around town.

Regular buses run from the **train station** into the centre of town (otherwise a fifteen-minute walk), stopping on the main thoroughfare, before continuing on to the beach. The **turismo** (Mon–Fri 9.30am–12.30pm & 2–5.30pm, Sat 10am–12.30pm; ☎256 572 215, ⓦwww.cm-ovar.pt) is near the main square, on Rua Elias Garcia.

The nicest **accommodation** is provided by the modern *Hotel Meia-Lua*, Quinta das Luzes (☎256 575 031, ⓦwww.hotel-meialua.pt; breakfast included; ❹), five minutes' walk east of the centre, which has a pool and private parking. The large *Albergaria São Cristóvão*, at Rua Aquilino Ribeiro 1 (☎256 575 105, ⓕ256 575 107; breakfast included; ❸), is closer to the middle of town, and also has parking, but is a little fusty. At the budget end of the scale, the **youth hostel** (reception 8am–midnight; dorm beds €11; ☎256 591 832, ⓦwww.pousadasjuventude.pt) is inconveniently sited about 2km out of town on the busy Avenida Dom Manuel I – the road has no footpath and you're a ten-minute walk to the bus stop for either Ovar or Furadouro. For something to **eat** in town, head to moderately priced *A Toca* on the central Praça da República (T 256 572 245; closed Sun), which does great fish kebabs.

Furadouro

The often-crowded resort of **FURADOURO** marks the northern extent of the system of waterways, and like its neighbours to the south boasts a long stretch of pine-fringed dunes. There's a small **tourist kiosk** on the main road back from the beach (Mon–Thurs & Sun 10am–1pm & 3–6pm, Fri 10am –3pm; no phone), while *Pensão Avenida* (T 256 591 435; breakfast included; ❷), right on the seafront, has basic **rooms** with shared bathrooms, some with great views out over the ocean; it can be noisy due to the bar below. The signposted **campsite** (T 256 596 010, W www.clubecampismo-sjm.pt) is pleasant and forested and has a restaurant. Otherwise, the best place for Portuguese **food** is *A Gaivota* (T 256 592 076; closed Mon) on the main road back from the beach. If you fancy testing out the surf, Animal Surf Shop, Rua Gonçalo Velho 282 (T 256 082 999), next to the market, runs a **surf school** and rents out gear.

Santa Maria da Feira

Easily reached by bus from Ovar or Espinho, and only a twenty-minute bus ride from Porto, **SANTA MARIA DA FEIRA** (or, more simply, Feira), is an odd mix of old and new. Attracting a growing number of commuters, its outskirts are filling up fast, but, hidden at the top of town, you'll find one of the most spectacular castles in Portugal.

The **Castelo da Feira** (Tues–Fri 9.30am–12.30pm & 1.30pm–6pm, Sat & Sun 10am–12.30pm & 1.30pm–6.30pm; closes at 5pm in winter; €2), a ten-minute climb up the hill on the southern side of town, has a sunken gateway that leads into the interior – part dilapidated, part overzealously restored. The principal room is the Great Hall, a magnificent Moorish structure. Beyond the keep, a tunnel links the two parts of the castle in such a way that no direct or easy access can ever have been offered to intruders – arrow slits and hidden entrances emphasize the point. In some of the walls you can see stones marked with Roman inscriptions, and you can make out the familiar straight Roman road through the wooded hills above. On the way down from the castle, you pass the grand **Convento de Loios**, set to become the town's municipal museum (check with the tourist office for details).

Located 3km out of town in the opposite direction to the castle, the **Vision-arium** (Mon–Fri 9am–6pm, Sat & Sun 10am–8pm; €6.50, discounted family tickets available; W www.visionarium.pt) is an impressive science museum. The interactive displays (in both Portuguese and English) cover subjects ranging from the Portuguese voyages of discovery to the insides of microchips. Set in expansive grounds the park also offers two open-air exhibits covering physics and astronomy.

An interesting time to visit Feira is during the annual **Festa das Fogaceiras** (Jan 20). Girls parade through the town carrying castle-shaped *fogaça* cakes to honour a vow made by St Sebastian in 1505 when the town was ravaged by plague. The cakes are available all year from *pastelerias* round town.

Practicalities

Buses stop at the bottom of the hill up to the castle; the helpful **turismo** (Mon–Fri 9am–6pm, Sat 10am–5pm; T 256 372 032, W www.cm-feira.pt)

is up the road on the left, on Praça da República. For **accommodation**, try *Residencial Tony*, on the third floor of an unattractive building at the top of Rua Jornal Correio da Feira at no. 22 (☎ & ℉256 372 593; no credit cards; breakfast included; ❷) – a left, then a right from Praça da República. It offers clean, nicely furnished rooms with bathrooms. With more money to spend, the best option is the outstanding *Casa das Ribas* (☎256 373 485, ℉256 374 481; breakfast included; no credit cards; ❹), an eighteenth-century manor house with large antique-filled rooms and gorgeous gardens, right next to the castle. Decent, inexpensive **meals** are to be had at *A Charrete*, Largo de Camões 7 (☎256 362 880; closed Mon), on the street at the bottom of the road up to the castle, where there are several other little **cafés**, too. At *Orfeu*, Rua Condes de Fijó (☎919 109 086), a converted old family residence, you can enjoy well-prepared meals in the expensive restaurant, cheaper bar food or a glass of wine on the peaceful terrace.

Arouca and the Serra da Freita

Picking up the N224 from Vale de Cambra, it's a splendid drive to **Arouca**, 20km to the east, a winding route through forested hills and small terraced slopes of tumbling vineyards, the air heady with the scent of pine resin and eucalyptus. There are regular buses from Santa Maria da Feira, and although there are no public transport links south from Arouca, through the magnificent **Serra da Freita**, buses do run on north to Porto.

Arouca

AROUCA is a small town entirely overshadowed by the vast **Convento da Arouca** (accompanied visits, sometimes in English; Tues–Sun 9.30am–noon & 2–5.30pm; €2), whose imposing walls loom across the busy main road that cuts through town. It was founded as early as 1091, though most surviving parts are from rather later medieval times. In the kitchen (closed for restoration at the time of writing) there are huge fireplaces along Alcobaça lines. The vast Baroque church (which you can see without buying a ticket; enter from the main road) holds richly carved choir stalls and a great organ with 1352 notes, played on rare occasions by one of the country's few experts, while off the central cloisters the airy Sala Capítula, lined with *azulejos*, is where the abbesses once held court.

The convent peaked in importance when Dona Mafalda, of whose dowry it had formed a part, found her marriage to Dom Henriques I of Castile annulled and retired here to a life of religious contemplation. In the extensive **museum** upstairs, you can see some of Queen Mafalda's most prized treasures, including an exquisite thirteenth-century silver diptych. In 1792, four centuries after Mafalda's death, villagers claimed to have witnessed her saving the convent from the ravages of a terrible fire. She was promptly exhumed and beatified.

The rest of town struggles to make a mark in the face of its prize exhibit, but it's a handsome little place with a certain sleepy appeal. The central square holds a couple of cafés with pavement seats, while in the medieval backstreets there are some beautiful old houses decked with wisteria.

Local heart rates increase slightly during the annual **Festa de Nossa Senhora da Mó** (Sept 7–8), when the whole town turns out for a picnic on the crown of a hill 8km to the east. **Holy Week** processions are a big deal here, too, starting on the Wednesday and culminating on the Saturday night, when most of the inhabitants parade behind the local saints' statues to the Misericórdia church, with candles lit in all the town's windows.

Practicalities

The **bus station** is at the entrance to the town on the main road. Head down to the main square, Praça Brandão de Vasconcelas, opposite the convent, where the **turismo** is on the right-hand side (July to mid-Sept daily 9.30am–12.30pm & 2–5.30pm; mid-Sept to June Mon–Fri 9.30am–12.30pm & 2–5.30pm, Sat 9.30am–12.30pm; ☎256 943 575, ⓦwww.rotadaluz.pt).

There's **accommodation** at *Residencial São Pedro*, Avenida Reinaldo de Noronha (☎256 944 580, ⓕ256 943 054; breakfast included; ❸), a five-minute walk up the main road from the square (take the left fork at the top). The rather tired rooms are due a renovation, but most have views over town, and the staff are very friendly. A better choice is the rustic *Quinta do Bóco* (☎256 944 169, ⓦwww.quintadoboco.com; breakfast included; no credit cards; ❸), in a lovely farmhouse dating from the fifteenth-century, which also has a pool; continue up from the *São Pedro* and it's on the left.

There are a couple of *casas de pasto* around town, while *Residencial São Pedro* has a good, expensive **restaurant** with mighty portions. *Restaurante Parlamento*, Travessa da Ribeira 2 (☎256 949 604; closed Tues eve), specializes in the local *arouquêsa* beef.

Serra da Freita

South of Arouca lies the beautiful, terraced countryside of the **Serra da Freita**, abundantly littered with dolmens, crumbling villages and waterfalls with ancient bridges. Arouca turismo can provide information on specific sights, while whitewater rafting, mountain biking and other activities are also on offer – contact Rios e Caminhos (☎256 941 205, ⓦwww.riosecaminhos.com) or the Arouca turismo to arrange these.

Perhaps the most extraordinary route over the peaks is the 43-kilometre drive to Vouzela. Head south from Arouca at the roundabout on the main street and take the first exit from the next roundabout. The road climbs to the radio mast on the heights of **São Pedro Velho** (1100m), from where views of the valley are tremendous. On the way, tiny settlements cling to the hillside, vines grow on precipitous terraces, while the road snakes first through pine forest and then high across the heather-dotted moorland.

At **ALBERGARIA DA SERRA**, a medieval hamlet, the road disappears altogether for an instant and degenerates into cart-rutted cobbles worn by centuries of use. After leaving Albergaria take the next available left and follow signs to **MANHOUCE**, a slightly larger village amid the pine forests and rocky uplands, where you can stay for the night at the beautifully restored *Quinta das Uchas* (☎232 700 800; breakfast included; ❸), about 1km from the village on the right. Staff can organize trips around the *serra* and also rent out mountain bikes; evening meals are available, if arranged in advance, for €7.50.

Beyond Manhouce, there's another 12km of incredible bends and views before emerging onto the N227 for Vouzela. It's a spectacular drive but be prepared to take evasive action along the whole route, against other drivers or, occasionally, against wandering cattle.

Travel details

Trains

Aveiro to: Braga (2–3 daily; 1hr 30min); Coimbra (hourly; 45min–1hr); Espinho (hourly; 35–50min); Lisbon (hourly; 2hr 30min–4hr 50min); Ovar (hourly; 25–40min); Porto (hourly; 1hr).

Coimbra to: Aveiro (hourly; 45min–1hr); Braga (2–3 daily; 2hr); Figueira da Foz (hourly; 1hr–1hr 20min); Guarda (4–7 daily; 3hr–3hr 20min); Lisbon (hourly; 1hr 50min); Lousã (Mon–Fri 17 daily, Sat 11 daily, Sun 8 daily; 50min); Luso-Buçaco (1–4 daily; 45min); Ovar (hourly; 50min–1hr 30min); Porto (hourly; 1hr 20min–2hr).

Figueira da Foz to: Caldas da Rainha (2–4 daily; 2hr–2hr 25min); Coimbra (hourly; 1hr–1hr 20min); Leiria (2–4 daily; 1hr–1hr 15min).

Buses

Arouca to: Porto (Mon–Fri 10 daily, Sat & Sun 2 daily; 1hr 30min); Santa Maria da Feira (Mon–Fri 3 daily, Sat & Sun 1 daily; 40min).

Aveiro to: Figueira da Foz (4–7 daily; 1hr 15min); Lisbon (4–9 daily; 3hr 30min); Mira (9–12 daily; 50min); Porto (Mon–Fri 8 daily; 2hr 45min); Praia da Barra (every 30min; 30min); Praia de Mira (Mon–Fri 1 daily; 1hr); Praia da Tocha (4–6 daily; 50min); Vouzela (1–3 daily; 1hr 10min).

Coimbra to: Braga (7 daily; 2hr 40min–3hr); Condeixa-a-Nova (Mon–Fri 7am–12.05am every 30min, reduced service weekends; 30min); Conímbriga (1–2 daily; 35min); Covilhã (1–2 daily; 4hr); Fátima (9–10 daily; 55min); Figueira da Foz (4–14 daily; 1hr–1hr 30min); Góis (1 daiy; 1hr 25min); Guarda (1–2 daily; 3hr 5min); Leiria (12–16 daily; 50min); Lisbon (12–33 daily; 2hr 30min); Lousã (4–6 daily;

45min); Luso via Buçaco (Mon–Sat 2–5 daily; 40min); Mira (1–2 daily; 1hr); Montemor-o-Velho (6–19 daily; 40min); Penacova (14–16 daily; 45min); Porto (9–14 daily; 1hr 30min–2hr 45min); Tondela (3–7 daily; 1hr 10–1hr 40min); Vila Real (2 daily; 3hr); Viseu (8–17 daily; 1hr 25min–2hr 15min); Vouzela (2 daily; 1hr 45min).

Figueira da Foz to: Aveiro (4–7 daily; 1hr 15min); Coimbra (7–12 daily; 1hr–1hr 30min); Leiria (9–11 daily; 1hr–1hr 25min); Lisbon (4 daily; 2hr 45min–3hr); Mira (2–5 daily; 1hr); Montemor-o-Velho (Mon–Fri roughly every 30min, Sat & Sun 4–8 daily; 30min); Quiaios (3–5 daily; 35min); Tocha (3–10 daily; 40min).

Góis to: Coimbra (Mon–Fri 2 daily; 1hr 30min); Lisbon (Sun 1 daily; 3hr); Lousã (Mon–Fri 1 daily; 1hr).

Lousã to: Góis (1 Mon–Fri; 1hr); Coimbra (4–6 daily; 45min).

Luso to: Coimbra (Mon–Sat 2–5 daily; 40min); Viseu via Buçaco (5–7 daily; 1hr 45min).

Mira to: Aveiro (9–12 daily; 50min); Coimbra (1–2 daily; 1hr); Figueira da Foz (2–5 daily; 1hr).

Ovar to: Furadouro (9–11 daily; 10min); Santa Maria da Feira (9–11 daily; 20–30min).

Penacova to: Coimbra (11–13 daily; 45min).

Praia de Mira to: Aveiro (1 daily; 1hr); Coimbra (1–2 daily; 1hr 15min).

Santa Maria de Feira to: Arouca (Mon–Fri 3 daily; 40min); Ovar (9–11 daily; 20–30min); Porto (every 30min; 20min).

Tondela to: Águeda (Mon–Fri 2 daily; 1hr); Caramulo (Mon–Fri 2 daily; 35min).

Vouzela to: Aveiro (1–3 daily; 1hr 10min); Lisbon (2–5 daily; 4hr 30min); Porto (1–3 daily; 1hr 50min); Viseu (1–6 daily; 1hr 10min).

Mountain Beiras

ATLANTIC OCEAN

N

SPAIN

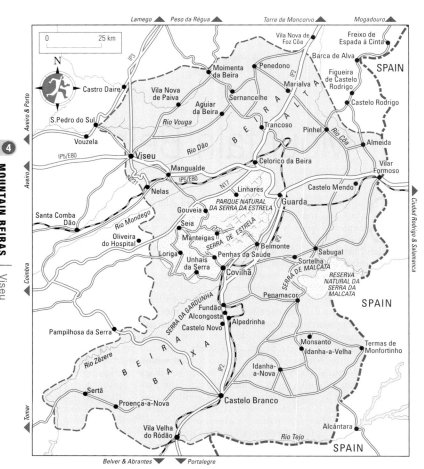

The whole Mountain Beiras region is little visited by tourists: if you've spent some days in the fleshpots of Lisbon, Porto or the Algarve, you'll find a very different atmosphere here. Bear in mind that – out of season at least – many hotels and restaurants shut sporadically. You'll rarely have trouble finding a bed for the night, but if you have a particular establishment in mind, be sure to phone ahead.

Viseu

From its high plateau, the dignified little city of **VISEU** surveys the surrounding countryside with the air of a feudal overlord. It's a place of great antiquity. There was a Roman town here, and on the northern outskirts you can still make out the remains of an encampment claimed to be the site where Viriatus

(Viriato in Portuguese) fought his final battle – it's marked by a monument to the Iberian warrior. The heart of the medieval city has changed little, though it's now approached through the broad avenues of a prosperous provincial centre. Parts of the walls survive and it is within their circuit, breached by two doughty gateways, that almost everything of interest lies.

The liveliest event in Viseu's calendar is the **Feira de São Mateus** which takes place from mid-August until its climax on September 21 (Dia do São Mateus) – it's largely an agricultural show, but is enlivened by occasional bull-fights and folk-dance festivals. The showground is at the top end of Avenida Dr. António José de Almeida, beyond the bus station and across the Rio Paiva.

The City

The approach to the old town, from the central Praça da República (also known as Rossio), up through the Porta do Soar, or along the shop-lined Rua Dr. Luís Ferreira, exhibits a certain amount of "beautification", but the jumble of alleys immediately behind the cathedral remains virtually untouched. You suddenly come upon sixteenth-century stone mansions proudly displaying their coats of arms in the middle of a street of run-down houses. The cathedral square, Praça da Sé, is lined with noble stone buildings, most striking of which is the **Igreja da Misericórdia** with its white Baroque facade. Silhouetted against a deep blue sky it looks like a film set without substance – you expect to walk around the back and find wooden props holding it up. There's some truth to that feeling: behind the symmetry of the facade, it's a very ordinary, rather dull church.

There's nothing two-dimensional, however, about the **Sé** (daily 9.30am –noon & 2–5.30pm; free), a weighty, twin-towered Romanesque base on which a succession of later generations have made their mark. The granite frontage, remodelled in the seventeenth century, is stern and makes the church look smaller than it actually is – inside it opens out into a great hall with intricate vaulting, twisted and knotted to represent ropes. The cathedral's Renaissance **cloister**, of which you get no intimation from outside, is one of the most graceful in the country. The rooms of its upper level look out over the tangled roofs of the oldest part of the town and house the treasures of the cathedral's art collection, including naive sculptures, two thirteenth-century Limoges enamel coffers and a twelfth-century Bible.

Museu de Grão Vasco

The greatest treasure of Viseu is the **Museu de Grão Vasco** (Tues 2–6pm, Wed–Sun 10am–6pm; €3, free Sun mornings) in the Paço dos Três Escalões – once the Bishop's palace – which backs on to the cathedral; the entrance lies on the northeastern side of Praça da Sé, near Calçada da Vigio. The museum celebrates the work of **Vasco Fernandes** (known always as Grão Vasco, The Great Vasco), who was born in Viseu and became the key figure in a school of painting that flourished here in the first half of the sixteenth century. The style of these "Portuguese primitives" was influenced heavily by Flemish masters and in particular by van Eyck, but certain aspects – the realism of portraiture and richness of colour – are distinctively their own. Vasco and his chief rival Gaspar Vaz have a fair claim to being two of the greatest artists Portugal has produced.

Centrepiece of the Vasco collection is the masterly *St Peter on His Throne*, one of Grão Vasco's last works. It shows considerably more Renaissance influence than some of the earlier paintings but its Flemish roots are still evident, a full-sized snooker table, an open fire in winter and a large pool in summer – perfect for a relaxing few days away from it all. Breakfast included. No credit cards. ➍

Quinta de São Caetano Rua Poça das Feiticeiras, on the outskirts of town ☏232 423 984, Ⓦwww.ed.ac.uk/~ptr/qsc/welcome.htm. A palm tree-flanked manor house of the seventeenth century, with six comfortable guest rooms. Breakfast included. ➎

Youth hostel and campsite

Orbitur Av. Jose Relvas, ☏232 436 146,

Ⓦwww.orbitur.pt. Fair-sized campsite with good facilities and adequate shade. It's adjacent to the municipal stadium, a 15min-walk northeast of Rossio. Closed Oct–March.

Pousada de Juventude Carreira dos Carvalhos, on the left beyond Portal do Fontelo ☏232 435 445, Ⓦwww.pousadasjuventude.pt. Modern hostel a 10min-walk northeast of Rossio, with five double en-suite rooms and fifteen mini-dorms with either four or five beds, as well as disabled facilities and a modest common room. Reception open 8am–1pm & 6pm–midnight. Dorm beds €10, rooms ➋

Eating, drinking and nightlife

Viseu is well known for its gastronomic delights, while the locally produced Dão wines, especially the mature reds, are some of the best you'll find in the country. For provisions, there's a **weekly market** on Tuesday, on the ring road by Largo Castanheiro dos Amores, and a weekday market in the **Mercado Municipal**, just west of Rossio. Most of Viseu's nightlife is to be found in the old town around Rua Augusto Hilário, Rua Dom Duarte and the Sé.

Restaurants

Bella Itália Rua Migel Bombarda 3 ☏232 982 189. A genuine Italian-owned place, with tasty favourites like *minestrone* and *maccheronie all'arabiatta*, while seafood lovers can sample the *zuppa pirata*, a spicy cream of tomato soup with shrimp. Closed Mon. No credit cards. Moderate.

Cacimbo Rua A. Herculano ☏232 642 264. Bustling, down-to-earth joint, regularly crammed with locals who come for the good-value Portuguese food and friendly service. The extensive menu covers enough meat and offal dishes to satisfy the most demanding carnivore while veggies can dine on omelettes for a mere €1.25. No credit cards. Inexpensive.

Casa dos Queijos Trav. Escadinha da Sé 9 ☏232 422 643. Located in the heart of the old town, the "House of Cheese" lives up to its name with a shop full of tempting mountain cheeses and – up a narrow, creaky staircase – a traditional restaurant with delicious meat and fish choices. Closed Sun. No credit cards. Moderate.

Claustros da Sé Rua Augusto Hilário 60–62 ☏232 426 452. Stylish, compact bar/restaurant run by an enthusiastic young Portuguese couple. The Brazilian cook can rustle you up a *picanha* (rice, black beans and pork) or try the excellent *bife a cervejeiro* (steak in beer – Super Bock, apparently – and mushroom sauce) for €8. Closed Mon. No credit cards. Moderate.

O Cortiço Rua Augusto Hilário 45 ☏232 423 853. This snug little restaurant boasts walls filled with messages of praise from customers heartily satisfied with the strictly traditional but creatively prepared food, named after figures who have passed into local folklore. Expensive.

Manga e Diospyrus Av. Emídio Navarro, Centro Comercial Académico II ☏232 421 991. Stuck inside a shopping mall and difficult to locate, this is nevertheless a proper vegetarian restaurant, albeit a self-serivce, canteen-style affair. The *prato do dia* – dishes such as tofu *feijoada* – comes with brown rice and vegetables, and there's a range of fresh fruit juices and mousses. Closes 9pm, and closed Sat & Sun. Inexpensive.

Rodízio Real Bairro Santa Eulália, 3km from town in Repeses, on the N2 (Coimbra road) ☏232 422 232. Suck on a *caipirinha* and tuck into some real *feijoada* at this highly regarded Brazilian restaurant, run by the same people behind *The Day After* and *Hotel Montebelo*. Expensive.

Bars and clubs

Galeria Bar Pr. Dom Duarte 37–39. Very stylish bar attracting a decent mix of people, with occasional live jazz alongside the obligatory DJs and theme nights.

Noitebiba Rua Conselheiro Afonso de Melo 39, behind the town hall. "NB" has long been a staple of the city's nightlife, its spacious dance floor and long, curving bar throbbing to Latin, pop and house sounds. Open Tues & Thurs–Sat only.

The Day After 1.5km north of town, N16. A huge entertainment/disco complex, featuring four dance floors and twelve bars, with DJs spinning everything from salsa, hip-hop and house to techno, indie and metal.

Listings

Banks Banks and ATMs are on Rua Formosa, just off Rossio, while you can change money at the Novo Mundo travel agency at the bottom of Rua Alexandre Herculano (Mon–Fri 9am–12.30pm & 2–5.30pm).

Hospital Hospital Distrital de São Teotónio, Av. Rei Dom Duarte ☎ 232 420 500.

Internet There's free access at espaçoInternet on Rua dos Andrades (Mon–Fri 10am–7pm, Sat 10am–1pm & 2–7pm, Sun 2–7pm), although online time is limited to 30min. Otherwise the nameless arcade/pool room next door to *Hotel Avenida* on Av. Alberto Sampaio (Mon–Fri 8am–midnight, Sun 9am–midnight) has internet access upstairs.

Pharmacy Farmácia Confiança Rua Formosa 10 ☎ 232 480 340.

Police Rua D. António Alves Martins ☎ 232 480 380.

Post Office Largo General Humberto Delgado ☎ 232 424 820 (Mon-Fri 8.30am-6.30pm, Sat 9am-12.30pm).

Celorico da Beira

CELORICO DA BEIRA, 50km east of Viseu, is an unprepossessing town; its one claim to Portuguese fame is as the birthplace of the aviator Sacadura Cabral, though it also has a long military history, forming, together with Trancoso and Guarda, a triangle of defensive fortifications against Spain. At just 20km from Linhares in the Parque Natural da Serra da Estrela, the town is one possible access point to the park, but it is certainly not the most attractive *serra* base, as the town is ringed by heavy traffic along the east–west road from Spain and the north–south route to Lisbon. It does, however, have a pretty enough old town hugging the slopes around its castle and, if you're passing through on the right day (see below), it's the best place to pick up a pungent *queijo da serra*, the famed round cheese of the Serra da Estrela district. A visit on June 13, meanwhile, will give you the chance to join in the **Santo António** festival when the whole town enjoys a riverside picnic; during other summer festivals locals indulge in the traditional game of climbing a greased pole to try and retrieve a flask of wine and some *bacalhau*.

It is no longer possible to enter the castle, although the views of the surrounding mountains from below the walls are stunning. Instead, it's the **feiras** – held on alternate Fridays for cheese, and on Tuesdays for the ordinary covered market – that are the times to come and enjoy the town's cheery provinciality. People arrive from the mountains to sell their *queijo da serra*, market-going being the only other available source of income to support their impoverished hilltop farms. If you miss the cheese market, you can visit the excellent old **cheese shop** on the main road through town, just down from the post office, or call in at the **Museu do Agricultor e do Queijo** (daily 9am–12.30pm & 2–5.30pm; free), adjacent to the bus station. As well as vintage cheese-making equipment and some fearsome-looking farm implements, the museum also contains some fascinating black-and-white photos of bygone *feiras*, including a priceless 1924 shot of a drunken man lying sprawled beside his donkey.

Practicalities

Celorico's **train station** is 6km north of town at Celorico Gare; bus connections are erratic, so take a taxi (if you can find one). It's far more convenient to

(Blacksmiths' Tower). In the **Museu da Guarda** on Rua Alves Roçadas (Tues–Sun 10am–12.30pm & 2–5.30pm; €2, free Sun morning) you can sift dutifully through the displays of local archeology, art and sculpture, though in the end it's the cobbled streets of the old town that provide the best diversion. The tangled, somewhat decaying area between the castle's other two portals – the **Porta da Erva** and **Porta d'El-Rei** – can have changed little in the past 400 years. You can climb the vertiginous steps of the latter for some great views, although you'll have to negotiate the litter and broken beer bottles.

In Guarda's covered **Mercado Municipal** on Rua Dom Nuno Álvares Pereira, busiest on Saturdays, you'll find delicious *queijo da serra*. On the other side of town, below Avenida Monsenhor Mendes do Carmo, is the open-air **Feira Ao Ar Livre**, held on the first and third Wednesday of every month and attracting agricultural folk from all around.

Practicalities

All **buses** depart and arrive from the terminal on Rua Dom Nuno Álvares Pereira, which is a fifteen-minute walk from the central square. Services are operated by a variety of companies to most of the neighbouring villages, the only problem being that many buses leave early in the morning and often don't return until late in the afternoon. Schedules are available at the bus station, but it's much easier to ask at the well-informed turismo (see below). Guarda's **train station** is 4km northeast and downhill from the centre of town, with daily services south to Covilhã, Castelo Branco, Abrantes and Lisbon, east to the border at Vilar Formoso and west to Coimbra and Porto. There's a regular bus service into town, leaving from a stop just outside the station entrance.

The **turismo** is in the old town hall building, just across from the Sé on Praça Luís de Camões (daily 9am–12.30pm & 2–5.30pm; ☎271 205 530, ⓦwww.mun-guarda.pt/turismo). As well as bundles of literature on Guarda and the region's picturesque villages (some if it in English) they sell Serra da Estrela books and maps, useful if you arrive at the weekend when the nearby **Serra da Estrela information office**, Rua Dom Sancho I (Mon–Fri 9am–12.30pm & 2–5.30pm; ☎271 225 454), is closed. This, however, has a much larger range of books, covering the botany and geology of the region, as well as walking guides and a mounted wall map.

Accommodation

You should have no trouble getting a room at one of the *pensões* or hotels detailed below although Guarda's growing popularity means that booking ahead at weekends in high summer is advisable. Guarda's **campsite** (☎271 221 200) is located in a park a short way from the youth hostel; it's open all year round, but beware that even in spring and autumn the nights can get extremely cold.

In town

Pensão Aliança Rua Vasco da Gama 8A ☎271 222 235, ☎271 221 451. Welcoming *pensão* with frayed but comfortable rooms with desk, TV, rudimentary balcony and private bathroom. It's especially good value for single travellers. Break-fast in the downstairs restaurant is included in the price while football fans can feast on the constant diet of televised games in the adjacent bar. Secure private parking. ❸

Casa da Sé Rua Augusto Gil 17 ☎271 212 501, ⓦwww.casa-da-se.com. *Azulejo*-decorated walls, and creaky wooden floors and shutters, make for an atmospheric night's stay. The small, bright rooms come with TV, although not all have a private bathroom. If you're after a bit of optical stimulation with your evening beer, there's the adjacent *Bar Salvador Dali*, open every night until 2am and featuring some outlandishly psychedelic wall murals. No credit cards. ❷

Hotel Filipe Rua Vasco da Gama 9 ☎271 223
659, ℱ271 221 402. The hotel itself favours
modern art and marble, although some of the
rooms are a little cramped and have garishly tiled
bathrooms, but all have TV and private facilities.
Rooms 103, 104 and 108 have the best views of
the church. Breakfast included. ❸

Dormidas Moreira Rua Mouzinho de Albuquerque
47 ☎271 214 131. Quiet, unassuming place with
friendly staff. The modern, peaceful rooms come
with spotless white bed linen and bathrooms, and
all have TV. Recommended. ❷

Residencial Santos Rua Tenente Valadim 14
☎271 205 400, ℯresidencial_santos@sapo.pt.
Great mid-range option incorporating part of the
original city walls into its intriguing stonework
interior. While the rooms themselves can be a little
box-like, views of the cathedral and the countryside beyond – framed within granite sills – more
than make up for it. Breakfast included. ❸

Solar de Alarção Rua Dom Miguel de Alarção
25–27 ☎271 214 392. Magnificent granite manor
house dating back to the seventeenth century. The
atmospheric rooms come with huge antique mirrors,
chandeliers, carved wooden ceilings and vintage
shutters, while secure parking is available in the
courtyard. Breakfast included. No credit cards. ❺

Hotel de Turismo Pr. do Município ☎271 223 366,
ℯsales@hotelguarda.com.pt. Formerly Guarda's
grandest hotel, now facing stiff competition from its
more modern peers. It's still comfortable enough,
with cable TV in the functional rooms, and there's
a swimming pool, disco and parking. Breakfast
included. ❹

Hotel Vanguarda Av. Monsenhor Mendes do Carmo
☎271 208 390, ℘www.hotelvanguarda.com. Out
on a limb at the edge of town, rooms in Guarda's
newest hotel look across the hills to Spain, and
feature plush carpets and gleaming baths. Breakfast
included. No American Express. ❺

Outside town

Quinta do Pinheiro Cavadoude, 15km north of
Guarda ☎271 926 162, ℘www.quintadopinheiro
.com. A pastoral idyll dating from the fifteenth
century and located near the Rio Mondego. Rooms
come with fearsomely Gothic four-poster beds and
good views, while the sprawling grounds allow
ample space for hammock-lounging, walking and
swimming. Breakfast included. ❹

Quinta da Ponte Faia, 12km northwest of Guarda
☎271 926 126, ℯponte@solaresdeportugal.pt.
Attractively situated near a Roman bridge in the
Mondego valley, this seventeenth-century manor
house boasts an impressive facade with attached
chapel, although the rooms themselves are more
ordinary. Nevertheless the lovely garden and
swimming pool help justify the price. Breakfast
included. ❺

Youth hostel

Pousada de Juventude Av. Alexandre Herculano
☎271 224 482, ℘www.pousadasjuventude.pt.
Beds in small four-bedded dorms, as well as four
double en-suite rooms available. Reception daily
8am–noon & 6pm–midnight. Dorm beds €11,
rooms ❷

Eating

Most of the town's **restaurants** are to be found in the area between Praça Luis
de Camões and the Igreja de São Vicente, with many huddled into the narrow
Rua Francisco dos Passos. There really isn't too much variety on offer, although
you'll be well served if you're eager to sample the regional cuisine.

Belo Horizonte Largo de São Vincente 1–2 ☎271
211 454. A Guarda institution for over sixty years.
A kindly old chef and matronly waitresses keep
locals supplied with regional specialities like spiced
sausage, while the extensive wine list features many
unusual varieties. Closed Sat. Moderate.

A Floresta Rua Franciso dos Passos 40 ☎271 223
746. Rustic decor, regional cuisine and red-checked
tablecloths provide an atmospheric old-town eating experience. The three-course *ementa turística*
is a bargain at €10 while the €15 *ementa da
mostra gastronómica* is a feast of local produce
including *requeijão come doce de abóbora e porto*
(fresh sheep's cheese with pumpkin jam and port).
Moderate.

A Mexicana Av. Monsenhor Mendes do Carmo 7
☎271 211 512. Nothing to do with Mexico, but
instead one of Guarda's best, presenting creatively
prepared and presented food – both regional and
national Portuguese fare with a twist. Their strawberry mousse is unforgettable. Closed Wed. Expensive.

O Monteneve Pr. Luís de Camões 24 ☎271 212
799. One half minimalist bar, one half stylish red
brick-walled restaurant with reasonably priced
meat and fish dishes. Try the shrimp omelette
appetiser and, if you're feeling homesick, you
could always follow up with *rosbbef à inglesa*.
Closed Mon. Moderate.

Oliveira Pizzeria Real Rua do Encontro 1 ☎271
214 446. About the only place in town where you

The turismo can point you in the direction of **private rooms** (❷), while the town offers a choice of two **pensions**. *Pensão Vale a Pena* (☎271 811 219, ℱ271 828 027; breakfast included; no credit cards; ❷), just outside the walls near the convent on Largo Senhora da Calçada, is a genial place with bright, modern rooms and bucolic views – although there's a sign on the side nearest to the town walls, the entrance is actually right around the corner in the next street. Otherwise, there's *Residencial Dom Dinis* (☎271 811 525; breakfast included; no credit cards; ❷), also outside the walls, above the post office in Estrada Nacional. While this puts on a great spread for breakfast – fresh orange juice, cake and home-made pumpkin jam – and the rooms are more tasteful than those at the *Vale*, a block of flats, power pylons and a warehouse do not make for inspiring views.

For **eating**, the renowned and correspondingly expensive *Área Benta* (☎271 817 180; closed Sun night & all Mon), in the old town's Rua dos Cavaleiros, offers handsomely prepared Portuguese food in an arty setting. More rustic is *O Museu* (☎271 811 810; closed Mon; no credit cards), a moderately priced seafood specialist on Largo de Santa Maria de Guimarães which does a memorable line in grilled trout and salmon. For something slightly cheaper and more unassuming head to *São Marcos* (☎271 811 326; closed Sun night; no credit cards), hidden away – but signposted – on Largo Luís Albuquerque, where you can dine on moderately priced fish and meat dishes.

Sernancelhe

Sited 30km northwest of Trancoso, four kilometres off the Guarda–Lamego road (N226), **SERNANCELHE** is a quietly impressive place with further reminders of the area's Jewish past and a fine riverside location. The village is also said to produce the *planalto*'s finest chestnuts, and its approach is dominated by the broad-boughed trees spreading across the road. If you coincide with the **Festa de Nossa Senhora de Ao Pé da Cruz** on May 1 you'll witness a curious mixture of religious devotion, springtime merrymaking and, above all, folkloric superstition. Aside from the usual religious procession there's a dance of the chestnuts, a blessing of the trees, and the exchange of handfuls of blossom by local lovers.

The old quarter of town is now semi-populated and comes alive only for the weekly Thursday market. En route, along the main road, you pass the **Igreja Matriz**, an attractive Romanesque church with a curious facade. Fixed into twin niches on either side of the main doorway are six weathered apostles – said to be the only free-standing sculptures of the period in the whole of Portugal. Inside the church are several sixteenth-century panels, including a magnificent *John the Baptist*. A wander around the old quarter will also reveal the same features of medieval **Jewish settlement** as in Trancoso – canted lintels, pairs of granite doorways of unequal size, the occasional cross for the converted. Equally noticeable are a number of large **town houses**, dating from the sixteenth and seventeenth centuries. One of these is the supposed birthplace of the Marquês de Pombal, another is the birthplace of Padre João Rodrigues, an influential missionary who founded a series of mission houses in Japan in the sixteenth century. Japanese tourists often make the pilgrimage here to see the building.

Practicalities

Buses to Lamego, Penedono and Trancoso (all Mon–Fri only) leave from the N226, 4km away – meaning that you'll have to walk or arrange a lift to the stop. There's a **turismo** in the centre of town on Rua Dr. Oliveira Serrão (Mon & Tues 11.30am–12.30pm & 3.45–5.30pm, Wed–Fri 9am–12.30pm & 2–5.30pm; ☎254 595 226), the limited opening hours of which can be explained by the fact that the staff also juggle the free **internet** facilities (Mon–Fri 9am–8pm, Sat & Sun 3–8pm) in nearby Rua Santa Cruz. There are clean, workaday **rooms** above the *Café Flora* (☎254 595 304; ❷), on the main road into town, whose large adjacent restaurant is the most reliable place for a moderately priced meal. However, the best place to stay is *Casa da Comenda de Malta* (☎254 595 166; breakfast included; ❸), a huge granite house in the middle of the old town, with comfortable rooms and an outdoor pool. With your own transport, you can also consider the *Hotel Rural Convento Nossa Senhora do Carmo* (☎254 594 080; breakfast included; ❺) in the nearby village of Freixinho. It's a restored sixteenth-century convent whose most alluring feature is the dining room, situated in the convent's former chapel and retaining some of the original frescoes.

Penedono

Sixteen kilometres northeast of Sernancelhe, **PENEDONO** is another one-horse town, though one with a fantastic castle, the **Castelo Roqueiro** (Mon–Fri 9am–5pm, Sat 10am–12.30pm & 3.30–5pm, Sun 2.30–5pm; free), visible from miles around. The *roqueiro* ("rock") part of the name is due to the castle's emergence from its granite base, as if the rock and the walls were one and the same. From the top there are grand views, with the village's old quarter laid out below, although the vertiginous turrets and sparsely railed walkways are not for the faint hearted.

The castle, in times of war, and the **Solar dos Freixos** (now the town hall), in times of peace, were supposed to have been home to Álvaro Gonçalves Coutinho, the legendary king **Magriço** ("Lean One"), sung of in Camões's *Os Lusíadas*. It's a claim fought over fiercely with the inhabitants of Trancoso, who likewise are prepared to swear he is their man. According to Camões, the Magriço led eleven men to England to champion the cause of twelve noble English ladies, who found themselves without knights, and fought a joust on their behalf. Such tales of chivalry made them the subjects of numerous allegorical murals and panels of *azulejos* around the country.

Buses run here from Trancoso and continue (Mon–Fri) to Vila Nova de Foz Côa, leaving from the centre of the village near the castle. There's a small **turismo** (Mon–Fri 9am–5pm, Sat 10am–12.30pm & 3.30–5pm, Sun 2.30–5pm; ☎254 509 030) opposite the castle, which stays open an hour later in summer. For **accommodation**, the *Residencial Flora* (☎254 504 411; breakfast included; no credit cards; ❷), on the main road into town, is a reliable if functional choice. Or there are homely rooms at the *Estalagem de Penedono* (☎254 509 050, ⓦ www.estalagempenedono.com; breakfast included; ❺), directly opposite the castle, whose expensive downstairs **restaurant**, *O Magriço*, serves suitably regal fare with prices to match – try the trout stuffed with ham or their delicious spin on *bacalhau*, roasted in the oven with local chestnuts. *Feiras* are held every other Wednesday, and there's a *romaria* on September 15–16.

Marialva

If you've got your own transport, it's worthwhile driving from Penedono to Pinhel via the tiny village of **MARIALVA**, some 25km to the southeast, which is dominated by the crumbling remains of a massive ruined **castle** (daily: June–Sept 10am–1pm & 3–6.30pm; Oct–May 9am–12.30pm & 2–5.30pm;

free) built by Dom Sancho I in 1200. Despite, or perhaps because of, its remoteness and state of disrepair, this is among the most atmospheric of all the region's many ruins, although it is currently being restored. A deserted old village is contained within the castle walls; the only intact building is the sixteenth-century Igreja Matriz.

The *Posto de Acolhimento*, a concrete box located in Largo do Cruzeiro near the Capel Nossa Senhora de Lourdes, functions as a de facto **turismo** (Mon–Fri 10am–1pm & 3–6pm). The only **accommodation** is in the nearby *Casas do Côro* (T917 552 020, Ecasa-do-coro@assec.pt; breakfast included; ❼), a mini-village of traditional granite houses, restored with painstaking attention to detail and design. Minimalist chic vies successfully with four-poster beds and stone walls in the rooms, while the outdoor pool is set amidst manicured lawns and olive trees. Rates drop by €25 at weekends.

Pinhel

PINHEL is big enough to run both a wine co-operative (producing an excellent red) and a cake factory (churning out *cavaca* sweetmeats). But it's also small enough to have left the narrow lanes of the old town centre virtually untouched inside its crumbling walls. From one corner of the walls you look down on the shell of a ruined Romanesque church; on another stretch sits what is left of the original fortress, two soaring towers, one of which boasts an intricately carved Manueline window.

Down in the town numerous manor houses cluster about magnificent gardens. One of the largest is now the Câmara Municipal (free internet access here), while an adjacent building houses the town **museum** (Mon–Fri 9am–12.30pm & 2–5.30pm; free), an unassuming collection of ex-votos and woodworm-eaten saints. The **turismo** opposite (T271 410 000) keeps the same hours and sells bottles of the local wine, a bargain at under €2.

Buses stop by the petrol station on the way into town, and both tickets and schedule information can be obtained at *Café Avenida* across the road. Guarda – 34km southwest, down the N221 – is best served, with four buses per day, and there's one bus to Almeida at 2.10pm, one to Figueira de Castelo Rodrigo at 3pm, and a solitary bus to Trancoso at 6.30am on Friday mornings. If you get stuck here, Pinhel has but one modest-priced **pensão**, the crumbling but comfortable *Residencial Falcão*, Avenida Carneiro de Gusmão 25 (T271 413 969; breakfast included; ❷), a short distance from the bus stop (look out for the sign). The inexpensive in-house restaurant offers, quite literally, meat-and-potatoes fare, although they will fry up omelettes on request. The local **Festa de Santo António** is held on the Sunday closest to June 13.

Almeida

Perhaps the most attractive of all the fortified border towns, **ALMEIDA** – 45km northeast of Guarda – is a beautifully preserved eighteenth-century stronghold. Its walls are in the form of a twelve-pointed star, with six bastions and six curtain walls within ravelins – a Dutch design, influenced by the French military architect Vauban. A four-kilometre walk around the walls – now overgrown with grass – takes in all the peaks and troughs, though you can only really appreciate the shape if you take a look at the aerial shot postcards sold around town. Despite the inevitable tourist development here, there's something irresistible about staying the night, watching the sun go down and the lights come on in a hundred tiny villages across the plateau of the Ribacôa.

This was one of the last stretches of land to be recognized as officially Portuguese in the Treaty of Alcañices with the Spanish in 1297, and it's easy to see why boundaries were not clearly staked out in the broad, flat terrain. Indeed, it was occasionally reoccupied by Spain – the last time was in 1762, after which the present stronghold was completed. Almeida later played a key role in the **Peninsular War** (1807–14), falling to the French in January 1808, though it was eventually reoccupied by the Portuguese. The Napoleonic army returned in 1810 and besieged Almeida, the Luso-Britannic forces holding out for seventeen days until, on July 26, a leaky barrel of gunpowder ignited and began a fire that killed hundreds. The survivors gave themselves up to the French, but Wellington, on his victorious return from Torres Vedras, subsequently took the fortress at Almeida with no bloodshed. The French army scuttled away during the night, probably making use of one of three *portas falsas* – narrow slits in the ramparts allowing for a discreet exit.

The Town

The original two double **gates** are among the town's most splendid features – long, shell-proof tunnels with emblazoned entrances – while the **Casamatas** (Mon–Fri 9am–12.30pm & 2–5pm; free), or barracks, are second in size only to those at Elvas, with a capacity for five thousand men and their supplies. The layout explains how Almeida withstood lengthy sieges. With its own water supply, rubbish chute, breathing holes, hidden escape routes, munitions chamber (there's a range of cannonballs and gunshot still on view) and dormitory space, the possibilities were limitless. Almeida's fortifications and military history tend to draw attention away from what the town walls actually enclose, which is an atmospheric warren of narrow, cobbled lanes and whitewashed houses, punctuated by airy squares. You're still as likely to see a horse-drawn cart lumbering up the street, as you are a car, while black-clad villagers live up to cliches by knitting on their doorsteps and gossiping togther at dusk. One other curiosity, opposite the *pousada* gateway in the walls, is an inscription on the side of a small house declaring it to be the dumping ground for illegitimate children. At the **Rodo dos Eispostos** (literally the "Circle of the Deserted"), anyone could come and claim an unwanted child for themselves – a convenient arrangement for both mother and foster parent.

If you can possibly do so, try to visit during one of the twice-monthly **feiras** (on the eighth day and last Saturday) or – best of all – come at Pentecost (fifty days after Easter) for the grand picnic in the grounds of the Franciscan **Convento da Barca**. It's the only time you can visit the convent grounds, which are now privately owned, but at other times of the year you can sample the excellent red wine, apples, peaches, nuts and various other produce for which it is famous, at shops in town.

Practicalities

There are two weekday **buses** to and from Guarda via Pinhel, as well as a solitary Sunday service. There are also a couple of weekday services south to the **Spanish border** at the town of Vilar Formoso, 12km away, which has good onward connections to Ciudad Rodrigo and, from there, to Salamanca. Schedules and tickets for all services are available from the green-and-yellow bar-kiosk, just down to the right from the main gate/car park at Largo 25 de Abril and opposite the BPI bank. The **turismo** is just inside the main gate within a former guardroom in the town walls (Mon–Fri 9am–12.30pm & 2–5.30pm, Sat & Sun 10am–12.30pm & 2–5.30pm; ☎271 570 020).

In addition to the options listed below you could ask about **accommodation** at the *Casa da Amelinha* on Rua Afonso de Albuquerque, adjacent to the square opposite the turismo, where *ginginha* (morello cherry liqueur) has been served since 1883. For unofficial **camping**, make your way to the Rio Côa, a two-kilometre stroll downhill on the Pinhel road. Just above the old Romanesque bridge (and its present-day equivalent), you'll find some idyllic spots.

Hotels and pensions

Casa do Cantinho Rua Afonso de Albuquerque, opposite *Casa da Amelinha* ✆ 271 574 224. Endearingly hospitable *turismo rural* offering two snug en-suite rooms in a family home. The same owners are also due to open *Casa do Marechal*, a guest house with library and internet facilities, although no prices were available at the time of writing. Breakfast included. No credit cards. ❹

Casa Pátio da Figueira Rua Direita 48 ✆ 271 571 133. Comfortable, refined rooms nestled in a back street near the *pousada*. The price is almost justified if you take into the account the charming gardens and secluded swimming pool. Breakfast included. No credit cards. ❺

Morgado Adjacent to the GALP station and opposite *A Muralha* ✆ 271 574 412. A more homely and frayed *residencial* than its counterpart across the road, run by an irrepressible old lady. Breakfast included. ❷

A Muralha A few hundred metres west of the fort's main entrance, opposite the GALP petrol station ✆ 271 574 357. Friendly, modern *residencial*, whose rooms have french windows and en-suite bathrooms (including bath), although its position

on the main road makes it noisier than the old town options. There's an attached unpretentious restaurant where hearty portions of meat and fish come in at around €7. Breakfast included. ❸

Pousada Senhora das Neves Rua das Muralhas ✆ 271 574 283, ⓦ www.pousadas.pt. Well signposted near the upper walls, this luxurious if slightly dated *pousada* boasts four-poster beds and glorious views to Spain. There's also a pricey restaurant and a terrace although the latter's preponderance of concrete renders it somewhat claustrophobic. Breakfast included. ❼

Cafés and restaurants

Granitus Largo 25 de Abril ✆ 271 574 834. A cheerful couple supply locals with *petiscos* such as sardines and chopped pig's ear at this popular, down-to-earth place, just outside the town walls. Inexpensive.

O Picadeiro d'El Rey ✆ 271 346 974. Well signposted and snuggled inside Almeida's northern fortifications, this slick equine-themed bar-restaurant allows you to dine on carefully prepared regional specialities such as wild boar, while gazing down at glossy maned horses ambling around their stables. No credit cards. Closed Tues. Expensive.

The Serra da Estrela

The peaks of the **Serra da Estrela** – the highest mountains in Portugal – rise to the southwest of Guarda. The range is basically a high plateau cut by valleys, from within which emanate two of the country's greatest rivers, the Rio Mondego and the Rio Zêzere – the only rivers to begin and end in Portugal rather than crossing the border from Spain. Over the last few decades the *serra* landscape has changed. Once, farmers lived in stone houses with straw roofs, dotted across the peaks and valleys, but they have now moved to more modern dwellings on the valley floor. Originally, too, the whole area was heavily forested, but these days the pines are widely cultivated for timber and shepherds now graze their sheep on the higher ground. Rye is grown lower down, where the land is more fertile.

The **Parque Natural da Serra da Estrela** was established in 1976 to preserve the rural character of the *serra* villages and landscape. The park covers around 1000 square kilometres, stretching for some 55km from its northern point near Celorico da Beira to its southernmost tip, southwest of Covilhã. All land over 1200m is designated "protected countryside", which means in effect that you're not allowed to camp wild, light fires or pick flowers. However, there are three major (and several minor) **hiking trails** through the park (see feature on p.272), which take in various authorized campsites and pass through villages with accommodation and other facilities.

From the west and north, access is down the N17 from Celorico da Beira, branching off on minor roads to enter the park at the quirky village of **Linhares**,

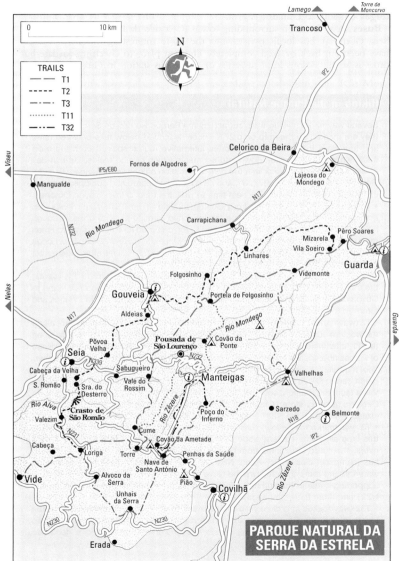

PARQUE NATURAL DA
SERRA DA ESTRELA

Fundão & Castelo Branco ▼

Gouveia

Another 20km southwest of Linhares by road, **GOUVEIA** has lost the rural *serra* feel that once constituted its charm, as it has developed into a fair-sized provincial town. However, there's a bustling Thursday market as well as several fine buildings, the most striking being the Baroque Igreja de São Pedro in the centre of town, which has an unexpectedly colourful *azulejo*-tiled exterior. Incongruously, the town also has a modern art museum, the **Museu de Abel Manta** (Tues–Sun 9.30am–12.30pm & 2–6pm; free), Rua Direita 45, with a broad selection of contemporary Portuguese pictures donated by Gouveia-born artist Abel Manta (1888–1982). Four kilometres northwards out of town, towards the main N17, the *Adega Cooperativa de São Pãio* (Mon–Fri 9.30am–noon & 2–5pm; free; ☎238 492 101) welcomes visitors to try its Dão wines.

Practicalities

Buses run here from Celorico da Beira, and there are three daily buses on to Seia, although services to Manteigas have been cut completely. Buses drop you by the bridge; walk up and veer right and you'll reach the centre of town. The very helpful **turismo** on Avenida 25 de Abril, a few minutes' walk uphill from the church (Mon–Sat 9.30am–12.30pm & 2–6pm, Sun 10am–12.30pm & 2–4pm; ☎238 490 243, ⓦwww.cm-gouveia.pt), can supply maps of the town although serious hikers will need to call in at the park **information centre**, a couple of blocks east of the church at Avenida dos Bombeiros Voluntários 8 (Mon–Fri 9am–12.30pm & 2–5.30pm; ☎238 492 411).

Gouveia itself offers a handful of decent **accommodation** possibilities but budget lodgings are nowhere to be found. The cheapest option is the *Residencial Monteneve*, Avenida Bombeiros Voluntários 12 (☎238 085 480, ⓕ238 490 371; breakfast included; ❸), a chic affair with inviting en-suite rooms, a bright dining room and a bar that's perfect for lounging. The flamingo-pink *Hotel de Gouveia* on Avenida 1º de Maio (☎238 491 010, ⓦwww.hoteldegouveia. com; ❹) fails to compete on either price or taste although the travel-lodge style rooms are comfortable enough and there's also a pool. On the northeastern outskirts of Gouveia – close enough to town to make it feasible without your own transport, but secluded enough to feel like you're in the middle of nowhere – the rambling *Casa da Mata da Cerca* (☎238 492 315, ⓔmaria. serpa@mail.telepac.pt; ❹), on Rua dos Marqueses de Gouveia, consists of two lovely houses surrounded by acres of mature woodland. The restored granite building with the balcony offers the best value. The local **campsite** (☎238 491 008; closed Dec–Feb) is at Curral do Negro, around 3km from the centre; turn right immediately after the Câmara Municipal, then right again, before finally forking to the left for 2km.

There's a surprisingly decent range of **cafes and restaurants** in town. For sheer value for money it's hard to beat *O Italiano* (☎238 493 026; no credit cards; closed Sun), a raucously popular lunchtime venue on Rua da Republica. Rustic *O Júlio* (☎238 498 016; closed Tues), Rua do Loureiro 11A, is strictly traditional, offering moderately priced dishes like wild boar with onions. For something a little different, the similarly priced *Restaurant Monteneve,* downstairs from the *residencial* of the same name and every bit as self-consciously stylish, offers French, Italian and Portuguese dishes.

Seia

Cut out the small town of **SEIA** (16km southwest of Gouveia) from your itinerary and you would miss little, but it is a useful park access point, with bus services from Coimbra. Moreover, the **Museu do Pão** (daily except Mon 10am–6pm; €2), about 2km from the centre of town at Quinta Fonte do Marrão, on the road to Sabugeiro (look for the signs), concentrates on the very stuff of life and, along with reconstructions of vintage bread-making equipment and a traditional mill, there are displays on the religious and political significance of bread.

Most are here, however, simply to press on into the park, after first visiting the **information office** in the centre of town at Praça da República 28 (Mon–Sat 9am–12.30pm & 2–5.30pm; ℡238 310 440) and nearby **turismo** on Rua Pintor Lucas Marrão (Mon–Sat 9am–12.30pm & 2–5.30pm; ℡238 317 762, ⓦwww.cm-seia.pt), two blocks to the south. There are two upmarket **hotels**: the excellent *Hotel Camelo*, Avenida 1º de Maio 16 (℡238 310 100, ⓦwww .camelohotel.pt; breakfast included; ❹), with comfortable, tartan-trimmed rooms, manicured grounds with swimming pool and good regional restaurant (closed Mon); or the *Estalagem de Seia* on nearby Avenida Dr. Afonso Costa (℡238 315 866, ℻238 315 538; breakfast included; ❹), which dates from the eighteenth century and boasts period furnishings, a granite staircase and a nice swimming pool. A cheaper option is the *Residencial Jardim* on Avenida Luís Vaz de Camões, in the environs of a shopping precinct (℡238 311 414, ℻238 310 091; breakfast included; no credit cards; ❷), whose rooms are clean but fairly spartan. The down-to-earth *Restaurante Regional da Serra,* Avenida dos Combatentes da Grande Guerra 12–14 (℡238 312 717), is a reliable place for a **meal**.

With transport, you could always stay instead at the wonderful *Casas da Ribeira* (℡238 311 221, ⓦwww.casadaribeira.com; no credit cards; ❸) in the ancient village of **Pôvoa Velha**, 5km or so outside Seia, signposted off the road to Sabugeiro. There are eight rustically restored stone houses to rent, some dating back more than six hundred years. Breakfast is included, in the form of a fresh loaf of bread delivered to your door in the morning.

Sabugueiro

SABUGEIRO, 10km east of Seia, is said to be Portugal's highest village, and is certainly one of the more interesting in the *serra*. Although the main road has succumbed to a rash of souvenir shops, much of the village remains essentially agricultural and, as well as being a good base for walking, Sabugueiro is one of the best places to pick up fresh rye bread, local spiced sausage and Estrela cheese. Drag yourself away from the shops and modern buildings lining the entire length of the main drag, and you'll find a typical mountain village populated by inhabitants with wind-whittled faces, bear-like mountain dogs and the odd squawking chicken. The slate-roofed stone cottages are in varying states of repair, although many have been restored and can be rented for a night's stay.

There is only one **bus** a week between Sabugueiro and Seia, departing Sabugueiro on Wednesdays at 8am, returning the same day at 1pm. There's no regular public transport from Sabugueiro into the rest of the park. There are plenty of identikit **rooms** above the souvenir shops (❷), but more attractive **accommodation** options include the traditional country houses in the old village, rented out by *Casas do Cruzeiro* (℡238 315 872, ℻238 315 282; ❸), whose office is on Rua da Igreja. There are thirty houses in total, most charmingly rustic, although some are slightly damp with tiny windows – ask to see a selection before choosing. A cheaper option is *Monte Estrela* (℡238 312 984; no credit cards; breakfast included; ❸), higher up on the outskirts of town towards Seia, with superb views from its otherwise unprepossessing back

Covilhã

Forty-four kilometres south of Guarda, **COVILHÃ** lies immediately below the highest peaks of the *serra*, and is the most obvious base for exploring the *parque natural*. It's a steeply terraced town with every thoroughfare looking out across the plain below or up to the crags of the Serra da Estrela. In summer, weekend picnickers and campers spread across the hillsides; in winter, ski enthusiasts take over, using Covilhã as a base for trips to the slopes.

A market town since the Middle Ages, it developed a textile industry in the seventeenth century using wool from the local sheep, which also provide the milk for the renowned local *queijo da Serra*. After industrialization, the woollen industry began to harness water power from the mountain streams; factories today, down on the plain below town, are powered by hydroelectricity. You can view the enormous vats used in the traditional wool-dyeing processes in the **Museu de Lanifícios** (Tues–Sun 9.30am–noon & 2.30–6pm; €2) on Rua Marquês d'Avila e Bolama, a short walk out of the centre. The vats were unearthed in the mid-1970s when Covilhã's university was renovating the old *Real Fábrica de Panos*, a woollen mill originally opened by the Marquês de Pombal in 1764.

Covilhã's favourite son is **Pêro de Covilhã**, who set out in 1487 on behalf of Dom João II, to search for Prester John (legendary Christian priest and king) in what is now Ethiopia. However, having reached Cairo, de Covilhã sailed instead to India before returning to Cairo and then heading south on his original errand. He never found Prester John and never returned to Portugal, though Vasco da Gama found his report about India useful when he made his own celebrated voyage there, around the Cape of Good Hope, in 1498. In front of the town hall there's a huge, polished granite slab depicting Pêro de Covilhã's voyages and a decidedly queasy-looking statue of the man himself.

Practicalities

The **train station** is 4km from the town, at the foot of the hill, as is the **bus station**. From here, you can catch a local bus into town or take a taxi (€4). The **turismo** (Mon–Fri 9am–5.30pm, Sat 9am–12.30pm & 2–5.30pm; ☎275 319 560) is in the pink building opposite the Jardim Publico. **Internet access** is available at Postweb at Rua Comendador Campos Melo 27 (Mon–Fri 9am –1pm & 2.30–7pm, Sat 9am–1pm). **Hikers or skiers** should contact the Club Nacional de Montanhismo, Rua Rui Faleiro (☎275 323 364), for up-to-date details of local conditions. Opening hours vary; you'll probably have a better chance of finding someone there in the evening. Covilhã also has plenty of shops for stocking up on provisions, as well as a daily **market** on Rua António Augusto d'Aguiar.

Although it's not immediately apparent upon arrival, the town does have a decent range of **accommodation**, most of which has great views to the surrounding mountains and valleys. Note that although prices given here are for high season (which, in Covilhã, means the winter skiing months), tariffs are usually around thirty percent cheaper in summer. The nearest **campsite** to town, *Pião* (☎275 314 312; open all year), lies 4km out on the road up to Penhas da Saudé. Covilhã doesn't have a huge choice of **restaurants**, although there are a few good options, as well as the various eating establishments attached to the hotels and *pensões*.

Hotels and pensions

Pensão Avenida Rua São Salvador 40 ℡275 322 140. A wonderfully tranquil whitewashed *pensão* tucked away behind the public gardens, with great views to the east. The rooms are sparsely furnished but full of character, with marble basins and high wooden ceilings, while the walls are adorned by the vivid paintings of the genial owner's son. Refurbishment is imminent, however, with a planned change of name to *Covilhã Jardim*. No credit cards. ❸

Hotel Covilhã Parque Av. Frei Heitor Pinto ℡275 327 518, ⓦwww.imb-hotels.com. Despite its grey exterior, this boasts the best views in town, at least from the easterly facing rooms which aren't quite as modern as the swish reception area suggests. A real bargain in summer nevertheless, and with parking available. Breakfast buffet included. ❹

Pensão Regional Rua das Flores 4–6 ℡275 322 596. Friendly *pensão* tucked away on a quiet side street. A steep flight of stairs leads up from the downstairs restaurant to peaceful rooms with heavy, dark wooden beds and amazing views. No credit cards. ❸

Residencial Solneve Rua Visconde da Coriscada 126 ℡275 323 001, ⓦwww.solneve.pt. Good-value businesslike rooms come with ochre-tiled bathrooms, internet access, DVD and cable TV, although there's a small charge for the car park. Although guests staying here tend to forego the cavernous downstairs restaurant and head elsewhere, they're missing some of Covilhã's best-value food. The grilled sole will set you back a mere €6, while the menu also extends to lasagne and cannelloni. Breakfast included. No credit cards. ❸

Hotel Turismo Acesso à Variante ℡275 330 400, ⓦwww.imb-hotels.com. The *Colvilhã Parque's* sister hotel is one of the flashiest in town, with a glass elevator, outdoor pool, health spa, jaccuzi and car park. Breakfast included. ❺

Estalagem Varanda dos Carquejais 6km north-east of town, on Penhas da Saudé road ℡275 319 120, ℮vc@turistrela.pt. The dowdy, overpriced rooms are stuck in an 1980s timewarp, but you can savour some breathtaking views over the Beira Baixa far below, especially from the lip of the large swimming pool. Mountain bike rental available, and parking. Breakfast included. ❺

Restaurants

Ovelhita Largo Infantaria 21 ℡912 509 659. The "Little Sheep" is a snug place serving *típico* food, with the mountain-style roasted kid goat highly recommended. Closed Sun & Mon. Moderate.

Montiel Pr. do Município 33–37 ℡275 322 086. Partly wood-panelled, slightly genteel, upstairs restaurant on the main square, filled to bursting with families at Sunday lunchtime. The menu concentrates on the usual regional specialities, although they also do grilled duck in orange sauce and a decent Spanish tortilla. No credit cards. Expensive.

Tania Rua das Flores 23 ℡275 087 699. Low-ceilinged, atmospheric little eaterie serving up plain portions of meat, fish and seafood. Try the grilled squid, or the good-value three-course *ementa turística*. Closed Sun night. No credit cards. Inexpensive.

Veranda Rua São Salvador ℡275 327 024. Unpretentious, reliable restaurant just below *Pensão Avenida*, providing hearty local fare from a menu that changes daily. Closed Sun. No credit cards. Inexpensive.

Penhas da Saúde and around

The mountain outpost and rudimetary ski station of **PENHAS DA SAÚDE** is right at the heart of the *serra* and close to the highest, most spectacular, ground. Getting here in the first place, however, is somewhat problematic. You can either hike the 11km up the glacial valley from Covilhã or catch the summer-season bus, either from Covilhã's bus terminal or from near its market (July–Sept only, daily at 8.50am, plus 2pm in Aug, 10min later at the market; the bus back leaves at 5.10pm). However, check bus times with the turismo, as they change frequently).

Penhas is a rather desolate-looking place, but makes a good base for summer hiking. Bear in mind that, despite the accommodation, it's not really a village and, apart from a few cafés, there are not many facilities. Cheapest place to stay is the 112-bed **youth hostel** (℡ 275 335 375, ⓦwww .pousadasjuventude.pt; dorm beds €8.50, rooms ❶), at the crest of a rise as you enter Penhas on the Covilhã road and with superb views across the plain to the Serra de Malcata. Reception is open daily from 8 to 10am and from 6pm to midnight. Just below the youth hostel is the overpriced *Hotel Serra da Estrela* (☎275 310 300, ✉hse@turistrela.pt; breakfast included; ❼), which is also responsible for a couple of newly constructed streets of wind-swept Swiss-style chalets (sleeping up to six; ❾) with pine-fresh interiors and limited views. If you're looking for somewhere with a bit more character try *Pensão O Pastor* (☎275 322 810, ℻275 314 035; breakfast included; ❸), whose green carpets, labyrinthine corridors and dark-wood rooms – with some of the best views in Penhas – are imprinted with forty years of service. It's located a few hundred metres from the youth hostel, on the road to Torre. In July and August there's also large-scale unofficial **camping** across the hillside, but the site is unpleasant and litter-strewn and you're much better off staying at *Pião* (see "Covilhã" above).

Torre

From Penhas, you are within striking distance of the chief beauty spots of the *serra*, with the highest peak in Portugal – **Torre** (1993m) – 10km up the road to the northwest. The stone *torre* (tower) here was added on the orders of Dom João VI, to raise the height to a more impressive 2000m. You can easily walk up from Penhas, but the road gets busy in summer and any sense of natural beauty and grandeur at the summit has been severely reduced by the disfiguring array of buildings, litter and broken-down ski-lifts, all in various stages of decay. There is a café, however, which is welcome if you've walked up.

En route you will pass the vast statue of **Nossa Senhora da Boa Estrela**, carved into a niche in the rock, to which there's a massive procession from Covilhã on the second Sunday in August. A little northeast of Torre, on the road to Manteigas, is the narrow rock cone known as the **Cântaro Magro** (Slender Pitcher), which conceals the source of the Rio Zêzere; there's an excellent summer campsite below it at Covão d'Ametade.

Manteigas

A few kilometres beyond Penhas da Saúde, you can strike north at Nave de Santo António, between Penhas and Torre, and follow the glacial valley of the Rio Zêzere down to the spa of **Caldas de Manteigas**. Its gushing waters run past a lovely old water mill (now a hotel training school), while the village spreads along one road on the bottom of the river valley, where a few hundred metres along on the left hand side, you'll find *Albergeria Berne* (see below). Caldas de Manteigas virtually merges with the larger *serra* town of **MANTEIGAS**, whose whitewashed houses and red roofs run along the contour above the Rio Zêzere. It is a popular tourist destination and an attractive base for exploring the *serra*, with two of the official trails passing through town and a wealth of other walking opportunities. Café terraces and hotel room windows offer pine-carpeted mountain views, which are rarely less than spectacular, while the invigorating mountain air is a welcome summer tonic if you've arrived from the coast or the scorching plains of the Beira Baixa.

Currently, **buses** run to and from Guarda, 45km to the northeast, passing through Belmonte and via the campsite at Valhelhas, but there's no service on to Seia. The bus stops on the main street, Rua 1 de Maio, outside the park's **main information office** (Mon–Fri 9am–12.30pm & 2–5pm; ☎275 980 060), where you can buy guidebooks. Nearby, next to the small park below the GALP service station, there's a very efficient **turismo** on Rua Dr. Esteves de Carvalho (Tues–Sat 9.30am–noon & 2–6pm; ☎275 981 129), which has a leaflet of circular walks from Manteigas, including the one detailed below.

For free **internet** access head to espaçoInternet (Mon–Sat 9am–12.30pm & 2–7pm), also on Rua 1 de Maio.

Hotels and pensions

Albergaria Berne Quinta de Santo António, Caldas de Manteigas ☎275 981 351, ⓦhttp:planeta.clix.pt/albergaria-berne/index.html. Modern, pine-furnished rooms and wall-mounted walking maps lend this place the air of an upmarket youth hostel, albeit one with a swimming pool. Breakfast included. ❸

Casa das Obras Rua Teles de Vasconcelos ☎275 981 155, ⓦwww.casadasobras.pt. This restored eighteenth-century mansion is a little difficult to find – follow the blue signs and, if you're driving, take a sharp left up the narrow lane beside *LusoPizza*. The faded dining room murals, giddy, uneven floorboards, and the tiny cellar-like bar are delightful, and there's an enchanting garden with fruit trees, great views, a big, soppy mountain dog and a secluded swimming pool. No credit cards. Breakfast included. ❺

Casa de São Roque Rua de St António 51 ☎275 981 125. A friendly *turismo rural* option, which feels more like an aged *pensão*, with characterful rooms – oak-panelled Room 8 has the most atmosphere – and a grand old dining room on the top floor. No credit cards. Breakfast included. ❸

Santa Luzia Rua Dr. Esteves de Carvalho ☎275 981 283. Tattered, slightly peeling rooms (with shared bathroom), but they are clean, afford good views and are among the cheapest you'll find in the whole region. No credit cards. ❶

Residencial Serradalto Rua 1 de Maio ☎ & ⓕ 275 981 151. Stylish, spotless rooms with wonderful views and wooden ceilings. The lofty guests' terrace is one of the best spots in Manteigas for a sunset beer, while full-length windows in the restaurant give on to the valley below. The most popular dish is steak cooked on a hot stone on your table. Breakfast included. Restaurant and hotel closed Tues. ❸

Pousada de São Lourenço N232, 12km west of Manteigas; follow the signs from town ☎275 980 050, ⓦwww.pousadas.pt. Reached by a series of careering switchbacks and perched at a height of 1290m, this marvellous *pousada* is best enjoyed in winter when log fires are roaring in the wood-panelled bar and the tartan curtains are drawn against howling mountain winds. That said, you can negotiate some serious discounts and last-minute deals in summer, when the views are superlative. The expensive restaurant has an innovative menu (try fried blood sausage with orange), including a surprising range of vegetarian options. Breakfast included. ❼

Restaurants

Cascata Rua 1 de Maio ☎275 982 511. A terrace with expansive views is the main selling-point although the food is hearty enough; the likes of mountain sausage and boiled potatoes, or steak with cheese, ham and egg, make it a reliable lunchtime stop. No credit cards. Moderate.

Dom Pastor Rua Sá da Bandeira ☎275 982 920. Tucked away in an idyllic little lane by the river, this fashionable restaurant recently scooped a regional first prize for its creative take on traditional cuisine. Dishes such as fillet of perch with shrimp sauce or *farinheira frita* (a local type of curled sausage) are eaten in a modern interior constructed using local materials. Closed Tues. No credit cards. Expensive.

LusoPizza Rua Teles de Vasconcelos 15–17 ☎275 982 928. The pizza – a rarity itself in the Beiras – at this tiny takeaway (room for two people eating in) is the genuine article, as is the humerous banter of the owner, a former professional footballer. No credit cards. Inexpensive.

A hike from Manteigas to the Poço de Inferno

There's a lovely round walk from Manteigas to the waterfall of Poço de Inferno and back, via Caldas de Manteigas, which takes around five to six hours. Begin at the GALP petrol station, and take the small road which goes steeply down to the right of the main road, behind the turismo. Follow this road downhill, bearing right, until you cross a small bridge. Bear left and you will start to pick up the yellow marker arrows, which head right into the woods. Keep your eyes peeled as these are not always easy to spot, but the arrows will eventually lead you to Poço de Inferno, 'hell's well', which is a great spot for a picnic and has good swimming potential. From here, continue along the paved road and you will arrive back in town at the top of Caldas de Manteigas.

Sabugal, Sortelha and the Serra da Malcata

The area east of Covilhã forms the upper boundary of the Beira Baixa, a landscape of undulating, heather-clad hills that extends to the Spanish border. The frontier town of **Sabugal**, 36km northeast of Covilhã, is unremarkable save for its impressive castle. It's nevertheless useful as a base for visiting nearby **Sortelha**, 10km away, whose amazing circuit of walls rises amid one of the bleakest locations in all Portugal: the unearthly landscape between Sabugal and Sortelha consists of undulating highland plateau strewn with giant glacial boulders, desolate but for a few trees and the shepherds who make their living here. If you're dependent on buses, you'll need to pick up connections from Guarda or Belmonte, but with your own transport the two towns make an easy circular tour, possibly combined with a trip into the wild terrain of the **Serra da Malcata** to the south and east. The **Reserva Natural da Serra da Malcata** is one of the last habitats of the Iberian lynx, and the town of **Penamacor**, just south of the reserve, makes a good base from which to explore the area.

Sabugal

SABUGAL, like most towns in Beira Alta, has a castle and it's a good one, too, with massively high walls and a pentagonal tower with three arched chambers piled one on top of the other. However, having seen this, and poked around the labyrinth of old streets surrounding it, there's very little reason to hang around Sabugal, which is otherwise modern and dull. Nonetheless, if you're travelling by public transport, you might well need to stay. Although there are regular weekday services to Guarda, Belmonte, Penamacor and Castelo Branco, buses are few and far between at weekends while public transport to Sortelha is limited to just two buses a week, on Tuesday and Thursday afternoons (plus a late-afternoon weekday school bus from September to June). If Sortelha is your aim, consider taking a taxi instead (€10–15) or even walk, no bad thing given the bizarre and breathtaking boulder-strewn scenery en route.

The **bus station** is at the upper end of Avenida Ismael Mota, around the corner from the *Albergaria Santa Isabel* (see below), with the **turismo** (daily 9.30am–1pm & 2–5.30pm; ☎800 262 788, ⓦwww.cm-sabugal.pt) located in the Câmara Municipal on Praça da Republica. There's a number of good-value **accommodation** options, including *Residencial Sol Rio* (☎271 753 197, ⓕ271 752 070; breakfast included; ❸), down by the bridge on Rua do Cárcere, whose tastefully finished rooms have french windows and balconies overlooking the river. *Albergaria Santa Isabel*, Largo do Cinema 9, 100m or so from the bus station (☎271 750 100, ⓔreservas@raihotel.pt; breakfast included; ❹), offers more conventional upmarket accommodation, and also operates all-inclusive two-night **tours** (€60 per person) to the surrounding medieval towns, otherwise difficult to access without your own transport. At *Hospedaria Senhora da Graça* (☎271 754 237, ⓔhospedaria.sradagraca@clix.pt; breakfast included; ❸), another 100m further on at Largo Padre Manuel Nabais Caldeira 4, rooms are modern and spruce with laminate flooring. For **meals**, it's hard to beat the moderately priced *Restaurante Dom Dinis* in the *Albergaria Santa Isabel*, though it's the *Restaurante Robalo* (☎271 753 566; closed Sun except in Aug) opposite the bus station that's the quality local choice, with pricey grilled trout from the nearby Rio Côa and a reputation for delicious *cabrito*.

△ Sortelha

Sortelha

SORTELHA is isolated and rather eerie – probably the most atmospheric town in the region, especially when mist drifts down from the *serra*. It is an ancient place, with Hispano-Arabic origins, and was also the site of the first *castelo roqueiro* ("rock fortress") to be built this side of the Côa. The number of permanent residents in the old town barely struggles into double figures, which only accentuates its ghostly feel and lends weight to the mystery and legend which have grown up with the castle and its fortifications (*sortelha* means "ring"): stories are spun around the figure of an old lady (*a velha*) whose profile you can see on rocks from outside the top gates.

At first sight the town seems nothing special. Walk uphill from the new quarters, however, and you arrive at the fantastically walled **old town**, a tight web of cobbled lanes wending between squat stone houses. Take a look at the **Igreja Matriz** (keys from the house next door) with its beautiful ceiling, executed by medieval Moors. Arabic script can be seen, too, on several house lintels near the top of town. The vivacious Viscountess who owns *Casa do Pátio* (see below) also runs an adjacent **antique shop**, O Ferrolho, which sells the handsome rugs woven by local women in their own homes.

Sortelha's major event is a **bullfight**, which takes place on August 15, once every two or three years, when the local council has the money to stage it. It retains the ancient and peculiar custom of the *forca* – a rudimentary defence against the bull, using branches – which has been handed down from generation to generation. The order of events for the day begins with a *forca* involving all the young boys of the town – at least 25 of whom are needed to carry the device to prevent it from being tipped up by the bull. Later, solo performers strut the stage with their red capes to take the bull's charges. Onlookers are also frequently involved – many a young bull has hopped up onto the terrace of rocks, only to find himself sniffing at discarded hats and bags while nervous laughter rises up from behind the safety of the nearest wall. In non-bullfight years there's still a *festa* on August 15, and a *romaria* in honour of **Santo António** takes place on June 13.

Practicalities

The two weekly **buses** back to Sabugal leave on Tuesday and Thursday mornings, though there's also a schoolbus running early on weekday mornings during term time – you can check up-to-date schedules at any of the restaurants. The bus drops you by a stop on the main road, which runs east to west through Sortelha's "new" town. There is a **turismo** signposted near the top of town, but it's more often closed than open. Sortelha is blessed with a surplus of enticing *turismo rural* **accommodation,** most of which is up in the old town. While most of it is well worth the money, budget travellers will be disappointed to learn that there's nothing at all at the cheaper end of the market, annoying given that a day-trip by bus from Sabugal is difficult. Note that there are no credit card or banking facilities in Sortelha.

Rooms

Casa da Calçada and Casa da Lagariça Calç. de Santo Antão 13, on the left-hand side on the road up to the old town ☎271 388 116, ⓦwww .casalagarica.com. Enquire at the nearby minimarket for these two adjacent modern *turismo rural* options. The former has more interior stonework,

although both are very comfortable, with natural fabrics and wooden floors. ❸

Casa da Cerca Largo de Santo António, at the edge of the main road into the new part of town ☎271 388 113, ⓔcasadacerca@clix.pt. Next to the antique shop, this rambling, restored house has six atmospheric bedrooms; the granite seats carved into the window sills are a nice touch. Breakfast included. **⑤**

Casa da Villa Rua Direita ☎271 388 113. Perhaps the most atmospheric and intimate choice, up in the old town near the castle. The air is permeated by the smell of ancient, reclaimed wood (old railway sleepers, inventively refashioned) while the patio affords some breathtaking views. **④**

Casa do Campanário Rua Mesquita, at the top of the old town ☎277 388 198. Enquire at the adjacent *Bar Campanário* (which has a spectacularly sited terrace) for these cosy, antique-stuffed rooms, although you'll have to mind your head on the precariously sloping ceilings. Breakfast included. **④**

Casa do Pátio Largo de Santo António ☎271 388 113. Forming part of the granite outbuildings of the Solar de Nossa Senhora da Conceição, this is a charming place to bed down, with wooden furniture, hot baths, a patio with logpile, ancient TV and cobwebs – all in all, a splendid mix of modern comforts and medieval surroundings. Breakfast is available for an extra €2.50. **④**

Restaurants

Restaurante O Celta Rua Dr. Vitor M.L.P. Neves, halfway along the main road in the new town ☎271 388 291. A functional but surprisingly pricey rendezvous for bus parties and day-trippers, though there's an *ementa turística* for €10. Closed Tues. Expensive.

Restaurante Dom Sancho I Largo do Corro, just inside the main gate ☎271 388 267. The only restaurant in the old town, with a typical low-beamed ceiling and rustic stone-walled interior. It's the perfect place to sample *javali* (wild boar), one of the cheaper items on the strictly traditional menu. Closed Tues. Expensive.

Restaurante Palmeiras On the western outskirts of the new town ☎271 388 261. Simple, friendly place with hearty dishes such as black beans with pork, and grilled chicken. Inexpensive.

Serra da Malcata

Running from northeast to southwest along the Portuguese-Spanish border, the 16,000 hectares of undulating, heather-clad hills and oak woodland which make up the **Reserva Natural da Serra da Malcata** are home to a diverse array of flora and fauna, none more famous than the **Iberian lynx**. A graceful spotted feline with the build of a domestic cat but the dimensions of a labrador, the animal is under serious threat of extinction: at the time of writing, it was the most endangered carnivorous species in Europe and the most endangered feline in the world. It's currently unknown how many lynx remain in the Portuguese side of the reserve – a joint Spanish-Portuguese project aims to reintroduce the creature from the Spanish side if necessary. The reserve's headquarters can be found at Penamacor (see below), 33km south of Sabugal, where the staff offers advice about how to approach the area and where best to go at different times of the year. They also sell an inexpensive booklet with information on wildlife and walking trails. If you're fortunate, you might just see a wild boar disappearing into the forests of black oak, or catch a glimpse of the magnificent golden eagle or black vulture. The reserve also contains a dam (near the village of Meimão, currently a scar on the landscape, though it will hopefully heal in time; it has good swimming spots).

Penamacor

PENAMACOR has another medieval castle, not as impressive as those in Sabugal and Sortelha but still offering great views over the Serra da Malcata towards Spain. The castle – along with a fascinating street of crumbling cottages – is situated in the old town, on a bluff high above the "new" part of town, reached by a punishing uphill hike. It's worth the effort for the spectacular views, though – sweeping vistas to the southern plains of the Beira Baixa. Down in the new town, the municipal **museum** (daily 9am–12.30pm & 2–5.30pm; free), at the back of the public gardens, is probably the only place you're going to get to see a lynx, sadly stuffed. There's also a collection of local archeological finds, agricultural tools, and banknotes from the Portuguese colonies.

The daily **buses** to Sabugal and Castelo Branco stop outside the public gardens; for up-to-date schedules ask in the garden café. The headquarters of the **Reserva Natural da Serra da Malcata** (Mon–Fri 9am–12.30pm & 2–5.30pm; ☎277 394 467, ✉msm@icn.pt) can be found on the corner of Rua dos Bombeiros Voluntários, just off the main road through town. There's a **turismo** (Mon–Fri 10am–1pm & 2–6pm; ☎277 394 316) on Rua 25 de Abril opposite the public gardens.

There are basic **rooms** at *Café Caninhas* (☎277 394 190; no credit cards; ❶), Rua de São Estevão 20, just down from the museum. Alternatively, you can stay up in the old part of town, where Jorge and Felicidade Goinhas have an atmospheric old house for rent (☎277 394 865; no credit cards; ❸) at Largo São Pedro 3. Enquiries can be made at their home, right at the end of Largo do Castelo (look for the *Arte* sign and the green iron gates), where – in exchange for some plant-watering work – you can also camp out in their magical garden and savour the views across the plain to Monsanto. *Estalagem Vila Rica* (☎277 394 311, ℱ277 394 321; breakfast included; ❹), 500m west of the centre on the main road, offers a more sumptuous alternative; the views from this ivy-cloaked eighteenth-century *solar* are marvellous and the rooms comfortable.

Penamacor is sorely lacking in decent **restaurants**, with the inexpensive *O Jardim* (☎963 411 980; no credit cards) in the public gardens being the least underwhelming of the limited options. There's no menu but you can dine on daily specials such as *bacalhau* or roast chicken, together with dessert, for around €6. Markets are held every first and third Wednesday of the month, and *feiras* on May 10, August 28, September 21, October 15 and November 30.

The Serra da Gardunha

The picturesque villages of **Alpedrinha** and **Castelo Novo** lie sunk into a ridge, the **Serra da Gardunha**, south of Covilhã. Both have magnificent views and are healthy, rural places, with delicious local fruit and, at Castelo Novo, healing waters. Without your own transport, a route through Castelo Branco is an easier approach to Monsanto (see p.290) than cutting across country from Sabugal and Penamacor.

Alpedrinha

ALPEDRINHA, 28km south of Covilhã, is set into the side of the *serra*, overlooking fields of olives and fruit trees. In spring the hillside flowers, fruit-tree blossoms and spring water oozing from every crack in the road make it as idyllic a spot as you could hope to find – notwithstanding the rumbling lorries crashing through the village on the main road to the south and the rather insular nature of its inhabitants.

A good first stop is at the museum in the former **Paços do Concelho** (daily 2–6pm; free), which displays a collection of tradesmen's tools – from cobbler to tinsmith – and traditional clothing, including a striking black wedding dress, the customary colour in this part of the world. A short way beyond, the **Capela do Leão** is in the courtyard of the Casa de Misericórdia; something of a mystery still surrounds the whereabouts of a series of valuable sixteenth-century panels that disappeared from the chapel during its renovation and which were last spotted at a Primitivist exhibition in Lisbon. At the top of the same street, above the plain Igreja Matriz, is the elaborate fountain known as the **Chafariz de Dom João V**. When the king passed through in 1714 he found the water so good that he commissioned the *chafariz* as a sign of royal approval. The little village flourished and grand houses such as the now-deserted **Palácio do Picadeiro**, which towers above the fountain, were constructed during the eighteenth century. In front of this spectre of a palace, the old **Roman road** begins to wind its cobbled way up the side of the *serra* toward Fundão.

A further point of interest is the work of **António Santos Pinto**, who crafted some of the most consummate single-handed marquetry ever produced. Pinto moulded Louis XV chair legs to Napoleonic dressers and threw the odd carved African pageboy into his structures for good measure. There's even a set of tableaux depicting the first six cantos of Camões's *Lusíadas* – all in the most incredible detail. His creations are displayed in the house where he used to live on Largo do Espírito Santo, although you'll have to ask for the key at the Junta de Freguesia (see below).

Practicalities

Alpedrinha is most easily reached by **train** from either Covilhã or Castelo Branco – the unstaffed station is a ten-minute walk away from the centre on the plain below. There are direct **buses** from Castelo Branco, but buses from Covilhã require a change at the market town of Fundão; timetables are available from the newspaper kiosk on the side of the main through-road in Alpedrinha. The **Junta de Freguesia** (Mon–Fri 9am–12.30pm & 2–5.30pm; ☎275 567 932) on Largo de Praça Nova, at the top of the road leading up from the train station, functions as a kind of de facto tourist office and can supply you with a rudimentary booklet on the village's architectural attractions, a regional map and transport timetables.

The best **accommodation** is the *Casa de Barreiro*, Largo das Escolas (☎275 567 120; no credit cards; ❸), a turn-of-the-century house with luxurious rooms and magnificent views, set amid bucolic gardens signposted at the northern end of the village. A cheaper option is the friendly *Pensão Clara* (☎275 567 391; no credit cards; ❷), on the right as you enter the village on the E802 from the north – ask at one of the town's cafés if you're having trouble finding it. Rooms are a bit tatty, if comfortable enough with great views, although noise from the downstairs bar – not to mention the busy main road – can easily put paid to an early night. Another option – good value if you're in a group – are the modern, four-bed bungalows at *Quinta do Anjo da Guarda* (☎275 567 126; no credit cards; ❺), located about 1km north of the village on the main Fundão road by the municipal swimming pool. The raucous poolside exploits of Alpedrinha's teenagers somewhat shatters the tranquility, but bungalow guests get free entry to the pool, which otherwise costs €4.

The *quinta* also has a bar (June–Sept) and an attractive, moderately priced **restaurant**, *Papo d'Ango* (closed Mon; lunch only Tues, Wed, Thurs; no credit cards), which prides itself on its daily fish specials. About the only other eating option is *Cerejal* (☎275 567 140; closed Tues in June; no credit cards), right on the northern edge of the village by the roundabout for the road to Fundão, an agreeable restaurant where you can dine on local produce on the garden patio – try the bean soup. Alpedrinha hosts a tremendous **feira**, on the first Sunday in every month, and a full-blown festival, the **Festa do Anjo da Guarda**, on the third weekend in August.

Castelo Novo

In northern Portugal **CASTELO NOVO** is best known as the source of *Alardo*, a bottled mineral water reputed to possess healing properties. At the

spa, marked by just a single café-restaurant, the water gushes from every crack in the earth's surface. The village proper has ancient origins, and a few crumbling remains to prove it: a castle (which – in summer at least – you'll have to share with a team of youthful amateur archeologists), an attractive Paços do Concelho (above the main square), and a Manueline *pelourinho*. Off to the sides of the square, narrow alleyways and heavy stonework constitute the village's principal charm.

Although there is no **bus** to the village, four daily run along the main N18 road (between Fundão and Castelo Branco), dropping you at the crossroads, 4km out. Unless you can arrange for someone to pick you up, or fancy an even longer hike into town, don't bother alighting at the "Castelo Novo" stop on the **train** line, it might as well be signposted "middle of nowhere". There's a small **turismo** on Largo da Bica (daily 9.30am–1pm & 2.30–6pm; ☎275 561 501), where you can pick up a leaflet on the town's history. The most enticing **accommodation** is the stately *Quinta do Ouriço* (☎275 567 256, ⓦwww .quintadoourico.com; no credit cards; ➎), whose atmospheric old rooms and tranquil library are complemented by a lovingly tended garden and swimming pool. Alternatively, there's the *Casa de Castelo Novo* (☎275 561 373, ⓦwww .castelonovo.web.pt; no credit cards; ➍) at Rua Nossa Senhora das Graças 7, a lovely seventeenth-century house in a shady lane. The four rooms are suitably antique in feel, while the graceful granite corner balcony offers good views. For **eating**, *Café Restaurante O Lagarto* (☎275 567 406; no credit cards) on Largo Dom Manuel I, supplies a cheap and tasty *prato do dia* as well as a mean omelette, and, of couse, endless bottles of *Alardo*. There's also a pleasant terrace with lovely views, frequented by gnarled old villagers.

Castelo Branco

Not much of **CASTELO BRANCO** has survived the successive wars of this frontier area and today it appears as a predominantly modern town. Set out around sweeping boulevards, squares and parks, the capital of the Beira Baixa has an air of prosperity and activity in contrast with the nearby somnolent villages, although it's not the most exciting of places. Typical of this vigour is the annual classical music festival (May and June), featuring national and international musicians.

What's left of the old town is confined within the narrow cobbled alleyways and stepped side streets leading up to the ruins of the **Castelo**. Around its twelfth-century walls, a garden *miradouro* has been laid out. Nearby is the **Palácio Episcopal**, the old bishop's palace, with its formal, eighteenth-century garden (daily 9am–7pm; €1.80), a sequence of elaborately shaped hedges, pools, fountains, flowerbeds, *azulejos* and orange trees. The balustrades of the two grand staircases are peopled with statues – on one, the Apostles; on the other, the kings of Portugal. Two of the latter are much smaller than the rest: the hated Spanish rulers, Felipe I and II. Elsewhere in the gardens other statues represent months of the year, signs of the zodiac, Christian virtues and the then-known continents.

The palace itself houses the **Museu Tavares Proença Júnior** (Tues–Sun 10am–12.30pm & 2–5.30pm; €2, free Sun morning), whose collections roam through the usual local miscellany, save for a large and splendid display of finely embroidered bedspreads, or *colchas*, a craft for which the town is known throughout Portugal. These lavish status symbols were originally produced in

India and China where wealthy Portuguese commissioned them from local artisans. The craftspeople duly incorporated motifs from their own myths and culture – typically animals, flowers and mythical figures – which subsequently influenced Portuguese manufacturers in Castelo Branco's newly created domestic *colcha* industry, each embroiderer coming to distinguish themselves through their own unique pattern. The museum has a room where you can still see women beavering away on these intricate works of art. You can even commission one yourself although you'd better have a fat wallet handy – a typical *colcha* costs thousands of euros. The elegant sixteenth-century **Câmara Municipal** on Praça Luís de Camões is another survivor of the town's turbulent past, as are the several seventeenth- and eighteenth-century mansions in the streets around it.

Practicalities

The **bus station** is on the corner of Rua Rebelo and Rua do Saibreiro, the latter leading straight up to the Alameda da Liberdade, the main avenue through town. It's a little further to the **train station**, but equally simple – straight down the broad Avenida de Nuno Álvares. There is a **turismo** (Mon–Fri 9.30am–5.30pm, Sat & Sun 9.30am–1pm & 2.30–6pm; ☎272 330 339 ⓦwww.cm-castelobranco.pt) right in the centre, though temporarily housed in a portacabin near the Câmara Municipal. At the time of writing the central area directly bordering the edge of Alameda da Liberdade was under major construction, with both pedestrian and traffic diversions. For **internet** access you'll have to head out to the suburbs to Kryptobyte (daily 10am–midnight) at Quinta do Dr. Beirão 30C, not far from the *Pequim* Chinese restaurant (see p.290); ask at the tourist office for directions.

Accommodation

Despite its position as the regional capital, the town is conspicuously lacking in good-value accommodation, while budget travellers will be hard pushed to find anything acceptable at all. The well-equipped municipal **campsite** (☎272 330 361; closed mid-Nov to Dec) is 3km north of town along the N18.

Residencial Arraiana Av. 1 de Maio 18 ☎272 341 634, Ⓕ272 331 884. White woodchip, brazenly blue-tiled bathrooms and cork floors lend this somewhat overpriced *residencial* a frumpish 1970s feel, although the rooms are clean, comfortable and quiet (ghostly even). Breakfast included. ❸
Residencial Império Rua dos Prazeres 20 ☎272 341 720. Smart and efficient, with functional, modern furnishings, gleaming bathrooms and a compact dining room where the inclusive breakfast is served. The downstairs rooms are gloomier but wonderfully cool in summer. No credit cards. ❸

Hotel Rainha Dona Amélia Rua Santiago 15 ☎272 348 800, ⓦwww.maisturismo.pt/hdamelia .html. Friendly and efficient, with a lovely *colcha* hanging in the reception, sunny rooms and parking facilities. Breakfast included. ❺
Hotel Tryp Colina do Castelo Rua da Piscina ☎272 349 280, Ⓔtryp.colina. castelo@solmeliaportugal.com. Glass-fronted hotel in a lofty location by the castle. The luxurious rooms have soft-focus interiors and the views from the balconies (and the bar and reception area) are breathtaking. There's also parking, a health club with sauna, Turkish baths and squash courts. Breakfast buffet included. ❺

Eating and drinking

Castelo Branco is better served by restaurants than hotels with a number of fine, if pricey, traditional choices and a good Chinese restaurant. For your own supplies, there's a large covered **market** on Avenida 1° de Maio.

Kalifa Rua Cadetes de Toledo 10 ☎272 344 246. Spacious, modern bar-restaurant with a lengthy menu featuring a particularly imaginative range of appetizers – try the sheep's cheese with banana. There's also sport on the big screen and a pleasant terrace at the back. Moderate.

A Muralha Rua de Santo Espiritu Santo Maria ☎272 322 703. Well-appointed first-floor restaurant with *azulejo*-tiled walls, tucked away in a courtyard on the fringes of the old town. Among the menu's local specialities, the green bean soup and the wild boar with duchess potatoes come recommended. Closed Mon. Expensive.

Pequim Quinta da Granja, Lote 172, Loja 3 ☎272 324 987. Out in Castelo's suburbs, this cheap and cheerful Chinese restaurant is nevertheless worth the trek. The service is speedy and the extensive range of meat, poultry and fish dishes – as well as a tasty vegetable chow mein – offer great value for money. No credit cards. Inexpensive.

Praça Velha Largo Luís de Camões 17 ☎272 328 640. Once the granary of Castelo Branco's Knights Templar, this fashionable restaurant now feeds the well-heeled and style-conscious townsfolk. For something different try the fondue or the *filet mignon*, although you can't go wrong with their grilled kid goat. Closed Mon. Expensive.

Monsanto

MONSANTO, 48km northeast of Castelo Branco, claims to be the most ancient settlement in Portugal, and it's almost certainly its most enchanting. It also holds the title of the "most Portuguese" village in Portugal, an award originally bestowed in 1948 and jealously guarded ever since. The old village – there's a newer settlement at the bottom of the hill where the bus drops you – looks as though it has barely changed in centuries. The houses huddle between giant granite outcrops, their walls carved from and moulded around the grey boulders, appearing to have grown organically from the hillside. It's all strikingly beautiful: flowers tumble from windows and the streets, barely wide enough for a mule, are cut out of the rock.

In common with most remote, traditional villages throughout the country, Monsanto has an ageing population and many houses now lie abandoned; look closely enough and you'll see cooking implements and other household items rusting poignantly among the rubble. One of the most remarkable ruins is the famous *Casa de Uma Só Telha* ("the house with only one tile"), consisting of a huge granite boulder. The remnants of the older generation nevertheless include an impressive array of characters and if you're lucky you may get to hear one of the old women playing the *adufe*, an ancient square-shaped drum of Arabic origin – Monsanto is one of only a handful of villages in Portugal where the instrument is still found. It's also one of the few villages where the women still make *marafonas*, rag dolls fashioned from a wooden cross and originally used as a defence against sorcery.

The **castle** is situated amid a desolate, windswept rockscape at a height of more than 700 metres. The site dates back to Lusitanian times although Gualdim Pais – Grand Master of the Knights Templar – and Dom Dinis fortified the structure in successive eras before it finally became the victim of cross-border warfare in 1810. One of the most interesting features is the central well, crisscrossed by stone arches which originally numbered seven – only two remain. Legend has it that a villager once tried to renovate the cistern but was buried alive by rocks after witnessing an apparition of a beautiful Moorish woman. A big celebration takes place every May 3, when the village girls throw baskets of flowers off the ramparts. The rite commemorates an ancient siege when, in desperation and close to starvation, the defenders threw their last calf over the walls: their attackers, so disheartened at this evidence of plenty within, gave up and went home.

As you hike your way up through the village you're quite likely to meet someone who'll insist on guiding you up, showing you the incredible views. The man known simply as Reinaldo is the town's resident expert, and you'll be hard pushed to find a more generous, knowledgeable or enthusiastic guide – you can usually find him in the homely *Café Montesino* at Rua do Castelo 4, the local's local.

Practicalities

Buses for Castelo Branco leave every day (except Sunday) at 6.15am from the parking area near *Café Jovem*, while a Sunday service departs at the more merciful hour of 2.30pm. On Mondays, Tuesdays and Thursdays there is also an afternoon service (2.45pm) departing from the nearby village of Relva. There's a small **turismo** (daily 10am–1pm & 2–6pm; ☎277 314 642) on Rua Marquês da Graciosa, just off to the right of the main square (itself a minute's walk uphill from the parking area), which also houses a display of traditional cooking implements.

The welcoming *Adega Tipica O Cruzeiro*, Rua Fernando Namora 4 (☎277 314 528; no credit cards; breakfast included; ❸), a rustically refurbished bar, has a couple of atmospheric upstairs **rooms** with stunning views. Although not essential, it's probably worth booking ahead as the only other **accommodation** in town is either the small ten-room *Pousada de Monsanto* (☎277 314 471, ⓦwww.pousadas.pt; breakfast included; ❻), a rather incongruous edifice amid the village's medieval charms, or the *Casa da Maria* (☎965 624 607; no credit cards; breakfast included; ❹), a spacious, open-plan house located some way down the hill from the main village at Avenida Fernando Rocha 11. The friendly proprietor speaks English, as do the amiable English/Portuguese couple who provide rudimentary **camping** facilities (☎277 312 614, ⓔana.rr.barrata@clix.pt; open all year) in a lovely garden located 6km or so from Monsanto on the EN239 road towards Termas de Monfortinho.

In Monsanto, the most upmarket **restaurant** is at the *pousada*, where you can try stewed wild boar or braised kid goat for around €18. However, the service is surly and the food a disappointment – you're better off having a cheap drink and snack at the *Adega Tipica O Cruzeiro*, which does delicious *pratos do dia*, or heading to the moderately priced *Café Jovem* (☎277 314 590; no credit cards), Avenida Fernando Ramos Rocha 21, which stays open for dinner with a menu centred on typical fare such as grilled kid goat and *feijoada*.

Idanha-a-Velha

IDANHA-A-VELHA is another tiny backwater, situated some 15km kilometres from Monsanto. There's no regular public transport to the village, although if you don't have a car you could try the cross-country walk from Monsanto, but make sure you get good directions before heading off. The village is certainly worth a little effort to reach. It's of a similar age to or even older than Monsanto, but has a considerably more illustrious history and is now regarded as a national monument. Known as Igaeditânia, it was once a major Roman city and, subsequently, under Visigothic rule, was the seat of a bishopric – which endured even Moorish occupation. Wamba, the legendary King of the Goths, is said to have been born here. During the reign of Dom Manuel, however, early in the fifteenth century, it is said that a plague of rats forced the occupants to move to Monsanto or nearby Idanha-a-Nova.

The village looks much as it must have done when the rats moved in, and not far different from when the Romans left, either. It retains a section of massive Roman wall, the **Roman bridge** is still in use, and odd Roman relics lie about everywhere. In the very ancient **Basilica**, which is at least part Visigothic, there's a collection of all the more mobile statues and lumps of inscribed stone found about the place; another small chapel contains an exhibition of coins, pottery and bones, all found more or less by accident. Nearby are the ruins of the **Bishop's Palace**. Ask in the village café for the key to the basilica, if it is locked. Perhaps the most fascinating restoration is the old oil press or *lagar de varas*, with an ingenious pressing system utilising a huge tree trunk. It's located near the Basilica although opening hours vary; ask in the turismo.

Even the **turismo** (daily 10am–12.30pm & 2–6.30pm; ☏277 914 280) is built atop ruins of a Roman dwelling on Rua da Sé, the excavations of which you can peer down into through glass panels in the floor. There's still no **accomodation** in the village although nearby Monsanto offers a decent range of options. There's a solitary, authentically local **café** near the turismo although they only serve light snacks; for a full meal, again, your only option is Monsanto.

Travel details

Trains

Castelo Branco to: Abrantes (5–6 daily; 1hr 20min–2hr); Alpedrinha (3-4 daily); Covilhã (5–6 daily; 1hr 25min); Lisbon (5-6 daily; 4hr 5min).
Celorico da Beira to: Coimbra (6-9 daily; 2hr 50min); Guarda (7-9 daily; 50min); Lisbon (3-4 daily; 4hr 15min); Vilar Formoso (4-6 daily; 2hr).
Covilhã to: Abrantes (5-6 daily; 2hr 25min–3hr 15min); Castelo Branco (5–6 daily; 1hr 25min); Guarda (2-3 daily; 1hr 15min); Lisbon (5–6 daily; 3hr 20min–4hr 30min).
Guarda to: Coimbra (7–8 daily; 2hr 30min–3hr 40min); Covilhã (2-3 daily; 1hr 15min); Lisbon (6-8 daily; 5hr–7hr 50min); Vilar Formoso (6-7 daily; 50min).
Vilar Formoso (Spanish border) to: Guarda (5 daily; 50min); Lisbon (4 daily; 6hr 30min); Salamanca, Spain (2 onward connections from Portugal daily; 2hr 30min).

Buses

Almeida to: Guarda (2 daily; 2hr); Pinhel (Mon-Fri & Sun 1 daily; 30min).
Alpedrinha to: Castelo Branco (Mon–Fri 4 daily; 30min); Covilhã (3 daily; 2hr 35min); Fundão (4 daily; 15–25min).
Belmonte to: Ginjal (2 daily; 5min); Guarda (3 daily; 45min); Manteigas (3 daily; 1hr 15min); Sabugal (2 daily; 1hr 30min).
Castelo Branco to: Alpedrinha (Mon-Fri 4 daily; 30min); Coimbra (3-4 daily; 3hr); Covilhã (4 daily;

40min–1hr 5min); Fundão (4 daily; 50min); Guarda (4 daily; 1hr 55min); Lisbon (7 daily; 3hr 45min–4hr 10min); Monsanto (1 daily; 3hr 30min); Penamacor (Mon-Fri 1 daily; 1hr 15min); Viseu (2 daily; 3hr 30min).
Celorico da Beira to: Coimbra (5 daily; 2hr 25min); Covilhã (5–6 daily; 1hr 15min); Gouveia (Mon-Fri 2 daily Sat & Sun 1 daily; 30min); Guarda (13 daily; 30min); Lamego (3 daily; 3hr 5min); Lisbon (2 daily; 5hr); Seia (Mon-Fri 3daily, Sat & Sun 1 daily); Trancoso (3 daily; 30min); Viseu (9 daily; 50min).
Covilhã to: Castelo Branco (7 daily; 1hr 5min); Fundão (7 daily; 20min); Guarda (7 daily; 50min); Lisbon (3 daily; 5hr 30min); Penhas da Saúde (July-September only: 1 daily; 2 daily during August, 3 daily on Sundays in August; 35min); Seia (1 daily; 2hr); Viseu (4 daily; 2hr 10 min).
Gouveia to: Seia (3 daily; 1hr).
Guarda to: Almeida (1 daily; 1 hr 10min); Alpedrinha (4 daily; 1hr 20min); Belmonte (4 daily; 45min); Braga (4 daily; 4hr 20min); Castelo Branco (6 daily; 1hr 55min); Celorico da Beira (12 daily; 30min); Coimbra (1 daily; 2hr 30min); Covilhã (15 daily; 50min); Gouveia (1-2 daily; 45min) Lisbon (4 daily; 5–6hr); Manteigas (Mon-Fri 2 daily; 1hr 45min); Pinhel (4 daily; 1 hr); Seia (2-3 daily; 1hr); Trancoso (5 weekly; 1hr 30min); Vilar Formoso (1 daily; 50min); Viseu (7 daily; 2hr 15min).
Sabugal to: Belmonte (1 daily; 1hr 30min); Castelo Branco (1 daily; 2hr 30min); Guarda (5 daily; 45min); Penemacor (2 daily; 1hr); Sortelha (2 weekly, plus 1 daily during term time; 30min).

Seia to: Celorico da Beira (1 daily; 45min); Coimbra (1-3 daily; 1hr 45min); Covilhã (Mon-Fri 1 daily; 2hr); Gouveia (3 daily; 1hr); Guarda (2 daily; 1hr 15min) Sabugeiro (1 weekly; 30min).

Trancoso to: Braga (2 daily; 4hr 10min); Bragança (2 daily; 3hr); Celorico da Beira (2 daily; 1hr 25min); Covilhã (2 daily; 1hr 45min); Guarda (2 daily; 1hr); Lamego (2 daily; 2hr); Lisbon (2 daily; 6hr 10min); Pocinho (2 daily; 1hr 20min); Viseu (2 daily; 1hr 50min).

Vilar Formoso to: Guarda (4 daily; 50min); Lisbon (4 daily; 5hr 40min–6hr).

Viseu to: Belmonte (Ginjal) (2 daily; 1hr 50min); Celorico da Beira (8 daily; 50min–1hr); Coimbra (10 daily; 1hr 25min); Covilhã (7 daily; 2hr 15min); Faro (9 daily; 11hr 35min–12hr 20min); Guarda (8 daily; 1hr 20min); Lisbon (11 daily; 4–5hr); Porto (12 daily; 1hr 50min); São Pedro do Sul (Mon–Fri 4–5 daily, 1–2 daily at weekends; 1hr); Sernancelhe (2 daily); Trancoso (2 daily; 1hr 25min).

Porto and the Douro

CHAPTER 5

Highlights

✱ **Festa de São João** The city's wildest annual festival, St John's Eve (June 23–24), sees riotous behaviour on an epic scale. See p.299

✱ **Douro river cruise** Let the countryside drift by on a trip along the country's historic "River of Gold". See p.304

✱ **Porto's riverfront** The cramped streets and alleys are an ideal introduction to this beguiling city. See p.314

✱ **Museu de Arte Contemporânea de Serralves** Housed in a building by Portugal's leading architect, this has a collection to delight all fans of contemporary art. See p.318

✱ **Port lodge visit** Sample some of the hundreds of varieties of port wine at Vila Nova de Gaia. See p.321

✱ **Citânia de Sanfins de Ferreira** The best preserved of the region's Celtic hilltop settlements, giving a vivid notion of daily life before the Romans. See p.346

✱ **Rock art at Foz Côa** Some of the world's oldest works of art, dating back over 20,000 years. See p.370

✱ **Castelo Rodrigo** An atmospheric hilltop village with stunning vistas and a superb restaurant. See p.372

△ Vinho do Porto

Porto and the Douro

P ortugal's second-largest city, **Porto**, is dramatically situated at the mouth of the Rio Douro, its old quarters scrambling up the rocky north bank in tangled tiers. As the de facto capital of the north, it's the hub of the region's road and railway system, and while you can't quite avoid it on any trip to the north of the country, nor would you want to. It's a massively atmospheric place, almost Dickensian in parts, though rather unfairly the attention of many visitors is focused firmly on the port-producing centre of **Vila Nova de Gaia**, across the river. For excellent beaches, the towns of **Vila do Conde** and **Póvoa de Varzim**, just to the north up the Porto coast, offer a taste of what's to come as you head into the Minho.

Inevitably, it's the **Rio Douro** ("River of Gold") that dominates every aspect of this region: a narrow, winding gorge for the major part of its long route from the Spanish border, with port wine lodges and tiny villages dotted about the hillsides. Historically a wild and unpredictable river with treacherous rapids, the construction of hydroelectric dams all along its course has tamed it considerably, making cruises from Porto a particularly relaxing way of getting a feel for this famous wine region. You can follow the river by road as well, though for many it's the **Douro railway line** that is the prime attraction. It joins the course of the river about 60km inland from Porto and sticks to it from then on, cutting into the rock face and crisscrossing the water on a series of rickety bridges. It's one of those journeys that requires no other justification but, if reason be needed, the amazing outdoor palaeolithic engravings around **Vila Nova de Foz Côa**, near the border with Spain, duly oblige.

About halfway along the Douro is **Peso da Régua**, the capital of Alto Douro ("Upper Douro") province, with more scope for visiting the wine lodges. Just to the south, the delightful Baroque town of **Lamego** is home of Portugal's champagne-like wine, Raposeira, as well as the magnificent shrine of Nossa Senhora dos Remédios. Rather less ostentatious is the twelfth-century Romanesque church at nearby **São João de Tarouca**, while there are even older churches near the town of **Penafiel**, north of the river.

Three narrow gauge railways follow the Douro's tributaries, all accessible from the Douro railway line. The Corgo and Tua lines provide access from the Douro to Trás-os-Montes (both covered in Chapter 7), while the **Tâmega line** runs to **Amarante**, a delightful riverside town around 50km east of Porto. Amarante makes the best approach to the **Serra do Marão**, whose stark, eroded granite slopes and pervasive scent of pine give a taste of the mountain scenery further north and east. Particularly attractive are the small towns of the **Terras de Basto**, named after curious life-size Celtic warrior statues found in the area.

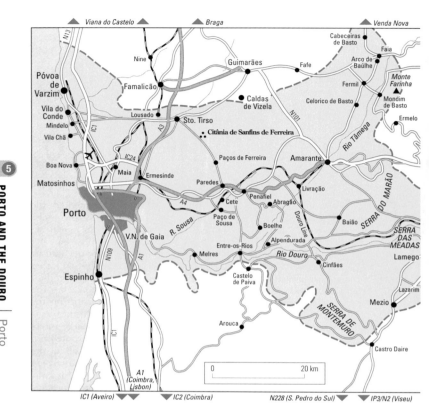

Map labels:

Viana do Castelo | Braga | Venda Nova

Cabeceiras de Basto
Faia
Nine
Guimarães
Fafe
Arco de Baúlhe
Póvoa de Varzim
Famalicão
Fermil
Monte Farinha
Caldas de Vizela
Celorico de Basto
Mondim de Basto
Vila do Conde
Lousado
Sto. Tirso
Ermelo
Mindelo
Vila Chã
Citânia de Sanfins de Ferreira
Rio Tâmega
Boa Nova
IC24
Paços de Ferreira
Amarante
SERRA DO MARÃO
Maia
Ermesinde
Paredes
Matosinhos
Cete
Livração
Porto
Penafiel
Abragão
Baião
SERRA DAS MEADAS
A4
R. Sousa
Paço de Sousa
Douro Line
V.N. de Gaia
Boelhe
Alpendurada
Lamego
Entre-os-Rios
Rio Douro
Melres
Cinfães
Espinho
Castelo de Paiva
Lazarim
SERRA DE MONTEMURO
Mezio
Arouca
Castro Daire

0   20 km

A1 (Coimbra, Lisbon)

IC1 (Aveiro) | IC2 (Coimbra) | N228 (S. Pedro do Sul) | IP3/N2 (Viseu)

Porto

As with Lisbon, it's hard not to like **PORTO**. A large city, maybe, but it's also an attractive, laidback destination, with a lengthy history – it was known in Roman times as *Portus Cale* (the "sheltered port"). However, there the comparison with the capital ends: as the saying goes: "Coimbra studies, Braga prays, Lisbon shows off and Porto works." In a city where the most obvious sights are its six bridges (four modern, two nineteenth-century, all spectacular), the fascination of Porto lies more in its day-to-day life. The prosperous business core – surrounded by well-to-do suburbs as well as depressed housing estates – is tempered by a kernel of cramped streets, ancient alleys, tiny bars and antiquated shops wholly untouched by the planners. Nonetheless, its status as European City of Culture in 2001 was the signal for a massive urban redevelopment, and Porto's streets and squares have subsequently been turned upside-down in a flurry of construction work, including the provision of a new metro system and tram lines. Many of the city's historic buildings are being restored, particularly in the riverside *bairro* of **Ribeira** – now a UNESCO World Heritage Site. This apart, there is only a handful of true tourist sights in the city, including a landmark Baroque tower, the cathedral, and a clutch of churches and good museums, most notably the **Fundação de Serralves** contemporary art gallery. For many visitors, though, it is the port wine trade that

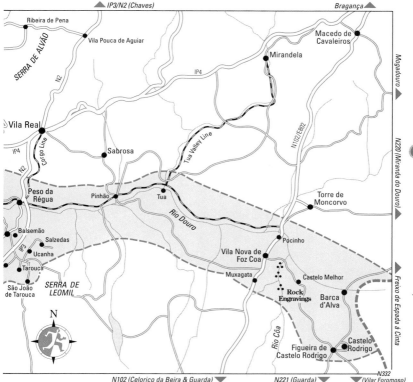

defines the city, with its centre of operations at **Vila Nova de Gaia** (just Gaia to locals), the home of the port wine lodges across the river.

The city is at its earthiest and finest for the riotous celebration that is the **Festa de São João**, St John's Eve (the night of June 23–24), when seemingly the entire population takes to the streets, hitting each other over the head with leeks, squeaky plastic hammers, or anything else to hand, whilst paper balloons illuminated by candles drift off into the night sky. There are many more festivals throughout the year, all detailed in the box on pp.332–333.

Arrival and information

The **airport** (information on ☎229 432 400 or 229 412 534) is 13km north of the city in Maia, where there's a bank, ATMs, 24-hour exchange bureau, car rental companies, and a tourist information counter (daily 8am–11.30pm; ☎229 412 534). The easiest way into town is by **metro** (Linha B; daily 6am–1am, departures every 8–15min), though there are also local buses as well as an **AeroBus** (7.30am–7pm, every 30min; €2.60, free for TAP passengers; ☎808 200 166), which stops at most central hotels and finishes its run at the central Avenida dos Aliados (40–60min journey). The last Aerobus back to the airport leaves Aliados at 6.15pm. The ticket remains valid for unlimited use on local buses until midnight. **Taxis** from the airport into the centre cost €15–20.

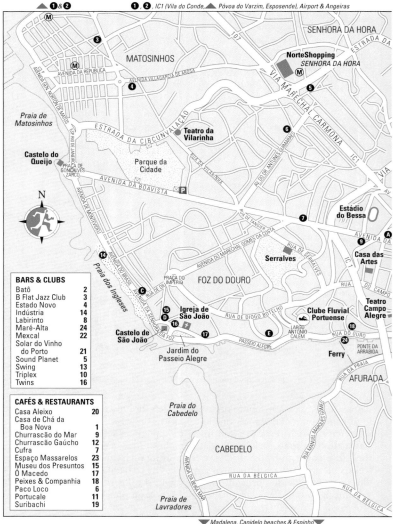

SENHORA DA HORA

MATOSINHOS

NorteShopping
SENHORA DA HORA

Praia de
Matosinhos

Teatro da
Vilarinha

Castelo do
Queijo

Parque da
Cidade

Estádio
do Bessa

Serralves

Casa das
Artes

BARS & CLUBS

Batô	2
B Flat Jazz Club	3
Estado Novo	4
Indústria	14
Labirinto	8
Maré-Alta	24
Mexcal	22
Solar do Vinho do Porto	21
Sound Planet	5
Swing	13
Triplex	10
Twins	16

FOZ DO DOURO

Teatro
Campo
Alegre

Igreja de
São João

Clube Fluvial
Portuense

Castelo de
São João

Jardim do
Passeio Alegre

Ferry

AFURADA

CAFÉS & RESTAURANTS

Casa Aleixo	20
Casa de Chá da Boa Nova	1
Churrascão do Mar	9
Churrascão Gaúcho	12
Cufra	7
Espaço Massarelos	23
Museu dos Presuntos	15
Ó Macedo	17
Peixes & Companhia	18
Paco Loco	6
Portucale	11
Suribachi	19

Praia do
Cabedelo

CABEDELO

Praia de
Lavradores

Most long distance trains from the south terminate at **Estação de Campanhã** (☎808 208 208), a few kilometres east of the centre but on metro Linha A. Alternatively, you can change at Campanhã for the five-minute ride to the central **Estação de São Bento** (☎222 051 714) on Praça Almeida Garrett. Taxis wait outside São Bento, and buses can be caught both here and in nearby Praça da Liberdade – the station is known for pickpockets and scammers, so take care, and be wary of people touting rooms.

International buses operated by Eurolines finish at Campo 24 de Agosto, less than 1km east of the centre (bus #34 to Bolhão); Internorte buses stop at Praça

PORTO

ACCOMMODATION

América	B
Boa-Vista	D
Meridien Park Atlantic	A
Portofoz	C
Pousada de Juventude	E

Hospital de São João

Parque de Campismo da Prelada

Balleteatro Auditório

PARANHOS

BOAVISTA

Casa da Música

CASA DA MÚSICA

Centro Commercial Brasília

Igreja da Lapa

ANTAS

Estádio do Dragão

Igreja de Cedofeita

Igreja do Bonfim

Teatro Helena Sé e Costa

TRINDADE

BONFIM

MASSARELOS

Museu do Carro Eléctrico

Casa Tait

Museu Nacional Soares dos Reis

Palácio de Cristal

São Bento Railway Station

São Lazaro

Museu Militar

Campanhã Railway Station

Museu Romântico

Igreja de Massarelos

Museu do Vinho do Porto

Alfândega

Botanical Garden

See Central Porto map for detail

PONTE DO INFANTE

PONTE DO FREIXO

PONTE D LUIS I

PONTE DE MARIA PIA

PONTE DE SÃO JOÃO

VILA NOVA DE GAIA

0   1 km

da Galiza between the Rotunda da Boavista and Palácio de Cristal, roughly 1.5km west of the centre (lots of buses from there to Pr. da Liberdade/Av. dos Aliados). **National and regional bus services** operate from stops and garages all over the city, though most are fairly central – see "Travel details", p.375, for full details.

Driving into the city from the north along the IC1 or A3/IP1, follow the signs for "Centro" or "Aliados" for the centre; following "Circunvalação" or "Hospital" will get you on the ring road; while "Antas" will spit you out on Avenida Fernão Magalhães in the northeast, close to FC Porto's Estádio do Dragão stadium, with loads of parking space and a rapid metro connection to the centre. From the south, the IC1 crosses the Douro on the Ponte da Arrábida, west of the centre; take the first exit immediately after the bridge and follow the signs for "Centro" or "Boavista". The IP1 crosses the Douro along Ponte do Freixo, east of the city; take the first exit and follow the river into town. A more spectacular approach is to follow the signs into Vila Nova de Gaia, from where the road passes over the top tier of Ponte Dom Luís I into Porto.

Porto has a convoluted one-way system and ongoing construction work, so it's best to park wherever you can and either walk or catch a bus or metro. The area around Campanhã railway station has plenty of parking, and there are rapid connections into the centre on the metro. Or there are large **car parks** under Praça dos Poveiros, east of the centre, under Praça de Lisboa to the west, and at the corkscrew-like "Silo Alto" garage at the top of Rua do Bonjardim.

Information

There are three city **turismos** where you can buy a detailed map (€1), and get information about hotels, restaurants, current events and port wine lodges. You can also pick up the *Rota do Vinho do Porto*, a driving itinerary detailing 54 wine-related attractions along the Douro. Turismos also sell guidebooks, walking itineraries and the **Passe Porto card** (€6.50 one day, €15.50 three days), which gives unlimited bus and tram transport plus discounts or free entry to many museums and monuments, theatre tickets and cruises.

The most helpful office is the **city-run turismo** at Rua Clube dos Fenianos 25 at the top end of Avenida dos Aliados (June–Sept daily 9am–7pm; Oct–May Mon–Fri 9am–5.30pm, Sat, Sun & hols 9.30am–4.30pm; ☎223 393 470, ✉turismo.central@cm-porto.pt), especially useful for transport-related questions and bookings, including river cruises and city tours. There's another city-run turismo in **Ribeira** at Rua Infante Dom Henrique 63 (Mon–Fri 9am–5.30pm, Sat, Sun & hols 9.30am–4.30pm; ☎222 009 770), and a **state-run turismo** at Praça Dom João I 43, just east of Aliados (Mon–Fri 9am–7.30pm, Nov–March until 7pm, Sat, Sun & hols 9.30am–3.30pm; ☎222 057 514), mainly useful for general queries about northern Portugal.

The best **website** is the town hall's matchless ⊛www.portoturismo.pt (also in English), with masses of up-to-date practical information and erudite sections on the city's history, culture and architecture.

City transport and tours

Although Porto sprawls for eleven kilometres from the coast inland, most sights lie within the compact and very hilly centre, and all are within **walking** – or perhaps more accurately, climbing – distance. For trips further afield, the city has an extensive **bus** network, and a brand new **metro** system, while lines for the city's **trams** (*eléctricos*) – many ripped up in the 1970s – are currently being relaid. In addition, a variety of **tours** and **cruises** show you the river and city by foot, water or sightseeing bus. For **transport enquiries**, visit the main turismo next to the town hall, or call ☎800 220 905 (free). Otherwise, the easiest way around is by **taxi**. Most squares have taxi ranks (or see "Listings", p.336, for cab companies) – fares should be no more than €5–7 for a cross-town ride.

Buses

Porto lacks a central bus station, though major termini include **Praça da Liberdade** at the bottom of Avenida dos Aliados, and **Jardim da Cordoaria**, 1km to the west. If you're heading west to the museum at Serralves or the coast, you may have to change at **Boavista**, meaning the huge Rotunda da Boavista

To Rotunda da Boavista: Buses #3, #20 or #52 (and #19 and #76 at night) from Pr. da Liberdade; and #34, #82 or #84 from Bolhão or Pr. da República.
To Vila Nova de Gaia: Buses #57 and 91 from Pr. Almeida Garrett (facing São Bento station); #32, #33 and #83 (and #33, #83 and #91 at night) from Av. dos Aliados.
To Foz do Douro and Castelo do Queijo: Bus #1 along the river from Pr. Almeida Garrett (São Bento station); #24 from Rotunda da Boavista and the Cordoaria; trams #1E and #18 from along the river bank west of Ribeira.
Nightbuses: the most useful, serving destinations north and west of the centre (#1, #7, #15, #19, #54 and #76) and Vila Nova de Gaia (#33, #83 and #91), start at Pr. da Liberdade /Av. dos Aliados.

5

roundabout at the eastern end of Avenida da Boavista, 2km northwest of Avenida dos Aliados. Bus stops are currently all around the *rotunda*; they should eventually relocate to an interchange beside the Casa da Música metro station.

Normal **hours of operation** are 6am to around 9pm, but there is an extensive nightbus network, running approximately hourly along fourteen routes. Most bus stops display detailed route maps, or check timetables and routes at either of the city-run turismos or the **STCP office** on Praça Almeida Garrett (☎808 200 166, Ⓦ www.stcp.pt), facing São Bento train station.

Single **tickets** cost €1.20 on the bus, but only €0.70 in advance from post offices, newsagents or kiosks at the main bus stops, and it's even cheaper to buy a *senha* – a ten-ride ticket. **Travel passes** include the three-day *Bilhete Porto 2001* (€5), which must be bought in advance and gives unlimited transport on all buses, including the AeroBus, and trams; the one-day *Bilhete Diário Rede Geral* (€2.60), can be bought when boarding. Also valid on buses is the metro's *Cartão Andante* – see below.

The metro

Since 1999, work has been underway on an ambitious, partly underground, **metro system** (☎808 200 444, Ⓦ www.metrodoporto.pt), whose completion date faded long ago into the realms of fantasy, thanks in part to Porto's famously hard granite. That said, one line is now open, and another partially functional (both daily 6am–1am, departures every 8–15 min).

Linha A or "Linha Azul" (drawn blue on route maps) runs between Matosinhos, 8km northwest of the city, to FC Porto's Estádio do Dragão in Antas, in the northeast, looping through the heart of town. Stops include Casa da Música at the Rotunda da Boavista, the central Trindade, just north of Avenida dos Aliados, Bolhão to the east of the Avenida, and Campo 24 de Agosto, Rua do Heroísmo and Campanhã, connecting with the national rail network. **Linha B** or "Linha Vermelha" (red) covers the same central stations as Linha A, but branches at Senhora da Hora towards the airport; the northward continuation to the seaside towns of Vila do Conde and Póvoa do Varzim is now slated for completion in 2006. The other lines – still far from ready – are Linha C ("Linha Verde") serving the northeastern suburbs, and Linha D ("Linha Amarela"), from the Hospital de São João in the north to Santo Ovídio in Gaia, crossing the river along the top tier of Ponte Dom Luís I.

Before your first journey you need to buy a rechargeable **Cartão Andante** (€0.50) from the metro station ticket office. Fares are credited to the card (there are no tickets), and vary according to zones and duration; they're also valid for STCP buses, trams and the Funicular dos Guindais. The minimum charge is €0.80 for one hour and two zones, covering the entire city. The **Tarifário Andante 24** gives 24hr of travel for €2.80 (two zones) or €3.50 (three zones, including Matosinhos). The card needs validating before travel; hold it close to the machine.

Trams

Porto currently has only two **tram routes** (every 30min, Mon–Sat 8.30am –7.30pm), utilising little wood-panelled, wicker-seated streetcars that are worth every cent of the fare (€0.50, STCP bus passes and metro's *Cartão Andante* also valid). Both are currently confined to a 4 or 5km route along the river, from just west of Ribeira to Passeio Alegre in Foz do Douro, but will be extended upon completion of construction work: **Linha #1E** from the bottom of Rua do Infante Dom Henrique to Matosinhos, 8km northwest of the city on the coast; and **Linha #18** along a loop from Hospital de Santo António, along the river to Foz, up the coast to the Castelo do Queijo and inland along Avenida da Boavista. A city centre loop is now under construction, linking the Jardim da Cordoaria with Praça da Batalha via Praça da Liberdade, with a link to the top of the Funicular dos Guindais (p.312).

Tours and cruises

There are numerous tour operators, but the town hall has made things easy by establishing **Porto Tours** (T222 000 073 or 222 000 045, Wwww.portotours .com), an information and bookings centre at the Torre Medieval, Calçada Dom Pedro Pitões 15, next to the Sé. The venture is a partnership between the authorities and tour and cruise operators; trips can also be booked through the main city-run turismo.

Porto's stock-in-trade is the **river cruise** along the Douro, with boats (from a variety of operators) leaving from the Cais da Ribeira in Porto, or from Avenida Diogo Leite in Vila Nova de Gaia, on the opposite shore. Note that services are much reduced or non-existent between November and February. The basic cruise is the fifty-minute **six bridges cruise** (€5–10), which can be extended by taking lunch or dinner (€30–40). The best are aboard wooden *barcos rabelo* (operated by Via D'Ouro, Rota Ouro do Douro and Douro Azul), traditionally used to transport port wine casks downriver. Lengthier **full-day cruises** (€50 –90) run to and from Crestuma dam, Peso da Régua, Pinhão or the Alpendurada monastery, sometimes with the return leg by bus, train or even helicopter. Alternatively, you can join the ships in Régua or Pinhão for day-trips to Barca d'Alva (reserve tickets beforehand). Two-day **weekend cruises** (€150–200), overnighting on the boat or in riverside hotels, also cover the Porto–Régua–Porto route, or Porto to the Spanish border at Barca d'Alva and back. All cruise ships have English-speaking guides and offer packages for special events like Valentine's, Carnaval, São João (23–24 June), Christmas and New Year's Eve.

Apart from the river cruises, the other mainstays from April to September are **road-train tours** from the Sé (1hr 45min; several departures daily; €6), which include wine-tasting in Gaia, and two-hour double-decker **bus tours** (10am, noon, 2pm & 4pm; €13), also with wine-tasting, looping around from Avenida dos Aliados via Bolhão, Batalha, Sé, Gaia, Ribeira and Clérigos. You can get on or off at any of these places and rejoin later. Both have English commentary; buy tickets onboard.

Year-round possibilities, requiring reservations, include **helicopter flights** over the city (€50 for ten minutes); thematic **architectural walks** (daily except April–June & Dec; €30); and **day-trips** into Minho province (upwards of €80–120) and as far as Santiago de Compostela in Galicia.

Accommodation

Porto has a wide range of **accommodation** to suit all tastes and pockets. However, budget travellers may have trouble finding anything under €40 in summer, when it's best to book ahead. The cheapest rooms are the *pensões* and *hospedarias* east of the centre, particularly along Rua da Alegria and Rua Alexandre Herculano; few are particularly enticing (the area is favoured by prostitutes) but they're handy if you're stuck. The upmarket suburbs of Boavista and Serralves, a fair distance west of the centre, contain most of the city's five-star hotels, but though amenities are well up to scratch, the suburban location and lack of any real atmosphere is the drawback. Overnight **parking** can be awkward in the centre, where only a few hotels have their own space, but a handful have negotiated deals with nearby car parks for their guests. Best value for single travellers is the **youth hostel** west of the centre, easily reached by bus. Unless you're staying at the hotels in Foz do Douro, **camping** is the only way to be on the coast – but the coastal sites are all a good 10km away from the city, and beyond the reach of nightbuses.

All the establishments listed below are marked on the Central Porto map, p.306, except for the hotels in Boavista and Foz de Douro, and the youth hostel – for all of which see the Porto map, p.300.

Ribeira and around

Hotel da Bolsa Rua Ferreira Borges 101 ☎222 026 768, Ⓦwww.hoteldabolsa.com. A modernized, well-placed three-star hotel with a classical facade, but rather spartan rooms, mostly twin-bedded, and similarly uninspiring restaurant and bar. The staff are friendly, though, and there are facilities for disabled visitors. Public parking next door. Breakfast included. ❹

Pestana Porto Hotel (Carlton) Pr. da Ribeira 1 ☎223 402 300, Ⓦwww.pestana.com. Enjoying the city's best location, atop the medieval wall next to the river. However, the expense and effort lavished on the restoration of this glorious cluster of sixteenth- to eighteenth-century buildings sadly eluded the bedrooms, which are modern but bland. Get a view to justify the expense; corner rooms also overlook the bridge. One room for wheelchairs. Breakfast included. ❼

Central Porto

Residencial dos Aliados Av. dos Aliados, entrance on Rua Elísio de Melo 27-2° ☎222 004 853, Ⓦwww.residencialaliados.com. Occupying a monumental late-nineteenth-century building, the 43 rooms – all with TV and phone – at this comfortable hotel fill quickly in summer. Front rooms give dizzying views over the avenue; ones at the back are quieter. There's also room service, bar and internet access. Rooms without a/c are considerably cheaper. Breakfast included. ❸

Hotel América Rua de Santa Catarina 1018 ☎223 392 930, Ⓦwww.hotel-america.net. Well-equipped mid-range choice with bright and relatively spacious rooms, some adapted for the disabled, plus 24hr reception and room service, and private underground parking. There's also a bar and restaurant, with tables in an attractive conservatory under a plexiglass roof. Bus #95 from Av. dos Aliados. Breakfast included. ❸

Residencial Brasília Rua Álvares Cabral 221 ☎222 006 095, Ⓦwww.residencialbrasiliaporto.com. Ten narrow en-suite rooms all with cable TV and old furniture, the better ones featuring Manueline-style beds and beautiful bathtubs. Might be a tad oppressive were it not for the warm family welcome. There's also an atmospheric lounge, and dining room with stuccowork ceiling and Persian carpets. Underground parking; bus #95 from Av. dos Aliados. Breakfast included. ❸

Pensão Residencial Duas Nações Pr. Guilherme Gomes Fernandes 59 ☎222 081 616, Ⓦwww.duasnacoes.com.pt. Tottering over a café, this is real gem, one of the cheapest in town. The modern rooms have central heating, some with bathrooms and TVs, while most have double-glazing. Also friendly English-speaking staff and internet access. No credit cards. ❶

Pensão Estoril Rua de Cedofeita 193-1° ☎222 002 751, Ⓦwww.pensaoestoril.com. En-suite rooms in varying shapes and sizes over a jewellers and café on a pedestrianized street (parking is some way away). Rooms are rather bare and have saggy beds, though five have balconies overlooking a lush garden at the back, and all have TVs. Breakfast included. ❸

Pensão Europa Rua do Almada 396 ☎222 006 971. Gloomy but very cheap, and with a lively bar

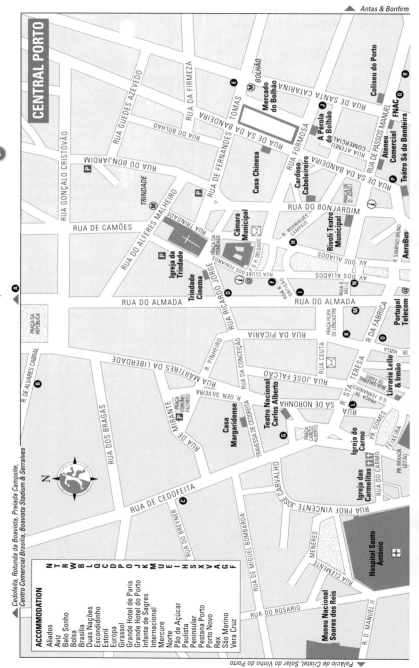

CENTRAL PORTO

PORTO AND THE DOURO

5

ACCOMMODATION

Aliados	N
Aviz	T
Belo Sonho	R
Bolsa	W
Brasília	B
Duas Nações	L
Escondidinho	Q
Estoril	C
Europa	D
Girassol	P
Grande Hotel de Paris	O
Grande Hotel do Porto	J
Infante de Sagres	K
Internacional	M
Mercure	U
Norte	I
Pão de Açúcar	H
Paulista	S
Peninsular	X
Pestana Porto	V
Porto Novo	A
Rex	G
São Marino	F

Antas & Bonfirm

Cedofeita, Rotunda da Boavista, Prelada Campsite,
Centro Comercial Brasília, Boavista Stadium & Serralves

Palácio de Cristal, Solar do Vinho do Porto

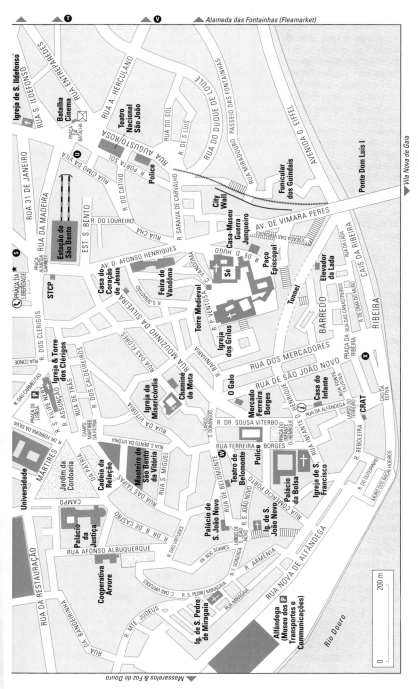

▲ Vila Nova de Gaia

Rio Douro

200 m

0

▲ Massarelos & Foz do Douro

▲ Alameda das Fontainhas (Fleamarket)

Igreja de S. Ildefonso

Batalha Cinema

Teatro Nacional São João

RUA S. ILDEFONSO

RUA ENTREPAREDES

RUA A. HERCULANO

RUA 31 DE JANEIRO

RUA DA MADEIRA

PRAÇA DA BATALHA

RUA CIMO DA VILA

RUA PORTA SOL

RUA AUGUSTO ROSA

RUA DO SOL

R. DE S. LUIS

RUA DO DUQUE DE LOULÉ

PASSEIO DAS FONTAINHAS

RUA MIRADOURO

Police

R. DO CATIVO

RUA CHÃ

EST. S. BENTO

R. DO LOUREIRO

Estação de São Bento

R. SARAIVA DE CARVALHO

City Wall

Casa-Museu Guerra Junqueiro

AV. DE VIMARA PERES

Funicular dos Guindais

AVENIDA G. EIFFEL

Ponte Dom Luís I

PRAÇA DA LIBERDADE ★

PRAÇA ALMEIDA GARRETT

STCP

AV. D. AFONSO HENRIQUES

Casa do Coração de Jesus

Feira de Vandôma

R. S. SEBASTIÃO

Sé

Paço Episcopal

C. VANDOMA

R. DE D. HUGO

Torre Medieval

Igreja dos Grilos

R. P. VENTOSA

Tunnel

Elevador da Lada

ESTRADA DAS VERDADES

BARREDO

CAIS DA RIBEIRA

RUA DA LADA

RUA DOS CLÉRIGOS

RUA CONDE

Igreja & Torre dos Clérigos

R. DE TRÁS

RUA DAS FLORES

RUA DOS CALDEIREIROS

RUA MOUZINHO DA SILVEIRA

RUA DA BAINHARIA

RUA DOS MERCADORES

RUA DE SÃO JOÃO NOVO

PRAÇA DA RIBEIRA

RIBEIRA

RUA DA ALFÂNDEGA

R. DE OMAR DO MURO

R. DA CANASTREIROS

R. DAS CARMELITAS

R. S. FILIPE NÉRI

R. ASSUNÇÃO

PRAÇA DE LISBOA

Igreja da Misericórdia

RUA DA VITÓRIA

Chaminé da Mota

LARGO S. DOMINGOS

O Galo

Mercado Ferreira Borges

Casa do Infante

CRAT

CASA DA ESTIVA

RUA DA FONTE TAURINA

LARGO DO FERREIRO

R. REBOLEIRA

R. DA FERREIRA DA SILVA

CAMPO MÁRTIRES DA PÁTRIA

MÁRTIRES

Universidade

Jardim da Cordoaria

CAMPO

Palácio da Justiça

Cadeia da Relação

Mosteiro de São Bento da Vitória

RUA DAS TAIPAS

RUA S. MIGUEL

RUA S. BENTO DA VITÓRIA

Teatro de Belomonte

RUA DR. SOUSA VITERBO

RUA FERREIRA BORGES

Police

Palácio da Bolsa

Igreja de S. Francisco

RUA INFANTE D. HENRIQUE

PALÁCIO RENATO D. HENRIQUE

RUA DA PÁTRIA

DA B. DE CASTRO

Cooperativa Árvore

Palácio de S. João Novo

RUA DE BELOMONTE

RUA JOÃO NOVO

R. S. JOÃO NOVO

Ig. de S. João Novo

RUA DO COMÉRCIO PORTO

R. ROC. SOARES

LARGO DE S. JOÃO NOVO

RUA NOVA DE ALFÂNDEGA

R. REBOLEIRA

R. DO OUTEIRINHO

MURO DOS BACALHOEIROS

RUA AFONSO ALBUQUERQUE

RUA DA RESTAURAÇÃO

RUA DA BANDEIRINHA

R. MTE. JUDEUS

Ig. de S. Pedro de Miragaia

R. S. PEDRO MIRAGAIA

RUA MIRAGAIA

C. DAS VIRTUDES

R. DAS VIRTUDES

R. T. GONZAGA

R. ARMÉNIA

Alfândega (Museu dos Transportes e Communicações)

and good restaurant; more expensive rooms come with showers. No credit cards. **❶**

Grande Hotel de Paris Rua da Fábrica 27–29 ⓣ 222 073 140, Ⓦ www.ghparis.pt. More modest than the name suggests, this popular *pensão* has friendly and helpful owners. Founded in 1888 and recently renovated, the building retains many of its original fittings, with period furniture and high ceilings in its en-suite bedrooms, some with balconies, plus a splendid drawing room for breakfast, a "pub", library and small garden. Breakfast included. **❸**

Hotel Infante de Sagres Pr. Dona Filipa de Lencastre 62 ⓣ223 398 500, Ⓦwww.hotelinfantesagres.pt. Luxurious five-star hotel on six floors, its public areas, restaurant and bar lavishly furnished with Persian carpets, crystal chandeliers, Carrara marble, Chinese porcelain and stained-glass windows. Sadly, the bedrooms – whilst more than comfortable – reflect little of this opulence. There's also an open-air patio for light meals, a cocktail bar and sundeck; public parking nearby. Breakfast included. **❼**

Hotel Internacional Rua do Almada 131 ⓣ 222 005 032, Ⓦ www.hi-porto.com. Behind an impressive nineteenth-century facade, this mid-range hotel conserves some of its original decor, including stonework and statues, and has comfortable rooms, those on the second floor (lift access) with balconies. Its restaurant – *O Almada* – is well regarded for traditional cuisine, and a bar occupies a granite-arched cellar. Breakfast included. **❹**

Residencial Pão de Açúcar Rua do Almada 262 ⓣ222 002 425, Ⓦwww.residencialpaodeacucar.com. Stylish and well-kept, if overpriced, 1930s Art Deco hotel close to the town hall. There are fifty reasonably large and quiet rooms, most with bathrooms, all with heavy furniture, phone, mini-bar and TV. Expensive parking nearby. Breakfast included. **❺**

Residencial Paulista Av. dos Aliados 214-2º ⓣ 222 054 692, Ⓔ residencial.paulista@iol.pt. Well-placed if modest and fusty pension popular with pilgrims en route to Santiago de Compostela. Comfortable en-suite rooms and TVs; ones at the back are quieter. Breakfast included. **❸**

Hotel Peninsular Rua Sá da Bandeira 21 ⓣ 222 003 012, Ⓔ hotel.peninsular@clix.pt. Comfortable and welcoming family-run *pensão* with a range of rooms, most with private bath and TV. The *azulejos* in the entrance reveal it to have been an outbuilding of the nearby church. Also has a bar and restaurant. Breakfast included. **❸**

Residencial Rex Pr. da República 117 ⓣ222 074 590, Ⓔr.rex@netcabo.pt. Facing the garden square, this refined 1845 town house has the

feel of a grand hotel, with spacious, old-fashioned en-suite rooms, some with great views over the city. Front rooms can be very noisy, but it's especially recommended for its unfailingly helpful staff. Access is up a staircase. Free parking; bus #95 from Av. dos Aliados. Breakfast included. **❹**

Residencial São Marino Pr. Carlos Alberto 59 ⓣ223 325 499, Ⓔresidencialmarino@sapo.pt. Facing a pleasant garden square near the Torre dos Clérigos, it's a friendly place with clean rooms, all with shower and most with TV; those at the back are quieter and cheaper. Breakfast included. **❸**

Residencial Vera Cruz Rua Ramalho Ortigão 14 ⓣ223 323 396, Ⓕ223 323 421. An elegant little *pensão* close to the main tourist office, with pleasant, calm rooms with new bathrooms, and efficient service. Breakfast included. **❸**

Batalha and eastwards

Pensão Residencial Aviz Av. Rodrigues de Freitas 451 ⓣ 222 008 937, Ⓔ aviz@netc.pt. Head along Rua de Entre Paredes from Batalha, and take the first right. Dozens of clean en-suite rooms in this calm and friendly pension, all with cable TV. Also a small bar. Breakfast included. **❸**

Residencial Belo Sonho Rua de Passos Manuel 186 ⓣ 222 003 389, Ⓕ 222 012 850. Basic rooms with not much in them – some (slightly more expensive) have en-suite showers. Breakfast included. No credit cards. **❷**

Residencial Escondidinho Rua de Passos Manuel 135 ⓣ 222 004 079, Ⓕ 222 026 075. Twenty-three spacious, if somewhat tired, en-suite rooms, though they do have polished wooden floors, bathrooms and TVs. Lift access. Breakfast included. **❸**

Pensão Girassol Rua Sá da Bandeira 131–133 ⓣ 222 001 891, Ⓕ 222 001 892. The central location is the main reason for staying here, though the rooms – all with baths and most with TVs – are perfectly adequate, and there's a good restaurant below. Breakfast included. **❸**

Grande Hotel do Porto Rua de Santa Catarina 197 ⓣ222 076 690, Ⓦwww.grandehotelporto.com. Along the pedestrian section of the shopping street, this is Porto's oldest and most delightful hotel, steeped in nineteenth-century mercantile style, with tons of polished marble, crystal chandeliers and uniformed valets. Rooms have all mod cons, some with wheelchair access, and there's also a restaurant, bar, room service, baby sitting and car park. Breakfast included. **❺**

Hotel Mercure Batalha Pr. da Batalha 116 ⓣ 222 043 300, Ⓦ www.mercure.com. The better but pricier of the two large conference-style hotels on this square, with bright and well-equipped rooms, lift access and disabled facilities, moderately priced car parking and a restaurant. Breakfast included. ⑤

Pensão do Norte Rua de Fernandes Tomás 579 ⊤222 003 503. Opposite an extravagantly tiled church, this pleasant, rambling old place has masses of rooms with and without bathrooms. The best have balconies overlooking the street, though these can be noisy. Breakfast included. ②

Residencial Porto Novo Rua Alexandre Herculano 185 ⊤222 055 739, ⓦwww.residencialportonovo .com. Clean and comfortable slightly old-fashioned rooms with TVs, phones and showers, those on the top floor with magnificent river views from their balconies. Friendly staff, but no English spoken. ②

Boavista

Le Meridien Park Atlantic Av. da Boavista 1466 ⊤800 880 424, ⓦ www.lemeridien-oporto.com. Extremely plush, well-run international five-star hotel, best of the bunch around Boavista, with over two hundred rooms, plus swimming pools, restaurants and health club. You'll pay more for rooms on the 14th and 15th floors. Wheelchair access and specially designed rooms and public bathrooms. Parking. ⑦.

Foz do Douro

Hotel Boa-Vista Esplanada do Castelo 58 ⊤225 320 020, ⓦ www.hotelboavista.com. A grand French Renaissance hotel at the mouth of the Douro with over seventy rooms – book ahead to be sure of a view over the ocean, river and fortress. The rooms are comfortable if unexceptional, but there's a nice rooftop pool and sun terrace, and a bar and restaurant. Parking available. Breakfast included. ⑤

Residencial Portofoz Rua do Farol 155 ⊤226 172 357, ⓦ www.portofoz.com. A characterful two-star *pensão* with good, if old-fashioned rooms, with heavy furniture, though modern creature comforts including sparkling bathrooms and cable TV, and there's a cosy bar. Reception is on the first floor; rooms are higher up, some with ocean views. Breakfast included. ④

Youth hostel

Pousada de Juventude Rua Paulo da Gama 551, Pasteleira, 4km west of the centre ⊤226 177 257, ⓦ www.pousadasjuventude.pt. Over 100 beds in four-bed dorms, plus 24 en-suite doubles. Facilities include a kitchen (meals available), bar, and arrangements for disabled guests. Reception open 9–10am & 6pm–midnight; it's essential to book ahead in summer. Bus #35 (from Campanhã and São Bento stations, Cordoaria and Pr. da Batalha) and #36 (from Rotunda da Boavista) pass by, or catch bus #1 (São Bento, also at night from Pr. da Liberdade) or #24 (Cordoaria) and get off at "Fluvial", 400m away. Dorm beds €15, rooms ③

Campsites

Marisol Rua Alto das Chaquedas 82 near Praia do Canidelo, 10km south of the city ⊤227 135 942, ⓦ www.roteiro-campista.pt. Fifty metres from the beach, and small by Portuguese standards (150 pitches). Bus #57 from São Bento.

Orbitur Angeiras, Lavra, 13km north of the city ⊤229 270 571, ⓦ www.orbitur.pt. Set 1km back from the beach, with good ocean views from its grove of pine trees; bus #45 from Boavista (no nightbuses).

Orbitur Praia da Madalena, 10km south of the city ⊤227 122 520, ⓦ www.orbitur.pt. Five hundred metres from the beach, with a swimming pool, tennis and volleyball courts, and some caravans for rent (③). Bus #57 from São Bento, or an Espírito Santo bus from Rua Mouzinho da Silveira, southwest of São Bento. Minimum stay 2 days, or 1 week in July & Aug.

Parque de Campismo da Prelada Rua Monte dos Burgos, 3km northwest of the centre ⊤228 312 616, ⓦ www.roteiro-campista.pt. The closest campsite to the city but, with 650 pitches, it's not exactly intimate; take buses #50, #54 or #87 from Cordoaria, #87 or the AeroBus from the airport, or #6 from Av. dos Aliados (last at 8.50pm).

Salgueiros Rua do Campismo, near Praia do Canidelo, 10km south of the city ⊤227 810 500, ⓦwww.roteiro–campista.pt. Similar to Marisol but a little larger; catch an Espirito Santo bus marked "Paniceiro - Praia de Salgueiros" from Rua Mouzinho da Silveira, southwest of São Bento. Closed Oct–April.

The City

Central Porto is perhaps best regarded as the sloping **Avenida dos Aliados**, the commercial hub of the city, with Praça da Liberdade at its southern end; just around the corner (reached via a pedestrian underpass) is São Bento train station, with the partially pedestrianized **Praça da Batalha** behind here. The streets leading off Avenida dos Aliados are the city's major shopping

Porto's architecture

An English-language pamphlet (€1) produced by Porto Tours (p.313) and also available from the Rua Clube dos Fenianos turismo, details four **architectural city walks**, each focusing on a particular style. All major sights are included, but there's a lot of uphill legwork involved.

The city's oldest secular building is the **medieval** Alfândega Velha (or Casa do Infante), built in 1324, while from the same period date parts of the city wall flanking the Cais da Ribeira, completed in the reign of Dom Fernando. The district of **Barredo**, clinging to the steep incline behind the wall, is in appearance probably very close to how the city looked in medieval times. Unfortunately, most churches and chapels were greatly altered in the eighteenth century, but the simple **Romanesque and Gothic** aesthetic remains apparent in the outward appearance of the Sé and the old church of Cedofeita – arguably Iberia's oldest Christian temple.

The bulk of Porto's churches date from the eighteenth century, and provide one of the country's richest concentrations of **Baroque** architecture. The style was brought to Portugal by Italian painter and architect **Nicolau Nasoni** (1691–1773), who arrived in Porto at the age of 34, and remained here all his life. Together with local stonemason António Pereira, Nasoni bequeathed the city a marvellous legacy, characterized by his masterful conception of space, clever use of local granite, and often theatrical facades. The church and tower of Clérigos is perhaps his greatest work; others include the interior of the Sé, the adjacent Paço Episcopal, the palace now housing the Casa-Museu Guerra Junqueiro, the facade of the Igreja da Misericórdia, and the churches of Carmo, Santo Ildefonso and São Francisco. All are remarkable for their decorative exuberance – notably cascading masses of intricate carvings, and lots of gold leaf – which reflects the wealth derived from Portugal's colonies.

In the second half of the eighteenth century, out went the luxuriant complexity of Baroque and in came the studied lines, pillars and capitals of ancient Rome and Greece. This **Neoclassical** period coincided with the booming port wine trade, which provided the necessary finance for the first concerted attempts at treating whole districts as architectural entities: the riverside **Praça da Ribeira** was entirely

areas: to the west, the busy Rua da Fábrica with its stationers and bookshops; to the east, Rua de Passos Manuel, which runs into Praça Dom João I, and beyond into **Rua de Santa Catarina** with its upmarket fashion shops and jewellers.

South of the landmark **Torre dos Clérigos**, a labyrinth of medieval streets and seedy alleyways tumble below the **Sé**, or cathedral, down to the waterfront **Cais da Ribeira**, which is lined with restaurants, bars, clubs and cafés. Here, the lower of the two tiers of **Ponte Luís I** runs across the river to Vila Nova de Gaia and its port wine lodges (see p.319). The other main points of interest are all to the west of the centre, particularly the religious art collections of the **Museu Nacional Soares dos Reis**, and the old streetcars at the riverfront **Museu do Carro Eléctrico**. You can walk around much of the city centre, and even out to outlying attractions like the **Solar do Vinho do Porto**, but you'll need to use public transport at some stage. The main outlying target is Porto's world-class **Museu de Arte Contemporânea de Serralves**, though trams and buses also run along the river to the former fishermen's suburb of **Foz de Douro** on the coast, or down Avenida da Boavista to the city's largest park, **Parque de Cidade**, and beyond to the stumpy seaside **Castelo de Queijo**.

redesigned, broad avenues were opened, and much of the city's medieval wall gave way to riverside esplanades. Neoclassicism also incorporated other art forms: hints of Gothic and Baroque, but most of all, Islamic, which reached its apotheosis in the Salão Árabe of the Palácio da Bolsa.

The Neoclassical period lasted over a century, by the end of which it had acquired a distinctly French Renaissance touch, thanks largely to the architect **José Marques da Silva** (1869–1947), who studied in Paris. His legacy includes two notable works: São Bento railway station (1900), and the Teatro Nacional São João (1909). Da Silva also designed the distinctly less elegant monument to the Peninsular War that dominates the Rotunda da Boavista. **Art Nouveau** saw little monumental expression in Porto, although several shops in this style survive, particularly the gaudy facade of the Pérola do Bolhão grocery (Rua Formsoa 279) and the beautiful Livraria Lello & Irmão (Rua das Carmelitas 144). The 1920s coincided with the establishment of the fascist **Estado Novo**, whose buildings acquired a heavy, morose character. The Palácio da Justiça (law court) facing the Cordoaria is a prime example, its monumental blank facade bearing angular "heroic" sculptures, not so different from the Soviet socialist-realism of the period.

Not until the 1950s did Porto see the emergence of a style of architecture that it could call its own, with the beginning of the so-called **Porto School**, centred on the city's School of Fine Arts. This proved fertile ground for many of Porto's **contemporary architects**, including Eduardo Souto Moura (Casa das Artes, and the conversion of the Alfândega), Alcino Soutinho (the conversion of the Casa-Museu Guerra Junqueiro; and Amarante's Museu Amadeo Sousa Cardoso), and – most famously – **Álvaro Siza Vieira**, best known for his redesign of Lisbon's fire-gutted Chiado district. In Porto, his masterpiece is the Museu de Arte Contemporânea de Serralves (1999), which uses natural light to its best effect. Also worth visiting are a couple of his works in Leça da Palmeira, north of the city: the imaginative *Casa de Chá da Boa Nova* (1958–63), unobtrusively built into the rocks and with a grand ocean vista, and the Piscina de Mar swimming pool, 2km before it and similarly hidden in the rocks by the shore.

Avenida dos Aliados to Batalha

The central Avenida dos Aliados is as good a starting point as any, with cafés at the foot of the avenue and the **Câmara Municipal** (1920–56), at its head, designed to look a good deal older than it is in order to fit in with the square's otherwise Neoclassical design. Off the southeastern side of the avenue, the **Estação de São Bento**, on Praça Almeida Garrett, is one of the city's grandest buildings. Designed by José Marques da Silva and opened in 1903, the entrance hall contains 20,000 magnificent *azulejos* painted by Jorge Colaço. These – somewhat arbitrarily – take on two great themes: the history of transport, and the history of Portugal, including the battle of Aljubarrota and the taking of Ceuta. North of the station, and just three blocks east of the avenue, along Rua Formosa, the **Mercado do Bolhão** (Mon–Fri 8am–5pm, Sat 8am–1pm) is a nineteenth-century wrought-iron construction selling meat and fish, fruit and veg, and flowers. On **Rua Formosa** itself, look for the few surviving antiquated *mercearias* (groceries), that hang their wares outside. *Bacalhau* (salt cod) is also bundled up in stacks around the counters, alongside just about every type of port available, plus cheeses and smoked sausages. Two blocks south of Bolhão, the **Ateneu Comercial do Porto**, Rua de Passos Manuel 44, is an opulent nineteenth-century mansion housing Porto's commercial association. Its gloriously decorated halls house temporary exhibitions of ceramics and postage stamps (daily 2–7.30pm; free).

At the top of the steep Rua da Madeira and Rua 31 de Janeiro, both leading from São Bento, the sunny **Praça da Batalha** is a pleasant resting point during the day, and there are several cheap restaurants around here, too. The square is dominated by the gorgeously over-the-top **Teatro Nacional São João**, built in 1909 and inspired by the Louvre and Charles Garnier's Paris Opera. At the north end of the square, the eighteenth-century **Igreja de Santo Ildefonso** (Mon–Fri 8.30am–noon & 3–6.30pm, Sat until 7.45pm, Sun 9am–12.45pm & 6–7.45pm) has more lovely *azulejo* panels by Jorge Colaço, livening up an otherwise graceless facade.

South of the square, down Rua Augusto Rosa, is the terminal for the new **Funicular dos Guindais** (every 10min, Tues–Sun 8am–7pm; metro tickets valid), reinstalled in 2004 after a 111-year hiatus. After a 90-metre dash through a tunnel, the two carriages clamber down a painfully steep 1-in-3 gradient beside the medieval city wall, emerging on Avenida Gustavo Eiffel, next to the lower level of the Ponte Luís I.

Clérigos, Cordoaria and around

The stifled streets of the old town make it difficult to get your bearings, so it's a good idea to climb the Baroque **Torre dos Clérigos**, on Rua São Filipe Nery, 300m west of the bottom end of Aliados (April–Oct 9.30am –1pm & 2–7pm, all day Aug; Nov–March 10am–noon & 2–5pm; €1), for a dizzying aerial view of the city. At 75.6 metres, it was the tallest structure in Portugal when completed in 1763. Like the curious oval **Igreja dos Clérigos** beneath it (Mon–Sat 9am–noon & 3.30–7.30pm, Sun 10am–1pm & 8.30–10.30pm), the landmark was designed by the Italian architect Nasoni, though the actual construction is the work of master stonemasons António Pereira and Miguel Francisco da Silva. Inside, the highlight is a polychromatic Baroque-Rococo marble retable by Manuel dos Santos Porto.

The area immediately below the tower comprises the older sections of the university and the **Jardim da Cordoaria**. At the southeastern corner of the gardens on Rua São Bento da Vitória is an imposing Neoclassical building distinguished by 103 – mostly barred – windows. This is the city's former prison, the **Cadeia da Relação** (Mon–Fri 9am–noon & 2–5.30pm; free). Restored in the 1990s, the cells can now be visited, including the ones that held the writer Camilo Castelo Branco and his lover, after their adulterous romance turned public (the couple later married). The ground floor houses the **Centro Português de Fotografia** (Tues–Fri 3–6pm, Sat & Sun 3–7pm; free), with both permanent and temporary exhibitions. The collection includes the work of Scotsman, Frederick William Flower (1815–1889), who spent much of his life in Porto and is considered a pioneer of Portuguese photography: his snaps – mostly of Porto and Gaia – are the country's oldest.

The area north and west of the Cordoaria is a fairly prestigious quarter housing most of the city's commercial art galleries, either on Rua Galeria de Paris, facing the Torre dos Clérigos, and along Rua Miguel Bombarda, off Rua de Cedofeita. Worth a particular mention is **Cooperativa Árvore** (Mon–Fri 9am–11pm, Sat 3–7pm & 9.30–11pm, Sun 3–8pm; ⓦwww.arvorecoop.pt), Rua Azevedo de Albuquerque 1, behind the Palácio da Justiça. It's a co-operative of painters, sculptors and designers who run their own art school in close competition with the official Escola das Belas Artes (itself housed in a nearby mansion). The artists pride themselves on the vitality of their teaching and the freedom they allow their pupils, the results of which are on view in a punchy summer show in June and July.

One hundred metres north of the Jardim da Cordoaria, at the corner of Rua do Carmo and Praça Carlos Alberto, lies the eighteenth-century **Igreja do Carmo** (Mon–Fri 8am–noon & 2–5pm, Sat 8am–noon, Sun 7.30am–1pm), with deliriously over-the-top *azulejos*, the work of Silvestre Silvestri (1910–12). Inside, the elegant gilt carvings – including all seven altars – are by Francisco Pereira Campanhã, and are among the finest examples of Portuguese Rococo. The older and rather more sober **Igreja das Carmelitas** (Mon–Sat 8.30–11am & 3–5pm, Sun 5–7pm) is almost adjacent, but not quite, as a law stipulated that no two churches were to share the same wall (in this case perhaps to hinder amorous liaisons between the nuns of Carmelitas and the monks of Carmo). As a result, what is probably the **narrowest house in Portugal** – barely a metre wide – was built between them, and remained inhabited until the 1980s.

The Sé and down to Ponte Dom Luís I

Set on a rocky outcrop, a couple of hundred metres south of São Bento station, the **Sé** (April–Oct Mon–Sat 8.45am–12.30pm & 2.30–7pm, Sun & hols 8.30am–12.30pm & 2.30–7pm; Nov–March closes 6pm; free) sports fine views over the rooftops of old Porto. Despite wholesale remodelling of its interior in the eighteenth century by António Pereira, the cathedral retains the austere, fortress-like lines of its twelfth-century origins. On the north tower, look for the bas-relief depicting a fourteenth-century ship – a reminder of the earliest days of Portugal's maritime epic, when sailors were still inching tentatively down the west Saharan coastline in fear of monsters. Inside, the blend of Baroque, original Romanesque and Gothic architecture is a strange marriage, not much aided by the prevailing gloom, and even Nasoni's vaunted silver altarpiece and the gilt retable by his collaborator, Miguel Francisco da Silva, fail to impress. However, for €2, you can escape into the neighbouring **cloisters** (April–Oct Mon–Sat 9am–12.15pm & 2.30–6pm, Sun & hols 2.30–6pm; Nov–March closes 5.15pm), with their magnificent *azulejos* designed by Baroque master António Vital Rifarto, and murals by Nasoni – some of his earliest work (circa 1725–31). Climb the staircase up to the dazzling chapterhouse (*Casa do Cabido*) for more of Rifarto's *azulejos*, plus sweeping views from the casement windows and a collection of sacred art, including a fourteenth-century image of Nossa Senhora da Vandôma.

On the north side of the Sé is the squat **Torre Medieval**, discovered in the 1940s during demolition work to clear the courtyard around the cathedral. Relocated, and completely rebuilt in the 1950s, the tower now houses the "Porto Tours" booking centre for trips and tours around the city (see p.302). On the south side of the Sé stretches the grandiose three-storey arched façade of the **Paço Episcopal** (not open to the public), the medieval archbishop's palace that was completely rebuilt in 1737. Opposite the palace, at Rua de Dom Hugo 32, is the beautiful **Casa-Museu Guerra Junqueiro** (Tues–Sat 10am–12.30pm & 2–5.30pm, Sun 2–5.30pm; €0.75, free at weekends). Framed by two low towers, this Baroque building later became home to the poet Guerra Junqueiro (1850–1923), who spent a lifetime collecting Portuguese and Islamic art, especially Iberian. Seljuk pottery, miniatures and glassware, painting and faience (glazed earthenware), are exhibited in rooms recapturing the atmosphere of the poet's last home. Close by, at Rua de Dom Hugo 15, is the **Multivisão** (every 40min, Tues–Sat except hols: July–Sept 2.30–6.05pm; Oct–May 2.30–4.55pm; €2), a 3D exhibition concerning Porto's history – basically, a thirty-minute 3D cinematic introduction to the city in several languages.

Rua de Dom Hugo curls around the south side of the cathedral to merge with the crumbling stairways and alleys that plunge down to the riverside through the most fascinating part of the city: a medieval maze of backstreets that would have been demolished or prettified in most other European cities. The tall, narrow and rickety houses have grown upwards into every available space, adapting as best they can to the terrain, while children try their best to play ball games on the steep staircases. The most atmospheric of them is the **Escada das Verdades** – the Staircase of Truths – which gives fantastic views of the girders of Ponte Dom Luís I as you descend.

Ponte Dom Luís I and east along the river

Porto's iconic bridge, **Ponte Dom Luís I**, is a real delight, and one of the city's most photogenic spots – at its most enchanting on mornings when the overnight mist is clearing. Designed by Belgian engineer Teófilo Seyrig, the bridge was inaugurated in 1886 to replace the short-lived Ponte Pênsil, part of whose obelisk-shaped pillars stand rather pointlessly beside it, topped by Doric capitals and bronze spheres. Local children have taken to leaping off the bridge's lower tier into the foul waters of the Douro for the benefit of tourists – watch out for pickpockets as you gape.

To the east of Ponte Dom Luís I are four more bridges, best seen from the comfort of a "six bridges" cruise; see p.304. The first, about 600m upriver, is also the newest: the 371-metre **Ponte Infante Dom Henrique** (or Ponte do Infante), whose central 280-metre reinforced concrete arch is the world's longest. Four hundred metres further upriver, around a bend, is the impressive **Ponte Dona Maria Pia**, an iron railway bridge, completed in 1876. Designed by Gustave Eiffel and named after Dom Luís I's wife, it remained in service until 1991, when it was replaced by Edgar Cardoso's adjacent triple-arched **Ponte de São João**. Another kilometre beyond here is the surprisingly elegant **Ponte do Freixo** road bridge. Close by, on the Estrada Nacional tracing the north bank of river, the **Museu Nacional da Imprensa** (daily 3–8pm; €1) is dedicated to the art of printing. Aside from dozens of presses that you're encouraged to play with, the museum has a great collection of newspaper caricatures, and hosts the annual PortoCartoon World Festival (mid-June to Sept). Bus #88 runs to here from the Alfândega, downriver, skirting Ribeira.

Ribeira

Not much commerce goes on down at the waterfront – the **Ribeira** – since the big ships stopped calling here a century ago, but along **Cais da Ribeira** – the area between Ponte Dom Luís I and the Praça da Ribeira – old men still sit around as if they expect to be thrown a line or set to work unloading some urgent cargo. There's some bustle around the weekday fruit and vegetable **market** but it's really at night that the riverfront comes alive, with dozens of cafés, clubs and restaurants to tickle your sensations. The area is best seen from the top of the iron **Elevador da Lada** (daily 8am–10pm; free) at the eastern end of the Cais, which climbs achingly close to the top of the Bairro da Sé, but as it's fenced in you won't be able to disembark.

Cais da Ribeira is flanked for the most part by the city's fourteenth-century **wall** and its four gates, completed in the reign of Dom Fernando. Behind the wall and arcades – apparently modelled on the City of London's medieval wharfs – is the mazelike warren of stairs and alleyways that form the Dickensian district of **Barredo**, much of it left untouched for centuries, and which lies at the heart of the city's historic centre. Close to the bridge, a bronze plaque commemorates the tragedy of the Ponte das Barcas when, in 1809, hundreds of people tried to flee the French siege of Porto by crossing the pontoon bridge to Gaia, which collapsed. Lighted candles in memory of the victims are still left there today.

At the western end of the Cais is the **Praça da Ribeira**, whose arcaded pavement bars and cafés provide the most popular spot in the city for a drink. Originally a medieval market, the square was transformed in the eighteenth century when the medieval wall was knocked down to open the place to the river. The northern facade is bounded by the **Fonte da Rua de São João**, a strange fountain bearing the Portuguese coat-of-arms and three empty niches that receive images of the local saints during the Santos Populares celebrations in June. In the centre of the square is another fountain, dominated by a 1970s bronze cube (*O Cubo*, by José Rodrigues) topped with metal pigeons; much loved by real pigeons, needless to say.

Heading west along the delightfully poky Rua da Fonte Taurina, with its stylish bars and restaurants, turn north up Rua da Alfândega for the **Casa do Infante** or Alfândega Velha (Tues–Sat 10am–12.30pm & 2–5.30pm, Sun 2–5.30pm; free), where Prince Henry the Navigator is said to have been born in 1394. It's an impressive mansion, constructed in 1324 by Dom Afonso IV following a dispute with the Bishopric over control of taxes, and for over five centuries it served as the Crown's customs house, extracting taxes from both river and marine traffic. Successively enlarged to cope with Porto's growth (the current facade conceals the original medieval one), it was finally abandoned in favour of the new Alfândega, a few hundred metres west. However, the building's original fabric has miraculously remained largely intact and now contains the city archives, a museum displaying finds from *in situ* excavations that revealed the remains of a large Roman palace, and – in the building's northern extension – a small turismo.

The Bolsa and around

Porto's stock exchange – the **Palácio da Bolsa** – is a pompous nineteenth-century edifice with a vast Neoclassical facade, whose keepers are inordinately proud of it. During the half-hour **guided tours** (daily: April–Oct 9am–7pm; Nov–March 9am–1pm & 2–6pm, Ⓦwww.palaciodabolsa.pt; €5) they dwell, with evident glee, on the enormous cost of every item, the exact weight of every piece of precious metal, and the intimate details of anyone with any claim to fame ever to have passed through the doors. The highlight is the Salão Árabe, an oval chamber designed by Gonçalves de Sousa who perhaps misguidedly attempted to copy Granada's transcendent Alhambra Palace; here the guide's superlatives achieve apotheosis. You can always see the elegant iron-and-glass-covered Pátio das Nações courtyard without having to buy a ticket.

Adjoining the Bolsa is the **Igreja de São Francisco** (daily: May–Aug 9am–7pm, March, April, Sept & Oct 9am–6pm; Nov–Feb 9am–5pm; €3), perhaps the most extraordinary church in Porto (now deconsecrated). From its entrance on Rua de São Francisco it looks an ordinary enough Gothic construction (indeed, the city's only truly Gothic survivor, dating from the fourteenth century), but the interior was completely transformed by a fabulously opulent eighteenth-century refurbishment. Altar, pillars, even the ceiling, drip with gilded Rococo carvings, reaching their ultimate expression in an interpretation of the Tree of Jesse on the north wall. Don't miss the church's small **museum**, housed in the catacombs below – although the entrance is opposite the church – which consists of artefacts salvaged from the former monastery. Beneath the flags of the cellar is an *ossário* – thousands of human bones, cleaned up and stored to await Judgement Day. Until 1839, public cemeteries didn't exist in Porto and the dead were buried in and around churches in an effort to bring them closer to God.

Two other churches in this neighbourhood also have small museums. Pride of the **Igreja da Misericórdia** (church Tues–Sun 8am–noon & 2.30–5.30pm, closed Aug; museum Mon–Fri 9.30am–noon & 2–5.30pm; €1.50), a couple of blocks north on Rua das Flores, is a remarkable *fons vitae*, depicting Dom Manuel I with his wife Leonor and eight children, richly clothed, kneeling before the crucified Christ. Donated to the church by the king in 1518, academics still dispute the nationality of the unknown artist, but no matter: it's an exceptional example of Flemish-style realism in the manner of Van Eyck and the School of Brussels. The church itself was constructed in the sixteenth century, and largely remodelled after its dome collapsed in 1748. The opulent facade – a painterly blend of Mannerism and Rococo – dates from 1750, and is the work of Nasoni.

Over to the west, in the **Igreja de São Pedro de Miragaia** (Tues–Sat 4.30–7.30pm, Sun 10–11.30am), on a *largo* of the same name, is another fine fifteenth-century Flemish triptych, depicting the descent of the Holy Spirit over the Apostles, flanked by St John the Baptist and St Paul. The Baroque high altar, sculpted in 1724 by António Gomes and Caetano da Silva Pinto, is noteworthy for being almost entirely gilded.

Museu Nacional Soares dos Reis and around

The **Museu Nacional Soares dos Reis**, Rua Dom Manuel II 44 (Tues 2–6pm, Wed–Sun 10am–6pm; Ⓦwww.mnsr-ipmuseus.pt; €3), was Portugal's first designated national museum, founded in 1833 to preserve works of art confiscated from dissolved monasteries and convents. The present building, into which the collection moved in 1940, is the Neoclassical Palácio das Carrancas, a royal residence that served as French headquarters in the Peninsular War. The museum contains excellent collections of glass, ceramics and gold jewellery, and a formidable display of eighteenth- and nineteenth-century Portuguese art. Highlights include sculptures by Soares dos Reis (*O Desterrado* – "The Exiled" – is probably his best-known work) and his pupil, Teixeira Lopes (who has his own museum across the river in Vila Nova de Gaia, see p.322). A more curious highlight is the huge Pedra de Eiró in the corridor behind the reception, a rock taken from a threshing ground close to Marco de Canavezes, along the Douro. The engraved spiral motifs are a typical if still deeply mysterious feature of western European megalithic art of the Neolithic period.

Follow the road for 100m or so past the Museu Soares dos Reis and you reach the **Jardim do Palácio de Cristal** (daily 8am–9pm), a beautiful park dominated by a huge domed pavilion, built in 1956 to replace an 1860s iron-and-glass "Crystal Palace". The pavilion now serves as a venue for all sorts of concerts and events, and there's also a children's playground and various hands-on activities with an environmental theme (daily 9am–5.30pm; free), including a "sound centre" with interactive recordings of natural sounds and instruments, and the great **Laboratório Micro-Mundo Vivo** with its microscopic views of fungi, bacteria, bugs and algae. The park itself offers peaceful shaded strolls along the wooded paths, though there's also an **art gallery** (Tues–Sun 10am –6pm) and a bandstand which, in summer, hosts pop and classical concerts.

Around the back of the park, accessed near the bottom of the steeply cobbled Rua de Entre Quintas, are the gardens of the Quinta da Macieirinha. The stately nineteenth-century country house here houses both the **Museu Romântico** (Tues–Sat 10am–12.30pm & 2–5.30pm, Sun 2–5.30pm; free) – dedicated to Carlos Alberto, exiled King of Piedmont and Sardinia, who died here in 1849 – and the elegant **Solar do Vinho do Porto** (Mon–Sat 2pm –midnight; closed Sun & holidays; Ⓦwww.ivp.pt). Relaxing in its comfortable lounge, or on the floral terrace overlooking Gaia and the river, you can sample one of hundreds of varieties of port wine. Nearby **Casa Tait**, Rua de Entre Quintas 219 (Tues–Fri 10am–12.30pm & 2–5.30pm, Sat & Sun 2.30–6pm; free), has attractive shaded botanical gardens, though it also contains a numismatic museum, tracing the history of Portugal through the coins of successive invaders, from the Greeks to the Spanish.

West along the river to Foz do Douro

The broad esplanade of Rua Nova da Alfândega takes its name from the imposing Neoclassical **Alfândega**, or customs house, partially constructed on stilts along the riverbank just west of Ribeira in 1860 to replace the old Casa do Infante *alfândega*. This has been turned into the excellent **Museu dos Transportes e Comunicações** (Tues–Fri 10am–noon & 2–6pm, Sat, Sun & hols 3–7pm; €3), which interprets its themes very liberally. Aside from a collection of old automobiles and an exhibit exploring "the expression of knowledge and imagination", there's also an engrossingly sensual tour (literally: vision, sound, smell and touch) around the building itself, using computers and other trickery to recount its history. Guided tours (€2) are available at weekends until 4pm, and there's a bar and restaurant.

A few hundred metres west of here at Rua de Monchique 45–52 is the elegant **Museu do Vinho do Porto** (Tues–Sun 11am–7pm; €0.75), occupying an eighteenth-century wine warehouse built for the Companhia Geral da Agricultura das Vinhas do Alto Douro. This traces the history of the port wine trade, and is not as dry as it sounds, with plenty of activities for kids, including multimedia puzzles and a "build your own *barco rabelo*" kit.

It's 600m further downriver to the *azulejo*-fronted **Igreja do Corpo Santo de Massarelos** (limited hours, but open Tues 6pm, with Mass at 7pm, plus Sat Mass 6pm, & Sun Mass 9am), dedicated to São Pedro Gonçalves Telmo (St Elmo), patron saint of sailors. Inside, a large painting of the Holy Trinity has Hope clutching an anchor whose cable is held by St Elmo, over the legend: "Triumph of Grace over Nature". Prince Henry the Navigator (depicted in an *azulejo* panel) was a member of the Almas do Corpo Santo brotherhood, founded in Porto by mariners who survived a storm when returning from England. The brotherhood kept a number of fighting ships, seeing action fending off north African pirates.

Carrying on along the riverbank, 200m beyond the Igreja de Massarelos is the **Museu do Carro Eléctrico**, the city's tram museum, situated in a former power station at Alameda Basílio Teles 51 (Mon 10am–noon & 2.30–5pm, Tues–Fri 9.30am–12.30pm & 2.30–6pm, Sat, Sun & hols 3–7pm; ⓦwww .museu-carro-electrico.stcp.pt; €2.50). Almost all the city's trams were phased out in the 1970s, though many are now being reinstated, and the museum includes delights like Iberia's oldest streetcar (1872). In summer on Thursdays, the museum hosts the "Noites de Massarelos" concerts (mostly chamber music but also some jazz), and there's also a café here.

The **Ponte da Arrábida** – just over 2km from Ribeira – is probably as far as most people will want to walk along the riverfront. It carries the A1/IC1 into Porto, and though it may be the least attractive of the city's six bridges, it represents a mean feat of engineering. Spanning 270 metres, and supported by a single arch, it was the largest such reinforced concrete bridge when inaugurated in 1963. The collapse of similar bridges previously had stirred something of a media frenzy and, when the final section was winched into place, everyone expecting it to tumble away. It didn't, and its designer, Porto's Edgar Cardoso, went on to receive worldwide acclaim.

A few hundred metres west of the bridge, small **ferries** (every 15min, 6am –11pm; €0.50), bedecked with Sandeman hoardings and pursuing erratic courses against the currents, cut across the river's mouth from Rua do Ouro to **Afurada** on the south bank. This was the centre of Portugal's *bacalhau* industry, until stocks were overfished, and cod was formerly strung out to dry in fields and along the shore all the way from here to the river's mouth at Cabedelo, 2km to the west. Afurada still contains one of the country's liveliest fish markets (best Tues–Sat mornings), and a number of cheap and cheerful restaurants, while it's possible to walk 4km back along the riverside road to the port wine lodges of Vila Nova de Gaia; there's not much traffic along the way, but take care at blind corners.

Foz do Douro, formerly a fishermen's quarter but distinctly more upmarket these days, is literally the "end of the Douro". It's around 5km from the city centre and best reached on bus #1 (from Praça Almeida Garrett) or #24 (from the Cordoaria), though trams #1E and #18 run this way too. The confluence of river and ocean is dominated by the squat Castelo de São João, still a military base, while the Baroque Igreja de São João da Foz lies hidden in the side streets behind the river on Largo da Igreja. For most locals, however, Foz is synonymous with the seaside and, more particularly, with its multitude of ocean-front esplanade bars, cafés, clubs and restaurants. Unless you want to swim (don't – the water's polluted), you won't be disappointed. The best way of getting to know Foz is by taking the imaginative **Coma Profundo audio walk** (May–Sept; English-language version available; €4; Ⓦwww.visoesuteis.pt), which provides you with headphones for a fifty-minute stroll around the back streets.

North of Foz lie Porto's beaches; not the cleanest in the world, being downcurrent from Matosinhos port and its ramshackle refinery, but no matter – you're likely to be drawn here instead by the beachfront cafés and bars along Avenida do Brasil, which becomes the hub of Porto's nightlife in summer. A couple of kilometres north along the Avenida, at a large roundabout where the Avenida da Boavista hits the coast, stands the **Castelo do Queijo** (Tues–Sun 1.30pm–7pm; €0.25), so-named (Cheese Castle) because it was built upon boulders that apparently looked like cheese. It's a typical star-shaped Vauban-esque fort, and is occupied by a social association of former commandos, but visitors are welcome and there's a small bar, plus good views. Buses covering this stretch are #1, 24, 37 and 78.

The Rotunda and Avenida da Boavista

Two kilometres northwest of Avenida dos Aliados (buses from Praça da Liberdade or Praça da República) is the traffic-filled Praça Mouzinho de Albuquerque roundabout, popularly known as the **Rotunda da Boavista**. It's overlooked by a huge column bearing a lion astride a much-flattened French eagle, celebrating the victory of the Portuguese and British in the Peninsular War.

Three blocks to the east, on Rua Aníbal Cunha, is the very simple **Igreja Românica de Cedofeita** (Mon–Sat 9am–noon & 4–7.30pm, Sun 9am–noon; free), whose name means "built quickly". Reputed to be the oldest Christian building in the Iberian peninsula (though the people of Balsemão, p.361, dispute this), it was supposedly built by the Suevian king Theodomir in 556 AD. However, the current Romanesque building is a thirteenth-century refashioning of a church whose existence can only be dated certainly to 1118. Cedofeita is unique, however, in being Portugal's only Romanesque church to have kept its original dome, supported by bulky exterior buttresses.

Heading west instead, it's 2km to the contemporary art collection of the **Museu de Arte Contemporânea de Serralves** (Tues–Thurs 10am–7pm, Fri & Sat 10am–10pm, Sun & hols 10am–8pm, closes 1hr earlier on Sun Oct –March; Ⓦwww.serralves.pt; €5, park only €2.50, free Sun morning), which is the best of the museums outside the city centre. It's on Rua de Serralves, reached by bus #3, #19, #21, #35 or #78. The permanent collection – from the 1960s to the present day – is housed in an ultra-modern building designed by local architect Álvaro Siza Vieira, and includes works by crowd-pullers like Rothke and Warhol, as well as contributions by less well-known artists such as Georg Baselitz, Christian Boltanski and Richard Serra. The museum is at pains to showcase Portuguese talent, so you'll also find works by Fernando Calhau, Alberto Carneiro, Ângelo de Sousa and Ana Vieira. Temporary exhibitions are held in the separate, pink **Casa de Serralves**, an Art Deco construction, and are usually well worth seeing; details are posted on the museum's fittingly minimalist website. The eighteen hectares of grounds contain both formal gardens and natural farmland, and are dotted with modern sculptures and art installations: don't miss the inventive scarecrows in the farm at the far end of the park, which appear towards the end of summer – made by schoolchildren from household garbage, they are ceremonially burned in October after the harvest period. There's also a tea shop, while summer sees a sequence of **jazz concerts** held in the gardens, known as "Jazz no Parque" (☎226 180 057 for details).

Four kilometres from Rotunda da Boavista is the main entrance of the **Parque da Cidade** (daily: June–Sept 9am–8pm; Oct–May 9am–6pm; free); take bus #24 from the Rotunda towards Castelo do Queijo. This is the largest remaining public space in Porto and perfect for an afternoon's ramble, with several duck ponds, woods and children's playgrounds. The other entrance is to the north, off Estrada da Circunvalação – the ring road that separates Porto from Matosinhos.

Vila Nova de Gaia

The suburb of **Vila Nova de Gaia** (or just Gaia) is dominated by the port wine trade. As you walk across Ponte Dom Luís I from central Porto, the names of the old port wine lodges, spelled out in huge letters across their roofs,

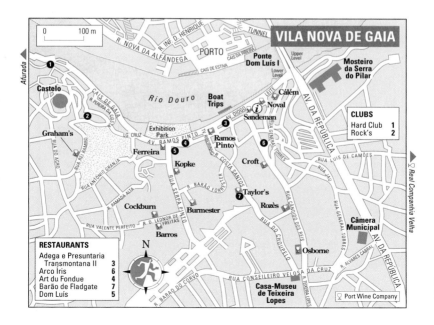

The making of port wine

Wine has been produced in the Douro valley ever since Roman times, but was probably little different from other Portuguese wines until the beginning of the eighteenth century, when Britain prohibited the import of French wine during the War of the Spanish Succession. In the absence of competition, and boosted by favourable trading terms established under the 1703 **Methuen Treaty**, Portuguese *vinhos de embarque* ("shipment wines") became increasingly popular in Britain. Indeed, so profitable was the trade that inferior wines, often adulterated and artificially coloured, were passed off as the genuine article, giving port a bad name. This led the future Marquês de Pombal to found the Companhia Geral da Agricultura das Vinhas do Alto Douro in 1756. The next year, he demarcated the area from which the best port wine – *vinho fino* – could legitimately come, making the Douro the world's oldest **demarcated wine region**. But it was only from 1820 to 1852 that port wine began to resemble the wine of today, when the use of *aguardente* grape spirit to stop fermentation was introduced, enabling the wines to be transported over even longer distances.

Today, the **grapes** for making port wine are grown in a 40,000-hectare demarcated region along both banks of the Douro and its tributaries, sheltered from the humid Atlantic climate by the Marão and Montemuro ranges. Grapes are harvested from September to October and then crushed; mechanically nowadays, not by foot as claimed by various lodges. The juice ferments for a few days and when the natural sugar level is sufficiently reduced, fermentation is arrested by the addition of *aguardente* – exactly when this is done determines the wine's sweetness. The wine then stands in casks in the *armazém* (cellar) of the company *quinta* (estate) until the following March, when it's transported downstream to the shippers' lodges at Vila Nova de Gaia, where it matures.

There are three basic **types of port** – white (*branco*), tawny (or *aloirado*, "blonde"), and red or ruby (*tinto* or *tinto aloirado*). Best among the reds are dated **vintages**, only declared in years when a *quinta's* wine is deemed sufficiently good; when this happens, the wine spends only two or three years in the cask before being bottled and left to mature – it's best drunk at least ten to fifteen years after bottling, when the flavours are at their most complex and delicate. Vintage port needs decanting for an hour before drinking. When serving, tradition dictates that glasses be filled in a clockwise direction using the right hand, starting with the most important person present; this apparently avoids the wrath of demons known to hide in people's left armpits!

Late Bottled Vintage (LBV) is not of vintage quality, but still good enough to mature in bottles, to which it's transferred after four to six years in the cask when already good enough to drink. All other ports are blended, and most are kept in the cask for much longer – at least seven years for a tawny. These light-coloured wines, intense, fruity and often with a woody taste, are perfect for dessert. They come in several categories: dated (10, 20, 30 or 40 years), Tawny Reserva, and Colheita (from a specific year). The flavour accentuates and becomes more complex as the wine ages; dated Tawnies and Colheita are the most intense.

Lastly, don't ignore the lesser known and often heavenly **white ports**; sweet and aromatic, they're best served chilled as aperitifs (even with ice – sacrilege for the other ports), or with smoked fish, cold meats or fresh cheese.

dominate the view. The most direct route there is across the bridge's lower level from Cais da Ribeira (walk, or take bus #32 from Avenida dos Aliados or Praça da Batalha, or #57 or #91 from Praça Almeida Garrett). However, if you've a head for heights it's an amazing sensation to walk over the upper level, some 60m above the river (or take buses #82, #83 or #84 from Praça

Almeida Garrett). In Gaia, there's a **turismo** on the waterfront at Avenida Diogo Leite 242, next to Sandeman (June–Sept daily 10am–7pm; Oct–May Mon–Fri 10am–6pm; ☎223 703 735), where you can pick up a useful map of the port wine lodges.

The port wine lodges

Most of the port wine lodges have long since been bought by multinationals, but still try hard to push a family image. Almost without exception, they offer **tastings and tours**, with a view to enticing you to buy their produce – worthwhile if you want top-quality stuff (not that they'll pour it out for the average visitor). You'll find it cheaper to buy the more basic plonk in town. Tours of the smaller, lesser known companies tend to be more personal than those of larger producers such as Croft, Osborne and Taylor's. There's also a noticeable difference between the "British" names and the Portuguese producers, mainly on account of the Portuguese having been forced to establish their cellars on the riverbank rather than higher up, out of reach of the Douro's annual floods. With dams nowadays straddling the length of the Douro, the river no longer floods as frequently as it once did, though the casks and barrels are still tethered down, just in case.

Where there's an **entrance fee**, the amount is deducted from anything you buy. All lodges have English-speaking guides. Arrive an hour before closing to be sure of a tour.

Barros, Almeida & Cª Rua Dona Leonor de Freitas 180 ☎ 223 752 395, Ⓦ www.porto-barros.pt. June–Sept daily 9.30am–7pm, Oct–May Mon–Fri 10am–6pm. One of only a handful of remaining family-owned companies, formed in 1913. Rated for its Tawnies, Colheitas and Vintages.

Burmester Rua Barão de Forrester 73 ☎ 223 747 290, Ⓦ www.burmesterporto.com. Mon–Fri 10am–noon & 2.30–5pm. Founded in 1730 by English merchants, and enjoys a reputation for fine Colheitas, Vintages and LBVs.

Cálem Av. Diogo Leite 26–42 ☎ 223 746 660, Ⓦ www.calem.pt. May–Oct daily 10am–7pm, Nov–April daily 10am–6pm. A small Portuguese lodge founded in 1859, with short but informative tours – they are happy to take just a couple of visitors at a time.

Cockburn/Martinez Rua Dona Leonor de Freitas 182 ☎ 223 776 545, Ⓦ www.martinez.pt. Mon–Fri 10am–noon & 2.30–4pm. Now owned by Spanish combine Martinez, Cockburn – founded in 1815 – is the most English of the lodges, offering personalized 1hr tours of its supremely atmospheric cellars.

Ferreira Av. Ramos Pinto 70 ☎ 223 746 107, Ⓕ 223 759 732. Daily 10am–12.30pm & 2–6pm; €6.50. Founded in 1751 and worth visiting for its lovely *azulejo*-decorated tasting hall; the wines are pretty good too, and they're happy taking just a couple of visitors around.

Graham's Rua Rei Ramiro 514 ☎ 223 776 330, Ⓦ www.symington.com. May–Sept Mon–Fri 9.30am–6pm, Oct–April Mon–Fri 9am–1pm & 2–5.30pm. An 1820 lodge with an impressive stone-arched reception under a wooden roof; the splendid tasting terrace overlooks the river.

Kopke Rua Serpa Pinto 183–191 ☎ 223 752 420, Ⓦ www.kopkeports.com. June–Sept daily 9.30am–7pm, Oct–May Mon–Fri 10am–6pm. The world's oldest port wine company (1638), now owned by Barros.

Ramos Pinto Av. Ramos Pinto 380, along the river ☎223 707 000, Ⓦwww.ramospinto.pt. June–Sept Mon–Sat 10am–6pm, Oct–May Mon–Fri 9am–1pm & 2–5pm. One of few Portuguese companies, founded in 1880, whose famous label – showing a couple kissing between a glass of wine – did much to popularize port in the 1900s. The 15min tour is free; the 50min version (€2) includes a visit to the museum with photographs, trinkets and posters.

Real Companhia Velha Rua Azevedo Magalhães 314 ☎ 800 205 905. April–Sept Mon–Fri 9.30am–7pm, Oct–Mar until 5pm; €2. Founded by Dom José I in 1756 to lead the Portuguese challenge to the British port monopoly; paintings from his reign are on display, including one of the all-powerful Marquês de Pombal. There's also a 6km tunnel, originally intended to form part of a rail link but, having been built at the wrong angle, now serves as a cold storage for Velha's famed sparkling wines and vintages. Popular with tour groups. Also has a *tapas* bar.

Rozès Rua Cândido dos Reis 526–532 ☏ 223 771 680, ⓦ www.rozes.pt. June–Sept Mon–Fri 10am–6pm, Oct–May by appointment. Founded in 1855 by a Bordeaux-based trader, this has one of the best tours, with six different ports to savour.

Sandeman Largo de Miguel Bombarda 3 ☏ 223 740 500, ⓦ www.sandeman.com. April–Oct daily 10am–12.30pm & 2–6pm, Nov–March Mon–Fri 9.30am–12.30pm & 2–5pm. One of the largest companies, founded in London in 1790; the lengthy tour (often packed) includes a good museum.

Taylor's Rua do Choupelo 250 ☏ 223 742 800, ⓦ www.taylor.pt. Mon–Fri 10am–6pm, also Sat July & Aug. Founded in 1692, this retains a rustic tasting room and has panoramic views from its salon, terrace and restaurant.

The rest of Gaia

If there's a beautiful view of the tiered ranks of Porto's old town from the bridge, there's an even better one from the terrace of the **Mosteiro da Serra do Pilar** just to the east. From this former convent, Wellington planned his surprise crossing of the Douro in 1809 and it's a barracks again today. The round church is open to the public on Saturday afternoon and Sunday morning, but sadly the unusual circular cloister rests in a sort of no-man's-land between church and army territory and cannot be easily visited.

You can make an easier visit to the **Casa–Museu de Teixeira Lopes** (Tues –Sat 9am–12.30pm & 2–5.30pm; July–Sept also Sun 3–7pm; free) – a very steep hike up Rua Cândido dos Reis from the waterfront just west of the turismo (or around €3.50 by taxi). Lopes was at the centre of an important artistic and intellectual set that lived in Gaia at the end of the nineteenth century. The circle is well represented in the second part of the museum's display, the first being devoted to Lopes' work – much of it preoccupied with the depiction of children. His masterpiece is considered to be the enigmatic portrait of an Englishwoman, *A Inglesa*.

Eating

Eating out, and eating well, is a long-standing tradition in Porto, whilst the cosmopolitan nature of the city ensures that there's something for all tastes. Many of the city's **cafés** in particular rival those of Lisbon, with some lovely old Art Nouveau and Art Deco survivors in the main shopping streets. For full meals, the cheapest eats are found in **workers' cafés**, many of which have a set menu (the *ementa do dia*) for under €5 a head, including drinks. These are mainly lunchtime places, though most serve an evening meal until around 7.30pm and a few stay open later; prime areas are the riverfront west of Alfândega (including the ultra-cheap *adegas* along Rua do Ouro), and the grid of streets north and south of the Cordoaria, especially Rua do Almada (north) and Rua de São Bento da Vitória (south). For atmosphere – and, more importantly, for fish – the **restaurants** of the Cais da Ribeira are hard to beat. There are several nameless places on Rua da Fonte Taurina and in the side streets back from the river, though nearer the water prices rise accordingly, with dozens of touristy establishments installed under the arches of the first tier of dwellings. For ocean views and esplanade cafés you can jump on a tram or bus to **Foz do Douro**, west of the centre, while around **Avenida da Boavista** are a series of well-regarded seafood and Brazilian-style grilled meat places.

You may not be over the moon to discover that the Porto's **speciality** is *tripas* (tripe) and that people are affectionately referred to by the rest of the country as *tripeiros* – tripe-eaters. The story goes that the inhabitants selflessly gave away all their meat for Infante Dom Henrique's expeditions to Ceuta (Sebta) in North Africa, leaving themselves only the tripe, and it's been on the menu ever since – most famously *à moda do Porto*, stewed with *chouriço* and white beans and best experienced with a glass or two of *vinho verde*. If you don't fancy chopped stomach lining, there are plenty of other local specialities: also typically Portuense is *caldo verde* (a thick vegetable soup), *cabrito assado* (roast goat – served particularly at Easter and during the São João *festa* in June) and sardines, whilst *papas de sarabulho* – a thick blood-based stew – is particularly tasty here. A heritage of returning emigrants is the *francesinha* ("little French thing"), a sort of *croque monsieur* – steak, sausage and ham covered with melted cheese and peppery tomato sauce.

Cafés

All Porto's cafés serve alcohol, snacks and cakes as well as coffee, and there are also some specialist cake shops (*pastelarias* and *confeitarias*) and tea houses worth keeping an eye out for. The most touristy but interesting location is down on Praça da Ribeira, whose few pavement cafés are packed in summer. Cake shops follow normal business hours; café opening times vary from place to place, though most tend to stay open until at least 10pm. The following are all marked on the Central Porto: restaurants, cafes, bars and clubs map, p.324.

Confeitaria Arcádia Pr. da Liberdade 63. Long-established sweet shop, famous for its chocolate bonbons, *ovos moles* (sticky UFO-shaped egg confectionery) and regional specialities.

Ateneia Pr. da Liberdade 58. For serious addicts: exquisite chocolates from the Costa Moreira company, plus quince *marmelada*, boiled sweets and cakes. There's a raised Art Deco seating area at the back in which to indulge your passion.

Café Guarany Av. dos Aliados 85. Bright and airy café with paintings inspired by Amazonian Indians. Also has cheap food.

Café Majestic Rua de Santa Catarina 112. Best known and most expensive of the old Belle Epoque cafés, with perfectly preserved decor (celestial cherubs, bevelled mirrors and wood panelling) dating from 1921. Plenty of outside tables, and a grand piano featuring in out-of-season recitals. Breakfast and light meals (€10–20) also available. Closed Sun except June & July.

Café na Praça Pr. de Lisboa. Trendy chrome-and-glass place popular at all hours. The outdoor tables are a great place to soak up the surroundings, and the *espetada de lulas* (squid kebab) is worth a try. Piano music evenings, and DJs most weekend nights (10pm–4am).

Café Progresso Rua Actor João Guedes 5, off Pr. Carlos Alberto. Founded in 1899 but now unrecognizable as such (the decor is modern), this remains popular with university types. Closes 2am on Thurs & Fri, otherwise 7pm; closed Sun.

Casa de Chá Actos Rua Sá de Noronha 76-1º, north of Pr. Gomes Teixeira. Offers a large variety of teas, cakes, tarts and scones. The unusual hours cater to a varied clientele: 5–7pm from Sept–June for a genteel atmosphere, followed by 10pm–2am, when it plays host to students, arty types and a gay crowd. Closed Mon.

Casa de Chá da Boa Nova Leça da Palmeira, 3km north of Matosinhos ☎229 951 785; bus #45 from Boavista (no nightbuses). Sophisticated seaside café and expensive restaurant with sweeping views (and comfortable chairs), and a small fishermen's chapel beside it. As architect Álvaro Siza Vieira's first work, the hike up here is worth it if you take your architecture seriously. The menu focuses on seafood, including a marvellous seafood soup, but it's possible just to while away an afternoon with drinks. Closed Sun.

Confeitaria do Bolhão Rua Formosa 339. Tranquil cake and coffee shop, repainted in Art Nouveau style, and rather popular with old ladies. They do good value *pratos do dia* in the restaurant above, too.

Storia del Caffè (*Il Caffè di Roma*) Rua Sá da Bandeira 75. The new incarnation of the famous *A Brasileira*, this dignified place remains popular with locals as much for its attractive Art Nouveau decor as for the wide selection of coffees, herbal teas, liqueurs and ice cream.

Tempo de Leitura no Porto Rua Ferreira Borges 86. A café that definitely doesn't mind students studying, this stylish place is also a bookshop and bar. Daily to 2am.

Restaurants

Reservations are always recommended for tables at good restaurants, and can be essential on Friday and Saturday nights at all but the most humble of places. The listings below have been coded into four price categories: inexpensive (less than €10), moderate (€10–18), expensive (€18–30), and very expensive (over

CENTRAL PORTO: RESTAURANTS, CAFÉS, BARS & CLUBS

CAFÉS & RESTAURANTS

Abadia	12
Adega Vila Meã	23
Antunes	2
Aquário	7
Arcádia	21
Ateneia	22
Café na Praça	20
A Canastra	41
Casa Cardoso	36
Casa de Chá Actos	6
Chinês	31
Confeitaria do Bolhão	8
Dom Tonho	39
Downing Street	32
O Escondidinho	18
Filha da Mãe Preta	42
O Ginjal	1
Guarany	14
Majestic	13
O Mal Cozinhado	43
Palmeira	10
Pinguim	26
Postigo do Carvão	34
Progresso	11
Regaleira	15
Solar Moinho de Vento	5
Storia del Caffé	16
Taberna dos Bêbobos	40
Tempo de Leitura no Porto	27
Tripeiro	17

Cedofeita, Rotunda da Boavista, Prelada Campsite,
Centro Comercial Brasília, Boavista Stadium & Serralves

Palácio de Cristal, Solar do Vinho do Porto

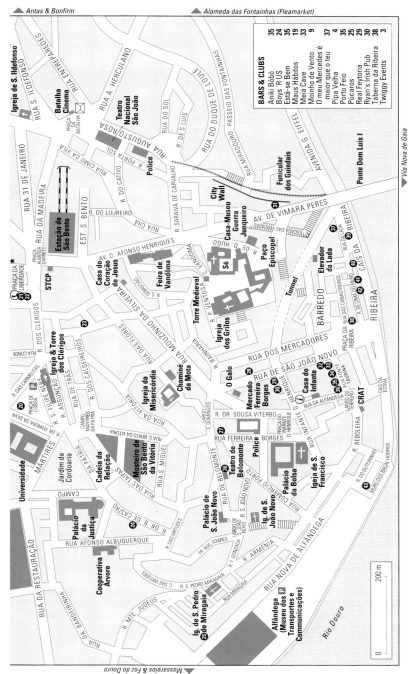

5

PORTO AND THE DOURO

▼ Vila Nova de Gaia

BARS & CLUBS
Aniki Bóbó	35
Boys R US	24
Está-se Bem	35
Maus Hábitos	19
Meia Cave	33
Moinho de Vento	9
O meu Mercedes é maior que o teu	37
Pipa Velha	4
Porto Feio	35
Púcaros	25
Real Feytoria	29
Ryan's Irish Pub	30
Taberna da Ribeira	38
Twiggy Events	3

Masserelos & Foz do Douro

0   200 m

€30) – the average price per person of a full meal, including drinks. Most of the following restaurants are marked on the map on pp.324–325 – exceptions are noted.

Ribeira and around

A Canastra Cais da Ribeira 37 ⊤ 222 080 180. A recommended under-the-arches option, particularly for seafood. It's a homely, local place, and a good deal cheaper than its neighbours. Closed Tues. Inexpensive.

Casa Cardoso Rua da Fonte Taurina 58 ⊤ 222 058 644. A simple *tasca* with excellent fish dishes, particularly scabbard fish (*peixe espada*). Closed Sun. Inexpensive.

Chinês Av. Vímara Peres 38–40 ⊤ 222 008 915. The city's best Chinese restaurant sports a stunning interior by the top-level entrance to Ponte Dom Luís I. Portions are large and dishes include tofu and other vegetarian options. Moderate.

Dom Tonho Cais da Ribeira 13–15 ⊤ 222 004 307. Swanky yet affordable place overlooking the river, combining chrome, pinewood and glass with the original granite walls. Despite the pretensions, the combination works well, extending to the modern twist given to traditional dishes such as bean soup. Fish is the focus (try wrasse or sea bass in a salt crust); other specialities include duck, veal and roasted kid. Enormous wine list. Expensive.

Downing Street Pr. da Ribeira 10 ⊤ 222 006 418. On two floors with granite walls, and a more genteel ambience than most. The pick from the refined menu includes seafood *cataplanas* and *caldeiradas*, and rabbit dishes, and there's also a vast selection of port wine. Usually has live music, including accordion. Reservations essential. Expensive.

Filha da Mãe Preta Cais da Ribeira 40 ⊤ 222 055 515. Built into the arches, the *azulejo*-decorated upper floor provides a river view whilst enjoying local favourites such as *arroz de marisco*, stuffed squid, *tripas* and *rojões* (roasted cubes of pork). The name ("daughter of the black mother") comes from the original establishment, Mãe Preta, popular with charcoal makers from upriver. It's not to be confused with the similarly named *taberna* nearby, which is an acquired taste. Closed Sun. Moderate.

O Mal Cozinhado Rua do Outeirinho 11–13 ⊤222 081 319. A splendid exception among Porto's handful of mainly touristic fado houses, housed in an atmospheric fourteenth-century cellar. The name means "badly cooked", not that you'll have cause to complain; the *bacalhau* and roast veal are well up to scratch. If you don't want to eat, entry is

€12, which gets you two drinks (additional beers are €5). Dinner only, open until 2am (music from 9.30pm); closed Sun. Very expensive.

Postigo do Carvão Rua da Fonte Taurina 24–26 ⊤ 222 004 539. Close to the fourteenth-century guardhouse of the same name, this unpretentious but classy place has live music Fri and Sat (fado, folklore and Brazilian), and a resolutely local menu, including shellfish *feijoada*, *francesinhas*, *rojões*, roast octopus, and roast pork with chestnuts; they also do grilled lobster and fondue. Dinner only, open until 2am, closed Mon. Moderate.

Taberna dos Bêbobos Cais da Ribeira 24 ⊤ 222 053 565. Established in 1876, this lovely old *adega* looks the part, with barrels of wine lining the walls of the downstairs bar; the name, happily mistranslated as "tavern of drunkards", actually means "drink eggs" – alluding to the house speciality, a gloopy eggnog made with port. In the cosy upstairs restaurant there's a fireplace and river views, while seafood, grills and regional dishes dominate – pork with wine sauce or with clams *à alentejana* are particularly good. Closed Mon. Moderate.

Central Porto

Abadia Rua do Ateneu Comercial 22–24 ⊤ 222 008 757. A big, busy (noisy) and unpretentious two-floor restaurant dishing out simple but delicious food – not just *bacalhau* and *tripas*, but less common dishes such as wild boar with chestnuts, and *porco preto* – a superior breed of pig from Alentejo. Inexpensive.

Adega Vila Meã Rua dos Caldeireiros 62 ⊤ 222 082 967. Rather cramped and tatty countrystyle decor, but the food – fresh, simple and tasty – comes in enormous portions, and includes an exceptional *cozido à portuguesa* (Thurs), roast octopus (Tues) and roast veal (Fri). Closed Sun & Aug. Moderate.

Antunes Rua do Bonjardim 525 ⊤ 222 052 406. Famously uses only wood-fired stoves, particularly auspicious for their oven-baked ham. Other good specialities include good *tripas* (Wed & Sat), and *cozido à portuguesa* on Thurs. It's very busy at lunchtimes, though you can also eat at the bar. Closed Sun and 4 weeks Aug–Sept. Inexpensive.

Aquário Marisqueiro Rua Rodrigues Sampaio 179 ⊤222 002 231. Supplying splendid well-priced seafood for over half a century – *aquário* refers to the tank in which your next meal is blissfully swimming or snapping. One of very few places to serve seafood soup. Closed Sun. Moderate.

Casa Aleixo Rua da Estação 216, by Campanhã train station ⓣ 225 370 462; see "Porto" map, p.300. Owned by the same family since 1948, and a decorative throwback to that period, this good-natured place enjoys a happy reputation for fine, uncomplicated food, as testified by numerous awards on the walls. Choose from fish fillets, octopus, roast veal, or roast pork chops. Closed Sun & Aug. Moderate.

O Escondidinho Rua de Passos Manuel 144 ⓣ222 001 079. "The little hidden place" has a cluttered, country-house interior (plus TV, unfortunately) and excellent French-influenced cuisine, popular with tourists. Wide choice of steaks, but fish is the main draw, including hake in Madeira sauce and shellfish soup. Closed Sun. Very expensive.

O Ginjal Rua do Bonjardim 724–726 ⓣ 222 000 661. Tripe, *bacalhau*, octopus and roasted kid served in a no-frills setting, and with a very cheap *prato do dia*. Closed Sun. Inexpensive.

Palmeira Rua do Ateneu Comercial 36 ⓣ 222 055 601. Small, cosy and friendly, long-known for good Portuguese food, from *tripas*, roast kid and other local favourites to lamprey and shad in season. Closed Sun. Inexpensive.

Portucale Rua da Alegria 598 ⓣ 225 370 717; see "Porto" map, p.300. On the thirteenth floor of the *Albergaria Miradouro*, proof that appearances – in this case, dated 1960s decor – aren't everything; this has both stupendous views and an unflagging reputation as the city's most refined restaurant. Regional dishes play second fiddle to aristocratic staples such as *foie gras* and truffles, wild boar with mussels, and partridge with chestnuts. Desserts gather up the best of northern Portugal's *doces conventuais*, and the wine list is top-notch. Very expensive.

Regaleira Rua do Bonjardim 87 ⓣ 222 006 465. One of the best places for fish and seafood, including platefuls of *perceves* (barnacles) and lamprey in season, plus *francesinhas*, *bacalhau* and *tripas*. Closed Sat. Moderate.

Solar Moinho de Vento Rua Sá de Noronha 81 ⓣ 222 051 158. A *típico* locale with somewhat formal service, offering everything from *bacalhau* and *arroz de polvo* to *tripas* and *cozido à portuguesa*. Closed Sun & August. Moderate.

Suribachi Rua do Bonfim 136–140 ⓣ225 106 700; see "Porto" map, p.300. Health food shop, 800m east of Praça da Batalha, concealing a vegetarian and macrobiotic restaurant (inventive tofu dishes, among others), with not a plate of chips in sight, though fish and seafood do feature. Open from 10am to after lunch; closed Sun. Inexpensive.

Tripeiro Rua de Passos Manuel 195 ⓣ 222 005 886. A consistently good bet for generous portions

of filling northern nosh, especially at lunch. This simple medieval-styled place is much loved for its tripe, but there's also *bacalhau*, meat and shellfish, and great soups, while you can eat in their cheaper bar next door too. Closed Sun. Moderate.

Boavista

The following are marked are on the Porto map, p.300.

Churrascão Gaúcho Av. da Boavista 313 ⓣ 226 098 206. Sophisticated Brazilian place specializing in shellfish as well as *rodízio* (€20), which involves waiters carving slices off skewers of grilled lamb and beef onto your plate until you beg them to stop. Free transport provided from hotels. Closed Sun and first 2 weeks Aug. Expensive.

Churrascão do Mar Rua João Grave 134–152, off Av. da Boavista ⓣ 226 096 382. Pure elegance in this century-old manor house, with a mainly Brazilian-style à la carte fish and seafood menu to match, or grills served *rodízio*-style. Free transport from hotels. Closed Sun and last 2 weeks Aug. Very expensive.

Cufra Av. da Boavista 2504 ⓣ 226 172 715. One of Porto's oldest shellfish *cervejarias*, now also popular for its famously good *francesinhas*, though you can also sample seafood, steaks and game, plus fancy cups of sorbet. Open to 2am; closed Mon. Moderate.

Paco Loco Av. Dr. Antunes Guimarães 1217, 1km north of Av. da Boavista ⓣ 226 189 480; bus #3 from Pr. da Liberdade or Cordoaria. Hot Mexican and Texan food in colourful surroundings, with music to match. Dinner only; closed Sun.

Massarelos and Foz do Douro

The following are marked are on the Porto map, p.300.

Espaço Massarelos Rua da Boa Viagem 3, Massarelos, behind the tram museum ⓣ226 008 732; buses and trams along the river. The terrace views over the Douro are the main attraction at this beautiful conversion of the 1830s headquarters of the Portuguese Legion. The seasonal menu covers most bases, and the food ranges from average to excellent (try the squid, or the wild boar carpaccio). Closed Sun dinner & all Mon. Expensive.

Museu dos Presuntos Rua Padre Luís Cabral 1070, Foz do Douro ⓣ 226 106 965. Surreal junkshop-decorated place with a pub-like feel that's popular with students – to find it, take the road to the right of the *Hotel Boa-Vista* and turn right. The main draws are the unusual *pratinhos* (small dishes), including stewed chicken innards and *tripas*, pickled *bacalhau* and smoked ham (*presunto*). Open to 4am; closed Mon. Inexpensive.

Ó Macedo Rua do Passeio Alegre 552, Foz do Douro ⓣ 226 170 166. Pleasantly refined establishment offering things like onion tart, *bacalhau*, even English roast beef, and a sophisticated wine list. Arrive early for views over the mouth of the Douro. Closed Sun & 2 weeks in Aug. Expensive.

Peixes & Companhia Rua do Ouro 133, on the riverbank west of Arrábida bridge ⓣ 226 185 655. Friendly and elegant atmosphere in a renovated town house, with views over the river. Different kinds of fish (no meat), depending on the day's catch. Nearby are several cheap *adegas*. Closed Sun. Moderate.

Vila Nova de Gaia

The following are marked on the Vila Nova de Gaia map, p.319.

Adega e Presuntaria Transmontana II Av. Diogo Leite 78–80 ⓣ 223 758 380. Lovely cool dining room with stone walls and a dozen smoked hams hanging over the bar. The menu features tasty specialities from Trás-os-Montes, whether as

snacks (particularly smoked meats) or more substantial meals: grilled veal is one speciality, octopus another. Open to 2am. Moderate.

Arco Íris Rua Cândido dos Reis 75–79 ⓣ 223 791 622. Popular *pão quente* ("hot bread") place, which has fresh, warm bread all day, as well as very reasonably priced snacks and full meals. Inexpensive.

Art du Fondue Av. Ramos Pinto 230 ⓣ 223 701 107. Upmarket restaurant with great views from its terrace, specializing in meat fondues (you dip the meat in boiling oil). Expensive.

Barão de Fladgate Rua do Choupelo 250 ⓣ 223 742 800. Inside Taylor's port wine lodge, the location is what counts here, with fine views of Porto from the terrace. The menu is international rather than local, but refined, while the interior dining room has tables around a central fireplace. Closed Sun. Expensive.

Dom Luís Av. Ramos Pinto 264–266 ⓣ 223 751 251. A calm, intimate, family-run place near the bridge, with all the local favourites, plus *tamboril com espargos* (monkfish with asparagus) and a wicked seafood *feijoada*. Closed Mon. Inexpensive.

Drinking and nightlife

Dozens of modish late-night **bars** are found in the streets around the Cais da Ribeira, as well as along the river in Vila Nova de Gaia. Out to the west in Foz do Douro, Avenida do Brasil (the coastal promenade facing Praia dos Ingleses) becomes the main evening drag in summer. Porto's **clubs** tend to be located way outside the city centre – we've mentioned nightbus connections (usually hourly) for these, though it's easier to get the club to ring a taxi for you when you leave. The majority really only get going well after midnight, and most stay open until 4 or 5am or later, with a standard €5–15 admission fee, whilst entrance to special events can cost €10–25. The entrance ticket acts as a voucher for free drinks, not that it'll last long – with beers and soft drinks averaging €3–5, and spirits €5–7, most people drink in bars before hitting the clubs. Ring ahead to check opening days and times and for special events; the scene changes constantly. The city's **gay scene**, until recently restricted to a couple of seedy suburban nightclubs, is now centred (by day) on Praça Carlos Alberto, which has a number of pleasant bars and cafés also popular with straight arty types, and at night on the *Boys 'R US* nightclub.

Bars

Unless stated otherwise, the following are marked on the Central Porto: restaurants, cafés, bars and clubs map, pp.324–325.

Está-se Bem Rua da Fonte Taurina 70–72, Ribeira. A nice little *tasca* where the arty pre-club crowd hang out, probably because it's cheap and there's no cover charge. Mon–Sat 9pm–4am.

Labirinto Rua Nossa Senhora de Fátima 334 ⓣ 226 063 665; see the "Porto" map, p.300; night

bus #19 or #76 to the Rotunda. Pleasant, friendly bar in a converted house, with a shaded back garden and gallery space. Occasional live music, poetry recitals and drama (usually starting at midnight; ring for details). Daily 10pm–4am.

O meu Mercedes é maior que o teu Rua da

Lada 30, Ribeira. Hands-down winner of the world's silliest bar name contest ("My Mercedes is bigger than yours") – although there's no name on the door – but inside it's a small and friendly joint which attracts regulars; tends to play alternative music. Daily from 8pm.

Moinho de Vento Rua Sá Noronha 78. Next to the restaurant of the same name, this gay and lesbian bar is busy weekends, dead midweek. Daily from 11pm.

Pinguim Rua de Belomonte 65–67. A laid-back arty venue, with live Brazilian or Portuguese music on Fri evenings starting at 11pm, and poetry readings on Mon at the same time.

Pipa Velha Rua das Oliveiras 75–77. Friendly, unpretentious bar in the Cedofeita area, plastered with old posters and popular with students and artistic folk. There's a piano for tinkling with, and appetizing and inexpensive *petiscos*. Mon–Sat 5pm–2am.

Porto Feio Rua da Fonte Taurina 52–54, Ribeira. Hi-tech art gallery and bar stocked with port wine; ring the bell for admission. Thurs–Sat, gallery 4–10pm, bar 10pm–2am.

Púcaros Bar Rua de Miragaia 55; nightbus #1. A relaxed and cosy cellar-like pub with medieval stone arches and bare walls bearing temporary art and photography exhibitions. Poetry night Wed, comedy Thurs. Mon–Sat 10pm–2am.

Ryan's Irish Pub Rua do Infante Dom Henrique 18. Irish music, Guinness (bottled), Jamesons and Bushmills, and Irish prices to match. There's a €2.50 cover charge after 11pm. Thurs & Sun 10pm–2am, Fri 9pm–4am, Sat 5pm–4am.

Solar do Vinho do Porto Quinta da Macieirinha, Rua de Entre Quintas 220; see the "Porto" map, p.300; nightbus #19. Laid-back venue for port-drinking (hundreds to choose from) in civilized surroundings, with views over the Douro. Mon–Sat 2pm–midnight.

Taberna da Ribeira Pr. da Ribeira. In a prime riverside location, this place has outdoor tables, *chouriço assada* (grilled with alcohol at your table) and home-made sangria to wash it down with. The perfect spot to while away a whole afternoon without realizing it. Daily until 2am.

Triplex Av. da Boavista 911 ℡ 226 063 164; see the "Porto" map, p.300; nightbus #19. Hard to categorize, this mellow place occupies three floors of a nineteenth-century villa. There's occasional live music (ring for details), and a restaurant. Daily 12.30pm–3am.

Clubs

Central Porto

The following are marked on the Central Porto: restaurants, cafés, bars and clubs map, p.324.

Aniki Bóbó Rua da Fonte Taurina 36–38, Ribeira ℡223 324 619. Named after a cult 1930s film about Ribeira's kids, this cool and spacious club (currently pop, house/rave, and drum 'n bass) is popular with fashionable darlings. Thurs may have live music or alternative theatre; ring for details. Cover €5. Tues–Sat 10pm–4am.

Boys 'R US Rua Dr. Barbosa de Castro 63 ℡917 549 988. Gay gay gay, with lashings of fashionable tunes and drag acts for a discerning public. No cover charge. Wed & Fri–Sun 11pm–4am.

Meia Cave Pr. da Ribeira 6–9, Ribeira ℡ 223 323 214. Drum 'n bass, breakbeat, acid-jazz and house to dance to in spartan environs. Prices rise after 2am. Fri–Sat 10pm–late.

Real Feytoria Rua Infante Dom Henrique 20 ℡ 222 000 718. Two floors, one for pop, rock and Brazilian, the other playing house. Cover is €2. Daily 9pm–2am.

Twiggy Events Rua do Bolhão 193 ℡ 222 054 732. Horrible 1960s retro "decor", but no matter – live music every day, plus karaoke Wed and fado Thurs. Daily 7pm–4am.

Boavista

Swing Rua Júlio Dinis 766 ℡ 226 090 019; night bus #19 or #76. See Porto map, p.300. The disco-goers' number one; five bars, a lively clientele, and a style a day, including the hugely enjoyable fancy-dress "Club Kitten". Busiest on Fri, but also good Mon. Daily midnight–6am.

Senhora da Hora and Matosinhos

The following are marked on the Porto map, p.300.

B Flat Jazz Club Rua Ló Ferreira 251, Matosinhos ℡ 223 744 194; nightbus #76. Porto's main live jazz venue, with plenty of tables in rather boring surroundings, but it's the music that counts. Thurs–Sat 10.30pm–3am; closed Aug.

Batô Largo do Castelo 13, Leça da Palmeira, north of Matosinhos ℡229 953 405; nightbus #76. Porto's oldest club, and with its original interior, too – a high camp pirates' galleon that just needs Errol Flynn sliding down one of the masts to complete the effect. Music covers everything from trashy 1980s pop to the latest flavours. Tues–Sat 11pm–4am.

Estado Novo Rua Sousa Arosa 722, Matosinhos Ⓣ229 385 989; nightbus #76. Converted sardine factory that's a current favourite for serious dancing (and drinking). There's no cover charge and free drinks for women on Thurs. Thurs–Sat 11pm–4am.

Sound Planet Av. Fontes Pereira de Melo 449, Senhora da Hora, close to NorteShopping centre Ⓣ226 107 232; nightbus #76. Popular club for pop and multi-flavoured house. Fri & Sat 11pm–4am.

Massarelos and Foz do Douro

The following are marked on the Porto map, p.300.

Indústria Av. do Brasil 843, Foz do Douro Ⓣ226 176 806; nightbus #1. A busy, sophisticated club in an unlovely shopping centre facing the beach. Gets packed in summer with a youthful, artistic crowd. Fri & Sat 11pm–6am.

Maré-Alta Bar Rua do Ouro Ⓣ226 162 540; night bus #1. A floating teepee moored on the river, west of Ponte da Arrábida, presenting a fashionable mix of Brazilian music and salsa (Fri from 11pm). The Sunday "House Breakfast" (7am–2pm) is usually accompanied by a live band. Cover charge €2.50. Tues–Sun 2pm–6am.

Mexcal Rua da Restauração 39, Massarelos Ⓣ226 009 188; nightbus #1. Very danceable mix of Latin American music. Cover is €3.50–5 though it's free for women on weekdays. Wed–Sat 10pm–4am.

Twins Rua do Passeio Alegre 994–1000, Foz do Douro Ⓣ226 185 740; nightbus #1. Lively mix of music, including Brazilian, popular with a youthful crowd. Tues–Sat 10pm–4am.

Vila Nova de Gaia

The following are marked on the Vila Nova de Gaia map, p.319.

Hard Club Cais de Gaia, Vila Nova de Gaia Ⓣ223 753 819; nightbus #91. Major venue for DJs and live music, including a good number of British and Stateside acts. Fri is more poppy.

Rock's Rua Rei Ramiro 228, Vila Nova de Gaia Ⓣ223 751 208; nightbus #91. Built in old port cellars, with a terrace overlooking the Douro, and barbecues in summer. Thurs–Sat 10pm–4am.

Theatre, music and the arts

The arts scene has undergone a veritable renaissance since Porto was made European Capital of Culture in 2001, and nowadays you're spoiled for choice, especially for music. **Classical concerts** are frequently held throughout the city, both full-scale orchestral works performed by Porto's Orquestra Nacional, and chamber ensembles (particularly Baroque) and choirs. Other **live music** performances are put on at a variety of venues, anything from fado in restaurants to experimental jazz in the clubs. Big names in **rock and pop**, both homegrown and international, tend to perform at the central Coliseu. The theatrical tradition remains strong, following a shaky period after the 1974 Revolution when Porto's underground dissident **theatres** lost ground to musicals, although standards remain variable. Performances are almost always in Portuguese, however, so either go with a local, or stick to ballet, contemporary **dance**, or other more visual or experimental genres, where dialogue isn't everything. There are major mainstream **cinema** screens at Central Shopping, Rua Santos Pousada; Cinema Charlot, Centro Comercial Brasília, Rotunda da Boavista; and Warner Lusomundo at NorteShopping centre, Senhora da Hora. The cinemas we've listed below are a better bet for Portuguese, art-house or independent movies.

Listings are given in the free monthly arts booklet, *cultura.norte*, and in the quarterly *Agenda do Porto*, both available at the turismos, and on the website Ⓦwww.agendadoporto.pt. Porto's leading newspaper, the *Jornal de Notícias*, and the local edition of the weekly *Público*, are also useful sources of information. **Tickets** for most shows (usually in the range €10–40) can be bought in advance for a €1 mark-up from FNAC on Rua de Santa Catarina (Mon–Fri 10am–10pm, Sat 9am–10pm, Sun 11am–8pm).

Cinemas

Casa da Animação Rua Júlio Dinis, Edifício Les Palaces 208–210 ☎ 225 432 770, ⓦ www .casa-da-animacao.pt. Animation and short films, and hands-on workshops by real fans of the genre. Casa das Artes see "Multipurpose venues" below. Screens art-house movies and productions by the long-established Cineclube do Porto/Clube Português de Cinematografia, mainly short "experimental" films. They also run film workshops and a small museum.
Cinema Batalha Pr. da Batalha 47 ☎222 022 407. Porto's oldest cinema, dating from 1908, when its crowd puller was a "cronomegaphone – the most modern perfection of talking cinema". Favours Portuguese and Brazilian films.
Cinema Passos Manuel Rua de Passos Manuel 137 ☎ 222030 706. Exclusively alternative cinema: art-house, experimental, documentaries, shorts, and foreign films.
Fórum FNAC NorteShopping centre, Senhora da Hora, northwest of the city; metro Linha A. A good venue for European art movies and debates, plus the better blockbusters.

Classical music and opera

Casa da Música Rotunda da Boavista. Yet to open at the time of writing, Porto's new opera house is destined to house the Orquestra Nacional do Porto (see below), and should become a prominent feature on the international music and arts circuit. Completion is scheduled for 2005.
Coral de Letras ☎226 094 559. Under the perfectionist leadership of José Luís Borges Coelho, the University of Porto's choir has become one of the best in Europe, particularly for its interpretations of works by Lopes Graça, and sacred music. There's no fixed venue, so ring ahead for details; best times to call are Tues–Thurs 4–7pm, Fri 9pm, or Sat 4pm.
Orquestra Nacional do Porto Rua de São Bento da Vitória ☎ 222 074 940, ⓦ www.onp.pt. One of Portugal's leading symphony orchestras, currently at home in the glorious former monastery of São Bento da Vitória.

Live music venues

Maus Hábitos Rua Passos Manuel 178-4º ☎ 222 087 268. "Bad Habits" is an in-crowd venue for alternative music and arts, including "interactive dance", jazz, funk, indie and world music, "retrokitchpop" parties and the like.
Coliseu do Porto Rua de Passos Manuel 137 ☎223 394 940, ⓦwww.coliseudoporto.pt. Inaugurated in 1941 as a cinema (hence the austere Art Deco exterior) it's now the main venue for international acts, from rock and pop to ballet and musicals.

Multipurpose venues and art centres

Casa das Artes Rua Ruben A 210, off Rua do Campo Alegre ☎ 226 006 153. Hub of the city's alternative arts scene, with daily art-house movies in addition to theatre, classical recitals and concerts. Bus #78 from Cordoaria or Bolhão.
Rivoli Teatro Municipal Pr. Dom João I ☎223 392 200. Home of the tireless Culturporto arts organization (ⓦ www.culturporto.pt): theatre, contemporary dance and music.
Teatro Carlos Alberto (TeCA) Rua das Oliveiras 43 ☎ 800 108 675. Theatre, contemporary dance, classical recitals, film shows and alternative music.
Teatro Helena Sá e Costa Rua da Alegria 503, entrance on Rua da Escola Normal 39 ☎ 225 189 982. Performances of variable quality by students of an arts school, plus classical ensembles, medieval music and acapella.
Teatro Sá da Bandeira Rua Sá da Bandeira 108 ☎222 002 550. Well over a century old, this played host to Portugal's first ever film screening in 1896, courtesy of Aurélio da Paz dos Reis and his amazing "Kinetograph". Nowadays it's a venue for live music (mostly alternative rock and pop), visiting music hall burlesque troupes from Lisbon, and porn movies.

Theatre and dance

Balleteatro Auditório Pr. 9 de Abril 76 ☎ 225 508 918. Contemporary and classical ballet and dance, and some theatre.
Teatro do Bolhão Pr. Coronel Pacheco, off Rua dos Mártires da Liberdade ☎ 222 089 007. Home to the respected Academia Contemporânea do

Popular traditions – feiras, festas and romarias

Passion Sunday (March/April; the second Sun before Easter). Celebrated with a feast, market and procession near Jardim de São Lázaro, opposite the church of Nossa Senhora da Esperança, east of Praça da Batalha.

Easter Day (March/April). Effigies of Judas are burnt in several locations around the Sé. Concerts at the Igreja da Lapa, north of Praça da República.

Corpus Christi (May/June). Processions of administrative and religious authorities through the centre of the city.

Santo António (closest Sat to June 13). Religious services in the churches of Massarelos and Bonfim districts, in honour of the protector of brides and newlyweds.

São João (June 23–24). The city's biggest popular festival (São João is the patron saint of lovers) sees folk and choral music performances, a marathon, and *cascata* competitions (displays of dolls in shop-windows depicting Santo António, São João and São Pedro, complete with miniature houses, trains and cars). The evening of June 23 culminates with fireworks and riotous celebrations, especially in Ribeira.

São Pedro (June 29). Street decorations, music and dancing celebrate the saint's day of the first Christian Pope.

São Bartolomeu (Sun after Aug 24). Procession in Foz do Douro of "puppets dressed in paper clothes", culminating in a health-giving bath (*banho santo*) in the rather polluted sea.

Nossa Senhora da Saúde (Aug 15). A month-long fair steeped in age-old harvest celebrations culminates with a procession and music at Paranhos, in the north of the city.

Nossa Senhora da Boa Fortuna (last weekend in Aug). In the parish of Vitória, west of Ribeira near Torre dos Clérigos/Rua de Ceuta, a procession of young children dressed as angels carry plastic baby dolls to the image of Nossa Senhora in Rua dos Caldeireiros.

Nossa Senhora de Campanhã (closest Sun to Sept 8). Market stalls are set up near Campanhã train station and there's live folk music and dancing.

Nossa Senhora do Ó (last Sun in Sept). A solemn procession from the Capela Nossa Senhora da Piedade do Cais to the river west of Alfândega in honour of the pregnant Virgin.

São Nicolau (Dec 6). Children wait for Santa Claus' arrival by boat at the Cais de Estiva in Ribeira, to escort him along Rua da Alfândega to the Igreja de São Francisco.

Nossa Senhora da Conceição (Dec 8 – national holiday). Feast held in Foz do Douro, centred on the Capela da Nossa Senhora da Conceição, followed by a night procession though Foz's streets.

Espectáculo theatre school, whose students put on frequent performances.

Teatro do Campo Alegre Rua das Estrelas 57 ☎226 063 017, ✉teatrocampoalegre@mail .telepac.pt. A superb auditorium worth checking out for performances from the Porto.Bando theatre company (an exuberant and acrobatic blend of music, theatre, burlesque and all-round weirdness). Also venue for the "Quintas de Leitura" poetry recitals on Thurs at 10pm. Bus #31 from Rotunda da Boavista.

Teatro de Marionetas do Porto Teatro de

Belomonte, Rua de Belomonte 57 ☎222 083 341, ⓦwww.marionetasdoporto.pt. Portugal's best puppet theatre, run by real fans of the genre, and producing children's productions in addition to thought-provoking commentaries on contemporary themes. Holds an excellent festival in December.

Teatro Nacional São João Pr. da Batalha ☎800 108 675, ⓦwww.tnsj.pt. Major plays by nationally acclaimed troupes or the resident company in this enchanting building, plus opera.

Teatro Universitário do Porto Rua Jorge Viterbo

Cultural and other festivals

For exact dates, times and venues, check with the turismos or at Ⓦwww.portoturismo.pt/en/eventos.

February Fantasporto international film festival Ⓦ www.fantasporto.online.pt, finishes early March. Portugal's window on international cult cinema, anything from Hitchcock and the *Wizard of Oz* to *Blade Runner, Frankenstein* and contemporary movies.

March–April Festival Intercéltico do Porto – Celtic sounds from Portugal, Galicia, Brittany, Wales, Ireland and Scotland.

April–May Fazer a Festa – international theatre festival in the gardens of the Palácio de Cristal Ⓦ www.teatroartimagem.org.

May Corta! Festival Internacional de Curtas Metragens do Porto (Ⓦ www.corta.com.pt), for short movies, usually at the Biblioteca Almeida Garrett in the gardens of the Palácio do Cristal.

May–June Book Festival at the Palácio de Cristal; International Festival of Youth Theatre in various open-air venues, and Festival Internacional de Teatro de Expressão Ibérica, highlighting theatre from all over the Latin world.

June Festival da Fábrica – contemporary dance at Teatro Helena Sá e Costa; Comer no Porto (food festival) next to the Alfândega.

June–September PortoCartoon World Festival at Museu Nacional da Imprensa.

July International Folklore Festival on last Saturday of July; Jazz no Parque at Serralves; Encontros com o Barroco (Baroque music) in churches.

July–August Festa da Cerveja (beer fest) in Foz do Douro.

August Noites Ritual Rock (rock music) at the Palácio de Cristal, on the last weekend – major Portuguese bands and some international acts.

September-October Porto Jazz Festival at the Rivoli Teatro Municipal; Festival Cómico da Maia, comedy in Maia, north of the city.

October International classical music competition held at the Rivoli Teatro Municipal; and the possibly unique Festa do Nabo (Turnip Festival) in Gondomar, Porto's eastern suburb.

October–November Fado Festival at the Coliseu.

October–December Contemporary Art Festival.

November Portugal Fashion; Encontro Internacional de Coros da Cidade do Porto (international choirs); and Ponti – the best of the annual theatre festivals – at the Teatro Nacional São João.

December Feira de Artesanato (crafts festival), a two-week bash at the Palácio de Cristal; Festival de Marionetas (puppet theatre festival) at the Teatro de Marionetas.

Ferreira 120, off Rua Dom Manuel II ☏ 226 090 103. Intimate venue for plays by theatre students. **Teatro da Vilarinha** Corner of Rua da Vilarinha and Circunvalação ☏226 108 924, Ⓔpevento@clix.pt. Home of the Pé de Vento theatre company (including occasional productions for kids). Bus #52 from Cordoaria.

Shopping

Porto's main shopping drag is Rua de Santa Catarina, with its fair share of designer boutiques, clothes shops, jewellers and elegant malls. However, one of the city's abiding pleasures is its surviving **traditional shops**, tucked away in side streets, in which you'll find anything from *bacalhau* and dusty bottles of vintage port to filigree gold jewellery and antiques. **Bookshops** are concentrated along Rua de Ceuta and Rua da Fábrica, running west from Avenida dos Aliados, though the most atmospheric – reviewed below – are to the south and west of here. A handful of Porto's old-style **markets** survive, though have largely been eclipsed by modern **shopping centres** – the biggest of which is NorteShopping, in the northwest at Senhora da Hora (metro Linha A).

Traditional **shopping hours** are Monday to Friday 9am to 6/7pm (some shops close for an hour at lunch), Saturday 9am to 1am. Some of the larger shops open all day until 8pm, even on Sundays, whilst the shopping centres tend to close at midnight. Unless otherwise stated, the shops listed below are closed Saturday afternoon and all day Sunday.

Arts, crafts and design

Casa de Ferragens Carvalho e Baptista Rua do Almada 79–83. Fashionable if not always useful designer objects, including items by renowned local architect Álvaro Siza Vieira.
Centro Regional de Artes Tradicionais (CRAT) Rua da Reboleira 37. In a beautiful seventeenth-century riverside building, this is the best place for regional crafts, especially ceramics, and it also stages temporary exhibitions. Try your hand at *azulejo* painting. Closed Mon.

Fernando Dias dos Santos Rua dos Clérigos 45–47. A touristy place in an eighteenth-century building, making and selling wonderful regional costumes (which you can have made-to-measure).
O Galo Rua Mouzinho da Silveira 68. Decorative ceramics, including ubiquitous Barcelos cockerels, and works by celebrated ceramic artists, the late Rosa Ramalho and her niece, Júlia.

Books and music

Chaminé da Mota Rua das Flores 28. Gorgeous secondhand bookshop (*alfarrabista*) complete with antique decorations, including *rialejos* – giant music boxes that play punched metal discs.
FNAC Rua de Santa Catarina; also at NorteShopping. The city's biggest selection of music CDs and books, plus computer and audio-visual hardware. Daily to 10pm.
Livraria Britânica do Porto Rua José Falcão 184. Good selection of English-language books.

Livraria Lello & Irmão Rua das Carmelitas 144. Probably *the* most beautiful shop in the country, this galleried Art Nouveau bookshop – designed in 1906 by Xavier Esteves – with its staircase just begging for a grand entrance, is a delight beyond words. Sells both new and secondhand books, plus CDs, and has a small café on the first floor. Closed Sun.

Food and drink

Casa Chinesa Rua Sá da Bandeira 343. One of Porto's best-known traditional groceries, going strong since the 1940s, now concentrating on health food, both imported (tofu, miso and other delicacies) and otherwise hard-to-find Portuguese produce like dried algae, herbal remedies, sweets and liqueurs.
Casa Margaridense Trav. de Cedofeita 20A. One of the oldest bakeries in the country, which uses traditional methods such as burning *carqueja* – a variety of broom which reaches high temperatures while producing very little ash. Best known as

purveyors of Porto's finest *pão de ló* – large spongy cakes containing precisely 24 egg yolks each, particularly sought after at Easter.
Loja do Infante Rua Infante Dom Henrique 83–85. A huge selection of vintage ports in this *garrafeira* ("bottle shop"), some over a century old, in a lovely sixteenth-century building.
A Pérola do Bolhão Rua Formosa 279, facing Bolhão market. A great little grocery, founded in 1917, loved as much for its garish Art Nouveau facade as for its cluttered stock of *bacalhau*, port wine, cheese and smoked hams.

Markets

Cais da Ribeira Fruit and veg are sold on weekday mornings along the riverbank.
Feira das Flores Pr. da Liberdade. An all-day Sunday flower fest between April and October.
Feira dos Passarinhos Campo dos Mártires da Pátria. Birds, cages, and birds in cages on Sunday mornings.
Feira de Vandôma Rua das Fontaínhas down to Alameda das Fontaínhas. A long-established Saturday-morning flea market overlooking the river. Some stalls sell food, but most have a splendid spread of unremitting if fascinating junk.
Mercado do Bolhão Three blocks east of Av. dos Aliados. Porto's largest surviving food and flower market, nowadays also dealing in handicrafts and dubious South American pep potions. Also has cafés. Mon–Fri 8am–5pm, Sat 8am–1pm.

Miscellaneous

Armazém dos Linhos Tecidos de Alcobaça Rua de Passos Manuel 19. Retail and wholesale linen from Alcobaça, plus decorative fabrics and embroideries, in a late nineteenth-century building.
Cardoso Cabeleireiro Rua do Bonjardim 105. Manufacturing quality wigs, hairpieces and other hairy stuff since 1906.
Casa do Coração de Jesus Rua Mouzinho da Silveira 302. A glorious collection of religious paraphernalia, from kitsch altar decorations and plastic figurines of Jesus and the saints, to incense, crosses and priests' gowns.
Cor do Tempo Largo Capitão Pinheiro Torres Meireles 25. A wide selection of antique bric-a-brac, including sports equipment and optical instruments.

Listings

Airlines Air France ⊤ 229 413 131, reservations ⊤ 808 202 800; Alitalia ⊤ 229 416 848; British Airways ⊤ 229 486 315, reservations ⊤ 808 220 125; Ibéria ⊤ 229 490 608, reservations ⊤ 808 261 261; KLM ⊤ 229 439 747; Lufthansa ⊤ 229 437 900; Portugália ⊤ 229 412 075; Sabena ⊤ 229 413 112; TAP ⊤ 226 080 200 or 226 080 255.
Banks and exchange The main banks and ATMs are concentrated around Pr. da Liberdade and around Pr. Almeida Garrett, at the lower end of Av. dos Aliados. Normal banking hours are Mon–Fri 8.30am–3pm, though exchange bureaux have longer hours (to 6pm weekdays, also Sat) and include: Intercontinental, Rua Ramalho Ortigão 10, around the corner from the main turismo ⊤ 222 005 557; Portocâmbios, Rua Rodrigues Sampaio 193, to the Câmara Municipal ⊤ 222 000 238; Nova Câmbios, Rua Sampaio Bruno 37 ⊤ 222 074 650; and Cotacâmbios at the airport, open 24hr ⊤ 229 419 518.
Buses Bus companies and their terminals, plus detailed frequencies to destinations country-wide, are given in "Travel details" on p.375.
Car rental Avis, Rua Guedes de Azevedo 125 ⊤ 222 055 947, airport ⊤ 229 449 525; Castanheira (agent for Budget, & also motorbikes), Av. da Boavista 918 ⊤ 808 252 627, airport ⊤ 229 443 714; Europcar, Rua de Santa Catarina 1158–1164 ⊤ 808 204 050, airport ⊤ 229 482 452; Guerin (agent for Alamo/National), Rua do Bolhão 182 ⊤ 222 002 363, airport ⊤ 229 484 250; Hertz, Rua de Santa Catarina 899 ⊤ 800 238 238; Rodalin (agent for Budget), Rua do Campo Alegre 290 ⊤ 226 001 905, airport ⊤ 229 416 534; Sixt, Rua Oliveira Monteiro 1058 ⊤ 228 328 574, airport ⊤ 229 483 752.
Consulates Consulates are usually open Mon–Fri mornings only. UK, Av. da Boavista 3072 ⊤ 226 184 789, Ⓔ consular.oporto@fco.gov.uk; USA, Av. da Boavista 3523 ⊤ 226 186 606, Ⓕ 226 186 625.
Football Futebol Clube do Porto, crowned European Champions in 2004, play at the Estádio do Dragão in Antas, off Av. Fernão Magalhães ⊤ 707 200 384, Ⓦ www.fcporto.pt (metro Linha A). Boavista FC play at Estádio do Bessa, Rua 1 de Janeiro, off Av. da Boavista ⊤ 226 071 000. Tickets cost €10–40 depending on the match and the seat location.
Hospitals The major hospitals are Hospital de Santo António at Largo Prof. Abel Salazar ⊤ 222 077 500, and Hospital de São João, on the Circunvalação ring road in the north ⊤ 225 512 100. In an emergency, call ⊤ 112.
Internet FNAC, Rua de Santa Catarina 73 (Mon–Fri 10am–10pm, Sat 9am–10pm, Sun 11am–8pm); NetPlay, Rua da Torrinha 111 (Mon–Sat 10am–midnight, Sun 2–7pm); Portoweb, Pr. General Humberto Delgado 291 (Mon–Sat 10am–2am, Sun

3pm–2am); Portugal Telecom (PT), Pr. da Liberda-de (Mon–Sat 10am–10pm, Sun 2–9pm).

Left luggage Coin-operated lockers at Campanhã and São Bento train stations (€1/24hr; maximum 72hr).

Library The state-of-the-art Biblioteca Municipal Almeida Garrett is at the Palácio de Cristal, Rua de Entre Quintas 328 (Tues–Sat 10am–6pm; ☎ 226 081 000); or there's the Biblioteca Pública Municipal do Porto, Rua Dom João VI, facing the Jardim de São Lázaro (Mon–Fri 9am–8pm, Sat 10am–6pm; ☎ 225 193 480).

Outdoor activities Arrepio, Rua Prof. Antão Almeida Garrett 229 ☎ & ℱ 228 303 940, orga-nizes canoeing, rafting, diving and caving, hiking, mountaineering, mountain biking, horse riding and paragliding. Contact Trilhos, Rua de Belém 94 ☎ 225 504 604, Ⓦ www.trilhos.pt, for canoeing and rafting, hiking, mountaineering, mountain biking and caving.

Pharmacies Late-night and 24hr pharmacies (*far-mácias de serviço*) operate on a rota basis; details at the back of *Jornal de Notícias*, or call ☎ 118 for information.

Police Polícia de Turismo, Rua Clube dos Fenia-nos, close to the main turismo (☎ 222 081 833). The PSP are at Rua Augusto Rosa, next to Teatro Nacional São João (☎ 222 088 518), and there's a station at the southwest corner of Mercado Ferreira Borges.

Post office The main post office, where poste restante ends up, faces the east side of the town hall on Pr. General Humberto Delgado (Mon–Fri 8am–9pm, Sat 9am–6pm).

Swimming pools The best is Clube Fluvial Portuense, Rua Aleixo Mota, on the riverbank in Pasteleira district near the youth hostel (Mon–Fri 8am–9pm; plus June-Sept Sat & Sun 9am–7pm, Oct-May Sat 9am–7pm, Sun 9am–1pm; ☎ 226 198 460. Bus #1 from Pr. Almeida Garrett or #24 from Cordoaria.

Taxis Radio Táxis ☎ 225 073 900, Taxis Invicta ☎ 225 022 693; Taxis Unidos ☎ 225 029 898. Rent-a-Cab, Rua de Santa Catarina 715 ☎ 222 001 530, has English-speaking drivers.

Telephones There are phone booths at the main post office (see above), and at Portugal Telecom, Pr. da Liberdade 62 (Mon–Sat 10am–10pm, Sun 2–9pm).

Trains Trains to Aveiro, Braga, Guimarães and Peso da Régua start at São Bento station, though these and all other services also call at Campanhã station – see "Arrival and information", p.300. Timetables and train information are available from the stations and on Ⓦ www.cp.pt. Always check departure times and stations in advance: many intercity services require a seat reservation (particularly to Coimbra/Lisbon), which you can do prior to departure, though allow yourself plenty of time.

Travel agencies Nortelândia, Rua de Ceuta 47 ☎ 223 393 320, Ⓦ www.nortelandia.com, is use-ful for budget/student travel, as is Abreu Jovem, Av. dos Aliados 221 ☎ 222 043 580, Ⓦ www .abreu.pt. Reliable general agents include Abreu's other branches at Av. dos Aliados 207 ☎ 222 043 500, Pr. da República 100 ☎ 223 391 940, and Av. da Boavista 1681 ☎ 225 430 160; and Portus, Rua Júlio Dinis 587 ☎ 226 004 254, Ⓦ www .portusviagens.pt.

Around Porto: the coast

The coastline around Porto is, for the most part, agreeably wild, though the chilly Atlantic is all too frequently polluted by discharges from the decrepit oil refinery at Leça da Palmeira, north of the city, and by untreated efflu-ent from Porto and the Douro. The good news is that things are gradually improving as water treatment plants are opened, though caution is still advised for bathers.

Before the Algarve developed into a major summer resort, the seaside town of **Espinho**, south of Porto, was the darling of northern Portugal's monied classes, but a rash of unchecked construction since the 1970s has destroyed much – if not all – of its charm. The town's famous casino offers little consolation, though surfers may well hit the jackpot. Trains run this way at least hourly, between Porto's São Bento station and Aveiro.

North of Porto, there's a distinct contrast in the beautiful seafaring town of **Vila do Conde**, which has managed to keep its historic centre intact. Just to the north of here, the burgeoning resort town of **Póvoa do Varzim** is distinguished by its profusion of excellent fish restaurants, a good museum and particularly colourful annual celebrations. Both Vila do Conde and Póvoa are due to be hooked up to Porto's metro network in 2006; in the meantime, catch the metro as far as it goes (currently the airport) and change to a shuttle bus (same ticket).

Espinho

ESPINHO, 18km south of Porto, is a decaying beach resort, littered with ugly high-rise buildings. Hot and overcrowded in summer, windswept and deserted in winter, it has a strangely suburban feel, a railway line right through the centre, and a dull grid of numbered (rather than named) streets. The water pollution doesn't help matters either; the cleanest beach is the Praia da Baía, next to the breakwater facing the casino, though its on-off Blue Flag status should be taken with a pinch of salt. Not that this deters surfers and bodyboarders since Espinho's breakers are pretty decent. Invert Surf Shop, 1km inland at Rua 32 no. 814 (T227 310 302, Wwww .surfshopnet.com), has advice and equipment. The surf shop faces the municipal swimming pool, and there's another pool, containing filtered seawater, at the north end of the esplanade on Rua 6 (Mon–Fri 8.15am –7.30pm, Sat–Sun 8.15am–12.30pm), which also offers a range of therapeutic and beauty treatments.

The coast road in from Vila Nova de Gaia becomes Avenida 20 in Espinho. The street numbers, incidentally, are even parallel to the sea, odd perpendicular. The **train station** lies in the thick of things on Avenida 8, close to the beach and next to the casino. The **turismo** is close by at Rua 6 (June–Sept Mon–Fri 9.30am–7.30pm, Sat & Sun 10am–1pm & 3–7pm; Oct–May Mon–Fri 9.30am–noon & 2–5.30pm, Sat 9.30am–noon; T227 340 911).

The cheapest **accommodation** is at the old-fashioned *Residencial de Espinho*, Rua 19 no. 326 (T227 340 002, F227 312 636; ❸). *Hotel Mar Azul*, Avenida 8 no. 676 (T227 340 824, F227 312 636; ❸) has more comfortable en-suite rooms; while, on the same street, *Hotel Nery* at no. 826 (T227 347 364, F227 348 596; ❸), has its own parking and a bar. Upmarket choices are the four-star *PraiaGolfe Hotel,* Rua 6, by the train station (T227 331 000, Wwww.praiagolfe .com; ❼), and the five-star *Hotel Solverde*, 2km north of town (T227 335 500, Wwww.solverde.pt; ❾), both with pools and sea views. The **campsite** is at Lugar dos Mochos (T227 343 718), 1km inland on the north edge of town, with plenty of shade.

Espinho might not be the greatest overnight stop, but a table at one of the promenade restaurants at least provides a view of the sea. The most famous **restaurant** is the moderately priced *Casa Marreta* on the esplanade at Rua 2 nos. 1355–1361 (T227 340 091; closed Mon), which serves sublime fish and seafood. Slightly cheaper is *Aquário*, Rua 4 no. 540 (T227 330 370), for fresh fish in refreshingly simple surroundings. The *Casa do Pescador* in the fishermen's quarter at the south end of town, just beyond Rua 2, is good deal more basic but also does superlative seafood. If you're around on Monday, don't miss the **weekly market** – one of the largest in the country – where you'll find an extraordinary selection of dried and crystallized fruits. It's held in the gardens one block east of Avenida 20, between streets 27 and 41.

En route to Espinho, it's well worth stopping at the small settlement of **Miramar**, 10km south of Porto, to see the Capela do Senhor da Pedra, a seventeenth-century chapel bizarrely situated on a rocky, wavebeaten headland jutting out from the beach.

Vila do Conde

VILA DO CONDE, 27km north of Porto, has become quite a significant resort over recent years, but has lost refreshingly little of its character in the process, helped along by some admirable restoration work on buildings that other town councils might simply have demolished. The old part of Vila do Conde, 1km back from the coast on the north bank of the Rio Ave, retains an active fishing port, modest ship-building yards and an atmospheric medieval quarter, whose cobbled alleys, whitewashed buildings and churches make for an attractive place to wander. The beaches on the other hand, boasting long stretches of fine sand, have been steadily developed right up the coast as far as Póvoa do Varzim. To the south, the sands come to an end at the mouth of the Rio Ave, marked by the stumpy Forte de São João Baptista, now a luxury hotel.

The old-town streets are at their best on **saints' days**, when the little street-corner votive chapels are illuminated by candles: the main ones are São João (night of June 23/24), Nossa Senhora do Socorro (end-Aug), and Nossa Senhora da Guia (Feb 2). Other events include an antiques market (third Sun of the month) and the town's **Feira Nacional de Artesanato** (crafts fair), held in the last week of July and the first week of August.

Arrival, information and accommodation

Vila do Conde's main metro station will be sited 300m east of the convent, close to the river and the Centro de Ciência Viva. In the meantime, **buses** shuttle between the last metro stop and the town, for which metro tickets remain valid. Other buses, run by Linhares and Auto-Viação do Minho, stop on the main north–south road at the small **turismo**, at Rua 5 de Outubro 207 (July–Sept Mon–Fri 10am–7pm, Sat & Sun 9.30am–noon & 1.30–6.30pm; Oct–June Mon–Fri 10am–7pm, Sat 9.30am–noon & 1.30–6pm; ☎252 642 700). The **main turismo**, an attractive ivy-clad house, is around the corner at Rua 25 de Abril 103 (mid–June to Aug daily 9am–7pm; rest of the year daily 9am–6pm; ☎252 248 473, ⓦwww.cm-viladoconde.pt), and is the best place for information about accommodation and day-trips in the region. It's also the starting point for a number of guided **audio walks** (*guias áudio*) around town – you'll need to leave your passport or other ID. Except on Friday mornings, when the weekly market is held, you'll always find shaded **parking** space in the enclosure just to the north of the market on Rua 5 de Outubro.

In summer, **accommodation** in town fills quickly, so if you haven't booked ahead you may need to contact the main turismo for their list of private **rooms** (❶). Out of season, prices everywhere can drop by a third. The nearest **campsite** (☎252 633 237, ℱ252 643 593) is 3km south of town and the river, in a pine grove next to the beach at Árvore. Slightly more intimate and also on the beach, with plenty of shade, is the one at Vila Chã, 4km further south (☎229 283 168).

Estalagem do Brazão Av. Dr João Canavarro 14 ☎252 642 016, Ⓔestalagembrazao@mail.telepac .pt. Grand if somewhat austere four-star hotel set in a partially modernized seventeenth-century mansion, and decked out in a strange mixture of period furnishings and 1960 and 70s decor. There's a bar and reasonable restaurant. Parking. Breakfast included. ❺

Forte de São João Av. do Brasil ☎222 240 600, ⓦwww.hotelfortesjoao.com. This airy conversion of the town's seventeenth-century pentagonal fortress is very well done, albeit in a minimalist IKEA-like style. The best rooms have ocean or river views – and the hotel's seven suites have aquariums – while there's also a library and wine bar. The chic *O Bartholomeo* restaurant (expensive; reservations advised) has a French-Portuguese touch, and serves a cultivated, seasonally

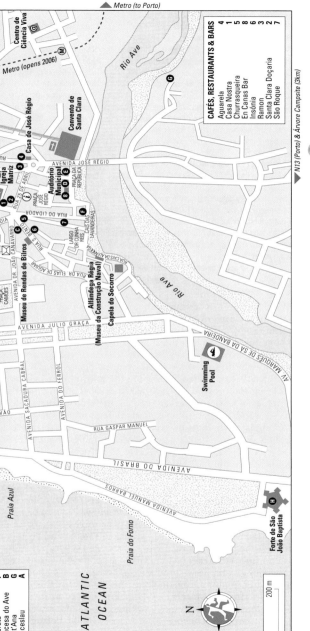

VILA DO CONDE

ACCOMMODATION

Brazão · · · · · · · · · · · C
Forte de São João · · · · · H
Le Villageois · · · · · · · · E
Manco d'Areia · · · · · · · D
Patarata · · · · · · · · · · F
Princesa do Ave · · · · · · B
Sant'Ana · · · · · · · · · · G
Venceslau · · · · · · · · · A

CAFÉS, RESTAURANTS & BARS

Aguarela · · · · · · · · · · 4
Casa Nostra · · · · · · · · 1
Churrasqueira · · · · · · · 5
En Canas Bar · · · · · · · 8
Insónia · · · · · · · · · · · 6
Ramon · · · · · · · · · · · 3
Santa Clara Doçaria · · · · 2
São Roque · · · · · · · · · 7

changing, menu of meat, game and seafood, plus fado on Wed evenings. Parking. ❽

Residencial Manco d'Areia Pr. da República 84 ⓣ & ⓕ 252 631 748. A motley assortment of rooms, some dingy, some better and with bathrooms – the best have nice river views, but are overpriced nonetheless. ❸, river-view rooms ❹

Pensão Patarata Cais das Lavandeiras 18 ⓣ 252 631 894. A basic *pensão* over a not-too-enticing restaurant and bar. There's a mixed bag of rooms, the better ones being big, airy and overlooking the waterfront. ❷

Residencial Princesa do Ave Av. Dr. António José Sousa Pereira 261 ⓣ 252 642 065, ⓕ 252 632 972. A pleasant and relatively cheap modern choice half-way between beach and town, with en-suite rooms with satellite TV. ❸

Quinta das Alfaias 2km inland of Mindelo, off the Santo Tirso road, 10km south of town ⓣ252 662 146, ⓦwww.quintadasalfaias.com. A wonderfully elegant early nineteenth-century country house set in extensive gardens and orchards, and with a comfortable verandah and large swimming pool. It has four rooms, plus one suite and three self-catering apartments, all with bathrooms, phone and TV. The decor throughout is simple, with plenty of bare granite. Breakfast included. Parking. ❺

Hotel Sant'Ana Monte de Sant'Ana ⓣ 252 641 717, ⓦ www.santanahotel.net. On the south side of the river, the appeal of this former motel lies in its views rather than the dull modern design. Staff are unfailingly friendly, though, and there's also an indoor swimming pool, sauna and solarium, and affordable restaurant. Parking. ❸

Hospedaria Venceslau Corner Rua 5 de Outubro and Rua das Mós ⓣ 252 646 362. Modern, comfortable rooms, most with TVs. ❷

Le Villageois Pr. da República 94 ⓣ 252 631 119. This is the best budget option in town, with clean, well-furnished, en-suite rooms, though some lack windows. The pretty restaurant below (closed Mon) serves huge portions of moderately priced food (skate a speciality), and has a few outside tables. ❷

The Town

Whichever way you approach town, the enormous hulk of the eighteenth-century **Convento de Santa Clara**, on a rise behind the old bridge, is unmistakable. It's currently a juvenile reformatory, and isn't open to the public, but you can visit the attached church, whose fourteenth-century Gothic origins have only partially been masked by its Renaissance additions, including a profusely decorated arch and multi-ribbed vault. The church contains two particularly fine Manueline tombs: that of the convent's founder, Dom Afonso Sanches, and his wife Dona Teresa Martins. Running into the north side of the complex is a well-preserved early eighteenth-century **aqueduct** – the country's second-longest – which starts at Terroso (p.345), north of town.

Completely overshadowed by the convent's west facade is a small row of houses, most of which are gradually crumbling away. The exception is the **Casa de José Régio**, Avenida José Régio 132 (Tues–Fri 9.30am–12.30pm & 2–6pm, Sat 10am–noon & 2–5pm, Sun 2–5pm; free), which displays popular art (particularly crucifixes) collected by Vila do Conde's most famous son, the writer and poet José Régio. A five-minute walk east of here along the river, past the new metro station, brings you to the **Centro de Ciência Viva** (Living Science Centre; Tues–Sun 10am–6pm; ⓦwww.viladoconde.cienciaviva.pt; €2.50), worth a visit for its bizarrely shaped glass-roofed building alone. It offers a series of interactive and educational exhibits in English and Portuguese, largely covering marine topics like tidal systems, the life cycle of water, or the food chain.

The town's **market** (Mon–Sat) is at its busiest on Friday, when you'll find everything from farm produce and shoes to traditional children's toys and articulated puppets. Overlooking the far side of the market is the sixteenth-century **Igreja Matriz**, a Manueline beauty with a soaring, airy interior and – thanks to the Basque workmen who helped with its construction – an unusual but very effective mix of Spanish and Portuguese styles, including a distinctly Moorish dome. The church contains a small museum of sacred art (June–Sept daily 10am–noon & 2–4pm; Oct–May daily 2–4pm; free), with a good selection of liturgical attire, effigies and other religious artefacts. The old town covers the area south of the church and en route you can call in at the **Museu de Rendas de Bilros** housed in an attractive eighteenth-century town house at Rua de São Bento 70 (Mon–Fri 9am–noon & 2–6pm, Sat & Sun 3–6pm; ⓦ www.mrbvc.net; free). This has displays of Vila do Conde's celebrated lacework (*rendas de bilros*) and embroidery, examples of which are on sale here or at the smaller turismo.

From the museum a series of narrow streets heads down to the elegant Praça da República on the river bank. The walk along the river through the old **fishing quarter** is punctuated by amusing sculptures and modest bars and *casas de pasto*, while on the other side of the river are the **ship yards**. Vila do Conde's shipbuilding industry is amongst the oldest in Europe, and fishing boats reminiscent of fifteenth-century caravels are still constructed here, albeit in metal rather than in wood. The old skills survive, though – it was here that a replica of Bartolomeu Dias' caravel was constructed in 1987 as part of the 500th anniversary celebrations of his epic voyage around the Cape of Good Hope. Another replica, of a sixteenth-century *nau* (larger than caravels and used for freighting and warfare), graces the interior of the **Museu da Construção Naval**, on Rua do Cais da Alfândega (Tues–Sun 10am–6pm; free). This also displays part of a massive archive of priceless documents from the golden era of the Portuguese Discoveries, including material relating to cartography, navigation, and life at sea. The museum is housed in the **Alfândega Régia** (royal customs house), founded in 1487 to wrest control of the lucrative taxes from the church.

Just along from here is the town's most memorable sight, the conspicuously Moorish white dome of the **Capela do Socorro**, built in 1603. Such domes are a typical feature of the tombs (*koubbas*) of North African saints, and this one bears witness to the conversion of Moorish craftsmen during the Inquisition. Inside, the *azulejos* depicting the Adoration of the Magi provide further proof of Moorish pragmatism, as several of the figures are wearing turbans.

Eating, drinking, nightlife and entertainment

The choice of **restaurants** pales in comparison to neighbouring Póvoa, but many are long-established and enjoy solid reputations. The best place in town is *O Bartholomeo* in the *Fort de São João* hotel, while *Le Villageois* also has a nice restaurant (see "Arrival, information and accommodation" above for both). Apart from seafood, a speciality is handmade *folar* or *pão doce* ("sweet bread"), traditionally given away at Easter and Christmas, particularly to people the giver had managed to annoy over the previous year. A good time to be around is at the end of August, for the nine-day **Feira de Gastronomia** (food fair) held in the gardens of Avenida Júlio Graça.

There's not much nightlife to speak of, though the handful of fashionable **bars** on Praça da República and along the river are worth trying. Sandwiched among the square's restaurants and bars is the **Auditório Municipal** (Tues–Fri 3–11pm, Sat & Sun 3pm–midnight), which shows temporary exhibitions of photography and local arts and crafts, and hosts performances of theatre, dance and music; there's also a pleasant bar. A six–day **European short-film festival** is held here (see ⓦ www.curtasmetragens.pt), beginning on the first Sunday of July.

Cafés and restaurants

Aguarela Rua de Santo Amaro 6 no phone. The favourite haunt of José Régio (it's three doors down from his house) and other artistic dissidents during the dictatorship, and still a good place for food at reasonable prices. Closed Tues. Inexpensive.

Casa Nostra Rua da Igreja ☏252 631 730. A classy *restaurante típico*, popular with tourists and locals alike, and specializing in *petiscos* (traditional snacks) and fish. Closed Sun. Moderate.

Churrasqueira (João da Ester) Corner Rua de São Bento and Rua do Lidador. A simple restaurant serving extremely cheap lunchtime *pratos do dia* at (€4), and not much more expensive à la carte dinners. The food's all right, if nothing special. Closed Sun. Inexpensive.

Ramon Rua 5 de Outubro 176 ☎ 252 631 334. An unfussy local restaurant, particularly good for shellfish. Closed Tues. Moderate.

Santa Clara Doçaria Conventual Rua 25 de Abril ☎ 252 647 892. A tea room with some of the best pastries and cakes in town, using recipes concocted in the convent. Inexpensive.

São Roque Rua do Lidador 128 ☎ 252 631 184. Hidden away in the old town, this is a modern place with reliably good food, from roast kid to fish. Closed Mon. Moderate.

Bars

Azenha Dom Zameiro Bar Ponte d'Ave, Vilarinho, 3km northeast of town. Live music (anything from grunge to salsa) can be heard here Thurs–Sat.

En Canas Pr. da República. Particularly enjoyable bar decked out with American road-trip memorabilia, busy most nights from around 10pm.

Insónia Rua de São Bento. A spartan, studenty feel in a cavernous, granite-faced building in the old town.

Listings

Hospital Hospital Distrital, Largo Dr. António José de Almeida ☎ 252 642 525.
Internet Free access at Centro Municipal da Juventude, Av. João Graça (Mon–Fri 10am -8.30pm, Sat 10am-7.30pm); Biblioteca Municipal, Av. Dr. António Sousa Pereira (Mon–Fri 10am–8pm, Sat 2–6pm); and Centro

de Ciência Viva, Av. Bernardino Machado 96 (Tues–Sun 10am–6pm).
Police PSP, Largo Dr. Cunha Reis ☎ 252 631 170.
Post office Av. Dr. João Canavarro (Mon–Fri 8.30am-6pm).
Swimming pool Av. Marquês de Sá da Bandeira, facing the river (closed Sept; ☎ 252 248 471).

Póvoa do Varzim

PÓVOA DO VARZIM is about 4km north of Vila do Conde, but the two couldn't be more different. Although Póvoa also retains a small harbour, along with the ruins of an eighteenth-century fortress, it's very much a large resort – brash and busy, and aimed firmly at beach-loving sun-worshippers. A casino and a line of modern hotels open onto the 8km-long beach (partly pebbly, so bring flip-flops or sandals), which is packed in summer with Portuguese holidaymakers. The crowds help to create a lively, enjoyable seaside feel, restaurants are excellent value, there's plenty of nightlife, and there usually seems to be enough accommodation to go round.

However, there's not all that much to do other than swim, lounge around on the beach and lose some coins at the casino. The **Museu Municipal de Etnografia e História**, Rua Visconde de Azevedo (Tues–Sun 10am–12.30pm & 2.30–6pm; €1, free Thurs) is the sole cultural draw, housed in an elegant eighteenth-century *solar* 300m east of the turismo. This contains well-presented displays of local archeological finds, plus an exhaustive collection of anything and everything connected to seafaring through the ages. There's also a room dedicated to a genetically transmitted muscle-wasting disease, familial amyloidotic polyneuropathy or *amyloidosis*, that's particularly common in Póvoa. Beyond its human impact, the disease is proof of early Viking contact with this part of the coast, as the only other hotspots are in Sweden, and among Swedish and Portuguese immigrants elsewhere. Indeed, northern Portugal's Viking heritage is apparent in the museum's fascinating display of fishermen's symbols – so-called *Siglas Poveiras* – which are in many instances identical to Scandinavian runes.

Póvoa's much-reduced historical centre is one of the focal points for a series of traditional festivals, the best of which is the **Romaria de Nossa Senhora**

da Assunção (August 15), when local fishermen carry life-sized images of Our Lady of the Assumption to the quayside to bless those who have perished at sea; the whole event is accompanied by fireworks let off from fishing boats. A similar event occurs for **Nossa Senhora das Dores** – the festivities culminate on the third Sunday of September, though the accompanying fair runs from the preceding Thursday to the following Tuesday. On the **Festa de São Pedro** (night of 28–29 June), the town enjoys a procession, an abundance of chargrilled sardines and the curious *saltar a fogeira* ("fire jumping"), in which locals take turns to leap over bonfires – the ritual dates back to pre-Roman times. The following day (June 29), various competing *rusgas* – musical groups in traditional garb, accompanied by their often rowdy supporters – congregate in exuberant procession at the town's bull ring on Avenida Vasco da Gama. Another procession follows in the evening.

Arrival, information and accommodation

The N13 highway from Porto and Vila do Conde to Viana do Castelo cuts through town about 1km inland. Most of the hotels lies between it and the coast. The beach can be reached from almost anywhere in town simply by heading west, with all roads eventually funnelling towards the coastal Avenida dos Banhos. **Parking** is easiest in the commercial lots along the Porto–Viana highway. By 2006, the town should be connected by metro to Porto; in the meantime, metro shuttle **buses**, and other buses from Porto (operated by Linhares), stop at Praça do Almada, a few blocks south of the turismo. Other buses finish at the **Central de Camionagem**, inconveniently located in the northern suburbs – head west from here along Avenida do Mar, turning left along Rua Gomes de Amorim for the turismo, or continue straight along Avenida Vasco da Gama to reach the coast.

The **turismo** (mid-June to mid-Sept daily 9am–9pm; rest of the year Mon–Fri 9am–1pm & 2–7pm, Sat & Sun 9.30am–1pm & 2.30–6pm; ☎252 298 120, ⓦwww.cm-pvarzim.pt) is in an unusual turreted building on Praça Marquês de Pombal, along the N13 highway, and distributes an excellent map (which includes most hotels and restaurants), lists of rooms, and booklet detailing bus timetables.

There are plenty of smart **hotels** around, while cheaper *pensões* are to be found mostly along Rua Paulo Barreto – the section of the N13 between the turismo and Praça do Almada. The nearest **campsite** is *Orbitur*, 8km north at Rio Alto and close to a beach (☎252 615 699, ⓦwww.orbitur.pt), which also has bungalows and caravans to rent (both sleep four; ❷); buses run every two hours or so from Praça do Almada.

Hotel Costa Verde Av. Vasco da Gama 56 ☎252 298 600, ✉hcvpovoa@mail.telepac.pt. A decent and well-kept mid-range choice at the north end of town, 200m back from the beach near the bull ring, with well-equipped rooms and a bar. Buffet breakfast included. ❹

Gett Residencial Av. Mouzinho de Albuquerque 54 ☎252 683 206, ✉residencial.gett@clix.pt. A pleasant, bright, modern place on the tree-lined avenue, 200m from the beach. Lift access, friendly and efficient staff, and large rooms with phones and satellite TV. Breakfast included. ❸

Hospedaria Jantarada Rua Paulo Barreto 8 ☎968 103 440. The best inexpensive option, with just five clean rooms above the popular *Don Egas Pais* restaurant, some with bathrooms. ❶

Hotel Mercure Largo do Passeio Alegre 20, next to the casino ☎252 290 400, ⓦwww.mercure.com. The best of the centrally located package-tour places comes complete with bar and restaurant. ❹, with breakfast and sea view ❺

Residência Rêve d'Or Pr. Marquês de Pombal 18, opposite the turismo ☎252 613 870. An antiquated and dark yet calm and attractive family run *pensão* in a green-tiled town-house. Rooms have cable TV and large bathtubs. ❷

Novotel Vermar Rua da Imprensa Regional, 2km north on the seafront ☎252 298 900, ⓦwww

.novotel.com. High-rise complex with almost 200 rooms (get one with a view), plus swimming pool, health club and bar. The *Vasco de Gama* restaurant (expensive) has good sea views, though the menu's influences are from the Minho rather than the coast – meaning plenty of pork (including *rojões*) plus duck and the inevitable *bacalhau*. ❻

Eating, drinking and nightlife

Póvoa has over fifty **restaurants**, most within a block or two of the seafront. There are Chinese restaurants and pizzerias, while if you're into fish, Póvoa is a treat – there's huge choice and competition keeps prices keen. The local speciality is *pescada à poveira* (slices of boiled whiting served with turnip leaves, eggs, potatoes and bread soused in olive oil, onion and paprika), while the adventurous might seek out *buchos de pescada* (boiled whiting stomachs stuffed with chopped whiting liver, onion and parsley), best eaten with olives. Póvoa's **bars and clubs** (they tend to function as both) change their names and styles every few years, though it's a safe bet to say that the best and busiest are invariably along the ocean-front Avenida dos Banhos.

There's a number of annual events and activities aimed at visitors, including a three-week **international classical music festival** in July; ask at the turismo for details, and pick up a copy of the monthly *Agenda Cultural* (free).

Restaurants

Adega Firmino Rua Dr. Caetano de Oliveira 100, two blocks back from the beach ☎ 252 684 695. A great local *adega* with bags of atmosphere and excellent marinated sardines and fish stews. Closed Tues. Inexpensive.

Belo Horizonte Rua Tenente Valadim 63 ☎ 252 624 787. Serves a wide variety of grilled fish, kid goat and other meats, and a great *açorda de marisco*. Moderate.

Casa Costa Rua Dr. Caetano de Oliveira 104 ☎ 252 684 139. A good local *adega*, particularly for *presunto* and fish. Closed Mon. Inexpensive.

Don Egas Pais (Jantarada) Rua Paulo Barreto 8 ☎ 968 103 440. On the unlovely highway but famed for its unique – and resolutely traditional – *bacalhau* dishes. Moderate.

São José Largo do Passeio Alegre 118 ☎ 252 622 339. A good place for seafood, particularly Póvoa's famous *pescada*, and with a fine sea view. Moderate.

Casino

Casino da Póvoa South end of the promenade ☎ 252 690 870, Ⓦ www.casino-povoa.com. Presents the usual concoction of games and cabarets (visiting stars have included the likes of Liza Minelli) – it's known countrywide and for many is the main reason to visit the town. Wed–Sat dinner 8.30pm, show 11pm; Sun lunch 1.30pm, show 3.30pm; prices from €25.

Listings

Bike rental Bikes can be rented in summer from people hanging around the Casino at the south of the promenade; around €10 a day.

Car rental Atlas, Av. Vasco da Gama ☎ 252 682 922; OTM, Rua Dr. Leonardo Coimbra ☎ 252 618 240.

Hospital Hospital São Pedro Pescador, Largo das Dores, two blocks east of the turismo ☎ 252 690 600.

Internet Free access (max 30min) at the Biblioteca Municipal, Rua Padre Afonso Soares, 650m inland off Rua Elias Garcia (Mon–Fri 10am–8pm, Sat 2–6pm); and at Casa da Juventude, Rua Dona Maria I 56, by the bus station (Mon–Sat 10am–8pm).

Police PSP, Pr. Marquês de Pombal, close to the turismo ☎ 252 298 190.

Post office The main post office is at Largo Elísio da Nova; handier is the branch at Av. dos Banhos, north of Rua Elias Garcia.

Scuba diving Clube Naval Povoense, Rua da Ponte 22 (☎ 918 119 106, Ⓔ antonio.vilas@mail.telepac .pt; Mon–Fri 9am–noon & 2–6pm), just off Pr. da República (southwest along Rua Manuel Silva from the turismo), offers PADI-accredited scuba-diving tuition

Taxis Ranks at the west end of Av. Mouzinho de Albuquerque, and at Pr. do Almada, south of the turismo. Or ring Rádio Táxis Varzim ☎ 252 612 288, Táxis Riba-Mar ☎ 252 621 066, or Taxis Unidos ☎ 252 611 800.

Around Póvoa de Varzim

There are four reasonably accessible sites located in or near villages close to Póvoa, which, given a spare day and rented bikes, or a car, would make a rewarding circuit – maps and information leaflets are available from the turismo in Póvoa. **LAÚNDOS**, 7km northeast, is notable for the windmills which stand on São Félix hill. Further on is **RATES**, boasting a splendid eleventh-century Romanesque church (São Pedro) built by the Benedictines in granite for Henry, Count of Burgundy, supposedly on the site of the martyrdom of the first Bishop of Braga. The three naves are timber-roofed while, inside, a series of fine pillars with carved capitals are lit by a colourful rose window. **RIO MAU**, 8km east of Póvoa, is the site of a smaller, but even better decorated, Romanesque church (São Cristóvão), also granite and completed in 1151. The carvings on the capitals are reminiscent of those in Braga cathedral and, in this case, are thought to illustrate the Song of Roland, a medieval French epic glorifying Charlemagne (Charles the Great).

The oldest of the settlements on this circuit is **TERROSO**, just 5km northeast of Póvoa, whose **citânia** – similar to the better-known ones at Sanfins de Ferreira (see p.346) and Briteiros (see p.397) – was excavated at the beginning of this century. Inhabited from around 800–700 BC to 200–300 AD, the double ring of ramparts and dozens of circular house foundations can still be traced. The spring here once fed the eighteenth-century aqueduct which carried water over 999 arches to the Convento de Santa Clara in Vila do Conde.

Santo Tirso and around

Travelling northeast from Porto towards the southern Minho towns of Guimarães and Braga, you pass through attractive, rolling countryside: a mix of market gardening in the valleys, vines on the gentle slopes, and wooded hill tops. The riverside textile town of **Santo Tirso** is the minor capital of this area, and can serve as a base for visiting the Romanesque church at nearby **Roriz** and the Celtic *citânia* of **Sanfins de Ferreira**.

Santo Tirso

Just under 30km northeast of Porto, **SANTO TIRSO** lies on the steep southern bank of the Rio Ave, which flows west to meet the sea at Vila do Conde. It's a pleasant-looking town with plenty of small shady squares and gardens, and its modern development has largely avoided the nineteenth-century kernel. Good times to visit are mid-July, for an international **guitar music festival**, and mid-May, for the *Feira das Tasquinhas* for an abundance of good local food and wine.

At the foot of the slope, by the bridge linking the town to its train station, is the former Benedictine monastery and church of **São Bento**, which now houses an agricultural college and a small municipal museum. This is less than gripping, fielding the usual motley collection of local archeological finds, but take the opportunity to visit the church (daily 8am–noon & 3–7.30pm; free), whose cloister features a fine double row of galleries dating from the fourteenth century, all beautifully restored.

Santo Tirso is served by Linhares **buses** from Póvoa, and Mondinense and Landim buses from Porto; all drop you at the bus station on Rua Infante Dom Henrique. On the plateau cresting the slope is the town hall, a charmless concrete building, with the **turismo** (Mon–Fri 9am–12.30pm & 2–5.30pm; ☎252 830 411, ⓦwww.santo-tirso.com) occupying an annexe. It provides a series of leaflets detailing walks in the surrounding area. If you need a **taxi** (handy for Sanfins and Roriz), call ☎252 850 888.

Central **accommodation** includes the homely *Pensão Caroço* at Largo Coronel Baptista Coelho 48 (☎252 852 823; ❶), or the more expensive *Residencial dos Carvalhais*, at the top of town on Praça Rodrigues Ferreira (☎252 857 894, ⓕ252 857 581; ❸). Much better than either, but needing your own transport, is the *Quinta da Picaria* in Guimarei, 6km south of town off the N105 to Porto (☎912 236 449 or 252 891 297, ⓦwww.turihab.pt; ❺), an eighteenth-century farmhouse with a rustic interior (plenty of bare granite, wood beams and fireplaces). It's run by an English-speaking family, and they have just four bedrooms; meals are available on request, and there are good hikes in the area.

The **restaurant** attached to *Residencial dos Carvalhais* (☎252 857 910) specializes in *arroz de pato*, and artery-clogging *bacalhau com natas* (smothered in cream and oven-baked). There's also a couple of good, inexpensive restaurants on Praça 25 de Abril: *Dona Unisco* at *Hotel Cidnay* (☎252 859 300) has curried squid, monkfish kebabs and excellent local desserts on the menu, including *jesuítas* (meringue-layered millefeuille); whilst at the *São Rosendo* at no. 6 (☎252 853 054), try the *cabrito assado* cooked in a wood-fired oven, finishing with *toucinho do céu* ("heavenly bacon") or *bolo lua de mel* ("honeymoon cake").

Roriz

RORIZ, 10km east of Santo Tirso, is much prettier, but poorly served by public transport. Any bus on the Santo Tirso–Guimarães route can set you down just after Rebordões, leaving a 4km walk to the church of São Pedro, at the top of the village.

The village itself is a mixture of old, rough granite cottages, whitewashed houses and several fairly kitsch creations built by returned emigrants – one is straight out of Disneyland, a Seven Dwarfs' cottage with brown concrete thatch. The date of the elegant Romanesque **Igreja de São Pedro** is disputed, but it's said to stand on the foundations of a Roman temple, later destroyed by the Moors. It was originally the church of the Benedictine monastery that once stood alongside, of which only one building still stands – and that's in private hands. The fine west door is embellished with an early Gothic rose window, adjacent to the solitary bell tower.

Citânia de Sanfins de Ferreira

Another 4km beyond the Igreja de São Pedro, along a track through shady woods and up a gentle slope (badly signposted), are the ruins of the **Citânia de Sanfins de Ferreira** (Mon–Fri 9am–6pm, Sat & Sun 10am–7pm; free), dating from the second century BC. It's a splendidly atmospheric place – perched atop its hill, the skyline to the south appears infinite and, even at the height of summer, the only sound is that of the broom pods popping out their seeds. The site has several rings of protective walls and the foundations of 160 circular huts, arranged in family compounds and separated by wide streets. One of the compounds (the *núcleo familiar* or "family nucleus") has been rebuilt, complete with thatched roof. If you want to go inside, ask for the guardian at the café next to the site, who has the key. He's also happy to show you the site's other attractions – a replica *basto* statue of a warrior (the original is in the archeological museum in Lisbon) standing guard on the crest of the hill, and the ruins of a bathhouse at one of the sources of the Rio Leça. The engraved *pedras formosas* ("beautiful stones") from the bathhouse are now held in the site **museum** (summer June-Sept Tues–Sun 10am–noon & 2–6pm; Oct-May Tues–Sun 10am–noon & 2–5pm; free), a glorious seventeenth-century Baroque mansion inconveniently located 3km from the *citânia*, and 1km from the village of Sanfins de Ferreira. Aside from the *pedras*, and a much older slab engraved with a hunting scene, the museum also displays three gravestones engraved with Celtic crosses, identical to those found in Ireland.

Penafiel and around

At **Penafiel**, 35km east of Porto, you enter *vinho verde* country. The wine's origins lie with the Benedictine monks, who were famed in this region for their laborious terracing of the valley slopes. A further legacy of the Benedictine presence is a dozen of the finest **Romanesque churches** in the country, each gorgeously sited in hamlets hidden away in folds of the countryside. The most impressive is at **Paço de Sousa**, southwest of Penafiel, though there are more churches to the southeast of town too. Although buses run to most areas of interest around Penafiel, they invariably leave at inconvenient times, making it difficult to visit more than one or two in a day – you'll see a lot more with your own transport.

Penafiel

Despite the motorway in the Sousa valley to the west, **PENAFIEL** itself is still split by main road traffic, around which most of the attractions are conveniently situated. Known as Arrifana de Sousa until 1770, Penafiel remains a pretty place, with a tightly packed old town of narrow streets and grand granite-walled houses. A magnificent Renaissance **Igreja da Misericórdia** faces the town hall, while the **Igreja Matriz** is on Rua Direita, built in 1569 by João Correia, whose tomb lies inside. The **Museu Municipal de Penafiel** (Mon–Fri 9.30am–noon & 2–5.30pm, Sat 9.30am–12.30pm; free), five minutes' walk downhill from here on Avenida Sacadura Cabral, next to the turismo, is worth a brief visit for its archeological and ethnological displays.

You'll find the fabulous local wine everywhere in bottles but to get it straight from the *pipa* (barrel), you'll either have to go to the *adega* near the train station or to the charming ivy-festooned **Quinta da Aveleda** (Mon–Fri 9am–noon & 2–5pm; ☎255 718 200, ⓦwww.aveleda.pt; bookings essential; €4 including wine tasting), where the stuff is made. To get there, go 2km down the Porto road, cross the motorway and turn right at the sign – it's 1km further on from this point. The guided tours include wine and cheese tasting, but it's really the gorgeously unkempt, wooded gardens that make the visit.

Practicalities

The **train station** is 3km down the hill from town, but there's no public transport into the centre; take a taxi (around €6) from the station car park. If coming from Porto, it's preferable to arrive by **bus**, which stops by the kiosk outside Penafiel's turismo and further along by the Igreja Matriz. For onward transport, VALPI runs buses to Amarante and Porto from its garage near the Igreja da Misericórdia; Santos, for services to Boelhe and Termas de São Vicente, has an office at Avenida Egas Moniz 69–71; and Asa Douro at Avenida Egas Moniz 125 operates services to Torrão and Paço de Sousa. The **turismo** is on the main street, at Avenida Sacadura Cabral 90 (Mon–Fri 9am–12.30pm & 2–5.30pm; ☎255 712 561), and can mark the location of the area's churches on a map. Beneath the turismo, there's a fine covered **market** (Mon–Sat).

The cheapest **accommodation** is *Casa João da Lixa*, in Largo do Padre Américo (☎255 213 158; **❶**), close to the Igreja Matriz and its bells, with good-value rooms in a friendly family house. A little more expensive is *O Cedro* on Rua do Cedro (☎255 213 551; **❷**), with unexceptional if comfortable en-suite rooms next to a restaurant. Penafiel's leading hotel is the surprisingly modest *Penahotel* facing Parque do Sameiro (☎255 711 420, **🖂**penahotel@mail.telepac.pt; **❸**), with some rooms overlooking the gardens and the modern Santuário de Nossa Senhora da Piedade. *Churrasqueira Central*, Avenida Sacadura Cabral 18 (☎255 214 439), between the turismo and Igreja Matriz, has tasty grilled chicken; just downhill from here, at Rua Engenheiro Matos 67, *Relógio do Sol* (☎255 213 270) serves good inexpensive **food** and has a fine view over the Sousa valley. *O Cedro*'s *churrasqueira* is an equally lively and inexpensive place to eat.

Paço de Sousa

The village of **PAÇO DE SOUSA** – 10km southwest of Penafiel off the N106 – was the former headquarters of the Benedictines in Portugal. It's set beside the Rio Sousa and is a popular picnic spot, easily reached by bus from Penafiel (not Sun), or on the Douro train line from Porto – slow trains on the line stop at Cête, a dozen stations out of Porto and just a kilometre or so away from Paço de Sousa.

The principal sight is the old **Igreja da Abadia** (abbey church), a dark and dank Romanesque-Gothic construction founded in 962 by the Knight, Godo Triutesindo Galendiz. In one corner is the tomb of his descendant, **Egas Moniz**, tutor and adviser to the first king of Portugal, Afonso Henriques, and a great figure of loyalty in Portuguese history. In 1127, shortly after Afonso Henriques had broken away from his grandfather, the King of León, Egas was sent to negotiate a settlement, thus enabling Afonso to concentrate his efforts on defeating the Moors in the south. Within three years, the King of León considered the treaty to be broken on the Portuguese side and threatened all-out war. Egas made his way to León, presented himself and his family and, as can be seen on the panels around the tomb, offered to receive the punishment due to his master. Impressed by his loyalty, mercy was granted and the King sent the minister home unscathed.

There are a couple of **cafés** in the village and an excellent old-fashioned *adega*, *O Moleira*, which serves wine straight from the barrel.

Boelhe, Abragão and Gandra

Apart from Paço de Sousa, the most accessible local church from Penafiel is at **BOELHE**, 10km southeast along the N312 minor road to Entre-os-Rios. São Gens is reputedly the smallest Romanesque church in the country, and it's a simple building, without much architectural detail, which gains its power from a stunning position on the brow of a hill overlooking the Tâmega valley. If it's closed, ask for the key at the nearest house. Note that the last bus back to Penafiel leaves Boelhe at 2.05pm.

At **ABRAGÃO**, 10km southeast along the N320 from Penafiel (last bus back at 6pm), all that survives of the Igreja de São Pedro is the vaulted chapel and transept arch with its rose window, while the Igreja de São Salvador or Cabeça Santa (Holy Head) at **GANDRA**, east off the N106, midway between Penafiel and Torrão, gets its name from the holy skull that used to be kept there. From Gandra, the last bus to Penafiel is at 9.05pm, 8.45pm at weekends.

The Tâmega: Amarante and the Serra do Marão

At Livração, about an hour east of Porto, the Tâmega train line branches off the Douro line for the 12km (half-hour) journey to the beautiful riverside town of **Amarante**. From the start it's a scenic ride, hugging the ravine of the **Rio Tâmega**, a tributary of the Douro, with pine woods and vines clinging to steep slopes, and goats scrambling across the terrace walls to nibble at haystacks. The Tâmega line terminates at Amarante, from where daily buses run up into the **Serra do Marão**, following the course of the Rio Tâmega. You soon feel the climb on the approach to the towns of **Celorico de Basto** and **Mondim de Basto**, both set astride the Tâmega with the Serra do Alvão rising immediately to the east. To the north – and technically in Minho province – is the larger, provincial town of **Cabeceiras de Basto**, which provides a useful link to Braga and Peneda-Gerês National Park. Together, the three Basto towns and their districts form the **Terras de Basto**, a region of fertile countryside that produces a strong *vinho verde* (and some excellent food to go with it). The region's name comes from a number of life-sized Celtic warrior statues – beautifully incised with Celtic emblems on the torso and a shield on the belly – which were originally laid on warrior's graves. *Eu basto* (I suffice) was their credo, expressing a willingness to face the enemy (Romans for the most part) single-handed.

Amarante

AMARANTE is immaculately set in a gorge of the Rio Tâmega, with the wooden balconies of its old houses leaning over the water. Much of the town's history revolves around the thirteenth-century hermit Gonçalo, later to become São Gonçalo, who is credited with just about everything positive about Amarante – most of the attractions bear his name or have some link to him. It's a fine place to stop, with innumerable bars and cafés along the south side of the river and a wide choice of accommodation. Sadly, the polluted river beaches are not recommended for swimming – though in summer you'll see some brave souls risking it – but *guigas* (pedal boats) or rowing boats can be hired for an hour or two and there's a swimming pool complex on the south bank with lots of slides and water chutes. Just past the complex is the peaceful, forested **Parque Florestal** which makes the perfect spot for a picnic. There's also a year-round Tuesday and Saturday morning **fair** held beside the river.

The church and former monastery of **São Gonçalo**, beside the very elegant town bridge, is Amarante's most prominent monument. Legend has it that the church marks the spot where Gonçalo's hermitage once stood, although it is almost certainly much older. It formed the heart of an ancient fertility cult – probably with pagan origins – which still persists here at the grand **Romaria de São Gonçalo**, celebrated on the first weekend (Fri–Sun) in June, with the large Sunday procession being the highlight. The event originally featured two sexually explicit carvings of the devil, which were appeased through offerings, a practice that was brought to an end in 1870 by a furious archbishop, who also ordered that the statues be castrated and sold off – to howls of local protest – to an English collector. When the statues were finally returned (they're now in the museum), the event was marked by much celebration. Perhaps local feelings were too much for the archbishop; he was unable to hinder the equally brazen practice of unmarried youth exchanging phallic cakes as tokens of their love, which still survives today. In the church, the saint's tomb is said to guarantee a

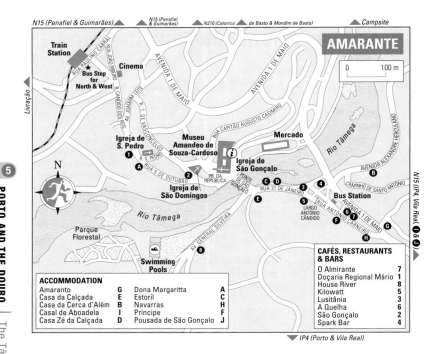

quick marriage to anyone who touches it – his face, hands and feet have been almost worn away by hopeful suitors. In another chapel, devoted to Gonçalo's healing miracles, are offered wax models of every conceivable part of the body, along with entire artificial limbs and bottles full of gallstones, although the offerings are removed at the end of each day.

Around the side of the church, in the cloister of the remodelled Dominican Convent of São Gonçalo, is the **Museu Amadeo de Souza-Cardoso** (Tues–Sun 10am–12.30pm & 2–5pm; €1). Dominated by the Cubist works of local boy Souza-Cardoso (1887–1918), one of few Portuguese painters to achieve international renown, this is a surprising exhibition to find out in the sticks. Temporary shows of modern painters and sculptors are displayed in the gallery, and there are also local archeology and history exhibits.

For **regional crafts**, look in Artesania, on Rua Teixeira de Vasconselos, selling shoes, rugs, weavings, and even string instruments – the viola Amarantina, also called *viola dos Corações* ("guitar of hearts"), is the town's speciality.

Practicalities

The **train station** on Rua Paulino António Cabral is a ten-minute walk northwest of the centre, while buses pull in on the other side of the river at the **bus station** on Rua António Carneiro. When leaving Amarante for the north and west buses leave from outside the train station. **Driving** to Amarante from Porto takes less than an hour if you take the fast A4; parking is easiest along the river beside the market, or in the gardens opposite the turismo. The **turismo** (daily 9am–12.30pm & 2–5.30pm; ☎255 420 246, ⓦwww.cm-amarante.pt) is next to the museum.

Bridge over troubled water

The north and south parts of town are linked by the Ponte de São Gonçalo, scene of a heroic stand-off in spring 1809 between the Portuguese, under General Francisco da Silveira, and the retreating French, under Marshall Sault. Fleeing Porto, having lost their brief tenure of Portugal, the French were ransacking villages along the way but when they reached Amarante they met with unexpected resistance. The bravery of the Portuguese army held up the French at the bridge, temporarily halting their rampage and allowing the people of the town to escape to safety. For two weeks there was a stalemate but on the night of May 2, under cover of darkness, the French planted explosives close to the Portuguese lines. The resulting explosions eventually caused enough panic to allow the French to cross the bridge and continue their plundering, but by then the people were safe. Today, canvases hanging inside the church of São Gonçalo still bear French bayonet marks from soldiers searching for treasure that may have been hidden behind.

Amarante itself has a good range of **accommodation**, as well as some lovely *turismo rural* places in the area, though you might need the help of the turismo in summer when rooms can be hard to come by. The municipal **campsite** (☎255 422 133) is on the river, 1.5km upstream at Penedo da Rainha. The town is also is quite a centre of gastronomic excellence, thanks in large part to the nuns of its former convent, who excelled in the art of cake- and pastry-making. Other specialities include *empadas de frango* (chicken pasties) and *cozido à portuguesa* (boiled meat stew), while the local hooch is *Gatão*, a fruity *vinho verde*. **Nightlife** is rather limited; try any of the bars and (usually short-lived) discos on the south side of the river, whose riverside terraces stay open till late in summer. Currently popular are *House River* on Avenida General Silveira, and *Spark Bar* on Avenida Alexandre Herculano.

Hotels and pensions

Aboadela Aboadela, 9km east of town, off the IP4 ☎255 441 141. A rustic farmhouse with central heating, log fires and three en-suite rooms, plus some self-catering apartments (minimum 2-night stay for the latter). Also a pool, playground, bicycles and farm activities for kids. Breakfast included. No credit cards. ❸

Hotel Amaranto Av. 1 de Maio ☎255 410 840, ⓦwww.hotelamaranto.com. A modern and rather uninspiring three-star hotel and restaurant with satellite TV and air conditioning in all rooms; the better ones have views over town. There are also some more expensive suites, and disabled access. Breakfast included. ❸

Casa da Calçada Largo do Paço 6, south side of the bridge, ☎255 410 830, ⓦwww.casadacalcada .com. The restored palace of the Counts of Redondo is set in magnificent parkland and stuffed with *objets d'art*. The best rooms go for €275–400 a night, though more modest ones are also available. Facilities include a swimming pool, tennis courts, and organized hiking, fishing and canoeing, while in the restaurant (very expensive;

reservations advised) the sky's the limit on the classic French-Portuguese à la carte menu – though the set menu costs around €30. Breakfast included. ❻

Casa da Cerca d'Além Av. Alexandre Herculano ☎255 431 449, f%254 732 149. Four rooms available in an atmospheric converted manor house with a small garden. It's beautifully decorated with antiques and boasts magnificent views. Meals available. Breakfast included. ❸

Casa Zé da Calcada Rua 31 de Janeiro 83 ☎255 422 023, ⓔzedacalcada@sapo.pt. Seven comfortable and good-value en-suite rooms, most with river views. The restaurant has a river terrace, and costly but superb local food, particularly its speciality, *Bacalhau à Zé da Calçada*. Also worth trying are *arroz de pato*, *pescada* fillets, roast kid and the *rojões*. Good *doces conventuais*, too, and an extensive wine list. ❷

Albergaria Dona Margaritta Rua Cândido dos Reis 53 ☎255 432 110, ⓦwww.albergariadonamargaritta.pa-net.pt. Comfortable and pleasantly sited overlooking the river, though it's a bit pretentious. Still, rooms

all have kitchenettes, TV, phone and air conditioning, there's lift access and a nice breakfast
terrace at the back. Breakfast included. No credit
cards. ❸

Residencial Estoril Rua 31 de Janeiro 49 ⓣ255
431 291, ⓕ255 431 892. A friendly budget choice by the old bridge, with double beds only. The
back rooms have river views. No credit cards. ❷

Hotel Navarras Rua António Carneiro ⓣ255 431
036, ⓦwww.maisturismo.pt/hnavarras. A large,
friendly and well-run three-star choice with a
good restaurant and bar, and attractive, comfortable air-conditioned rooms with satellite TV.
Private parking and disabled access. Breakfast
included. ❸

Residencial Príncipe Largo António Cândido 53
ⓣ 255 432 956. The front rooms have balconies,
though the views aren't up to much. No credit
cards. Breakfast included. ❷

Pousada de São Gonçalo Curva do Lancete,
Ansiães, 20km east of town ⓣ255 461 113,
ⓦwww.pousadas.pt. Along the IP4 to Vila Real
and perched on a clifftop, the views over the
Serra do Marão (walking trips can be arranged)
are unbeatable, and there's an excellent (if expensive) restaurant, covering international cuisine
in addition to regional highlights, like pork with
chestnuts, trout stuffed with *presunto*, and a
good selection of *doces conventuais*. Breakfast
included. ❺

Cafés and restaurants

O Almirante Largo António Cândido ⓣ 255 432
566. A welcoming, family-run place with a great
reputation for shellfish and also for regional
dishes, including octopus, lamprey and *cozido
à portuguesa*. Good desserts and wine list, too.
Expensive.

Doçaria Regional Mário Rua Cândido dos Reis
ⓣ 255 433 044. The best place for convent
cakes and pastries – ask for *doces conventuais*.
Inexpensive.

Kilowatt Rua 31 de Janeiro ⓣ 255 433 159. A
characterful *adega* with hams hanging from the
roof and carafes of wine around the walls, specializing in *pestiscos*, including succulent *presunto*.
Full meals around €5. Inexpensive.

Lusitânia Rua 31 de Janeiro 65 ⓣ 255 426 720.
A simple and informal *casa de pasto* with a river
terrace next to the bridge, well known for its perfect oven-roasted kid and veal. Or try the *bacalhau
à Narcisa*, the Porto-style *tripas*, and the nice
apple tart. Inexpensive.

A Quelha Rua de Olivença ⓣ 255 425 786. This
adega's well-spiced dishes are a meat-eater's
dream, especially when washed down with jugs of
the rich local wine. There's also fish. Inexpensive.

Café São Gonçalo Pr. da República ⓣ 255 432
707. Drinks and snacks throughout the day, and
filling evening meals, best sampled from the tables
outside. Moderate.

Celorico de Basto

Thirty kilometres northeast of Amarante, **CELORICO DE BASTO** is proud
of its neatly laid out lawns, formal flowerbeds and sweeping views into the
Serra do Alvão. There's also a weekly Saturday *feira* and an annual round of
festivals, including two big annual fairs (Aug 21 and Nov 25) and – oddest of
the lot – the Romaria de São Bartolomeu (Aug 24) which features a parade of
dogs. Celorico is fast becoming a favourite with **outdoor sports** enthusiasts:
the experts at Trilhos, based in Porto (p.336), can help arrange mountain-biking, rock-climbing, canyoning and rafting. For a brief foray into the woods, a
labyrinth of paths heads off from behind the village church, while in the distance lies the prospect of Monte Farinha, the region's highest peak (more easily
approached from the village of Mondim de Basto; see below).

There's no turismo as yet, although the industrious town hall has one
planned, together with a campsite and tourist-class hotel. In the meantime,
there's **accommodation** at the central *Pensão Progresso*, 200m south of the bus
stop on Praça Albino Alves Perreira (ⓣ255 321 170; ❶), with six rooms and a
decent restaurant; or at the more modest *Pensão Maia* (ⓣ255 321 220; ❶) on
the same square. The best **restaurant** is the moderately priced *Quinta do Forno*
1km north of town at Venda Nova (ⓣ255 322 255), set in an old farmhouse
and specializing in home-reared *vitela* (veal).

Frequent Mondinense **buses** run on to Mondim de Basto, though to really
explore this wonderfully rural valley, you could always walk along overgrown
trails to Mondim, a pleasant two-hour hike through woods and over viaducts.

❺

Fermil

On the main road, halfway between Celorico and Mondim, lies the small, pleasant village of **FERMIL**; buses on their way between Cabeceiras and Amarante pass through three to four times daily. The attraction is a couple of a wonderful *turismo rural* properties. The *Casa do Barão de Fermil* (☎255 361 211; breakfast included; no credit cards, ❹; closed Nov–Feb, Easter & Sept) is the cheaper of the two, a slightly decaying mansion fronted by amusing box-woods, with an outdoor swimming pool and English-speaking owners. More magnificent is *Casa do Campo* (☎255 361 231, ⓦwww.turihab.pt; breakfast included; ❺), an eighteenth-century manor house complete with outdoor pool and traditional *espigueiro* granary, stone threshing ground (*eira*) and an aromatic camellia garden. Unlike many such properties, it has a **restaurant** that is also open to the public (dinner only; closed Sun, also closed Mon Nov–May), where, alongside cherished local favourites such as *alheira* sausages with young cabbage leaves, you'll find dishes normally only made at home, including *roupa velha* ("old clothes") – a delicious pan-fried mixture of potatoes and *bacalhau* that traditionally uses the remains of *cozido à bacalhau*.

Mondim de Basto and around

Nine kilometres along the main road northeast of Celorico, **MONDIM DE BASTO** has a small, but well-preserved old town in the centre of a modern sprawl. There's nothing specific to see here, but it's a handy hiking base (see below), while you might also consider exploring the nearby **Parque Natural do Alvão** from town; there's a park information office (daily 9am–12.30pm & 2–5.30; ☎255 381 209) 800m down the Celorico road by the Barrio primary school. Guided walks in the park can be arranged here, while the office also has details of a 50km walk to and from the park. In addition, outdoor special-ists Basto Radical operate park tours from the town – all the park details are on p.458.

Mondim's **bus station** is by the central Mercado Municipal and there are regular connections to Vila Real (Mon–Sat 7am, 12.30pm & 5.30pm), a spec-tacular ride that skirts the Parque Natural de Alvão, as well as to Guimarães, Coimbra and Lisbon. Alternatively, catch a bus to Fermil and then on to the lively provincial town of Cabeceiras de Basto (see p.354), from where there are regular buses to Braga; you can also change at Fermil for Celorico and Ama-rante. The **turismo** (daily: July–Sept 9am–9pm; rest of the year 9am–12.30pm & 2–5.30pm; ☎255 381 479), on Praça 9 de Abril, provides maps, a list of hotels, information on local *turismo rural* properties and somewhat illegible handwritten sheets detailing walking routes. Good times to visit are the 2nd or 22nd of each month for the *feira*.

The best **accommodation** in Mondim is *Casa das Mouroas* on Rua José Carvalho Camões (☎255 381 394; ❸), a charming granite house with just three rooms. Otherwise, choose between two good-value modern places: *Resi-dencial Arcadia*, Avenida Dr. Augusto de Brito (☎255 381 410; ❷), which can be a touch noisy as it's above a café and games arcade; or the friendly *Residencial Carvalho* (*Sossego*) by the petrol station on the same road (☎255 381 057; ❷). There's also an excellent **campsite** (☎255 381 650; closed mid-Dec to mid-Jan) 1km from the centre along the N304 Vila Real road, near the banks of the Rio Cabril; the river is clean enough to swim in.

Rua Velha is the main drag for **bars** and **restaurants**. Food tends to be sim-ple and filling, in the style of Trás-os-Montes; the local beef is particularly good, especially as *bife na pedra* – grilled on a hot stone. Good inexpensive choices include the homely *Adega São Tiago* (☎255 386 957) and equally affable *Adega Sete Condes* (☎255 382 342), both open daily. On Avenida da Igreja, *Churrasqueira Chasslik* is a busy chips–with–everything sort of place. On the same street, the moderately priced *Transmontano* (☎255 381 682) has specialities from beyond the Serra do Alvão, including roast boar and a filling *feijoada*. Also recommended is the moderately priced *Casa do Lago* at the swimming pool (☎255 381 800; closed Mon), prized for its octopus; it also has an esplanade. The main **nightlife** focus is *Bar da Vinha* on Rua Velha and the sometimes rowdy *Bar Net's* on Avenida da Igreja. Try also *Koton Club* at Vilar de Viando, 1km out towards Vila Real.

Monte Farinha and the Cabril valley

Monte Farinha (996m) is surprisingly easy to climb from Mondim – less than three hours' easy walking – and, if the times coincide, you can get a head start by taking a Cabeceiras bus to the foot of the ascent, 3.5km from town. Follow the N312 Cerva road east out of Mondim, then take a path up to the right shortly after Pedra Vedra. Once on the mountain, follow the road which zigzags up to the summit (Mondim's turismo has a map). An alternative but more tiring route is to take the mountain track towards Carazêdo, turning left after 2km onto the path for Pegadinhas. At the hamlet of Campos, a further 2km on, turn left again and continue north to Pegadinhas, after which you've a good ninety-minute hike up steep terrain to join the zigzags to the top. The panoramic views well repay your efforts, and at the top is the attractive late eighteenth-century parish church of **Nossa Senhora da Graça**, centre of a major *romaria* on the first Sunday in September. Another *romaria* is held on July 24, in honour of São Tiago.

Another good hike from Mondim is into the valley of the **Rio Cabril**. Only about twenty minutes beyond the village campsite, the Cabril – more a stream than a river – is crossed by a Roman bridge, set near a little waterfall where there's a good swimming hole. From here, follow the Cabril upstream to a working watermill or take the stone track (about 200m upriver) along what must have been a Roman road. Follow this, cross a road, and you're at the start of a maze of small paths cutting between the fields and vineyards of the Cabril valley, and leading higher into the slopes.

Cabeceiras de Basto

CABECEIRAS DE BASTO – under 30km north of Mondim – is the largest and most interesting Basto town. If you can, it's worth timing your visit to coincide with the Monday *feira*, when traders sell clothes and food in the square above the bus station. The annual *Feira* and *Romaria de São Miguel* (Sept 19–30) also features a market, as well as traditional choirs, dancing and a colourful procession on the last day.

The old centre is dominated by the twin towers of the Baroque **Mosteiro de São Miguel de Refojos** (daily 7am–8pm). Although you should be able to organize access if your Portuguese is good, staff at the turismo (see below) may well be more successful in convincing the busy *padre* to let you visit the monastery's locked treasury (a collection of statues and religious garments) and access the clock tower, from which you can view the church's highlight – the 33-metre-high *zimbório* (dome). The monastery was most likely founded early in the seventh century by the Visigoths, just before the first Moorish invasion.

Opposite the monastery, in the immaculate gardens of the Praça da República, is a rather curious *basto* statue that probably covered the tomb of one Hermígio Romarigues, successful defender of Cabeceiras de Basto from Moorish attacks on three occasions. The *basto*'s original head disappeared somewhere along the line (no one's sure where or when), and the figure stood headless for many years until 1892, when somebody added a dapper mustachioed head complete with French-style kepi and a new pair of legs and boots.

On the hill above the town is the **Centro de Educação Ambiental** (daily 9am–noon & 2–5.30pm; park always open; free), which contains a small zoo of native wildlife, along with picnic areas, a children's park and sports facilities. An equestrian centre is planned; details from the tourist office.

Practicalities

Buses pull in at the terminus by the market in the new section of town. There are services to and from Celorico and Mondim de Basto, Póvoa de Lanhoso in central Minho, Braga and Porto (Mon–Sat only). Change in Arco de Baúlhe for Chaves. The **turismo** faces the monastery on Praça da República (mid-June to mid-Sept daily 9am–12.30pm & 2–5.30pm; mid-Sept to mid-June Mon–Fri 9am–12.30pm & 2–5.30pm; ☎253 669 100), and distributes the beautifully produced *Guia das Aldeias* booklet (free) with details of tours in the region.

Most of the **accommodation** is in the newer part of town, close to the bus station, though the compact nature of Cabeceiras means that nothing is more than a short walk away. A reliable, inexpensive option is the *Residencial São Miguel*, above the equally good restaurant on Largo Barjona de Freitas (☎253 661 034; ❷), on the road connecting the market square with Praça da República. There's also a superb rural property at Lugar da Tojeira in Faia, 5km back towards Mondim, the *Casa da Tojeira* (☎253 663 169, ⓦwww.casadatojeira.com; breakfast included; minimum 2-night stay; ❻). This is a grand country manor with a sweeping facade and very comfortable rooms in the side wings; its other attractions include a heated indoor swimming pool, Turkish bath and sauna, horse-riding and bicycle hire. Four kilometres north of Cabeceiras, off the road to Venda Nova at Rio Douro, there's a small, thirty-pitch **campsite**, *Parque de Campismo Valsereno* (☎253 662 047). The site is close to a small river and has its own bar and swimming pool.

Good cheap **meals** in town can be had at the *Cozinha Real Basto* on Avenida Sá Carneiro (☎253 661 795), a short way up the road to Arco de Baúlhe from the monastery. Classier and more expensive is *O Barão* (☎253 661 602), at the narrow end of Praça da República, facing the monastery, famed for its roast veal.

Lamego and around

Although technically in Beira Alta, the beautiful town of **Lamego** is isolated at the tip of its mountain province, and much more accessible from the Douro, with which it shares a passion for wine. Indeed, port wine may have its origins in the vineyards that drape the length of the Balsemão valley, from below town to the Douro. Although the demarcated wine region now excludes Lamego, it makes up for lost pride in the form of *Raposeira* – Portugal's answer to champagne – and produces celebrated smoked hams and sausages. But the region **around Lamego** is perhaps best known for its churches and monasteries, a legacy of the twelfth-century Reconquista, which attracted a number of religious orders to these lands. Lamego was among the first towns to be retaken from the Moors, and the surrounding verdant valleys are full of ancient chapels, churches and monasteries.

Lamego

LAMEGO is a wealthy place, and long has been, as evidenced by the graceful white *quintas* and villas on the hillsides, and the luxuriant architecture of the many *solares* and churches. Much of the wealth stems from the town's geographical position astride a valuable trade route from Beiras to the Douro, which saw trade in satin and velvet and, later, port wine. But the town's real importance stems from its history: in 1143, less than a century after its reconquest from the Moors by Fernando Magno and Rodrigo de Vivar (the famous "El Cid"), Lamego hosted Portugal's first parliament, when a group of clergy and noblemen assembled to recognize Afonso Henriques as the nation's first king. As such, Lamego lays claim to being the birthplace of both country and crown, something hotly disputed by Afonso Henriques' birthplace, Guimarães. The town also has one of the very greatest Baroque structures in Europe – the dominant shrine of **Nossa Senhora dos Remédios** – which plays host to an annual pilgrimage from late August to early September. Other notable *festas* and events include *Santa Cruz* (May 3), with its displays of horsemanship and

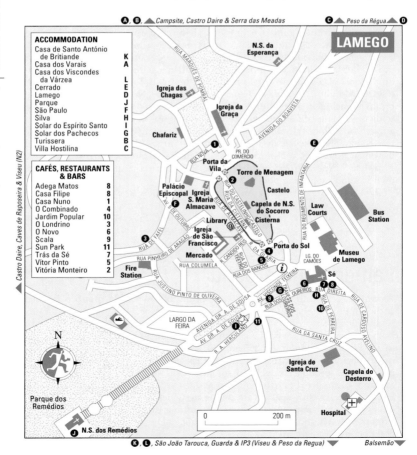

cattle, and Easter, for magnificent religious processions and a curious ceremony where an effigy of Judas goes up in smoke amid a blaze of fireworks. The weekly **market** is on Thursdays, a colourful combination of local farmers, trailers with grilled chicken, and gypsies selling clothes.

Arrival, information and accommodation

The **bus station** is behind the museum, a stone's throw from the main sights. **Taxis** wait outside and around the corner along Avenida Visconde Guedes Teixeira, and can be called on ☎254 612 351 or ☎254 612 898. The helpful **turismo** is also on the Avenida (July–Sept Mon–Fri 10am–12.30pm & 2–6pm, Sat & Sun closes at 5pm; Oct–June Mon–Fri 9.30am–12.30pm & 2–5.30pm, Sat 9.30am–12.30pm; ☎254 612 005, ✉douro.turismo@mail.telepac.pt), and can provide information on festivals and other special events. It's also the place to find out more about day-trips and Douro cruises from nearby Peso da Régua. The town's **road train** (daily mid-May to mid-Sept: hourly 2-7pm; €3) is perfect for seeing the sights without the legwork. It covers pretty much everything except the castle (too steep), and starts at the west end of Avenida Visconde Guedes Teixeira by the statue of the soldier.

Accommodation can be tricky to find, so book ahead if possible. The turismo can help with private rooms and also has details of rural accommodation in manor houses and *quintas*, for which you'll need your own transport. The closest **campsite** (☎254 612 090; closed mid-Sept to May) is at the *Complexo Turístico Turissera*, 5km northwest of town in the Serra das Meadas (see "Out of town", below).

In town

Albergaria do Cerrado 400m along the Régua road from the Sé ☎254 613 164, ✉alberga .cerrado@mail.telepac.pt. Business-class hotel with parking, lift access and good, air-conditioned rooms; the best also have bathtubs and balconies. Breakfast included. ❹

Albergaria Solar dos Pachecos Av. Visconde Guedes Teixeira ☎254 600 300, ✉albergariasolarpachecos@clix.pt. A grandiose granite-walled *solar* renovated in modern, minimalist style. The comfortable rooms, with baths or showers, have cable TV and air conditioning, and there's also a bar. Note that rates almost halve in low season. Breakfast included. No credit cards. ❺

Hotel Parque Parque dos Remédios ☎254 609 140, ℱ254 615 203. A lovely three-star hotel in an unbeatable location next to the shrine, set in its own gardens, with suitably elegant if sober en-suite rooms, plus a bar, restaurant, games room and parking. Breakfast included. ❸

Pensão Silva Rua Trás da Sé 26 ☎254 612 929. A friendly place up a long flight of stairs next to the cathedral; the bells might disturb, but are not as loud as you might expect. Rooms, sharing bathrooms, are decent if a little antiquated, but it's cheap, especially for couples. No credit cards. ❷

Residencial São Paulo Av. 5 de Outubro 22 ☎254 613 114, ℱ254 612 304. Excellent rooms in this modern building, including enormous twin-bedded ones, all with TV and shower or bath. Rooms at the back give lovely views of the old town and the Igreja de Almacave. Lift access; parking for guests. Breakfast included. No credit cards. ❸

Residencial Solar do Espírito Santo Rua Alexandre Herculano, entrance also on Av. Dr. Alfredo de Sousa ☎ & ℱ254 655 060. The comfortable if smallish en-suite rooms in this modern hotel are equipped with cable TV and air conditioning. Ones overlooking the avenue have balconies. Lift access and private parking. Breakfast included. ❸

Out of town

Casa de Santo António de Britiande Britiande, 5km southeast, along the N226 ☎254 699 346, ⓦwww.turihab.pt. A sixteenth-century manor complete with chapel, so it's the atmosphere you're paying for, as the bedrooms aren't all that special. However, there is a swimming pool, tennis court and bicycles; meals on request. Breakfast included. Closed a fortnight in mid–Aug. ❻

Casa dos Varais Cambres, 9km northwest along the Estrada Florestal ☎254 313 251, ⓦwww .turihab.pt. This eighteenth-century mansion, perched on the northern flank of the Serra das Meadas, overlooking Régua and the Douro, has three guestrooms decked out in Victorian style, complete with old wallpaper. Meals on request. Breakfast included. Closed Nov–Mar. **⑤**

Casa dos Viscondes da Várzea Várzea de Abrunhais, 10km southeast, signposted off the N226 at Britiande ⓣ254 690 020, ⓦwww .hotelruralviscondesvarzea.com. A palacial nineteenth-century *quinta* set in 180 acres of farm and gardens, with elegant decor in the common areas, and less special, but still comfortable, bedrooms. Meals, taken in a romantic *azulejo*-lined dining room, are a treat, and there's a pool. Breakfast included. **⑤**

Complexo Turístico Turissera 5km northwest along the Estrada Florestal towards Avões ⓣ254 655 882, ⓕ254 656 152. A large motel, campsite and good restaurant rolled into one, occupying a lofty position in the Serra das Meadas. Rooms are comfortable, and there's a tennis court and mini-golf. No buses;

the owners may give you a lift up from town. Breakfast included. **❸**

Hotel Lamego Quinta da Vista Alegre, 2km out of town on the Régua road ⓣ254 656 171, ⓦwww .hotellamego.pt. Large and affordable four-star hotel favoured by tour companies, with two pools (one indoor), squash and tennis courts, health club, bar, restaurant and disabled facilities. Rooms are large, and those at the back overlook the Balsemão valley. Free transfer from Régua. Breakfast included. **❹**

Villa Hostilina Ortigosa, 2km north, off the N2 to Régua ⓣ 254 612 394, ⓕ 254 655 194. Set in vineyards and orchards, a grand nineteenth-century house stuffed with period trappings, contrasting oddly with its ultra-modern "Instituto Kosmos" health club, tennis courts and pool. Meals by arrangement. Breakfast included. **❹**

The Town

Lamego's cathedral – the **Sé** – dominates the centre of town (daily 8am–1pm & 3–7pm), basically a Renaissance structure, though a thirteenth-century tower survives from a previous building. The mixture works well and the cloister is a beauty. Facing the Sé, occupying the eighteenth-century Episcopal Palace, is the excellent **Museu de Lamego** (Tues–Sat 10am–12.30pm & 2–5pm, Sun 10am–12.30pm; €2, free Sun), whose exhibits include five of the remaining panels of a polyptych commissioned from Grão Vasco by the Bishop of Lamego in 1506. Also on show are a series of huge sixteenth-century Flemish tapestries, some curious statues of a conspicuously pregnant Virgin Mary (a genre peculiar to this region), a fine assembly of *azulejos*, and piles of other ecclesiastical treasures.

Across the square, the narrow and very steep Rua da Olaria leads up from beside the turismo to the castle, passing an array of antiquated shops and *casas de pasto*: hams and smoked sausages feature strongly, as do handmade shoes and – at no. 54 – a place selling traditional wooden toys. A right turn at the top takes you to the castle's Porta do Sol (see below), whilst straight ahead is Rua de Almacave, which follows the walls of the medieval town. This takes you past two notable churches: **Igreja de São Francisco** (daily 7.30am-10.30am & 5.30-6.30pm, closes 6pm Sun; free), a seventeeth-century reconstruction on earlier foundations whose highlight is an altar painting of the death of Saint Francis of Assisi, and **Igreja de Almacave** (daily 7.30am–noon & 4–7.30pm), a simple Romanesque church said once to have been a mosque.

The top of Rua de Almacave opens out on Praça do Comércio, where two alleys on the right head up along the town's massive thirteenth-century walls to the castle's north gate – the beautiful **Porta da Vila** (or Porta dos Fogos), straddled by a sorry-looking wooden oratory constructed in the 1700s. This gives access to the **Castelo** – a cluster of medieval houses huddled around the twelfth-century **Torre de Menagem** (mid-June to Sept Tues–Sun 10am–noon & 3–6pm; Oct to mid-June Sun 10am–noon only; free). The castle has been inhabited since at least the fifth century BC, while a number of Roman engraved stones and stelae can be seen inside and just outside the walls. The tower itself was cleaned up and restored by boy scouts in the 1970s after a long period of neglect, and it's the scouts who'll show you around. It's worth clambering up the rickety stairs onto the roof for the stunning views, and afterwards you can unwind in the lovely *casa de pasto* next to the tower at Rua do Castelinho 25.

Heading south along Rua do Castelo, the small **Capela da Nossa Senhora do Socorro** was built – according to the inscription – on the site of Lamego's first Sé, founded by the Suevian Idácio, who crowned himself Bishop of Lamego in 435. Further down the street is a small circular *praça* at the junction with Rua da Cisterna. To the right of the *praça*, behind the wall, lies a thirteenth-century subterranean **cisterna** (water cistern) – apparently one of the most beautiful in the country, with a church-like Romanesque interior, but unfortunately closed to visitors. The enclosing wall is remarkable in that virtually every stone contains a different stonemason's mark; some of the designs are uncannily similar to symbols found in Iron Age rock art. The castle's southern gate – the **Porta do Sol** – gives two ways back into town: turn right to join the top end of Rua da Olaria, or left for steps down to the bottom.

Nossa Senhora dos Remédios

The celebrated shrine of **Nossa Senhora dos Remédios** (daily: May–Sept 7.30am–8pm; Oct-Apr 8am–6pm) is a major point of pilgrimage in late August and early September, when a reputation for healing miracles draws devotees from all over the country. Standing on a hill overlooking the city, at the end of a wide avenue of shady chestnut trees, it's approached by a magnificently elaborate eighteenth-century stairway, modelled on the one at Bom Jesus near Braga. Its 611 steps – which the most committed ascend on their knees – are punctuated by a *via santa* of *azulejo*-lined devotional chapels and allegorical fountains and statues. The church itself is surprisingly bright and airy, more colourful than many in the region and a pleasant assembly hall for the ever-present faithful. To escape the crowds, stroll back along the forested tracks of the **Parque dos Remédios** on either side of the steps; early in the morning the air is filled with cuckoo calls and warbling birdsong, although the arrival of picnicking families later in the day can make the park almost as crowded as the steps themselves.

The **Festas de Nossa Senhora dos Remédios** (nicknamed *Romaria de Portugal*) kick off on the last Thursday of August, and continue for eleven days, concluding on the second Monday. The opening day sees a popular fair, whilst the pilgrimage itself climaxes over the last three days, when the image of Our Lady leaves Remédios in procession to the Igreja das Chagas in town, where it stays in adoration for two days. The main procession takes place on the last day, with cavalcades of young children in white, and bulls pulling the carriage that transports Our Lady between the Igreja das Chagas and Igreja de Santa Cruz. In addition to the pilgrimage, there's a traditional "Battle of Flowers", torchlit parades, dances, car races, performances from some of the country's top rock bands and a fair on the Recinto da Feira, below the sanctuary.

Eating and drinking

Lamego has plenty of **restaurants**, some rather touristy and expensive, others – mainly characterful *adegas* tucked away from the main avenidas – serving excellent food at low prices. Lamego produces excellent *fumeiros* (smoked meats), particularly *presunto* (ham) and *salpicão* sausages, which even find their way into unleavened *bôla* cakes. Buy these from the shops along Rua da Olaria, up from the turismo, where you'll also find good bread and cheese. The town's food **market** is along Avenida 5 de Outubro. The esplanade **bars and cafés** scattered along either side of Avenida Visconde Guedes Teixeira and its western continuation, Avenida Dr. Alfredo de Sousa, are the hub for summertime evening drinkers (and ice cream addicts), and the trees here provide ample shade for a midday rest.

The **Caves da Raposeira** (☎254 655 003), 2km out of town on the N2 Castro Daire road, are open on weekdays for free guided tours around the cellars and a tasting of Portugal's "champagne". However, you should call in advance or ask at the turismo to ensure that tours are operating before heading out there. Lamego's **nightlife** is limited; the main venue for younger folk (also by day) is the trendy *Café Bar Sun Park*, with its large esplanade, at the eastern end of Rua Alexandre Herculano.

Adega Matos Rua Trás da Sé 52 ☎254 612 967. Characterful *casa de pasto* behind the Sé, always busy (more tables upstairs) and with a wide range of dishes, including pickled eels, sardines and *arroz de salpicão* (rice with smoked sausage). Closed Sun dinner. Inexpensive.

Café Scala Av. Visconde Guedes Teixeira ☎254 612 699. Smart, cool café that's a popular refuge from the midsummer heat. Good pastries, including *bolo de presunto*, plus *Raposeira*, other local wines and herbal teas. Closed Wed. Inexpensive.

Casa Filipe Rua Trás da Sé 58 ☎254 612 428. Established for over a century, this is quieter but less atmospheric (especially upstairs) than *Adega Matos* next door. Specialities include roast kid and veal, anything grilled, and various *bacalhau* concoctions. Closed Sun evening, & Mon in summer. Inexpensive.

Casa Nuno Rua Nova, off Pr. do Comércio ☎254 623 500. This first-floor *casa de pasto* near the castle rustles up some great local nosh, including *feijoada*, *cozido à portuguesa* and various oven-baked meats. Inexpensive.

Casa de Pasto Vítor Pinto Rua da Olaria 61 ☎254 612 974. Very cheap eats, with fine *presunto* figuring strongly, together with *bacalhau*. Closed Sun. Inexpensive.

Casa de Pasto Vitória Monteiro Rua do Castelinho 25 ☎968 434 816. Inside the castle, an intimate and atmospheric little place offering simple meals, plus snacks and drinks. Eels are a speciality, and Wednesday is *feijoada* day. Closed Sun dinner. Inexpensive.

Jardim Popular Rua da Perreira ☎254 655 636. A rather strange construction in a walled garden, but the grills and salads are good. Closed Mon. Moderate.

O Combinado Rua da Olaria 84 ☎254 612 902. A good local *tasca* where you can eat well for under €6. Apart from grilled pork chops and trout, a speciality is *arroz de cabidela* – rice with blood and seasoning. Closed Sun in winter. Inexpensive.

O Londrino Rua de Fafel 36 ☎254 655 314. A *churrasqueira* and bar with good grills. Closed Tues. Inexpensive.

O Novo Largo da Sé 9 ☎254 613 166. A swanky mix of old *azulejos* and modern design, though the big draw here is dining at an outdoor table. Specialities include grilled kid goat on weekends, and the inescapable *bacalhau*. Closed Sat in winter. Moderate.

Trás da Sé Rua Trás da Sé 12 ☎254 614 075. Excellent place often packed with locals, who have adorned the walls with messages of congratulation. Specialities include *rancho à Lamecense*, a very filling stew incorporating pasta and chick peas, and *chanfana de cabra* – a stew of goat blood and innards. Closed Wed evening. Inexpensive.

Listings

Bike rental At the swimming pool, see below, for around €10 a day.

Car rental Avis, Av. 5 de Outubro ☎254 612 345.

Hospital Hospital Distrital de Lamego, Lugar da Franzia ☎254 609 980.

Internet The Biblioteca Municipal on Rua de Almacave offers 30min of free access (Mon-Fri 10am-12.30pm & 2.30-6pm).

Police Av. António Osório Mota ☎254 612 022.

Post office Av. Dr. Alfredo de Sousa ☎254 609 250 (Mon-Fri 8.30am-6pm).

Swimming pool Facing the Recinto da Feira at the west end of town (mid–June to mid–Sept Mon–Sat 10am–6pm; €2.50, including a small water park).

Travel agent Lima Júnior Viagens e Turismo, Largo da Vitória 3 ☎254 609 020, ☎limajunior@mail.telepac.pt. For tours around Lamego; see next section.

Around Lamego

The country around Lamego is characterized by a series of wild, sparsely inhabited mountain ranges – **Leomil** in the southeast, **Montemuro** to the southwest, and **Meadas** in the northwest – whose fertile valleys are marked by strings of picturesque villages. All sport long traditions of local handicraft industries, including weaving, knitting, basketry, honey and cheese production, pottery and cape-making. There's still a thriving cultural life, too – from folk dancing to religious festivals – but the tourist infrastructure is minimal.

These lands were among the earliest to be relinquished by the Moors in the face of the Christian Reconquista, and are also deeply associated with Afonso Henriques, the first king of Portugal, who, it is said, laid the first stone of the monastery of **São João de Tarouca** after his victories at Trancoso and Sernancelhe in Beira Alta. The region's three other rewarding sights – the monastery of **Salzedas**, the fortified bridge at **Ucanha** and the church at **Tarouca** – were also founded at this time. Even older is a seventh-century Suevi chapel at **Balsemão**, within walking distance of Lamego, whilst pre-Christian traditions survive in exuberant form at **Lazarim** to the south, which holds one of the most colourful Carnaval celebrations in the country.

The region is infrequently visited, thanks in part to patchy bus services, which tend to follow school timetables, if there's a service at all; Lamego turismo and the EAVC/Joalto counter at Lamego's bus station will fill you in on what's feasible. It's far easier with your own transport, or you can take one of the **guided tours** operated by Lima Júnior Viagens e Turismo (see Lamego "Listings", above), who have well thought-out itineraries covering all the places below (day-trips around €50–100 depending on group size and transport), including church amd monastery tours, wine tastings and visits to *quintas* for the September and October grape harvest. For tours with a more adventurous flavour, contact Naturimont, Rua Nova 26, Lamego (☎254 613 918, ⊛www .naturimont.com), or Arrepio in Porto (see "Listings", p.336), both of which lay on **adventure activities** – from rafting to hiking – tailored to individual requirements.

North of Lamego: Balsemão and the Serra das Meadas

At the hamlet of **BALSEMÃO**, a 3km hike from the back of Lamego's cathedral, is the ancient **Capela de São Pedro de Balsemão** (Tues 2–6pm, Wed–Sun 10am–12.30pm & 2–6pm, closed on the third weekend of the month). The route requires three left turns in all: the first at the Capela do Desterro, down into the old quarters of town and across a bridge; the second, a fork on to the hillside road; the third a little later, taking you down into the valley and above a rushing river. Believed to have been founded in the seventh century by the Suevi, the present foundations were actually laid in the tenth century during the Reconquista. The undistinguished granite facade and dark interior give it the air of a family vault, an impression strengthened by the imposing fourteenth-century **sarcophagus** of the Bishop of Porto, Dom Afonso Pires, who was born in Balsemão. The florid capitals encircling the tomb make the few remaining Suevi curls on the archway into the choir seem subdued by comparison. Look out for the restored, profoundly pregnant statue of Nossa Senhora do Ó (that's Ó as in the shape of her belly, though others ascribe it to the exclamation uttered when seeing it: *Ó! Nossa Senhora, Mãe de Deus...*). After your visit, you could eat at the smart *Quinta Ferra Bordão* **restaurant** (closed Tues; ☎254 615 961), 2.5km away, which also has a bar with good views over the Balsemão valley.

The **Serra das Meadas**, a few kilometres northwest of Lamego, makes for a refreshing change from the permeating religious atmosphere. The range contains a newly opened **Parque Biológico** (June–Sept Wed & Thurs 10am–5pm, Sat & Sun 3–6pm; Oct–May Sun 2–5pm; €1; ⓦwww.cm-lamego .pt/parquebio), a 50-hectare patch of unspoiled forest 7km along the road to Avões. This contains 3km of walking trails around what's basically a miniature safari park; denizens include deer, boar, foxes and wild fowl.

Lazarim and Lalim

A left turn off the N2 Lamego–Castro Daire road leads to the small and normally unremarkable village of **LAZARIM**, 20km from Lamego. Sleepy for 364 days of the year, it plays host to one of the oddest rituals to survive in Portugal, the **Entrudo dos Compadres**, a carnival that has taken place every Shrove Tuesday since the Middle Ages. Revellers celebrate the end of winter and the beginning of spring (Lent in the Christian calendar) by taking to the streets wearing beautifully carved wooden masks, symbolic of the event's licentiousness. Despite the lewd masquerades, Entrudo dos Compadres is also a time of castigation for the year passed: from a balcony on Largo do Padrão, two colourful dolls loaded with fireworks are presented to the crowd – the *compadre*, carried by two young women, and *comadre*, toted by two young men. The couples proceed to recite insulting rhymes centring on sexual behaviour, which, in the manner of Punch and Judy, are often maliciously aimed at certain unnamed people in the crowd below. After the recital, the fireworks are lit and the dolls disintegrate in an explosive fury of smoke and flame, marking the end of the festival and the old year and the beginning of the new. A *feijoada* is then served to the waiting crowd.

If you can't coincide with the Entrudo, another worthwhile date is Easter, when **LALIM** – 5km east of Lazarim – holds the **Queima do Judas**, in which an effigy of the bad guy is ceremonially burned. Accommodation is available at the *Quinta do Terreiro* in Lalim (☏254 697 040, ⓦwww.geocities .com/quintadoterreiro; breakfast included; ❺), an impressive eighteenth-century farmhouse with ten granite-walled rooms, some with fireplaces. A lovely period dining room and cosy cellar-bar complete the picture, and there's a swimming pool, tennis court, and trips to the Serra de Santa Helena on offer.

São João de Tarouca

The small village of **SÃO JOÃO DE TAROUCA**, off the N226 Moimenta da Beira road 40km southeast of Lamego, was the site of the first Cistercian monastery to be founded on the Iberian peninsula, the earliest known reference to it dating from 1139. Rebuilt in the seventeenth century, it was thoroughly trashed after the 1834 dissolution, leaving only a vast ruined shell and lone belltower. However, the Romanesque **church** (May–Sept Tues 2.30–6pm, Wed–Sun 9.30am–12.30pm & 2–6pm; Oct–April Tues 2–5.30pm, Wed–Sun 10–12.30pm & 2–6.30pm; closed third weekend of each month) remains fully intact. Consecrated in 1169, this is a real delight, as much for the subtle light suffusing the simple interior as for the works of art that adorn its walls. The focal point is Grão Vasco's sixteenth-century painting of the first pope, St Peter (the sombre-looking gentleman in red), similar to the one in Viseu's Museu de Grão Vasco. More amusing is the undated painting of a saint smiting a cute-looking demon as his brethren look on in horror, while *azulejos* in the transepts depict the life of Saint Bernard, including one of him standing in a wine barrel (a pre-Christian symbol of abundance). Later Baroque additions include a colourful organ (1766), whose central figure marks time with his arm. He can be seen in action during Mass (Tues & Thurs 5.30pm, Sun 10.30am).

Entry to the church is free, though the (optional) guide expects a tip. Ask for him in the small exhibition room above the toilets outside the church. There's a local café-bar nearby, and five minutes' walk downhill is a lovely Roman bridge over the Rio Varosa – a pleasant spot for a picnic.

Getting here by bus is best on Tuesdays to Fridays, with services leaving Lamego at 8.25am, 12.50pm, 1.45pm and 4.50pm, returning at 11.10am, 1.05pm and 6.05pm. The journey takes 20min. On Sundays, you only have time for a quick look, as the 4.50pm bus returns just after 6pm. There's nothing on Saturday. Times change, so ask at the EAVC/Joalto counter in Lamego's bus station, ensuring you ask for São João de Tarouca, not just "Tarouca", which is a different place. **Drivers** should follow the N226 as far as Alvarinho (past Mondim da Beira), and turn right at the signpost.

Ucanha

In **UCANHA** – north of Tarouca, on the opposite side of the N226 – life revolves around the water. Down below the main road, two ingenious ducts have been made to tap the river upstream in order to provide adequate washing facilities in the centre of the village. The wash houses are practically in ruins, but the system of one tank for suds and another for rinses, common to the Mediterranean, has been preserved. Running below the pools, the river looks so tempting that on a sunny day, regardless of what trash might be floating by, village children are constantly splashing around.

The real beauty of the scene stems from the majestic **tollgate** and single-arched **bridge**. They date from the 1160s, when the diocese of Salzedas was awarded to Teresa Afonso, erstwhile nursemaid to Afonso Henriques' five sons and heirs and widow of Egas Moniz, the first king's tutor and closest adviser. Besides marking and protecting the border of her domain, these structures were also, of course, an ostentatious mark of manorial power. Today, clothes are hung out to dry under the arches.

Salzedas

SALZEDAS lies 4km further along the Ucanha road, its **monastery** (Tues–Sun 10am–12.30pm & 2–6pm) once the greatest of its kind, grander even than São João de Tarouca. In 1168, when the order was Augustinian, the complex was rebuilt with money donated by Teresa Afonso; it became Cistercian during a later period of administration from Alcobaça.

Unfortunately, eighteenth-century renovation has largely altered its original appearance into a clumsy mixture of Baroque and pseudo-Classical styles. The monastery's main facade presides over the small square of the diminutive village. As at Tarouca, students work here in the summer and, though they may seem surprised to see casual visitors, they will follow you around and open the relevant doors. The smell of decay is strong inside, and the two dark and dusty **paintings** of St Peregrine and St Sebastian by Grão Vasco, either side of the choir, are easily overlooked. More conspicuous are the fifteenth-century tombs of the Coutinho family – dominant nobles in these parts in the early years of the Portuguese nation – near the entrance. Out through a side door, a succession of courtyards, once fronting formal gardens, bear the scars of a period of extensive pillage and decay, which began in 1834 with the dissolution of the monasteries.

△ A traditional Barco Rabelo

Practicalities

The **train station** is centrally located, near the waterfront on Avenida da Galiza, close to the main hotels. The **bus station** is on the same street. Buses to Lamego run every hour until 8pm, and the last train to Vila Real pulls out at 7.15pm. Avenida de Galiza turns into Avenida João Franco along the river, while running parallel to it inland is Rua José Vasques Osório, which turns into Rua dos Camilos to the west, then Rua João de Lemos, and finally Rua de Ferreirinha, which contains the small **turismo** (July & Aug Mon–Fri 9am–12.30pm & 2–5.30pm, Sat & Sun until 6pm; Sept–June Mon–Fri 9am–12.30pm & 2–5.30pm; ℡254 312 846, Ⓦwww.cm-peso-regua.pt), about 1.5km west of the train station, which provides an excellent *Rota dos Vinhos do Porto* map of wine-related sites along the Douro.

Accommodation is usally easy to come by, and there are plenty of **bars and restaurants** along the riverfront Avenida João Franco, where you'll also find Lugar do Vinho, opposite the cruise ship jetty, a good shop for buying wines, cheese, olive oil and other rarefied victuals.

Hotels and pensions

Pensão Borrajo Rua dos Camilos ℡254 213 396. Above a restaurant, this is the cheapest by far in town, clinging to its defiantly unmodernized rooms, including free-standing washbasins for which you're brought hot water by the staff. No credit cards. ❶

Residencial Dom Quixote Av. Sacadura Cabral, west of the turismo ℡254 321 151, Ⓕ254 322 802. A little way out of town, with modern en-suite rooms costing not much more than the *Borrajo*. It's owned by the folks at *O Maleiro* restaurant, who are happy to take you out there. Breakfast included. ❷

Residencial Império Rua José Vasques Osório 8, by the train station ℡254 320 120, Ⓔresidencial.imperio@mail.telepac.pt. The main mid-market option, with comfortable, well-appointed rooms (smelling somewhat of disinfectant); buffet breakfast included. ❸

Hotel Régua Douro Av. da Galiza, facing the train station ℡254 320 700, Ⓦwww.hotelreguadouro.pt.

A four-star high-rise eyesore that improves substantially inside, with a pool on a river-view terrace, jacuzzi and health club, and top-floor restaurant. There are river views from the fractionally more expensive "Deluxe" rooms, though all have balconies. Also has rooms suitable for disabled access. Breakfast included. ❺

Restaurants

Arco Íris Av. Sacadura Cabral, west of the turismo ℡254 313 524. Understated family-run place offering superlative regional cooking – particularly roast kid. Inexpensive.

O Maleiro Rua dos Camilos 108 ℡254 313 684. Friendly, bustling place with tables in a vine-draped inner courtyard. Inexpensive.

Restaurante Panorâmico *Hotel Régua Douro*, Av. da Galiza ℡254 320 700. The best views in town from the top-floor restaurant, and not as expensive as you might fear. Sundays feature an eat-all-can-eat brunch. Moderate.

Singing in the train

Tourist interest in the Douro has rekindled the state railway company's interest in keeping alive the narrow-gauge railway lines that branch off from the Douro train line. Sadly, most of the wonderful old wooden carriages that used to cover the routes have been retired, though certain exceptions are lovingly cared for by the **Comboios Históricos do Douro** (Historic Douro Trains). From May to October, the venerable old dames are hauled out for scenic afternoon trundles between **Régua and Tua** on the Douro line (pulled by 1926 steam loco or 1967 diesel), and from **Régua to Vila Real** up the Corgo line (1923 steam loco or 1975 diesel), accompanied by *viola* and *guitarra* players and a singer. Times and dates change annually, though Saturdays are likely, but details are available from CP (℡211 021 129, Ⓦwww.cp.pt). Return tickets cost €30.

Pinhão and Pocinho

After Régua the country continues craggy and beautiful, with the softer hills of the interior fading dark green into the distance. **PINHÃO**, 25km east, is the main centre for quality ports. Trains pull in at the attractive *azulejo*-decorated station east of town near the river, an area awash with advertising signs for the local port wine *quintas*; the closest is Quinta do Panascal, a few kilometres back along the N222 (see listing in Peso da Régua). Between March and October you can also reach Pinhão on a **river cruise** from Porto (see p.302) or Régua; aside from the usual packages, most companies offer bargain one-way fares to make up the numbers. If you need a taxi, call ⓉT 254 732 244.

Accommodation isn't a problem. Cheapest is *Pensão Ponto Grande* at Rua Central 103–105 (Ⓣ254 732 456; ❸), with rather small and dated en-suite rooms, but a good inexpensive restaurant. Almost identical, but €10 more, is *Pensão Douro*, two doors down facing the train station (Ⓣ & Ⓕ254 724 404; breakfast included; ❸). Both have splendid river views. However, if your budget can stretch to it, consider *Quinta de la Rosa* (Ⓣ254 732 254, Ⓦwww.quintadelarosa.com; breakfast included; ❺), a working wine estate 1.5km west of Pinhão, with six double rooms and a swimming pool, as well as wonderful river views and the chance to see at first hand the early processes of port wine making. Top-of-the-range is *Vintage House* (Ⓣ254 730 230, Ⓦwww.hotelvintagehouse.com; breakfast included; ❽), a sumptuously decorated former warehouse beside the train station, owned by cruise company Douro Azul (Ⓣ223 402 515, Ⓦwww.douroazul.com), in whose packages it features – a three-day cruise with two nights here costs €365. Bedrooms are comfortable, and common areas are tastefully decked out in period furniture and wine- and river-related art. Wine tours can be arranged, and there's also a swimming pool, a broad riverfront esplanade, and a shop selling some of the region's rarest tipples.

The Douro continues on its journey eastwards, through the village of **TUA**, where sleek green carriages toil uphill along the scenic Tua valley line to Mirandela in Trás-os-Montes (see p.461). The Douro line train continues on to its terminus, 45km east of Pinhão, at the isolated station of **POCINHO**, which is little more than its railway station, a hydroelectric dam and a couple of restaurants. Trains are met by buses to Vila Nova de Foz Côa, 8km south, and to Torre de Moncorvo, 10km northeast. The last bus to either town leaves at 6.30pm, but stay alert as they don't hang around. If you get stuck, call a cab from Foz Côa (Ⓣ279 762 651) or Torre de Moncorvo (Ⓣ279 252 432); the ride to either place shouldn't cost more than €5.

Vila Nova de Foz Côa

Sitting high above the Côa valley, 8km south of Pocinho, the small town of **VILA NOVA DE FOZ CÔA** was awarded the status of a city on account of an astonishing collection of Palaeolithic rock art, discovered nearby in 1992. Rescued from imminent submersion under a proposed dam, three of the sites are now open to the public (see next section). However, other than the Igreja Matriz, with its impressive Manueline doorway, leaning walls, painted wooden ceiling and sixteenth-century pillory outside, there's little else to Foz Côa. Although the blistering midsummer heat and winter cold makes it hard to believe, the town benefits from a Mediterranean microclimate, proof of which is provided by local produce: aside from almonds, olives and fruit, the town and its region is famed for cheese, wine and – especially – olive oil, among the country's finest. Stock up at the *Adega Cooperativa* (daily 9am–12.30am & 2–6pm), 200m back along the Pocinho road from the bus station.

Good dates to coincide with include the self-explanatory *Feira de Cebolas* (Onion Fair; May 8), the *Festa de Nossa Senhora da Veiga* on August 8, the *Feira de São Miguel* (also with an oniony theme) on September 29, and *Festa de São Martinho* on November 11, with more parades, music and a couple of oxen pulling a 200-litre barrel of wine whose contents become lighter as the day wears on. The **monthly market** is on the first Tuesday of the month next to the football field, and the blossoming of **almond trees** draws the crowds in late February and early March.

Practicalities

Foz Côa is most easily reached by the Douro train to Pocinho, from where connecting **buses** pass through town on the way to Castelo Rodrigo or Lisbon via Guarda and Viseu. Returning to Pocinho or Torre de Moncorvo, buses leave daily at 2.54pm and 4.06pm, with additional weekend and night services. The **bus station** is along the road in from Pocinho; tickets and timetables are available from the café. From the bus station, walk south 250m to reach Avenida Gago Coutinho, the town's main thoroughfare. Turn left for the old town and the park office (see next section) or right, where the avenue is called Avenida Cidade Nova, to bring you to the **turismo**, Avenida Cidade Nova 2 (daily 9am–12.30pm & 2–5.30pm; ☏279 765 243). In the same complex is a library (free internet access), theatre, cinema, and the **municipal museum** (same hours; free), with all sorts of temporary exhibitions, from art to archeology and geology. **Taxis** have their HQ on Praça da República (aka Largo do Tabulado; ☏279 762 651), and there's also a rank on Avenida Gago Coutinho facing the park office. For **trips** around the area, including to rock art sites not covered by the park's tours, plus mountain biking and canoeing, contact Impactus (☏962 838 261, ⓦwww.impactus.pt), based in nearby Castelo Melhor.

Finding **accommodation** isn't difficult, though the cheaper places leave something to be desired. In summer, ensure the room is airy; in winter, check for heating. Aside from the **restaurants** covered below, there are more at Praça da República, at the east end of Rua São Miguel, the pedestrian eastern continuation of Avenida Gago Coutinho. The town's speciality is *acelgas*, a starter made with a special kind of spinach, cooked with eggs and garlic. To cool down with a **drink** or five, the shaded terrace of *Gaiteiro Bar* (daily to 2am), Avenida Gago Coutinho 12, next to *Residencial Avenida*, beckons. Try also *Bar do Jô*, Rua do Olho 35, which mutates into the *Foz-Club* at night.

Hotels and pensions

Albergaria Vale do Côa Av/ Cidade Nova 1A, facing the turismo ☏ 279 760 010, ⓦ www .albergariavaledocoa.net. The best hotel in town, with spacious air-conditioned rooms, all with satellite TV and polished wooden floors, most with balconies, double glazing (noisy bars nearby) and spotless bathrooms with bathtubs. There's also the excellent *Rota das Gravuras* restaurant (moderate; closed Mon), with regional specialities like carp *açorda*, grilled kid, and *bacalhau* stuffed with ham, plus wine from their own *quinta*. No credit cards. Breakfast included. ❹, suites ❺

Quinta do Chão d'Ordem Off the N102 towards Guarda, just south of Muxagata ☏279 762 427, ⓦwww.chaodordem.com. One of the nicest and

friendliest places to stay in northern Portugal, with eight bedrooms on a working farm. The hand of its artistically minded owners shows up everywhere, from the tasteful decor to superlative cooking in the restaurant (expensive; reservations essential), featuring ingredients – many grown on the farm – you won't find elsewhere, including wild asparagus, *beldroegas* (a kind of watercress) and homemade sausages, together with superb desserts and sheep's milk cheese. There's also a cosy lounge and bar, library, tennis court and pool, and wine cellar in a converted dovecot. Breakfast included. ❹

Residencial Avenida Av. Gago Coutinho 8–10 ☏271 762 175. The best budget choice, with large rooms, kitted out with satellite TV and bathtubs in their bathrooms, though it can get noisy at night if *Gaiteiro Bar* is on form. No credit cards. ❷

Residencial Marina Av. Gago Coutinho 2–4 ⓣ 271 762 112. Loses out to the *Avenida* next door; rooms in the main house are good, but those at the back are stuffy and dilapidated, if still acceptable. All have bathrooms and local TV. No credit cards. ❶

Youth hostel

Pousada de Juventude 1.5km northwest of town off the Pocinho road ⓣ 279 768 190, ⓦ www .pousdasjuventude.pt. Awkwardly sited, while its en-suite doubles are more expensive than some hotels for couples, but redeemed by great, windswept views. There are washing machines,

kitchen, restaurant and disabled facilities. Dorms €12.50, rooms ❸

Restaurants

A Marisqueira Rua de São Miguel 35, just off Pr. da República ⓣ 279 762 187. Good food and snacks in a bar-like *tasca*, specializing in shellfish; particularly successful is their *arroz de marisco*. Open to 2am; closes every other Sun. Inexpensive.

A Terrinca Rua de São Miguel 37. Superb bread and pastries, and a first-floor tea room. Daily to 2am. Inexpensive.

A Tentação Pr. da República ⓣ 279 764 301. A bakery, pastry shop and restaurant rolled into one (dining room on the first floor); the speciality here is *bacalhau*. Inexpensive.

Parque Arqueológico do Vale do Côa

The Rio Côa near Vila Nova de Foz Côa became the centre of one of the greatest archeological finds in recent memory with the discovery in 1992 of the most extensive array of outdoor **Palaeolithic art** in Europe. Engravings of horses, deer, goats and other animals (some extinct, such as the auroch bison), as well as later, Neolithic, images of people, were found along 17km of the river's steep, rocky schist valley. The engravings themselves are of a similar style to those found in caves across Europe, but their uniqueness lies in the fact that they are outside on exposed rock faces and invariably near water. With the oldest dated at around 22,000 years (there may also be older, undatable ones), it is remarkable that the engravings survived to be discovered at all, but even more remarkable perhaps is that they continued to survive after their discovery.

The proposed building of a controversial dam threatened to submerse the site and the engravings under 90m of water. Archeologists and environmental groups joined forces with local people, schoolchildren and students from across the country in an incredible "people's campaign" against the proposed dam. Success came in 1995 when the sites were declared a National Monument. The **Parque Arqueológico do Vale do Côa** was created the following year, and in December 1998 became a UNESCO World Heritage site. The bulk of the rock art is now protected by the park, which covers much of the area east and south of the town. The park contains thousands of engravings on several hundred rocks, a good number of which are clustered around three major sites. A museum is planned at a fourth rock art site, Vermelhosa, in Foz Côa's former railway station at the confluence of the Côa and Douro.

Visits (daily except Mon) must be booked through the **park headquarters** in Foz Côa at Avenida Gago Coutinho 19A (Tues–Sun 9am–12.30pm & 2–5.30pm; ⓣ 279 768 260, ⓦ www.ipa.min-cultura.pt/pavc). Bookings can also be made by telephone; in summer, reserving two or three days in advance is recommended. The €5 per-site fee includes a guide and 4WD transport from the appropriate visitor centre (see below); each trip has a maximum of eight visitors, and children under three are not allowed. Bear in mind that it can get extremely hot in the sheltered valleys and there is some walking involved, so it's a good idea to bring a wide-brimmed hat, sun cream and plenty of water. Umbrellas and parasols are prohibited to avoid accidental damage to the engravings.

The sites

Without your own transport, **Canada do Inferno** – the site of the half-built dam, whose construction scarred the landscape – is the easiest option, as you're picked up from the park office in Foz Côa (daily: May–Sept 9.15am–10.30am; Oct–April 10am–2.30pm; tour lasts 1hr 30min). The site contains a wide variety of engravings, from bisons to horses (many more are underwater since the construction of Pocinho dam), but be prepared for an hour's difficult walk down the steep slopes to the Côa and back.

For the other two sites, you have to make your own way to the respective visitors centres, each with a cafeteria, books and souvenirs for sale, and computers containing multimedia presentations (you can see the same on the park's website). Access is easiest by taxi (around €5 each way). **Ribeira de Piscos** (daily: May–Sept 9.30am–3pm; Oct–April 10am–2.30pm; 2hr 30min) – whose engravings are spread out along the eponymous *ribeira* down to its confluence with the Côa – is a beautiful place, but there's a lot of walking involved and it gets extremely hot in summer. The highlights are several: a tender engraving of two horses "kissing"; exceptionally fine engravings of auroch bisons; and a very faint and exceptionally rare Palaeolithic engraving of a man. Trips head out all day (mornings are best) from **MUXAGATA**, 1km off the N102 to Guarda, which has a bar beside the visitor centre with meals and good olives, a sixteenth-century pillory, and not much else.

Another beautiful place, and the least strenuous to visit as the jeeps park right next to it, is **Penascosa** (daily: May–Sept 2–5.30pm; Oct–April 1–3.30pm; 1hr 30min), with trips starting at the visitor centre in **CASTELO MELHOR**, just off the N322 to Figueira de Castelo Rodrigo. The route is covered by Lopes & Filho buses, so can be visited by public transport (Tues–Fri only): catch the bus out of Foz Côa just before midday, and head back on the 5.55pm service (or the 7pm run on to Figueira). The village itself has a gorgeous tenth-century ruined castle, and a couple of café-restaurants, one opposite the visitor centre. Penascosa's highlights include an engraving of a fish (one of very few such depictions worldwide), and a wonderful rock containing over a dozen superimposed animals, the meaning of which archeologists are at a loss to understand.

More archeological interest is at the **Quinta da Ervamoira** (closed Mon; visits by appointment: ☎279 759 229 or 279 759 313, ✉museuervamoira@mail .telepac.pt; €5), a secluded vineyard on the west bank of the Côa between Ribeira de Piscos and Penascosa, accessed from Muxagata. Founded in 1880 by the Ramos Pinto port wine company, the attractive granite estate house here is now a museum housing finds from Roman times and displays on geomorphology and ecology, olive oil-making, and of course port wine. Wine tasting (included in the entrance fee) is on a terrace, where you can also enjoy sumptuous meals (€20 excluding wine, €35 "VIP" with wine). Access is by 4WD only, though the *quinta* may be able to provide transport.

Castelo Rodrigo

The only settlement of any real size east of Foz Côa is sleepy **FIGUEIRA DE CASTELO RODRIGO**, sitting at the junction of the N332 from Foz Côa and N221 between Vilar Formosa and Barca d'Alva. It's an attractive enough place, with a broad central square, large Romanesque church, and storks' nests atop both church and fire station, while a decent range of accommodation makes it a good base for exploring the southern stretches of the Parque Natural do Douro Internacional (see p.488). However, it's not Figueira but diminutive

CASTELO RODRIGO, 2km to the south, that constitutes the main reason for coming here. Cresting an isolated hill with splendid views over into Spain, this is a fortified medieval settlement, whose original roots go back even further, when the mysterious Túrdulos people established a *castro* (hilltop settlement) here around 500 BC. Although now inhabited only by a few dozen families, settled around the ruins of a palace, it's a perfect place to spend an afternoon: the views are superb, and its poky cobbled alleys conceal one of the best restaurants in Portugal.

The Castelo

What was, until the end of the 1990s, an all-but-forgotten and abandoned settlement – typical of the urban drift that has emptied so many places in the interior – is now almost vibrant. The reason is the large amounts of money pumped in by the EU to fund Portugal's *Aldeias Históricas* ("Historic Villages") scheme for restoring particularly important or picturesque villages, mostly in Beiras. Whilst the old ladies and their cats are still to be seen, so too are an increasing number of returnees from the cities, which is tipping the population back towards a hundred. Money from the scheme has been put to good use: the ruined palace has been cleaned up, the rough cobbled streets now also sport smooth pathways suitable for wheelchairs and frailer citizens, while dozens of formerly abandoned houses are slowly being restored, a number of which are earmarked to become *turismo rural* accommodation.

Access is easiest by **taxi from Figueira** (under €4), as the steep walk – though short – will also leave you short of breath. The village is surrounded by a road, so you can enter it through any of its three surviving thirteenth-century gates. The southeastern **Porta do Nascente** is identifiable by the graveyard outside, whose inscription warns:"Consider with attention this place of terror, the end of this duplicitous world's vanities", a possible allusion to the castle's long and often violent history. Suitably chastened, enter the village through the gate, where the gatehouse now contains the **Loja dos Sabores** grocery (10am–7pm: June–Sept closed Tues; Oct–May closed Mon–Wed). Besides cheese and smoked meats, it also sells local wines, spirits and liqueurs, plus age-old delicacies like honey vinegar and honeycombs. It also has a small terrace and bar, and plans to open a restaurant.

The **turismo** (daily: May–Sept 8am–8pm; Oct–April 9am–5pm; ☏271 311 277) is just around the corner, beside the palace. The **palace** itself (same hours as the turismo; €1 paid at the turismo), built on a rocky outcrop, remains impressive despite having been torched and sacked by locals in 1640, furious at the oppressive rule of the Spanish-leaning Count, Manuel de Moura y Corte Real. Indeed, the defensive nature of the palace – evidently intended to defend against locals rather than Spain – is evident from the arrow slits that open out over the village.

Practicalities

The local Lopes & Filhos **bus** company (services between Pocinho and Barca d'Alva, via Foz Côa) drops you in the large Largo Mateus de Castro in the centre of town. Leaving town, their buses to Foz Côa depart at 7.40am (except Sun) and 5.10pm (except Sat). Heading south to Lisbon via Guarda, Viseu and Coimbra, there's a daily bus (Mon–Sat 8.20am, 3.30pm Sun), leaving from the ticket kiosk in the southwestern corner of the square, in front of the *Residencial Transmontano*. **Taxis** are based at an office on the north side of the Largo, near the turismo (☏271 312 112).

The **turismo** in Figueira is in a prefab at the north end of the main square (May–Sept Mon–Fri 9.30am–12.30pm & 2–6pm, Sat & Sun 10am–1pm & 2.30–6.30pm; Oct–April daily 9.30am–12.30pm & 2–6pm; ℡271 311 365, Ⓦwww.cm-fcr.pt), and sells arts and crafts as well as handing out information and maps for the **Parque Natural do Douro Internacional**. The same practical advice can be had from the park's regional office, Rua Artur Costa 1 (℡ & Ⓕ271 313 382).

Staying overnight is easiest in Figueira, as bedspace in Castelo Rodrigo is currently limited. There are good **restaurants** in both Figueira and Castelo Rodrigo, with the latter winning out in terms of locations. Local specialities include pork, known locally as "*reco*", and all sorts of game. For **drinking**, try any of the places reviewed below, or the *Casa da Cultura* on the central Largo in Figueira.

Accommodation and food

Cantinho dos Avôs Rua da Sinagoga 1, Castelo Rodrigo ℡271 312 643, Ⓔumcantinho@hotmail .com. Currently only one room here, though more are planned. But it's a delightful little place with great views of the Serra da Marofa from its shady terrace. More importantly, it has a seriously good restaurant – quality olive oil and vinegar on the table, equally good cheeses to start, sublime home-made smoked meats and sausages, lots of choice and low prices (mains are around €5–7) make this one of Portugal's best. Breakfast included. ❷

Casa do Baldo Castelo Rodrigo ℡271 313 148. Reservations are essential if you want to stay in this restored house over the village's southern fortifications. ❸

Estalagem Falcão de Mendonça Rua Álvaro Castelões 20, Figueira, one block north of the turismo ℡271 319 200, Ⓦwww.falcaodemandonca.com. A splendidly refurbished 1820 mansion with lots of stonework and modern glass separations. Facilities include "hydromassage" in the bathrooms, a small covered swimming pool and sundeck, while half-day trips are included in the price. There are good meals and bags of atmosphere at the hotel's surprisingly good-value restaurant, whose speciality is a seafood *cataplana* at €12 a head. Breakfast included. ❺

Pensão Figueirense Av. 25 de Abril, Figueira, 1km south of the Largo ℡271 312 517. Basic plain rooms above a none-too-inviting bar. Breakfast included. ❷

Residencial Transmontano Av. 25 de Abril 66, Figueira, at the south end of the Largo ℡271 312 244, Ⓔtransmontano@iol.pt. Large and comfortable hotel on three floors (lift access). Its large air-conditioned rooms have bathtubs, some with balconies. Also has a good, inexpensive restaurant – the short menu changes daily, though at least one dish features something regional, for instance grilled rabbit. Buffet breakfast included. ❸

Barca d'Alva

Twenty kilometres to the north of Figueira de Castelo Rodrigo (around €15 by taxi), and less than 2km from the Spanish border, is the last Portuguese village along the Douro, **BARCA D'ALVA**. The route is a delight – agricultural land dotted with boulders, storks' nests and conical, stone-roofed houses – and Barca d'Alva itself is an attractive place, overlooked by mountains on all sides and with a row of whitewashed cottages facing the river. It is the final destination of some of the river cruises from Porto, but it's looking a little neglected now since the railway line across the border was discontinued in the 1980s.

The settlement's appeal is the tranquil atmosphere and attractive countryside, which also makes it a good local hiking base. A lovely walk along a quiet road starts by crossing the road bridge into Trás-os-Montes; then you can follow the Douro through olive and orange groves, and past the terraced vineyards still providing grapes for the port companies in Porto.

Accommodation is at *Baga d'Ouro* (℡279 315 126; ❶), above a restaurant on the main road along the river; the unnamed *casa de pasto*, a few doors along, also has cheap rooms. The *Baga d'Ouro* is also a good place to eat, and does a fine set meal and excellent breakfasts of coffee, fresh bread and local honey. **Onward transport** is restricted as there are no bus services north to Freixo de Espada à Cinta; if you want to continue on to Trás-os-Montes by bus your only option is to catch a Lopes & Filho bus back to Pocinho (Mon–Fri 7.30am & 4.30pm, Sat 7.30am, Sun 4.30pm), from where there are three daily buses to Torre do Moncorvo and beyond.

Travel details

Trains

Amarante to: Livração (6–8 daily; 30min); Porto (6–8 daily; 1hr 40min).

Espinho to: Aveiro (1–2 hourly; 25–45min); Braga (1–2 daily; 1hr 10min); Coimbra (1–2 hourly; 55min–1hr 45min); Fátima (3–5 daily; 1hr 55min–2hr 50min); Lisbon (6–12 daily; 2hr 45min–4hr 40min); Porto (3–6 hourly; 15–40min); Santarém (6–12 daily; 2hr 20min–3hr 40min).

Livração to: Amarante (6–8 daily; 30min).

Penafiel to: Peso da Régua (4 daily; 1hr 15min); Porto (2–3 hourly; 45–55min).

Peso da Régua to: Penafiel (3–4 daily; 1hr 15min); Pinhão (6 daily; 30min); Pocinho (3–4 daily; 1hr 30min); Porto (3–4 daily; 2hr–2hr 25min); Tua (6 daily; 45min); Vila Real (3–5 daily; 50min).

Pinhão to: Pocinho (4 daily; 1hr); Régua (5–6 daily; 30min); Tua (2–3 daily; 15min).

Pocinho to: Pinhão (4 daily; 1hr); Régua (4 daily; 1hr 30min); Tua (4 daily; 40min).

Porto to: Aveiro (39–46 daily; 40–75min); Barcelos (4 daily; 1hr); Braga (14–25 daily; 50–70min); Caminha (3 daily; 1hr 45min); Coimbra (20–30 daily; 1hr 10min–2hr15min); Espinho (4–6 hourly; 15–35min); Faro (Sun; 8hr 40min); Fátima (3–5 daily; 2hr 10min–3hr 10min); Guimarães (9–14 daily; 1hr 15min); Lisbon (10–16 daily; 3–5hr); Ovar (4–6 hourly; 25–55min); Penafiel (1–2 hourly; 45min–2hr); Peso da Régua (4 daily; 2hr); Santarém (6–12 daily; 2hr 35min–4hr); Santo Tirso (9–14 daily; 40min); Valença (3 daily; 2hr 10min); Viana do Castelo (4 daily; 1hr 30min); Vigo, Spain (2 daily; 3hr); Vila Nova de Cerveira (2 daily; 2hr); Vila Praia de Âncora (3 daily; 1hr 40min).

Santo Tirso to: Guimarães (9–14 daily; 35min); Porto (9–15 daily; 45min).

Tua to: Mirandela (2 daily; 1hr 35min); Pinhão (5–6 daily; 20min); Peso da Régua (5–6 daily; 45min); Pocinho (3–4 daily; 40min).

Buses from Porto

Porto lacks a central bus station, and its bus companies operate from various locations: companies running to given destinations are noted as abbreviations after the journey times; order reflects frequency of service. Refer to the list opposite for contact numbers and departure point in Porto.

To the Douro region: Amarante (10 daily; 1hr 30min; AVT, SA, RN); Espinho (18 daily; 30min; AVE); Lamego (3–5 daily; 4hr; AD, RE); Mondim de Basto (7 daily; 3hr 30min; MO); Penafiel (24 daily; 1hr; VA, AD, AVT, AVL); Peso da Régua (3–5 daily; 3hr; AD); Póvoa de Varzim (hourly; 50min; LI, AVM, RE); Santo Tirso (8 daily; 1hr; MO, AVL, AR, RE); Vila do Conde (hourly; 40min; LI, AVM, RE).

To the Alentejo and Algarve: Elvas (3 daily; 10hr; RE); Estremoz (2 daily; 8hr 30min; RE); Évora (6 daily; 6hr 30min; RE); Faro (6 daily; 8–10hr; RE, RX); Portalegre (daily; 7hr 30min; RE).

To the Beiras: Arouca (2 daily; 2hr 30min; CA, AVF); Aveiro (4 daily; 2hr 30min; CA); Castelo Branco (3–4 daily; 5–6hr; SA); Coimbra (8–10 daily; 1hr 30min; RE, RN, SA, AVT); Covilhã (2 daily; 4hr 15min; SA); Guarda (7 daily; 2–3hr; SA, MA); Seia (daily; 4hr 15min; MA, RE); Viseu (8 daily; 2hr; MA, RE).

To Lisbon, Estremadura and the Ribatejo: Abrantes (daily; 4hr 30min; RE, RN); Caldas da Rainha (3 daily; 4hr 30min; RE, RN); Fátima (6 daily; 3hr 30min; RE, RN); Leiria (6 daily; 2hr–2hr 30min; RE, RN); Lisbon (hourly; 3hr–3hr 30min; RX, RE, AVT); Nazaré (3 daily; 4hr; RE, RN); Peniche (3 daily; 5hr 30min; RE, RN); Santarém (2 daily; 4hr 30min; RE, RN); Tomar (daily; 4hr; RE, RN).

To Minho: Barcelos (7 daily; 1hr 45min; LI, AR, RE); Braga (17 daily; 1hr 10min; REDM, RE, AR, RX); Caminha (5 daily; 2hr; AVM, RE); Esposende (8 daily; 1hr 20min; LI, RE, AVM); Guimarães (12 daily; 2hr; RE, MO, AR); Melgaço (2 daily; 3hr; AVM); Monção (5 daily; 3hr; AVM, RN, RE); Ovar (5 daily; 1hr; AVE, CA); Valença (5 daily; 2hr 30min; AVM, RN, RE); Viana do Castelo (hourly; 2hr; RE, AVM, LI).

To Trás-os-Montes: Bragança (6 daily; 2–4hr; AVT, SA, RE); Chaves (6–12 daily; 3hr 30min; AVT,

AR	*Arriva* Rua Fons Cardoso ☏222 051 383
AD	*Asa Douro* Campo 24 de Agosto ☏225 376 737
AVA	*Auto Viação Almeida e Filhos* Campo 24 de Agosto ☏225 104 939 or 225 370 377
AVE	*Auto Viação Espinho* Garagem Atlântico, Rua Alexandre Herculano ☏222 007 544
AVF	*Auto Viação Feirense* Parque da Camélias ☏222 007 408
AVL	*Auto Viação Landim* Pr. General Humberto Delgado ☏222 005 532
AVM	*Auto Viação do Minho* Pr. da República ☏222 006 121
AVT	*Auto Viação do Tâmega* Rua Alexandre Herculano 68 ☏222 083 019, ⓦwww .avtamega.pt
CA	*Caima* Garagem Atlântico, Rua Alexandre Herculano ☏222 002 660
LI	*Linhares* Garagem Linhares, Rua José Falcão ☏222 000 427
MA	*Marques* Rua da Restauração ☏222 039 889
MO	*Mondinense* Campo 24 de Agosto ☏225 376 737
RED	*REDM* Rua Dr. Alfredo Magalhães 94 ☏222 003 152
RE	*Rede Expressos* Garagem Atlântico, Rua Alexandre Herculano ☏222 006 954, ⓦwww.rede-expressos.pt
RX	*Renex* Jardim da Cordoaria, next to Palácio da Justiça ☏222 003 395
RN	*Rodonorte* Rua Ateneu Comercial 19 ☏222 004 398, ⓦwww.rodonorte.pt
SA	*Santos* Campo 24 de Agosto ☏225 104 915, ⓦwww.santosviagensturismo.pt
VA	*Valpi* Pr. General Humberto Delgado ☏222 007 555 or 224 157 960

5

PORTO AND THE DOURO | Travel details

RN, RE); Freixo de Espada-à-Cinta (daily; 7hr; SA); Miranda do Douro (1–2 daily; 8hr; SA, RN); Mirandela (2–4 daily; 2hr 45min; SA, RN); Vidago (7 daily; 3hr–3hr 30min; AVT, RN); Vila Pouca de Aguiar (7 daily; 2hr 30min–3hr; AVT, RN, RE); Vila Real (9 daily; 2hr; AVT, RN, RE, SA).

Regional buses

Amarante to: Braga (5–8 daily; 1hr 20min); Cabeceiras de Basto (3–4 daily; 1hr 35min); Celorico de Basto (5 daily; 40min); Fermil (3–4 daily; 1hr); Guimarães (5–8 daily; 50min); Porto (3–7 daily; 1hr); Vila Real (hourly; 1hr 40min).
Figueira de Castelo Rodrigo to: Barca d'Alva (1–2 daily; 40min); Guarda (daily; 1hr 30min); Lisbon (1 weekly; 7hr); Pocinho (1–2 daily; 1hr 50min); Vila Nova de Foz Côa (1–2 daily; 1hr 20min).
Lamego to: Braga (daily; 2hr 50min); Celorico da Beira (daily; 3hr); Lisbon (2–4 daily; 6hr); Penafiel (3–5 daily; 1hr 40min); Peso da Régua (19 daily; 30min); Porto (4–6 daily; 4–4hr 30min); São João de Tarouca (4 daily; 20min); Sernancelhe (2–6 daily; 2hr); Trancoso (1–2 daily; 2hr); Viseu (5–7 daily; 1hr 20min–2hr).
Penafiel to: Abragão (Mon–Fri 7 daily, Sat & Sun 2–3 daily); Amarante (3–9 daily; 30min); Boelhe (6 daily; 45min); Gandra (every 30min; 30min); Lamego (3–5 daily; 1hr 40min); Paço de Sousa (Mon–Fri

6 daily, Sat 2 daily); Porto (28 daily; 30min–1hr 20min); Torrão (7 daily; 45min–1hr 30min).
Peso da Régua to: Coimbra (1–2 daily; 3hr 40min); Guarda (daily; 2hr 30min); Lamego (16 daily; 25min); Vila Real (hourly; 40min); Viseu (6 daily; 1hr 30min).
Pocinho to: Barca d'Alva via Foz Côa (Mon–Fri 2 daily; Sat & Sun 1 daily; 2hr 30min); Bragança (2 daily; 1hr 40min); Celorico da Beira (2 daily; 1hr 45min); Coimbra (2 daily; 4hr 55min); Lisbon (2 daily; 7hr 25min); Torre de Moncorvo (3 daily; 30min); Trancoso (2 daily; 2hr 30min); Viseu (2 daily; 2hr 45min).
Póvoa do Varzim to: Barcelos (4–5 daily; 45min); Braga (9 daily; 1hr 15min); Esposende (9–12 daily; 40min); Guimarães (8–10 daily; 1hr 45min); Porto (hourly; 50min); Santo Tirso (12 daily; 1hr); Viana do Castelo (2 hourly; 1hr); Vila do Conde (2 hourly; 15min).
Vila do Conde to: Porto (hourly; 40min); Póvoa do Varzim (2 hourly; 15min); Santo Tirso (5–10 daily; 40min); Viana do Castelo (hourly; 1hr 20min).
Vila Nova de Foz Côa to: Bragança (daily; 2hr); Celorico da Beira (daily; 1hr); Coimbra (daily; 4hr); Guarda (daily; 1hr 30min); Leiria (3 daily; 5hr); Lisbon (4 daily; 6hr 30min); Macedo de Cavaleiros (daily; 1hr 30min); Miranda do Douro (4–5 daily; 2hr 10min); Mogadouro (4–5 daily; 1hr 30min); Moncorvo (4–5 daily; 30min); Trancoso (2 daily; 40min); Viseu (daily; 2hr).

The Minho

ATLANTIC
OCEAN

SPAIN

N

CHAPTER 6

Highlights

✳**Guimarães** The country's first capital is an attractive maze of cobbled streets, medieval monuments and hidden squares. See p.381

✳**Bom Jesus do Monte** Join the pilgrims and the penitents on a wonderful Baroque stairway to heaven. See p.395

✳**Citânia de Briteiros** Step back to pre-Roman times at the magnificent Celtic hill fort. See p.397

✳**Feira de Barcelos** The spectaclar Thursday *feira* is one of Europe's biggest weekly markets. See p.400

✳**Costa Verde beaches** There's always space to lay your towel on the golden sands of the rugged Atlantic coast. See p.404

✳**Valença do Minho** Gaze across the Rio Minho to Spain from the ramparts of the ancient walled town. See p.417

✳**Ponte de Lima** Stay in a manor house or rural property near the peaceful riverside town. See p.424

✳**Parque Nacional da Peneda-Gerês** A wild and solitary part of the country offering spectacular hiking and outdoor pursuits. See p.430

△ Ponte de Lima

6

The Minho

With good reason, many Portuguese consider the **Minho** – the province north of Porto – to be the most beautiful part of their country. A rolling province of lush river valleys, forested hillsides, trailing vines and long, sandy beaches, it is immensely pleasing on the eye, while much is made of the Minho's traditional aspect, especially in the mountainous east, where you can still see wooden-wheeled ox-carts creak down cobbled lanes. Here age-old customs are maintained at dozens of huge country markets, *festas* and *romarias*. In summer, especially, you're likely to happen upon these carnivals and it's worth trying to plan a trip around the larger events if you're keen to experience Minho life at its most exuberant.

It's not all a rural backwater, however, and as you travel around the region you'll see new buildings in even the smallest and most isolated villages; things are starting to change. This is explained by a raft of new initiatives which have sprung up to capitalize on the tourism potential of the region, but also by the new-found prosperity of returned emigrants keen to put something back into their home towns. Starting in the late 1950s, Minho, more than any other area of Portugal, suffered severe depopulation as thousands migrated to France, Switzerland, Germany and the United States in search of more lucrative work. The tide of emigration has slowed in recent years as European Union money has provided inward investment, but many still choose to at least start a career abroad.

The largest towns are concentrated in the southern Minho and any trip should allow time to examine the competing historic claims of **Guimarães**, first capital of Portugal, and neighbouring **Braga**, the country's ecclesiastical centre. Between them lie the extensive Celtic ruins of the **Citânia de Briteiros**, one of the most impressive archeological sites in Portugal, while from Braga it's also easy to visit **Barcelos**, site of the best known and biggest of the region's weekly markets. It takes place on Thursdays, although for the full experience reserve a room in advance and arrive on Wednesday evening.

At Barcelos, you're only 20km from the **Costa Verde**, the Minho coast, which runs north all the way to the Spanish border. Although this boasts some wonderful beaches along the way, the weather is as unpredictable as the sea, with cool temperatures possible even in midsummer. The principal resort is **Viana do Castelo**, a lively town with an elegant historic core and, if you're seeking isolation, beaches to the north and south that scarcely see visitors. The coast ends at **Caminha**, beyond which the **Rio Minho** runs inland, forming the border with Spanish Galicia. This is a delightful region, featuring a string of compact fortified towns flanking the river on the Portuguese side. Their fortresses, in various stages of disrepair, stare across at Spain, with perhaps the most compelling stop at the quaint old town of **Valença do Minho**.

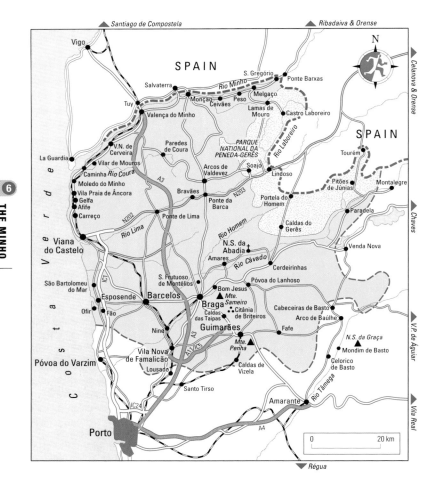

Inland from Viana, the Minho's other major river, the beautiful **Rio Lima**, idles east through a succession of gorgeous small towns where there's little to do but soak up the somnolent scenery. Indeed, it's in the Lima valley, particularly around the town of **Ponte de Lima**, that you'll find the pick of the region's famous rural-tourism and manor-house accommodation. Further east, the gentle Minho scenery eventually gives way to the mountains, waterfalls, river gorges, reservoirs and forests of the protected **Parque Nacional da Peneda-Gerês**, Portugal's only national (as opposed to natural) park. This is superb camping and hiking territory, stretching from the main town and spa of **Caldas do Gerês** north as far as the Rio Minho and the Spanish border and east into Trás-os-Montes. It's possible to dip into the park from nearby towns, but you really need to devote several days if you're going to see the more isolated regions as bus services are limited. Even by car the going's slow and on foot you could spend weeks exploring the trails.

Southern Minho

The southern Minho's two chief towns, Guimarães and Braga, are both small enough to walk around in a busy day's sightseeing, although a night's stay brings greater rewards. This is especially true if you want to explore the series of religious attractions around Braga, none more extraordinary than the pilgrimage site of Bom Jesus do Monte, while you'll need to set aside another half-day at least to see the Celtic remains of Citânia de Briteiros. For shoppers, the best overnight stop is undoubtedly at Barcelos, provided you can find a room on a Wednesday night before the weekly market.

Braga is on a branch of the main train line from Porto to Viana do Castelo; for non-direct **trains** you need to change at Nine. Direct but dawdling trains travel to Guimarães from Porto on a separate branch line. Regardless of this, it is far quicker to use the direct **bus** between Braga and Guimarães rather than fiddle about with connections between train lines.

Guimarães

GUIMARÃES never misses an opportunity to remind you of its place in Portuguese history. Birthplace of the first king, Afonso Henriques, in 1110 and first capital of the fledging kingdom of "Portucale", it has every right to be proud of its role in the formation of the nation. It was from here that the reconquest from the Moors began, leading to the subsequent creation of a united kingdom that, within a century of Afonso's death, was to stretch to its present borders. Although Guimarães subsequently lost its pre-eminent status to Coimbra (elevated to Portuguese capital in 1143), it has never relinquished its sense of self-importance, something that's evident from the careful preservation of an array of impressive medieval monuments and the omnipresent reminder "*Portugal nasceu aqui*" (Portugal was born here). Today, despite its industrial outskirts, the centre of Guimarães retains both a grandeur and a tangible sense of history in a labyrinth of attractive, narrow streets. If you can afford to stay at one of the two local *pousadas* – one in the centre, the other in a former monastery at Penha, 2km southeast – then the experience is complete. Otherwise, decent budget accommodation is hard to come by, although Braga (24km), or even Porto (55km), is close enough to be used as a base to visit on a day-trip.

The major event is the **Festas Gualterianas** (for São Gualter, or St Walter), which has taken place on the first weekend in August every year since 1452. If you miss this you can catch most of the same stallholders and something of the atmosphere on the following weekend in Caldas de Vizela, a spa town 10km south of Guimarães. Next in importance is the long-established *romaria* to **São Torcato**, 6km northeast of town, on the first weekend in July, while a well-timed visit in winter will enable you to see one or more of the festivals of **Nicolinas** (Nov 29 to Dec 7), **Nossa Senhora da Conceição** (Dec 8) and **Santa Luzia** (Dec 13).

Arrival and information

Guimarães's historic centre is pedestrianized, although metered **parking** is available in the streets adjacent to the Convento do Carmo; there's also an underground car park beneath the shopping centre on Largo da República do

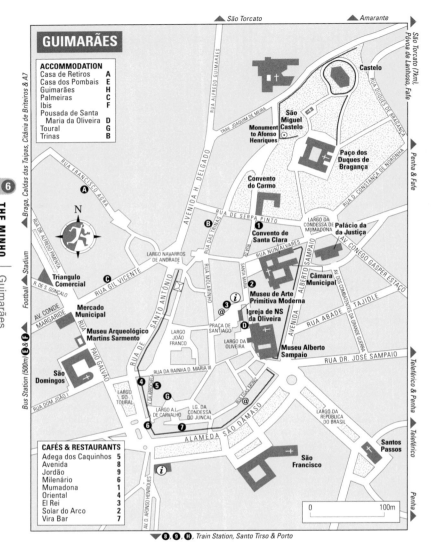

GUIMARÃES

ACCOMMODATION
Casa de Retiros	A
Casa dos Pombais	E
Guimarães	H
Palmeiras	C
Ibis	F
Pousada de Santa Maria da Oliveira	D
Toural	G
Trinas	B

CAFÉS & RESTAURANTS
Adega dos Caquinhos	5
Avenida	8
Jordão	9
Milenário	6
Mumadona	1
Oriental	4
El Rei	3
Solar do Arco	2
Vira Bar	7

Brasil. The **bus station** is fifteen minutes' walk southwest of the town centre at the bottom of Avenida Conde Margaride. It's part of the Guimarães shopping complex, unmarked but identifiable by the Continente supermarket or McDonald's sign above the entrance. There are express bus services from Porto and Lisbon, and regular weekday connections with Braga, Amarante, Cabeceiras and Mondim de Basto, and Póvoa do Lanhoso. Guimarães train station is ten minutes' walk south of the centre; to get into town, bear left from the station and take the first right down Avenida Dom Afonso Henriques, which takes you to the leafy boulevard of Alameda São Damaso.

The **main turismo** is at Alameda São Damaso 83 (Mon–Fri 9.30am–12.30pm & 2–6.30pm; ☎253 412 450, ⓦwww.cm-guimaraes.pt). It produces the *Manual de Informação Turística* (available in English), a work of Biblical proportions containing almost every piece of contact information a visitor could ever need, although, understandably, they are in short supply, so you may have to make do with consulting the office copy. There's also a **branch turismo** in the old town at Praça de Santiago 37 (Mon–Fri 9.30am–6.30pm, Sat 10am–6pm, Sun 10am–1pm; ☎253 518 790).

Accommodation

Accommodation in town is scarce – nearby Braga has a much better choice. Consequently, it's best to book ahead, especially if you're planning to stay in the *pousadas* or in one of a number of superb manor houses in the vicinity. The turismo has details of these (ask for *turismo rural*), but we've highlighted a couple of the best below.

In Guimarães

Casa de Retiros Rua Francisco Agra 163 ☎253 511 515, ⓕ253 511 517. A pilgrims' hostel and as a result one of the cheaper places in town – at peak times it may be booked up by groups. Be prepared for a simple existence: spartan surroundings, bland breakfasts and a strict 11.30pm curfew. Single rooms offer good value. No credit cards. ❸

Casa dos Pombais Av. de Londres ☎253 412 917, ⓦwww.solaresdeportugal.pt. Opposite the bus station and marooned by a busy road, this eighteenth-century manor house is an oasis with attractive gardens. There are only two guest rooms, with grand furniture but homely touches, though they have received mixed reports from readers. There's no reception, so phone ahead to ensure owners are in. ❹

Hotel de Guimarães Rua Dr. Eduardo Almeida, 100m from the train station ☎253 424 800, ⓦwww.hotel-guimaraes.com. The smartest modern hotel choice, quietly stylish and with four-star comforts, including health club, jacuzzi, pool, sauna and restaurant. Breakfast included, and there's parking for guests. ❻

Hotel Ibis Av. Conde Margaride 12 ☎253 424 900, ⓦwww.ibishotel.com. Bland but adequate modern rooms in a chain hotel, next to the bus terminal. Rates includes breakfast. ❸

Albergaria das Palmeiras Centro Comercial das Palmeiras, Rua Gil Vicente ☎253 410 324, ⓕ253 417 261. On the fourth storey of a commercial mall, which can make it difficult to find, but the modern rooms in this *albergaria* are more comfortable than the drab surroundings suggest. Also has a restaurant and its own parking. ❸

Pousada de Santa Maria da Oliveira Rua de Santa Maria ☎253 514 157, ⓦwww.pousadas.pt. Converted from a row of sixteenth-century houses, right in the medieval centre, this sixteen-room *pousada* is beautifully furnished with antiques and worth every euro. Breakfast is included and the restaurant (reservations required; expensive) is the finest in town, with traditional Minho dishes served in a wonderful antique dining room or at outside tables in summer. ❽

Hotel Toural Largo do Toural, entrance in Largo A.L. de Carvalho at the back ☎253 517 184, ⓔhoteltoural@netc.pt. Once an elegant town house, this has been completely renovated into a modern four-star establishment – not particularly cheap, but rooms are spacious and very comfortable and it has parking. Breakfast included. ❺

Residencial das Trinas Rua das Trinas 29 ☎253 517 358, ⓕ253 517 362. This old-town *residencial* has eleven modest rooms and is one of the best budget options. Rooms overlooking the street have the atmosphere – rear rooms are noisier, although are double-glazed – and all have private bathrooms and satellite TV. Breakfast included. ❸

Outside Guimarães

Casa de Sezim Nespereira, 6km south of Guimarães off the Santo Tirso road – turn right at Covas ☎253 523 000, ⓦwww.sezim.pt. Ten rooms in a delightful aristocratic country estate owned by the same *vinho verde*-producing family for over six centuries – the current incumbent is charming. Rooms in the main powder-pink eighteenth-century *solar* (manor) are furnished with Murano chandeliers and *objets d'art*, with four-posters in many. There's also a swimming pool and walking and horse-riding trips are available. Breakfast included. ❻

Paço de São Cipriano Taboadelo, 6km south of Guimarães off the Santo Tirso road – turn left at Covas ☎253 565 337, ⓦwww.solaresdeportugal.pt. Stun-

ning eighteenth-century country palace, complete with chapel and medieval tower. There are five guest rooms, plus orchards, vineyards and a swimming pool. Breakfast included. Closed Nov–March. **⑥**
Pousada de Santa Marinha da Costa 2km southeast of Guimarães along Rua Dr. José Sampaio ☎253 511 249, ⓦwww.pousadas.pt. Occupying a convent at the foot of Monte Penha, parts of which date from the ninth century, this is reckoned to be one of the top *pousadas* in the country. Elegant, comfortable rooms gather around a serene courtyard; the original rooms have more character than the new additions. There's also an outdoor pool with splendid views and an excellent restaurant. Breakfast included. **⑧**

Campsites

Caldas das Taipas 7km northwest of Guimarães ☎253 576 274. By the banks of the Rio Ave, off the N101. Pricier but arguably more attractive, with a swimming pool and a thermal spa nearby. Closed Oct–May.
Parque de Campismo da Penha 2km southeast of Guimarães ☎253 515 912, ⓕ253 516 569. The nearest site to town is a pleasant place on the slopes of Penha and accessible by the cable car at the end of Rua Dr. José Sampaio. There's a small swimming pool and some bungalows for rent (**②**). Officially open April–Oct, though worth ringing ahead at other times.

The Town

The old centre of Guimarães is an elongated kernel of small, enclosed squares and cobbled streets dominated by warm, honey-coloured buildings. Bounded at its southern end by the town gardens and overlooked from the north by the imposing castle, it is an enduring symbol of the emergent Portuguese nation. In between lie a series of medieval churches, convents and buildings that lend an air of dignity to the streets – two of the convents provide an impressive backdrop to a couple of the country's more illuminating museums. The presence of the University of the Minho gives local cafés and bars a lively, student-orientated feel, particularly in the old town.

Around the Castelo

The imposing Castelo (daily 9.30am–5pm, Oct–May closed 12.30–2pm; free) was originally built in the tenth century by the Countess of Mumadona to protect the people of Guimarães from attack by Moors and Normans. It was extended by Afonso Henriques, who established the first Portuguese court here in the twelfth century. After falling into disrepair, and being used as a debtor's prison in the nineteenth century, the castle was rebuilt in the 1940s. Afonso is reputed to have been born in the great square keep, which is surrounded by seven fortified towers. You can wander the ramparts and check out the views of town, or climb the 77 steps to the top of the central keep (€1.50), which opens out onto a narrow tower, but take care because stonework is uneven and narrow in places. The castle is juxtaposed with the diminutive Romanesque chapel of São Miguel do Castelo (daily 9am–12.30pm & 2–5pm; free) on the grassy slope below, in whose font Afonso is said to have been baptised.

Just across from the chapel is the **Paço dos Duques de Bragança** (July & Aug daily 9.30am–12.30pm & 2–7pm; Sept–June daily 9.30am–12.30pm & 2–6pm; €3, free Sun mornings). Built in the fifteenth century by the illegitimate son of Dom João I, Dom Afonso, it was constructed along Burgundian lines by a French architect, reflecting Afonso's cosmopolitan tastes. It served as the medieval palace of the all-powerful Bragançan duchy until it fell into decline at the end of the sixteenth century. Under the Salazar dictatorship, its ruins were "restored" as an official residence for the president (the second floor is still reserved for this function), but today it looks faintly ludicrous, like a mock-Gothic Victorian folly. Inside is an extensive collection of portraits (including a room of colourful paintings and sculptures by modern artist José de Guimarães), tapestries, furniture, weapons and porcelain, around which lengthy guided tours perambulate. Free concerts are occasionally held here on summer weekends as part of the annual "Encontros da Primavera" season of concerts; enquire at the turismo for details.

Along Rua de Santa Maria

From the castle, Rua de Santa Maria leads down into the heart of the old town, a beautiful thoroughfare flanked by iron grilles and granite arches. Many of the town's historic buildings have been superbly restored and as you descend to the centre you'll pass one of the loveliest, the sixteenth-century convent of Santa Clara, with its Baroque facade. Today, this serves as the Câmara Municipal. Many of the convent's furnishings were removed after the dissolution of the monasteries and are now displayed in the Museu Alberto Sampaio (see below).

On a much more intimate scale are the buildings ranged around the delightful central squares at the end of the street, **Praça de Santiago** and **Largo da Oliveira**. The latter is dominated by the **Igreja de Nossa Senhora da Oliveira** (daily 7.15am–noon & 3.30–7.30pm; free), a convent-church built (like the great monastery at Batalha) to honour a vow made to the Virgin Mary by João I prior to his decisive victory over Castile at Aljubarrota. Its unusual dedication to "Our Lady of the Olive Tree" dates from the fourteenth century, when an olive tree from the shrine of São Torcato was replanted in the monastery to provide oil for the lamps of the church. The tree died and remained lifeless until September 8, 1342, when a cross, hung from one of its branches, made it grow again. Before it stands a curious Gothic **canopy-shrine**, erected in 1340 to commemorate the Battle of Salado, another one of many disagreements with the Castilians. It also marks the legendary spot where Wamba, unwilling king of the Visigoths, drove a pole into the ground swearing he would not reign until it blossomed. Naturally, it sprouted immediately, in keeping with remarkable growth rates hearabouts. João I, interpreting this as indication of divine favour, rode out to meet the Castilian forces from this very point.

Next door is the convent's simple Romanesque cloister with varied, naively carved capitals. This, and the rooms off it, house the **Museu Alberto Sampaio** (Tues–Sun 10am–6pm, July & Aug open until midnight as Museu à Noite; €2, free Sun mornings), essentially the treasury of the collegiate church and convent but, for once, outstandingly exhibited and containing pieces of real beauty. The highlight is a brilliantly composed silver-gilt *Triptych of the Nativity*, said to have been found in the King of Castile's tent after the Portuguese victory at Aljubarrota in 1385, although it was more probably made from melting down the king's silver measuring weights. Close by is the tunic worn by João I in the battle and beginning to show its age.

Opposite the museum, and housed in a heavy arched structure that was formerly the council chambers, the **Museu de Arte Primitiva Moderna** (Mon–Fri 9am–12.30pm & 2–5pm; free) contains over 300 works by self-taught artists. This provides a fascinating excursion through daily, secular and ritual life and ranges from pure kitsch to the odd masterpiece.

Museu Martins Sarmento

Across to the west, over the main Largo do Toural, the Museu Arqueológico Martins Sarmento (Tues–Sun 10am–noon & 2–5pm; €1.50) is another superb collection, named after Martins Sarmento, an archeologist, born in the town, who discovered the Celtic citânia of Briteiros (see p.397). Finds from the site are displayed in the fourteenth-century Gothic cloister of the Igreja de São

Domingos. They include a remarkable series of bronze votive offerings (among them, a "coach", pulled at each end by men and oxen) and ornately patterned stone lintels and door-jambs from the huts. Most spectacular of all are the Pedras Formosas ("beautiful stones"). Once assumed to be sacrificial altars or portals to funerary monuments, it's now agreed that these were more likely to have been taken from the interiors of bathhouses.

The **Colossus of Pedralva**, a vast granite hulk of a figure with arm raised aloft and an oversized phallus, once the museum's prize exhibit, now stands guard at the pedestrian precinct outside the bus station. More enigmatic and considerably more ancient than the Pedras Formosas, it shares the bold, powerfully hewn appearance of the stone pigs found in Trás-os-Montes and, like them, may date from pre-Celtic fertility cults of around 1500 to 1000 BC.

Penha and Santa Marinha da Costa

Two kilometres southeast of Guimarães on the slopes of Penha (617m), the locals' favourite spot for a Sunday picnic, stands the region's best-preserved medieval building, the former monastery – and now *pousada* – of Santa Marinha da Costa. It can be reached by taking the São Roque bus (Mon–Sat 6am–10pm, Sun 6am–8pm; every 30min) from the main turismo; alight at "Costa" and follow the signs.

The monastery was founded in 1154 by order of Dona Mafalda, the wife of Afonso Henriques, in honour of a vow to Santa Marinha, patron saint of pregnant women. Originally Augustinian, the foundation passed into the hands of the Order of St Jerome in the sixteenth century. In the **chapel** (official hours July–Sept 9am–1pm & 2–7pm, but often closed), Jerome's twin emblems of the skull and the lion are recurring motifs. They are surrounded by an oddly harmonious mixture of styles – tenth-century doorways on the south wall, sixteenth-century panels in the sacristy (including one depicting Jerome beating his breast with a stone against the temptation of women) and an eighteenth-century organ and stone roof in the choir. A catastrophic fire ravaged the monastery in 1951, but careful restoration and its transformation into a *pousada* have returned it to some semblance of its former glory. Strictly speaking, the rest of the monastic buildings are off limits except to guests of the *pousada*, but you can peek into the magnificent **cloister**, with a Mozarabic doorway, while the beautiful **gardens** are open to the public, too.

The peak of Penha is crowned by a statue of Nossa Senhora. By far the most fun way to reach it is to take the ingenious **Teleférico da Penha**, a cable car whose hi-tech bubbles leave from the end of Rua Dr. José Sampaio (Mon–Fri 10.30am–7pm, Sat & Sun 10.30am–8pm; €2.50 return), a five-minute walk from Largo da República do Brasil.

Eating, drinking and entertainment

Guimarães has no shortage of cafés and restaurants which, in contrast to much of the accommodation, are quite reasonably priced. Local specialities to look out for – or avoid – include *chispalhada de feijão* (beans, sausage and pig's trotters), *papas de sarabulho* (a blood and bread stew) and *rojões de porco* (roast pork, blood-sausage and potatoes). Desserts include *melindres* (honey cakes), *aletria* (like vermicelli) and *toucinho do céu* ("heavenly bacon"), actually a super-sweet concoction of sugar, almonds, eggs and lemon.

Bars around central Praça de Santiago and the adjacent Largo da Oliveira are aimed at a youthful clientele, but all have outdoor tables and are very popular, particularly on summer Saturday nights. Other **clubs** besides those listed below make mayfly-like appearances in summer, only to disappear without trace in winter – ask at the turismo for details or (more reliably) collar a student at a Largo da Oliveira bar.

Outside festival time, at the beginning of July and August, the only time the town erupts into spontaneous celebration is when the local football team, **FC Guimarães**, wins at home. The stadium is located to the northwest of the centre, along Rua de São Gonçalo; tickets may be available depending on the status of opponents – consult the turismo.

Cafés and restaurants

Adega dos Caquinhos Trav. da Arrochela ☎253 516 917. Good, reasonably priced food – around €12 for a full meal and drinks – in a traditional *adega* whose name reflects its decor; walls are covered in broken crockery (*caquinhos*). Moderate.

Avenida Av. Dom Afonso Henriques 141 ☎253 414 774. Snacks and basic dishes such as pork cutlets in an unassuming, no-frills place, a five-minute walk from the main turismo. Eat at tables (you may have to share) or at the bar. Inexpensive.

Jordão Av. Dom Afonso Henriques 55 ☎253 516 498. Near the train station, this offers well-priced regional specialities such as roast veal and *rojões de porco* in a hall-like traditional dining room. Closed Mon eve and all Tues. Moderate.

Milenário Largo do Toural ☎253 412 526. Large and airy traditional café serving decent snacks. It's always busy with young and old exchanging gossip over a coffee. Inexpensive.

Mumadona Corner of Rua Serpa Pinto and Rua Santa Maria ☎253 416 111. Reliable, friendly and unpretentious, serving all the usual dishes plus a two-course set menu for €12.50. Closed Sun. Moderate.

Oriental Largo do Toural ☎253 414 048. Atmospheric dining beneath a nicely worn stucco ceiling, or three balcony tables which offer superb views over the square. Try the *truta grelhada com presunto* (grilled trout stuffed with ham). Moderate.

El Rei Praça de Santiago 20A ☎253 419 096.

Small, cosy restaurant in a prime location serving consistently good-quality food, although prone to close at lunch if custom is slow. Closed Sun. Moderate.

Solar do Arco Rua de Santa Maria 48–50 ☎253 513072. The daily specials here are always worth sampling – try the *feijoada de camarões* (bean stew with shrimps) if it's on – as are the home-made desserts. It's in a central position, and priced accordingly, at around €12–14 for main dishes. Closed Sun eve. Moderate.

Vira Bar Largo da Condessa do Juncal 27 ☎253 518 427. A well-regarded church-like place with stone walls, a barrel-vaulted ceiling and a subdued ambience. Spending around €20 will get you the full works. Closed Sun. Moderate.

Bars and clubs

Patri Mónio At foot of the *Teleférico da Penha*. The closest club to the town centre plays Euro-pop, Latin and house. Fri & Sat 10pm–4am.

Seculo Off Av. da Universidade, a continuation of Rua Alfredo Guimarães. House sounds, beefed up by techno and spiced with Latin tunes, in a stylish garden club. Wed–Sun 10pm–4am.

Sitio Praça de Santiago 10. Currently the hangout of choice for stylish bar-hoppers.

Ultimatum Jazz Café Rua Francisco Agra, off Rua Dr. Alfredo Pimenta. An atmospheric café-cum-restaurant, occasionally with live music, that metamorphoses into a disco after-hours.

Listings

Ambulance Call ☎253 515 444.

Banks Banks and ATMs line Rua Gil Vicente and Largo do Toural.

Hospital Accident and emergency services are available in the hospital opposite the bus station ☎253 512 612.

Internet Net Pr@ca Online at Pr. de Santiago 11 (daily 10am–midnight). Busier, free municipal terminals are at Rua Egas Moniz 31 (Mon–Sat 10am–10pm, Sun 10am–3pm).

Police PSP headquarters is 500m northeast of the market on Rua Dr. Alfredo Pimenta ☎253 513 334.

Post office On the corner of Largo Navarros de Andrade, at the top of Rua de Santo Antonio (Mon–Fri 8.30am–6.30pm, Sat 9am–12.30pm).

Taxis On Largo do Toural and Alamdea São Dâmaso, or call ☎253 522 522 or 253 515 515.

Braga

BRAGA is a small city with ecclesiastical pretensions. Even the turismo pamphlet hails it as the Portuguese Rome, although the Portuguese Canterbury is more appropriate. One of the country's most ancient towns, it was probably founded by the Bracari Celts (hence the name), later falling into Roman hands and being christened Bracara, capital of Roman Gallaecia. Its history is then one of conquest and reconquest, being occupied at various times by the Suevi, Visigoths and eventually the Moors. Braga was an important Visigothic bishopric and by the end of the eleventh century its archbishops were pressing for recognition as "Primate of the Spains", a title they disputed bitterly with archbishops of Toledo and Tarragona over the next six centuries.

The city is still Portugal's religious capital. Look around and you soon become aware of the weight of ecclesiastical power, embodied by an archbishop's palace built on a truly presidential scale. At **Easter**, Braga is the scene of spectacular celebrations which climax in the three days before Easter Sunday, when the priest blesses each house with a crucifix and holy water, while torchlit processions of hooded penitents known as *farricocos* parade spinning large rattles. The city's outlying districts also boast a selection of important religious buildings and sanctuaries, notably that of **Bom Jesus** (see next section), one of the country's most extravagant Baroque creations.

Not surprisingly, perhaps, Braga retains a reputation as a bastion of reactionary politics. It was here, in 1926, that General Gomes da Costa appealed to "all citizens of dignity and honour" to overthrow the democratic regime, kickstarting the process that eventually led to Salazar's dictatorship, while in the more recent past, after the 1974 Revolution, the Archbishop of Braga personally incited a mob to attack local Communist offices. Desperate to escape its traditionally conservative image, Braga is keen to acquire a new energy that reflects less of the Church and more of its status as a fast-growing commercial centre. This is most clearly evident in the scores of fashion boutiques scattered liberally among the churches and stores peddling religious paraphernalia. However, the network of fast roads, underpasses and big, modern tower blocks in and around the ancient town has angered many residents who feel that the old centre of Braga (the phrase "as old as the cathedral of Braga" is the Portuguese equivalent of "as old as the hills") should have been better preserved. They point, in particular, to the digging up of the gardens around Praça da República and Avenida Central to make an underground car park. The excavations uncovered, and promptly destroyed, a number of Roman houses.

In addition to the costumed parades of the **Semana Santa** (Holy Week) celebrations, the city is illuminated for the **Festas de São João** (June 23–24), which provides the excuse for ancient folk dances, a fairground and general partying. There's also a festival of *gigantones* (giant carnival figures; June 18–20). The main **pilgrimage to Bom Jesus** takes place over Whitsun (six weeks after Easter).

Arrival and information

Braga is a fair-sized city, although the old town – an oval of streets radiating out from the Sé – is a compact area. The uneasy alliance of old and new is never more apparent than when driving – a confusing one-way system does its best to keep you out if you're trying to enter and keep you in when you're trying to leave. If you don't want to pay for the undergound car park on Praça Conde

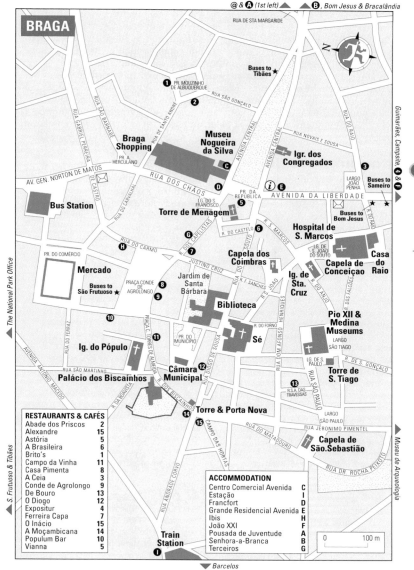

BRAGA

@ & **A** (1st left) ▲   ▲ **B**, Bom Jesus & Bracalândia

RUA DE STA MARGARIDE

N

Buses to
Tibães ★

RUA SÃO GONÇALO

1 PR. MOUZINHO
DE ALBUQUERQUE

2

RUA DE SANTO ANDRÉ

RUA GABRIEL PEREIRA

RUA SÃO BARNABÉ

**Braga
Shopping**

PR. A.
HERCULANO

**Museu
Nogueira
da Silva**

C

AVENIDA CENTRAL

AVENIDA CENTRAL

RUA DO RAIO

RUA NOVAIS E SOUSA

**Igr. dos
Congregados**

3

Guimarães, Campsite, **4** & **F** ▶

AV. GEN. NORTON DE MATOS

RUA DO CARVALHAL

DE CASTRO

RUA DOS CHÃOS

D

IG. DOS
FRANCISCO

PR. DA
REPÚBLICA
5

LARGO
JOÃO
PENHA

**Buses to
Sameiro**

Bus Station

i E

AVENIDA DA LIBERDADE

**Buses to
Bom Jesus**

★ ★

RUA DO RAIO

Torre de Menagem

R. DO CASTELO

R. S. MARCOS

6

**Hospital de
S. Marcos**

RUA DO CARMO

R. S. CAPELISTAS

H

6

7

JUSTINO CRUZ

**Capela dos
Coimbras**

LG. DE
S. JOÃO
DO SOUTO

**Capela de
Conceiçao**

**Casa
do
Raio**

◀ The National Park Office

PR. DO COMÉRCIO

Mercado

**Buses to
São Frutuoso** ★

PRAÇA CONDE
DE
AGROLONGO

8

9

**Jardim de
Santa
Bárbara**

R.F. SANCHES

RUA DR. JOÃO

R. DO ANJO

**Ig. de
Sta.
Cruz**

RUA DOS TALÉOES

Biblioteca

R. DOM AFONSO HENRIQUES

**Pio XII &
Medina
Museums**

LARGO
SÃO TIAGO

10

RUA DO FERRAZ

11

PRAÇA C. TORRES DE ALMEIDA

PR. DO
MUNICIPIO

R. DO FORNO

Sé

**Torre de
S. Tiago**

◀ S. Frutuoso & Tibães

AVENIDA ANTÓNIO MACEDO

Ig. do Pópulo ✝

RUA SÃO MARTINHO

Palácio dos Biscaínhos

R. DA BISCAÍNHA

**Câmara
Municipal**

12

RUA DOM PEDRO DE SOUSA

RUA DOS BISCAÍNHOS

LG. DE S.
PAULO

RUA SÃO PAULO

RUA DE S. GONÇALO

R.S.A. DAS
TRAVESSAS

13

LARGO
SÃO PAULO

◀ Museu de Arqueologia ▶

Torre & Porta Nova

14

15

CAMPO DAS HORTAS

RUA DO MATADOURO

RUA JERÓNIMO PIMENTEL

i

**Capela de
São.Sebastião**

RUA DR. ROCHA PEIXOTO

RESTAURANTS & CAFÉS

Abade dos Priscos	2
Alexandre	15
Astória	5
A Brasileira	6
Brito's	1
Campo da Vinha	11
Casa Pimenta	8
A Ceia	3
Conde de Agrolongo	9
De Bouro	13
O Diogo	12
Expositur	4
Ferreira Capa	7
O Inácio	15
A Moçambicana	14
Populum Bar	10
Vianna	5

RUA ANDRADE CORVO

**Train
Station**

D

▼ Barcelos

ACCOMMODATION

Centro Comercial Avenida	C
Estação	I
Francfort	D
Grande Residencial Avenida	E
Ibis	H
João XXI	F
Pousada de Juventude	A
Senhora-a-Branca	B
Terceiros	G

0   100 m

de Agrolongo, the side streets around the pedestrianized centre are your best
hope for free parking.

From the **train station**, west of the centre, it's a fifteen- to twenty-minute
walk to the old town, reached down Rua Andrade Corvo. The main **bus
station** is a bit closer in, under ten minutes' walk from the central Praça

da República. Here, on the corner of Avenida da Liberdade, you'll find the **turismo** (June–Sept Mon–Fri 9am–8pm, Sat & Sun 9am–12.30pm & 2–7pm; Oct–May Mon–Fri 9am–12.30pm & 2–6.30pm, Sat & Sun till 9am–12.30pm & 2–5.30pm; ☎253 262 550, ⓦwww.cm-braga.pt), which offers an impressive large-scale map of the city and displays bus and train timetables.

If you're heading for the Peneda-Gerês national park, it's worth calling at the **national park headquarters** (Mon–Fri 9am–12.30pm & 2–5.30pm; ☎253 203 480, ⓕ253 613 169), a large, white house on Avenida António Macedo in the Quinta das Parretas suburb, a twenty-minute walk from the centre, where you can buy a useful map and booklet, and pick up information on walking trails.

Accommodation

Braga has plenty of hotels and *pensões*, and a good central youth hostel, though it's unwise to turn up without a reservation during religious events and local festivals. If none of the options in town appeals, you can always stay out at the hilltop pilgrimage site of Bom Jesus (see p.395), 5km from the centre, which makes a peaceful and attractive place to spend the night.

In Braga

Residencial Centro Comercial Avenida Av. Central 27–37 ☎253 616 363, ⓔgeral @hotel-recavenida.com. On the second floor of the Braga shopping complex, which is open late for easy access. Big, comfortable rooms with TVs and baths, although some at the back lack windows and can be a bit dingy. Breakfast included. ❸

Hotel Estação Largo da Estação 13 ☎253 218 381, ⓔhotelestacao@mailtelepac.pt. A modern hotel next to the train station, which, claims the brochure, will engender a "feeling of peace and eternity". Jacuzzis in some of the rooms may go some way to achieving this desirable state, even if the occasional rumble of daytime trains seeps through the double-glazing. Breakfast included. Parking available. ❹

Pensão Francfort Av. Central 1–7 ☎253 262 648. A *pensão* dating from 1879 and run by a pair of vintage grande dames. Opinions are divided, and it's either beginning to show its age but full of character, or is simply tatty. Some simple rooms have a bath, while those at the front have the best views in town. No credit cards. ❸

Grande Residencial Avenida Av. da Liberdade 738–2° ☎253 609 020, ⓔr.avenida@netcabo.pt. Far from grand nowadays, but a fine old *pensão* nevertheless and in a great location. Rooms are spacious and high-ceilinged, if rather dowdy, and those at the rear are quieter than the front rooms, which overlook the underpass and the avenue. Reservations advisable in summer. No credit cards. ❷

Hotel Ibis Rua do Carmo 13 ☎253 610 860, ⓦwww.ibishotel.com. Clean and modern, this is a

decent option when space elsewhere is limited in peak season. Includes breakfast. ❸

Hotel João XXI Av. João XXI 849 ☎253 616 630, ⓔreservas@hoteljoaoxxi.com. Off Avenida da Liberdade, 1km from Pr. da Republica, this six-storey hotel has a top-floor restaurant and neat, en-suite rooms, plus parking. It's good value and the price includes breakfast. ❸

Albergaria Senhora-a-Branca Largo da Senhora-a-Branca 58 ☎253 269 938, ⓦwww .albergariasrabranca.pt. Facing a garden and attractively furnished, this is one of Braga's smarter choices, with parking for guests. It's about a kilometre from the centre; keep going out of town down Av. Central. Breakfast included. ❸

Residencial dos Terceiros Rua dos Capelistas 85 ☎253 270 466, ⓕ253 275 767. A well-located modern *residencial* whose unspectacular but keenly priced rooms all have TV and private bathroom. ❷

At Bom Jesus

Pensão Águeda Behind the park at the back of the church ☎253 676 521, ⓕ253 281 220. At the budget end of the scale, this friendly *pensão* has basic rooms with shared bathrooms, but breakfast is included and the downstairs restaurant is excellent. ❷

Casa dos Lagos On the road just below the top of the steps ☎253 676 738, ⓔcasadoslagosbom jesus@ominet.pt. One of the most charming local places – a lovely old house, with two spacious traditionally furnished rooms, four modern apartments that sleep four, and a swimming pool. Views are sensational from all quarters. ❺, apartments ❼

Hotel do Parque Next to the church ☎ 253 603 470, ⊛ www.hoteisbomjesus.web.pt. A superb nineteenth-century hotel furnished in 1920s style. The nearby *Hotel Elevador* (☎ 253 603 400), under the same management, is of a similar standard but more modern in style, the best rooms boasting sweeping views over the valley. Views from its restaurant are just as spectacular. Breakfast included. ❺

Youth hostel

Pousada de Juventude Rua de Santa Margarida 6 ☎ 253 616 163, ⊛ www.pousadasjuventude. pt. Braga's excellent youth hostel, very popular in summer with hikers, has some double rooms, as well as a good noticeboard, lockers for valuables, a kitchen, and a common room with satellite TV and a pool table. Reception open 9am–noon & 6pm–midnight. Dorm beds €10, rooms ❷

Campsite

Camping Parque da Ponte 2km south of the centre, next to the municipal swimming pool ☎ 253 273 355. Passable, but far from inspiring, city-based site – officially, you need an international camping carnet to stay here. Closed Nov–March.

The City

The obvious point from which to start exploring Braga is Praça da República, a busy arcaded square at the head of the old town, marked by an impressive trio of fountains. It's backed by the former town keep, the Torre de Menagem, while in the arcade itself you'll find two fine coffee houses which look out down the length of the long central square. From here, almost everything of interest is reached down narrow Rua do Souto, the main pedestrianized street which runs past the Sé. The street is also Braga's principal shopping district, though few commercial centres are like this one, where shoe shops rub shoulders with those selling candles and religious icons.

The Sé

The old centre is dominated by the **Sé**, a rambling structure founded on the site of a Moorish mosque in 1070 after the Christian reconquest. The original Romanesque building encompasses Gothic, Renaissance and Baroque additions, though the cathedral's south doorway is a survival from the building's earliest incarnation, carved with rustic scenes from the legend of Reynard the Fox. However, the most striking element of the cathedral is the intricate ornamentation of the roofline, commissioned by Braga's great Renaissance patron, Archbishop Diogo de Sousa, and executed by João de Castilho, later to become one of the architects of Lisbon's Mosteiro dos Jerónimos, the greatest of all Manueline buildings. Inside, the cathedral complex is disorientating and, with the exception of the Baroque organs, somewhat disappointing.

You enter through a courtyard fronting three Gothic chapels, a cloister and, most prominently, a ticket desk, where you can gain access to the **Tesouro da Catedral** and Capela dos Reis (daily 8.30am–6.30pm; €2). The cathedral's treasury is one of the richest such collections in Portugal, containing representative pieces from the tenth to the eighteenth centuries, but visits are accompanied by a guide, who locks every room behind you and offers a rather cursory commentary on the age and value of each piece. After several rooms of very similar, unlabelled displays, light relief comes with the shoes of the diminuitive Archbishop Dom Rodrigo de Maura-Teles. Measuring just 1m 20cm high, he commissioned 22 monuments during his term of office at the beginning of the eighteenth century, among them the fabulous shrine at Bom Jesus. Eventually you emerge alongside the magnificent twin Baroque organs in the **Coro Alto**, supported by life-sized figures of satyrs, mermen and monstrous fish.

Of the three outer chapels, the fourteenth-century **Capela dos Reis** (King's Chapel) is the most significant, built to house the tombs of the cathedral's

Conde de Agrolongo Pr. Conde de Agrolongo 74 ☎253 261 134. Typical Portuguese restaurant serving good rice dishes for under €11. Head for the large, cool basement rather than the deserted ground floor. Moderate.

Diogo Rua Diogo da Sousa 83 ☎253 262 297. Reasonably priced food, including *cabrito* (roast kid), though a house-special octopus dish is a €19.50 splurge. Closed Sun. Moderate.

Expositor Parques de Exposições, at the end of Av. da Liberdade, 15min walk from Pr. da República ☎253 217 031. Traditional Minhota cooking, served in epic portions at low prices. It's strong on grilled meats and fish, all displayed in window cases. Closed Tues. Moderate.

O Inácio Campo das Hortas 4 ☎253 613 235. Rather pricey, but this offers atmospheric dining in a rustic old stone house, beneath log beams. The menu encompasses both Portuguese and Spanish dishes. Closed Tues. Expensive.

A Moçambicana Rua Andrade Corvo 8 ☎253 262 260. As the name suggests, *bacalhau*, veal and beef here have African accents. A three-course *menu turística* (€15) is good value despite the rather rough house wine. Closed Sat. Moderate.

Bars and clubs

Populum Bar Pr. Conde de Agrolongo 115. Large central club, with two dance floors and a penchant for karaoke nights.

Sardinha Biba Bar Rua Galos S. Lázaro. Riverside hangout with a pool, 2km from the centre, southeast of the bypass Av. João Paulo II.

Listings

Ambulance Call ☎253 264 077 or 253 200 430.

Banks and exchange Banks with ATMs are located on pedestrianized Rua dos Capelistas. Caravela Travel, Rua Francisco Sanches 47 ☎253 200 500 offers reasonable rates of exchange and doesn't usually charge commission.

Books and newspapers English-language books from Livraria Cruz, Rua Dom Diogo da Sousa 129. International newspapers are available from the tobacconists at Rua Dr. Justina Cruz 149.

Hospital São Marcos, Largo Carlos Amarante ☎253 209 000.

Internet Netstation, Rua de Santa Margarida 13, just past the youth hostel (Mon–Sat 9am–8pm); or free at espaçoInternet, Pr. Conde de Agrolongo 177 (Mon–Fri 9am–7.30pm, Sat 9am–1pm).

Pharmacy Farmacia Central, Rua dos Capelistas 34.

Police The PSP headquarters is at Campo Santiago 6 ☎253 200 420.

Post office Avenida da Liberade (Mon–Fri 9am–6pm, Sat 9am–12.30pm).

Swimming pools Both are 2km from the centre: the Complexo Desportivo da Rodovia ☎253 616 773, at the junction of the main ring road and Av. João Paulo II, before Bracalândia (most easily reached down Av. Central, turning right onto Av. Padre Julio Fragata); and the municipal Piscina da Ponte ☎253 264 424, open July only, at the far end of Av. da Liberdade by the campsite.

Taxis Central Rádio Táxi ☎253 683 228.

Tours One-day canoeing and hiking tours (from €25) are offered by Gota Verde, at the Instituto da Juventude, Rua de Santa Margarida 215 ☎253 616 836, ☎253 616 835. One-day walking trips in Peneda-Gerês operate roughly once a week and cost €25 per person, including transport.

Travel agents Abreu, Av. Central 171 ☎253 200 540; Atlas, Pr. Conde de Agrolongo 129 ☎253 613 731.

Around Braga

Having soaked up the religious atmosphere in Braga itself, a number of fascinating sites are within easy reach, most of which can be visited by public transport. The Baroque stairway and pilgrim church of **Bom Jesus do Monte**, 5km east of Braga, is a good enough reason to come to the city in the first place and is within striking distance of the massive (if distinctly oppressive) **Santuário do Sameiro**. To the northwest easy visits can also be made to the Visigothic church of São Frutuoso and the ruined Benedictine monastery at Tibães. However, if you only have time for one more trip apart from to Bom Jesus, it should be to the fascinating Celtic hill settlement of **Citânia de Briteiros**, halfway between Braga and Guimarães.

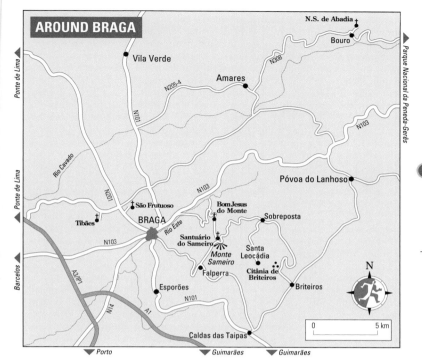

There are also daily buses from Braga to the small provincial town of **Póvoa do Lanhoso**, 20km to the northeast, worth a side trip for its castle and Romanesque church. Drivers are probably more likely to make the effort, en route along the N103 to the Peneda-Gerês park (see p.430). Of more peripheral interest – though revered in Portugal – is the shrine of **Nossa Senhora da Abadia**, to the north of the Braga–Gerês road, turning off at Santa Maria do Bouro. You'll need your own transport to visit this.

Bom Jesus do Monte and Santuário do Sameiro

Bom Jesus do Monte is one of Portugal's best-known images. Set in the woods high above the city, the glorious ornamental stairway of granite and white plaster is a monumental homage, commissioned by Braga's vertically challenged archbishop Maura-Teles in 1723 but which took sixty years to complete. There is no particular reason for its presence – no miracle or vision – yet it remains the object of devoted pilgrimage, with many penitents climbing up on their knees. It is a very pleasant place to spend an afternoon or, best of all, early evening. There are wooded gardens, grottoes and miniature boating pools behind the church and, at the far end, just outside the park up the hill, horse rides are available at negotiable rates.

Buses (#2, at 10min and 40min past the hour) run the 5km to the foot of the stairway at Bom Jesus from Avenida da Liberdade, close to the post office.

At weekends they are packed, as seemingly half the city piles up to picnic in the woods. Most of the local families, armed with immense baskets of food, ride straight to the top in a rickety hydraulic **funicular** (daily 8am–8pm; every 30min and usually timed to coincide with buses; €1). If you resist the temptation to ride the funicular and make the climb up the stairway, Bom Jesus's simple allegory unfolds. Each of the **stairway** landings has a fountain: the first symbolizes the wounds of Christ, the next five the Senses, and the final three represent the Virtues. At each corner, too, are chapels with larger-than-life wooden tableaux of the Life of Christ, arranged chronologically, leading to the Crucifixion at the altar of the church at the top of the steps. As a design it's a triumph – one of the greatest of all Baroque architectural creations – and was later copied at Lamego.

A handful of lively **restaurants** at Bom Jesus come into their own on Saturdays, when they're filled with day-trippers and parties from a seemingly constant stream of weddings. Note, however, that most open only at weekends during winter. A good option is the moderately priced *Restaurante Águeda* (☎253 676 521) beneath the *pensão* of the same name, at the back of the church, which serves large portions and local wines. *Restaurante Portico* (☎253 676 672; closed Thurs) just beyond the bottom of the steps, is a traditional-style building serving high-quality food, but at a price.

The domed **Santuário do Sameiro** – 1.5km by road from the bottom of the staircase or reached by a 20-minute walk uphill beyond the pine woods at the top – is impressive for its size and its grimly monolithic monumental stairway, which affords fantastic views across the city. Although built in 1837, it bears the heavy marks of interference during Salazar's regime in its swathes of concrete and enormous statues. Like it or loathe it, it's a powerful monument to the might and authority of the Roman Catholic Church in Portugal and the church is the second most venerated shrine in the country after Fátima. There's a very good, if somewhat pricey, restaurant here, too, the *Restaurante Maia Sameiro* (☎253 675 114).

São Frutuoso and Tibães

Three and a half kilometres northwest of Braga, the church of **São Frutuoso** (April–Sept daily 9.30am–12.30pm & 2–5.30pm; otherwise keys are kept in a nearby house; tours available on request, €1) was built by the Visigoths in the seventh century, adapted by the Moors, then restored to Christian worship after the reconquest. It's a gem of a church, flanked by an eighteenth-century chapel but its previously tranquil setting has now been engulfed by Braga's ever-expanding suburbs. Buses for São Frutuoso leave every thirty minutes from Praça Conde de Agrolongo (they are marked "Sarrido"); get off at the hamlet of São Jerónimo Real, from where it is a five-minute walk.

Half a kilometre beyond the São Frutuoso turning, a road left leads in 3km to Mire de Tibães and the monastery of **Tibães**, formerly the grandest Benedictine establishment in the land. A vast and partly ruined hulk, its abandoned medieval buildings, cloisters and rambling gardens have been reopened to the public after extensive renovation; the church is now a favourite for local weddings. A small local-history **museum** (daily 10am–6.30pm; €4) provides a fascinating window on the past, while exhibition rooms house temporary displays of photography and art. Guided tours of the monastic buildings are available but you can also explore the gardens and ruins of the stables and kitchens at your leisure. Hourly buses for Tibães, marked "Padim da Graça", leave from Braga's Avenida Central.

Citânia de Briteiros

Midway between Guimarães and Braga is one of the most impressive and exciting archeological sites in the country, the **Citânia de Briteiros**. Citânias – Celtic hill settlements – lie scattered throughout the Minho: remains of 27 have been identified along the coast, plus sixteen more in the region between Braga and Guimarães alone. Most date from the arrival of northern European Celts in

▲ Braga

N

CITÂNIA DE
BRITEIROS

○ 14

13

11

12

15

10

8

16

17 18

P

9

5

7

6 3

19 20

1

4

0   100 m

2
Visitor
Centre

Bath House ▼   Briteiros and Guimarães ▼

P

1 Area reserved for cattle	11 Gateway
2 Early fountain	12 Gateway
3 Cross and Christian cemetery	13 Well for water provision
4 Circular house belonging to community	14 Single, isolated house outside inner walls
5 Chapel of S.Romão	15 Water source (now defunct)
6 House with helix	16 Houses with stone benches
7 Houses reconstructed by Martins Sarmento	17 Law courts (?), prisons (?)
8 Small paved area	18 Ingenious method of transporting water
9 Inside wall	19 House with various rooms
10 Second (of four) walls	20 Cistern

the Iron Age (c.600–500 BC), though some are far older, their inhabitants having merged with an existing local culture established since Neolithic times (c.2000 BC). The site at Briteiros, straddling the boulder-strewn hill of São Romão, was probably the last stronghold of the Celt-Iberians against the invading Romans, finally being taken around 20 BC and eventually abandoned in 300 AD.

The Roman historian Strabo gave a vivid description of the northern Portuguese tribes, who must have occupied these *citânias*, in his *Geographia* (c.20 BC). They organized mass sacrifices, he recorded, and inspected prisoners' entrails without removing them. Otherwise, they liked to:

live simply, drink water and sleep on the bare earth … two-thirds of the year they live on acorns, which they roast and grind to make bread. They also have beer. They lack wine but when they have it they drink it up, gathering for a family feast. At banquets they sit on a bench against the wall according to age and rank … When they assemble to drink they perform round dances to the flute or the horn, leaping in the air and crouching as they fall.

Entrails aside – and they may have been literary licence – none of this seems far removed from the Minho and Trás-os-Montes of recent memory.

Getting there

Drivers from Braga have an enjoyable 16km journey, twisting through villages beyond Bom Jesus to the site. Coming from Guimarães, it's 7km to Caldas das Taipas, from a small road winds 5km to the small town of Briteiros – here, signs direct you to the *citânia* on the hill above town. There is limited parking on the road before the site and by the entrance.

Getting there by bus is more convoluted, at least **from Braga**. Frequent buses from the city to Guimarães stop in Caldas das Taipas, where you can either wait for one of the infrequent local buses to Briteiros or take a taxi (around €8). If you can rustle up a group, by far the easiest direct option from Braga is to hire a taxi for the trip, and ask it to wait outside the *citânia* while you visit – this should cost around €30–35. It's much easier by bus **from Guimarães**, as plenty of Arriva buses travel to and from Briteiros, via Caldas das Taipas. Once in Briteiros, you can either walk the 2km up to the site, or catch a taxi from the village square (around €4).

The excavations

The excavations (daily 9am–6pm; €2) have revealed foundations of over 150 huts, a couple of which have been rebuilt to give a sense of their scale and design. Most of them are circular, with benches around the edges and a central stone that would have provided support for a pole holding up a thatched roof. A few are rectangular in shape, among them a larger building which may have been a prison or meeting house – it is labelled the *casa do tribunal*. There's also a clear network of paved streets and paths, two circuits of town walls, plus cisterns, stone guttering and a public fountain (the *fonte*). Most of these features are identifiable as you wander around the place, though the site is more evocative in its layout and extent than for any particular sights. However, one feature not to be missed is the bathhouse (a fair walk downhill to the left of the settlement entrance), with its geometrically patterned stone doorway. This was believed to be a funerary chamber until recently, when it was pointed out that because much of the hill's run-off flowed into the site, it wouldn't have been the best place to lay-out bodies. Carved lintels from the huts and other finds from the *citânia* are displayed at the Museu Martins Sarmento in Guimarães. However, there's a smaller hoard of finds exhibited in the Museu da Cultura Castreja in nearby Briteiros (Tues–Sun 9.30am–12.30pm & 2–6pm; €3, joint ticket with excavations €4).

Póvoa do Lanhoso

The small town of **PÓVOA DO LANHOSO** is famed for its gold jewellery, produced in traditional workshops (*ourivesarias*) and bearing clear traces of Moorish influence, especially in the filigree work. This aside, the modern quarters of the town don't have much to offer, but they do lie sandwiched between two ancient sites. At the northern end of town (the approach from Braga), a steep mound – the Monte do Pilar – rises up to one of the smallest castles in Portugal, amid a scattering of chapels and picnic tables. In the fourteenth century, the lord of the shire was reported to have locked up his adulterous wife, her lover and their servants in the castle and ordered it to be burned; it was substantially rebuilt in the eighteenth century. The *Panorâmico* restaurant nearby keeps a set of keys and offers reasonable food and good views, if you can squeeze in between their regular parties of christening and wedding guests. In the opposite direction, 3km out of town, the small church of **Fonte Areada** is a short walk from the main road (past the white statue). The simple interior, characteristic of the Romanesque style, is in marked contrast to the complications of the doorway with its centrepiece relief of a large sheep.

If you have your own transport, it's also worth paying a visit to one of two local *vinho verde* quintas that offer free tastings and tours: **Quinta do Minho** (contact Maria Teresa Martins on ☏253 633 240); and **Quinta Villa Beatriz** in Santo Emilião (☏253 631 523 or 253 631 292), an imposing blue-tiled four-towered mansion in the "Brazilian" style of the early twentieth century, constructed by emigrants who made their fortune in the New World. There are superb gardens, as well as cows and horses for children to admire.

The town is a useful transport junction, with regular bus services to Braga, Caldas do Gerês, Guimarães and Porto, as well as to destinations in Trás-os-Montes and the Douro.

Nossa Senhora da Abadia

Drivers can follow an alternative route into Gerês from Braga, along the minor N205-4 via Amares, after which the road becomes the N308. Some 13km along you come to **Santa Maria do Bouro** (Bouro to the locals) – which has a shell of a monastery and a large Baroque church. Turning off from here, you arrive at the shrine of **Nossa Senhora da Abadia**. This is said to be the oldest sanctuary in Portugal and, like Bom Jesus, is a centre of pilgrimage: the main festival is on August 15. The focus of devotions is a twelfth-century wooden statue of the Virgin and Child and, while the church itself was largely rebuilt in the eighteenth century, outside are two earlier, elegant wings of monks' cells and, usually, some market stalls. There's no accommodation here but you can eat well with the pilgrims at the sizeable *Restaurante Abadia* (no phone), which can seat up to 500 people.

Barcelos

It's worth making plans to arrive in **BARCELOS**, 20km west of Braga, for the Thursday market, the **Feira de Barcelos**. The great weekly event of southern Minho, it takes place from around dawn until late afternoon on the Campo da República – known colloquially as the Campo da Feira – a vast open square in

△ Feira de Barcelos

peoples to have lived in Barcelos: both Celtic and Catholic crosses, six-point Jewish Stars of David, and five-point Islamic pentagrams. Finally, if you wanted to pursue an interest in the local ceramic wares, you could visit the **Museu de Olaria** (Tues–Sun 10am–5pm; €1.40, free Sun), in the Casa dos Mendanhas on Rua Conego Joaquim Gaiolas, 300m from the archeological museum.

Practicalities

The **train station** is at the drab eastern edge of town; follow Avenida Alcaides de Faria straight ahead for fifteen minutes until it becomes Avenida Combatentes da Grande Guerra and you'll emerge on the Campo da Feira. There are two main **bus** companies: Linhares, Rua Dr. Julio Vieira Ramos, off the eastern end of Avenida dos Combatentes Guerra, for local services within Minho and to Vila do Conde and Póvoa do Varzim; and REDM, Avenida Dr. Sidónio Pais 245, facing the Campo, for main towns in the region and beyond (also agents for Rede Express, Renex and Internorte for long-distance services). Both run frequent services to Braga. Buses heading east to Ponte de Lima depart from a stop on Avenida Dom Nuno Álvares Pereira.

The **turismo** (March–Oct Mon–Fri 9am–12.30pm & 2.30–6pm, Sat 10am–12.30pm & 2.30–5.30pm, Sun 2.30–5.30pm; Nov–Feb Mon–Wed & Fri 9am–12.30pm & 2.30–5.50pm, Thurs 9am–5.30pm, Sat 10am–5pm; ☎253 811 882) is housed in the Torre da Porta Nova, just off the Campo. In addition to its information counter, it features a permanent display and sale of Barcelos handicrafts. The river is too polluted for **swimming** but there are two municipal pools under one roof, on Rua Rosa Ramalho, just upstream from the bridge.

Accommodation

There's a fairly limited choice of cheap accommodation in Barcelos, and you will definitely need to book ahead if coinciding with the market (Wed & Thurs nights), as rooms fill up quickly.

Residencial Arantes Av. da Liberdade 35-1° ☎253 811 326, ℱ253 821 360. An eccentric mix of rooms in a rambling, family-run place on the west side of the Campo da Feira, above a good *pastelaria*. Ask for a room with a view and avoid the cell-like rooms overlooking a central well. Cheaper rooms are without facilities, but shared bathrooms are clean. Breakfast included. ❸

Pensão Bagoeira Av Dr. Sidónio Pais 495 ☎253 811 236, ℱ253 824 588. A former market inn facing the Campo, with a modernized annexe tacked on behind. Rooms, all with bathrooms, are bright, clean and comfortable. The ever-busy restaurant (moderately priced) retains its old market inn atmosphere, with stone nooks to dine in; be sure to have lunch here on market day, when a stream of stallholders enter with pans for a takeaway. Specialities include *polvo*, *arroz de frango* and *bacalhau*. ❸

Casa do Monte Abade de Neiva, 3km west of Barcelos on the N103 (Viana do Castelo road) ☎253 811 519, ℠www.solaresdeportugal.pt. Delightful country manor house with three double and three twin rooms dressed with charming Alentejo furniture painted with floral designs. Large gardens and a verandah give wonderful panoramic views and there's a swimming pool and tennis court – advance reservations recommended. Breakfast is included, parking available. ❸

Residencial Dom Nuno Av. Dom Nuno Álvares Pereira 76 ☎253 812 810, ℱ253 816 336. Comfortable if unspectacular rooms with bath, telephone and TV in a characterless modern *residencial*. Breakfast included. Visa only. ❸

Residencial Solar da Estação Largo da Estação ☎253 811 741. Nothing special, but this place above a restaurant opposite the railway station at least has spacious and spotless modern rooms, all with bathroom and TV. Includes breakfast. No credit cards. ❷

Eating and drinking

Aside from the *Bagoeira* (see "Accommodation" above) – the place for a market-day meal – there is a row of three bargain-basement café-restaurants

The miracle of Moure

If you want to witness a miracle, head for the **Igreja de Moure**, 7km southwest of Barcelos off the road to Vila Nova de Famalicão and reachable on REDM buses from Barcelos. The church has become a minor centre of pilgrimage since May 18, 1996, when a ghostly "shadow of the top half of Christ" first appeared. The miracle has since returned every year on May 18, and during its 1998 appearance the congregation entered "total delirium and nervosity" according to a newspaper report: some circled the image, others clapped, while others begged forgiveness for their sins. Sadly, the archbishop of Braga pooh-poohed the miracle, declaring to the press "it is a singular event generated from sentiments of faith and piety but explainable by the laws of optical physics". Further tests concluded that the "miracle" was indeed caused by a mere trick of the light. However, science has not dissuaded the faithful, who still flock here every May to witness what the *Diário de Notícias* calls the "marvellous half-bodied manifestation of Moure".

around the corner from the Campo, in the alleyway opposite the Templo; the central one offers the best value. Other good local cafés and restaurants are highlighted below, while the finest place for a beer while catching the last of the day's sun is *Turismo*, a bar at the bottom of Rua Duques de Bragança, with a terrace overlooking the river.

Casa dos Arcos Rua Duques de Bragança 185 ☏ 253 881 975. The traditional old stone house is a local favourite for Sunday lunch. Regional specialities include suckling pig, while the house-special steak and *bacalhau* are always popular. Closed Mon. Moderate.

Pastelaria Confortio Rua Dom António Barroso 104 no phone. Pleasant pastry shop with outdoor tables, serving very sweet egg-and-peanut sweets among other goodies. Inexpensive.

Dom António Rua Dom António Barroso 87 ☏ 253 812 285. Rather tourist-orientated, but serving good-value meat dishes – most under €10 – with many available in huge portions for two. Wild boar from Montesinho is on the menu and the *rojões de porco* (roast pork, sausages and potatoes) is good. Moderate.

Furna Largo da Madalena 105 ☏ 253 861 879. The queues for the takeaway charcoal-grilled chicken stretch out of the door, which gives a good clue as to the best dish here – €3.25 for a whole bird. Closed Mon. Inexpensive.

The Costa Verde

The Minho's long sandy coastline is promoted as the **Costa Verde**, but despite the enticing promises of "unpolluted beaches with a high iodine content … health for the whole year", Costa Verde is green for a reason. It can be drizzly and overcast even in summer and the Atlantic here is never too warm. That said, pick almost any road, any village, and you'll find a great beach virtually to yourself. The coast between Póvoa de Varzim, north of Porto, and Caminha, at the mouth of the Rio Minho, is virtually one long beach, with the road running, for the most part, 1km or so inland. Much of the coast is protected from development by law, including the 18km from Apúlia to the mouth of the River Neiva, which has been designated the Área de Paisagem Protegida do Litoral de Esposende (Esposende Protected Coastal Area). Along this stretch and beyond, local people have perfected the art of dune agriculture. Small "fields" are created by digging out depressions in the sand dunes, which trap moisture from the Atlantic mists and protect crops from wind. Dried seaweed is used as fertilizer, which over the centuries has created a soil so fertile that many believe these dune fruits and vegetables to be among the best in the country.

The attractive resort of **Viana do Castelo** is very much the main event on the coast, with frequent daily buses chugging north from Porto to Viana, via the beach at **Ofir**, the resort of **Esposende** and the small fishing village of **São Bartolomeu do Mar**. Note that trains north from Porto run inland via Barcelos and do not reach the coast until Viana. **North of Viana**, though, the train line follows the coast all the way to Caminha, with trains stopping at all the villages en route – notably at Carreço, Afife, Gelfa, Vila Praia de Ancora and Moledo do Minho – offering easy access to a sequence of largely deserted beaches. Buses cover the same route, while it is even possible to **walk** along the northern coast from Viana's Praia do Cabadelo, covering the whole stretch in a couple of days, stopping overnight among the sheltered dunes or in one of the small villages.

Esposende

ESPOSENDE, a breezy, sunbleached seaside resort, 20km north of Póvoa on the estuary of the Rio Cávado is a more intimate chill-out spot than touristy Viana do Castelo. Passing the rather drab sprawl of buildings on the town's outskirts, things brighten up in the compact centre, which has some lovely old buildings and squares, including a small **museum** on Largo Dr. Fonseca Lima (Tues–Fri 10am–6pm, Sat & Sun 3–6pm; free), which contains displays of local ethnography, items from nearby *antas* (megalithic Bronze Age tombs), and ceramics and tools from the 2000-year-old *castro* of São Lourenço, a local Bronze Age settlement. If you'd like to explore the sites themselves, ask at the turismo (see below) for the leaflets containing directions to the *antas* and to the *castro*.

The town's **beach** is a 2km walk to the north, accessed via the lighthouse that protrudes from the late-seventeenth-century Forte de São João Baptista. Much less enticing is the beach at **Ofir**, 6km by road on the south side of the estuary, where impressive pine-backed dunes have been ruined by the addition of several ugly high-rise buildings.

Practicalities

Buses drop you at the Largo do Mercado, on the riverfront beside the market. Two hundred metres south along the river is the **turismo** (Mon–Sat 9.30am–12.30pm & 2.30–6pm, Sun 9.30am–12.30pm; closed Sun in winter; ℡253 961 354), which gives out a good local map and publishes an excellent guidebook to the district. There's a **swimming pool** complex on the riverbank opposite the turismo (daily 10am–10pm; €5), with waves in its indoor pool and great views over the Rio Cávado from the outdoor one. **Canoeing** and **rafting** trips (€25 including transport) are organized by the Associação de Defesa do Ambiente do Rio Neiva (℡253 872 562, ℮cm.esposende@mail.telepac.pt), based at Antas, 12km north of Esposende.

Accommodation

The only really cheap accommodation is at Fão, 3km away, where there's a **youth hostel** (see below) and a decent **campsite** (open all year; ℡253 981

777). Otherwise, the turismo may be able to help you find rooms in town in private houses. Note that during the off-season (mid-Sept to mid-June), room rates at many hotels are often reduced by as much as fifty percent.

Hotels and pensions

Residencial Acrópole Pr. Dom Sebastião, near the turismo ☎ 253 961 941, ⓦ www .residencialacropole.com. A cheapish option close to the action – the modern rooms are comfortable, all en suite and with TVs, telephones and air con. Breakfast is excellent. ❸

Clube Pinhal da Foz Rua João Ferreira da Silva, 1km north of the turismo ☎ 253 961 098, ⓕ 253 965 937. Modern self-catering apartments, equipped with TVs, and with access to a swimming pool. ❹

Estalagem Zende Corner of the N13 and Rua José de Alpoim, 1km north of the turismo ☎ 253 964 663, ⓕ 253 965 018. En-suite rooms, all with television, air conditioning and balconies, and a pleasant lounge. The location isn't great, but a rated restaurant with good shellfish is some compensation. ❸

Residencial Mira Rio N13, 1km south of the turismo ☎ 253 964 430, ⓦ www.residencial -mirario.com. A small block of ten traditionally furnished rooms, each with bathroom, satellite TV and telephone. It's close to the river but 3km from the beach, though there's a restaurant on-site. ❸

Hotel Nélia Av. Valentim Ribeiro ☎ 253 966 244, ⓔ isabelmanfer@oil.pt. Three blocks behind the turismo is this central three-star hotel with decent facilities – an indoor swimming pool, gym, squash courts and nightclub. Rooms are rather frumpy, but are air-conditioned and en suite. ❸

Hotel Suave Mar Rua 27 de Maio ☎ 253 969 400, ⓕ 253 969 401. Large resort hotel that's the closest of any to the beach (though still 1km away). The air-con rooms have satellite TV and balconies, and there's a huge restaurant, outdoor swimming pool, tennis court and gym. ❺

Youth hostel

Pousada de Juventude Foz do Cávado, Fão, 3km south of Esposende ☎ 253 981 790, ⓦ www .pousadasjuventude.pt. On the south bank of the Rio Cávado. Has a swimming pool, kitchen, bar, bicycles for rent, and can arrange canoeing trips. Dorm beds €11, rooms ❷

Eating, drinking and nightlife

Esposende's restaurants are geared towards wooing the tourist euro and none is particularly outstanding. The main local speciality is *arroz de lampreia* (lamprey cooked with rice, *chouriço*, wine, onion, pepper and cloves). For dessert, try *clarinhas de Fão*, pastries filled with sweet marrow (*chila*) vermicelli. The town's bars gather on the seafront, though more enjoyable are the cafés located on the town's small squares. Aside from hotel discos, *Bar Big Osses*, Rua João Ferreira da Silva, near Clube Pinhal de Foz, is the main nightlife venue, a late-night music bar sporadically open during the day.

Adega Regional O Barrote Largo Dr. Fonseca Lima, facing the museum ☎ 253 963 884. A charming nook, with tiled table tops and dried vines strung over the bar. *Bacalhau* and *rojões* are reliable standbys, although the daily specials are always worth exploring. Inexpensive.

Dom Sebastião Rua 19 de Agusto ☎ 253 961 414. Try the steak, stewed rabbit or a tasty *arroz de marisco* in a simple restaurant behind the *turismo*. Inexpensive.

Foz do Cavado Av. Eng. Eduardo Abrantes de Oliveira 56 ☎ 253 966 755. The finest restaurant in Esposende, 100m south of the turismo and with a terrace overlooking the river. Seafood is highly rated and if you want to splash out, go for the grilled tiger shrimps. Moderate.

Pasteleria Nélia Rua 1 de Dezembro no phone. Award-winning gateaux and pastries by the hotel of the same name. Inexpensive.

São Bartolomeu do Mar

North of Ofir, you probably won't see another tourist all the way to the little fishing village of **SÃO BARTOLOMEU DO MAR**, which is on the N13,

1km back from one of the best stretches of the Costa Verde. It's just 15km south of Viana do Castelo, but there is still refreshingly little to the place: just a church, shop and café (with a few rooms to let), and good unofficial camping amid the pines. As well as fishing, the local economy revolves around gathering seaweed. Traditionally, whole families harvest it on the beach using huge shrimping nets, which are then hauled across the sands by beautiful wooden carts pulled by oxen. Although the methods are changing and tractors are supplanting beasts, the seaweed is still stacked at the edge of the village to dry before being spread as fertilizer on the coastal fields.

If you're here on August 24, you'll catch the *romaria* that takes place at the end of the **Festas de São Bartolomeu**. The festivities draw thousands of people from the area, many of them families with sick children who come in the hope that they will be cured by taking the traditional Banho Santo – a bizarre ritual in which the child circles the church three times with a black cockerel tied to his or her head before being thrown into the ocean three times by an attendant. The **menhir** (standing stone), in the field immediately behind the church, is believed by many archeologists to be a fertility symbol and could well have something to do with the roots of the ritual, as many Portuguese parish churches tended to be built adjacent to pre-Christian ritual sites, or else were constructed on top of them.

Viana do Castelo

VIANA DO CASTELO is the Minho's principal resort town and a highly appealing one it is, too, with a historic old centre, above-average restaurants and, some distance from the town itself, one of the best beaches in the north. As a prosperous seafaring town, Viana produced some of the greatest colonists of the "discoveries" under Dom Manuel, and was later a departure point for fishing expeditions to Newfoundland's Great Banks. In the eighteenth century, the town was the first centre for the shipment of port wine to England. The most interesting buildings are a throwback to these times where, unusually for the north, you'll notice Manueline mouldings around the doors and windows of the local mansions. The town is also beautifully positioned, spread along the north bank of the Lima estuary and shaped by the thick wooded hill of Monte de Santa Luzia, which is strewn with Celtic remains and crowned by an imposing basilica. If this wasn't enough of an incentive to come, Viana's romaria at the end of August (see box on p.410) is the biggest and most exciting festival in the Minho, while the weekly Friday market is another mass of Minho produce and artefacts.

Arrival and information

The **train station** is at the north end of the main Avenida dos Combatentes da Grande Guerra, which runs right through the town and down to the river at Largo 5 de Outubro. The **bus station** is more inconveniently located at the top end of Rua da Bandeira, twenty minutes' walk northeast of the centre. You might find it easier to catch services from the more central bus stops along the main avenue, at the southern end of Largo 5 de Outubro, or further east by the marina. Buses to Spain (not Sun) head up the coast to Vigo in Galicia, and leave at noon and 5.30pm. The **turismo** is in the centre on Rua do Hospital Velho, off Praça da Erva (Mon–Fri 9am–7pm, Sat 9.30am–1pm & 2.30–6pm, Sun 9.30am–1pm; ☎258 822 620, ⓦwww.cm-viana-castelo.pt) walk down the

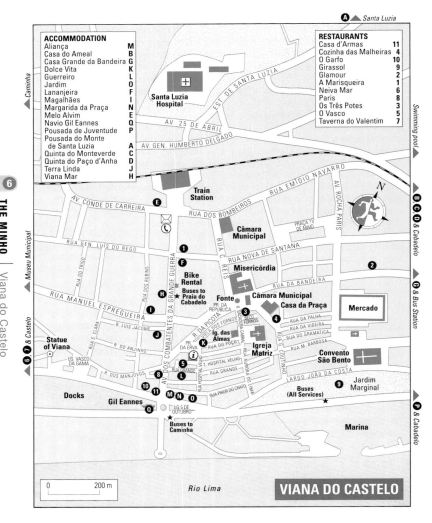

ACCOMMODATION

Aliança	M
Casa do Ameal	B
Casa Grande da Bandeira	G
Dolce Vita	K
Guerreiro	L
Jardim	O
Lananjeira	F
Magalhães	I
Margarida da Praça	N
Melo Alvim	E
Navio Gil Eannes	Q
Pousada de Juventude	P
Pousada do Monte de Santa Luzia	A
Quinta do Monteverde	C
Quinta do Paço d'Anha	D
Terra Linda	J
Viana Mar	H

RESTAURANTS

Casa d'Armas	11
Cozinha das Malheiras	4
O Garfo	10
Girassol	9
Glamour	2
A Marisqueira	1
Neiva Mar	6
Paris	8
Os Três Potes	3
O Vasco	5
Taverna do Valentim	7

VIANA DO CASTELO

main avenue and look for the sign pointing to the left. The building dates from 1468 and was first used by pilgrims travelling to Santiago de Compostela in Spain. Today's helpful staff hand out a good map-booklet and pamphlets detailing walks in the city and trips in the surrounding countryside.

Accommodation

Hotels and pensions – mostly ranged down and off the main avenue – are easy enough to find, although in summer private rooms (**2**, **3** during the *romaria*) offer the best deals. They are generally of good quality and the chances are that you'll be offered one on arrival – otherwise look for signs in house windows or try the turismo. You can also ask the turismo about accommodation at farms and manor houses in the surrounding villages – an ideal way to get to know the countryside, provided you have transport; a clutch are listed below.

In Viana

Hotel Aliança Av. dos Combatentes da Grande Guerra ☎258 829 498, ℱ258 825 299. Eighteenth-century building retaining some period charm, with pleasant, comfortable rooms; those on the top floor boast balconies and views. Breakfast included. ❺

Casa Grande da Bandeira Largo das Carmelitas 488, Rua da Bandeira ☎258 823 169, ⓦwww .solaresdeportugal.pt. This charming seventeenth-century house near the bus station has a small enclosed garden containing camellias and Chinese black bamboos. Only three rooms with traditional furnishings, so book ahead. Breakfast included. ❺

Residencial Dolce Vita Rua do Poço 44 ☎258 824 860, ℮pizzeriadolcevita@iol.pt. A little pricey, but with bright, modern, spotless rooms, all en suite and air-conditioned, and well located in a quiet square above a great, inexpensive restaurant (opens at 7pm, busy by 8pm), serving excellent freshly baked pizzas, and good pasta and wine. Breakfast included. ❹

Pensão Guerreiro Rua Grande 14-1º ☎258 822 099, ℱ258 820 402. A fairly run-down place at the bottom of the main avenue, with a boarding house feel; all rooms have a sink but share bathrooms. Still, it's clean and friendly, and the restaurant (closed Thurs) here is good, serving moderately priced traditional favourites either in the upstairs dining room or, better, at outside tables. No credit cards. ❶

Residencial Jardim Largo 5 de Outubro 68 ☎258 828 915, ℱ258 828 917. Overlooking the river, at the bottom of town, with nicely furnished rooms with bath and TV. Front rooms with a balcony have good views but can be noisy in summer. Excellent value, especially considering the huge breakfasts. ❸

Residencial Laranjeira Rua General Luís do Rego 45 ☎258 822 261, ℮resid.laranjeira@mail. telepac.pt. A reasonable choice just off the main avenue, with small, but pleasant rooms, all with bath and air conditioning. Friendly, comfortable and with breakfast included in the price. ❸

Residencial Magalhães Rua Manuel Espregueira 62 ☎ & ℱ258 823 293. Twin and triple rooms, with or without bath, furnished in the best Minho tradition, with dark, carved headboards on the beds. Rooms at the back can be noisy. Includes breakfast. ❸

Hotel Margarida da Praça Largo 5 de Outubro 58 ☎258 809 630, ⓦwww.margaridadapraca .com. A simple and stylish hotel, hewn from an eighteenth-century building, whose rooms sport pale wood floors and modern fabrics. Includes breakfast. ❹

Melo Alvim Av. Conde da Carreira 28 ☎258 808 200, ⓦwww.meloalvimhouse.com. A sixteenth-century *solar* superbly renovated to provide twenty elegant but individually furnished rooms. Service is faultless, and breakfast is included, while a good restaurant serves a polyglot of international flavours. Parking. ❽

Residencial Terra Linda Rua Luís Jácome 11–15 ☎258 828 981. The cheapest rooms in Viana, with and without private facilities – all fairly dowdy but adequate, while the owner tries hard to please. No credit cards. ❶

Pensão Viana Mar Av. dos Combatentes da Grande Guerra 215 ☎ & ℱ258 828 962. High-ceilinged *pensão* rooms create a feeling of spaciousness. Cheaper rooms are available with shared facilties, while a summer overflow of guests is accommodated in two nearby annexes. ❸

Outside Viana

Casa do Ameal Rua do Ameal, Meadela, 1km east off N202 (Ponte de Lima road) ☎258 822 403 ⓦwww.solaresdeportugal.pt. A stone-walled noble mansion whose rooms are furnished with dark-wood Minho furniture. There's a pool, and breakfast is included. ❺

Pousada do Monte de Santa Luzia Monte de Santa Luzia ☎258 800 370, ⓦwww.pousadas .pt. Showpiece *pousada* at the top of the hill, just behind the basilica, in a 1918 hotel refurbished in elegant but relaxed style, with chandeliers and comfy sofas. Beg for a room at front to enjoy the best views in Viana. Breakfast and taxis into town included, parking available, and there's a good restaurant, too. ❽

Quinta do Monteverde Sendim de Cima, Castelo do Neiva, 10km south off IC1 ☎258 871 134 ⓦwww.soalresdeportugal.pt. A beautifully restored seventeenth-century manor house, cocooned from modernity behind walls and located just 2km from a lovely sand beach; it also has a pool. Period rooms – two doubles and a twin – are spacious and elegant and there are three two-person apartments available for the same price. Includes breakfast. ❻

Quinta do Paço d'Anha Vila Nova de Anha, 3km south off N13 ☎ 258 322 459. Once a hiding place for Dom António from the invading Spanish in 1580, this manor house on a peaceful wine-producing estate maintains six comfortable apartments in the outbuildings (one sleeps 2, others 3 or 4), lifted by cheerful fabrics and equipped with kitchenettes. ❻

Youth hostels

Navio Gil Eannes Doca Comercial ☎ 258 821 582, ⓦ www.pousadasjuventude.pt. Part of a former hospital ship has been turned into use as a youth hostel, with dorm beds, and single and double cabins. Facilities are pretty basic – there's only a common room – but it's hugely atmospheric. Dorms beds €11, cabins 2x

Pousada de Juventude Rua da Argaçosa ☎ 258 800 260, ⓦ www.pousadasjuventude.pt. Viana's

other hostel is a modern affair with dorm beds, nine en-suite double rooms, plus kitchen, bar and internet access. Rent its bicycles if you can't face the 15-minute walk back into town. Dorm beds €12.50, rooms ❸

Campsite

Orbitur Praia do Cabedelo ☎ 258 322 167, ⓦ www.orbitur.com. Overcrowded in summer (there's a minimum stay of one week in July and August and two days at other times) and over-priced for what you get. However, it does at least have the advantage of an attractive, pine-shaded beach location and has also some six-bed bungalows for rent (❸). The bus to the beach passes the site or, if the Viana ferry runs again, cross the river and walk from there. Closed Dec to mid-Jan.

The Town

At the heart of Viana's old town is the distinctive **Praça da República**, enclosed by an elegant ensemble of buildings. You'll see copies of its showpiece Renaissance fountain in towns throughout the Minho, but few structures as curious as the old **Misericórdia** (almshouse) that lines one side of the square. Built in 1589, this is one of the most original and successful buildings of the Portuguese Renaissance, its upper storeys supported by deliberately archaic caryatids. The adjacent sixteenth-century **Câmara Municipal** has been brightly restored and stands foursquare above a medieval arcade, while just off the square is the **Igreja Matriz**, Viana's parish church, which retains a Gothic door of some interest as well as some unusual sculpturework on the towers.

The **Museu Municipal** (Tues–Sun 9am–noon & 2–5pm; €2) adds further to these impressions of Viana's sixteenth- to nineteenth-century opulence. It's at the far end of Rua Manuel Espregueira, ten minutes' walk east from the square, housed in an eighteenth-century palace. The interior has been

The Viana romaria

Viana's main *romaria*, dedicated to **Nossa Senhora da Agonía** – Our Lady of Sorrows – takes place for three days around the weekend nearest to August 20. A combination of carnival and fair, and fulfilling an important business function for the local communities, it's a great time to be in town.

Events kick off with an impressive **religious parade** on the Friday. But the best day is **Saturday**, when there's a massive parade of floats with every village in the region providing an example of a local craft or pursuit: a marvellous display of incongruities, with threshers pounding away in traditional dress while being pulled by a new Lamborghini tractor. If you want a seat in the stands, get a ticket through the turismo well in advance.

On each of the three days there are lunchtime **processions** with *gigantones* (carnival giants), folk dancing, loud drum bands, pipe bands and, needless to say, concerted drinking. The blessing of the fishing boats on Monday morning is rather moving – women in the fishing quarter, east of the centre and behind the docks, decorate their streets with pictures in coloured sawdust on religious and quotidian themes, and there are spectacular nightly **firework displays** too.

maintained close to the original and displays beautifully a large collection of ceramics and furniture, alongside more modern temporary exhibitions and some simple paintings of nineteenth-century Viana.

If you continue past the museum, you'll eventually reach the **Castelo de Santiago da Barra**, commissioned by Philip II of Spain for the defence of the port. Outside the walls, in the area known as Campo do Castelo, Viana's **Friday market** takes place. It's much smaller than the famous one at Barcelos but attracts many of the same stallholders and always turns up a few surprises.

On the waterfront, moored in the dock off Largo 5 de Outubro, is the **Gil Eannes**, Portugal's first hospital ship, returned to its home port after mouldering as scrap in Lisbon. It's a floating museum dedicated to the ship's history as a hospital and supply ship for cod fishermen on the Newfoundland and Greenland seas from 1955 to 1973 (July–Sept daily 9am–noon & 2–7pm, rest of year Sat & Sun 9am–noon & 2–7pm; €1.50). Part is now also in service as a youth hostel (see "Accommodation").

Monte de Santa Luzia

Wherever you stand in Viana, the twentieth-century basilica atop **Monte de Santa Luzia** makes its presence felt. It's a lengthy (2km) but pleasant walk to reach it along the Estrada Santa Luzia, up through the pines and eucalyptus trees, but shorter and far more punishing if you take the stairs. However, the effort is worth it because from the top are fantastic views of the coast and Rio Lima. A taxi up will cost around €6.

At the summit there's a café and plenty of wooded walks. While the **basilica** itself is of little interest, look for the side entrance (marked *Zimbório*; April–Sept daily 8am–7pm; Oct–March daily 8am–5pm; €0.50), where a narrow winding staircase climbs right through the building, past traffic lights laid on during summer to keep tourist hordes in check, and out on top of the dome itself. It's very narrow, very steep and – at the top – pretty hair-raising when the wind picks up, but the magnificent views were once acclaimed by National Geographic Magazine as "the most beautiful in the world".

Behind the *pousada*, at the crown of the hill (see "Accommodation"), lie the ruins of a Celto-Iberian **citânia** (Tues–Sun 9am–noon & 2–5pm; €0.70). The ruins are viewed from a raised walkway and include the foundations of dozens of small, circular stone huts, a thick village wall and partly paved streets. Occupied from around 500 BC, the settlement was only abandoned with the Roman pacification of the north under Emperor Augustus (c.26 BC) and is worth a look, particularly if you can't get to any of the larger *citânias* in the region.

Praia do Cabedelo

Viana's town beach, **Praia do Cabedelo**, lies across the river. At the time of writing the ferry service, which formerly left from the harbourside at the southern end of the main avenue, had been suspended, although hopes are high that it will resume. Check with the turismo before resorting to the road access from town to beach, over a bridge east of the centre. Buses (Mon–Fri 6 daily, plus weekends July–Sept, last bus back to Viana at 5.10pm) leave from a stop in the centre of Avenida dos Combatentes da Grande Guerra, or from the stop by the marina. More frequent buses to Cabedela can be caught across the river from Viana, at the end of the bridge, although it's a stiff 2km walk to get there. However, since these run at weekends they can be the only option out of season.

Given sun, the beach is more or less perfect – a low, curving bay with good (but not wild) breakers and a real horizon-stretching expanse of sand. Praia do Cabedelo is ideal for watersports – several companies rent out equipment and offer lessons (see "Listings", p.413). There's a bar, *Aquario*, at the windsurf school and a couple of others close to the ferry dock, but there is nowhere else to buy food or drink, so take a picnic. From Viana, the beach extends northwards, virtually unbroken, to the Spanish border at Caminha and south to Póvoa de Varzim.

Eating, drinking and nightlife

There's a wide choice of cafés and restaurants in town, as you might expect from a busy resort, including a number of cheap places with outdoor tables in Rua Prior do Crato, one road back from the river. Many of the restaurants serve extremely good food since they cater mostly for demanding Portuguese visitors rather than foreigners. Several of the *pensões* also incorporate restaurants, and a couple are definitely worth considering, including the *Dolce Vita* and *Guerreiro* (see "Accommodation" p.409). For general provisions, there is a permanent morning market at the eastern end of town on Rua Martim Velho.

Romaria time aside, there's not an awful lot going on after dark in Viana, though a couple of cafés at the bottom of the main drag are good places for a beer or late-night coffee. For **cultural** events, consult the *Agenda Cultural*, a monthly diary issued by the Câmara Municipal; the turismo holds copies and can provide information on regional festivities.

Cafés and bars

Girassol Café Jardim Marginal. A lovely spot for a *bica,* among the trees of this small park. Shame it closes at 7pm.

Glamour Rua da Bandeira 183. Glamour, indeed, for small-town Viana – a stylish metropolitan-style bar, also serving food, which morphs into a nightclub (10pm–4am) with live jazz, blues and salsa during the week and house tunes at weekends.

Pastelaria Paris Av. Combatentes da Grande Guerra. Great cakes, pastries and biscuits, plus thickly sliced hot-buttered toast for breakfast. Closed Mon.

Restaurants

Casa d'Armas Largo 5 de Outubro 30 ☎258 824 999. A quality restaurant in a lovely building, but high prices as a result. It's strong on seafood – choose your lobster from the tank – but carnivores are well catered for too. Closed Wed. Expensive.

Cozinha das Malheiras Rua Gago Coutinho 19 ☎258 823 680. A well-priced place – main courses are €7.50–10 – serving a number of local specialities. Try the roast wrasse (when available), goat, *arroz de marisco* or *papas de sarrabulho*. Closed Tues. Moderate.

O Garfo Largo 5 de Outubro ☎258 829 415. Friendly, small place, as popular with locals for an afternoon gossip over brandy and a *bica* as

with tourists dining on seafood on the waterfront. Moderate.

A Marisqueira Rua General Luís do Rego 36 ☎258 823 225. Generous portions – try a house special *rojões* – go some way towards making up for the brusque service. The €6 *ementa turística* is a bargain. Inexpensive.

Neiva Mar Largo Infante D. Henriques 1 ☎258 820 661. Superb seafood, off the road on the seafront near the castle. *Bacalhau* dishes are well worth a try here, while the *arroz de tamboril* (monkfish rice) feeds two for €23. Closed Wed except July & Aug. Moderate.

Os Três Potes Beco dos Fornos 7 ☎258 829 928. In a converted sixteenth-century bakery, this restaurant is hugely popular in high season (book ahead), when national costumes are worn and music played at weekends. Good traditional food – try the chargrilled *polvo* (octopus) and a locally produced ewe's cheese – but relatively pricey, with full meals running to at least €18. Closed Mon. Expensive.

O Vasco Rua Grande 21 ☎258 824 665. Simple, tasty Portuguese dishes – try the stewed kid or lamprey in season – at reasonable prices. Moderate. Closed Sun.

Taverna do Valentim Rua Daniel Machado 180 ☎258 827 505. Excellent seafood restaurant in a former fisherman's tavern, secreted away in a backstreet (one block back from the dock-side road) and without a sign; a menu beside the door gives the game away. The speciality is a seafood stew. Closed Sun. Moderate.

Listings

Banks Banks are on Pr. da República and along the main avenue.

Bike rental Stress Off, Av. dos Combatentes da Grande Guerra 38 ☎258 821 302, rents mountain bikes from €5/hr.

Boat trips Departures from the pier at the bottom of the avenue for trips up the Rio Lima. Prices are negotiable but expect to pay around €15 per person.

Books and newspapers English-language books are available at Livraria Bertrand, Rua Sacadura Cabral, while international newspapers are sold in the newsagents on the corner of Praça da República and in the *tabacaria* on the corner of Rua Luís Jácome and Av. Combatentes da Grande Guerra.

Car rental Avis, Rua do Gontim ☎258 817 540; Hertz, Av. Conde da Carreira 3 ☎258 822 250.

Hospital Hospital Santa Luzia, Estrada Santa Luzia ☎258 829 081.

Internet The post office (see below for hours) and library (Mon–Fri 9.30am–12.30pm & 2–9pm) have public online access, otherwise you can pay for terminals at esp@ço.net at Rua General Luis do Rego 23 (Mon–Sat 9am–8pm).

Pharmacy Nelsina, Pr. da República ☎258 822 235; Central, Rua Manuel Espregueira ☎258 822 527. The turismo has details of late-night openings.

Police Headquarters at Rua de Aveiro ☎258 822 022.

Post office Av. dos Combatentes da Grande Guerra 66 (Mon–Fri 8.30am–6pm, Sat 9am–12.30pm); you can make phone calls from the Portugal Telecom office next door.

Swimming pool The municipal pool is on Av. Capitão Gaspar de Castro, 700m along the eastern continuation of Rua Emídio Navarro. The Foz Health Club, Cabadelo ☎258 331 274, also has a pool.

Taxis Available from ranks along Av. Combatentes da Grande Guerra. To call Taxi Vianeses try one of three numbers: ☎258 826 641, ☎258 333 971 or ☎258 822 061.

Watersports Several companies at Praia do Cabedelo rent windsurfing gear for around €30 per day with wetsuit, including the Associação de Windsurf do Norte ☎919 048 379, and the Escola Zurf School ☎966 221 092, ⓦwww.surfingviana. nortenet.pt, which also features kitesurfing and lessons for €30/hr (June to mid-Sept only). Dive trips – €35 one dive, €160 for five – are available through Cavaleiros do Mar, Edifício do Parque, Estrada da Papanata 204 (15min walk beyond the marina) ☎258 824 455 or ☎964 397 293, ⓦwww.cavaleirosdomar.com.

Carreço, Afife and Gelfa

The small village of **CARREÇO**, 5km north of Viana, is set back a couple of kilometres east of its beach, where there's a café-bar, toilets and showers. **AFIFE**, another 2km further north, is also a good goal with a fort, several cafés and even a casino. The modern *Residencial Compostela* (☎258 981 590, ⒻF258 981 244; includes breakfast; no credit cards; ❷) is on the main road just north of the turning to the beach; it also has a restaurant, although the two on the beach are preferable. If you're looking for a more dramatic place to stay, *Casa do Penedo* (☎258 980 000, ⒻF258 980 009; includes breakfast; no credit cards; closed Nov–March; ❸) is a typically attractive stone Minho home with a garden, 1km south of the station, up a hillside with sea views. The dunes – and a particularly wonderful expanse of beach – are fifteen to twenty minutes' walk from the village, the least frequented parts being to the south. On Praia do Bico you can hire surfboards and wetsuits (€15/hr each) from Escola Zurf School (☎966 221 092, ⓦwww.surfingviana .nortenet.pt), which also offers surfing lessons (€30/hr) if you pre-book.

At the village of **GELFA**, between Afife and Vila Praia de Âncora, there's a **campsite** in the pinewoods (☎258 911 537; mid-March to mid-Oct daily; rest of year weekends only), but it's on the inland side of the train station and hence some distance from the beach.

Vila Praia de Âncora and around

Six kilometres up the coast from Afife, the next major stop on the train line is **VILA PRAIA DE ÂNCORA**, a medium-sized resort popular with locals at weekends and Portuguese tourists in summer. Sitting on the basin of the River Âncora, there is a superb beach right alongside the train line, sheltered by the surrounding hills and drifting back into the river's estuary. Here you can swim enjoyably even when the Atlantic breezes are blowing towels around the sands. For good measure there are two **forts** guarding the bay: the Fortim de Cão, south of the estuary, and the better-preserved Forte de Lagarteira, to the north by the little fishing harbour. Legend has it that the river, and indeed the town, owe their name to a punishment doled out to the adulterous Queen Urraca of Navarre, drowned in the river by her jealous husband King Ramiro II of Asturias, Galicia and Leon with an anchor (*âncora*) around her neck. Four kilometres north of Vila Praia de Âncora, Moledo do Minho is the train traveller's last chance to swim in the sea. Very much in the same mould as Vila Praia, it too has a fort – this time half-ruined, guarding the river from a long, sandy spit. If you're heading for Caminha, Valença, or even Spain, you could easily stop off here or at Vila Praia, wander down to the beach and catch the next train.

The **train station** for Vila Praia is Âncora-Praia, and is the only station between Viana do Castelo and Caminha at which express trains stop. Just down the road on Largo da Estação, the well-signposted **bus station** also houses the **turismo** (Mon–Sat 9.30am–12.30pm & 2.30–6pm; ☎258 911 384), from where you can get leaflets detailing a five-kilometre walking circuit to the **Cividade de Âncora**, the ruins of a first-century AD Bronze and Copper Age settlement; the walk starts from the main square of Santa Maria de Âncora, 2km inland.

Finding accommodation for a few days here shouldn't be hard. The turismo has a list of **private rooms** (❷), while **hotel** choices include the popular, mid-range *Hotel Meira*, Rua 5 de Outubro 56 (☎258 911 911, ✉hotel.meira@mail.telepac.pt; breakfast included; ❺), with parking and a pool, and the more reasonably priced *Albergaria Quim Barreiros*, on the seafront behind the train station (☎258 959 100, ⊕www.albergariaquimbarreiros.com; breakfast included; ❹), with pleasant, modern rooms, the priciest with balconies. Apart from **camping** unofficially by the Fortim de Cão, there's the *Parque de Campismo do Paço* (☎258 912 697, ✆258 951 228; closed mid-Oct to mid-March) 1.5km from town on the south bank of the Rio Âncora, which also offers canoes and rafting.

Restaurants are plentiful, as is fresh fish. *Fonte Nova*, Rua Miguel Bombarda (☎258 911 191), along from the church, serves good meals, while *Park Café* on leafy Praça Republica (no phone) offers light lunches as well as tasty *pastéis de nata*. Beach restaurant *Gelfa Mar* (☎258 911 213; closed Oct–June), twenty minutes' walk south down the beach, is recommended for its moderately priced food (try the lamprey) and sunsets.

Along the Rio Minho

At Moledo do Minho, the train line moves inland along the south bank of the **Rio Minho**, which forms the country's border with Spain. **Caminha** is the first river town, a pleasant stopover, while beyond here several small fortified towns guard the Portuguese side of the river, with the Minho train line terminating in perhaps the best of the lot, **Valença do Minho**. This is a major crossing-point into Spain and also the site of a splendid weekly market. However, the most scenic section of the river is from Valença east to **Monção** and **Melgaço**, which can both be reached by bus. Both towns are also minor border crossings, with buses running onwards from the Spanish side. Food is a highpoint along the Minho, especially the local eels (*enguias*), shad (*savel*) and the rich, eel-like lamprey (*lampreia*), in season between January and March; Minho trout and salmon are always tremendous, too.

Caminha

At the mouth of the Rio Minho, and straddling the Rio Coura, **CAMINHA** is a quiet river port that was at its peak in the seventeenth century. A few reminders of more prosperous days remain, principally in and around the main square, Praça Conselheiro Silva Torres, known locally as Largo Terreiro. Here a battlemented town hall, Renaissance clock tower and large fountain vie for your attention. However, Caminha's most distinguished building is the magnificently restored **Igreja Matriz**, a couple of minutes' walk from the square towards the river; take the street through the arch by the clock tower, past the turismo (see below). The church was built towards the end of the fifteenth century, when the town was reputed to rival Porto in trade, and it still stands within part of the old city walls. Inside there's a superb inlaid ceiling, intricate *azulejos* and a carved granite pulpit. Note also the figures carved on the two Renaissance doorways, one on the north side giving the finger to Spain across the river. Nearby, a small **museum** in the library opposite the **turismo** (daily 9.30am–2.30pm & 2–6pm; free) houses a collection of items plundered from local archeological sites.

A couple of kilometres south of town, the island of **Fortaleza da Ínsua** makes an enjoyable trip – local fishermen run trips across on Sundays from the spit of sand at Foz do Minho, on the river side of its fine beach. If you want to arrange something during the week (for the next morning), ask in the *Café Valadares* at the road's end for directions to António Garrafão's house. He will go only if there is a reasonably large – or affluent – group gathered. Five kilometres east of Caminha at Lanhelas, Afluente Desporto e Natureza, Lugar da Sentinela (☎258 727 017, ✉safari@afluente.com) offers **boat trips**, plus "canoe safaris" (daily at 10am & 3pm), mountain biking, rafting, sailing and surfing; each activity costs around €20 per person.

Practicalities

The bus terminal is out of town at Vilharelho, 2km northeast of the centre, but all buses stop on the central artery of Avenida Manuel Xavier. This runs 500m north to the train station on Avenida Saraiva Carvaero. The **turismo** (Mon–Sat 9.30am–12.30pm & 2–6pm; ☎258 921 952, ⓦwww.caminha.pt), on Rua Ricardo Joaquim Sousa, reached via the clock tower, provides good town maps. The town also has a ferry link to La Guardia in Spain, which leaves from beside the bridge over the Rio Coura. There are daily services throughout the year (April–Sept on the hour 8am–9pm; €0.60; cars €2.50), but winter times are variable.

A few hotels and pensions provide **accommodation**, or consult the turismo or restaurant *Pero de Camina* (see below) to locate the few **private rooms** in town. Bar a couple of notable exceptions listed below, **restaurants** and **cafés** cluster around Caminha's showpiece *praça*. **Bars** gather along Rua Ricardo Joaquim de Sousa, which threads from the main square beneath the clock tower and down towards the Igreja Matriz.

Hotels and pensions

Residencial Arca Nova Largo Sidónio Pais, 200m left of the train station ℡ 258 721 590, ℻ 258 728 120. A dreary building hides bright and pleasant rooms, all en suite and with a television. Breakfast included. ❸

Casa de Esteiró Rua Benemérito Joaquim Rosas ℡ 258 721 333, ℻ 258 921 3546. Originally an eighteenth-century hunting lodge, this charming house – crammed with family mementoes – is set in lovely gardens behind the *Hotel Porta do Sol*. There are two homely doubles and a single room, all en suite, plus two self-catering apartments. Breakfast included. ❹, apartments ❼

Residencial Galo d'Ouro Rua da Corredoura 15 ℡ & ℻ 258 921 160. Just off the main square. It's rather tatty but friendly and full of character, as some rooms in the eighteenth-century building have stucco ceilings or chunks of original stone wall. No credit cards. ❸

Quinta da Graça, Vilarelho, 2km northeast of town ℡ 258 921 467 ⓦ www.solaresdeportugal .pt. Grandstand views over the river – breakfast (included) is served on the balcony – and four cosy rooms of heavy Minho furniture in a seventeenth-century *quinta* snug against the town walls. ❺

Hotel Porta do Sol Av. Marginal ℡ 258 710 360 340, ⓦ www.hotel-portadosol.com. Spacious modern rooms, some with river views, in Caminha's most modern hotel, a four-star which boasts a pool, sauna and gym. It's located by the southern entrance to town. Prices drop by a third outside July–Sept. Breakfast included. ❺

Campsites

Parque de Campismo Natural Vilar de Mouros, 4km west ℡ 258 727 472, ℮ pnvm .anta@cartaopostal.com. A little way inland and

nicely positioned by a small river gorge. It has a swimming pool, tennis court and some bungalows for rent (❷ or ❸); two buses daily (Mon–Fri) travel to the site from outside the café 200m left of the train station.

Orbitur Mato do Camarido, 2km south of town at Foz do Minho ℡ 258 921 295, ⓦ www.orbitur .com. At the river mouth opposite the Fortaleza da Ínsua and 200m from the beach; buses (Mon–Fri 3 daily) from the town hall stop close by. Tends to be crowded in summer. Closed Dec to mid-Jan.

Cafés and restaurants

Adega do Chico Rua Visconde de Sousa Rego 30, off the main square ℡ 258 921 781. Choose the catch of the day or, for a real blow-out, the chef-special *arroz do marisco*. Moderate.

Duque de Caminha Rua Ricardo Joaquim de Sousa 111–113 ℡ 258 722 046. Top-notch cuisine, which gives a nod to its Spanish neighbours, and an excellent wine list in a classy, rustic-styled restaurant by the Igreja Matriz. Closed all Sun & Mon evening. Expensive.

Pastelaria Riviera Pr. Conselheiro Silva Torres ℡ 258 922 993. The best place for breakfast and a sandwich lunch – try the *francesinha*, a Portugese-style croque monsieur with *choruriço* and home-made sauce. Inexpensive.

Pêro de Caminha Pr. Conselheiro Silva Torres no phone. All the usual *bacalhau* and *frango* standards, plus pizzas and pastas for around €5. Closed Tues. Moderate.

Petisqueria Rua Ricardo Joaquim de Sousa 32 no phone. Snug locals' choice for a weekday set-menu lunch, a bargain at €6. Or try the *porco á alentejana* from the weekend menu. Inexpensive.

Vila Nova de Cerveira

The small town of **VILA NOVA DE CERVEIRA**, 11km northeast of Caminha, huddles behind the walls of a castle that peers across the Rio Minho to Spain. Its popularity, however, is due more to the car and passenger ferry (actually, little more than a floating platform) that drifts across the river to Goyan in Galicia. The **ferry** (every 30min: April–Sept 8.30am–8.55pm; Oct–March 8.30am–7.25pm; passengers €0.40, cars €1.50) has transformed the town into something of a minor shopping centre for Spaniards, but it remains a pleasant place, far more relaxed and less commercial than Valença further upstream. The town is also home to an art school, which has spawned a surprising prevalence of modern works around town.

Vila Nova's most impressive building is the **Solar dos Castros** on Praça da Liberdade, once a manor house and now a library and cultural centre. Behind, facing a beautifully manicured garden, is the **Câmara Municipal**, alongside which, in a small garden, is a striking sculpture of a tripod holding aloft a rock. This has become the symbol of the **arts festival** held here in August on alternate (odd) years.

Practicalities

The train station is at the far western end of Vila Nova de Cerveira, a 15-minute walk from central Praça da Galicia. The ferry crossing is halfway between the two, abutting the town's riverside park. Adjacent to the Câmara Municipal is the **turismo** (Mon–Sat 9.30am–12.30pm & 2.30–6pm, Sun 10am–12.30pm; ☎251 708 023, ⓦ www.cm-vncerveira.pt), which has free internet access.

Although there is little in the way of **accommodation**, there is something to fit every budget. The cheapest option is the pleasant **youth hostel** at Largo 16 de Fevereiro 21 (☎251 796 113, ⓦ www.pousadasjuventude.pt; dorms €10, rooms ❷), which boasts its own kitchen and a terrace. Anyone with a fat wallet can do no better than stay in the excellent *Pousada de Dom Dinis* (☎251 795 601, ⓦ www.pousadas.pt; breakfast included; ❼), built hard against the sixteenth-century fortress walls and ramparts. Although not a historic building itself, it has been charmingly modernized and would provide a memorable first or last night in Portugal; not surprisingly, it also has the best restaurant in town featuring Minho specialities. In between these two extremes, rather dated but comfortable rooms are available at the *Residencial Rainha de Gusmão*, Avenida Heróis do Ultramar (☎& ⓕ 251 796 227; Visa only; 3x), some of which have river views.

For **food**, the *Café Restaurant Central* (no phone) in the main square is a good choice for light lunches, while *Abrigo das Andorinhas*, Rua Querirós Riberio 76 (☎251 795 335) offers solid cooking at moderate prices, with specials like monkfish or roast octopus. *Cerva Bar* and *Barril Bar*, off the main square, are the hubs of the evening action.

Valença do Minho and around

Get beyond the uninspired modern surroundings of **VALENÇA DO MINHO** (or just Valença), 17km northeast of Vila Nova de Cerveira, and you'll discover an absurdly quaint old town clumped amid perfectly preserved seventeenth-century ramparts on a hillock above the river. The fortress has repelled innumerable Spanish and French invasions over the centuries, and it stands as the backdrop to some lovely local walks, down by the river and along the ramparts (watch out for hidden stairwells), the design of which was influenced by the work of the seventeenth-century French military architect, Vauban. However, during the day, the town's undoubted charms are exploited by a myriad of souvenir shops that cater for Spanish day-trippers who cross the border to pick up inexpensive baby clothes, bed linen, towels and ceramics. Increasingly, the extent of this commercialism is reducing the appeal of the town and even the regional tourist office describes Valença as a "shopping fortress". But by late afternoon the crowds have gone and by evening you have old Valença to yourself, and can lazily explore what is almost a ghost town.

On foot, you're likely to approach the old town from the Largo da Trapichera roundabout at the bottom of the hill, where Rua das Antas, which runs from the train station, enters the new part of town. Climb the hill straight ahead, turn right at the top and you enter through the **Portas da Coroada**, further along from which a causeway leads over a dry moat to the **Portas do Meio**, the bastion's middle gates. Throughout the area around Largo de São João, a rich diversity of buildings lines the narrow, cobbled streets, with sudden views of the surrounding countryside appearing over the lower reaches of the walls. The new town, to the south of the ramparts, has nothing of historical interest but it's here that you'll track down all the basic necessities. Come on Wednesday and you'll encounter the huge weekly **market**, held on the wooded slopes below the walls. The other local point of interest is over the river, just a mile from Valença, across the iron bridge designed by Eiffel, where Spanish **Tuy** is an ancient, pyramid-shaped town with a grand battlemented parish church. It, too, is partly walled and it looks far sturdier than Valença, though the first English guidebook to Portugal (*Murray's* in 1855) reported that "the guns of Valença could without difficulty lay Tuy in ruins".

Practicalities

Trains from Spain rattle over the bridge to Valença, or you can simply walk across from Tuy – there's no passport control, and walking from the centre of one old town to the other takes around thirty minutes. There are also three daily trains to Vigo in Spain, which is within easy reach of Santiago de Compostela, the beautiful ancient pilgrimage town of Galicia.

Domestic **trains** from Viana do Castelo end their run in Valença, and to head further east or south you'll have to take a local **bus** – the terminus is in front of the train station. There are no obvious signs to the old town but it's easy enough to find: turn right at the avenue that leads away from the station, then head uphill after the crossroads. You'll see the **turismo** (Mon–Sat 9.30am–12.30pm & 2.30–6pm, Sun 9.30am–12.30pm; ☎251 823 329, ⓦ www.cm-valenca.pt) in a wooden chalet opposite a small park; the free town map is helpful and you can also buy an information pack (€2.50) detailing the Romanesque churches and monuments of the Rio Minho.

Accommodation

The best of the accommodation options are listed below and, bar the two upmarket choices, they are located in the new town. For cheaper old-town accommodation in private rooms (❷) ask at restaurants or consult the turismo.

Casa do Poço Trav. da Gaviarra 4 ☎251 825 235, ⓦ www.casadopoco.fr.fm. The connoisseur's choice is this former doctor's home in the old town, near the *pousada*, which it surpasses in atmosphere and antique furnishings. There are only six rooms so book ahead. Breakfast included. American Express only. Closed Jan. ❻

Hotel Lara Av. dos Bombeiros Voluntrários, 300m uphill from Largo da Trapichera ☎251 824 348, ⓕ251 824 358. Smart and efficient hotel facing the walls on the main Spain road. Its thirty modern, spacious rooms all have a balcony and TV. Breakfast included. ❸

Residencial Ponte Seca Av. Dr. Tito Fontes ☎ & ⓕ251 822 580. East on the Monçao road, on the fringes of the new town, this is spotless and good value, if a little isolated from the main attractions – expect a 10min walk to the old town. No credit cards. ❸

Pousada de São Teotónio Inside the fortress ☎251 800 260, ⓦ www.pousadas.pt. Although a largely modern building within the walls, many of the *pousada* rooms have balconies and sensational views. If you don't stay, at least have a drink in the bar or dine in the excellent restaurant (around €18–25 a head). Breakfast included, parking available. ❻

Residencial Rio Minho Largo da Estação ☎251 809 240, ℱ251 809 248. Opposite the train station and the cheapest option in town, with basic but high-ceilinged en-suite rooms and a budget restaurant. Visa only. ❷

Residencial Val-Flores Av. dos Bombeiros Voluntários, 200m uphill from Largo da Trapichera ☎251 824 106, ℱ251 824 129. A friendly, modern high-rise with spotless rooms, which all have bath and satellite TV. Breakfast included. ❸

Eating and drinking

You should be able to eat well in any of the old town's restaurants, although sharing the experience with the day-trippers can make lunch anything but peaceful. Local specialities include *lampreia* (lamprey) and *enguias* (eels), *cabrito à Sanfins* (a goat dish prepared at Easter) and *sável frito* (fried shad). The best place to stock up on wine, port, cheese and chocolate is Garrafeira Vasco da Gama, on Largo da Esplanada in the new town.

Baluarte Rua Apolinária da Fonseca ☎281 842 042. Old-town restaurant with lamprey on the menu (€18), though also more basic food for those on a budget. Moderate.

Fortaleza Rua Apolinário da Fonseca 5 ☎251 823 146. Just outside the Portas do Meio and not as pricey as it looks. House special is roast goat, although the chef also prepares an excellent *arroz de marisco*, best enjoyed at the outdoor tables. Moderate.

Os Gallegos Av. Doutor Tito Fontes Valença ☎251 824 152. A snack-bar located just off Av. de Espanha, south of the old town, that's popular with

day-trippers from across the border because of a Spanish-orientated menu. Moderate.

Mané Av. Miguel Dantas 5, by Largo da Trapichera ☎251 823 402. On the road from the station towards the old town, Valença's finest restaurant is not overly expensive (mains around €14), so it's the place to try *arroz de lampreia* (lamprey with rice). Closed Mon. Expensive.

Monumental Just inside the Portas da Coroada ☎251 823 557. There's a wonderful, spicy *arroz de marisco* served in this reasonably priced restaurant built into the bastion walls. Moderate.

Inland: Paredes de Coura

PAREDES DE COURA, 28km south of Valença, claims to be the oldest village in Portugal, an assertion that's rendered a little hard to believe by the new emigrant-financed houses surrounding what's really quite a sizeable town. Still, if you're headed for Ponte da Barca or Ponte de Lima, it warrants a detour. You can climb up to the top of the town for views over an almost Swiss landscape, with chalet-style houses and white church spires, or follow the track down beyond the football field to the river for the town's best swimming spot. Every year, over the first weekend in August, the **Festas do Conselho** features the usual Minho mix of dance, costumed procession and music.

   Buses run here from Valença (Mon–Fri 1 daily), Monção (Mon–Fri 1 daily) and Ponte de Lima (2–5 daily), stopping on Rua 25 de Abril in the east of town. The best **accommodation** is at *Pensão Miquelina*, on the central Rua Conselheiro Miguel Dantas (☎251 782 103; no credit cards; ❷), with a number of good restaurants on the same street – try *Arcada* for huge portions of good local food. The **turismo** (Mon–Sat 9.30am–12.30pm & 2.30–6pm; ☎251 782 105) is housed in an old prison in Largo Visconde Mouzelos in the east of town, off Rua Conselheiro Miguel Dantas.

Monção

MONÇÃO, 16km east of Valença, is home to yet another border fortress, although little remains of it except a doorway, a section of wall above the bus

At other times, the only likely reasons for visiting Melgaço are that it is so obviously off the usual tourist track and that it provides easy access to the remote northern part of the Parque Nacional da Peneda-Gerês. Its one historic feature is the ruined tenth-century **fortress**, much fought over during the Wars of Restoration but now little more than a tower and a few walls handy for hanging out washing. However, there are attractions in the vicinity, including a couple of Romanesque churches and the local spa resort (see below), while the **Spanish border** is only 11km to the east. Following the Minho into Spain – or Miño as it becomes known – you'll find it becomes more placid in the further reaches, as it is dammed shortly after the point when both of its banks are within Spain. Nearby targets include Ribadavia (along the river, and with superb local red wine) and Celanova (on the route to Orense, dwarfed by a vast medieval monastery), two of the most lovely and characteristic towns of Spanish Galicia.

Practicalities

All **buses** leave from Largo da Calçada – 300m east of the central Praça da Republica – with daily services to Monção (for connections to Braga), plus direct services to Porto, Coimbra and Lisbon. Auto Viação Melgaço buses to Lamas de Mouro and Castro Laboreiro (for the Peneda-Gerês park) leave on weekdays at 7.30am (with an additional 12.50pm service on Fri). Buses to São Gregório, for the Spanish border, leave four times a day, in the afternoon and early evening; the same journey by taxi costs around €6. The border itself is at Ponte Barxas, 1km east of São Gregório, and from across the frontier buses leave twice daily (Mon–Fri) for Ribadavia and Orense.

The town's helpful **turismo** (Mon–Sat 9.30am–12.30pm & 2.30–6pm, closed Wed Oct–April; ℡251 402 440, ⓦwww.cm-melgaco.pt) is just out of town in the stone Casa Castreja, on the road to Monção near the Parque Nacional da Peneda-Gerês turning. It has details on the local *vinho verde quintas* (estates) that welcome visitors, and can provide details of inexpensive **rooms** in private houses. Near the turismo, on Rua Rio do Porto, those in the home of Maria Helena Morais are good (℡251 402 188; ❶). Otherwise, there's inexpensive **accommodation** at the *Pemba,* on Praça Amadeu Abilio Lopes (℡251 402 555; no credit cards; ❶), and the *Miguel Pereira,* Rua Dr José Candido Gomes de Abreu 16, near the cinema (℡251 402 212; no credit cards; ❷), which between them offer a range of rooms. The most charming property, however, is the seventeeth-century *Quinta da Calçada* (℡251 402 547; ⓦwww. solaresdeportugal.pt; breakfast included; ❸), a rural house 1km east of the turismo on the São Gregorio road, which also has a swimming pool.

In the alleys below the fort, a couple of café-restaurants offer good food at reasonable prices and there's a café in the attractive castle gardens overlooking the Minho valley. But best **restaurant** of all is the *Panorama* in the Mercado Municipal, 150m northeast of the fortress (℡251 410 400), whose unexceptional decor belies excellent food (mains around €11), including roast pork leg with pineapple or lamprey cooked in rice. Another local dish is *bifes de presunto de cebolada* (gammon steak fried with onions), while for dessert you might be able to try *bucha doce*, made with eggs and port wine and traditionally served at carnival time. In the newer part of town there are a couple of pizzerias and the *Adega Regional Sabino* on Largo Hermenegildo Solheiro (℡251 404 576), a modern cafe-restaurant that serves food in generous portions.

Melgaço Radical (℡251 402 155, ⓔmelgacoradical@clix.pt) offers half-day **rafting and canoeing trips** on the Rio Minho, and canyoning in the

Peneda-Gerês park (each activity €25), plus walking trips (€20), although groups can be a rather over-subscribed in peak season. The turismo stocks their leaflets and has links on its website to Melgaço Radical and other local adventure sports operators.

Around Melgaço

Short excursions from Melgaço might include the two thirteenth-century Romanesque churches of **Paderne** (3km west, off the road to Monção) and **Nossa Senhora da Orada** (1km east, off the road to the border).

Thermal spa enthusiasts might want to stop at **PESO** – also known as Termas de Melgaço – 4km west of Melgaço. This is a tiny spa town, spread along the old main road (the new one passes just below) and looking down on a magnificent curve of the river. The spa itself is a delight, with shaded, landscaped gardens and a fountain room (baths usually open summer Mon–Sat 8am–noon & 4–7pm), and there's a **campsite** nearby (☎251 403 282), which also has bungalows (❸) for rent. The only **hotel** is the plush, modern *Albergaria Boavista* (☎251 416 464, ⓦwww.albergariaboavista.com; includes breakfast; ❹), which has a swimming pool, tennis courts and a good restaurant. On the other side of the road, the *Adega do Sossego* (☎251 404 308; dinner only) is also an excellent place to eat, with lamprey and roast goat as house specials.

A historic incident in Anglo-Portuguese relations took place on the fragile-looking bridge over the Rio Mouro just before **CEIVÃES**, another 10km west of Peso along the road to Monção. This is the spot where John of Gaunt, the Duke of Lancaster, arranged the marriage of his daughter Philippa to King Dom João I in 1386, an arrangement that resulted in the signing of the **Treaty of Windsor** between the two countries. It gave rise to an alliance lasting over six hundred years and to the naming of numerous public places in honour of "Filipa de Lencastre".

The Lima valley and Parque Nacional da Peneda-Gerês

The **Rio Lima**, whose valley is perhaps the most beautiful in Portugal, was thought by the Romans to be the Lethe, the mythical River of Oblivion. Beyond it, they imagined, lay the Elysian Fields; to cross would mean certain destruction, for its waters possessed the power of the lotus, making the traveller forget country and home. The forces of Roman Consul Decimus Junius Brutus were so convinced of this that they flatly refused to cross, despite having trekked across most of Spain to get there. Brutus had to seize the standard and plunge into the water shouting the names of his legionaries from the far bank – to show his memory remained intact – before they could be persuaded to follow.

From Viana do Castelo, where the river meets the sea, there are roads along both banks, connecting a cluster of peaceful little settlements on the banks of the Lima and its tributaries. Regular bus services along the main N202 and N203 pass through two highly attractive towns – **Ponte de Lima** and **Ponte da Barca** – both excellent bases for exploring the dramatic countryside. Ponte de Lima, in particular, is known for its quality rural accommodation in historic buildings and manor houses. Many of the small villages hereabouts, notably **Bravães**, harbour Romanesque churches of simple and rustic design, featuring naive carvings on the doorways and columns. Most were built in the twelfth and thirteenth centuries under the supervision of Cluniac monks, who brought their architecture to Spain and Portugal along the pilgrimage routes to Santiago de Compostela in Galicia; the main Portuguese route ran through Braga and so Minho has the highest concentration.

Further east, the Lima runs into the heart of the astonishingly beautiful **Parque Nacional da Peneda-Gerês**, which encompasses the dramatic mountain ranges of the Serra da Peneda to the north and the Serra do Gerês to the east. The park is no longer a secret, and the main town of **Caldas do Gerês** probably attracts more tourists than anywhere else in the Minho – at weekends, when Portuguese campers arrive in force, parts of it can seem a bit too close to civilization. However, the park as a whole is large enough to absorb the great numbers of visitors, and trippers and hikers alike can be sure of finding some quiet corner.

Ponte de Lima

PONTE DE LIMA – 23km east of Viana do Castelo – is a delightful place, whose old centre has no specific attraction other than its air of sleepy indifference to the wider world. You might disagree if you visit in July or August, when Ponte de Lima begins to show worrying signs of midsummer tourist strain, a phenomenon that the local authorities have tried to capitalize on by building an eighteen-hole golf course. Outside these times though, Ponte de Lima remains one of the most pleasing towns in the region and visitors are seldom disappointed. The river's wide sandbank beaches provide the venue for the town's bi-monthly Monday market, the oldest in Portugal, held since a charter was first granted in 1125. A ramshackle collection of items is on sale, from mobile phone accessories to trussed chickens. Also held here is the curiously named "New Fair" (second and third weekend of September), a festival and market seemingly attended by half of the Minho, with fireworks, fairground rides, wandering accordionists, gigantones (enormous carnivalesque statues), and a brass band competition. More tradition is on display in early June, with the Vaca das Cordas festival (see box opposite).

The town takes its name from the low stone **bridge** that crosses the river, rebuilt in medieval times but still bearing traces of its Roman origin. It is said to mark the path of the first hesitant Roman crossing of the river and was part of a military route leading from Braga to Astorga. Besides the bridge, the town's main focus is the long riverside Alameda (promenade), shaded by magnificent plane trees, which threads past the rambling old convent of **Santo António** (Tues–Sun 2–5.30pm; free), whose small museum of ecclesiastical treasures is found inside its church. Across the bridge lie the immaculately manicured **Jardims Tematicos** and the small **Museu Rural** (Tues–Sun 2–6pm; free), which houses an uninspired collection of archaic tools and farming acoutrements. Handsome buildings in town include several sixteenth-century mansions with stone coats of arms, and the interesting remains of the old

If you're in Ponte de Lima in early June (the day before Corpus Christi), you might witness the rather odd spectacle of the **Vaca das Cordas** (literally, "Cow of the Ropes"), which involves an enraged and rather reluctant bull being dragged down through the town's streets to the beach.

Like Pamplona's famous *corrida*, this is one of many Iberian traditions that stem back to pre-Christian times, with its origins in the ancient Egyptian cults brought to the Iberian peninsula by the Phoenicians a few centuries before Christ. According to mythology, Jupiter, angry that his attempts to kidnap the beautiful Io had been repelled by her mother, turned his love into a cow and commanded a bumble bee to repeatedly sting her. Understandably perturbed, Io fled to Egypt, where she regained her human form, and promptly married the god Osiris. In her honour, the Egyptians erected altars to Isis in the image of an errant cow, a symbol which became a popular goddess of fertility in both Egypt and, later on, in Portugal. The Igreja Matriz in Ponte de Lima was presumably erected over such a temple, after which time the newly converted Christian citizens – to show their renunciation of idols – dragged their old bovine image around town until finally it fell into pieces. Since then, a live cow – actually now a bull – has been used.

Echoes of the original rite still remain. At around 3pm, the bull is led to the church, where it is stabbed with a small dart in order to madden it. At 6pm, two millers arrive, tie the bull by its horns and lead it three times around the church – a common feature of pre-Christian rituals – whilst jabbing it with goads in reference to the mythical bee described above. Following this, and depending upon whether anyone can keep a grip on its ropes, the unfortunate animal then stumbles or charges through the town's streets (mimicking Io's flight to Egypt) before finishing up at the beach. It is then led off to the abattoir, as the good people of Ponte de Lima prepare for the more sedate procession of **Corpo do Deus** the following day, which sees the streets covered with flowers carefully arranged into ornate patterns.

fourteenth-century keep, the **Torre da Cadeia**, now an exhibition space for temporary art displays.

Wandering through some of the villages on both sides of the river is a joy, while more energetic walkers can climb to **Santo Ovídio chapel** (about half an hour to the top) – a bizarre shrine to the patron saint of ears – for glorious views of the Lima valley, before ambling back to Ponte de Lima along cobbled and vine-covered lanes. The turismo has a few illustrated leaflets detailing more attractive local walks, including those around the protected Lagoas de Bertiandos e São Pedro de Arcos wildlife wetlands, 5km to the east.

The river would offer fine swimming were it not so polluted. However, there is a municipal **pool** in Rua Francisco Sá Carneiro (Mon–Fri 10am–10pm, Sat & Sun 9am–noon & 5pm–10pm), or you can take to the water on a canoe, rented from the **Clube Náutico** (☎258 944 449; €3 for 90min), 2km from the Alameda on the other side of the river by the new bridge.

Practicalities

The **bus station** is behind the market, just a minute or so from the river. There are daily services to Arcos de Valdevez, Viana do Castelo, Barcelos, Ponte da Barca, Paredes de Coura, Braga and Porto. A few minutes' walk away from the river, on Praça da República, the **turismo** in the Paço do Marquês (Mon–Sat 9.30am–12.30pm & 2–5.30pm, Sun 9.30am–12.30pm; ☎258 942 335, ⊛www.cm-pontedelima.pt) is extremely helpful, and provides free maps of the town. **Internet** access is available at espaçaoInternet (Mon–Fri 1–8pm, Sat 10am–noon) at Avenida Antonio Felio 143, 100m up from the turismo.

Accommodation

The town is famous for its rural tourism properties – manor houses and the like, offering bed-and-breakfast accommodation. Most belong to one of several agencies promoting such accommodation, under the umbrella of the Central Nacional de Turismo no Espaço Rural (or CENTER – see "Basics", p.36), through whom you can make bookings. You can also make reservations directly with the properties concerned (see reviews below) or contact Solares de Portugal in Ponte de Lima (⊕258 742 827 or 258 741 672 ⊛www .solaresdeportugal.pt), whose office is at Praça da República, opposite the turismo. You will need your own transport to reach most of the properties. Considering Ponte de Lima's appeal, the selection of *pensãos* is limited and booking ahead in peak season is a good idea. Alternatively, the turismo holds a list of private rooms, while there's also an excellent **youth hostel** out of town.

In town

Casa das Pereiras Largo das Pereiras ⊕258 942 939, ⑤258 941 493. Wonderful eighteenth-century stone *solar* in a hidden square, with a pool and splendid dinners served every Friday evening. The garden is a delight, at its best when 100-year-old camellia shrubs bloom. Closed Nov–May. Breakfast included. ❹

Hotel Império do Minho Av. Dom Luís Filipe (aka Av. dos Plátanos), on the riverfront ⊕258 741 510, ⑤258 942 567. The largest and most modern place in town, offering fifty en-suite rooms with three-star comforts. There's also a spacious bar and swimming pool. Breakfast included. ❺

Pensão Morais Rua da Matriz 8 ⊕258 942 470. A rather tatty *pensão* with simple, traditionally furnished rooms, some with balconies overlooking a quiet street. The shared bathrooms are basic. No credit cards. ❷

Pensão São João Largo de São João ⊕258 941 288. The best budget option in town, near the bridge and with airy, clean en-suite rooms, though front rooms can suffer minor traffic noise. Breakfast included. No credit cards. ❸

Outside town

Casa de Crasto 1km east of town along the N203 to Ponte de Barca ⊕258 941 156 ⓔCrasto@sola resdeportugal.pt. A beautiful seventeenth-century property in verdant grounds, which – legend has it – was partly demolished by the owner in 1896 while looking for hidden treasure. The kitchen and tower managed to evade his attention. Breakfast included. ❺

Casa da Lage São Pedro Arcos, 9km west, off N202 to Viana do Castelo ⊕258 731 417 ⓔLage@solaresdeportugal.pt. Ten rooms with period features – a stone arch or antique furniture – in

a magnificent seventeenth-century manor house, secluded among vineyards. Also has its own chapel, bar and indoor pool. Breakfast included. ❻

Casa do Outeiro Arcozelo, 2km north of Ponte de Lima ⊕258 941 206 ⓔouteiro@solaresdeportugal. pt. Stately decor in a manor house that dates from the seventeenth century – its vast kitchen fireplace is original – and is surrounded by a garden and woods. Has a swimming pool and three homely twin rooms for rent. Breakfast included. ❺

Casa de Sao Gonçalo Arcozelo, 1km north of Ponte de Lima ⊕258 942 442, ⓔSaoGoncalo@so laresdeportugal.pt. Views of the town are oustanding from this nineteenth-century house, 500m from the bridge. Although elegant and furnished with antiques, it's very much a family home, and the charming garden is a lovely place for breakfast (included). Since there's just one double room and a two-person apartment (same price), booking ahead is recommended. ❹

Moinho de Estorãos Estorãos, 7km northeast of Ponte de Lima ⊕258 941 546 ⓔMoinhoEstoraos @solaresdeportugal.pt. Low-key rustic charm in a converted seventeenth-water mill. The location is an escapist's idyll – next to a Romanesque bridge and with walking, fishing and swimming all at hand. Book in advance for the single double room. Closed mid-Oct to mid-May. Breakfast included. ❺

Paço de Calheiros Calheiros, 7km northeast of Ponte de Lima ⊕258 947 164, ⓔCalheiros@sola resdeportugal.pt. An elegant, seventeenth-century mansion, the country retreat of none other than the Count of Calheiros, founder of the Turihab scheme. Set in beautifully landscaped gardens with views over the Lima valley, it has nine tastefully decorated bedrooms and six apartments (same price, available by the night) plus a swimming pool and tennis courts. Breakfast included. ❻

Quinta da Roseira Lugar da Roseira, 1km west, via N203 towards Darque ℡ 258 941 354 Ⓔ Roseira@solaresdeportugal.pt. Modest but charming, this lovely nineteenth-century converted farmhouse is set among vineyards and fruit trees, and offers a swimming pool and horse-riding. Views over Ponte de Lima are exceptional. Breakfast included. **❺**

Youth hostel

Pousada de Juventude Rua Agostinho José Taveira, 2km southeast of the centre on Viana do Castelo and Barcelos road ℡ 258 943 797, Ⓦ www.pousadasjuventude.pt. Excellent modern hostel with comfortable rooms, a kitchen and living room. Dorm beds €12.50, rooms **❸**

Campsite

Camping Rural e Albergue São Pedro de Arcos, 5km east of town ℡ 258 733 553. The nearest official site to Ponte de Lima; also offers horse-riding.

Eating and drinking

As well as the places picked out below, there are a few inexpensive cafés and restaurants along the riverfront, especially in Praça de Camões, by the old bridge. Local dishes include *arroz de sarabulho com rojões* (rice cooked with blood and pieces of roast pork) and lamprey (usually available from January to March).

To sample *vinho verde* straight from the barrel, try either *Tasca de Isac* in Largo São João 26 (no sign, beside *Tasquinha*) or *Os Telhadinhos* at Rua Do Rosário 24, off the square. An unnamed daytime bar before the Jardins Tematicos offers splendid views of the bridge and town, and a respite from peak-season crowds. At night, popular **bars** include *Cervejaria Rampinha* and *Bar S.A. Galeria*, both at the foot of Rua Formosa, while the liveliest place in town is *Lethes Bar* (till 2am, midnight Sun) on the more northern of the two alleys off Largo das Pereiras.

Açude Centro Naútico de Ponte de Lima ℡ 258 944 158. A sophisticated option across the river and part of the sailing club. Food is good – house specials include monkfish and roast kid – but you're also paying for the attractive surroundings. Expensive.
Alameda Largo da Feira ℡ 258 941 630. A snug cabin, by the bridge on the town side of the river, with splendid views, serving dishes in eipc portions – there's *sarabulho* and *feijoda* for culinary explorers. Closed Wed. Inexpensive.
Brasão Rua Formosa 1 ℡ 258 911 890. A quietly classy reataurant in an old stone building, tucked away in a back-alley. *Arroz de marisco* is delicious, the wine list long. Closed Wed. Moderate.

Encanada Alameda ℡ 258 941 189. Tasty, well-priced dishes, including salmon and trout. The soulless interior is nothing special, but the terrace boasts grandstand views of the river and bridge. Closed Thurs. Moderate.
Parisiense Alameda ℡ 258 942 159. A simple *tasca* with a limited menu but a good view of the river from its first- and second-floor tables. Inexpensive.
São João Largo de São João ℡ 259 941 288. Smarter and a touch more stylish than its neighbours, so a little more expensive – regional dishes cost around €12 – though with a bargain €6.50 lunch menu. Moderate.

Ponte da Barca

From Ponte de Lima, the N203 runs 18km east to **PONTE DA BARCA**, another Minho market town with a bridge so attractive it, too, has been incorporated into the town's name. The Barca part refers to a boat that once ferried pilgrims across the Rio Lima, presumably before the bridge was built. If you ignore the modern suburbs and head to the river, the old town is a treat. The Lima is spanned by a lovely sixteenth-century bridge, beside which there's a superb fortnightly Wednesday market (it alternates with Arcos de Valdevez), spreading out by the river in an almost medieval atmosphere and drawing hundreds of people from outlying hamlets. Just across from the bridge is the

– turn uphill from the river at the fountain – you can buy a park map (€3) although the turismo has just as much information, including leaflets (in Portuguese) detailing numerous walks.

Hotels and pensions

Pensão Dom António Rua Dr. Germano Amorim ☎ 258 521 010, ⓕ 258 521 065. A friendly place at the south end of the riverside road whose rooms – all with TV, some with phones and minibars – are far brighter than the drab exterior suggests. **❸**

Pensão Flôr do Minho Largo da Valeta ☎ 258 525 216. Small and unpretentious *pensão* in a northwestern square, with basic accommodation. No credit cards. **❶**

Isabel Campo do Trasladário ☎ 258 520 380, ⓕ 258 520 389. Small but up-to-date en-suite rooms on the opposite side of the bridge, above a good restaurant. Double-glazing helps reduce traffic noise in the front rooms, which boast the best views. **❸**

Hotel Ribeira Largo des Milagres ☎ 258 515 174, ⓔ hotelribiera@mail.pt. A modern hotel in a rebuilt historic house on the east side of the old bridge – rooms are spacious, the finest with balconies overlooking the river. Breakfast included. No credit cards. **❹**

Residencial Tavares Rua Padre Manuel José da Cunha Brito, off Largo da Lapa ☎ & ⓕ 258 516 253. Dated and rather gloomy, but it is central, all

rooms have TV, and parking is available. Breakfast included. **❸**

Cafés and restaurants

Churrascaria Arco dos Caneiros Rua São João 92 ☎ 258 516 291. Good and cheap, offering hearty pork and *bacalhau* dishes at around €7, plus *tripas à la moda de Porto* (tripe) on Wednesdays and a bargain €5 *ementa turística*. Inexpensive.

Floresta Campo do Trasladário ☎ 258 515 163. Before the bridge, and one of the few options in town for eating al fresco. Regional meats feature, but ask for the unlisted house special of roast *cabrito*. Moderate.

Minho Verde Rua Prof. Dr. Mário Julio Almeida Costa ☎ 258 516 296. Try the grilled octopus or squid with prawns for a €14 splurge in an excellent, stylish eaterie, a short distance away from the turismo. Moderate.

Violeta Rua Prof. Dr. Mário Julio Almeida Costa no phone. No-nonsense bar with scant choice, but usually heaving with lunching locals tucking into the dish of the day – always a good sign. Closed Sun. Inexpensive.

Parque Nacional da Peneda-Gerês

The magnificent **Parque Nacional da Peneda-Gerês** divides into three regions: the central area, based around the spa town of **Caldas do Gerês**, the wilder northern section around the **Serra da Peneda** and the far eastern section of **Serra do Gerês**, which spans the border into Trás-os-Montes. Both mountain ranges remain largely undiscovered by tourism, especially in the eastern reaches of the Serra do Gêres where the spectacular mountain terrain is still remote and often impenetrable.

The roads into the park, and to the main settlements, are pretty decent, but **bus** services are limited during the week and often non-existent at weekends. The main public transport connections are: Melgaço (on the Rio Minho) to Lamas de Mouro and Castro Laboreiro in the north; Arcos de Valdevez to Soajo and Lindoso in the centre; and Braga to Caldas do Gêres and the route east to Montalegre. Once in the park, **walking** is generally the only option for getting around. Waymarked trails and paths cover large areas and there are dozens of hiking opportunities, from short strolls to two- and three-day treks across whole sections of the park.

Apart from in the main centre of Caldas do Gerês, **accommodation** is limited to a handful of *pensões* in other villages and **camping** at designated sites, run either by the park or by private operators. Small groups might find renting one of the ten self-catering *casas abrigos* (converted farmhouses) to be better value. Although occasionally basic, and sometimes even lacking electricity, these houses offer excellent value for money – you'll generally pay around €40 in winter and €70 in summer for a four-bed house, including firewood. They must be booked and partly paid for in advance at the ADERE park office in Ponte da Barca (see p.428) and there is a minimum stay of two nights. The office also lists other park accommodation options, such as apartments or rooms in private *quintas*.

Caldas do Gerês

The national park is centred on the old spa town of **CALDAS DO GERÊS** (usually referred to simply as Gerês), which can be reached easily from Braga on regular buses operated by Empresa Hoteleira do Gerês. The town consists

6

Park practicalities

Information, maps, brochures and walk leaflets for the **Parque Nacional da Peneda-Gerês** (Ⓦwww.adere-pg.pt) can be obtained from the **park offices** in towns surrounding the park, most usefully at Braga (p.390) and Ponte da Barca (p.428), but also in Arcos de Valdevez (p.429) and Montalegre (p.469). **Entrance** to the park is free, and there are also **visitor centres** at the park entrances, in Mezio, on the road in from Arcos de Valdevez (24hr emergency telephone service ☏258 526 751), at Britelo, on the road from Ponte da Barca (☏258 576 160), and in Lamas de Mouro, on the road from Melgaço (see p.438), as well as in Caldas do Gerês (see above). These visitor centres (9.30/10am–12.30pm & 2/2.30–5/6pm; closed Wed) are geared more towards their immediate vicinity, with photographic displays and information on local walks, agriculture, flora and fauna.

An invaluable series of leaflets in English detailing **footpaths** (*trilhos*) are available from the visitor centres and park offices. The official **park map** (€3), on the other hand, shows roads but omits footpaths, making it of little use to walkers, although it may suffice for drivers. A more useful alternative (with footpaths shown) are the "Série M888" 1:25,000 **topographical maps** produced by the Instituto Geográfico do Exército (Ⓦwww.igeoe.pt), which you can buy online from the Institute or from shops in Portugal (see "Basics", p.26). For an excellent **guidebook** to walking in the park (amongst other regions), buy Brian and Eileen Anderson's *Landscapes of Northern Portugal* (Ⓦwww.sunflowerbooks.co.uk/norport.htm).

Organized hikes and other **outdoor activities** in the park are provided by various companies, including PlanAlto (among others) in Campo do Gerês (☏253 311 807 or 917 540 903, Ⓦwww.planalto.com.pt), and Trilhos in Porto (Rua de Belém 94 ☏225 504 604, Ⓦwww.trilhos.pt). You can expect to pay around €12 for a simple guided walk, or more like €40 for day-long kayaking adventure. You might also want to consider hiring a **private guide**, since those approved by the park are an invaluable source of information, assistance and support: the park office in Ponte da Barca retains a list of officially approved guides, with fees of around €12 per person, or €75 for a group (minimum five people) per day.

As far as **equipment** goes, you'll need good boots, warm, waterproof clothes, a compass (beware fog in spring and winter), food and a water bottle – there are plenty of streams but it's good practice to purify water with iodine or chlorine tablets. Also bear in mind that night falls a lot quicker in the mountains than on the coast, temperatures can drop quickly in fog, during rain and at night, and that in winter you're likely to find plenty of snow, which makes following trails a much riskier business. Finally, note that picking flowers and **lighting fires** are forbidden – the Portuguese have an alarming habit of lighting them whenever and wherever they picnic, with terrible consequences in the dry summers.

Life in the Parque Nacional de Peneda-Gerês

The **Parque Nacional de Peneda-Gerês** was established in 1971, not only to protect the region's landscape, archeology and wildlife, but also to safeguard the traditional rural way of life of its inhabitants.

The most common vestiges of **early human occupation** are *antas* (or dolmens), tombs constructed from upright stones that were topped with roof slabs and then covered with soil; unexcavated *anta* mounds are called *mamoas*. Less frequent are *menhirs* (tall standing stones with a phallic appearance that archeologists inevitably ascribe to fertility cults), *cromeleques* (stone circles) and *arte rupestre* (rock art, usually engraved symbols such as concentric circles, little cup-like depressions possibly used for sorting or crushing seeds, boxed crosses and hand axes). The locations of some are marked, very approximately, on the park's maps.

Unique **domestic animals** – primitive breeds long extinct elsewhere like *cachena* and *barrosa* cattle, *bravia* goats, *garrano* ponies and the powerful *Castro Laboreiro* sheepdog – continue to be the mainstay of the local economy. In distant forested corners, remnants of the **wildlife** that once roamed all Europe still survive: wild boar, otters, polecats and some of the continent's last surviving wolves exist side by side with more familiar species like badgers, foxes and roe deer. Birds are numerous in both numbers and breeds, from majestic raptors such as goshawks, eagles and kites to mountain passerines like rock buntings and aquatic dippers, while on the ground lizards and snakes, though common, are rarely seen.

The variety of **vegetation** that gives the park its lush greenness is equally impressive. A total of eighteen plant species – including the Serra do Gerês iris – are found nowhere else on earth. In the valleys oak and laurel line the riverbanks, replaced by holly, birch, pine and juniper at higher elevations.

But while the park boundaries afford some security to the natural wonders, the **traditional communities** are less easily protected. The lure of the city proves irresistibly attractive to many youngsters and village populations throughout the region are slowly shrinking. They are also ageing; in some areas as many as three-quarters of the inhabitants are of pensionable age. Tourism may go some way towards providing incentives for locals to stay in the area and thereby preserving ancient customs and traditions, but with the influx of tourists comes a responsibility to protect the delicate ecosystems and uniqueness of the environment. Time will tell if the right balance can be achieved.

of little more than two roads running either side of a babbling brook and, weekends aside, when Portuguese picnickers arrive en masse, it's a relaxed base from which to explore. "The Spa of Gerês" became fashionable in the early years of the nineteenth century – an epoch convincingly evoked by a row of grand period hotels (some now in a sorry state) along the sedate main Avenida Manuel Francisco da Costa. Considerable recent development has somewhat marred the town's nostalgic charm, but it's not all bad and you'll probably appreciate the public outdoor swimming pool (reached through the park), tennis courts, boating lake and countless cafés.

Practicalities

Buses stop at two stops on the main drag, Avenida Manuel Francisco da Costa, which is also where you can catch local buses to Rio Caldo. Pick up information either at the **turismo** (Mon–Sat 9.30am–12.30pm & 2.30–6pm, Sun 9.30am–12.30pm; ☎253 391 133), at the top end of the main avenue, or at the national park office just around the corner (Mon, Tues & Thurs–Sun 9.30/10am–12.30pm & 2/2.30–5/6pm; ☎253 390 110).

△ Grain stores, Lindoso

your footsteps to the sign, continue around the mountain in an anticlockwise direction, following the signs back to Gerês.

South to Rio Caldo and São Bento da Porta Aberta

The village of **RIO CALDO**, 8km south of Caldas do Gerês, lies on the west bank of the Barragem da Caniçada; change here for buses from Caldas to São Bento. The reservoir is a watersports centre for windsurfing and waterskiing, and the swimming is fine, too. The English-run AML (☎253 391 740 or ☎968 021 142, ⓦwww.aguamontanha.com) rents out mountain bikes, canoes (€4/hr), and motorboats (€18/hr). It also maintains three stone houses, which are available by the night (although often booked up for weekly stints); they sleep two to six and all have balconies overlooking the lake (❹ or ❻).

Otherwise, there's plenty of **accommodation** along the edge of the reservoir, as well as along the road to Caldas do Gerês – a good bet is the *Pensão Pontes do Rio Caldo* (☎253 391 540, ⓕ253 391 195; includes breakfast, no credit cards; ❷), a stone building with a garden bar at the road junction with the bridges. More modern, but in an unbeatable reservoir location, is the friendly *Casa Beira Rio* (☎253 391 197; includes breakfast, no credit cards; ❷), on the north side of the bridge to Gerês, where rooms have bathrooms and TVs. Alternatively, you could drive (or catch a bus) uphill towards Cerdrinhas to the *Pousada de São Bento* (☎253 647 190, ⓦwww.pousadas.pt; includes breakfast; ❼), in a superb position overlooking the reservoir from the east. This timber-beamed former hunting lodge has its own swimming pool and a superb restaurant, with great views.

Three kilometres northwest of Rio Caldo, in the Covide direction, **SÃO BENTO DA PORTA ABERTA** is a small village high above the reservoir, commanding more excellent views. Its austere sanctuary is a favourite spot with pilgrims, who gather here at the beginning of July and again a month later (and on most Sundays throughout the year) – at such times the traffic makes it a place best avoided. The former monastery, hidden under an ugly modern facade, is now the *Estalagem de São Bento da Porta Aberta* (☎253 391 106, ⓕ253 391 117; includes breakfast; ❸), a little severe inside but comfortable nevertheless and with a good restaurant. Cheaper **rooms** may be available in the *Restaurante Mira Serra* (☎253 391 362; includes breakfast, no credit cards; ❷) at the western end of the village, and at the charming turn-of-the-century *Pensão São José*, halfway between São Bento and Rio Caldo (☎253 391 120; includes breakfast, no credit cards; ❷).

The northern section: Serra da Peneda

Thanks mainly to the limited public transport and scant accommodation, the wild **Serra da Peneda**, in the north of the park, sees far fewer tourists than the central zone, and this sense of isolation can be an advantage. You'll often have the prehistoric sites, steep forested valleys, and exposed, wind-blown *planaltos* dotted with weird rock formations entirely to yourself – not to mention the marvellous views. Weekday **buses** to Lamas de Mouro and Castro Laboreiro leave from Melgaço on the Rio Minho (see p.445 for details), returning at around 6.30pm.

Lamas de Mouro

There's a national park visitor centre (Mon, Tues & Thurs–Sun 9.30/10am–12.30pm & 2/2.30–5/6pm; ☎251 465 563) in the hamlet of **LAMAS DE MOURO**, 19km southeast of Melgaço. However, the only accommodation is at the beautifully situated **campsite** (℡251 465 129; ring ahead in winter), just inside the park, past the visitor centre, which has hot showers, a bar, a nearby natural pool for swimming and a restaurant. There's also a good **guide** here, who covers the Trilho da Peneda circuit northwest of Peneda village (see below, access from Lamas by jeep), in addition to several other park trails. For food, the *Churrasqueiria Vidoeiro* (no phone) makes up for above-average prices with generous portions.

Castro Laboreiro

The left-hand fork at Lamas leads 8km up to the ancient village of **CASTRO LABOREIRO**, best known for the breed of mountain dog to which it gives its name. Once used to protect sheep from marauding wolves, the breed has become rare as wolf numbers have declined and is now hardly seen outside the region. Before the arrival of tourism, the village was practically deserted every summer, when the pastoral community would leave to find greener fields and build *brandas* (temporary homes with stone walls and "soft" roofs made of branches and twigs) elsewhere for the warmer months, returning in winter to their *inverneiras* (winter houses) in Laboreiro. To reach the ruins of the castle, you have a steep twenty-minute walk: left at the roundabout on the other side of the village, then left up a path where the road drops to the right, past a large rock known as the *Tartaruga* (Tortoise), and through heather and between boulders, with sheer drops to each side and steps hacked out of the rock face. The village itself is nothing special but there are superb walks in the area, especially to the east and south. The *Trilho Castrejo* leaflet (in Portuguese), available from the turismo in Melgaço, is helpful here.

For budget **accommodation** the *Miradouro do Castelo* (℡251 465 465; includes breakfast; ❷) at the far end of the village is a good choice, overlooking a magnificent valley. For views from balconies, though, you'll need to stay at the smarter, modern *Albergaria Miracastro* (℡251 460 020, ⓦwww.miracastro. com; includes breakfast; ❸) opposite. You'll also find good, modern rooms plus an apartment at *Casa São José* (℡251 465 134; ❶), 500m out on the Lamas road. Both the *Miradouro do Castelo* and *Albergaria Miracastro* have good **restaurants**, serving solid mountain food such as *cabrito serrano* (mountain kid goat).

Peneda

Nine kilometres south of Lamas de Mouro, along a stunning forested valley topped on either side with vertiginous boulders, you arrive at the small village of **PENEDA**, most famous for its **Santuário da Nossa Senhora da Peneda**, a miniature version of the pilgrimage church at Bom Jesus near Braga. It's full of devotees at the beginning of September (especially on September 7 and 8), but pretty much deserted for the rest of the year. The original focus of adoration was a curious stone which natural forces had sculpted into the form of a woman, who some said was pregnant. Come Christianity, the cult and its stone was adopted as the Virgin Mary and was duly incorporated into the late eighteenth-century church. There she remained until the 1930s, when somebody stole her; a gaudy plastic replacement now stands in place of the original.

The village itself has cafés and religious artefact shops clustered around the main square. There are good **rooms** in a modern house 100m before Peneda: contact Isolina Domingues Fernandes at the *Casa de Artigos Religiosos*, on the corner of the main square (℡251 465 139; no credit cards; ❷). Otherwise, ask at *Café Perada* in the main square (℡251 465 568 or 251 465 275; no credit cards; ❷), whose owner has basic rooms usually used by pilgrims. There's also a classy *turismo rural* property, the *Anjo da Guarda* (no phone; ❹), in the main square.

and two spacious suites, all with good views, plus a pool. *Lindo Verde*, 1km east of Lindoso on the road to Spain (☏258 578 010, ⓕ258 578 011; ❷), has eight modern rooms with bathrooms over its restaurant.

Parada

PARADA, clinging to the hillside 3km west of Lindoso, is perhaps an even more attractive place, with two clusters of *espigueiros* and vines draped over its cobbled streets. There's a superb circular walk, the Trilho do Penedo do Encanto (4km, 2hr), which heads uphill behind the village passing age-old houses and forests of chestnut and cork. For some of the way up, it follows a rocky stream bed, remarkable for the ruts worn into the stones over the centuries by ox carts. After about 1km, with forest plunging down to your right, look for a rusty metal gate straight in front of you, and a wall to your right covered with bundles of branches. Hop over the wall some 40m before the gate, and walk 30m straight on through the bushes. The large flat boulders in the clearing (not visible from the track) are the **Peneda do Encanto** (the "enchanted rocks"), of which the largest is covered with numerous (but faint) Bronze Age engravings. Mainly concentric circles and circular depressions, these are most visible about two hours before sunset, when the shadows are long. No one knows for sure what they represent, though similar designs can be found elsewhere in Minho and in Trás-os-Montes. Further up, the track loses itself in an exposed rocky area with superb views. To descend back to Parada, hug the forest wall to your right.

    Accommodation is limited to *Café Mó* (☏258 576 150; no credit cards; ❶), on the main road 1km west of Parada, which has six modern but musty rooms with ancient TVs, shared bathrooms, and a macho ambience in the bar, though a friendly owner. Nearby is a natural pool for swimming, popular with local kids.

The eastern section: Serra do Gerês

The eastern section of the park really allows you to get off the beaten track, though you'll have to be prepared to tackle some long walks or tricky driving conditions. Easiest access is via Caldas do Gerês to Ermida and on to Cabril. From Cabril, drivers and hikers can move on to Paradela, Outeiro, Paredes do Rio and Pitões das Júnias, any of which would make an ideal base for a leisurely exploration of this little-known corner of the Minho. There's no public transport along this route, and infrequent traffic, but the gorgeous countryside is well suited for walking, and people are friendly. Alternatively, from Cabril or Paradela you can strike for Montalegre (see p.469), which provides a suitably remote and dramatic link with the Trás-os-Montes region. Daily buses from Braga pass through Venda Nova to Montalegre and Chaves, passing the hydroelectric plant of Pisões in this otherwise very remote region. The appeal lies as much in the road there as in the place itself. Bumpy and narrow, it makes for one of those journeys that seem to trigger madness in bus drivers, simultaneously delighting and terrifying unaccustomed passengers.

Ermida to Cabril

Despite its proximity to Caldas do Gerês (a two- to three-hour walk away), the farming community of **ERMIDA** has an air of true isolation about it – be warned that driving beyond the village involves some extremely steep sections, in parts badly pitted by floods. Driving in or after heavy rain is unwise without a four-wheel drive. However, if you're looking for a quiet hiking base, this is a good choice, with a scattering of *dormidas*, accommodation and food at *Casa do Criado* (T 253 391 390; includes breakfast; no credit cards; ❷), an orchard to camp in and a couple of cafés.

East of Ermida, along a dirt-track, you'll pass a group of small waterfalls – paradise to swim in – and cross a sturdy but unsafe-looking bridge before coming to the farming hamlet of **FAFIÃO**. A restaurant here, *Retiro do Gerês*, has rooms (T 253 659 860; no credit cards; ❶). Beyond, the countryside becomes more fertile, terraced with vines and maize, the road winding down to another hamlet, **PINCÃES**, and through it (turn right at the end of the houses) to the slightly larger village of Cabril.

A lovely, isolated place, sat on the Rio Cabril and surrounded on all sides by mountains, **CABRIL** flaunts odd attempts at modernity, although its centre is still sauntered through by oxen, goats and sheep. Parts of the locality have been submerged because of the Salamonde dam and, consequently, the old bridge is half under water, making for great swimming through the bridge arch. There's a **campsite**, *Outeiro Alto* (T 253 659 860), 1km out on the Pincães road, which is fine provided it's not too busy – there are only two toilets. It also rents out bicycles and canoes and offers horse-riding. Alternatively, the *Cafe Snack-Bar* (T 253 659 752; no credit cards; ❶) on the Paradela road has a few basic rooms. You can get a good **meal** at the *Restaurante Ponte Novo* (no phone) beside the bridge, which serves a hearty meat stew, or at the *Café 1º de Maio* (no phone) further up the road, which serves snacks and more substantial food given advance warning.

Paradela to Pitões de Júnias

The signposted path from Cabril to Paradela – around 23km – is stunningly dramatic, winding along the river valley through the handsome villages of Sir-vozelo, Lapela and Xertola. At **PARADELA**, a particularly attractive mountain village whose cobbled streets are lined with vines, you're rewarded by fine views over the dam and mountains from a cluster of cafés and hotels. The mod-ern *Restaurant Flôr do Rio* (T 276 566 122; includes breakfast; no credit cards; ❷) has ten rooms, most with views, bathrooms and TVs. More characterful, and set in shaded gardens with views, *Pensão Pousadinha* (T 276 566 165; no credit cards; ❷), 200 metres down the road to Cabril, has the feel of an English B&B, with some self-contained rooms and excellent breakfasts included in the rates. The *pensão* is also the base for horse-riding trips run by Trote Gerês (T 253 659 860). A further 100m downhill is the friendly *Hospedaria Restaurante Dom Dinis* (T 276 566 253; no credit cards; breakfast included; ❷), where all rooms have views, TVs, showers and heating. The homely restaurant here is good, too, with Barrosã specialities like veal and *cozido* in winter.

The small village of **OUTEIRO**, a charming cluster or roofs 4km north of Paradela, is home to a bizarre seventeenth-century twin-towered church with a heavily decorated facade. Accommodation is at the upmarket *Estalagem Vista Bela* (T 276 560 120, Ⓦ www.estalagemvistabela.co.pt; includes breakfast; Visa only; ❺), with sweeping views over the dam, and good meals (mains around €12) – try the veal or roast goat for dinner.

PAREDES DO RIO, 3km east, is the next stop, notable for the excellent *Hospedaria Rocha* (T 276 566 147; breakfast included; no credit cards; ❷). All rooms have bathrooms, but the restaurant is the main draw, cooking meat from its own farm. Main dishes cost around €7.50: try the duck, or *cabidela de frango* – chicken cooked with blood and rice – or, in winter, go for the warming *feijoada* or *cozido*. They can also arrange four- to six-hour **walking trips** to Pitões de Júnias for the price of a picnic or lend photocopies of maps with the route marked on. On the hill above the *hospedaria* is the rustic *Casa da Travessa*

(☎276 566 121; no credit cards; ❸), which has only two rooms, but also offers bikes if your legs are up to it, horse-riding and fishing.

PITÕES DE JÚNIAS, 10km northwest, is set in one of the remotest corners of Portugal, close to the Spanish border. This is lovely walking country, with a ruined monastery and waterfall nearby, and the jagged peaks (*pitões*) of Gerês tantalizingly close to the west. The monastery was founded in the ninth century, and the following century became part of the Cistercian Order; the Romanesque facade and most of the walls still stand. There's modern family-run **accommodation** at the *Casa do Preto* (☎276 566 158; no credit cards; ❶), which also houses one of Pitões' two excellent restaurants, the other being the *Pitões do Gerês*.

Venda Nova

The village of **VENDA NOVA** has some lovely walks in the vicinity and bracing swimming in the Barragem da Venda Nova. There are two rather pricey **accommodation** options: the better is the classy *Estalagem do Morgado*, 4km to the west, almost on an island in the reservoir at Lugar de Padrões (☎253 659 906, www.hotelmorgado.com; includes breakfast; ❻), with a swimming pool, tennis courts, water sports marina and shaded gardens. It also has lakeside cottages that sleep four and cost €220 a night. Cheaper is the *Motel São Cristóvão* (☎253 659 387; ❸), an ugly modern building at the corner of the reservoir, 1km beyond Venda Nova at the junction to Salto, which also has tennis courts and rents out boats.

Travel details

Trains

Barcelos to: Valença do Minho (7 daily; 1hr 15min–1hr 50min); Viana do Castelo (11–12 daily; 30–40min).

Braga to: Nine – change for Viana and Valença (12–15 daily; 12–28min); Porto (11–14 daily, some change at Nine; 1hr–1hr 45min).

Caminha to: Valença do Minho (7–8 daily; 20–40min); Viana do Castelo (6–8 daily; 20–40min).

Guimarães to: Porto (hourly; 1hr 10min).

Valença do Minho to: Afife (4–6 daily; 55min); Barcelos (7–8 daily; 1hr 15min–2hr); Caminha (6–8 daily; 20–45min); Nine – change for Braga (5–7 daily; 2hr 20min); Vigo, Spain (3 daily; 1hr 10min; connections to Santiago de Compostela and La Coruña); Vila Nova de Cerveira (6–8 daily; 12–18min); Vila Praia de Âncora (6–7 daily; 20min–1hr).

Viana do Castelo to: Afife (4 daily; 20min); Barcelos (12 daily; 25–45min); Caminha (7–8 daily; 20–40min); Porto (10–12 daily; 1hr 36min–2hr); Vila Nova de Cerveira (7 daily; 30min–1hr); Vila Praia de Âncora (7 daily; 15–35min).

Vila Nova de Cerveira to: Valença do Minho (6–8 daily; 12–18min); Viana do Castelo (6–7 daily; 30min–1hr).

Buses

Arcos de Valdevez to: Braga (10 daily; 1hr 15min); Lindoso (Mon–Fri 1–3 daily; 30min–1hr); Monção (4–6 daily; 45mins); Ponte de Lima (5–8 daily; 50min); Porto (2–4 daily; 2hr); Soajo (Mon–Fri 1–3 daily; 30min); Viana do Castelo (5–8 daily; 1hr 45min).

Barcelos to: Braga (Mon–Fri every 30min, Sat & Sun hourly; 50min); Chaves (Mon–Fri 13 daily, Sat & Sun 3–6 daily; 6hr); Ponte de Lima (Mon–Fri 8 daily, 1–2 at weekends; 40–55min); Porto (Mon–Sat 9–12 daily, Sun 1–2 daily; 1hr 45min).

Braga to: Arcos de Valdevez (10–12 daily; 1hr 30min); Barcelos (Mon–Fri every 30min, Sat & Sun hourly; 30–50min); Bragança via Porto (3–5 daily; 6hr); Cabaceiras de Basto (4–5 daily; 1hr 45min); Caldas do Gerês (Mon–Fri hourly, Sat & Sun 8–10 daily; 1hr 30min); Campo do Gerês (3–7 daily; 1hr 30min); Cerdeirinhas (5–9 daily; 45min); Chaves (4 daily; 4hr); Coimbra (6 daily; 2hr 40min); Covide (3–4 daily; 1hr 10min); Guimarães (every 30 min; 30min–1hr); Leiria (6–9 daily; 4hr 5min); Lisbon (8–11 daily; 5hr 30min); Monção (3–5 daily; 2hr 20min); Montalegre (4–7 daily; 2hr 40min); Pisões (4–5 daily; 2hr 15min); Ponte da Barca (4 daily;

1hr 15min); Ponte de Lima (Mon–Fri 9 daily, Sat 5 daily, Sun 1 daily; 1hr); Porto (every 30min; 1hr 10min); Póvoa do Lanhoso (5–7 daily; 35min); Póvoa do Varzim (11 daily; 1hr 25min); Terras do Bouro (3–7 daily; 50min); Venda Nova (5–10 daily; 1hr 50min); Viana do Castelo (4–10 daily; 1hr 40min).

Caldas do Gerês to: Braga (6–10 daily; 1hr 30min); Rio Caldo (4-7 daily; 25m).

Campo do Gerês to: Braga (3–6 daily; 1hr 20min).

Guimarães to: Braga (every 30 mins; 30min–1hr); Cabeceiras de Basto (6–8 daily; 1hr 15min); Lisbon (4–6 daily; 5hr 30min–6hr); Mondim de Basto (2 daily; 1hr 5min); Porto (6–8 daily; 2hr 30min–3hr); Vila Real (Mon–Fri 5–7 daily, Sat & Sun 1–3 daily; 1hr 30min).

Melgaço to: Castro Laboreiro (Mon–Fri 1 daily; 1hr); Coimbra (1–3 daily; 5hr); Lamas de Mouro (Mon–Fri 1 daily; 40min); Lisbon (1–3 daily; 6hr); Monção (Mon–Fri 5 daily, Sat & Sun 1 daily; 40min); Porto (1–3 daily; 3hr); São Gregório (Mon–Fri 3 daily; 30min).

Monção to: Braga (3–6 daily; 1hr 45min); Melgaço (Mon–Fri 5 daily, Sat & Sun 1 daily; 40min); Paredes de Coura (Mon–Fri 1 daily; 50m); Porto Mon–Fri 3 daily; 2h 30m); Valença do Minho (10 daily; 20min); Viana do Castelo (5 daily; 1hr 20min).

Ponte da Barca to: Arcos de Valdevez (hourly; 15min); Braga (14 daily; 1hr); Lindoso (2 daily; 45min); Ponte de Lima (3–4 daily; 20–30min); Viana do Castelo (6–8 daily; 1hr 30min).

Ponte de Lima to: Arcos de Valdevez (5–8 daily; 50min); Barcelos (Mon–Fri 8 daily, 1–2 daily at weekends; 40–55min); Braga (Mon–Fri 10 daily, Sat 6, Sun 3; 1hr); Paredes de Coura (2–5 daily; 1hr 20min); Ponte de Barca (3–4 daily; 20–30min); Porto (7 daily; 2hr); Valença (1 daily; 1hr); Viana do Castelo (Mon–Fri 21 daily, Sat & Sun 9 daily; 50min).

Valença do Minho to: Lisbon (4 daily; 6hr 30min); Melgaço (8 daily; 40min); Monçao (10 daily; 20min); Ponte de Lima (1 daily; 1hr); Porto (7 daily; 2hr 30min); Viana do Castelo via Caminha (7 daily; 1 hr); Vila Nova de Cerveira (6 daily; 15min); to Spain: Sat to Vigo/Santiago (2hr/4hr 15min); Tues, Thurs and Fri via Monção and Melgaço for Ponte Barxas.

Viana do Castelo to: Afife (5–14 daily; 15min); Arcos de Valdevez (3–7 daily; 1hr 50min); Braga (4–8 daily; 1hr 40min); Caminha (Mon–Fri 13 daily, Sat & Sun 5 daily; 35min); Esposende (Mon–Sat 7–13 daily, Sun 4 daily; 40min); Lisbon (2 daily; 6hr); Moledo do Minho (Mon–Fri 13 daily, Sat & Sun 5 daily; 30min); Ponte da Barca (6–8 daily; 1hr 30min); Ponte de Lima (Mon–Fri 21 daily, Sat & Sun 7 daily; 50min); Porto (Mon–Sat 10–14 daily, Sun 4 daily; 2hr 5min); Póvoa de Varzim (Mon–Sat 10–15 daily, Sun 4 daily; 1hr 5min); Vila do Conde (Mon–Sat 7–13 daily, Sun 4 daily; 1hr 40min); Vila Praia de Âncora (Mon–Fri 13 daily, Sat & Sun 5 daily; 30min).

Trás-os-Montes

Fast daily bus services from Porto run to the main towns of Vila Real, Chaves, Mirandela and Bragança; while Chaves can also be reached by daily buses from Braga in the Minho (via the Peneda-Gerês national park). However, the finest approach to the region by public transport is along the Douro train line (from Porto to Pocinho), off which branch two narrow-gauge rail lines. At Peso da Régua, 108km east of Porto, the **Corgo train line** – one of the country's joys – cuts north through a spectacular winding gorge to Vila Real. Although the trains are modern, the landscape is centuries old, with every last vertiginous inch of terrace given over to vine cultivation. In amongst it all, tiny white villages somehow cling to the hillsides, oblivious to the small trains rattling past. Around 38km further along the Douro line, the **Tua train line**, from Tua to Mirandela, affords equally spectacular scenery.

The routes between the main towns apart, **travel within the region** can be a slow business, as minor roads often meander along the contours, while local buses generally operate on weekdays only, being aimed at local schoolchildren as much as paying customers.

Vila Real and around

VILA REAL is the one break from the pastoralism of the beautiful Rio Corgo, a tributary of the Douro. The name means "Royal Town" and, as home to the largest concentration of nobility outside Lisbon, it was once very apt, although today it has more of an industrial role, as well as being the home of the University of Trás-os-Montes. Founded and named by Dom Dinis in 1829, its setting is magnificent, with the twin mountain ranges of Marão and Alvão (the so-called "Gateway to Trás-os-Montes") forming a natural amphitheatre behind the town. Walkers may well want to make Vila Real a base for an exploration of these ranges, while other visitors concentrate on the Roman site at **Panóias** and the **Solar de Mateus** – the country house featured on the Mateus Rosé wine label. Compared with the somnolent villages further north and east, Vila Real is actually quite a lively place – especially during the major **festivals** of Santo António (June 13–21) and São Pedro (June 28–29), when you should book your accommodation well in advance. Other *feiras* include those of São Brás (February 3) and Santa Luzia (December 13), and there's also a procession for Corpus Deus on June 3. The *feiras* are the best time to buy the distinctive pewter-grey earthenware crockery made in the nearby village of Bisalhães.

The Town

The old quarter of Vila Real is built on a promontory above the confluence of the Corgo and Cabril rivers, with the main avenue running down its spine; the view from the fourteenth-century **Capela de São Brás** at its southern end is not one for vertigo sufferers. Despite its noble heritage, there's little of architectural merit in town, save the turismo building – formerly the palace of the Marquês of Vila Real, and fronted by four Manueline windows – and the **Sé**, over the way, which has modern stained-glass windows and a simple, fifteenth-century interior. At the bottom of the hill near the Câmara Municipal, a plaque on the wall of the café opposite commemorates the **birthplace of Diogo Cão**, who discovered the mouth of the Congo River in 1482. Otherwise, there's only the small **Museu de Arqueologia e Numismática** on Rua do Rossio (Tues–Fri 10am–12.30pm & 2.30–6.30pm, Sat & Sun 2.30–6.30pm;

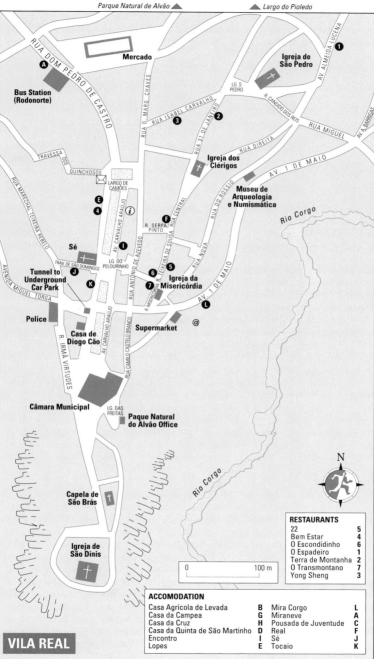

RESTAURANTS

22	5
Bem Estar	4
O Escondidinho	6
O Espadeiro	1
Terra de Montanha	2
O Transmontano	7
Yong Sheng	3

ACCOMODATION

Casa Agrícola de Levada	**B**	Mira Corgo	**L**
Casa da Campea	**G**	Miraneve	**A**
Casa da Cruz	**H**	Pousada de Juventude	**C**
Casa da Quinta de São Martinho	**D**	Real	**F**
Encontro	**I**	Sé	**J**
Lopes	**E**	Tocaio	**K**

VILA REAL

free) to delay you, featuring a selection of Neolithic stone engravings from the Parque Natural do Alvão and a numismatic collection that contains Roman and Visigothic coins.

Around town

You can see both sites outside town by bus, with regular weekday services along the Sabrosa road to the east. Santos buses run from the station on Travessa dos Quinchosos to **Mateus**, 4km east of Vila Real (Mon–Fri 9 daily) – there's only a solitary midday bus at weekends and it doesn't return to Vila Real. The same weekday service will also get you to **Panóias**, 4km further east of Mateus and signposted a few hundred metres north of the road. There are only two return buses to Vila Real, the last of which leaves Sabrosa at 3.25pm, passing Panóias about fifteen minutes later; wait by the main road below the site.

Solar de Mateus

The **Solar de Mateus** (signposted "Palácio de Mateus") was described by Sacheverell Sitwell as "the most typical and the most fantastic country house in Portugal". It's certainly the most familiar, being reproduced on each bottle of Mateus Rosé, one of Portugal's major wine exports. The facade fits in well enough with the wine's soft-focus image, its twin wings "advancing lobster-like", as Sitwell put it, across a formal lake. The architect is unknown, though most authorities attribute it to the Italian, Nicolau Nasoni, who built the landmark Clérigos church in Porto. The palace is dated to around 1740 – the heyday of Portuguese Baroque.

Ticket prices include a thirty-minute **tour of the interior** (daily: June–Sept 9am–7.30pm; Oct & March–May 9am–1pm & 2–6pm; Nov–Feb 10am–1pm & 2–5pm; house and gardens €6.25, gardens only €3.50; ☎259 323 121), which are popular – it's best to call in advance to reserve a place. Although there are no special treasures, the building is an enjoyable evocation of its period, full of aristocratic portraits and rural scenes. The **gardens**, too, are a delight, the spectacular box avenue forming an impressive tunnel about 50m long, and there's a small gift shop and café in the grounds. On summer weekends (mid-May to early September) classical **concerts** are held here, part of the work of the foundation which administers the house and which also sponsors musical workshops, seminars and even an annual literary award for Portuguese writers. Performances usually begin late (9–10pm), so you'll need your own transport.

Panóias

The Roman site of **Panóias** (Tues 2–5pm, Wed–Sun 9am–12.30pm & 2–5pm; €1.50 with a guided tour and brochure, free Sun morning) is the sole remnant of the once powerful settlement of Vila de Constantim de Panoyas. First appearances aren't encouraging, consisting of a wire fence enclosing a few boulders with odd-shaped cavities, though the site has a long history, initially as the location of the temple of a particularly bloody pre-Roman cult, later adopted by the Romans and dedicated to Serapis (a cult of Egyptian origin), and possibly also to Jupiter. The rickety viewing tower (closed at the time of writing) at the top end gives you a good view of the three coffin-shaped **sacrificial cavities** on the largest boulder, which used to have a filter system for the blood and viscera created by the offerings. The much-eroded inscriptions to this effect on nearby boulders are in a strange mixture of Greek and Latin, lending weight to the theory that the temple may have been constructed well before the Romans arrived.

Practicalities

Vila Real is the hub of Trás-os-Montes' regional transport with frequent **buses** leaving to all major destinations. Rodonorte services to Amarante, Braga, Bragança, Chaves, Coimbra, Guimarães, Porto, Peso da Régua and Viseu run from the bus station on Rua Dom Pedro de Castro, just north of the centre. The Santos bus terminal on Travessa dos Quinchosos has services eastwards to Mirandela, Miranda do Douro and Torre de Moncorvo; Auto-Viação do Tâmega is also based here, with regular services to Chaves and Peso da Régua. The Corgo line **train station** is 500m east of the centre, on the opposite bank of the river; to reach the town centre, follow the road into town, over the bridge, and turn left. There's no ticket office, but you can pay on the train for the daily service to Peso da Régua, with the last train leaving at 7.10pm. Save for the one-way system around Avenida Carvalho Araújo, driving should be fairly straightforward. There's a large underground **car park** at the southern end of the avenue, where it meets the eastern end of Avenida Miguel Torga.

The central **turismo**, Avenida Carvalho Araújo 94 (June–Sept Mon–Fri 9.30am–6pm, Sat & Sun 9.30am–12.30pm & 2–6pm; Oct–May Mon–Sat 9.30am–12.30pm & 2–6pm; ☎259 322 819, ⓦwww.rtsmarao.pt), can help with local bus timetables, while anyone planning a visit to the Parque Natural do Alvão should also head for the **park headquarters** on Largo das Freitas behind the Camâra Municipal (Mon–Fri 9am–12.30pm & 2–5.30pm; ☎259 302 830, ☎259 302 831, ⓦwww.icn.pt).

Accommodation

The pick of the town's accommodation is reviewed below but be warned, most of it is underwhelming and the more basic places can get distinctly chilly and damp in winter, and unbearably hot in summer. For directions on how to get to the various *turismo rural* properties in the area, which on the whole provide much nicer accommodation, consult the turismo.

In town

Residencial Encontro Av. Carvalho Araújo 76–78 ☎259 322 532. Family-run place with a mixed bag of rooms above a restaurant, which means it can be a bit noisy at night. Breakfast included. No credit cards. ❸

Residencial Lopes Av. Carvalho Araújo 91 ☎259 324 690. Tucked away off the main road, a corridor-full of spotless, high-ceilinged old rooms, some of which have modern bathrooms and good views of the hills. Especially good value for single travellers. Breakfast included. No credit cards. ❷

Hotel Mira Corgo Av. 1 de Maio 76–78 ☎259 325 001, ⓔmiracorgo@mail.telepac.pt. Vila Real's swankiest hotel is an ugly modern building but its rooms overlook the stepped terraces of the Rio Corgo, far below, and there's an indoor swimming pool and solarium. There's also a disco, guaranteed to disturb many a peaceful night, as well as secure parking. Breakfast included. ❹

Hotel Miraneve Rua Dom Pedro de Castro ☎259 323 153 ⓔreservas.miraneve@clix.pt. Modern functional comforts with secure parking, although if you're looking for a regular hotel, this is more expensive than the *Mira Corgo* and lacks a pool. Breakfast included. ❺

Residencial Real Rua Serpa Pinto ☎259 325 879, ⓕ259 324 613. Clean, cool and fresh rooms with white walls and varnished wooden floors, sited above the *pastelaria* of the same name. Breakfast included. No credit cards. ❸

Residencial da Sé Trav. de São Domingos 19–23 ☎259 324 575. Promises more than it delivers, with a welcoming pine stairway but rather musty en-suite rooms. It's nevertheless very popular with French and German tourists in summer, when you'd be better off booking ahead. Breakfast included. ❸

Hotel Tocaio Av. Carvalho Araújo 45–55 ☎259 371 675. Large and rather dark 1960s hotel, past its prime despite the international flags flapping outside. All rooms come with a private bathroom and clunky old telephone, while the slightly kitsch reception area is decked out with red carpets and leather armchairs. Breakfast included. ❸

Outside town

Casa Agrícola da Levada Timpeira, 2km northeast ☏259 322 190, ⓦwww.casadalevada.com. Take the Mateus bus or follow Avenida 1 de Maio towards Bragança for 2km until the road descends towards a stone bridge; on the left you'll see this impressive farmhouse set in its own grounds. Rooms are fairly modest in comparison to the grand exterior, with dark wood furniture, white bed linen and small shuttered windows. The owners breed wild boar and produce their own sausages and honey. Breakfast included. ④

Casa da Campeã 10km west, 2km before Campeã, just off the IP4 ☏259 979 604, ⓔquality.vilareal@mail.telepac.pt. Modern chalet-cum-motel set-up with a pool and good restaurant, which warrants inclusion for the activities offered in the nearby Vale da Campeã (Serra do Marão), including rafting, paragliding, bungee jumping and hiking. Breakfast included. ③

Casa da Cruz Campeã, 12km west, signposted along the road to Mondim de Basto ☏259 979 422 ⓔcasadacruz@mail.telepac.pt. Six simple rooms with lovely carved beds at this eighteenth-century granite farmhouse, overlooking the Vale de Campeã. There's a rustic sitting room and free use of the kitchen, although the highlight is the secluded swimming pool. Fishing and cycling trips can be arranged. Breakfast included. No credit cards. ③

Casa da Quinta de São Martinho Mateus, 4km east, 300m from Solar de Mateus ☏259 323 986, ⓔquinta.s.martinho@clix.pt. Idyllic seventeenth-century granite country house swathed in ivy and containing a comfortable clutter of old and new furniture. In addition to the two bedrooms there are also two self-contained apartments (sleeping up to four) in the garden, complete with spiral staircase and exposed stone walls. Fringe benefits include a secluded pool, and port wine tasting in the bar (the friendly proprietor being president of the Douro wine trail). Breakfast included. ⑤, apartments ⑦

Youth hostel

Pousada de Juventude Av. Dr. Manuel Cardona, 1km northeast of the centre ☏259 373 193, ⓦww.pousadasjuventude.pt. Modern hostel with four private en-suite rooms and fourteen four-bed dorms, as well a kitchen and common room. Dorm beds €10, rooms ②.

Campsite

Parque de Campismo 700m northeast of the centre ☏259 324 724. There's adequate shade at this site, and a swimming pool, but arrive early if you want a riverside pitch. Follow Av. 1 de Maio and its continuations Av. Aureliano Barrigas and Rua Dr. Manuel Cardona, a 15min walk; if you're coming from the train station, turn right after crossing the bridge.

Eating, drinking and nightlife

For inexpensive local meals, try any of the **cafés** in the streets behind the turismo. Local dishes include roast kid goat and veal, *cozido à portuguesa*, and *tripas aos molhos* ("sheaves" of tripe, no less). For those with a sweeter tooth, **pastries** to ask for are *pastéis de Santa Clara* (stuffed with very sweet egg goo), *toucinho do céu* ("heavenly bacon", because it supposedly looks like it) and *tigelinhas de laranja* ("orange bowls"). Also worth a try is the delicious *nata do céu*, a very sweet, cheesecake-like dessert, drizzled with a sugary egg mixture. There's a weekday **market** opposite the Rodonorte bus station, a **supermarket** hidden in the shopping centre next to *Hotel Mira Corgo* on Avenida 1 de Maio, and a good **wine shop** on Largo de Pelourinho.

The liveliest nightspots are the **café-bars** along Largo do Pelourinho, although you'll have to arrive early if you're after a pavement seat. For a less family-orientated atmosphere, head to the numerous late-night drinking dens on Largo do Pioledo such as *Kopos* and *Ex-bar*, while those in search of a more mature vibe should head to *Minister*, the disco in *Hotel Mira Corgo*.

Bem Estar Av. Carvalho Araújo ☏259 322 343. Family-run place offering good value, no-nonsense plates of steak, as well as *bacalhau* fried with chips and onions. No credit cards. Moderate.

O Escondidinho Rua Teixeira de Sousa 7 ☏259 325 535. Portugese meat and fish dishes as well as a range of pastas are served at this perennially popular wood-panelled eaterie. The outdoor tables fill quickly in summer with both tourists and locals, although it's largely the latter who tuck into the chef's special tripe. Moderate.

△ Wine grower, Douro valley

O Espadeiro Av. Almeida Lucena ☎ 259 322 302. Highly renowned regional restaurant that's been going for over 30 years. Trout stuffed with ham and the roast kid are both good, while the desserts are irresistibly tempting. There's a good wine list. Closed Wed. Expensive.

Terra de Montanha Rua 31 de Janeiro 16–18A ☎ 259 372 075. Huge antique barrels, stacks of slowly maturing wine and stone walls set the tone for this determinedly rustic restaurant. The menu is upmarket traditional, featuring dishes such as *bacalhau* and corn bread, and there's a rotating selection of hearty *pratos do dia*. Closed Sun. Expensive.

O Transmontano Rua da Misericórdia 37 ☎ 259 323 540. Caters for big groups and can be a bit touristy, but it's good value nonetheless for standard Portuguese meals, with the *bolinhas de bacalhau* (salt cod balls) offering something slightly different. No credit cards. Moderate.

22 Rua Teixeira de Sousa 16 ☎ 259 321 296. First-floor retreat from the bustle below, with discerning lunchtime diners tucking into the various *bacalhau* specialities and great value €4 *pratos do dia*. Closed Sun. Moderate.

Yong Sheng Rua Isabel de Carvalho 30 ☎ 259 322 088. Authentic, friendly and great-value Chinese restaurant which does a lovely sweet and sour pork. There's also a free after-dinner shot of fruit liquor, served in glasses that can only be described as unconventional, and probably not for the easily offended. Inexpensive.

Listings

Banks There are banks and ATMs scattered throughout the town's small centre. For exchanging money, head to the branch of Caixa Geral de Depositos, near the turismo.

Hospital Hospital de São Pedro, 2km north of the centre ☎ 259 300 500.

Internet At espaçoInternet (Mon–Sat 10am–7pm & Sun 2–7pm), tucked away behind the shopping centre/supermarket off Av. 1 de Maio.

Pharmacy Farmácia Almeida, Av. Carvalho Araújo ☎ 259 322 874.

Police Av. Miguel Torga ☎ 259 322 022.

Post office Av. Carvalho Araújo (Mon–Fri 8.30am–6pm, Sat 9am–12.30pm).

Taxis Rádiotáxis Expresso ☎ 259 321 531 will take you into the Parque Natural do Alvão.

Parque Natural do Alvão

The boulder-strewn and pine-covered **Parque Natural do Alvão** is Portugal's smallest natural park. Although just 5km west of Vila Real, it's not easy to see without your own transport, and there's a distinct lack of accommodation, but partly because of these limitations it's one of the few remaining places in Portugal where you really feel you're in the wild. The handful of settlements are mostly constructed on rocky terrain to conserve the little arable land that is available, and almost everywhere basks in the scent of pine. Locals remove the bark on parts of the tree trunks and use a series of channels to collect the sap in sticky plastic bags for use in solvent production. Birds to look out for include golden eagles, buzzards, screech owls and the remarkable dipper, a sparrow-sized diving bird that makes its living on turbulent rocky streams. Other wildlife isn't so easy to spot, and you'd be extremely lucky to see any of the wolves, roe deer or wild boar that live in the park, while the numerous snakes tend to disappear at the sound of approaching footsteps.

Park practicalities

Access is along the N304, which branches off the IP4 about 5km before Campeã and heads towards Mondim de Basto, running through the western tip of the park itself, via Ermelo. This route is served by three daily Rodonorte **buses** from Vila Real to Aveção do Cabo (currently Mon–Fri only at 7.50am, 1.20pm and 6.10pm), where you'll have to pick up a Mondinense bus connection on to Mondim de Basto. There is also a regular service from Vila

Real to Agarez (Mon–Fri 7 daily, Sat & Sun 3 daily), just outside the park's southeastern boundary, and a more limited service along the minor N313 to Lamas de Ôlo (Sept–June Mon–Fri only, 3 daily), in the middle of the park. The helpful turismo in Vila Real stocks up-to-date bus timetables for all routes, or taxis are another possibility; the Vila Real to Lamas do Ôlo trip shouldn't cost more than €15.

There's little **accommodation** within the park itself, while **camping** is prohibited to avoid the very real risk of forest fires. Serious walkers intending to cross the whole reserve should obtain information and maps in advance from the park headquarters in Vila Real (see p.455). There's also a park office in Mondim de Basto, which is often used as an alternative base for seeing the Parque Natural (see p.353). Leaflets detailing walking circuits (available from both offices) are currently available only in Portuguese. For **organized tours**, contact Basto Radical (℡255 381 296, ⓦwww.basto-radical.pt/zbr/index. shtml), based in Mondim de Basto, who feature two-hour guided walking trips to the waterfalls of Fisgas de Ermelo (€20) as well as a day's rafting on the Rio Ôlo (€50). Other outdoor activities in the park can be arranged through Trilhos in Porto (see p.336).

The western side of the park

By public transport the easiest circuit to make from Vila Real is in the west of the park, giving you gorgeous views of mountains, pine trees and plunging valleys (allow 5–7 hours). Take the early morning bus from Vila Real to the junction for **ERMELO**, 1km off the main N304, a sleepy little hamlet with the proud title of "largest village in the park". Ermelo comes alive for just two days a year (August 7–8) during the Feira de São Vicente, a joint celebration also marking the annual return of Ermelo's emigrants. The place has a few cafés, but nothing more in the way of services. From the village, a track leads up the mountain, running high above the right bank of the Rio Ôlo – a tributary of the Tâmega – past the hamlet of **FERVENÇA**, where a 3km detour takes you to **BARREIRO**, with superb views westwards. Back on the track, you cross the river at **VARZIGUETO**, before following it back westwards, crossing the Ôlo river bridge and heading back to the Ermelo junction. Here, you can catch the late-afternoon bus back to Vila Real or on to Mondim.

For an alternative circuit (also 5–7hr), take the track 1km west of Ermelo, on the main Vila Real–Mondim road (signposted "Fisgas"), and head uphill along the forestry track, with the Rio Ôlo hidden in the ravine to your right. A couple of kilometres along, a right turn by a café-restaurant takes you on a 2km detour to a spectacular rocky ledge overlooking the waterfalls of **Fisgas de Ermelo**. Back at the restaurant, the track continues uphill among more rugged terrain for another 3km before joining the track from Varzigueto back to Ermelo.

The eastern side of the park

To explore the eastern side of the park on foot, catch a bus from Vila Real towards Chaves, getting off after 5km at the turning for the N313 to Mondim de Basto. From here it's a strenuous 8km hike to **LAMAS DE ÔLO**, a quiet rural hamlet around 1000 metres above sea level. It's notable for its peculiar granite houses (many now abandoned) with tent-like thatched roofs and, above the village, a watermill with a primitive aqueduct. Look out also for the eccentric, bus shelter-style construction where the villagers collect their post from small, individual mail boxes. The kindly old proprietress of *Café Albina de Olo* (☎ 250 341 950; no credit cards; reservations essential; 2x) has four decent en-suite rooms to rent above the café, itself without a sign but located near the main bus stop on the edge of the village.

An attractive walking circuit (around 3hr) begins in **AGAREZ**, 10km northwest of Vila Real. It loops anticlockwise via the waterfall and working watermill of **Galegos da Serra** on the Arnal stream, and past a bleakly situated cottage, which was once home to forestry workers but is now used primarily by school groups. Nonetheless, it is possible to rent spartan **rooms** here for €20 per person, although you'll have to book in advance at the park office in Vila Real. The cottage has a fully equiped kitchen and a living room with open fire. From here, the path takes you upstream to **ARNAL**, where a women's cooperative produces linen clothing and sheets for sale. From Arnal, there's a minor road back to Agarez.

The Corgo valley

From Vila Real, Auto-Viação do Tâmega buses run regularly along the IP3 through the spectacular **Corgo valley**, where everything from cowsheds to vine posts is made from granite, and where the luscious green of the vines belies the apparent barrenness of the earth. You'll also see the strange *espigueiros* or corn sheds, long and improbably thin granite constructions perched atop stone or wooden stilts to protect the contents from rats. The old Linha do Corgo train line once ran as far as Chaves, though it stops now at Vila Real, with the remaining track long since abandoned to the elements. But the road makes for a handsome enough route, following the valley fairly closely as far as the village of **Vila Pouca de Aguiar**, with the spa town of **Vidago** beyond providing easily the most attractive stop en route to Chaves.

Vila Pouca de Aguiar

VILA POUCA DE AGUIAR, 28km from Vila Real, is famous in the north for its bread and there's a spa, Pedras Salgadas (May–Nov only), whose waters are apparently good for disorders of the digestive system, but these are hardly essential experiences. A handful of small hotels line the main road but if you wanted to stop in the area you'd be far better off lodging at the *Quinta dos Ferreiros* (☎ 259 469 329, ℻ 259 469 140; breakfast included; ❸), a rambling eighteenth-century country house set in the tiny hamlet of **Vila Chã**, signposted off the main road, 9km to the south. If you're feeling energetic you can pitch in with the grape and chestnut harvests or simply chill out by the pool and admire the granite and grey-white scree of the magnificent Serra da Falperra. The *quinta* also has a particularly fascinating *espigueiro*; carved into its granite facade are some unusual markings relating to fertility and the agricultural cycle.

Beyond Vila Pouca, the road cuts through the edge of the Serra da Padrela, before reaching the upper valley of the Rio Tâmega at Vidago, which it then traces for the rest of the route to Chaves.

Vidago

The spa town of **VIDAGO**, some 16km north of Vila Pouca and about 17km south of Chaves, has some lovely walks in the surrounding pine forests, while the **spa** itself (early May to late-Oct daily 8am–noon & 4–7pm) is set in the beautiful grounds of the *Vidago Palace Hotel* (see below), an astonishingly opulent Edwardian pile with a magnificent pump room, a bandstand amid the trees, boating lake, pool, tennis courts and nine-hole golf course. Buses drop you by the summer **turismo** (irregular hours; ☎276 907 470) on the main road and from here it's only a short walk to the spa and hotels – follow the flurry of signs. It's important to note, however, that the spa closes in winter, as do most of the hotels and *pensões*.

Top **accommodation** choice is of course the *Vidago Palace Hotel* (☎276 990 900, ✆vidagopalace@unicer.pt; breakfast included; ❼), but even if you don't stay here you could try the restaurant – the prices are less scary than you might imagine, and you can have a drink on the balcony. Otherwise, *Hotel Parque*, Avenida Teixeira de Sousa (☎276 909 666, ✆hotelparque.vidago@clix. pt; breakfast included; ❺), is the contemporary rival of the *Vidago Palace*, with tennis courts and a pool, but it lacks its grace and character. The best of the less expensive options include *Pensão Alameda*, Rua Padre Adolfo Magalhães 2 (☎276 907 246; breakfast included; no credit cards; ❷), a small, friendly, family-run place, with old-fashioned rooms and a lovely big garden with a willow tree and vines; and the ageing *Pensão Primavera* at Avenida Conde de Caria 2 (☎276 907 230, ✆276 909 378; €30), facing the *Vidago Palace*, with wooden-shuttered rooms and another charming garden.

For **eating**, head to the moderately priced *Restaurant-Pizzeria Gomes & Gomes* (☎276 909 703), tucked away but signposted on Rua José António Costa, behind the main road heading out to Chaves. The pizzas are pretty authentic, while locals pile in for their *bacalhau* and *vitela*, although the vinegar-like house wine is best avoided.

Mirandela

It's around 65km from Vila Real to **MIRANDELA**, an odd little town on the Tua river that's not to everyone's taste. Certainly, it's not as attractive as some of the nearby towns – only a few remnants of the former medieval centre survive, making the town's most striking feature its **Roman bridge**, renovated in the fifteenth century and stretching a good 200m across seventeen arches. It's only open to pedestrians, with traffic forced to use the concrete bridge beside it, or the Ponte Europa upstream. The riverside gardens and lawns are pleasant places to lounge around, while you can rent kayaks and pedaloes in summer to splash up and down the Tua. Mirandela has also been making an improbable name for itself in recent years as one of the world's jet-ski hotspots, hosting the world championships in 2004 (it also hosts the annual national championships).

River antics aside, much of the old town is decaying or has been demolished, and attempts at renovation have yielded mixed results. The chapel near the Câmara Municipal, at the summit of the ancient citadel, simply fell down in 1985. Scavengers pilfered the best of the stonework, and what was left was rebuilt in a foursquare style topped with an ugly glass pyramid that contrasts awkwardly with the grandiose **Câmara Municipal** itself. Formerly the Palácio dos Távoras, this was one of several flamboyant Baroque town houses associated with the Távora family, which controlled the town between the fourteenth and seventeenth centuries. The only other attraction, as such, is the modern art gallery, the **Museu Armindo Teixeira Lopes** (Mon–Fri 10am–12.30pm & 2–6pm; free), combined with the town's library, which has a section dedicated to images of Mirandela and Lisbon by local artist Armindo Teixeira Lopes.

Weekday **markets** are held in Mirandela as close as possible to the 3rd, 14th or 25th of every month. Otherwise, the best time to visit is during the **Festa da Senhora do Amparo** (July 25 to the first Sunday in August) – the Friday night is the *Noite das Bombas*, or "Night of the Drums", while the final Saturday is the big day, with a procession and fireworks. Traditional music and dance can be sampled at the **Festa dos Reis** (January 6) at Vale de Salgueiro, 12km north on the Vinhais road, when a "king" visits the village's houses distributing *tremoços* (pickled beans) and wine to the sound of bagpipes.

Practicalities

Mirandela is the terminus of the **Tua train line** (departures from Tua on the Douro train line); **buses** drop you at the terminal next to the train station. To reach the town centre, turn right, then right again and, with the river on your left, it's a five-minute walk to the Roman bridge, from where the road veers into the main Rua da República. The informative **turismo** (Mon–Fri 9.30am–12.30pm & 2–6pm; ☎278 200 272, ⓦwww.cm-mirandela.pt) is located nearby in the public gardens, Jardim Dr. Trigo de Negreiros, and can supply a useful town map. Also nearby, in the upper tier of the municipal market, there's free **internet** access at espaçoInternet (daily 9am–12.30pm & 2–6pm).

Accommodation in Mirandela is pretty easy to find, except in late-July during the summer *festa* and annual jet-ski championship. The local **campsite** (☎278 263 177) is 3km north of town on the Bragança road and, as well as a restaurant and shop, has a **swimming pool** open to the public in summer (July–Sept). Mirandela is famed for both its olive oil and its delicious *alheira* **sausages**, a legacy of the Jewish community that has long since disappeared. Made primarily from chicken and bread (though pork is now also added), they're cooked quickly and served with rice or potatoes. Most restaurants in Mirandela serve them, and in fact there's a fair bit of controversy as to who makes the best.

Hotels and pensions

Hotel Dom Dinis Rua Nossa Senhora do Amparo ☎278 260 100, ℗278 260 101. Mirandela's showpiece hotel although, the swanky reception area and great river views aside, the rooms really aren't much more impressive than those at the various *residenciais* and certainly aren't worth double the money. Breakfast included. Parking. ⑤

Residencial Globo Rua Cidade de Orthez 35 ☎278 248 210, ℗278 248 871. Located over the old bridge near the hospital, this comes with cork floors, gleaming modern bathrooms and red telephones rescued from another decade. Views aren't so great though, offering a perfect perspective on the apartment building opposite. Breakfast included. ③

Pensão Residencial O Lagar Rua da República 120 ☎278 262 712. One of the few places in town with any character, featuring homely, comfortable rooms, some with old wooden shutters. The friendly owner serves refreshments from an ageing bar. Breakfast included. No credit cards. ②

Hotel Miratua Rua da República 38 ☎278 200 140, ℗278 265 003. Slick if unremarkable and overpriced high-rise, with carpets in poor taste but otherwise comfortable enough. There are some good views from the upper rooms. Breakfast included. ③

Pensão Praia Largo 1 de Janeiro 6, off Rua da República ☎278 262 497. Offers a mixed bag of rooms (some en-suite) and attractive river views from its upper floor. The central location is appealing, as is the fact it's set back from the main road, although you'll have to find your own breakfast in the morning. No credit cards. ②

Restaurants

D. Maria Rua Dr. Jorge Pires ☎278 248 455. Locally renowned restaurant that's one of the main contenders for the best *alheira*. It specializes in spruced-up traditional fare, although you can also dine on fondue and Jamaican-style pork. Expensive.

O Jardim Rua da República 20 ☎278 262 712. Around the corner from the tourist office in the public gardens, you get four different types of *bacalhau* here, as well as good-value grilled chicken, beef and pork, plus a hearty vegetable soup. Closed Sun. Moderate.

Pizzeria Diablo Rua Vasco da Gama ☏ 278 263 952. A hidden gem, signposted near the bus station and attracting a neighbourhood clientele. The mushrooms don't come from a tin, and they even provide chilli oil and freshly ground black pepper. For dessert, choose the delectable home-made chocolate mousse. Closed Mon. No credit cards. Inexpensive.

Vila Flôr

Like so many of the towns in the area, **VILA FLÔR** (Town of Flowers), 24km south of Mirandela, was given its name in the thirteenth century by Dom Dinis who, on his way to meet Isabel of Aragon, was clearly in a romantic frame of mind. His favouritism was short-lived, though, for soon Vila Flôr was forced to contribute a third of its revenue to rebuilding the walls of rival Torre de Moncorvo, 30km to the south. Vila Flôr still has a piece of old wall known as the Arco Dom Dinis as well as a so-called "Roman" fountain.

With its tree-lined squares, attractive location and striking church, the town warrants at least a night's stay, and the wonderfully eccentric **Museu Municipal de Berta Cabral**, just south of the main square (daily 9am–12.30pm & 2–5.30pm; free), certainly merits a visit. Three eminent Vilaflôrians donated the contents of their houses to the museum when it was founded in 1946, and the result is an incredible hodge-podge, encompassing not just local relics – like the town's first telephone – but all kinds of bizarre curios, from an embalmed Angolan rat to an ensemble of antelope-horn-and-zebra-hide furniture. The museum's amiable director takes great pride in enthusiastically explaining each and every item, although you may have to ask him to open the upstairs rooms, which are normally kept closed.

An extensive street **market** is held on the weekday closest to the 15th and 28th of every month, and the town *festa* (August 22–28) can be counted upon for live music and open-air stalls. However, the main event in the region is the **Romaria de Nossa Senhora da Assunção**, which takes place every August 15 to the hilltop sanctuary of Vilas Boas), 8km northwest of Vila Flôr. Held on the site of an apparition of the Virgin in 1673, this is one of the largest *romarias* in Trás-os-Montes, where ten saintly images are carried through the multitude, headed by an image of Nossa Senhora carried on the backs of over a hundred men.

Practicalities

Buses stop by the GALP petrol station on Avenida Marechal Carmona; there are regular weekday services to Torre de Moncorvo and Mirandela, but weekends are very restricted with no Saturday service and only one or two buses on Sundays. The town's **turismo** (Mon–Fri 9am–noon & 2–5pm; ☏ 278 512 411) is on Largo Dr. Alexandre de Matos, opposite the Museu Municipal, and there's free **internet** access at espaçoInternet (daily 9am–10pm) near the cinema on Avenida Marechal Carmona.

There's only one **pension** in town, the very underwhelming *Casa Roças* at Avenida Marechal Carmona 4 (☏ 278 516 277; no credit cards; ❷), whose basic, no-frills rooms possess only slightly more charm than the owner. Vila Flôr's **campsite** (☏ 278 512 350), 2km southeast of town on the N213 Torre de Moncorvo road, at least partly makes up for this, as it's attractively wooded and located right next door to the municipal outdoor swimming pool.

For **meals** the best place by a country mile is the informal and moderately priced *Restaurante Dom Dinis* (☏ 278 576 696; no credit cards), secluded behind a lush garden and signposted up a side street off Avenida Marechal Carmona. There's no excuse not to delve into their renowned *posta à Vila Flor* (braised veal) and lovely table wine, a red sourced from the local Adega Cooperativa. Another good choice is the modern *Restaurante e Adega da Casa do Turismo* (☎278 516 532; closed Mon), below the tourist office, with good-value meat and fish dishes including a tasty *bacalhau com presunto*.

Out of town, *Quinta do Reboredo* (☎278 516 872, ✉arqueiroverde@clix .pt; breakfast included; ❸), 8km northwest near **Vilas Boas**, is a rural retreat with comfortable rooms and horse-riding facilities. Nearby *Quinta da Veiguinha* no longer offers accommodation but does sell gourmet cheese and olive oil produced on the premises. Alternatively, head for the village of **Assares**, 12km to the northeast and signposted off the main IP2, where the eighteenth-century *Quinta do Barracão da Vilariça* (☎278 536 200, ⓦwww.terra-sa.com; breakfast included; no credit cards; ❸), sits in a lovely location.

Carrazeda de Ansiães

CARRAZEDA DE ANSIÃES, 16km southwest of Vila Flôr, is a modern town of little intrinsic interest. However, three and a half kilometres to the south (a taxi should cost around €3 each way) are the intriguing ruins of a medieval walled town, known as **Ansiães**. Little remains within the perimeter of walls except rocks and boulders, but two chapels stand outside, the better preserved of which – the twelfth-century **São Salvador** – has a Romanesque portal, extravagantly carved with leaves, animals and human figures. Local myth has it that a tunnel connects Ansiães to another castle beyond the Rio Douro, 12km away; a gaping, fly-ridden hole beneath an impressive slab is the principal piece of supporting evidence. What is undoubtedly true, however, is that the town was a base for five different kings, including the King of Léon and Castile, before Portuguese independence; they're listed by the gateway on a plaque unveiled by President Mário Soares in February 1987.

The last inhabitants of old Ansiães left in the mid-eighteenth century. The gradual depopulation resulted from the decision, in 1734, of a gentleman named Francisco de Araújo e Costa, to transfer the official council seat to the new town below (known by then as Carrazeda de Ansiães). In response to local protests he ordered the castle *pelourinho* to be destroyed; with this symbol gone and deprived of a sufficient supply of water, the hill community had no hope of putting up effective resistance. The medieval town went into decline and was soon totally abandoned.

A good time to visit Carrazeda de Ansiães is on January 3 for the *Cantar os Reis* (night-long music and dance in honour of the Three Kings) or, in the summer, for the **Festa de Santa Eufémia** (August 15–16), in which pilgrims stuff themselves with weaned sow and the local wine, the latter famed for its supposed ability to be imbibed in vast quantities without the drinker falling over. Should you still be in a fit state to drive, the most enticing accommodation is in the nearby village of Pombal at the *Hotel Rural Flor do Monte* (☎278 660 010, ⓦwww.flordomonte.com; breakfast included; no credit cards; ❹), where there are modern rooms and a pool, as well as activities such as hunting and fishing.

Chaves

CHAVES stands just 12km from the Spanish border and its name, which means "keys", reflects a strategic history of occupation and ownership. Founded by the Romans in 78 AD, their name for the town, Aquae Flaviae, comes from a dual reference to the famous spa waters, and Flavio Vespasianus, who

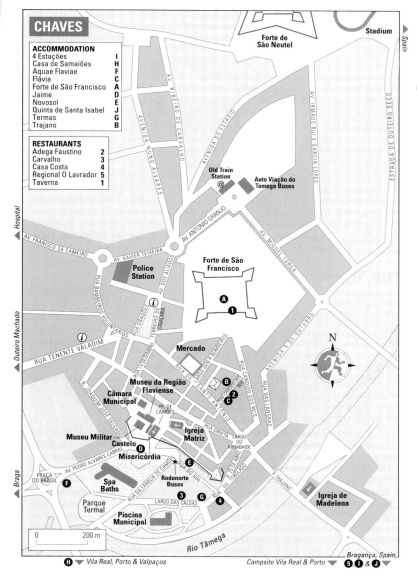

CHAVES

ACCOMMODATION
4 Estações	I
Casa de Samaiões	H
Aquae Flaviae	F
Flávia	C
Forte de São Francisco	A
Jaime	D
Novosol	E
Quinta de Santa Isabel	J
Termas	G
Trajano	B

RESTAURANTS
Adega Faustino	2
Carvalho	3
Casa Costa	4
Regional O Lavrador	5
Taverna	1

Spain

Stadium

Forte de São Neutel

AV. RIBEIRO DE CARVALHO

AVENIDA DO ESTÁDIO

AV. IRMÃOS RUI E GARCIA LOPES

ESTRADA DE OUTEIRO SECO

AVENIDA NUNO ALVARES

AV. ANTONIO GRANJO

AV. MIGUEL TORGA

Old Train Station @

Auto Viação do Tamega Buses

Hospital

AV. FRANISCO SÁ CAMEIRO

AV. XAVIER TEIXEIRA

AV. DOS ALIADOS

Police Station

Forte de São Francisco

A **1**

RUA BAMBEIROS VOLUNTARIOS

Outeiro Machado

RUA TENENTE VALADIM

RUA DIAGO

TERREIRO DE CAVALARIA

RUA DA CADEA

Mercado

RUA DE LARGO GEN E BOMBEIROS

RUA CANDIDO DOS REIS

AVENIDA 5 DE OUTUBRO

RUA DAS LANGRAS

N

Museu da Região Flaviense

RUA SANTO ANTONIO

B
C

Câmara Municipal

R. JOAQUIM JOSE DELGADO

PR. DE CAMÕES

RUA DIREITA

LARGO DO ARRABAIDE

Museu Militar

Castelo **D**

Igreja Matriz

Misericórdia **E**

AV. PEDRO ALVARES CABRAL

Braga

PRAÇA DO BRASIL **F**

Spa Baths

RUA DA FAMILIA DE CAMÕES

RUA DO SOL

Rodonorte Buses **3**

G **4**

RUA DO TOBELADO

R. 25 DE ABRIL

P. TRAJANO

Igreja de Madelena

Parque Termal

LARGO DAS CALDAS

Piscina Municipal

0   200 m

Rio Tâmega

H ▼ Vila Real, Porto & Valpaços   Campsite Vila Real & Porto ▼   Bragança, Spain, **5** **I** & **J** ▼

Albergaria Jaime Rua Joaquim José Delgado
Ⓣ276 301 050, Ⓕ276 301 051. This place was
operating as a *pensão* as far back as the late
1800s, although its recent makeover has placed
it firmly in the upmarket hotel category. Its apricot
facade and strange, often rather naughty artwork
aside, rooms are plush without ever being remarkable, while the downstairs minimalist cyber-bar
has pricey internet access and a concrete terrace.
Breakfast included. ⑤

Hospedaria Novosol Rua do Sol 56 Ⓣ276 325
385. An elderly couple has some spotless, modern
rooms for rent at the back of their otherwise
engagingly antiquated house. Although they're
rather dark, the cool interiors are a perfect anti-
dote to the merciless heat in summer. Breakfast
included. No credit cards. ②

Residencial Termas Rua do Tabolado Ⓣ276 333
280. It's a bit of a concrete hulk, but it's centrally
located and friendly, with pleasantly cool air-
conditioned rooms with varnished wooden floors.
Breakfast included. ②

Hotel Trajano Trav. Cândido dos Reis Ⓣ276 301
640, Ⓕ276 327 002. Modern and comfortable,

if a bit dull, though some of the pleasant rooms
have traditional local furniture and good views.
There's a renowned restaurant (closes 9.30pm)
in the basement, not too expensive and just the
place for Chaves ham and local trout. Breakfast
included. ③

Outside town

Casa de Samaiões Samaiões, 5km south of
Chaves Ⓣ276 340 450,
Ⓔhotel-casadesamaioes@clix.pt. A cross
between an upmarket hotel and a *turismo rural*,
this combines traditional four-poster beds with
contemporary furnishings, while the rural setting
and landscaped grounds – complete with swimming pool and full-sized football pitch – supply all
the open space and fresh air you could wish for.
Breakfast included. ⑥

Quinta de Santa Isabel Santo Estévão, 7km east
of Chaves Ⓣ & Ⓕ276 351 818. A traditional Trás-
os-Montes country house with vineyards, 500m
off the N103 to Bragança. Queen Isabel is said to
have slept here the night before she married Dom
Dinis. Breakfast included. No credit cards. ③

Eating, drinking and nightlife

Some of the *pensões* and hotels have reasonable restaurants attached (the *Trajano*
in particular), but wherever you eat you shouldn't have any difficulty finding
good Chaves smoked ham, tasty local sausages and fine red wine. Over Christmas, look out for the traditional speciality of octopus (*polvo*), brought up dried
from the coast, then boiled with potatoes and greens. The **restaurants** along
Rua do Sol near the river tend to be particularly cheap and serve good hearty
portions. Despite the number of elderly spa-clients in town, there are several
fashionable **bars** in Chaves, many lining Largo das Caldas.

Restaurants

Adega Faustino Trav. Cândido dos Reis
ⓉT276 322 142. An old converted wine cellar-
cum-art gallery, filled with huge wooden
barrels, which serves great bean salads and
a selection of *petiscos*, which you can turn
into a reasonable meal. And, of course, it has
terrific wines. Closed Sun. No credit cards.
Moderate.

Carvalho Largo das Caldas Ⓣ276 321 727.
Some of the region's best food is served here, as
testified by the numerous awards on the walls.
Service is excellent – efficient and unobtrusive
– and the food uniquely prepared and presented.
Try the grilled conger eel or lobster. Closed Thurs.
Moderate.

Casa Costa Rua do Tabolado Ⓣ276 323 568. Tre-
mendously popular place serving huge portions of
excellent home cooking; the speciality is *bacalhau
à Costa*, ideally followed by one of their desserts.

There's a pleasant vine-covered rear garden with
bench-style tables. Moderate.

Regional O Lavrador Rua Dom Afonso III Ⓣ276
332 838. Located around 1km out of the centre,
off a very busy main road, but frequented by
locals in the know. Both decor and menu are
in the traditionalist vein, and the chef is big
on seafood, with fried fish, lobster and prawns
featuring prominently. Closed Thurs. No credit
cards. Moderate.

Taverna At the *Forte de São Francisco* Ⓣ276
333 700. Built into the fort's outer walls by the
main gate, this dimly lit replica of a traditional
rural tavern has enough suspended hams,
exposed granite and taped fado to at least get
your imagination working. The food is excellent,
centered on *petiscos* such as mushrooms in
garlic sauce and cod balls, though there's also
a small selection of main dishes. Closed Sun &
Mon. Moderate.

Bars and clubs

Bar Garage Trav. Cândido dos Reis. There's no mistaking it – there are bits of cars protruding from the walls.

Biblioteca Trav. Cândido dos Reis. The town's only central club, with a regular rotation of local and guest DJs.

Espelho d'Agua Largo das Caldas. Plays Brazilian and Portuguese sounds until late.

Triunfo 4km out of town on the road to Valpaços. Chaves' main club – take a taxi, or get a ride with other clubbers from around the Largo dos Caldas at around 10pm.

Listings

Banks Banks and ATMs can found in the main thoroughfare of Rua de Santo António and on Largo do Arrabaide, where you can also exchange money at Caixa Geral do Depositos.

Hospital Av. da Raposeira ☏276 300 900.

Internet Free access at espaçoInternet (Mon–Fri 9am–12.30pm & 2–5.30pm), behind the old train station.

Pharmacy Farmácia Mariz, Rua Santo António 32 ☏276 322 270.

Police Av. Xavier Teixeira ☏276 323 125.

Post office Largo General Silveira (Mon–Fri 8.30am–6pm, Sat 9am–12.30pm).

Montalegre

The historic frontier town of **MONTALEGRE** – 45km west of Chaves, and a 10km detour off the N103 – looms up suddenly, commanding the surrounding plains. Despite its relative isolation, there's a fair amount of modern development that is gradually encroaching on the medieval centre, though age-old traditions remain strong here. Bread is still baked in communal ovens in local villages, while the nearby settlements of the Serra do Barroso have long been known for their *Vinhos dos Mortos* – Wines of the Dead – so called because of the practice of maturing the wine in bottles buried underground. This originated in 1809 when villagers, keen to protect their wine stocks from the invading French hordes, hid their bottles, only to find that the contents tasted considerably better when they dug them up again. Curiosities like this, as well as the impressive fourteenth-century **Castelo** (Tues–Sun 9am–12.30pm & 2–5.30pm; free), make the town an atmospheric stopover, especially in winter when snow covers the mountains to the north.

It's also excellent **hiking** country around Montalegre, scattered with dolmens and the odd Templar or Romanesque church. If you've escaped from the summer heat of Chaves, you'll find the pure air invigorating. The local turismo (see below) provides free leaflets detailing the various marked circuits, most of which start a few minutes' walk from the town's hotels and which wind up to within sight of the Spanish border. Or contact NaTurBarroso (☏276 511 337, ✆naturbarroso@hotmail.com) in town, up near the castle at Terreiro do Açougue, which offers organized **walking tours**, most based on themes like "Trail of the Wolves" or "Mushroom Hunting". The tours start at €40, rising to €160 for a fully inclusive two-day hike. For many people, though, Montalegre simply makes a useful overnight stop, especially if you're bound for the Peneda-Gerês park.

Practicalities

The **bus station** is at the far end of Rua General Humberto Delgado, and a five-minute walk west brings you to the main square, Praça do Município, and the **turismo** (Mon–Fri 9am–12.30pm & 2–5.30pm; also June–Sept Sat

10am–12.30pm & 2–5.30pm, Sun 10am–12.30pm & 2–4pm; ⓣ276 511 010). There's also a useful **Peneda-Gerês national park office** at Rua Reigoso 17 (Mon–Fri 9am–12.30pm & 2–5.30pm; ⓣ276 518 320), off to the left of the roundabout in the middle of the main Avenida Dom Nuno Álvares Pereira.

Montalegre has a decent range of **accommodation**, the best value being the comfortable en-suite rooms at the *Restaurante Hospedaria Girrasol* (ⓣ276 512 715; no credit cards; breakfast included; ❶), located up a quiet, leafy cul-de-sac at the end of Rua da Portela, itself running off to the northeast of the main roundabout on Avenida Dom Nuno Álvares Pereira. More central is the large *Albergaria do Castelo* on Rua 1 de Dezembro (ⓣ276 511 376; breakfast included; no credit cards; ❸), with modern, boxy rooms, some with good views of the castle. *Hotel Quality Inn* on Rua do Avelar (ⓣ276 510 220, Ⓔquality. montalegre@mail.telepac.pt; breakfast included; ❺), 200m or so north of the turismo, heading towards Braga, is the upmarket choice, where you'll find it hard to believe that jail cells once lined the corridors. This Salazar-era prison has been well and truly transformed, with indoor pool, sauna, gymnasium and Turkish bath, while the hotel has a programme of outdoor activities, from paragliding to horse riding.

Restaurante O Castelo (ⓣ276 511 237; no credit cards), up by the castle at Terreiro do Açougue, makes for a rustic **dining** experience, strangely pitched halfway between a Mexican cantina and a traditional Portuguese tavern – try the grilled trout or salmon. *Restaurant Terra Fria* (ⓣ276 512 101; no credit cards) on Rua Vitor Branco, northeast of the main square, is another good restaurant choice, perennially popular with locals and offering hearty, moderately priced Portuguese dishes, including an unusual seafood *feijoada*. Meat-eaters are also in for a treat – the Barroso region is famed for its smoked meats (*fumeiros*) and ham (*presunto*), best bought at the shop opposite the GALP service station, down from Praça do Município, or at the **market** (Mon, Tues & Thurs) below the bus station. There's even a whole festival dedicated to the products, the annual **Feira do Fumeiro e Presunto**, which takes place in the fourth week of January.

East to Vinhais

The twisting 96km white-knuckle ride from Chaves to Bragança takes in some of the most awe-inspiring scenery in Portugal. The road passes through broad-leaved forest, pine forest and, at its greatest altitude, rocky moorland, blanketed by yellow gorse and purple heather at certain times of year. Interspersed amongst these are the smallholdings of traditional farmers, with tiny fields still ploughed with the assistance of reluctant donkeys.

Two-thirds of the way along the route is the pleasant village of **VINHAIS**, whose main sight is the Baroque convent of **São Francisco**, a vast building incorporating a pair of churches in its facade. It is situated at the Chaves end of the main street, which runs for 1km or more, and offers staggering views away to the south. A minor road from Vinhais leads north into the Parque Natural de Montesinho, making this a useful access point for motorists, but there's no reason to stop for long otherwise – and certainly no reason to get off the Chaves–Bragança bus.

There is a well-stocked **turismo** (Mon–Fri 9am–6pm, Sat 10am–1pm & 2–6pm; ⓣ273 770 309) in the centre of the village on Largo de Arrabalde, and park information available from the **Delegação do Parque** at the Casa do Povo (Mon–Fri 9am–12.30pm & 2.30–5pm; ⓣ273 772 416). Park-bound visitors might be glad of the **accommodation** options, namely *Pensão Ribeirinha*, Rua Nova 34 (☎2373 771 490; breakfast included; no credit cards; ❷), halfway between the main square and the convent, with lovely old en-suite rooms, some with balconies overlooking the valley; and the more upmarket but rather clinical *Residencial Cidadela Transmontana* on Rua dos Frades (☎273 770 112, ✉rescidtrans@mail.telepac.pt; breakfast included; no credit cards; ❸), 200 metres west of the *Ribeirinha*, whose expensive **restaurant** serves wild boar, rabbit and other rustic delights. Alternatively, you can grab a bite to eat at *Restaurante Comercial* (☎273 772 169) on Rua da Calçada, serving moderately priced Portuguese fare, including their speciality *francesinhas*, a cheese-and-ham combo with an over-the-top sauce made from whisky, port, beer, white wine, tomato and butter.

Bragança

On a dark hillock above **BRAGANÇA**, the remote capital of Trás-os-Montes, stands a circle of perfectly preserved medieval walls, enclosing a white medieval village and rising to a massive keep and castle. Known as the Cidadela, this is one of the most memorable sights in Portugal, as well as the embodiment of the town's dynastic history. The Bragançans were the last line of **Portuguese monarchs**, ruling from 1640, when they replaced the Spaniards, until the fall of the monarchy in 1910. To the British, the name is most readily associated with Catherine, queen to Charles II, though for the Portuguese the town represents the defence of the liberty of the people, because the Bragançans were the first to muster a popular revolt against Junot in 1808, and always defended their power to make their own decisions.

The citadel provides the principal reason for a visit, though the nearby Parque Natural de Montesinho (see p.476) is an additional draw, while Bragança is also a useful stop for anyone crossing the nearby border into Spain. It's certainly worth staying for a night or two, especially to experience early evening in the Cidadela, when the tourists have gone for the day and peace returns to the ancient streets. Looking out over the castle walls into Spain brings home the very real isolation that Bragança endured until recent times, a location taken advantage of by the Jews in the sixteenth century, who escaped over the border from the terrors of the Spanish Inquisition. Despite the common rule by Spaniards over the two countries during this period, the Inquisition in Portugal was relatively inefficient and only spread slowly northwards with ever-decreasing zeal.

Bragança's **Festa de Nossa Senhora das Graças** (August 12–22) offers another very good reason to be in town, featuring lots of cultural events and traditional music. Shortly after follows the religious **Romaria de São Bartolomeu** (August 24), while other notable dates include the **Feira das Cantarinhas** (May 2–4), a crafts fair dedicated to the clay water jug (*cantarinha*) which was once used to store the gifts given to a bride on her wedding day. On **Ash Wednesday** (usually February or early March) people dressed as devils run around town whipping penitents – the origins probably lie in an ancient fertility cult, when it was believed that Pan impregnated women simply by smacking them.

The Town

Modern Bragança, set along the valley below the Cidadela, is a pleasant enough place, despite an eruption of concrete apartment buildings on the outskirts. It's

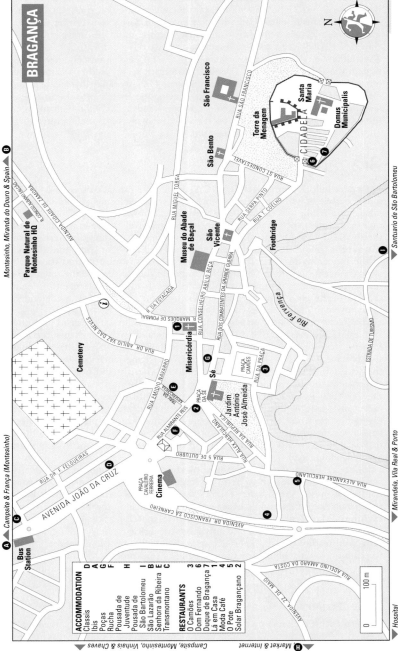

BRAGANÇA

N

▲ Campsite & França (Montesinho) **C**

A ▲ Montesinho, Miranda do Douro & Spain **B** ▲

▼ Market & Internet **H** ▲

▼ Campsite, Montesinho, Vinhais & Chaves

▼ Santuário de São Bartolomeu

▼ Mirandela, Vila Real & Porto

▼ Hospital

Parque Natural de Montesinho HQ

Cemetery

Bus Station

Cinema

ACCOMMODATION

Classis	D
Ibis	A
Poças	G
Rucha	F
Pousada de Juventude	H
Pousada de São Bartolomeu	I
São Lazarão	B
Senhora da Ribeira	E
Transmontano	C

RESTAURANTS

O Camões	3
Dom Fernando	6
Duque de Bragança	7
Lá em Casa	1
Moda Café	4
O Pote	5
Solar Bragançano	2

Museu do Abade de Baçal

São Vicente

São Bento

São Francisco

Santa Maria

Torre da Menagem

CIDADELA

Domus Municipalis

Misericórdia

Sé

Footbridge

Rio Fervença

0   100 m

a twenty-minute walk from the centre up to the Cidadela – the obvious place to start your exploration of town – though for an overall view of the citadel and town, there's no beating the vantage-point of the **Santuario de São Bartolomeu**; to get there, follow the signs to the *pousada*, which is next to the church – a half-hour walk from the town centre.

At the heart of the **Cidadela** stands the thirteenth-century council chamber, the **Domus Municipalis**. Very few Romanesque civic buildings have survived, and no other in Europe has this pentagonal form. Its meetings – for solving land disputes and the like – took place on the arcaded first floor; below was a cistern. Ask around for the key at the nearby houses if peering through the keyhole isn't enough for you. Rising to one side, and almost blocking the doorway of the Domus, is the **Igreja de Santa Maria** (daily 9.30am–6.30pm; free), whose interior is distinguished by an eighteenth-century, barrel-vaulted, painted ceiling – a feature of several churches in Bragança.

Facing these buildings is the town keep, the **Torre de Menagem** (Mon–Wed & Fri–Sun 9–11.45am & 2–4.45pm; €1.50, free Sun morning), which the royal family rejected as a residence in favour of their vast estate in the Alentejo. It was one of the first works of restoration by the Society of National Monuments in 1928, and now houses a collection of military odds and ends as well as offering great views from the top. At the side of the keep, a curious **pelourinho** rises from the back of a prehistoric granite pig. The town's museum has three more of these crudely sculpted *porcas* (though the most famous example is to be seen at Murça, halfway between Vila Real and Mirandela). They are thought to have been the fertility idols of a prehistoric cult, and it's easy to understand the beast's prominence in this province of wild boars and chestnut forests, where the staple winter diet is smoked sausage.

From the Cidadela, the narrow, stepped Rua Serpa Pinto leads to the **Igreja de São Vicente**, where Dom Pedro I claimed to have secretly married Inês de Castro (see p.173); while a small diversion east of here, along Rua São Francisco, brings you to the **Igreja de São Bento**, the town's finest church – a simple Renaissance structure with three contrasting ceilings.

Continuing into town, along Rua Conselheiro Abílio Beça, you will find the **Museu do Abade de Baçal**, the town's distinguished museum (Tues–Fri 10am–5pm, Sat & Sun 10am–6pm; €2, free Sun morning), installed in the eighteenth-century former Bishop's Palace. In its gardens Celtic-inspired medieval tombstones rub shoulders with a menagerie of *porcas*, while, inside, the collection of sacred art and the topographical watercolours of Alberto Souza are the highlights, along with displays of local costumes – especially the dress of the *Pauliteiros* ("stick dancers"), who hail from the area around Bragança and Miranda do Douro. Further down the street is a fine Renaissance-style **Misericórdia** dating from 1873.

Practicalities

Most buses operate from the shiny new **bus station** at the northern end of Avenida João da Cruz, where you'll find offices for Rodonorte (services to Mirandela, Vila Real, Vinhais and southern Trás-os-Montes), Auto-Viação do Tâmega (Chaves), Santos (Miranda do Douro and Mirandela) and Rede Expresso (national services). **Parking** is easy by the bus station or up in the citadel itself.

From the bus station it's a short walk to Praça da Sé, essentially the centre of town, with the English-speaking **turismo** (June–Sept Mon–Fri

10am–12.30pm & 2–6.30pm, Sat 9am–12.30pm & 2–5pm, Sun 9am–1pm; Oct–May Mon–Fri 9am–12.30pm & 2–5pm, Sat 10am–12.30pm; ☎273 381 273, @www.cm-braganca.pt) located a couple of hundred metres to the north on the wide boulevard of Avenida Cidade de Zamora. Another 200m down the avenue, in a modern development on the left, is the headquarters of the **Parque Natural de Montesinho**, Rua Cónego Albano Falcão, Lote 5, Apartado 90 (Mon–Fri 9am–12.30 & 2–5.30pm; ☎273 381 444, @www .icn.pt), where the very helpful English-speaking staff can provide you with information about visiting the park, including the ever changing accommodation situation.

Accommodation

Pensões and hotels are scattered around town, with generally decent standards and offering good value for money; even in summer you shouldn't find it too difficult to find a good room. There are a lot more rural options nearby, within driving distance of Bragança, particularly within the Parque Natural de Montesinho (see next section). The two nearest **campsites** are also convenient for exploring the park.

Hotels and pensions

Residencial Classis Av. João da Cruz 102 ☎273 331 631, @273 323 458. A friendly, if slightly ageing, motel-style *residencial* with good views from its third- and fourth-floor rooms. It's not bad value most of the year although prices go up in August. Breakfast included. ❸

Hotel Ibis Rotunda do Lavrador Transmontano ☎273 302 520, @www.ibishotel.com. Located to the north of town, and with great views to the Montesinho park, though the cabin-style rooms boast challenging colour schemes. ❸

Pensão Poças Rua Combatentes da Grande Guerra 200 ☎273 331 428. A reliable, cheap and characterful town-centre *pensão*, though pick your room with care – some are very bare and in winter this place is freezing. Rooms with or without bathroom available. Prices are per person, so it's very good value for singles. You check in at the associated restaurant, which is a great place for no-nonsense meat and fish dishes – family-run and popular enough to fill a couple of floors. Breakfast included. ❶

Pensão Rucha Rua Almirante Reis 42 ☎273 331 672. More of a family home than a *pensão*, run by a friendly couple, with rooms on the first floor along corridors lined with antiques, pottery and flowers. The eight rooms (with shared bath) have a little more character than most places in town, with big wooden shutters and hand basins. No credit cards. ❶

Pousada de São Bartolomeu Estrada de Turismo ☎273 331 493, @www.pousadas.pt. South of the river, about 1km by road from the centre – drivers should follow the signs off Rua Alexandre Herculano. Purpose-built in 1959, it's got wood panelling throughout, cork ceilings, great views and a good restaurant (with a reputation for wild game) as well as an inviting swimming pool. ❽

Hotel São Lazaro Av. Cidade de Zamora ☎273 302 700, ✉hotelsaolazaro@mail.telepac.pt. Mammoth new hotel looming over the motorway on the northern edge of town. Rooms are perfectly acceptable, if a bit ho-hum, with varnished wood floors instead of carpets, their saving grace being the uninterrupted views to the Montesinho park. Breakfast included. ❺

Residencial Senhora da Ribeira Trav. da Misericórdia ☎273 300 550, ☏273 300 555. On an alley off Rua Almirante Reis, offering conspicuously spotless rooms – some with good views of the citadel – and friendly service for a very good price. In the words of their own brochure, "please visit Residencial Senhora da Ribeira, the best hotel in that king, at North East of the province of Trás-os-Montes. Thank You". Breakfast included. ❸

Residencial Transmontano Av. João da Cruz 168 ☎273 331 899. On the doorstep of the bus station. Rooms are bare-board basic but bright and fresh, with TV and a choice of en-suite bathroom. Good value. Breakfast included. No credit cards. ❶

Youth hostel

Pousada de Juventude Av. 22 de Maio ☎273 304 600, ✇ww.pousadasjuventude.pt. Roughly 1km west of the centre, this swanky new hostel has ten double rooms and sixteen four-bed dorms, as well a six-bed family room (€82.50) and a couple of two-person apartments with kitchen (€60). Also internet, laundry service and bar. Open 24hr. Dorm beds €12.50, rooms ❷

Campsites

Cepo Verde 8km west of town, on the N103 Vinhais road ☎273 999 371. All the usual facilities, plus a pool. Closed Oct–March.

Parque de Campismo 6km north of town on the França road no phone. The nearest campsite to town is the municipal one, perched on the banks of the Rio Sabor. It's had a refit, with new showers, toilets and a bar. Closed Oct–April.

Eating and drinking

Bragança has a promising array of **restaurants**, most of them pretty good value. The municipal **market** is open daily for food, although its distance from town means that the central groceries are an easier option. Most of the town's **café** culture, meanwhile, unfolds along Avenida João da Cruz, where there are any number of places with pavement tables.

Restaurants

O Camões Pr. Camões 45–47 ☎273 324 040. Stylish restaurant offering alfresco dining, a tempting selection of grilled fish and seafood, and an impressive array of pasta dishes. Closed Sat. Moderate.

Dom Fernando Cidadela 197 ☎273 326 273. Good location just inside the walls of the old town, although the quality of the food varies and service is as eccentric as the proprietor. The snug, vaguely medieval, azulejo-tiled interior is nice though. No credit cards. Moderate.

Lá em Casa Rua Marquês de Pombal 7 ☎273 322 111. A convivial place, decked out in the kind of faux-rustic style so beloved of northern restaurateurs. You might need the Portuguese menu to figure out what you're ordering, since the English-language menu offers such things as "grilled sideburns of lamb" and "threads of blond octopus". Moderate.

O Pote Rua Alexandre Herculano ☎273 333 710. Good cheap tasca, serving petiscos of chouriço,

ham, cheese, olives, and bacalhau fish balls, as well as budget pasta dishes. No credit cards. Closed Sun. Inexpensive.

Solar Bragançano Pr. da Sé 34 ☎274 323 875. Upmarket casa típica, where you dine in chandelier-hung, oak-panelled rooms to the accompaniment of classical music. The food is good, although not quite as special as the prices might suggest, and it's the place to try more unusual regional dishes, like pheasant prepared with chestnuts or partridge cooked with grapes. There's a nice arzine bar. Expensive.

Bars

Duque de Bragança Cidadela. Nightlife in town is rather limited, though this extremely popular bar inside the walled town is always a good bet – it sometimes has live music, or magic and poetry evenings, and it's open until 2am.

Moda Café Av. Dr. Francisco Sá Carneiro. The place for serious dancing, where the music keeps on coming until 5am.

Listings

Banks Branches of most of the major banks are clustered on Av. Dr. Francisco Sá Carneiro, including Caixa Geral de Depósitos for exchanging money.
Hospital Av. Abade Baçal ☎273 310 800.
Internet Cyber Centro (Mon–Fri 10am–11pm & Sun 2–8pm) in the municipal market behind the town hall.

Pharmacy Farmácia Confiança, Av. João da Cruz 76–80 ☎273 323 226.
Post office Rua Almirante Reis (Mon–Fri 8.30am–6pm, Sat 9am–12.30pm).
Taxis There's usually a fleet of taxis parked on Av. João da Cruz, on the opposite side from the cafés.

Parque Natural de Montesinho

Occupying the extreme northeastern tip of Portugal, the **Parque Natural de Montesinho** is the only sector of the Terra Fria where the way of life and the appearance of the villages have not yet been drastically changed by the incoming wealth of emigrant workers. That's not to say that the park is completely untouched – once pristine villages are slowly being defaced by ugly red terracotta brickwork – but on the whole the Serra de Montesinho's heather-clad hills, wet grass plains and thick forests of oak look much as they have done for centuries. The park covers 751 square kilometres, and has a population of 9500 distributed between 92 villages, many of which retain their old Roman or Visigothic names. Tradition hangs heavy here – the inhabitants' black capes and cloaks of straw as much a protection against heat as cold – though change, of course, is inevitable. Most of the curious round pigeon houses (*pombal*), a feature of the region, are now deserted, despite efforts by conservationists to entice the birds back. The pigeons, it seems, like many from Trás-os-Montes, prefer an easier existence in the cities than eking out a living in the countryside.

The two main access points for the park are Bragança and Vinhais, and there are **park information offices** in each, where you can pick up brochures on the local flora and fauna. In addition to the **walk** detailed in the box (see p.478), the park offices can also supply you with leaflets on other marked routes, including circuits around Moimenta and Quintanilha.

The **eastern section** of the park is the only one you can really see by public transport, with buses running north from Bragança along the N103-1 to the sleepy village of **França** and on to Portelo, just before which you can divert to the spectacularly situated border village of **Montesinho**. Another minor road (and regular bus service) runs northeast from Bragança to the fascinating medieval village of **Rio de Onor**.

Obviously, having your own transport opens up many more possibilities, and that's especially true of the more remote **western section** of the park, which is home to countless little villages waiting to be discovered if you have the time and patience to negotiate the poor and often confusing road system. However, a new hilltop-hugging stretch of tarmac between Mofreita and the once isolated village of Moimenta has opened up the possibility of a fine circuit into the park from Bragança to Vinhais, taking in the timeless villages of Gondosende, Vilarinho, Dines and Moimenta en route.

Accommodation is scattered throughout the park, with the lion's share in Montesinho, though there are rustic lodgings to be had in Gimonde, Vilarinho, França, Gondosende and Moimenta. In addition, various restoration projects are underway in other villages (including Pinheiro Nova, Travanca, Zeive, Baçal and Meixedo), aimed at supplying tourists with traditional, but

PARQUE NATURAL DE MONTESINHO

N

Barragem de
Serra Serrada

Guadramil
Petisqueira
Quintanilha
Deilão
Vila Meã
Réfega
Velgas
Labiados
Caravela
Palácios
Milhão
Babe
Rio de Onor
Varge
Sarcoias
Vale de
Lamas
Gimonde
Calabor
Portelo
Aveleda
Baçal
França
Rabal
Montesinho
Oleirinhos
Vila
Nova
Bragança
Soutelo
Cova de Lua
Meixedo
Vilarinho
Carragosa
Donai
Castro de Avelãs
Paramio
Terroso
Carragosa
Espinhosela
Oleiros
Grandais
Zeive
Maçãs
Gondesende,
Cepo
Verde
Portela
Mofreita
Fresulfe
Soeira
Castrelos
Dine
Quintela
Santa
Cruz
Paço
Prada
Vila
Verde
Moimenta
Travanca
Carvalhas
Montouto
Rio de
Fornos
Manzalvos
Landedo
Salgueiros
Vinhais
Casares
Quadra
Vilar de
Ossos
Peleias
Cerdedo
Tuizelo
Zido
Lagarelhos
Contim
Santalha
Nuzedo de
Cima
Sobreiró
de Baixo
Pinheiro
Velho
Seixas
Cabeça
da Igreja
Pinheiro
Nova
Sernande
Edroso
Penso
Vilarinho
de Lomba
Quirás
Gestosa
Cisterna
Passos de
Lomba
Vilar Seco
Sandim

⊼	Camping
	Asphalt road
⋯	Four-wheel drive only
	Scenic Routes

0 ——————— 10 km

The best **trail** in the park is a moderately easy two-day walk beginning and ending at França (see p.480). Start by turning left off the main road after the bridge and walk along the track which follows the Rio Sabor. This is rarely used by vehicles and winds through a steep gorge, where you can spot many species of birds and, in summer, maybe some wild boar. The track passes a hydroelectric power station and a disused trout farm (on your left), then after about 4km there's a turning off to the left marked "Soutelo". Ignore the turning and continue for about 6km along the track towards the **Barragem de Serra Serrada**, near the Spanish border, where there's a mountain hut (currently closed; check with the park office in Bragança) – just past the reservoir take a right-hand path signposted "Lama Grande". For alternative accommodation, head instead to Montesinho (p.480) – there's a signposted turning off to the left about 2km before the reservoir. It's a worthwhile detour in any case, and if you do spend a day or two here you can tackle the new **circular walk** up to the *barragem* and back (3hr, 7km), involving a climb of about 400m. The route – marked by red-and-yellow painted crosses, which are sometimes difficult to follow – takes you up from the eastern side of the village and back down the western side.

To rejoin the track to the reservoir, retrace your steps to the Montesinho junction. About 2km after the reservoir, the track splits in two; take the right-hand turning for the mountain hut (see above) and the left-hand turning to start the return journey to França. The track leads over a high plateau covered with expanses of heather and rock formations, and giving spectacular views over to Bragança in the distance. Follow the track, descending steadily for a few kilometres, then take a left-hand turning. A couple of kilometres further on, you'll see a right-hand turning – clearly signposted to França – and, if you take this, after about 4km you'll rejoin the track in França where the walk started.

high-quality accommodation – check at the park office in Bragança for up-to-date information. Wild **camping** in the park itself is prohibited, although there are two official sites located on the southern boundary (see Bragança, p.471) and another in Rio de Onor. Note that there are no credit card facilities for accommodation payment anywhere in the park.

Gimonde

Seven kilometres east of out of Bragança, along the N218, is **GIMONDE**, a rural village of traditional wooden houses beautifully sited on the edge of the Montesinho park which would make a fine base should you want to stay somewhere quieter than Bragança. The rivers Onor, Sabor and Igrejas all meet here near a Romanesque bridge, a favourite spot for stork-watching in early summer. The village also boasts one of the regions's most famed restaurants, the multi-prize winning *Restaurante Típico Dom Roberto* (☎273 302 520). The decor is convincingly rustic with a roaring log fire and a small wood-panelled bar, while both the menu and the adjacent delicatessen deal in fine cuisine sourced from natural, chemical-free ingredients, including home-made jams and a bewildering array of *chouriço* and *alheira*. The various wild boar and stuffed rabbit dishes may be expensive but they're worth a splurge. The peaceful *Quinta das Covas* (☎273 044 000; ✆qcovas@amontesinho.pt; breakfast included; ❸) is run by the same people, located amidst cherry trees, 1km or so out of the village. Rooms are en suite with homely white bed linen and simple furniture, while the *azulejo*-tiled dining room is equipped with an open fire, perfect for huddling up to after a stroll around the huge gardens.

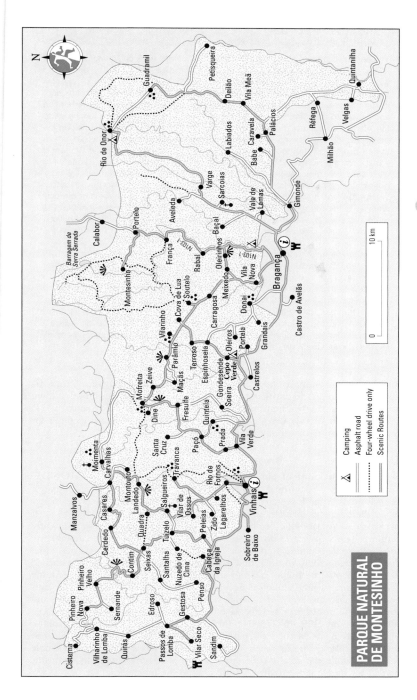

PARQUE NATURAL DE MONTESINHO

△	Camping
	Asphalt road
....	Four-wheel drive only
	Scenic Routes

0 — 10 km

The best **trail** in the park is a moderately easy two-day walk beginning and ending at França (see p.480). Start by turning left off the main road after the bridge and walk along the track which follows the Rio Sabor. This is rarely used by vehicles and winds through a steep gorge, where you can spot many species of birds and, in summer, maybe some wild boar. The track passes a hydroelectric power station and a disused trout farm (on your left), then after about 4km there's a turning off to the left marked "Soutelo". Ignore the turning and continue for about 6km along the track towards the **Barragem de Serra Serrada**, near the Spanish border, where there's a mountain hut (currently closed; check with the park office in Bragança) – just past the reservoir take a right-hand path signposted "Lama Grande". For alternative accommodation, head instead to Montesinho (p.480) – there's a sign-posted turning off to the left about 2km before the reservoir. It's a worthwhile detour in any case, and if you do spend a day or two here you can tackle the new **circular walk** up to the *barragem* and back (3hr, 7km), involving a climb of about 400m. The route – marked by red-and-yellow painted crosses, which are sometimes difficult to follow – takes you up from the eastern side of the village and back down the western side.

To rejoin the track to the reservoir, retrace your steps to the Montesinho junction. About 2km after the reservoir, the track splits in two; take the right-hand turning for the mountain hut (see above) and the left-hand turning to start the return journey to França. The track leads over a high plateau covered with expanses of heather and rock formations, and giving spectacular views over to Bragança in the distance. Follow the track, descending steadily for a few kilometres, then take a left-hand turning. A couple of kilometres further on, you'll see a right-hand turning – clearly signposted to França – and, if you take this, after about 4km you'll rejoin the track in França where the walk started.

high-quality accommodation – check at the park office in Bragança for up-to-date information. Wild **camping** in the park itself is prohibited, although there are two official sites located on the southern boundary (see Bragança, p.471) and another in Rio de Onor. Note that there are no credit card facilities for accommodation payment anywhere in the park.

Gimonde

Seven kilometres east of out of Bragança, along the N218, is **GIMONDE**, a rural village of traditional wooden houses beautifully sited on the edge of the Montesinho park which would make a fine base should you want to stay somewhere quieter than Bragança. The rivers Onor, Sabor and Igrejas all meet here near a Romanesque bridge, a favourite spot for stork-watching in early summer. The village also boasts one of the region's most famed restaurants, the multi-prize winning *Restaurante Típico Dom Roberto* (☎273 302 520). The decor is convincingly rustic with a roaring log fire and a small wood-panelled bar, while both the menu and the adjacent delicatessen deal in fine cuisine sourced from natural, chemical-free ingredients, including home-made jams and a bewildering array of *chouriço* and *alheira*. The various wild boar and stuffed rabbit dishes may be expensive but they're worth a splurge. The peaceful *Quinta das Covas* (☎273 044 000; ✉qcovas@amontesinho.pt; breakfast included; ❸) is run by the same people, located amidst cherry trees, 1km or so out of the village. Rooms are en suite with homely white bed linen and simple furniture, while the *azulejo*-tiled dining room is equipped with an open fire, perfect for huddling up to after a stroll around the huge gardens.

Rio de Onor

RIO DE ONOR, 25km north of Bragança and right on the Spanish border, provides perhaps the most fascinating insight into village life in the Serra de Montesinho. There are in fact two Rio de Onors – one in Spain (called Rio-honor de Castilla) and one in Portugal – but two stone blocks labelled "E" and "P", and a change from cobbles on the Portuguese side to smooth concrete on the Spanish, are all that delineate the frontier. The villagers have come and gone between the two for generations, operating essentially as an independent state and speaking, until recently, a hybrid Portuguese-Spanish dialect known as *Rionorês*. Their extreme isolation engendered a mutual cooperation that was independent of their respective nations, something considered so unusual that it inspired an anthropological study in the 1950s. In the past, communal meetings fined troublemakers and miscreants in wine, while today's ageing villagers (most of the youth have left for the cities) still share land, flocks, winepresses, mills and ovens. Nevertheless, there's an undeniable sense of traditions slowly dying here. A steady trickle of tourists has begun and it's difficult to imagine how Rio de Onor's medieval charm can survive indefinitely.

The two villages are set on either side of a stream: the granite steps and wooden balconies of rough schist houses line narrow alleyways, while straw creeps out across the cobbles. Hidden sheep bleat behind tattered barn doors and the ancient streets are splattered with animal dung. The old bar in the Portuguese "half" of the village – complete with ancient, wall-mounted glass cigarette case and 1970s photographs of the local football team – contains a long stick on which locals once marked the number of cattle and sheep they owned. There's some good **hiking** to be had in the surrounding hills – if you haven't had time to pick up any routes from the park office you could try asking the locals, although don't be too surprised when they express disbelief that you want to walk anywhere rather than take your car.

Rio de Onor's **Festa dos Reis** – mainly an excuse to feast on *chouriço* – is on January 6. More traditional though is the **Lenha das Almas** ("Firewood of Souls") celebration on November 1, where the boys of the village gather firewood, which is then hauled into the village by ox carts (or, more commonly now, by tractors) and auctioned off, the proceeds going to the "souls" of the dead (ie the church). The ritual has its roots in a pre-Roman cult of ancestors, as well as marking the time when boys become adults, and ends with a communal feast and a binge on roast chestnuts.

Practicalities

STUB **buses** currently leave Bragança daily at 12.40pm and 5.50pm (plus additional Rodonorte services on schooldays at 2pm), returning from Rio de Onor at 7am, 3pm and 7pm (none on weekends), with a journey time of roughly an hour. However, at the time of writing the STUB schedule was due for revision, check at Bragança turismo or bus station for details. Alternatively, a return trip by taxi from Bragança costs around €20. As you wend your way here, you'll begin to realize how isolated Rio de Onor is – the road has existed for only twenty years, before which the locals had to walk across open country to and from Bragança.

There's simple **accommodation** available at the *Casa do Povo* (parish rooms; ❶), which has a couple of clean and comfortable double rooms complete with kitchen, bathroom and washing machine; contact António Jose Preto (☎273 927 128), the friendly and accommodating village *presidente*, who lives in the last house on the right before the bridge. The *Casa*'s central location means you'll be of great interest to the villagers who congregate on the granite benches below: dig out your Portuguese phrasebook and be ready for their earthy sense of humour. There's also a new **campsite** (contact the *presidente* on the above number; closed Oct–April), located on the left at the entrance to the village. If you are staying the night you can pick up some supplies from Rio de Onor's sole **shop**, a grocer's located just over the border and down to the right in the Spanish side of the village.

França

Ten kilometres north of Bragança, up the 103-1 road, the unassuming village of **FRANÇA** is locally famous for its chestnuts and *chouriço*, though visitors use it as a base for exploring the park. While it's not difficult to spot emigrant-inspired construction clashing with the traditional schist cottages, the village still has a number of untouched, tumbledown streets which remain rooted in the distant past. França was once home to a small gold and lead mining industry (the last lead mines at nearby Portelo closed only fifteen years ago) and, if you ask around, someone might show you some of the vintage pumping equipment. Keep an eye out, too, for the old metal trolleys scattered around, once used for transporting lead but now put to more prosaic use. The local **riding centre** (daily 9am–noon & 2.30–7pm; ☎273 919 141), signposted on the right on the road out to Portelo, offers either tuition or guided trips for €10 per hour, as well as longer expeditions into the park.

There are currently two STUB **buses** daily (Mon–Fri only) from Bragança to França/Portelo, though the timetable is liable to change. França is home to the *Promise of Portugal* (☎273 919 258, ⓦwww.promise-of-portugal.com; breakfast on request), which consists of a number of charmingly restored **cottages** rented out by an hospitable English couple. Both the *Casa da Montanha* (❹) and *Casa da Castanha* (❸), sleeping four and two people respectively, are tucked away up a country track at the back of the village (look for the sign), with rustic, unpretentious interiors and cheerful kitchens. Great walking and river bathing are literally on your doorstep, although if you fancy lodging in the heart of the village, they also rent out a lovingly renovated, 250-year-old cottage, *Casa Pequena* (❹), which can sleep five. Dorm-style accommodation for cyclists and walkers should be available, too, in the near future, though for now there's the possibility of unofficial **camping** by the river and village picnic area, located just over the bridge and down to the left.

There's a small café/bar in the village down by the bridge, but for a full **meal** head to the moderately priced *Restaurante Turismo* (☎273 919 163; no credit cards) out on the left on the outskirts of the village, heading towards Portelo. It's best to give them some notice if you want to eat in the evening, when you can enjoy tasty, no-frills servings of trout, pork or omelette outside on the vine-covered patio. With your own transport, you could also drive to the *Restaurante Típico O Javali* (☎273 333 898), 6km or so south of França near the village of Rabal. It's expensive, but authentically traditional, with dishes like stewed partridge and wild boar all cooked with the ubiquitous chestnuts native to the region.

Montesinho

Flanked by wind-whipped pine plantations and dramatic granite outcrops – as well as some ugly Spanish wind farms – the border outpost of **MONTESIN-HO** (permanent population 35) packs centuries of history into its manure-mottled streets. The magnificently knotted chestnut tree towering over the main square is claimed by some villagers to be two thousand years old, while inscriptions on the doors of the houses date back to the sixteenth century. The village is roughly 8km northwest of França and walking alongside the **Rio Sabor** is idyllic, with wonderful deserted spots for swimming along the way.

The refreshingly rustic *Café Montesinho* (℡273 919 219) is the hub of village life and its genial, enterprising owner has **accommodation** available in a plainly fitted stone house (room ❶, whole house ❹) with kitchen and wooden balcony. If it's occupied, he can direct you to his brother who runs *Casas da Eira* (℡273 919 227; ❷–❹), a trio of traditional dwellings around a secluded, if rather scrappy, yard. The interiors are all very similar: comfortably modern-rustic with basic kitchens. The pick of the bunch is the small house looking onto a potato field; it comes with a small strawberry patch, which you can dig into if temptation gets the better of you. The woman known as Tia Maria Rita (℡273 919 229; room ❸, whole house ❹) also rents a place beside the café, with a charming stone-and-wood kitchen, as well as a petite cottage (❷) complete with private courtyard nestled away at the back of the village.

Montesinho's flagship accommodation looks set to be the *Lagosta Perdida* (℡933 125 106, ⓦwww.lagostaperdida.com; breakfast and dinner included; 5x), a painstaking restoration of an old granite house masterminded by a convivial Dutch/English couple. Chestnut-wood floors, an amazing central space with glass roof and encircling staircase, vintage bread oven, ecofriendly almond husk-fired power and a swimming pool with bucolic views were all under construction at the time of writing. It plans to cater for walking groups and hikers, as well as general tourists, so don't be scared to turn up with muddy boots. There is in fact a new, marked circular hiking route from Montesinho up to the dam above the village, details of which can be found in the walking box on p.478.

The western park

The gentle chestnut- and oak-wooded hills of the central and western expanses of the park are easily accessed via the pretty five-hundred-year-old hamlet of **GONDOSENDE**, 8km west of Bragança, just off the main N103 to Chaves. Nestled among the tranquil streets and flower-festooned window ledges is the *Casa do Passal* (℡273 323 506, ⓦwww.casadopassal.no.sapo.pt; no credit cards; ❺) a rustically restored cottage. Reservations are advised, though if this is full the irrepressibly jovial owner also rents out the nearby, and almost identical, *Casa de Pomar* (no credit cards; ❺). Just around the corner is *Casa da Bica* (℡273 999 454, Ⓔcasadabica@braganca.pt; breakfast included; no credit cards; ❸), that's not quite as charming as its competitors but significantly cheaper. There's also some engaging accommodation available at the 300-year-old *Casa dos Marrões* (℡273 999 550, ⓦwww.casadosmarroes.com; breakfast included; ❹) in the tiny hamlet of **VILARINHO,** some 6km to the north. While its chief attraction is the reed-cleansed, biological swimming pool, the house boasts some remarkable architectural features, notably the dizzyingly high stone walls and open space in the bar/dining area.

Eight kilometres or so further to the northwest is the enchanting village of **DINE**, constructed on descending cobbled streets that afford sweeping views of the valley. These lead down to an eerie, bat-inhabited *gruta* (cave), discovered, bizarrely enough, by a Danish diplomat in 1984, with the resulting excavations unearthing various bones, cooking implements, flints and arrowheads dating back to 4000 BC. While there's a small museum up beside the church, ostensibly designed to display the finds, the cabinets are currently empty, with

Europarques Portugal (☎273 432 396, ⓦwww.europarques.com) runs **boat trips** along the length of the river that marks the border between Spain and Portugal. Trips operate throughout the year (Mon–Fri 1 daily; Sat & Sun 2 daily; 1hr cruise €12, 2hr €18), though there's a minimum group size of twenty – check at the turismo whether you're likely to get on or not.

Accommodation

Given the high volume of tourists it receives, Miranda unsurprisingly boasts a sizeable range of places to stay, although most of the accommodation is disappointingly modern and clustered into a few streets in the new part of town.

Pensions and hotels

Residencial Cabeço do Forte Rua Cabeço do Forte 10 ☎273 431 423, ⓕ273 431 126. Nestled on a rise at the back of town, the reception area is resplendent with leather sofas while the well-appointed rooms lead off a red-carpeted corridor. The proprietors are friendly, the ambience peaceful and the views from the terrace fabulous. Private parking. Breakfast included. ❸

Pensão Flor do Douro Rua do Mercado Municipal 7 ☎273 431 186. Hemmed in on all sides by the tourist boutiques, the main selling point here is the view over the gorge, although the rooms are comfortable enough. Breakfast included. No credit cards. ❸

Residencial Planalto Rua 1 de Maio 25 ☎273 431 362, ⓦwww.hrplanalto.pt. A quaint and quietly ageing *residencial* with views of the Sé and beyond. Parking. Breakfast included. No credit cards. ❸

Estalagem Santa Catarina Largo da Pousada ☎273 431 255, ⓔsanta.catarina@mail.pt. The rooms aren't invested with any more character than those in an average upmarket hotel, although the marble balconies have dizzying views into the gorge, and a swimming pool and gardens – also poised above the dam – are planned. Breakfast included. ❻

Residencial Santa Cruz Rua Abade Baçal 61–61A ☎273 431 374, ⓕ273 431 341. Miranda's oldest *residencial* with almost seventy years under its belt. It's also the only place to stay in the old town, an attraction in itself although the immaculately clean rooms are almost of hotel standard and the owners welcoming. Breakfast included. ❷

Campsite

Santa Luzia ☎273 431 273. It's signposted on the southern side of town by the stadium and municipal swimming pool, a 2km hike from Largo da Moagem. Closed Oct–May.

Eating

Locals maintain that Miranda is home to some of the most tender meat in Portugal, which they proudly prepare in the form of *posta à Mirandesa*, basically braised calf or veal. You can sample it at just about every restaurant in town, although there's the usual local debate as to which place serves the best.

Capa d'Honras Trav. do Castelo 1 ☎273 432 699. Announced by a wrought-iron sign, this upmarket but friendly restaurant takes as its theme the flowing medieval capes traditionally worn by local dignitaries during important events. As for the food, it's aimed at well-heeled tourists – there are no less than twelve varieties of *bacalhau* on the menu, none of them under €10. Expensive.

O Mirandês Largo da Moagem ☎273 431 418. A longtime local favourite with a flurry of cooks beavering away in full view of the busy dining room. They're justly proud of their *posto à Mirandesa*, and the grilled lamb is also highly recommended. Closed alternate Sundays in winter. No credit cards. Moderate.

O Moinho Rua do Mercado 47 ☎273 431 116. Great value pizza and pasta, plus good views of the reservoir. There's a surprising array of vegetarian options (well, at least three, which qualifies as surprising in Portugal), including a delicious *spaguetti picante* prepared with chilli and garlic. Inexpensive.

São Pedro Rua Mouzinho de Albuquerque ☎273 431 321. Huge first-floor restaurant in the old town, known for its grilled kid and lamb, as well as *tamboril* and other seafood. The place is so popular in fact, that it's effectively closed on Saturdays in summer when it's usually block-booked for weddings and baptisms. Moderate.

Mogadouro

For an unkempt and authentic picture of town life in the Terra Fria, you need look no further than **MOGADOURO**, and specifically its castle. This is unexceptional as a monument, but the ground in front is common land where children play and farmers sort out their produce. During the harvest period the area is stacked high with dried *tremoços* bushes, whose seeds are consumed as beer-time snacks and used in soups. The castle hill also commands terrific views over a long, low horizon and a patchwork of fields and traditional pigeon houses. The feeling persists of a town caught between past and present, not quite ready to embrace tourism, though it does have at least one conventional attraction in its tiny **Sala Museu de Arqueologia** (daily 9am–12.30pm & 2–5.30pm; free), a sparse display of tools, coins, ceramics, arrowheads, rock paintings and other archeological miscellany unearthed from various local sites. It's located underneath the Câmara Municpal, and signposted from the main square, Largo Trindade Coelho.

The main tree-lined Avenida Nossa Senhora do Caminho has a leafy walkway and views over the hills on one side, a row of shops and cafés on the other. The avenue ends at Praça Duarte Pacheco and the adjacent main square, with the old town and ruined castle beyond. Mogadouro is 46km southwest of Miranda do Douro, and **buses** drop you on Largo Trindade Coelho, where there's a Santos bus office for onward services to Freixo de Espada à Cinta, Torre de Moncorvo or Vila Real. At the time of writing the **turismo** was closed indefinitely, its windows cobwebbed and its walls graffitied. However, there is a helpful information office for the **Parque Natural do Douro Internacional** (daily 9am–12.30pm & 2–5.30pm; ☎279 340 030, ⊛www.icn.pt), at Rua de Santa Marinha 4, just off Largo Trindade Coelho, which sells a basic park map as well as leaflets for individual walks.

Given the proximity of the Douro river, Mogadouro is one of the few places in the region where mosquitoes can seriously disrupt a good night's sleep; it's a good idea to keep your window closed from dusk onwards. The best **hotel** in town is the three-star *Hotel Trindade Coelho* (☎279 340 010, ⓔhotelcoelho@nerba.pt; breakfast included; ❸), on the Largo. Several other places lie just off the square: there are reasonable balconied rooms at *Pensão Russo* on Rua 15 de Outubro (☎ & ⓕ279 342 134; breakfast included; no credit cards; ❷), while *Residencial 2000* (☎279 342 450; breakfast included; no credit cards; ❸) in Bairro de São Sebastião (signposted off the main roundabout) has clean, bright rooms with cork floors in a quiet apartment building. The municipal **campsite** (☎936 989 213; open all year) is situated 1km or so from the centre, adjacent to the sports complex and **swimming pool** (June–Sept only; €1.50).

While almost every *residencial* in town has a **restaurant** attached, or vice versa, the moderately priced *Restaurante A Lareira*, Avenida Nossa Senhora do Caminho 58–62 (☎279 342 363; closed Mon), deserves special mention for its French-speaking chef, who personally attends to every table and cooks his delicious *posta de vitela* on a roaring fire in the corner. *Restaurante Kalifa* (☎279 342 115; closed Sun), on Rua Santa Marinha, opposite the national park office, is another local favourite, with red-checked tablecloths, wood-panelled ceiling, delicious steak and superb red wine.

Be warned that the town is busy (and rooms at a premium) in August, when the emigrants are back home with their families. There is an annual **festa** in honour of Nossa Senhora do Caminho (August 7–23), with a special *emigrante* weekend on the last weekend of August, before they leave the country again. There's more entertainment in mid-June, with processions, music and exhibitions during the annual cultural week, the **Semana Cultural**.

Torre de Moncorvo and around

There's little to see in **TORRE DE MONCORVO**, 58km southwest of Mogodouro, though its network of handsome, narrow medieval streets makes the town a pleasant place to spend the night. There's an imposing sixteenth-century Igreja Matriz – the largest church in Trás-os-Montes, which took a century to build – while the turismo (see below) is housed in the yellow-and-blue **Casa da Roda**, a reconstructed dwelling complete with its own underground well. Staff can advise you on how to track down the remains of the old town walls, though more complicated questions may see you directed to the library. In the **Oficina Vinaria** on Travessa das Amoreiras (May–Sept Tues–Sun 10am–12.30pm & 2–6.30pm; Oct–April Tues–Sun 9am–12.30pm & 2–6.30pm; free) there's an array of ageing wine-producing equipment, while the **Museu de Ferro** in Largo Balbino Rego (May–Sept Tues–Sun 10am–12.30pm & 2–5.30pm; Oct–April Tues–Sun 10am–12.30pm & 2–6.30pm; free), records the region's former iron industry. That, basically, is your lot, making the town's main attraction its almond trees, the blossoming of which draws crowds of Portuguese visitors in late February and early March. Later, the nuts are gathered and sugared, and sold locally; a good place to try them is Flormêndoa at Largo Diogo Sá 5–7, by the Igreja Matriz. Local **festivities** include the Festa de Nossa Senhora da Assunção (second weekend of August), the Feira do Ano (December 23), and the Feira das Cerejas (May 10), in honour of Moncorvo's locally produced cherries.

Practicalities

The **bus station** is on the main road, the N220, next to the telecom building near the hospital, while the **turismo** is hidden away behind the Camâra Municipal at Travessa Campos Monteiro 21 (Mon–Fri 9am–12.30pm & 2–5.30pm; ☏ 279 252 265).

   Best of the cheaper **accommodation** options is the basic *Residencial Café Popular*, Rua Tomas Ribeiro 66 (☏ 279 252 337; breakfast included; no credit cards; ❷), off the main Praça Francisco Meireles, with good views from the concrete terrace. More upmarket is *Residencial Campos Monteiro*, Rua Visconde de Vila Maior 55 (☏ 279 254 055, ℻ 279 254 280; breakfast included; ❸), featuring modern rooms with attractive balconies, plus parking and free internet access. The lovely *Quinta das Aveleiras* (☏ 279 258 280, ⓦ www.quinta-das-aveleiras.com; breakfast included; no credit cards; ❺), 300m from the bus station on the Pocinho road, has spacious rooms in four restored farmhouses, each with kitchenettes, log fires and bicycles for rent. They also make their own wine.

   The moderately priced **restaurant** at *Residencial Campos Monteiro* is a decent choice, though the menu is a bit workaday (steak, pork chops and fried fish). For more variety, *Restaurante Regional O Lagar* (☏ 279 252 828), Rua Adriano Leandro 16, down from the Igreja Matriz, serves very moderately priced regional food – try the stewed wild boar, washed down with a fruity table wine.

Around Moncorvo

The surrounding hills of the **Serra do Reboredo** make for a scenic drive east along the N220 – the first road on the right takes you within sight of the range's main peak, a distance of some 7km. Back on the main road, the next turning on the left leads to the small village of **FELGAR**, 13km east of Torre de Moncorvo and home to the remarkable *Casa de Santa Cruz* (℡279 928 060, Ⓦwww.casasantacruz.com; breakfast included; no credit cards; ❺). Located in a corner of the main square, this eighteenth-century manor house has been imaginatively restored, while retaining its huge old chimney and heavy oak doors. The dining room furniture has been recycled from the original beams.

At **CARVIÇAIS** – 16km east of Moncorvo – there's one of Trás-os-Montes' best restaurants, the moderately priced *O Artur* (℡279 939 184; closed Mon), famed for its genuine *alheira* sausages – it's almost the only place left in Portugal which hasn't succumbed to mixing pork into the stuffing. As if to underline their *típico* status, the walls are hung with antique farm implements, while the menu features other earthy staples such as fried sardines with rice and beans. They also have a few modern, functional en-suite **rooms** available (breakfast included; ❷).

Turning north for Mogadouro along the N221 you reach **LAGOAÇA**, a very old village whose houses feature Manueline stone-arched windows, and where some of the older women still wear traditional dress. Pass through the village, beyond the cemetery, and there's a superb viewing platform, looking over the deep Douro valley into Spain.

Freixo de Espada à Cinta

The southernmost town in Trás-os-Montes is **FREIXO DE ESPADA À CINTA**, 46km south of Mogadouro. The name is something of a mouthful, translating as "ash-tree of the sword" and supposedly referring to Dom Dinis hacking at a nearby ash tree as he announced the founding of the town. It feels end-of-the-worldish, as the road winds down to its valley, the town hidden on each side by wild, dark mountains, a backdrop against which you might glimpse the occasional hawk or black kite. You're unlikely to come across any other tourists – in fact the town was once considered so remote that prisoners who had been granted an amnesty were allowed to settle here – and it's this sense of isolation that makes the town worth a visit.

Curiously for such a remote outpost there is a very rich **Igreja Matriz** (Tues–Sun 9.30am–12.30pm & 2–5pm; free) – part Romanesque, part Manueline – with a *retábulo* of paintings by the famous Viseu artist, Grão Vasco. The church is at the heart of the town's **Romaria de Sete Paços**, which takes place at midnight on Good Friday; a sombre cortege of chanting, hooded penitents dressed in black, with their faces covered, proceeds from the church and wends its way through town. Across the way from the church is a magnificent heptagonal **keep** (ask for the key in the Igreja Matriz), a landmark for miles around, which affords great views from its bell tower for those who brave the very steep steps. The only other attraction is a mansion in Largo do Outeiro that maintains a **garden** (Mon–Fri 9am–12.30pm & 2–5.30pm, Sat & Sun 10am–noon & 2–5pm; free) of mulberry bushes complete with worms for silk production.

The town is served by daily Santos **buses** from Miranda do Douro, Moncorvo and Mogadouro. To the south, the N221 follows a beautiful stretch of the Douro to Barca d'Alva, 20km southwest, but there are no buses along this route. The town's small **turismo** (daily: July & Aug 9.30am–7.30pm; Sept–June 9am–6pm; ☎279 653 480) is on Avenida do Emigrante, just off the main Avenida Guerra Junqueira, where the buses drop you. One block northeast of Avenida do Emigrante is Largo do Outeiro, site of the regional office for the **Parque Natural do Douro Internacional** (Mon–Fri 9am–12.30 & 2–5.30pm; ☎ & ℉279 658 130, ⓦwww.icn.pt), which is worth a visit if you plan to visit the park.

Accommodation options include the rather soulless *Hospedaria Fatibel* (☎279 658 090, ℉279 652 268; breakfast included; no credit cards; ❷), just around the corner from the turismo, or the more characterful *Hospedaria Cinta de Ouro* (☎279 652 550, ℉279 653 470; breakfast included; ❸), opposite the cinema on the way out of town to the south. The brightly painted walls here are hung with the owners' own artwork, and the upstairs **restaurant** (with pleasant terrace and wicker chairs) is the best place in town for quality Portuguese meals, although portions can be on the small side. Try their *alheira* with egg and potato. The town's most charming choice is *Casa do Conselheiro* (☎279 653 439, ℮albusquerqus@yahoo.com; breakfast included; no credit cards; ❹), a lovely old house on Rua das Moreirinhas in the old part of town to the north, with lots of exposed stone and a covered patio. There's also a free, if rather bleak and dusty, municipal **campsite**, the *Congida* (☎279 653 371; open all year), 4km east down a series of hairpin bends on the banks of the Rio Douro; follow the signs or take a taxi. The complex also houses the municipal swimming pool (June–Sept only; €1), a couple of cafés and a restaurant. **Boat trips** are also available from here at weekends, either to the nearby Barragem de Saucelle (€4), or further north to the Barragem de Aldeiadávila (€10), both of which straddle the Spanish border.

Parque Natural do Douro Internacional

The **Parque Natural do Douro Internacional** covers a vast tract of land along the west bank of the Rio Douro as it flows along the Spanish border from Miranda do Douro in the north to Barca d'Alva (p.373) – the point at which the river officially enters Portuguese territory. It also encompasses a stretch of the Rio Águeda further south in Beira Alta. The upper Douro is ecologically important because it has a Mediterranean microclimate, in marked contrast to the harsher, mountainous terrain of the surrounding Terra Fria. The combination of mild winters and its isolation from large human populations has led to the survival of a number of animal and plant species now extinct in the south. To the visitor, this quirk of geography is most visible in the region's famous **almond trees**, explained in the legend of a Moorish prince who married a northern European princess. Though happy in summer, she grew sad and wistful in winter, and ached for the snow-clad hills of her homeland. The prince hurried to the Algarve, from where he brought back the almond trees, so that from then on, every February when the trees blossomed, the princess beheld white as far as the eye could see.

Despite some river pollution (mild in comparison with further downstream), and industrial sand extraction on the Spanish side, the area has been left largely untouched by the more damaging aspects of modern agriculture and industry. The park preserves a rich, if endangered, variety of local **fauna**, including wolves, wild cats and otters, as well as various species of bats and amphibians.

The area is also home to over 170 **bird species**, including rare peregrine falcons, black storks and, in summer, Europe's largest concentration of Egyptian vultures. In common with all natural parks, its success depends on achieving a fine balance between the encouragement of much-needed investment in the agricultural infrastructure on its margins, and the development of ecotourism within the park itself to benefit the local population.

The main **park office** is in Mogadouro (see p.485), which produces an excellent map (€3.50) with a brief rundown of the points of interest in the park (in Portuguese). Other offices are found at Miranda do Douro, Freixo de Espada à Cinta and Figueira de Castelo Rodrigo, any of which could be used as a base to visit the park. There are a number of waymarked **walking circuits** in the park, ranging in length and difficulty, at least two of which are accessible without your own transport, starting from Miranda do Douro and Freixo de Espada à Cinta respectively. Leaflets with detailed route maps are available from the park offices. Scattered down the eastern side of the park are a number of viewing platforms, where you can gaze down from the canyon-like cliffs into the Douro far below, although you'll need your own transport to reach these.

Impactus (☎962 838 261, ⊛www.impactus.pt) is an **ecotourism** outfit operating out of Castelo Melhor, near Vila Nova de Foz Côa, offering a wide variety of nature walks and activities in the park, including a three-day/two-night tour, travelling by 4WD and focusing on bird-watching (€235 with all food and board). Otherwise, Torre de Moncorvo-based Sabor, Douro e Aventura (☎279 258 270, ⊛www.sabordouro.com) organizes **adventure tours**, including walking trips, boat trips, rock-climbing and canoeing. A day's boat trip, or a day's kakaying on the Douro will set you back around €35, while guided day-walks into the park cost €17.50.

Travel details

Trains

Peso da Régua to: Livraçao (for Amarante; 9–10 daily; 1hr 15min); Pocinho (5 daily; 1hr 30min); Porto (9–10 daily; 2hr–2hr 30min); Tua (2 daily; 40min); Vila Real (3–5 daily; 50min).
Pocinho to: Livraçao (5 daily; 2hr 20min–3hr 20min); Peso da Régua (5 daily; 1hr 30min); Porto (5 daily; 3hr 45min–4hr 45min), via Tua (5 daily; 45min).
Tua to: Livraçao (5 daily; 1hr 50min); Mirandela (2 daily; 1hr 50min); Peso da Régua (5 daily; 45min); Pocinho (5 daily; 45min); Porto (5 daily; 3–4hr).
Vila Real to: Peso da Régua (3–5 daily; 50min).

Buses

Bragança to: Braga (10–17 daily; 5hr); Chaves (Mon–Fri & Sun 3 daily; 2hr 10min); Coimbra (5–7 daily; 5hr); Lamego (Mon–Fri & Sun 3 daily; 4hr); Lisbon (Mon–Fri & Sun 12–15 daily, Sat 7 daily; 9–10hr); Miranda do Douro (Mon–Fri 3–4 daily; 1hr 30min–2hr 15min); Mirandela

(13–19 daily; 1hr); Mogadouro (Mon–Fri 1–2 daily; 1hr 40min); Peso da Régua (Mon–Fri & Sun 3 daily; 3hr 45min); Porto (Mon–Fri & Sun 19–30 daily, Sat 11 daily; 5hr–5hr 20min); Vila Nova de Foz Côa (2 daily; 2hr); Vila Real (Mon–Fri 15–23 daily; 2hr); Vinhais (2–3 daily; 35min); Viseu (Mon–Fri & Sun 3 daily; 5hr 15min).
Chaves to: Braga (Mon–Fri 6 daily, Sat & Sun 1 daily; 3hr); Bragança (1–2 daily; 2hr); Coimbra (5–10 daily; 2hr 40min); Fronteira (Mon–Fri 5 daily; 1hr); Lamego (Mon–Fri 6–7 daily, Sun 2–4 daily; 2hr); Lisbon (5–10 daily; 8–10hr); Mirandela (Mon–Fri 3 daily; 2hr); Montalegre (Mon–Fri 4 daily, Sun 1 daily; 1hr 20min); Porto (Mon–Fri 16–18 daily, Sat & Sun 5–11 daily; 3hr); Vila Real (Mon–Fri 20–23 daily, Sat & Sun 9–15 daily; 1hr 10min–2hr).
Freixo de Espada à Cinta to: Miranda do Douro (Mon–Fri 1 daily; 2hr); Mogadouro (Mon–Fri 1 daily; 1hr); Torre de Moncorvo (Mon–Fri 3 daily; 1hr).
Miranda do Douro to: Bragança (Mon–Fri 2 daily; 1hr 30min–2hr 15min); Freixo de Espada à Cinta

(Mon–Fri 1 daily; 2hr); Mirandela (Mon–Fri 2 daily; 1hr 30min); Mogadouro (Mon–Fri 5 daily, Sat & Sun 2 daily; 50min); Torre de Moncorvo (1 daily Mon–Fri & Sun 1hr 45min).

Mirandela to: Bragança (14–22 daily; 1hr 25min–2hr 45min); Chaves (Mon–Fri 3 daily; 2hr); Miranda (Mon–Fri 2 daily; 2hr–2hr 30min); Vila Flôr (4 daily; 40min); Vila Real (14–22 daily; 1hr 10min).

Mogadouro to: Freixo de Espada à Cinta (Mon–Fri 3 daily; 1hr 15mins); Miranda do Douro (Mon–Fri 5 daily, Sat & Sun 2 daily; 50min); Pocinho (2 daily; 1hr 30min); Torre de Moncorvo (Mon–Fri 3 daily, Sat & Sun 2 daily; 1hr); Vila Real (Mon—Fri 3 daily, Sat & Sun 2 daily; 2hr 45min).

Montalegre to: Braga (2 daily; 2hr 40min); Chaves (Mon–Fri 4 daily, Sun 1 daily; 1hr 20min).

Torre de Moncorvo Freixo de Espada à Cinta (Mon–Fri 3 daily; 1hr); Miranda do Douro (1 daily Mon–Fri & Sun; 1hr 45min); Mogodouro (2 daily; 1 hr); Pocinho – for trains running along the Douro line (see p.368) – (3 daily; 15–30mins); Vila Real (Mon–Fri & Sun 2 daily; 1hr 45min); Vila Nova de Foz Côa (3 daily; 35–40min).

Vila Flôr to: Carrazeda de Ansiães (Mon–Fri & Sun 2 daily; 1hr); Mirandela (Mon–Fri 4 daily; 40min); Torre de Moncorvo (Mon–Fri 1–2 daily; 30min); Tua (Mon–Fri & Sun 2 daily; 1hr).

Vila Real to: Amarante (Mon–Fri 18 daily, Sat & Sun 9–12 daily; 1hr 25min); Braga (Mon–Fri 9–12 daily, Sat & Sun 5–8 daily; 2–3hr); Bragança (Mon–Fri 26–32 daily, Sat & Sun 18—21 daily; 2hr); Chaves (Mon–Fri 22–25 daily, Sat & Sun 10–12 daily; 1hr 10min); Coimbra (11–18 daily; 3hr 20min); Guimarães (Mon–Fri 5–6 daily, Sat & Sun 1–4 daily; 1hr 30min); Lamego (1–3 daily; 1hr 30min); Lisbon (9–18 daily; 7hr); Mirandela (Mon–Fri 23–29 daily, Sat & Sun 15–17 daily; 1hr); Peso da Régua (4–12 daily; 45min); Porto (Mon–Fri 38 daily, Sat & Sun 18–25 daily; 1hr 40min); Viseu (Mon–Fri 7 daily, Sat & Sun 1–3 daily; 1hr 45min).

Alentejo

ATLANTIC
OCEAN

N

SPAIN

CHAPTER 8

Highlights

✳ **Templo Romano, Évora**
Enjoy a sunset drink near
Évora's most impressive
Roman remain. See p.498

✳ **Cromeleque dos Almendres** The Iberian peninsula's
largest Neolithic stone circle, near Évora, is a hugely
atmospheric site. See p.504

✳ **Saturday market, Estremoz** A classic Portuguese
market, selling everything
from earthenware to
cheese, all locally made.
See p.506

✳ **Monsaraz** Stay the night in
one of the traditional houses in this fortified hilltop
village. See p.510

✳ **Serpa** Defensive walls
entirely surround one of
the region's most delightful
small towns. See p.529

✳ **Mértola** The Alentejo's
best-kept secret – a quiet
riverside town of great
charm and antiquity.
See p.533

✳ **Miróbriga** Visit the Alentejo's
most extensive Roman
remains. See p.536

✳ **Vila Nova de Milfontes**
The Alentejo coast is quite
distinct from that of the
Algarve, with the estuary
town of Vila Nova its finest
resort. See p.539

△ Tiles, Estremoz train station

8

Alentejo

The sparsely populated plains of the **Alentejo** are overwhelmingly agricultural, dominated by vast cork and olive plantations – the two crops that are well suited to the low rainfall, sweltering summer heat and poor soil. The region covers a huge area, almost a third of the whole country, stretching south from the Rio Tejo to the northern mountain ranges of the Algarve. Much of the interior landscape, it has to be said, is tedious to travel through, with long bus and train rides, or car journeys, the norm between the sparse population centres. However, it's a region that repays exploration, offering unexpected surprises – from superbly sited castles and remote walled towns to Roman ruins and sweeping Atlantic beaches. The Alentejo is also home to hundreds of species of birds, from black storks to great bustards, all finely adapted to the mix of varied agriculture and marginal wilderness.

It's still one of the poorest parts of Europe in many respects, much of whose population derives a living from the huge agricultural estates known as *latifúndios*, which have been in place since Roman times. Handed down from generation to generation, these estates remained largely feudal in character until the 1974 revolution, when much of the land was collectivized. However, the workers possessed neither the financial means nor the technical know-how to cope with a succession of poor harvests, and increasingly the original *latifúndio* owners have been clawing back their estates at depressed prices. Moreover, mechanization has done away with much casual farm labour – a move hastened by EU grants for modernization programmes and the introduction of new agricultural methods.

For most visitors, understandably, the region's major draws are its few towns and cities, with the outstanding attraction being **Évora**, whose Roman temple, medieval walls and cathedral have put it very much on the tourist map. Elsewhere in **Alto Alentejo** (Upper Alentejo), few towns see more than a handful of visitors a day. Yet there is much to see and enjoy: the spectacular fortifications of **Elvas**; the district capital of **Portalegre**; the hilltop villages of **Monsaraz** and **Marvão**; and the marble towns of **Estremoz** and **Vila Viçosa**, where even the humblest homes are made of fine stone from the local quarries. This region is also scattered with **prehistoric remains**, including over a dozen megalithic sites with dolmens, standing stones and stone circles.

South of Évora, in the plains of **Baixo Alentejo** (Lower Alentejo), the attractions lie further apart and, without a car, it's difficult to construct a quick sightseeing route – limited daily bus departures mean spending nights in places you might otherwise simply stop in for a couple of

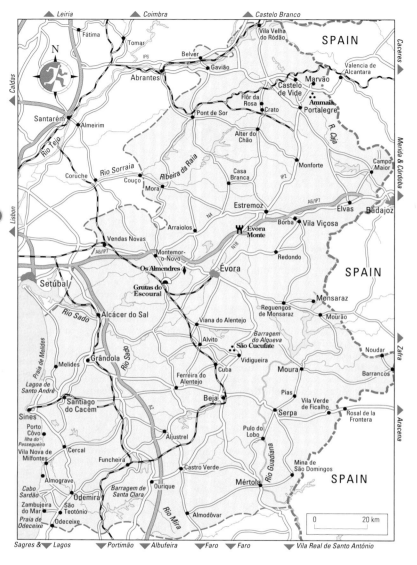

▲ Leiria   ▲ Coimbra   ▲ Castelo Branco

Fátima
Tomar   Vila Velha
                          do Ródão   SPAIN   Caceres
          IP6
                   Belver
                        Gavião   Valencia de
      Abrantes   Alcantara
                                         Marvão
                              Flôr da   Castelo
                              Rosa   de Vide   Ammaia
Santarém   Pont de Sor Crato   Portalegre
        Almeirim   Campo
                             Alter do   Maior
Rio Tejo   Chão
      Coruche   Rio Sorraia   Monforte
                         Couço   IP2
              Mora
                                         Casa
                         Ribeira da Raia Branca
                                                        A6/IP7
                                  Estremoz   Elvas   Badajoz
                   Arraiolos   Borba Vila Viçosa
          Vendas Novas   Évora
                                            Monte
      A6/IP7   Montemor-   SPAIN
Setúbal   o-Novo   Redondo
                  Os Almendres   Évora
                  Grutas do   Reguengos
                  Escoural   de Monsaraz   Monsaraz
Alcácer do Sal   Mourão
Rio Sado   Viana do Alentejo
                          Alvito   Barragem
              Grândola   do Alqueva
      Melides   São Cucufate   Noudar
Lagoa de   Cuba   Vidigueira
Santo André   Santiago   Ferreira do Moura   Barrancos
Sines   do Cacém   Alentejo   Pias
Porto   Beja   Vila Verde
Côvo   de Ficalho
Ilha do   Aljustrel   Serpa Rosal de la
Pesseigueiro   Frontera
Vila Nova de   Cercal   Pulo do
Milfontes   Funcheira   Lobo
Cabo   Castro Verde   Mina de
Sardão Almograve Ourique   São Domingos SPAIN
Odemira Barragem de   Mértola
Zambujeira Santa Clara   Almodôvar
do Mar São Teotónio
Praia de Odeceixe
Odeceixe

Sagres & ▼ Lagos   ▼ Portimão ▼ Albufeira ▼ Faro ▼ Faro   ▼ Vila Real de Santo António

0   20 km

hours. However, there are some good overnight targets, including the main
town of **Beja**, as well as nearby **Serpa**, **Moura** and **Mértola**, enjoyable
historic towns all, with a wealth of good accommodation. To the west, the
Alentejo **coastline** is almost as extensive as that of the Algarve, though it
is considerably less developed. Only a few small resorts – prime among
them **Vila Nova de Milfontes** – attract summer crowds, but the beaches
are superb.

Alto Alentejo

Évora provides the easiest starting point in Alentejo, with frequent buses and trains from Lisbon. Give yourself at least two days here, if you can, and allow another day to see the surrounding sights, most notably the carpet town of **Arraiolos** and the extraordinary stone circle of **Os Alemendres**. From Évora, you're within striking distance of the handsome market town of **Estremoz**, which sits at the heart of Alto Alentejo's "marble country". Here, as well as in neighbouring Borba and particularly in the regal retreat of **Vila Viçosa**, the most mundane streets and buildings are given the kind of luxurious finish you generally see only in the grandest churches and houses. South of Estremoz, the fortified village of **Monsaraz** rises from the plains, while to the east lie the superbly preserved walls of **Elvas**, close to the Spanish frontier. To the north, **Portalegre** is the capital of Alto Alentejo, though the better overnight stops are in its surroundings – either at the fine *pousada* near rural **Crato** or in the upland district north of Portalegre, whose tree-clad mountain ranges hide a series of gorgeous hilltop towns and villages. Among these, the best targets are **Castelo de Vide** and **Marvão**, the former with a historic Jewish quarter, the latter with views to rival those of Monsaraz.

Évora

ÉVORA is one of the most impressive and enjoyable cities in Portugal, full of memorable monuments. A Roman temple, Moorish alleys, a circuit of medieval walls, and a rather grand ensemble of sixteenth-century palaces and mansions are all in superb condition, spruced up by a long-term restoration programme and placed under UNESCO protection. Inevitably, they attract a great number of summer tourists but, despite the crowds, the city is far from spoiled. It's still a relatively small place – the population of 50,000 is only half its medieval number – and the streets contained within its walls are a pleasure to stroll, with none of the hustle associated with larger tourist centres. The university, re-established here in the 1970s, adds an independent side to city life, while Évora emphasizes its agricultural roots with a huge open-air market held on the second Tuesday of the month in the Rossio, just south of the city walls. However, Évora's big annual event is the **Feira de São João**, a folklore, handicraft, gastronomic and musical festival, whose origins date from pre-Christian times and which takes over the city during the last ten days of June.

Arrival and information

Évora's **train station** is 1km southeast of the centre – if you walk up through the Rossio and follow Rua da República, straight ahead, you'll reach Praça do Giraldo, the city's main square, or it's a €4 taxi ride. The **bus terminal** is five minutes' walk from the western city walls along the Lisbon road; it's a ten-minute walk in total to Praça Giraldo, or you can take one of the regular green buses running into town. Drivers should park in one of the many (mostly free) **car parks** at the walls and walk in, as the centre is confusing to drive around and has few parking places.

The **turismo** is at Praça do Giraldo 73 (daily: April–Oct 9am–7pm; Nov–March 9am–6pm; ℡266 730 030), and posts transport timetables, gives out a city map and can help with accommodation. You can also pick up **tour** leaflets here – for more on which, see "Listings". At the office of the **Rota dos Vinhos do Alentejo**, Praça Joaquim António d'Aguiar 20 (℡266 746 498, Ⓦ www.vinhosdoalentejo.pt), a marketing organization for the Alentejan wine industry, there's a wine route booklet available detailing all the region's vineyards – you need to contact this office in advance to arrange vineyard visits, and they are very helpful and speak English.

Accommodation

Accommodation prices in Évora are higher than in the rest of the Alentejo, more or less comparable with Lisbon. That said, there's a more agreeable choice of places here than virtually anywhere else in the south, from simple rooms in family houses to ducal palaces. Outside the city, a large array of country houses and estates also offer accommodation, most within a short drive. In summer you're advised to book in advance to guarantee a bed anywhere, though the turismo may be able to help if you arrive without a reservation. There is a campsite reasonably close to the centre, but note that the city's youth hostel is currently closed for renovation.

In Evora

Residencial O Alentejo Rua Serpa Pinto 74 ℡266 702 903. Spacious en-suite rooms in a well-kept house, though if you want the air-con remote control you pay another €5. It's probably the best value in this category. No credit cards. ❸

Residencial Diana Rua Diogo Cão 2 ℡266 702 008, ℻266 743 101. Feeling its age a bit now, which means the rooms (either in the *residencial* or over the road in a dusty annexe) are adequate, not inspiring. You can save yourself €10 by taking a room with a shower cubicle but sharing a toilet. Breakfast included. ❸

Pensão O Giraldo Rua dos Mercadores 27 ℡266 705 833. A real mix of rooms – some are far better than others – means it pays to have a good look around if possible. Prices have edged up and rooms with bath are a bit overpriced, but you'll still score a relative bargain if you're prepared to share facilities. No credit cards. ❷, en-suite ❹

Casa Palma Rua Bernardo Matos 29A ℡266 703 560. First-floor *quartos* in a scrupulously clean family house, featuring fine old pieces of furniture, polished floors and brass bedsteads. A couple of rooms (€5 cheaper) share a bathroom. No credit cards. ❷

Alojamento Particular Rua Romão Ramalho 27 no phone. Apart from the street number and a small "quartos" sign it's unmarked, but upstairs is a nice family home with four reasonably sized modern rooms available, sharing two clean bathrooms. No credit cards. ❷

Residencial Policarpo Rua Freiria de Baixo 16 ℡266 702 424, ℻266 702 424. The hands-down mid-range winner, this former ducal summer palace has sixteenth-century *azulejos*, a granite staircase and fine views from many rooms. Staff are helpful and English-speaking and, if the rooms are fading a little, they still have bags of charm. There's parking, but good luck trying to find the place by car. Breakfast (on the terrace) included. No credit cards. ❸, en-suite ❹

Pousada dos Lóios Largo do Conde de Vila Flor ℡266 730 070, Ⓦ www.pousadas.pt. One of the country's finest *pousadas*, housed in the former Convento dos Lóios. It really warrants its prices, as rooms are lovely – many with traditional furniture, including some dramatic four-poster beds – and there's a pool. Also elegant dining (from €40 a head; reservations required) in the cloisters, where fine Alentejan specialities (tomato soup, squid with chickpeas, rabbit stew) are served. Winter rates (Nov–Feb) cut around €50 from the bill. Breakfast included. ❾

Residencial Riviera Rua 5 de Outubro 49 ℡266 737 210, Ⓔ res.riviera@telepac.pt. A makeover has transformed this central *residencial* into something rather nice – 21 individually styled rooms with stripped wooden floors, Alentejan rugs, pretty bedspreads and little marble bathrooms. Some rooms are more attractive (and bigger) than others, but it's not a bad deal at all for the price. Breakfast included. ❹

Hotel Santa Clara Trav. da Milheira 19 ℡266 704 141, Ⓦ www.hotelsantaclara.pt. The rooms (all en-suite) are none too exciting, but they are mod-

ÉVORA

Estremoz

Arraiolos

ESTRADA DA CIRCUNVALAÇÃO

0   200 m

Mosteiro do Calvario

LG CHÃO DAS COVAS

LARGO DE AVIZ

Spain

Antiga Universidade

Rota dos Vinhos

Palacio Duques de Cadaval

Teatro García de Resende

PRAÇA J. A. AGUIAR

RUA MENINO JESUS

São João Evangelista

Police

Jardim do Paço

Convento dos Lóios

Câmara Municipal

Templo Romano

Santa Clara

Museu Municipal

Sé

Santo Antão

Misericórdia

Olimpia Laundry

PRAÇA DO GIRALDO

Lisbon

Bus Station & Lisbon

São Francisco

N. S. da Graça

Mercado Municipal

Ruined Palace

Palácio de Dom Manuel

Temporary Market

Hospital & Beja

Jardim Público

AV. MARECHAL CARMONA

N

Campsite

Praça de Touros

ROSSIO DE S. BRÁS

Ermida de São Brás

Train Station

Beja

ALENTEJO | Évora

8

ACCOMMODATION				CAFÉS & RESTAURANTS		O Fialho	3	BARS & CLUBS	
Alentejo	F	Policarpo	B	Arcada	8	O Forcado	11	Bar UE	
Alojamento		Pousada dos Loíos	A	Botequim da Mouraria	4	Pane & Vino	14	Café Alentejano	16
Particular	I	Riviera	C	A Choupana	13	Quarta-Feira	2	Oficina	12
Casa Palma	J	Santa Clara	D	Cozinha do		Repas	18	Praxis Clube	15
Diana	E	Solar de Monfalim	G	Santo Humberto	10	O Sobreiro	1		
Giraldo	H			Jardim Diana	7	Violeta	5		
				Taverna	6	Zoka	17		

ern, relatively spacious and air-conditioned. They are also quiet – the backstreet location, behind the convent, a real boon – and there's a little roof terrace. Breakfast included. ❹

Albergaria Solar de Monfalim Largo da Misericórdia 1 ☏ 266 750 000, ⓦ www.monfalimtur.pt. To

step inside this restored summer ducal palace is to enter a haven – elegant, spacious and relaxed. There are 25 handsome rooms, with pretty Alentejo furniture and furnishings, while breakfast is taken on the terrace, which has superb views. Parking available (for a daily fee). Breakfast included. ❺

Outside Évora

Estalagem Monte das Flores 5km southwest, on the N380 (Alcáçovas road) ☎ 266 749 680. A rustic farm offering lots of activities, including horse-riding, as well as tennis courts, pool and a decent restaurant. ❺

Monte da Serralheira 3km east, beyond Bairro Almeirim ☎ 266 741 286, ⓦ www.monteserralheira.com. Dutch-owned farm with six good-value apartments (sleeping two or four people) each with terrace, sitting room, small kitchen and TV. It's very peaceful, there's a nice communal pool, and you can rent a bike or ride a horse. Breakfast also available (€6). 2 people ❸, 4 people ❺

Quinta a Espada 4km north, Estrada da Arraiolos ☎ 266 734 549, ⓦ www.softline .pt/quintadaespada. Seven country-style rooms in a *quinta* set in pretty grounds, through which the Évora aqueduct runs. There's a sun terrace and pool, and plenty of space. ❺

Campsite

Orbitur 2km southwest of town, N380 (Alcáçovas road) ☎ 266 705 190. Clean and well equipped, with a restaurant and swimming pool. Bus #5 from Pr. do Giraldo runs nearby, or take a taxi (around €3). Open all year.

The City

Évora was shaped by its **Roman** and **Moorish** occupations: the former is commemorated by a temple, the latter by a characteristic tangle of alleys, rising steeply among the whitewashed houses. Most of the city's other monuments, however, date from the fourteenth to the sixteenth century, when Évora prospered under the patronage of the ruling **House of Avis**. To them are owed the many noble palaces scattered about the city, as is the Jesuit university and the wonderful array of Manueline and Renaissance buildings. That the city's monuments have survived intact is due, in large part, to Évora's decline after the Spanish usurpation of the throne in 1580. Future Portuguese monarchs chose to live nearer Lisbon, and the university was closed down. For the next four hundred years, Évora drifted back into a rural existence as a provincial market centre.

Praça do Giraldo is the central hub, with the main historic kernel just to the east. Within the surrounding city walls are several distinct old-town areas, with another concentration of sights in the streets between the main square and the public gardens. Meanwhile, to the north of the touristed centre you can follow the course of the medieval Aqueduto do Água Prata (Silver Water Aqueduct), into whose ever-rising arches a row of houses has been incorporated. Wherever you wander, nothing is more than a ten-minute walk from Praça do Giraldo.

Templo Romano and Termas Romanas

The graceful **Templo Romano** stands at the very heart of the old city. Dating from the second century AD, it is the best-preserved temple in Portugal, despite its use as an execution-ground during the Inquisition and a slaughterhouse until 1870. The remains consist of a small platform supporting fourteen granite columns with Corinthian capitals and a marble entablature. Its popular attribution to Diana is apparently fanciful; Jupiter is the more likely alternative. The little garden in front of the temple has a kiosk-bar, while from the terrace you can look north across the rooftops – and see just how small contemporay Evora is, with the fields beginning only a few hundred metres away.

The other significant Roman remain was uncovered beneath the nearby town hall, the **Câmara Municipal** (Mon–Fri 9am–5.30pm), where during office hours you can walk in to view the **Termas Romanas** (Roman baths), which date from a century earlier than the temple. These include an arched brick doorway, the entrance to an extraordinary room with a circular hot and steam bath that's 9m in diameter.

Convento dos Lóios and São João Evangelista

Directly opposite the temple, the magnificent fifteenth-century **Convento dos Lóios** is now a top-grade *pousada*. Hotel staff can be sniffy about allowing in non-residents (or non-diners) to look around, but those that are able to proceed beyond the doors encounter dual horseshoe arches, slender twisted columns and intricate carvings on the doorway to the chapterhouse. All are fine examples of the so-called Luso-Moorish style and have been attributed to Francisco de Arruda, architect of Évora's aqueduct and the Belém tower in Lisbon.

Adjoining the *pousada* is the former conventual church, dedicated to **São João Evangelista** (Tues–Sun 10am–12.30pm & 2–5pm; €3). This is still the private property of the Duques de Cadaval, who occupy a wing or two of their adjacent ancestral palace. You are ushered through the Gothic church doorway to see the extraordinary floor-to-ceiling *azulejos* within, the masterpiece of one António Oliveira Bernardes and created early in the eighteenth century. They show scenes from the life of São Lourenço Justiniano, founder of the Lóios order. Hidden among the pews two small trapdoors stand open to reveal both a Moorish cistern (the church and convent were built over an old castle) and a grisly ossuary containing the bones of the convent's monks. You can buy a combination ticket (€5) at the church if you also want to see the private art collection of the Cadaval dukes, housed in a few rooms of the **Palácio dos Duques de Cadaval**, but it's probably one to skip.

The Sé and around

Évora's cathedral, the **Sé** (daily 9am–12.30pm & 2–5pm; free; entrance on Largo Miguel de Portugal), was begun in 1186, about twenty years after the reconquest of Évora from the Moors. The Romanesque solidity of its original battlemented towers and roofline contrasts sharply with the pointed Gothic arches of subsequent and less militaristic additions, such as the porch and central window. The interior is more straightforwardly Gothic, although the choir and high altar were remodelled in the eighteenth century by the German, Friedrich Ludwig, architect of the palace-monastery at Mafra. A desk at the entrance sells tickets for the cathedral **museum** (Tues–Sun 9am–noon & 2–4.30pm; €3), stuffed with treasures and relics, the prize exhibits being a reliquary studded with 1426 stones and a carved statue of the Madonna, whose midriff opens out to display layered scenes from the Bible. The ticket will also get you into the marvellous Gothic **cloister** (also open Mon, when museum closed; €1.50), and allows you to clamber onto a terrace above the west entrance and take an unusually close look at the towers.

Immediately adjacent to the Sé is the former archbishop's palace, now the **Museu de Evora**, unfortunately closed for major renovations until 2006. Its important collection centres on fifteenth- and sixteenth-century Flemish and Portuguese paintings assembled from the city's churches and convents, reflecting the strong medieval trade links between the two countries. While the museum remains closed, representative selections of its works are on display in the **Igreja de Santa Clara**, across town down Rua Serpa de Pinto (Tues noon–6pm, Wed–Sun 10am–6pm; €1.50).

From the cathedral, a couple of other sights warrant a quick detour. In nearby Largo da Misericórdia, the **Igreja da Misericórdia** (Mon–Fri 9am–12.30pm & 2–5.30pm, Sat 9am–1pm; free) sports wooden Baroque bas-reliefs and fine *azulejos*, while at the end of the street in **Largo da Porta de Moura** there's a pretty, but well-worn, Reniassance marble fountain.

A quick stroll from here will take you to the **Antiga Universidade**, whose beautiful courtyard is entered from Rua Cardeal Rei. Founded in 1559 by Cardinal Henrique, the future "Cardinal King", the university was closed down by the Jesuit-hating Marquês de Pombal during the eighteenth century, but since reopening in the 1970s it is now one of the liveliest corners of the city. You are free to wander in and view the brazilwood ceiling, *azulejos* and double cloister of marble columns.

Igreja de São Francisco and around

Situated on the eastern side of Praça 1 de Maio, the **Igreja de São Francisco** contains perhaps the most memorable monument in Évora – the **Capela dos Ossos** (Chapel of Bones; daily 9am–1pm & 2.30–5.30pm; €1). A timeless and gruesome memorial to the mortality of man, the walls and pillars of this chilling chamber are entirely covered in the bones of more than 5000 monks. During the fifteenth and sixteenth centuries, there were 42 monastic cemeteries in town which took up much-needed space. The Franciscans' neat solution was to move all the remains to one compact, consecrated site. There's a grim humour in the ordered, artfully planned arrangement of skulls, tibias and vertebrae around the vaults, and in the rhyming inscription over the door which reads *Nós ossos que aqui estamos pelos vossos esperamos* (We bones here are waiting for your bones).

Praça 1 de Maio itself has been remodelled, along with its **Mercado Municpal**, though the market building itself isn't expected to be open until well into 2005. In the meantime, the daily market (closed Mon) is held on two floors of the old bus terminal, a block away on Rua da República, and if you walk this way you might as well nip around the corner afterwards to see the exterior of the mid-sixteenth-century **Igreja Nossa Senhora da Graça**. At each of the corners of its Renaissance pediment, grotesque Atlas-giants support two globes – the emblem of Dom Manuel and his burgeoning overseas empire.

Dom Manuel's palace stood just to the south, its reconstructed gallery – incorporating inventive horseshoe arches with strange serrated edges – now forming part of the **Jardim Público**, at the foot of Praça 1 de Maio. It was from here, historians believe, that Vasco da Gama received the commission that changed the direction of the Portuguese empire, as the explorer established the sea route to India. The resultant wealth found its expression in the flamboyant style of architecture known as Manueline – after the king – and an echo of this can be seen from the garden walls, which look out over the southern edge of the city. The **Ermida de São Brás**, visible just outside the city walls on the road to the train station, has been identified as an early work by Diogo de Boitaca, pioneer of the Manueline style. Its tubular, dunce-capped buttresses and crenellated roofline bear scant resemblance to his masterpieces at Lisbon and Setúbal, but they certainly foreshadow the style's uninhibited originality.

Eating, drinking and nightlife

Finding a place to eat is no problem, with a range of decent **restaurants** to suit most budgets located in the centre. Many are geared towards tourists, but you don't have to venture too far to find something a bit more down-to-earth. For the cheapest eats, good streets to look along are ruas Mercadores and Moeda, off Praça do Giraldo, and those around the market on Praça 1 de Maio. **Cafés** are widespread, too, though anywhere on or near Praça do Giraldo tends to hike its prices, as you might imagine. For **picnic** supplies, best place is the municipal market (Tues–Sun mornings), currently on Rua da República (but due to move to its renovated home in Praça 1 de Maio).

Concerts and **cultural events** are advertised in the *Agenda Cultural* booklet, available from the turismo. When the students aren't around, Évora goes to bed pretty early, as if exhausted by the attentions of the tour groups, but a few **bars** can provide a bit of late-night drinking – keep an eye out for flyers for club nights. At *Café Alentejano*, Rua Raimundo 5, off Praça do Giraldo, there's **fado** on Thursday nights – you'll have to eat but the food isn't particularly expensive.

Cafés

Café Arcada Pr. do Giraldo, at Rua João de Deus. The nicest perch in town, by the fountain at the top of the square, for perusing the comings and goings.
Quiosque Jardim Diana Largo do Conde Vila Flor. The outdoor kiosk by the temple is the finest place in the city for an over-the-yardarm beer, as the fading sun dapples the cathedral and temple columns. Given its location, it's amazingly low-priced. It closes by 8pm-ish though.
Pastelaria Violeta Rua José Elias Garcia 47. Mouth-watering cakes and pastries. Opens for breakfast from 7.30am; closed Sept.
Gelateria Zoka Rua Miguel Bombarda 14. Lots of lovely ice cream – you can sit at tables in the pretty square outside.

Restaurants

Botequim da Mouraria Rua da Mouraria 16A ☏ 266 747 775. This tiny bar with counter-seating serves excellent regional food at surprisingly high prices (mains €12–14). You can snack, lunch or dine off the finest cuts of cured or grilled meat, earthy salads and stews, and choose from the extensive wine list. This is a place that knows its food and drink. Closed Sun. Expensive.
A Choupana Rua dos Mercadores 16–20 ☏ 266 704 427. Close enough to the main square to attract tourists aplenty, but good enough to appeal to locals, who tend to eat at the counter rather than in the adjacent tiled dining room. Plenty of choice at middling prices and while you can eat very cheaply (dish of the day, at the counter), full meals soon add up (most mains €8–10). Closed Sun. Moderate.
Cozinha de Santo Humberto Rua da Moeda 39 ☏ 266 704 251. Top-notch establishment, highly recommended by locals. Downstairs, in a converted cellar, choose from a fine menu of regional dishes for around €30 a head; try the *arroz de pato* (duck with rice) or the seasonal game dishes (wild boar and pigeon stew among others). Closed Thurs & all Nov. Expensive.
O Fialho Trav. das Mascarenhas 16 ☏ 266 703 079. Up a cobbled alley off Pr. J.A. Aguiar, this

is reckoned to be one of the best restaurants in Portugal, and it boasts it's the "most traditional" in town. The regional cuisine is excellent, appetizers particularly, the wine list is good and prices, unsurprisingly, are high. Reservations advised. Closed Mon. Expensive.
O Forcardo Rua dos Mercadores 26 ☏ 266 702 566. A modestly priced old-town restaurant (mains €7–8) with reliable food, where the TV keeps you reassuring company. Closed Sun. Moderate.
Pane & Vino Patio do Salema 22, entrance on Rua Diogo Cão ☏ 266 749 960. Once the stables of a town house, now an amenable Italian restaurant. It's a popular local night out and, though hardly authentic, pizzas (from €6) are filling, prices are reasonable and staff well-used to tourists. Moderate.
Restaurante Repas Pr. 1 de Maio 19 ☏ 266 708 540. The tables outside on the square are the big draw, opposite São Francisco church – and you can just sit down for a drink (the locals order snails as an appetizer) – but it's also a cheap place to eat a steak and chips or all the other usual standards. Inexpensive.
O Sobreiro Rua do Torres 8 ☏ 266 709 325. A bit off the beaten track, and all the better for it, this rustic restaurant shouts its rural credentials – wood-panelling, hanging yokes, a milk pail on the air-con unit, the traditional TV in the corner. But the food is good and cheap – grilled chicken and lamb particularly – with a *meia-dose* for €4 big enough for most appetites. Closed Sun. Inexpensive.
Taberna Tipica Quarta-Feira Rua do Inverno 16 ☏ 266 707 530. Moorish Quarter tavern with moderate prices for mostly meaty Alentejan classics – *borrego, bife, lombinhos, rojões*. Closed Sun. Moderate.
Restaurante Taverna Trav. de Santa Marta 5 ☏ 266 700 747. Good little tavern for out-of-the-ordinary Alentejan dishes – lamb stewed with mint, *migas* with asparagus and pork, or spinach with fried pork. Dishes are all around €7 and, in the case of the daily changing *pratos do dia*, you can eat for €6, soup to coffee. Closed Sun dinner. Moderate.

Bars and clubs

Bar Oficina Rua da Moeda 27. Chilled-out cellar-style bar, open from 8 or 9pm – there's no guarantee you'll see people in black polo-neck sweaters saying "nice jazz" but it's a fair bet. Closed Sun.

BarUE Rua Diogo Cão 21. The official student union bar, tucked into a leafy courtyard near the cathedral, with a garden-terrace. The night starts here.
Praxis Clube Rua de Valdevinos. This is it – the town's only central club, open Mon–Sat until very late.

Listings

Banks There are banks with ATMs on and around Pr. do Giraldo.
Bike rental Silvano Manuel Cagado, Rua Cândido dos Reis 66 ☎ 266 703 434. Bikes from €15 a day.
Hospital Hospital do Espirito Santo, Largo Sr. da Pobreza ☎ 266 740 100.
Internet Cyber Center, Rua dos Mercadores 42 (Mon–Fri 9am–8pm, Sat & Sun 2–8pm).
Laundry Olímpica, Largo dos Mercadores 6 ☎ 266 705 293, closed Sat afternoon and Sun, does a lovely wash and iron, very cheaply.
Police Police station on Rua Francisco S. Lusitano, near the Roman temple ☎ 266 702 022.

Post office Rua d'Olivença (Mon–Fri 9am–6pm, Sat 9am–noon).
Taxis You'll find them in Pr. do Giraldo, or call ☎ 266 734 734.
Tours Aventur, Rua João de Deus 21 ☎ 266 743 134, ✉ turaventur@mail.pt, operates 4WD "safaris" (€35 half-day/€60 full-day), 4WD-plus-kayak tours (€40/75) and bike tours (€40), all on varied itineraries, visiting local vineyards, historic sites and megaliths. Policarpo, Alcarcova de Baixo 43, off Rua 5 de Outubro ☎ 266 746 970, ✉ incoming-alentejo @sapo.pt, runs regular city tours (€18), as well as minibus tours to the megaliths (€24), or to Monsaraz and local vineyards (€25).

Around Évora

Évora's environs have some significant attractions, and it's worth extending your stay by a day or so to see them. Some, like the castles at **Évora Monte** or **Montemor-o-Novo**, perhaps just warrant a quick stop en route elsewhere, though the famed carpet town of **Arraiolos**, just to the north, is a popular day-trip from the city. The administrative district of Évora also contains over a dozen megalithic sites – dolmens, standing stones (menhirs) and stone circles – which have their origins in a culture that flourished here before spreading north as far as Brittany and Denmark. These might seem a more specialized attraction on the face of it, but the stones of **Os Almendres**, in particular, west of the city, provide one of the country's most extraordinary sights. With your own car, you can combine a visit to Os Almendres with the Neolithic caves at **Escoural**, also an easy drive from the city. However, the other major megalith in the area, the dolmen of Zambujeiro – sited down a rough track – is really only feasibly seen on a guided 4WD tour (see Évora "Listings" above).

Évora Monte

Twenty-nine kilometres northeast of Évora, along the N18 towards Estremoz, the sixteenth-century castle at **ÉVORA MONTE** occupies a spectacular position, atop a steep mound high above the main road and modern village. It stands on fortifications going back to Roman times, though the current keep was constructed in Italian Renaissance style, with four robust round towers, and is adorned with a simple rope-like relief of Manueline stonework. It was here in 1834 that the regent Miguel was finally defeated and the convention signed that put Pedro IV on the Portuguese throne. Legend has it that the signing took so long that there was only stale bread left to eat, causing the invention of the well-known Portuguese dish *açorda* (a soup of bread, water, coriander, garlic and olive oil). Inside the **castle** (daily: June–Sept 10am–1pm & 2.30–6.30pm; Oct–May 10am–1pm & 2.30–5pm; €1.50) are three vaulted chambers, each displaying intricately carved granite capitals, though if you're going to pay for entrance it's really for the views obtained from the terrace.

The upper medieval village rings the castle mound and, with care, you can clamber around the walls and gate-towers, and then wander down the cobbled main street to the small church and cemetery. There's a **restaurant**, *A Convençao* (☎268 959 217; closed Mon), next to the castle, which has an outdoor terrace, and more cafés down by the modern settlement on the main road. The Estremoz bus from Évora can drop you off on the main road, but it's a long uphill hike to the castle – realistically, only drivers are going to make a halt here.

Arraiolos

ARRAIOLOS, 21km north of Évora (and connected to it by bus twice a day), is famed for its superb **carpets** (*tapetes*), which have been handwoven here since the thirteenth century. Based on elaborate Persian imports, they have been much prized for centuries and adorn the interiors of any Portuguese manor or palace worth its salt – the most luxuriant eighteenth-century creations hang on the walls of the Palácio de Queluz, near Lisbon. For carpet enthusiasts, Arraiolos is a dream – every second shop sells them, and you can spend €40 on a small square or €1500 or more on a fine example. The best ones are indeed expensive, but a lot less so than elsewhere.

Carpets aside, it's a very pretty small town, with a ruined hilltop castle, brightly whitewashed houses trimmed in lavender, and a sixteenth-century pillory in the paved central square, Praça Lima e Brito. Antique dye chambers, 500 years old, are preserved under glass in the square, and the **turismo** here (daily 9.30am–12.30pm & 2–6pm; ☎266 490 254, ⓦwww.cm-arraiolos.pt) can provide a map if you want to know where you're strolling and what you're looking at. A few **cafés** provide drinks and meals, while some visitors are tempted to stay longer at the lovely *Pousada Nossa Senhora da Assunção* (☎266 419 340, ⓦwww.pousadas.pt; breakfast included; ❾), whose contemporarily styled rooms have been inserted into a refashioned sixteenth-century convent a kilometre or so out of town on the Pavia road.

Montemor-o-Novo

Thirty kilometres northwest of Évora along the N114 lies the sleepy white town of **MONTEMOR-O-NOVO**, birthplace of São João de Deus, patron saint of the sick. Its outskirts appear anything but appealing, but it's worth persevering to encounter a largely unvisited old town of cobbled streets and crumbling mansions, topped by a castle where Vasco da Gama finalized his plans for opening up the sea route to India. This was Montemor's heyday, in the fifteenth century – it's hard to resist the impression it's been all downhill since then. Climb up the steep street for the views and then wend your way back into the old town, where the main square sports a statue of São João de Deus carrying an injured beggar in need of care.

There are a couple of cafés and *tascas* in the old town, and more restaurants in the newer part of Montemor, lined along the main road through town. **Buses** drop you at the station on Avenida Gago Coutinho, with the **turismo** three minutes' walk away along the avenue and off to the left in Largo Calouste Gulbenkian (Mon–Sat 9.30am–1pm & 2.30–6pm; ☎266 898 103). There are two places to stay, a little way further down the avenue, but no earthly reason why you should. **Lunch** is another matter, either in the dining room of the *Residencial Monte Alentejano* (☎ 266 899 630) on the avenue – good but relatively pricey – or around the corner on Rua do Poço do Paço where *Restaurante 8 de Março* (closed Sun) is a simple diner with €5 *pratos do dia*.

Grutas do Escoural

Twelve kilometres south down the N2 from Montemor are the **Grutas do Escoural** (Tues 1.30–5.30pm, Wed–Fri 9am–noon & 1.30–5.30pm, Sat & Sun 9am–noon & 1.30–5pm; €2), a cave system discovered in 1963 and showing evidence of human habitation for the last 50,000 years. Early man would have used the caves as a mere shelter, but from around 30,000 years ago primitive rock art was being scratched out on the walls, and in Neolithic times (5000 BC) the caves were used as a burial place. A short tour (in patchy English) lights up the weird leathery interior of the caves and points out the very faint drawings. The caves are 2.5km east (signposted) of the small village of Santiago do Escoural, where a local museum has some photographs and finds from the site. There's also a café or two here.

For the stone circle of Os Almendres, you take the very minor country road east to São Brissos (6km) and Valverde (14km) from Santiago do Escoural, in which case you'll pass the chapel at **São Brissos** (usually locked), built from the stones of an ancient dolmen.

Os Almendres

The Iberian peninsula's largest and most impressive stone circle lies just to the west of Évora, south of the small village of Guadalupe, 13km from the city. To get there directly from Évora, take the N114 towards Montemor/Lisbon and follow the signs from Guadalupe. If you're approaching from the south, from Escoural and Valverde, you need to turn left in Guadalupe, at the *Café Barreiros*.

You are directed out along a dirt road (largely flat and in good condition, fine for cars), reaching the **Menir dos Almendres** after 2km. This is a single, three-metre-high standing stone set in a quiet olive plantation. Despite its obvious Neolithic origins, the local legend has it that it is the tomb of an enchanted Moorish princess, who appears once a year on the eve of São João and can be seen combing her hair.

This is simply the taster, since another 2.5km along the dirt road there's a parking area beside the extraordinary **Cromeleque dos Almendres**, where no less than 92 stones are aligned in concentric enclosures for seventy metres down a dusty hillside. Placed here in several phases, between six and seven thousand years ago, they are thought to have been erected as some kind of astronomical observatory and site of fertility rituals – though no one really knows. However, what's immediately clear, even today, is the power of the site, the stones resembling frozen figures, standing impassively, gazing down across the surrounding cork plantation to Évora gleaming in the distance.

Estremoz

ESTREMOZ, 46km northeast of Évora, is the largest and liveliest of the three so-called "marble towns" – nearby Borba and the far more interesting Vila

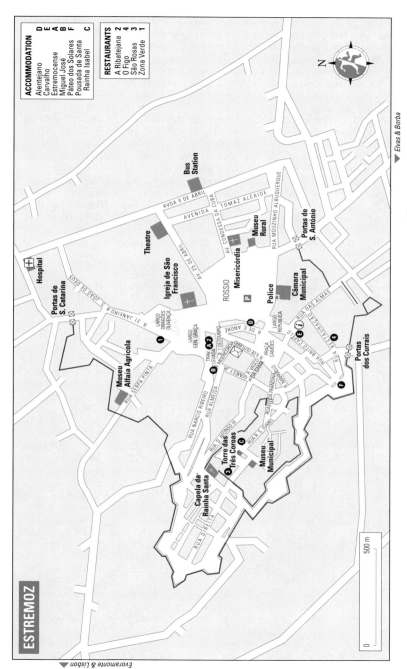

ESTREMOZ

ACCOMMODATION
Alentejano   D
Carvalho   E
Estremocense   A
Miguel José   B
Páteo dos Solares   F
Pousada de Santa
Rainha Isabel   C

RESTAURANTS
A Ribatejana   2
O Figo   4
São Rosas   3
Zona Verde   1

N

▼ *Elvas & Borba*

Hospital
Portas de
S. Catarina
Museu
Alfaia Agrícola
RUA SERPA PINTA
Theatre
Bus
Station
AVDA 9 DE ABRIL
AVENIDA
Igreja de São
Francisco
AV 23 DE ABRIL
AV. CONDESSA DA CUBA
AVENIDA TOMAZ ALCAIDE
Museu
Rural
RUA MOUZINHO ALBUQUERQUE
Portas de
S. António
Misericórdia
ROSSIO
Police
Câmara
Municipal
RUA DAS ALMAS
LARGO
GEN GRAÇA
LARGO
DRAGÕES
OLIVENÇA
R 31 JANEIRO S. JOÃO DE DEUS
RUA NARCIS RIBEIRO
RUA ALMEIDA
LARGO
D DE S ANDRÉ
PRAÇA
CAMÕES
RUA
REPUBLICA
LARGO
Capela da
Rainha Santa
Torre das
Três Coroas
Museu
Municipal
RUA DIREITA
RUA D AFONSO III
RUA R S. ISABEL
Portas
dos Currais
500 m

▲ *Évoramonte & Lisbon*

8

ALENTEJO | Estremoz

505

Viçosa are the others. The area is so rich in marble that it replaces brick or concrete as a building material, and is used extensively in the most commonplace surroundings. This is immediately obvious in the marble streets and fountains of Estremoz, a strategically sited walled market centre that in its heyday was ten times its current size (today's population is around fifteen thousand). On the hill within the star-shaped ramparts of the upper town stands the former palace of Dom Dinis, the king famous for his administrative, economic and military reforms. Meanwhile, below, on the Rossio, the vast main square of the lower town, the Saturday **market** still drives the local economy, a classic Alentejan event selling – among many other things – what are renowned as some of the best cheeses in Portugal, mainly made from ewe's and goat's milk. It starts and finishes early, so it pays to stay over on Friday night if you can. Otherwise, Estremoz's annual festival takes place in the Rossio over the first weekend in September, with bull-running, concerts, fireworks and roll-baking contests; while at the start of May it sees a cattle and handicraft fair, including displays of the earthenware pottery for which the town has been celebrated since the sixteenth century. All in all, Estremoz makes a great stopover – it's certainly the best base from which to explore the area, not least because of the number and quality of the pensions and restaurants that cater for the market crowds.

The Town

Dom Dinis' palace is now a *pousada* (see "Accommodation" below), but you're free to wander in and look around. In particular, there's a splendid panoramic view from the thirteenth-century **Torre das Três Coroas** (Tower of the Three Crowns), so called because three kings took part in its construction, namely Afonso III, Sancho II and Dom Dinis. With its Islamic-style battlements and Gothic balconies, it bears a close resemblance to the great tower of Beja, its exact contemporary. From this part of town the castle of Évora Monte is clearly visible on the horizon, 15km to the southwest. Dom Dinis' queen, Isabel, devoted her life to the poor, giving away food and money with unseemly enthusiasm for a monarch. A famous episode saw her challenged by her husband to reveal what was beneath her skirt. The bread she had hidden there was miraculously turned into roses – as the modern statue of Isabel, in front of the tower, clearly shows.

Opposite the tower, in an old almshouse, is a small **Museu Municipal** (Tues–Sun 9am–12.30pm & 2–5.30pm; €1.10), with displays of Alentejan life and, particularly, Estremoz pottery. This is characterized by simple floral and leaf patterns, sometimes inlaid with marble chips; the most distinctive products are the porous water coolers known as *moringues*, globe-shaped jars with narrow bases, two short spouts and one handle. Although nowadays largely ornamental, the pottery used to play an important role in gypsy weddings: the procession would march into town, whereupon the bride made a sudden dash for freedom across the market place, hotly pursued by the groom. When the groom finally caught up with his bride, a fine Estremoz dish was thrown into the air. The couple were pronounced man and wife at the moment that the dish fell to the ground in pieces.

Down in the lower town, the **Rossio** – properly the Rossio Marquês de Pombal – is dominated on its southern side by the twin-towered marble facade of a former convent, which now houses the Câmara Municipal, as well as a police station and a little ecclesiastical museum – duck in at least to see the handsome *azulejos*. Royal attentions in the past aside, Estremoz is still clearly an agricultural town at heart, with not only the market but two rural museums, the Museu Rural on the Rossio and the Museu Alfaia Agricola down Rua de Serpa Pinto (currently closed), neither, to be honest, worth the time – certainly not if you've witnessed the real thing in the market at first hand.

Practicalities

Buses stop on the eastern edge of town on Avenida 9 de Abril, outside the old train station. From here, it's a two-minute walk down Avenida Condessa da Cuba to the Rossio. There's plenty of **parking** in the Rossio, except on market day. The **turismo** is a short walk from the square, around the corner at Largo da República 26 (daily 9.30am–12.30pm & 2–6pm; ☎268 333 541). Unless you're stopping over on Friday night, before the market, **accommodation** should be easy enough to find – there's plenty of it, particularly at the budget end of the scale. A good area to look is in the streets off Largo General Graça, where four or five *residencais* are gathered. This is also the area to hunt for **restaurants**, most of which are very good value. For **picnic** supplies, the place to go is the Saturday-morning market on the Rossio where a wide array of cheeses, spicy sausages and olives are on sale.

Hotels and pensions

Pensão-Restaurante Alentejano Rossio Marquês de Pombal 14 ☎268 337 300. A lovely place overlooking the Rossio whose dozen rooms come with flowery painted Alentejan furniture, brass beds, marble bathrooms, satellite TV and air conditioning – a steal at the price. There's a bar and café downstairs and a proper old country-style restaurant on the first floor, serving excellent moderately priced food, including a fine *arroz de marisco*. Breakfast included. ❸

Residencial Carvalho Largo da República 27 ☎268 339 370. An elderly tiled *residencial* that has seen better days, but the rooms are in good enough shape, and some have private bathroom and air conditioning. Breakfast included. ❸

Residencial Estremocense Trav. da Levada 19 ☎268 333 002. Decent rooms on the edge of a nice square, with cafés and restaurants right on the doorstep. No credit cards. ❸

Residencial Miguel José Trav. da Levada 8 ☎268 322 326. Simple old-town rooms available with and without private bathroom. Breakfast included. No credit cards. ❸

Páteo dos Solares Rua Brito Capelo ☎268 338 400, @pateo.solares@clix.pt. A very genteel ambience in this beautiful town mansion, with a swimming pool, well-regarded terrace-restaurant, and gardens for guests to enjoy. Room rates vary (some are classed "luxo"), and drop a category from Nov to March. Parking. Breakfast included. ❽

Pousada de Santa Rainha Isabel ☎268 332 075, @www.pousadas.pt. Rooms with grand beds and heavy drapes, plus some scintillating views from the lavish thirteenth-century palace of Dom

Dinis. The pool and gardens are a treat, set within the battlemented walls, and the restaurant (very expensive) offers a variation on the usual Alentejan cuisine, with specials like *arroz de pato*, leg of pork with garlic and coriander, or monkfish wrapped in *presunto*. Breakfast included. Parking. ❾

Restaurants

O Figo Rua da Restauração 36 ☎268 324 529. The *pratos do dia* here are always good value (€6.50), and while other dishes are pricier they are worth it, like the excellent *arroz de marisco* (€20, minimum two people). Moderate.

A Ribatejana Largo General Graça 41 ☎268 323 656. Back-room *churrasqueira* that delivers the goods – principally a plate of spit-roast chicken or *leitão* (suckling pig) and chips at value-for-money prices. It's a bit rough and ready, but the food's tasty – and you may have to wait for a table at weekends if you leave it late. Inexpensive.

São Rosas Largo de Dom Dinis 11 ☎268 333 345. The *pousada* and *Pateo dos Solares* aside, this is the town's best restaurant. Once a medieval inn, now beautifully restored, it serves excellent regional cuisine, though at a price – there's a €21.50 *ementa turística*, but otherwise expect to pay €30–40 a head. Smoked salmon, or clams with garlic, are fancy appetizers, and the *açorda* is well thought of. Closed Mon. Very expensive.

Zona Verde Largo Dragões de Olivença 86 ☎268 324 701. No real menu surprises here, but good honest food at middling prices (mains €6–8) draws the locals. Closed Thurs. Moderate.

Vila Viçosa

Seventeen kilometres southeast of Estremoz, the ducal palace in the small town of **VILA VIÇOSA** was the last residence of the Portuguese monarchy. The dukes of Bragança were descended from the illegitimate offspring of João I of Avis and established their seat here in the fifteenth century. For the next two centuries they were on the edge of the Portuguese ruling circle but their claims to the throne were overridden in 1580 by Philip II of Spain. Sixty years later, while Spanish attention was diverted by a revolt in Catalunya, Portuguese resentment erupted and massive public pressure forced the reluctant João, eighth Duke of Bragança, to seize the throne; his descendants ruled Portugal until the foundation of the Republic in 1910. Despite a choice of sumptuous palaces throughout Portugal – Mafra, Sintra and Queluz are the most renowned – the Bragança kings retained a special affection for their residence at Vila Viçosa, a relatively ordinary country home, constructed in various stages during the sixteenth and seventeenth centuries. Dom Carlos spent his last night here before his assassination on the riverfront in Lisbon in 1908, and it was a favourite haven of his successor, Manuel II, the last king of Portugal.

It's a pretty town, dominated entirely by its palace – and by the coachloads of tourists who descend upon it for a quick visit before being whisked off again. Because of that, it's actually quite a pleasant place to spend the night, with an unhurried small-town atmosphere that survives the daily imposition of visitors. As at Estremoz and nearby Borba, marble is the dominant building material: the road from Borba, 5km away, is lined on either side with enormous marble quarries, and in town everything from the pavements to the toilets in the bus station are made of the local stone.

The Town

The wide palace square, Terreiro do Paço, is backed by the **Paço Ducal** (Tues–Sun 9.30am–1pm & 2.30–5.30pm; 1hr guided tour; €5), which has a simple, rhythmic facade. Most of it dates from the sixteenth to the eighteenth centuries, and while the regal trappings of the more formal chambers are rather tedious, the private apartments and mementos of Dom Carlos and his wife Marie-Amélia have a *Hello!* magazine fascination. Faded family photographs hang on the walls, changes of clothing are laid out, and the table is set for dinner: the whole scene seems to await the royals' return. In reality, Dom Duarte, heir to the nonexistent throne, spends his days in experimental eco-farming at his estate near Viseu. The guided tour of the palace is obligatory, and none too revealing – you might well pass up on the opportunity to visit the armoury and coach museum (separate charges for both) that form part of the complex.

The Bragança dukes were buried opposite the palace in marble tombs in the chapel of the **Mostéiro dos Agostinhos**, while the duchesses had their own mausoleum in the **Convento das Chagas**, just to the side of the palace – part of this is now the *pousada* (see below). Before you leave the square, walk a little way up the road out of town (to Borba), where on the left you can see the **Porta do Nós** – a Manueline stone gateway formed into the knot symbol of the Bragança family.

The modern town spreads back from the palace, but the original population of Vila Viçosa was based within the walls of the **old town**, whose castle was built by Dom Dinis at the end of the thirteenth century. Avenida dos Duques de Bragança runs from the palace square past the hilltop **Castelo** (Tues–Sun 9.30am–1pm & 2–5.30pm; €2.50), which was the seat of the Bragancas before the construction of their palace. Its interior has been renovated beyond recognition, and houses an indifferent museum dedicated to hunting and archeology, but you don't need to pay to climb the outer castle walls for views over town. Behind lies the Braganças' old **Tapada Real** (Royal Hunting Ground), set within its own eighteen-kilometre circuit of walls. A few old houses and a sixteenth-century *pelourinho* are all that remain of the old town itself – if it's open, take a look at the eighteenth-century *azulejos* inside the church of **Nossa Senhora de Conceição**, the pick of Vila Viçosa's 22 churches.

Practicalities

The **bus station** is opposite the municipal market at the foot of Largo Dom João IV – cross the square and it's a 200m walk up any of the streets ahead of you to the extraordinarily elongated Praça da República, which marks the centre of town. This slopes from São Bartolomeu church at the top to the castle mound at the bottom, with the palace another five-minute walk beyond, down either Rua Dr. Couto Jardim or Rua Florbela Espança. The **turismo** is near the upper (church) end of Praça da República, in the town hall (daily: May–Sept 10am–1pm & 2.30–6.30pm; Oct–April closes at 5.30pm; ☎268 881 101, Ⓦwww.cm-vilavicosa.pt), and takes indifference to visitors' needs to new levels – you might, at best, be given a map and allowed a peek at the list of accommodation phone numbers.

Budget **accommodation** can be hard to find. The *Hospedaria Dom Carlos* at Praça da República 25 (☎268 980 318; ❸), over the square from the turismo, is the most obvious choice, but rooms are pricier than they warrant. That just leaves a handful of places advertising *quartos* (❷), all found off the main square: the nicest, at Rua Couto Jardim 7, around the corner from the Dom Carlos; but also on Rua Florbela Espança (on the corner by *Café Regional*); and – across the square, down past *Café Restauração* – at Rua Dr. Gomes Jardim 19. At all, ring the bell and hope for the best. Other options in and around Vila Viçosa are far grander, starting with the *Pousada de Dom João IV*, by the palace on Terreiro do Paço (☎268 980 742, Ⓦwww.pousadas.pt; breakfast included; ❽), which has kept intact its sixteenth-century convent cells and cloister. One kilometre out of town, there's the antique-laden seventeenth-century *Casa dos Peixinhos* (☎268 980 472; breakfast included; ❻), which has half-a-dozen elegant rooms available; follow the signs for Alandroal.

Cafés are found lining the lower half of Praça da República, but if you stay the night and don't eat at the *pousada*, seek out somewhere with a bit more local character. Any of the streets from the square on the turismo side lead down to Largo Dom João IV, where there are some cheap places around the market. At the top of this square, in the Mata Municipal (town gardens), *Os Cucos* (☎268 980 806) is a popular grill-house with good fish and a changing list of daily specials – you'll eat well for around €15.

South to Monsaraz

The region south of Vila Viçosa is the Alentejo at its most rural, the roads running past scattered farming communities, protected at one time by the castles that still stand in places like Redondo, Alandroal and Terena. The ultimate target is the dramatic hilltop village of **Monsaraz**, close to the Rio Guadiana and the Spanish border, a 65-kilometre drive from Vila Viçosa, via the market and wine-growing town of **Reguengos de Monsaraz**. Monsaraz is one of those places that's worth the trip for the views from its walls alone, but it also has some excellent accommodation and a local circuit of megalithic stones and circles. Travelling by bus, you have to come from Évora down the N256 to Reguengos, where you change for Monsaraz.

Reguengos de Monsaraz

The small market town of **REGUENGOS DE MONSARAZ**, around 40km from either Évora or Estremoz, is known for its fine local wines, and you can visit the *adegas* outside town – though you'll need to contact the office of the Rota dos Vinhos do Alentejo in Évora (see p.496) to arrange this. There isn't, in fact, a great deal to delay you on your way to Monsaraz, though the **turismo** in the Câmara Municipal on Rua 1° de Maio (Mon–Fri 9am–12.30pm & 2–5.30pm, Sat & Sun 10am–12.30pm & 2–5.30pm; ☎266 508 040), just off the main Praça da Liberdade, might be able to persuade you otherwise. They can certainly give you a map of the megalithic monuments sited between São Pedro do Corval and Monsaraz (see below), and rather hopefully proffer an enormous map of Reguengos itself.

There are places to stay in town, but with Monsaraz only 17km away and regular **bus** services from Évora (as well as direct from Lisbon), plus weekday connections on to Monsaraz, it's unlikely you'd get stranded. *Pensão Gato* (☎266 502 353; ❸) on Praça da Liberdade would do the honours if it came to it, and if you're looking for lunch you can eat well at the **restaurant** here or next door at the slightly pricier *Café Central* (☎266 502 219).

The minor road on to Monsaraz passes through **São Pedro do Corval**, 5km to the east, known for its score or more ceramics workshops, all clearly signposted from the road. Some of these might tempt you to stop for a browse around – a few of the workshops and galleries also stock the hand-woven woollen scarves, rugs and blankets in which the region specializes.

Monsaraz

MONSARAZ – known locally as Ninho das Águias (Eagles' Nest) – is perched high above the border plains, a tiny village, fortified to the hilt and entirely contained within its walls. From its heights, the landscape of Alentejo takes on a magical quality, with absolutely nothing stirring amid a sensational panorama of neatly cultivated sun-baked fields, dotted with cork and olive trees. To the east, the Rio Guadiana, delineating the frontier with Spain, has swollen in great pools following the building of the Alqueva dam (see p.532) – it presents a waterlogged panorama, crossed by the snaking bridge to Mourão to the west, at odds with the aridity to the west.

There's something peculiarly satisfying about such a small village. It's entirely pedestrianized, and there are only two main streets, parallel to each other, Rua Direita and Rua de Santiago, with the **Igreja Matriz** at the heart of the village. Here in the square is the turismo (see below) and an unusual eighteenth-century **pillory** topped by a sphere of the universe. A few stepped alleys invite exploration, while *artesanato* shops hang colourful ceramics and blankets from their walls.

The **Torre das Feiticeiras** (Witches' Tower) looms from the castle at the far end of the village, part of a chain of frontier fortresses continued to the south and north. The views from the walls are magnificent. When the Moors were ejected in 1167 the village was handed over to the Knights Templar, and later to their successors, the Order of Christ. Their fort has now been converted, rather extraordinarily, into a bullring – the annual village festival, in the second week of September, features bullfights, concerts, dancing and, of course, spectacular fireworks.

Practicalities

If you time the service right from Évora to Reguengos, there are two or three **buses** a day on to Monsaraz, though there's no service at weekends. You're dropped right outside the gates. Drivers can't enter the village – use the spacious **car parks** outside the gates. The **turismo** in the square (daily 10am–1pm & 2–5.30pm; ☎266 557 136) can help with bus timetables, and has information on all the local accommodation possibilities – though by the time you reach the office, you've already passed most of them. There's not much else in Monsaraz, but amazingly there is an ATM.

Half a dozen houses along Rua Direita and its continuation advertise **rooms**, sheltered behind thick walls in traditional Alentejan homes – cool in summer, warm in winter – many with stone floors, painted furniture, terraces and balconies. Prices are broadly similar (€50 a room, breakfast included), though soften a little outside peak summer season and might be €10 less or so if you are on your own or forgo a room with a view – though the sensational panoramas are half the attraction. Good choices include our favourite, *Casa Dom Nuno* (☎266 557 146), as well as *Casa Pinto* (☎266 557 388), *Casa Dona Antónia* (☎266 557 142) and *Casa do Paço* (☎266 557 306), all within a few seconds walk of the church. Booking in advance in summer is advisable – get someone to call for you if necessary, as not much English is spoken. There's also a rather fancy small **inn**, the *Estalagem de Monsaraz*, in Largo São Bartolomeu (☎266 557 112; ❺, panoramic suite ❼), just outside the castle walls but still very close to the village, with half a dozen lovely rooms, plus a garden and pool. Below the village, a few **rural tourism** places also provide comfortable accommodation, including *Monte Alerta* (☎266 5510 150, @www.montealerta.pt; breakfast included; ❺), at Telheiro, a couple of kilometres from Monsaraz, which has eight pretty rooms, plus a pool, spa and fine gardens.

A couple of cafés and three or four **restaurants** feed the visitors. First among equals is the *Santiago* (☎266 557 188), by virtue of its outdoor terrace with the best views in Monsaraz – you can just have a drink here too. But *Casa do Forno* (☎266 557 190; closed Tues) and *O Alcaide* (☎266 557 168) offer equally good food, all moderately priced (mains €9–10), with Alentejan meat specialities much to the fore – things like *borrego assado no forno* (roast lamb), pork and lamb chops, and *migas*.

Megaliths around Monsaraz

Four thousand years ago, the region around Monsaraz was an important centre of megalithic culture, and various dolmens (covered temples or tombs), menhirs (standing stones) and stone circles survive today. A good driving circuit from the village takes in four such examples, about an hour and a half's round trip.

Closest to Monsaraz, 1.5km away, is the most impressive, the **Cromeleque do Xerez**, a square "circle" of 49 granite stones with a towering four-metre-high central menhir, probably the site of Neolithic fertility rites. Leave Monsaraz and follow the signs at the first roundabout for the Convento do Orata, park by the low walls near the convent and it's a 200-metre walk to a flat red-earth area where the stones have been re-erected – they were moved from their original site when the Alqueva dam was flooded.

Back at the roundabout, follow the sign for Telheiro and then take the Outeiro road (from Telheiro it's easiest to follow the "O Convivio" restaurant sign), where, just before Outeiro itself a blue "Menhir" sign indicates the **Menhir da Belhoa**, a five-metre-high standing stone visible from the road. It's 50m up a track, and on it you can trace zigzags, whorls and other faint symbolic markings. Next, follow the back-country road round through Outeiro, Barrada and Motrinos to the main Reguengos–Monsaraz road and turn right, towards Reguengos. Just before São Pedro do Corval, opposite the dusty football ground, there's roadside parking at the signpost for the **Rocha dos Namorados** (Lovers' Rock), a large, squat, naturally standing, mushroom-shaped stone used for thousands of years in fertility rites. If you can lob a rock on top of the stone, the stork is on its way (though you have to do it on Easter Monday to be sure).

Finally, turn back along the main road towards Monsaraz and, 7km from the fertility rock and just 1.5km from Telheiro, there's an "Anta" sign pointing 200m up a dirt road. This marks the **Antas do Olival da Pega**, a 4000-year-old dolmen nestled in an olive grove.

Elvas

The hilltop town of **ELVAS**, 40km east of Estremoz, was long one of Portugal's mightiest frontier posts, a response to the Spanish stronghold of Badajoz, just 15km to the east across the Rio Guadiana. Its star-shaped walls and trio of forts are among the most complex and best-preserved military fortifications surviving in Europe. In addition, the town itself is a delight – all steep cobbled streets and mansions.

Elvas was recaptured from the Moors in 1230 and withstood periodic attacks from Spain throughout much of the following three centuries. It succumbed just once, however, to Spanish conquest, when the garrison was betrayed by Spanish bribery in 1580, allowing Philip II to enter and, for a period during the following year, establish his court. The town subsequently made amends during the war over the succession of Philip IV to the Portuguese territories. In 1644, the garrison resisted a nine-day siege by Spanish troops, and in 1658, with its numbers reduced by an epidemic to a mere thousand, saw off a fifteen-thousand-strong Spanish army.

During this period, the fortifications underwent intensive rebuilding and expansion, and they were later pressed into service twice more: in 1801, when the town withstood a Spanish siege during the War of the Oranges, and ten years later, during the Peninsular War, when the fort provided the base from which Wellington advanced to launch his bloody but successful assault on Badajoz. Perhaps out of tradition as much as anything, a military garrison is still stationed in the town.

Elvas's weekly event is its **Monday market** – a vibrantly chaotic affair attracting people from miles around, held just outside town behind the aqueduct. Otherwise, the town's big annual bash is its **Festa de São Mateus**, which lasts for six to eight days, starting on September 20, and encompasses a programme of agricultural, cultural and religious events, including the largest procession in southern Portugal.

Arrival and information

The walls make Elvas a pretty easy place to get your bearings. There's **parking** at various signposted points by the entrances to the old town, though you can also follow the "Castelo" signs up though town – the narrow streets are a bit hair-raising at times, but there's lots of parking by the castle. **Buses** drop arrivals at the foot of town by the outer wall, at Praça 25 de Abril, where there's a hole-in-the-wall ticket kiosk. Shuttle buses (and taxis, €4) also run into the centre

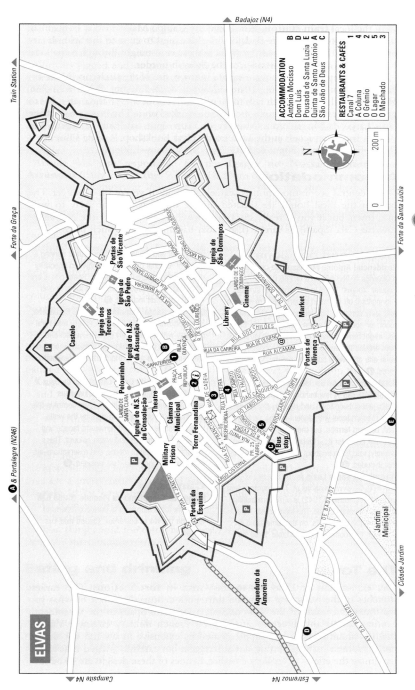

ELVAS

▲ *Badajoz (N4)*

◄ *Train Station*

◄ *Forte da Graça*

◄ ▲ & *Portalegre (N246)*

ACCOMMODATION
António Mocisso .... B
Dom Luís .... D
Pousada de Santa Luzia .. E
Quinta de Santo António .. A
São João de Deus C

RESTAURANTS & CAFÉS
Canal 7 1
A Coluna 4
O Grémio 2
O Lagar 5
O Machado 3

N

0 ————— 200 m

▼ *Forte de Santa Luzia*

Portas de São Vicente

Igreja de São Pedro

Igreja dos Terceiros

Castelo

Igreja de N.S. da Assunção

Pelourinho

Igreja de N.S. da Consolação

Theatre

Câmara Municipal

Torre Fernandina

Military Prison

Praça da República

Portas da Esquina

Library

Cinema

Igreja de São Domingos

Market

Portas de Olivença

Bus stop

Jardim Municipal

Aqueduto da Amoreira

RUA DOS CHILÕES

RUA DA CARREIRA

RUA DE OLIVENÇA

RUA ALCAMIM

RUA DE CADEIA

RUA DA FEIRA

RUA CABRITO

RUA JOÃO CASQUEIRO

AVENIDA GARCIA DE ORTA

AV DE BADAJOZ

AV. D. PELOPIDE

AVIDA LI ZANEIRO

LARGO CISTERNA

RUA DE ÉVORA

8

ALENTEJO | Elvas

513

▼ *Cidade Jardim*

▼ *Estremoz N4*

◄ *Campsite N4*

△ Pillory, Elvas

A Coluna Rua do Cabrito 11 ☎ 268 623 728. Locally considered one of Elvas's best restaurants, and deservedly so. Housed in whitewashed old stables with *azulejo* tiles, it specializes in *bacalhau* dishes, but there's plenty more besides. Moderate.

Canal 7 Rua dos Sapateiros 16 ☎ 268 623 593. A grill-house that's the best of the budget places, always popular. Inexpensive.

O Grémio Pr. de República ☎ 268 622 711. Simple café with outside tables on a perch above the square, and basic, no-nonsense food. Inexpensive.

O Lagar Rua Nova da Vedoria 7 ☎ 268 624 793.

Blessedly air-conditioned restaurant for good regional cuisine. You probably won't sample the *orelha em vinagreta* (pickled pig's ear), but clams, cuttlefish, *bacalhau*, *açordas* and *cataplanas* sit alongside the usual grills – and the *porco alentejana* is excellent. Closed Thurs. Moderate.

O Machado Rua de Cadeia ☎ 268 628 155. A bit pricier than usual but lunching locals think it's worth it – and it has the advantage of shaded streetside tables. The *pratos do dia* are always the best deal, highlighting the best regional dishes. Moderate.

Portalegre

PORTALEGRE is the capital, market centre and transport hub of Alto Alentejo. It is an attractive town, crouched at the foot of the Serra de São Mamede and endowed with a typically whitewashed old quarter that, for once, isn't dominated by a castle – only three towers and a few sections of wall remain of the thirteenth-century fortification. Instead, it's a bustling place of shops, cafés, churches, tiled houses and little squares, reached up the pedestrianized Rua 5 de Outubro, which runs steeply uphill from the main Rossio square.

Portalegre's industrial history looms large. Reminders include a cork factory, whose great twin chimneys greet you on the way into town, and the town's single surviving tapestry factory, housed in the former Jesuit **Colégio de São Sebastião** on Rua Guilhermo Gomes Fernandes in the lower town – the last remnant of a great textile industry that peaked in the seventeenth and eighteenth centuries. The factory is still in operation, though not open to the public, but you can trace the history of local tapestry-making instead in the **Museu da Tapeçaria Guy Fino** (daily except Wed 9.30am–12.30pm & 2.30–6pm; €2), housed in a superbly adapted eighteenth-century mansion in Rua da Figueira, up in the old town. None of the background information is in English, but you can see examples of old looms and a selection of the five thousand shades of wool used in the reproduction of centuries-old patterns. Exhibitions change, and there may be classical designs on show or contemporary recreations of paintings by Portuguese artists.

The wealth produced in the town's boom years, in particular from the silk workshops, has a further legacy in the collection of grand mercantile mansions and town houses. These are especially apparent as you walk along Rua 19 de Junho – the main thoroughfare at the top of the old town – which is lined by a spectacular concentration of late-Renaissance and Baroque mansions. Facing Praça do Municipio, and dominating the quarter, is the **Sé**, an austere building save for a flash of fancy in the pyramidal pinnacles of its towers. To one side of this an eighteenth-century palace houses the **Museu Municipal** (daily except Tues 9.30am–12.30pm & 2–6pm; €2). It's not exactly a compelling visit, with much routine furniture and fittings on display, though there are some lovely ceramics and ivories as well as early Arraiolos carpets.

At the foot of the old town, all the main roads converge on the **Rossio**, the nineteenth-century square with fountain that's at the heart of modern

Portalegre. Beyond here the town **gardens** flank Avenida da Liberdade, the lower part featuring stepped polychromatic cobbled tiles and a renowned plane tree (*plátano*), planted in 1848, whose spreading branches are now so long they have to be supported by pillars.

Practicalities

The **bus station** is set just back from the Rossio on Rua Nuno Álvares Pereira. Shuttle buses to and from here (15min) meet **trains** at the Estação de Portalegre, 12km out of town to the south, on the Lisbon–Badajoz line. There's lots of **parking** by the gardens, near the Rossio, some of it free. The helpful **turismo** (Mon–Fri 10am–7pm, Sat & Sun 10am–1pm & 3–6pm; ☎245 331 359, ⓦwww.cm-portalegre.pt) is in the Palácio Póvoas, right on the Rossio, though it's not clearly signposted – it's the green-shuttered building with wrought-iron balconies. It's also due for a move within the next two years, to the revamped city council offices which will form part of the Colégio de São Sebastião on Rua Guilhermo Gomes Fernandes. There's a regional tourist office, the **Região de Turismo de São Mamede**, Estrada de Santana 25 (daily 10am–2pm & 3–6pm; ☎245 300 770, ⓦwww.rtsm.pt), on the southern edge of town.

Accommodation

There is only limited accommodation available in town, and it's advisable to book ahead to be sure of a bed. The well-equipped *Orbitur* **campsite** (☎245 331 736, ⓦwww.orbitur.pt; closed Nov–Feb) is at Quinta da Saúde, 3km into the hills.

O Cortiço Rua Dom Nuno Álvares Pereira 17 ☎245 202 176. The bar-restaurant opposite the bus station is usually full of good old boys, but persevere with the bar staff and you should be escorted around the corner, up Rua 1 de Maio, to an apartment building with smart, modern en-suite air-conditioned rooms that are good-value for money. Back at the *Cortiço*, you can eat cheaply with the locals. No credit cards. ❷

Hotel Dom João III Av. da Liberdade ☎245 330 192, ⓕ245 330 444. The town's only proper hotel, which means it's often busy. Reasonable rooms, many with balconies overlooking the gardens; breakfast included. ❹

Residencial Mansâo Alto Alentejo Rua 19 de Junho 59 ☎245 202 290, ⓔmansaoaltoalentejo@netc.pt. Nicest choice up in the old town, with traditional Alentejan decor (including painted headboards) in twelve en-suite, air-conditioned rooms. Breakfast included. No credit cards. ❸

Pensão Nova Rua 31 de Janeiro 28–30 ☎245 331 212, ⓕ245 330 493. Friendly place with simple rooms, nicely turned out, with private bath and TV. The same management runs the nearby *Pensão São Pedro*, Rua da Mouraria 14, which offers more of the same at similar prices. No credit cards. ❶

Quinta da Saúde Estrada de São Mamede, 3km northeast of town ☎245 202 324. An attractive rural property with a great view over the surrounding hills and a good restaurant. ❹

Residencial Rossio Rua Dom Nuno Álvares Pereira 10-1° ☎245 201 975. The budget rooms on offer, some windowless, all small and stuffy, are adequate for a night if all else fails. It's next to the bus station, so expect some noise. No credit cards. ❶

Solar das Avencas Parque Miguel Bombarda ☎245 201 028. Five rooms in an elegant, antique-laden, eighteenth-century town mansion. Breakfast included. ❹

Eating and drinking

There's no shortage of **cafés** and **restaurants**, mostly concentrated in the upper old town, particularly along and near Rua 19 de Junho. Three or four budget places are found near the bus station, close to the Rossio, fine if you're not too concerned about ambience. During the day the nicest place for a drink is the terrace-café at the top of the Avenida da Liberdade gardens. In the evening the

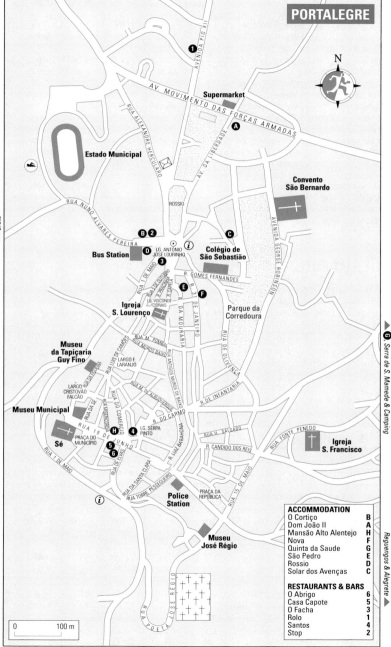

Castelo de Vide & Marvão

PORTALEGRE

AV. MOVIMENTO DAS FORÇAS ARMADAS

Supermarket

A

N

AVENIDA PIO XII

RUA ALEXANDRE HERCULANO

AV. DA LIBERDADE

Estado Municipal

ROSSIO

Convento
São Bernardo

Crato

RUA NUNO ALVARES PEREIRA

B **2**

C

Bus Station

D

LG. ANTÓNIO
JOSE LOURINHO

i

Colégio de
São Sebastião

AVENIDA GEORGE ROBINSON

3

R. GOMES FERNANDES

RUA 1 DE MAIO

RUA DE OLIVENÇA

RUA 5 DE OUTUBRO

R. PARREIRA

R. DA CORREIA

E

F

LG. VISCONDE
CIDRAIS

RUA 31 DE JANEIRO

Parque da
Corredoura

Igreja
S. Lourenço

RUA DA MOURARIA

Museu
da Tapiçaria
Guy Fino

RUA M.ª POMBAL

RUA AMEIXAS BAIXO

RUA ANTIGOS MINIS DE BAIXO

Serra de S. Mamede & Camping

RUA LUIS DE CAMÕES

LARGO F.
LARANJO

RUA M. DE ALBUQUERQUE

RUA DE INFANTARIA

LARGO
CRISTOVÃO
FALCÃO

RUA DA SÉ

RUA VISCONDE

RUA DO COMERCIO

R. DO CARMO

Museu Municipal

H

4

LG. SERPA
PINTO

RUA H. SALGADO

RUA FONTE PENEDO

Sé

PRAÇA DO
MUNICIPIO

5

6

RUA 19 DE JUNHO

RUA LUZ BARRAHO

R. CANDIDO DOS REIS

Igreja
S. Francisco

RUA 1 DE MAIO

RUA DE ELVAS

RUA DA SANTA CLARA

RUA 15 DE MAIO

Reguengos & Alegrete

i

RUA TORRE PISSEGUEIRO

Police
Station

PRAÇA DA
REPÚBLICA

Museu
José Régio

RUA POETA JOSÉ RÉGIO

0   100 m

Train Station, Évora, Elvas & Lisbon

8

ALENTEJO | Portalegre

ACCOMMODATION
O Cortiço   **B**
Dom João II   **A**
Mansão Alto Alentejo   **H**
Nova   **F**
Quinta da Saude   **G**
São Pedro   **E**
Rossio   **D**
Solar dos Avenças   **C**

RESTAURANTS & BARS
O Abrigo   **6**
Casa Capote   **5**
O Facha   **3**
Rolo   **1**
Santos   **4**
Stop   **2**

action, such as it is, switches to the old town, where the *Café Central*, facing Largo Frederico Laranjo, and others in the same area, are open until late.

Restaurante O Abrigo Rua de Elvas 74 ⊕245 331 658. A favourite with local families, serving locally inspired Alentejan dishes, meat and fish. Closed Tues. Moderate.

Casa Capote Rua 19 de Junho 56 ⊕245 201 748. Swing-door tavern on one side, nice local restaurant the other, where a full meal is likely to set you back under €10. Closes early at night sometimes, so get there before 8pm. Inexpensive.

O Facha Largo António José Lourinho 3–5 ⊕245 203 161. Glass and brass Art Deco joint, a bit on the faded side, though popular at lunch – there's a wide menu of snacks and meals, pricier than usual but hardly bank-breaking. Moderate.

Rolo Av. Pio XII ⊕245 205 676. The best place in town is a bit of a hike from the old centre – beyond the top of the gardens – but it's renowned

for its grilled meats and northern Alentejan specials. Expensive.

Santos Largo Serpa Pinto 4 ⊕245 203 066. Eat on the outdoor deck in a pretty square, or in the rustic dining room. The menu is strong on *açorda* and *arroz* specials involving *mariscos* or *bacalhau*, but otherwise it's the usual grill menu in big servings, complemented by a decent regional wine list. The mention of *sobremesas* brings out a mini photo album of amateur shots of puds on tables. You'll eat for well under €15, all in. Closed Wed. Moderate.

Restaurante Stop 11–15 Rua Dom Nuno Álvares Pereira ⊕245 201 364. One of the better options just off the Rossio, serving typical Alentejan cuisine in pleasant surroundings; a slap-up meal will cost under €10. Inexpensive.

Crato and around

CRATO – 21km west of Portalegre – is an ancient agricultural town that has clearly seen better days and larger populations. It's hardly an essential stop, though it is an interesting diversion, and has a terrific *pousada* just out of town to the north, set in the honey-stone convent of Flôr da Rosa. Horse enthusiasts will also want to make the 13km drive south of Crato to Alter do Chão, home of a prestigious *coudelaria* (stud farm).

In town, a trio of imposing, ornate churches and the elegant **Varanda do Grão Prior** in the pretty main Praça do Municipio attest, like Portalegre's monuments, to the textile boom years of the sixteenth century. The *varanda* is the most interesting of the structures – an arcaded granite balcony built for the outdoor celebration of Mass. Also worth a look is the town mansion around the corner, which houses a small **Mueu Municipal** (theoretically open Tues–Sun 10am–12.30pm & 2–6pm) of Alto Alentejo handicrafts and domestic traditions. Well into the last century, alms were handed out to the local poor from a balcony-chapel upstairs.

Wind up through the streets to the town **castle**, once among the mightiest in the Alentejo, but today a pastoral ruin, overrun by farm animals, fig trees and oregano plants. There's no access, but from the cobbled square in front there is a splendid view across the countless rows of olive trees to the hills of Portalegre. On the way back into the centre you can marvel at the dominant colour scheme in town – white with mustard-yellow trim – that adorns every single house, mansion to cottage.

Buses run intermittently from Portalegre to Crato, while the **Estação de Crato**, south of town, gives access to the Lisbon–Badajoz train line. Realistically, though, Crato is a car-and-coffee stop – a kiosk in the town gardens, by the roundabout, does the honours. And if you've diverted out this way, you may as well then drive out west along the N363 towards Aldeia da Mata. After 7km you'll see the sign for the **Anta do Tapadão**, which is reckoned to be the best-preserved dolmen in Portugal. The leaning stones are visible atop a small rise in the middle of grazing land away to the left; access is along a farm track.

Flôr da Rosa

Two kilometres north of Crato lies the village of **FLÔR DA ROSA**, tradi-tionally a centre for pottery. Off the main road, a dusty square lined with simple whitewashed cottages is overshadowed by the dour battlemented walls of the **Convento de Flôr da Rosa**, founded in the fourteenth century and much endowed over the next two hundred years. It was abandoned in 1897, due to leaking roofs and a decaying structure, and after extensive restoration (begun in 1940) the fortress monastery finally reopened in 1995 as the *Pousada de Flôr da Rosa* (☎245 997 210, ⓦwww.pousadas.pt; breakfast included; ❾). It's a magnificent building, marrying contemporary style with the convent buildings – there's a games room in the upper cloister and a lovely restaurant. Visitors are welcome to have a look around the main building, and trace the plan of the gardens, laid out in the insignia of the Order of Malta, in honour of the warlord **Nuno Álvares Pereira**, whose father founded the monastery. His tomb (dated 1382) is prominent in the narrow, soaring convent church.

There's a small **turismo** on the main road through Flôr da Rosa (Tues–Sun 10am–12.30pm & 2.30–5.30pm; ☎245 997 341). Next door, *O Recanato* is a popular local **lunch** spot, with tables in the back dining room or on a covered outdoor terrace.

Alter do Chão

ALTER DO CHÃO, 13km to the south of Crato, is another town that did well from textiles, particularly during the sixteenth century, as indicated by its attractive Renaissance marble fountain and an array of handsome town houses. There is a castle, too, whose central tower can be climbed for an overview of the region, but the chief reason for a visit is the **Coudelaria de Alter-Real** stud farm, 3km out of town. It was founded in 1748 by Dom João V of the House of Bragança, and remained in the family until 1910 when the War Office took it over. Today, maintained by the state, it is open for public visits (daily 9am–5.30pm), though to see the horses in action it's best to arrive in the morning, between 10am and noon, when you can watch them filing in from the fields to feed, accompanied to the ringing of forty bells. Alter-Real horses have been sought after since the stud's foundation – one is depicted in the equestrian statue of Dom José in Lisbon's Praça do Comércio, for example – and they remain the favoured breed of the Portuguese mounted police and the Lisbon Riding School at Queluz.

Castelo de Vide

Twenty kilometers north of Portalegre, the small town of **CASTELO DE VIDE** covers the slopes around a fourteenth-century castle, its blindingly white cottages delineated in brilliant contrast to the greenery around. Mineral springs pepper the local hills and the town is one of public fountains and gardens, its cobbled streets and placid squares lined with well-watered pots of geraniums and two-metre-high sunflowers.

From the main road through town, half a dozen narrow parallel streets make a sharp climb up to the aptly named **Praça Alta** on the northern edge of town, from where there are sweeping views across the plain. The main road, meanwhile, peters out into a cobbled lane, descending past a tranquil Renaissance marble fountain to the twisting alleyways of the **Judairia** – the extra €3 for room 15, with its own terrace with extensive views; or, two doors, down, *Casa do Arvore*, a gleaming private house flanking Largo de Camões (☎245 993 854; includes breakfast; ❹), whose genteel rooms have wooden floors, carved pine beds and great views. Up a rung there's the *Albergaria El Rei Dom Manuel*, Largo do Terreiro (☎245 909 150, ⓦwww.turismarvao.pt; breakfast included; ❹) – in the first square through the gate – whose appealing rooms have more expansive views, tasteful decor and monogrammed towels. Top choice is the superb *Pousada de Santa Maria* at Rua 24 de Janeiro 7 (☎245 993 201, ⓦwww.pousadas. pt; breakfast included; ❽), converted from a couple of former village houses – not all the rooms have views, but those that do are blessed.

For budget **meals**, you can eat well at the *Varanda do Alentejo* (☎245 993 272), in the middle of the village in Praça do Pelourinho, and less well at *Casa do Povo* (☎245 993 160), just down Rua da Cima off the square – though the latter does have an outdoor terrace. The more upmarket choices are the restaurants at the *albergaria* (moderate) and the *pousada* (expensive), both good, both with menus that venture from the standard. The odd little **bar** and café tucks into quiet corners and old town houses: at *O Castelo* (marked "Café-Bar), opposite *Dom Dinis*, you can snack on scrambled egg or smoked ham *petiscos*, and sit outside under the spreading trees.

Baixo Alentejo

There are two main routes south into the Baixo Alentejo. From Évora, the main highway runs down to **Beja**, 80km away, which is arguably the most interesting southern Alentejo town, and certainly the only one of any real size. If you're not in any hurry, you could always follow the minor roads instead and head for Beja via **Viana do Alentejo** and **Alvito**, both small towns of some charm. Beja sits at the heart of the Baixo Alentejo and from here there are easy routes to the old Moorish town of **Moura**, close to the **Alqueva** dam, and to the classic walled town of **Serpa**, while further south – en route to the western Algarve – riverside **Mértola** really demands a night of its own.

Approaching the Alentejo from Lisbon and Setúbal, however, the obvious route south loops around the Rio Sado estuary via the old port of **Alcácer do Sal** and runs on through the agricultural town of **Grândola**, 25km further south – the latter not worth a stop, though legendary in Portugal through the song *Grândola vila morena*, the broadcasting of which was the prearranged signal for the start of the 1974 revolution. From here, Beja is a straight run to the east, while motorway and highway speed south through interminable parched tracts of wheat fields towards the central Algarve. The highlight of this side of the Alentejo, though, is its long Atlantic coastline, which begins in earnest just to the west of **Santiago do Cacém**. Resorts like **Porto Covo**, **Vila Nova de Milfontes** and **Zambujeira do Mar** provide an attractive alternative to the summer crowds on the Algarve. Their only disadvantage – and the reason for a very patchy tourist development – is their exposure to the Atlantic winds, which at times create huge breakers and dangerous swimming conditions.

Flôr da Rosa

Two kilometres north of Crato lies the village of **FLÔR DA ROSA**, traditionally a centre for pottery. Off the main road, a dusty square lined with simple whitewashed cottages is overshadowed by the dour battlemented walls of the **Convento de Flôr da Rosa**, founded in the fourteenth century and much endowed over the next two hundred years. It was abandoned in 1897, due to leaking roofs and a decaying structure, and after extensive restoration (begun in 1940) the fortress monastery finally reopened in 1995 as the *Pousada de Flôr da Rosa* (☎245 997 210, Ⓦwww.pousadas.pt; breakfast included; ⑨). It's a magnificent building, marrying contemporary style with the convent buildings – there's a games room in the upper cloister and a lovely restaurant. Visitors are welcome to have a look around the main building, and trace the plan of the gardens, laid out in the insignia of the Order of Malta, in honour of the warlord **Nuno Álvares Pereira**, whose father founded the monastery. His tomb (dated 1382) is prominent in the narrow, soaring convent church.

There's a small **turismo** on the main road through Flôr da Rosa (Tues–Sun 10am–12.30pm & 2.30–5.30pm; ☎245 997 341). Next door, *O Recanato* is a popular local **lunch** spot, with tables in the back dining room or on a covered outdoor terrace.

Alter do Chão

ALTER DO CHÃO, 13km to the south of Crato, is another town that did well from textiles, particularly during the sixteenth century, as indicated by its attractive Renaissance marble fountain and an array of handsome town houses. There is a castle, too, whose central tower can be climbed for an overview of the region, but the chief reason for a visit is the **Coudelaria de Alter-Real** stud farm, 3km out of town. It was founded in 1748 by Dom João V of the House of Bragança, and remained in the family until 1910 when the War Office took it over. Today, maintained by the state, it is open for public visits (daily 9am–5.30pm), though to see the horses in action it's best to arrive in the morning, between 10am and noon, when you can watch them filing in from the fields to feed, accompanied to the ringing of forty bells. Alter-Real horses have been sought after since the stud's foundation – one is depicted in the equestrian statue of Dom José in Lisbon's Praça do Comércio, for example – and they remain the favoured breed of the Portuguese mounted police and the Lisbon Riding School at Queluz.

Castelo de Vide

Twenty kilometers north of Portalegre, the small town of **CASTELO DE VIDE** covers the slopes around a fourteenth-century castle, its blindingly white cottages delineated in brilliant contrast to the greenery around. Mineral springs pepper the local hills and the town is one of public fountains and gardens, its cobbled streets and placid squares lined with well-watered pots of geraniums and two-metre-high sunflowers.

From the main road through town, half a dozen narrow parallel streets make a sharp climb up to the aptly named **Praça Alta** on the northern edge of town, from where there are sweeping views across the plain. The main road, meanwhile, peters out into a cobbled lane, descending past a tranquil Renaissance marble fountain to the twisting alleyways of the **Judaria** – the old Jewish quarter. A signpost points you up the precipitous Rua da Fonte, past cottages with Gothic doorways and windows, to the thirteenth-century **Sinagoga** (daily: June–Sept 8am–7pm, Oct–May 8am–5pm; free), the oldest surviving synagogue in Portugal. From the outside it doesn't look very different from the cottages – it's the corner building almost at the top of the street – and inside the plain room only the tabernacle survives. Keep on up Rua da Fonte for another 200m or so to the **Castelo** itself (daily: June–Sept 8am–7pm, Oct–May 8am–5pm; free), whose dour foursquare keep squats within the wider fortifications of the original medieval village.

Practicalities

Arriving by **bus** (direct from Portalegre and Lisbon, change at Portagem from Marvão) you'll be dropped right in the centre at the *pelourinho* by the town hall clocktower, on Rua Bartolomeu Álvares da Santa. A little shop, just across the road and around the corner on Rua 5 de Outubro, posts timetables in the window. The **turismo** (daily: June–Sept 9am–7pm; Oct–May 9am–5pm; ☎245 901 361) is just behind the town hall, in the middle of the large paved Praça Dom Pedro V, in the shadow of the Santa Maria church whose bulk dominates the lower town. There's ample free **parking** in clearly marked bays all around the main square and street.

Given its size, the town has a surprising amount of **accommodation**, much of it very central – there are three or four places alone by the town gardens, at the eastern end of Rua Bartolomeu Álvares da Santa. The turismo has a full list. Good **restaurants** are thinner on the ground – our favourites are picked out below – but there's no shortage of **cafés** for drinks, cakes and snacks. You can sit outside those along Rua Bartolomeu Álvares da Santa and the parallel Rua de Olivença.

Hotels and pensions

Casa Amarela Pr. Dom Pedro V 11 ☎245 905 878, ℱ245 901 228. Lovely yellow mansion, its carved stone windows overlooking the main square. Beautiful rooms with plenty of space, spacious marble bathrooms, antiques and polished wood. Parking outside. There may be a short wait as the elderly *senhora* summons the *padron*, who arrives screeching to a halt in his car to show you in. Breakfast included. ❻

Casa de Hóspedes Melanie Largo do Paço Novo 3 ☎245 901 632. Best value of the bunch at the western (town-centre) end of the public gardens is provided by this friendly, English-speaking place with five nice spacious rooms. No credit cards. ❸

Residencial Isabelinha Largo do Paço Novo ☎245 901 896. Old-fashioned place virtually next door to *Melanie* – there's a slight smell of camphor, plenty of nickknackery and old furniture, but there are views onto the public gardens, and it's very clean. Breakfast included. ❸

Casa Machado Rua Luís de Camões 33 ☎245 901 515. Three modern spotless rooms, and shared patio, at the western (bottom) edge of town, 300m from Porta São João. No credit cards. ❸

Albergaria El Rei Dom Miguel Rua Bartolomeu Álvares da Santa 45 ☎245 919 191, ℱ245 901 592. Seven elegant air-conditioned rooms with polished floors and nice bathrooms, plus a baronial salon – breakfast included. ❹

Hotel Sol e Serra Estrada S. Vincente 73 ☎245 900 000, ⊛www.grupofbarata.com. Just off the top of the gardens at the eastern end, it's a large hotel with nicely turned out rooms with balconies over town and hills, plus pool, connections with the local golf course (10min drive away), bar and restaurant. Prices are very reasonable too. ❹

Restaurants

O Alentejano Largo Mártires da República ☎245 901 355. Simple budget meals, in a little restaurant at the top of a sloping square next to the town gardens. Closed Wed. Inexpensive.

Dom Pedro V Pr. Dom Pedro V ☎245 901 236. A good place for quality regional dishes, with mains costing €7–10. Moderate.

Marino's Pr. Dom Pedro ☎245 901 722. Tucked away at the back of the main square, and specializing in Italian dishes (pastas, grilled veg and carpaccio) as well as regional food. You'll be able to eat well for €20. Closed Sun, & Mon lunch. Expensive.

Marvão

Beautiful as Castelo de Vide is, nearby **MARVÃO** surpasses it. The panoramas from its remote eyrie site are unrivalled and the atmosphere even quieter than a population of less than a thousand would suggest. No more than a handful of houses – each as scrupulously whitewashed as the rest – lies outside the seventeenth-century walls, which encircle a dramatically sited rocky outcrop high above the undulating *serra*. There was a Roman settlement on the plains below, later abandoned in the face of the Moorish advance in around 715, under whose rule the first fortifications were built – and named after Marvan, the Moorish Lord of Coimbra. Marvão fell to the Christians in 1166, and the castle was rebuilt by Dom Dinis around 1229 as another important link in the chain of outposts along the Spanish border.

The **castle** (always open; free) stands at the far end of the village, its walls blending into the slopes of the *serra*. It's dauntingly impenetrable, and was provided with a huge cisterna, just inside the main entrance, still full of water, designed to supply the entire village. Indeed, the castle was captured only once, in 1833, when the attackers entered through a secret gate. In the village, stepped and cobbled streets switchback along the contours, the terraces planted with impeccably kept gardens and the houses sporting granite windows and pitched red roofs. Just walking around is enjoyment enough, though there is a **Museu Municpal** (daily 9am–12.30pm & 2–5.30pm; €1), in the Igreja de Santa Maria, which has an interesting range of Roman remains and other local finds.

Some of the archeological exhibits come from the **Cidade Romana de Ammaia** (Tues–Fri 9am–1pm & 2–5pm, Sat & Sun 110am–1pm & 2–5pm; €2), around 7km south of the village on the Portalegre road; follow the signs for São Salvador de Aramenha from the Portagem junction. It's a beautiful site in a wooded hollow, Marvão high on its bluff in the distance. Sheep graze across the Roman remains, which include parts of the south gate, a bath complex, forum and temple, while a small museum occupies the kitchen and basement of an old Roman house.

Practicalities

Marvão is 12km from Castelo de Vide and about 17km from Portalegre. There are buses from both places, though only a couple in each direction – and coming from Castelo de Vide, you may have to change at the road junction of Portagem. At Marvão, **buses** stop just outside the main villlage gate, the Portas de Rodão. You can park here as well, or drive further into the village, where there's more **parking** in the first square you come to. You can drive onwards and upwards, too, following signs for the turismo and castle, but it's narrow, cobbled and unnerving – you might want to park early and get your bearings first.

The village makes a superb night's stop, as several houses within the walls are rented out under a scheme organized by the **turismo**, in Largo de Santa Maria, very near the museum and castle (June–Sept Mon–Fri 9am–7pm, Sat & Sun 10am–12.30pm and 2–7pm; Oct–May daily 9am–12.30pm & 2–5.30pm; ☎245 993 886, ⓦwww.cm-marvao.pt). In some of these you can get just a room, while others are rented out as a unit; prices, consequently, are extremely varied. Otherwise, **accommodation** is pricier than in Castelo de Vide, but includes the characterful *Dom Dinis* on Rua Dr. António Matos Magalhães (☎245 993 957, ⓦwww.casaddinis.pa-net.pt; ❹), on the corner across from the turismo – pay the extra €3 for room 15, with its own terrace with extensive views; or, two doors, down, *Casa do Arvore*, a gleaming private house flanking Largo de Camões (☎245 993 854; includes breakfast; ❹), whose genteel rooms have wooden floors, carved pine beds and great views. Up a rung there's the *Albergaria El Rei Dom Manuel*, Largo do Terreiro (☎245 909 150, ⓦwww.turismarvao.pt; breakfast included; ❹) – in the first square through the gate – whose appealing rooms have more expansive views, tasteful decor and monogrammed towels. Top choice is the superb *Pousada de Santa Maria* at Rua 24 de Janeiro 7 (☎245 993 201, ⓦwww.pousadas. pt; breakfast included; ❽), converted from a couple of former village houses – not all the rooms have views, but those that do are blessed.

For budget **meals**, you can eat well at the *Varanda do Alentejo* (☎245 993 272), in the middle of the village in Praça do Pelourinho, and less well at *Casa do Povo* (☎245 993 160), just down Rua da Cima off the square – though the latter does have an outdoor terrace. The more upmarket choices are the restaurants at the *albergaria* (moderate) and the *pousada* (expensive), both good, both with menus that venture from the standard. The odd little **bar** and café tucks into quiet corners and old town houses: at *O Castelo* (marked "Café-Bar"), opposite *Dom Dinis*, you can snack on scrambled egg or smoked ham *petiscos*, and sit outside under the spreading trees.

Baixo Alentejo

There are two main routes south into the Baixo Alentejo. From Évora, the main highway runs down to **Beja**, 80km away, which is arguably the most interesting southern Alentejo town, and certainly the only one of any real size. If you're not in any hurry, you could always follow the minor roads instead and head for Beja via **Viana do Alentejo** and **Alvito**, both small towns of some charm. Beja sits at the heart of the Baixo Alentejo and from here there are easy routes to the old Moorish town of **Moura**, close to the **Alqueva** dam, and to the classic walled town of **Serpa**, while further south – en route to the western Algarve – riverside **Mértola** really demands a night of its own.

Approaching the Alentejo from Lisbon and Setúbal, however, the obvious route south loops around the Rio Sado estuary via the old port of **Alcácer do Sal** and runs on through the agricultural town of **Grândola**, 25km further south – the latter not worth a stop, though legendary in Portugal through the song *Grândola vila morena*, the broadcasting of which was the prearranged signal for the start of the 1974 revolution. From here, Beja is a straight run to the east, while motorway and highway speed south through interminable parched tracts of wheat fields towards the central Algarve. The highlight of this side of the Alentejo, though, is its long Atlantic coastline, which begins in earnest just to the west of **Santiago do Cacém**. Resorts like **Porto Covo**, **Vila Nova de Milfontes** and **Zambujeira do Mar** provide an attractive alternative to the summer crowds on the Algarve. Their only disadvantage – and the reason for a very patchy tourist development – is their exposure to the Atlantic winds, which at times create huge breakers and dangerous swimming conditions.

South from Évora

While it's temping to take the fast road to Beja and the south, there's an attractive detour to be made into deepest rural Alentejo, via the small historic towns of **Viana do Alentejo** and **Alvito** and the Roman ruins of **São Cucufate**. From Évora the first stop, Viana do Alentejo, is a simple twenty-minute drive down the ruler-straight N254. There's no public transport along this route – at least, none that makes any sense in terms of jumping off for a quick look around and heading swiftly on. You'll need a car.

Viana do Alentejo

VIANA DO ALENTEJO is a typically dozy southern Alentejan town – village really – which nonetheless preserves a highly decorative castle, full of Mudejar and Manueline features. The walls were built on a pentagonal plan by Dom Dinis in 1313, and the interior ensemble of buildings was expanded under Dom João II and Dom Manuel I in the late fifteenth century. To this latter period belong a sequence of elaborate battlements, with their witch's hat towers and pinnacles, and the beautiful parish church which has a superbly carved door, mottled with lichen. You can grab a quick coffee down the street from the castle in the Praça da República before moving on.

Alvito

ALVITO, 10km further south, has altogether more to delay you, being a small town of great charm with an abundance of Manueline features. It's dominated, as is the way, by its castle – now a *pousada* (see below) – but in the few streets between here, the parish church and the town hall clocktower is plenty of interest. The castle itself (built in 1494) is a curious Manueline-Mudejar hybrid, a style seen also in the much smaller Ermida de São Sebastião, on the edge of town, from there are fine views across the cultivated plains below. In addition, many of the houses have carved sixteenth-century windows and door-frames, and if you seek out the town gardens, small market and typical *pelourinho* in the handsome main square, Praça da República, you've easily occupied an hour or two.

There's no need to stay longer though there's a feeling that the presence of the *Pousada do Castelo de Avito* (☎284 480 700, Ⓦwww.pousadas.pt; breakfast included; ❾) – and the money it brings in – has raised the town's game. Certainly, it's a pleasant night's stop and, if you can't run to **accommodation** at the *pousada*, then *Residencial A Varanda* (☎284 485 135; breakfast included; ❹), right opposite the castle on Praça da República, has much the same outlook. Who could resist a drink in its "Lady Di" bar in any case? The **turismo** (Tues–Sun 9.30am–12.30pm & 3–7pm; ☎284 485 440) in Largo do Relógio, behind the town hall, next to the market, can also point you in the direction of rural guest houses, like *Horta da Lameira* (☎284 475 286, Ⓦwww.hortadalameira.com; breakfast included; ❹), 7km northwest of town near Vila Nova da Baronia, which has pretty rooms and a pool. Dinner can be arranged here, and it's much better value if you stay more than one night.

São Cucufate

Heading east from Alvito to the Beja road, you'll pass the **Ruinas Romanas de São Cucufate** (Tues 2.30–5pm, Wed–Sun 9am–12.30pm & 2–5pm; €2), 19km from Alvito and around 1km before Vila de Frades. It's a peaceful, rural spot, shrouded in landscaped grounds of rosemary, thyme and lavender, where the history of three separate Roman villas is laid bare in a series of extensive excavations and reconstructions. The first villa was built here in the middle of the first century AD, but replaced by two successively grander constructions, with baths, grain stores, oil presses and servants' quarters. The third villa was abandoned in the fifth century and later reoccupied in medieval times as a monastery – the old wine cellar was eventually decorated with frescoes in the late-sixteenth century, after which the whole complex was abandoned once more. There is a small exhibition detailing the site's history, but it's all in Portuguese – you'll need to buy the English-language leaflet to make much sense of the ruins, though they are atmospheric enough without explanation.

Beja

On the inland route through southern Alentejo, **BEJA** appears as a welcome oasis amid the sweltering, featureless wheat fields. Commanding a strategic position in the centre of the plains, it has long been an important and prosperous city. Founded by Julius Caesar in 48 BC it was named Pax Julia, in honour of the peace accord signed here between Rome and the Lusitanians, but later became Pax Augusta and then just Pax, from which it gradually corrupted to Paca, Baca, Baju, and finally Beja.

South of Évora, it's the only major town en route to the Algarve, and once past the modern suburbs Beja reveals an unhurried old quarter with a cluster of churches, a beautiful convent and a thirteenth-century castle. You can take in the sights in this compact historic centre in half a day, though in summer the heat will slow you down – and it's not a bad night's stopover in any case, with plenty of good cafés and restaurants. Annual events and **festivals** include Ovibeja (March), a big agricultural and handicrafts fair, and the *feira* for São Lourenço and Santa Maria (second week of August).

The Town

In Portugal Beja is best known for the love affair of a seventeenth-century nun who lived in the **Convento de Nossa Senhora da Conceição**, right in the centre of today's town. Sister Mariana Alcoforado is believed to have fallen in love with Count Chamilly, a French cavalry officer, and is credited with the notorious (in Portugal anyway) *Five Love Letters of a Portuguese Nun*, first published in Paris in 1669. The originals have never been discovered, and a scholarly debate has raged over the authenticity of the French "translation". Nonetheless, English and Portuguese editions soon appeared and the letters became internationally famous as a classic of romantic literature.

Sentimental associations aside, the convent is an impressive building, first founded in the fifteenth century. It has a panoply of Manueline fripperies, including elaborate portals and a rhythmic roofline decorated with balustrades and pinnacles. The walls of the cloisters and chapterhouse are completely covered with multicoloured sixteenth- and seventeenth-century *azulejos*, and present one of the finest examples of this art form. The other highlight is a magnificent Rococo chapel, sumptuously gilded and embellished with flying cherubs.

The convent was dissolved in 1834 and today houses the **Museu Regional** (Tues–Sun 9.30am–12.30pm & 2–5.15pm; €2, includes entry to Museu Visigótico, free on Sun), entered from Largo de Conceição. Compared with the architecture of the building, the museum pieces are comparatively lacklustre,

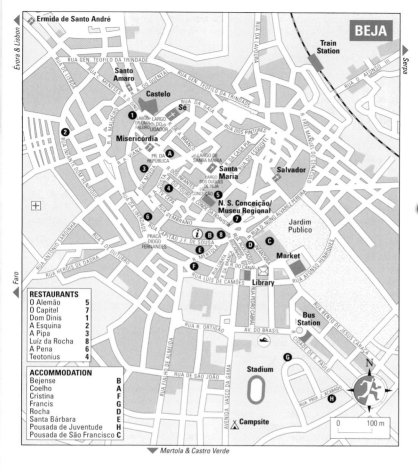

Mertola & Castro Verde

though they include wide-ranging displays on the town's past eras – including items as diverse as Roman and Visigothic stonework, fifteenth- to eighteenth-century Dutch and Portuguese painting, and even the grille through which the errant nun first glimpsed her lover.

From the convent it's a quick walk up to attractive **Praça da República** and its *pelourinho*, while at the head of the square is the distinctive mid-sixteenth-century **Igreja da Misericórdia**. Its huge projecting porch served originally as a meat market and the stonework is deliberately chiselled to give a coarse, rustic appearance; handicrafts are sold just inside the entrance. Beyond, past the unassuming cathedral, Beja's **Castelo** (Tues–Sun 10am–1pm & 2–6pm; tower €1.50) rises decoratively on the edge of the old quarter. It was built – yet again – by Dom Dinis and is remarkable for the playful battlements of its Torre de Menagem.

In the shadow of the keep stands the small, whitewashed, Visigothic **Igreja de Santo Amaro** (Tues–Sun 9.30am–12.30pm & 2–5.15pm), today a small archeological museum. The building is a rare survival from pre-Moorish Portugal; the interior columns are carved with seventh-century geometric motifs.

Practicalities

The old quarter is a circular tangle of streets, enclosed within a ring road that has largely replaced the town walls. You can get fairly close to the historic centre by car, and there's signposted **parking** at various points (some of it metered) – anywhere around the gardens or bus station is convenient.

The **bus station** is five minutes' walk southeast of the old centre, the **train station** five minutes northeast. Beja has good transport connections to the rest of central and southern Portugal, as well as a bus link to Seville. For Lisbon and the western Algarve, it's usually quickest to take the train, whereas for Évora, Vila Real de Santo António (for the eastern Algarve) and Santiago do Cacém (for the Alentejo coast) it's better by bus.

The **turismo**, right in the centre at Rua Capitão João Francisco de Sousa 25 (Mon–Sat: May–Sept 9am–7pm; Oct–April 10am–1pm & 2–6pm; ☎284 311 913, Ⓦwww.cm-beja.pt, Ⓦwww.rt-planiciedourada.pt), is fairly useless, though you'll get a nice big map with everything marked on it.

Accommodation

Most of the town's accommodation is to be found within a few blocks of the turismo, and in summer it's worth booking ahead to make sure of a room at the better places. The turismo might be able to help – don't count on it – but there are also various simple **rooms** places around town, including *Santa Maria*, Rua da Casa Pia 8, and *Rosa do Campo*, Rua da Liberdade 12; you should find something. Parking near your hotel is often difficult as many of the central streets and squares are pedestrianized.

Hotels and pensions

Residencial Bejense Rua do Capitão J.F. de Sousa 57 ☎284 311 570, Ⓕ284 311 579. The best budget choice in town, clad in inviting bougainvilla and nicely tiled within, has tasteful, high-ceilinged, air-conditioned rooms with newish bathrooms and satellite TV. It's a welcoming place, which hangs its family photos on the landings and serves breakfast (included) in a rustic first-floor dining room. ❸

Residencial Coelho Pr. da República 15 ☎284 324 031. It's a lovely square, and some rooms have balconies opening directly onto it, but they have all seen lots of better days. Rooms are plain and worn, with functional shower-rooms, but would do for the night. Breakfast included. No credit cards. ❸

Residencial Cristina Rua de Mértola 71 ☎284 323 035, Ⓕ284 329 874. Rooms (en-suite, air-con) are disappointingly austere, but spacious enough – and there are views from those on the fourth floor. If you like padded leather, the 1970s period piece of a bar will delight. Breakfast included. Some parking available. ❹

Hotel Francis Pr. Fernandes Lopes Graça ☎284 315 500, Ⓦwww.hotel-francis.com. Flashy in the public areas – in the way of Portuguese three-stars – not quite so grand in the rooms, but still nice enough, with colour-coordinated rooms, many with big balconies. Best of all, there's a sauna, Turkish bath, gym and hot tub, plus parking (and a pizzeria) right outside. It's right by the bus station, down the steps off Rua da Conde São Paulo – driving, follow the signs. Breakfast included. ❻

Pensão Rocha Rua da Infantaria 17 ☎284 324 271. It faces the *pousada*, which is all the class you're going to get in this faded, decrepit old place. But it's clean and cheap. No credit cards. ❷

Residencial Santa Bárbara Rua de Mértola 56 ☎284 312 280, Ⓕ284 312 289. Trim, good-value, air-conditioned rooms with tile floors and a small en-suite shower/toilet. Rooms either overlook the street, with pocket-sized balconies, or are internal, a bit quieter and with perhaps a glimpse of the sky. Check out the bar – a veritable wooden pulpit. Breakfast included. ❸

Pousada de São Francisco Largo Dom Nuno Álvares Pereira ☎284 313 580, Ⓦwww.pousadas.pt. Imposing *pousada* inside a former convent, where rooms have been fashioned from the monastic cells. They are, of course, extremely comfortable, while the public areas make the same enterprising use of the space – an enclosed cloister with grand restaurant (high-quality Portuguese cuisine with

Alentejan specialities; expensive), bar and esplanade, attractive gardens and pool, and your very own Gothic chapel. Parking. ⑥

bike rental. Dorms are four-bedded, though there are also six en-suite doubles. Dorm beds €11, rooms ②

Youth hostel

Pousada de Juventude Rua Prof. Janeiro Acabado ☎284 325 458, ⓦwww.pousadasjuventude.pt. Newly built hostel, close to the bus station, with a good-sized common room, internet facilities and

Campsite

Parque de Campismo Av. Vasco da Gama ☎284 324 328. The municipal site, on the south side of town, past the stadium. It's fairly pleasant and shaded, and adjoins the local swimming pool.

Eating and drinking

Beja has a lot of cafés and restaurants, all signposted at every turn by the enthusiastic city authorities. There are plenty of places where you can sit outside with a coffee, while meals tend to be of the traditional variety – big portions, meat-orientated.

Churrasqueira O Alemão Largo dos Duques de Beja 11 ☎284 311 490. The queues out the door at lunch are for the takeaway side of the operation – slip though into the simple tiled dining room for cheap charcoal-grills, sausages to steaks, though the chicken is in a league of its own. Inexpensive.

Esplanada O Capitel Jardim Eng. Duarte Pacheco ☎284 325 708. The nicest place in town for an outdoor beer and snack is this open-air café in the gardens opposite the Tribunal building. Inexpensive.

Restaurante Dom Dinis Rua Dom Dinis ☎284 325 937. An upmarket grillhouse where meat is very definitely the thing – the butcher's is right next door. It's pretty good, but with mains at €10 or €11 the bill soon mounts up. Closed Wed. Expensive.

Restaurante A Esquina Rua Infante Dom Henrique 26 ☎284 389 238. Not far from the castle, but a bit off the normal route. Your reward is a thoroughly good locals' place, with a wide-ranging menu (meat and fish) – enormous portions for around €8. Closed Sun. Moderate.

Luíz da Rocha Rua do Capitão J.F. de Sousa 63 ☎284 323 179. In business for over a century, the café and tearoom downstairs is one of Beja's big meet-and-greet destinations, popular with elderly matrons, garrulous blokes and giggling teenagers. Pop in for a *bica* and a pastry or an evening brandy, or head upstairs for the cheap meals. Inexpensive.

Restaurante Pena Praça de Diogo Fernandes de Beja 19A ☎284 323 714. Come here if you fancy fish – there's more choice than on most local menus (mackerel, sardines, swordfish, squid) and the prices aren't too high. Closed Sun. Moderate.

Adega A Pipa Rua da Moeda 8 ☎284 327 043. Typically casual rustic tavern with decent prices – around €7 for most main courses, or a *meia dose* is a steal at €5. Closed Sun. Inexpensive.

Restaurante Teotonius Rua do Touro 8 ☎284 328 010. Grills a speciality in this old-town restaurant – the *picanha a Teotonius* is the house-recipe veal steak, though there are also good lamb cutlets and game in season. There's a chatty owner and an outdoor patio. Closed Mon. Moderate.

Listings

Banks There are banks and ATMs along Rua do Capitão J.F. de Sousa; also an ATM at the bus station.
Bikes Available for free use around town – you'll see the racks – though you have to go through a tortuous form-filling procedure first (take ID) at the turismo, the Câmara Municipal or the Casa da Cultura.

Hospital Rua Dr. António F.C. Lima ☎284 310 200.
Internet At the Biblioteca Municipal, Rua Luís de Camões (Mon 2.30–11pm, Tues–Fri 9.30am–12.30pm & 2.30–11pm, Sat 2.30–8pm).
Police PSP, Largo Dom Nunes Álvares Pereira ☎284 322 022.
Post office Largo dos Correios (Mon–Fri 8.30am–6.30pm).

Serpa

Thirty kilometres east of Beja, on the road to Spain, the small market town of **SERPA** offers the classic Alentejan attractions – a walled centre,

Accommodation is easy to find, unless you coincide with the two big annual fairs, in May and September (both second weekend). Best value is *Residencial Alentejana*, Largo José Maria dos Santos (☎285 250 080; breakfast included; ❸), a block down from the bus station – on the right-hand side of the gardens – which has modern, air-conditioned rooms with tile floors, good bathrooms and a buffet breakfast. Another couple of blocks down towards the centre, *Hotel de Moura*, on the peaceful Praça Gago Coutinho (☎285 251 090, ⓕ285 254 610; ❹), is more traditional, its facade completely covered with *azulejos*, and within, patios, mirrored doors and a rambling garden. Or there's the *Pensão Residencial Santa Comba*, right on Praça Sacadura Cabral (☎285 251 255, ⓕ285 251 257; breakfast included; no credit cards; ❸), by the castle, which is the cheapest of the lot, but as it's right on a road junction front-facing rooms can be noisy.

A few pleasant **cafés** face the gardens and castle on Praça Sacadura Cabral, and there are plenty of **restaurants** in the streets running back from here. *O Trilho*, Rua 5 de Outubro 5 (☎285 254 261; closed Mon), serves moderately priced regional dishes, while *O Túnel*, Rua dos Ourives 13 (☎285 253 384; closed Sun), is more in the way of an inexpensive neighbourhood bar and grill house. It's popular at lunchtime, though you may find yourself eating in splendid isolation at night.

The Barragem de Alqueva

In February 2002 the floodgates opened on the controversial **Barragem de Alqueva (Alqueva Dam)**, a project started decades ago under the Salazar regime. At 250 square kilometres (of which 69 square kilometres is in Spain), it's created Europe's largest reservoir from the waters of the Rio Gaudiana and several tributaries, which – the government claims – will provide reliable irrigation in this arid region, satisfy the increasing need for domestic water supplies in the neighbouring Algarve and provide jobs in the agricultural and tourism industries. There are many who still dispute these claims and strongly decry the destruction of over a million oak and cork trees, the threats to the habitats of golden eagles and the even rarer Iberian Lynx, plus the submerging of over 200 prehistoric sites. The World Wildlife Fund has described the project as an ecological disaster, while the inhabitants of the former village of Luz on the east bank of the Guadiana, now submerged, have had to be relocated to a facsimile village above the waterline.

The government, in turn, points to the benefits of the dam, not least the hydro-electric plant, switched on in 2004, which will provide enough electricity to supply the Évora and Beja districts combined. The dam is also designed to irrigate vast tracts of land which can then be exploited by farmers, while tourism projects in this previously underdeveloped area of Portugal are also underway now that a secure source of water is on hand. Primarily, of course, this means resort hotels and golf courses, something Alentejan farmers seem to have managed well without for hundreds of years.

You can drive right on to the **dam wall** from Moura – just follow the signs from town for 12km. Whatever you think of it, it's an extraordinary engineering project, whose viewing platforms offer sweeping vistas of the now-submerged river valley. The road continues up to Portel, on the Beja–Évora highway, while there's another road-bridge crossing, much further north, at Mourão, just south of Monsaraz (p.510), where the rising waters have completely changed the Guadiana river's environs.

Mértola and around

MÉRTOLA is as beautifully sited as any town in the south, set high on a spur above the confluence of the Guadiana and Oeiras rivers, guarded by the ruins of a Moorish frontier castle. It makes a fine place to stay the night, or longer – either en route to the Algarve, or just as a destination in its own right – sporting a compact, somnolent old town full of discoveries and quiet back-country surroundings that form part of the **Parque Natural Vale do Guadiana**. The region is home to the rare black stork and other endangered species, and the local hills, riverbanks and valleys have some excellent walks.

Mértola's history goes back as far as Phoenician times, when it was an important river port, and it was later fortified and expanded by both Romans (as Myrtilis) and Moors (Martulah), before being taken by Dom Sancho II in 1238 as part of the Christian Reconquista. With the walled town occupying such a small area, successive conquerors and settlers simply built on what they found, which provides Mértola with its current fascination – the evidence of thousands of years of habitation visible in almost every building and street.

The Town

If you start with the **Castelo** (daily 9am–5.30pm; free) all becomes clear, not least the layout of the walled old town and modern settlement beyond. The arched main door and winding entrance into the central keep area are Moorish, though the rest of the castle dates from the thirteenth-century Christian reconquest, when for a century it became the headquarters of the Order of Santiago. The earlier Islamic inhabitants lived within the castle walls and, later, in the Moorish quarter, just outside, which is still being excavated. The parish church at the foot of the castle, the **Igreja Matriz** (Wed–Sun 10am–1pm & 3–7pm), started life as a mosque and was barely altered after the reconquest. Its Moorish arched doorways are still visible and it retains its *mihrab* (prayer niche) behind the altar on the eastern wall.

The archeological finds from the various sites could simply have been placed in a municipal museum, but to the eternal benefit of Mértola, the whole town instead has been designated a "vila museu", allowing you to trace its art and history in a series of small, well-designed **exhibitions**. They are all open roughly the same hours (Tues–Sun 10am–1pm & 3–7pm, unless otherwise stated) and a single ticket (€5) gets you in them all, or you can pay €2 to visit a single exhibition.

Each deals with a single facet of the town's history, like the **Núcleo Romano** (Mon–Fri 9am–12.30pm & 2–5.30pm, Sat & Sun 10am–1pm & 3–7pm), the foundations of a Roman house discovered under the Câmera Municipal. In the **Museu Islâmica** are gathered the inscribed funerary stones, glazed tableware and decorated urns discovered within the Moorish quarter, while the **Museu de Arte Sacra** concentrates on religious art, notably the three retables from the parish church depicting Sancho's ousting of the Moors. A cooperative set up to revive the traditional weaving industry showcases its methods and products in the **Oficina de Tecelagem**, while even the town's former blacksmiths' workshop, the **Forja do Ferreiro** (key available from adjacent cottage if locked), is open for visits. All these lie in the old walled town, signposted and easily found, though the most moving exhibit is five minutes' walk away in the modern part of town, where the **Basílica Paleocristã**, in Largo do Rossio do Carmo, preserves thirty funerary stones in a partial reconstruction of an early Christian temple. These inhabitants – a "servant of God", "a man of social standing", or simply "son" or "daughter of" – were buried here, outside the city walls, over 1500 years ago.

Around Mértola

Cross the old bridge south of town (the Vila Real road), spanning the Ribeira de Oeiras, and it's a fifteen-minute walk up to the former **Convento de São Francisco** (Fri–Sun 2–6pm; €4; ⓦwww.conventomertola.com), whose Dutch owners have turned into an artistic retreat, with organic gardens, bird sanctuary, open-air and water installations, and a contemporary art gallery in the old church. Whether you think this is worth four euros to see is another matter.

North of town, across the new bridge, the bumpy country road to Serpa winds for 17km to **Mina de São Domingos**. The copper mines here were, until recent decades, the principal source of the town's employment, and until World War II they were owned by a British company, which employed a private police force and treated the workers with appalling brutality. There's nothing to see, but there is a very attractive river beach on the small reservoir here, with plenty of shade – it's very popular on summer weekends.

Practicalities

Mértola is around 50km from Beja or Serpa, an easy drive, and only 72km north of Vila Real de Santo António on the eastern Algarve, which means it sees progressively more tourist traffic. If you're heading south to Vila Real afterwards, you won't want to miss Alcoutim (p.570) on the way. Don't, incidentally, even think of driving into the walled town – **park** anywhere you like close to the walls or by the bus stops.

Buses come either from Beja, or stop in Mértola on the express run between Lisbon and Vila Real, with a limited local service on to Vila Real via Alcoutim. You're dropped at the bus stops by the main Serpa/Beja traffic circle in the new town – follow the signs for "Mértola/Vila Real" for the five-minute walk down the road to Largo Vasco de Gama at the foot of the old town. The **turismo** (daily 10am–1pm & 3–7pm; ☎286 610 109, ⓦwww.cm-mertola.pt) is just inside the walls (signposted), and hands out a very useful map, plus accommodation and restaurant lists. You can access the **internet** for free here too.

Although the walled town is handsome in the extreme, all the services are in the modern town, not unattractive itself, which sits in a tight clump between the castle walls and traffic circle. For **accommodation**, it's hard to conceive of a better – or friendlier – budget choice than the *Residencial Beira Rio*, Rua Dr. Afonso Costa 108 (☎286 611 190, ⓦwww.beirario.co.pt; breakfast included; ❸), down the left-hand fork as you come towards the old town, whose best rooms (all modern and en-suite, most air-conditioned) have balconies directly overlooking the peaceful river. A good buffet breakfast can be eaten on the terrace, and there's parking. The *Oásis*, immediately adjacent (☎286 612 404; no credit cards; ❷), though cheaper, isn't half the place. Some prefer the only choice within the walls, *Casa das Janelas Verdes*, Rua Dr. Manuel Francisco Gomes 38–40 (☎286 612 145; breakfast included; ❹), up from the turismo, a town house of some character, though it only has three rooms available. *Casa Rosmaninho*, Rus 25 de Abril 23 (☎963 019 341 ⓔcasa.rosmaninho@clix.pt; no credit cards; ❸), just outside the walls up from Largo Vasco de Gama, is also a small, pretty house with comfortable rooms. There are simpler "quartos" available at various locations, including at the *Restaurante Boa Viagem*, by the traffic circle, and above the *Café Campaniço* on Rua José Carlos Ary dos Santos – up the garden-avenue from the traffic circle and turn left at the fountain.

The best local **restaurants** are all ranged along Avenida Aureliano Mira Fernandes, the garden-avenue beyond the traffic circle in the modern town. First choice is the *Alengarve* (☎286 612 210; closed Wed), run by an affable bunch of young guys, serving a varied menu at highly reasonable prices. You'll eat very well for around €12 (try the *atum cebolada*), and can sit outside on the raised terrace. *O Repuxo* (☎286 612 563; closed Sun), at the end, is also well thought of, while a bit grander – though no more expensive – is *O Nautico*, Rua Dr. Serrão Martins (☎286 612 596; closed Sun), the sailing club restaurant, with panoramic windows and terrace. It's just before you get to Largo Vasca de Gama and the old town.

Alcácer do Sal

Coming from Lisbon and the west, **ALCÁCER DO SAL** is the first town of the Baixo Alentejo, just 52km from Setúbal. It is one of Portugal's oldest ports, founded by the Phoenicians and made a regional capital under the Moors – whence its name (*al-Ksar*, the town) derives. The other part of its name, *do Sal*, "of salt", reflects the dominance of the salt industry in these parts; the Sado estuary is still fringed with salt marshes.

Few stop longer than to stretch the legs – either Beja or the coast are less than an hour away – but it's an attractive enough place to do just that, particularly along the waterfront promenade. A couple of roads back from the promenade, at its western end, lies a charming quarter of medieval houses, centred on Rua Rui Salem. Further uphill, above the town, stands the part-ruined Moorish **castle**, from where there are striking views of the lush green paddy fields which almost surround the town, and of the storks' nests on the church rooftops. The castle is now home to the fabulous *Pousada Dom Afonso II* (☎265 613 070, ⓦwww.pousadas.pt; breakfast included; ❾), whose contemporary rooms, swimming pool and restaurant make dramatic use of the buildings. There are more modest hotels in town, but none provide as good a reason to stop as the *pousada*. For quieter country surroundings, you could always drive the 30km east along the minor N5 to Torrão, past the **Barragem de Vale do Gaio**, whose *Pousada de Vale do Gaio* (☎265 669 610, ⓦwww.pousadas.pt; breakfast included; ❽) – sited on the edge of the reservoir – is a fairly simple conversion of the lodge used by the dam engineers.

Santiago do Cacém

South of Alcácer, the only place that might tempt you to stop before the Alentejo coast is **SANTIAGO DO CACÉM**, a pleasant little provincial town overlooked by a castle, with the fascinating Roman ruins of Miróbriga on its outskirts. You certainly don't need to stay the night, even travelling on public transport – there are regular bus services west and south to the local beaches.

The modern town centres on its market, with what's left of the old town (not much) spreading up one of the hills to the **Castelo** (April–Sept Mon–Sat 8.30am–7pm, Sun 8.30am–12.30pm; Oct–March Mon–Sat 8.30am–4.30pm, Sun 8.30am–12.30pm; free), Moorish in origin but later rebuilt by the Knights Templar. It now does rather odd duty as a cemetery for the neighbouring church, but you can climb up to the battlements for distant views to the coast. The castle is a steep fifteen-minute walk up from town. Back down in the centre, it's worth having a look around the covered market, before making your way to the **Museu Municipal**, facing the municipal gardens off Avenida Álvares Pereira (Tues–Fri 10am–noon & 2–5pm, Sat & Sun 2–5pm; free).

Housed in one of Salazar's more notorious prisons, one of the spartan cells has been preserved while two others have been converted into a "typical country bedroom" and "a rich bourgeois bedroom".

Miróbriga

The archeological section in Santiago's museum should whet your appetite for a visit to the **Ruinas Romanas de Miróbriga** (Tues–Sat 9am–12.30pm & 2–5.30pm, Sun 9am–noon & 2–5.30pm; €2). It's a short drive from town or around half an hour's walk – follow the Lisbon road, Rua de Lisboa (N120), as far as the windmill on the hill, turn sharp right at the signpost and keep on down the country lane for another ten minutes. The site, which lies isolated amid arcadian green hills, was first inhabited during the Iron Age, but the Roman city here dates from the first century AD. For 200 years Miróbriga thrived on trade, a planned town set around its forum and temple, with recreational zones and residential areas – a "new town" of its era. By the fourth century AD it was in decline, and was then lost to history until the sixteenth century, and only first excavated in the nineteenth century.

The ruins are extensive, scattered over the gullies and hills below the small interpretation centre. At the highest point a **Temple of Jupiter** has been partly reconstructed, overlooking the forum with a row of shops built into its supporting wall. A house below here retains some second-century **wall paintings**, protected by a wooden hut. A paved street descends to a huge **bath complex** whose underground central heating system is still intact, while alongside sits a beautifully preserved Roman **bridge** from the first century AD.

Practicalities

The **bus station** is in the square just above the market, and there are regular services from Lisbon, as well as south to Porto Covo and Vila Nova de Milfontes. There's also a regular summer (May–Sept) service west to the lagoon beach at Lagoa de Santo André, the nearest sands to town, though this becomes less reliable out of season. The **turismo**, 100m from the station, in the side of the market building, (Mon–Fri 9am–7pm, Sat 9am–1pm & 2–6pm; ☎269 826 696), hands out a useful town map.

There really is no need for **accommodation**, though the *Pousada da Quinta da Ortiga* (☎269 822 871, Ⓦwww.pousadas.pt; breakfast included; ❻), 1km out of town on the Lisbon road, attracts some – set on a typical Alentejan rural estate, with a pool and a decent restaurant. If you were stuck in town, the best budget choice is *Residencial Gabriel*, Rua Professor Egas Moniz 24 (☎269 822 245, Ⓕ69 826 102; breakfast included; ❸), on the main road through Santiago. There are simple **restaurants** between the bus station and market where you can get an inexpensive meal, though if you're heading out to Miróbriga you might as well combine seeing the ruins with lunch at the moderately priced *Restaurante Refúgio do Mirante* (☎269 826 622; closed Sun & Dec), opposite the entrance to the site. It excels for fish – *massa do peixe*, a soupy dish of minted maccaroni and mixed poached fish is recommended.

The Alentejo coast

The long **Alentejo coast** stretches for over 150km, from Setúbal bay to the western Algarve. For the most part it's undeveloped, as its beaches can seem pretty wild – whipped by the Atlantic winds, many are strictly local in character, often only reached on minor roads or tracks. The northern section has really only one realistic target, the lagoon beach of **Lagoa de Santo André**, northwest of Santiago do Cacém. South of the lagoon, the industrial town of **Sines** dominates the coast for some distance around, its oil refinery, towers and pipelines adding more than just an unattractive smell to the air – the sea in the vicinity is polluted as well. The centre of Sines is actually better than you'd imagine, but there's no reason to visit – not even on the trail of Vasco da Gama, who was born here but left no trace. Buses instead run directly from Lisbon and Santiago do Cacém to **Porto Côvo**, the first place on the coast you could call a resort, with its low cliffs backed by a rash of villas.

It's further south that things really improve, particularly at **Vila Nova de Milfontes**, the main – and by far the nicest – Alentejan resort. **Almograve** and **Zambujeira do Mar**, further south, are both much less developed seaside villages with stupendous beaches, while **Odemira** – about 15km from the coast – is the only inland stop worth making. Zambujeira is the southernmost Alentejo beach, and an attractive road twists its way into the hills of the Algarve from the river crossing at Odeceixe. For the most dramatic approach, however, take the road from Odemira through the Serra de Monchique, descending to the Algarve coast at Portimão.

All the resorts are accessible by local **buses** from Santiago do Cacém or Odemira, but you can also simply head straight for them from Lisbon on the daily express routes – in which case it's wise to buy your ticket in advance. From Vila Nova de Milfontes and Zambujeira do Mar there's a daily express bus service on to the Algarve (to Sagres, Lagos or Portimão).

Lagoa de Santo André

Fifteen kilometres northwest of Santiago do Cacém a beautiful sand beach separates the **Lagoa de Santo André** from the sea. The wide lagoon itself, only a couple of metres deep, is backed by an extensive *reserva natural* of pinewoods and reeds, and development is consequently limited, at least adjacent to the lagoon and beach. There's a beach café and a couple of restaurants at the road's end, while beyond is the sand – miles and miles of it. The sea is very enticing with high waves and good surf, but be warned: the undertow can be fierce and people drown here every year.

In summer, up to five **buses** a day run out here from Santiago do Cacém (30min), stopping right at the road's end. You can stay, but there's only one **hotel**, the apartment-style *Al Tarik* (☎269 708 600, ⓦwww.hoteltarik.com; ❹, Oct–May ❸), and a large, well-equipped **campsite**, the *Parque do Campismo* (☎269 708 550), both found on the road in, but set well back from the beach on the northern side of the lagoon, where some development has been allowed. Otherwise, it's the kind of place Portuguese families come to rent villas and apartments – you may find "quartos" advertised – but as there's no real village centre, it's not the greatest overnight stop.

Porto Côvo

The coast south of Sines is undeniably pretty, with a minor road hugging the coves and high dunes as far as **PORTO CÔVO**, a former fishing village now entirely surrounded by modern holiday villas. However, the centre – just a few cobbled, whitewashed streets around a restored square – remains highly attractive, while boats still bob around in the minuscule deep cove harbour, almost Cornish in aspect. It's busy in summer, but at night it's still a recognizably old-fashioned village, the predominant sound the whistle of the Atlantic breeze and the crashing of the waves. Clifftop paths run north and south of town providing access to the coves and beaches. **Praia do Somouqueira** just to the north is named after the extraordinary rock formations and is popular at low tide when temporary new beaches are created.

The pedestrianized Rua da Vasco da Gama runs from the cliffs above the sea up to the main Largo Marquês de Pombal. There's an ATM along here, as well as most of the village's dozen cafés and restaurants, plus various shops selling beach gear, souvenirs, Peruvian jewellery and newspapers. **Buses** connect Porto Côvo with Santiago do Cacém, Vila Nova de Milfontes, Almograve and Zambujeira. There's a **turismo** (Mon–Sat 9am–noon & 1–5pm; may close in winter; ℡269 959 124, Ⓦwww.freguesiadeportocovo.com) at the car park above the square, next to the small daily **market** (mornings only).

The turismo has a list of local **accommodation**, but it's just a matter of strolling the few central streets and checking out the options. You'll see "quartos" and "apartamentos" signs all over town, and more posted in the turismo windows. Prices given below are for July and August – you'll get much better deals everywhere out of season. For simple whitewashed rooms with tile floors and private bathrooms, *Quartos Abelha*, Rua Vasco da Gama 44 (℡934 755 293; no credit cards; ❷), can be recommended – *Pensão Zé Inácio*, next door (℡269 959 136; ❹), is smarter but overpriced. A cheaper, more old-fashioned place is *Pensão Boa Esperança*, Rua Conde Bandeira (℡269 905 109; no credit cards; ❷), two blocks west, which offers no-frills accommodation with shared bathrooms. A block over from the *Boa Esperança*, basic **apartments** are available at *Apartamentos Rosa*, Rua da Farmacía 6 (℡269 905 125; no credit cards; ❷), and over the road at *Apartamentos Campos*, Rua da Farmacía 11 (℡269 905 144; no credit cards; ❷), though you may have to get the turismo to call as there's often no one at the actual addresses. There's a bit more comfort all round at *Aparthotel Porto Côvo*, Rua Vitalina da Silva (℡269 959 140, Ⓦwww.hotelportocovo.com; ❹), a litte way inland, above the turismo – the air-conditioned studios and one-bed apartments come with kitchen and the use of a pool. There's also a good year-round **campsite**, *Parque de Campismo* (℡269 905 136), on the Vila Nova road out of town.

Restaurants, on the whole, are aimed at well-to-do Portuguese holidaymakers. The two in the square, and others, specialize in seafood and are not a cheap night out. However, they are good, particularly the *Marquês* (℡269 905 036; open for drinks until 1am), which is more like a classy Lisbon *cervejaraia* than a local restaurant, with stand-at-the-bar beers, oysters, fresh-from-the-tank lobsters and other delights. They also have a good cakes-and-ice cream **café** across the square.

Ilha do Pessegueiro

The next beach south of Port Covo is at **Ilha do Pessegueiro** (Peach Tree Island), reached by car off the Porto Côvo–Vila Nova de Milfontes road. However, it's much nicer to walk, following the coastal path south from Porto Côvo. It's only a couple of kilometres and en route you'll pass the remains of a Bronze Age burial site.

The name actually applies to the mainland beach, another typically duned stretch of sand sitting below a small sixteenth-century fort. The island itself – with the matching ruins of another fort – is a few hundred metres offshore, clearly visible from Porto Covo and reachable from there on local fishing boats (ask at the turismo).

At the dusty car park by the beach there's the *Restaurante A Ilha* (☎269 905 113), while the **campsite** (☎269 905 178) is a fair way inland, back up the road to Vila Nova de Milfontes.

Vila Nova de Milfontes

VILA NOVA DE MILFONTES – 20km south of Porto Côvo – lies on the estuary of the Rio Mira, whose wide sandy banks gradually merge into the coastline. It is an advantageous spot for sailors (the port is reputed to have harboured Hannibal and his Carthaginians during a storm) and, while the resort is not exactly undiscovered, it remains an attractive place – at least it does below

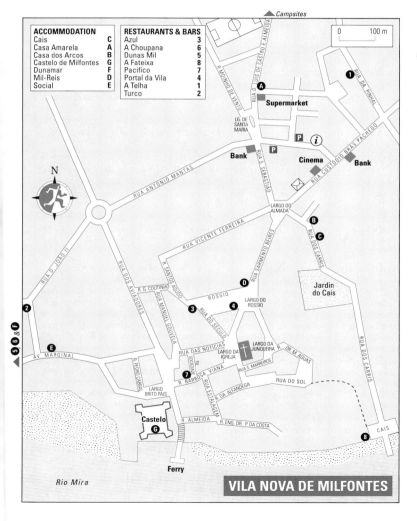

ACCOMMODATION		RESTAURANTS & BARS	
Cais	C	Azul	3
Casa Amarela	A	A Choupana	6
Casa dos Arcos	B	Dunas Mil	5
Castelo de Milfontes	G	A Fateixa	8
Dunamar	F	Pacifico	7
Mil-Reis	D	Portal da Vila	4
Social	E	A Telha	1
		Turco	2

VILA NOVA DE MILFONTES

the sprawl of the new town that has developed since the 1980s. Portuguese families on holiday from the big cities of the north give it a homely atmosphere quite distinct from that of the cosmopolitan Algarve. The few whitewashed streets of the old town huddle around a striking, ivy-wreathed castle, with the long river beach just a few minutes' walk to the west. The beach road, Avenida Marginal, ends at a lighthouse, fifteen minutes from the centre, from where you can see the full force of the Atlantic crashing waves down onto the rocks below. Even though the beach is spacious, it gets busy in July and August, when you might want to take the **ferry** (every 30min, daily 10am–7pm; €2 return) instead from the town jetty at the foot of the castle. This runs to the far side of the estuary, to another long duned swathe of river beach. Swimmers in the river need to be aware of the strong currents – the town beach has a roped-off swimming area that you should heed.

Practicalities

Buses come in down the main Rua Custódio Brás Pachego in the newer, upper part of town, and drop you off in a small lot near the **turismo** on Rua António Mantas (July & Aug daily 10am–7pm; Sept–June 10am–1pm & 2–6pm; ☎283 996 599). There's a daily morning service to the Algarve, several express services to Lisbon, and local connections to Odemira, Porto Côvo and Zambujeira do Mar, with times posted on the ticket office door. Apart from providing a range of useful lists and brochures, the turismo is the place to find out about local **activities and tours**, from river trips and kayak rental to scuba-diving and horse-riding.

Accommodation is spread all over town, with a few traditional *pensões* in the centre and lots of apartments along the beach road and in the surroundings. Prices peak in August, but are far more reasonable in low season (Sept–June), when you should be able to do better than the rates indicated below. There are two **campsites** just north of town, both also with bungalows for rent as well as tent space: the *Parque Campismo de Milfontes* (☎ & ☎283 996 104) has excellent facilities, while the nearby *Parque Campismo Campiférias* (☎283 996 409; closed Dec) is more modest.

Hotels and pensions

Casa Amarela Rua D. Luís de Castro e Almeida ☎283 996 632 or 934 204 610, ✉casa_ama @hotmail.com. The "yellow house" is the highly personal project of a gregarious backpacking owner, who has decorated seven stylish en-suite rooms (some with terrace) with art from his trips. Some rooms sleep up to four, and there's a kitchen and lounge, with free internet access for guests. A separate mews-style block a couple of minutes' away has eight more en-suite rooms (one of them a dorm; €10–15 a bed, depending on season) arranged around a large terraced area and kitchen. Laundry facilities available. No credit cards. ❸

Pensão Casa dos Arcos Rua dos Carris ☎283 996 264, ☎283 997 156. A very pleasant small hotel with crisp tiled bathrooms and stand-up balconies in most of the modern-looking rooms – however, the views are only partial. Breakfast included. No credit cards. ❹

Pensão do Cais Rua dos Carris 9 ☎283 996 268.

This is the first choice in town for *pensão* rooms, primarily because of the estuary views – even if your room (fairly spacious with traditional furniture and modern bathrooms) doesn't have the best aspect, there's always the lovely vine-covered patio or first-floor terrace. Breakfast included. No credit cards. ❹

Castelo de Milfontes Largo do Brito Pais ☎283 998 231, ☎283 997 122. Vila Nova's finest lodgings, inside the fortress – cross the drawbridge to enter. The seven rooms have terrific views, while surroundings are baronial to say the least. Dinner is available. Breakfast included. ❽

Apartamentos Dunamar Rua dos Médos 2, off Av. Marginal ☎283 998 208, ☎283 998 508. In a prime location, high above the estuary, these smart air-conditioned studio and one-bedroom apartments (with balconies and kitchenette) have great views and are just a few minutes' walk from the beach and town, with the *Dunas Mil* restaurant on your doorstep. Parking available. ❺

Residencial Mil-Réis Largo do Rossio 2 ☎283

998 233, ⓕ283 998 328. Smart, clean, central rooms with TV, looked after by kindly owners. Breakfast inlcuded. No credit cards. ❸

Hotel Social Av. Marginal ☎283 996 517, ⓕ283 996 324. A bit plain and institutional, but from inside the rooms all you see is the views – though there's a premium for sea-view rooms with a balcony (the cheaper rooms face the pool). High-season prices are steep – it's a much better deal once the summer crowds have left. There's parking outside. Breakfast included. ❹

Restaurants

Restaurante A Choupana Av. Marginal ☎283 996 643. Beachcomber-style bar and restaurant, down the cliff steps at the far (lighthouse) end of the beach road. An outdoor barbecue dishes up fish and meat grills, but while the food's fine it's not really the main event – the views and the sunsets are the thing. Moderate.

Restaurante-Marisqueira O Dunas Mil Av. Marginal ☎283 997 104. The best fish restaurant in town, five minutes' along the coast road and high up on the right. There's a big outdoor terrace, and they specialize in *arroz* dishes, *açordas* and *cataplanas*, as well as excellent shellfish, but none of this comes cheap. Grilled fish and meat are more reasonably priced. Expensive.

Restaurante A Fateixa Rua dos Carris ☎283 996 415. A superb location on the riverbank below town, and a shady terrace, makes this a good bet for lunch. It's pretty fair value too – platters of squid, sardines, mackerel, swordfish and tuna, all cost around €8. Closed Wed. Moderate.

Churrasqueira A Telha Rua da Pinhal 3 ☎283 996 138. Simple grillhouse menu at reasonable prices, especially the charcoal-grilled chicken. Inexpensive.

Portal da Vila Largo do Rossio ☎283 996 823. With every internal inch covered in tiles, and the ceiling dripping in greenery, it doesn't look much like a local restaurant – and you're unlikely to find many Portuguese in here. But the kebabs suspended on hangers and the sizzling hot-stone dishes (*da pedra*) of pork and veal are different enough to attract a tourist crowd for an enjoyable night out. Around €25 a head for a full meal and drinks. Closed Mon. Expensive.

Bars

Café Azul Rossio 20. Relaxed bar playing a mix of jazz, rock and blues, washed down with frozen tequila margaritas. Busy Fri and Sat and open from 9pm till 4am.

Bar Pacífico Rua Barbosa Viana. Dance-bar playing a mixture of chart, techno and reggae music. Open 10pm–6am (closed Oct & Nov).

Café Turco Rua Dom João II. Mock-Moorish café-bar, a favourite with Lisboans, featuring live music at the weekend. Open 10pm–4am, though weekends only in winter.

Almograve

The coast south of Vila Nova de Milfontes becomes ever more rugged and spectacular. At the tiny resort of **ALMOGRAVE**, 10km south of Vila Nova (west of the Odemira–Vila Nova de Milfontes road), huge waves come crashing down on the rocks and for most of the day swimming is impossible. It can get very crowded at high tide, too, when the beaches are reduced to thin strips with occasional waves drenching everybody's belongings; but, for all that, it's an exhilarating place. There are miles of high dunes to north and south, riddled with tracks, where – according to the local tourist brochure – "flora and fauna meet in perfect harmony".

Buses stop in the modern village, basically just a block of houses and villas which sits back from the beach – a road and boardwalk runs over the dunes to a huge car park above the sands. There are several bars and restaurants by the roundabout in the village, while the beach road passes the *Residencial Duna Praia* (☎283 647 115, ⓕ283 647 112; ❹), which has a terrace and grill.

South of Almograve, drivers can make for the promontory of **Cabo Sardão**, a dead-end road that culminates in a cliff-top lighthouse, from near where there are magnificent panoramas of the rocky coastline.

Zambujeira do Mar

The southernmost Alentejan resort is the small village of **ZAMBUJEIRA DO MAR**, which is 29km south of Vila Nova de Milfontes and slightly less

CHAPTER 9

Highlights

* **Ilha de Tavira** Sandspit island with an enormous stretch of dune-backed beach – the best in the eastern Algarve. See p.565

* **Rio Guadiana** The river marking the border with Spain offers some of the region's least spoilt scenery. See p.569

* **Albufeira** Simply the most enjoyable all-round resort on the Algarve. See p.574

* **Silves** The historic Moorish capital of the Algarve is overlooked by the grandest of castles. See p.588

* **Serra de Monchique** The woods around Monchique's mountains offer superb walking terrain. See p.590

* **Boat trip, Lagos** Explore the extraordinary rock formations and grottoes on a boat trip from Lagos. See p.596

* **Sagres** Iberia's most south-westerly point, complete with fortress, lighthouse and great surfing beaches. See p.601

* **West coast beaches** A stunning variety of wave-battered sandy swathes between Sagres and Odeceixe. See p.605

△ Tavira

9

The Algarve

With its spectacular sandy beaches and picturesque rocky coves, it is not surprising that the **Algarve** is Portugal's most popular region for holidaymakers. This has inevitably led to some heavy development. Large segments of the coast from Faro west to Albufeira have suffered most, with endless villa complexes creating a rather depressing Mediterranean-style suburbia. But at least the facilities are first rate, as are the beaches. Elsewhere in the Algarve, especially around Sagres and Tavira, the surroundings are far more attractive, with relaxed, small-scale resorts located near superb beaches or island sandbanks.

The coastline in fact has two quite distinct characters. To the west of Faro you'll find the classic postcard images – namely a series of tiny bays and coves, broken up by weird rocky outcrops and fantastic grottoes. They're at their most exotic around the major resort towns of **Lagos** and **Albufeira**, while smaller resorts include the former fishing villages of **Salema** or **Burgau**, or the historic cape of **Sagres** – site of Henry the Navigator's naval school. The string of villages along the rougher west (Atlantic) coast, as far as **Odeceixe**, are quieter still, with limited facilities but fantastic wild beaches.

East of Faro, there's a complete change as you encounter the first of a series of sandy offshore islets, the **ilhas**, which front the coastline virtually all the way to the Spanish border. The resorts here have a more Portuguese feel than those in the central stretch, and first-choice bases here would be **Faro** itself – capital of the entire region – **Olhão, Fuzeta** or **Tavira**, all of which offer access to the sandbank islands.

Inland Algarve is still relatively undeveloped, especially around **Alcoutim** on the Spanish border, and there are other scattered attractions in the Roman ruins of **Estói** and the market town of **Loulé**, both north of Faro, and the old Moorish town of **Silves**, easily reached from Portimão. The outstanding area, however, is the **Serra de Monchique**, the highest mountain range in the south, with cork and chestnut woods, remote little villages and a beautiful old spa in **Caldas de Monchique**.

The Algarve is a year-round destination, and in many respects the region is at its best in **spring** or **winter**, when the sunshine is still warm and there are far fewer visitors. Indeed, off-season travel in the Algarve will get you some of the best deals in the country, with luxury hotels offering all-in packages at discounts of up to seventy percent; check out the latest deals at the local tourist offices. But if you come in high **summer** without an advance booking, finding accommodation can be a real struggle, though you'll usually find something. It's essential to reserve in advance if you want to stay at a particular

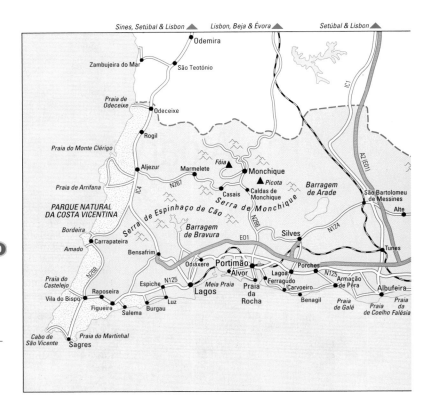

establishment, and you should also be prepared for very high summer prices relative to the rest of the country – pensions and hotels can cost up to twenty percent more on the Algarve.

Getting around by public transport is easier here than anywhere else in Portugal and, since the coastline is only 240km long from east to west, you can see an awful lot in just a few days. The **Algarve rail line** runs from Lagos in the west to Vila Real de Santo António on the Spanish border, calling at most major towns en route (you may have to change at Tunes, Faro or Tavira, depending on your destination); while **buses** link all the resorts and main inland villages. With a car, you'll be able to reach the more out-of-the-way inland villages and inaccessible cove beaches. The main east–west E01 highway from Lagos to the Spanish border offers fast and easy access to the region, linking with the A2/E01 motorway to Lisbon just north of Albufeira.

Finally, a comprehensive calendar of **cultural events** can be found in *Agenda*, available free from tourist offices, cultural centres and larger hotels – perhaps the biggest affair is the Algarve International Music Festival (early summer), hosting major artists.

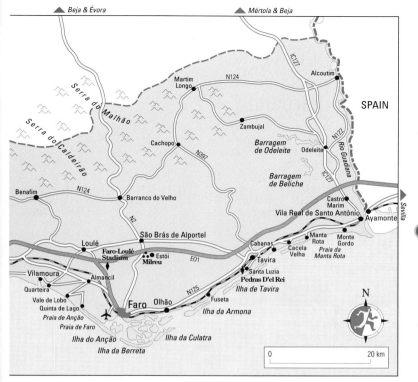

The eastern Algarve

All flights to the Algarve land at **Faro**, the administrative capital of the region since 1776 and by far the largest town along the coast. Although no great holiday destination in itself, the centre of town is considerably more attractive than the concrete suburbs might suggest, and there are some fine beaches within easy reach, as well as possible day-trips inland to the Roman remains at **Estói** and the small country town of **São Brás de Alportel**. Faro is also a useful transport hub, connected to Lisbon by fast express coaches and to most Algarve towns by bus or – a little slower – on the Algarve rail line.

The coastline east of Faro as far as **Manta Rota**, en route to the Spanish border, is protected by thin stretches of mud flats, fringed in turn by a chain of magnificent long sandbanks, or *ilhas*, the shores thick with wading birds in winter and spring. The sandbank beaches are usually far less crowded than the small rocky resorts of the western Algarve and visitors have the option of basing themselves at enjoyable little towns like **Olhão**, **Fuzeta** and, above all, **Tavira**. Most of the other resorts on this stretch – with the exception of **Monte Gordo** – are fairly small-scale, while the Portuguese coast peters out at **Vila Real de Santo António**, a historic small town that preserves a fair bit of character. Vila Real lies near the mouth of the **Rio Guadiana**, which forms the Spanish border, and from here there's a fine route to be followed upstream to the small fortified river towns of **Castro Marim** and **Alcoutim**.

Faro and around

With its international airport, impressive shopping centre and ring of high-rise apartments, **FARO** boasts something of a big city feel. However, the central area is a manageable size, boasting attractive mosaic-paved pedestrianized streets and harbourside gardens, while its university contributes to a lively nightlife, during termtime at least. In summer, boats and buses run out to some excellent local beaches. Originally a Roman settlement, the city was named by the Moors, under whom it was a thriving commercial port, supplying the regional capital at Silves. Following its conquest by the Christians, under Afonso III in 1249, the city later experienced a series of conquests and disasters. Sacked and burned by the Earl of Essex in 1596, and devastated by the Great Earthquake of 1755, it is no surprise that modern Faro has so few historic buildings. What interest it does retain is contained within the pretty **Cidade Velha** (Old Town), which lies behind a series of defensive walls, across the harbour from the main part of town.

Arrival, information and transport

Flights land at Faro's international **airport** (flight information ☎289 800 800), 6km west of town, where there's a bank, ATMs, post office and tourist office (daily 8am–11.30pm; ☎289 818 582), as well as shops and restaurants. A number of car rental companies also have offices at the airport. There are no direct public transport services to other resorts from the airport, which means heading first into central Faro.

A **taxi** into the centre of town (15min) should cost about €8, plus €1.50 for any luggage that goes in the boot; there's also a twenty-percent surcharge between 10pm and 6am, and at weekends. Local **buses** #14 and #16 also run from the airport to the centre (25min), costing €1.20 (departures roughly every 45min, 7.10am–9pm, 8pm at weekends; buy tickets on board). Both stop outside the bus terminal in town (see below) and, further on, at the Jardim Manuel Bivar ("Jardim" on the timetables) by the harbour.

Faro's **bus terminal** is on Avenida da República, behind and beneath the *Hotel Eva*, just back from the harbour. There's an English-speaking information office inside, though it is not always staffed. The **train station** is a few minutes' walk further north up the avenue, facing Largo da Estação. The compact town is simple to negotiate on foot, and all the *pensões*, hotels, restaurants and bars are extremely central. There is a **town bus service**, but you'll only need it to get to the beach (for which, see below) and back to the airport.

Faro's **turismo** is at the end of the town gardens at Rua da Misericórdia 8 (May–Sept daily 9.30am–7pm; Oct–April Tues–Thurs 9.30am–5.30pm, Fri–Mon 9.30am–12.30pm & 2–5.30pm; ☎289 803 604, ⓦwww.cm-faro.pt), and provides town maps and posts local and long-distance bus, boat and train timetables. The regional tourist office – **Região de Turismo do Algarve** – east of the old town at Avenida 5 Outubro (Mon–Fri 9.30am–12.30pm & 2–5.30pm ☎289 800 400, ⓦwww.rtalgarve.pt) is a source of information on the area as a whole.

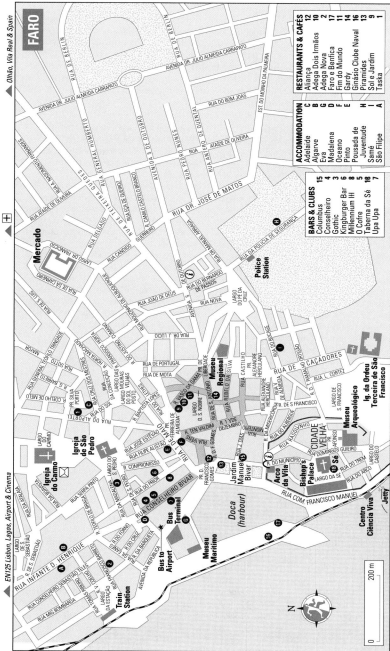

FARO

◀ Olhão, Vila Real & Spain

◀ EN125 Lisbon, Lagos, Airport & Cinema

Ferries to Farol & Ilha Deserta ▶

RESTAURANTS & CAFÉS

Aliança	12
Adega Dois Irmãos	10
Adega Nova	2
Faro e Benfica	17
Fim do Mundo	11
Gardy	14
Ginásio Clube Naval	16
Piramides	13
Sol e Jardim	9
Taska	1

ACCOMMODATION

Adelaide	C
Algarve	G
Eva	B
Madalena	D
Oceano	F
Pinto	E
Pousada de Juventude	H
Samé	I
São Filipe	A

BARS & CLUBS

Columbus	15
Conselheiro	4
Gothic	3
Kingburger Bar	6
Millennium III	8
O Cofre	5
Taberna da Sé	18
Upa Upa	7

9

THE ALGARVE | Faro and around

551

Accommodation

If you arrive without a room reservation, it's worth asking the airport tourist office to try and help you book you a place, though it's not officially part of their job and you'll have to pay for any calls they make on your behalf. Most of the city's *pensões* and hotels – the best of which are picked out below – are concentrated in the area just north of the harbour. Faro's basic **campsite** at Praia de Faro was closed at the time of writing – call for the latest details (T289 817 876) or check with the turismo.

Hotels and pensions

Residencial Adelaide Rua Cruz das Mestras 7–9 T289 802 383, F289 826 870. The friendly owner offers the best-value rooms in town, with attached bathrooms and cable TV, and there's an airy breakfast room. Some rooms sleep three or four, and in summer the roof is opened for dorm beds at €10 per person. Breakfast included. ❸

Residencial Algarve Rua Infante Dom Henrique 52 T289 895 700, W www.residencialalgarve .com. Very popular *residencial*, with bright if sparsely furnished rooms on several floors (there's a lift). Bathrooms are spotless, the rooms have air-con and cable TV, while breakfast (included) is served in the downstairs dining room or on the tiled internal patio. Parking on nearby streets is usually easy. ❺

Hotel Eva Av. da República 1 T289 001 000, e❊va@tdhotels.pt. The town's top hotel offering slightly fusty rooms with balconies looking across to the old town or the marina. There's a rooftop pool and restaurant, and a courtesy bus to the local beach. Parking. Breakfast included. ❼

Pensão Madalena Rua Conselheiro Bivar 109 T289 805 806, F289 805 807. A mixed bag of rather characterless en-suite rooms with phones and TVs, but it's very central. ❸

Pensão-Residencial Oceano Trav. Ivens 21-1° T289 823 349, %289 805 590. A promising *azulejo*-lined stairway leads to clean – if fairly bland – rooms with bathrooms and TVs. ❸

Residencial Pinto Rua 1 de Maio 27 T and F289 807 417. Welcoming *residencial* with spartan but characterful rooms, with shiny wooden floors and old-fashioned doors. Bathrooms are shared. ❷

Residencial Samé Rua do Bocage 66 T289 824 375, F289 804 166. Small rooms in a neat, modern hotel just outside the old town. Some have balconies and all come with bathrooms and TV. There's an appealing lounge downstairs. Breakfast included. ❺

Pensão São Filipe Rua Infante Dom Henrique 55-1° T & F289 824 182. Run by the same owners as the *Residencial Algarve*, with similarly smart rooms, each with cable TV and en-suite facilities. Rooms are small but have high ceilings with spinning fans, though the front ones contend with the traffic of a busy through road. Breakfast included. ❹

Youth hostel

Pousada de Juventude Rua da Policia de Segurança Pública T289 826 521, W www.pousadasjuventude.pt. A quiet place next to the gardens, on the left past the police station. Book well in advance as it's often filled with groups. Dorms sleep four or six people, and twin rooms, with and without bath, also available. Dorm beds €10, rooms ❷

The Town

The only part of town to have survived the various violent historic upheavals is the **Cidade Velha**, facing the harbour, an oval of cobbled streets and brightly painted buildings set within a run of sturdy walls. The houses are fronted by decorative balconies and tiling, with the odd one serving as an antique shop, café or art gallery. You enter through the eighteenth-century town gate, the **Arco da Vila**, next to the turismo. From here, Rua do Município leads up to the majestic Largo da Sé, flanked by the cathedral and a group of palaces – including the former bishop's palace – and lined with orange trees. The **Sé** itself (Mon–Sat 9am–12.30pm & 1.30pm–5pm, Sun open for Mass at 10am & noon; €1.50) is a squat, white mismatch of Gothic, Renaissance and Baroque styles, all heavily remodelled after the 1755 earthquake. However, there's fine eighteenth-century *azulejo* tiling inside, while you can climb the bell tower for views over the old town and the mud flats beyond.

More impressive is the **Museu Arqueológico** (May–Sept Tues–Fri 9.30am –5.30pm, Sat & Sun 11.30am–5.30pm; Oct–April Tues–Fri 10am–6pm, Sat & Sun 2–6pm; €2) in nearby Praça Afonso III, installed in a sixteenth-century convent with a beautiful cloister – one of the oldest in Portugal. In front of the building stands a forthright, crucifix-carrying statue of the conqueror Afonso himself, king between 1249 and 1279. The most striking of the museum's exhibits is a superb third-century AD Roman mosaic of Neptune surrounded by the four winds, unearthed near the train station. Other items include a collection of Roman statues from the excavations at Estói (see p.556), exquisite Moorish lamps, vases and bowls, and a variety of Baroque and Renaissance paintings. There are also Futurist works by Carlos Porfírio, one of the country's leading twentieth-century artists.

South of the Cidade Velha and marked by an impressive fountain, **Largo de São Francisco** serves as a giant car park for most of the year, but is cleared in late October for the Feira de Santa Iria, an enormous market-cum-fairground with live entertainment over the best part of a week. The square is overlooked by the **Igreja da Ordeu Terceira de São Francisco**, rebuilt in the eighteenth century on the site of an earlier church. It's plain on the outside, but the interior contains Baroque tiles and some beautiful Rococo woodwork.

At the **harbour**, the town gardens and a cluster of outdoor cafés overlook the rows of sleek yachts and at the end of the day much of Faro gathers to promenade here. Continuing around the harbour to the west you'll pass the small **Museu Marítimo** (Mon–Fri 2.30–4.30pm; free), a modest maritime museum with displays of model boats and local fishing techniques. Heading southwards on Rua Comandante Francisco Manuel, you can follow the railway line for an attractive walk along the seafront, with the town walls on one side and the mud flats on the other. A small arch through the old town walls offers another approach to the Cidade Velha, while from the jetty opposite here, ferries depart to the local sandspit beaches (see below). Just before the jetty, the **Centro Ciência Viva** (July to mid-Sept Tues–Sun 4–11pm; mid-Sept to June Tues–Fri 10am–5pm, Sat & Sun 3–7pm; €2.50), housed in Faro's former electricity station, is a good wet-weather attraction. There are several low-tech interactive exhibits that explain various scientific principles, while the permanent displays include a rock pool and a flight simulator.

Most of the town centre is devoted to shops, bars and restaurants, though there are a couple of other sights. At the end of Rua de Santo António, on Praça de Liberdade, the **Museu Regional** (Mon–Fri 9am–12.30pm & 2–5.30pm; €1.50) has a display of local crafts and industries, including reconstructions of typical cottage interiors, and models of the net systems still used for tuna fishing. By far the most curious attraction in town, however, is the twin-towered, Baroque **Igreja do Carmo** (Mon–Fri 10am–1pm & 3–6pm, Oct–April until 5pm, Sat 10am–1pm, Sun only for Mass at 9am; free), near the central post office on Largo do Carmo. A door to the right of its altar leads to the sacristy where you buy a ticket (€1) to view the macabre **Capela dos Ossos** (Chapel of Bones), set in an overgrown garden at the rear, its walls decorated with human bones disinterred from the adjacent monks' cemetery. Nearby, in Largo de São Pedro, the sixteenth-century **Igreja de São Pedro** is infinitely more attractive as a church, its finest decorative work an altar (to the left of the main altar) whose central image is a gilded, wooden *Last Supper* in relief.

The beaches

Faro's "town beach" – **Praia de Faro** – is typical of the sandspit *ilha* beaches of the eastern Algarve; a long sweep of beautiful sand with both a sea-facing and a more sheltered lagoon-facing side. However, as it's so close to both airport and Faro, it is rather overdeveloped, with bars, restaurants and villas jammed onto a sandy island almost too narrow to cope – though out of season you'll probably have the sands to yourself. The beach is situated on the Ilha de Faro, southwest of town; buses #14 and #16 run from the harbour gardens, or the stop opposite the bus station, calling at the airport en route (every 45 min, 7.10am–9pm, until 8pm at weekends), stopping just before the narrow bridge to the beach itself.

Alternatively, in summer, **ferries** shuttle through narrow marshy channels to a couple of other local sandbar beaches, between Faro and Olhão. They depart from the jetty below the old town, either to **Farol** (described on p.560) on the Ilha da Culatra (June to mid-Sept 4 daily, first boat 9.30am, last return 7pm; €4 return; ☎917 634 813), or to the so-called **Ilha Deserta** (June to mid-Sept 4 daily; €12 return; ☎917 811 856, ⓦ www.ilha-deserta.com), part of the Parque Natural da Ria Formosa. The island's official name is Ilha da Barreta, the most southerly point of mainland Portugal. Once there, you'll find one pricey café and a great beach.

Eating, drinking and nightlife

The heart of the town is an attractive pedestrianized shopping area on either side of Rua de Santo António, where you can find innumerable **restaurants**, **cafés** and **bakeries** – the latter stocked with almond delicacies, the regional speciality. Most of the pavement restaurants have similar menus and similar prices; if you're prepared to scout around the back streets, you can often find cheaper, better food, though without the accompanying streetlife that makes central Faro so attractive. As you'd expect, the cuisine is predominantly sea-food-based, the highlight the ubiquitous *arroz de mariscos* (a stew of shellfish and rice).

The best of Faro's nightlife is concentrated along two or three central pedestrianized streets – in particular Rua Conselheiro Bivar, with its café-bars with outdoor seating, and the parallel Rua do Prior, where many of the **bars and clubs** feature DJs, live bands and video screens; there are rarely cover charges. Few places open much before 11pm and things get going around midnight; soon afterwards, as the bars fill up, drinkers spill out onto the cobbled alleys to party. Faro also occasionally hosts big-name rock and pop **gigs** at the football stadium – check posters around town, or ask at the turismo.

Cafés

Café Aliança Rua Dr. F. Gomes 6–11 ☎282 458 860. Once the favoured haunt of the literary set – including Simone de Beauvoir – this faded coffee house is said to be one of the oldest cafés in Portugal, dating from 1908. It has seats outside, and a full menu of breakfasts, burgers, salads, omelettes, pastries and ice cream.

Gardy Rua de Santo António 16 ☎289 824 062. Popular local *pastelaria* whose seats are always at a premium – excellent cakes, pastries and coffee.

Café Piramides Jardim Manuel Bivar ☎289 822 964. Set in a glass pavilion with a pyramid-shaped roof, this all-purpose café has tables in the attractive gardens facing the harbour. You can enjoy anything from breakfast and coffee to inexpensive pizzas, or ice cream and beer.

Restaurants

Adega Dois Irmãos Largo Terreiro do Bispo 13–15 ☎289 823 337. Opened in 1925 by two brothers (*dois irmãos*) in a former welder's shop, this attractive tiled place is one of the oldest of the city's fish restaurants. The day's catch can be expensive (around €15), though the *pratos do dia* are usually better value. Despite the number of tourists passing through, service remains courteous and efficient. Expensive.

Marisqueira Faro e Benfica Doca de Faro ☎289 821 422. One of the town's best spots for a splurge on fish and seafood, with tables facing across the harbour. The pricey specialities include *cataplana, feijoada* and various rice dishes. Closed Tues & all Nov. Expensive.

Fim do Mundo Rua Vasco da Gama 53 ☎289 826 299. A bustling place mostly filled with locals enjoying good-value grilled fish and meat dishes – *frango piri-piri* is the house speciality. Closed all day Mon & Tues lunch. Inexpensive.

Restaurante Ginásio Clube Naval Doca de Faro ☎289 823 869. Set on a raised terrace right on the harbour, this is one of the few restaurants in town where you can dine with a sunset view over the tidal mud flats. There are well-priced fish dishes and grilled meats. Closed Mon. Moderate.

Adega Nova Rua Francisco Barreto 24 ☎289 813 433. This old-fashioned *adega* seats diners along long shared benches. It's a buzzy place, serving big portions of traditional Portuguese food and jugs of local wine or sangria. Order *bife na pedra* and you can cook your own steak on a sizzling stone, brought to your table. Moderate.

Sol e Jardim Pr. Ferreira de Almeida 22–23 ☎289 820 030. Characterful place with a barn-like "garden" dining room serving moderately priced Portuguese food. Live folk music on Fridays. Moderate.

Taska Rua do Alportel 38 ☎289 824 739. Friendly place serving traditional Algarve fare to a mostly Portuguese crowd. The house specialities include

corn mash with cockles and prawns, accompanied by an excellent range of regional wines. Closed Sun. Moderate.

Bars and clubs

Columbus Jardim Manuel Bivar, corner with Rua João Dias ☎289 813 051. Jazzy local haunt with outdoor seats under the arcades opposite the harbour gardens. There's a dartboard inside. Closed Mon.

Conselheiro Rua Conselheiro Bivar 72–78 ☎289 803 191. Disco bar with indoor tables, swirling lights and occasionally some good sounds, plus karaoke on Wednesdays. Minimum consumption policy most nights.

Gothic Rua da Madelena 38, near Igreja de São Pedro ☎289 807 887. Goths are alive but looking distinctly unwell at this dark club with cheap beer and wicked shots. Closed Sun.

Kingburger Bar Rua do Prior 40. A small and relaxed bar, one of the first to open up along here, and one of the last to close. Closed Sun–Tues.

Millennium III Rua do Prior 21 ☎289 823 628. Large club with an industrial-warehouse feel, playing all the latest sounds. There are good DJs and regular performances by local bands. Open until 5am; closed Mon–Wed.

Taberna da Sé Largo da Sé 26 ☎965 827 662. Arty tavern in the old town with outdoor tables attracting a friendly, young crowd. A popular spot for spontaneous jamming sessions on a summer's evening. Closed Sun.

Upa Upa Rua Conselheiro Bivar 51 ☎289 807 832. Laid back and relatively early opening music bar with a mixed clientele spilling onto outdoor tables on the widest stretch of this pedestrianized street.

Listings

Car rental All the following agencies have offices at the airport: AutoJardim ☎800 200 613, ✆www.auto-jardim.com; Avis ☎800 201 002; Hertz ☎800 238 238.

Cinema There's a multiplex (☎289 889 300) at the Fórum Algarve shopping complex, on the airport road (N125), a brisk fifteen-minute walk from town up Rua Infante Dom Henrique.

Consulate The only British consulate in the Algarve is in Portimão (p.584). In Faro itself, there are the following: Canada, Rua Frei Lourenço Santa Maria 1-1º, Apt. 79 ☎289 803 757; Denmark, Rua Conselheiro Bívar 10-1º ☎289 805 561; and Netherlands, Largo Francisco Sá Carneiro 52 ☎289 820 903.

Football The Algarve's top soccer team, Farense,

plays at the 30,000-seater Faro-Loulé stadium (☎289 990 360, ✆www.parquecidades-eim.pt), the centrepiece of a cultural, sports and medical park called Parque das Cidades, 6km north of Faro on the Loulé road. It can be reached by a special bus service for matches (including some internationals), concerts and events.

Hospital Hospital Distrital de Faro, Leão Penedo ☎289 891 100. In emergencies call ☎112.

Left luggage At the bus terminal (Mon–Fri 9am–1pm & 2–6pm); €2.50 per item per day.

Police Rua da Policia de Segurança Pública 32 ☎289 822 022.

Post office Largo do Carmo (Mon–Fri 8.30am–6.30pm, Sat 9am–12.30pm). It has *poste restante*

facilities, and you can make international telephone calls from here too.

Taxis There's a rank in Pr. Dr. Francisco Gomes, by
the town gardens, otherwise call ℡289 822 275
or 289 895 795.

Travel agencies Abreu, Av. da República
124 ℡289 870 900; Top Tours, Edifício Hotel
Eva, Doca de Faro Av. da República
℡289 895 340.

Around Faro: Estói and São Brás de Alportel

Apart from the beach, other worthwhile day-trips from Faro are to the couple
of villages in the gentle hills to the north. At **Estói**, you can divide your time
between the gardens of a delightful eighteenth-century country estate and
the remains of a Roman settlement at **Milreu**, just below the village. Further
north is the hilltop town of **São Brás de Alportel**, whose *pousada* provides a
more refined base for the region than staying in Faro. Travelling by bus, unless
you make a fairly early start it's difficult to see both villages on the same day.
However, it's perfectly feasible to take the bus to São Brás and walk the 7km
down to Estói, catching the late-afternoon bus back to Faro from there.

Estói

Regular buses make the twenty-minute journey 11km north of Faro to
ESTÓI, which basically consists of a main street, a little square and a small
white church. Buses drop you in the square, just off which you'll find the
delightful peach-coloured **Palácio do Visconde de Estói**, a diminutive
version of the Rococo palace of Queluz near Lisbon. It's currently being converted into a *pousada* (Ⓦwww.pousadas.pt), but the attractive grounds are still
open to the public (Mon–Sat 9am–12.30pm & 2–5.30pm; free), the terraces
lined with spectacular *azulejos* and tropical plants.

The main reason for a visit to Estói, however, is the Roman site at **Milreu**
(Tues–Sun: April–Sept 9.30am–12.30pm & 2–6pm; Oct–March 9.30am–12.30
& 2–5pm; €2), a ten-minute walk downhill from the square. Known to the
Romans as Ossonoba, the town that once stood here predated Faro and was
inhabited from the second to the sixth century AD. The surviving ruins are
associated with a peristyle villa – one with a gallery of columns surrounding a
courtyard – and dominated by the apse of a temple, which was converted into
a Christian basilica in the third century AD, making it one of the earliest of
all known churches. The other recognizable remains are of a bathing complex
southwest of the villa, with its fragmented fish mosaics, and the *apodyterium*, or
changing room, sporting stone benches and arched niches below for clothes.
The site was finally abandoned in the eighth century AD, after which date the
Moors founded Faro to the south.

Back in the village, there's good **food** at *Casa do Pasto Victor*, Rua Vasco da
Gama 41 (closed Sun), just off the square on the Olhão road, where you'd be
hard pushed to spend more than €10 a head. There are also no fewer than
eleven **café-bars** along and around the main street; the two on the main square
are good bets.

São Brás de Alportel

Seven kilometres north of Estói, the quiet country town of **SÃO BRÁS
DE ALPORTEL**, in a valley of the Serra do Caldeirão, also makes an
appealing detour for anyone with an hour to spare. Buses pull up in the
main square and, just off it, at Rua Dr. José Dias Sancho 61, lies the **Museu
Etnográfico do Trajo Algarvio** (Mon–Fri 10am–1pm & 2–5pm, Sat

2–5pm; €1), much the best reason to come to São Brás. Housed in an old mansion, the museum's alcoves and corridors are full of traditional costumes, and farming and domestic equipment. A series of buildings around an outside courtyard shelter cork-cutting equipment, ancient donkey carts and looms, while in the courtyard itself you can walk down a partially excavated traditional well. From the museum, cut down Rua Nova de Fonte to the **Jardim da Verbena** (May–Sept 8am–8pm; Oct–April 8am–5pm; free), a wonderful little garden with an open-air swimming pool (hours as park; free). Just west of here lie the narrow streets of the oldest part of town, clustered round the **Igreja Matriz**, from where there are lovely views of the surrounding valleys.

There's a small **turismo** on the main square (Mon–Fri 10am–1.30pm & 2.30–6pm; ☏289 843 165), and – just off the square – the *Residencial São Brás*, Rua Luís Bivar 27 (☏ & ℱ289 842 213; ❹), which has large if musty rooms in a fine old town house. However, if you were going to stay out here, it might as well be at the very comfortable *Pousada de São Brás* (☏289 845 171, ⓦwww.pousadas.pt; breakfast included; ❼). The views from the comfortable rooms' balconies are splendid, and there's a pool, tennis courts, games room and (expensive) restaurant. Advance booking is essential in summer. **Restaurants** in town are sparse but try the *Savoy*, Rua Luís Bivar 40 (closed Wed), past the *Residencial São Brás*, which offers well-cooked international cuisine and a children's menu. There are also plenty of café-bars round the main square.

Olhão and its ilhas

OLHÃO, 8km east of Faro, is the largest fishing port on the Algarve and an excellent base for visiting the surrounding sandbank *ilhas* of Armona and Culatra or the Quinta da Marim environmental centre. There are no sights in town as such, but with a vibrant market, attractive riverfront gardens and atmospheric back streets, it makes a great place to visit on a day-trip or to stop for a night or two. The flat roofs, outdoor stairways and white terraces of the old town are striking and give a North African look to the place. No surprise, then, that Olhão has centuries-old trading links with Morocco, as well as a small place in history for its uprising against the French garrison in 1808. Following the French departure, the local fishermen sent a small boat across the Atlantic to Brazil to transmit the news to the exiled king, João VI. The journey, completed without navigational aids, was rewarded after the king's restoration to the throne by the granting of a town charter.

The old town's most prominent building is the seventeenth-century parish church of **Nossa Senhora do Rosário** (Tues–Sun 9.30am–noon & 3–6pm), right in the middle of town. Outside, at the back of the church, an iron grille protects the chapel of **Nossa Senhora dos Aflitos**, where townswomen traditionally gathered when there was a storm at sea to pray for their sailors amid candles and curious wax ex-voto models of children and limbs.

The other obvious focus of the town is the **market**, held in the two modern redbrick buildings on the harbourside. Open from the crack of dawn (Mon–Sat), there's meat, fruit and vegetables on one side, fish on the other, the latter hall full of such delights as swordfish heads propped up on the marble counters and squid ink running off the tables into the gutter.

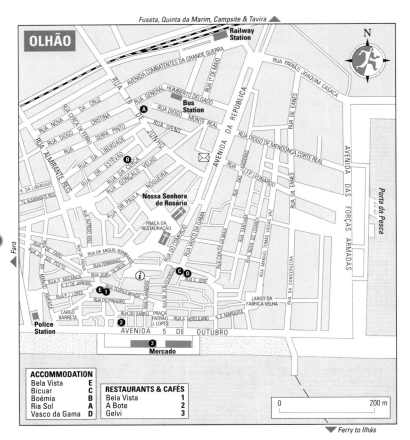

Fuseta, Quinta da Marim, Campsite & Tavira ▲

OLHÃO

Railway
Station

N

ACCOMMODATION

Bela Vista	E
Bicuar	C
Boémia	B
Ria Sol	A
Vasco da Gama	D

RESTAURANTS & CAFÉS

Bela Vista	1
A Bote	2
Gelvi	3

0   200 m

▼ Ferry to Ilhás

Practicalities

The **train station** is at the northern edge of town, off Avenida dos Combatentes da Grande Guerra, with the **bus terminal** a few minutes away on Rua General Humberto Delgado. From either, it's a quick walk down to the main Avenida da República, a wide boulevard which leads into the town centre, a further five minutes' walk away. At the parish church, the avenue forks: follow Rua do Comércio to find the **turismo** on Largo Sebastião Martins Mestre (June to mid-Sept daily 9.30am–7pm; mid-Sept to May Mon–Fri 10am–1.30pm & 2.30–6pm; ☎289 713 936, ⓦwww.cm-olhao.pt), which can provide sailing times of boats to the *ilhas*.

  Accommodation can be hard to find in the height of summer, despite a fair scattering of *pensões*, but the turismo also has a list of private **rooms** (❸). There are plenty of inexpensive cafés and bars around the market buildings, while the riverfront Avenida 5 de Outubro is lined with more expensive **fish restaurants**. Up by the ferry stop is another clutch of budget cafés and fast-food restaurants.

Hotels and pensions

Pensão Bela Vista Rua Teófilo Braga 65–67 ℡ & ℱ 289 702 538. A longstanding favourite, with a range of bright rooms arranged around a tiled, flower-filled courtyard. ❸
Pensão Bicuar Rua Vasco da Gama 5 ℡ 289 714 816, ⓦ www.pension-bicuar.net.Very central, recently refurbished *pensão* with a variety of rooms, including family rooms and dorms sleeping up to four (€15 per person). All are well furnished, with private bathrooms and cable TV. From the roof terrace there are great views over the town. ❸
Pensão Boémia Rua da Cerca 20 ℡ & ℱ 289 714 513. A friendly, quiet choice. Rooms come with shower and balcony. Breakfast included. ❸
Ria Sol Rua General Humberto Delgado 37 ℡ 289 705 267, ℱ 289 705 268. A decent two-star hotel with its own bar and small rooms. Recently renovated and handy for the bus and train stations. Breakfast included. ❹
Pensão Vasco da Gama Rua Vasco da Gama 6 ℡ 289 702 785. Big, airy but simple rooms in an old building right in the centre of the old town. Shared facilities. ❷

Campsite

Camping Olhão Pinheiros de Marim, 3km east of town, next to Quinta da Marim ℡ 289 700 300, ⓦ www.sbsi.pt/camping. The upmarket site, served by regular bus from Olhão, is set in substantial grounds with use of its own pool (for a small fee), playground, tennis courts, mini-market, restaurant and bars.

Cafés and restaurants

Restaurante Bela Vista Rua Dr. Teofilio Braga 59 ℡ 917 879 361.Simple, cheap restaurant with mammoth servings of grilled meats. Closed Sun. Inexpensive.
A Bote Av. 5 de Outubro 122 ℡ 289 721 183. The best place for a lively meal, serving superb grilled meat and fish dishes. Closed Sun. Moderate.
Café Gelvi Mercado, Av. 5 de Outubro. Bustling *pastelaria*, *geladaria* and *croissanteria* in the corner of the fish market, with outdoor seats facing the water. Inexpensive.

Armona and Culatra

Separate **ferries** leave for the *ilhas* of Armona and Culatra from the jetty at the eastern end of Olhão's municipal gardens, five minutes' walk from the market. There's a timetable posted at the kiosk; if it isn't open, you can buy tickets on the ferries. The **Ilha da Armona** (15min) is accessible all year round, as are the villages of Culatra (35min) and Farol (45min) on the **Ilha da Culatra**. Note that in summer you can also get the boat to Farol from Faro (see p.554).

Ilha da Armona

Ferries (June & early Sept 9 departures daily; July & Aug first departure 7.30am, then hourly 9am–8pm; late-Sept to May 4 daily; €2 return) drop their passengers at the southern end of the single settlement on **Ilha da Armona** – a long, crowded strip of holiday chalets and huts that stretches right across the island on either side of the main path. It's a fifteen-minute walk to the ocean, where the beach disappears into the distance. A short walk will take you to attractive stretches of sand and dune – the further you go, the greater the privacy. Continue east for two hours up the beach and you end up at Praia da Fuzeta opposite Fuzeta town (see p.560).

There are a few **bar-restaurants** by the jetty, though most are closed once summer is over. There are no *pensões* or hotels on Armona, and camping on the beach is frowned upon, but *Orbitur* (℡ 289 714 173, ⓦ www.orbitur.pt) operates a series of beachside holiday **bungalows** sleeping up to four (❹; closed Nov–March; reservations advised).

Ilha da Culatra

The **Ilha da Culatra** (ferries June & Sept 6 daily; July & Aug 7 daily; rest of year 4 daily; €2 return to Culatra, €2.60 to Farol) is another huge sand spit, though quite different in character from Armona. Its northern shore is dotted with a series of fishing settlements, mixed with an incongruous sprinkling of holiday chalets. The ferry's first port of call, **Culatra**, is the largest settlement, though **Farol**, the second stop, is far more agreeable, with its fisherman's huts and holiday homes gathered below a lighthouse, edged by beautiful tracts of beach on the ocean side – the mainland-facing beach is rather grubby. If you're considering staying, the best you can do is to ask around in Farol's market where you might be able to pick up a private **room** for around €30; camping is not allowed. In Farol, *A-do-João Restaurant* (Oct–April weekends only) serves good seafood dishes, including *cataplana*, as well as less expensive snacks and sandwiches.

Quinta da Marim

Three kilometres east of Olhão, just off the N125 Olhão–Tavira road (and served by regular bus from Olhão and Fuzeta), **Quinta da Marim** (daily: centre 9.30am–12.30pm & 2.30–5.30pm; park 8am–8pm, Oct–May until 6pm; €1.50) is an environmental educational centre within the **Parque Natural da Ria Formosa**. It's a lovely quiet spot, set amid scrubby dunes and mud flats dotted with pines and gorse, well worth a half-day's visit. The reserve is best known for being the refuge of bizarre aquatic poodles that were formerly bred to dive into the water to help chase fish into the local fishermen's nets. More modern, less enterprising, methods were adopted in the 1950s, though the shaggy dogs still thrive here in their pure-bred form. The poodles can be seen in an enclosure as part of a 3km-long **nature trail** that leads from the car park past the visitor centre, along which you'll also be able to view storks' nests, and the remains of Roman salt pans. The highlight is one of the country's last remaining tidal mills, complete with a rooftop organic café; there's also a restaurant at the visitor centre.

Fuzeta

Around 10km east of Olhão, and served by regular bus as well as the main Algarve rail line, the fishing town of **FUZETA** (or Fuseta) is one of the Algarve's least "discovered" resorts, probably because of its shortage of accommodation. It is not the region's most beautiful town, but it does retain some character as a working fishing port. Indeed its daily routine revolves around the fishermen, whose colourful boats line up alongside the river in town, though in summer Fuzeta also attracts a lively community of backpackers. The two communities usually mingle at the line of lively kiosk-cafés spreading down from the ferry stop towards the river beach.

The town's back streets straddle a low hill facing the lagoon, sheltered by the eastern extremity of the Ilha da Armona. Many of the local fish find their way to the small covered **market** on Largo 1 de Maio, on the road running parallel to the river; the quayside behind the building is often lined with drying octopus. On Saturdays the market expands into a weekly flea market that lines the adjacent pedestrianized Rua Tenente Barrosa. Continue up this road to reach the town's little palm tree-lined central square and Rua da Liberdade.

The waterfront of modern shops and apartments faces broad gardens that are largely taken over by the campsite (see below). Beyond this is the **river beach**, a fine stretch of white sand that weaves up to a wooden lifeboat house. Many people splash about in the calm waters of the river, though more exhilarating and cleaner waters are found over the river on the Ilha da Armona (see p.559).

Regular **ferries** (April–Oct roughly every 15min, 9am–7pm and often later; Nov–March 4 daily; €1.10 return) shuttle from the fishing quay at the back of the campsite across the lagoon to **Praia da Fuzeta** on the eastern end of the Ilha da Armona. The beach immediately opposite the ferry stop gets fairly crowded in high summer, but you only have to walk ten minutes or so either way from the holiday beach huts and seasonal drinks kiosks to have beautiful, low dune-backed sands all to yourself.

Practicalities

Buses drop you at the waterfront gardens, opposite the campsite. There are **rooms** (*quartos*) advertised in private houses, but most visitors stay at the waterside **campsite**, the *Parque de Campismo da Fuzeta* (☎289 793 459, ⓕ289 794 034), beautifully positioned under the trees. It gets pretty full in high summer. Around 2km northwest of Fuzeta – signposted Bias Sul – *Monte Alegre* (☎289 794 222, ⓔmonte.alegre@iol.pt; ⑨) consists of three well-equipped apartments sleeping up to five, and a superb double room with its own terrace. It's set in countryside with great coastal views, there's an outdoor swimming pool, stables for horse rides and a pond full of resident frogs; rooms all have satellite TV and kitchenettes.

There are plenty of **cafés and restaurants** on and around the main Rua da Liberdade. *Capri*, at Praça da República 4 (☎289 793 165; closed Wed) is a lively bar-restaurant with tables on the main square, serving inexpensive fish dishes and reliable grills. Out on Praia da Fuzeta, just back from the sands, *Restaurante Caetano* (☎919 962 048; daytime only) is open all year for excellent salads, snacks and full meals.

Tavira and around

Situated 30km east of Faro, **TAVIRA** is one of the most beautiful towns in the Algarve and a clear winner if you are looking for a base on the eastern stretch. It's sited on both sides of the broad Rio Gilão, which is overlooked by balconied houses and straddled by two low bridges, one of Roman origin. Despite ever-increasing numbers of visitors and encroaching development Tavira continues to make a living as a fishing port, and its seafood restaurants along the palm-lined river are a powerful incentive to stop. Indeed, many stay longer than planned – particularly those intent on lounging around on the superb island beach of the **Ilha de Tavira**, which lies within easy reach of the town by year-round ferry. There are also several quieter spots in the area, such as the holiday village of **Pedras d'el Rei** and nearby beach at **Barril** and, for some excellent seafood, the tiny fishing village of **Santa Luzia**.

The Town

Founded as long ago as 400 BC, Tavira was an important port trading with North Africa until the Great Earthquake of 1755, when the town was largely rebuilt with the graceful eighteenth-century town houses and mansions that you see today. In the old town streets on both sides of the river, numerous houses retain fine old doorways and coats of arms.

From the arcaded **Praça da República**, by the river, it's a short climb up into the old town following Rua da Galeria. Ahead stands the **Igreja da Misericórdia** with its once fine carved stone doorway (1541) depicting a series of mermaids, angels and saints, though the most visible carvings are a couple of lute-playing figures in the doorframe. Inside there's a striking *azulejo* interior showing scenes from the life of Christ, below a wooden vaulted ceiling, but unfortunately the church is almost always locked. Turn left here and a couple of hundred metres up the cobbled street are the ruins of the **Castelo** (Mon–Fri

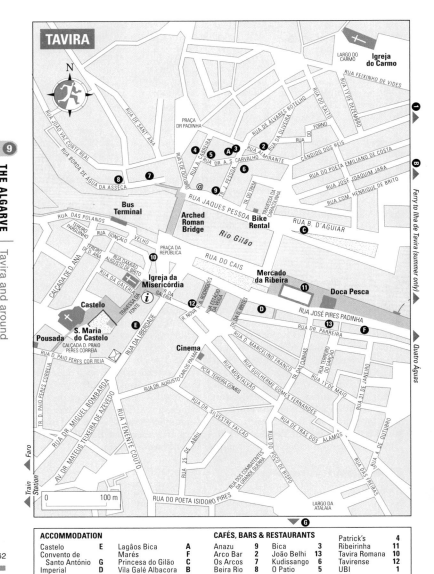

ACCOMMODATION			
Castelo	E	Lagâos Bica	A
Convento de		Marés	F
Santo António	G	Princesa do Gilão	C
Imperial	D	Vila Galé Albacora	B

CAFÉS, BARS & RESTAURANTS				Patrick's	4
Anazu	9	Bica	3	Ribeirinha	11
Arco Bar	2	João Belhi	13	Tavira Romana	10
Os Arcos	7	Kudissango	6	Tavirense	12
Beira Rio	8	O Patio	5	UBI	1

8am–5pm, Sat & Sun 9am–5.30pm; free), half hidden amid landscaped gardens on a low hill in the centre of town. From the walls you can look down over the peculiarly hipped terracotta rooftops and the town's numerous church spires. Adjacent to the castle, the impressive, whitewashed **Santa Maria do Castelo** is open daily, and contains the tomb of Dom Paio Peres Correia, who reconquered much of the Algarve, including Tavira in 1242, from the Moors. Fittingly, the church stands on the site of the former mosque.

With its tranquil vistas and palm-lined gardens, the **riverfront** is the best part of Tavira for a wander. There are no sights as such north of the river, though the old streets hide many of the town's best restaurants. South of the river, the former town market building, **Mercado da Riberia**, has become a "cultural centre" – actually a handful of small boutiques and waterfront cafés. The old market walls are also used for temporary exhibitions, usually the work of local artists and photographers.

Beyond the market lies the fish market (for the trade only) and the fishing boats, lined up as far along as the flyover – this part of the river is also where most of the touristy fish restaurants are. In summer, you can catch direct ferries to the Ilha da Tavira (see p.565) from here. Head under the bridge and you'll see the large new town **market** (Mon–Sat 8am–1.30pm), whose bustling interior is filled with an array of fruit and vegetables.

Practicalities

Tavira's **bus terminal** is by the river, from where it's a two-minute walk to the old bridge and Praça da República. The **train station** is 1km from the centre of town, straight up the Rua da Liberdade and at the end of Avenida Dr. Mateus Teixeira de Azevedo. Up the steps just off Praça da República is the **turismo**, at Rua da Galeria 9 (daily: May–Oct 10am–1pm & 2–6pm; Nov–April 9.30am–1pm & 2–6pm; ☎281 322 511, ⓦwww.cm-tavira.pt). Drivers will encounter a complicated one-way system in the central area; there's metered parking in and around Praça da República though it's probably best to head for the free **car park** under the flyover – follow signs to Quatro Águas. A fun way to get your bearings is by taking the **road train**, which does a circuit from Praça da República out to Quatro Águas (daily every 45min, 10am–dusk; €2.50). *Sport Nautica*, Rua Jacques Pessoa 26 (☎281 324 943), offers **bike rental** from €5 a day. **Taxis** line up in Praça da República.

The town has a growing number of places to stay and finding **accommodation** is only a problem in high season. The tourist office can help with **private rooms** (❸) if you have no luck at any of the places listed below. The nearest campsite is on the Ilha da Tavira, for which see p.565. There are **cafés and restaurants** all over town, though for the seafood restaurants that characterize Tavira you need to stroll down the partly pedestrianized Rua José Pires Padinha, where the tables edge out on to the riverside.

Hotels and pensions

Pensão do Castelo Rua da Liberdade 22 ☎281 320 790, ⓕ281 320 799. Very centrally located, this rambling place has spotlessly clean en-suite rooms with TVs. There's also disabled access. ❹
Convento de Santo António Rua de Santo António, 1km southeast of town ☎281 321 573, ⓕ281 325 632. Book well ahead (by fax only) for one of the seven elegant double rooms in this converted convent with swimming pool and roof terrace. It's

located just out of town in a residential suburb. There's a minimum four-night stay in summer, two in winter. Closed Jan. Breakfast included. ❽
Residencial Imperial Rua José Pires Padinha 24 ☎ & ⓕ281 322 234. Small *residencial* above a restaurant. Opt for one of the rooms overlooking the gardens and river rather than the noisy street-facing ones. Breakfast included. ❹
Residencial Lagãos Bica Rua Almirante Cândido dos Reis 24 ☎281 322 252. On the north side

of the river, this has simple but attractive rooms clustered round a rooftop patio. It's above the top-notch budget restaurant, *Bica* (see below). Breakfast included. ❸

Residencial Marés Rua José Pires Padinha 134 –140 ☎ 281 325 815, ✉ maresresidencial@mail .telepac.pt. Extremely pleasant rooms, some facing the river, with tiled floors and *azulejos* in the bathrooms; there's also a roof terrace and sauna. Breakfast included. ❺

Residencial Princesa do Gilão Rua Borda d'Àgua de Aguiar 10–12 ☎ & ℻ 281 325 171. A white modern building with *azulejo*-decorated interior, located right on the quayside. The rooms are small, and fairly simply furnished, but the front ones are enhanced by balconies overlooking the river. Breakfast included. ❸

Vila Galé Albacora 2km east of town, opposite Quatro Águas ☎ 281 380 800, ⊕ www.vilagale .pt. This former tuna-fishing village has been tastefully converted into a four-star hotel, with rooms in the old houses either facing the river estuary or the enormous central courtyard (though some face the car park). The village's chapel is still used, and the former school is now a children's club. The flower-filled courtyard also contains a large pool, games room, restaurant and bar; inside there's another pool and health club. A courtesy bus serves Tavira and the beach. The downside of its riverside position is a colony of voracious mosquitoes. Parking. Breakfast included. ❽

Cafés

Anazu Rua Jacques Pessoa 11–13 ☎ 281 381 935. A lovely, tiled riverfront café, which seems to catch the sun all day – a good place for breakfast or a sunset drink. There's a games-room/cyber café attached. Inexpensive.

Tavira Romana Pr. da República ☎ 281 323 451. The café by the pedestrianized bridge does superb ice creams.

Tavirense Rua Marcelino Franco 19. For some of the best cakes in town, try this old-fashioned *pastelaria* opposite the cinema.

Restaurants

Os Arcos Rua João Vaz Corte Real 15 ☎ 281 324 392. Good-value local tavern serving fine grills, soups and salads. In summer, tables are placed in a superb riverfront position facing the old bridge. Full meals around €10. Inexpensive.

Beira Rio Rua Borda da Àgua de Assêca 46–48 ☎ 281 323 165. Arty and airy riverside bar-restaurant with tree-shaded tables. It's a tranquil

venue for pizza, pasta and salads; closed Nov. Moderate.

Bica Rua Almirante Cândido dos Reis 22–24 ☎ 281 323 843. Excellent-value Portuguese meals in a bustling little restaurant on the north side of the river. Mains around €5. Inexpensive.

João Belhi Rua José Pires Padinha 96 ☎ 965 449 557. There are no outdoor tables, but this is less expensive and more locally inclined than most of the restaurants on this stretch. The menu features the usual fish and meat dishes and there's good house wine. Moderate.

Kudissango Rua Dr. Augusta da Silva Carvalho 8 ☎ 281 321 670. A cheerful spot to sample some cuisine from Portugal's former African colonies. There is a good range of vegetarian food, as well as the speciality – boiled mandioca fish with *escabeche*. Dinner only, though also lunch on Sat; closed Thurs. Inexpensive.

O Patio Rua Dr. António Cabreira 30 ☎ 281 323 008. Pricey fish restaurant with French-influenced dishes and an attractive summer roof terrace. Specialities include a terrific lobster *cataplana*. Closed Sun. Expensive.

Quatro Águas Quatro Águas ☎ 281 325 329. Out by the ferry stop, this highly rated seafood restaurant specializes in dishes such as *açorda* and *cataplana de marisco*, or try the *bife de frango com molho roquefort* (chicken with roquefort sauce). Closed Mon. Expensive.

Ribeirinha Mercado da Ribeira, Loja 3 ☎ 965 384 464. One of the best positioned of the old market café-restaurants, a fine spot for a beer or a simple meal overlooking the river. Closed Thurs Oct–May. Inexpensive.

Bars and clubs

Arco Bar Rua Almirante Cândido dos Reis 67 ☎ 918 504 200. One of a few fashionable spots north of the river, this is a gay-friendly place attracting a laid-back crowd. Closed Mon.

Patrick's Rua Dr. António Cabreira 25–27 ☎ 281 325 998. A welcoming *adega*-style English-run bar-restaurant where, along with some familiar beers, you can enjoy bar food such as *piri-piri* prawns and curries. Closed Sun, Mon & Nov.

UBI Rua Vale Caranguego ☎ 281 322 555. Follow Rua Almirante Cândido dos Reis to the outskirts of town Tavira's only club is housed in a huge metallic warehouse. The locals warm up with a few pre-clubbing drinks in the *Bubi Bar* in the same building, open from 10pm. Club open July–Sept Tues–Sun midnight–6am; Oct–June Fri and Sat only.

Ilha de Tavira

The Ilha de Tavira stretches southwest from Tavira almost as far as Fuzeta, some 14km away, and the beach is enormous, backed by tufted dunes. In summer you can catch ferries direct from the riverfront in town (July–Sept daily 8.30am–8pm, roughly hourly; €1.50 return). Otherwise, you get there by ferry from the jetty at **Quatro Águas**, 2km east of town – it's a thirty-minute walk, or you can take the road train from Tavira (see "Practicalities", p.563) or a bus from the terminal (July to mid-Sept Mon–Fri roughly hourly). There's a huddle of cafés and restaurants next to the ferry terminal, while the **ferries** themselves (daily: Easter–June 8am–8pm; July–Sept 8am–9pm; Oct–Easter 9am–dusk; €1 return) take just five minutes to cross to the island. In high season they run every fifteen minutes or so, often until much later than 9pm; at other times they run roughly hourly – always check with the ferryman what time the last boat returns. Alternatively, **aquataxis** (daily from 8am; ☎964 515 073) from Quatro Águas do the ride for €6 per person one-way (take up to six people).

On the **Ilha de Tavira**, the main path on the island runs from the jetty through a small chalet settlement to the beach, where there are umbrellas and pedaloes for rent, and half a dozen bar-restaurants. In high summer this part of the beach is packed with families and beach dudes, though you only have to walk fifteen minutes or so to be clear of the crowds, and out of season you'll probably have the place entirely to yourself. Alternatively, pick up an attractive path heading west from the ferry stop, parallel to the coast, where there are picnic tables dotted under fragrant pines.

The **campsite** (☎281 321 709, ⓦwww.campingtavira.com; closed Oct –Easter) is just a minute from the sands, with a well-stocked mini-market. Between here and the beach *Pavilhão da Ilha* (☎281 324 131; closed Nov–Feb) is the best place on the island for a full **meal,** with moderately priced fish and grills and a lively bar area.

Santa Luzia, Pedras d'el Rei and Barril

Along the coastal road from Tavira, regular weekday buses (three on Sat) run the 3km west to the fishing village of **SANTA LUZIA**, which bills itself as the "King of the Octopus". It's an earthy working fishing village with a number of seafood restaurants catering to day-trippers, who saunter around the palm-lined waterfront and small fishing harbour. Having admired the octopus traps on the jetty, and the bright, whitewashed buildings, most people settle for a leisurely meal. Best bet is *Capelo* (☎281 381 670; closed Wed), a slightly pricey joint on the main Avenida Engheneiro Duarte Pacheco, with a spacious *azulejo*-lined interior and an outdoor terrace.

A kilometre west down the river, 4km from Tavira, **PEDRAS D'EL REI** is served by six buses daily from Tavira's bus station (Mon–Fri only). This is a fairly upmarket holiday complex, which offers access to another stretch of the Ilha da Tavira at Barril (see below). The **apartments and villas** here (☎281 380 600, ⓦwww.pedrasdelrei.com; from ❺) are perfect for families, set in beautifully landscaped grounds. There's a central lawned area focused on an outdoor pool and overlooked by a café, bar and restaurant. Facilities include a playground, children's club, aviary and well-stocked shop, and residents have free passes for the train to the beach.

From the bus stop and car park next to Pedras d'El Rei, you cross the causeway to the terminal of a rather ancient-looking **miniature train** (daily, except in bad weather, 8am–dusk, roughly every 15–30min; €1 one-way). This shuttles across the mud flats, past thousands of fiddler crabs, to the beach of **Barril** on the Ilha de Tavira. You can also walk alongside the tracks (10–15min). At the beach, attractive former fishermen's houses have been turned into a cluster of slightly pricey café-restaurants; there's also a small shop, showers and toilets. A few minutes' walk right or left of the terminus – past lines of anchors wedged into the dunes – there are miles of peaceful, dune-fringed beach.

East of Tavira: to Monte Gordo

Just to the east of Tavira, beyond the resort of **Cabanas**, the sand spit that protects much of the eastern Algarve from the developers starts to thin out and merges with the shoreline beach at **Manta Rota**, 12km away. Manta Rota itself and neighbouring **Altura** have been intensively developed, although the beaches are still alluring, and there are more sandy stops further to the east at **Praia Verde** and the resort of **Monte Gordo**. However, there is one surprise on this part of the coast: for some reason, the small hamlet of **Cacela Velha** (not to be confused with Vila Nova de Cacela, 2km inland) is barely touched by tourism.

You can reach Cabanas, Altura and Monte Gordo by bus from Tavira; for Manta Rota, the only services are from Vila Real (or Monte Gordo); and for Cacelha Verde and Praia Verde, the best you can do is get off any bus to Vila Real on the highway and walk down the side roads. You can of course always **walk** along the beach: from Manta Rota it's around thirty minutes to Altura, another twenty minutes to Praia Verde, and forty more to Monte Gordo.

Cabanas

Six kilometres east of Tavira – past the golf course at Benamor – lies **CABANAS**, with a kernel of back streets made up of pretty fishermen's houses and a line of low-rise shops, cafés and bars facing a picturesque river estuary. Moored fishing boats testify to the village's former mainstay, though nowadays the economy is largely driven by tourism thanks to the glorious sands on **Praia de Cabanas** over the estuary and to the ruins of an old sea fort just east of town. Ferries shuttle passengers to the beach from a small jetty at the eastern edge of town (April–Oct, every 15min; €1 return). Cross the dunes and you're faced with miles of golden sand, plus a couple of seasonal beach cafés.

Eight weekday **buses** (only two on Saturday) run from Tavira to Cabanas, stopping at the west end of the waterfront. The town is also is just 1km south of Conceição on the Tavira to Vila Real **train** line, though you'll have to walk into the centre from the station. **Accommodation** options are mainly limited to apartments and villas, although you can always ask at bars and cafés for private **rooms**. *Pastelaria Jerónimo*, on Avenida 28 de Maio (☎281 370 649; ❹), opposite the ferry jetty, rents out decent apartments with sea-facing balconies, while on the sloping main road into town *Pedras da Rainha* (☎281 380 680, Ⓦwww.pedrasrainha.com; from ❺) has apartments and villas (sleeping up to ten) clustered around pleasant lawns, tennis courts and a large pool, all with disabled access. **Cafés**, **bars** and **restaurants** spread along the riverfront and a block or two inland, best the *Restaurante A Rocha* (☎281 370 239) by the jetty on Avenida 28 de Maio, an attractive place with a breezy terrace where you can enjoy moderately priced omelettes, salads and fresh fish.

Cacela Velha

Ten kilometres from Cabanas, and perched on a low cliff facing the estuary, the whitewashed village of **CACELA VELHA** is a reminder of how the Algarve must have looked half a century ago. Apart from a couple of simple café-restaurants, there are no tourist facilities, just a pretty church and the remains of an eighteenth-century fort, and even that is a GNR station and closed to the public. Surrounded by olive groves, and offering exhilarating views from its clifftop, it is spectacularly pretty and, despite the new golf courses just to the west, rarely overrun by visitors. The beach below the village is a delight. To get to it, follow signs to "Fábrica", just west of the village, around 1km downhill. Here a ferryman can take you over to the beach for €1 return (daily in summer but only during good weather the rest of the year).

To reach Cacela Velha by public transport, ask to be let off the Tavira–Vila Real bus on the highway, just before Vila Nova de Cacela, from where it's a fifteen-minute walk down a side road to the village. There are a few private rooms that get snapped up quickly in summer, or try *Cantinho da Ria Formosa* (☎281 951 837, ⓦwww.cantinhoriaformosa.com; breakfast included; ❺), around 1km from the beach and the golf course. Rooms in this blue-edged *residencial* are clean and modern, and have views over the garden or fields. There are stables attached, and horse rides are on offer for around €15 an hour.

Manta Rota, Altura and Praia Verde

Two kilometres further along the coast at **MANTA ROTA**, a group of half a dozen restaurants, all serving platters of sardines and grilled swordfish or tuna, cluster at the entrance to a superb, broad beach. There's not much else to hang about for; the main road is a fifteen-minute walk up from the beach. The next resort east, **ALTURA**, is more developed, backed by white villas and apartments facing another fantastic beach, Praia de Alagoas. Here, there's a line of beach umbrellas and beach bars, drinks kiosks and water sports on hand. Further east, towards Monte Gordo, the beach becomes more unkempt, backed by scrubby dunes, but the sands are much less likely to be crowded in summer. Four kilometres east of Altura, **PRAIA VERDE** is the nicest stretch, with just one beach café.

Monte Gordo

MONTE GORDO is the last resort before the Spanish border and the most built-up of the eastern holiday towns. White hotels overlook the wide, clean sands, on which are scattered a profusion of café-restaurants with studiously similar menus and inflated prices; the *Mota* (☎281 512 340) is the best, a huge place serving fish and grills on the sands. For something a little less expensive, *Jaime*, further west up the beach, serves lunchtime snacks.

Buses from Vila Real and Tavira pull up on Rua Pedro Àlvares Cabral, by the parish church. From here it is a short walk down the main Avenida Vasco de Gama to the seafront and the casino. Just east of the casino is the **turismo** (May–Sept Mon & Fri–Sun 9.30am–1.30pm & 2.30–7pm, Tues–Thurs 9.30am–7pm; Oct–April Mon–Fri 10am–1.30pm & 2.30–6pm; ☎281 544 495), which has details of private rooms in town. However, if you want **accommodation** right on the beach, look no further than the *Vasco da Gama*, Avenida Infante Dom Henrique (☎281 510 900, ⓦwww.hotelvascodagama .com; breakfast included; ❻), a highrise with tennis courts and kids' facilities. It's cheaper at the *Pensão Monte Gordo*, Avenida Infante Dom Henrique (☎281

542 124, ⓔpensao-montegordo@clix.pt; breakfast included; ⑤), set back from the main drag just west of the casino, where some of the large en-suite rooms have sea views. Monte Gordo is also the site of the last – and largest – **campsite** (ⓣ281 510 970) on this stretch of the Algarve, a huge place set under pines near the beach on the Vila Real road.

Vila Real de Santo António

The border town and harbour of **VILA REAL DE SANTO ANTÓNIO** used to be the main crossing point into Spain, but has declined since the opening of a road bridge over the Rio Guadiana, 4km to the north. Still, you may want to call in anyway, not least because it's one of the more architecturally interesting towns in the Algarve. The original settlement was demolished by a tidal wave following the earthquake of 1755 and the current town was rebuilt on a grid plan by the Marquês de Pombal, using the same plans he had already pioneered in the Baixa quarter of Lisbon. Remarkably, the whole project only took five months.

The central grid built by Pombal radiates out from the handsome square that bears his name, ringed by orange trees and low, white buildings, a couple of which are pleasant outdoor cafés. On the north side of the square is Rua Teófilo Braga, the pedestrianized main drag that leads inland from the riverfront Avenida da República. The former market building along here has been reborn as the **Centro Cultural António Aleixo** (Mon–Fri 10am–1pm & 3pm–7pm; free), an innovative space used for temporary exhibits, installations and occasionally even films. The centre also embraces the **Museu de Manuel Cabanas**, displaying the works of a local painter and wood engraver. The surrounding streets have a certain low-key charm, bristling with linen shops, electrical retailers and grocers, and the riverside **gardens** offer fine views across to the splash of white that is Ayamonte in Spain.

Practicalities

Vila Real is the eastern terminal of the Algarve railway, and **trains** pull up at the station, five minutes north of the riverfront. **Buses** either stop by the river or at a terminus just north of the train station, while the **turismo** (Mon–Fri 10am –1.30pm & 2.30–5pm; ⓣ281 542 100) is situated in a corner

ACCOMMODATION
Guadiana · · · · · · · · · · · · A
Pousada de Juventude · · B

CAFÉS & RESTAURANTS
Arenilha · · · · · · · · · · · · · 1
Caves do Guadiana · · · · · · 2

of the Centro Cultural on Rua Teófilo Braga. There's really no need to stay the night, though the *Hotel Guadiana* at Avenida da República 94, overlooking the gardens and river (☎281 511 482, ⓦwww.hotelguadiana.com; breakfast included; ❺), is a National Monument with a fine old Art Deco frontage, an ornate breakfast room and river views, though the rooms are nothing special. Alternatively, there's a simple **youth hostel**, the *Pousada de Juventude* at Rua Dr. Sousa Martins 40 (☎281 544 565, ⓦwww.pousadasjuventude.pt; dorm beds €10, doubles ❶); it's open all year but fills quickly in summer.

Half-a-dozen similarly priced **cafés and restaurants** line the riverfront, all with outdoor seats. *Caves do Guadiana*, Avenida da República 89–90 (☎281 544 498; closed Thurs), has long been considered the best in town. It's got a tiled and vaulted interior, and you'll pay around €16 for a full meal. For less expensive fish and grilled meats try the *Churrasqueira Arenilha* on Rua Cândido dos Reis (☎281 544 038).

Crossing the border: Ayamonte

Daily buses run from Vila Real across the bridge to **Ayamonte** in Spain (15min), which has onward connections to Huelva (1hr) and Seville (4hr). There are timetables posted at the Vila Real bus terminus, and remember that Spanish time is one hour ahead of Portuguese. If you just want to make a day-trip to the Spanish border town – with its tapas bars and palm-lined squares – it's more fun to use the **ferry** from Vila Real's harbour (daily every 40min from 8.40am, last return 7pm, which is 8pm Spanish time; €1.10 each way). This is a twenty-minute ride across the Rio Guadiana, with the forts of Castro Marim visible to the west and the impressive bridge to the north.

Inland: along the Rio Guadiana

North of Vila Real, the **Rio Guadiana** forms the border with Spain and provides a little-travelled diversion. Buses from Vila Real follow the N122, which runs inland of the river, with regular weekday services to **Castro Marim** and less frequent services to **Alcoutim**, each with a castle and a smattering of historic interest. Best of all, though, is a **boat trip** up the river itself. Summer tourist charters are offered in Monte Gordo or Vila Real: at around €50 per person they're not especially cheap, but you do get a barbecue lunch and plenty of swimming opportunities along the way.

Castro Marim

The little village of **CASTRO MARIM**, 5km north of Vila Real, was once a key fortification protecting Portugal's southern coast. Marim was the first headquarters of the Order of Christ (1319) and is the site of a huge **castle** (daily: April–Oct 9am–7pm; Nov–March 9am–5pm; free), built by Afonso III in the thirteenth century. The massive ruins are all that survived the earthquake of 1755, as well as those of the smaller fort of São Sebastião across the village, but it's a pretty place with fine views of the bridge to Spain. A small museum inside the castle walls displays local archeological finds.

The marshy area around Castro Marim has been designated the **Reserva Natural do Sapal**, so there's little danger of its being despoiled. The village turismo (see below) has information about local walks and can direct you to the remote **park headquarters** (Mon–Fri 9am–12.30pm & 2–5.30pm; ℡281 510 680). One of the area's most unusual and elusive inhabitants is the ten-centimetre-long, swivel-eyed, opposing-toed, Mediterranean **chameleon** – a harmless, slow-moving lizard that's severely threatened elsewhere by habitat destruction.

The **turismo** is in Praça 1 de Maio (Mon–Fri 10am–1.30pm & 2.30–6pm; ℡281 531 232), just below the castle. There are several **cafés** on Rua de São Sebastião, west of the turismo, or eat at the *Eira Gaio* (℡281 351 358; closed Sun evening) on Rua 25 de Abril opposite the turismo.

Alcoutim

Some 40km north of Vila Real – and best approached by car along the road that hugs the Guadiana river – **ALCOUTIM** is extremely attractive. It has a long history as a river port, dominated in turn by Greeks, Romans and Arabs who all fortified the heights with various structures; the **castle** (daily 9am–1pm & 2–5pm; €2.50) dates from the fourteenth century and offers fine views over the town and the Rio Guadiana. The entrance fee includes access to a small archeological **museum** by the main gates, which traces the history of the castle, its active service in the War of Restoration and the Liberal Wars, and the remnants of ealier structures on the site. The fee also covers entry to the so-called Núcleos Museológicos, tiny craft museums that have been set up in many of the villages in the region. For further diversion, a ferry (daily 9am–1pm & 2–7pm; €1 single) crosses the river to the Spanish village of **Sanlúcar**, a mirror image of Alcoutim, with its own ruined castle.

A couple of buses a day (not Sun) run back down to Vila Real, and there's a twice-weekly service north to Mértola and Beja in the Alentejo. A small **turismo** (May–Oct Mon–Fri 10am–1.30pm & 2.30–7pm; Nov–April closes at 6pm; ℡281 546 179) is located in the main Praça da República, right in the centre of the village. They're helpful people and can point you in the right direction for private **rooms**, or try at the modern *Pensão Afonso*, Rua João Dias 10 (℡281 546 211; ❷), just uphill from the main square, which has some pleasant en-suite rooms. The smart fifty-bed **youth hostel** (℡281 546 004, ⓦwww.pousadajuventude.pt; dorm beds €14, rooms ❸) is around 1.5km north of the village, across the Ribeira Cadavais; cross the bridge beyond Praça da República and follow the signs. It has its own canteen, bar and laundry, as well as disabled access. For upmarket lodgings, head north out of Alcoutim and follow the signs to the *Estalagem do Guadiana* (℡281 540 120, ⓦwww .grupofbarata.com; breakfast included; ❺), a very swish modern inn with its own pool, tennis court and restaurant. The spacious rooms come with satellite TV, baths and fine river views.

Alcoutim's inexpensive **cafés** cluster around the square, though the best positioned place in town is *O Soeiro* (℡281 546 241), with outdoor tables facing the river, a bustling downstairs café (closed Sun) and an upstairs restaurant serving fine local specialities such as lamprey (lunch only, closed weekends).

The western Algarve

The western Algarve stretches for a hundred kilometres from Faro to Sagres, and encompasses some of the region's best beaches but also Portugal's most intense tourist development. Much of the stretch between Faro and Albufeira, for example, consists of purpose-built resorts that feature marinas, golf links and tennis centres – "Sportugal" – as the tourist board promotes the leisure complexes – which are fine if you've booked a package holiday, but with little promise for anyone simply in search of a quiet beach and an unsophisticated meal.

Albufeira itself is one of the biggest – and *the* most enjoyable – resorts, while other decent stops include **Alvor**, **Portimão** and **Lagos**, the last of which still retains some character as a town in its own right. All of these places are packed to the gills in summer and, particularly if you have transport, you might do better to seek a base inland at the interesting old market towns of **Loulé** or **Silves** and drive down to the nearest beach for the day. **Caldas de Monchique**, a nineteenth-century spa town, and the neighbouring market town of **Monchique** are other inland options, though these are a good forty-minute drive from the sea.

West of Lagos, development has been restricted by the Parque Natural do Sudouste Alentejano e Costa Vicentina, which embraces most of the coastline. As a result, erstwhile fishing villages such as **Luz**, **Burgau** and **Salema** still retain a fair amount of charm, while beyond the road cuts high above the sea across a cliff-edged plateau and down to **Sagres**, with its dramatic scenery and busy nightlife. The coast north of Sagres, heading towards the Alentejo, is the least developed part of the Algarve – partly because the sea (the Atlantic) is distinctly colder and often pretty wild. Low-key villages such as **Vila do Bispo**, **Carrapateira**, **Aljezur** and **Odeceixe** all have magnificent local beaches that attract a rather more "alternative" crowd than resorts on the Algarve proper, with plenty of beach parties, nude sunbathing and surfing.

Loulé

LOULÉ, 18km inland of Faro, has always been an important market town and has recently grown to a fair size, though its compact centre doesn't take long to look around. Its most interesting streets, a grid of whitewashed cobbled lanes, lie between the remains of its Moorish castle (now a museum) and the thirteenth-century Gothic **Igreja Matriz**, with its palm-lined gardens in front. Here you'll see traditional craftsmen labouring in workshops, producing copper *cataplanas* (cooking vessels) and leatherwork for the region's restaurants and souvenir shops.

The remains of Loulé's castle enclose a mildly interesting **Museu Arqueológico** (Mon–Thurs 9am–5.30pm, Sat 10am–2pm; €1.10), housing a range of Roman, Moorish and early Portuguese finds from Loulé and the surrounding area. The largest exhibit is a giant sixteenth-century stone urn, retrieved from the castle itself. Loulé's most atmospheric sight, however, is the covered fruit and vegetable **market** (Mon–Sat 8am–3pm) on Rua José Fernandes Guerreiro, a couple of minutes' walk southeast off the main Praça da República, set in a red onion-domed building with Moorish-style windows. Try and visit on a Saturday morning, when the market spreads into the surrounding streets – a medley of stalls selling everything from pungent cheese to cages of live chickens and rabbits. There's also a Saturday **morning market** (from 9.30am), which takes place around fifteen minutes' walk northwest of the centre – follow the signs to IP1/Boliquieme – on a patch of ground beautifully framed by a pair of dazzling white churches, including the curious modern beehive-shaped **Nossa Senhora da Piedade**. At Easter, the church is the starting-point of a procession into town for *Mãe Soberana*, one of the Algarve's most important religious festivals.

Practicalities

The **bus station** is on Rua Nossa Senhora de Fátima, a couple of minutes' walk north of the old town area; there are regular services from Quarteira and Faro. The **turismo** (May–Sept Mon–Fri 9.30am–7pm, Sat 10am–6pm; Oct–April Mon–Fri 9.30am–5.30pm, Sat 10am–2pm; ☎289 463 900, ⓦwww .cm-loule.pt) is due to move from its position inside the castle walls to an office on Avenida 25 de Abril, close to the bus station. For **accommodation**, try *Casa Beny*, at Rua São Domingos 13 (☎289 417 702; breakfast included; ❸), on the main through road. It's not the quietest of spots, but the tastefully renovated town house offers neat rooms with TV and bathroom. Better is the comfortable *Loulé Jardim Hotel* at Praça Manuel de Arriaga 23 (☎289 413 094, ⓕ289 463 177; breakfast included; ❹), a block south of Rua Nossa Senhora da Piedade, which boasts a bar, a small pool and comfortable rooms with cable TV.

Just around the corner from the castle, *Café Calcina* (closed Sun) is a great traditional **café** with outdoor tables, dark wood fittings, and black-and-white photos of old Loulé on the walls. Downhill below the castle, *A Muralha*, Rua Martim Moniz 39 (☎289 412 629; dinner only except Sat; closed Sun) is housed in a former bakery, and has an attractive flower-filled patio and pleasant interior – the meat and seafood dishes are elaborate and pricey. For simpler local fare, try *Flôr da Praça*, Rua José Fernandes Guerreiro 44 (☎289 462 435; closed Sun), opposite the food market.

Quinta do Lago and Vale do Lobo

Around 12km northwest of Faro, right on the Almancil turn-off from the N125, the church of **São Lourenço** (Mon 2.30–6pm, Tues–Sat 10am–1pm & 2.30–6pm; €1.50) comes as a surprise amid the development. Built in the eighteenth century, it survived the earthquake of 1755 and retains its superb tiled interior depicting the life and martyrdom of St Laurence.

Almancil itself is served by regular buses from Faro, and is also the turn-off point for the first of the resorts west of Faro, **QUINTA DO LAGO**, which is a vast, luxury holiday village with its own golf courses and sports complex. One or two daily buses run here directly from Loulé and Almancil. The *Hotel Quinta do Lago* (☎289 350 350, ⓦwww.quintadolagohotel.com; ❾) is typical of what's on offer, popular with celebrities who appreciate the privacy offered by its sprawling wooded grounds. The rooms are truly splendid, and there are restaurants, bars, an indoor and outdoor pool, and spa and sports facilities, though a night here will set you back close to €500. Most day visitors, however, head straight for the great beach, the **Praia do Anção**, reached over a wooden bridge from the car park at the end of Avenida André Jorge, the main

9

drag. The bridge heads across the western extremity of the Parque Natural da Ria Formosa; it also marks the start of two marked nature trails that lead either side of the inland waterways.

Facilities are similar at **VALE DO LOBO**, just to the west, where a great beach is backed by more serious-money hotels; there is a 24-hour reception as you enter the complex (☎289 353 000, ⓦwww.valedolobo.com), which can help with booking accommodation. Nearby are golf courses, a riding school, and the **Vale de Lobo Tennis Academy** (☎289 396 991), the most famous in the country. You can book lessons and coaching sessions, though as even Tim Henman comes here to practise, courts do get booked up well in advance.

Quarteira

QUARTEIRA, 22km west of Faro, has a very different feel to the deluxe resorts on either side. It was one of the first fishing villages to be developed in the Algarve, and remains high-rise and downmarket. Stick to the palm-lined seafront promenade and the attractive stretch of beach – Praia de Quarteira – and it's a pleasant enough destination, and at least it remains largely Portuguese in character. The main attraction is the bustling fish and vegetable **market** (Mon–Sat 8am–3pm, Sun vegetable market only 8am–2pm) by the working fishing harbour, to the west end of town, though there's also a good weekly flea market each Wednesday, a couple of blocks back from the tourist office. From May to September you can tour Quarteira on a **road train** which trundles along the seafront and around the town every hour or so (daily 10.15am–1pm & 3pm–midnight; €2).

The **bus terminus** is a couple of blocks back from the beach, on Avenida Dr. Sá Carneiro, with the **turismo** right by the beach on Praça do Mar (May –Sept Mon & Fri–Sun 10am–1.30pm & 2.30–7pm, Tues–Thurs 9.30am–7pm; Oct–May same hours until 6pm; ☎289 389 209). They should be able to help with finding **accommodation** if there's no room at the very pleasant *Pensão Miramar*, Rua Gonçalo Velho 8, off the seafront (☎289 315 225, ⓕ289 314 671; breakfast included; ❹) – some rooms here have sea views, while others face a charming plant-lined internal terrace. *Pensão Romeu*, on the same street at no. 38 (☎289 314 114; breakfast included; ❹), is similar in style but lacks the views. There's also a well-equipped **campsite** (☎289 302 821, ⓕ289 302 822) 1km east of town; any bus to or from Faro will stop outside it.

Quarteira boasts one of the Algarve's top seafood **restaurants**, *O Jacinto* at Avenida Dr. Sá Carneiro (☎289 301 887; closed Mon), which is on the north side of the main road through town; it's the best place to try Quarteira prawns, rated as some of the best in the world. For something decidedly less expensive, *Rosa Branca* (☎289 314 430), at the market end of the seafront, has decently priced fish and grilled meats and outdoor tables facing the sands.

Vilamoura

Now virtually merged with Quarteira, **VILAMOURA** is a complete contrast, a constantly expanding resort with a bewildering network of roads signposted to upmarket hotels and exclusive leisure facilities, including five renowned **golf courses**. It's perhaps *the* place in the Algarve to come and practise your swing, while another indication of the kind of clientele Vilamoura attracts is the ritzy **marina**, bristling with yachting hardware and lined by pricey international cafés. Various stalls offer **boat trips** which range from local excursions (from €15 for a two-hour trip) to dolphin-watching (up to €50 for a full-day excursion).

The only historical sight in Vilamoura is just to the northwest of the marina, where the **Museu Cerra da Vila** archeological site and museum (May–Sept Tues–Sun 10am–1pm & 3–8pm; Oct–April Tues–Sun 9.30am–12.30pm & 2–6pm; €2) displays the vestiges of a late Roman, Visigothic and Moorish colony. You can make out the foundations of a Roman mansion, baths and a fish-salting tank, together with well-preserved Roman mosaics laid out in a scrubby field.

The bus drops you next to the casino, one block from the impressive beach, the **Praia da Marina**. The enormous *Tivoli Marinotel* (☎289 303 303, Ⓦ www .tivolihotels.com; breakfast included; ❾) is typical of the accommodation here, a five-star place with every conceivable comfort, overlooking the marina. For a drink, meal or late-night action, *Sete* (☎289 313 943) in the marina is a fashionable chrome-and-steel **café–bar** part-owned by Portuguese soccer star Luís Figo, and named after his shirt number (*sete*, seven). Meanwhile, on the outskirts, opposite the Mobil garage on the Vilamoura–Albufeira road, *Kadoc* (11.30pm–6am: June–Sept daily; Oct–May Fri & Sat only) – the Algarve's biggest **club** – pulls in up to eight thousand revellers a night, and often hosts guest DJs from all over Europe.

Albufeira and around

ALBUFEIRA tops the list of package-tour destinations in the Algarve. The old centre remains an unusually pretty village, with narrow, twisting lanes of whitewashed houses crisscrossing the high ochre-red cliffs above a beautiful spread of beaches. Beyond, hundreds of apartment buildings lie strung across the hillsides that spread west around the town's marina. If you're looking for unspoiled Portugal, this isn't it – whatever the brochures might say. Nevertheless, Albufeira is undeniably a fun resort, attracting a varied mix of holidaymakers, notably a well-heeled clientele that frequents the more expensive restaurants, and a younger contingent who devote themselves to consuming as much alcohol as is humanly possible.

Although the 1755 earthquake did for much of the town, there's still a Moorish feel to parts of central Albufeira, as well as the more tangible remnants of a Moorish castle – the original Arabic name of the town, *Al-Buhera*, means "Castle-on-the-Sea". There are some fine beaches either side of the town, too. **Praia da Oura** and those further east towards **Praia da Falésia** are the more developed, while the cove beaches to the west, up to the swathe of sands at **Praia de Galé**, tend to be quieter. Inland, Albufueira is the nearest base for a couple of the Algarve's best family-orientated **theme parks**, while day-trips also run north into the hills to the pretty village of **Alte**.

Arrival and information

Albufeira's **bus terminal** is on Avenida da Liberdade, a five-minute walk from the central square, Largo Engenheiro Duarte Pacheco. Albufeira's nearest **train station** is 6km north of town at Ferreiras; a bus connects it with the bus terminal every 45 minutes or so (daily 7am–8pm), or a taxi will set you back about €8. There's a large, free **car park** just back from the bus station; any closer in

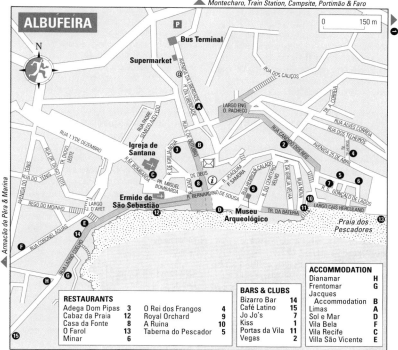

and you have to pay to park, though there are usually free places to the west of town – follow signs to "Albufeira Ponte".

If you're in Albufeira on a package holiday, you might well be staying in one of the handful of small resort-villages on either side of town. The largest of these, **Montechoro** is a downmarket suburb to the northeast, known as "the strip", with a gaudy Eurotrashy appeal. The easiest way to get in and out of town is on the **road train** which circles Albufeira and runs out to Montechoro (every 20min, 9.20am–midnight; €2 a trip, or €3/6 for half/full-day pass).

The **turismo** (Oct–May Mon & Fri–Sat 9.30am–12.30pm & 1.30–5.30pm, Tues–Thurs 9.30am–5.30pm; June–Sept same hours until 7pm; ☎289 585 279, ⓦwww.cm-albufeira.pt) is on Rua 5 de Outubro, close to the tunnel to the beach.

Accommodation

In high season most of the hotels and *pensões* are block-booked by package holiday companies. Those listed below may have "independent" vacancies, otherwise the tourist office can help you find a **private room** (❸), though they'll charge you for any phone calls they make. Alternatively, accept the offer of a room from one of the touts at the bus station; you can always look around on your own later if it's not up to scratch.

Hotels and pensions

Pensão Dianamar Rua Latino Coelho 36 ☏289 587 801, ⓦwww.dianamar.com. Well-run Swedish-owned *pensão* in the nicest part of town, a block from the beach. The simple en-suite rooms are pristine and breezy, and those at the top have great sea views, as does the communal roof terrace. Breakfast available, but costs extra. ❸

Pensão Residencial Frentomar Rua Latino Coelho ☏289 512 005, ⓔfrentomar@sapo.pt. Simple, clean rooms on a quiet side road. Get one with a sea view and you won't be disappointed, though these are usually snapped up quickly. ❸

Jacques Accommodation Rua 5 de Outubro 36 ☏969 584 933. Lovely town house with large, airy rooms – each with their own bathrooms – right on the main street to the beach. Closed Nov–March. ❹

Residencial Limas Rua da Liberdade 25–27 ☏289 514 025. Ten decent rooms in an attractive, yellow-faced building. Avoid the front ground floor rooms or it'll feel as if you're sleeping on the street. Breakfast included. ❹

Hotel Sol e Mar Rua Bernardino de Sousa ☏289 580 080, ⓦwww.grupofbarata.com. With its entrance above the tunnel to the beach, this somewhat characterless four-star hotel stretches down five floors to exit right on the beach. The balconies overlook the sands, while there's live entertainment, a small covered swimming pool and a large buffet breakfast. Parking. ❻

Residencial Vila Bela Rua Coronel Águas 32–34 ☏289 512 101, ⓔctr@mail.telepac.pt. Attractive *residencial* with its own bar and balconied rooms overlooking a small swimming pool and the bay. Breakfast included. April–Oct. ❹

Residencial Vila Recife Rua Miguel Bombarda 6 ☏289 583 740, ⓔvila.recife@iol.pt. This rambling *residencial* has its own garden and small pool. The communal areas are lined with *azulejos*, and while the en-suite rooms are on the small side they are comfortable, and the best have fine views. Breakfast included. Closed Nov–April. ❺

Villa São Vicente Hotel Largo Jacinto d'Ayet 4 ☏289 583 700, ⓦwww.hotel-vila-sao-vicente .com . A modern three-star hotel built in traditional style with tiled floors and whitewashed walls. It has its own small pool and a terrace facing the beach. You pay less for rooms facing the street, but it is worth the extra for the sea views. All rooms are en suite with TVs and air conditioning. Breakfast included. ❻, sea-view rooms ❼

Campsite

Camping Albufeira 2km to the north of town, off the N396 ☏289 587 629, ⓕ289 587 633. Expensive but well-appointed, complete with swimming pools, restaurants, bars, shops and tennis courts. There are regular connections from the bus station (any bus to Ferreiras passes it).

The Town

The focus of Albufeira is the main square, **Largo Engenheiro Duarte Pacheco**, a pretty, pedestrianized space with a small fountain and benches beneath palms and exotic trees. After dark, it's a magnet for families and promenaders, often serenaded by live performers and buskers. From the square, Rua 5 de Outubro leads down to the town **beach** – reached through a tunnel – as good as any in the region, flanked by strange tooth-like rock formations and with a particularly fine grotto at the west end; there are usually plenty of companies on the seafront offering **boat trips** (from around €5) up and down the neighbouring coastline. If it's too crowded here, a relatively short bus (or taxi) ride can open up a number of other good beaches, the best of which are detailed on pp.579–580.

Just above the tunnel to the beach, in the old town hall, the **Museu Arqueológico** (Tues–Sun: mid-Sept to May 10am–5pm; June to mid-Sept 2.30–8pm; free) presents a rather sparse but well laid out collection of artefacts gathered from the area from Neolithic times to the present. There are fragments of mosaics from a Roman villa, Visigothic rock tombs and jars, and even an Islamic silo excavated *in situ* beneath the museum.

Albufeira's other historic sites lie up the steps to the west of the tunnel, around Praça Miguel Bombarda. The **Ermide de São Sebastião** is one of the region's oldest churches with a distinctive Manueline door, though most of the building was constructed in the early eighteenth century. The church houses the **Museu Arte Sacra** (July–Oct daily 10am–midnight; free) a picturesque if

△ Cove beach, Central Algarve

uninspiring museum containing plaster images of saints; its most valuable items are a silver crown and chalice for Nossa Senhora Ourada, a local saint. Nearby, from the patio at the front of the whitewashed, domed **Igreja de Santana**, there are lovely views over the distinctive filigree chimneys of the old town and across the other church spires to the sea.

Eating

Albufeira has **restaurants** to match every budget – and most tastes. As well as Portuguese restaurants, there's also a whole range of places serving pizzas, Chinese and Indian food, even fish and chips. The morning-after-the-night-before is well catered for in most restaurants and bars, with massive **English–style breakfasts** available until the sensible hour of 3pm.

Adega Dom Pipas Trav. dos Arcos 78 ☎ 289 588 091. The mock olde-worlde decor and standard Portuguese menu are nothing special, but there are outdoor tables in an attractive narrow alley usually strung with coloured ribbons. Moderate.

Cabaz da Praia Pr. Miguel Bombarda 7 ☎ 289 512 137. With a roof terrace overlooking the beach, this French-inspired place has an excellent menu – feast on things like duck breast with quince and honey, or carpaccio of salmon, and finish off with one of the long list of desserts. Expensive.

Casa da Fonte Rua João de Deus 7 ☎ 289 514 578. A popular spot set around a beautiful Moorish-style courtyard complete with *azulejos*, lemon trees and a resident parrot – get there early if you want a courtyard table. There's a long menu but it boils down to the usual range of fish and meat. Moderate.

Restaurante O Farol Praia dos Pescadores ☎ 289 513 552. Simple beachside cafe-restaurant right behind the boats on the fisherman's beach. It's refreshingly unpretentious – though service can be excessively laid back – and the fresh fish and grilled meat come in generous portions. Moderate.

Minar Trav. Cais Herculano ☎ 289 513 196. Good-value Indian restaurant, where you'll eat for around

€15 – or €10 if you stick solely to the vegetarian dishes. Moderate.

A Taberna do Pescador Trav. Cais Herculano ☎ 289 589 196. A genuinely authentic Portuguese *taberna* that attracts as many locals as tourists, with an outdoor terrace where most of the barbecuing takes place. The fish, seafood and meats are grilled to perfection and portions are huge. Inexpensive.

O Rei dos Frangos Trav. dos Telheiros 4 ☎ 289 512 981. A first-rate *churrasqueira* – the chicken comes smothered in *piri-piri* and there's grilled steak, swordfish and a speciality meat *cataplana*. Inexpensive.

Royal Orchard Beco Bernardino de Sousa ☎ 289 502 505. Thai restaurant with sumptuous decor and tables laid out in a leafy courtyard. The long menu features noodle and rice dishes with fish, meat or seafood, though there's also a range of vegetarian options. Moderate.

A Ruina Largo Cais Herculano ☎ 289 512 094. Rustic old restaurant built into the cliffs over the beach. The lower, beachside area is the best place for those with kids, as they can play in the sand while you have a meal. The waiter will show you the latest fish catch, but check the price when ordering as there is no menu. Expensive.

Drinking and nightlife

At night, the focus switches to Albufeira's pedestrianized streets. **Rua Candido dos Reis** is the focal point of a writhing mass of humanity parading past handicraft and souvenir stalls, or sitting at bars and cafés which vie with each other to play the loudest music and offer the most over-the-top cocktails. Like the restaurants, Albufeira **bars** and **clubs** are into promotion and, since there's not much to choose between them, you may as well frequent those offering the cheapest drinks at the time – Happy Hour is an extremely flexible concept here. The other main areas for carousing are along Rua São Gonçalo de Lagos, around Largo Engenheiro Duarte Pacheco and on Rua Alves Correira. Most bars stay open until around 3am, the clubs until 6am or later in summer.

Bizarro Bar Esplanada Dr. Frutuosa Silva 30. This attractive bar is high above the eastern end of the beach, with superb views over the sands from its front terrace. Closed Sun.

Jo Jo's Rua São Gonçalo de Lagos 1. Friendly family-run pub with British soccer and other sports on satellite TV – the owner proudly recalls the day Paul Gascoigne and his mates got hopelessly drunk here. The bar food always includes a vegetarian option.

Kiss Rua Vasco da Gama, Areias de São João. Out of town, this glitzy place is regarded as the best club around. It often hosts foreign guest DJs (keep an eye out for flyers), but tends to be overcrowded.

May–Sept open nightly from midnight, Oct–April Sat & Sun only.

Café Latino Rua Latino Coelho 59. A superb spot to start off an evening with a cocktail – the back terrace has fantastic views over the town and the beach, while inside there are spinning ceiling fans and a snooker table. Closed Mon.

Portas da Vila Rua da Bateria. High-ceilinged cocktail and sangria bar, just above the old fish market, next to the site of the old gates to the castle.

Vegas Rua Candido dos Reis 22–26. Café, bar and club offering everything from milkshakes to rudely named cocktails, live soccer to thumping dance sounds.

Listings

Banks and exchange Banks and ATMs are grouped around Largo Eng. Duarte Pacheco.
Bike/motorbike rental Vespa Rent ☎289 542 377, ⓦwww.vesparent.com will deliver to your hotel; scooters from €60 for 3 days.
Bookshop Julie's, Rua Igreja Nova 6 (Mon–Fri 10am–6pm, Sat 10am–1pm, Sun 10am–3pm) stocks a large range of English-language books, most of them secondhand.
Bullfights Take place weekly from May to October, usually on Saturdays. The bullring is a five-minute taxi ride to the east. Tickets (available from travel agents round town or at the arena) start at around €30.
Car rental Avis, Rua Igreja Nova 13 ☎289 512 678; Hertz, Rua Manuel Teixeira Gomes Bloco 1, Areias de São João ☎289 542 920.
Health Centre Urbanização dos Caliços, 2km north of the centre ☎289 588 770 or 289 587 550 (open 24 hours). The nearest hospital is in Faro or Portimão.

Internet access Augusto's, Av. da Liberdade 81 (Mon–Sat 10am–midnight), just south of the bus terminal.
Markets A lively flea market takes place to the north of the centre at Urbanização dos Caliços, 2km north of the centre, on the first and third Tues of each month.
Pharmacy Farmácia de Sousa, Rua 5 de Outubro 40.
Police Contact the local police on ☎289 512 205.
Post office Rua 5 de Outubro (Mon–Fri 8.30am–5.30pm).
Supermarket Alisuper, Av. da Liberdade, near the bus station (daily 8am–8pm).
Taxi There's a taxi rank next to the bus station. To order a cab call ☎289 583 230.
Travel agents Rua 5 de Outubro has row upon row of travel agents offering everything from tickets to bullfights to tours (inland Algarve, Lisbon, Spain or Gibraltar).

The local beaches

Immediately **east of Albufeira**, ochre-red cliffs divide the coastline into a series of bays and beaches, all reached on local buses (8–12 daily) from the bus station. You can also walk to the first, **PRAIA DA OURA**, just 2km away, by heading down Albufeira's beach and up along a rocky bluff along a coastal path. This, though, has been extensively developed and you might want to push on by bus to **OLHOS DE ÁGUA**, 7km further east, an erstwhile fishing village with an attractive beach. If this, too, is crowded, there is generally space at **PRAIA DA FALÉSIA**, 10km east of Albufeira, which is one tremendous stretch of sand backed by unbroken red cliffs topped with sprawling villa complexes.

Most of the development behind the red headlands **west of Albufeira** is set back from a series of cliff-backed cove beaches. There are no direct buses to these resorts, though the Albufeira–Portimão service drops passengers on the main road, a steep 2km walk away. **SÃO RAFAEL**, 2km west of Albufeira, and

cafés above a narrow gully. The road loops down over a dried up river valley, at the bottom of which is a fine beach under high cliffs. *Vila Linda Mar* (℡282 352 812, ⓦwww.algarve-paradise.com; breakfast included; ❺), 1.5 kilometres back from the beach, is a tasteful, traditionally decorated guest house with gardens and a small pool. The restaurant here (moderate; closed Tues) serves superb Algarvian dishes, including smoked ham from Monchique and *gambas com espinafres* (prawns with spinach).

West of Benagil, the scenery changes again with coastal development crowding in around another appealing beach at **PRAIA DE CENTIANES**, 3km away. From here, the road is lined with villas and apartments all the way to Carvoeiro.

Carvoeiro

Cut into the red sea cliffs, the small resort of **CARVOEIRO** must once have been an attractive fishing village, but now its small cove beach has to support the prostrate bodies of hundreds of tourists shipped in to what has become an overblown resort. The beach is pleasant enough, though it's rockier and less impressive than many along this stretch, and most accommodation is in the form of block-booked apartments. Out of season, perhaps, the town has more appeal, and at least it is within range of a couple of superb neighbouring beaches, Praia de Centianes and Benagil (see above). Accessible by the coast road, and by a road train that trundles out every 20 minutes or so (€3 round trip) a kilometre east, are the impressive rock formations of **Algar Seco**, where steps lead down low cliffs to a series of dramatic overhangs above blow holes and grottoes.

The **turismo** (mid-Sept to May Mon–Fri 9.30am–1pm & 2–5.30pm; June to mid-Sept daily 9.30am–7pm; ℡282 357 728), just behind the beach, can help with **private rooms**. *Hotel Carvoeiro Sol* (℡282 357 301, ⓔcarvoeirosol@mail.telepac.pt; breakfast included; ❼, sea-view rooms ❽) is the most comfortable hotel, a four-star property right by the beach. Rooms come with small balconies, and there's also a pool, courtyard bar and a babysitting service. The best budget option is *O Castelo,* Rua da Casino 59–61 (℡ & ℻282 357 416, ⓔcasteloguesthouse@clix.pt; ❸), which has three clean, modern rooms with a superb view over the beach – take the road that overlooks the beach uphill above the tourist office and it's a five-minute walk.

For slides, pools and aquatic fun, **Slide & Splash** theme park (daily April–Oct 10am–5pm; €15.50, children €12.50; ⓦwww.slidesplash.com) is just a short drive just outside Estômbar, signposted off the N125 at Vale de Deus.

Portimão and around

Portimão is one of the largest towns on the Algarve, with a population of more than thirty thousand. Sited on the estuary of the Rio Arade, it has made its living from fishing since pre-Roman times and today remains a sprawling port, as well as being a base for the construction industries spawned by the tourist boom. Most visitors are just here for a day's shopping, taking time out from the full-blown resort of **Praia da Rocha**, 3km south of Portimão. Just across the estuary to the east is the more traditional village of **Ferragudo**, which has a castle right on a small beach. The coast road west of Praia da

Rocha, towards Lagos, has been engulfed by a series of massive and graceless tourist developments fronting more sweeping beaches; only **Alvor**, slightly inland, retains its original charm.

Portimão

As a town, **PORTIMÃO** is fairly undistinguished – most of the older buildings were destroyed in the 1755 earthquake. Its most historic building is the **Igreja da Nossa Senhora da Conceição**, rebuilt after the earthquake, but retaining a Manueline door from the original fourteenth-century structure; the interior is more impressive, covered in sevententh-century *azulejos*. The encircling streets are pleasant enough, filled with shops selling lace, shoes,

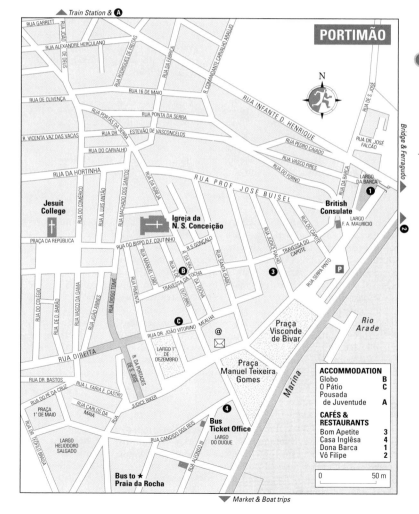

▼ *Market & Boat trips*

ACCOMMODATION

Globo	B
O Pátio	C
Pousada de Juventude	A

CAFÉS & RESTAURANTS

Bom Apetite	3
Casa Inglêsa	4
Dona Barca	1
Vô Filipe	2

0   50 m

jewellery, ceramics and wicker goods; the main shopping streets are around the pedestrianized Rua Diogo Tomé and Rua da Portades de São José. Just off the latter street lies Largo 1 de Dezembro, an attractive square with seats inlaid with *azulejos* depicting historical scenes.

However, the best part of town is undoubtedly the **riverfront**, where a series of squares – Largo do Duque, Praça Manuel Teixeira Gomes and Praça Visconde de Bivar – are filled with outdoor cafés beneath shady trees. You'll be approached by people offering **boat trips** along the coast to see the grottoes (2hr; €15), while three-hour trips (around €20) also go up the Rio Arade to Silves (departure times depend on the tides).

Heading up the river and under the road bridge you'll find a series of open-air restaurants serving inexpensive grilled sardine lunches. The streets just back from the bridge – off **Largo da Barca** – are Portimão's oldest: narrow, cobbled and with more than a hint of their fishing-quarter past. Other reasons to come to town are the huge **market** on the first Monday of each month, selling secondhand clothes, ceramics, CDs and junk; it's held near the riverfront on Estrada da Rocha, just southwest of town towards Praia da Rocha. On the morning of the first and third Sunday of each month, a **flea market** spreads out past the railway station in the Parque das Exposições.

Practicalities

The **train station** is inconveniently located at the northern tip of town but a bus runs into the centre every 45 minutes (Mon–Fri only); a taxi costs about €4 or it's a fifteen-minute walk. **Buses** (including those to and from Praia da Rocha) pull up in the streets around Largo do Duque, close to the river. There's a **post office** in Praça Manuel Teixeira Gomes while the Algarve's only **British consulate** is further up the quayside at Largo Francisco A. Mauricio 7-1° (☎282 490 750).

Portimão has a good *Pousada de Juventude* at Lugar do Coca, Maravilhas (☎282 491 804, ⓦwww.pousadasjuventude.pt; dorm beds €10, rooms ❷), a large modern place with its own small swimming pool, bar, canteen and sports facilities – it's a twenty-minute walk out of the centre. Otherwise, the better-value **accommodation** options include the modern *Hotel Globo*, Rua 5 de Outubro 151 (☎282 416 350, Ⓕ282 483 142; breakfast included; ❺), and the *Residencial O Pátio*, Rua Dr. João Vitorino Mealha 3 (☎282 424 288, Ⓕ282 424 281; breakfast included; ❸), with simpler rooms but a groovy bar. *Vô Filipe* is the best of the row of inexpensive fish **restaurants** north of the old bridge, on the riverfront – they all specialize in grilled sardines, though other fish and meat dishes are available. Nearby are some more expensive fish restaurants, such as the highly rated *Dona Barca* in Largo da Barca (☎282 484 189), or try friendly *Bom Apetite*, Rua Júdice Fialho 21 (closed Sun), which serves authentic Portuguese cuisine, including a splendid *arroz de marisco*. Finally, *Casa Inglêsa* in the riverside Praça Manuel Teixeira Gomes is a thoroughly pleasant café with outdoor tables.

Praia da Rocha

PRAIA DA ROCHA, five minutes' south of Portimão by bus, was one of the first Algarve tourist developments and it's easy to see why. The beach is one of the most beautiful on the entire coast, the wide expanse of sand framed by jagged sea cliffs and the walls of an old fort built in 1691. The **Fortaleza da Santa Caterina** once protected the mouth of the Rio Arade and its terrace offers splendid views at sunset – beach and ocean on one side, Ferragudo, river

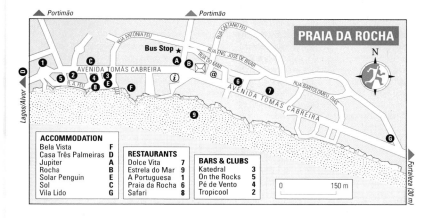

and marina on the other. The effect is only spoiled by the high-rise hotels, discos and casino that sit on the clifftop behind the beach, all but swamping the town's original *fin-de-siècle* villas. Most of the development lies channelled in a strip just two blocks wide, with the beach reached down steep steps from the elevated main street, Avenida Tomás Cabreira – which means that from virtually every bar, restaurant and hotel terrace the views are of the sands and sea. There's little that is traditionally Portuguese, of course, but it is lively enough to be fun at whatever time of year you visit.

Practicalities

There's a **bus** from Portimão every fifteen to thirty minutes (7.30am–11.30pm) and it stops in front of the *Hotel da Rocha* on Avenida Tomás Cabreira. If you plan to do much to-ing and fro-ing, buy a block of ten tickets from the bus-stop kiosk in Portimão, which will save you around fifty percent. Drivers should note that the main coast road is one-way west to east; it is best to **park** on the main drag in from Portimão. The **turismo** (May to mid-Sept daily 9.30am–7pm; mid-Sept to April Mon & Fri–Sun 10am–1.30pm & 2.30–6pm, Tues–Thurs 9.30am–6pm; ☎282 419 132) is opposite the bus stop by the beach. Cyberspace, just east of the tourist office on Avenida Tomás Cabreira, has **internet** access (daily 2–8pm).

Finding **accommodation** is rarely a problem; ask at the turismo about the array of private rooms to rent (❸), or try one of the following *pensões* or more expensive hotels, all of which offer sea-facing rooms, pools and heavily reduced winter rates. **Restaurants** are plentiful and the half a dozen down on the beach mean that you don't have to leave the sands during the day. For a civilized **drink**, the lovely bar of the *Hotel Bela Vista* is open to the public (8.30pm–midnight), though there are plenty of far more rowdy places too.

Hotels and pensions

Hotel Bela Vista Av. Tomás Cabreira ☎282 450 480, ⓦ www.hotelbelavista.net. The most stylish place to stay on the seafront, a pseudo-Moorish mansion built in 1903 by the wealthy Magalhães family as a wedding gift. The rooms and communal areas are an exquisite mixture of carved wood, stained glass, and yellow, white

and blue *azulejos*. Breakfast included. Parking. ❻

Casa Três Palmeiras Praia do Vau, 2km west of Praia da Rocha ☎282 401 275, ⓦ www .casatrespalmeiras.com. In a sublime position on a clifftop above a little beach, this sleek villa is a superb example of 1960s chic. Glass-fronted rooms curve around a terrace with a pool, where breakfast is served in summer. Rooms and communal areas are spacious and tastefully furnished in traditional Portuguese style. Services available include manicures, reflexology and massages, and discounts are available for local golf courses. Breakfast included. Parking. Closed Dec & Jan. ⑥

Hotel Jupiter Av. Tomás Cabreira ☏ 282 415 041, ✉ hoteljupiter@mail.telepac.pt. A modern hulk on the wrong (land) side of the Avenida, but with all mod cons including a bar and swimming pool. Breakfast included. ⑥

Hotel da Rocha Av. Tomás Cabreira ☏ 282 424 081, ✉ hoteldarocha@clix.pt. Affordable three-star, well positioned, with its own bar, restaurant and comfortable rooms. Breakfast included. ⑥

Solar Penguin Rua António Feu ☏ & ☏ 282 424 308. On the cliffs above the beach, just off the main avenue, this delightful old *pensão* has faintly shabby but airy rooms overlooking the sea. In the antiquated lounge there's a portrait of Queen Elizabeth, which was painted by the late husband of the owner. Closed mid-Nov to mid-Jan. ③

Residencial Sol Av. Tomás Cabreira 10 ☏ 282 424 071, ☏ 282 419 944. Standard rooms in a modern block opposite the *Katedral* nightclub – so pick from noisy rooms with sea views or quieter ones without much to look at. ③

Residencial Vila Lido Av. Tomás Cabreira ☏ 282 424 127, ☏ 282 424 246. Beautiful blue-shuttered building with original decor in its own small grounds facing the fort. Front rooms have superb views over the beach. Breakfast included. ⑤

Cafés and restaurants

Estrela do Mar On the beach ☏ 282 427 495. Has a terrace facing the sands and serves good-value fish, salads, meat dishes and ice cream. Inexpensive.

La Dolce Vita Av. Tomás Cabreira ☏ 282 419 444. Owned and run by Italians, so the home-made pastas and pizzas are authentic and pretty good value; set lunch €7. There's live music at weekends. Moderate.

A Portuguesa Av. Tomás Cabreira ☏ 282 424 175. Good for Portuguese grills, backed by gentle jazzy sounds. Closed Sun. Inexpensive.

Cervejaria Praia da Rocha Edifício Colunas, off Av. Tomás Cabreira ☏ 282 416 514. Attracts a largely Portuguese crowd for excellent daily specials and seafood. Moderate.

Safari Rua António Feu ☏ 282 423 540. The restaurant overlooks the beach and while it's a mainly Portuguese menu, there are a few dishes with an Angolan influence. Moderate.

Bars and clubs

Katedral Av. Tomás Cabreira. Housed in a futuristic cube on the clifftop, this is the largest and highest-profile club in town, with a lightshow and the latest dance sounds. The downstairs bar, *Nicho*, is a good place to start the evening. Open midnight–6am, June–Sept daily, Oct–May Thurs–Sat only.

On the Rocks Av. Tomás Cabreira, Lojas B & C. A modern dance bar with a sunset terrace. Live soccer on TV sometimes vies for attention in the bar; there's also a dance floor and live music on Fridays. Daily 10am–4am.

Pé de Vento Av. Tomás Cabreira, Loja A. Popular disco-bar on two floors. The upstairs bar has a beach-facing terrace, next to a large dance floor which features live music on Wednesdays. Daily 3pm–4am.

Ferragudo

Surprisingly, **FERRAGUDO**, facing Portimão across the estuary, has made relatively few concessions to international tourism. It is centred on a strip of palm-fringed gardens which spread alongside a narrow riverlet up to the cobbled main square, Praça Rainha Dona Leonor, a wide space dotted with cafés. The riverlet ends at the Rio Arade estuary, where there is a small fishing harbour and a few fish restaurants backed by a waterfront promenade. South of here, the old town spreads up the side of a hill, a warren of atmospheric cobbled backstreets gathered around the town church; from its terrace there are great views over the estuary. Below the church – accessible from the fishing harbour or by taking the road that skirts the old town – lies the town beach, which gets progressively more appealing as it approaches the **Castelo de São João do Arade**, one of the only forts in Portugal that lies right behind a sandy beach. The fort (closed to the public), a partner to that in Praia da Rocha, is a tremendous site – built in the sixteenth century to defend Portimão against attack.

The town is connected to Portimão by a regular **bus** service (hourly 7.30am–7.30pm), which drops you on the main road by Praça Rainha Dona Leonor. **Accommodation** is somewhat limited, and the best option is *Quinta da Horta* (T282 461 395, Eart-ferragudo@clix.pt; ❹, apartment ❻) just out of town – follow the concrete riverlet east for ten minutes and it is on the right. Run by a British artist, who runs art courses and the occasional naturist meeting, it sports a series of tasteful studios, as well as a two-room apartment, set round a hacienda-style garden full of tropical plants. There's also a small plunge pool, sauna, TV room and tennis court; the price includes a superb organic breakfast.

There are a number of lively cafés and bars on the main square, while *Sueste* on the riverfront Rua da Ribeira (T282 461 592; closed Mon) is the most arty and buzzy of a row of fish **restaurants** facing the harbour. Better value, though far more basic, is *O Velho Novo*, Rua Manuel Teixeira Gomes 2 (dinner only), five minutes' walk from the main square – cross the riverlet along the road signed to Belavista and it's on the left – where good-value fish and meat is grilled on an outside barbecue.

The town beach stretches below the castle, and there's another at **Praia Grande** around the headland, about a kilometre south of town, which also has a scattering of restaurant-bars. A large **campsite**, the *Parque Campismo de Ferragudo* (T282 461 121), lies 3km out of Ferragudo beyond Praia Grande, but it is only open to members of the International Camping Club. It has a pool, kids' play area, large supermarket and restaurant, and is just fifteen minutes' walk from two superb cove beaches, **Praia Pintadinho** and **Praia da Caneiros**, both with beachside bar-restaurants (closed Nov–March).

Alvor and Quinta da Rocha

The resorts immediately west of Praia da Rocha – Vau and Praia Três Irmãos – have good beaches but little else going for them, and it is better to push on to historic **ALVOR**, 6km west of Praia da Rocha. The ancient port briefly achieved fame as the place where Dom João II died in 1495 and, though much of the town was razed in the 1755 earthquake, it still boasts a sixteenth century Igreja Matriz with Manueline doors, arches and pillars carved into fishing ropes and plants. It remained a sleepy fishing village until the 1960s, when tourism began to take hold, and today the old town has been outgrown by a sprawl of modern – though largely low-rise – buildings. Nevertheless, the old town around the church and the central Praça da República retains its character, while the harbour itself is a delight, lined with colourful fishing boats and aromatic fish restaurants.

The town's **turismo** is in the centre of town at Rua Dr. Alfonso Costa 51 (daily: July–Sept 9.30am–7pm; Oct–June 10am–1.30pm & 2.30–6pm; T282 457 540). From here it is a short walk uphill to the leafy ruin that is Alvor's **castle**, which dates back to the thirteenth century but now houses a children's playground. From here, Rua Padre David Neto leads onto Rua Dr Frederico Romas Mendes, the main drag lined with bars and restaurants. This stretches down to the riverside **Largo da Ribeira**, marked by a modern statue of a fish, where you'll find the former market building. Half a dozen fish restaurants here, most with outdoor seating, overlook the picturesque estuary of the Rio Alvor. Head right as you face the river and a path leads up the estuary for a tranquil walk; bear left and it is a ten-minute stroll past fishermen's huts to the **Praia de Alvor**, an enormous beach backed by café-bars.

Rooms can be hard to come by, though there are plenty of expensive **hotels** around 1km east of Alvor, facing the beach. The best bet in town is *Hospedaria*

Buganvilia, Rua Padre Mendes Rossio de 5 Pedro (T 282 459 412; breakfast included; ❹), just down the hill from the turismo, a modern place above a decent restaurant. Most rooms have balconies and there's also a roof terrace. *Campismo Dourado* (T 282 459 178, F 282 458 002) lies around 1km north of Alvor, near the N125, a pleasant, leafy **campsite** with a small shop.

One of a row of decently priced fish **restaurants** on the harbourfront Largo da Ribeira, *Casa da Maré* (T 282 458 191; closed Sun) has tables spilling out onto the square. Even better is the inexpensive *Tasca do Margadinho* at Largo da Ribeira 9 (T 282 459 144; closed Thurs), an atmospheric place opposite the old fish market serving grilled fresh fish. Down on the sands, *Restaurante Restina* (T 282 459 434; closed one month in winter) sits on the cusp of a large dune and offers great views to go with its moderately priced fish and grills.

Quinta da Rocha lies on the peninsula between the mouths of the rivers Alvor and Odiáxere, northwest of Alvor's huge beach. It is an extensive area which, in the parts not given over to citrus and almond groves, consists of copses, salt marshes, sandy spits and estuarine mud flats, forming a wide range of habitats for different species of animals and birds – including twenty-two species of wading bird. You can follow paths and tracks around the reserve by taking the turning off the main N125 opposite Mexilheira Grande; there are no marked trails, but follow any of the tracks into the wetlands.

Silves and around

Eighteen kilometres northeast of Portimão, **SILVES** – the medieval residence and capital of the Moorish kings of the al-Gharb – merits a half-day's detour. It has a superb castle and a highly dramatic approach, with its red ring of walls gradually revealing their course as you emerge from the wooded hills. Under the Moors, Silves was a place of grandeur, described in contemporary accounts as "of shining brightness" within its three dark circuits of guarding walls. Such glories and civilized splendours came to an end, however, in 1189, with the arrival of **Sancho I**, at the head of a mixed army of Portuguese and Crusaders. Sancho, desperately in need of extra fighting force, had recruited a rabble of "large and odious" northerners, who had already been expelled from the holy shrine of St James of Compostela for their irreligious behaviour. The army arrived at Silves toward the end of June and the thirty thousand Moors retreated to the citadel. There they remained through the long, hot summer, sustained by huge water cisterns and granaries, until September when, the water exhausted, they opened negotiations.

Sancho was ready to compromise, but the Crusaders had been recruited by the promise of plunder. The gates were opened after Sancho had negotiated guarantees for the inhabitants' personal safety and goods; all were brutally ignored by the Crusaders, who duly ransacked the town, killing some six thousand Moors in the process. Silves passed back into Moorish hands two years later, but by then the town had been irreparably weakened, and it finally fell to Christian forces in 1249.

The Town

The **Moorish Fortaleza** (daily: July–Aug 9am–8pm; Sept–June 9am–6pm; last entry 30min before closing; €1.25) remains the focal point of Silves, dominating the town centre with its impressively complete set of sandstone walls and detached towers. It is currently undergoing extensive renovation, which will eventually re-create a Moorish-style garden, a traditional well and the governor's palace, but this is unlikely to be completed until 2006. Renovation also restricts access to the wonderful vaulted thirteenth-century water cistern, the **Cisterna Grande**, which once served the town. Some 10m in height and supported by six columns, the cistern is said to be haunted by a Moorish maiden who can be seen sailing across the underground waters during a full moon. However, you can still clamber onto the castle walls for impressive views over the town and surrounding hills.

Silves's **Sé** (Mon–Fri 8.30am–6.30pm, limited hours on Sun; free) sits below the fortress, built on the site of the Grand Mosque. Flanked by broad Gothic towers, it has a suitably defiant, military appearance, though the Great Earthquake and centuries of impoverished restoration have left their mark within. The tombs lining the cathedral walls are of bishops and of Crusaders who died taking Silves back from the Moors. Opposite the Sé, it is worth a quick look in the newer **Igreja da Misericórdia** (Mon–Fri 9.30am–1pm & 2–5.30pm; free), a sixteenth-century church with a fine Manueline doorway and hung with seven impressive religious paintings, some of them dating back to the seventeenth century.

Below the Sé, in Rua das Portas de Loulé, is the town's **Museu Arqueologia** (Mon–Sat 9am–6pm; €1.50). It's engaging enough, despite a lack of English-language labelling, and romps through the history of Silves from the year dot to the sixteenth century with displays of local archeological finds. At the centre of the museum is an Arab water cistern, which boasts a ten-metre-deep well.

Silves's other main attraction is the **Fabrica de Inglês** (Tues–Sun 12.30–3pm & 7–10.30pm; free except during special events; @www.fabrica-de-ingles.com), near the riverfront, five minutes' walk east of the road bridge. A series of cafés, bars and fountains are clustered round a large central courtyard filled with outdoor tables below scented orange trees. It is a lovely space, most animated when it hosts the annual summer **Silves Beer Festival**, usually in July. At this time – and on Friday evenings in summer – the cafés and bars are heaving, and a spectacular light show illuminates the fountains. The one permanent attraction is the **Museu da Cortiças** (daily 9.30am–12.45pm & 2–6.15pm; €2), a cork museum in the northwest corner of the complex, which won the European Industrial Museum Award in 2001. But unless you have a keen interest in the cork industry its displays are unlikely to get your pulse going.

There's a **market** (Mon–Sat 8am–1pm) on the riverfront, near the narrow thirteenth-century bridge. This is a fine place to sit outside at one of the grill-cafés and watch life go by.

Practicalities

The **train station** – an easy approach from either Lagos or Faro – lies 2km out of town; there is a connecting bus, or you can walk if you're not weighed down with luggage. **Buses** stop on the main road, next to the market, near the riverfront at the foot of town. The town **turismo** is in a small kiosk below the town hall on Largo de Município (Mon–Fri 9.30am–1pm & 2–5.30pm; ☏282 442 325, @www.cm-silves.pt), while just around the corner in the heart of town at Rua 25 de Abril 26–28 is a **regional turismo** (Mon–Sat 10am–1.30pm & 2.30–6pm, until 7pm in July–Sept; ☏282 442 255).

Apart from **private rooms** (ask at the town turismo), there are a couple of basic **pensões**, including the faded but central *Residencial Sousa*, Rua Samora Barros 17 (☏282 442 502; ❷), and, across the river, the somewhat poky but nicely positioned *Restaurante Residencial Ponte Romana* (☏282 443 275; breakfast included; **②**). A more upmarket option is *Hotel Colina dos Mouros* (☎282 440 420, ☎282 440 426; breakfast included; **⑤**), a prominent modern hotel over the road bridge opposite the fortress, which has an outdoor pool, and rooms with superb views over the town. Or you can drive out to *Quinta do Rio*, at Sitio São Estevão (☎ & ☎282 445 528; breakfast included; **③**), around 5km out of town off the road to São Bartolomeu de Messines, a country inn with six rustic-style rooms with shaded terraces facing orange groves and grazing horses. The Italian owners can supply evening meals on request.

In town, the *Restaurante Marisqueira Rui*, Rua Comendador Vilarinho (☎282 442 682; closed Tues), is rated one of the Algarve's finest seafood **restaurants**; it's pricey but recommended. Alternatively, *U Monchiqueiro* (closed Wed) is one of the best of a handful of inexpensive grill-cafés on the riverfront road in front of the market. Sit outside and tuck into *piri-piri* chicken, fries, salad and wine for around €10. *Café Inglês* on Escadas do Castelo (☎282 442 585; closed Mon evening, Sat lunch & all day Sun), by the fortress, is a fashionably restored town house which sells delicious home-made snacks, ice cream and fruit juices, as well as full meals, including pizzas on the roof terrace in summer; it also has seats outside, live music at weekends and the occasional art exhibition. For something simpler, *Pastelaria Rosa*, in Largo do Município, is a superb old *pastelaria* with a cool *azulejo*-lined interior and a counter smothered in cakes and goodies. Outdoor tables spill onto the pretty main square next to a small fountain.

Barragem do Arade

Around 8km northeast of Silves, signed off the road to São Bartolomeu de Messines, the **Barragem do Arade** makes a good excursion for watersports, a swim or a walk. This is one of the area's main sources of water, set amongst rolling, tree-lined hills. It's an attractive spot, popular with campervanners and migrating birds, though when the water level falls its scarred sides spoil the picturesque effect.

Just as the dam itself comes into view, take the left hand fork to *Café Coutada*, which offers slightly pricey drinks and meals on an outdoor terrace filled with twittering caged birds. The café can organize boat trips (€7.50 per person) to a scraggy, tree-lined offshore islet known as **Paradise Island**; the fee covers the return trip together with use of canoes, sunloungers and swimming in a cordoned-off area of the reservoir. You can also hire jet skis at the café.

The Serra de Monchique

Nine weekday buses – five at weekends – leave Portimão for the 24km journey north to the market town of **Monchique** via the spa town of **Caldas de Monchique**. These both lie in the **Serra de Monchique**, a green and wooded mountain range of cork, chestnut and eucalyptus that provides the western Algarve with a natural northern boundary. This area bears the brunt of summer fires that seem to rage annually, but the woodland is generally quick to recover and it remains ideal hiking country. Cyclists or drivers have the option of cutting across afterwards to the wilder reaches of the western Algarve coast, along the minor N267, which passes through the little mountain village of Marmelete and continues all the way to Aljezur (see p.606). It's a fine route, heading through tranquil countryside before swinging down through the hills and forests to the west coast.

Caldas de Monchique

CALDAS DE MONCHIQUE, set in a ravine and surrounded by thick woods, has been a celebrated spa since Roman times. In 1495 Dom João II came here to take the waters (though he nevertheless died soon afterwards in Alvor), and in the nineteenth century the town became a favourite resort of the Spanish bourgeoisie. In 2000, virtually the entire village was purchased by the Monchique Termas company, who set about sympathetically restoring the run-down buildings round the main square into hotels and guest houses, revitalizing the cafés and shops and completely modernizing the spa itself. In doing so they have transformed a somewhat ramshackle spa resort into a tourist village – but the results, so far at least, have been fairly successful.

Caldas is 19km north of Portimão, and the centre is reached by a looping, one-way side road off the main Monchique road. Halfway down the hill on the left you'll see the cobbled, tree-shaded main square, fronted by the pseudo-Moorish windows of the former casino – now a *pensão* – and surrounded by lovely nineteenth-century buildings. The setting is as beautiful as any in the country, though the tiny village's peace and quiet is shattered daily by busloads of day-trippers.

Head downhill and you pass the **Bouvet** – a little stone building where you can sample the waters straight from the ground. The modern **thermal spa** (Mon 9am–1pm, Tues 10.30am–1pm & 3–7pm, Wed–Sun 9am–1pm & 3–7pm; €23; ⓦ www.monchiquetermas.com) sits below here, on the edge of a ravine, flaunting its well-kept gardens and housing various specialist water treatments on the ground floor of a modern hotel. The entrance fee gives access to the sauna, steam room, gym, water massage facilities and pool, with extra sessions ranging from 40-minute "tired leg" treatment (€25) to full body massages from €50. Discounts are available to hotel guests.

Climbing up from the spa, above the square, you can follow the stream to sit under giant eucalyptus trees – a wonderful spot for a picnic. Take along some of the local drink – *medronho* – a kind of schnapps made from the arbutus (or strawberry tree) that grows on the surrounding hills.

Practicalities

Not all **buses** from Portimão call into the centre of Caldas, some stopping instead on the main road just out of town before continuing up to Monchique. Still, it's only a minute's walk downhill to the main square. There's a four-star **inn** just above the main square, the *Albergaria do Lageado* (☎ 282 912 616, Ⓕ 282 911 310; closed Nov–April; breakfast included; ❹), which has twenty smart en-suite rooms, a bar and a pool in the garden, and an excellent restaurant where you can eat for around €15. Apart from this, the rest of the **accommodation** is owned by the Monchique Termas company (☎ 282 910 910), including the *Pensão Central* (breakfast included; ❺), a very comfortable three-star *pension* partly set in the former casino building on the main square; and *Estalagem Dom João 11* (breakfast included; ❺), opposite, a four-star inn in another converted nineteenth-century building, with marginally larger rooms. Monchique Termas also rents out apartments (sleeping up to four people; ❻) overlooking the main square, with small living rooms and kitchenettes.

Good places to eat include *Restaurante 1692* (☎ 282 910 910), named after its year of construction, with tables set out under the square's trees – the food's not particularly cheap, but the menu has some interesting appetizers such as *morcelo* (spicy sausage) and melon with ham. For something simpler, *O Tasco*, on the far side of the main square, below the path up to the picnic tables, is a darkened **bar** set in sixteenth-century stables, the oldest building in the village. Specialities include bread rolls with sausage meat inside, baked in the traditional exterior oven.

Monchique

MONCHIQUE, 6km to the north of Caldas de Monchique, and 300m higher up the range, is a small hill town whose large market on the second Friday of each month is famous for smoked hams and locally made furniture – especially the distinctive x-shaped wooden chairs. The most impressive building in town is the **Igreja Matriz** (Mon–Sat 10am–5.30pm; free), up a steep cobbled street from the main square, Largo 5 de Outubro, but the rest of Monchique is worth a wander too – it's dotted with beautifully crafted metal sculptures of local characters made by a contemporary Lisbon artist. The most evocative local sight, though, is the ruined seventeenth-century monastery of **Nossa Senhora do Desterro**, which you can walk to up a wooded track – brown signs point you up here from Rua do Porto Fundo, the road leading uphill from the bus station. Only a rickety shell of this Franciscan foundation survives, apparently quite uncared for, but it's in a great position overlooking the town and shows a beautiful blend of classical Renaissance facade with Moorish-influenced vaulting.

Practicalities

Buses arrive at the terminal in the main square, Largo 5 de Outubro. Opposite here, Monchique's helpful **turismo** (Mon–Fri 10am–1.30pm & 2.30–6pm; ℡282 911 189, ⓦwww.cm-monchique.pt) sits on a pretty, pedestrianized part of the square. There are a couple of budget **places to stay** in town, first choice the very welcoming *Estrela de Monchique*, Rua do Porto Fundo 46 (℡282 913 111; ❸), a stone's throw to the right of the bus terminal. Otherwise, facing the main Largo 5 de Outubro, the *Bela Vista* (℡282 912 252; ❷) offers basic comforts above a decent café. The front rooms have balconies facing the square, but these can be noisy.

Better by far are the **inns** on the road up to Fóia (see below), though you'll need your own transport to reach them. The *Estalagem Abrigo da Montanha*, a couple of kilometres from the centre (℡282 912 131, Ⓔabrigodamontanha@ hotmail.com; breakfast included; ❺), has a lovely garden, a pool and views, as well as a fine dining room; while 4.5km from Monchique on the same road, the *Quinta de São Bento* (℡ & Ⓕ282 912 143; breakfast included; ❹) has just five rooms stuffed with period antiques in a home owned by the Bragança family, the former monarchs of Portugal. It is also one of the best places in this part of the Algarve for high-quality, but reasonably priced Portuguese cooking, featuring traditional recipes (restaurant closed Mon).

Monchique itself also has a handful of **restaurants** that soak up the passing tourist trade. *A Charrete*, Rua Samora Gil 30–34 (℡282 912 142), is recommended, specializing in award-winning "mountain food" – meat and fish cooked with beans, pasta and rice and the like – while *Restaurante Central,* near the church at Rua da Igreja 5 (℡282 913 160), offers basic but inexpensive Portuguese cuisine. It's a tiny place virtually smothered under the weight of thousands of photocopied notes and postcards detailing past visitors' comments – most of them complimentary.

Fóia and Picota

Fóia, 8km west of Monchique, is – at nearly 900m – the highest of the *serra*'s peaks; on Mondays and Thursdays, two buses (11am & 3.30pm) make the delightful run up here from Monchique. Bristling with antennae, and capped by an ungainly modern complex sheltering café-restaurant, shop and inn – the *Estalagem de Santo António* (☎282 912 158, ⓕ282 912 878; breakfast included; ❹) – the summit itself can be an anticlimax, especially if clouds obscure the views or you have to share the experience with the midsummer crowds. Get here early if you can. On a clear day, the panoramic view of the Algarve takes in Portimão, Lagos, the foothills stretching to the Barragem da Bravura, and west across to Cabo de São Vicente.

East of Monchique, **Picota** (770m) comes second in altitude to Fóia, though it's much more interesting in terms of its botany, and easier to reach without transport. You can get to the peak from Monchique in around one and a half hours, a walk that takes in cork trees (and cork collection points), eucalyptus and pines, peach, lemon and orange orchards, and even wild goats scurrying about the heights. From Monchique, take the N266 Caldas de Monchique road, and turn left onto the N267, signposted Alferce. Picota is the second turning, signposted around 800m along this road off to the right. At the top there's nothing save a rickety watchtower occupied by a solitary guardian with a pair of binoculars. From here you can see the coastline stretching all the way to Sagres, and take in another magnificent view of the Monchique mountain range.

Lagos and around

LAGOS is one of the Algarve's most attractive and historic towns, its historic centre enclosed in largely fourteenth-century walls at the mouth of the Ribeira de Bensafrim. It was from here that many of Portugal's great explorers set off for the New World, including Gil Eanes, who was born here. In 1577, Lagos became the administrative capital of the Algarve, though much of the town was destroyed in the 1755 earthquake and Faro took over as capital in 1776. Lagos went into long decline, until tourism revived the town in the 1960s, since when it has developed into a major resort – though it also remains a working fishing port and local market centre. For all its historical significance, Lagos's main attraction is its proximity to some of the best beaches on the Algarve coast. To the east of the town is the long sweep of **Meia Praia**, while to the west – from **Praia de Dona Ana** to **Porto do Mós** – is an extraordinary network of coves, pierced by tunnels and grottoes and studded by extravagantly weathered outcrops of purple-tinted rock. Popular boat trips run along the west coast all year round, while other popular side trips are inland to the **Barragem de Bravura**, a pretty hillside reservoir, or to **Lagos Zoo**.

Arrival and information

Lagos is the western terminal of the Algarve railway line and its **train station** is across the river, a fifteen-minute walk from the centre via a swing bridge in the marina; taxis are usually available if you can't face the walk. The **bus station** is a bit closer in, a block back from the main estuary road, Avenida dos Descobrimentos, and almost opposite the bridge to the train station. The **turismo** (May–Sept Mon–Fri 10am–7pm, Sat & Sun 10am–1pm & 2.30–6pm; Oct–April same hours until 6pm; ☎282 763 031, ⓦwww.cm-lagos.pt) is inconveniently positioned at Sítio de São João, which is the first roundabout as you come into the town from the east. From

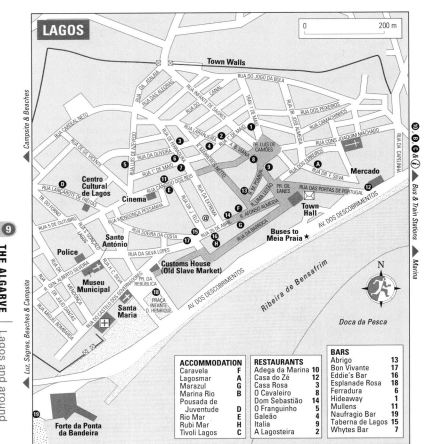

LAGOS

0   200 m

Town Walls

◄ Campsite & Beaches

⑩, ⑧, ⑥ & ⓘ ► Bus & Train Stations

► Marina

Centro Cultural de Lagos

Cinema

Santo António

Police

Museu Municipal

Santa Maria

Customs House (Old Slave Market)

Town Hall

Mercado

Buses to Meia Praia ★

◄ Luz, Sagres, Beaches & Campsite

N

Ribeira de Bensafrim

Doca da Pesca

⑲ Forte da Ponta da Bandeira

ACCOMMODATION	
Caravela	F
Lagosmar	A
Marazul	G
Marina Rio	B
Pousada de Juventude	D
Rio Mar	E
Rubi Mar	H
Tivoli Lagos	C

RESTAURANTS	
Adega da Marina	10
Casa do Zé	12
Casa Rosa	3
O Cavaleiro	8
Dom Sebastião	14
O Franguinho	5
Galeão	4
Italia	9
A Lagosteira	2

BARS	
Abrigo	13
Bon Vivante	17
Eddie's Bar	16
Esplanade Rosa	18
Ferradura	6
Hideaway	1
Mullens	11
Naufragio Bar	19
Taberna de Lagos	15
Whytes Bar	7

the centre, it's a twenty-minute walk; keep going down Rua Vasco da Gama, past the bus station.

Most of Lagos can be explored comfortably on foot, but the best way to see the outlying sights in summer is on the **road train** (May–Sept hourly, 10.30am–7pm; €3), which trundles from the marina along Avenida dos Descobrimentos and out via the beaches of Praia de Dona Ana and Porto de Mós to the headland at Ponta da Piedade.

Accommodation

Most of the town's hotels and *pensões* are fully booked through the summer so if you turn up without a reservation, your best chance of a bed will be a **room** in a private house (❷-❸). The tourist office may phone around and try to find you a space, though you'll probably be met by touts at the bus or train station. There's a **youth hostel** in town, while Lagos also has a **campsite**, to the west of the centre, near Praia de Dona Ana.

In town

Pensão Caravela Rua 25 de Abril 16 ☎ 282 763 361. Reasonable rooms on the town's main pedestrianized street. Doubles come with or without bath. Breakfast included. ❸

Pensão Lagosmar Rua Dr. F. Silva 13 ☎ 282 763 523, ✉ dfhoteis@inoxnet.com. Upmarket *pensão*, where some rooms have small balconies. Breakfast included. ❹

Residencial Marazul Rua 25 de Abril 13 ☎ 282 770 230, ✉ pensaomarazul.hotmail.com. Beautifully decorated *residencial*, with bright rooms and communal areas tiled in *azulejos*. The en-suite bedrooms vary in size, but all come with TVs and some have terraces with sea views. Closed Oct–March. Breakfast included. ❸

Albergaria Marina Rio Av. dos Descobrimentos 388 ☎ 282 769 859, ⓦ www.marinario.com. A large, modern inn facing the harbour (though back rooms face the bus station). It's a decent enough place with modern facilities, including satellite TV, a games room and rooftop pool. Breakfast included. ❺

Hotel Rio Mar Rua Cândido dos Reis 83 ☎ 282 770 130, ⒻⒶⓍ 282 763 927. Smart, medium-sized hotel with its own bar, tucked into a central street. Most rooms have a balcony – the best overlook the sea at the back of the hotel, others overlook a fairly quiet main street. Breakfast included. ❹

Pensão Rubi Mar Rua da Barroca 70–1° ☎ 282 763 165, ✉ rubimar01@hotmail.com. Wonderful old *pensão* with spacious rooms, most en-suite and some with balconies, the best with harbour views. Also has rooms sleeping up to five. Breakfast included. ❸

Tivoli Lagos Rua Nova da Aldeia ☎ 282 790 079, ⓦ www.tivolilagos.com. Lagos's most upmarket central hotel (5min from the market) is built "village-style", with paths linking the rooms and public areas. Not all the rooms are spacious, and some overlook a busy street, but the best have terraces facing the outdoor pool – all are air-conditioned. There are two restaurants, bar, indoor and outdoor pool, and health club, plus a courtesy bus to its own beach club at Meia Praia. Parking available. Good buffet breakfast included. ❼

At the beaches

Pensão Dona Ana Praia de Dona Ana ☎ 282 762 322. Small, white *pensão* situated above one of Lagos's finest beaches, a 20-minute walk from town across the clifftops. Breakfast included. ❷

Meia Praia Beach Club Meia Praia ☎ 282 789 400, ⓦ www.dompedro.com. A 10min drive from Lagos, just back from one of the best stretches of beach, this tasteful three-star is set in attractive grounds; the best rooms have sea-facing balconies. Apartments for 4–6 people are also available, there are tennis courts and a pool, while guests are entitled to discounts at the Palmares Golf Course. Breakfast included. Parking. ❻

Sol e Praia Praia de Dona Ana ☎ 282 762 026, ⒻⒶⓍ 282 760 247. The best option on this stretch, close to the steps down to the beach and with a pool, gym and games room. Most rooms have coastal-facing balconies. Breakfast included. ❺

Youth hostel

Pousada de Juventude Rua de Lançarote de Freitas 50 ☎ 282 761 970, ⓦ www.pousadasjuventude.pt. Modern, well-designed youth hostel, just up from the Centro Cultural de Lagos, with several dorms plus a few en-suite doubles (book in advance for these). There's a pleasant courtyard plus internet access and currency exchange. Dorms €15, rooms ❸

Campsite

Campismo da Trindade Rossio da Trindade ☎ 282 763 893, ⒻⒶⓍ 282 762 885. Wedged up by the Clube de Futebol Esperança de Lagos on the way to Praia de Dona Ana, this is a basic and cramped campsite with a small shop. In season a bus marked "D. Ana/Porto de Mós" runs to the site from the bus station. On foot, follow the main Sagres road around the old town and it's 10-15min from the Forte Ponta da Bandeira to the site.

The Town

Lagos was a favoured residence of Henry the Navigator, who used the town as a base for the new African trade, to which is owed the town's least proud relic – Europe's first **slave market**. This opened in 1444, and its arcades survive alongside the old **Customs House** in Praça da República near the waterfront. It was from this part of town that the youthful Dom Sebastião is said to have roused his troops before the ill-fated Moroccan expedition of 1578. Fired up by militant Catholicism, the dream-crazed king was to perish on the battlefield

outdoor seating, a traditional, cobbled-floor interior, good seafood, and a fabulous selection of appetizers. A full meal runs to about €30, though with careful selection you could get away for less. Expensive.

O Franguinho Rua Luís de Azevedo 25. Bustling *churrasqueira* with a tiny first-floor dining room. This is the place to come for barbecued chicken or *febras de porco* (grilled pork steaks). There are daily changing specials, too. Closed Mon. Inexpensive.

Galeão Rua de Laranjeira 1 ☎ 282 763 909. A bit hidden away, and consequently quieter than many, this nice little formal restaurant offers black-tie service and a traditional Algarvian menu (smoked swordfish, excellent *cataplana*), plus superb steaks and lobster thermidore. There's a good local wine list too. Closed Sun. Expensive.

Italia Rua Garrett 26–28 ☎ 282 760 030. Bright, cheery restaurant run by Italians: pizzas come from a wood-burning oven, there's Italian wine, pasta and a full menu besides. Moderate.

A Lagosteira Rua 1 de Maio 2 ☎ 282 762 486. Upmarket, blue-tiled restaurant specializing in *camarão flambé* (flambéed prawns), fish cooked in a *cataplana* and, of course lobster. Daily specials too. Expensive.

Drinking and nightlife

There is no shortage of bars around town, many of them owned by expatriates – in particular Irish and British. Cocktails are extremely popular in Lagos and measures are almost universally generous; look out for the places offering two-for-one deals and special events. Most bars stay open until at least 2am, some even later if the party is in full flow.

Cervejaria Abrigo Rua Marquês de Pombal 2. Laid back place with outdoor tables under scented orange trees – beer, cocktails, snacks and meals all day. Closed Sun.

Bon Vivante Rua 25 Abril 105. This late-night den at the top of the street has drinking on three floors, gaudy marble "cactus" pillars and a superb roof terrace, that's a great spot to watch the sun go down. Open till 4am.

Eddie's Bar Rua 25 de Abril 99. Small, friendly bar with good selection of sounds. Attracts a surf /bike/skate dude kind of crowd.

Esplanade Rosa Pr. Infante Dom Henrique. This kiosk café-bar has outdoor tables sprawling across the leafty square adjacent to Praça da Republica. Serves inexpensive pastries, pizzas, coffees, beer and ice creams.

Cervejaria Ferradura Rua 1 de Maio 26A. Atmospheric *cervejaria* with stools around a horseshoe-shaped bar, walls covered in soccer posters (who on earth gave them the one of Wigan Athletic?) and stacks of inexpensive shellfish *petiscos*. Closed Sun.

Hideaway Trav. 1 de Maio 9, off Praça Luís de Camões. Cheap beer, more than fifty cocktails, laid-back sounds and food till 2am.

Mullens Rua Cândido dos Reis 86. This cavernous *adega* is the most appealing late-night choice in town. The drinks are inexpensive – there's Guinness, sangria and *vinho verde* on tap – while excellent, moderately priced meals are served to a jazz and soul soundtrack.

Naufragio Bar Av. dos Descobrimentos. Pleasant bar with a youthful clientele, jazzy sounds and moderately priced bar snacks. Out the back there's a great terrace facing the town beach and the Forte da Ponta da Bandeira.

Taberna de Lagos Rua 25 de Abril. Lovely, high-ceilinged town house converted into a sophisticated bar-restaurant that attracts a laid-back, arty crowd. Superb cocktails include caipirinhas and alcohol free fruit cocktails, and bar meals too, things like pizza, pasta and salads.

Whytes Bar Rua do Ferrador 7A. Positively thrives on drunken behaviour and offers a dodgy combination of darts, cocktails and lethal measures of spirits. The brave commit the "Nine Deadly Sins" in the downstairs bar to win a free T-shirt.

Listings

Banks and exchange Banks and ATMs are grouped around Pr. Gil Eanes, and you can exchange money in almost every travel agency.

Bike and motorbike rental Motor Ride, Rua José Afonso 23 ☎ 282 761 720, in the new town towards Ponta da Piedade, rents out bikes from €8.50 and motorbikes from €35 a day.

Bullfights These take place most Saturdays throughout the summer, usually at 5.30pm (€35) at the Praça de Touros de Lagos, out on the Portimão road.

Car rental Auto Jardim, Rua Vítor da Costa Silva 18 ☎ 282 769 486, ⊛ www.auto-jardim.com; Avis, Largo das Portas de Portugal 11 ☎ 282 763 691;

Hertz, Rossio de São João ☎282 769 809; Luz-Car-Sociedade, Largo das Portas de Portugal 10 ☎282 761 016 (also does motorbikes).

Hospital Rua do Castelo dos Governadores, adjacent to the Santa Maria church ☎282 770 100.

Internet Império do Mar, Rua Cândido dos Reis 199 (Mon–Sat 10am–4am, Sun 2pm–4am), opposite the cinema.

Police Rua General Alberto Silveira ☎282 762 930.

Post office Next to the town hall, just off Av. dos Descobrimentos (Mon–Fri 8.30am–6pm).

Taxis There are ranks in front of the post office or call Lagos Central Taxi ☎282 762 469.

Telephones It's easiest to make long-distance calls at the Telecom office, next to the post office.

Travel agency Tickets (including bus tickets) and tours from Tourlagos, Rua Infante de Sagres 31 ☎282 767 967.

West to Sagres

The coast west of Lagos, to Vila do Bispo and Sagres, remains one of the least spoiled parts of the Algarve, largely thanks to the Parque Natural do Sudoeste Alentejano e Costa Vicentina which prohibits large-scale building on the coastline west of Burgau. As a result, the resorts – **Luz, Burgau** and **Salema** – remain largely low-rise and low key.

In summer there are frequent **bus** services from Lagos to Luz and Burgau, and a regular service to Salema. Connections are less frequent during the winter, but you should always be able to get to at least one of the villages and back in a day-trip, even if it means walking to the highway on occasion to pick up the bus. You could also plan a day that involved walking between the villages: Burgau to Luz to Lagos, in particular, is a nice, relatively easy stretch. Other local beaches, near **Figueira** and **Raposeira**, can't be reached by public transport, but they are much less visited as a consequence – great if you're looking for some solitude.

Luz

Five kilometres west of Lagos, the mass of white chalets and villas that is the resort of **LUZ** pile up behind a fine, sweeping beach set below towering cliffs. There's a palm-lined beachside promenade that leads from the sands to a *miradouro* beneath the village's old fort – now a restaurant – and the church. Along the promenade there are any number of bar-restaurants with advantageous terraces, including *O Poço*, which serves moderately priced fish and seafood, including a tasty *espadarte de tamboril* (monkfish kebab). *Restaurante Fortaleza da Luz* (☎282 789 926), above the west end of the beach, opposite the church, is a pricier choice for Algarvian and international cuisine, served inside the old fort or on a lovely sea-facing terrace. Luz has just one **hotel**, *Belavista da Luz* (☎282 788 655, ✉hoteldaluz@mail.telepac.pt; breakfast included; ❸), around 1km uphill on the road out of town towards Sagres – it's a modern pink four-star with restaurant and pool, but little in the way of character. The rest of Luz's accommodation consists of **apartments** and villas, often block-booked in summer, though you can try the main agency, *Luz Bay Club*, Rua do Jardim (☎282 789 640, ⓌWww.lunahoteis.com; ❻), some of whose apartments have balconies and views of the sea. *Luz Bay Club* also offers tennis, squash, a sauna and pool for a day membership fee of €11. **Campers** like the *Valverde* site (☎218 117 070), close to the highway but a good 1.5km or so from the seafront, which has a restaurant, bar, supermarket and kids' playground.

Incidentally, the **path to Lagos** starts at the eastern end of the beach. At the Algarve Sports Club, follow the private road uphill and make the steep scramble up to the obelisk on the cliffs, from where a gentle path careers along the tops to Porto do Mós, Ponte das Piedade and Lagos.

Burgau

It's another 5km or so to **BURGAU**, a resort that still displays vestiges of its former fishing village life. The cobbled main street, with its side alleys and terraces, retains some charm, running right through the village and tumbling down to a wide sweep of sand backed by crumbling cliffs. Out of season, it's truly attractive, the beach deserted and the shutters down in most of the shops and restaurants, leaving the streets to echo to your own footsteps and little else. In July and August, there's no mistaking Burgau for the out-and-out resort it is. Note that not all the **buses** from Lagos and Sagres call into Burgau itself, though all pass the turn-off on the highway, from where it's a 2km walk to the village through arid farming country.

Unless you're here on a pre-booked holiday, you'll find it tough to locate **accommodation** in summer, though signs scattered around the village advertise rooms in private houses. The best choice is *Casa Grande* (☎282 697 416, @casagrande@mail.telepac.pt; breakfast included; ❸–❺ depending on size of room), at the top end of town on the road towards Luz, which is a characterful old manor run by Brits. Set in its own grounds, the rooms have soaring ceilings, each decorated with a motley assortment of old furniture, and there's a fine restaurant attached, the *Adega Casa Grande* (evenings only, closed weekends & Nov–Feb). Failing that, *Hotel Praia do Burgau* (☎282 690 160, @dfhoteis@inoxnet.com; breakfast included; ❻), on a hillside to the east of town, is a friendly three-star place with a small pool. The top rooms with balconies have superb views (€15 extra).

Burgau is well served with **bars and restaurants**, including the *Beach Bar Burgau* with a splendid terrace-bar (open till 2am, closed Mon evenings) and good, if pricey, food in the restaurant (closed Mon). Slightly less expensive, *A Barraca*, Largo dos Pescadores 2 (☎282 697 748), sits on the clifftop and does fine *cataplanas*.

Salema

SALEMA remains one of the most popular resorts along this stretch, certainly for independent travellers who have numerous accommodation options. Just 20km west of Lagos, the turn-off from the N125 snakes down a delightful semi-cultivated valley, the sea creeping ever closer. The bus parks just above the beachside promenade, much of it cluttered with brightly coloured boats. The fairly homogenous white splodge of apartment and villa construction spreads back up the valley, leaving the old village to the east of the harbour largely untouched. The beach – a wide, rock-sheltered bay – is magnificent: in winter, the sea comes crashing right up to the edge of the village.

There are plenty of **rooms** to let round the old town (just look for the signs: you should be able to secure something with a terrace and kitchen). There's also the fair-sized *Hotel Residencial Salema* (☎282 665 328, @hotel.salema@clix.pt; breakfast included; closed Nov–Feb; ❺), plonked rather unceremoniously by the cobbled square just back from the beach. There are cheaper rooms at *A Mare* (☎282 695 165, @johnmare@telepac.pt; breakfast included; ❹), on the hill above the main road into town, where the small rooms have bath, sea views and terraces with sun loungers. More upmarket – and steeply uphill – is the *Estalagem Infante do Mar* (☎2282 690 100, @www.infantedomar.com; breakfast included; ❺), around 1km from the seafront on the road to Figueira, a smart four-star inn with many rooms offering panoramic views over the coast; there's also a restaurant, bar and pool. The pleasantly landscaped **campsite**, *Quinta dos Carriços* (℡282 695 201, Ⓔquintacarrico@oninet.pt), is 1.5km back up towards the main highway – the bus passes it on the way into the village.

Best of the **restaurants** is *Mira Mar*, Travessa Mira Mar 6 (℡919 560 339), with a sea-facing terrace and excellent fresh fish at moderate prices; try the bream. The nearby *Boia Bar Restaurante*, Rua das Pescadores 101 (℡282 695 382), is a swish place with snappy service; *caldeirada* (fish stew) is the speciality and full meals here cost around €18. *Bar Aventura*, Rua das Pescadores 80, is an attractive bar open until 2am (and has internet access).

Figueira and Raposeira

At the village of **FIGUEIRA** on the N125, around 3km northwest of Salema, there's the very welcoming *Bar Celeiro* by the bus stop. Opposite here, a rough farm track (signed Forte da Figueira) leads off to the isolated sands of **Praia da Figueira** (a 20–30min walk through lovely countryside), one of the least visited beaches along this stretch, below the ruins of an old fort.

Between Figueira and Raposeira, a sign points off the main N125 to the chapel of **Nossa Senhora de Guadalupe**, reached down the old road which runs parallel to the highway. Built in the thirteenth century by the Knights Templars, and said to have been frequented by Henry the Navigator, the chapel stands in rural solitude. It is usually kept locked, but it's a pleasant place to stroll around or have a picnic.

Two other little visited beaches are accessible by road from the village of **RAPOSEIRA**, 3km further west, sliced through by the speeding highway. The turn-off to the beach ("Ingrina") is signposted at the traffic lights on the highway: go through Hortas do Tabual and take the left fork, and after 3km you'll reach **Praia do Zavial**, a rocky beach popular with surfers and with a decent café-restaurant (closed Mon). Another couple of kilometres around the bay, **Praia da Ingrina** is more sheltered and sandy, good for beachcombing amid the rock pools, with another beachside café (closed Tues). There's also a rural **campsite** (℡82 639 242) here, 1km up from the sea, with its own bar-restaurant. There are no public transport connections with either beach from the main road.

West of Raposeira the road passes Vila do Bispo and the turn-off for the west coast, before heading across the flattened landscape for Sagres.

Sagres and Cabo de São Vicente

Sagres and its wild and windswept cape were considered by the Portuguese as the far limit of the world. It was on these headlands in the fifteenth century that Prince Henry the Navigator made his residence and it was here, too, that he set up a school of navigation, gathering together the greatest astronomers, cartographers and adventurers of his age. Fernão de Magalhães (Magellan), Pedro Álvares Cabral and Vasco da Gama all studied at Sagres, and from the beach at Belixe – midway between the capes of Sagres and **São Vicente** – the first long caravels were launched, revolutionizing shipping with their wide hulls, small adaptable sails, and ability to sail close to the wind. Each year new expeditions were dispatched to penetrate a little further than their predecessors, and to resolve the great navigational enigma presented by the west coast of Africa, thereby laying the foundations of the country's overseas empire.

After Henry's death here in 1460, the centre of maritime studies was moved to Lisbon and Sagres slipped back into the obscurity from which he'd raised it. Now, the main highway from Lagos has put Sagres on the tourist map, and it attracts a growing number of families, young backpackers and surfers, drawn by the string of magnificent local beaches. It's not a handsome town, but it can still be a great place to stay, with an ever-growing array of rooms, restaurants and bars, along with a smart *pousada*, which overlooks the village.

Sagres

SAGRES village, rebuilt in the nineteenth century over the earthquake ruins of Henry's town, has nothing of architectural or historical interest. Its small sixteenth-century Fortaleza de Baleeira was damaged by Francis Drake in 1587 and further ruined in the 1755 earthquake; the rest of the town is little more than a main road – Rua Comandante Matoso – connecting the lively fishing harbour and Praia da Baleeira at one end with the main square at the other, all backed by a new town of white villas and apartments. The small square, **Praça da República**, is the main focus of town, an attractive cobbled space lined with squat palms and whitewashed cafés, swooped over by swallows. From here, it's a short walk southeast to Sagres's best beach, Praia da Mareta (see below).

Henry the Navigator's **Fortaleza** (daily: May–Sept 10am–8.30pm; Oct–April 10am–6.30pm; €3) dominates the whole village, with Rua da Fortaleza running directly up the headland towards its massive bulk; it is better to walk this way than to follow the road signs which take you on a detour to a giant car park set well back from the fort. An immense circuit of walls – only the north side survives intact – once surrounded the vast, shelf-like promontory, high above the Atlantic.

After the formidable tunnel entrance is spread a huge pebble **Rosa dos Ventos** (wind compass), unearthed beneath a church in 1921. Wind compasses are used to measure the direction of the wind, but most are divided into 30 segments. This is unusual in that its 43-metre diameter is divided into 40 segments. No one is sure whether the compass dates back to Henry's time, though the simple, much-restored chapel of **Nossa Senhora da Graça** besides the compass is accepted as dating from the fifteenth century.

Over the last few years there has been an attempt to beef up the contents of the fortress with new buildings within the walls – a shop, café and exhibition space showing maps of Portugal and other nautical memorabilia – but, gracelessly constructed with concrete, they have done little to enhance the beauty of the site. Still, it's pleasant enough to wander around the walls or out to **Ponta de Sagres**, a headland with a small lighthouse beacon offering fine views along the coast.

Local beaches

Most people's days in Sagres are spent on one of the excellent beaches, five of which are within easy walking distance of the village. Three of them are on the more sheltered coastline east of the fortress, with the nicest, **Praia da Mareta**, just five minutes' walk southeast of the main square. The small **Praia da Baleeira** is by the working fishing harbour, around fifteen minutes' walk from the main square along Rua Comandante Matoso. From the cliffs above the harbour it's another five- to ten-minute walk to the longest, and generally least crowded, beach, **Praia do Martinhal**, an ideal spot for windsurfing (there's a rental outfit here). West of the fortress, **Praia do Tonel** is a wilder location, popular with surfers, while it's a longer walk to the beautiful **Praia de Belixe**, 2km down the road from Sagres to Cabo São Vicente, where you are usually guaranteed plenty of sand to yourself.

Whichever beach you choose, be cautious when swimming – there are some very strong currents, especially on the west side of the fortress. Before setting off for the more distant strands, stock up with drinks and picnic supplies at the village supermarket on the main Rua Comadante Matoso as there are virtually no beach facilities, especially out of season.

Practicalities

Buses from Lagos stop just by Praça da República and then continue to the harbour. The **turismo** (Tues–Sat 9.30am–12.30pm & 2–6pm; ☎282 624 873) is by a dusty square just up from the *praça*, while on Praça da República, in the *Residencial Dom Henrique*, there's also a privately run information office, **Turinfo** (daily 9.30am–1pm & 2–5.30pm; ☎282 620 003, ℻282 620 004), which can arrange room rental, book you on a local jeep or boat tour, organize surf lessons or mountain bike rental, and provide internet access.

There are places to stay in and around Sagres village, and in high season, at least, it's basically a question of turning up and seeing what **accommodation** you're offered. Generally, you'll be approached by people offering **rooms** (❷) and, if you want it, access to a kitchen too. There is also a scattering of regular *pensões* and hotels; as with the private rooms, prices come down considerably out of season. The nearest **campsite**, *Parque de Campismo de Sagres* (☎282 624 351, ℻282 624 445), is 2km northwest of the village, along (and off) the main road; it sits in rural solitude.

Hotels and pensions

Hotel da Baleeira Porto da Baleeira ☎282 624 212, ⓔhotel.baleeira@mail.telepac.pt. This smart hotel is the spot for harbour views, complete with pool, restaurant and tennis courts. Breakfast included. Parking. ❻

Casa Sagres Pr. da República ☎282 624 358. Behind the main square, on the road down to Praia da Mareta, this is primarily a restaurant that also lets out decent en-suite rooms. The best ones have sea-facing balconies (€5 extra). Breakfast included. ❹

Residencial Dom Henrique Pr. da República ☎282 620 000, ℻282 620 001. In a great position right on the square – there's a terrace and bar, while the front rooms have superb sea-facing balconies (which you pay €7 more for). Breakfast included. ❺

Motel Gambozinhos Praia do Martinhal ☎282 620 160, ℻282 620 169. Out of town, this is a very attractive but simple motel with a line of low rooms and apartments set in peaceful gardens just back from the sands of Praia do Martinhal. Parking. ❹

Pousada do Infante ☎282 620 240, ⓦwww .pousadas.pt. The best choice in town – an attractive clifftop mansion with Moorish elements and splendid views of the fortress from its bar-terrace. Rooms are large and comfy with luxurious bathrooms. There are also tennis courts and a games room. Parking. Breakfast included. ❽

Cafés and bars

Bubble Lounge Rua Nossa Senhora da Graça ☎282 624 497. This groovy surfers' bar has comfy chairs, a screen showing surf movies and ambient sounds. Closed Mon Oct–April.

Last Chance Saloon Sítio da Mareta ☎282 624 113. In a wooden shack overlooking the beach, this is a laid-back place to down an early evening beer or two, and also has internet access. Closed Mon.

Pastelaria Marreiros Pr. da República 12 ☎282 624 861. Very popular tourist spot, thanks to the attractive outside tables on the main square. There's a good range of snacks, including croissants, *tostas* and sandwiches.

Rosa dos Ventos Pr. da República ☎282 624 480. Atmospheric bar in an old town house on the main square, which also does simple food. Gets packed most evenings with a young, drunken crowd. Closed Tues.

Restaurants

Bossa Nova Rua Comandante Matoso, corner with Rua da Mareta ☎282 624 566. Lively place just off the main drag with a little courtyard, noted for its pizzas, pasta, salads and imaginative vegetarian meals. Closed Mon. Inexpensive.

Dromedário Rua Comandante Matoso ☎282 624 219. Fashionable little bistro with Egyptian-inspired decor, serving pizzas, great breakfasts and a mean range of cocktails and juices. Inexpensive.

A Grelha Rua Comandante Matoso. At the fishing harbour end of the road, this is a simple place with a modest menu of grills which attracts a largely local crowd. Inexpensive.

Mar á Vista Sítio da Mareta ℡ 282 624 247. On a scrubby patch of ground just off the road to Praia da Mareta, this pleasant eatery serves a long list of good-value fish, omelettes and salads (around €15 for a full meal), with fine views from its outdoor tables. Closed Wed. Moderate.

Nortada Praia da Martinhal ℡ 282 624 147. Jazzy bar and restaurant with a terrace right on the sands. Serves a good range of international dishes and baguettes along with the usual Portuguese fare. Also does fine milkshakes and fresh juices, and is the base for the local watersports school. Closed Tues Sept–April. Moderate.

Raposo Praia da Mareta ℡ 282 624 168. Lovely wood and chrome beach bar-restaurant right on the sands. Food is good value if you steer clear of the pricey seafood. By day it's full of surfers enjoying a drink. Moderate.

A Tasca Porto da Baleeira ℡ 282 624 177. Sagres's best fish restaurant, with a few meat dishes but superb fish straight from the harbour. Tables outside face the Atlantic, though it's just as fun in the barn-like interior, its walls encrusted with pebbles and old bottles. Expect to pay upwards of €20. Closed Wed Oct–April. Expensive.

Vila Velha Rua Patrão António Faustino ℡ 282 624 788. Excellent upmarket restaurant near the *pousada* which gives an international twist to Portuguese ingredients in a rustic-style interior. Has vegetarian options and a children's menu. Evenings only, closed Mon Oct–April. Expensive.

Cabo de São Vicente

The exposed **Cabo de São Vicente** – Cape St Vincent – across the bay from Sagres, was sacred to the Romans, who called it Promontorium Sacrum and believed the sun sank hissing into the water beyond here every night. It became a Christian shrine when the relics of the martyred St Vincent arrived in the eighth century (see box below). Today the sea off this wild set of cliffs shelters the highest concentration of marine life in Portugal, including rare birds such as Bonelli's eagles, white storks, white herons, kites and rock doves.

It was almost certainly at the cape that Henry established his School of Navigation, founded a small town, and built his Vila do Infante. Today only a **lighthouse** – the most powerful in Europe – flanked by the ruins of a sixteenth-century Capuchin convent, are to be seen. The other buildings on the cape, already vandalized by the piratical Sir Francis Drake in 1587, came crashing to the ground in the Great Earthquake of 1755, the monks staying on alone until the Liberal suppression of the monasteries in 1834.

St Vicent

St Vicent was born in Zaragoza in Spain in the fourth century AD and became the town's deacon during the early days of Christianity in Iberia. He was later imprisoned in Valencia and sentenced to death in 304 during the days of Christian persecution. It is said that while he was being burned alive, the room filled with flowers, light and the voices of angels, and he was proclaimed a martyr and then a saint. In the eighth century, his remains – which had somehow survived the fire – were miraculously washed up in an unmanned boat piloted by ravens at what is now Cabo de São Vicente. Perhaps more credible is the theory that Christians took whatever was left of Vincent with them to flee invading Moors, arriving at the safe outpost of the Cape where they later built a chapel to house his remains. In 1173, Afonso Henriques, Portugal's first Christian monarch, had the saint's remains moved to Lisbon. Legend has it that the faithful ravens followed to the capital, and guarded over him in the cloisters of Lisbon's Sé (cathedral), until the last one died in 1978. Today São Vicente remains Lisbon's patron saint.

It's a dramatic and exhilarating 6km (2hr) walk from Sagres to the cape, a path skirting the cliffs for much of the way. In spring and early summer you should be able to spot blue rock thrushes and peregrines nesting on the cliffs. Walking on the road is easier – it'll take less than an hour and a half, with glorious views all the way. Try to be at the cape for sunset, which is invariably gorgeous.

The west coast

Unlike the southern stretches of the Algarve, the west coast, stretching north from Sagres to Odeceixe, is still relatively undeveloped. There are several reasons: the coast is exposed to strong Atlantic winds; the sea can be several degrees cooler than on the south coast; and swimming can be dangerous. In addition, the designation in 1995 of the stretch of coast from Burgau to Cabo de São Vicente and up through the Alentejo as a nature reserve – the Parque Natural Sudoeste Alentejano e Costa Vincentina – should go even further to protect this dramatic and rugged scenery from potentially harmful development. The nearest bases to the beaches are at the uneventful villages of **Vila do Bispo** and **Carrapateira** or the livelier **Aljezur** and **Odeceixe**, all of which have an inexpensive network of private rooms and accommodation options. Like Sagres, these resorts attract a predominantly young crowd of surfers and campervanners.

Vila do Bispo

VILA DO BISPO, at the junction of the west and south coast roads, is a fairly scrappy traditional little town whose kernel of old white houses centres on a lovely seventeenth-century parish **church** (Mon–Sat 10am–1pm & 2–6pm; free), every interior surface of which has been painted, tiled or gilded. The town has no other sights, but it makes a pleasant spot for a coffee or a meal in one of the bars and restaurants by the town garden, or to look out over the hills from the terrace outside the church.

If you have your own transport, the town could make a reasonable accommodation base, ideally suited for day-trips to the surrounding beaches. The nearest stretch of sand, **Praia do Castelejo**, is reached via the bottom of town – from the main square, take the road downhill past the post office, turn left and then bear right – along a narrow road leading 5km west. The beach is a huge swathe of sand (though covered in high tides) lashed by heavy waves below dark grey cliffs, with a fine café-restaurant (closed Wed & Oct–April) to add a touch of civilization.

Buses from Sagres or Lagos drop you right at the bottom of the village, five minutes' walk from the church. There are **rooms** advertised here and there, or try the *Pensão Mira Sagres*, Rua 1 de Maio 3 (☎282 639 160; breakfast included; ❷, en-suite ❸) – opposite the church – which has its own basic bar-restaurant downstairs. There are several other places to **eat**: the best is *Restaurante Correia* (closed Sat), down Rua 1 de Maio from the church, with a decent inexpensive menu and a friendly, local feel. The village also has a small supermarket, bakery and even a couple of **bars** that see some late-night action; the *Convivio* on the central square, Praça da República (closed Sun), serves a wicked range of cocktails until 2am.

Carrapateira and its beaches

Fifteen kilometres to the north (connected by occasional weekday bus from Vila do Bispo) is the village of **CARRAPATEIRA**, which is better positioned for the beach. It's possible to get **accommodation** in a private room if you ask around the main square or at the *Bar Barroca*, or try for space at the best budget place, *Pensão das Dunas*, Rua da Padaria 9 (T & F 282 973 118; breakfast included; ❷), a very pretty building on the beach-side of the village, which has a number of simple rooms overlooking a flower-filled courtyard; there are also two apartments sleeping two or four (❸).

Carrapateira's local beach, a kilometre's walk from the *Casa Fajara*, is the **Praia da Bordeira**, a spectacular strand with dunes, a tiny river and crashing surf. The sandbanks provide shelter from the wind for a sizeable unauthorized community, who seem to be tolerated by the local police. There is a moderately priced restaurant just back from the beach, *O Sitio do Rio* (T 282 997 119; closed Tues & Nov), which uses largely organic produce – fresh soup, simple grills or stir-fried veggies offer a change from usual Portugese seaside food.

Four kilometres south of Praia da Bordeira, along the coast road, lies **Praia do Amado**, which is also signed off the main road just south of Carrapateira. This fantastic, broad sandy bay backed by low hills with a couple of seasonal cafés is particularly popular with surfers. There's also a **surf school** here (T & F 282 624 560) which offers equipment rental and surf courses from €35.

Aljezur and around

Fairly regular buses run from Lagos and Portimão to the village of **ALJEZUR**, 16km north of Carrapeteira, which is both the prettiest and liveliest town along the west coast of the Algarve. The main coast road passes through a prosaic, modern lower town where you find banks, the post office and a range of cafés and restaurants. The more interesting historic centre spreads uphill beyond the bridge over the Aljezur river, a network of narrow cobbled streets reaching up through whitewashed houses to the remains of a tenth-century Moorish **castle**. It's a lovely walk with sweeping views over the valley, via a trio of dull museums; the only one worth a visit is the **Casa Museu Pintor José Cercas** (Mon–Fri 10am–12.30pm & 2–5.30pm; €1), which displays the works and collections of local artist José Cercas, who lived in the house until his death in 1992. His well-observed landscapes and religious scenes are complemented by the attractive house and pretty garden.

At the foot of the old town, the **turismo** (May–Sept Mon & Fri–Sun 10–1.30pm & 2.30–5.30pm, Tues–Thurs 9.30am–7pm; Oct–April Mon–Fri 9.30am–1pm & 2.30–6pm; T 282 998 229) in Largo do Mercado, by the river, does its best to help with private **rooms**. Most places to stay are in the suburb of Igreja Nova, one kilometre from the tourist office, just off the Monchique road – the bus from Lagos loops through Igreja Nova on its way out of Aljezur. Best bet is the modern *Residencial Dom Sancho*, Largo Igreja Nova 1 (T 282 998 119, ✉turimol@mail.telepac.pt; breakfast included; ❸), which overlooks a pedestrianized street. Rooms are large and comfortable and come with bath and TV. The local **campsite**, *Parque de Campismo do Serrão* (T 282 990 220, ✉camping-serrao@clix.pt), has its own pool, supermarket and tennis courts amongst dense trees; it's 7km northwest of Aljezur, and 4km from the beach of Praia Amoreira.

There are several inexpensive **cafés and restaurants** in Aljezur, most of them along the main through-road, Rua 25 de Abril. *Restaurante Ruth* at no. 14 (T 282 998 534; closed Sat) is highly regarded, specializing in regional dishes such as *arroz de tamboril com camarão*. Also moderately priced, but in a better position, *Pont a Pé*, near the tourist office on Largo da Liberdade 16 (☎282 998 104; closed Sun), offers grills in a cosy diner or on the riverside terrace. Live music most weekends competes with the sound of the resident frogs.

Arrifana and Monte Clérigo
From May to September, two buses daily run to a couple of superb beaches within a few kilometres of Aljezur. The largest of these is **Praia da Arrifana**, 10km to the southwest, a fine, sandy sweep set below high, crumbling black cliffs. The beach is popular with surfers and surf competitions are sometimes held here. The clifftop boasts the remains of a ruined fort, just up from a half a dozen cafés and holiday villas. *Oceano* (☎282 997 300; ❷) will cater to most of your needs, a café, restaurant and guest house on the clifftop above the beach. The simple rooms come with shower and fine views, while the upstairs restaurant (closed Tues) does fine mid-priced fish and grills.

MONTE CLÉRIGO, 8km northwest of Aljezur, is a pretty little holiday village of pink- and white-faced beach houses. A cluster of café-restaurants face a superb, family-oriented beach tucked into the foot of a river valley. There is also a decent **campsite**, *Parque de Campismo de Aljezur* (☎282 998 444, ✉vale.telha@clix.pt) at Vale da Telha, less than 1km from Monte Clérigo beach.

Odeceixe

ODECEIXE tumbles down a hillside opposite the broad valley of the Odeceixe river, below the winding, tree-lined main coast road. Sleepy out of season, its character changes in summer when it attracts a steady stream of surfers, campervanners and families, lured by a superb beach and some of the cheapest rooms in the region. Most of the action is centred on the main square, Largo 1 de Maio, with some good café-bars, and from where the beach is signposted to the west. Around here you'll also find the post office, banks, supermarkets, café-restaurants and plenty of places letting out **rooms**. Most central is *Residêncio do Parque*, Rua da Estrada Nacional 11 (☎282 947 117; breakfast included; ❹), a huge place with a mixed bag of en-suite rooms – the best are on the top floor with small balconies overlooking the valley. Better value is *Hospedaria Firmino Bernardinho*, on the way to the beach on Rua da Praia (☎282 947 362; ❸), with modern en-suite rooms each also with small balconies that overlook the valley. The best place for food is *O Retiro do Adelino* at Rua Nova 20, which serves inexpensive grilled chicken, fish with tomato rice and *feijoda*.

Praia de Odeceixe lies some 4km to the west, reached down a verdant river valley. It's a lovely walk, following the river to a broad, sandy bay framed by low cliffs. It is one of the most sheltered beaches on this stretch of coast, offering superb surfing and relatively safe swimming, especially when the tide is out. A pretty cluster of traditional houses and cafés lie banked up to the south of the bay. *Restaurante Café Dorita* (☎282 947 581; breakfast included; ❸) serves decent grills and snacks on a terrace above the beach, and also lets out simple rooms – the best are en suite with sweeping views over the waves. There are plenty of private rooms available too; look for signs saying *quartos*.

Travel details

Trains

Along the Algarve train line, the IC (Intercidades) trains are considerably faster than the stopping IR (Interregional) and snail-like R (Regional) trains.
Faro to: Albufeira (14 daily; 15–45min); Lagos (7 daily; 1hr 40min); Lisbon (4 daily; 5hr 30min–6hr); Monte Gordo (3–4 daily; 1hr–1hr 15min); Olhão (16 daily; 10min); Portimão (7 daily; 1hr 15min–1hr 35min); Silves (7 daily; 1hr–1hr 15min); Tavira (12–17 daily; 35–45min); Vila Real de Santo António (10–13 daily; 1hr–1hr 20min).
Lagos to: Albufeira (8 daily; 1hr 10min); Faro (7 daily; 1hr 40min); Loulé (8 daily; 1hr 25min); Portimão (10–13 daily; 15–20min); Silves (13 daily; 30–50min); Tunes (13 daily; 50min–1hr).
Tunes to: Lisbon (4 daily; 4hr 15min, add on 2hr or so for connections from Vila Real, 1hr from Faro or Lagos); Beja (3 daily; 3hr).

Local buses

Albufeira to: Areias de São João (8–11 daily; 10min); Armacão de Pêra (Mon–Sat 12 daily, Sun 5 daily; 15–20min); Faro (8 daily; 40min–1hr 15min); Montechoro (8–11 daily; 10min); Olhos d'Água (hourly; 10min); Portimão (Mon–Fri 11 daily, Sat & Sun 4 daily; 45min); Quarteira (Mon–Fri 15 daily, Sat & Sun 9 daily; 40min); Silves (3–7 daily; 45min); Vila Real (1 daily; 3hr).
Faro to: Albufeira (8 daily; 40min–1hr 15min); Estói (Mon–Fri 14 daily, Sat & Sun 9 daily; 25min); Évora (3–4 daily; 4hr–4hr 30min); Huelva (for connections to Sevilla, Spain; 2–4 daily; 3hr 30 min); Loulé (Mon–Fri hourly till 7.30pm, Sat 8 daily, Sun 6 daily); Monte Gordo (Mon–Fri 9 daily, Sat & Sun 4 daily; 1hr 35min); Olhão (Mon–Fri every 15–30min, Sat & Sun roughly hourly; 20min); Quarteira (Mon–Fri hourly, Sat & Sun 3 daily; 25min); Tavira (7–11 daily; 1hr); Vilamoura (Mon–Fri hourly, Sat & Sun 9 daily; 30–40min); Vila Real (6–9 daily; 1hr 40min).
Lagos to: Albufeira (12 daily; 1hr 15min); Aljezur (2–5 daily; 50min); Alvor (6 daily, Sat & Sun 4 daily; 15min); Armacão de Pêra (12 daily; 45min–1hr); Burgau (8–11 daily, 4 daily on Sun; 25min); Faro (8 daily; 1hr 45 min); Luz (8–11 daily, 4 daily on Sun; 15min); Odeceixe (Mon–Fri 4 daily, Sat 1 daily; 1hr 20min); Portimão (hourly; 15min–35min); Sagres (7–11 daily; 1hr); Salema (5 daily; 40min); Vila do Bispo (7–11 daily; 45min).
Portimão to: Albufeira (Mon–Fri 11 daily, Sat & Sun 4 daily; 45min); Alvor (Mon–Fri hourly, Sat & Sun roughly every 2hr; 20min); Caldas de Monchique (Mon–Fri 9 daily, Sat & Sun 5 daily; 30min); Faro (8 daily; 1hr 25min–1hr 45min); Ferragudo (hourly; 10min); Lagos (hourly; 15–35min); Monchique (Mon–Fri 9 daily, Sat & Sun 5 daily; 45min); Praia da Rocha (every 15–20min; 5min); Silves (Mon–Fri 9 daily, Sat & Sun 7 daily; 35–45min).
Sagres to: Lagos (Mon–Fri 7–11 daily; 1hr); Salema (Mon–Fri 7–9 daily, Sat & Sun 3–4 daily; 35min); Vila do Bispo (hourly; 15min).
Vila Real de Santo António to: Albufeira (1 daily; 3hr); Alcoutim (Mon–Fri 2–3 daily, Sat 1 daily; 1hr 15min); Ayamonte, Spain (2–4 daily; 15min); Castro Marim (Mon–Fri 12 daily, Sat & Sun 2 daily, 15min); Faro (6–9 daily; 1hr 40min); Huelva, Spain (2–4 daily; 1hr); Manta Rota (Mon–Fri 4–5 daily, Sat 2 daily; 30min); Monte Gordo (Mon–Fri at least half-hourly, Sat & Sun in winter 10–13 daily; 7min); Tavira (9–10 daily; 40min).

Long-distance buses

Several companies operate regular daily express buses between Lisbon and the Algarve. Ask at any travel agency or bus terminal for details, though note that the Rede Expressos buses (Ⓦ www .red-expressos.pt) are slightly cheaper than EVA buses (Ⓦ www.eva-transportes.pt). EVA also runs a number of international buses from the Algarve, the most useful being the service from Lagos to Seville (€17).
Lagos to: Seville (2 daily, at 7am and 2.15pm; 6hr), via Faro (1hr 20min) and Vila Real de Santo António/Ayamonte (2hr 35min). Connections from Seville to Malaga, Cádiz, Algeciras and Grenada.
Linha Litoral express service: runs from Lagos to Vila Real/Ayamonte (Mon–Fri 1 daily; 4hr); on the Lagos–Albufeira leg of the route, there are more like seven weekday departures and four at weekends.
Lisbon to: Albufeira (3hr 35min); Faro (4hr 20min); Lagos (4hr 45min); Olhão (4hr 30min); Tavira (4hr 45min); Vila Real (4hr 30min).

Contexts

Contexts

History

T he early history of Portugal – as part of the Iberian Peninsula – has obvious parallels with that of Spain. Indeed, any geographical division is somewhat arbitrary, since independent development only really occurred following Afonso Henriques' creation of a Portuguese kingdom in the twelfth century.

Early civilization

The human presence in Portugal dates back at least 30,000 years, when ice covered much of northern and central Europe. Some time around 22,000 years ago, Palaeolithic hunter-gatherers, concentrated in the sheltered river valleys of the upper Douro and Tejo, began to leave **animal engravings** on the rocky river flank, most famously around Vila Nova de Foz Côa. The purpose of the etchings remains a mystery, although their unerringly lifelike nature suggest that shamanic ritual may have been involved. Over the following millennia as the ice receded, through the Mesolithic and **Neolithic** era, early man extended his range further into Portugal. The first man-made stone structures made their appearance 6000 to 7000 years ago in the form of communal tombs or **antas** (dolmens), most of which follow a basic design of a circular stone-walled chamber, roofed with flat slabs and originally covered with soil and rubble. Associated with the *antas* is a fertility cult, whose most obvious remains are a series of vertically planted stone **menhirs** (heavy cylindrical stones, some carved into unarguably phallic forms) scattered all over the country. Analogous to these are what are believed to be female equivalents, egg-shaped boulders bearing vaginal symbols.

How long this so-called "granite civilization" lasted is unknown, though certainly by 2000 BC it was well integrated into a broader western European megalithic culture, as testified by a series of **stone circles** in the Alentejo (most dramatically at Os Alemendres, near Évora) and the development of symbolic rock art. Particularly fine examples of Neolithic art are the carved shale funerary plaques from Alentejo and Algarve, mostly in the form of stylized owls or other birds of prey, probably a divinity; the plaques may also have been symbols of tribal power or affiliation.

The end of the Neolithic era, roughly around 1000 BC, saw the development of northern Portugal's **Cultura Castreja**, based around fortified hilltop towns – called **citânias** – and villages (*castros*). The potential for new trading outlets and the quest for metals, in particular tin for making bronze, attracted a succession of peoples from across the Mediterranean but most of their settlements lay on the eastern seaboard and so fell within "Spanish" history. The **Phoenicians**, however, established a series of outposts along Portugal's Atlantic coastline around 900 BC, and there were contacts, too, with Mycenaean Greeks: a curious testament to this cultural mingling is found at Panóias, close to Vila Real, where an engraved text next to a massive sacrificial altar bears a bilingual Latin and Greek inscription dedicated to the Greco-Egyptian deity of Serapis.

The Cultura Castreja was further developed and refined after the arrival of **Celtic peoples**, between 700 and 600 BC. The most impressive remains are at the Citânia de Briteiros, near Braga, and Citânia de Sanfins de Ferreira, north life developed, with prosperous local craft industries: Lisbon, Évora, Beja and Santarém all emerged as sizeable towns.

The Christian renconquest, the **Reconquista**, began – at least by tradition – at Covadonga in Spain in 718, when Pelayo, at the head of a small band of Visigoths, halted the advance of a Moorish expeditionary force. The battle's significance has doubtless been inflated but from the victory a tiny kingdom of the Asturias does seem to have been established. It expanded over the next two centuries to take in León, Galicia and the "lands of Portucale", the latter an area roughly equivalent to the old Swabian state between the Douro and the Minho.

By the eleventh century **Portucale** had the status of a country, its governors appointed by the kings of León. In 1073 Afonso VI came to the throne. It was to be a reign hard-pressed by a new wave of Muslim invaders – the fanatical Almoravids, who crossed over to Spain in 1086 after appeals from al-Andalus and established a new Muslim state at Seville. Like many kings of Portugal after him, Afonso was forced to turn to European Crusaders, many of whom would stop in at the shrine of St James in Compostela. One of them, Raymond of Burgundy, married Afonso's eldest daughter and became heir-apparent to the throne of León; his cousin Henry, married to another daughter, Teresa, was given jurisdiction over Portucale. With Henry's death Teresa became regent for her son, **Afonso Henriques**, and began to try to forge a union with Galicia. Afonso, however, had other ideas and having defeated his mother at the battle of São Mamede (1128), he established a capital at **Guimarães** and set about extending his domains to the south.

The reconquest of central Portugal was quickly achieved. Afonso's victory at Ourique in 1139 was a decisive blow and by 1147 he had taken Santarém. In the same year Lisbon fell, after a siege in which passing Crusaders again played a vital role. Many of them were English and some stayed on; Gilbert of Hastings became Archbishop. By now Afonso was dubbing himself the **first King of Portugal**, a title tacitly acknowledged by Alfonso VII (the new king of León) in 1137 and officially confirmed by the Treaty of Zamora in 1143. His kingdom spread more or less to the borders of modern Portugal, though in the south, Alentejo and the Algarve were still in Muslim hands.

For the next century and a half Afonso's successors struggled to dominate this last stronghold of the Moors. **Sancho I** (1185–1211) took their capital, Silves, in 1189, but his gains were not consolidated and almost everything south of the Tejo was recaptured the following year by al-Mansur, the last great campaigning vizier of al-Andalus. The overall pattern, though, was of steady expansion with occasional setbacks. Sancho II (1223–48) invaded the Alentejo and the eastern Algarve, while his successor **Afonso III** (1248–79) moved westwards, taking Faro and establishing the kingdom in pretty much its final shape.

The Burgundian kings

The reconquest of land from the Muslims also incorporated a process of **recolonization**. As it fell into the king's hands, new territory was granted to such of his subjects that he felt would be able to defend it. In this way much of the country came to be divided between the church, the Holy Orders – chief among them the **Knights Templar** – and a hundred or so powerful nobles (*ricos homens*). The entire kingdom had a population of under half a million, the majority of them concentrated in the north. Here, there was little displacement of the traditional feudal ties, but in the south the influx of Christian peasants blurred the distinction between serf and settler, dependent relationships coming instead to be based on the payment of rent.

Meanwhile a **political infrastructure** was being established. The land was divided into municipalities (*concelhos*), each with its own charter (*foral*). A formalized structure of consultation began, with the first **Cortes** (parliament) being held in Coimbra in 1211. At first consisting mainly of the clergy and nobility, it later came to include wealthy merchants and townsmen, a development speeded both by the need to raise taxes and by later kings' constant struggles against the growing power of the church. The capital, which Afonso Henriques had moved to Coimbra in 1139, was transferred to **Lisbon** in about 1260 by Afonso III.

The Burgundian dynasty lasted through nine kings for 257 years. In the steady process of establishing the new kingdom, one name stands out above all others, that of **Dom Dinis** (1279–1325). With the reconquest barely complete when he came to the throne, Dinis set about a far-sighted policy of strengthening the nation to ensure its future independence. Fifty fortresses were constructed along the frontier with Castile, while at the same time negotiations were going on, leading eventually to the Treaty of Alcanizes (1297) by which Spain acknowledged Portugal's frontiers. At home Dinis established a major programme of forest planting and of agricultural reform; grain, olive oil, wine, salt, salt fish and dried fruit became staple exports to Flanders, Brittany, Catalunya and Britain. Importance, too, was attached to education and the arts: a **university**, later transferred to Coimbra, was founded at Lisbon in 1290. Dinis also helped entrench the power of the monarchy, forcing the church to accept a much larger degree of state control and, in 1319, reorganizing the Knights Templar – at the time being suppressed all over Europe – as the **Order of Christ**, still enormously powerful but now responsible directly to the king rather than to the pope.

Despite Dinis's precautions, fear of **Castilian domination** continued to play an important part in the reigns of his successors, largely owing to consistent intermarrying between the two royal families. On the death of the last of the Burgundian kings, Fernando I, power passed to his widow Leonor, who ruled as regent. Leonor, whose only daughter had married Juan I of Castile, promised the throne to the children of that marriage. In this she had the support of most of the nobility, but the merchant and peasant classes strongly opposed a Spanish ruler, supporting instead the claim of João, Grand Master of the House of Avis and a bastard heir of the Burgundian line. A popular revolt against Leonor led to two years of war with Castile, finally settled at the **Battle of Aljubarrota** (1385) in which João, backed up by a force of English archers, wiped out the much larger Castilian army.

The great abbey of **Batalha** was built to commemorate the victory. **João I**, first king of the **House of Avis**, was crowned at Coimbra the same year, sealing relations with England through the 1386 Treaty of Windsor and his marriage to Philippa of Lancaster, daughter of John of Gaunt, the following year.

Dom Manuel and the maritime empire

Occupying such a strategic position between the Atlantic and the Mediterranean, it was inevitable that Portuguese attention would at some stage turn to **maritime expansion**. When peace was finally made with Castile in 1411,

Spain. As it turned out, however, the Spanish were so preoccupied with wars elsewhere that they had little choice but to accept the situation, though they did not do so formally until 1668 under the **Treaty of Lisbon**. João IV used the opportunity to rebuild old alliances and although the Portuguese were often forced into unfavourable terms, they were at least trading again. Relations with Britain had been strained during the establishment of that country's Commonwealth, especially by Oliver Cromwell's particular brand of Protestant commercialism, but were revived by the marriage of Charles II to Catherine of Bragança in 1661.

At home Portugal was developing an increasingly centralized administration. The **discovery of gold and diamonds in Brazil** during the reign of Pedro II (1683–1706) made the crown financially independent and did away with the need for the Cortes (or any form of popular representation) for most of the next century. It was **João V**, coming to the throne in 1706, who most benefited from the new riches, which he squandered in an orgy of lavish Baroque building. His massive convent at Mafra, built totally without regard to expense, virtually bankrupted the state. The infamous **Methuen Treaty**, signed in 1703 to stimulate trade with Britain, only made matters worse: although it opened up new markets for Portuguese wine, it helped destroy the native textile industry by letting in British cloth at preferential rates.

The accession of João's apathetic son, **José I** (1750–77), allowed the total concentration of power in the hands of the king's chief minister, the **Marquês de Pombal**, who became the classic enlightened despot of eighteenth-century history. It was the **Great Earthquake of 1755** that sealed his dominance over the age; while everyone else was panicking, Pombal's policy was simple – "bury the dead and feed the living".

Pombal saw his subsequent mission as to modernize all aspects of Portuguese life, by establishing an efficient and secular bureaucracy, renewing the system of taxation, setting up export companies, protecting trade and abolishing slavery within Portugal. It was a strategy that made him many enemies among the old aristocracy and above all within the Church, whose overbearing influence he fought at every turn. Opposition, though, was dealt with ruthlessly and an assassination attempt on the king in 1758 (which some say was staged by Pombal) gave him the chance he needed to destroy his enemies. Denouncing their supposed involvement, Pombal executed the country's leading aristocrats and abolished the Jesuit order, which had long dominated education and religious life in Portugal and Brazil.

Although Pombal himself was taken to trial (and found guilty but pardoned on the grounds of old age) with the accession of Maria I (1777–1816), the majority of his labours survived him, most notably the reform of education along scientific lines and his completely rebuilt capital, Lisbon. Further development, however, was soon thwarted by a new invasion.

French occupation and the Miguelite years

With the appearance of **Napoleon** on the international scene, Portugal once more became embroiled in the affairs of Europe. The French threatened to invade unless the Portuguese supported their naval blockade of Britain, a demand that no one expected them to obey since British ports were the destination for most of Portugal's exports. Only the protection of the British fleet, especially after the victory at Trafalgar in 1805, kept the country's trade routes open. General Junot duly marched into Lisbon in November 1807.

On British advice the royal family had already gone into exile in Brazil, where they were to stay until 1821, and the war was left largely in the hands of British generals **Beresford** and **Wellington**. Having twice been driven out and twice reinvaded, the French were finally forced back into Spain in 1811 following the Battle of Buçaco (1810) and a long period of near starvation before the lines of Torres Vedras.

Britain's prize for this was the right to trade freely with **Brazil**, which, together with the declaration of that country as a kingdom in its own right, fatally weakened the dependent relationship that had profited the Portuguese treasury for so long. Past roles were reversed, with Portugal becoming effectively a colony of Brazil (where the royal family remained) and a protectorate of Britain, with General Beresford as administrator. The only active national institution was the army, many of whose officers had absorbed the constitutional ideals of revolutionary France.

In August 1820, with Beresford temporarily out of the country and King João VI still in Brazil, a group of officers called an unofficial Cortes and proceeded to draw up a new **constitution**. Inspired by the recent liberal advances in Spain, it called for an assembly – to be elected every two years by universal male suffrage – and the abolition of clerical privilege and the traditional rights of the nobility. The king, forced to choose between Portugal and Brazil, where his position looked even more precarious, came back in 1821 and accepted its terms. His queen, Carlota, and younger son **Miguel**, however, refused to take the oath of allegiance and became the dynamic behind a reactionary movement which drew considerable support in rural areas. With João VI's death in 1826, a delegation was sent to Brazil to pronounce Crown Prince Pedro the new king. Unfortunately Pedro was already Emperor of Brazil, having declared its independence some years earlier. He resolved to pass the crown to his infant daughter, with Miguel as regent provided that he swore to accept a new charter, drawn up by Pedro and somewhat less liberal than the earlier constitution. Miguel agreed, but once in power promptly tore up any agreement, abolished the charter and returned to the old, absolutist ways. This was a surprisingly popular move in Portugal, certainly in the countryside, but not with the governments of Britain, Spain, or France who backed the liberal rebels and finally put Pedro IV (who had meanwhile been deposed in Brazil) on the throne after Miguel's defeat at Évora-Monte in 1834.

The death of the monarchy

Pedro didn't survive long. The rest of the century – under the rule of his daughter Maria II (1834–53) and his grandsons Pedro V (1853–61) and Luís (1861–89) – saw almost constant struggle between those who supported the charter and those who favoured a return to the more liberal constitution of 1822. In 1846 the position deteriorated virtually to a state of **civil war** between Maria, who was fanatical in her support of her father's charter, and the radical constitutionalists. Only a further intervention by foreign powers maintained peace, imposed at the Convention of Gramido (1847).

Revolution

By 1974 the situation in Africa was deteriorating rapidly and at home Caetano's liberalization had come to a dead end; morale, among the army and the people, was lower than ever. The **MFA**, formed originally as an officers' organization to press for better conditions, and which had become increasingly politicized, was already laying its plans for a takeover. Dismissal of two popular generals – Spínola and Costa Gomes – for refusing publicly to support Caetano, led to a first chaotic and abortive attempt on March 16. Finally, on April 25, 1974, the plans laid by **Major Otelo Saraiva de Carvalho** for the MFA were complete and their virtually bloodless coup – known as the **Revolution of the Carnations** – went without a hitch, no serious attempt being made to defend the government.

The next two years were perhaps the most extraordinary in Portugal's history, a period of continual **revolution**, massive politicization and virtual anarchy, during which decisions of enormous importance were nevertheless made – above all the granting of independence to all of the overseas territories. At first there was little clear idea of any programme beyond the fact that the army wanted out of Africa. Though the MFA leadership was clearly to the left and at first associated with the PCP (Portuguese Communist Party), the bulk of the officers were less political and **General Spínola**, whom they had been forced to accept as a figurehead, was only marginally to the left of Caetano and strongly opposed total independence for the colonies. Spínola's dream was clearly to share the conservative nationalist policies that General de Gaulle had imposed in France, while the army was above all determined not to replace one dictator with another.

In the event their hands were forced by the massive popular response and especially by huge demonstrations on May Day. It was clear that whatever the leadership might decide, the people, especially in the cities, demanded a rapid move to the left. From the start every party was striving to project itself as the true defender of the "ideals of April 25". Provisional governments came and went but real power rested, where it had begun, with the MFA, now dominated by Saraiva de Carvalho and Vasco Gonçalves. While politicians argued around them, the army claimed to speak directly to the people, leading the country steadily left. It was a period of extraordinary contradictions, with the PCP, hoping to consolidate their position as the true revolutionary party, opposing liberalization and condemning strikes as counter-revolutionary, while ultra-conservative peasants were happily seizing their land from its owners.

Sudden **independence** and the withdrawal of Portuguese forces from the former colonies – while generally greeted in Portugal with relief – did not always work so well for the countries involved. Guinea-Bissau and Mozambique, the first to go, experienced relatively peaceful transitions, but **Angola** came to be a serious point of division between Spínola and the MFA. When independence finally came, after Spínola's resignation, the country was already in the midst of a full-scale civil war. The situation was even worse in **East Timor**, where more than ten percent of the population was massacred by invading Indonesian forces following Portuguese withdrawal. In Portugal itself the arrival of more than half-a-million colonial refugees – many of them destitute, most bitter – came to be a major problem for the regime, though their eventual integration proved one of its triumphs.

At home, the first **crisis** came in September 1974, when Spínola, with Gonçalves and Saraiva de Carvalho virtual prisoners in Lisbon's Belém Palace, moved army units to take over key positions. The MFA, however, proved too strong and Spínola was forced to resign, General Costa Gomes replacing him as president. By the summer of 1975 more general reaction was setting in and even the MFA began to show signs of disunity. The country was increasingly split, supporting the Revolution in the south, while remaining deeply conservative in the north. The Archbishop of Braga summed up the north's traditional views, declaring that the struggle against communism should be seen "not in terms of man against man, but Christ against Satan". Nevertheless the Revolution continued to advance; a coup attempt in March failed when the troops involved turned against their officers. The Council of the Revolution was formed, promptly nationalizing banking and private insurance; widespread land seizures went ahead in the Alentejo; and **elections** in the summer resulted in an impressive victory for Mário Soares' Socialist Party (PS).

On November 25, 1975, elements of the army opposed to the rightward shift in the government moved for yet another **coup**, taking over major air bases across the country. Otelo Saraiva de Carvalho, however, declined to bring his Lisbon command to their aid; nor did the hoped-for mass mobilization of the people take place. Government troops under Colonel Ramalho Eanes moved in to force their surrender and – again virtually without bloodshed – the Revolution had ended.

Democracy and Europe: the 1980s

In 1975, the ruling Socialist Party helped to shape the post-revolutionary constitution – a mildly Socialist document, though providing for a fairly powerful president. Early fears of a right-wing coup led by Spínola failed to materialize, helped by the election of **Colonel Eanes**, a man whom the army trusted, as president. He above all was a figure of stability, with enormous popular support and happy to concentrate on developing Portugal's links with Africa, Asia and Latin America and overseeing a gradual normalization process. The Socialists had effective control until 1980 when Dr. Sá Carneiro managed to create the **Democratic Alliance**, uniting the larger groupings on the right. But within a few months he died – some say suspiciously – in a plane crash.

In elections held on the ninth anniversary of the Revolution, April 25, 1983, Mário Soares' Socialist Party again became the largest single party in the national assembly. Soares' premiership was dogged by the unpopularity of his **economic austerity measures** (in part insisted on by the IMF) and by constant delays and breakdowns in the talks over Portuguese and Spanish **entry into the European Community**. These problems did have one positive result, however, namely closer relations with the traditionally hostile government in Madrid. But the government's economic problems led eventually to the withdrawal of Social Democratic support and to the collapse of the coalition.

Soon after the inconclusive elections of October 1985, the revolutionary leader Otelo Saraiva de Carvalho was arrested and put on trial in Lisbon accused of being the leader of 73 suspected terrorists in the **FP–25** urban guerrilla group. Proceedings were postponed following the shooting of one of the wasn't helped either by the **enlargement of the European Union** in 2004, from fifteen to twenty-five member states. This hails the end of the "free lunch" period of EU structural funding, which has played a dominant role in Portugal's development – mostly visibly in its road network. Worse, the bulk of Portugal's industries remain small or medium-scale, and have now to compete with eastern European enterprises, who have the advantage of lower labour costs and fresh EU funding. In fact, even within the enlarged European family, Portugal finds itself at the bottom of many comparative lists of economic factors.

Internationally, Barroso looked uncomfortable in the international spotlight, doing himself no favours by agreeing to host the 2003 Azores **Iraq War Conference** between Bush, Blair and Spain's Aznar. This did little to bolster Barroso's standing within Portugal, so when the post of European Commissioner within the EU became vacant, Barroso was only too glad to oblige, and resigned the premiership in July 2004. His replacement, former mayor of Lisbon, **Pedro Santana Lopes**, failed to lift the economy and called fresh elections in February 2005, but few expect things to change soon. A survey in early 2004 determined that Portugal was Europe's second-most pessimistic nation, after Slovakia. Yet, looking back, it's apparent that Portugal has progressed immensely since the Revolution, now thirty years ago. The installation of **democracy** has been an unmitigated success, and whilst excesses, corruption and other kinks remain, they're minor. **Infrastructure** has also developed beyond recognition, particularly the roads, but also ambitious bridges, transport systems in Lisbon and Porto, new stadiums built for the 2004 football championships, and many other more local developments.

However, the country's biggest challenges – ones that each government since 1974 has failed to adequately address – remain unanswered. Despite massive social change, economic restructuring and external funding, the economy remains ill-equipped to compete successfully in the international arena. Real spending power has fallen; the Portuguese still earn much less per capita than their more industrialized European partners. **Unemployment** is on the increase, currently hovering around 500,000 (from a working population of around five million), and **education** remains a slumbering catastrophe, with Europe's highest school drop-out rates. A slightly alarming shift, too, has been the takeover of large areas of banking, real estate and the financial sectors by Spanish companies. It looks unlikely that any solution will be found to these problems during this government's lifetime.

Chronology of
monuments and arts

22,000–8000 BC ▶ **Palaeolithic** hunter-gatherers sheltering from the Ice Age in the tributaries of the Douro and Tejo rivers leave behind thousands of engravings of animals: some of the world's oldest art.

7000–2000 BC ▶ **Neolithic** "granite civilization". Portugal's first man-made stone structures, belonging to a fertility cult; rock art spreads across country, beginning of metal ages.

1000–700 BC ▶ **Cultura Castreja** based around fortified hilltop settlements; Phoenicians establish first Atlantic trading posts around 900 BC; culture begins to adopt elements of classical mythology, including veneration of bulls.

700–200 BC ▶ **Celtic migrants** along Europe's Atlantic seaboard intermingle with locals; impressive towns at Briteiros and Sanfins. Local religion centred on wild sows and boars, of which statues remain.

210 BC ▶ **Romans** begin colonization; Conímbriga, 4th century BC Celtic town near Coimbra, adapted to Roman occupation (survives until 5th c AD).

193 BC ▶ **Lusitani uprising,** led by Viriatus, against Roman occupation; Viriatus is betrayed in 139 BC; northern Portugal not pacified until 19 BC.

60 BC ▶ **Julius Caesar** establishes a capital at Lisbon and towns at Beja, Braga, Évora, Santarém, etc. Walls and other remains at Idanha, in Beira Baixa; temple and aqueducts of Évora; bridges at Chaves, Ponte de Lima, Leiria and elsewhere.

1st to 4th century AD ▶ **Christianity** reaches Portugal's southern coast towards the end of the first century AD; bishoprics founded at Braga, Évora, Faro and Lisbon.

5th to 7th century AD ▶ Declining Roman Empire unable to resist **Barbarian invasions**. The Suevi establish courts at Braga and Porto in the north. Visigoths incorporate Suevian state into their Iberian empire in 585. Isolated churches, mainly in the north: São Pedro de Balsemão, near Lamego, and São Frutuoso at Braga.

711 ▶ **Moors** from North Africa invade and conquer peninsula within seven years. Christian **Reconquista** begins in 718, but will take more than 500 years to retake all Portugal. Moorish fortresses/walls survive at Silves, Lisbon, Sintra, Elvas, Mértola and Alcácer do Sal. Portuguese language emerges, heavily influenced by Arabic.

9th century ▶ **Al-Gharb** (Algarve) becomes an independent Moorish kingdom, governed from Silves. Porto reconquered by the Christian kings of Asturias-León in 868.

11th century ▶ Country of **Portucale** ("the sheltered port") emerges and in 1097 is given to Henry of Burgundy. Cluniac monks, administering pilgrimage route to Santiago, bring Romanesque architecture from France: 12th-century churches at Bravães, Tomar and around Penafiel, and council chamber at Bragança.

12th century ▶ **Afonso Henriques** recognized as first king of Portucale at the Treaty of Zamora of 1143. Guimarães castle built. In 1147, Afonso takes Lisbon and Santarém from the Moors; followed in 1162 by Beja and Évora. Fortress-like Romanesque cathedrals of Lisbon, Coimbra, Évora, Braga and Porto constructed.

13th century ▸ First assembly of the Cortes (parliament) at Coimbra in 1212. **Gothic architecture** enters Portugal at the Cistercian abbey of Alcobaça and several churches, most notably in Coimbra, and Porto's Sé. In 1249, **Afonso III** completes reconquest of the Algarve.

1279–1325 ▸ Reign of **Dom Dinis** sees construction of chain of fortresses along Spanish border.

1385 ▸ Battle of Aljubarrota: **João I** defeats Castilians to become first king of House of Avis. The great triumph of mature Portuguese Gothic – the abbey of Batalha – is built in celebration. Paço Real built at Sintra.

1415 ▸ **Infante Henriques** (Prince Henry the Navigator) active at the Navigation School in Sagres. Madeira discovered in 1419, and Azores in 1427. Flemish-influenced "Portuguese Primitive" painters include Nuno Gonçalves.

1434–1487 ▸ The **Portuguese Discoveries**: Gil Eanes opens the sea route around Africa. Cape Verde Islands discovered 1457; Ghana 1475; Congo 1482; and Cape of Good Hope rounded in 1487 by Bartolomeu Dias. Development of *Romanceiro* ballads.

1495–1521 ▸ Reign of **Dom Manuel I** ("The Fortunate"). Two years into his reign, the flotilla of **Vasco da Gama** reaches India; Cabral discovers Brazil in 1500; and in 1513, Portuguese reach China. New riches finance **Manueline** architectural style, with greatest examples at Tomar, Batalha and Belém. By 1530s Renaissance forms are introduced and merged.

1521–57 ▸ Reign of **João III**. Celebrated contemporary painters include Grão Vasco.

1557–78 ▸ Reign of boy-king **Dom Sebastião**. Important sculptural school at Coimbra (1520–70) centred on French Renaissance sculptors Nicolas Chanterenne, Filipe Hodart and Jean de Rouen. **Luís de Camões** publishes *Os Lusíadas* (1572), Portugal's national epic in verse.

1578–1640 ▸ Sebastião's disastrous expedition to Morocco, loss of king and mass slaughter of nobility at Alcácer-Quibir. **Philip II** steps into the void in 1581 and brings Spanish occupation under Habsburg rule.

1640 ▸ **João IV**, Duke of Bragança, restores independence. Severe late-Renaissance style: eg São Vicente in Lisbon designed by Felipe Terzi.

1706–50 ▸ Reign of **Dom João V**. Gold and diamonds discovered in Brazil, reached peak of wealth and exploitation in the 1740s, reflected in opulence of **Baroque** style. Highlights include Porto's church and tower of Clérigos, the palace-monastery of Mafra, Queluz palace, Coimbra university library, and the more rustic Baroque style at Lamego and Bom Jesus.

1755 ▸ **Great Earthquake** destroys Lisbon and parts of the Alentejo and Algarve. "Pombaline" Neoclassical style employed for rebuilding of Lisbon (Baixa) and Vila Real de Santo António in the Algarve. Regulation of port wine industry by Pombal guarantees Porto's success and flourishing of the arts.

19th century ▸ **Maria II** (1843–53) holds throne with German consort, Fernando II. Pena Palace folly built at Sintra. Extensive mercantile construction throughout the country in Neoclassical and Renaissance styles. Birth of fado music in Lisbon's popular *bairros*.

1900–10 ▸ **Assassination of Carlos I** in Lisbon in 1908; exile of Manuel II ("The Unfortunate") two years later marks end of Portuguese monarchy.

1910–26 ▸ "Democratic" Republic. Works by writer **Fernando Pessoa**. Fado's popularity spreads, particularly among Coimbra's students.

1932–68 ▶ **Salazar** dictatorship. Goa is seized by India; colonial wars in Africa. Traditional music, bearer of North African and Celtic heritage, recorded by Michel Giacometti and composer Fernando Lopes Graça from 1950s onwards; influences Lopes Graça's own choral output.

1974 ▶ **April 25 Revolution.** "New Song" movement of singer-songwriters associated with the change, but trashy "Pimba pop" replaces fado – scarred by Salazar's support – as the nation's most popular music. **European Community** (1986) kicks off massive road-building programme.

1994–1998 ▶ **Lisbon** is European Capital of Culture (1994).

Permanent gallery of modern Portuguese artists opens at Lisbon's Gulbenkian Foundation. Lisbon hosts Expo 98; becomes a showcase for the work of national and international architects.

1999 ▶ Porto's Serralves Museum of Contemporary Art opens. Death of fado singer **Amália Rodrigues** sees three days of national mourning and marks revival of the genre.

2001 ▶ **Porto** is European City of Culture; signals massive programme of urban regeneration.

2004 ▶ Portugal hosts European Football Championships. Fado music celebrates the centennial of its first recording.

Music

M usically, Portugal is best known as the home of the passionate and elegant vocal and instrumental fado of Lisbon and Coimbra but, away from the cities, a rich variety of regionally distinct music and a wide range of traditional instruments can still be encountered. Even though social and economic change has diminished its role in everyday life, you are still likely to come across traditional music during local festivals and public performances. This inheritance invests much of what is distinctively Portuguese in the music coming out of the country today, as it did in the "new song" movement of singer-songwriters associated with the political change of the 1974 revolution. Portuguese democracy has matured to an eclectic soundtrack: vibrant music from the country's former colonies and Lusophone variants of global pop, rock, rap, electronic dance music and jazz have developed alongside the home-grown kitsch known as *pimba*.

Portuguese instruments

Portugal is home to a remarkable variety of instruments, most of them associated with particular regional traditions.

Guitarra Portuguesa

The best-known Portuguese music is fado, and be that the Lisboa or Coimbra tradition its dominant instrument is the **guitarra**. Though sometimes called the Portuguese guitar, its body isn't "guitar-shaped", but that of an Arabic lute (*ud* or *'aoud*), introduced over a thousand years ago during the Moorish conquest. Two designs evolved – the Lisbon *guitarra*, usually used for accompanying singers, and the larger body and richer bass of the version more suited to Coimbra fado, with its strong *guitarra*-virtuoso strand. Both have six pairs of steel strings tuned by knurled turn-screws on a fan-shaped metal machine head.

Violas

In fado, the *guitarra* is usually accompanied by a six-string guitar of the Spanish form which, like all fretted instruments of that waisted body-shape, is known in Portugal as a *viola*. Though the **viola de fado** is usually a normal Spanish guitar, there is a remarkable range of other specifically Portuguese *violas*. They are virtually always steel-strung, and most have soundboards decorated with flowing tendril-like dark wood inlays spreading from the bridge, and soundholes in a variety of shapes.

The version encountered most often, particularly in the north, is the **viola braguesa**, which has five pairs of strings and is usually played *rasgado* (a fast intricate rolling strum with an opening hand). A slightly smaller close relative, from the region of Amarante, is the **viola amarantina**, whose soundhole is usually in the form of two hearts. Other varieties include the ten- or twelve-stringed **viola campanica alentejana** which has a very deeply indented waist, almost like a figure of eight; a notable modern player is **José Barros** of the Alentejo duo **Cantesul**. Another version is the **viola beiroa**, which is distinctive in having an extra pair of strings which are played in a way similar to the high fifth string on an American banjo.

Cavaquinhos and bandolims

One popular Portuguese stringed instrument has taken root across the world. The **cavaquinho** looks like a baby viola with four strings, and is played with an ingenious

Regional traditions

Each region of Portugal has its own characteristic songs, ensembles and instruments but the vocal and instrumental traditions survive most strongly in the rural areas away from the sea – regions like Trás-os-Montes, Beiras and Alentejo. Villages and towns throughout Portugal have folklore troupes known as **ranchos folclóricos** who perform at festivals and sometimes on concert stages and help perpetuate the musical traditions of the country. These were encouraged by the dictatorship as exemplars of the happy colourful peasantry, and were therefore somewhat disapproved of by musicians who were opponents of the regime, but emerging from those associations some continue to exist. Recently there has also been an increase in the number of musicians and bands performing traditional material, making new music with a roots heritage.

Portuguese tradition is rich with song, some of it drawing on the **oral ballad** repertoire that was once widespread across Europe. Iberia has its own specific group of ballads – the *Romanceiro* – which were sung in the royal courts from

fast strum akin to the braguesa's *rasgado*. It spread from Portugal to the Azores and Madeira, and travelled onwards with Portuguese migrants from the Atlantic islands to Hawaii, where it became, with very few changes, the ukulele. The Portuguese form of mandolin, the **bandolim** or *banjolim*, is much used; a particularly fine player is **Júlio Pereira** (⊛ www.juliopereira.pt), who is also an expert exponent of *cavaquinho* and the range of *violas*.

Pipes

The **gaita-de-foles** is the Portuguese bagpipe, in form similar to the Scottish Highland war-pipe but closest to the *gaitas* of Spanish Galicia and Asturias, all of which are drawn from the Moorish tradition (*ghaita* being the Moroccan word for a pipe), itself perhaps evolved from Celtic influence two thousand years ago. It is the main melody instrument of Trás-os-Montes music, accompanied by *bombo* and *caixa*. Each *gaita* has the tuning its player chooses, the scale in which he sings, rather than the fixed, mathematical scale developed for classical harmony that has come to prevail in much of the western world.

Percussion

A feature of Beira Baixa music, and found elsewhere too, is the **adufe**. Introduced by the Arabs a millennium ago, it is a square double-headed drum usually containing pieces of wood or pebbles which rattle. Held on edge and tapped with the fingers, it's played by women, often in groups, to accompany their singing. Also found in several traditions is the clanking **ferrinhos** (triangle), played pretty much as in Cajun music.

Bombo, *caixa*, *adufe*, *pandeiro* (small drum) and *pandeireta* (tambourine) or occasionally *cântaro com abano* (a clay pot struck across its mouth with a leather or straw fan) provide the thump of Portuguese traditional music, while the clatter comes from the likes of the *cana* (a split cane slap-stick), **trancanholas** (wooden "bones"), *castanholas*, *reco-reco* (a scraped serrated stick), *conchas* (shells rubbed together), *zaclitracs* (a form of rattle) and *genebres* (a wooden xylophone hung from the neck (a feature of the *dança dos homens* (men's dance) in Beira Baixa).

the fifteenth until the seventeenth century, but continued in the fields and villages long after that. Many other traditional songs – of love, religion or the cycles of nature – remained part of life until the 1970s, but with migration, changing ways of work, and mass media, the need and occasions for singing them have dwindled. Many now exist only in field recordings or in the repertoire of the revival folk bands.

Singers are sometimes joined by others in a refrain, perhaps accompanied by a stringed instrument or percussion. In the south, particularly **Alentejo**, there is a long tradition of *a cappella* vocal groups, a vibrant Mediterranean sound comparable to that of the vocal ensembles of Corsica and Sardinia. These are generally single-sex with a lead singer who delivers the first couple of verses before being joined by harmonizing lines from a second singer and then full-group vocal. Performing and recording ensembles exist, such as **Ensemble Vidigueira**, **Cantadores de Redondo**, **As Ceifeiros de Pias** or the female group **As Camponesas de Castro Verde**. **Vozes do Sul**, a group led by Alentejo singer-songwriter **Janita Salomé**, combines the singers from some of these groups and from his own family with new arrangements on acoustic instruments. An unexpected commercial success in 2004 was the Alentejan-style *As Meninas da Ribeira do Sado*, performed by folk group **Adiafa** (⊛www.adiafa.com).

Trás-os-Montes in the northeast is the heartland of *gaita-de-foles* (bagpipes), and the old tradition – inherited from both Celtic times and Moorish occupation – survives principally in the easternmost tip, Miranda do Douro, hard up against the Spanish border. Of the surviving handful of traditional Mirandês *gaiteiros*, two of the best are in the quartet **Galandum Galundaina**, fine musicians and singers whose activity shows signs of creating new interest. They play regularly for the *dança dos paulitos*, a stick dance for men which is strongly reminiscent of an English morris dance. Its music is provided by the standard Trás-os-Montes line-up of a *gaita-de-foles* accompanied by a *bombo* (bass drum) and *caixa* (snare drum), or sometimes by a solo musician playing a three-hole whistle (*flauta pastoril*) with one hand and a small snare drum (*tamboril*) with the other.

Bombos and *caixas* also feature in other northern and central regions as the thud and snap driving various ensembles playing for ceremony or celebration, such as the *zés-pereiras* of the **Minho** region, where they join flutes and sometimes clarinets and *gaitas*. Another style of Minho ensemble is the *rusga*, a variable line-up of stringed instruments such as *viola braguesa*, *cavaquinho* and perhaps violin, with accordion, flutes, clarinet, perhaps ocarina, and a clattering rhythm section.

Every region of Portugal has its own traditions – songs and ways of singing them, instruments, types of ensemble – and social or festival events at which they occur. Wherever you are, you might well stumble across something interesting. For more detail, sound samplers, festival listings and links, take a look at these websites: ⊛www.attambur.com, run by the group At-Tambur, and ⊛www.juliopereira.pt.

Roots revival

In the 1970s, young performing groups began to form to devote their attention either to the performance of traditional music, or to the construction of new music with folk roots. They used material that was still being sung or played, or could be enticed from the memories of their elders. Another source of inspiration was the material preserved in the **field recordings** made by enlightened individuals earlier in the 20th century, notable among them being Michel Giacometti (1929–90), a Corsican-born Frenchman who together with Fernando Lopes Graça made field recordings throughout Portugal that were released on various labels from the late 1950s onwards.

The number of new revival bands appears to be increasing, while several of the pioneers are still around, including **Brigada Victor Jara**, formed in Coimbra in 1975, which, while containing none of its original members, continues to be a major force. A particularly innovative recent arrival is **Gaiteiros de Lisboa**, which makes dramatic new music with deep roots, using raw percussion, voices, *gaitas* and other reeds plus quirky invented instruments. Another such inventive project is the group **Adufe**, inspired by Japanese Taiko drumming and formed by José Salgueiro, which makes a dramatic show focused on four giant *adufes*.

Well worth tracking down, too, are performances by accordion group **Danças Ocultas**, who – fed up with the accordion's usual fairground repertoire – reinvented the genre and, some would say, the instrument, with some extraordinarily atmospheric and at times haunting sounds. In similarly uncategorizable vein is the flute playing of **Rão Kyao**, fusing the formal beauty of Indian *raga* with frequent collaborations with Moroccan drum and lute players, and classical fado guitar.

Fado

Portugal's most famous musical form, **fado** ("fate") is currently experiencing a boom in popularity at home and abroad. It's an urban music, a thing of nighttime and bars, the origins of which are debatable but certainly involve influences from Portugal's overseas explorations. The essence of fado is *saudade* (inadequately translatable as "yearning" or "beautiful melancholy"), which is carried in the lyrical and sentimental expression of a solo singer, usually accompanied by the *guitarra* and *viola de fado*. There are two distinct traditions of fado: Lisbon, which is very much a vocal form, male and female, and Coimbra, which in addition to its songs has a purely instrumental, *guitarra*-led aspect and is a male-only preserve. Portuguese are often mystified as to what a non-Portuguese speaker could get from fado, since so much of its meaning is in the poetic lyrics, but the beauty of the soaring vocals over the silvery *guitarra* is certainly seductive.

By far the most famous of the fado singers, and arguably its greatest performer, was **Amália Rodrigues** who had an immeasurable impact upon the direction of the fado through her recordings. Born in 1920 in the Alfama district of Lisbon, her death in October 1999 saw three days of official mourning announced in Portugal. Though in the course of her long singing career she ventured into other musical forms, her style and most celebrated recordings have become a central reference point in what people mean by fado.

Two working class districts of Lisbon – Mouraria and Alfama – are considered the birthplace of fado, and the music can still be found in both, but the main focus of fado clubs these days, is the Bairro Alto (see pp.117–118). Some are expensive, some are tourist-traps, some are both; as with the elusive *duende* of Spain's flamenco, you may find the most memorable fado of all is performed by an unadvertised performer and, whether the performer is famous or not, when you're present at a special, real moment of fado you'll know it. Fado clubs are social places, with eating, drinking and informality, but during a song set in a good club the waiters don't serve, and the music is treated with due reverence. It's also not unusual for well-known fadistas to run their own clubs. **Maria da Fé** owns the Lisbon fado house *O Senhor Vinho*, where she and other notables perform. Seated at the long tables in the Clube de Fado in Alfama, you might well hear the owner **Mário Pacheco** himself, a fine *guitarrista* and the last to play with Amália, accompanying **Ana Sofia Varela**.

On the concert stage and on recordings, the band line-up may be larger and use a wider range of instruments, including piano, strings or wind instruments. This isn't a new phenomenon – Amália and others of her generation did it – but the elegant simplicity of the traditional line-up is the key in the work of many of today's leading young international performers, such as **Mariza** (a truly delectable voice; her version of *Barco Negro* is spine-chilling), **Mísia**, **Cristina Branco**, **Kátia Guerreiro**, **Mafalda Arnauth** and male singers (currently in a minority among the new wave) **Helder Moutinho** and **Camané**. At the same time, **Dona Rosa**, unaccompanied save for her gently tinkling triangle, as stark as a rural ballad-singer, is now receiving international acclaim after years of performing her very personal fado on the streets of Lisbon.

Many performers move in and out of fado, or mix aspects of it with other genres. For example **Dulce Pontes** began in the world of rock-pop ballads, then for her second CD, *Lágrimas*, she performed fado and while she explores other genres it has remained a strong thread in her music, including on her 1999 release, *O Primeiro Canto*. The music of the equally well-known Lisbon band **Madredeus** – a manicured blend of classical guitars and keyboards surrounding the songbird vocals of **Teresa Salgueiro** in songs largely by band leader Pedro Ayres Magalhães – while not fado as such is, nevertheless, replete with the reflective melancholy of *saudade*.

Coimbra fado has a very different style: reflecting that city's ancient university traditions, and typically performed by students and Coimbra graduates, it's an exclusively male domain. As well as more formal songs that are less personally expressive than in Lisbon fado, there is also a strong aspect of *guitarra*-led instrumentals. The most famous Coimbra *guitarra fadista* of the latter half of the twentieth century was **Carlos Paredes**, who combined enviable technical mastery with genuine feeling and expression, placing the fado guitar centre-stage alongside the singers it traditionally accompanied. Coimbra's instrumental fado continues to evolve in skilled hands in both traditional and new combinations: most of **Pedro Caldeira Cabral**'s compositions aren't fado as such, but they and his immense virtuosity on the *guitarra* can be seen as part of the legacy of Coimbra fado.

For an excellent and detailed introduction to fado, "the people's soul", see ⓦhttp://paginas.fe.up.pt/~fado.

Nova Canção and música popular

It was an attempt to update the Coimbra fado that resulted in the modern Portuguese **ballad** (the term in this context meaning a set of poetic – usually contemporary – lyrics set to music, rather than the epic story-song that is the traditional folk-ballad).

The great figure in this movement was **José Afonso**. He had a classic, soaring fado-style voice and his first recording, with Luís Góes in 1956, comprised fados from Coimbra together with a couple of his own songs. It was principally Afonso's songs, his choice of those by others, and his music drawing on regional traditional musics and fado, that during the last years of the dictatorship, became known as **nova canção** (new song). Together with the songs and performances of a gathering cast of others such as **Fausto**, **Luís Cília**, **Sérgio Godinho** and **Vitorino**, this provided a rallying point in the development not only of new Portuguese music but also of a new democratized state. In the final years of dictatorship, censorship and the restriction of performing opportunities caused some songwriters to move and record abroad, but Afonso remained, when necessary masking social and political messages with allegory.

In the years after the 1974 revolution *nova canção* broadened to a movement known as **música popular** – essentially contemporary singer-songwriter music with folk roots. As in fado, the lyrics were as significant as the music, but unlike the more personal and emotional subject matter of fado they dealt with contemporary social and cultural issues. The music drew on popular tradition, both rural and urban, as well as reflecting Latin American, European and North African influences. Though he died in 1987, Afonso's albums keep his music and ideas very much a touchstone in Portuguese musical thinking, and many of his contemporaries are still performing. Younger singers and songwriters, such as **Amélia Muge**, continue in a similar spirit of drawing on a mixture of rural and fado traditions, and you'll frequently hear songs by Afonso, Godinho and other *nova canção* leaders in the repertoire of fado singers.

Rock and pop

Although the music of the likes of **Madredeus**, **Brigada Victor Jara**, **Dulce Pontes**, **Cristina Branco**, **Mísia** and **Mariza** has an identifiably Portuguese international profile, pop bands like **Coldfinger** have come onto the scene in recent years and, as they sing mainly in English, are easily marketable abroad as pop rather than world music. Among other mainstream rock and pop groups to keep an ear out for in Portugal are Os Delfins, GNR, Santos e Pecadores, Clã, the REM-influenced Silence 4, and all-round rockers Xutos e Pontapés.

On a national level, the acknowledged "father of Portuguese rock" is guitarist and singer-songwriter **Rui Veloso** (⊛www.ruiveloso.net), now into his third decade of performing. Combining elegant bluesy guitar sounds in the manner of Eric Clapton and Bob Dylan with down-to-earth lyrics by Carlos T, he remains popular across the generations and his albums regularly go platinum within a week of release. Rap singer **Pedro Abrunhosa** – who never takes his shades off in public – is the other big star. On its release, his first record, *Viagens*, broke sales records and opened the doors for many groups. One of the main achievements of his music was to make **rap** more acceptable and its decidedly jazzy feel has provided an alternative to a music scene previously dominated by FM-style hard rock. In fact Portuguese rap and hip-hop from General D, Da Weasel, Boss AC and others now dominate the underground music and club scene.

Dance music took a while to catch on, but in 1991 the first ever Portuguese house track, *Deep Sky* by Matrix Run, stimulated a wave of new interest and Lisbon has become a major clubbing destination. Though most dance music you'll hear in clubs is still imported, major home-grown exponents include **DJ Vibe** and **X-Wife (DJ Kitten)**.

You're unlikely to get through a visit to Portugal without hearing some **música pimba** – unrepentantly tacky music of the sort that usually enters the charts around Christmas time. Despite the wholesale snubbing of this style by the Portuguese media, *pimba* – which has its roots in a popular oom-pa-pah brand of music played at fairs – has succeeded in conquering the whole country, as well as being big in countries with large Portuguese communities. Mixing traditional and modern elements, its success was previously limited to rural areas (where most bars have a selection of cassettes for sale), but the introduction of satirical jokes and sexual references in the lyrics found new support among college students, and endless performances on morning and afternoon TV shows means *pimba* is now firmly established. The main names are effeminate singer/songwriter **Marco Paulo**, the raunchy **Ágata**, half-Brazilian **Roberto Leal**, and **Quim Barreiros**, much loved for his scurrilous lyrics; if you get a chance to see him, take it – the atmosphere at his shows is contagious.

Music from former colonies

Touring musicians and bands from all over the world perform in Portugal, but naturally it's a good place to encounter those from the world's biggest Luso-phone country, **Brazil**. An exciting and relatively recent development in the Portuguese music scene has been the appearance of groups from the **former colonies** of Angola, Mozambique, Cabo Verde, Guinea-Bissau and São Tomé e Príncipe. Following the colonial wars and independence many African musi-cians settled in Lisbon, while some spend part of the year based in Portugal while they tour Europe or record.

Cabo Verde music in particular has achieved great acclaim, with the reflec-tive, melodic fado-like *morna* – whose most internationally famous exponent is **Cesária Évora** – and the more danceable *moradeira*. Another fine Lisbon resident Cabo Verdean singer is **Celina Pereira**. Among the **Lisbon Cabo Verdean** community, some women, such as the twelve-strong group **Voz de África**, gather on Sundays and at celebrations to play, sing and dance *batuc* – a social music banned in colonial times in which lively singing is accompanied by clapping, slapping on plastic-covered pillows and a dance in which two women circle and bump hips. Taking some influences from *batuc* **Sara Tavares**, who made a reputation in her teens as a pop singer, is now turning to what she describes as her personal tradition, with roots in Cabo Verde, Portugal and elsewhere, delivering live performances of freshness, beauty and subtlety.

Soft-voiced Angolan singer-guitarist **Waldemar Bastos** was imprisoned in his native country in the 1970s, and defected to Portugal in 1982. Now an internationally esteemed performer with influences from Brazilian and Portuguese as well as Angolan forms, he runs a small restaurant with his wife in Lisbon's Barrio Alto (*Água do Bengo*; see p.109) where you can dine to an Angolan-inspired soundtrack. New resident African-rooted formations arise and visiting bands arrive frequently, so it's worth keeping an eye on the posters and papers for promising-looking live shows and festivals.

Discography

This list is just a pointer to some of the recordings available, many of them internationally. Investigation of small music shops and chain stores in Portugal will turn up the many CDs that don't have international distribution, and there's a steady stream of new releases and re-issues too. In particular, there are a large number of Lisbon fado CDs – new and historic recordings, single artist releases (including vast numbers by Amália) and compilations (which often include tracks from great singers, particularly from the past, who have no whole album extant). Better than any CD, though, go and experience the music live – follow that sound echoing down the street.

Traditional

Alentejo
Ensemble Vidigueira *Portugal: Voices of Alentejo* (Auvidis)
Grupo Coral e Etnográfico *As Camponesas de Castro Verde – Castro Verde: Vozes das Terras Brancas* (EMI Valentim de Carvalho), *Os Camponeses de Pias – Pias: O Cante na margem Esquerda* (EMI Valentim de Carvalho)
Vozes do Sul *Vozes do Sul* (Capella)
Various *Portugal: Musique de l'Alentejo* (Ocora)
Various *Portuguese Folk Music. Vol 4: Alentejo* (field recordings by Giacometti and Lopes Graça) (Strauss)

Algarve
Various *Portuguese Folk Music. Vol 5: Algarve* (field recordings by Giacometti and Lopes Graça) (Strauss)

Beiras
Grupo de Cantares de Manhouce *Cantares da Beira* (EMI Valentim de Carvalho)
Various *Idanha-a-Noca: toques e cantares da vila* (EMI Terra)
Various *Portuguese Folk Music. Vol 3: Beiras* (field recordings by Giacometti and Lopes Graça) (Strauss)

Estremadura
Various *Tradições Musicais da Estremadura* (Book & 3 CDs) (Tradisom)

Minho
Various *Portuguese Folk Music. Vol 1: Minho* (field recordings by Giacometti and Lopes Graça) (Strauss)

Trás-os-Montes
Various *Música Tradicional: Terra de Miranda* (Tecnosaga)
Various *Portugal: Trás-os-Montes: Chants du Blé et Cornemuses de Berger* (Ocora)
Various *Portuguese Folk Music. Vol 2: Trás-os-Montes* (field recordings by Giacometti and Lopes Graça) (Strauss)

Collections
Various *Musical Traditions of Portugal* (Smithsonian/Folkways)
Various *Musical Travel: Portugal and the Islands* (Auvidis)
Various *Sons da Terra: A tradição é o que é* (Series of 10 CDs) (Sons da Terra/Edições e Produções Musicais)
Various *Portugal: Sons da Tradição* (BMG Classics/RCA)
Various *Women's Voices of Portugal* (Auvidis)

Roots revival and development

Brigada Victor Jara *Danças e Folias* (Farol)

Danças Ocultas *Ar* and *Danças Ocultas* (both EMI Valentim de Carvalho)

Gaiteiros de Lisboa *Bocas do Inferno*, *Invasões Bárbaras* and *Dançachamas* (all Farol)

Né Ladeiras *Traz os Montes* (EMI Valentim de Carvalho)

Realejo *Cenários* (Movieplay)

Sétima Legião *Sexto Sentido* (EMI Valentim de Carvalho)

Vai de Roda *Polas Ondas* (Alba)

Various *Novas vos Trago* (a modern interpretation of medieval *Romanceiro* ballads, with Amélia Muge, Brigada Victor Jara, Gaiteiros de Lisboa, João Afonso and Sérgio Godinho) (Tradisom)

Fado

Lisbon fado

João Braga *Cantar ao Fado* (Strauss)

Camané *Pelo Dia Dentro* (EMI Valentim de Carvalho)

Katia Guerreiro *Fado Maior* (Ocarina)

Mafalda Arnauth *Esta Voz Que Nos Atrevessa* (EMI Valentim de Carvalho)

Mariza *Fado em Mim* (World Connection), *Fado Curvo* (EMI)

Mísia *Ritual* and *Fado: Garras dos Sentidos* (both Erato)

Helder Moutinho *Sete Fados e Alguns Cantos* (Ocarina)

Amália Rodrigues *The Art of Amália* (EMI Hemisphere), *The First Recordings* (EPM), *Clássicos da Renascença* (Rádio Renascença/Movieplay)

Dona Rosa *Histórias da Rua* (Jaro)

Various *Portugal: The Story Of Fado* (EMI Hemisphere)

Various *Arquivos do Fado* (Heritage) (Series of CDs; recordings from the 1920s and 1930s)

Various *Um Parfum de Fado* (Playasound) (Series of CDs)

Coimbra vocal fado

Fernando Machado Soares *The Fado of Coimbra* (Auvidis)

Coimbra instrumental fado

Carlos Paredes *Guitarra Portuguesa* (EMI Valentim de Carvalho), *O Melhor de Carlos Paredes e Rão Kyao* (Universal Music Portugal)

Nova canção and música popular

José Afonso *Cantigas do Maio* (Movieplay), *Fados de Coimbra e Outras Canções* (Movieplay), *Best of José Afonso* and *José Afonso* (Movieplay)

Sérgio Godinho *Lupa* (EMI Valentim de Carvalho)

Vitorino *Alentejanas e Amorosas* (EMI Valentim de Carvalho), *Clássicos da Renascença* (Rádio Renascença/Movieplay)

Fado-influenced developments

Amélia Muge *Todos os Dias* (Columbia)

Carlos Paredes & Charlie Haden *Dialogues* (Antilles)

Dulce Pontes *Caminhos* (Movieplay)

Fernando Lameirinhas *Live* (Munich)

Filipa Pais *L'Amar* (Strauss)

Júlio Pereira *Acústico* (Sony)

Madredeus *Antologia* and

Movimento (both EMI Valentim de Carvalho)
Pedro Caldeira Cabral *Variações - Guitarra Portuguesa* (World Network)

Rão Kyão *Fado Virado a Nascente* (Universal), *O Melhor de Carlos Paredes e Rão Kyao* (Universal Music Portugal)

Rock and pop

Coldfinger *Lefthand* (Nortesul)
Rádio Macau *Onde o Tempo Faz a Curva* (BMG)

Rui Veloso *Ar de Rock* (Valentim de Carvalho)
Silence 4 *Only Pain is Real* (Universal)

Music from former colonies

Waldemar Bastos *Pretaluz* (Luaka Bop)
Justino Delgado *Casamenti D'Haos* (Lusafrica)
Cesária Évora *Miss Perfumado* and *Cesária* (Lusafrica/Melodie),

Anthologie: Mornas & Coladeras (BMG)
Celina Pereira *Nõs Tradições* (Lusafrica)
Various *The Soul of Cape Verde* (Tinder)

Compilations

Various *Music from the Edge of Europe: Portugal* (EMI Hemisphere). Compiled from EMI Valentim de Carvalho's catalogue. Amália Rodrigues, Carlos Paredes, Vitorino, Sérgio Godinho, Né Ladeiras, António Pinho Vargas & Maria João, Madredeus, Danças Ocultas, Lua Extravagante, Trovante et al. Fado, *guitarra*, *nova canção/música popular*, *guitarra* and jazzish, but no rural traditional music.

Various *The Rough Guide to the Music of Portugal* (World Music Network). Compiled from Movieplay's catalogue; fado, *nova canção*, *guitarra*, roots revival but again no traditional rural music. José Afonso, Dulce Pontes, Carlos Paredes, Vai de Roda, Carlos Zel, Vitorino, Maria Teresa de Noronha, Maria da Fé, Teresa Silva de Carvalho et al.

Fiction

António Lobo Antunes *An Explanation of the Birds, The Natural Order of Things, Act of the Damned, The Return of the Caravels* and *South of Nowhere.* Psychologically astute and with a helter-skelter prose style, Antunes is considered by many to be Portugal's finest contemporary writer after Saramago. His recent *The Return of the Caravels,* a modern "take" on the Discoveries, is a good place to start.

Maria Isabel Barreno, Maria Teresa Horta and Maria Velho da Costa *New Portuguese Letters: The Three Marias.* Published (and prosecuted) in 1972, pre-Revolution Portugal, this collage of stories, letters and poems is a modern feminist parable based on the seventeenth-century "Letters of a Portuguese Nun".

José Cardoso Pires *Ballad of Dog's Beach* (o/p). Ostensibly a detective thriller but the murder described actually took place during the last years of Salazar's dictatorship and Pires' research draws upon the original secret-police files. Compelling, highly original and with acute psychological insights, it was awarded Portugal's highest literary prize and made into a film.

Lídia Jorge *The Migrant Painter of Birds.* Born near Albufeira in 1946, Lídia Jorge is one of Portugal's most respected contemporary writers. This beautifully written novel describes a girl's memories as she grows up in a small village close to the Atlantic, and in doing so poignantly captures a changing rural community.

Ray Keenoy, David Treece and Paul Hyland *The Babel Guide to the Fiction of Portugal, Brazil and Africa.* A tantalizing introduction to Portuguese literature, with a collection of reviews of the major works of Lusophone fiction since 1945.

Eugénio Lisboa (ed) *The Anarchist Banker and Other Portuguese Stories* and *Professor Pfiglzz and His Strange Companion and Other Portuguese Stories.* A fabulous two-volume collection of twentieth-century short stories, which gives more than a taste of the exuberance and talent currently proliferating in Portuguese literature. Stories by old favourites – Eça de Queirós, Pessoa, José Régio and Miguel Torga – are included too, mostly for the first time in English.

Eugénio Lisboa and Helder Macedo (eds) *The Dedalus Book of Portuguese Fantasy.* A rich feast of literary fantasy comprising short stories by the likes of Eça de Queirós and José de Almada Negreiros.

José Rodrigues Miguéis *Happy Easter.* A powerful and disturbing account of the distorted reality experienced by a schizophrenic, whose deprived childhood leads him to a self-destructive and tragic life in Lisbon; evocatively written and a gripping read.

Fernando Pessoa *Book of Disquiet* and *A Centenary Pessoa.* The country's best-known poet wrote *The Book of Disquiet* in prose; it's an unclassifiable text compiled from unordered fragments, part autobiography, part philosophical rambling. Regarded as a Modernist classic, the Penguin edition is the most complete English version. *A Centenary Pessoa* includes a selection of his prose and poetry, including his works under the pseudonym of Ricardo Reis.

Eça de Queirós *The Sin of Father Amaro* (o/p), *Cousin Bazilio, The Maias* and *The Illustrious House of Ramires.* One of Portugal's greatest writers, Eça de Queirós (or

Queiroz; 1845–1900) introduced realism into Portuguese fiction with *The Sin of Father Amaro*, published in 1876. Over half a dozen of his novels have been translated into English; always highly readable, they present a cynical but affectionate picture of Portuguese society in the second half of the nineteenth century. His *English Letters*, written during his long stint as consul in England, is also well worth investigating.

Erich Maria Remarque *The Night in Lisbon*. Better known as author of *All Quiet On The Western Front*, German author Remarque writes with a similar detachment in this tale of a World War II refugee seeking an escape route from Europe. One night in Lisbon, he meets a stranger who has two tickets, and within hours their lives are inextricably linked in a harrowing and moving tale.

Mário de Sá-Carneiro *The Great Shadow* and *Lucio's Confessions*. *The Great Shadow* is a collection of short stories set against the backdrop of Lisbon in the early 1900s as the author describes his obsession with great art. Sá-Carneiro, who committed suicide at 26, writes with stunning intensity and originality about art, science, death, homosexual sex and insanity. Similar themes appear in *Lucio's Confessions*, in which a menage-a-trois between three artists ends in a death.

José Saramago *All the Names, Baltasar and Blimunda, Blindness, The History of the Siege of Lisbon, The Year of the Death of Ricardo Reis, The Gospel According to Jesus Christ, The Stone Raft, The Tale of the Unknown Island, Manual of Painting and Calligraphy*. Saramago won the Nobel prize for literature in 1998 and is Portugal's most famous living writer. His novels have come thick and fast and are mostly experimental, often dispensing with punctuation altogether; *Blindness* even avoided naming a single character in the book. The one to start with is *Ricardo Reis*, a magnificent novel whose theme is the return of Dr. Reis, after sixteen years in Brazil, to a Lisbon where the Salazar dictatorship is imminent and where Reis wanders the streets to be confronted by the past and the ghost of the writer Fernando Pessoa. In *Baltasar and Blimunda*, Saramago mixes fact with myth in an entertaining novel set around the building of the Convent of Mafra and the construction of the world's first flying machine.

Antonio Tabucchi *Declares Pereira, Requiem: A Hallucination* and *Fernando Pessoa* (with Maria José de Lancastre). Tabucchi is a highly regarded Italian author and biographer of Pessoa, who lived in Portugal for many years. In *Declares Pereira* he has re-created the repressive atmosphere of Salazar's Lisbon, tracing the experiences of a newspaper editor who questions his own lifestyle under a regime which he can no longer ignore. The book has recently been made into a film by Roberto Faenza. *Requiem: A Hallucination* is an imaginative and dream-like journey around Lisbon. The unifying theme is food and drink, and the book even contains a note on recipes at the end.

Miguel Torga *The Creation of the World* and *Tales from the Mountain*. Twice nominated for the Nobel Prize before his death in 1995, Torga lived and set his stories in the wild Trás-os-Montes region. His pseudonym "Torga" is a tough species of heather which thrives in this rural, unforgiving landscape, where the fiercely independent characters of his books battle to survive in a repressed society. Torga's harsh views of rural life in *Tales from the Mountain* led to the book being banned under the Salazar regime.

Language

More common is **ÃO** (as in *pão*, bread — *são*, saint — *limão*, lemon), which sounds something like a strangled yelp of "Ow!" cut off in midstream.

Portuguese words and phrases

Basics

sim; não	yes; no	lavabo/quarto de banho	toilet/bathroom
olá; bom dia	hello; good morning		
boa tarde/noite	good afternoon/night	banco; câmbio	bank; change
adeus, até logo	goodbye, see you later	correios	post office
hoje; amanhã	today; tomorrow	(dois) selos	(two) stamps
por favor/se faz favor	please	O que é isso?	What's that?
tudo bem?	Everything all right?	Quanto é?	How much is it?
está bem	it's all right/OK	fala Inglês?	Do you speak English?
obrigado/a*	thank you	sou Inglês/Inglesa	I am English
onde; que	where; what	Americano/a	American
quando; porquê	when; why	Australiano/a	Australian
como; quanto	how; how much	Canadiano/a	Canadian
não sei	I don't know	Irlandês/Irlandesa	Irish
não compreendo	I don't understand	Neozeelandês /Neozeelandesa	New Zealander
sabe...?	do you know...?	Escocês/Escosesa	Scottish
pode...?	could you...?	Galês/Galesa	Welsh
desculpe; com licença	sorry; excuse me	Como se chama?	What's your name?
aqui; ali	here; there	(chamo-me...)	(my name is...)
perto; longe	near; far	Como se diz isto em Português?	What's this called in Português?
este/a; esse/a	this; that		
agora; mais tarde	now; later		
mais; menos	more; less		
grande; pequeno	big; little		
aberto; fechado	open; closed		
senhoras; homens	women; men		

* Obrigado agrees with the sex of the person speaking — a woman says obrigada, a man obrigado.

Getting around

Para ir a...?	How do I get to...?	a estação de comboios	the railway station
esquerda, direita	left, right	Qual é o destino deste comboio?	What is the destination of this train?
sempre em frente	straight ahead		
Onde é a estação de camionetas?	Where is the bus station?		
a paragem de autocarro para...	the bus stop for...	É este o comboio para Coimbra?	Is this the train for Coimbra?
Há uma camioneta para...?	Is there a bus to...?	A que horas parte?	What time does it leave?
Donde parte o autocarro para...?	Where does the bus to ... leave from?	(chega a...?)	(arrive at...?)
		bilhete (para)	ticket (to)

ida e volta	round trip	Para onde vai?	Where are you going?
Qual é a estrada para...?	Which is the road to...?	Vou a...	I'm going to...
		Pare aqui por favor	Stop here please

Finding accommodation

Há uma pensão aqui perto?	Is there a pension near here?	É caro, não quero	It's expensive, I don't want it
Queria um quarto	I'd like a room	Posso/podemos deixar os sacos aqui até...?	Can I/we leave the bags here until...?
É para uma noite (semana)	It's for one night (week)		
É para uma pessoa (duas pessoas)	It's for one person (two people)	Há um quarto mais barato?	Is there a cheaper room?
Posso ver?	May I see/look around?	Com duche (quente/frio)	With a shower (hot/cold)
Está bem, fico com ele	OK, I'll take it	Pode-se acampar aqui?	Can we camp here?
Quanto custa?	How much is it?	chave	key

Food shopping

biológico/produtos biológicos	Organic/organic produce	mercearia	Grocery
fatias/fatiado	Slices/sliced	metade de/da...	Half of...
fresco	Fresh	padaria	Bakery
gramas	Grammes	peso/pesar	Weight/to weigh
lata, em lata	Can, tinned	queria um saco	I'd like a bag
litro	Litre	quilo	Kilo
mercado	Market	supermercado	Supermarket
		unidade	Unit

Days of the week

domingo	Sunday	quinta-feira	Thursday
segunda-feira	Monday	sexta-feira	Friday
terça-feira	Tuesday	sábado	Saturday
quarta-feira	Wednesday		

Months

janeiro	January	julho	July
fevereiro	February	agosto	August
março	March	setembro	September
abril	April	outubro	October
maio	May	novembro	November
junho	June	dezembro	December

The time

Que horas são?	What time is it?	A que horas?	(At) what time?
é/são...	it's...	à/às...	at...

Soups (Sopas)

Caldo de castanhas	Chestnut soup	Gaspacho	Chilled vegetable soup
Caldo verde	Cabbage/potato broth (with or without *chouriço*)	Sopa à alentejana	Garlic/bread soup with poached egg on top
Canja de galinha	Chicken broth with rice and boiled egg yolks	Sopa de feijão verde /grão/legumes /marisco/peixe	Green bean/chickpea /vegetable/shellfish /fish soup

Fish (peixe) and shellfish (mariscos)

Ameijoas	Clams	Linguado	Sole
Anchovas	Anchovies	Lulas	Squid
Atum	Tuna	Mexilhões	Mussels
Besugo	Bream	Ostras	Oysters
Camarões	Shrimp	Pargo	Snapper
Caranguejo	Crab	Peixe Gale	John Dory
Carapau	Mackerel	Perceves	Goose barnacles
Cherne	Sea bream	Pescada	Hake
Chocos	Cuttlefish	Polvo	Octopus
Corvina	Meagre	Robalo	Sea bass
Dourada	Bream	Salmão	Salmon
Enguia	Eel	Salmonete	Red mullet
Espada	Scabbard fish	Santolas	Spider crabs
Espadarte	Swordfish	Sapateiras	Common crabs
Gambas	Prawns	Sarda	Mackerel
Garoupa	Garoupa (like bream)	Sardinhas	Sardines
Lagosta	Lobster	Tamboril	Monkfish
Lagostim	Giant prawns	Truta	Trout
Lampreia	Lamprey (similar to eel)	Vieiras	Scallops

Meat (carne), poultry (aves) and game (caça)

Alheira	Sausage (bread and chicken mix)	Costeleta	Chop
		Dobrada	Tripe
Almôndegas	Meatballs	Enchidos	Smoked sausages
Borrego	Lamb		
Bucho	Haggis	Escalope	Escalope
Cabrito	Kid goat	Espetada mista	Mixed meat kebab
Carne de porco	Pork		
Carne picada	Mince meat	Farinheira	Floury sausage
Carneiro	Mutton	Fiambre	Boiled ham
Chouriço	Cured sausage	Figado	Liver
Coelho	Rabbit	Frango	Chicken
Cordeiro	Lamb	Fumeiros	Smoked meats
Cordoniz	Quail	Javali	Wild boar

LANGUAGE | Menu reader

Leitão	Spit-roast suckling pig	Pato	Duck
Linguiça	Cured sausage	Perdiz	Partridge
Lombo	Loin, fillet or tenderloin	Perna	Leg
		Perú	Turkey
Medalhão	Medallion	Pomba	Pigeon
Miolos	Brain	Presunto	Smoked ham
Moela	Gizzard	Rim	Kidney
Morcela	Black pudding, blood sausage	Salpicão	Smoked sausage
		Salsicha	Sausage
Paio	Cured sausage	Tripas	Tripe
Pata/Pé	Leg	Vitela	Veal

Vegetables (legumes or hortaliças) and salad (salada)

Abacate	Avocado	Couve	Cabbage
Abóbora	Pumpkin	Couve-flor	Cauliflower
Agriões	Watercress	Ervilhas	Peas
Aipo	Celery	Espargos	Asparagus
Alcachofra	Artichoke	Espinafres	Spinach
Alface	Lettuce	Favas	Broad beans
Alho	Garlic	Feijão	Beans
Alho Francês	Leek	Grão-de-bico	Chickpeas
Batatas (fritas /cozidas/a murro)	Potatoes (French fries /boiled/jacket)	Lentilhas	Lentils
		Nabo	Turnip
Berlingela	Aubergine	Pepino	Cucumber
Beterraba	Beetroot	Pimento	Sweet pepper
Cebola	Onion	Salsa	Parsley
Cenoura	Carrot	Tomate	Tomato
Cogumelo	Mushroom		

Fruit (fruta)

Ameixas	Plums	Manga	Mango
Ananás	Pineapple	Maracujá	Passion fruit
Castanhas	Chestnut	Melancia	Water melon
Cerejas	Cherries	Melão	Melon
Damascos	Apricots	Meloa	Cantaloupe or Car margue melon
Figo	Fig		
Framboesas	Raspberries	Morangos	Strawberries
Frutas silvestres	Berries	Pêra	Pear
Goiaba	Guava	Pêssego	Peach
Groselhas	Red currants	Romã	Pomegranate
Laranja	Orange	Tangerina	Tangerine
Limão	Lemon	Toranja	Grapefruit
Maçã	Apple	Uvas	Grapes

General terms

Adega	Wine cellar or winery, often also a wine bar or restaurant.
Alameda	Promenade.
Albufeira	Reservoir or lagoon.
Aldeia	Small village or hamlet.
Artesanato	Handicraft shop.
Bairro	Quarter, area (of a town); *alto* is upper, *baixo* lower.
Baixa	Low; used to mean commercial/shoping centre of town.
Barragem	Dam.
Cachoeira	Waterfall.
Caldas	Mineral springs or spa complex.
Câmara municipal	Town hall.
Campo	Square or field.
Centro comercial	Shopping centre.
Chafariz	Public fountain.
Cidade	City.
Correios	Post office, abbreviated CTT.
Cruzeiro	Cross.
Eléctrico	Tramcar.
Elevador	Elevator or funicular railway.
Espigueiro	Grain shed on stilts, common in the north.
Esplanada	Seafront promenade.
Estação	Station.
Estrada	Road; Estrada Nacional is a main road.
Farmácia	Pharmacy.
Feira	Fair or market.
Festa	Festival or carnival.
Fonte	Fountain or spring.
Freguesia	Parish (*Junta da Freguesia* is the local council).

Grutas	Caves.
Ilha	Island.
Jardim	Garden.
Lago	Lake.
Largo	Square.
Miradouro	Belvedere or view point.
Paço	Palace or country house.
Paços do concelho	Town hall.
Palácio	Palace or country house; *palácio real*, royal palace.
Paragem	Bus stop.
Parque	Park.
Parque nacional /natural	National/Natural Park or Reserve.
Pelourinho	Stone pillory.
Poço	Well.
Pombal	Pigeon house.
Ponte	Bridge.
Praça	Square.
Praça de touros	Bullring.
Praia	Beach.
Quinta	Country estate, farm or villa.
Ria	Narrow, open-ended lagoon where sand bars block a river's mouth.
Ribeiro	Stream.
Rio	River.
Romaria	Pilgrimage-festival.
Serra	Mountain or mountain range.
Solar	Manor house or important town mansion.
Termas	Thermal springs or spa complex.
Tourada	Bullfight.
Vila	Town.

Rough
Guides

advertiser

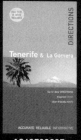

Rough Guide Maps, printed on waterproof and rip-proof Yupo™ paper, offer an unbeatable combination of practicality, clarity of design and amazing value.

CITY MAPS

Amsterdam · Barcelona · Berlin · Boston · Brussels · Dublin
Florence & Siena · Frankfurt · London · Los Angeles
Miami · New York · Paris · Prague · Rome
San Francisco · Venice · Washington DC and more...

COUNTRY & REGIONAL MAPS

Andalucía · Argentina · Australia · Baja California · Cuba
Cyprus · Dominican Republic · Egypt · Greece
Guatemala & Belize · Ireland · Mexico · Morocco
New Zealand · South Africa · Sri Lanka · Tenerife · Thailand
Trinidad & Tobago · Yucatán Peninsula · and more...

US$9.99   Can$13.99   £5.99

small print and

Index

A Rough Guide to Rough Guides

In the summer of 1981, Mark Ellingham, a recent graduate from Bristol University, was travelling round Greece and couldn't find a guidebook that really met his needs. On the one hand there were the student guides, insistent on saving every last cent, and on the other the heavyweight cultural tomes whose authors seemed to have spent more time in a research library than lounging away the afternoon at a taverna or on the beach.

In a bid to avoid getting a job, Mark and a small group of writers set about creating their own guidebook. It was a guide to Greece that aimed to combine a journalistic approach to description with a thoroughly practical approach to travellers' needs —a guide that would incorporate culture, history and contemporary insights with a critical edge, together with up-to-date, value-for-money listings. Back in London, Mark and the team finished their Rough Guide, as they called it, and talked Routledge into publishing the book.

That first *Rough Guide to Greece*, published in 1982, was a student scheme that became a publishing phenomenon. The immediate success of the book – with numerous reprints and a Thomas Cook prize shortlisting – spawned a series that rapidly covered dozens of destinations. Rough Guides had a ready market among low-budget backpackers, but soon also acquired a much broader and older readership that relished Rough Guides' wit and inquisitiveness as much as their enthusiastic, critical approach. Everyone wants value for money, but not at any price.

Rough Guides soon began supplementing the "rougher" information about hostels and low-budget listings with the kind of detail on restaurants and quality hotels that independent-minded visitors on any budget might expect, whether on business in New York or trekking in Thailand.

These days the guides – distributed worldwide by the Penguin group – offer recommendations from shoestring to luxury and cover more than 200 destinations around the globe, including almost every country in the Americas and Europe, more than half of Africa and most of Asia and Australasia. Our ever-growing team of authors and photographers is spread all over the world, particularly in Europe, the USA and Australia.

In 1994, we published the *Rough Guide to World Music* and *Rough Guide to Classical Music*; and a year later the *Rough Guide to the Internet*. All three books have become benchmark titles in their fields – which encouraged us to expand into other areas of publishing, mainly around popular culture. Rough Guides now publish:

- Travel guides to more than 200 worldwide destinations
- Dictionary phrasebooks to 22 major languages
- History guides ranging from Ireland to Islam
- Maps printed on rip-proof and waterproof Polyart™ paper
- Music guides running the gamut from Opera to Elvis
- Restaurant guides to London, New York and San Francisco
- Reference books on topics as diverse as the Weather and Shakespeare
- Sports guides from Formula 1 to Man Utd
- Pop culture books from *Lord of the Rings* to Cult TV
- World Music CDs in association with World Music Network

Visit **www.roughguides.com** to see our latest publications.

Rough Guide credits

Text editor: Jules Brown
Layout: Ajay Verma
Cartography: Katie Lloyd-Jones
Picture research: Mark Thomas, JJ Luck, Harriet Mills
Proofreader: Amanda Jones
Editorial: **London** Martin Dunford, Kate Berens, Helena Smith, Claire Saunders, Geoff Howard, Ruth Blackmore, Gavin Thomas, Polly Thomas, Richard Lim, Clifton Wilkinson, Alison Murchie, Sally Schafer, Karoline Densley, Andy Turner, Ella O'Donnell, Keith Drew, Edward Aves, Andrew Lockett, Joe Staines, Duncan Clark, Peter Buckley, Matthew Milton, Daniel Crewe; **New York** Andrew Rosenberg, Richard Koss, Chris Barsanti, Steven Horak, AnneLise Sorensen, Amy Hegarty
Design & Pictures: **London** Simon Bracken, Dan May, Diana Jarvis, Mark Thomas, Jj Luck, Harriet Mills, Chloë Roberts; **Delhi** Madhulita Mohapatra, Umesh Aggarwal, Ajay Verma, Jessica Subramanian, Amit Verma

Production: Julia Bovis, Sophie Hewat, Katherine Owers
Cartography: **London** Maxine Repath, Ed Wright, Katie Lloyd-Jones, Miles Irving; **Delhi** Manish Chandra, Rajesh Chhibber, Jai Prakash Mishra, Ashutosh Bharti, Rajesh Mishra, Animesh Pathak, Jasbir Sandhu, Karobi Gogoi
Online: **New York** Jennifer Gold, Suzanne Welles, Benjamin Ross; **Delhi** Manik Chauhan, Narender Kumar, Manish Shekhar Jha, Lalit K. Sharma, Rakesh Kumar
Marketing & Publicity: **London** Richard Trillo, Niki Hanmer, David Wearn, Chloë Roberts, Demelza Dallow; **New York** Geoff Colquitt, Megan Kennedy, Milena Perez
Custom publishing and foreign rights: Philippa Hopkins
Finance: Gary Singh
Manager India: Punita Singh
Series editor: Mark Ellingham
PA to Managing Director: Megan McIntyre
Managing Director: Kevin Fitzgerald

Publishing information

This eleventh edition published March 2005 by **Rough Guides Ltd**,
80 Strand, London WC2R 0RL.
345 Hudson St, 4th Floor,
New York, NY 10014, USA.
Distributed by the Penguin Group
Penguin Books Ltd,
80 Strand, London WC2R 0RL
Penguin Putnam, Inc.
375 Hudson St, NY 10014, USA
Penguin Group (Australia)
250 Camberwell Rd, Camberwell
Victoria 3124, Australia
Penguin Books Canada Ltd,
10 Alcorn Ave, Toronto, Ontario,
Canada M4V 1E4
Penguin Group (New Zealand)
Cnr Rosedale and Airborne Roads
Albany, Auckland, New Zealand
Typeset in Bembo and Helvetica to an original design by Henry Iles.
Printed and bound in China

688pp includes index
A catalogue record for this book is available from the British Library

ISBN 1-84353-438-X

The publishers and authors have done their best to ensure the accuracy and currency of all the information in **The Rough Guide to Portugal**, however, they can accept no responsibility for any loss, injury, or inconvenience sustained by any traveller as a result of information or advice contained in the guide.

1   3   5   7   9   8   6   4   2

Help us update

We've gone to a lot of effort to ensure that the fourth edition of **The Rough Guide to Portugal** is accurate and up-to-date. However, things change – places get "discovered", opening hours are notoriously fickle, restaurants and rooms raise prices or lower standards. If we've got it wrong or left something out, we'd like to know, and if you can remember the address, the price, the time, the phone number, so much the better.

We'll credit all contributions, and send a copy of the next edition (or any other Rough Guide if you prefer) for the best letters. Everyone who writes to us and isn't already a subscriber will receive a copy of our full-colour thrice-yearly newsletter. Please mark letters: "**Rough Guide Portugal Update**" and send to: Rough Guides, 80 Strand, London WC2R 0RL, or Rough Guides, 4th Floor, 345 Hudson St, New York, NY 10014. Or send an email to **mail@roughguides.com**

Have your questions answered and tell others about your trip at **www.roughguides.atinfopop.com**

Index

Map entries are in colour.

INDEX

Map symbols

maps are listed in the full index using coloured text

▬ ▬ ▬	International boundary	🏛	Stately home
▬ ▬ ▬	Chapter boundary	⊤	Gardens
▬▬▬	Motorway	⊙	Statue/monument
═══	Road	⌂	Casa abrigo
▬▬▬	Pedestrianized road	∩	Arch
------	Path	⊠—⊠	Gate
⊞⊞⊞⊞⊞	Steps	———	Wall
═•═•═	Railway	Å	Campsite
··········	Funicular	P	Parking
— —	Ferry route	✈	Airport
———	Waterway	★	Bus stop
✦	Point of interest	Ⓜ	Metro station
⚑	Church (regional maps)	⚑	Golf course
+	Chapel	@	Internet access
⛪	Monastery	⊞	Hospital
✡	Synagogue	ⓘ	Tourist office
∴	Ruins	Ⓒ	Telephone
⌓	Cave	⊠	Post office
▲	Peak	⬗	Swimming pool
〽	Mountains	▬	Building
⬐	Viewpoint	⊞	Church (town maps)
☗	Lighthouse	⊡	Cemetery
⚗	Waterfall	▢	Park
〰	Spring	⣿	Forest
♇	Castle	⣀	Beach